THE WAR
ILLUSTRATED

FIELD-MARSHAL THE VISCOUNT ALEXANDER OF TUNIS, G.C.B., D.S.O.

To him, as Supreme Allied Commander, Mediterranean, the German armies in Italy and Western Austria on May 2, 1945, made the first major surrender of the War at Caserta.

Portrait by Captain Neville Lewis. Exhibited at the National Portrait Gallery, London, Summer 1943: reproduced by permission of the Government of South Africa

THE WAR Illustrated

Complete Record of the Conflict
by Land and Sea and in the Air

Edited by

SIR JOHN HAMMERTON

Volume Nine

The NINTH VOLUME of THE WAR ILLUSTRATED contains the issues numbered 206 to 230, covering the period May 1945 to April 1946. Through swift crescendo of stirring events to the climax of total Victory it carries on the story of six years of fighting told phase by phase in preceding volumes.

The link-up of the Allies from West and East in the heart of Germany was speedily followed by the Russian capture of Berlin, the capitulation of German armed forces, and the final passing from the stage of Adolf Hitler himself, of Goebbels and Himmler. The capture of Goering, Ribbentrop and other of the Nazi war criminals led to the opening, at Nuremberg, of the greatest crime trial in world history. Allied triumph in Italy was proclaimed only a few days after the ignominious downfall, and execution by his own countrymen, of Benito Mussolini. Then came those memorable celebrations at Home and elsewhere which crowned the dramatic last days of War in the West.

On the Pacific front we recorded one victory after another. British prowess in Burma secured the reoccupation of Rangoon. Australians cleared the Japanese from New Guinea. American feats of island-hopping culminated in 82-days' battle for Okinawa, springboard for the invasion of Japan, whose mainland was being subjected to Allied air attacks growing rapidly in intensity. Then, changing the whole conception of warfare, came the dropping of the two atomic bombs, the first on Hiroshima, and the second on Nagasaki, followed in a few days by the capitulation of Japan and, in due course, the release and repatriation of large numbers of Far Eastern prisoners of war.

In the realm of politics came the death of Franklin Delano Roosevelt and the accession to the American presidency of Harry S. Truman. A general election in Britain resulted in a change of Government during the last of the "Big Three" conferences (at Potsdam). Buoying up with bright hope all peoples of good will there gathered together at San Francisco the "architects of the better world"—and there came into being the United Nations Organization, whose First General Assembly was held at Westminster in London whilst Britain was striving mightily to swing her productive efforts once more into the channels of Peace. It is on that high note of optimism that we close this penultimate volume of THE WAR ILLUSTRATED.

Published 2000

TRIDENT PRESS INTERNATIONAL
ISBN 1-58279-108-2 Single Edition
ISBN 1-58279-023-X Special Combined Edition*
*Contains Volume 9 & 10 Unabridged
Printed in Croatia

General Index to Volume Nine

This Index is designed to give ready reference to the whole of the literary and pictorial contents of THE WAR ILLUSTRATED. *Individual subjects and people of importance are indexed under their own headings, while references are included to general subjects such as Atomic Bomb; Commandos; Food. Page numbers in italics indicate illustrations.*

C

D

E

H

I

List of Maps and Plans

Index of Special Drawings and Diagrams

Errata and Corrigenda

Page 54, Col. 3. Last sentence should read: Their example of integrity will endure for all time.

Page 76. Illus. No. 1. Aircraft shown are Short Stirlings and not Wellingtons.

Page 262. Line 3 of caption. *For* 18-in. shells *read* 8-in.

Page 408. Line 3. *For* Nottinghamshire, *read* Lancashire.

Page 454. War risk money: *For* weekly, *read* monthly. (See footnote to page 518).

Page 468. Line 2 of caption. *For* St. Stephen's Cathedral *read* the Votiv Church.

Page 551. Line 3 of caption. *For* seven read *five*.

Printed in Great Britain by The Amalgamated Press, Ltd., London

Vol 9 The War Illustrated Nº 206

SIXPENCE Edited by Sir John Hammerton MAY 11, 1945

HOISTING HIS TROOP FLAG AT OSNABRUCK, W. K. Laidler of No. 1 Commando Brigade climbed a street lamp after the town had been entered by Field-Marshal Montgomery's 11th Armoured Division on April 3, 1945. This famous Prussian industrial and railroad centre, with a peacetime population of 107,000, offered little resistance: chief task of the Commandos was picking off stray snipers in the heart of the city, whilst loudspeakers gave orders to the remaining civilians. *Photo, British Official*

NO. 207 WILL BE PUBLISHED FRIDAY, MAY 25

Unspeakable Horrors of Nazi Prison Camps

AT BUCHENWALD, overrun by Gen. Patton's U.S. 3rd Army on April 11, 1945, a thousand citizens of nearby Weimar were marched six miles to witness the horrors of the notorious Nazi concentration camp where 21,000 emaciated and disease-ridden captives were found still alive; among the appalling sights was this lorry (1) loaded with skeleton-like corpses.

Headed by General Eisenhower, high-ranking Allied officers visited another vile concentration camp at Ohrdruf, near Gotha, captured by the U.S. 3rd Army on April 13; a Dutch prisoner in the camp related his experiences to the Allied C.-in-C. (2). At Nordhausen, east of Gottingen, where troops of the U.S. 1st Army, on April 10, found over 2,000 unburied dead (political prisoners) a few survivors were discovered on a floor among the bodies of other victims (3). Six hundred German civilians from the town were ordered to dig graves and remove the corpses for burial (4).

Photos, U.S. Official, L.N.A.

IN THE WAKE OF THE VICTORS

Another chapter from Our Own Correspondent's impressions of his visit to the British Front

by Captain NORMAN MACMILLAN, M.C., A.F.C.

Many of the roads in Belgium and Holland are surfaced with stone, cut in the shape of cubes and laid close together, without mortar or cement, on top of the levelled soil. Such roads stand up reasonably well to normal traffic, but they were subjected to terrific strain by the enormous mechanized convoys that poured in unending succession towards the Front. The severe frost had frozen the water in the soil beneath them and the expanding ice had thrown the stone sets upward; when the thaw came the weight of traffic destroyed the surface. Wherever we went we found stretches of road under repair, causing the flow of traffic to slow down at one-way bottlenecks.

American and British white troops and darkies worked on the roads. It was hard, unremitting toil, whether the surfaces were of pavé or of clay and broken stone. The pavé had to be reset accurately; macadam and dirt roads were resurfaced with the debris of shattered buildings, where these were at hand. I cannot say that the men engaged on this work looked happy. Most wore miserable expressions, especially the white Americans. Here was no glory, no fame, but disillusionment arising from realization of the chores of war. Yet there was honour in the sweaty toil, for without it the all-important convoys could not go through to their destination.

By day and night we passed lines of amphibious vehicles: buffaloes, 8-wheeled naval ducks, 6-wheeled army ducks; followed and preceded by supply transport and armour of all kinds, wherever possible moving up in a double row, for the great assault on the Rhine barrier. By day, vehicles on urgent priority used blinking red lights to distinguish them and give them right of way. At night, headlights blazed, dipped to ours, then blazed again as they passed. But one long convoy of amphibious craft, on urgent call, moved lightless through the night; military traffic police stopped all transport going the other way and warned the drivers to turn off their headlights to avoid dazzling the drivers of the oncoming amphibians.

Tree-trunk Signs Warn Drivers

Traffic Control utilized almost every roadside tree-trunk to display instructions and warnings to drivers. The more important signs were repeated every few miles. Roads were code-named or numbered, and the words UP or DOWN distinguished direction to or from the front. One road might be 305 DOWN; another MAPLE LEAF DIAMOND UP. Tanks or heavy trucks were scheduled to a speed limit over soft or worn roads. Sometimes all traffic had to be speed restricted, as at approaches to temporary bridges where single line traffic was compulsory.

Many signs, painted in black letters on large white boards, were repeated every few miles. Among them were IF YOU MUST STOP GET OFF THE ROAD . . IF YOU CAN'T GET OFF THE ROAD DON'T STOP . . . THE CAREFUL DRIVER HAS NO REGRETS . . . NO DOUBLE BANKING . . . DON'T OVERTAKE IN FOG . . . OBEY THE SIGNS AND HELP TRAFFIC CONTROL . . . VEHICLES MUST KEEP THIRTY YARDS APART . . . NO OVERTAKING. And on one tree-trunk, I CAN'T THINK OF ANYTHING TO PUT ON THIS ONE. In the front zones the signs became less official in tone. Two I noted were inscribed on white cardboard nailed to convenient tree-trunks, south of the Reichswald Forest, where at that time the 51st (Highland) Division was in action. They read:

Drive on the verges
And break up the route,
We'd sure like to give you
A kick with our boot.

Wave at the girls
To help your nerves,
But remember the road
Has dangerous curves.

In the towns, traffic signposts to indicate the location of units' headquarters looked like totem poles. They were covered from top to street-level with little plates of diverse colours, signs, queer letters, and abbreviated names; and when the face of the post was filled more plates were mounted on the sides until the indicator looked like a brilliantly coloured, scaly, tropical animal. Everywhere prominent among the signs were the Maple Leaf and the Scottish Lion.

We stopped for a few minutes in 'S-Hertogenbosch (it means Duke's Wood) to see the magnificent Gothic cathedral, much less damaged than some of our English cathedrals; indeed, almost unhurt. The interior, which reminded me of Milan cathedral, felt damp and cold. There was no heating. But a number of worshippers knelt in the quiet building, most of them in the chapels alongside the choir and altar, intent upon their devotions, while outside the dull boom of U.S. "Long Tom" guns of big calibre broke the silence with the reminder that war waged over the land. When we returned to the car, Dutch children ran up to ask us if we were Canadians.

GAS BOMBS READY FOR USE, to the number of 50,000, each weighing 500 lb. and filled with paralysing cyanogen chloride, were shown by Nazi officers to their captors of the U.S. 1st Army at Losa, Germany, in mid-April 1945. Masks were worn as a precaution. *Photo, Associated Press*

Before we reached the Grave bridge—protected by light A.A.—a flying bomb flew past us at about 1,500 feet, its roar sounding above that of the traffic. Throughout Holland the Bailey bridge was almost the most conspicuous feature of the landscape.

TO BREMEN THROUGH SMOKE AND FLAMES, a British dispatch-rider speeds past a burning building near the famous river port. On April 16 armour of the British 2nd Army moving up from Quakenbruck had broken out from the Aller bridge-head at Rethem; eight days later they had entered the Bremen suburbs. *Photo, British Official.*

This prefabricated bridge must have saved immense labour and much time during the advance over a countryside so cut by waterways. See page 564, Vol. 8.) We crossed the Maas-Wahl canal by Bailey bridge, and entered Nijmegen, where a fair-haired, curly-topped Dutch girl of about five stood on a chair in a window watching the traffic and singing at the top of her voice.

We pushed on towards the forward zone, and after traversing an appalling road of mud reached the main road to Krannenburg, a small town eight miles from Nijmegen and the railway frontier station within Germany. It had been captured the previous evening by the H.L.I. Medium bombers of 2nd T.A.F. had softened up for the attack, bombing both sides of the Nijmegen-Krannenburg road where defence points were sited. In a length of several miles I found only one bomb crater on the road itself, evidence of remarkable accuracy of aim despite poor visibility.. This one crater was being filled in by Pioneers, to restore the roadway which was there reduced to one-way traffic.

The Jerrican Cooking-Stove

Before reaching Krannenburg I saw two undamaged German frontier radiolocation towers—of an early pattern—apparently anti-aircraft radar posts. Krannenburg was badly smashed up by the guns, bombs and rockets of the Typhoon squadrons. I went into a doctor's house. On one side of the lobby was his waiting-room, opposite was his surgery. Behind was his combined dining-room and lounge. A picture frame hung on one wall, but the picture it had contained was out of the frame. Tables were overturned, windows smashed, plaster gone; books lay about the floor and sideboard. The house looked as if a gigantic impish child had been let loose in it. Yet it had every appearance of having been lived in until the bombardment began a few hours before.

Krannenburg, with a pre-war population of just under 4,000, has considerable remains of ancient ramparts, and near it were the newer ones of the Siegfried Line. Its 13th-century church had an attractive tall steeple, but the sky showed through a few war-made holes in it. On a plot of open ground facing the main street some troops sat on wooden chairs brought out from the houses, cooking their rations on a petrol fire that burned in a torn-open jerrican; the thought struck me that last time I warmed myself at such a fire was on the Transjordanian desert, east of the Dead Sea; here it was in a dead town, through which poured a never-ending stream of armoured and unarmoured vehicles.

Lieut.-Gen. B. G. HORROCKS, C.B., D.S.O., commanding the 30th Corps, (left) gives Capt. Norman Macmillan, Special Correspondent for "The War Illustrated" with the British Forces (centre) a message for our readers (see foot of next column).

We drove on to the beginning of the Siegfried defence system, and then walked forward. The road was camouflaged from the farther bank of the Rhine—five miles away, on the other side of floods that lapped to the edge of the road—by cut branches of fir trees placed between the trunks of the trees that grew in an avenue along the verges. The main German position was visible on the wooded slopes ahead, and for some way back the road was open to enemy observation.

I could hear our bombers passing high above the clouds. Austers spotted amid flak. I saw the tank crews stiffen and look up. Two specks grew swiftly in the eastern sky. I recognized them quickly. "Spits," I said. Simultaneously the tank crews knew them. "Good thing, too!" they said. What a target that road was for fighter bombers! If the enemy had possessed air superiority it would have been impossible to use it as it was being used.

At the first anti-tank ditch of the Siegfried Line we met Lieut.-Gen. B. G. Horrocks, the 30th Corps Commander, inspecting the position. I asked him for a message for readers of The War Illustrated. He hesitated. But when I told him the articles could not possibly appear for several weeks, he realized that security questions could not be endangered, as they sometimes are by quick publication of messages which may be useful to the enemy. And General Horrocks said: "Our soldiers have fought magnificently against considerable opposition. We have definitely broken through now. Our trouble is roads and communications. Yesterday we bulldozed over the country"—he waved one arm towards the land that lay behind us to the right of the road. "I won't say that we won't have our little set-backs, but we should be all right." Events have proved his forecast, made at the opening of the Rhine offensive, to be correct.

LOOTERS SWARMED THE STREETS OF HANOVER after its capture by Gen. Simpson's U.S. 9th Army on April 10, 1945. Handcarts and bicycles piled with stolen goods were wheeled through the shell-shattered thoroughfares before the Allied Military Control took over after the flight of the Reich police authority. During this operation the U.S. 9th Army cut the highly important autobahn which runs through Magdeburg (captured April 18) and the heart of Prussia to Berlin. See story in page 25. *Photo, Keystone*

THE BATTLE FRONTS

by Maj.-Gen. Sir Charles Gwynn, K.C.B., D.S.O.

WRITING on the eve of the great battle which is bound to be fought between the Elbe and the Oder the task of the commentator is not easy. Before what I write is published the results of the battle will probably be known. That it will be the final major battle of the war is practically certain, although it is impossible to predict how long hard and bitter fighting may be necessary if fanatical and desperate groups maintain a suicidal struggle. Apart from the action of such groups it remains to be seen whether the German Army will go down fighting desperately or whether there will be a sudden unexpected collapse such as has occurred in the Ruhr pocket.

There can be no doubt that the Germans have deployed the bulk of their available forces on their Eastern Front, hoping that they would at least be able to limit the area to be overrun by the Red Army whose vengeance they naturally feared. Now that the Allies have closed up from the west the Germans may decide that protracted resistance is useless and would entail only further devastation of the country. German historians will find it hard to explain away the ignominious surrenders in the Ruhr pocket. If the 300,000 prisoners taken there in the course of a fortnight had fought with the determination the situation demanded, a large part of the U.S. 9th and 1st Armies could probably have taken no share in the battle beyond the Elbe. Not until a "cease-fire" had been ordered by the highest authority could surrender on such a scale and under such circumstances be excused.

Red Army would cause. Personally, I doubt whether the German Army as a whole will fight with the desperation Hitler has demanded now that the arrival of the western Allies on the scene makes it impossible to stem the Russian advance; and I should not be in the least surprised if we see some tame surrenders on a large scale.

DECLARED German Intention Was to Hold Vienna at All Costs

It is now quite clear that the renewal of the Russian offensive on the Oder-Neisse line was deliberately postponed till the Anglo-American Armies had reached the Elbe, in order to give the best prospects of securing decisive results. It is equally evident that the threat of the Russian offensive immensely facilitated the Allied advance from the Rhine. Not till the line of the Elbe was reached did the Germans dare to withdraw reserves from the Eastern Front to oppose it, and the fact that those reserves sufficed to offer considerable resistance goes to prove the strength of the army facing the Russians.

IN previous articles I have commented on Tolbukhin's remarkable record, and his capture of Vienna (see illus. page 9) in a six-day attack is another notable achievement, for the Germans had not only declared their intention to hold the city at all costs, but had placed one of their most fanatical leaders in charge of the defence. Malinovsky's operations, of course, contributed greatly to the speed and completeness of the achievement, and there is no doubt that collaboration between these two generals has reached an exceptionally high standard.

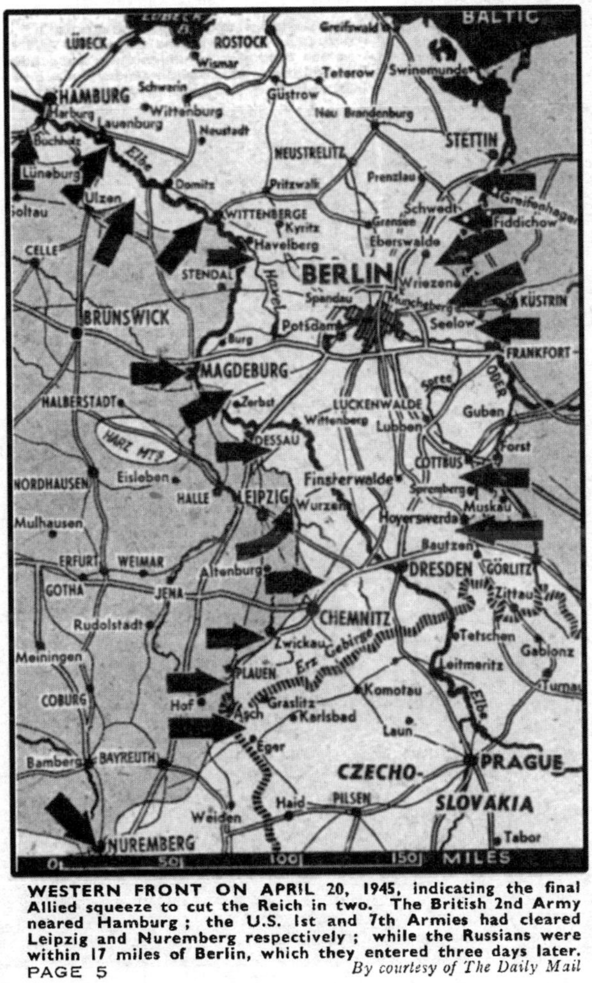

Looking back on the course of the war since the winter offensive began and passed into the spring campaign, one is even more impressed by the perfection of the Allied plans and by the way the whole complex structure of the operations has been fitted together than by the performances of individual generals or armies, brilliant as they have often been. Astonishingly little has apparently been unforeseen or unprovided for. Yet it is obvious that the programme was never so rigid as to cramp initiative or lead to the loss of opportunities. It is less surprising that the operations on the Western Front should have been admirably co-ordinated, for there the Allied armies have fortunately a single directing head, but few could have believed the Western and Eastern offensives should not only have been so well synchronized but that their component parts should have fitted together so remarkably.

IT was of course obvious that Berlin would be a lodestar dictating the direction of the advance from each side, and it might have been foreseen that the left of the Russian invading armies and General Eisenhower's right would probably meet in the neighbourhood of Dresden. But was it by chance or by brilliant collaboration that the Russian drive through Rumania and Hungary (at one time criticized as an unwise dispersion of effort) and General Patch's 7th Army from Alsace should arrive practically simultaneously at Vienna and Nuremberg respectively, with good prospects of meeting in the upper Danube valley and of interposing between Hitler's main armies in the north and the mountain strongholds of the south?

Furthermore, there is every probability that Malinovsky's Army advancing into Moravia has a rendezvous with General Patton's troops in Bohemia. There is little likelihood, therefore, that Bohemia (as has been suggested) will provide Hitler with a stronghold in which part of his army could offer prolonged resistance. As a further blow to Hitler's hopes of continuing the struggle in the mountains of the south, Field-Marshal Alexander has again found himself in a position to launch a major offensive which seems likely to prove annihilating and to make it impossible for the Germans to withdraw into the Alpine passes. Within a fortnight from the start of the attack on April 12, the 8th and 5th Armies had driven the enemy from his long-held positions, captured Bologna, Ferrara and Modena, crossed the Po and reached the line of the Adige and Verona, gateway to the Brenner.

WHAT we are watching is an outstanding example of the correct development of exterior lines strategy: a strategy which demands unrelenting pressure by widely separated forces, giving the enemy no chance of concentrating such offensive power as he possesses against any one of them. Obviously, this entails difficulties which increase with the number of separate fields of action. The problem of maintaining each force at sufficient strength and with such assurance of supplies as to give it the requisite offensive potentialities is by no means simple. Synchronization of intensive efforts may not always be necessary or desirable—alternating blows may be at times more effective—but the correct timing of blows is perhaps the highest test of the skill of the co-ordinating authority. In this case where there are two co-ordinating authorities, nothing is more remarkable than the way the timing on both sides has been harmonized.

I DO not often hark back to views I have previously stated, but I think I may claim that a suggestion I made when the Allied winter offensive was pending has to a considerable extent been justified. I held then that the German Regular Army, though convinced that the war was lost, would fight desperately in the defence of the frontiers, and in order to maintain the prestige and traditions of the Army; but that, realizing the devastation it entailed, it would not lend itself to Hitler's plans for prolonging the struggle in the heart of the country.

In the frontier fighting I thought it probable that German commanders might attempt gambling operations, fully realizing that should they fail the end would come sooner. I rank Rundstedt's offensive in that category, although it was more formidable than anything I had expected. The counter-offensive in Hungary was in the same class, though with less prospect of achieving a success of real importance. The episode of the Ruhr pocket, and many others, on the other hand tend to show that the remnants of the Regular Army have no intention of sacrificing themselves to prolong the struggle if they can avoid it.

LIKE all generalizations, what I suggested could only be partially true, and there can be no doubt that the Wehrmacht of all classes was prepared to fight desperately to prevent the Russians advancing beyond the Oder. But the Oder for all practical purposes had become a frontier of Germany, and there was an immense incentive to save the country from the devastation it was naturally expected invasion by the

WESTERN FRONT ON APRIL 20, 1945, indicating the final Allied squeeze to cut the Reich in two. The British 2nd Army neared Hamburg; the U.S. 1st and 7th Armies had cleared Leipzig and Nuremberg respectively; while the Russians were within 17 miles of Berlin, which they entered three days later.

By courtesy of The Daily Mail

Wondrous Rescue for Airmen in Peril on the Sea

AIRBORNE LIFEBOAT SUSPENDED FROM PARACHUTES was dropped (1) by a 2,000-h.p. Warwick heavy transport aircraft of R.A.F. Coastal Command during the dramatic rescue of the U.S. crew of a Catalina flying-boat on April 3, 1945 : as the sea-marker gave off its column of smoke, supplies also were floated down. The lifeboat righted itself (2) and the Catalina's crew clambered into it (3) from their dinghy.

The Catalina, searching for the pilot of a Mustang which had been forced down into the sea, had itself got into difficulties and force-landed. The crew were driven to take to their dinghy, in which they were adrift for six days. Soon after the dropping of the lifeboat, the Catalina's crew were picked up by a rescue launch of the Royal Navy. See also story in page 731, Vol. 8. *Photos, British Official*

THE WAR AT SEA

by Francis E. McMurtrie

By the time this is published, the German fleet, apart from submarines and small craft, may no longer exist as a fighting force. Already several of its few remaining large ships have been eliminated, and the fate of the remainder cannot long be delayed. First to be accounted for was the heavy cruiser Seydlitz, of 10,000 tons. Though launched as long ago as January 1939, this ship, for some unknown reason, had never been completed for service. Laid up in harbour at Königsberg, she is believed to have been blown up by the Germans before the Soviet forces entered the city.

Another incomplete ship, the aircraft carrier Graf Zeppelin, of 19,250 tons, was last reported as laid up in a dismantled state in the estuary of the Oder, below Stettin. That port is likely to be in Russian hands at any moment, and the fate of Germany's only aircraft carrier, launched with great ceremony at Kiel in December 1938, will doubtless be that of many another enemy ship—scuttling. A sister ship, the Peter Strasser, though laid down at Kiel in 1936 or 1937, seems never to have been launched.

At Gdynia, former Polish naval base, which the Soviet armies entered late in March, the only surviving German battleship, the Gneisenau, was under refit. She had been reduced to a hulk, the gun turrets and entire superstructure having been removed in order that the ship might be rebuilt. Though nothing is known positively of the damage which she had sustained, it is well to recall that when, on February 12, 1942, this ship passed through the Straits of Dover in company with the battleship Scharnhorst and the heavy cruiser Prinz Eugen, on their way from Brest to Wilhelmshaven, a series of determined attacks was made on the enemy by the Royal Navy.

Six Swordfish aircraft, led by Lieutenant-Commander (A) Eugene Esmonde, who had won the D.S.O. for torpedoing the Bismarck nine months earlier, flew through a storm of anti-aircraft fire, and, in spite of being attacked by German fighters, are believed to have got at least one torpedo home before all were destroyed. Esmonde was posthumously awarded the Victoria Cross for this gallant action (see page 567, Vol. 5).

Motor torpedo boats based on Dover next delivered a torpedo attack at long range, and finally, two flotillas of our destroyers in the North Sea pressed home attacks off the Dutch coast, managing to get within close range through squalls of rain. Altogether it is estimated that half-a-dozen torpedoes may have found their marks, though the Germans asserted that a minesweeper, one of some 30 small craft which were endeavouring to screen the three big ships, was the only casualty.

ADMIRAL Scheer at Kiel Presumed Sunk by a Magazine Explosion

Though both the Scharnhorst and Prinz Eugen were soon in service again, the Gneisenau has never been reported at sea since, and it seems reasonable to conclude that she suffered such severe structural injuries from torpedo hits that it was necessary to strip her completely to get at the damage. What has now become of her does not very much matter ; but probably she was destroyed by the Germans before Gdynia fell.

Next it was the turn of the 6,000-ton cruiser Köln, survivor of three sisters. Both the other two were lost during the German invasion of Norway five years ago, the Karlsruhe being torpedoed off Kristiansand by H.M. submarine Truant, and the Königsberg being dive-bombed in harbour at Bergen by the Fleet Air Arm. Towards the end of March last, bombers of the Royal Air Force scored two or three direct hits on the Köln as she lay at her moorings in Wilhelmshaven, Germany's principal naval base on the North Sea coast. When photographed a day or two later she was seen to be lying on the bottom, with her upper deck submerged. She may therefore be safely written off as an effective warship.

On the night of April 9-10 a heavy attack was made by Bomber Command on the dockyard at Kiel. Several bombs were dropped in the vicinity of a large ship lying in the dockyard basin, and a heavy explosion followed. Photographic reconnaissance disclosed that the ship was the Admiral Scheer, one of the so-called "pocket battleships." She was lying under water, completely capsized, and is presumed to have been sunk by a magazine explosion.

Her only remaining sister ship, the Lützow (formerly named Deutschland) was spotted shortly afterwards at the entrance to the port of Swinemünde, in the Baltic. Swinemünde bears much the same relationship to Stettin, at the mouth of the Oder, as Gourock does to Glasgow. On the afternoon of April 16 a determined attack was made on the ship by R.A.F. bombers, as the result of which she now lies on the mud with her stern under water, a helpless wreck.

FLEET AIR ARM RATINGS in Ceylon find it no hardship to do their own washing, outside their quarters. The F.A.A. has played a big part in clearing the Indian Ocean of U-boats.
Photo, British Official

This completes the inglorious saga of the "pocket battleships," an inaccurate and non-technical description of a type which has failed to live up to the flamboyant advertisement which accompanied its production by the Germans 15 years ago. Designed to evade the restrictions placed on German naval construction by the Versailles Treaty, this type of ship combined an armament of six 11-in. and eight 5·9-in. guns with an armour belt of from four to five-and-a-half inches in thickness and a speed of 26 knots.

It was the enemy's boast that these ships were too powerful to be tackled by the heaviest British cruisers, which carried no weapon more powerful than the 8-in. gun ; while the speed of 26 knots was in excess of that of any British capital ship then existing, other than the battle cruisers Hood, Renown and Repulse. It was Commodore (now Vice-Admiral Sir Henry) Harwood who exposed the weakness of the "pocket battleship" design. With three cruisers, one mounting 8-in. guns and the others 6-in. guns, he fought the Admiral Graf Spee with such fury and determination, tempered with a high degree of skill, that the German ship was glad to slink into the neutral port of Montevideo. She emerged again on December 17, 1939, only to scuttle herself rather than face a renewal of the action.

Since then the other two ships of this discredited design discreetly refused action on every occasion when it was offered, except on November 5, 1940, when the Admiral Scheer descended on a convoy in the Atlantic. At that date the Royal Navy was so short of escorts that the convoy's only protector was the armed merchant cruiser Jervis Bay. Though hopelessly outmatched, she resolutely attacked the Admiral Scheer, and before she sank had the satisfaction of knowing that she had given the convoy time to scatter. Captain E. S. F. Fegen, commanding officer of the Jervis Bay, received the V.C. posthumously (see page 567, Vol. 3). On Christmas Day, 1940, another convoy, this time escorted by the cruiser Berwick, armed with 8-in. guns, was attacked by an enemy ship, believed to have been the Admiral Scheer. After an exchange of gunfire with the Berwick, the German ship prudently withdrew.

SUBMARINE RESCUED AIRMEN ditched in the Indian Ocean, when a Super-Fortress was shot down by Japs. American survivors from the blazing plane are here seen transferring from the Royal Navy submarine which picked them up to the rubber dinghy of a R.A.F. Catalina of Eastern Air Command, which flew them back to base.
Photo, British Official

Australian Pathfinders in New Guinea Waters

To help make possible the advance of big Allied forces against Japan through hundreds of miles of enemy-controlled waters of which no adequate charts were available, little ships set forth to survey the way. How hydrographers of the Royal Australian Navy carried out this supremely difficult task, taking millions of soundings, in the face of offensive action by the Japanese, is specially described for "The War Illustrated" by GORDON HOLMAN.

UNCHARTED seas are just as big a menace in wartime as in peace. On occasions, in the desperate situations of war, ships must take risks that they would not be called upon to face in more normal times; but, for any well-planned operation, good charts are even more essential than for ordinary peacetime passage.

The main shipping routes across the wide oceans are like great highways, and the coasters that carry supplies in all parts of the world in peacetime have their well-marked channels. Still there remain thousands of square miles of sea that are, to all intents and purposes, "unknown," in the sense that no reliable charts of their depths and shallows have ever been made.

So it was many months ago, when General MacArthur sat down to plan for his promised return to the Philippines. "We will go northabout round New Guinea," he said, "leapfrogging the Japanese positions by sea." Almost the first consideration, once this decision had been made, was the setting down of the exact course the advance was to follow. Staff officers, studying their maps, saw at once that uncharted waters lay in the path of progress.

Better known to sailors, proceeding on their lawful occasions, were the Torres Strait and the Arafura Sea to the south of New Guinea. Going this way to or from Australia, they avoided passing round the great length of the island and were able to pay their calls in the busy Moluccas area and keep in line with the gateway of Singapore.

PLENTY of ships had passed through the China Straits, off the south-eastern tip of New Guinea, from the days when the old convict ships used to turn round and head for China and the valuable cargoes to be found there. It was after one had turned the corner and faced the long run up by what used to be the German part of New Guinea—not unexpectedly named Kaiser Wilhelm's Land—that the existing charts began to look more than a trifle sketchy. But this was the way the Allied advance on Japan had to go. Hundreds, perhaps thousands, of ships had to pass through those waters and they could not be committed to their task until adequate charts were available. The problem was simple, but the solution was going to call for great skill, enterprise and courage.

The Royal Australian Navy had its own hydrographic branch, and a number of the officers serving in it had had experience before and during the war, with the Royal Navy. It was to these naval surveyors that General MacArthur and his staff turned at this critical moment. The United States Navy had many commitments in other spheres, and the Australians were only too glad to undertake anything that would help to carry the war to the enemy. The chief hydrographer was a Royal Australian Navy officer with a curious Norwegian name, Commander Karl Eric Oom. A naval surveyor of wide experience, he wore the rare white ribbon of the Antarctic medal. At the beginning of the war, and for some months subsequently, he was in this country and saw service in one of the Royal Navy's famous survey ships, H.M.S. Franklin.

Ahead of Allied Naval Forces

It was in this ship, incidentally, that I had the honour, much later, to enter Cherbourg, the first great port to fall into our hands after the Allied armies returned to Europe. Apart from the small minesweepers and motor launches, Franklin led the way for British shipping into the harbour which the Germans had done everything in their power to make untenable for vessels. As a passing tribute to our own splendid naval survey service, I can record from personal knowledge that, for days before the first Liberty ship slowly nosed its way into the harbour at Cherbourg, officers and men of the Franklin worked day and night surveying and producing their meticulous charts. Mines were being exploded by the sweepers as the small boats used for the survey moved backwards and forwards across the harbour, but the hydrographers never faltered.

For the big task on the other side of the world, Commander Oom organized his small force with all the scientific exactitude that accompanied his own peacetime surveys. The ships, with their special gear, included H.M.A.S. Moresby, Shepparton, Benalia, Warrego and Polaris. Their commanders, and those who served in them, knew that they would have to face offensive action by the Japanese, because, first, they would be working ahead of the Allied invading forces, and, secondly, the enemy could not fail to recognize the importance of what these little ships were doing.

There were other handicaps, too. Every day was valuable and much of their labour had to be done during periods of intense heat. Heavy responsibilities rested on the men in the engine-rooms. If there was a breakdown or a ship was disabled in any way, there was not only increased danger for those who served in her, but she became a big liability on the rest of the small fleet. With their eyes open to all this, the Australian hydrographers went forth with hundreds of miles of enemy controlled sea ahead of them.

IT did not take the Japanese long to discover that "the pathfinders" were out, mapping the way for the big forces that were to thrust up towards the centre of the Jap empire. There were attacks by aircraft and, although every effort was made to give protection to the survey ships, the hydrographers had to be as ready to man their guns as they were to make their soundings. For those actually engaged on the survey there could be no distraction. Every echo had to be carefully recorded, and it is probable that the total number of recordings taken ran into millions.

And when the record books were full, every sounding had to be entered with the utmost exactness on the big charts. Sheet by sheet, as the little ships advanced more than a thousand miles along the northern coast of New Guinea, the figures shaded the sea areas and the deep-water channels became apparent Not content with this magnificent contribution to the great return of Allied sea power in the south-west Pacific, the survey men put down buoys to mark rocks and other dangerous obstructions. Sometimes the Japanese came out and destroyed these markers, but the tireless hydrographers always returned to mark afresh the dangers of the seas.

HOW the big ships followed in the wake of these heroic little vessels of the Royal Australian Navy is now a matter of history. When the immense strides of the advance began there was only one enemy to be faced —the Japanese. The uncharted seas, which might have proved an equally dangerous enemy, had already been beaten. H.M. the King has recognized the work of the Australian hydrographers with a number of awards to all ranks. Commander Oom receives the O.B.E. (Mil.). The D.S.C. goes to Commander C. G. Little, R.A.N., Lieut. Commanders S. F. Bolton, R.A.N., D. T. Gale, R.A.N., C. R. K. Roe, R.A.N., G. D. Tancred, R.A.N., Lieutenants C. H. McGee, R.A.N.R., H. M. Knight, R.A.N.V.R., and C. L. Crook, R.A.N.V.R. A D.S.M. and other awards have been granted to ratings.

H.M.S. FRANKLIN, 850-TON SURVEY SHIP of the Royal Navy (left) in which Commander K. E. Oom, chief hydrographer of the Royal Australian Navy, saw service. H.M.A.S. Moresby (right), 1,320 tons, combining minesweeping with surveying since the commencement of the war, is one of the famed "little ships" of the Royal Australian Navy whose soundings in the hitherto uncharted Pacific—as described in this page—have helped to pave the way for the ultimate invasion of the Japanese mainland.

New Soviet Tactics Saved Austrian Capital

VIENNA WAS CAPTURED BY THE RED ARMY, little damaged, in less than a week (finally cleared on April 13, 1945), thanks to new tactics by Marshals Malinovsky and Tolbukhin. Instead of advancing along the streets and there engaging in fighting, the Russians moved through spacious courtyards, smashing down walls to neutralize enemy firepoints. The Parliament House, seen (top) with Soviet artillery rumbling by, was unscathed. Red Army troops laid a wreath on the memorial to Johann Strauss of "Blue Danube" fame (bottom).

Photos, Pictorial Press, Planet News

Restored to the Freedom They Had Fought For—

OVER 9,000 RUSSIANS WERE RELEASED AT ESELHEIDE, between Münster and Hamm, on April 2, 1945. Wild with joy (1) they broke through the gates of Stalag 326 following the swift advance of the British 6th Guards' Tank Brigade and the U.S. 17th Airborne Division. Two Russian soldiers shared a cup of tea (2) with their British liberators. Freed Russian "slaves" (3) tramped to the repatriation centre, as U.S. officers inspected the trench-like communal graves of 30,000 Soviet victims of privation (4).

Photos, British Official. Keystone

–Allied Ex-Prisoners Hit the Homeward Trail

AWAITING THE BLIGHTY-BOUND PLANES, BRITISH EX-PRISONERS rested on a wrecked Nazi airfield (top) after their rescue from Oflag 12B at Lollar, near Giessen, which troops of the U.S. 3rd Army overran on March 28, 1945. At Soest, 15 miles south-east of Hamm, Maj.-Gen. Henry Twaddle, commanding the 95th Infantry Division of the U.S. 9th Army, on April 7 took the salute from 4,000 liberated French officers (bottom), many of them prisoners for five years. *Photos, British Official, Keystone*

ROOSEVELT January 30, 1882 April 12, 1945 A TRIBUTE 

by JAMES LANSDALE HODSON

NOT in modern history has the loss of a great leader of men been so profoundly felt by all right-thinking humanity as the sudden death of Franklin Delano Roosevelt, when within sight of the final triumph of that herculean task to which he had so completely dedicated his life. We have invited a brilliant English journalist, but recently returned from the U.S.A., author of "And Yet I Like America," to write this special tribute to the memory of the greatest President since Lincoln.

FRANKLIN DELANO ROOSEVELT, four times President of the United States—a burden no man had ever borne so long and which no man will ever endure for so many years again—was one of the great men of our time. Great in his statesmanship and vision, in his fight for the downtrodden and oppressed, in his personal courage.

Because of this the world is right to mourn him, for the world is darkened by his loss. But we in this country mourn him for other and additional reasons. Without the generous help of the United States, and the United States led by Franklin Roosevelt as none other could have led it, we might not have held out against Hitler when we stood alone through that long year in 1940–41. This was friendship in excelsis. It is true, of course, that we were fighting not only for ourselves but for men everywhere who prize dignity and freedom. Had we been overthrown, it is probable that in due time the United States would have fallen to Nazism also. We stood and the earth abided.

IT was Roosevelt's genius that, being 2,000 miles farther from the peril than ourselves, he saw what it meant as clearly as we did. And he acted accordingly. I have met those in America who believe that when Mr. Churchill was about to take office as Prime Minister, he rang up the President, who told him plainly that he, the President, would be behind him. Whether that is true or not, we know that within six days of the fall of France we began to receive on these shores the first of those 80,000 machine-guns, those millions of rounds of rifle ammunition, those old French 75s that were the first flowing of the rivulet that swelled to a mighty river of munitions and materials and food that have run to us across the broad Atlantic from that day onwards. In due time we sent a river flowing back, reverse Lend-Lease. But it does not diminish what America did for us, America led by Roosevelt.

How Should We Have Borne It?

Of course, when one looks at Roosevelt's career it is not surprising that he acted in this way. He was born wealthy and of what may be called America's aristocracy. Gay, gifted, clever, educated at Harvard, rather dilettante in politics and affairs, he yet had instinctive roots and feelings. He became a Democrat, and Democrats, although a mixed party with rich and poor in it, stand rather more with the workers than with the financiers and bankers. Broadly, Roosevelt was a Liberal. When he was 40 years old and was already known as a coming man he was stricken with infantile paralysis, this disease which made his legs almost useless to him. If you and I ask ourselves how we should have borne it, whether we should have refused to be dismayed, whether we could have struggled on in the arena of politics with its strains, its trials, its humiliations, its giving and taking of heavy and sometimes dirty verbal blows (for America is a violent nation), then we may know what a conquest of spirit it was for Franklin Roosevelt to do what he did. For he fought on and triumphed. Twelve years later he was President.

But what a time it was to go to the White House! Again, a lesser man might have quailed. For that great nation of 120,000,000 people was lying like a battered ship on a stagnant sea, a ship whose engines would not turn over. America had 16 millions of unemployed (and no State unemployment schemes such as ours to take care of them). The banks had almost foundered, agriculture was in ruins, and widespread despair was eating like a canker into men's hearts. Roosevelt began that series of measures known as the New Deal—to which many adjectives have been applied, such as courageous, fine, revolutionary, faulty, extravagant. But those measures restored some faith, they did something if not everything to put the United States back on her feet; and in such schemes as the T.V.A., which stopped soil erosion and flooding in Tennessee and made that valley more prosperous than ever before, they stand vindicated with a kind of splendour.

ROOSEVELT was not only leader of the party of Democrats in America; he was a leader of democrats, as we understand that word, throughout the entire world. Democracy was his faith. He believed in and fought for the common man; and the common man of America trusted him in return. Roosevelt saw with magnificent clearness that were Hitler and Mussolini and what they represented to succeed, then democracy would perish and with it all that British folk and Americans prize, yea, all that free men everywhere prize—independence of spirit, the dignity of man, and the sacredness of the individual. So that he, personally, was in the fight against Hitler from the first. While America was still neutral he said: "Even a neutral cannot be asked to close his mind or his conscience."

Before war began he had spoken of the ugly truculence of autocracy, and of those who were threatening a breakdown of all international law and order. It was plain who he meant. When war threw its black shadow over the earth he took, in succession, bold measures that followed inexorably one on the heels of the other—amended the Neutrality Act, sent us 50 over-age destroyers in exchange for air bases, invented Lend-Lease, dispatched troops to Iceland, guarded more and more of the Atlantic, and in August 1941 began that series of historic meetings with Mr. Churchill which, following on this first one where they compiled the Atlantic Charter, were to take Roosevelt to Casablanca, Teheran and Yalta, bring these two men into close living contact in four continents and during 120 days, and to result, from the war's early days to Roosevelt's death, in an exchange of messages numbering 1,700. (It was at Casablanca he first used the phrase Unconditional Surrender.)

HE saw the path that America ought to take and, holding up his own torch, guided her along it. Doing so, he rendered another enduring service. He clothed his vision, from time to time, in statements and speeches of singular power and nobility—as, for example, when he spoke of the Four Freedoms, freedom of speech and writing, freedom of worship, freedom from want and freedom from fear. This speech was to illuminate men's minds almost as brightly as passages in the Declaration of Independence and Lincoln's address at Gettysburg; it was in the line of descent. He was thinking not only of the freedom of Americans or Englishmen but of Poles and Chinese, of Africans and Australians, of all men apart from race or colour or creed.

WAS this man, then, respected, admired and loved by all Americans in his time—did he command the almost universal admiration in the United States that Churchill does here? By no means. One of his reputations has been that of being "the best-hated man" ever to occupy the White House. His enemies said he was vain, a poor administrator, the perfect politician who didn't know what truth was, that he could never sack anybody, that he was a prima donna, that he kept in office by courting Negroes and Labour and blandishing the downtrodden. We may note the charges without taking them too seriously. America is a violent country and politics is a violent business. Business and money-making are idealized and any man who thinks human beings count higher than dollars is bound to make enemies. But even as Roosevelt was widely hated so was he widely loved. He was returned to power time after time by the inarticulate millions who ignored the newspapers' advice—for more than three-fourths of the Press was usually against him. He could inspire affection just as he could give affection; he took affection to his meetings with Mr. Churchill and other leaders and could bring it away in return.

Wit and Humour and Blarney

During even a brief meeting with him, one could perceive this power. His face was strong but fine, with no atom of coarseness in it; the eyes were bluish grey, the forehead noble, and when he shook hands you saw the hands were as distinguished as the face. When I met him he had a trick of puffing out his cheeks and pursing his mouth—a trick that might have been a nervous trick—but he could control a Press conference in masterly fashion, using wit and humour and blarney and, when desirable, being grave and even piercing in his answers.

HIS enemies said he left papers on his desk unattended for long periods, but, in truth, no man could have borne his burden without possessing an immense capacity for work. One item: every day he signed a hundred or two hundred State documents. He was Commander-in-Chief; first citizen; holding powers in some respects near to a dictator's. In private he could be jovial and mix a cocktail that was dynamite. A score of Washington newspapermen feel a really personal friend has gone. He was Mr. President to them, but a lot of them were Christian names to him.

It was his privilege to harness a fight for the downtrodden to the fight to restore America's prosperity; to harness his fight for democracy and the common man to the fight against the greatest evil—Hitlerism—we have known in our time or our father's time. Nobly he did it. As one of the Three—Roosevelt, Churchill, Stalin—he had already achieved military conquest. But his other great task is unfinished—to help to weld the world into a unity for peace that none will dare break. He saw the need for that as clearly as he saw the other two perils. The lesson is for us who survive to carry on the Torch, and the road lies by way of ever stronger and better relations with America on the one hand and Russia and China on the other. What each of us can do seems small; but it is worth doing. In a war in which so many of our best men have perished, he has given his life alongside them in the same cause. It is for us who survive to make the new world worthy of them.

Heart of the Empire Mourns America's President

IN ST. PAUL'S CATHEDRAL BRITAIN PAID TRIBUTE to the memory of President Roosevelt at a solemn memorial service on April 17, 1945. Among those who had assembled to mourn the loss of the great American statesman were Their Majesties the King and Queen, Princess Elizabeth, the Archbishop of Canterbury, the Prime Minister and Cabinet, Dominion leaders, high officers of the British and U.S. Services, Queen Wilhelmina of the Netherlands, King Haakon of Norway, King George of Greece, and King Peter of Yugoslavia. *Photo, P.N.A.*

Scandinavia's Post-War Position and Policy

It may be said, without any reflection on his good sense, that the average reader is not too well informed concerning the present or the future of the chief Baltic countries which have played such widely different rôles in this war—Norway, Sweden, Denmark and Finland—but in the coming resettlement of Europe their importance cannot be overstated. This article, which has been written at the suggestion of the Editor by Mr. HENRY BAERLEIN, will help the reader to a better understanding of the problems awaiting solution in Scandinavia and the Baltic generally.

THERE used to be some idea that a Scandinavian Federation would be very desirable from every point of view, since the three Scandinavian realms would thus strengthen their international position. This view the statesmen of those countries no longer hold, for they have no quarrel with Russia and no desire to antagonize her. This they might do by coming together in such a Federation, or by adhering to an Atlantic Union.

If, unhappily, we are going to see the formation of West and East blocks, then it will be necessary for the Scandinavians to continue with their old policy of neutrality, avoiding a too close association with either side. They intend to keep out of such blocks, always excepting that of an international peace organization.

There was a time—not so far distant—when Sweden and Finland, owing to the many conflicts of the past, were filled with suspicion of Russia. The moderation which Russia has displayed towards Finland, despite the grave injury done her in recent years by the subservience of the now discredited Finnish rulers to the Germans, has had an excellent effect in Sweden.

The reparations Finland will have to make are onerous, and understandably so, for Russia has demanded not merely wood and the other ordinary Finnish products, but machinery and ships that will oblige the Finns to borrow capital in Sweden. Be it noted here that Swedish credits for reconstruction amount now to nearly 20 per cent of her annual income. Most of her neighbours are in need of much reconstructive work.

SCANDINAVIA AND THE BALTIC. Map illustrating the geographical relationship of the North European countries whose post-war position is discussed in this page.

WHAT the Swedes desire is the establishment of firm trade relations with Russia, from whom they wish to import flax, hemp, linseed, and so forth, while Russia wants to purchase Swedish electric machinery and railway rolling stock. Arrangements to send vast quantities of wood-pulp to Britain from Sweden have already been made, but cargoes of this bulk cannot slip through on those small, swift vessels whose runs from Sweden to this country have aroused such admiration.

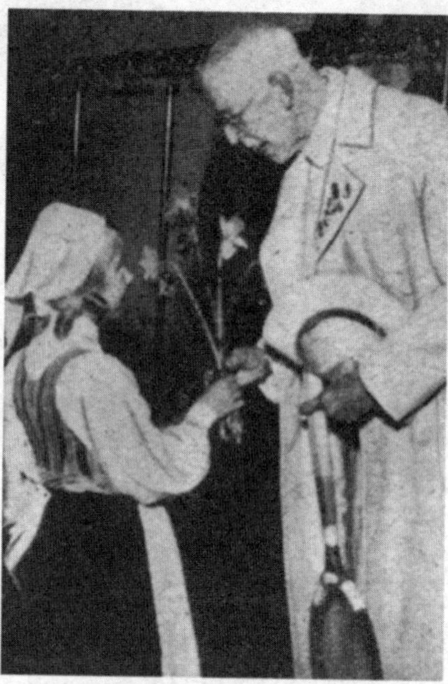

KING GUSTAV V of Sweden, 87 years old in June 1945, has been a monarch for over 37 years—a record for his country. Still an ardent tennis player, he is seen being congratulated by a Swedish girl. *Photo, Planet News*

There used to be some notion that, while the Norwegians are a most democratic people, the Swedes are not, and that they incline towards totalitarian ideals. There can be no greater mistake. Less than two per cent of the Swedes are pro-Nazi; their champion, the old explorer Sven Hedin, is now a very lonely person in Stockholm. At the last General Election to the Riksdag in 1940, when the Germans were at the height of their success, the Swedish Nazis did not dare to put up a single candidate. The present Government is a coalition, predominantly Social-Democratic, and embracing all parties except the Communists, who with 15 members out of 230 are now fairly strong, and, of course, full of enthusiasm for any closer connexion with Russia.

A FORMAL union between all the Scandinavian countries does not appear to them to bring with it any great advantages. But they are resolved on the most intimate co-operation. For instance, Sweden will give all possible assistance in the rehabilitation of Norway. It is not yet known how much will be required, though the Germans have threatened to destroy every harbour, power-station and factory in Norway. Anyhow, in Denmark it seems that Sweden's task will be easier; there, less fighting and bombing have taken place, though sabotage has caused a good deal of devastation.

Instead of a formal federation, a monetary and customs union is within the range of possibilities. There is also a very strong feeling for the removal of labour barriers, so that anyone in search of work shall be free to go from his own Scandinavian country to any other country. Before this war a start had been made to standardize the equipment and co-ordinate the war industries of these northern countries; and this will be taken up again and further developed, as one branch of the economic co-operation that is the aim of all Scandinavians.

With regard to the attitude of these countries to the post-war Germany, it seems doubtful as to whether Norway or Denmark will have men to spare for the occupation of that country. Sweden, as a non-belligerent, will not be called upon to do so, though she may be asked to police the areas of plebiscites, as she did in the Saar after the 1914-18 war. But problems will arise owing to the non-existence of an active and productive Germany. Fortunately the Polish coal-mines have not been injured, and if transport can be found we may soon see shipments taking place from Poland's new port of Danzig.

Kiel Canal Internationalized?

As for measures for the future security of these regions: in 1918, despite the defeat of Germany, the Baltic remained a German inland sea. Versailles reduced the German navy so that it could not compete with the navies of the Western Powers on the high seas, but it left it strong enough to make the Danish straits inaccessible and to rule the Baltic. The annexation of Slesvig-Holstein in 1866 had eliminated the chance of that province being used by an enemy for an attack on Germany, while the Kiel Canal doubled the strength of the German fleet by enabling it, unseen and unmolested, to pass into the North Sea or the Baltic.

By her control of the Baltic, Germany has been able to separate Western Europe from the East, the industrialized regions that would be an arsenal of any anti-German coalition from Eastern Europe, the reservoir of man-power and raw materials. (Of course, in this war such considerations have become rather out of date, owing to Russian industry in the Urals and beyond, and because of the man-power of the United States, a condition of affairs which the Nazis protest against as utterly unfair.)

The Kiel Canal will have to be internationalized after the war. Russia, Poland and Czechoslovakia are greatly concerned in maintaining this direct communication with Western Europe, while Britain will need to have this route to Central Europe. Both commercial and political considerations will therefore call for a mixed defence of the Baltic route. Not only will Germany have to surrender Bismarck's loot of Slesvig-Holstein, but islands in the Baltic and the North Sea, where military bases must be created to control German ports and protect Denmark and the rest of Scandinavia from another invasion. Airfields will have to be at the disposal of the occupying Powers.

DENMARK will understand the geopolitical similarity between Egypt, the Republic of Panama and herself. The Allied Powers cannot allow these canals to fall under enemy influence; and there are reasons to believe that Denmark, after the experiences of this war, will realize that the Powers concerned cannot allow Germany, because of Denmark's weakness, to control straits which are so important to the security of Europe. She will therefore, one supposes, grant necessary rights in her territory to the Powers capable of maintaining the defence of that region.

Slesvig-Holstein, owing to its size and position, would be the natural centre of the whole system. Use would be made of the various islands in the North Sea and the Baltic, while the Danish island of Bornholm could be an intermediary base; its size and position make it suitable for the anti-invasion defence of Sweden and for the naval and air protection of convoys passing to and fro

Photos, British Official, Keystone

No More are Our Bombers Interested in Hamm

Heavy bomber raids on Münster's railway yards and sidings caused vast damage: a locomotive and tender reacted to one bomb in this grotesque fashion (1). The town, administrative centre of Westphalia, was entered by Allied troops on April 2, 1945. After many visits the R.A.F. used 10-ton bombs on the famous marshalling yards at Hamm, railway nerve-centre in the Ruhr, where civilians took refuge in this massive concrete shelter (2); the town (3) was finally cleared on April 6.

The R.A.F. Went Many Times to Essen and—

Remains of the great Krupps plant, a prime target in the Ruhr, were taken over by the U.S. 9th Army on April 9, 1945. Bomber Command had already been there—with 14 saturation raids. A 1,000-lb. bomb hurled the bronze statue of frock-coated Herr Alfred Krupp (1812–1887) from its granite plinth to the bottom of a crater (1). No complete gun of any kind left the works after the raid of July 26, 1944: one of the many unfinished pieces (2).

Photo

—Left Krupps Armament Works Like This

Official

Covering an area of 2¼ miles by 1,500 yards, the factory, with its 50,000 workers, turned out high-grade steel—at one time 42,000 tons a day—and guns, locomotives, crankshafts for aero engines, and other armaments. After the last R.A.F. raid, in daylight on March 11, 1945, production ceased entirely. This air view of the tangled devastation that was Krupps shows no sign of life: the power, if not the will, to give birth to more death is crushed.

Both Sides of the Picture in Beaten Germany

Photos, British Newspaper Pool, Keystone

The Nazi military machine loses its cogs in very large numbers and with great rapidity: above are a few of the 2,000,000 prisoners taken by the Allies between the Normandy landings and April 1945. At a ceremonial parade (top) the same American flag which flew over Fort Ehrenbreitstein during the Occupation after the last war, was hoisted there again on April 6, in the presence of Gen. Omar Bradley; in the background is Coblenz, and the Moselle where it joins the Rhine.

VIEWS & REVIEWS Of Vital War Books

by **Hamilton Fyfe**

High Adventure in the Desert War

"WAR is hell!" said Sherman, one of the most famous American generals of last century, and in a broad way everyone would now admit that to be true. But for some few who take part in it war provides a good deal of fun. If, as Alan Moorehead once put it, a man "has a taste for piracy and high adventure," war offers him opportunities which he could not hope for in peacetime.

Moorehead was writing about a force that operated in North Africa, leading a life of its own, engaged on duties that had to be kept secret, contributing valuably all the time to the defeat of the Nazis and Italians which was completed in Tunisia. At the time Moorehead wrote, very little could be told about this force; but now the censorship has been lifted and in Long Range Desert Group (Collins, 12s. 6d.) Major W. B. Kennedy Shaw, who was its able Intelligence Officer, tells almost the whole story of its doings between 1940 and 1943.

It is not altogether creditable to our military chiefs. Neither at the War Office nor at British headquarters in Cairo was the need for a force of this rapidly moving daredevil kind foreseen. "Had the Germans been in our place," says Major Kennedy Shaw, "would they not have seen war with Italy as at least a very considerable probability" and have gathered together men who knew the desert well already, so that they might be ready when the moment came? One of these men who had done a great deal of exploration in Libya was Major (now Brigadier) Bagnold. Three times Bagnold had to suggest that such a force should be formed. Only after Italy had come into the war was his scheme accepted. He set to work to collect men and machines for the task. One of the first he roped in was the author of Long Range Desert Group.

He also secured the loan of a number of New Zealanders, and "there can be no doubt whatever that much of the early and continued success of L.R.D.G. was due to the speed and thoroughness with which the New Zealanders learned desert life and work." There was a great deal to be learned even by these Dominion farmers "with a maturity and independence not found in Britishers of similar age, and with that inherent superiority which in most of a man's qualities the countryman will always have over the townsman." They had to master not only the technics of desert warfare but the art of keeping alive, of overcoming "the appalling difficulties of Nature—heat, thirst, cold, rain, fatigue."

HEAT was probably most trying of all. When a certain wind blows over the sand . . .

> You don't merely feel hot, you don't merely feel tired, you feel as if every bit of energy has left you, as if your brain was thrusting its way through the top of your head and you want to lie down in a stupor till the accursed sun has gone down.

Scarcity of water, dust storms, a glare that "shrivels you to a cinder in summer and puts but little warmth into the winter winds," were worse enemies than the Italians, worse even than the Nazis. In some places flies were "beyond belief," though camp cleanliness could keep them down. "Scorpions and snakes added to the hazards of existence." Air attack was the one real danger from man. To take cover in the desert is impossible unless there are rocks or gullies into which a car can be wedged. But if the aircraft could be heard or seen while you were out on the flat, the thing to do was to stop. A motionless vehicle is very hard to spot from the air. Unfortunately, some cars were spotted by R.A.F. planes and mistaken for an enemy patrol.

The first task the L.R.D.G. undertook was to watch what the Italians were doing in the interior of Libya. They were, as a rule, doing nothing. The Italians had no maps of their own territory—at any rate, none which were of any use to them, or to us when we captured them. They were purely imaginary. "The mountains were all high, as became the dignity of Fascist Italy. Making our way anxiously towards an obviously impassable range of hills, we would find we had driven over it without feeling the bump." One outstanding example of this was a map supposed to represent a place called Jalo. The map-maker, an officer of the Survey Department, was, says the author sarcastically, "a realist I am sure. Jalo, he felt, was a one-eyed hole, of which no map was really needed. The sand was soft and the day was hot, so why worry? He put his feet up on the mess table, shouted for another drink, and drew his map." Its inaccuracies were so absurd that it might have been thought to be a ruse to mislead our forces, but "it seems hardly likely the Italians were thinking of that as long ago as 1931!"

THE author shows nothing but contempt for Mussolini's troops. They tried to win the war by using catchwords, slogans, hot-air phrases. Everywhere on forts, barracks, houses were such words as "Believe, obey, fight!" . . . "The Duce is always right," . . . "With the Duce we shall conquer." But few of them put up much of a fight even when there were 500,000 of them against about 10,000 of us. Their officers simply did not know what to do with them.

Very different were the French—"these outlaws from France, the officers of the Senegalese Fusilier Regiment from Lake Chad; reckless, gay in spite of their misfortunes, and with one object in life—to get their teeth into the Boche."

> Yet for all their dash and courage one could not but notice some of the traits which must have helped to bring France to the Armistice in 1940, a spirit of *je m'enfoutisme* about the dull things like discipline, good Q-work, and the maintenance of vehicles, aircraft and equipment, which go so far to win modern battles.

THE Q problem—that is, the problem of supplies for the L.R.D.G.—was handled by a New Zealander named Barrett, a forty-year-old lawyer in peacetime, with magnificent ability. He had a very difficult task. Instead of sending twenty or thirty miles for what he needed, which was the usual distance for ordinary units, he had to send two or three hundred. Where other Quartermasters thought in days, he had to think in weeks or months. Yet he never failed the Desert Group. They got pretty nearly all they asked for, including sheepskin coats and sandals such as are worn on the Indian North-West Frontier. Wearing these on their feet, with month-old beards thick with sand and a month's dirt, since the water ration allowed none for washing; with skin burned to the colour of coffee, and clad only in a pair of torn shorts, they "looked like creatures from some other world."

Keeping the Group supplied with petrol was one bad headache in itself. "The loss by leakage was very high. Enough petrol must have been wasted in the Western Desert to run all the buses in London for months or years." Why was this? Because "the Army had unfortunately equipped itself in peacetime only for a war in England where petrol-pumps abound." The Germans used a strong, unleaking tin container with a good pouring lip, which was soon copied, but in the copying the pouring lip was forgotten or deliberately left out. So the German container was still the best.

That the Group did most useful work admits of no doubt. Commanders-in-Chief have thanked them profusely. Did they also get more fun out of life than men belonging to more ordinary units? Summing up, Major Kennedy Shaw puts on the credit side that they had the best food in the Middle East, their work was always interesting and often exciting, they were almost completely free from drills, guards and fatigues, and endured a minimum of being "mucked about." Against that was the strain of operating almost continually behind the enemy's lines, never returning to base for a long refit and rest, and suffering as a result from weariness, desert sores, and occasional irritation. It is clear that in spite of these heavy debit items a favourable balance was struck.

NEW ZEALAND PATROL of the famous Long Range Desert Group, the story of whose exploits in the Western Desert between 1940 and 1943 is revealed in the book reviewed in this page. Staffed by picked troops, all experts in guerilla tactics, these motorized columns performed magnificent deeds. *From a drawing by Captain Peter McIntyre (New Zealand Official artist) reproduced by courtesy of the New Zealand Government.*

All Reichsbank's Bullion Seized in Salt Mine

GERMANY'S ENTIRE GOLD RESERVE, millions of pounds in other currencies, and priceless art treasures, were seized by Gen. Patton's U.S. 3rd Army, in a salt mine 700 yards deep at Merkers, 30 miles south of Mulhausen, it was disclosed on April 8, 1945. An illuminated sign announced "Heil Hitler!" (1). A U.S. officer inspected valuable paintings (2) which had not even been crated; while a Reichsbank official, left in charge, helped troops to count the sacks of gold (3) which had been so craftily and carefully hidden away.

Photos, Sport & General, Associated Press

How the Airborne Men of Arnhem Were Avenged

THE FAMOUS BRIDGE at Arnhem (1), which the British 1st Airborne Division fought so valiantly to hold in September 1944, fell to our 2nd Army when the Netherlands town was cleared on April 15, 1945, after the bridge had been blown up by the Nazis. Against this final assault Arnhem was defended with the utmost ferocity; before our men reached the centre it had been set ablaze by the Nazis in retreat.

Armed with Sten guns, and against the background of a burning hotel (2), our troops had a tough task winkling-out snipers left to infest the smouldering ruins. Near the bridge, a Netherlands policeman laid flowers on the grave (3) of a British parachutist, killed in the September fighting, whose steel helmet crowns the simple wooden cross on which is inscribed in German, "An Unknown English Soldier." In readiness for the onslaught our troops embarked on landing craft (4) before sailing up the Rhine. (See also pages 366-370, Vol. 8.)

Photos, British Official, British Newspaper Pool, Associated Press

EAST AFRICA—Its Warriors Aid the Empire

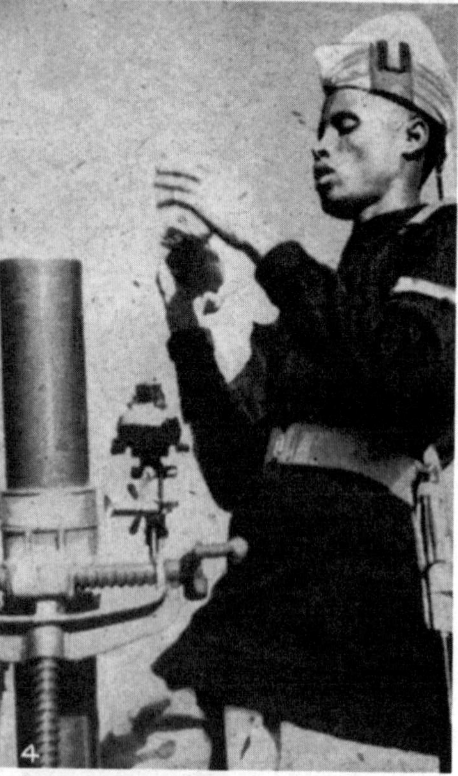

MOBILE PROPAGANDA UNIT of East Africa Command became bogged in a rain-swollen river and had to be hauled ashore by men and oxen (1). This unit travelled nearly 60,000 miles in 2½ years, teaching more than 750,000 people how to help the war effort. It consists of 24 African Askaris led by two white officers and two N.C.O.s. A corporal of the King's African Rifles demonstrates (2) the uses, for war purposes, of the water buffalo ; contrast between old and new East African warriors was emphasized by the striking figures of a Nyasaland Ngoni in tribal dress (3), and a Somali operating a 3-in. mortar (4). Askaris of the 11th E. African Division distinguished themselves at Kalemyo and Kalewa, on the Burma front. See also page 619, Vol. 7. *Photos, British Official*

8th Army Men and Mules in Mountain Warfare

FIGHTING IN THE HEIGHTS OF NORTHERN ITALY, troops of the 8th Army were specially trained in mountain warfare. While pack-mules —seen above being loaded with supplies for forward positions—carried food and ammunition, each man of this battalion bore a pack of 100 lb. in addition to a Bren gun weighing 25 lb.—half the load carried by a mule. Bologna, opening the way to the central plains, fell on April 21, 1945, to the 5th and 8th Armies, who three days later forced a crossing of the River Po. See also story in p. 602, Vol. 8. *Photo, British Official*

From Arakan to Arnhem Their Valour Won V.C.s

Cpl. J. W. HARPER
In Holland on September 29, 1944, leading the assault by his platoon of the Hallamshire Battalion of the York and Lancaster Regiment against a strong enemy post and defying heavy spandau and mortar fire, Corporal Harper was mortally wounded. But the position was taken.

Capt. J. H. C. BRUNT, M.C.
During fierce counter-attacks against his battalion of the Sherwood Foresters in Italy on December 4, 1944, Capt. Brunt "was always to be found moving from one post to another, encouraging the men and firing any weapon he could find." He was killed next day.

Sqd.-Ldr. R. A. M. PALMER, D.F.C.
Bomber-pilot hero of over 100 dangerous missions, Squadron-Leader Palmer was missing after a hazardous daylight operation over Cologne in December 1944, when he led his formation to raid the marshalling yards. Utterly ignoring risk, he pressed home the attack, his plane ablaze.

L/Cpl. H. E. HARDEN
Against almost hopeless odds, this N.C.O. of the R.A.M.C. three times led a stretcher party to the rescue of Royal Marine Commandos wounded in action in north-west Europe on January 23, 1945, and brought them in. He was fatally wounded.

Sepoy BHANDARI RAM
In the Arakan on November 22, 1944, this young Sepoy of the 10th Baluch Regt., though severely wounded by bullets and grenade splinters, crawled to within five yards of a Japanese position, killing the occupants with a grenade and securing the enemy outpost.

Capt. L. E. QUERIPEL
On the road to Arnhem, Capt. Queripel of the 1st Airborne Division was last seen on September 19, 1944, covering the withdrawal of his men. Although badly wounded, he insisted on remaining behind, armed with only his pistol and a few grenades.

Fusilier DENNIS DONNINI
This 19-year-old private of the Royal Scots Fusiliers, though wounded in an assault on enemy positions between the Rivers Roer and Maas on January 18, 1945, with superb self-sacrifice drew the enemy fire from his comrades to himself. He died from wounds.

Flight-Sergeant G. THOMPSON
Trapped in a blazing Lancaster, in which he was the wireless operator, during the raid on the Dortmund-Ems Canal on January 1, 1945, he rescued two of his companions overcome with fumes and flames, later dying from his injuries.

Lieut. J. H. GRAYBURN
Ordered to seize and hold the Rhine bridge at Arnhem on September 18, 1944, Lieut. Grayburn of the Parachute Regiment, though badly wounded, for three days led his men "with supreme gallantry and determination." He was killed directing a withdrawal.

Photos, British Official, Gilbert Bowley, Daily Mirror, G.P.U., Topical Press

I WAS THERE! Eye Witness Stories of the War

The Germans Cringed to Us in Captured Hanover

This great provincial city of 250,000 Germans, 60,000 slaves and 300 British prisoners of war fell on April 10, 1945, to a company of U.S. infantrymen, and the Americans lost fewer than ten men in taking it. James Wellard's story is given by arrangement with The Daily Express.

We drove into Hanover along the 80 ft. wide Reichsautobahn, which sweeps across the rolling countryside in two double lane traffic highways separated by a wide strip of grass. The Germans had only blown one bridge on the road, but snipers were still in the woods on either side. This was all the resistance we met going into this great city.

We travelled at 70 miles an hour until we came to the city limits. Here vast multitudes of slave workers were pouring out of the factories to welcome us. They had already acquired hundreds of bicycles and were starting down the road westwards. Some were riding in German cars until they ran out of petrol. Hundreds were swarming over the smashed marshalling yards looting the railway trucks of leather and canned foods.

They had raised the flags of Russia, Belgium and France in their concentration camps. In the heart of the city along the miles of streets I saw not one undamaged house, except for the great Rathaus (Town Hall). There are 60 deep shelters in the city and most of the remaining 250,000 civilians were still in them, not yet daring to come out. The American military governor, a young Jewish captain, Herbert Fried, of Chicago, told me that there is a minor epidemic of diphtheria and smallpox in the city

Driving down one of Hanover's wide, rubble-lined streets I saw a company of 60 Germans marching west without a guard. In a public square 15 high-ranking officers lay on the grass, guarded by an American soldier. Other U.S. infantrymen were looking for General Lohring, who was reported to be hiding in a cellar.

Sniping, except for stray shots outside the city, was negligible. We drove all over Hanover without difficulty, welcomed with cheers and gifts from slave workers, who had practically taken over the city. Outside the Rathaus, where the Allied Military Government had just moved in, I met two British Tommies standing guard, on the orders of Captain Fried. The Tommies escaped yesterday from a British prisoners' camp along the road. One said, "My greatest moment was when Captain Fried told me to guard a German major who had just been brought in from a cellar!"

Inside the palatial town hall, where Oberburgermeister Bouenner worked, I saw a number of cringing Germans waiting outside Captain Fried's door. Most of them were in the smart green uniform of the German security police. They said they had come for orders and wished to work with the Americans. Captain Fried sent them out with their arms full of proclamations to stick up on walls.

The chief of the Nazi police still wore a Wehrmacht field cap, which, together with his Nazified uniform, looked to me like the wrong kind of garb to be wandering round Hanover in, as infantrymen with rifles cocked were still strolling through the town. Captain Fried said: "We have not had time yet to get them out of their uniforms. They will just have to hope for the best."

The Nazi police chief kept doffing his Wehrmacht cap to the young Jewish captain. The German was true to type and had a square, shining bald head and heavy face. He went off with his load of proclamations, which announced that the Americans had "come as conquerors." The police chief told us that 60 per cent of Hanover had been destroyed by bombing. All of us agreed this was an under-estimate.

The food situation was said to be very bad—only enough for three days. Electricity was still on, so was water. There was one large military hospital with thousands of wounded, including Americans and British. Hanover's entire police force of 800 had been told by the Nazis to stay behind. They were almost crawling on their stomachs before Captain Fried and his three assistants.

It appears that the Nazis are now abandoning even their high officials in their eagerness to get away, and in Hanover we have captured the entire administration and practically every piece of civilian and military machinery. So the city is full of Nazis.

The 300 British prisoners of war we found were in the notorious death march from Poland. They were all safe, though two days ago four men died of dysentery, and were left by the Germans unburied. Two prisoners told me their treatment during the last months had been "terrible and inhuman." Men were dying from dysentery and were given no adequate food or medical attention. These two were like skeletons.

I Saw World's Biggest Armament Plant in Ruins

Krupps was the most important part of Essen, the biggest city of the industrial Ruhr. It was knocked completely out of the war, when Ronald Knox, News Chronicle correspondent, visited the great works—a series of husks—and wrote this story on April 11. See also illus. pages 16-17.

We walked, in the glorious sunshine of a clear spring day, through the almost indescribable destruction to which this vast factory had been reduced by bombing. Driving into the Ruhr, where the horizon is striped with tall chimneys, no longer smoking, you sniffed the wind, already heavy with the smell of gasworks, mines and burnt-out buildings and dead things. But on the green strips of earth amid the

AT HANOVER THE NAZIS CAMOUFLAGED A LARGE LAKE, the Machsee, by covering it with floating wooden slats strung closely together to resemble solid earth, and dotting this foundation with imitation trees. The ingenious, if laborious, ruse failed, however, to deceive the keen eyes of R.A.F. aircrews, and part of it was blown up. Hanover fell to troops of the U.S. 9th Army, who rode into it on captured enemy half-tracked vehicles. See story above, and illus. page 4; also page 654, Vol. 8. *Photo, British Official*

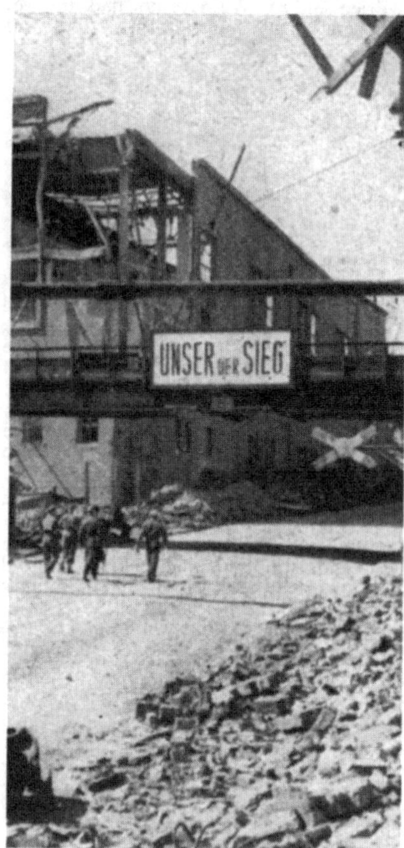

INSIDE CAPTURED KRUPPS, Allied officers on a tour of inspection passed under a foot-bridge bearing a painted Nazi slogan—"Victory is Ours." *Photo, British Official*

factory wastes fruit trees blossomed in defiant beauty, and there were larks singing like mad overhead. The roads were lined with German people returning to their homes, wheeling or carrying their possessions, and with groups of released slave workers heading for their homes in many lands.

Essen itself was not easy to get at until you found the way, for many streets were blocked by railway bridges that had fallen into them and often the road bridges had fallen into the canals. This kind of German demolition has been on the grand scale. But we nosed a way through it at last, and drove under the trailing electric wires and past a covey of shattered trams into the wreckage of Essen. Essen is another story of a German city blasted and burned almost out of existence.

It was Krupps we had come to see, so we drove on through the rubble-blocked streets, where white flags hung from the windows. If we were not sure of the route there was always a German eager to direct us. How these people respect conquerors! When you reach the sprawling Krupp plant there is a sort of ornamental entrance at one side, something like the Admiralty Arch, in London, only in brick.

At the top of some steps there are the remains of a plinth on which stood a bronze Herr Alfred Krupp, 1812-1887. Alfred now lies flat on his back at the bottom of a large bomb crater beside the granite plinth. It is a fine monument in reverse (see illus. p. 16). After a visit to Alfred you come to the workshops. It is useless to go on attempting to describe endless destruction. Every one of the shops is wrecked.

The walls have fallen and everywhere steel girders, roofing, chimneys and machinery lie in tangled masses. You can see where repairs have been made and this reconstruction has in turn been wrecked. In places intricate machinery has been oiled, but most of it is broken, derelict and rusty. Huge masses of machinery for shaping steel in one way or another rear out of the wreckage.

Here and there a great gun barrel 60 feet in length stands rusting on its trestles. The picture of one shop is the story of them all, and there are one hundred of them. In the administration block, where all the offices are blast-wrecked, we found some of the company officials. We soon found that they remembered the dates of our bomb raids very, very well indeed.

One of the reasons for R.A.F. Bomber Command developing the system of sky marking and ground marking targets which could not be seen by the bomber crews was to get at Krupps. The plant had been bombed from March 1942, but it was not until the night of March 5-6, 1943, that the battle of the Ruhr really began. Krupps officials tell the rest of the story. Full-scale production ceased from March 5, 1943.

From then on repair work enabled production to be maintained at a varying level, but after October of 1944 only small-scale production was achieved in small parts of the works. Krupps were reduced to making parts and doing repairs. The 5,000-ton daylight raid by Bomber Command on March 11 last knocked out Krupps entirely except for some coal mining.

We found today that the gate-keepers were still guarding their gates and doors, if they were lucky to have a door or a gate left. The manager of the labour office who showed me some of the shops solemnly presented his pass, and the guardian solemnly examined it. We passed a group of grinning Russians.

The manager gave them a glance which displayed unrest, and said the Russians were becoming dangerous. They had, he said, got hold of guns. Last night he had 1,000 bottles of wine. Now—with such a shrug—he had none. He was visibly hurt when I asked him whether he was aware what the Germans had done to the Russians, and that these Russians had been brought into Germany by the Germans.

He thought that the military should deal with them. At the end of our tour of defeat and destruction this manager faced us, stared hard through his thick glasses; and said, "You comprehend. I do all you want of me, but there is no peace between us. I shall do my duty to the end."

How I Helped to Clear Messina's Depth Charges

Disinclined to kill, a young physics master volunteered for bomb disposal work. Since then, as Lieut. John Bridge, R.N.V.R., he has achieved fame as the only holder of the George Cross and George Medal with Bar. His story is reproduced by courtesy of the London Evening News.

I would certainly kill a German today and I would kill him with a great deal of satisfaction. It was my experience during the Plymouth blitz that completely altered my views. I was the second person to attempt to clear Messina Harbour of depth charges. The first was killed in the attempt.

I started my investigations of the depth charges on Wednesday, August 25, 1943. The point about these depth charges was that they contained a mechanism not previously encountered. Having located them successfully I sent for a diving suit, which arrived on Sunday night. I started diving early on Monday morning, cleared all the depth charges and succeeded in recovering two of them with their new mechanism intact by 11 o'clock on Thursday morning.

I learned my diving in South Africa. My longest spell was one of 20 hours. I did not suffer any particular discomfort. You see, when I am working on an important job I always feel 100 per cent fit and never get tired. I leave that to afterwards.

There wasn't very much shelling at the time. In fact, it never became necessary to suspend diving operations because of enemy shell-fire. I was the only man diving, but I had an assistant and a number of men working above water. Two of them got George Medals. One was Acting Petty Officer Woods, of London; the other, Able Seaman Thomas Peters, of Liverpool.

Lieut. JOHN BRIDGE, R.N.V.R., of Warrington, Lancs, whose courageous deeds have won him the unique distinction of being the only recipient of the George Cross and George Medal with Bar. Some of his exploits are recorded above. *Photo, Daily Mirror*

As the result of clearing Messina Harbour we were able to work the ferry to the Italian beaches, which meant that three landing-ship tanks were got across safely. In view of the circumstances it was one of my most difficult jobs, but I don't regard it as the most dangerous. That was during the Plymouth blitz, when I spent two hours on a time-bomb that was ticking away all the time.

It was Lieutenant Bridge—so far referred to only as "a British Naval lieutenant"—whose courage prevented the Germans at Nijmegen from carrying out one of the most daring acts of the war. This was the German attempt on the night of September 28, 1944, to destroy the bridges spanning the River Waal and so cut communication between the British troops fighting north of the river and the supply areas south of it. Two twin-torpedoes of floating high-explosive charges, equipped with time fuses, were sent against the road bridge. Lieutenant Bridge stripped to his underpants and dived in after the first charge had exploded. He explored the piers supporting the bridge until he found the second charge, which was hauled out and rendered harmless a few seconds before it was timed to explode. And so the bridge was saved.

It was the first time this type of sabotage had been used. My main difficulty was to find where the charge was located.

We Are the Royal Navy's Pioneer Rocketeers

That is the unofficial title conferred upon Lieut.-Cmdr. C. W. T. Blackman, R.N.V.R., and Lieut. C. L. P. Moore, R.N.V.R., both associated with the Navy's rocket craft from the first experimental stage. Lieut.-Cmdr. Blackman, who took part in the invasion of Sicily, when these craft first went into action, tells his story, followed by Lieut. Moore.

We were all a little nervous as to how the craft were going to behave in actual battle. With thousands of our invasion troops already approaching the beaches as we went in to saturate with high explosive enemy territory only a few hundred yards ahead of them, we knew there was not the slightest margin for error. We were the happiest men in the Navy after the success of the Sicilian operations, and we went on with a new-found confidence to repeat the success at Reggio, Salerno, Anzio and the South of France.

Not only the enemy were surprised by the new weapon. One naval captain taking part in the Sicilian invasion was overheard to remark "Thank goodness they're here, but what are they?" After their first performance the rocket craft were a source of inspiration to the troops in subsequent landings. It became a much safer proposition for them to put foot on enemy soil after they had seen enemy defences blown to pieces by the rocket salvos.

A battery of 80-millimetre cannon, concealed in a wood, was giving our troops a great deal of trouble. We brought the rocket craft into position and poured our salvos into the trees. The effect was immediate. All opposition ceased and what few of the enemy survived could be seen scurrying like scared rabbits out of the wood. When a rocket craft goes into action all the ship's company, with the exception of the commanding officer who controls the firing mechanism from a protected position on the bridge, go below decks.

As the salvos are fired there is a deafening roar like that of an express train and a blinding sheet of red flame envelops the steel deck. Sometimes it is not possible to see the rockets reach their target because of the overhanging cloak of smoke and the choking cordite fumes. The decks would get red-hot from the back-fire but for the automatic water spray. After a succession of salvos the decks are steaming—with boiling water!

Interesting episodes in the early development of rocket craft were recalled by Lieut. Moore, who, as gunnery officer, has been concerned with the study and development of the rocket-firing apparatus both in experiments and actual battle:

We had no known gunnery rules to guide us in the behaviour of the new weapon. During the tests everybody was clad in asbestos suits. Now only one man remains above deck controlling the fire from the protection of something which looks like a telephone kiosk. We had a few casualties in those early days—one of them an Army colonel collaborating with the Royal Navy. Although he was sheltering behind the flash screen, the back-flash found him and whipped off his luxuriant moustache. All he suffered was a loss of dignity!

The first six rocket craft to go into battle made their own way for 3,000 miles from England to the scene of operations. One of the most anxious times for the ship's companies was not in battle at all.

They had to load up with rockets at a North African base. The heat was terrific and the rockets became so hot that the men had to handle them wearing gloves. The rockets were already fused ready for firing, but they were safe to handle so long as the temperature kept below 130 degrees. When the thermometer rose to 127 degrees a strange silence fell over the loading party, but they went on working as though no danger threatened. Fortunately, the thermometer did not rise further and the job in due course was completed.

For the practice shoot preceding the Sicilian invasion a small island in the Mediterranean was chosen as target. The only difficulty was presented by the sole occupants, an aged man and his wife who had never left the island and refused to do so when requested by the Navy! Compromise was reached when the couple transferred themselves and their possessions to the other side of the island—and stayed there until the completion of the shoot.

As to the rocket crafts' part in the D-Day assault on the Normandy beaches, in the space of three or four minutes one flotilla fired such an immense number of rockets that practically all enemy resistance was wiped out on that particular sector. And we ran in so close to the shore during the assault on Walcheren that the six-in. guns of an enemy battery, although at maximum depression, were unable to hit us. But after firing our rockets we had to run the gauntlet.

We crammed on so much speed in making our getaway that the exhaust heat in some of the craft burned holes in the funnels. Only one craft, which struck a mine, was lost, but some of the others were so peppered with shot that they looked more like colanders.

OUR DIARY OF THE WAR

APRIL 11, Wednesday *2,048th day*

Western Front.—9th Army reached the Elbe near Magdeburg and entered Brunswick. Coburg captured by 3rd Army. 7th Army entered Schweinfurt. Canadians captured Deventer and made assault crossing of Ijssel.

Air.—Allied bombers attacked rail targets, airfields and oil storage depots in southern Germany.

Russian Front.—In Vienna, Soviet troops forced the Danube canal.

Italy.—8th Army troops broke out from Senio bridge-head and reached River Santerno.

General.—Von Papen, former German Chancellor, captured in Ruhr pocket.

APRIL 12, Thursday *2,049th day*

Western Front.—9th Army crossed the Elbe, S.E. of Magdeburg. Weimar and Neustadt occupied by 3rd Army; Erfurt cleared. Troops of 2nd Army captured Celle. 7th Army took Heilbronn.

Italy.—8th Army crossed Santerno River in strength.

Japan.—Super-Fortresses bombed aircraft works at Tokyo and industrial targets at Koriyama.

General.—President Roosevelt died suddenly.

APRIL 13, Friday *2,050th day*

Western Front.—Jena captured by 3rd Army, Duisburg by 9th.

Air.—U.S. fighters destroyed 266 German aircraft near Neumunster. R.A.F. bombed Kiel at night.

Russian Front.—Vienna captured by Marshal Tolbukhin's forces.

Japan.—Super-Fortresses made incendiary raid on Tokyo

Far East.—Carrier-aircraft of British Pacific Fleet attacked airfields on Formosa.

APRIL 14, Saturday *2,051st day*

Western Front.—Arnhem captured by British troops. Canadians entered Groningen. Dortmund cleared. 3rd Army captured Bayreuth.

France.—U.S. bombers made heavy attack on German positions in Gironde estuary.

Air.—R.A.F. bombers heavily attacked Potsdam.

APRIL 15, Sunday *2,052nd day*

Western Front.—In Holland, Canadian units reached North Sea. U.S. 1st Army captured Leuna.

France.—Land and sea attacks by French forces on Gironde pocket. 2nd Armoured Division entered Royan.

APRIL 16, Monday *2,053rd day*

Western Front.—Groningen surrendered to Canadians. 7th Army entered Nuremberg.

Air.—Lancasters bombed naval units at Swinemunde, sinking pocket-battleship Lützow.

Italy.—5th Army launched attack south of Bologna.

Burma.—Taungup, last Japanese coastal supply base in Arakan, captured.

Japan.—Tokyo again attacked by Super-Fortresses with incendiary bombs.

APRIL 17, Tuesday *2,054th day*

Air.—Allied bombers attacked railway targets near Dresden, Nuremberg and Pilsen, and oil depot near Prague. Mosquitoes made low-level attack on Gestapo H.Q. at Odense, Denmark.

Russian Front.—Soviet troops captured Austrian oil centre of Zistersdorf.

Japan.—Six airfields on Kyushu bombed by Super-Fortresses.

APRIL 18, Wednesday *2,055th day*

Western Front.—Canadian spearheads reached Zuider Zee. U.S. 3rd Army crossed Czech frontier. All Magdeburg west of Elbe fell to 9th Army. 1st Army entered Düsseldorf.

Netherlands.—German breached dyke west of Zuider Zee, causing floods in North Holland.

Air.—Nearly 1,000 R.A.F. bombers attacked Heligoland and airfield on Dune, and at night bombed railway yard at Komotau in Czechoslovakia.

Italy.—8th Army captured Argenta.

General.—Spanish Govt. prohibited landings of German aircraft.

APRIL 19, Thursday *2,056th day*

Western Front.—Leipzig finally fell to U.S. 1st Army. Resistance ended in Halle.

Air.—R.A.F. dropped 12,000-lb. bombs on Heligoland.

Russian Front.—Soviet High Command announced crossing of Neisse in Dresden direction, and setting up of bridge-head on Oder west of Kustrin. Polish troops captured Rothenburg.

Japan.—Mustangs made first attack on Atsugi air station, S.W. of Tokyo.

APRIL 20, Friday *2,057th day*

Western Front.—All organized resistance ended in Nuremberg. French 1st Army reached Rottweil.

Air.—Flying Fortresses attacked railway yards in Berlin area, Liberators in Munich-Prague area. At night Mosquitoes made six raids on Berlin; Soviet bombers also attacked the city.

Italy.—Units of 5th Army entered Po Valley west of Bologna.

APRIL 21, Saturday *2,058th day*

Western Front.—3rd Army captured Asch, Czechoslovakia. Troops of U.S. 1st Army entered Dessau.

Air.—Railway yards in Munich area bombed by U.S. aircraft from Britain and Italy.

Russian Front.—Zhukov's troops entered suburbs of Berlin. Koniev attacked N.E. of Dresden.

Italy.—Bologna captured by troops of 8th and 5th Armies.

General.—Twenty-year pact of mutual assistance signed by U.S.S.R. and Polish (Lublin) Government.

Burma.—All oilfields in Allied hands except for minor wells, with capture of Yenangyaung, main centre of production; two other centres, Chauk and Magwe, were cleared on April 18 and April 19 respectively.

APRIL 22, Sunday *2,059th day*

Western Front.—3rd Army launched drive into Bavaria towards Regensburg. 7th Army captured Danube bridge at Dillingen. French occupied Stuttgart and Freiburg and advanced to Swiss frontier.

Air.—R.A.F. Lancasters bombed Bremen.

Russian Front.—Soviet High Command announced capture of many Berlin suburbs, including Weissensee in the north-east, little more than three miles from Unter den Linden.

France.—Gen. de Gaulle visited French troops who cleared Gironde pockets at Royan and Pointe de Grave.

General.—Mr. Molotov, Soviet Foreign Commissar, arrived in Washington on way to San Francisco Conference.

APRIL 23, Monday *2,060th day*

Russian Front.—Zhukov's troops broke into Berlin from east after capturing Frankfort-on-Oder. Koniev's forces broke into Berlin from south after taking Cottbus, and also reached the Elbe.

Air.—Mosquitoes twice bombed Kiel and shipping at Travemunde.

Japan.—Super-Fortresses attacked aircraft works at Tashikawa, west of Tokyo.

Home Front.—Lighting restrictions removed over most of Britain.

General.—Czech Govt. called on army and civilians to rise.

APRIL 24, Tuesday *2,061st day*

Western Front.—British troops entered suburb of Bremen. U.S. and French troops captured Ulm.

Russian Front.—Troops of Zhukov's and Koniev's commands linked up in southern suburbs of Berlin.

Air.—R.A.F. bombers attacked rail centre of Bad Oldesloe, nr. Hamburg.

Italy.—Ferrara occupied by 8th Army, Modena and Spezia by 5th. Allied troops across the Po.

Flash-backs

1940

April 13. *Second battle of Narvik; seven German destroyers sunk.*

April 15. *Announced that British forces had landed in Norway.*

1941

April 13. *Germans occupied Belgrade,*

April 14. *Siege of Tobruk began.*

April 17. *Yugoslavia capitulated.*

April 23. *Greek Government moved from Athens to Crete.*

1942

April 16. *H.M. the King awarded the George Cross to Malta.*

April 18. *U.S. bombers from aircraft carrier Hornet raided Tokyo.*

April 24. *Exeter bombed in first of "Baedeker" reprisal raids.*

1943

April 12. *Sousse, port on Tunisian coast, occupied by 8th Army.*

April 21. *Enfidaville and Takrouna, Tunisia, captured by Allies.*

JET-PROPELLED ME 262, captured by U.S. 7th Army troops at Giebelstadt, near Frankfort-on-Main (cleared by March 28, 1945). Powered by two Junkers Jumo jet engines, it mounts four 30-mm. cannon and carries about 475 gallons of fuel. Speed is estimated at 500 m.p.h. Though primarily a fighter it is used for reconnaissance and can also carry two 500-lb. bombs. Tricycle landing-gear is fitted with front wheel well forward. *Photo, Associated Press*

THE WAR IN THE AIR

by Capt. Norman Macmillan, M.C., A.F.C.

THE climacteric in the war occasioned by the Allied advance deep into Germany from the West has brought new revelations and confirmed past theories. Knowledge denied to the German people is now known to the Allies from the indisputable evidence of materials accumulated in overrun dumps and factories.

Immense in value is this penetration of German war secrets, for through it the Allies gain information, while their own secrets remain undiscovered by the enemy. In the post-war years the Allies will have available to them the pool of world knowledge of armaments, whereas the Germans will know only what they themselves learned, and that was not good enough to win the war.

AT the German town of Losa, troops of the U.S. 1st Army found a depot containing more than 50,000 filled 550-lb. gas bombs, with a large number of bomb cases waiting to be filled. (See illus. p. 3.) Some of these bombs were reported to be filled with cyanogen chloride, reputed to be a nerve-paralysing gas. Others contained lung-injuring gas, phosgene, and tear gas. These bombs were brought to the Losa depot late in 1944. Faced with the complete air superiority of the Allies, the enemy dared not employ his gas weapon against the United Kingdom or Russia, for had he done so it must have resulted in the most terrible retaliation. It will be remembered that Mr. Churchill on more than one occasion has stated that if Germany used gas the R.A.F. was ready to make swift rejoinder. At Losa there was proof that Allied air power saved the world from the terror of aerial gas warfare.

FUSELAGES Constructed in a Salt Mine 900 Feet Underground

Second in importance is the proof of German underground factories. I remember before the war how sceptical many people were that Germany had then constructed factories underground. But at Tarthun the U.S. 9th Army discovered a factory equipped to manufacture Heinkel 162 jet-planes at the rate of 500 to 700 a month. This aircraft was stated by the director of the factory to have a speed of about 600 m.p.h. and a flight duration of about an hour. The factory was 900 feet underground in a salt mine. Here were built complete fuselages. Lifts brought them to the surface at night, and railways took them 15 miles to another secret factory, at Bernberg, for the installation of wings and engine. Above the Tarthun factory were peaceful-looking farms; the 2,000 factory workers were dispersed, and transport movement by road was kept to a minimum to escape detection by air reconnaissance.

THE capture of flying bombs and rocket bombs and launching ramps and sites; the seizure of multiple rocket-firing batteries on the French coast that were intended to bombard London with V3 120-lb. shells carrying a 40-lb. explosive charge at the rate of ten a minute; the capture almost intact of Messerschmitt 262 jet-plane fighters (see illus. above); and the seizure of archives of immense value must combine to devalue the secrecy of the German war effort.

There is now no doubt that the enormous effort expended by Germany to protect herself within the "Fortress of Europe" was denied opportunity of achieving success by the pounding of the enemy factories from the air during the tremendously steepened Allied air offensive from the spring of 1943 onwards. This delayed the German programme, and so gave the Allies time to build up for the invasion of Europe before the German defensive plans were completed. The great deflection of German man power into anti-aircraft defensive measures meant a further loss of man-hours in useful work to the German defence scheme.

THE last two years of war in the air have been significant for the victory of Allied orthodox air war over the German new-weapon air war. It is probable that this victory came just in time; in a few more years it might have been too late for the orthodox to challenge and defeat so decisively the new methods which have been evolved and which will affect future war—if the world does not abstain from this recurrent spectacle.

By April 12 more than half the aerodromes used by the Luftwaffe were in Allied hands; enemy aircraft had been evacuated during the preceding three weeks from west of Bremen to Sleswig-Holstein and Bavaria. At this date it was considered that Germany could put 1,000 aircraft into the air on the Western Front in sorties of 150–200 daily, if fuel were available. But already a great programme of daylight assaults on enemy aerodromes was in hand. On April 10, 5,600 Allied sorties were flown; 40 aircraft were lost (mostly due to flak), but 406 enemy aircraft were destroyed, 342 on the ground. By April 17, the Luftwaffe had lost 3,900 aircraft in 17 days; 3,214 on the ground (1,016 on the previous day); and 485 in the air; Allied air losses were the same as the German losses in combat—485. It was then estimated that the Luftwaffe had only 3,000 aircraft of all types left.

In addition to this strategic assault on airfields, the aircraft continued to give full tactical support to all the surface forces, in Germany, in Italy, and in France, where the U.S.A. 8th A.F. supported the French forces attacking the Germans in the Gironde area. On April 14, 1,150 bombers dropped 3,500 tons of bombs there, and next day over 1,300 Fortresses and Liberators deluged the German positions with 460,000 gallons of a new inflammable liquid contained in tanks (each of which splashes its contents over 60 square yards), plus 1,000 H.E. bombs and 6,000 large incendiaries. These fire tanks are the air equivalent of flame-throwers on the ground.

NIGHT Attack Plays Havoc with Shipping in the Kiel Canal

On April 9, Bomber Command made a night attack on Kiel, using some ten-ton bombs. The Admiral Scheer, pocket battleship, had been found there two days before by recce-planes. Bomber Command sank her in their first attack. In addition, Bomber Command may have damaged the Hipper and Emden cruisers, and did damage the liner Osorio, which was listing heavily when later photographed. In the afternoon of April 16, a small force of Lancasters with 12,000-lb. bombs, sank the pocket battleship Lützow at Swinemunde. A new rocket-propelled bomb, design-sponsored by the British Admiralty, was used for the first time by Flying Fortresses against E-boat pens at Ijmuiden. Hitting the target at 1,100 feet per second, this bomb can penetrate several layers of concrete before it explodes.

IN the night of April 20, Berlin was bombed by a large force of Russian bombers. That day it was announced that British air-raid casualties from the beginning of the war totalled 146,760 killed and seriously injured. Almost daily Super-Fortresses bomb Japan. On April 16 it was announced that 27 square miles of Tokyo had been burnt out. One great raid from 11 p.m. on April 13 to 3 a.m. on April 14 was Tokyo's greatest fire-bomb raid. The Japs counter-attacked the Super-Fortresses with jet-planes, but 10 square miles of arsenal and factory were left as smoking rubble. More Allied attacks have been made along the China coast, the Philippines and Formosa. On April 19, American Mustangs from Iwojima swept over central Japan and destroyed 85 Jap aircraft on the ground, making a round trip of 1,500 miles. Over 20,000 Jap aeroplanes were destroyed from America's entry into the war to March 11, 1945, by U.S. Army, Navy and Marine Corps pilots and A.A. gunners. The 14th Army in Burma is now supplied by a British and U.S. air transport armada, which flies the equivalent of three trainloads daily to the front line.

Rockets that Will Never be Fired at Britain

EN ROUTE FOR HOLLAND thirteen wagons of V2s, attached to a train at a wayside station, were seized by Gen. Hodges' U.S. 1st Army near Bromskirchen, between Cassel and Giessen, on April 7, 1945. It was the first time any of these rocket projectiles had been captured intact.

The top of one of the nine V2s found in the train (1); this part of the rocket was divided by wooden partitions into four compartments (3), containing the radio direction-controlling device (4), a compressed-air power unit and other instruments. Dimensions of the aluminium shell of the rocket were taken (2) and were recorded as length 46 feet and diameter 5½ feet. The Bromskirchen V2s were without their 2,000-lb. explosive warheads. Part of the train with its camouflage covers removed (5).

British forces of the 21st Army Group cut the last direct railway supplying the Dutch V2 coast when they took Nordhorn on April 13.

Photos, Fox, Associated Press

Our Roving Camera Bids Raid Shelters Farewell

NAVY WEEK CELEBRATION in London, April 15-21, 1945, in aid of the Lord Mayor's National Fund for Seamen, included in its many features a motor torpedo boat lying alongside Westminster pier (right). Twenty metropolitan boroughs took part, the display of naval gear and equipment providing popular centres of attraction.

DISPLACED PERSONS, mainly French and Belgians rescued from Nazi horror-camps and numbering over 1,000, have been flown in Dakotas of R.A.F. Transport Command to Brussels, and from there dispatched to their homes. A pilot (below) makes sure his passengers are comfortable before taking-off.

DRIVERS FOR OVERSEAS lined up for their first military meal. Manned by volunteer British personnel and under the auspices of the Ministry of War Transport, heavy goods vehicles are being sent to liberated areas in north-west Europe.

DEMOLISHING AIR RAID SHELTERS in London, this 3-ton sledge (left) swung from an excavator operated by Royal Engineers is dropped repeatedly on the concrete roof from a height of ten feet, then swung against the walls. Two R.E.s do in under an hour a task which would occupy five men working with pneumatic drills a whole week.

Photos, British Official, G.P.U., Planet News, Fox Photos

Editor's Postscript

WHEN I read of historic German towns being badly battered my regret is tempered by the ruins which I see daily in the once lovely old courts of the Temple and the shells of famous London churches, and although I do not subscribe to the old Jewish *lex talionis,* which exacted an eye for an eye and a tooth for a tooth, I could easily have withstood the shock of learning that some of our ten-ton bombs had accidentally been dropped on Heidelberg —much as I enjoyed a stay there long ago. Thus I thought more about the Temple round the corner from my office than I did of Vienna when I read the other day that the historic buildings of the Austrian capital had suffered more damage than was at first announced. Vienna was never an outstandingly beautiful city, like Paris or Rome, but the small inner city within the circle of that handsome boulevard, the Ringstrasse, had as much history packed into the square mile as most cities could hope for, even though some of the minor palaces of the imperial régime had been turned latterly into rather humdrum hotels. The opera house on the Ringstrasse has been reported gutted. It was one of the resorts of the Emperor Francis Joseph, who had a secret entrance into the royal box. After the last war it was run as a state enterprise at moderate prices. They took over the entire cellar of the famous Imperial Tokay, the wine that Noel Coward made such a song about in Bitter Sweet; and every night during the intervals stalwart republicans, Herr Schmidt and his frau, used to roll this golden wine of the Hapsburgs round their tongues in the lounge bar—also at moderate prices. But I expect Hitler's thugs claimed all that was left.

IF I know the Viennese, they will not brood unduly over the loss of their opera house or the reputed damage to the Schönbrunn and S. Stephen's cathedral. Temperamentally they are not unlike Londoners. They have the same sense of humour in that they laugh at themselves, a thing your typical German was never able to do. Between the end of the last war and that day in 1938 when Hitler's tanks first rumbled into the Ringstrasse, shabby old Vienna, a capital far too big for its country, like an enormous head with hardly any body, and buffeted by insoluble political and economic troubles, had contrived to put up a brave enough imitation of her former sparkle. She danced and sang and made the whole world welcome. Presumably that was just the trouble!

THE other day I was looking at a reproduction of Sir William Orpen's famous picture of the signing of the Versailles Treaty. It seemed a topical thing to do. Orpen painted a number of peace conference pictures. One that I recall with particular delight is a less formal bit of portraiture showing Clemenceau in vigorous argument with Lloyd George, while Woodrow Wilson sits impassive and aloof. These arguments were a frequent occurrence. Before the present war the guides at Versailles used to point out a great gash on the conference table, made, they said, when Lloyd George flung down his pen in anger during a disagreement. I have been told that the story was altered for American visitors so that it was Wilson who did the damage. For all I know, it was actually the cleaners.

BUT the picture of which I now write is the official one commissioned by the Government and shown at the Royal Academy in 1920. It provoked criticism at the time, because the artist seemed to have been more impressed by the beauty of the Hall of Mirrors than by the little frock-coated history-makers, whom he relegated to the bottom of his canvas. What impressed me most in studying the picture was the fact that Lloyd George, who sits in the very centre of the group, was by several years the last survivor of the twelve semi-heroic figures who sat at the historic table. One by one through the years they have all added their

MR. HARRY S. TRUMAN, former Vice-President of the United States, succeeded Franklin D. Roosevelt as President on the latter's sudden death on April 12, 1945. *Photo, Pictorial Press*

names to the obituary lists. Bonar Law, on Lloyd George's immediate left, was the first to go. That was in 1923. Wilson died the following year. The others were Viscount Milner (1925), Henry White, of the U.S. delegation (1926), Robert Lansing (1928), Clemenceau (1929), Earl Balfour, and the U.S. General Bliss (1930), Colonel House (1938), G. N. Barnes, Prince Saionji, the Japanese delegate (1940), and Lloyd George (1945). The lesser groups standing behind the table have thinned out, but among those still flourishing are Signor Orlando, W. M. Hughes of Australia, and the present Lord Hankey, then secretary to the Cabinet. On the other hand, Louis Botha outlived the Versailles conference by only a few weeks.

R.A.F. Middle East—one of H.M. Stationery Office's wholly admirable booklet war-histories—lies before me. Prepared for the Air Ministry by the M.O.I., it is described baldly as "the official story of Air Operations, February, 1942–January, 1943," yet what glorious reading it makes! Indeed I am not sure that when the Gibbon of the future comes to write of the Decline and Fall of the Third Reich he won't take this 150 page booklet (costing one-and-ninepence, by the way) as providing material for his most illuminating chapters. For it was in the Middle East—an area roughly one-third larger than the United States—that the tide of battle began to turn in our favour when Monty thwarted Rommel's bold bid for Egypt and carried out, from El Alamein to Tripoli, in three months to a day, the greatest single advance in history—1,400 miles in blinding sun and sand. As the anonymous author so rightly points out, the war in the Middle East was a struggle for airfields. So long as our main air force was based in Egypt wide stretches of the Mediterranean were beyond our fighter control. With our fighters based at Benina, near Benghazi, we could (and did) sail our shipping convoys successfully and in reasonable safety to Malta. I wonder, by the way, how many of our amateur tacticians are aware that the R.A.F. fighter-bomber and tank-buster were the direct outcome of this epic desert war when at one dark hour in 1942 all seemed lost?

A RECENT gossip paragraph told a story of Montgomery asking Eisenhower why he pronounced "schedule" as "skedule." This can scarcely be true, for I suspect that Monty is scholar enough to know that the American version is the more consistent. The word is derived, though in a roundabout way, from the Greek *skizo,* meaning "split." Our pronunciation of it illustrates one of the many illogicalities of the English tongue; for of three words derived from this same Greek root, schedule is pronounced as *shedule,* schism as *sizzum,* and schizophrenia as *skizophrenia.* The confusion probably arises from the familiar German *sch,* which is soft. This again differs from the Dutch, which is usually hard, as in Scheldt. I know that Dr. Percy Scholes, the well-known writer on music, feels justifiably aggrieved because so many people call him Sholes. Justifiably, because Scholes, like Schofield, is a good old Yorkshire name, which no one north of the Trent would dream of mispronouncing. Indeed, there is a village of Scholes, with a station on the L.N.E.R., between Leeds and Wetherby

When Men Saw Victory Written in the Skies

DARKENING THE REICH SKIES, THE ALLIED AIR ARMADA, watched breathlessly by British troops, swept across the Rhine during all-out operations on March 24, 1945. Our complete air supremacy, which enabled the glider and parachute troop landings to be carried out, is shown by the fact that in the first sixteen days of April as many as 3,462 enemy planes were destroyed, the record single day's kill being 879, on April 16, all for the loss of 52 Allied aircraft. See also illus. pages 776-77, 786, Vol. 8. *Photo, Planet News*

Printed in England and published every alternate Friday by the Proprietors, THE AMALGAMATED PRESS, LTD., The Fleetway House, Farringdon Street, London, E.C.4. Registered for transmission by Canadian Magazine Post. Sole Agents for Australia and New Zealand: Messrs. Gordon & Gotch, Ltd.; and for South Africa: Central News Agency, Ltd.—May 11, 1945. S.S. *Editorial Address:* JOHN CARPENTER HOUSE, WHITEFRIARS LONDON, E.C.4.

Vol 9 The War Illustrated No 207

SIXPENCE Edited by Sir John Hammerton MAY 25, 1945

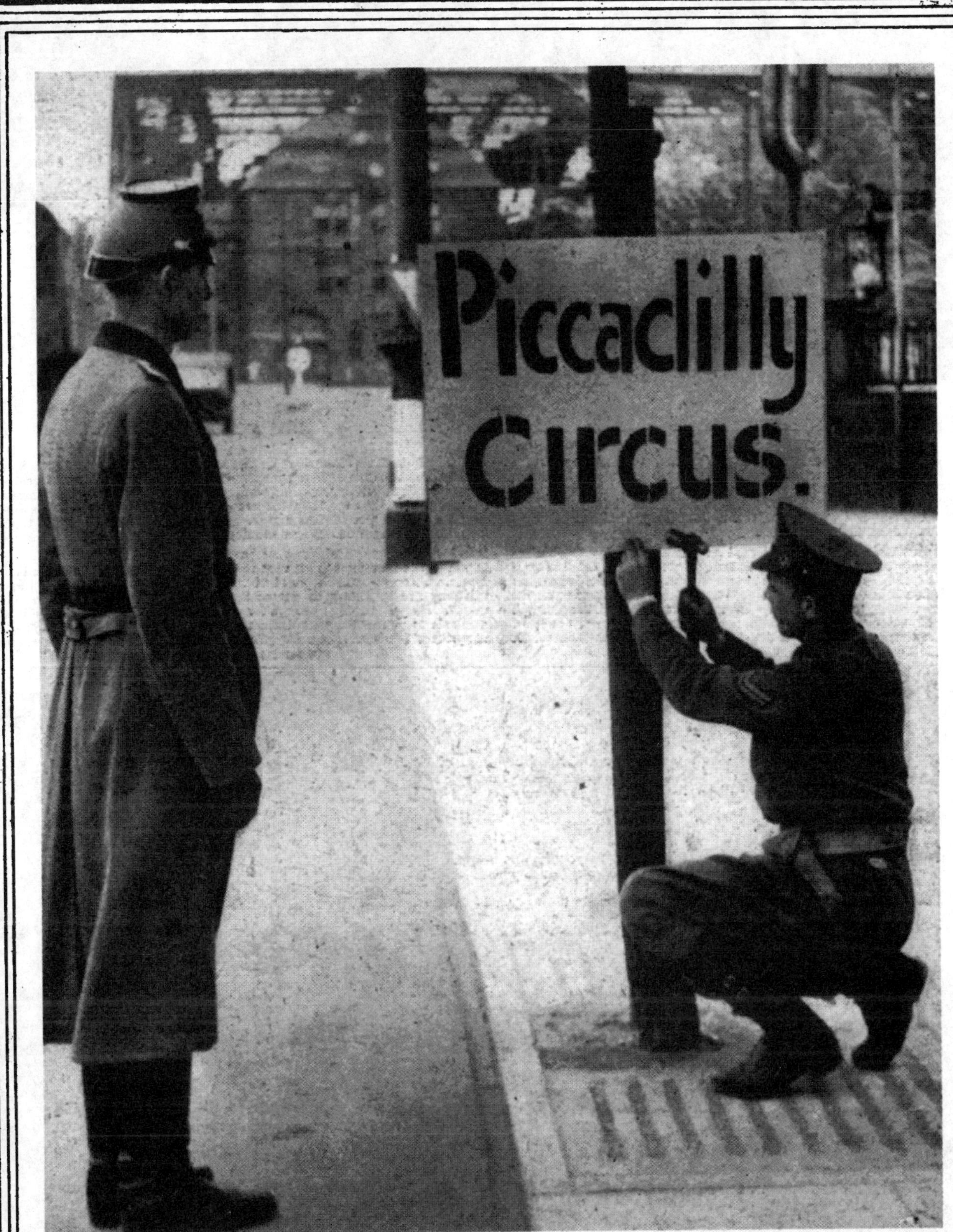

IN HAMBURG, FOUR DAYS BEFORE GERMANY'S UNCONDITIONAL SURRENDER, a corporal of the British 2nd Army, watched closely by a German policeman, erected new street-signs: the Grosse Allee became "Piccadilly Circus." Germany's second largest city, with a peacetime population of over 1,700,000, surrendered to General Dempsey's troops on May 3, 1945; the vast dockyards were less badly crippled than had been anticipated, and many U-boats were found on the stocks. *Photo, British Official*

Alexander Rings Down the Curtain in Italy

UNCONDITIONAL SURRENDER to Field-Marshal Sir Harold Alexander, Allied Supreme Commander, Mediterranean, of nearly 1,000,000 Germans fighting in Italy was announced on May 2, 1945, and hostilities ceased that day at noon. The territory involved—that of the German South-West Command—included all northern Italy to the Isonzo River in the north-east, the Austrian provinces of Vorarlberg, Tirol and Salzburg, and portions of Carinthia and Styria.

The instrument of surrender was signed on April 29. at Caserta, by two German plenipotentiaries and Lieut.-General W. D. Morgan, Chief of Staff of Allied Force H.Q. Both German representatives were in civilian attire ; one signed on behalf of General von Vietinghoff-Scheel, the other on behalf of Obergruppenfuehrer Karl Wolff, Supreme Commander of the S.S. and police and the German general plenipotentiary of the Wehrmacht in Italy. One of the German agents signs the document (left). Lieut.-Gen. W. D. Morgan (right) signs for the Allies. Scene at the ceremony (below).

TO HIS VICTORIOUS TROOPS, in an Order of the Day issued on May 2, Field-Marshal Alexander declared : "After nearly two years of hard and continuous fighting which started in Sicily in the summer of 1943, you stand today as victors of the Italian campaign. You have won a victory which has ended in the complete and utter rout of the German armed forces in the Mediterranean. By clearing Italy of the last Nazi aggressor, you have liberated a country of over 40,000,000 people.

"Today the remnants of the once proud army have laid down their arms to you—close on 1,000,000 men with all their arms, equipment, and impedimenta. You may well be proud of this great, victorious campaign, which will long live in history as one of the greatest and most successful ever waged. No praise is high enough for . . . your magnificent triumph. My gratitude to you and my admiration are unbounded and only equalled by the pride which is mine of being your commander-in-chief."

Photos, Allied Official

V Day & The War Illustrated

By The Editor

TWENTY-SIX years and six months ago saw me preparing the issues of THE WAR ILLUSTRATED (1914-19) in which were recorded the total collapse of the Imperial German Army, the shameful surrender of the German Grand Fleet, the ignominious flight of the All Highest War Lord Kaiser Wilhelm.

Today, 8th May 1945, for the second time in an editorial life, I have a similar task in hand . . . but with a difference in circumstance beyond all imagining in November 1918. As the First Great War was ending we who had lived and worked through it trusted that the world would be spared any comparable tragedy at least for generations to come: some had even believed that we had been fighting "a war to end war." The Allies in 1918 had humbled to its knees one of the most aggressive and flashiest empires since that of Jenghiz Khan and his barbarians had disintegrated in the thirteenth century. But following the defeat of Germany, and thanks in large measure to lack of co-ordination between the victorious powers; also to the ill-judged clemency with which the victors treated the vanquished but revengeful Germanic tribes—who still remained as barbaric as the hordes of Jenghiz—these predatory people were able to reorganize themselves under a new and vastly more ruthless leadership, and by 1939 to challenge again the peaceable peoples in a yet more desperate bid for "world dominion."

A NEW March of the Barbarians began: these dehumanized Huns of the West were soon to over-run Europe, and dreaming of a new Empire of Barbarism under the maniac leadership of Adolf Hitler, threw themselves with all their fury and fanaticism against Soviet Russia, on June 22, 1941, precipitating that Anglo-Russian alliance which after Britain's year of lone defiance proved the next great obstacle to the March of the Barbarians.

In France, and throughout its empire, men whose names had once been honoured had now thrown in their lot with the invader to their everlasting shame: most shameful of all Marshal Pétain, General Weygand and Admiral Darlan, who, but resolute against the common foe in the summer of 1940, might well have helped to change the subsequent course of the War, had they believed in Britain's power of recovery after Dunkirk.

We British must never forget that the true turning point of the war was the Battle of Britain: the most glorious epic of our race. Had not the splendid youth of the R.A.F. so superbly acquitted themselves in that tremendous encounter with the boasted Luftwaffe, when in the historic three months beginning August 8, 1940, they "clawed down" no fewer than 2,375 enemy planes out of British skies, the Hitlerian Empire might well have had a longer run, Russia's resistance and heroic resurgence would surely have provided strangely different chapters for the historian, and the United States would have seen the war carried into their own land.

NOR at this historic moment of stupendous victory should we hesitate to remind the world that it was British valour, British skill, British endurance that made incomparably the noblest contribution to the resurgence of the democratic countries which we are now celebrating.

Every nation of Europe, including Russia, and by the same token the U.S.A., would have had its history "changed for a thousand years," as Hitler had promised his Germanic tribes, had the British peoples lost faith in their own high destiny. Let us ask ourselves, therefore, what would have happened had Hitler won, and having contemplated the horror which the question implies, every loyal Briton can reflect with pride that it was his or her country *alone* that held up the march of the modern barbarians, until Russia was forced in, and Japan on December 7, 1941, struck the blow at Pearl Harbour which stung the United States into participation under the leadership of President Roosevelt—a leadership that will rank with Lincoln's at one of the other crises in American history.

THE short-lived Hitlerian Empire which was to bring wealth with power to the *Herrenvolk*; and was to endure for a thousand years as the majority of these square-head Germans no doubt believed, has crumbled to dust before the eyes of its creator; the chief breeding places of the whole of this pestiferous race have been rubbed from the face of Europe. Hitler promised his people that he would "erase" the cities of Great Britain while protecting those of his beloved Germany from harm. Dire has been our own suffering from his piloted planes, and those "secret weapons" the flying-bomb and rocket; but not comparable with what Germany has had to endure at the hands of Anglo-American air attacks.

This overwhelming superiority in the air has been a determining factor in the Second Great War—just as the British air power proved in the First—a factor that could never have reached the dimension necessary in this mightier conflict without the magnificent contribution of America in men and machines.

HOW abysmal has been the failure of the Germans can best be measured by recalling their war aims. In THE WAR ILLUSTRATED, December 7, 1918, we printed an extract from the *Kolnische Zeitung*, September 1914, reprinted again in this page together with some typical examples of Hitler's threats and promises. These ought to be accepted as having had the endorsement of every Nazi and of most Germans who are now eagerly assuring us they never sympathized with the National Socialist Party which has brought their country to irretrievable ruin.

With the end of the European War, our task in THE WAR ILLUSTRATED is not yet complete. There remains Japan, whose military chiefs went one better than Hitler by declaring their preparedness to "fight for a hundred years." But Japan, I am persuaded, will collapse sooner than is generally believed.

It would seem, therefore, that the time is not distant when, as in 1919, I shall have to frame some announcement about bringing our picture-record of events to an end. It can at least be promised that there will be no abrupt closing down of THE WAR ILLUSTRATED: we shall continue until the declared object with which No. 1 was issued on Sept. 16, 1939—to provide "a permanent picture-record of the Second Great War"—has been achieved. J. A. H.

1914. GERMANY'S THREAT

THERE will be no such country as Great Britain in existence at the end of the war. In its place we shall have Little Britain, a narrow strip of island territory, peopled by loutish football kickers living on the crumbs that Germany will deign to throw to them. Certain it is that the laughable and childish military system of Britain will shortly fall to pieces.

Then the once mighty Empire, with her naval strength represented by the few old tubs which Germany will have left her, will become the laughing-stock of the nations, the scarecrow at which children will point their fingers in disdainful glee.

Cologne Gazette, Sept. 1914

卐 卐 卐

1941 HITLER'S THREATS

THIS struggle can end only with the complete annihilation of one or other of the two adversaries. Mr. Churchill may believe that this will be Germany. I know it will be Britain.

Speech to Reichstag, July 19, 1940

If the British attack our cities we will simply erase theirs. The hour will come when one of us two will break up and it won't be Nazi Germany. If the British drop two or three thousand bombs on us, we will unload 150, 180, yes, 200,000 on them.

Broadcast, Sept. 4, 1940

When the hour strikes we shall dea decisive blows against Britain. These gentlemen will be taught by history this year.

Nazi Party meeting, Berlin, Jan. 30, 1941

MY VISIT TO WARTIME HOLLAND

by Captain NORMAN MACMILLAN, M.C., A.F.C.

CONTROL of the waterways is so important in Holland that a Government minister of public works (Waterstaat) is responsible for this feature of Dutch life, and each district in Holland has its own waterways engineer. In the area around Nijmegen and Arnhem, where flow the Maas, the Waal, and the Neder Rijn, the problem is aggravated by the very low level of the land contained within the courses of the three rivers, known as "the island." During the late winter, when the rivers are in flood, their water level may run twenty feet above that of the surrounding countryside.

The Germans had blown the dykes to flood the flanks of the British positions east of Nijmegen. Here was a great inland sea. Between Krannenburg and Beek (Dutch railway frontier town) it washed right over the road, but vehicles continued to drive through it with great bow waves sending the water rippling in all directions. On the opposite side of the road the ground rose to a wooded hill clear of the flood; there summer villas stood untouched by war or flood, but without occupants.

FACING the river I surveyed a scene of desolation. Water rushed through a gap in the dyke that ran outwards from the road like a breakwater. Some houses were almost submerged. Villages that stood on slightly higher ground were cut off like islands. Greenhouses showed their top lights above the water. The upper framework of a glider rose from the water half a mile away, like the skeleton of an antediluvian monster. A church spire stood sentinel amid the waters half-way between us and Germany, over there beyond the Rhine.

A squadron of buffaloes, returning from patrol, came splashing roadwards from the east. Seated in one were two prisoners of war who looked both materially and spiritually damp. In all were British troops whose land tanks had been caught by the floods. The amphibious tanks churned their way over the water with the thrust of the little cupid's bow-shaped steel paddles that projected transversely from their tracks; when they reached the land these paddles gripped the mixture of gravel and mud and hauled the buffaloes on to the tar macadam road. They were manned by cheerful Canadians, who said they would rather go to battle in buffaloes than in any other way.

Amphibians Foiled the Germans

Each buffalo is a self-contained unit with one officer and its crew; there is a large open-well interior, wherein there is plenty of room if not much comfort, and crews can eat and sleep aboard. They are lightly armed with cannon and machine-guns. With the Ducks (wheeled vehicles driven on the water by a screw propeller) these amphibians foiled the German attempt to break the 1st Canadian Army flank by flooding, and made the flooded area more of a nightmare to the Germans than ourselves. Later they were the spearhead that crossed the Rhine. The only infantry I saw on the march in this zone were the sections of a company of Canadians moving up in single file to join the buffaloes and go into action with them. All the other troops rode to war.

After driving along the flooded road our car engine died, due to a flooded ignition system. After an abortive attempt to cure the trouble on the roadside, we were nosed out of a traffic jam we had created by a little armoured scout car, whose driver then tried to start us up by towing, but without success. A M.T. section in the woods could not help us, and the car had to be towed back to Nijmegen, where a mechanic who knew the engine design stripped the distributor and dried it so that the plugs would spark.

Gen. KURT DITTMAR, Wehrmacht radio commentator, who surrendered to the U.S. 30th Division on the Elbe on April 25, 1945, chatted nonchalantly with a French war correspondent. *Photo, Keystone*

MEANWHILE, I walked into Beek with R. J. Montgomery of the B.B.C. Two Free Dutch soldiers guarded the Customs control post. For us there were no formalities; for those in civilian clothes there were. (In many parts of Holland I saw Dutchmen on road control work, some wearing only armlets to indicate they were traffic controllers.) Beek was surrounded by 25-pounder guns that barked incessantly from between the houses, among the trees, beside the floods.

The prisoner-of-war cage—in this case an erroneous term, for there was no wire—was in the restaurant of a small hotel that stood back from the road; a wood building, with a veranda. The room was bare, with painted wood walls. On a raised portion of the floor, where, perhaps, once a band had played in peacetime, about 40 German soldiers sat on benches. They were mostly young men up to 20 years, but about a quarter of their number were oldish men. All looked extremely docile. The Canadian sergeant, who spoke German, said they had had one very arrogant chap earlier.

TO the right, on the lower floor, two German officers sat on chairs. One, tall and fair-haired, wore a voluminous macintosh and a peaked cap. The other, shorter and swarthy, was coatless, rather dapper despite his unshaven chin, dressed in tunic, breeches and field boots, with a forage cap; he smoked a pipe. Both belonged to the infantry. Their clothes were soiled with dried mud. About every minute the room shook like a jelly when a 25-pounder fired just outside.

Montgomery, an Afrikaans-speaking South African, had been in Germany before the war and spoke fluent German. I do not speak fluent German, but I understood most

ROYAL MARINE COMMANDO of the British No. 1 Commando Brigade, carrying a tommy-gun, looks back over the famous north German river Elbe which he and his comrades crossed on April 29, 1945, establishing a broad bridge-head and capturing Lauenburg. Quick-firing A.A. gun in the foreground was not needed. *Photo, British Official*

ACROSS THE DANUBE BY TANK-DESTROYER rode these U.S. 7th Army infantrymen; General Patch's troops crossed without opposition when they captured the bridge at Dillingen on April 22, 1945, forging swiftly towards Munich, which fell eight days later. *Photo, U.S. Official*

of what was said. Both men went straight from school to the army. They were now 23 and had known nothing in adult life but war. From the age of about 10 they had been schooled in the Nazi outlook, and one certainly had it indoctrinated within his mind; the other seemed puzzled by its results, and was less assertive about its values, but nevertheless it obviously affected his judgement.

One had fought two years and a half on the Russian front, and said he was happier to be taken prisoner in the west. As he talked he grew more vehement, especially about German *lebensraum*. The Sudetenland, Danzig and Memel were German; the souls of Danzigers had cried out to belong to the Reich. It was wrong that Germany had been forced into war because she desired only what was German. That was his theme. These two men could see no viewpoint but their own. The silent one nodded approval of all his comrade said. They had no thought for the nations ravished by the Wehrmacht. All was reserved for Germany, past, present, and future. They said that if the war would only finish, and the Germans were allowed to go back to Germany, they would soon rebuild everything that had been destroyed there.

I said to them, "We once had a king who came from Herrenhausen, so by your argument Hanover should belong to Britain!" The macintosh-clad officer, who appeared to know as much English as I knew German, laughed and translated to his companion, who shrugged his shoulders. They said they knew Germany could not then win the war, but as the Allies would give the Germans no terms they must go on fighting to the end. By doing so they would lose no more, and might gain something. At least the Allies would have to pay for their policy. How Goebbels would have applauded his disciples!

A lorry drew up outside. The Canadian sergeant ripped out a command. The German soldiers rose and ran to the door and stopped in a bunch just inside. Then they got the order to get in. They scrambled quickly on to the lorry, and stood packed tight one against another in its open truck. The officers ended their conversation, rose, bowed, and left the room, climbed into the cab beside the driver, and that group of prisoners left the forward cage.

Nijmegen, with 81,686 population, is the largest town in Gelderland. For a Dutch town it stands high, on a slope that rises steeply from the south bank of the Waal, and on the level ground above. The old town has narrow streets and close-set houses, the newer part wide roadways and spacious gardens. It has seen war throughout the centuries. Captain Churchill of the Grenadiers—later the Duke of Marlborough, ancestor of our present Premier—attracted the attention of General Turenne by his bravery at the capture of Nijmegen in 1672.

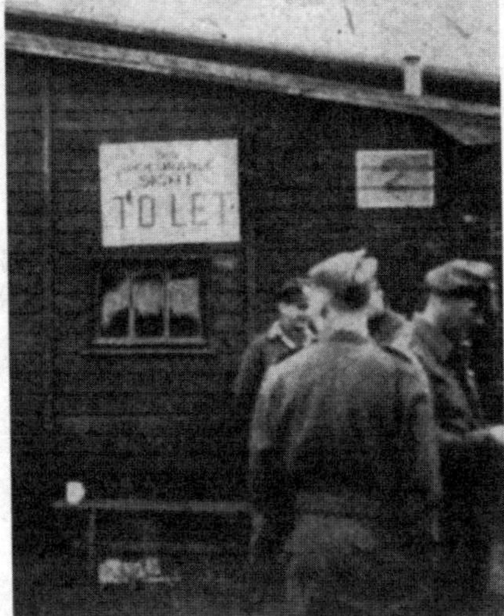

P.O.W. CAMP AT WESTERTIMKE, north-east of Bremen, was labelled with a "to let" notice by British troops—including Scots and Welsh Guards—when they overran it on April 27, 1945. *Photo, British Official*

The scout car driver stopped on a rising street outside a row of houses to ask where the M.T. depot was, and, as usual, some Dutch children came up to look into the car. One boy of about eight—Toni Neppelbuerger—said he and his younger sister slept in a loft at the top of the three-floored house he pointed out. Toni said he was afraid of nothing, not even when two nights before the bombers came and went "boom-boom!"—the night when Bomber Command bombed Cleve. While the car was being serviced, another Dutch boy came up to ask if we needed billets. He said his mother had a room that could sleep ten. They were expecting Canadians, who so far had not arrived, so if we were held up he proudly announced that we could have a room to sleep in there.

Nijmegen was packed with men, armour and transport. Tanks and trucks stood in every side street. Long lines of vehicles, guns, and their attendant soldiers moved through the town. What a target for night bombers! Cleve and Goch must have been like that when our heavies struck. Here, in Nijmegen, but for the sound of our own guns, and as night fell the motionless searchlight fingers that cut the sky as direction markers for night patrols, there was little to suggest that one was in a front line town.

A NAAFI canteen and an ENSA cinema were housed in one building that must have been a place of amusement before the war. The canteen was a rotunda. There was scarcely a vacant seat. Dutch girls worked at the counter and in the kitchen and served the tables. Montgomery and I joined two soldiers at a table. For them and ourselves we ordered four cups of tea, and ten finger-roll sandwiches for the car journey we had still to make; for these we paid one Dutch guilder 45 cents—two shillings and eightpence-halfpenny at the ruling rate of exchange. We were asked to produce paper to enwrap our sandwiches for the car.

ON THE KRANNENBURG-BEEK ROAD, almost submerged in the Rhine-Waal floods in February 1945, Capt. Norman Macmillan, Special Correspondent for "The War Illustrated" (left), and R. J. Montgomery, of the B.B.C., watched supplies move up to the line.

THE BATTLE FRONTS

by Maj.-Gen. Sir Charles Gwynn, K.C.B., D.S.O.

MAY 2, 1945, will, I think, always be remembered as the day on which major operations in the European theatre of the World War came to an end, and therefore may be even more important than the day on which Germany's unconditional surrender was accepted. The former may be looked on as the military, the latter as the political winning post.

Apart from its great military and political importance no event, however great, will I think give more universal satisfaction than the unconditional surrender of the Axis forces in Italy and an immense extent of territory to Field-Marshal Alexander. Mr. Churchill, as usual backed by the applause of Parliament, evidently feels, and has given expression to, what we all, I hope, recognize was due to the Field-Marshal and his very gallant, efficient and long-suffering armies. They have had an immensely difficult and often a heart-breaking and thankless task. They have had to operate in a terrain and under weather conditions which gave a strong and highly efficient enemy every advantage and caused great hardships. When victory appeared to be in sight they saw some of their best troops transferred to other theatres.

ASSORTMENT of Nationalities Welded Into Winning Team

Nothing, surely, could be more likely to suggest the idea that their job was of secondary importance and did not demand wholehearted effort or extreme sacrifices. Yet they stuck to their task and there was no relaxation of effort, even when only small scale operations were feasible. When conditions became more favourable and the time arrived for the decisive effort it lacked nothing in energy, speed and willingness to drive home the blow. Immense as is the credit due to the troops I feel certain that they would be the first to acknowledge how much they owe to the leadership of Field-Marshal Alexander and General Mark Clark. Few men could have welded such an amazing assortment of nationalities into a team of such quality.

For the Empire it must always be a particular source of gratification that the 8th Army has added yet another great victory to the record of its achievements, and that its traditions have not been lost in spite of many changes in its commanders and constituent elements. If German die-hards ever really hoped that they would be able to prolong resistance in their "Southern Redoubt" the surrender in Italy finally quenched the hope. When Kesselring decided, or more probably was ordered by Hitler, not to withdraw across the Po after his Gothic line was broken, it was clear that he had burnt his boats. For with ever-diminishing transport it was certain that withdrawal would become increasingly difficult as weather conditions improved and favoured pursuit. By the time Vietinghoff-Scheel had replaced Kesselring it was apparent that the only alternatives open to him were a suicidal last struggle where he stood, or a last minute attempt at retreat.

THE fact that Field-Marshal Alexander's forces were so greatly weakened and of such strange composition may have raised hopes of at least saving part of his force by retreat covered by determined rearguards. If such were his hopes they were probably finally shattered by the very effective action of the Italian patriots. It was not the least of Alexander's achievements that the sympathy he had shown to the underground movement and the steps he had taken to ensure that the rising should be well organized and well-timed bore fruit, and made an important contribution to the completeness of his victory.

It was a remarkable coincidence that the cease fire in Italy, the surrender of Berlin, and of the Army which had apparently been ordered to relieve the city, and the arrival of the British 2nd Army on the shores of the Baltic should all have occurred on the same day. The surrender of Berlin was clearly an event that equalled if it did not exceed the Italian surrender in importance, and it undoubtedly resulted from perhaps the bitterest fighting in the war. Here more than anywhere else the Germans carried out their intention of making a last-ditch stand and they fought with a fanatical determination only exceeded by the fury of the Russians' relentless attack. Every weapon in the German armoury was brought into play to stimulate resistance and fanaticism. The Hitler myth was exploited by Goebbels with his usual skill and disregard of truth. Promises of relief were continued after all hope had vanished, and even the Luftwaffe appeared to drop ammunition to the defenders.

MEN OF THE QUEEN'S REGIMENT, on armour and transport, move through the centre of Hamburg, Germany's leading port, which surrendered on May 3, 1945.
Photo, British Official

To Zhukov's and Koniev's Armies, which broke the really formidable German defences on the Oder and engaged at Berlin the greater part of the German forces still willing to fight, the Western Powers certainly owe the comparative ease with which their final advances were carried out. In counting our own losses and our own captures the sacrifices the Russians made in these last battles should not be forgotten. The 2nd Army's advance to the Baltic, well designed to link quickly with Rokossovsky's advance, although it had very important strategical results in defeating any plans the Germans may have had of establishing a northern stronghold, was achieved more by skilful and energetic execution than by hard fighting. It certainly gave no indication of relaxation of effort. The surrender of Hamburg unexpectedly on the following day testified to the success of the operation.

The annihilation or surrender of all enemy forces caught between Dempsey's and Rokossovsky's armies had become a certainty, but that Field-Marshal Montgomery should immediately receive the unconditional surrender of the whole of the enemy opposing him could not have been expected. It is surely a matter for legitimate pride that he and Field-Marshal Alexander should have been the first of all the Allied commanders to finish the war on their respective fronts.

OF all the surrenders which took place in the week before the fall of Berlin the voluntary surrender of General Dittmar seemed to be one of the most significant. His frank and realistic broadcasts had for long marked him as the mouthpiece of the General Staff rather than of Goebbels. His surrender therefore was a clear indication of the state of mind of an important section of highly placed professional officers. The interview a B.B.C. representative had with Dittmar threw an interesting light on a number of points. For instance, he asserted that Rundstedt realized that his counter-offensive was strategically unsound and that the reserves he employed in it should have been kept for use elsewhere, but that he was forced into the enterprise by Hitler. Moreover he revealed that Rundstedt's objectives were in reality less ambitious than those proclaimed. This bit of information, if correct, gives me I admit some satisfaction, since it seems to agree with the views I expressed at the time. What is more important is Dittmar's evident desire to throw all the blame for Germany's military defeat on to Hitler's interference and suppression of all generals who showed signs of outstanding ability and independence.

After the last war it is notorious that the German officer class denied military defeat and attributed the collapse to the home front. This time it looks as if they had already decided to make Hitler the sole scapegoat for military defeat, and Himmler's S.S. for atrocities committed. One can trust a German to invent excuses and even to believe in them! In this case they are to some extent justifiable, for if Hitler's death had occurred some years earlier the strategic blunders for which he was undoubtedly responsible would probably not have been made by professional soldiers.

BURMA

While such great events were happening in Europe perhaps too little attention was being paid to the great achievements of General Slim's 14th Army in Burma. I confess that I, and many others better qualified by local experience to judge, have always considered that it would be impossible to effect the liberation of Burma and the recapture of Rangoon by an army invading from the north. Even allowing for the potentialities of air transport, advance as far as Mandalay seemed hardly practicable. Now General Slim has conclusively proved us wrong, for undoubtedly he would have recaptured Rangoon without the assistance of the force landed in the Irrawaddy Delta just as he was closing in on the city, welcome as no doubt the assistance was. The Japanese have suffered such a heavy defeat that it seems probable they will not make determined efforts to retain the southern strip of Burma, but will concentrate on holding Malaya and covering Thailand where there are greater possibilities of maintaining communications with Japan.

The landing of an Australian force on Tarakan island close to Borneo is another notable event, and it will, I hope, give general satisfaction that Australian forces have now been allotted a more interesting and congenial task than that of liquidating the by-passed Japanese detachments in New Guinea and the Bismarck Archipelago.

How Dempsey's Scottish Troops Cleared Bremen

KING'S OWN SCOTTISH BORDERERS picked off Nazi snipers down a street in the great north German port of Bremen, which troops of Gen. Sir Miles Dempsey's British 2nd Army cleared on April 27, 1945. In the background, a crowd is assembled outside one of the city's vast air-raid shelters. Constructed of solid blocks of concrete, each shelter had its own telephone, lighting, heating and air-cooling system. Sixteen U-boats, almost completed, were seized in Bremen's famous Deschimag shipyards (see illus. p. 42).

Photo, British Official

Allied Link-Up on the Elbe Split the Reich

HANDSHAKES AT TORGAU, 30 miles north-east of Leipzig, on April 26, 1945, sealed the link-up between the Allied armies advancing from the west and the Soviet forces who had battled the long road from Stalingrad, the historic meeting cleaving the Reich in two. Maj.-Gen. E. F Reinhardt, commanding the 69th Division, U.S. 1st Army (1, third from right), chatted with the Russian general (second from right) commanding the 58th Guards' Division of the Soviet 1st Ukrainian Front.

Outside Torgau, a U.S. Army lieutenant talked with a girl of the Soviet armed forces and a member of the Russian Guards Division (2). Balancing on the fragments of a bridge, men of the Allied armies stretched out welcoming hands to one another (3). U.S. and Red Army troops discussed the position (4), with a map spread on the bonnet of a jeep.

See also story in page 57.

Photos, U.S. Official, Associated Press, Keystone, Pictorial Press

Proudly the Red Flag Flies on the Reichstag

POUNDED HEART of the dying Third Reich, Berlin was entered on April 23, 1945, by troops of the Red Army; Soviet tanks and infantry move on through one of the central streets (1). The capital was entered simultaneously by forces of Marshal Zhukov's 1st White Russian Front from the north and east and of Marshal Koniev's 1st Ukrainian Front from the south. On April 30 the Red Flag was hoisted above the shattered Reichstag building (2), Soviet tanks looming in the foreground. On that memorable day thousands of German prisoners passed under the famous Brandenburg Gate (3).

Soviet advance into the German capital was led by 162 generals and spear-headed by tanks. Cannon- and rocket-firing fighters of the 2nd T.A.F., R.A.F., flying alongside bombers of the Red Air Force, struck at German convoys with men and supplies for the centre of the city.

Photos, U.S.S.R. Official, Planet News, Pictorial Press

THE WAR AT SEA

by Francis E. McMurtrie

So far as Germany is concerned the war at sea is at an end. With the surrender of submarines at British ports, the experience of 1918 is being repeated. The only important warships that have so far fallen into our hands appear to be the Prinz Eugen and the Nürnberg, at Copenhagen.

Having regard to all the circumstances, a "last ditch" stand in Norway was never a really practical proposition. By the time this is in print, the Norwegians will again be in control of their country and be engaged in disarming the German hordes who have so long defiled it. Those who credited Grossadmiral Dönitz with the intention of carrying on submarine warfare from Norwegian bases were deceived by his blustering words when he assumed the now empty office of Fuehrer. However truculent he may have sounded, he was not quite such a fool as to carry on a hopeless struggle with all the odds against him at this stage.

Though few people in this country have met Dönitz, I was recently lucky enough to obtain a personal estimate of him from the man who accepted his surrender towards the end of the last war. Commodore Humphrey W. Best, C.B.E., D.S.O., R.N., describes him as being "a typical Prussian," with a surly and bad-tempered demeanour when taken prisoner.

This occurred on October 4, 1918, when Dönitz was in command of the submarine UB 68, operating from an Adriatic base. He was lying in the path of a convoy, for the escort of which Lieut.-Commander Best (as he then was) commanded a force comprising his own ship, the 1200-ton sloop Snapdragon, and four armed trawlers. One of the trawlers sighted the submarine on the surface and gave the alarm; it was then six o'clock in the morning. Forced to make a crash-dive, the U-boat appears somehow to have damaged her hydroplanes (the diving rudders which force a submarine below), and again emerged on the surface astern of the convoy. Here she was attacked by the Snapdragon and the other ships, whose combined gunfire inflicted irreparable damage on the enemy. Dönitz and his men hastened to abandon the crippled submarine before she sank, and were mostly picked up, to the number of 30 or more.

In spite of his arrogant manner, the drenched Dönitz was lent a spare suit of uniform by the captain of the Snapdragon; this he returned, with an abrupt note of thanks in broken English, after he had been landed at Malta.

U-BOAT Menace Was the Greatest Peril This Country Has Faced

His circumstances in 1945 were very much the same as in 1918; he was in a sinking ship, and chose to give up rather than go down with her. For the 200 or more U-boats in Norwegian ports to continue their attacks on shipping would have offered nothing better than the prospect of being hunted down and exterminated like rats; while the duration of their operations would have been severely limited by the extent of their resources in fuel, torpedoes and other supplies. Nor is it likely that the officers and men of the German submarine service, with their country occupied and no idea of what is happening to their homes, displayed any enthusiasm for a continuance of the fight, even if Dönitz ever tried to put forward the idea seriously.

Yet the fact must never be ignored that the U-boat menace has been the greatest peril this country has faced in this war, as in the last. If the enemy could have contrived to cut all communication by sea between Britain and the rest of the world, we should have been beaten. Food, petroleum and munitions would have been denied us, and, without these, all resistance would speedily have been overcome.

There is no doubt Hitler fully appreciated this, having studied the history of the previous Great War. In 1935, when he ordered submarine building to be resumed, it was with the design of undermining British sea power, which was otherwise bound to overcome Germany. On the very first day of the war the sinking without warning of the liner Athenia gave the cue to what was to follow.

Fortunately, anti-submarine methods had not been neglected by the Royal Navy in the interval between the two wars, and all plans had been prepared to put in force a general system of convoy within a few days of the outbreak of hostilities. It was this which held and then parried the initial submarine attack.

When France fell out of the war and Italy came in on the other side, the odds in favour of the U-boats were much improved. Not only were the Allied naval forces reduced in numbers and faced with the fresh task of opposing the Italian fleet, but the occupation by the enemy of the French Atlantic harbours gave him a series of submarine bases from which attacks could be launched on the Atlantic trade routes with far better prospects of success.

Thus 1940-41 were the most critical years of the conflict. Losses of shipping ran into millions of tons, and the situation was grave in the extreme. Yet in the later months of 1941 the augmenting of escorts by the large numbers of corvettes ordered in 1939-40 began to yield results, and the U-boats found themselves sinking fewer merchant vessels at greater cost. Moreover, as British aircraft output increased, it was found possible to spare more aircraft for operation by Coastal Command in the narrow seas, which soon became unhealthy for the enemy.

Japan's entry into the war imposed a further strain on British naval resources. Until the United States Navy had recovered from the initial shock administered at Pearl Harbour, and had implemented its matchless capacity for reinforcement, the situation again became threatening. The U-boats found a new harvest awaiting them in the Western Atlantic, with American coastal traffic almost unprotected from the assault that was launched against it. A convoy system had to be organized with the aid of experienced British personnel and escort vessels, but it took some months for the situation to be restored.

VISTA OF U-BOATS ON THE STOCKS AT BREMEN was the satisfying sight which greeted this soldier of the 52nd Lowland Division after they had cleared the famous port on April 28, 1945. First U-boat to give itself up in British home waters, under the unconditional surrender terms, was U 249 which, flying the German naval ensign at half-mast with the British flag above it, sailed into Weymouth Bay on the morning of May 10. *Photo, British Official*

After this the submarine wolf-packs concentrated as far as possible on the mid-Atlantic area, where there was a gap between the extreme ranges of aircraft operating from British, Newfoundland or American shore bases. To overcome this weakness, convoys were reinforced with escort aircraft carriers, whose planes were able to patrol the danger zone. Many a U-boat fell victim to this counterstroke, and in time it was proved that to attack a convoy was apt to be suicidal.

Hitler's replacement of his Commander-in-Chief, Grossadmiral Raeder, by the U-boat specialist Dönitz was a fresh confession by the enemy that everything depended on the success of the U-boat campaign. Its failure has long been apparent to the world, for the Germans have never attempted to disprove the figures of their losses, amounting at the height of the conflict to a submarine every day. New devices such as the *Schnorkel*, or airpipe to enable a submarine to remain submerged for a much greater time, may have extended the lives of U-boats, but this has done no more than delay the inevitable end.

From Her Decks Our Planes Can Strike Japan

H.M.S. ILLUSTRIOUS ENTERED SYDNEY'S NEW GRAVING DOCK for repairs (1) before the dock was officially opened by H.R.H. the Duke of Gloucester and named "Captain Cook" on March 24, 1945. The aircraft carrier's giant propellers (2). A carrier force led by the Illustrious, and a task force of the British Pacific Fleet, commanded by Vice-Admiral Sir Bernard Rawlings (3, right, seen with Capt. H. Howden, commanding H.M.A.S. Hobart), attacked, on March 26, the Sakishima Group. See illus. pages 582, 751, Vol. 8.

Photos, Sport & General

Final Tragic Throw of the Dice for the Duce

MUSSOLINI and his 25 years old mistress, Clara Petacci, and 12 members of his Cabinet, were executed by Italian partisans at a Lake Como village on April 28, 1945, after being arrested in an attempt to cross the Swiss frontier. The bodies were brought to Milan and exhibited to public view.

The ex-Duce and Signorina Petacci sprawled in death in Milan (1), and the crowds spat upon them. News of the execution was followed by an outburst among the population, who overthrew all the remaining statues of the ex-Duce: one was flung into a dog kennel (2). During the final hours in Milan these patriots picked off Fascist snipers (3). Troops of the U.S. 5th Army entered Genoa on April 27 after its liberation by partisans; jeep-riding American soldiers passed German prisoners (4). See also illus. page 34.

Photos, U.S. Official, Evening Standard, Keystone

Dramatic Last Days of the War in the West

With bated breath the civilized world awaited the final dissolution of the Third Reich, which Hitler had boasted was to endure 1,000 years. One by one, day by day, the ignoble figureheads in this tragedy of a nation passed from the limelight. To the inexorable demand of Unconditional Surrender the Realm of Germany drew violently to its close.

APRIL 24, 1945.—The rot sets in. The Reich is crumbling. At his own request Himmler, chief of the S.S. and C.-in-C. the Home Army, meets Count Folke Bernadotte of the International Red Cross, at the Baltic port of Luebeck, and expresses the wish to meet General Eisenhower, to surrender the whole Western Front. He admits that Germany is finished, and that Hitler is so ill that he might already be dead—in any case cannot live more than two days. Gen. Schillenburg, Hitler's confidential staff officer, declares the Fuehrer is suffering from brain haemorrhage but does not indicate his whereabouts.

Mr. Herschel Johnson, the American Minister to Sweden, and Sir Victor Mallet, the British Minister, are summoned by M. Guenther, the Swedish Foreign Minister, and informed of Himmler's overtures.

APRIL 25.—President Truman and Mr. Churchill discuss the offer and agree to notify Marshal Stalin that it is proposed to reject it and to tell Himmler that the only acceptable one will be unconditional surrender to Britain, the U.S.A. and Russia. Meanwhile, the Russians complete the encirclement of Berlin.

APRIL 26.—Marshal Stalin's reply received by Mr. Grew, U.S. Acting Secretary of State, thanks President Truman for the information and agrees to the proposed message. The President telegraphs the reply to the American Legation at Stockholm: insisting on unconditional surrender to all the three Governments on all fronts, that the German forces should surrender to local commanders in the field, and where resistance continued the Allied Armies would press the attack. On this date Russian and U.S. forces link up at Torgau on the Elbe. (See illus. p. 40.)

APRIL 27.—The U.S. Minister reports that Count Bernadotte has left for Flensburg, on the German-Danish Frontier, to take the message to Himmler. At night it is reported from Stockholm that the Count has returned there but that no reply has been received from Himmler—who is heard of no more in connexion with these negotiations.

APRIL 28.—In London a statement, drawn up by Mr. Churchill, comes from 10, Downing Street: ". . . At a time like this all kinds of proposals for German surrender from various parts of the German Reich are rife as these are in harmony with the enemy's desperate situation. His Majesty's Government have no information to give about any of them at this moment. But it must be emphasized that only unconditional surrender to the three major Powers will be entertained." Mussolini and members of the Fascist Cabinet are executed by Italian partisans at Lake Como. (See illus. p. 44.)

APRIL 29.—German Armies in N. Italy and W. Austria capitulate; hostilities to cease on May 2. Hitler is reported dead in a suicide pact with Goebbels.

APRIL 30.—Russians capture ruins of the Reichstag in Berlin. Marshal Stalin, in an Order of the Day, says, "Seeking a way out of their hopeless plight, the Hitlerite adventurers resort to all kinds of tricks, down to flirting with the Allies in an effort to cause dissension in the Allied Camp. These fresh tricks are doomed to utter failure. They can only accelerate the disintegration of the German Army." (See illus. p. 41.)

MAY 1.—Count Bernadotte, expected in Stockholm today, had contact on April 29 (reports the London Times) with one of Himmler's representatives. "It is generally believed that if Himmler gave the order to lay down arms he would be obeyed by what remains of the Wehrmacht and the party formations of which he is head."

Hitler's death in Berlin is announced by Hamburg radio at 10.20 p.m.—"It is reported from the Fuehrer's Headquarters that our Fuehrer, Adolf Hitler, has fallen this afternoon at his command post in the Reich Chancellery, fighting to the last breath against Bolshevism and for Germany."

Admiral Dönitz goes to the microphone: "German men and women, soldiers of the Wehrmacht! Our Fuehrer, Adolf Hitler, has fallen . . . The Fuehrer has appointed me as his successor. Fully conscious of the responsibility, I take over the leadership of the German people at this fateful hour. It is my first task to save the German people from destruction by the Bolshevists and it is only to achieve this that the fight continues. As long as the British and Americans hamper us from reaching this end we shall fight and defend ourselves against them as well . . ." An Order of the Day by Admiral Dönitz is then read: "The Fuehrer . . . died the death of a hero." Our 8th Army makes contact with Tito's Yugoslavs west of Trieste.

THE PRIME MINISTER'S HISTORIC PEACE MESSAGE

Extracts from the historic speech Mr. Churchill made to the world before the microphone, at 3 p.m. on May 8, 1945, and later repeated in the House of Commons:

YESTERDAY morning, at 2.41 a.m., at General Eisenhower's headquarters, General Jodl, the representative of the German High Command and of Grand-Admiral Dönitz, the designated head of the German State, signed the act of unconditional surrender of all German land, sea and air forces in Europe to the Allied Expeditionary Force, and simultaneously to the Soviet High Command . . . Today, this agreement will be ratified and confirmed at Berlin . . .

Hostilities will end officially at one minute after midnight tonight (Tuesday, May 8), but, in the interests of saving lives, the Cease Fire began yesterday to be sounded all along the front, and our dear Channel Islands are also to be freed today . . .

We may allow ourselves a brief period of rejoicing, but let us not forget for a moment the toils and efforts that lie ahead. Japan, with all her treachery and greed, remains unsubdued. The injury she has inflicted upon Great Britain, the United States and other countries, and her detestable cruelties, call for justice and retribution.

We must now devote all our strength and resources to the completion of our tasks both at home and abroad. *Advance Britannia! Long live the cause of freedom! God save the King!*

MAY 2.—Gen. Eisenhower explodes the "death of a hero" fantasy. From the Headquarters of the Supreme Commander Allied Expeditionary Force comes the refutation, "Admiral Dönitz's statement that Hitler met a hero's death is in contradiction with the facts given by Himmler and Gen. Schillenburg . . . nothing which either Admiral Dönitz or Himmler may say or do can change in any way the agreed operations of the Allied Armies."

"Berlin has fallen!" is announced from Moscow, the remnants of the defeated garrison surrendering to the Red Army at 2 p.m. British double summer time, after a battle which has lasted little more than a fortnight.

In Italy, at the same hour, nearly 1,000,000 men, comprising all enemy land, sea and air forces commanded by Gen. Vietinghoff-Scheel, cease fighting. This surrender of the whole of the German Armies in Italy and parts of Austria to Field-Marshal Alexander is the first made unconditionally in this war. The Baltic ports of Luebeck and Wismar fall to the British, Rostock and Warnemunde to the Russians. (See illus. p. 34.)

MAY 3.—The enemy collapses in Northern Germany and is surrendering in thousands. Hamburg is being occupied by the British 2nd Army.

MAY 4.—Field-Marshal Montgomery accepts surrender of German forces in Holland, North-West Germany and Denmark, including Heligoland and the Frisian Islands—"a battlefield surrender involving the forces now facing the 21st Army Group on their northern and western flanks." This is announced from Supreme Headquarters at 8.15 p.m., six weeks after the British crossing of the Rhine. The German plenipotentiaries who have arrived at Montgomery's camp at Luneburg Heath, south of Hamburg, to surrender include Admiral Von Friedeburg, C.-in-C. of the German Navy, who succeeded Admiral Dönitz in that post when Dönitz became the new Fuehrer, Gen. Dietel, and Rear-Admiral Wagner.

MAY 5.—Demoralization and disintegration of the enemy on the west front continues: on the south flank the German 1st and 19th Armies surrender to Gen. Devers.

MAY 6.—Admiral Dönitz, presumed to have fled to Norway, broadcasts to all German ships, "Crews of all ships flying the flag of the German Merchant Navy or the State service flag are to abstain from any act of war in the ports and waters affected by the truce. They are forbidden either to scuttle the ships themselves or to render them unserviceable. The crews will remain on board ship."

MAY 7.—The war in Europe is over. After five years and eight months "complete and crushing victory" has, in the words of H.M. The King, crowned Britain's unrelenting struggle against Nazi Germany. Germany has surrendered unconditionally to Great Britain, the United States and Russia, at 2.41 a.m. in the technical college at Rheims, where Gen. Eisenhower has his headquarters. Gen. Bedell Smith, Gen. Eisenhower's Chief of Staff, signed for the Supreme Allied Command; Gen. Ivan Susloparov for Russia; Gen. François Sevez for France. Acting jointly on behalf of Adml. Dönitz as head of the Reich, the German delegates were Adml. Hans George Von Friedeburg, C.-in-C. the German Navy, and Col.-Gen. Gustav Jodl, Chief of Staff of the Wehrmacht. Signing for Germany, Jodl said, "With this signature the German people and armed forces are, for better or worse, delivered into the victors' hands."

MAY 8.—This is V-Day, together with tomorrow a national holiday. Tremendous scenes of rejoicing in London begin in the afternoon with the Prime Minister's announcement of the end of hostilities (see panel in this page).

MAY 9.—Germans have signed capitulation in Berlin, Moscow radio announces shortly after one a.m. (B.D.S.T.). It states, "The German High Command will immediately issue orders to all forces on sea, land and air under the German High Command to cease military operations after 11.01 p.m. (Moscow time)." The announcement added that the capitulation was signed by Field-Marshal Keitel, commanding all the German armed forces, Adml. Von Friedeburg, and Gen. Stumpf, commanding the Luftwaffe, in the presence of Marshal Zhukov, commanding the Russian forces in the field, and Air Chief Marshal Tedder, Allied Deputy Supreme C.-in-C.

Fleet Air Arm Service Under the Red Ensign

Urgent need arose for aircraft carriers of a new type, to safeguard our lifelines and protect officers and men of the Merchant Navy. How British tankers and grain-ships were ingeniously adapted to serve this purpose whilst still functioning as freighters, with F.A.A. personnel aboard, is told by Capt. FRANK H. SHAW. See also illus. page 615, Vol. 8.

It used to be a commonplace in the Merchant Navy that if you called down a ship's engine room skylight: "Are you there, Mac ?" a Scots voice was certain to reply, "Ay, I'm here !" Today the title has another significance, though no doubt the majority of merchant aircraft carriers (M.A.C. for short) are of Scots origin, the Clyde shipbuilding yards being mainly responsible for their production.

The M.A.C. is a natural development of the Catafighter-carrying freighter (see page 214, Vol. 8). I have seen Hurricane fighters catapult off from tankers in convoy and engage long-range enemy bombers in mid-Atlantic with satisfactory results ; but the limitations of such air defence were obvious, as the aircraft concerned had the brief life of a moth. They shot up, they fought desperately and, even when victorious, were compelled to sacrifice themselves by crashing into the sea, the pilots parachuting clear to be picked up by escorting destroyers. What was needed, plainly, was a type of ship from which the aircraft could take-off and to which, duty completed, they could return for further service. The merchant aircraft carrier supplied the effective answer.

A "Woolworth carrier" (see illus. page 104, Vol. 7) is a warship. She flies the White Ensign, is manned by naval personnel, and must be ready to take part in any operations deemed necessary. It was this need for ubiquity on the part of the pocket-carriers that brought the M.A.C. into service. The Murmansk convoys were a thorn in Germany's flesh. Consequently every effort was made by the Norwegian-based Luftwaffe to destroy the armadas on which Russia relied. The Woolworth carriers embodied themselves in these vital convoys and defeated the enemy's plans, but by doing so left the Atlantic convoys—equally vital to Allied survival—more or less unguarded for a gap of five hundred miles in mid-ocean.

And the Catafighters were not protection enough. Fleet carriers were too important—and in too short supply—to be thus utilized. Enemy U-boats were reported to carry aircraft—more, perhaps, for spotting convoys than for direct attack ; but attacks were made by such wasps in mid-sea. Our invaluable convoys could not be left to the protection of anti-aircraft fire, good and improving though it was.

It was a simpler matter to adapt certain types of merchantmen than to build new carriers in the numbers requisite to afford sufficient protection. Not that such adaptation was easy. The average merchantman is designed for carrying, and working, cargo. That means the provision of many wide hatches, of derrick-bearing masts, Samson-posts, winches and the like ; all obstacles to maintaining a clear unbroken deck such as aircraft require for taking-off and landing. If such impedimenta were removed, it meant that the freighter's usefulness as a cargo-carrier was destroyed or severely handicapped. The questions of funnels and engine-room superstructures could be overcome—there were motor-ships in plenty, requiring no funnels, only escape-pipes over the stern. There was the business of the navigating bridge, of course ; but when steam replaced sail the point of command was shifted from the poop aft to the Monkey Island amidships.

Tankers and grain-carriers supplied the solution (see illus. page 615, Vol. 8). These vessels required no complicated gear to handle their freights , oil could be shipped or discharged by pipes shackled on to connexions practically anywhere. Grain in bulk is normally pumped out into the receptive elevators. It can be shipped by a canvas hosepipe pouring a powerful stream downwards. Wide hatches are unnecessary.

Masts, derricks, winches were all redundant to such craft. These long-waisted, ugly ships were ideal for the purpose, except as regards size. The maximum length of flight deck attainable was roughly 400 feet. But Fleet Air Arm pilots are accustomed to taking risks. At a height, the deck of even a 27,000-ton Fleet carrier looks minute in its framing of boisterous sea. Not that 400 feet affords much of a run when taking off ! But as the F.A.A. pilots didn't object—who could ? It was their lives with which the gamble was made.

THE M.A.C. ANCYLUS, a British merchant ship equipped with flight deck for the launching and landing-on of Fleet Air Arm fighter aircraft during the most critical period of the Battle of the Atlantic, as described by Capt. Frank H. Shaw in this page. *Photo, British Official*

Flight decks were consequently superimposed on selected tankers and grain-carriers. The navigating bridges were shifted to the side of the top deck. This gave the craft a lopsided, unsightly appearance, but a ship could be as ugly as sin so long as she performed her designed function. The M.A.C. came into being soon after the theory was advanced, for Clyde shipbuilders can make even the most fantastic dream come true.

It must be stressed that the conception of the M.A.C. was for defence only. The ships were to fly the peaceful Red Ensign. Registered as men-of-war they would not be permitted by International Law to remain in a neutral port for longer than 24 hours. But they were to carry cargoes, the loading and discharge of which would occupy much more time than 24 hours. Still, "Defence" is capable of wide interpretation.

To attack an enemy aircraft before it can deliver its own attack on peaceful merchantmen is defence, authorized by law. To dive on a surfacing U-boat about to torpedo a convoy is also defence. These considerations being taken into account, the merchant ship rolé was quite permissible. But the F.A.A. personnel, the pilots, navigators, riggers, and engineers, were naval as to one hundred per cent. Thus the paradox came about of commissioned officers serving under Red Ensign captains, being amenable to Red Ensign discipline. The Junior Service for once outranked the Senior ! Yet contentment and happiness resulted. It meant adaptation, certainly ; but the F.A.A. is in the main recruited from "hostilities only" men, who are not steeped in the Royal Navy's hoary traditions. The resultant liaison between Red and White Ensigns was a happy omen for the future.

The smaller the ship the more boisterous she becomes in a sea-way. A 10,000-ton tanker can be tossed about like a cockboat in an Atlantic storm ; the U-boats preferred plenty of white-caps on the water when they closed in to attack. Such waves hide the feather of the periscope and the track of the hurrying torpedo. It is impossible to give adequate praise to the daring young flying-men of the F.A.A. No weather conditions appalled them when taking-off or landing-on the miniature flight decks. Often those decks were slanted at a forty-five degree angle, and washed by sluicing brine. True, they were fitted with trip-wires to bring alighting fighters up short ; but the take-off run could be very precarious.

During the ocean crossing aircraft from the M.A.C.s maintained a tireless overhead patrol. Especially was this so when crossing the great gap ; for though our giant bombers can cross the Atlantic in one furious hop, they cannot carry fuel enough to permit of giving continuous cover to the ships they sight beneath them. The weather was foul indeed that kept the M.A.C. airmen "grounded." Whether the aircraft were fitted with rockets capable of sinking a U-boat outright is a State secret. But the best way to defend a convoy is to sink the predatory submarines stalking it. True, an unarmed aircraft could spot U-boats and direct the attention of the surface escort to them ; but when the relative speeds of aircraft and destroyers are taken into account, it will be seen that the former is peculiarly adapted to deliver shattering blows whilst the enemy is still remote from his target.

It can readily be imagined how cordial a welcome was offered to these new sea monsters by the men of the Merchant Navy. The conviction was drilled into these—often sceptical—"toughs" that the Admiralty was determined to give them maximum protection. That is why, when at a Master's conference the Commodore of Convoy announced that an M.A.C. or two would sponsor the armada on its eastward run, every shipmaster present got to his feet and cheered himself hoarse.

Just how much farther the development of this peculiar type of winged freighter will go it is difficult to estimate. Imagination pictures liners of the future equipped with flight decks from which passengers can take-off to effect a rendezvous ahead of the parent ship's arrival in port. Delayed passengers will be able to join ship far out at sea. Cases of illness can be transported to a hospital ashore with minimum delay. But the future will take care of itself.

Photos, Keystone

On Hitler's Birthday Nemesis Came to Nuremberg

Medieval city of Bavaria, where in the great Zeppelin Stadium the Fuehrer was wont to rant at the annual Nazi party congress, Nuremberg was entered by the U.S. 7th Army on April 16, 1945. Fierce fighting went on until the 20th (his 56th birthday) when the Stars and Stripes fluttered over the Adolf Hitler Platz and the Stadium (top) stood desolate save for a disabled Allied tank and two jeeps. At the same time our armour moved into the old walled inner city (bottom).

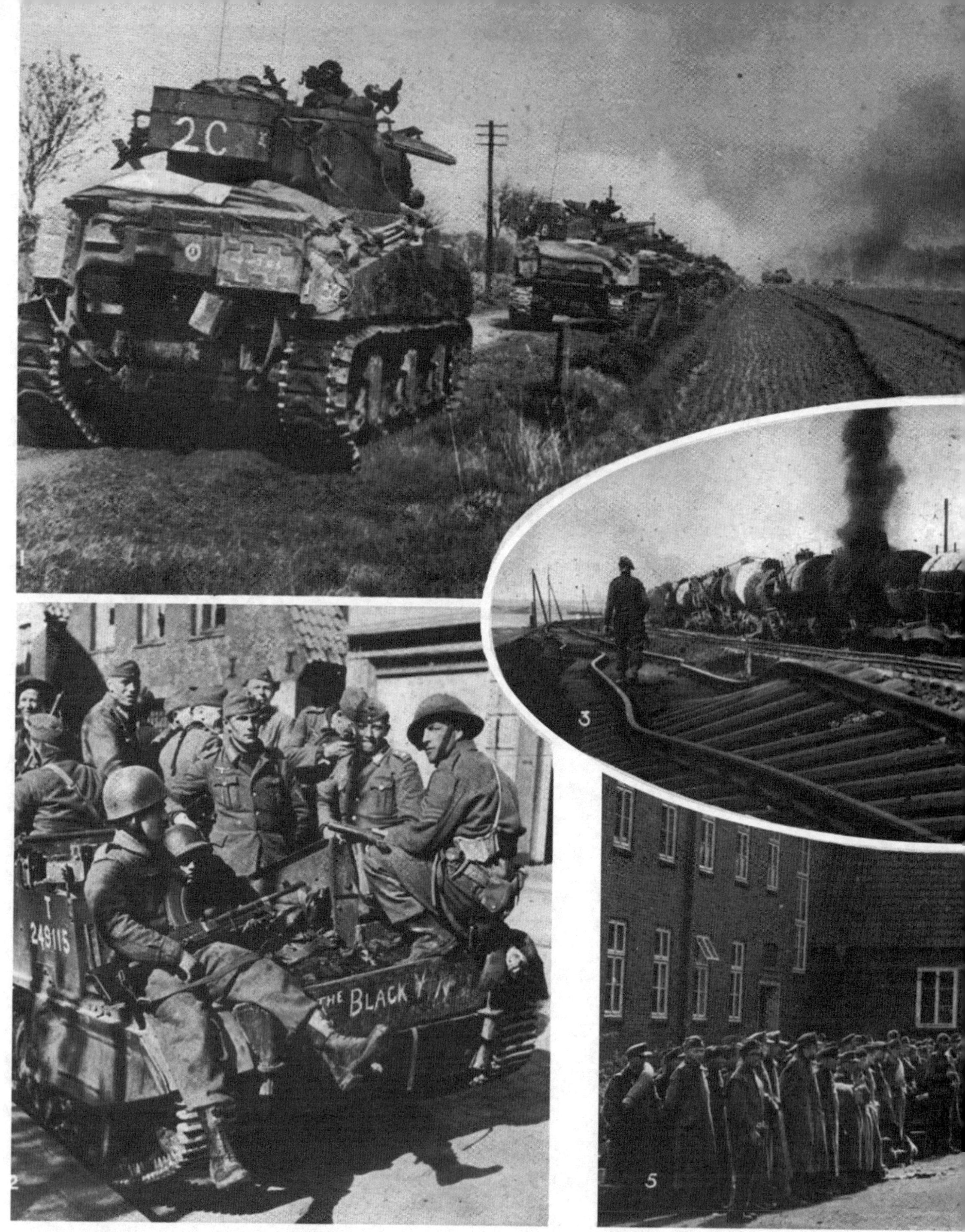

British Bid for Nazi Ports in Full Swing—

Nearing Bremen, tanks of the Coldstream Guards fired into woods where the enemy were still holding out (1); the city fell to the 52nd (Lowland) Division on April 27, 1945. Previously Verden, S.E. of Bremen, had been taken by Royal Scots Fusiliers; troops bringing in prisoners on a Bren carrier (2). South of Hamburg, Uelzen was cleared by men of the 15th Scottish Division: a bombed German oil train was still burning when Stederdorf, beyond Uelzen, was entered (3).

Photos, ... Asso...

—As War Flames Flicker Out in the West

One of the last strongholds in Leipzig to hold out (April 19) was the huge monument commemorating the defeat of Napoleon in 1813, garrisoned by 150 fanatics with ammunition and foodstuffs sufficient for three months. After bombardment by U.S. 1st Army artillery, American infantry moved up to accept the surrender; white flags flutter above (4). The naval base of Buxtehude, Hamburg, was taken by British forces on April 22; garrison troops after their mass surrender (5).

Starvation and Torture Behind Barbed Wire

Photos, British and U.S. Official, Central Press

Revolting details came to light in the overrunning by the Allies of huge concentration camps in Germany. At Belsen, 60,000 disease-ridden civilian prisoners had been without water for six days; under compulsion, S.S. guards removed bodies for burial (1). At Gardelegen, carrying crosses prepared by themselves under Allied orders, Germans marched to a burial site (2). At Buchenwald (3) British M.P.s saw pitiful victims. British P.O.W.s at Stalag 11B greet their liberators (4).

VIEWS & REVIEWS Of Vital War Books

by Hamilton Fyfe

If a butcher said to a customer in Warsaw while the Nazis were in occupation of the city, "Put your steak on ice directly you get home," the customer knew there was a secret newspaper, printed by the Underground Movement, inside the meat parcel. Or perhaps newsboys would be shouting at street corners, "Latest news! Great German victories!" which told passers-by who loathed the Germans that within the Nazi sheet was a copy of the Voice of Poland or Polish Freedom. With the production of these journals a Mr. Jan Karski was concerned. He tells about them and many other Underground activities in his country in Story of a Secret State (Hodder and Stoughton, 7s. 6d.), which gives the best account I have seen anywhere of what Polish patriots did to outwit Germans, to keep alive the national spirit, and to prepare for the establishment of a genuinely democratic system.

Mr. Karski's story begins with the last gay days in Warsaw, before the invasion began on September 1, 1939. A week before that, surprise and some anxiety were caused by the issue of mobilization orders, but the general feeling was one of utterly foolish optimism. Mr. Karski reports a remark by the major of the battery to which he belonged: "England and France are not needed this time. We can finish this alone." An official high up in the civil service, familiar with "well-informed circles," declared that "Hitler was bluffing." As soon as the Nazis saw the Poles were strong, united and prepared, they would back down. With such poisonous soothing syrup the nation was dosed. The collapse of their army and the widespread bombing of their homes plunged most of them into hopeless despair. They have never forgotten how they were deceived then, and with what disastrous consequences. That is why the remnants of the old ruling classes are distrusted.

General Sikorski, Polish Prime Minister and C.-in-C., whose death in an aircraft accident near Gibraltar on July 4, 1943, was most unfortunate for Poland and the world, understood this well. He told Mr. Karski that the past could not be recreated. "Our pre-war rulers," he said, "thought that Poland should develop, not according to democratic ideals, but through the so-called 'strong hand system.' The men responsible for that cannot come to power again. Post-war Poland will not be built up again by any privileged group. It must be a free democratic state."

Someone Might Crack Under Torture

By the Underground activities foundations were actually laid for parliamentary government. The leaders met together and debated; they were a national assembly in miniature. But they met always under the shadow of death. Work in the Underground Movement meant suffering constant tension, never-relaxing alertness to possible dangers.

> No one could ever tell when a leak might occur, when someone who had been caught might have cracked under torture, so that one's identity and the address to which one was going might become known to the Gestapo.

Those who were engaged in printing the secret newspapers were often surprised by the police. If knocking brought nobody to the door, grenades were thrown through windows, machine-gun bullets sprayed into the house. Survivors, if captured, were shot. So were the owners of the house, and sometimes those of neighbouring houses as well. Yet there never seems to have been any lack of people—women as frequently as men—to carry on. Women, says Mr. Karski,

> despite the world-wide opinion that they are loquacious and indiscreet, are on the whole, better conspiratorial workers than men . . . quicker to perceive danger and less inclined to avoid thinking about misfortunes. They are indubitably superior at being inconspicuous, and generally display much caution, discretion, and common sense . . . Men are often prone to exaggeration and bluff, are unwilling to face reality, and in most cases are subconsciously inclined to surround themselves with an air of mystery that sooner or later proves fatal.

That, the author might have added, applies especially to excitable, romantically minded, emotionally effervescent Polish men. But, though he does not say it bluntly, he lets it be seen plainly enough. Still, there were sufficient workers with Mr. Karski who, like him, were calm and not in the least theatrical. They carried on their activities by the simplest, most prosaic methods. The greatest law of underground work is 'Be inconspicuous.' The quality we valued more highly than any other was the ability to melt into

Underground Patriots at Work in Poland

the landscape, to seem humdrum and ordinary." Many people suppose that anti-Nazi plotters met usually at night in eerie surroundings, illumination being supplied be flickering candles, the conspirators wearing masks and speaking in whispers. Nothing could be further from the truth. The motion pictures I have seen and the fiction I have read about the Underground in Europe have invariably been products of purely sensational imagination."

Mr. Karski, by the way, declines to believe in the existence of any widespread or vigorous Underground plotting in Germany.

> I have come to know Nazi Germany rather well from many angles during this war. I have had occasion to travel in the Reich and I have never encountered a trace of any important movement hostile to the Nazi regime . . . I believe that all accounts of such movements are either pure fiction or wishful exaggeration.

POLISH PATRIOT FIGHTER exemplified on the military side the courage and resource of those whose desperately heroic struggles are described in the book reviewed here. *Photo, Keystone*

It was his employment as a courier to keep the Polish Government in London in contact with the patriots in Poland that gave him an insight into what was going on in Germany. He was lucky enough only to be caught once by the Gestapo, who applied their usual barbaric methods to him, but let him slip through their fingers. He had at the beginning of the war an experience as prisoner in Russian hands. He contrasts the behaviour of Soviet soldiers with that of the Germans. "They were lenient, within the limits of military discipline. I never saw a Russian guard strike or curse at a prisoner, no matter how enraged he might become. The worst threat they ever employed was the standard, 'Quiet, or you'll be sent to Siberia!' They knew Siberia had been a Polish bugaboo for generations." It was where the Tsars used to send Poles who struggled against their tyranny.

The Tsars failed to Russianize Poland as signally as the Germans failed to Prussianize the country. In Posen "everything possible was done to spread German influence and culture" from the time of Frederick the Great Scoundrel. Bismarck tried to turn the Polish farmers into serfs. When the independence of Poland was restored in 1919 "every vestige of German influence disappeared." There were, however, a good many Poles who unfortunately decided to Nazify themselves when the Germans once more terrorized the country.

Quislings Liquidated Without Mercy

In the book there is an account of the execution of one such renegade. He was found hanging to the branch of a tree, with a letter sticking out of his pocket which said he had repented of acting as a Nazi spy. He had, of course, been hanged by Poles, and no doubt the Germans knew this. But they had to keep it quiet. Though they gave out that the man had gone mad, the incident had its effect; it made them more jumpy and it made the peasants think that if the spy had lost faith in the enemy, the hated Huns could not be as strong as was supposed.

Polish "quislings" who attempted to give active aid to the Nazis or who were proved to have put obstacles in the way of Underground workers were sentenced to death and "liquidated" without mercy. Others who had merely failed to behave stiffly and coldly towards Germans were summoned by the secret court of justice and asked to justify their conduct if they could. They were usually pronounced "infamous," which meant that they were boycotted socially and held liable to have criminal proceedings taken against them after the war.

Hatred of such "vermin" increased as living conditions became harder. In 1942 prices of bread and potatoes were thirty times as high as they had been three years before; bacon cost sixty times as much. The Underground workers fared no better than the rest of the population. For twelve months Mr. Karski tasted neither butter nor sugar. "A plate of cereal a day was considered a luxury. We were all hungry nearly all the time." The result was that "any trick to get more food was moral." A priest, for instance, "dug up two birth certificates of dead babies born about twenty-eight years before, and I managed to obtain two more fake identity papers and ration cards." His papers were always fakes while he worked Underground, and they had to be changed often. The number of disguises he assumed while he was on his final journey to London make up a most amusing story.

After this adventure he was taken off active service and sent to the United States as a kind of unofficial ambassador. There he wrote this book, as is made plain by the American terms he uses, such as "bills" (currency notes), and "dry goods store."

'Architects of Better World' at San Francisco

CONFERENCE OF ALLIED NATIONS at San Francisco—to establish "a general international organization to maintain peace and security"—was first mooted in the joint statement issued at the conclusion of the Crimea Conference in February 1945 (see pages 682-683, Vol. 8). Held in the city's new Opera House, the Conference was opened by an address broadcast from Washington by President Truman in which he designated the delegates as "architects of the better world." All the United Nations were represented, with the exception of Poland—about the formation of whose new Government the Western Allies and the U.S.S.R. were still deliberating when the Conference opened. At the first session, as the delegates took their seats in the stalls, arc-lamps for the cine-cameras were focused on the stage, where the flags of the Allied Nations hung. A band played "The World is Waiting for the Sunrise," whereupon U.S. soldiers and Servicewomen marched on to the stage to stand to attention, while Mr. Edward Stettinius, Jnr., U.S. Secretary of State, took his seat. Then delegates heard the President speak from Washington by radio.

MEETING PLACE OF THE ALLIED NATIONS' HISTORIC CONFERENCE which opened on April 25, 1945—the Opera House, San Francisco (1). Contrasts in oratory: Mr. Anthony Eden, Britain's Foreign Minister (2), and Mr. Molotov, Soviet Foreign Commissar (3). The brilliant opening scene (4); against a background of 46 Allied flags, and men and women representatives of the U.S. armed forces, sat Mr. E. R. Stettinius, Jnr., U.S. Secretary of State (2nd from right, on dais). See also page 63.

Photos, British and U.S. Official, British Combine Photos, Black Star

'Beacon of Fresh Hope in a Sadly Torn World'

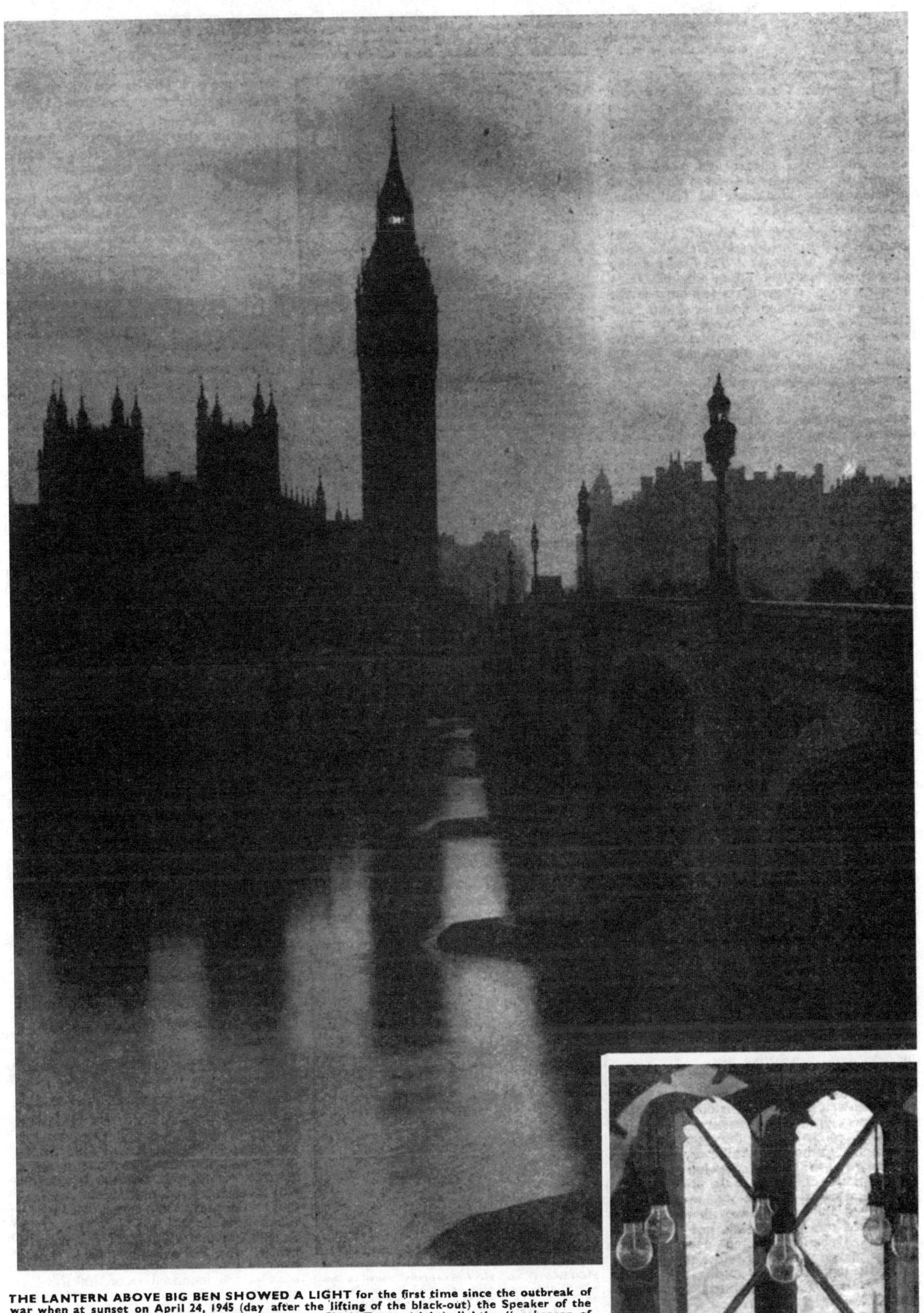

THE LANTERN ABOVE BIG BEN SHOWED A LIGHT for the first time since the outbreak of war when at sunset on April 24, 1945 (day after the lifting of the black-out) the Speaker of the House of Commons switched on the lamps in the Clock Tower (right), lighting " a beacon of fresh hope in a sadly torn and distracted world." *Photos, G.P.U. and Keystone*

Tremendous Struggle of the Heroic Netherlands

With the surrender of all German forces in Holland on May 4, 1945, the Dutch regained their freedom after five years of enemy occupation. One of their most valiant struggles against this Nazi tyranny had its inception on the eve of Arnhem, when 30,000 Dutch railwaymen obeyed the official Netherlands Government order to strike. The story of this great and long-sustained blow against the foe and its consequences is told by HAROLD A. ALBERT, from official sources. See also p. 780, Vol. 8.

UNESCORTED Lancasters of R.A.F. Bomber Command, flying low over Holland on April 29, 1945, dropped food to the starving people of the occupied western districts. Sacks containing meat, vegetables, flour, milk, margarine, dried eggs, sugar, tea, cheese and yeast—even pepper, salt and mustard—were dropped at airfields and a racecourse at The Hague, Rotterdam and Leyden.

Before the Lancasters set out, a message from SHAEF was broadcast in Dutch, German and English. It stated: "The food-carrying aircraft will first drop bright coloured flares to guide them. These flares will burst in the air and will be coloured red or green. The flares will make a distinctive noise while they are falling." A second broadcast announced: "Allied aircraft are now on their way. The next aircraft you hear overhead will be carrying food, not bombs."

The International Red Cross had previously contacted the Germans in Holland, and were given an assurance that the planes would not be attacked provided they kept to an agreed route. This R.A.F. operation, unique in the history of Bomber Command, was followed on May 1 by an announcement from SHAEF that a meeting between Allied and German representatives (the former headed by Lieut.-Gen. W. B. Smith, Chief of Staff to Gen. Eisenhower, the Germans by the notorious Austrian quisling Seyss-Inquart, Reichskommissar for the Netherlands) had been held to arrange for importation of food into N.W. Holland not only by air but by sea and road. By air, ten dropping zones were agreed, for use from 7 a.m. to 3 p.m. daily. By sea, foodships to enter Rotterdam, the Germans to meet them at a prearranged rendezvous and guarantee safe conduct to port. One main road was made available, the supply scheduled to start on May 2 with 1,000 tons.

Behind all this there lies one of the most stirring chapters of the war—the story of how 6,000,000 Dutch civilians stood shoulder to shoulder in support of a sustained great strike while Allied armies fought their way to final victory.

On the evening of Sept. 17, 1944, the day that the Dakotas and Horsa gliders spilled their loads around Arnhem, an official announcement was broadcast to the people of Holland that the Netherlands Government after consultation with the Allied High Command deemed the moment had come to call a general strike of all railway workers, and 30,000 railwaymen promptly stopped work. Six-and-a-half months later the strike was still 100 per cent complete. And in early April 1945, when many of the Nazis were on the run no Dutch railwayman lifted a finger to speed the parting pests.

THE strike was total, nation-wide. At zero hour, drivers left their trains standing; signalmen walked out of their boxes; booking clerks and station-masters left their offices. Even the railway directors left their desks and their homes. And every manjack had to go into hiding, knowing that the penalty, if caught, would be the firing squad. Then thousands of factory workers in Amsterdam and other centres downed tools and walked out in sympathy, and remained absent. Operatives closed down power stations and repair shops rather than assist the Nazis in any degree during the bitter fight for the Lower Rhine, and the results were far-reaching.

BOMB-BAYS OF A LANCASTER being loaded with sacks of food for the starving Dutch—enough to provide a balanced ration for over 3,000 people for a day. *Photo, Keystone*

If the Germans could have made use of the Dutch railways during the critical second half of September 1944, for instance, the struggle for the bridge across the Waal might not have been decided in favour of the Allies, and the British 2nd Army might perhaps have been held at Nijmegen. If the railways had been working efficiently as late as April this year, Field-Marshal Montgomery might have been delayed in his push beyond the Rhine.

Instead, Reich German railway staff had to deplete the already tenuous manpower of German lines to clear the Dutch main lines of goods trains which had come to a standstill and to operate the few military trains that circulated. The imported railwaymen were unfamiliar with the Dutch signalling system—itself now liable to sabotage—and the trains had to run "on sight," crawling from point to point and presenting an easy target to Allied aircraft. The points had to be operated by hand, and military trains took twelve hours to complete the 23-minute run from Amersfoort to Utrecht. Eventually this was "improved" to four hours, and the 20-minute Utrecht-Amsterdam journey—so vital to V-supplies—was "reduced" to three hours. But for the strike, obviously

HOLLAND and N.W. Germany, showing (in white) the areas still occupied by the Nazis on May 1, 1945, when food was being delivered by the Allies to the Dutch civilians as described in this page.

many more V-bombs carried on this line would have fallen on southern England.

The Germans alternately cajoled, threatened, and tried reprisals in attempts to make the strikers return. They offered coal-trains in return for co-operation, and the Dutch refused, preferring to shiver through one of the bitterest winters Europe has ever known. In Utrecht, headquarters of the Dutch rail administration, the Occupation authorities offered double wages and double rations to strike-breakers, a powerful inducement in a land reduced to direst poverty and hunger. Although 1,000 railway families lived in the town only four men came forward, and these were Dutch Nazis. In the whole of Holland only fifty Dutch Nazis offered to perform blackleg work.

Some resistance leaders were captured and shot, and many strikers' families were seized as hostages. Others saw their homes destroyed, their furniture confiscated. It made no difference. The strikers of course drew no official pay and none were allowed rations. The contingency was foreseen and provided against by the strike-leaders, and thousands of key men—traffic controllers and dispatchers, locomotivemen, signalmen and shunters—were allocated their hiding places weeks before Arnhem.

THE hiding places had to be secure against prying eyes. One man lived with eight others in a secret cellar under a barn; another spent four weeks in a cupboard. Forty families from Oldenzaal took to the woods with their children and lived in tents until better quarters could be found. "One half of occupied Holland was in hiding—the other half kept it hidden!" That is how a Dutch transport official described the situation to me. And he added, "many were living on the ration cards of the rest."

After twenty days the Germans once again tried to induce the railwaymen to give in, by promising that no action would be taken against them and that coal and food would be available for the population. By now the Allied setback at Arnhem (see page 366, Vol. 8) had become known, the future was uncertain, and strikers and supporters alike could foresee only grave consequences for their own people. From Radio Orange, however, came the call for the stoppage to go on, and there was no wavering.

Normally, Holland's food supplies were transported in barges and lorries; railways conveyed only a small proportion. Now the unscrupulous enemy confiscated lorries and barges and stole most of the remaining food stocks as part of a deliberate policy, and blamed the famine upon the strikers. But public opinion remained unaltered. Upon the walls of Rotterdam and the Hague appeared a slogan that proclaimed the motif of the struggle, "To the end, now!"

By April this year, British and Canadian troops had liberated north-east Holland and cut the escape-route of the Germans left in the west; but the trickle of food from the north-eastern provinces to the west was also abruptly cut off. The German flooding of the rich farmlands south and east of Amsterdam and of the great north-west polder rendered the plight of the Dutch in The Hague, Utrecht, Amsterdam and Rotterdam still more desperate. But the strike still held. Looking back at the immortal record of the "two hundred days," we can see that the suffering of the Dutch people bore due fruit. Their

Cheers for the 1st Canadian Army in Holland

WEST OF FAMOUS ARNHEM, inhabitants of the Netherlands town of Ede (1) acclaimed Yorkshire troops of the British 49th Division, fighting as part of the 1st Canadian Army, as they rode in on April 17. Also near Arnhem, two young Canadians talked (2) with veterans from the famous 17th-century Bronbeek Institute for Netherlands Colonial Soldiers where the Dutch tricolour was flown for the first time since May 10, 1940 (see also facing page).

Inside Germany, police—the only enemy officials allowed to wear uniform—passed a Canadian provost in Meppen (3), on the Dortmund-Ems canal, captured on April 9 by the 4th Canadian Division. Dutch nurses and patients at a hospital near Otterloo, ten miles north-west of Arnhem (4), cheered when troops of the 1st Canadian Army on April 17 captured the village after fierce fighting in which a Canadian H.Q. staff took part.

Photos, British and Canadian Official, Planet News

THE FAMOUS AVA BRIDGE AT SAGAING, NEAR MANDALAY, in Burma—one of the world's biggest—partly demolished by our troops during the 1942 retreat, was retaken on March 17, 1945, by a patrol of the Royal Worcester Regiment and a mixed striking force of all-Indian troops aided by Burmese irregulars. After its capture, troops and transport of the 14th Army stand by at a bridge-head alongside (1). A zig-zag catwalk (2) was the sole link across the shattered section of the bridge which was the only road-rail structure spanning the Irrawaddy. A 25-pounder of the 36th Division (3) laid a protective barrage for troops crossing the Shweli River north-east of Myok (taken on March 20). Commanding the 26th Division, Maj.-Gen. C. E. N. Lomax watched Rajputs embark at Ramree (4). *Photos, British Official*

I WAS THERE! Eye Witness Stories of the War

How East and West Met at Torgau on the Elbe

Russian and American forces "officially" made contact when on April 26, 1945, units of the two Armies shook hands. By that union of Eastern and Western Allies Germany had been cut in two. Stanley Baron, News Chronicle war correspondent with Koniev's 1st Ukrainian Army, tells of the wild day that followed a fantastic night. See also illus. page 40.

BEFORE THE "OFFICIAL" LINK-UP, these men of the U.S. 69th Division claim to have made the first contact with Soviet Forces near Torgau—on April 25, 1945. Sec.-Lieut. W. D. Robertson (second from right) tells his story in this page. *Photo, Associated Press*

SEC.-LT. William D. Robertson, of Los Angeles and the Headquarters C.O. of the First Battalion of the 273rd Infantry, U.S. 69th Division, looks at the moment like being officially credited as the first man to shake hands with a soldier of Koniev's First Ukrainian Army, but I do not suppose we shall ever be sure. This has been a wild day following a fantastic night, during which at least a couple of rival claims to be first in the field, have come in from two different places.

All I am personally certain of is that I am here in the mess hall of a German barracks with the Elbe flowing fast about 250 yards behind, that I have just had lunch and drunk "victory and death to the Fascist invader" with the cropped-headed commander of the 173rd Regiment of the Ukrainian 58th (Honour Guard) Division, that Torgau, once the location of one of the biggest stalags in Germany, with thousands of British prisoners, is now an empty shell behind me with scarcely half a dozen Germans showing their heads, and that the American front lines are 25 miles to the rear.

AT ANOTHER ELBE CROSSING, troops of the U.S. 9th Army at the southern end of their line scrambled across a pontoon bridge to shake the hands of the Russians on the east bank. In the foreground, right, is a Red Army woman interpreter. *Photo, Pictorial Press*

Jeep Out on a Lonely Sortie

I came into Torgau this morning with a platoon of riflemen, the second to cross no man's land after Robertson's jeep, out on a lonely sortie, had made one contact at 4.20 last night. We drove into the market square—I shall go back to the journey in a minute—and found it completely empty. For a minute we circled round. Then from under an arch walked three Russian soldiers, Lt. Ivan Feodor Kuzminski, Pte. Peter Melehen, and another. They paused, and then they ran with arms outstretched, grabbing at any American's hand they could see.

KUZMINSKI spun round with a G.I. Joe clutching each hand. They thumped each other on the back. We all wrung hands. We all thumped. If there had been any lurking suspicion that any political decision on zones of interest would get in the way of our rapture at this meeting, it was gone in a second. We were allies, we met and rejoiced, and I can think of nothing so exciting, so warm, so human as this encounter in this alien square. Kuzminski began to make a little speech, but it was drowned in exclamations and shouts. Out came the cameras for the inevitable arm-in-arm pictures. Then we saw a couple of Russian fighter planes weaving overhead.

Kuzminski pointed out the road to the river, and we drove on down the street past the Rose Gasthaus, set on fire by shelling when Koniev's men arrived on the opposite bank on Tuesday, and still flaming. There ahead was the Elbe, 100 yards wide and flowing fast, both girder bridges north and south down in the river, and the ancient castle, with a hole in its roof, rising up to the right of the cobbled quay. Here I will insert a little bit of story about that castle, as it was told to me last midnight by Sec.-Lt. Robertson when he got back to the U.S. 69th Division command post with the three Russian officers whom he had brought along, Maj. Anaphim Larinov, Capt. Vassili Petrovich Nedov and Lt. Alexander Silvacho—the first man from the east to enter our lines.

Robertson's mission had been to go out with Cpl. James McDonnell and Ptes. Paul Staub and Frank Huff in an armed jeep from the First Army's bridge-head over the River Mulde at Wuerzen, east of Leipzig, to help bring some sort of order into the masses of German refugees streaming in from the east, with liberated prisoners of war and German soldiers by the thousand, hurrying to give themselves up to the Americans. His surprise was all his own when he found himself 25 miles eastward in Torgau. Robertson said:

I had just found 30 Allied prisoners in a barracks, when some Krauts came up and said the Russians were just over the river. I got out of the jeep and went down on foot with a white flag to a big castle in the town. Other Krauts said the Russians were 500 yards away over the river. I broke into a drug-store, found some paint, painted the white flag with U.S. red stripes on blue field, went up to the top of the castle tower and began to wave and shout—"Tovarich Kamerad!"

The Russians on the other side bellowed something back to me, but I don't understand Russian. Then they fired up two coloured flares. I hollered that I hadn't got any flares, but apparently they got tired of listening, or thought I was a German, so they fired a couple of anti-tank gun shells. I came down and found a Russian prisoner to tell them who I was, and after that everything was friendly. Once across the river we sat round saying: "Hi, there!" and smiling at each other and drinking toasts. Then three Russian officers with Pte. Nikolai Andreev climbed on the jeep, one on the bumper, one on the bonnet and the other inside, and here we are.

UNDER their eyes, waiting at the river edge, to cross by skiffs, were hundreds of their fellow-people who have been taken into slavery. For 25 miles I passed them on this extraordinary journey. Most jogged along in high-sided farm carts, some drawn by oxen, some by horses, in an apparently endless cavalcade which, by this time, had little interruption to fear from Germans trying to escape from north to south through the slender corridor which was still technically enemy-occupied territory.

Some flew white flags, and were obviously nervous as we raced up alongside them. Then, when they saw the white stars on the jeeps, they waved and cheered. Down by the river, I spoke to 23-year-old Capt. Alexander Siderenko, while some of his men, fine-looking soldiers, young, bronzed, exceptionally well dressed and equipped, kept the party going with accordion music, somewhat alarmingly punctuated with close-by explosions as their comrades on the other side practised panzerfaust fire.

Only Way to Control Germany

Siderenko said, "I went out into the woods last night to tell the German civilians that they had nothing to fear, and that we had not come as murderers but as soldiers fighting for a just cause. Stalin's order is that we shall not molest civilians, we must take prisoners of war without injury or danger to their lives, and that this is a war for the right to enjoy life and to respect the rights of other people. That is what we are here for, and that is what we must stick to."

I asked him what he thought of the proposed joint control of Germany. "I think it is the only way to control Germany," he said, "and we Russians will willingly stay here until she has learned that other people have rights equal to their own." Lt. Arnold Gonorowski chimed in heartily, "That goes for me too!"

'The Target, Gentlemen, is Berchtesgaden !'

Down on Hitler's lair in the Bavarian Alps rained 12,000-lb. earthquake bombs—a present from Britain. Trees were thrown like straws to the sky, the ground spewed rocks and earth. V. Brown, News Chronicle war correspondent in one of the Lancasters, wrote this story on April 25, 1945.

It was dark and cold at the R.A.F. station in England this morning when the Lancaster bomber crews filed in for their briefing. The wing-commander stood up. With a half-smile he said: "The target, gentlemen, is Berchtesgaden!"

All knew the significance of the raid. Berchtesgaden, Hitler's mountain home, was the nerve centre of the Redoubt, headquarters of any final resistance by the enemy. It was still dark when we climbed into the laden Lancasters. The engines roared. Flt.-Lt. L. E. Marsh, of Dunfermline (awarded the D.F.C. for helping to sink the Tirpitz and veteran of 30 missions), piloted the bomber in which I flew. He put his thumb in the air—and we were off to Berchtesgaden. About 350 heavies took part in the attack.

As we flew over England, over the Channel, over Belgium—still black, before the April dawn had risen—I tried to remember what I had heard about Berchtesgaden, the Eagle's Nest. Francois Poncet, the former French Ambassador to Berlin, in an official book described how from a distance it looks like an observatory perched 6,000 ft. up (twice the height of Snowdon) on the crest of a mountain. He told how he drove along a winding road cut through the rock, and then entered a long tunnel. Next he entered a large, copper-plated lift, and was carried 300 ft. up to the top. And there was Hitler's home. He had a vivid phrase. When you looked out, he said, it was like being in an aeroplane in flight. Now real aeroplanes in deathly flight were on their way to this strange abode.

Dawn came and we saw the Rhine. Over the Continent we made rendezvous with our escort of United States Mustang fighters, emerging from the sunrise like a cloud of midges. In one great formation we flew on to the Bavarian Alps. Around me the crew were busy. It was a symbolic moment when they examined the recognition signals which would be shown by any Russian planes we might meet in the course of our flight.

Germany unrolled below us. The countryside was brown and green and peaceful. Lake Constance came in view, shimmering like a mirror. There was no flak, no sign of enemy fighters. We avoided Swiss territory and flew on to the Bavarian Alps. The navigator, Flying Officer A. Brown, of Toronto, pointed them out to me. Said the bomb-aimer, Flying Officer J. A. Carr, of Vancouver, "I've never before seen anything quite so beautiful!" But the target was near. As we approached Berchtesgaden, "The Eagle's Nest" could be easily seen, on its pinnacle in its picture-postcard setting.

Six Lancasters headed towards it. I saw their bombs fall as we flew alongside to drop our load. It was horrific. Into this scene below, which had the prettiness of a Victorian postcard, burst some of the most powerful bombs ever devised by man—12,000 lb. earthquake bombs. Our plane rocked.

Below, the ground spewed rocks and earth and bricks, and even trees were uprooted and thrown like straws in the sky. Planes were above, below and alongside us. The huge bombs went down at regular intervals. Said the engineer, Pilot Officer L. Harrison, of London, "Not one must be wasted. We've either to be certain to hit the target or bring them back."

I saw 30 bombs go down—there may have been more—on the target area, which included the large S.S. barracks where Hitler's Storm-troopers are stationed. There were at least two direct hits on the Eagle's Nest. As I write, great clouds of smoke roll to the sky. All the target is now covered in smoke: you can smell it inside the plane. There are no enemy fighters. Even the flak is not so heavy as anticipated . . .

We are nearing our English base. We have been in the air almost nine hours and flown 1,600 miles. Below us lies the glory of the English landscape in spring, but I keep thinking of that mountain grandeur we have just visited. Hitler's home, "like an aeroplane in flight," will soar no more on its mountain top.

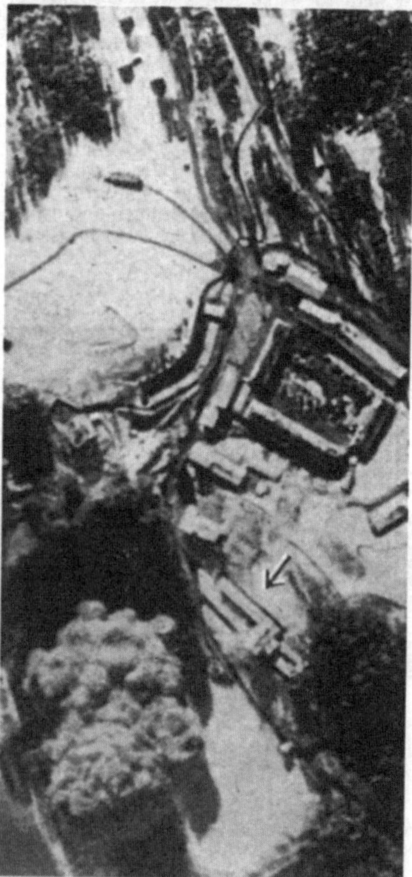

BOMBS FOR HITLER'S CHALET at Berchtesgaden (top) are seen (bottom) falling near their target during the daylight raid by R.A.F. Lancasters described in this page.
Photos, British Official and New York Times Photos

Stalingrad Banners Waved on Berlin Hills

Making for the heart of the Third Reich, with lips blackened and parched with thirst and dust, the Soviet Guards, some of whom had fought all the way from Stalingrad, carried red flags to plant on the heights dominating Berlin, as narrated in Soviet War News by V. Vishnevsky and I. Zolin.

None of us will ever forget that night. Twenty-three bridges had been thrown across the swollen Oder. Engines roared in unison. Pillars of heavy dust hung in the air. The glow on the western horizon grew bigger and bigger as our parachute flares exposed every nook and cranny of the German lines. Shell-bursts lit up the sky. The earth trembled, and over the German positions rose an immense fountain of smoke, earth and rocks.

The aircraft added their noise to the general din; their targets were the enemy's front line rail communications. By the time they had finished the steel rails were twisted into hoops. We found a German armoured train called "Berlin" standing intact in Seelow station, unable to move in either direction. The gunfire made all conversation impossible.

A Guards unit brought its Stalingrad banner to the forward trenches. That banner had been borne from the Volga to the very approaches of Berlin. Senior Sergeant Mosolov, Junior Sergeant Shmokov and Sergeant Shapovalov, all of them cavaliers of the Order of Glory, carried the colours. The folds opened in the breeze: the face of Lenin was turned to the west, towards the enemy. Flashes of gunfire lit up the assembly of red banners.

The colours were paraded slowly through the narrow trenches, and the Guards, on bended knee, kissed the fringe. The ceremony was conducted in silence. There was no need for words, here before Berlin. As they advanced the Soviet Guards carried red flags to plant on the heights that cover Berlin. The flags were carried in front of the troops, borne by the boldest and bravest. When one standard-bearer fell the flag was immediately taken by another. Corporal Igor Ivanov was badly wounded. The flag he carried was erected on a hill far to the west.

By seven in the morning it was fully light. Dust and smoke lay over us like a blanket, getting thicker every moment. An intricate trench system was buttressed by pillboxes, blockhouses, tanks dug into the earth, cleverly sited artillery, machine-guns and light field guns emplaced in cellars, attics and sheds. In short, every square foot of the soil of Brandenburg—cornfields and gardens, greenhouses, railway embankments, woods, parks and cemeteries—had been fortified.

Every building was a link in the scheme of defence—a link that had to be flattened, battered or destroyed by an artillery barrage, by a sudden infantry attack, or by an encirclement manoeuvre. We stumbled over a wilderness of smashed bricks. This was once a German village that had been converted into a solid fort. The Soviet guns had obliterated it. Trees had been uprooted. The pond was filled in with debris and dust.

Now and then a Messerschmitt would fly over the battlefield at 600 ft., hunting for field hospital units. That is what these "knights of the air," these "Richthofen" heroes have come to. It was pleasant to see one of these jackals brought down by the Soviet A.A. guns.

I have just visited a battery commanded by a Georgian, Captain Ushuradze of the Guards, which has fought its way to Berlin all the way from Stalingrad . . . The great toilers of war, the sappers, pass by us. They blow up everything the Germans can build, even their trickiest fortifications, lying underground to a depth of 300 ft. or more. There is a dull yellowish haze over the sun.

The battle rages ever more fiercely. There is a cloud of dust over the Berlin autobahn. Russia, the Ukraine, Byelorussia, Georgia, Armenia, Azerbaidjan, Uzbekistan, Kazakhstan, Kirghizia, Lithuania, Latvia and Estonia are marching on Berlin.

Dust, dust, dust . . . Nothing to drink, everything dried up, burnt out. But nothing matters. We are going on to Berlin with lips black and parched. The distance grows less on the signposts. The heavy guns go by to fire their first salvos into Berlin.

LIGHT MACHINE-GUNNER from one of the Red Army units which made contact with the forces of the Western Allies on the Elbe, during the last week of April 1945.

I Went With the Green Berets to Osnabruck

Senior Brigade Chaplain and R.C. Chaplain to the 1st Commando Brigade, the Rev. Terence Quinlan, R.N. (known throughout the Brigade as "The Bish"), tells how he stopped a sniper's bullet—and made his captors his captives. Osnabruck was cleared of the enemy on April 5, 1945.

At a fork in the road to Osnabruck I took the wrong turning. I was in my jeep with my driver. The first we knew anything was wrong was a sniper's bullet. It was a rotten shot and missed us by miles. We decided it was just an odd sniper, and pushed on, but 100 yards down the road a fusillade broke out from all sides. The hail of bullets shot the tires to pieces and we had to stop. We baled out pretty promptly and crouched down behind the jeep looking for cover. Then I was hit in the back of the leg and bled profusely.

I made a dash for a house by the road, but the door was locked. I hammered on the door with my stick, and a woman opened it. She looked alarmed, but I limped in and my driver joined me. The Jerries must have been rotten shots, or we should have been cut to pieces. While my wound was being attended to, ten or fifteen Germans walked into the basement. They let my driver finish dressing the wound, then told us to get outside. It was then I noticed a row of the German field grey hats poking up behind a hedge.

We were led across country, through gardens and over railway embankments. They were a most disorderly crowd. There were at least 100 of them, and they just straggled along. I told them they were completely surrounded and they might just as well give up. Some were muttering among themselves and appeared quite willing, but two N.C.O.s ordered them on. They told me their officers had left them the day before.

I had walked about a mile when my leg began to bleed again, so an escort of two Germans was left to guard my driver and me. We entered the south of Osnabruck. We were the first British to enter that part of the town, and I asked the escort if there was a church nearby. He pointed to one, and I sat on the steps to rest my leg. Immediately a large crowd of foreign workers gathered, attracted by British soldiers with green berets. I asked one of the workers to fetch a priest, who offered me the hospitality of his house. He gave us lunch—my escort as well—and told me he could be shot for harbouring British soldiers.

I then turned to the two German soldiers and asked them: "Are we with you, or you with us?" and they replied: "With you." They threw away their ammunition and rifles and became our prisoners. It was then reported that some British troops with guns were in the south of the town, so I asked them to send for a doctor and ambulance. The doctor arrived, patched me up, and drove me and my prisoners to the centre of the town to meet up with my Commandos who were in the north-west of Osnabruck.

We began to walk through Osnabruck, and the populace gazed in wonderment, for we were the first British troops in that part. We met my Commandos and handed over our prisoners. The next day I saw a number of other prisoners brought in and I recognized many of them who had been among my captors the previous day.

OUR DIARY OF THE WAR

APRIL 25, Wednesday *2,062nd day*
Air.—Hitler's Berchtesgaden chalet attacked by Lancasters with 12,000-lb. bombs. U.S. bombers attacked Skoda armament works at Pilsen.
Russian Front.—Zhukov's and Koniev's forces joined up near Potsdam, completing encirclement of Berlin.

APRIL 26, Thursday *2,063rd day*
Elbe.—American and Russian forces linked up at Torgau, N.E. of Leipzig.
Western Front.—U.S. 3rd Army crossed Danube both sides of Regensburg.
Russian Front.—Stettin on Baltic, and Brno, Czechoslovakia, captured by Soviet troops. In Berlin, districts of Dahlem and Siemensstadt were taken.
Italy.—5th Army captured Verona and crossed the Adige; Mantua and Parma also captured.
Japan.—Super-Fortresses attacked airfields on Kyushu and Shikoku.
Germany.—Announced that Goering, owing to heart disease, had relinquished command of Luftwaffe.

APRIL 27, Friday *2,064th day*
Western Front.—Bremen captured by British troops. 3rd Army captured Regensburg and crossed into Austria.
Russian Front.—Potsdam, Spandau and Rathenow captured by Soviet troops. Neukölln and Tempelhof occupied in Berlin. Wittenberg on the Elbe captured.
Italy.—Genoa occupied by 5th Army troops after Italian partisans had seized control from Germans. Milan also taken over by partisans.

APRIL 28, Saturday *2,065th day*
Western Front.—Augsburg captured by U.S. 3rd Army.
Italy.—Mussolini and members of his cabinet executed by Italian partisans. Bergamo, Brescia, Vicenza and Padua occupied by Allied troops.
Germany.—First news of Himmler's offer to surrender to Britain and U.S.A. through Swedish intermediary.

APRIL 29, Sunday *2,066th day*
Italy.—German armies in North Italy and West Austria capitulated; surrender terms signed at Naples, effective from May 2. 8th Army troops entered Venice.
Western Front.—British troops crossed lower Elbe near Lauenburg. Troops of 7th Army captured Oberammergau.
Russian Front.—In street battles in Berlin, district of Moabit and Anhalter station were captured.
Netherlands.—First supplies of food dropped from R.A.F. aircraft to Dutch civilians in western Holland.
General.—Formation of provisional government in Austria announced by Moscow radio.

APRIL 30, Monday *2,067th day*
Western Front.—Munich captured by U.S. 7th Army.
Russian Front.—Reichstag building in Berlin captured by Soviet troops. In Czechoslovakia, Moravaka Ostrava was carried by storm.
Italy.—Turin entered by U.S. troops after its capture by Italian partisans. Tito's Yugoslav forces broke into Trieste.
Indian Ocean.—Andaman and Nicobar Is. bombarded by E. Indies fleet.

MAY 1, Tuesday *2,068th day*
Germany.—Death of Hitler in Berlin announced by Admiral Dönitz, who succeeded him as Fuehrer.
Russian Front.—Soviet troops captured Stralsund on the Baltic and city of Brandenburg; inside Berlin Charlottenburg and Schoeneberg were cleared.
Italy.—N.Z. troops of 8th Army made contact with Tito's troops at Monfalcone, west of Trieste.
Burma.—14th Army troops occupied Pegu. Parachute troops landed south of Rangoon.
Pacific.—Australian troops landed on Tarakan Island off Borneo.

MAY 2, Wednesday *2,069th day*
Western Front.—Baltic ports of Luebeck and Wismar captured by British.
Russian Front.—Berlin's last defeners surrendered to Russians. Baltic ports of Rostock and Warnemunde also captured.
Burma.—Allied forces landed from sea on both banks of Rangoon river.
Italy.—German garrison in Trieste surrendered to 8th Army. Germans still fighting Tito's troops.

MAY 3, Thursday *2,070th day*
Western Front.—German defences collapsed in the north; Hamburg surrendered to British. Passau and Braunau (Hitler's birthplace) captured by U.S. 3rd Army advancing in Austria.
Russian Front.—Teschen, on Czech-Polish frontier, occupied by Russians.
Burma.—Rangoon entered by Allied land forces. Prome also captured.
Japan.—Super-Fortresses bombed airfields on Kyushu.
Netherlands.—First land-borne supplies of food handed over to Dutch.

MAY 4, Friday *2,071st day*
Western Front.—German land, sea and air forces in North-west Germany, Holland and Denmark surrendered to 21st Army Group; terms effective 8 a.m. May 5.
Italy.—Troops of 7th Army occupied Innsbruck and Salzburg, drove through Brenner Pass and linked up with 5th Army troops at Vipiteno.
Japan.—Super-Fortresses attacked airfields on Honshu and Kyushu.

MAY 5, Saturday *2,072nd day*
Western Front.—German Army Group "G" surrendered to Gen. Devers' 6th Army Group. In Austria U.S. 3rd Army captured Linz.
Russian Front.—Swinemunde and Peenemunde on the Baltic captured by Red Army.
Czechoslovakia.—Street fighting in progress in Prague between Germans and Czech patriots.
Denmark.—First Allied troops entered Copenhagen.

MAY 6, Sunday *2,073rd day*
Western Front.—Pilsen, Czech arms centre, captured by U.S. 3rd Army, advancing on Prague on wide front.
Russian Front.—Rokossovsky's troops captured and cleared Baltic Island of Rügen.

MAY 7, Monday *2,074th day*
General.—Gen. Jodl, representative of German High Command and of Adm. Dönitz, signed at Rheims act of unconditional surrender of all German land, sea and air forces in Europe.
Western Front.—Canadians entered Emden, Polish armour entered Wilhelmshaven. British and Canadian troops moved into Denmark and Holland.
Russian Front.—Breslau capitulated to Russians after 82 days' siege.
Italy.—Troops of 8th Army crossed Italian frontier into Austria.

MAY 8, Tuesday *2,075th day*
General.—Ratification of German surrender signed in Berlin at midnight by Field-Marshal Keitel, chief of German High Command, Marshal Zhukov and Air Chief Marshal Tedder.
Russian Front.—Dresden, last large German city, occupied by Russians after two days' battle.
Czechoslovakia.—German C.-in-C. in Bohemia surrendered in Prague: groups of Germans still fighting Russians.
Balkans.—Zagreb, capital of Croatia, liberated from Germans.
Burma.—First deep-water ships sailed up Rangoon river to Rangoon.
Home Front.—Mr. Churchill proclaimed end of war in Europe.

★ *Flash-backs* ★

1940

May 2. *Allied troops left Aandalsnes and Namsos, Norway.*

1941

April 26. *Germans crossed Egyptian frontier at Sollum.*
April 27. *Athens, capital of Greece, occupied by Germans.*
May 2. *Evacuation of Imperial forces from Greece completed.*

1942

May 1. *In Burma, British troops evacuated Mandalay.*
May 3. *Battle of Coral Sea began.*
May 5. *British troops landed on French island of Madagascar.*
May 6. *Corregidor, Philippines, fell after five months' siege.*

1943

May 7. *In Tunisia, cities of Bizerta and Tunis were captured.*

1944

April 26. *Australians captured Alexishafen in New Guinea.*
May 7. *Russians began final assault on Sebastopol, Crimea.*

THE WAR IN THE AIR

by Capt. Norman Macmillan, M.C., A.F.C.

FROM September 3, 1939, to April 28, 1945, the Royal Air Force Commands in the United Kingdom lost 11,449 aircraft and destroyed 7,911 enemy aircraft. Bomber Command lost 7,997 and destroyed 759; Fighter Command lost 2,998 and destroyed 6,977; Coastal Command lost 454 and destroyed 175. To these figures have yet to be added the losses of the Tactical Air Forces serving overseas in Western Europe, Italy, and the Far East, and of the Fleet Air Arm—together with their scores of victory—before we shall know the complete cost of the war in aircraft up to the moment of impending German defeat. And there should also be added the losses in training aircraft and gliders, and in Army Air Observation Posts and Transport Command. But, already, the figures announced show that the numerical first-line aircraft strength of the R.A.F. at the outbreak of the war has been destroyed five-and-a-half times in the losses of these three Commands alone. The compensation for this heavy price of victory in the air is the knowledge that it has helped to reduce the cost of the war on land and at sea, both in lives and materials. Indeed, it is problematical if Germany could have been defeated without the use of air power on a lavish scale. But there can be no doubt that our air losses would have been reduced, and the duration of the war curtailed, if the R.A.F. had been adequately prepared for war when it began. This is a lesson to be learnt for the future—always to be fully insured against loss.

DIVERSE Conditions With Which Tactical Air Forces Contended

In these days of victory over Nazi Germany it is appropriate to discuss the Tactical Air Forces which have given such magnificent close support to the armies in the field.

The degree of comfort of squadrons of the Tactical Air Forces varied tremendously. Sometimes they had to work under improvised conditions on airstrips where they had landed during the day, returning to rear bases at night. Once the armies gained a foothold of sufficient extent, the Tactical Air Forces began to operate from bases which they did not regard as forward airstrips, although they were often little more.

When the Continent had been well secured, by the autumn of 1944, there was room for more squadrons. But some units of 2nd T.A.F. were still operating from United Kingdom bases at the beginning of February 1945. Those that were on the Continent had a great variety of conditions to contend with. Some Wings were based on airfields which had been permanent airfields of our Allies before they were occupied and used by the Germans; in some cases the Luftwaffe improved these bases, but in other cases R.A.F. Bomber Command damaged them very seriously, while the U.S. Army Air Forces damaged others, with the result that what had once been excellently equipped air bases housed the Tactical Air Squadrons in very draughty and often overcrowded conditions.

THE Luftwaffe also used camouflage fairly effectively on their airfields, disguising hangars as houses by means of painting, and often trying to make an airfield look like a farmstead; they built quarters and offices accordingly, and these were sometimes as uncomfortable as farm outbuildings can be. The messes of some airfields were several miles away, located perhaps in a château, or in a building in a town, while in other cases they were housed in newly erected wooden buildings put up by local labour in wet weather from local standing timber that was still green and damp. One airfield I visited was like a scene from a cowboy film. It was sited in a forested piece of country about six miles behind the front. Runways had been cut through the fir trees which grew on sand as real as that of the desert or the seashore. On top of the sand were laid the hinged perforated steel plates that were needed to make a surface suitable for Typhoons to take off and alight and taxi upon. Dispersal points were surfaced in the same way. Great mounds of sand had been thrust up to form shelters, and there was water in the trough from which it had been taken, forming a natural swimming pool, in which the men swam. Recce cars of the R.A.F. Regiment were posted on top of the mounds as A.A. defence. On this airfield one could hear the guns firing in the fighting line, and an occasional shell came down not far off.

Glades, like shooting brakes, were cut through the forest to serve as roads. Soon the jeeps cut up the loose sand, and when the rain came these roads were several feet deep in soft mud and impassable; new roads had then to be cut through the trees.

HUTS were built under the fir branches, which gave them natural camouflage; they were a local shape, which gave the camp an appearance foreign to the R.A.F.; they were built of planks sawn from the felled trees; one reached them by footpaths in the forest. The officers' mess had a floor of square, red Dutch tiles; damp sweated upon them in a heavy film of moisture; trestle tables and collapsible benches gave seating accommodation: crockery and cutlery were coarse. In the ante-room was a bar that might have come from a film of the Yukon in the gold rush, except that there were no women.

There were few W.A.A.F.s in 2nd T.A.F., and none in the field squadrons. This made a striking difference between Home and Continental air stations. But the very conditions of the overseas units brought the war home closer than it seemed to be on stations in the U.K. Typhoons, Tempests, Spitfires, Meteors, Mitchells and Mosquitoes made up the formidable array of 2nd T.A.F., a force that scourged the enemy by day and night, and contributed in no small measure to the success of the armies they supported.

When the bombed enemy troops came out dazed by concussion, the troops called them "bomb happy." The 51st Highland Division had an unfortunate experience of close support bombing in Normandy. They refused further such support until the beginning of the attack on the Rhine, where the support given by 2nd T.A.F. bombers was so effective that they asked for it to be given on all occasions thereafter.

DEFEAT of German Army Ascribed Mainly to the Effect of Bombing

In the five days preceding the surrender to Field-Marshal Montgomery of the North-West German forces on May 4, 1945, 2nd T.A.F. destroyed 150 ships, including submarines, trying to get away to Norway, 116 aircraft, and 4,500 vehicles involved in the German military traffic jam in Denmark.

Rundstedt, a prisoner of war, ascribed the defeat of the German Army mainly to the effect of the Allies' strategic bombing, especially the cutting of communications. The destruction of railways and bridges prevented supplies from reaching the German armies; that caused the failure of the Ardennes offensive, which had been designed to advance the German defence line to the river Meuse from Liége, and so protect the Ruhr.

SIKORSKY R4B HELICOPTERS OF THE R.A.F., photographed for the first time flying in formation, at an R.A.F. training school. Capable of rising vertically, flying backwards, forwards or sideways, and hovering to drop or pick up passengers, these aircraft are expected to play an important part in Britain's post-war aerial development. *Photo, Planet News*

As the strategic air assault died away with the overrunning of Germany, Bomber Command and the U.S.A. 8th A.F. were diverted to humanitarian ends, proof, were such needed, that the aeroplane can be a blessing and not alone a curse. These Commands dropped supplies of food to the starving Dutch people in Western Holland, releasing over 800 tons daily from April 29 above the large cities. (See illus. p. 54.)

WHEN the forces of Montgomery drove into Hamburg, May 3, they found nine square miles of that great city destroyed by the attacks of Bomber Command in July and August 1943. Japan will watch reports of this nature with the keenness of despair.

Rangoon was entered on the same day as Hamburg. The final advance of the 14th Army on the Burmese capital was assisted by the advance dropping of paratroops south of Rangoon, on May 1, and by a landing from the sea under the support of ships and aircraft on the next day. The landings were preceded by bombing attacks on military installations and troops in Rangoon city area.

At 3 p.m. on May 2 Berlin surrendered to the Red Army. Next day it was announced in the U.K. that no more air raid warnings would be sounded. The Civil Defence Service was to be disbanded

This Was a London Market Until a V2 Fell

FARRINGDON MARKET IN LONDON, one morning in early March 1945, was crowded with shoppers when a rocket bomb fell amongst the street stalls. The dead numbered 110, and the seriously injured 123. Many victims, trapped in the debris of masonry and girders, were traced with the aid of bloodhounds. In the background is the world-famous Smithfield Meat Market. On April 27 it was revealed that the total number of rocket bombs that reached this country was 1,050. The first fell at Chiswick on Sept. 8, 1944.

Photo, Topical

Our Roving Camera Sees First Fruits of Victory

HASTINGS PREPARED FOR INVASION—this time, according to this entertaining poster, by an onrush of holiday-makers following the announcement of Victory Day in Europe.

BRIGHTON IS ITSELF AGAIN and youngsters take full advantage of the Children's Bathing Pool, reopened in late April 1945, after having been closed since 1940. The foreshore from Black Rock to Saltdean was reopened on March 8.

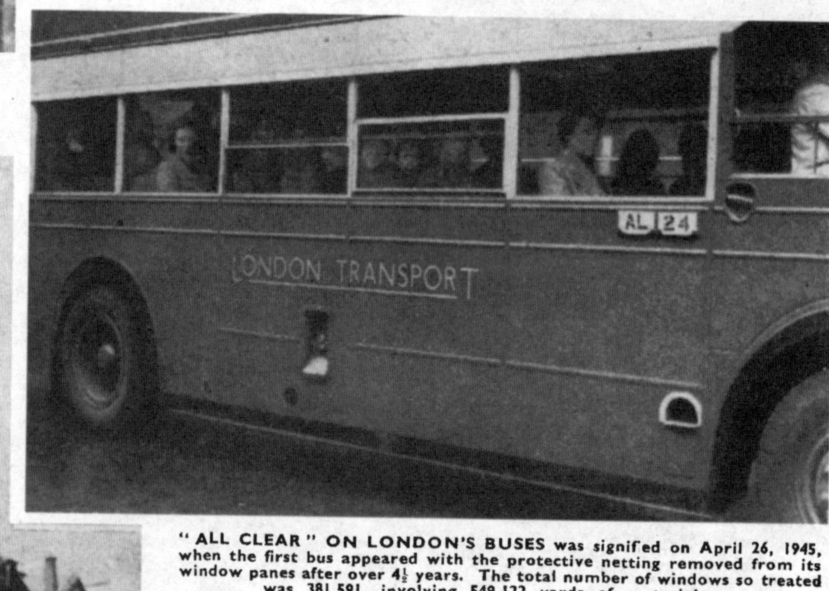

"ALL CLEAR" ON LONDON'S BUSES was signified on April 26, 1945, when the first bus appeared with the protective netting removed from its window panes after over 4½ years. The total number of windows so treated was 381,591, involving 549,122 yards of material.

LEGLESS RAILWAY WORKER sits down to his job in this special chair provided by the Southern Railway. He is Mr. F. J. Clarke, a welder. Formerly an employee of the company, he had both legs amputated—one above and the other below the knee—while serving with the Royal Armoured Corps in France in 1944.

BLITZED BUILDINGS BULLDOZED AWAY in London (right), where the scars left by the Luftwaffe are being swiftly removed by these "mechanical navvies." On April 27 it was announced that over 5,400 firms were employed in rebuilding the Capital.

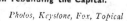

Photos, Keystone, Fox, Topical

Editor's Postscript

THE Opera House at San Francisco, where the Allied Nations Conference (see illus. page 52) is being held as I write, is one of the most interesting buildings in the New World. Not only is it a masterpiece as regards its seating and acoustics, but it also represents San Francisco's solution of the war memorial problem with which she was faced after the cessation of hostilities in 1918. The Opera House and the Veterans' Hall adjoining it, together with the beautifully laid-out courtyard in between, are probably the most "practical" war memorial in existence. It will surprise many of my music-loving readers—especially those who imagine that America is the musician's paradise—to learn that it is the only municipally owned opera house in the United States. The Philistines will be equally surprised to learn that since it was built in 1932 it has shown an appreciable margin of profit at the end of each season. A well-known English baritone who has sung there tells me that its acoustics are at least as good as Covent Garden's—which is to say, as good as any in the world—and the accommodation for just over 3,000 is exactly the same. On the other hand, the atmosphere, especially at an important début, is as delirious as at the San Carlos in Naples, where I once watched an infuriated audience storm the stage because the tenor skidded badly off his top notes. The account of the highly theatrical opening of the Conference suggests that the stage manager at least has not been axed for the duration of international deliberations in the stalls.

I SHALL be interested to read the comments of the Dominions Press on Mr. Lionel Curtis's new book, World War: Its Cause and Cure, a copy of which has been delivered to me from the Oxford University Press. For Mr. Curtis—who will be remembered for his activities on behalf of Federal Union—here puts forward the startling suggestion that Quebec should be the future defence H.Q. of the British Empire! Mr. Curtis contends that "the British Commonwealth is in jeopardy (and so is the peace of the world) until it is armed so strongly that no one thinks of attacking it." The solution he offers is that Britain should establish a vast defence union with the Dominions—a Commonwealth Defence Union, he calls it—to secure adequate security for the Empire as a whole, the cost of maintaining it to be a "first charge on all the resources of the self-governing Dominions, no less than on those of Great Britain and Northern Ireland." In other words, "an international Government of British democracies." It is his contention—with which few will disagree—that the best place to train such vast mechanized forces as would be needed by the Defence Union would be the almost boundless plains of Canada, where they could be so widely dispersed as to be virtually invulnerable to air attack from Europe. Hence the proposal to make Quebec the H.Q. of the Empire's defences. Mr. Curtis is plainly no blind optimist when it comes to plain thinking about the possibility of future wars. Some of our airy-minded pacifist gentry could do worse than spend 7s. 6d. on his stimulating book.

SOMEHOW "V Day" sounds better than "VE Day," though the latter is more correct as signifying Victory in Europe; but I still prefer to call it V Day! And, retaining vivid memories of the mob behaviour on Mafeking night, of being caught in the crowd at Ludgate Circus when the C.I.V. returned from South Africa and fought their way up to St. Paul's as single stragglers through a shrieking mass of hysterical humanity, and of the scenes in Fleet Street and the Strand when the Armistice was announced on November 11, 1918, I was apprehensive of what I might encounter in London when V Day was officially announced. But the declaration of the two National holidays came sooner than I expected by at least twenty-four hours and made needless my return to town during these celebrations. For this I was thankful, as I have an ingrain dislike of popular celebrations where order and good sense are so often abrogated. At my country home in Downland—where I could look on the pitiful wreckage of a Dakota which two nights earlier missed hitting my chimney-stacks and smashed into a small hill less than a mile beyond—here, I was tempted to follow Professor Gilbert Murray's plan of celebrating the great event by having a peaceful sleep, after five years of troubled nights! Only the need to do some urgent writing and the loveliness of the weather made me refrain. I returned to my job in London on the Thursday fresher and happier I am sure than if I had gone through the two days of Saturnalia; but I gather that the exciting occasion was marred by hardly any of the rowdyism of Mafeking night or Armistice Day. The manners of the populace are evidently improving.

Admiral KARL DÖNITZ, who on May 1, 1945, proclaimed himself Fuehrer of the Third Reich in succession to Adolf Hitler, who was reported to have died in Berlin on that day (See also page 45.) *Photo, Sport & General*

IT is a melancholy reflection that while wars have diminished the "expectation of life" (as the insurance companies call it) for the young—especially young men—that expectation is becoming longer, through the healthier manner in which we live, for the old. In the last forty years there has been so marked a change in the United States that both men and women can now expect to live fifteen years longer than their 19th-century forerunners. Exactly the same tendency is visible here. If you read the deaths column in The Times newspaper you will find that on most days of the week the average length of years recorded is well over seventy. Turn back to the files of the paper for half-a-century ago and the figure will turn out to be between fifty and sixty. Something must be allowed for the fact that those who appear in The Times as having departed this life are people who have been well looked after. But, taking the population all round, there is no doubt that the span of life has been extended. Fortunately those whom we used to call old have brisked up so heartily that a very large number of them seem no more than middle-aged. That makes the prospect less gloomy than it might have been.

ALL predictions and even probabilities may be knocked sideways by changes that may alter the population problem entirely. When the Rev. T. R. Malthus deplored the increase in numbers in England during the early part of last century and said there would soon not be enough food to go round, he was made to look foolish by the enormous supplies of food which we received from across the Atlantic. His reasoning was sound enough according to the state of things at the moment, but it was quickly falsified by new events. So it may be again. The warning of the experts that in a hundred years' time Britain may have a population of no more than 12 millions may be dissipated in the same way. Families may become larger again. I was surprised, by the way, to see that the National Council of Women think "public opinion tends to pity, even to jeer at, mothers of large families." Nearer the mark, I should say, is the finding that women feel they cannot keep up companionship with their husbands if they have too many children to look after. It is all a question of personality. You can't lay down any hard and fast rules.

Flames and Fanatics Subdued on the Elbe

DRIVING INTO BLAZING BORN, shock troops of the U.S. 9th Army on the Elbe front encountered fanatical enemy remnants in the doomed village. General Simpson's was the first Allied Army to reach and cross the Elbe, on April 11-12, 1945. Farther north on April 29 the British 1st Commando Brigade and the 15th Scottish Division crossed the river and took Lauenburg, all but isolating Denmark; which, with North-West Germany and Holland, was surrendered unconditionally to Field-Marshal Montgomery on May 4. *Photo, Planet News*

Printed in England and published every alternate Friday by the Proprietors, THE AMALGAMATED PRESS, LTD., The Fleetway House, Farringdon Street, London, E.C.4. Registered for transmission by Canadian Magazine Post. Sole Agents for Australia and New Zealand: Messrs. Gordon & Gotch, Ltd.; and for South Africa: Central News Agency, Ltd.—May 25, 1945. S.S. *Editorial Address:* JOHN CARPENTER HOUSE, WHITEFRIARS LONDON, E.C.4.

Vol 9 The War Illustrated No 208

Edited by Sir John Hammerton

SIXPENCE JUNE 8, 1945

ANGLO-RUSSIAN LINK-UP ON THE BALTIC COAST On May 2, 1945, British troops of the 6th Airborne Division made contact at Wismar, due north of Schwerin on Lubeck Bay, with a Russian armoured squadron which had swung 30 miles westwards from Rostock, hastening the final debacle on Germany's fast-crumbling northern front when escape routes into Denmark had been all but cut off. The following day the port of Travemunde fell to the British 11th Armoured Division. *Photo, British Official*

NO. 209 WILL BE PUBLISHED FRIDAY JUNE 22

Last Stages of the Japanese Retreat in Burma

RANGOON, famed capital of Burma, was swiftly entered from the sea by troops of the 15th Indian Corps, supported by ships of the East Indies Fleet, on May 3, 1945. Priest guns of the 14th Army (1), advancing on the capital from the north, blazed into action against a Japanese stronghold. On the day Rangoon fell Prome (see map) was captured, thus cutting the only escape route left for the enemy in the Arakan and west of the Irrawaddy: natives turned out to welcome their liberators (2).

Hampered by mines, demolitions and heavy rains, men of the East Yorkshire Regiment in full kit (3) entered Rangoon from the north. Allied heavy bombers and fighter-bombers cleared the way to the capital for troops landing by sea and air on the banks of the Rangoon River. See also story in page 91.

Photos, British Official. Map by courtesy of The Daily Mail

THE BATTLE FRONTS

by Maj.-Gen. Sir Charles Gwynn, K.C.B., D.S.O.

VICTORY over Germany has been as complete and satisfying as anyone could wish, although it leaves innumerable political problems to be settled. Among other things it is necessary to bring conviction and genuine admission of defeat home to the mass of the German people, and more especially to the German Army. One might imagine that an army that has been driven out of positions of immense strategical and tactical strength and has surrendered by the million would be prepared to admit defeat, but already there are unmistakable signs that the myth that the German Army was undefeated and will always be invincible may again be accepted by an amazingly gullible people. Naturally, excuses have to be found to account for the situation in which Germany finds herself.

Hitler is marked down as an obvious scapegoat, but what may be more dangerous is the assertion by German generals that Allied air superiority was the sole cause that prevented Germany maintaining the struggle. That the Russian Army time and again defeated the bulk of the German Army without air superiority, and even when air superiority lay with the defeated side, is conveniently forgotten, as are also defeats suffered when weather conditions deprived both sides of air support. No one in his senses would seek to deny the immense contribution air power, both over sea and land, made to victory, especially in the final stages of the war. But the danger of accepting the German thesis is that the belief may be engendered that air power alone can achieve decisive victory.

RUSSIAN Army's Advance Deprived Germany of Natural Oil Supply

Nothing should shake us from the true belief that victory depended on the harmonious co-operation and co-ordination of all the elements of military power, of which air power has obviously become a vitally important one. Nevertheless, nothing can alter the fact that, for a country separated by the sea from its potential enemies, the foundation of military action, especially offensive action, must always be sea power, however much aircraft are developed as weapons in the armoury of sea power. Without control of sea communications neither air nor land power can be sustained or brought into full offensive action.

Land power is required to secure bases needed for the full exploitation of both sea and air power, and its action when fully developed, more than any other form of force, compels the enemy to develop and expend his military resources; thereby, among other things, forcing him to present vulnerable and vital targets to air attack. Land forces, moreover, alone can occupy enemy territory and deprive him permanently of the sources of his military strength. For instance, in the war just ended it was the Russian Army's advance that deprived Germany of her sources of natural oil supply and compelled Germany to expand her synthetic oil industry, which in turn presented targets to air power far more vulnerable and accessible than natural oil sources.

INCIDENTALLY, it may be noted that it was the advance of the Allied Armies that so narrowed the area in which the German Armies operated, and, from which they drew their resources, that air power could be concentrated with devastating effect. While, therefore, although a headline proclaiming that "without air mastery there could have been no victory" is undoubtedly true, yet "sea mastery" or "land mastery" might have been substituted with equal truth. That mastery in not one of these three elements could have been secured without the assistance of Allies and without the full co-operation of all three fighting Services and the exertions of the civil population, is the undoubted fact that all of us, and more especially our political leaders, should bear in mind in this hour of victory.

JAPAN

How are such considerations applicable to our war with Japan, a country protected by immense spaces of sea, and which, though having possessed in the earlier stages of the war a strong navy and air force, ultimately has been forced to rely mainly on her great army? The conditions of the war are obviously very different from those in the war with Germany, but there are points of resemblance, and now that the initial stages of the Allied counter-offensive have been carried through with such unexpected speed and success the points of resemblance become more apparent. In particular, we are faced with the problem of defeating Japan's army or of capturing or destroying the sources from which it draws its warlike supplies.

THE question arises now that sea power, using its air weapon, has secured control of sea communications, and land forces, in limited strength, have secured bases from which sea and air power can effectively operate, whether air power will be able alone to achieve decisive victory. So far, success has evidently been attained by the close co-operation of the three forms of power, although air power has perhaps made its greatest contribution as a weapon of sea power rather than in an independent role. Sea power has certainly been by now firmly established as the foundation of victory, and air power is evidently well on the way to have the bases from which it can fully develop its effectiveness. It remains to be seen, however, whether its destructive action combined with control of sea communications will reduce the Japanese Army to an impotent mass, or whether land power in strength will have to be summoned in order to compel Japan to expend her reserve resources and to deprive her of areas in which she can maintain the struggle.

Land power has been employed with remarkable success in co-operation with air power in the Philippines, in New Guinea and in Burma, but it has not yet come to grips with the main forces of Japan, in China and in her Home islands, or with the large detachments occupying the Netherlands East Indies islands. Is it possible that air action alone directed against the Home islands will force all that mass of power to surrender unconditionally under the orders of, or due to the breakdown of, the Central Government; and that land power will not have to be employed to the full to secure victory?

IT would seem that in this case the Japanese Central Government, unlike the Nazi regime, might lose its will to continue resistance under the full weight of air attack; but can we assume that the Army leaders, as in Germany, will acknowledge that the war is lost and consent to surrender? In the case of Germany our fears were that the war might be prolonged by the fanaticism of the Central Government in power; but in the case of Japan the prolongation of the war in face of obvious defeat might depend on the fanaticism of the Army and its leaders. We have seen that fanaticism displayed time and again in the suicidal resistance of isolated detachments, but does any Westerner understand Japanese mentality sufficiently to say with confidence what is the basis of that fanaticism? Is it ultimately based on the deification of the Emperor and a willingness to obey what are believed to be his orders, or is it based on a belief in the supernatural status of the Japanese people?

AT KIEL GERMAN PRISONERS DISEMBARKED from two German destroyers which had brought them there after the unconditional surrender. Royal Navy forces, travelling overland from Ostend, took over the famous port and dockyard, where they found the 8-in.-gun cruiser Admiral Hipper and the 6-in.-gun cruiser Emden, both beached, 11 destroyers, and 12 U-boats scuttled. (See also illus. in page 73.) *Photo, British Official*

Assuming, as seems possible, that the Central Government induced the Emperor to sanction surrender, as they induced him to sanction the war, would the Japanese Army obey orders or would it still retain the fanatical spirit it has so often displayed? Japan has already lost the war almost as conclusively as Germany lost it when the landing in Normandy was successful, but her isolated detachments have shown what fanatical resistance can achieve. China also has shown what can be achieved by forces cut off from sources of warlike supplies. However great our air superiority may become, will it not still be necessary to call on our armies in strength to finish the business?

THE outlook is certainly far from clear. Personally, I believe that the Japanese Government under air attack may realize the hopelessness of their position and agree to unconditional surrender. But I am far from confident that the Japanese Army is as yet in a condition to accept defeat. Too large a part of it has as yet not experienced a reverse of any sort. The danger of prolonged sporadic and unauthorized resistance is therefore much greater than it was in Germany.

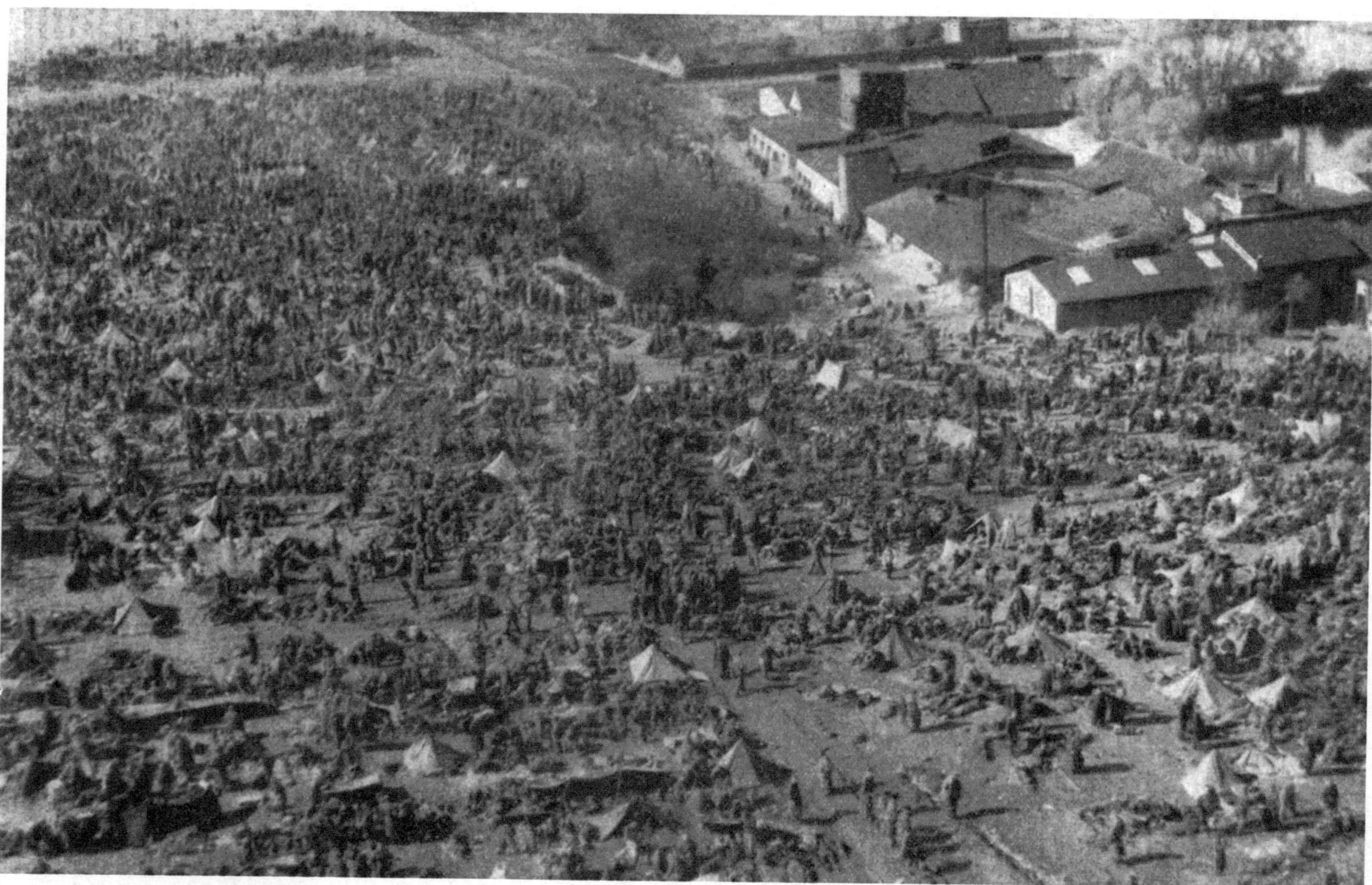

STUPENDOUS PROBLEM OF THE PRISONERS, their provisioning and employment demanding all the Allies' ingenuity to solve, is exemplified by this vast P.O.W. camp near Hamburg after the city's surrender on May 3, 1945. So anxious were German troops to get out of the war that they streamed into this and other "cages" on lorries, tractors and ambulances (driven by themselves), on bicycles and afoot. It was estimated that between D-Day 1944 and May 6, 1945, well over 4,000,000 were taken on the Western Front alone. It was announced from Paris on May 13 that 30,000 were to work in the French mines, another 100,000 were to be employed on heavy repairs. Up to mid-May about 50,000 German prisoners were employed in Britain, mainly on agricultural work.

Photo, British Official

ALONG the CROWDED ROADS of WAR

Last Impressions of My Visit to the Western Front

by Captain NORMAN MACMILLAN, M.C., A.F.C.

In this, the last article of this series, I will describe briefly some of the many things I saw for which there is no space to give a full description. Follow me in imagination on long journeys across Germany, Holland, Belgium and France, along the crowded roads.

One of the few forward cemeteries I saw was just outside Nijmegen, beside a country lane bordered with elms, whose sandy surface led to the gated entrance to a wood: a quiet spot. Six graves were in a single row in a wired-off rectangle of ground. A large central cross stood higher than the humbler wooden crosses that marked the burial place of each man. I noted the names. Almost all were of men of different regiments. If any of their relatives should read these lines, they may be glad to know that the cemetery was well kept. These were the inscriptions on the crosses:

5506369 Pte. Pease, E. A., The Hampshire Regt.
4862780 Pte. Mellors, W., Leicester Regt. 11/10/44.
5504337 Pte. Newton, S. N., The Hampshire Regt. 11/10/44.
6406521 L/Cpl. Ashdown, H., C.M. Police. K/A. 12 Oct., 1944.
1231054 W/O Wilks, R.A.F., 11/10/44.
1144509 Gnr. Oades, F. Born Sept. 10, 1920. Killed in Action, 25 Oct., 1944. C. of E.

A long column of German prisoners of war trudged along a lane, their boots squelching in the mud. There were about a thousand of these disconsolate-looking men in mud-bedrabbled greatcoats and uniforms, their windy pride deflated, their future dim, but not, like that of some of their foes and comrades, extinguished. We drove on to visit an Army Air Observation Post. Here half the personnel were Army and half R.A.F. The soldiers ran the transport, the R.A.F. flight mechanics serviced the Auster aeroplanes. The squadron had 19 officers and 16 aeroplanes. All the pilots were gunner officers. Their Austers were unarmed. They generally flew between 800 and 4,000 feet, and came down to land if they saw enemy aircraft below 10,000 feet. They relied on the R.A.F. fighter screen shooting the enemy out of the sky. Flak was another matter.

The Auster is simply an elevated artillery observation post from which the plan view of the target enlarged the vision obtainable by the surface forward observation officers. Sometimes the air view is superior to the ground view, sometimes it is the other way about, and sometimes the air view is the only one. Both views are needed for modern artillery fire, and both posts must be manned by gunner officers. The Austers carry radio telephones, and cameras when tactical photographs are required.

Dead Were Used to Kill the Living

The day before my visit five Messerschmitt 109s swooped down on this airfield and shot up a visiting Auster that was about to alight. The pilot was killed. In the plane were Major J. R. E. Harden and Captain D. C. M. Mather. The pilot fell over the controls. Mather was wounded. Harden had never piloted a plane, but he leant forward, pulled the pilot's body away from the controls, seized the stick and got down without a catastrophic crash, in which he received slight head injuries and Mather broke an arm.

A few dead Germans lay huddled in slit trenches concealed between the houses of Riethorst village, untouched because their bodies had not been examined for booby traps. An ugly war in which the dead were used to kill the living! The village street was strewn with rubble and rubbish of all kinds. A petrol pump lay on its side. A private motor-car lay upside down upon a bank beside the Bondshotel. German hand grenades still lay about the slit trenches. A dead German soldier lay in the gutter like a dead dog. More corpses lay in the fields, which were not yet cleared of mines; one British soldier was blown up and badly wounded when crossing over to two German soldiers' bodies. About 50 Germans still held out in a factory behind us to the right. Ahead they were in strength. Somewhere in between there was an indeterminate line.

The retreating enemy blew up the bridge across the stream at the end of the village. During the night the Royal Engineers were unable to build a new bridge because of snipers. When daylight came the snipers were dealt with. A wooden bridge was built and single line traffic got across. They were now making a wider and stronger crossing. They had laid a corrugated iron culvert in the stream bed beside the bridge to carry the water. Bulldozers were nosing it over, with soil and the rubble of demolished buildings, to make a road. When that was done the bridge would come down, for use elsewhere, and that part of the stream be similarly treated to widen the road. It was dangerous work; three engineers were killed by mines while building the bridge. But no British casualties were to be seen. All had been borne back. Only the booby-trapped Germans lay about, and they, too, would soon be removed beyond sight if not memory.

CEREMONIAL VICTORY PARADE IN OCCUPIED GERMANY was held at Bremerhaven—the port of Bremen—on May 13, 1945, when men of the 51st Highland Division marched through the streets with skirling pipes. Lieut.-Gen. B. G. Horrocks, C.B., D.S.O., M.C., Commander of the 30th Corps, took the salute. Wearing the kilt of his old regiment, the Argyll and Sutherland Highlanders, Major-Gen. G. H. A. MacMillan, C.B., D.S.O., M.C., the Divisional Commander, led the march past. German civilians were confined to their houses during the parade. *Photo, British Newspaper Pool*

A dog platoon cleared the mines at Riethorst. They had been trained at the Dog School, north of London, after having been given to the Service by their owners. The dogs were in the charge of Sappers dressed in anti-gas coat, rubber boots and steel helmet. Those I met were gamekeepers in civil life.

LADDIE was worked by Sapper Wilfred Crick of Cambridgeshire, keeper to the late Earl of Ellesmere ; he had transferred to this job from the Ack-Ack. Bruce jumped up excitedly at Sapper Robert Coote, another Cambridgeshire gamekeeper, who had a tin mug tied to his belt with enticing pieces of dog food to be given as reward for good work. Evidently Bruce thought he had done good work already. In charge of the platoon of dogs was Sergeant Terence Maguire, who was a coal miner in County Durham before war turned him into a sapper.

Roads or tracks cleared of mines were marked out with white tape—which probably explains the British housewife's shortage of this material. While the dogs worked eastwards, in Riethorst were notices : ROAD VERGES NOT CLEARED OF MINES, and outside the houses were other placards : HOUSES NOT CLEARED OF BOOBY TRAPS. But due to the skill of both men and dogs there have been comparatively few casualties in the dog platoons.

In Holland and Belgium I frequently found myself in flying bomb alleys. Frequency varied. Some days there were many, other days few bombs. Sometimes they came over at the rate of about six an hour. Their height seemed to vary between 1,200 and 3,000 feet. I also spent some time at various receiving ends, where I found that the use of V1 and V2 weapons against the Allies on the Continent was almost inconsequential in its effect upon the military effort. It did not hold up the work of the great port of Antwerp, where I saw many ships discharging their military cargoes, although it drove many of the civilian inhabitants out of the city and caused superficial damage to housing, and here and there destruction.

ANTWERP was as quiet as Brussels was busy. If, as at least once did happen, an oil store was hit, Messerschmitt 262 jet-planes flew over and photographed the result ; but the quantity of oil lost was so small that no hold-up was involved in the supply of either road transport or high octane aviation petrol. If, occasionally, billets were hit, other billets could be found. The V-weapons were, at their then stage of development, merely a nuisance.

Ack-Ack batteries were stationed on the line of flight of the flying bombs and brought down not a few of them. On a dripping wet

IDENTIFICATION TELESCOPE being operated at night by A.T.S. girls of No. 484 Battery, his visit to which Captain Norman Macmillan describes below. *Photo, British Official*

Flanders day I visited No. 484 Battery. Regimental H.Q. Mess was in the château of a Belgian baron, whose rooms had old wood panelling and massive Flemish furniture. Senior Commander Elizabeth Elwes, second cousin of Simon Elwes, the portrait painter, greeted us, and we drove over to a gunsite, where slippery duckboards kept one's feet off the muddy soil. Four 3·7-in. guns sited in the field were shrouded in waterproof covers. Nearer were the predictor, radiolocation posts, and Nissen huts.

THIS was the first mixed battery to cross the Channel. There were 500 men and 800 girls in the regiment. There were 70 men and 120 girls in a section. The section I met was commanded by Captain L. Povey, who was a Mayfair ladies' hairdresser before the war. With a charming smile he said he thought that was why he could handle the girls so well. It certainly seemed a happy unit. The A.T.S. did 24 hours on duty and 24 hours off. They were divided into four sections, one section manning, one on relief, one in bed, and one on fatigues and daily leave. Men manned the guns, the girls the predictor and signals. They had then shot down 19 flying bombs in Belgium. They classified their results as Category A, bomb blown up in flight ; Category B, bomb brought down. "Smack on" was their slang for a direct hit.

The manning hut was made locally as an annexe to the Nissen control-room. Within it there were a round iron stove, eight beds, washstand, looking-glass, chairs—primitive but liveable. There was a constant supply of hot water from a tank heated by the exhaust pipe of the generator. Subalterns Jean Vernon and Susan Inglis told me they did one night's duty in every four. There were organized parties, and dances four to five miles away. They could get into Brussels by tram in slightly under two hours, and got 48 hours leave every month. But officers had to go alone, whereas the other ranks went sociably in parties of six. When the non-commissioned girls arrived in Brussels they went to the Montgomery Club for a hair-set, manicure and lunch ; then they would go on to a cinema and the Montgomery or A.E.F. Club for tea-dance ; and in the evening find excellent entertainment at an E.N.S.A. theatre or the 21 Club.

IN the manning hut, Corporal Dorothy Strain, of Chorley, said it was "a bit lonely when there were no doodle-bugs around." Some of the girls wrote letters, some read, others talked, one brushed her long blonde hair before the glass. They were happy in spite of the depressing weather, and the inelegant hut which was like a contractor's workmen's shed. Cheerfullest among them was L/Cpl. Margery Cloud, nicknamed "Sunshine." Dancing, oh yes, there were weekly dances at a café ; "rat racing" they

"THUMBS UP" SIGNAL to passers-by was given by this electrically-operated sign of the 6th British Armoured Division's mailed fist insignia, which our troops set up on the Austro-Italian border. *Photo, British Official*

called it. Each girl could get two bottles of beer a month, but very few used it. Cosmetics were scarce ; the Mess notice read, "Month's Allocation : strict rota will be drawn for."

They were against conscription for girls for overseas service. "We volunteered, and we can rough it," they said. "But a girl should not be forced to come out here and rough it like this if she does not want to." Suddenly the siren sounded ; instantly the girls were off at the double to their action stations, in the rain, out in the muddy field, or in the control-room—without fuss or excitement.

THE girls of this battery composed their own songs. And here are verses from two of them :

Oh ! Merry oh ! Merry oh ! merry are we.
We are the girls of the Artillery ;
Sing high, sing low, wherever you go,
The girls of the Ack-Ack they never say no.

Down in buzz bomb alley,
You'll find us every night,
Shooting down the buzz bombs
Is surely our delight.
Every night you'll find us standing there,
We curse and swear : but we don't care.
Down in buzz bomb alley, the Gunner's Paradise.

They were first-class soldiers, those Ack-Ack girls ; but they were neither toughened nor roughened by their work for the Army.

RUSSIAN GUARD OF HONOUR was inspected by General Sir Miles Dempsey, British 2nd Army Commander (left), accompanied by General Grishin, commanding the 49th Russian Army, when by invitation of the Soviet general he visited the Red Army lines in May 1945, at the ancient town of Parchim in Mecklenburg. *Photo, British Official*

Germany's Biggest Port Under New Management

HAMBURG'S FIRST ALLIED-CONTROLLED NEWSPAPER, the Hamburger Nachrichten-Blatt, printed under the direction of the Allied Military Government, was anxiously read by German troops and civilians (1): "The War is Finished!" proclaimed its headlines. Hamburg surrendered to General Dempsey's British 2nd Army on May 3, 1945: British armour parked outside the Rathaus (2). The vast dock area, so frequently a target for the R.A.F., seen rom the air after the city's capitulation (3). *Photos, British Official, New York Times Photos*

In Ignoble Surrender their Evil Mission Ends

TWO E-BOATS PUT INTO FELIXSTOWE HARBOUR (1) on May 13, 1945, bringing the E-boat fleet commander, Adml. F. Bruening. First U-boat to give itself up, under the terms of surrender, was U 249; She arrived in Weymouth Bay on May 10, the crew lining the deck (2) and guarded by Polish naval ratings. Her commander, Ober-Lieut. Kock (3, right) took his orders from Cmdr. N. J. Weir, R.N. (3, left). Flying the black flag, another was sighted from the air off the north-west coast of Scotland.

Photos, British Official, G.P.U. Planet News

THE WAR AT SEA

by Francis E. McMurtrie

To judge from the particulars so far published of those that have been surrendered at British and American ports, the majority of the U-boats at sea when war with Germany ended were of fairly recent construction. Probably a high proportion of the older submarines were either destroyed or relegated to training duties. From the fact that nearly 70 are reported to have been operating in the Atlantic at the cessation of hostilities, it may be inferred that perhaps 150 more may have been at various bases, undergoing minor refits or waiting to relieve those at sea. As a rule, not more than one-third of the total of immediately available submarines would be actively employed at one time.

Though a full list of numbers is not yet available, the following are reported to have been handed over: U 236, 249, 293, 485, 532, 541, 776, 802, 805, 825, 826, 858, 889, 956, 1005, 1009, 1010, 1023, 1058, 1105, 1109, 1231, 1305. The majority of them are of the 500-ton design, but several are of 740 tons, and one or two are understood to be of the 1,600-ton supply type. A coastal submarine of 250 tons which arrived at Dundee is said to have been numbered U 2326, but this may prove to be another version of U 236.

How the Surrendered U-Boats Are Likely to be Disposed Of

In German harbours and in the ports of France and Norway which had been occupied by the enemy large numbers of U-boats were found. In some cases these were either incomplete or scuttled, but it seems likely that the total is not less than 200. What is to become of them all? Probably the precedent of the First Great War will be followed, and the majority broken up or used for targets or other experimental purposes. Some may be given to France and other Allied countries to replace losses, as was done in 1919.

Reports have also been received of most of the surviving surface ships of importance. In Kiel are the damaged cruisers Admiral Hipper and Emden, both beached, with 11 destroyers. The cruisers Prinz Eugen and Nürnberg, with three destroyers and two torpedo boats, were captured at Copenhagen, undamaged. The cruiser Köln is lying in Wilhelmshaven, sunk in shallow water, together with a single torpedo boat. Another cruiser, the Leipzig, is at the Danish port of Aabenraa, disabled.

Several ships were found in ports taken by the Russians, but all were either sunk or wrecked. They include the cruiser Seydlitz, at Königsberg; the battleship Gneisenau and coast defence ship Schleswig-Holstein, at Gdynia; the incomplete aircraft carrier Graf Zeppelin, at Stettin; and the "pocket battleship" Lützow and coast defence ship Schlesien at Swinemünde. At various other ports occupied by the Allies are 19 more destroyers and torpedo boats, with some 1,200 smaller craft, such as motor torpedo boats, escort vessels, landing craft, trawlers, and minesweepers of various classes.

Thus the German Navy has ceased to exist, save for such stray U-boats as have still to surrender; these will probably have come in by the time this is printed. This time it is to be hoped that the Germans will not be allowed to retain a single ship capable of being used for warlike purposes. In 1919, it will be remembered, they kept a certain number of their older and smaller ships, which were used as a nucleus for building up a fresh fleet, and for training large numbers of recruits who ultimately manned that fleet.

It has been suggested in Merchant Navy circles that the German mercantile flag should be banished from the seas, in view of the many breaches of the laws of humanity committed by U-boats in this war and the last. It is advocated that for this purpose Germany should be deprived of the whole of her seaboard. Ports could be administered for the time being by an international commission, but ultimately they could be given to the neighbouring countries which the Germans have despoiled and maltreated. Hamburg, Bremen, Cuxhaven, Bremerhaven, Wilhelmshaven and Emden might be offered to the Dutch; Brünsbüttel, Kiel and Lübeck to the Danes; and Rostock, Sassnitz, Stralsund, Swinemünde, Stettin and Danzig to the Poles. In any case, it may be assumed that Schleswig-Holstein, which formed part of the kingdom of Denmark before the Germans appropriated it in 1866, will revert to its former ownership; and it has been long understood that Poland is to be compensated for her lost territory farther East by the cession of most of Pomerania.

GERMAN ADMIRALS Von Friedeburg and Kummetz, leaving the British flagship after calling on Rear-Admiral Baillie-Grohman, R.N., who commanded the British ships at Kiel. The Royal Marine sentry was not impressed. *Photo, British Official*

Those who object that such transfers of territory would involve the migration of the coastal population may be reminded that the Germans did not hesitate to transfer people from occupied areas in Poland and Russia without notice or consideration. There is a great deal to be said for making the punishment fit the crime, though it may not always be possible to work on this principle.

Japanese Suicide Attacks Made Against British Pacific Fleet

In the Far East, the Japanese are still resisting fiercely in Okinawa, though a desperate counter-attack was broken after 12 hours' hard fighting, in which every man who could hold a weapon, including many auxiliary troops such as cooks, bakers, and so on, was thrown into the struggle on the American side. Up to May 14 the U.S casualties in this island totalled 20,950. Those of the enemy, so far as could be ascertained, were 47,543.

The task of the British Pacific Fleet has been to smother Japanese intervention by aircraft from fields in Formosa and the Sakishima group, lying between that island and Okinawa. Tons of bombs have been dropped by aircraft from British carriers on Miyako and Isigaki, two islands from which enemy planes were suspected to be coming. In the course of these operations a number of suicide attacks were made upon our warships, seven of which were actually struck by aircraft carrying 500 or 1,000-lb. bombs, deliberately crash-dived on to their decks. Casualties were caused and fires started, but not a single ship was out of action for more than a couple of days.

Japan's impotence at sea enabled British troops to be landed without interference in the neighbourhood of Rangoon. Unfortunately the monsoon breaks this month, and the consequent deterioration in the weather may slow up further amphibious operations in this region for some time. Otherwise there is no doubt that it would be possible to effect landings on the narrow part of the Malay Peninsula, south of the Isthmus of Kra, so as to cut off land communication with the Japanese in Singapore.

Command of the sea has also facilitated the landing of Australian and Dutch forces at Tarakan, off north-east Borneo. Here opposition has been far lighter than in Okinawa, the garrison retreating to the hills and abandoning the port to the invaders. The importance of this place lies in its oil production. Allied ships will soon be able to fuel at Tarakan, as the installations are reported to be capable of being restored to working order in a short time.

TWO-MAN MIDGET U-BOAT was inspected by British experts in its assembly shelter. This prefabricated type has an overall length of 39 ft. and a displacement of 16 tons, with approximate endurance of 275 miles at 8 knots surfaced, plus about 50 miles at 3 knots submerged. Eighty-one midget U-boats were sunk, probably sunk, or captured. *Photo, British Official*

Royal Navy and Airborne Men Shared Honours—

FIRST TROOPS TO ENTER FREED DENMARK were men of a South Lancashire parachute battalion escorting the SHAEF military mission on May 6, 1945; on the Kastrup aerodrome at Copenhagen crowds cheered them from their Dakotas (1). Two days later King Christian and Queen Alexandrine (2) drove through the capital to open the first Riksdag (State Parliament) since the Nazi Occupation in 1940. British cruisers Birmingham, nearer to camera, and Dido berthed at Copenhagen received a tumultuous welcome (3).

Photos, British Official, Sport & General

–With Monty Riding in Triumph in Copenhagen

AT THE INVITATION OF DENMARK'S LEADERS, Field-Marshal Montgomery visited Copenhagen on May 12, 1945, and drove along a six-mile route of cheering citizens. He was received at the aerodrome by the Danish Cabinet, headed by the Premier, Hr. Buhl, who expressed to the British Field-Marshal the Danish people's gratitude. Later, Monty lunched with King Christian and Queen Alexandrine at Amalienborg Castle, where he was invested with the Grand Cross of the Order of Dannebrog with Diamond Star.

Photo, Associated Press

Our Sky-Men of Arnhem Take Over in Norway

FLOWN FROM ENGLAND by R.A.F. Transport Command, airborne veterans of Arnhem, together with 140 Norwegian parachute troops, arrived in Norway on May 11, 1945, as vanguard of the Allied liberation forces. Headed by a piper (1) they left their Wellington aircraft on Gardemoen Aerodrome for Oslo. Their duties included supervising the withdrawal of 400,000 German service personnel to reservation areas. At Oslo they were given a tremendous reception when, headed by their Norwegian comrades-in-arms, they marched through the Karl-johansgaten, the capital's main thoroughfare (2), on their way to a parade at the town hall.

Four days later the Crown Prince Olaf, in British battle-dress, arrived from England in a Royal Navy destroyer ; two small Norwegian girls broke from the crowds to greet him as he left the quayside at Oslo (3). He was welcomed by Maj.-Gen. R. Urquhart, commanding the 1st Airborne Division.

General Boehme, the German C.-in-C. in Norway, broadcast the " cease fire " to his troops on May 7. After five years, the Occupation was ended: Norway was free.

Photos, British Official, Sport & General

Hun Bonds Struck From the Channel Islands

BRITISH FLAGS FLYING from their houses, the people of Guernsey turned out to welcome the band of the Duke of Cornwall's Light Infantry as it marched along the esplanade after the liberation of the Channel Islands (1). Admiral Huffmeier, German C.-in-C. in the Islands, followed by his diminutive aide-de-camp (2), strutted from his former H.Q. after he had surrendered the island, with its garrison of 10,000, to a token force of 22 men of the Royal Artillery on May 9, 1945.

Ever since the Occupation in June 1940, the Islanders had concealed British flags in anticipation of liberty celebrations; when the great day dawned they displayed them lavishly, as did this cheering Guernsey housewife (3). On the steps of Elizabeth College, Guernsey (used by the Germans as their administrative H.Q.), crowds listened to Brigadier A. E. Snow, R.A., commander of the relief forces (4), reading the King's Proclamation on May 12. That same day a convoy unloaded 2,000 tons of foodstuffs. See also page 622, Vol. 8.

Photos, British Official, British Newspaper Pool, G.P.U.

Mr. Churchill Retreads the Path to Victory

To mark his five years as Prime Minister—he was commissioned by H.M. the King on May 10, 1940, to form a National Government—Mr. Churchill broadcast on May 13, 1945 (ten days before his resignation), a stirring review of the achievements and ordeals that led to victory in Europe and pointed to great tasks lying ahead. A condensation of his speech is given here.

For a while our prime enemy, our mighty enemy, Germany, overran almost all Europe. For ourselves, the British Commonwealth and Empire, we were absolutely alone. In July, August and September, 1940, 40 or 50 squadrons of British fighter aircraft broke the teeth of the German air fleet at odds of seven or eight to one in the Battle of Britain. Never before in the history of human conflict was so much owed by so many to so few. I was never one to believe that the invasion of Britain would be an easy task. With the autumn storms, the immediate danger of invasion in 1940 had passed.

Then began the blitz, when Hitler said he would rub out our cities. This was borne without a word of complaint or the slightest signs of flinching, while a very large number of people—honour to them all—proved that London could take it, and so could the other ravaged centres.

But the dawn of 1941 revealed us still in jeopardy. The sense of envelopment, which might at any moment turn to strangulation, lay heavy upon us. We had only the north-western approach between Ulster and Scotland through which to bring in the means of life and send out the forces of war. Owing to the action of Mr. de Valera, so much at variance with the temper and instinct of thousands of Southern Irishmen who hastened to the battlefront to prove their ancient valour, the approaches which the Southern Irish ports and airfields could so easily have guarded were closed by the hostile aircraft and U-boats.

These Kept the Life-line Open

This was indeed a deadly moment in our life, and if it had not been for the loyalty and friendship of Northern Ireland, we should have been forced to come to close quarters with Mr. de Valera or perish for ever from the earth. However, with a restraint and poise to which I venture to say history will find few parallels, we never laid a hand upon them.

We will not forget the devotion of our merchant seamen, the vast inventive, adaptive, all-embracing and, in the end, all-controlling power of the Royal Navy, with its ever more potent ally, the air, which have kept the life-line open. We were able to breathe; we were able to live; we were able to strike. Dire deeds we had to do.

The destruction or capture of the French Fleet which, had it ever passed into German hands would, together with the Italian Fleet, have perhaps enabled the German Navy to face us on the High Seas. The dispatch to Wavell all round the Cape at our darkest hour, of tanks—practically all we had in the island—enabled us as far back as November 1940 to defend Egypt against invasion and hurl back with the loss of a quarter of a million captives the Italian armies at whose tail Mussolini had planned a ride into Cairo or Alexandria.

Great anxiety was felt by President Roosevelt, and by thinking men throughout the United States, at what would happen to us in the early part of 1941. He feared greatly that we should be invaded in that spring, and he sent Mr. Wendell Willkie to me with a letter in which he had written the famous lines of Longfellow:

> Sail on, O Ship of State!
> Sail on, O Union strong and great!
> Humanity with all its fears,
> With all the hopes of future years,
> Is hanging breathless on thy fate!

We were in a fairly tough mood by the early months of 1941 and felt very much better about ourselves than in the months immediately after the collapse of France. Our Dunkirk army and field force troops in Britain, almost a million strong, were nearly all equipped or re-equipped. We had ferried over the Atlantic a million rifles and a thousand cannon from the United States, with all their ammunition, since the previous June. In our munition works, which were becoming very powerful, men and women had worked at their machines till they dropped senseless with fatigue. Nearly one million of men, growing to two millions at the peak, at their work all day, had been formed into the Home Guard. They were armed at least with rifles and also with the spirit, "Conquer or Die."

We Marched and Never Knew Defeat

Later in 1941, when we were still all alone, we sacrificed our conquests of the winter in Cyrenaica and Libya in order to stand by Greece, and Greece will never forget how much we gave, albeit unavailingly, of the little we had. We repressed the German-instigated rising in Iraq. We defended Palestine. With the assistance of General de Gaulle's indomitable Free French we cleared Syria and the Lebanon of Vichyites and of German intrigue.

On June 22, 1941, Hitler, master as he thought himself of all Europe, nay, soon to be master of all the world, treacherously without warning, without the slightest provocation, hurled himself on Russia and came face to face with Marshal Stalin and the numerous millions of the Russian people. And then at the end of the year Japan struck her felon blow at the United States at Pearl Harbour, and at the same time attacked us in Malaya and at Singapore.

Never since the United States entered the war have I had the slightest doubt but that we should be saved and that we had only to do our duty to win. From Alamein in October 1942, through the Anglo-American invasion of North Africa, of Sicily, and of Italy, with the capture of Rome, we marched many miles and never knew defeat.

And then in June last year, after two years of preparation and marvellous devices of amphibious warfare, we seized a carefully selected little toe of German-occupied France and poured millions in from this island and from across the Atlantic until the Seine, the Somme, and the Rhine all fell behind the advancing Anglo-American spearheads. France was liberated. She produced a fine army of gallant men to aid her own liberation. Germany lay open. And now from the other side, from the East, the mighty military achievements of the Russian people, always holding many more German troops on their own front than we could do, rolled forward to meet us in the heart and centre of Germany. At the same time, in Italy, Field-Marshal Alexander's army of so many nations, the largest part of which was British or British Empire, struck their final blow and compelled more than a million enemy troops to surrender.

We have never failed to recognize the immense superiority of the power used by the United States in the rescue of France and the defeat of Germany. For our part we have had in action about one-third as many men as the Americans, but we have taken our full share of the fighting as the scale of our losses shows. Our Navy has borne incomparably the heavier burden in the Atlantic Ocean, in the narrow seas and Arctic convoys to Russia, while the United States Navy has used its massive strength mainly against Japan. It may well be said that never have the forces of two nations fought side by side and intermingled in the line of battle with so much unity, comradeship and brotherhood as in the great Anglo-American Army.

Some people say, "Well, what would you expect, if both nations speak the same language and have the same outlook upon life with all its hope and glory." Others may say, "It would be an ill day for all the world and for the pair of them if they did not go on working together and marching together and sailing together and flying together wherever something has to be done for the sake of freedom and fair play all over the world."

There was one final danger from which the collapse of Germany has saved us—various forms of flying bombs and rockets—and our Air Force and our Ack-Ack batteries have done wonders against them. But it was only when our armies cleaned up the coast and overran all the points of discharge, and when the preparations being made on the coasts of France and Holland could be examined in detail that we knew how grave was the peril. Only just in time did the Allied Armies blast the viper in his nest. Otherwise the autumn of 1944, to say nothing of 1945, might well have seen London as shattered as Berlin. For the same period the Germans had prepared a new U-boat fleet and novel tactics which, though we should have eventually destroyed them, might well have carried anti-U-boat warfare back to the high peak days of 1942.

The Craven Fear of Being Great

I wish I could tell you that all our toils and troubles were over. On the contrary, I must warn you, as I did when I began this five years' task—that there is still a lot to do and that you must be prepared for further efforts of mind and body and further sacrifices to great causes if you are not to fall back into the rut of inertia, the confusion of aim, and the craven fear of being great. You must not weaken in any way in your alert and vigilant frame of mind.

On the Continent of Europe we have yet to make sure that the simple and honourable purposes for which we entered this war are not brushed aside or overlooked in the months following our success, and that the words freedom, democracy and liberation are not distorted from their true meaning as we have understood them. There would be little use in punishing the Hitlerites for their crimes if law and justice did not rule, and if totalitarian or police governments were to take the place of the German invaders. It is the victors who must search their hearts in their glowing hours and be worthy by their nobility of the immense forces that they wield.

We must never forget that beyond all lurks Japan, harassed and failing, but a people of a hundred millions for whose warriors death has few terrors. We, like China, so long undaunted, have received horrible injuries from them. We must remember that Australia, New Zealand, and Canada were and are all directly menaced by this evil power. They came to our aid in our dark times, and we must not leave unfinished any task which concerns their safety and their future.

I told you hard things at the beginning of these last five years. You did not shrink, and I should be unworthy of your confidence and generosity if I did not still cry, "Forward! Unflinchingly, unswerving, indomitable, till the whole task is done, and the whole world is safe and clean."

The Great Surrender

Photo, British Official

To Field-Marshal Sir Bernard Law Montgomery, at his headquarters at Luneburg Heath, near Hamburg, came on May 3, 1945, representatives of Admiral Dönitz and Field-Marshal Keitel to ask for surrender terms for all the German forces in Holland, N.W. Germany and Denmark. The delegates were Admiral Von Friedeburg, C.-in-.C. German Navy (nearest the Union Jack), Gen. Kinzel, Chief of Staff to Field-Marshal Busch, Rear-Admiral Wagner, and a S.S. staff officer. How they attempted to discuss conditions, were told " Nothing doing ! " and were brought to heel by a stern ultimatum, is described by Montgomery in his own story in page 88. Other pictures, of the actual signing on the following day, and of the historic Instrument of Surrender, are in pages 80-81.

Monty Dominated the Scene—

In his tent at 21st Army Group H.Q., on May 4, 1945, grimly satisfied, Montgomery watched General Kinzel (1) and Admiral Wagner (2) sign the Instrument of Surrender (4), after the German delegates had anxiously conferred among themselves at a distance in a grove of silver birch (3).

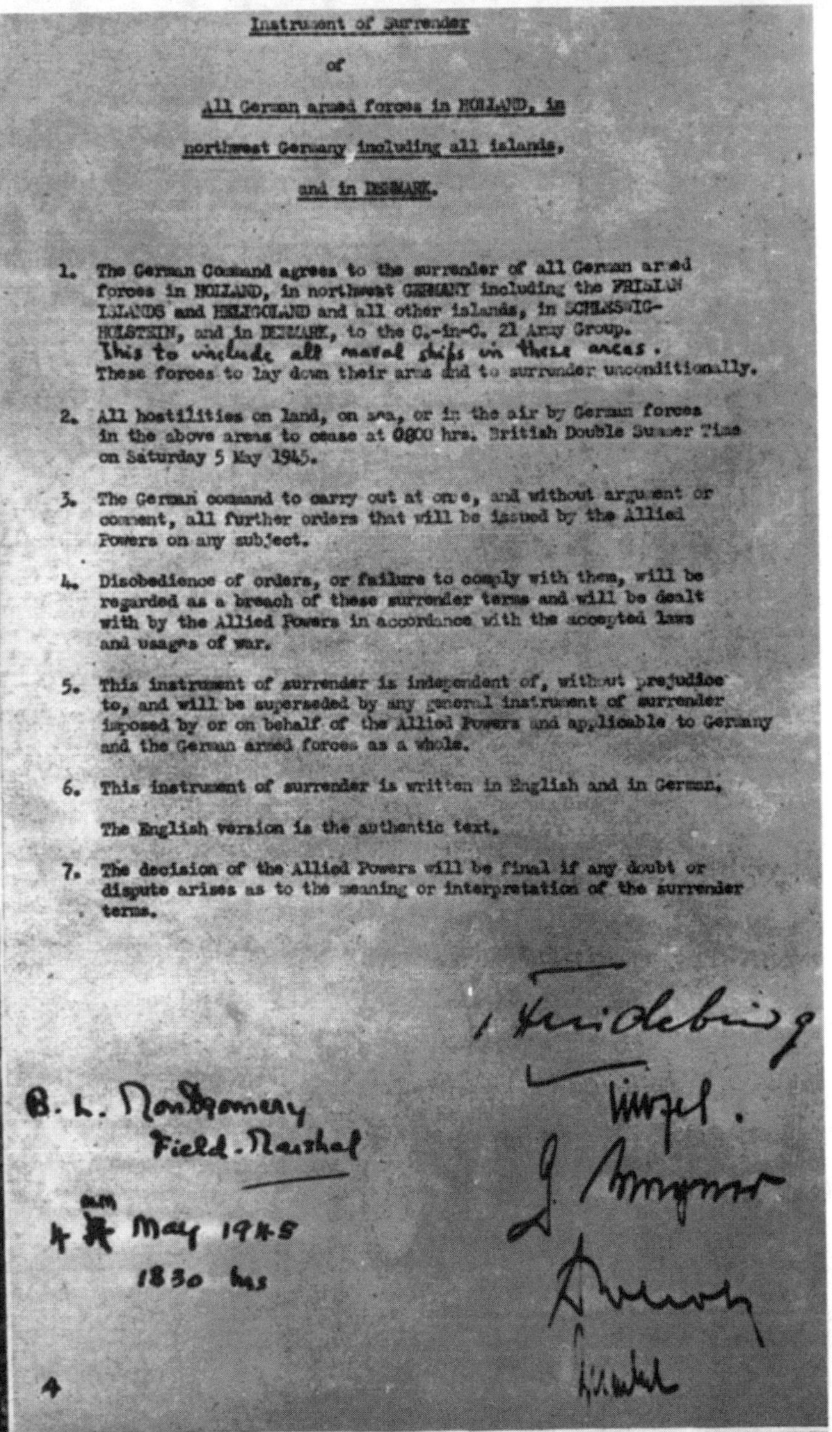

Instrument of Surrender

of

All German armed forces in HOLLAND, in

northwest Germany including all islands,

and in DENMARK.

1. The German Command agrees to the surrender of all German armed forces in HOLLAND, in northwest GERMANY including the FRISIAN ISLANDS and HELIGOLAND and all other islands, in SCHLESWIG-HOLSTEIN, and in DENMARK, to the C.-in-C. 21 Army Group. This to include all naval ships in these areas. These forces to lay down their arms and to surrender unconditionally.

2. All hostilities on land, on sea, or in the air by German forces in the above areas to cease at 0800 hrs. British Double Summer Time on Saturday 5 May 1945.

3. The German command to carry out at once, and without argument or comment, all further orders that will be issued by the Allied Powers on any subject.

4. Disobedience of orders, or failure to comply with them, will be regarded as a breach of these surrender terms and will be dealt with by the Allied Powers in accordance with the accepted laws and usages of war.

5. This instrument of surrender is independent of, without prejudice to, and will be superseded by any general instrument of surrender imposed by or on behalf of the Allied Powers and applicable to Germany and the German armed forces as a whole.

6. This instrument of surrender is written in English and in German.

The English version is the authentic text.

7. The decision of the Allied Powers will be final if any doubt or dispute arises as to the meaning or interpretation of the surrender terms.

B. L. Montgomery
Field-Marshal

4 May 1945
1830 hrs

4

7

—As Germany Fell Asunder

Twenty-four 3·7-in. A.A. guns fired 21 rounds each at Monty's headquarters to celebrate the occasion (5). Men who escorted the surrender delegation through our lines (6). Two high-ranking German officers led the march of the surrendering troops later in an ancient landau (7).

'*Delivered Into the Victors' Hands*'

Photos, British Newspaper Pool, Keystone

On May 7, 1945, at Rheims, was signed the unconditional surrender of the remainder of Germany's stricken forces. Col.-Gen. Gustav Jodl, Chief of Staff (top right, centre) with Adm. H. G. Von Friedeburg, signs for Germany. Afterwards Gen. Jodl rose and declared, " With this signature the German people and German armed forces are, for better or worse, delivered into the victors' hands ! " At the table (bottom), facing the Germans, are representatives of the U.K., U.S.A., France and Russia. In Rheims, Gen. Eisenhower (with Air Chief Marshal Sir A. Tedder, top left) broadcast his thanks to his staff.

VIEWS & REVIEWS Of Vital War Books

by Hamilton Fyfe

How well New Zealanders have fought on land we all know. Many of them have in the Navy given equally good service to the Commonwealth. Now we have a tribute to their prowess above ground ; a record, not complete, but sufficiently full to make a satisfying picture, of the exploits of New Zealanders in the Air War (Harrap, Cloth 5s. : Paper 2s. 6d.).

Mr. Alan W. Mitchell, the author, would be the last to claim that they have done better than other Allied airmen. Where all have shone so brightly it would be invidious—indeed, it would be impossible—to pick out particular acts of cleverness and courage. But this can be claimed for the members of the R.N.Z.A.F., which is the Dominion's own service (though many of its boys are in the R.A.F. and have been since before war began), this can be said without fear of any doubt being cast on the claim : they have been second to none in their skill and bravery. As Sir Archibald Sinclair, Secretary of State for Air, declares in his Foreword to the book, the reader is " left with a profound sense of admiration and gratitude for the grit and the abounding cheerfulness and unflinching courage " of all those who are mentioned in it—and of those who are not mentioned also, for all contributed their share to the common pool of audacity, devotion to duty, and readiness to undergo any trial of endurance.

There is little that could be called spectacular, for instance, in the jobs that night fighters are given to do. They search for enemy bombers in a vast, empty sky. " It's something between blind-man's buff and hunt-the-thimble," a C.O. at a night-fighter station once said. " The pilots are groping for their prey all the time and it's as though someone were saying to them ' You're getting warmer—warmer. Now, can you see him ?' " Often the search is monotonous. The look-out man can't see anything. But " it always demands the highest order of patience, concentration and skill." No relaxation is possible, and after hours of battling with cloud, rain and ice, the pilot may return tired out, with nothing to show for his pains. For this job a certain temperament is needed, unemotional, even, perhaps phlegmatic. That does not sound like the New Zealand temperament, but the routine tasks of the night fighter were undertaken as cheerfully and carried out as carefully as those which were more exciting, more " fun."

The most striking single figure here commemorated was " Cobber " Kain, who flew prominently into public notice during the early part of the war (see pages 366 and 367, Vol. 2). Mr. Mitchell suggests that during this period there was little for the war reporters to chronicle and therefore Kain's single combats were seized on and made the most of for newspaper purposes. But he does not in the least belittle what Kain actually did. His bag of German planes was exaggerated ; sometimes it was put as high as forty. It seems to have been about half that number. That was a fine record, especially at that stage of the war. Kain was killed by accident in June 1940, when practising the aerobatics which gave him his reputation as a " mad devil " among his fellow airmen ; he stunted once too often.

Kain always carried about with him as a mascot a large greenstone Maori charm. This superstitious belief in the power of certain objects to protect their possessors from harm was general. Almost every man, Mr. Mitchell noticed, when he was with bomber crews about to start for the Ruhr, took some sort of mascot with him—" a tiki, a scarf, a helmet, or a pair of gloves. I remember Frank Denton wore a tattered flying-suit which he had used on forty operations, over one pocket of which was sketched a skull and cross-bones, and over the other a shamrock. There was good-natured chaff among the crews concerning the values they placed on the mascots." They seemed to guard them quite as carefully as they did their flight rations, which consisted of a tin of orange juice, barley sugar, biscuits and cheese, chocolate and chewing gum.

In War Skies With the R.N.Z.A.F.

Two Victoria Crosses have been won by the R.N.Z.A.F. The first was awarded to the twenty-two-year-old second pilot of a Wellington—Sgt.-Pilot James Allen Ward. Attacked on July 7, 1941, by a Messerschmitt, which it destroyed, the machine caught fire. A petrol pipe had been split and the flames became more fierce every minute. Ward reached them with the greatest difficulty, braving the most hideous dangers ; exposed himself to the ninety-mile wind created by the aircraft, risked being swept off, worked his way towards the fire against agonizing obstacles, and subdued it. Two months afterwards he disappeared during a raid on Hamburg and was not heard of again (see page 71, Vol. 5).

The other V.C. was won by Flying-Officer L. A. Trigg, D.F.C., who did not survive the deed for which it was awarded in peculiar, maybe unique, circumstances. The only evidence of that deed was provided by enemy members of a submarine crew. In August 1943 their U-boat was sunk and the Liberator which Trigg commanded went down into the sea in flames. Some of the Germans after their vessel had gone under found the Liberator's dinghy and climbed into it. They were rescued a couple of days later by one of our naval corvettes and they described so vividly the valour shown by the pilot of the aircraft which attacked them that the authorities decided to act upon their testimony and decorate him posthumously with the V.C.

IN NEW GEORGIA a marker keeps tally on this score-board of Jap aircraft shot down by New Zealand fighters, the prowess of whose comrades is extolled in the book reviewed here. *Photo, Sport & General*

One of the specially daring efforts of the Commonwealth Air Forces in which the R.N.Z.A.F. took part was the freeing of a large number of Frenchmen from the prison at Amiens. These men had been prominent in the Underground Movement and were under sentence of death. It was decided to save them. Eighteen crews from British, New Zealand and Australian squadrons were picked and told what they must do. First, the wall round the prison had to be broken down in at least two places, so that the captives, when released from their cells, could get out. This was the part of the operation allotted to the New Zealanders. Next, the wing of the building in which the German guards were housed had to be smashed up. Then the ends of the main building must be blown open, but with as little force as possible, so that the prisoners might not suffer. If these separate actions were exactly timed and carried out with no hitch, the escape of the prisoners under sentence could be made.

'A Death-or-Glory Show, Boys!'

The weather on the day chosen for the attack—February 18, 1944—was vile. It snowed and rained and blew. Any other operation would have been " scrubbed " (postponed) ; but on the immediate carrying-out of this depended perhaps the lives of a hundred men, who might be bumped off at any moment. So a start had to be made. " It's a death-or-glory show, boys," said Group-Captain P. C. Pickard, D.S.O. and two bars, D.F.C., who was in command. " If it succeeds, it will be one of the most worth-while ' ops ' of the war. If you never do anything else you can still count this as the finest job you have ever done." It did succeed, though that commander lost his life, and the Air Ministry called it " one of the most memorable achievements of the Royal Air Force " (see pages 502, 503, Vol. 8).

That was a daylight operation. Whether these are preferable to night raids is a matter on which airmen are not all agreed. But they all say the same about the unpleasant sensation of being caught in searchlights. One told Mr. Mitchell, after he had taken part in bombing Munich, " When we got into the centre of a searchlight cone nearing the target it was like being in a gigantic bird-cage, but with searchlights surrounding us instead of wires." From a little distance the rays looked like " a grotesque lattice-work " and formed part of a fantastic, unforgettable scene. " Against a cloth of flames, sometimes white from new incendiaries, but more often growing red as the flames began to get a hold, we could see, hanging in the sky, our own flares. Then the Germans sent up a firework like an orange ball. It exploded at 15,000 ft., dribbling down in orange streaks, the scene surrounded by probing searchlights."

Like our airmen, the New Zealanders are drawn from all sorts and conditions of families, but a larger proportion come from open-air occupations. Many of them have been engaged in farming or sheep ranching, but they include numbers also who are town-bred boys—sons of professors, shopkeepers, and office workers. They did not like the English weather—or the Scottish weather. One wrote from Scotland : " Fog in the morning, sunshine for an hour, mist in the afternoon. Mother, oh mother, what a climate ! " But they liked the people of Britain and were well liked by them. They have helped to weld fresh links between us in our island and their own folk in their islands—links that are strong already and will grow stronger and stronger with time.

Fallen Leaders of Germany as Prisoners of War

VON KESSELRING, once German C.-in-C. in Italy, then on the West Front, and finally in North-West Germany, gave himself up on May 10, 1945, to Maj.-Gen. Maxwell D. Taylor, U.S. 7th Army (1, right) with whom he is seen at Berchtesgaden, where the surrender took place. Reichsmarshal Hermann Goering (2), ex-Luftwaffe chief and first on the official list of war criminals, surrendered on the same day to Brig.-Gen. Stack, Assistant Commander, U.S. 36th Division. Seyss-Inquart (3, centre), notorious Reichskommissar of the Netherlands during the Occupation, was guarded after his arrest in Hamburg by Royal Welch Fusiliers.

Conqueror of Poland in 1939, Field-Marshal Von Kleist (4) after his capture at Mittenfels. Field-Marshal Von Rundstedt (5, with walking-stick), former German Supreme Commander in the West, caught at his Bavarian retreat by the U.S. 7th Army, was accompanied by his son (centre) and a medical attendant (right).

Photos, British and U.S. Official, Associated Press

Last Act of the Drama in Conquered Berlin

WEARING THE NAZI " ORDER OF BLOOD," FIELD-MARSHAL KEITEL, Wehrmacht C.-in-C. (1), signed at the Soviet H.Q. in Berlin (announced on May 9, 1945) the Instrument ratifying the unconditional surrender of German power signed previously at Rheims (see illus. page 82). Red Army signatory was Marshal Zhukov (2), Anglo-American representative was Air Chief Marshal Sir Arthur Tedder (3, second from left), who with Admiral Sir Harold Burrough, (extreme right), inspected Berlin's ruins with their Russian hosts. See story in page 89. *Photos, U.S. Official*

How Europe's Capitals Hailed the Great News

PARIS BECAME AGAIN THE "CITY OF LIGHT" when she celebrated Germany's unconditional surrender: even the fountains in the Place de la Concorde (1) were illuminated. Victory crowds in Moscow's Red Square carried a young Red Army officer shoulder-high (2). At the Hague, as R.A.F. Lancasters droned overhead with food supplies, Dutch children clustered on an Allied motor vehicle (3). In Brussels, Allied bombers dipped in salute over the Hotel de Ville (4). See also story in page 90, and illus. page 94.

Photos, British Newspaper Pool, Planet News

Story With an Echo All Over Our Fair Land

HOMECOMING OF SERGEANT F. G. TUCKER to Oreston, in Devon, from a prison camp in Germany has its happy parallel wherever the war has touched the families of Britain. The small village turned out in force to greet him—arm-in-arm with a proud wife, and a wondering small son to whom a new and miraculous world has suddenly opened. Waiting to be repatriated (May 25, 1945) were some 30,000 British captives in Russian-occupied Eastern Germany, Austria and Czechoslovakia. See also illus. in page 92.

Photo, Central Press

I WAS THERE! Eye Witness Stories of the War

Montgomery's Own Story of the Great Surrender

An hour before the signing of the capitulation at Luneburg Heath in N.W. Germany, Field-Marshal Sir Bernard Montgomery told war correspondents, in his own inimitable style, of German moves leading up to the surrender. How this was made later is also described here.

THERE is a German general called Blumentritt who, as far as I know, commands all forces between the Baltic and the Weser river. On Wednesday he sent in and said he wanted to come in on Thursday and surrender what they call the army group Blumentritt. It is not an Army group as we know it—but a sort of brigade group. He wanted to surrender it so that it was done to the British 2nd Army. He was told, "You can come in. That's O.K. We are delighted."

Now the next thing that happened was yesterday morning (Thursday). Blumentritt did not come. He said, "As far as I know there is something going on just above my level and therefore I am not coming in." He did not come in. But instead there arrived here to see me four German people—Gen.-Adml. Friedeburg, who is commander-in-chief of the German navy (I think Dönitz was commander-in-chief German navy until he became Fuehrer); Gen. Kinzel, chief of staff to Field-Marshal Busch (he is here in camp now); Rear-Adml. Wagner, staff officer to Friedeburg; and Major Friede, who is staff officer to Kinzel, so the party really was just two chaps—Friedeburg and Kinzel.

Now this is extremely interesting. They lined up above my caravan and I said, "What do you want?"—I am telling you the whole story because it is very interesting. They said, "We've come here from Field-Marshal Busch to ask you to accept the surrender of the three German armies that are now withdrawing in front of the Russians in Mecklenburg between Rostock and Berlin. They are the 3rd Panzer, the 12th and 21st Armies." They said, "We want you to accept the surrender of these armies. We are very anxious about the condition of the civilians who are driven along as these armies flee from the advancing Russians and we want you to accept their surrender."

I said "No, certainly not. These armies are fighting the Russians and therefore if they surrender to anybody it must be to the Russians—it has nothing to do with me and I am not going to have any dealings with anything on my eastern flank from Wismar to Domitz on the Elbe, on which flank we are now in closest contact with the Russians. This is the Russians' business. A Russian peace, therefore you surrender to the Russians. Now the subject is closed." I then said to them, "Are you prepared to surrender to me the German forces on my western and northern flanks—that is to say, all the German forces between Luebeck and Holland, and all those forces that they have in support of them? These forces include the German army in Denmark—will you surrender those?"

They said, "No." So far it had been a very good discussion. Then they said, "We are most anxious about the condition of civilians in the areas of Luebeck and on the northern flank—we are very anxious about them and we would like to come to some agreement with you by which these civilians can be saved slaughter in battle. We thought perhaps you would make some plan with us whereby you would advance slowly and we would withdraw slowly and all the civilians would be all right." So far we had not got very far.

READING THE SURRENDER TERMS to the German delegation on May 4, 1945, Field-Marshal Montgomery—who tells his own story in this page—was stern and implacable. Round the table, left to right: Major Friede, Rear-Admiral Wagner, Admiral Von Friedeburg, Field-Marshal Montgomery, General Kinzel and Col. Polleck. On May 23 Friedeburg committed suicide at Flensburg. **See also pages 79-81.**
Photo, British Official

I said, "No. There is nothing doing. I am not going to discuss any conditions at all as to what I am going to do. I wonder whether you officers know what is the battle situation on the Western Front? In case you don't I will show it to you." I produced a map which showed the battle situation. That situation was a great shock to them. They were quite amazed and very upset. I was perfectly frank and held back no secrets. They were in a condition—and in a very good, ripe condition—to receive a further blow, which they got. I said to them, "You must clearly understand three points.

"One. You must surrender to me unconditionally all the German forces in Holland, in Friesland, including the Frisian Islands, Heligoland, and all other islands, in Schleswig-Holstein and in Denmark.

"Two. Once you have done that I am then prepared to discuss with you the implications of the surrender—that is to say I am prepared to say to you how we will dispose of the German forces, how we will occupy the area concerned, how we will deal with the civilians and so on. Once you have done Point Number One I will discuss Point Number Two. (You see, they wanted me to do Point Number Two first.)

"Three. If you don't agree to Point Number One I shall go on with the war and will be delighted to do so and am ready. All your soldiers will be killed. These are the three points—there is no alternative—one, two, three, finished!"

They then said to me, "We came here entirely for the purpose of asking you to accept surrender of these German armies on your eastern flank and we have been given powers to agree to that subject only. We have no power to agree to what you now want. That is a new one on us. But two of us will now go back again to where we came from, get agreement and come back again. Two will stay here with you."

So yesterday afternoon between 3.30 and 4 o'clock the Gen.-Admiral, accompanied by Major Friede, went back. We sent them through our lines into Hamburg and I sent with them my personal assistant, Col. Warren. He took them right up the road until they met the Germans—they had a special flag. The other two stayed in my camp all night. The arrangement was that the Gen.-Admiral would be back here tonight at five o'clock and here he is back.

He was to come back here with the doings. He was to get agreement to my Point Number One; after that, I would agree to Point Number Two and Point Number Three. That is the story that is going to unfold itself in the next business. Now they have arrived—they are up top somewhere, and my present intention is that they will sign what I have prepared. This piece of paper is really the Instrument of Surrender of the forces in accordance with my demands. I am dealing with the commander of the forces facing me and that is why I am doing it alone like this. I am demanding from him the tactical surrender of the forces fighting me and any ones in close support like the ones in Denmark.

Very Tricky Problems Involved

I have absolutely excluded anything which would be an Allied thing and would require the presence of our Allied Russians and Americans and so on. The forces which surrender will total over 1,000,000—that is their own statement. It will involve some very tricky problems getting them from these places—from West Holland and Denmark. We know there are in Schleswig-Holstein 2,000,000 civilians over and above the normal population. They came into it as the battle surged from Eastern Germany right across Germany and up into Schleswig-Holstein. I have given you absolutely the whole story. The next scene will be up top in the tent.

The narrative is continued by R. W. Thompson, special correspondent of The Sunday Times:

He left us, and for a short time we waited, and then, just before six, we walked up to where above the small cluster of caravans that is Monty's headquarters the Union Jack fluttered in the still cold breeze. A square table with a plain grey army blanket showed under the rainflaps of a tent, around it six brown hard chairs. In this tent we knew this "piece of paper" would be signed.

Presently Monty walked down the steps of his caravan, the "piece of paper," in one hand, the other hand stuffed deep into his battle-dress pocket. And then they came through the woodland. Two British staff officers walked with Friedeburg and behind them followed in pairs Kinzel and Wagner, Friede and a new arrival, Col. Polleck. Von Friedeburg climbed the steps of the Field-Marshal's caravan alone and entered. It was 6.20 when he emerged from the caravan and the small cavalcade led by two British staff officers walked across to the tent with the simple table. There they stood each at his chair, waiting. Two minutes later Field-

Marshal Montgomery followed. The five German officers saluted stiffly and seated themselves after the Field-Marshal.

Montgomery, who wore his tortoiseshell spectacles, read clearly the text of the " piece of paper." " The German Command agree to surrender all German forces to the C.-in-C., 21st Army Group. All hostilities to cease at 8 a.m. British double summer time, May 5, 1945. The decision of the Allied Powers final." Then Montgomery said, " The German delegation will now sign. They will sign in order of seniority. Gen.-Adm. Von Friedeburg first."

The admiral rose, walked to the place, and with the simple army issue pen signed. Then Kinzel, then the others as the Field-Marshal called their names. Only Montgomery's voice rose above the sibilant click of the cameras, and then he said : " Now I will sign on behalf of the Supreme Commander, Gen. Eisenhower." As he finished signing he sighed faintly sat back, removed his tortoiseshell rims, completely master of himself and his enemies in this great moment. " That concludes the formal surrender." The tent flaps were let down as details were discussed and we walked away.

Field-Marshal KEITEL, Wehrmacht C.-in-C., arrogantly raised his baton before signing the unconditional surrender terms in Berlin. Story in this page. *Photo, U.S. Official*

Keitel Was Furious As He Signed in Berlin

How the final act of surrender was signed on Germany's behalf by the chiefs of her Army, Navy and Air Force, in Berlin, is told by Clifford Webb of the Daily Herald. Present at the ceremony, he describes it as " probably the most uproarious surrender scene in history." See also p. 85.

WE met our first Russians at Stendal airfield, close to the Elbe, where the planes carrying the official British party under Air Chief Marshal Tedder, General Eisenhower's Deputy, touched down by arrangement. There we had to await the arrival first of a plane from Flensburg, bringing Field-Marshal Keitel, the chief German signatory, and then an escort of Russian fighters to escort us to the Tempelhof aerodrome in Berlin. Eventually we became airborne again and flew on with a swarm of fighters, circling, zooming and diving all around in the most exuberant fashion.

At Tempelhof Sir Arthur Tedder's party was warmly welcomed by high-ranking Russian officers and all but mobbed by uniformed Russian Press photographers. Then the British party inspected the guard of honour of young, smart-looking Red troops, and took up position for a march past.

This was a grand spectacle. The Russians held their bayoneted rifles in the forward lunge position, each point only inches from the neck of the man in front. They marched stiffly and with wonderful precision to martial music in a manner that would have " brought the house down " in any part of the world.

Hustled into waiting cars, we were driven at breakneck speed through the ruins of Berlin. We came to Karlshorst and were shown into neat, typically suburban villas, for rest and refreshment. Wine, vodka, cognac, red and black caviare, fish, ham and cheese, were brought in by trim Russian waitresses. At 7 p.m. we went to the school. Interpreters and secretaries were deep in the throes of their struggles to convey precisely the same meaning to technical paragraphs in Russian, English and German. Cases of beer were brought to the building.

Meanwhile, Sir Arthur Tedder, puffing away at his pipe, roamed around obviously enjoying the informality as much as anybody. It was 11.1 p.m. British time when all was finally ready, and we filed into the large, lofty conference-room, whose main adornment was the Russian, British, United States and French flags on the wall above the table reserved for Marshal Zhukov, Sir Arthur Tedder and the other Allied signatories.

Zhukov, shortish, broad, hair slightly thinning in front, gave an immediate impression of immense power and obvious intelligence. His eyes are steely, blue, deep set and unwavering. His jaw juts, but his mouth is that of the good-humoured man. He was in Russian Marshal-of-Armies uniform, white stars on his epaulettes.

THERE was a buzz of conversation, which was hushed as through the wide open doors the three German delegates, Keitel, Stumpff and Friedeburg appeared. Keitel strode to his seat, looked towards the top table, clicked his heels and raised his Field-Marshal's baton in his right hand in salute. The other two bowed stiffly and were seated. Keitel, a typically arrogant-looking Prussian Junker, thin-lipped, grey moustached, and pink-faced, screwed a monocle into his left eye to read papers set in front of him.

Marshal Zhukov put on steel-rimmed spectacles and looked sternly in front of him. Sir Arthur Tedder, composed and absolutely at ease, was probably the most unmoved person in the whole room. Keitel was directed to the top table to sign Germany's final surrender. And then an astonishing thing happened. The eager crowd of Russian photographers could contain their enthusiasm no longer.

They surged forward until they all but engulfed the top table, pushing and struggling among themselves to thrust their cameras within inches of Keitel's furious face while he signed. Reporters stood on chairs until other reporters pushed them off. It was probably the most uproarious surrender scene in history and yet the top table somehow managed to retain a calm dignity and the signings proceeded as arranged.

Keitel returned to his former seat and began expostulating to interpreters about some detail in the surrender terms with which he did not agree. It was a small point and, anyway, he had already signed. After a while he tried to cover his humiliation with some light conversation to his aides. The signings complete, the documents were carefully stored away in blue folders, and everybody repaired to the largest ante-room for conversation and beer, Marshal Zhukov among them.

Meanwhile, a small crowd of waitresses descended on the conference-room, whipped away pens, pencils, papers, and all the paraphernalia of surrender, and swiftly transformed the room into a banqueting-hall. And then a full five hours of eating, drinking, toasting and music. Marshal Zhukov became more and more smilingly expansive as the night wore on, and the top table quickly became the scene of much back-slapping, hand shaking, and general good humour, with all the other tables following suit. Sir Arthur Tedder scored a great personal triumph with just the right note in his speeches and with his informal easy-going manner. He did a grand job.

Air Chief Marshal SIR ARTHUR TEDDER, as Deputy Allied Supreme Commander was a signatory of the surrender document in the German capital. *Photo, U.S. Official*

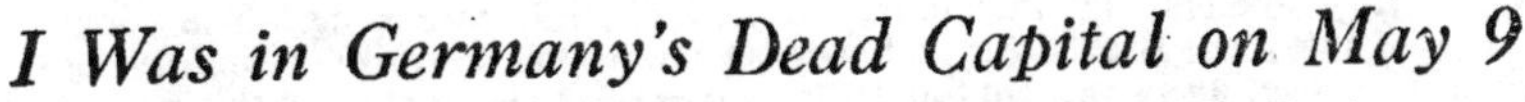

I Was in Germany's Dead Capital on May 9

Touring Berlin in company with Air Chief Marshal Tedder and the Russian Military Commander of the capital, Gen. Berzanin, on the day capitulation was announced there, Reuters correspondent Harold King saw grimly contrasting scenes in a metropolis which " had simply ceased to exist."

I HAVE seen Stalingrad, I have lived through the entire London blitz, I have seen a dozen badly damaged major Russian towns. But the scene of utter destruction, desolation and death which meets the eye in Berlin as far as the eye can rove in all directions is something that almost baffles description. Dozens of well-known thoroughfares, including the entire Unter den Linden from one end to the other, are utterly wrecked. The town is literally unrecognizable.

The Alexanderplatz, in the East End, where the Gestapo headquarters were, is a weird desert of rubble and gaping smoke-blackened walls. From the Brandenburg Gate everything within a radius of from two to five miles is destroyed. There does not appear to be one house in a hundred which is even useful as shelter. Among hundreds of well-known landmarks which have disappeared or been irreparably damaged are the former Kaiser's palace, the Opera House, the French, British, American and Japanese Embassies, Goering's Air Ministry, Goebbels' Propaganda Ministry, the Bristol and Adlon hotels. Hitler's Chancellery in the Wilhelmstrasse is like some vast, abandoned ancient tomb of the dead. It has had several direct hits, and it is impossible yet to tell who lies buried beneath the rubble—perhaps Hitler himself.

"If you want to know what war means, come to Berlin ! " was Air Chief Marshal

FROM THE RUINS OF THE FRANKFURTERALLEE clouds of smoke arose as the remnants of Berlin's garrison, under General Weisering, surrendered on May 2, 1945, to Marshal Zhukov's and Marshal Koniev's troops, elaborate barricades and street trench-systems failing to stay the Red Army's advance. A tour of the dead capital is described below. *Photo, Planet News*

Tedder's comment, after he had stood for five minutes on his tour of inspection, making a quick sketch of the scene at the Brandenburg Gate for his famous sketchbook. The only people who look like human beings in the streets of what was Berlin are the Russian soldiers. There are 2,000,000 inhabitants in the city, the Russian authorities told me, but they are mostly in the more remote suburbs. In the central part of the city you only see a few ghost-like figures queueing up to pump water.

If Stalingrad, London, Guernica, Rotterdam and Coventry wanted avenging, they have had it and no mistake about it. All observers this morning agreed that it would probably be impossible to rebuild the centre of Berlin for many years, if ever. Fires are still burning here and there, and the dull sound of a mine exploding or dynamite being sprung can be heard every few minutes. The Red Flag flies on top of the Reichstag (see illus. page 41) which is burned hollow—really burnt this time. The Tiergarten opposite the Reichstag looks like a forest after a big fire.

I MOTORED from Tempelhof Airport in a fast car, driven with dash and determination by a Russian who had come all the way from Stalingrad. During thirty minutes' driving I spotted only six houses which I was not able to see straight through and in which there were signs of habitation. The population and Red Army soldiers are attempting to clear some of the main streets, but it looks like trying to shovel away the sand and the Pyramids in Egypt. One has the impression that if placed in the midst of one of a network of smaller streets without any guidance one might wander around for hours, lost as if in a desert. The Russian command has already erected huge sketch maps at all main squares and crossings. Without these it would be impossible to find one's way about.

Except for the noise of an occasional Russian Army car, or the gentle trot of the small horse-drawn Russian carts, there is complete silence, and the air is permanently filled with rubble dust. One sign of life, however, is the interminable columns of displaced persons of all European nationalities who seem to be marching through Berlin in various directions, carried forward by a homing instinct more than by any clear idea of where they are going.

The Russian military command is already feeding hundreds of thousands of Berliners. The Red Army has seized what food stocks the city had, and has added from its own supplies. Berliners receive 500 grammes of bread a day (more than many people got in Moscow in the winter of 1942), a little meat, sugar, coffee, potatoes. Attempts are being made to get the water supply working. The Russians are obviously not wreaking any vengeance on the population. Notices in Russian, the only spot of bright colour in this place of desolation, are all over the town. In many respects, one has the impression, on arriving in Berlin today, that one is back in some war-scarred region of the Soviet Union. Russian troops are everywhere, cheerful, enduring, good-natured. With them they have brought their girl army traffic control "cops," who signal with red and yellow flags and salute smartly every time, as they have been doing all the way from the Volga to the Spree.

When the Allied Delegation arrived at the Tempelhof Airport yesterday there were compact squads of tough little Siberians lined up to honour their arrival. And practically the only Germans within sight were the surrender envoys, with their aides, who marched across the airport accompanied by Russian and Allied officers.

The German chief executives of gas, transport, electric light, water and other public utility organizations, have voluntarily placed themselves at the disposal of General Berzanin, and Berlin workers have reported to Russian command posts, I was told, with the words: "We are your soldiers. We work for you." Many wounded German soldiers, who were lying in underground hospitals, have been sent to Russian-organized hospitals, and are looked after by German doctors and German nurses. Every day thousands of Berliners are coming back, but there is nothing much to come back to.

While the Russians told me they hoped to have part of the underground working again by the middle of this month, at present hundreds of burnt-out trams stand on the tram tracks, dead horses are still lying in the streets, and parts of the city are very dangerous because of the risk of tens of thousands of walls collapsing in a final spasm of death.

I Saw Joyous London Blaze Up on V Day Eve

Suddenly, spontaneously, deliriously the people of London on May 7, 1945, held their own jubilations—before Victory Day was officially declared. "V Day may be tomorrow," they said, "but the war is over tonight!" Guy Ramsey, of The Daily Mail, tells what it was like—a staggering contrast to the scenes in conquered Berlin. **See also illus. p. 94.**

THE sky once lit by the glare of the blitz shone red with the Victory glow. The last trains departed from the West End unregarded. The pent-up spirits of the throng, the polyglot throng that is London in wartime, burst out, and by 11 o'clock the capital was ablaze with enthusiasm.

Processions formed up out of nowhere, disintegrating for no reason, to reform somewhere else. Waving flags, marching in step, with linked arms or half-embraced, the people strode down the great thoroughfares—Piccadilly, Regent Street, the Mall, to the portals of Buckingham Palace. They marched and counter-marched so as not to get too far from the centre. And from them, in harmony and discord, rose song. The songs of the last war, the songs of a century ago. The songs of the beginning of this war—Roll out the Barrel, and Tipperary; Ilkla Moor and Loch Lomond; Bless 'em All and Pack Up Your Troubles.

Rockets—found no one knows where, set-off by no one knows whom—streaked into the sky, exploding not in death but a burst of scarlet fire. A pile of straw filled with thunder-flashes salvaged from some military dump spurted and exploded near Leicester Square. Every car that challenged the milling, moiling throng was submerged in humanity. They climbed on the running-boards, on the bonnet, on the roof. They hammered on the panels. They shouted and sang.

Against the drumming on metal came the clash of cymbals, improvised out of dustbin lids. The dustbin itself was a football for an impromptu Rugger scrum. Bubbling, exploding with gaiety, the people "mafficked." Headlights silhouetted couples kissing, couples cheering, couples waving flags. Every cornice, every lamp-post was scaled. Americans marched with A.T.S. Girls in civvies, fresh from their workbenches, ran by the side of battle-dressed soldiers. A handful of French sailors lent a touch of Cosmopolis to the scene. Wherever one went, song was in the air. Half-way up Regent Street the shouts of Piccadilly smote on the ear like a ceaseless machine-gun fire of sound.

Over Buckingham Palace soared aircraft, their navigation lights like coloured stars, while a throng, convinced the Royal Family would *not* appear, still chanted monotonously and happily, "WE WANT THE KING!"

The police in their wisdom took no steps to check the gaiety the people had earned. Only here and there did a kindly hand fall on an obstreperous shoulder and shift somebody on. The American M.P.s—"Snowdrops"—stood about grinning humorously, good-humouredly, and . . . helplessly. Flashes of Press cameras stabbed the lurid sky. The whir of rattles—once to warn us against gas, the single terror-weapon not used—confounded the confusion.

And yet—and yet, what a good-humoured crowd! No violence, no stampede, no rough stuff. A kindly crowd, a little drunk, but incredibly more intoxicated with victory than alcohol, cheered and laughed and broke into dance. Ships in the river sounded their sirens continuously. It went on for two hours. Wherever there was a piece of derelict land there was a bonfire.

Floodlights blazed at Stage Door Canteen, where a score of flags shone scarlet; Big Ben shone steady through the night; the County Hall—also floodlit—added its quota of brilliance to the scene. London University students formed a mile-long procession that traipsed up and down the Strand. Fire engines clanged and clattered—summoned by false alarms. Lights swung brilliantly in Admiralty Arch.

On Hampstead Hill a huge throng gathered to look down over London. And one woman, who had lost the irreplaceable in the blitz, looked out across the glaring lights and murmured: "I never want to see London glow again—even tonight!" Aircraft flung down multi-coloured balls of fire, and from the highest church in London—Christ Church, Hampstead—a V in living light, wrought by skilfully adjusted flood-lighting, blazoned its message that *Victory is won.*

In the Nightmare City of Rangoon Today

The Burmese capital was reoccupied by British forces on May 3, 1945, after nearly three years' occupation by the Japanese. How the once lovely city had been transformed by the enemy to a horror almost beyond belief is told by Arthur Helliwell, the Daily Herald's special correspondent.

THE Japanese have left their ugly trade-mark smeared heavily across the face of this once lovely city—the trade-mark of filth and degradation and misery they left in their wake across half Burma as we chased them down to the sea.

All the way from the Chindwin we have seen the same thing in their abandoned jungle camps that looked more like pigsties than human habitations. But here in Rangoon, where traces of the city's former beauty still shine through the dirt and decay, the trade-mark of Japanese bestiality is much more horrifying.

The refuse of months is piled up feet high along the broad, tree-lined, sun-drenched boulevards. Gutters are clogged with it and over the whole city there hangs a cloying and nauseating stench that sticks in your gullet—the vile odour of decay.

Rangoon today is a nightmare city—a city where the streets are paved with millions of worthless Japanese currency notes, where beggars squat on piles of paper money and beg for alms, where ownerless buffaloes roam the pavements of a city riddled with loathsome disease.

The still smouldering vaults of the impressive white Bank of India building, the bodies of native looters stabbed to death in a crazy fight for money lie sprawled among the litter of bloodstained Japanese notes.

People who remained here through the Japanese occupation are hungry. The children have that peaked, hollow-eyed look that comes from months of semi-starvation. And when you see them another tragedy of this sad city hits you. In Rangoon today children never laugh or play games. Most of them seem to have forgotten how to smile.

They simply squat and stare with their wizened little faces puckered in bewilderment, and once again you recognize another trade-mark of the "sons of heaven"—the stamp of fear.

Reconstruction work has already begun, and out in the dirty river trim Royal Navy minesweepers are weaving to and fro among the gently bobbing sampans, clearing the waterway for the big freighters that will soon come sailing up to Rangoon again with supplies for more Allied victories.

LANDING CRAFT RUSHED THE BANKS OF RANGOON RIVER, south of Burma's capital, on May 3, 1945, in one of the greatest amphibious operations to date under South-East Asia Command; blinding rain and smoke from the great strike of the Allied Strategic Air Force obliterated the defences. It was the first Allied full-scale invasion without naval bombardment, but so heavy was the air attack that the British and Indian sea-borne troops, with Gurkha paratroops, went in almost unopposed. **See also illus. page 66.** *Photo, British Official*

OUR DIARY OF THE WAR

MAY 9, Wednesday
1,249th day of War against Japan

Channel Islands.—Final surrender of German garrison signed on board H.M. destroyer Bulldog.

Sea.—Last remnants of German fleet, including Prinz Eugen and Nürnberg, surrendered in Copenhagen harbour.

Home Front.—Home Secretary announced revocation of many Defence Regulations, including 18b.

MAY 10, Thursday *1,250th day*

Sea.—First U-boats to give themselves up entered British ports.

Japan.—Super-Fortresses attacked aviation fuel centres near Tokuyama on Honshu and on Oshima island.

MAY 11, Friday *1,251st day*

Russian Front.—Marshal Koniev arrived in Prague. Russian forces converged on last Germans holding out in Czechoslovakia.

Philippines.—Fresh landing of U.S. forces on Mindanao announced.

MAY 12, Saturday *1,252nd day*

Channel Islands.—British force and relief expedition arrived in Jersey and Guernsey.

Mediterranean.—Unconditional surrender of German garrison in Crete signed at Heraklion.

Ryukyu Islands.—U.S. troops occupied Tori island, E. of Okinawa.

MAY 13, Sunday *1,253rd day*

Germany.—British troops, including Scots Guards, occupied Heligoland.

New Guinea.—Australians captured Wewak peninsula and airfield.

Japan.—Nine square miles of Nagoya laid waste in attack by more than 500 Super-Fortresses.

Home Front.—King George and Queen Elizabeth drove through London to Thanksgiving Service at St. Paul's.

MAY 14, Monday *1,254th day*

Mediterranean.—First contingent of British troops landed in Crete.

Philippines.—In Luzon, U.S. troops captured Balete Pass.

MAY 15, Tuesday *1,255th day*

Ryukyu Islands.—Fierce fighting in Naha, capital of Okinawa.

Japan.—Japanese Cabinet decided to abrogate all treaties with Germany and other European nations.

MAY 16, Wednesday *1,256th day*

Channel Islands.—British naval and military expedition reoccupied Alderney, last island to be freed.

Malacca Straits.—Japanese cruiser sunk by ships and aircraft of East Indies Fleet west of Penang.

Japan.—Nagoya again attacked by Super-Fortresses with incendiaries.

Home Front.—Mr. Bevin announced Government's plan for re-allocation of man-power; group releases from Army to start June 18; ballot for "Bevin boys" for mines to be suspended.

MAY 17, Thursday *1,257th day*

Indian Ocean.—Allied heavy bombers attacked the Andaman Islands.

Home Front.—Minister of Fuel and Power announced basic petrol ration to come into operation June 1.

General.—H.M. the King announced creation of seven new medals for War service.

MAY 18, Friday *1,258th day*

China.—Treaty port of Foochow recaptured by Chinese troops.

Japan.—Super-Fortresses attacked Hamamatsu, south-east of Nagoya.

MAY 19, Saturday *1,259th day*

Japan.—Super-Fortresses from the Marianas bombed Tokyo. Philippines-based Fortresses attacked Hamamatsu.

Formosa.—Allied aircraft from the Philippines attacked Formosa.

MAY 20, Sunday *1,260th day*

Ryukyu Islands.—Japanese in U.S. Marine uniforms counter-attacked on Okinawa, but were repulsed.

China.—Allied patrol bombers attacked railway installations along the Yangtse near Nanking.

MAY 21, Monday *1,261st day*

Netherlands.—Canadian 1st Army held victory march through The Hague.

U.S.A.—War Dept. announced that U.S. 1st Army under Gen. Hodges was on its way to the Pacific via U.S.A.

MAY 22, Tuesday *1,262nd day*

U.S.A.—War and Navy Depts. revealed that for some time Japanese balloons carrying bombs had fallen in isolated spots in U.S.A. and Canada.

Germany.—Field-Marshal Montgomery appointed C.-in-C. British Forces of Occupation in Germany.

Home Front.—Food Minister announced cuts in civilian rations of fats, bacon, meat and soap.

Flash-backs

1940

May 10. *Germans invaded Holland, Belgium and Luxembourg. Mr. Churchill became Premier.*

May 14. *Rotterdam heavily bombed by Luftwaffe. Dutch surrendered. Formation of Local Defence Volunteers announced by Mr. Eden.*

May 15. *Germans broke through French lines south of Sedan.*

1941

May 10. *Last heavy bomber raid on London. Hess landed in Scotland.*

May 20. *First German airborne troops landed in Crete.*

1943

May 12. *All organized Axis resistance ended in Tunisia.*

May 16-17. *R.A.F. mine-laying Lancasters breached Mohne and Eder dams in the Ruhr basin.*

1944

May 11-12. *5th and 8th Armies opened offensive against the Gustav Line in Italy.*

May 18. *Cassino town captured by British, Monastery Hill by Poles. U.S. and Chinese troops in Burma under Gen. Merrill captured Myitkyina airfield.*

THE WAR IN THE AIR

by **Capt. Norman Macmillan, M.C., A.F.C.**

I MET a friend a few days ago who was just back from the East, where he has spent a good deal of the last 25 years from Bengal eastwards. He is inclined to think the Japs may sue for peace. He had come home in a Sunderland flying boat, taking five days for the journey from the farther side of India. Himself a pilot of great experience, he found the journey comfortable. His one doubt was that the sudden transition, with stops at diverse places, placed an undue strain on the stomach, because it entailed a rapidly varying diet, with a complete change of food between the two terminal ends of his journey. If my friend were not accustomed to flying in many different climates one might suppose it was the method of travelling, or the change of climate, that caused his trouble.

But he was quite sure it was simply the different food. Here is a new problem which will have to be investigated by medical dieteticians if fast world air travel is to become popular and it would be wise to investigate it in view of the transport of thousands of troops home by air on leave from Burma, and elsewhere. It is, of course, possible that only a small percentage of air travellers would be affected by very sudden change of food, but it seems likely that these could be aided by knowing what to eat and what to avoid eating until their digestive organs had readjusted themselves.

MEDICAL Aspect of Flying in Tropical Climates is Involved

Fortunately, this question of change of diet does not affect the aircrews who are operating within the Commands of the Far East and Pacific war area, for the air forces there, including the transport aircraft, are geographically zoned. But there is little doubt that the medical aspect of flying in tropical climates will receive more attention than it obtained before the war, due to the enormous strides that have been made in aviation, especially in the Burmese theatre of war, where from April 1, 1944, to March 31, 1945, transport aircraft delivered more than 550,000 tons of supplies. During the first three months of 1945 more than 250,000 tons lift was made by air ; 236,000 men were transported, and over 70,000 sick and wounded evacuated from battle areas. In March, alone, the rising effort in this theatre lifted 98,000 tons.

These figures of tonnage are not to be regarded as rivalling the lift of ships. They represent a shuttle service over stages of about 250 miles from base to advanced airfield, but fuel must be carried for the return journey, so that they are not comparable with commercial air transport journeys either. The difference between air lift and sea lift cannot be discussed on such short haul runs, for ships are capable of conveying large cargoes over long sea routes where aircraft making a similar passage would have to reduce cargo seriously to take on fuel for the flight. The fact is that sea and air transport are complementary, and most of the supplies run into Burma by air must first reach India by sea.

THE comparison is between what is now done in air lifts and what was formerly done. This cannot be compared with earlier military air transport lifts, because pre-war military air transport was on a puny scale. But I have turned up the ton mileage figure for Imperial Airways for 1938 and find it was 8,353,618 ton miles. Taking the Burmese campaign figure for the 12 months given in a previous paragraph, and for one way only (that is, the inward run to the battle area) the figure is 137,500,000 ton miles, or more than 16 times the lift of Imperial Airways for 1938. If one were to take the return lift into account, it is probable that the figure would rise to a ratio of 30 to one.

REMEMBER that Imperial Airways' ton mileage was flown on Empire-wide routes, from England to South Africa and Singapore, whereas the Burma battle lift was concentrated into one relatively small area ; then it becomes possible to visualize how big this air transport operation is. There is no doubt that the Burma counter-campaign, directed, as it was, with all the geographical factors favouring the Japanese, could not have been the success it has proved without the large-scale use of air transport. For it is characteristic of air transport more than of any other form of transport that it can swiftly overcome geographical handicaps which present otherwise impassable barriers.

In Burma air power was tactically employed to cut Japanese communications after the pattern used in Europe against the Germans. Surface communications in Burma are dependent upon bridges in many parts of the interior, and these were selected as a priority target. From December 27, 1944, to April 30, 1945, 124 bridges in Burma and Siam were destroyed by the Strategic Air Force 7th Bombardment Group. And as a counter to the breaking of Jap communication lines, the transport aircraft of the Allies flew narrow-gauge railway locomotives into Burma to aid the surface communications of the Allied armies.

IN the Japanese home zone the air war has been directed to secure complete air supremacy for the Allies by (1) elimination of the Japanese air forces (Navy and Army) and (2) the congestion of the industrial communications of Japanese industry. On March 27, 1945, the U.S. 21st Bomber Command began a sea-mining operation with Super-Fortress bombers flying from Tinian. Each aircraft dropped 10 tons of mines in one sortie. The plan was to seal up the entrances to the 240-miles long Inland Sea, whereon lie the large ports of Kobe and Osaka, and others of smaller size. Other mines were dropped in Tokyo and Nagoya harbours, by parachute, from below 10,000 feet. Twelve of these night operations had been completed by May 11. Seventy-five per cent of Japanese communications depend on her waterways, hence their importance.

ON May 4, British carrier aircraft bombed airfields, flak positions and radio installations in the Sakishima group. The following night Super-Forts bombed airfields in South Japan three times, these raids making a total of 16 in eight days. On May 10, 400 Super-Forts, without loss, bombed Japanese navy and army main refuelling points near the Inland Sea, and at Oshima ; hit a large refinery ; and attacked airfields on Kyushu.

On May 11 between 100 and 150 Super-Forts bombed two airfields in Kyushu and the Kawanishi aircraft plant at Fukai on Honshu, the leading Japanese naval aircraft factory. Two days later 900 aircraft from carriers and a small force of Super-Forts attacked airfields and military installations on Kyushu ; Admiral Nimitz reported that 71 Japanese planes were destroyed in combat and over 100 on the ground, while many more were damaged. On May 13 more than 500 Super-Forts dropped 570,000 incendiary bombs on Nagoya, Japanese aircraft manufacturing centre ; the bomb load weighed 3,300 tons, and over 5,500 aircrews were engaged in the operation. This raid was estimated to have added another nine square miles of ruins to the five miles and a half burned out on two previous raids. Pacific strategy thus follows European methods.

HOME FROM GERMANY BY AIR, ex-prisoners of war cheered as they landed from an R.A.F. Lancaster at a Southern England aerodrome ; the journey normally takes from two to two-and-a-half hours. On May 13, 1945, No. 46 Group R.A.F. Transport Command brought 4,407 ex-prisoners to England from the Continent ; three days later the total since the service started on April 4 was announced as 95,000. See also illus. p. 87. *Photo, Barratts*

ON May 5, R.A.F. Dakotas landed British forces at Kastrup airfield, Copenhagen, to take over from the Germans (see illus. page 74). The fighter escort did not land with the unarmed transports. On May 8—V-day—Bomber Command Lancasters landed in Germany for the first time, to fly back relieved prisoners of war ; Juvincourt airfield, near Rheims, is a P.O.W. flight staging station whence about 5,000 fly daily to the U.K. after having been flown from Germany the day before. The U.S. Air Transport Command will fly combat troops from Europe to the U.S.A. in the next few months. A round-the-world R.A.F. Lancaster has made experimental flights over the Magnetic and Geographic North Poles to test radio and radar, compass and other navigational equipment.

Far East Air Force Shatters Japanese Targets

SAILING IN CONVOY, this Japanese vessel (1) was trying to reach Ormoc, main enemy port and base on western Leyte in the Philippines (which General MacArthur's men seized on Dec. 10, 1944), when a 3,000 h.p. B-25 of the U.S. Far East Air Force chose it for a target. During this engagement B-25s sank at least three transports and six escort ships, damaging others. In Ormoc Bay a B-25 roared in over an enemy destroyer (2), which was broken in two by hits amidships (3). The bombers were escorted by P-37s and P-38s, which shot down between 16 and 20 intercepting planes.

Following unconditional surrender in the West, a spectacular start was made to reduce Japan's war machine as Germany's had been dealt with. On May 13, 1945, over 500 Super-Fortresses, flying from the Marianas, dropped 570,000 incendiary bombs on Nagoya, biggest centre of Japan's aircraft industry, which was attacked again three days later and left blazing furiously.

Photos, New York Times Photos

Victory Day in London With Our Roving Camera

FROM THE BALCONY OF BUCKINGHAM PALACE their Majesties, accompanied by the Princesses and the Prime Minister (1), acknowledged the roar of the crowds on May 8, 1945. At night the Palace blazed with floodlighting (5). Trafalgar Square (2) was packed to hear the King's speech broadcast at 9 p.m. There were victory fires for miles around ; at Eynsford, Kent, youngsters hauled fuel (3). The royal procession on Ludgate Hill after the Thanksgiving Service at St. Paul's (4) on May 13.

Photos, P.N.A, Fox, Sport & General, Planet News

Editor's Postscript

LONDON taxi-drivers are asking for alterations to the design of their cabs, some of which, it must be confessed, go back almost as far as my earliest motoring days when many pedestrians, when they saw a car go by, still looked for the man in front with the red flag. At a recent conference the drivers urged that in the ideal cab the doors should be narrower and lighter and the taxi have a standard non-fading colour and a more distinctive sign, an all-enclosed driver's cabin—and lots more. No one will grudge the London taxi-man his cramped comforts after five years of blacked-out streets and crippling petrol-control, but it is surely time that the taxi-users were allowed to state their side of the transaction. I for one would demand an immediate change in the size and angle of the "For Hire" flag. As things are, I defy anyone not of abnormal eyesight to ascertain by its flag at more than 30 yards whether a cab is plying for hire. The hours and energies I, with countless others, must have spent on London kerbs signalling in vain to taxis under the impression that they were disengaged—when all that was needed was a flag of discernible proportions, tilted in such a way as to preclude all doubts at a reasonable distance. Before he can ply in the metropolis a taxi-driver has to pass a stiff course in London topography. Does this apply only to London, I wonder? I ask this because an acquaintance, a commander in the R.N.R., just demobbed and set up as a taxi-owner in the country, has been telling me with undisguised amusement how by mistaking his route the other night he took an hour to drive a "fare" a distance of less than six miles. He blamed the "fare" for insufficiently directing him. I (I'm afraid) blamed the driver for faulty navigation. The old London cabbies' trick of taking passengers round-about ways in order to run up the fare has entirely lost its point owing to petrol shortage; but it may be renewed when ampler supply is available.

AN American building expert visiting this country declares that though Britain is making a "magnificent effort" to solve her housing problem she is "hampered by tradition" in the use of materials. Such a remark—if its author be correctly reported—betrays a shallow knowledge of the English countryside and of English country architecture. For the rural English builder, ever since he abandoned "wattle-and-daub" for stone, has never ceased to exploit to the full the local material, dug from nearby quarries, creating not only major and minor masterpieces of church and domestic architecture—from the simple dower-house to the ducal palace, the spireless parish-church to the lofty cathedral—but buildings which, whatever their dimensions, fit into the landscape as unobtrusively as a wild flower or an ancient oak. One thinks of the oolite limestone of the Cotswolds and Somerset, especially round Bath; of the Devon and Hereford sandstone; of the millstone-grit of Yorkshire; of the Cornish whinstone; and, farther north, of Aberdeen granite—all stealing into their surroundings like the hand to the glove, warm and kindly, and anything (thank heaven!) but prefabricated.

HOW many innocent babes are now destined to bear lifelong evidence of the times into which they were born, by being given the baptismal names of Montgomery, Alexander, or Eisenhower, or, perhaps, more subtly, names that fit the momentous initials V.E.? This sort of thing is liable to occur at the climax of every war. The years 1940 and 1941 provide a fairly excusable crop of little Winstons—not forgetting the real Winston's own grandson. I doubt if the 1918 news paragraph about a child called Armistice Brown was ever verified. But a schoolmaster once told me of six boys in his Form all with the initials D. H., for Douglas Haig. Another, called Verdun Smith, was in a higher Form, as befitted his seniority in chronological significance. Recently I heard a broadcast by an American jazz expert with the odd Christian name of Woody. This, I gathered, was short for Woodrow, which put a date to him at once. An older acquaintance once shyly confessed to me that the modest initials R. B., by which he invariably prefixed the surname in his own signature, stood for nothing less than Redvers Buller. General Sir Redvers Buller was the British commander in the field at the outbreak of the South African war. That fixed my man at 1899 or early 1900, for poor Buller was soon superseded, and somewhat ignominiously. People are usually more careful to avoid saddling a daughter with any name that may betray an age too exactly. Yet there must be many women, now aged either forty-eight or fifty-eight, who have long ago dropped from their signatures that tell-tale name of Victoria which would reveal them as the Jubilee babies of parents whose loyalty outran their discretion.

BEFORE the war one of the surest signs that the Silly Season was upon us—it was the newspaper man's name for that arid period, usually in the dog days, when fantastic stories of seaside monsters, practical jokes and the like were vamped up to provide news for holiday-makers—was the hardy annual that snuff-taking was once more becoming popular, not to say fashionable. There being no space for Silly Seasons for the past five years I take it that the story in my evening paper about the Snuff Revival is no Fleet Street fabrication but a matter of hard fact, especially when one considers that cigarettes and pipe-tobacco, to say nothing of cigars, now cost about twice-and-a-half what they cost in 1938. Snuff, being a by-product of tobacco, has increased in cost proportionately; quite ordinary blends, I am told, fetch as much as three-and-sixpence an ounce. In the old days this would have caused a revolution among craftsmen of most callings, especially among printers, the majority of whom kept a well-stocked snuff-box at the side of their type-cases. That was when you could buy an ounce for tuppence! Even to this day you will find snuff on the side-tables in many West-End clubs, where it is usually kept in a silver-mounted ram's horn known as a "mull." There used to be a particularly fine example in the Caledonian in St. James's Square, though I doubt whether many of even your true Caledonians patronize it nowadays, the perils and price of handkerchief laundering being what they are. Dr. Johnson himself in such circumstances would have needed all his philosophy.

Gen. DWIGHT D. EISENHOWER, Allied Supreme Commander in Western Europe, had every reason to smile as he left his London hotel, on May 15, 1945, during a brief Victory celebration in this country. On May 24 it was announced that the honorary freedom of the City of London, together with a sword of honour, was to be conferred on him.

Photo, Topical Press

IN the days of my youth we called it a Debating Society, usually prefaced with the words "Literary and ——." Today they call it a Discussion Group, and it would be easy to add "a distinction without a difference." But there is a difference, a big difference, between the starchy-collared Victorian debating society and its modern counterpart; it lies chiefly, I think, with the subject-matter for discussion. Nowadays all sorts of subjects are aired and threshed out by young discussion groups which could scarcely have been whispered in the old days. I listened to only a few of the recent B.B.C. discussion-group series "To Start You Talking," but fortunately they included the last one on Sex; which I don't hesitate to describe as one of the frankest and most spontaneous broadcasts I have ever heard, though what the black-mitten gentry thought about it I shudder to think. The scripts of this series, introduced by Charles Madge, have now been published by the Pilot Press, with a most enlightening section by Inez Madge on how listening groups reacted to them. The speakers, all of them under eighteen and chosen from all over the country, were given *carte-blanche* as to the expression of their opinions. The result is a book of printed broadcast material unique in history—in other words, it makes as stimulating reading as it made listening. For discussion groups just starting let me recommend What Do You Think?, a shilling pamphlet issued by the National Council of Social Service and crammed with highly practical hints on how to organize discussions on such subjects as Good Neighbours, Good Health, A Living Wage.

WAR stimulates invention to such an extent that nothing appears to be beyond the power of science to achieve. Astonishing claims are being made for discoveries and inventions that would, if they were ever to survive the newspaper stage, alter completely our whole lives. From New York comes a method of producing electricity without dynamos, engines or machinery of any kind, and the American Physical Society seems to think there is something in it. In France, a prominent figure in the field of Scientific Research thinks he can do away with electricity, as well as gas and petrol, by making atoms provide us with light and heat. Then I read in an American scientific magazine a forecast of the family aircraft of the future, which will require no engine but be operated by "beam," and will be controlled merely by pushing buttons instead of using what pilots call the joy-stick for steering and going up or down. All such reports I read with the same caution as that with which I used to regard some announcements of cures for this, that and the other disease, which were at one time frequent in the Press.

This Was the Prime Minister's Finest Hour

LONDON "MOBBED" OUR GREAT WAR LEADER on the afternoon of May 8, 1945, when, after broadcasting at 3 p.m. the news of Germany's unconditional surrender, Mr. Churchill passed through tumultuous crowds from Downing Street to the House of Commons, there to make to Parliament the formal announcement of Victory in Europe. Having done so, he moved that the House—following the precedent at the end of the First Great War—should proceed to St. Margaret's Church, Westminster, for a thanksgiving service.

Photo, Sport & General

Printed in England and published every alternate Friday by the Proprietors, THE AMALGAMATED PRESS, LTD., The Fleetway House, Farringdon Street, London, E.C.4. Registered for transmission by Canadian Magazine Post. Sole Agents for Australia and New Zealand: Messrs. Gordon & Gotch, Ltd.; and for South Africa: Central News Agency, Ltd.—June 8th, 1945. S.S. *Editorial Address:* JOHN CARPENTER HOUSE, WHITEFRIARS, LONDON, E.C.4

Vol 9 The War Illustrated Nº 209

SIXPENCE Edited by Sir John Hammerton JUNE 22, 1945

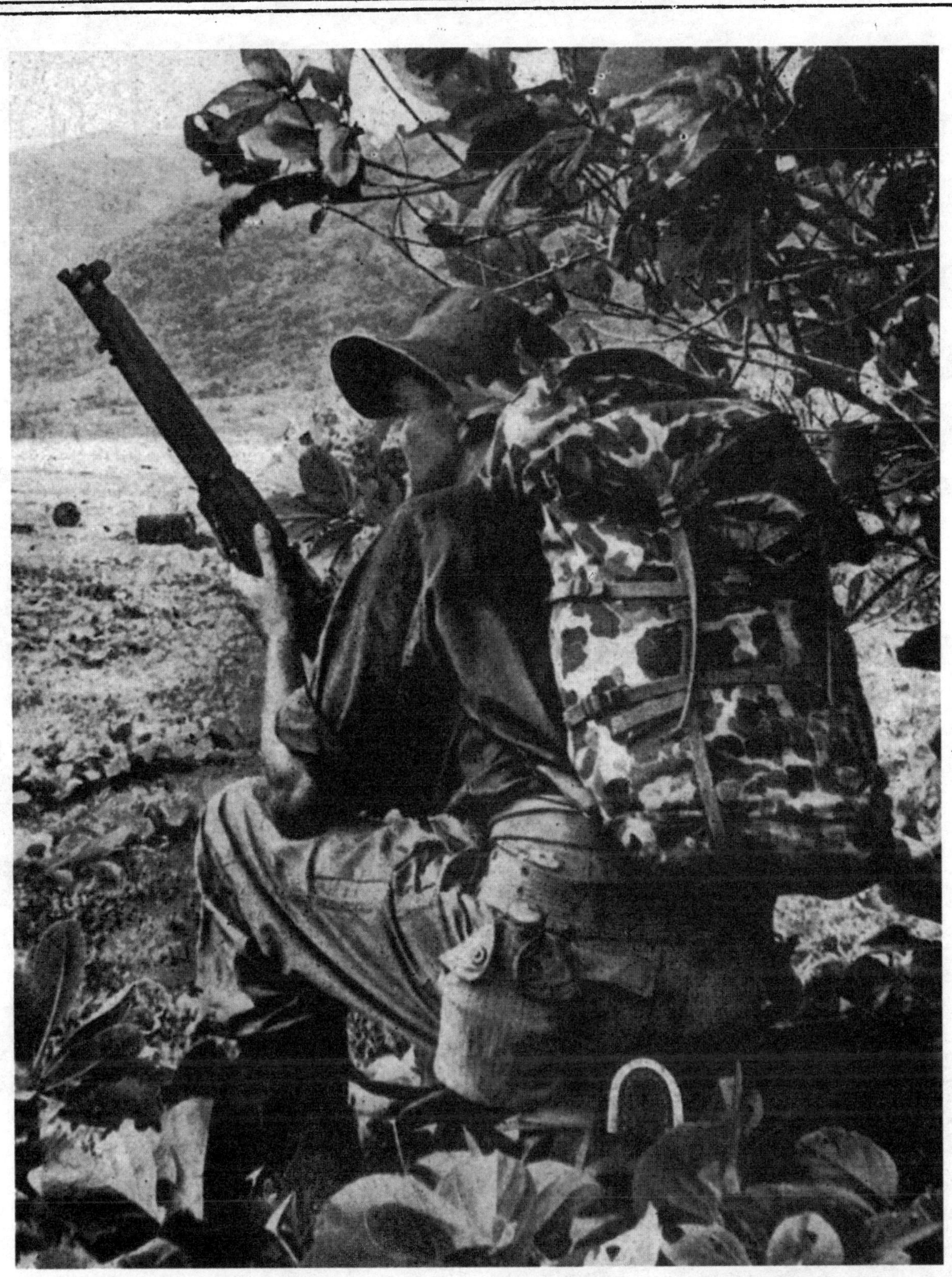

AUSTRALIAN SOLDIER IN NEW GUINEA prepared to advance at But in the Aitape sector (captured early in April 1945), where the Japanese, in caves and foxholes, had to be exterminated with flame-throwers. Cape Moem, last enemy stronghold in Wewak, fell on May 24. Aussies have been fighting the Japanese on New Guinea since the enemy invasion in January 1942; the famous 6th Australian Division was engaged in specially desperate coastal and inland fighting during the first five months of this year. See also illus. page 103.

Inglorious Was Their Exit from the Netherlands

BY LAND AND WATER THE DEFEATED WEHRMACHT LEFT HOLLAND, some on foot, some in horse-drawn vehicles, across the great causeway linking Den Helder and Harlingen ; others were waterborne over the Zuyder Zee (1). They were the remnants of the Nazi Netherlands occupation army of 110,000, making their way to the Reich for demobilization. British landing craft helped in the evacuation (2 and 3). Less fortunate wayfarers were only too glad to "thumb" a lift on circus trailers (4)

Photos, Planet News

With Our Armies Today

By MAJOR-GENERAL
SIR CHARLES GWYNN
K.C.B., D.S.O.

I PROPOSE in this article to try to give a connected account of the brilliant and elaborate campaign which has resulted in the reconquest of the greater part of Burma and the capture of Rangoon, for it has not been easy to follow. It will be remembered that by the end of the monsoon in the late autumn last year, General Stilwell's Chinese troops in the north, assisted by Lentaigne's long-distance penetration group and Merrill's Marauders, had captured Myitkyina and were well on their way to Bhamo covering the construction of the new road from Ledo. West of the Irrawaddy his 36th British Division had also advanced down the Myitkyina-Mandalay railway to the neighbourhood of Indaw.

In the centre, the Japanese offensive into Manipur had been heavily defeated and driven across the Chindwin by General Slim's 14th Army ; and in the Arakan district the end of the monsoon had made a resumption of operations practicable for his troops in that area. It was evidently the intention to continue the offensive during the dry season on an increased scale ; but few believed that, with ever-lengthening lines of difficult communications, it would be possible to employ sufficient forces to effect the reconquest of Burma without a concurrent amphibious operation in the south, for which shipping was not available.

IT was generally believed that the main object would therefore be to reconquer northern Burma in support of Stilwell's operations and possibly reach Mandalay. It is now clear, however, that S.E.A.C. envisaged from the first the recapture before the next monsoon not only of Mandalay but of Rangoon, over 300 miles to the south. The immense expansion of air transport services was the trump card relied on to overcome lack of adequate land communications.

General Slim's command included Stopford's 33rd and Messervy's 4th Corps in the centre, and in the Arakan district Christison's 15th Corps and West African Divisions. A strong Allied air force was available to co-operate, and native levies provided a valuable partisan force. His plan, broadly, was for the 15th Corps and West African Divisions, assisted by a number of amphibious operations organized by the Royal Navy, to clear the Arakan coast ; the first objective being the capture of the port and airfields of Akyab in order to provide a base from which air transport could work at shorter range. The 33rd Corps was to clear north Burma between the Chindwin and Irrawaddy, closing on to Mandalay. The 4th Corps advancing west of the Chindwin apparently formed a strategic reserve to be used as the situation developed. On the left, Stilwell's forces were to capture Bhamo and open the road thence to the old Burma Road about Lashio. It would then operate westwards to clear the road and railway towards Mandalay.

DESPERATE Jap Efforts to Cover the Approaches to Mandalay

In October 1944 the 19th Indian Division (Rees) crossed the upper Chindwin and struck eastwards across the mountains to the Irrawaddy, which it reached south of Indaw, making contact with Stilwell's 36th Division by mid-December. Thence it worked southwards along the Irrawaddy and established two bridge-heads on the east bank 60 miles north of Mandalay by mid-January.

Meantime, the 11th East African Division had captured, on Dec. 2, Kalewa, the last Japanese stronghold on the west bank of the Chindwin, and two days later established a bridge-head on the east bank, to which the sappers soon constructed a 300-yard Bailey bridge—a notable feat. The 2nd and 20th Divisions crossed over, and working through hilly country by the New Year emerged into the north Burma plain where tanks could operate. The 20th Division (Gracey) took Yeu, at the terminus of a branch railway from Mandalay, and then struck south-west along that line to Monywa, an important Japanese centre on the Chindwin.

It had been expected that the Japanese would fight desperately here to cover the approaches to Mandalay, and actually it took some days to drive them out of Monywa ; but it now became plain that their main stand would be made on the Irrawaddy where it runs from east to west passing Mandalay. And in pursuance of that policy they made violent but fruitless attempts to drive the 19th Division out of the bridge-heads it had established across the river.

EMPIRE'S WAR CASUALTIES

FROM Sept. 3, 1939, to the end of Feb. 1945 (a total of 66 months) the armed forces of the British Commonwealth and Empire suffered 1,128,315 casualties, that figure including 307,201 deaths, stated Mr. Churchill on May 29. This compares with the First Great War total (for 52 months) of 3,286,090, including 996,230 deaths.

Additional losses in this war, caused to the civilian population of Great Britain by enemy bombardment : 60,585 killed ; 86,175 seriously injured ; slightly injured, upwards of 150,000.

By the end of January, Stopford's three Divisions were in position to initiate a converging attack on Mandalay. The 20th Division, working down the Chindwin from Monywa, reached the Irrawaddy and forced a crossing on the night of Feb. 13, 40 miles below Mandalay, by a surprise attack.

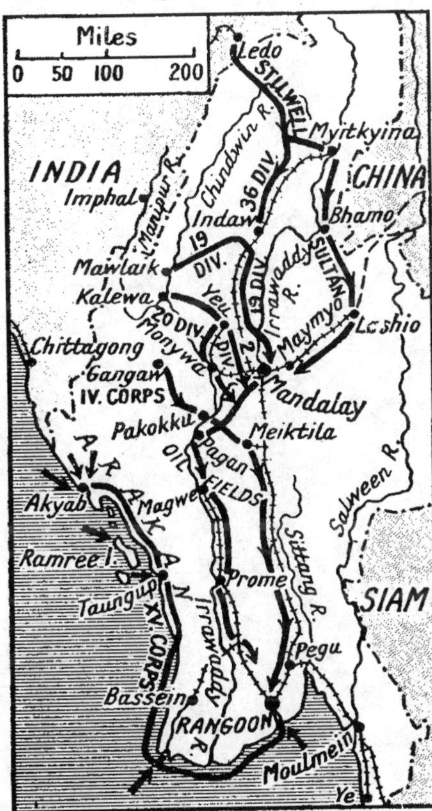

RANGOON, capital of Burma, fell on May 3, 1945—after being over three years in Japanese hands—as the result of a combined operation involving the landing of seaborne and airborne troops and units of the 14th Army advancing from the north. A description of the campaign which led to the fall of this great port is given in this page.

Having already had their river position turned on the right by the 19th Division, the Japanese Command fully realized the imminent danger of this threat to their left, and for six days counter-attacked violently. But while they were thus occupied the 2nd Division (Nicholson) closed up to the river and crossed still nearer to Mandalay. Thus all three divisions were across the river and in a position to encircle and close in on the city. The 19th Division early in March broke out of its bridge-head and reached the outskirts of the city by March 8. Fully occupied with opposing the other two divisions, the Japanese could only spare troops to hold its moated and fortified citadel of Fort Dufferin.

GENERAL SULTAN'S Successes Led to Great Slaughter of the Enemy

There they held out till March 20, when they withdrew in consequence of a new danger that threatened their whole army. While they had been engaged by the 33rd Corps, the 4th Corps (Messervy) advancing down the Gangaw valley had reached the Irrawaddy at Pakokku, where the river turns south below its confluence with the Chindwin. After crossing the river here and capturing Pagan, the ancient capital of Burma, Messervy thrust an armoured column eastward to Meiktila. Airfields were captured and the column was reinforced by airborne troops.

Caught in a trap, the Japanese fought desperately throughout March in what was the decisive battle for central Burma. They attempted to hold off the 33rd Corps, while at the same time they tried to recover the airfields Messervy had seized, and on which he depended for the supply of his force. Their position was made all the more desperate by successes General Sultan (who had succeeded Stilwell) had gained. Having captured Bhamo and Lashio and linked up with the Burma Road he had turned westwards towards Mandalay and taken Maymyo, cutting Japanese escape routes eastward. The slaughter was now on, and the Japanese Army was soon reduced to a number of separate ill-equipped groups seeking escape.

IT will be seen that the 4th Corps was across the front of the 33rd Corps, and when the latter was ready to advance south it passed behind the 4th Corps and undertook the capture of the oilfields in the Irrawaddy valley. The 4th Corps—more highly mechanized—on the other hand, was ready to push south from Meiktila by the main road to Rangoon ; and in the second half of April its advance began at all speed in order to capture the port before the monsoon broke—a matter of vital importance, for supply by air transport during monsoon weather would have been impossible. Leap-frogging his divisions Messervy brushed aside opposition, captured Pegu and reached the Rangoon area three weeks before the monsoon.

There, however, he was held up by elaborate minefields and other defences, and it was a well-timed landing by troops of 15th Corps that actually captured the port. Thus this Corps rounded off the great contribution it had made in co-operation with the Navy, to the general success of the campaign. By capturing Akyab early in January it had ensured the supply by air transport of the troops inland, and by a subsequent advance southwards and a series of landing operations had cleared the coastal area, depriving the Japanese of sources of supply and disturbing the disposition of their forces. There remains much mopping up to be done, but seldom has an elaborate plan of campaign been carried through with such brilliant success in all its main features, and although most of the formations employed belong to the Indian Army, yet it should be remembered that British troops provide more than one-third of their strength.

Great Swoop by Australians on a Borneo Isle

JAPANESE-HELD TARAKAN, important oil centre off the Borneo coast, was successfully invaded on May 1, 1945, by the 9th Australian Division, assisted by Dutch East Indies troops, under Maj.-Gen. G. F. Wootten. A Matilda slipped into a tank-trap (1) but was soon hauled into action; in the background a L.C.T. discharged its cargo. This gargantuan enemy periscope interested Aussie infantrymen (2). The stronghold of Tarakan Hill bristled with bunkers which all had to be winkled out (3).

Photos, Associated Press

Gurkha Paratroops Dropped to Battle in Burma

FROM DAKOTAS OF EASTERN AIR COMMAND hundreds of Gurkha parachute troops were dropped on May 1, 1945, to capture coast defences at the mouth of Rangoon River and clear the way for seaborne forces that were to storm Rangoon itself (see illus. page 66). They are seen (1) preparing to emplane. Enemy destruction was rife in the oilfields (2). In Burma's third city, Prome (captured May 3), men of the 15th Indian Corps attacked across the railway (3). Rangoon civilians turned out to thank the victorious troops (4). On June 4 was announced the end of Eastern Air Command, its mission splendidly achieved. It was formed in Dec. 1943 to supply the 14th Army.

Photos, British Official

U 776 SAILED UP THE THAMES on May 22, 1945, under the White Ensign, to be on show at Westminster Bridge, which she is seen approaching. Said to be capable of travelling 10,000 miles at a surface speed of 10 knots, she had been commissioned one year, had survived only one patrol of 54 days when she surrendered, and had fired one torpedo—which missed. On her upstream voyage (see story in page 121) she was under the command of Lieut.-Comdr. P. B. Marriott, R.N., who commanded the U-boat U 570 captured in 1941 and renamed H.M.S. Graph (see page 497, Vol. 8).

Photo, Daily Mirror

GERMAN CRUISER NÜRNBERG sailed from Copenhagen to Wilhelmshaven along with the Prinz Eugen after the surrender, her escort including R.A.F. Liberators of Coastal Command. Together with four destroyers and about 130 warships of various types, the cruisers were taken over on May 22, 1945, from Admiral O. Wurmach, Senior German Naval Officer in Denmark, by Rear-Admiral Reginald V. Holt, Senior British Naval Officer in Denmark, who on that day restored the Royal Danish Dockyard at Copenhagen to its lawful owners. *Photo, British Official*

With Our Navies Today

By
FRANCIS E. McMURTRIE

A LITTLE more information has been forthcoming recently concerning the British Fleet in the Pacific. Ships which have been taking an active part in the covering operations connected with the occupation of Okinawa are reported to have included, amongst others, H.M.S. King George V, flagship of Vice-Admiral Sir Bernard Rawlings; the Fleet aircraft carriers Indefatigable, Indomitable, Illustrious and Victorious; the Dominion cruisers H.M.C.S. Uganda and H.M.N.Z.S. Gambia; and the destroyers Troubridge, Tenacious and Termagant.

Repeated attacks have been made on the Sakishima group by the above squadron. American naval forces off Okinawa were thus able to pursue their operations without being seriously troubled by air attacks from the Sakishima direction; but as soon as the British ships were ordered elsewhere to refuel, Admiral R. A. Spruance, commanding the U.S. Fifth Fleet, was obliged to detach other forces to cover the Sakishima area. This was mentioned in the course of some remarks addressed to the ship's company of H.M.S. King George V by Fleet Admiral Chester Nimitz, U.S.N., Commander-in-Chief of all Allied naval forces in the Pacific, when that ship was at Guam, the operational headquarters.

BRITISH Naval Launchings and New Ship Construction Now Disclosed

With the termination of the war in Europe, a corner of the veil which has enveloped British naval construction since 1939 has been lifted by the Admiralty. It has been disclosed that a number of ships described as light fleet carriers, specially designed for operations in the Far East, with air conditioning and other exceptional features, are building or completing. One of these, H.M.S. Powerful, was launched from the shipyard of Harland & Wolff, Ltd., at Belfast, on February 27, being named by Mrs. A. V. Alexander; and another, H.M.S. Leviathan, will have been launched from the yard of Swan, Hunter & Wigham Richardson, Ltd., at Wallsend-on-Tyne by the time this is in print. In the latter case, the naming ceremony was to have been carried out by H.R.H. the Duchess of Kent; and from the fact that this is stated to be the second ship of the type built by Messrs. Swan Hunter, it may be assumed that they belong to a numerous class.

Other ships whose existence had not previously been revealed include the "Battle" class of destroyers. Two names have so far been mentioned, the Alamein, launched by Lady Alexander, wife of the Field-Marshal, from the yard of Messrs. R. & W. Hawthorn, Leslie & Co., Ltd., on May 28; and H.M.S. Corunna, which went afloat the following day from the Swan Hunter establishment. Thus both are Tyne-built ships, and as it is usual for destroyers to be built in pairs, it may be supposed that at least four have been put in hand in the Tyne district. Assuming that other shipbuilding areas are participating to a similar extent, it seems probable that this also is a fairly numerous class.

GERMAN Surrendered Cruisers Not Suitable for Service Out East

Nothing more has been heard of new cruisers since it was stated a month or two ago that H.M.S. Ontario was completing at Belfast for the Royal Canadian Navy; but again, it may be pointed out that as it is customary for ships of the Royal Navy to be built in classes, other cruisers are most likely to be under construction. Possibly it will not be long before the Admiralty revert to their pre-war practice of announcing the number, names and principal characteristics of all new warships under construction. Such information could be of no material assistance to the Japanese at the present stage, and should indeed be a source of further discouragement to our Eastern enemies. It is not as if Japan retained sufficient naval strength to undertake any major operation. In fact, Fleet Admiral Nimitz has declared publicly that he does not think there is any prospect of the Japanese fleet coming out from its ports of refuge.

IN some quarters it appears to be imagined that surrendered German warships may be recommissioned by the Allies for service against Japan. Of this there does not, in fact, seem much likelihood. There are only two undamaged ships of any size, the cruisers Prinz Eugen, of 10,000 tons, and Nürnberg, of 6,000 tons, and neither of these is at all suitable for service in Eastern waters. Nor is it to be expected that any of the surrendered destroyers will go East, for the United States Navy alone now possesses between 400 and 500, to say nothing of those belonging to the Royal Navy, Royal Australian Navy, Royal Canadian Navy and Royal Netherlands Navy.

It seems also to have been supposed that surrendered U-boats would be turned to account in Pacific operations. Here again it has to be pointed out that together the British and United States Navies should be able to dispose of ample submarine strength without the need of reinforcement, especially now that there is a tendency for targets to get fewer owing to the tremendous losses inflicted on enemy shipping. Rear-Admiral James Fife, commanding the submarines of the U.S. Seventh Fleet in the Pacific, declared on June 1 that Japan had lost practically all her shipping. On the same date President Truman estimated that the Japanese mercantile fleet had been reduced to less than a quarter of its pre-war size. It is not as though the German vessels possessed any features of particular value for this purpose, for the much-boosted Schnorkel, or breathing pipe, is essentially a defensive weapon of which Allied submarines, being very much on the offensive, have no need. (See pages 680-681, Vol. 8.)

What, then, is to become of all German tonnage, both naval and mercantile? It is possible that certain of the countries which have lost warships through enemy action, notably Norway, Denmark and the Netherlands, might be able to find a temporary use for some of the German cruisers, destroyers and minesweepers, the two former categories for training their personnel, and the latter for dealing with enemy-laid minefields. But for permanent service, each nation would undoubtedly prefer to employ ships built according to its own ideas. An undesirable characteristic of German naval design is a tendency to sacrifice the comfort of the ship's company with the object of making the vessel harder to sink.

ADVANTAGE to the World if German Mercantile Fleet Were Broken Up

It is improbable that any Allied Navy will wish to take over U-boats, except perhaps for experimental purposes, such as target practice. Of course, some may be retained for a while for exhibition purposes, as in the case of U-776 in the London Docks recently; but the ultimate destination of the U-boat fleet, as in 1919, is likely to be the scrapheap. (See illus. page 102, and story in page 121.)

German mercantile tonnage offers a more complicated problem. There are a few modern ocean liners, of which the Europa is the largest, which will be useful as troopships pending the winding up of the war with Japan. Some vessels of special type, such as those with refrigerated holds for carrying food, can also be utilised to advantage for the time being. But it is to the advantage of the whole world that, as soon as it can be spared, the German mercantile fleet should be broken up and its place in the world's transport services taken by vessels belonging to nations which have not abused the laws and customs of the sea as Germany has. This would have the added advantage of keeping Allied shipyard workers regularly occupied in the replacement of discarded tonnage.

British East Indies Fleet in Action off Sumatra

BOMBARDMENT OF SABANG AND KOTA RAJA was included in an offensive sweep off Sumatra which began on April 11, 1945. Three destroyers of the British East Indies Fleet (1, left to right), Venus, Virago and Vigilant, steam into action. A dense smoke-screen (2) was put up for an escort-carrier after one of her fighters had shot down the ship's first Japanese aircraft. Kota Raja under fire (3). Destroyers under Captain M. L. Power, R.N., in H.M.S. Saumerez, sank an enemy cruiser off Penang on May 16. See also illus. in pages 751-754, Vol. 8. *Photos, British Official*

Activity Without Fraternization is the Order

DISARMING NAZI TROOPS crossing the Danish frontier into the Reich after the great surrender, Allied soldiers stacked weapons by the roadside (1). First batch of 300,000 of the Wehrmacht on this British 2nd Army front were sent home to work on the land on June 4, 1945 ; stripped of all badges, their uniforms became utility suits. Field-Marshal Montgomery's proclamation to the German people on May 30 had told them, in effect, " No work, no food ! "

Tanks of the British 7th Armoured Division—the Desert Rats (2)—swept across the bridge spanning the Kaiser Wilhelm canal near Steenfeld. The no-fraternization order was strictly observed by these British soldiers (3) resting by the Elbe near Hamburg. Warning his troops against fraternization, Field-Marshal Montgomery on March 3 said, " Be just : be firm : be correct : give orders—and don't argue." Tough-looking S.S. man vainly pleaded with his captors of the 9th Durham Light Infantry (4). Members of the 8th Railway Construction Corps of the R.E.s watched the first passenger train cross the 250-ft. bridge with which they had spanned the Ilmenau River in four days (5).

Photos, British Official, British Newspaper Pool, Keystone

The Problem of Trieste—Port of Contention

The great cosmopolitan port of Trieste, at the head of the Adriatic, was freed from the Germans by Marshal Tito's Yugoslav forces and New Zealand troops of the 8th Army at the beginning of May 1945. Its future, however, is still conjectural in view of the dispute as to its status, some of the reasons for which are explained here by HENRY BAERLEIN

In Italian possession since the break-up of the old Austrian Empire in 1918, Trieste, owing to its geographical situation and past history, has long been a subject of dispute. The war of words which has already arisen since its liberation might, if steps be not taken, turn into something so serious that Italo-Yugoslav relations, to mention no others, would be poisoned for years to come.

Yugoslavia and Italy have for some time been claiming the town with equal insistence. Thus the Giornale del Mattino, the non-party and purely informative Rome paper, asserts that it would be difficult, nay, impossible, to deny the wholly Italian character of the town. And in the monarchist Italia Nuova, Signor Enzo Salvaggi, speaking of Trieste and the entire district around it, Venezia Giulia and Istria, accuses the Yugoslavs of imperialist manoeuvres which go beyond the limits of a healthy nationalism.

He does not contest that in the territories in question there may be some infiltration of Slavs and economic interests gravitate to those zones, interests which are not solely either Italian or Slav. In view of this fact, Salvaggi declares that Italy will be able to serve the interests of the Danube Basin through these territories, and particularly through the port of Trieste. On the other hand, Marshal Tito and his spokesmen have announced that the non-inclusion of Trieste in Yugoslavia is unthinkable.

Signor Vivante, a native of Trieste, in his book L'irredentismo Adriatico (1912) came out as a determined adversary of the Italian occupation, his opinion being shared by all the town's inhabitants except the extreme nationalists; and the Italian economist Signor Giorgio Roletto, says in his book The Harbour of Trieste (1941) that the town belongs morphologically to the vast Karst-Dinaric system, that is to say the mountain-chain of South-East Europe, which finds in Trieste its natural outlet to the sea.

Roletto's compatriot of to-day, Salvaggi, who alludes to "some infiltration of Slavs" would win a big prize for understatement. Not only has the entire district outside the town been, from of old, almost exclusively Slav, but the town itself had its population largely recruited from that hinterland. It was the custom of the Austro-Hungarian Empire to have a variety of official languages, and the one prescribed for Dalmatia, the maritime province, was Italian. Thus it came about that a good many Slovenes, for reasons of convenience or snobbery, returned themselves as Italians. Most of Trieste's "Italians" towards the end of the nineteenth century were Slovenes by origin. Geographically, Trieste and its neighbourhood are an integral part of purely Slav territories; and it must be remembered that when statistics gave the town a marked Italian majority these Austrian statistics were compiled on the language basis, so that Germans, Greeks, Levantines and others were included, as Italian-speaking, among the Italians.

It has been argued by some that, in order to resist the powerful suction of Hamburg, Trieste must be backed by a government with a sufficient weight in economic resources, industry, size of population, naval power and diplomatic influence; and doubt is expressed as to whether Yugoslavia can fill such a bill. In the past, whenever Italy has lost a war she has added another province to her possessions; but let us assume that the coming Peace Conference will not allow itself to be ruled entirely by precedent.

YUGOSLAV FLAG was presented by a Partisan to a New Zealand tank man at Trieste, which after the surrender of the German garrison was occupied by Yugoslavs and troops of the 8th Army. *Photo, British Official*

There seems to be no reason why the vigorous young Yugoslav nation should not make just as much of a success in its administration of Trieste as the Greeks at Salonika, where they granted a free harbour to Yugoslavia, an arrangement which worked extremely well. Similarly the Yugoslavs would, one thinks, invite both the Czechoslovaks and the Austrians to have a part of Trieste harbour, thus eliminating Hamburg's semi-monopoly, and, in the case of Austria, causing any future talk of another Anschluss to become less strident.

TRIESTE, showing its position in relation to the Italo-Yugoslav frontier. *By courtesy of News Chronicle*

But if it is considered that neither Yugoslavia nor Italy should be in sole possession of this great port, what other method can be adopted? The experience of Danzig does not induce us to maintain that an outside body, however well intentioned, is the best of governments for an international port. However, in Tangier, with the component nationalities joining in the administration, there was far less fault to find, prior to Franco's abolition of the international control in 1940. A system analogous to Tangier's might be the best solution for Trieste, with Yugoslavia, Italy, Britain, Russia, the United States and France sharing in the government. It is to be hoped that, pending the permanent settlement, an Allied Military Government will be set up.

For a certain time the situation in and around Trieste was disconcerting. It appeared as if Marshal Tito was unable or unwilling to restrain his ebullient followers, whose treatment of all those of whom they disapproved (and whom they indiscriminately charged with being Fascists) was less tolerant than the Marshal's words. But happily he determined to translate these diplomatic words into acts, obliging his men—as one says in the Balkans—to pour some water into their wine. They took to playing football with the Anglo-American troops and at the same time to being less critical when these troops occupied commanding positions outside Trieste, positions that would enable the communications between the port and Central Europe to be kept open. All the troops concerned seem to have comported themselves well in a situation that called for the utmost tact.

Marshal Tito's Note to London and Washington, indicating his approval of Allied administration of Trieste, and proposing Yugoslav participation, seems to have convinced the citizens that the tension is finally over, and there is a general feeling that the result of negotiations must be patiently awaited. There is now considerably more fraternization between troops, after the difficult period following the movement of Anglo-American forces into the new zones east of the Isonzo. It has always been a Yugoslav contention that the Isonzo is the ethnic, and should be the national, boundary between themselves and the Italians.

It is true that there are few Italians to the east of that river; and the Yugoslavs, who have for so many years waited to have this frontier assigned to them, were unwilling to wait any longer. Why, they asked, could not this territory be granted them at once? Now they have reconciled themselves to the necessary delay, and their reasonableness will surely be taken into account when the final dispositions are made at the Peace Conference. They will certainly be given an expanded frontier in Istria and Venezia Giulia, even if the city of Trieste itself is placed under a mixed administration. We and the United States have, in the friendliest fashion, informed the Yugoslavs that we cannot countenance any unilateral decision.

As Storm Clouds Gathered in the Adriatic

NEAR MUCH-DISPUTED TRIESTE, Lieut.-Gen. Sir Bernard Freyberg, V.C., commander of the 2nd New Zealand Division, met Marshal Tito's representative, Gen. Borstnar (1, right), commanding the Yugoslav 9th Corps, at Monfalcone, for discussions on May 16, 1945. In Trieste—where the Nazi garrison surrendered to New Zealand troops of the 8th Army on May 2, while continuing to resist Tito's partisans—townspeople cheered Gen. Freyberg's armoured columns (2). On V Day, in the Piazza Unità, the Slav population gathered for a Partisan demonstration (3) at which no Allied troops were present. See also facing page.

Photo, British Official

In the Last European Capital to Be Set Free

AFTER SIX GRIM YEARS OF NAZIDOM, CZECHOSLOVAKIA welcomed the U.S. and Red Army troops : outside the 16th-century town hall of Pilsen (entered by the U.S. 3rd Army on May 6, 1945) children in national dress assembled with traditional tokens of friendship—gifts of bread and salt (1). Pilseners sought every possible vantage point to secure a view of the U.S. soldiers (3). Marshal Koniev in Prague, last European capital to be freed, drove through streets of rejoicing (2) on May 11.

Photos, L.N.A., Pictorial Press, The Evening Standard

After the Cease Fire Had Sounded in Italy

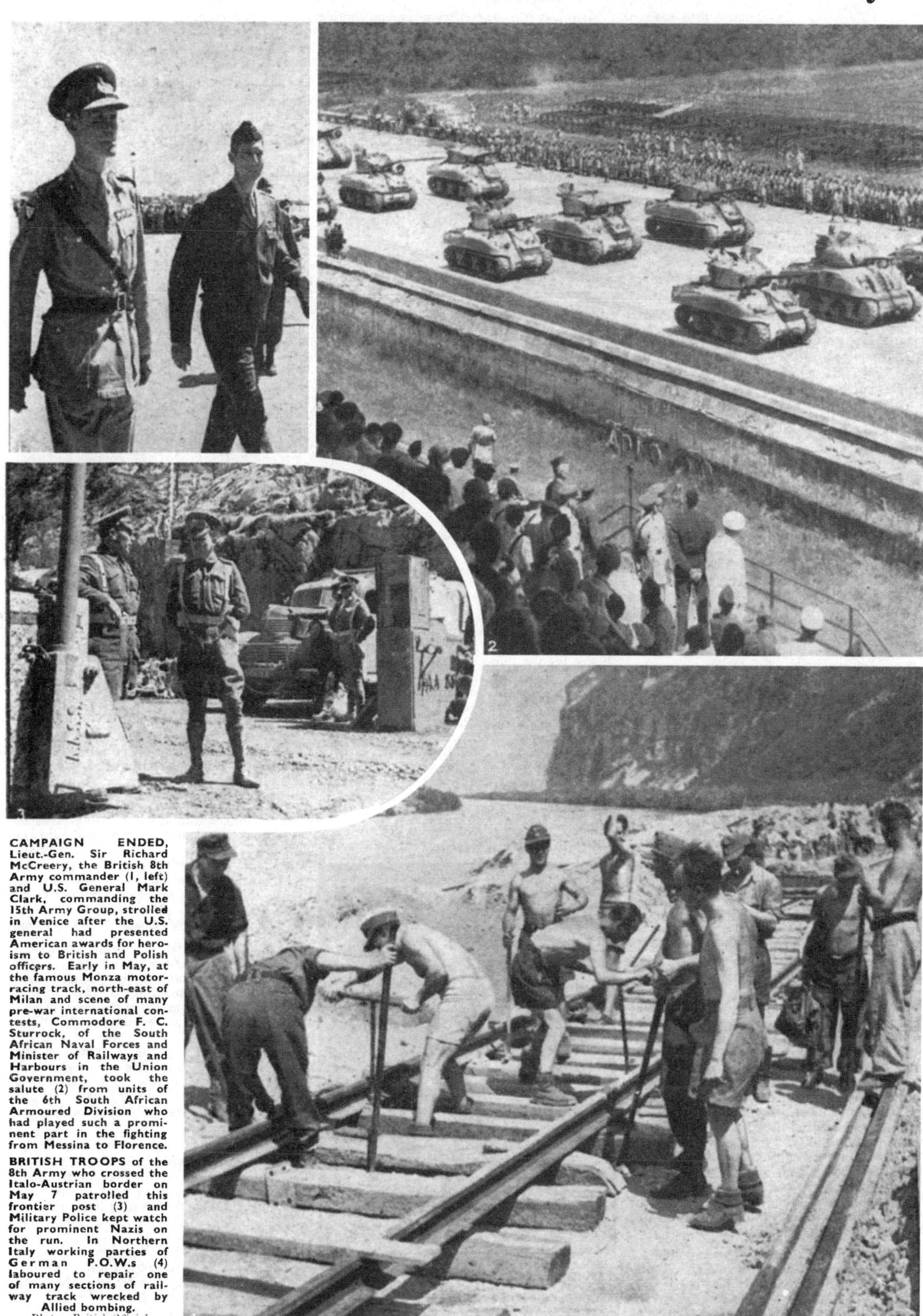

CAMPAIGN ENDED, Lieut.-Gen. Sir Richard McCreery, the British 8th Army commander (1, left) and U.S. General Mark Clark, commanding the 15th Army Group, strolled in Venice after the U.S. general had presented American awards for heroism to British and Polish officers. Early in May, at the famous Monza motor-racing track, north-east of Milan and scene of many pre-war international contests, Commodore F. C. Sturrock, of the South African Naval Forces and Minister of Railways and Harbours in the Union Government, took the salute (2) from units of the 6th South African Armoured Division who had played such a prominent part in the fighting from Messina to Florence.

BRITISH TROOPS of the 8th Army who crossed the Italo-Austrian border on May 7 patrolled this frontier post (3) and Military Police kept watch for prominent Nazis on the run. In Northern Italy working parties of German P.O.W.s (4) laboured to repair one of many sections of railway track wrecked by Allied bombing.

Photos, British Official

How the P.O.W. Problem is Being Solved

"Eating their heads off!" has been the general cry of our people in connexion with enemy prisoners of war brought to this country. What is to be done with them all? How is this drain on the country's resources to be met? Facts of their feeding and useful employment in Britain are given here by ALEXANDER DILKE, who also discusses the situation in Germany itself.

MANY millions of men and women in Britain have now had glimpses of German prisoners of war, either behind the barbed wire of their camps or working on farms. The sight of them is likely to become familiar in the near future, for although no exact figures have been issued the possibility of employing up to a quarter of a million Germans on the reconstruction of cities blitzed by the Luftwaffe has been mentioned. The few gangs that started work in Southern England in the middle of May are the forerunners of thousands who will be given work when arrangements for housing and guarding them have been made.

Just how many German prisoners there are in Britain has not been revealed. The last official figure was given in March by Mr. Arthur Henderson (Financial Secretary to the War Office), when he stated that of the 150,000 of them then in Britain one quarter were employed. Since then the British Armies roped in more than a million, and although only a small fraction of the total have been brought here, the available accommodation is full to overflowing. Guarding, accommodating and feeding them in accordance with the Geneva Convention is a considerable drain on the country's resources; and, other considerations apart, it was obvious the Germans would have to "pay their way."

THE conditions under which they are kept are strictly in accord with international agreement on prisoners of war. The fact that the Germans systematically flouted these agreements has not made the British authorities depart from their determination to keep them in the letter and in the spirit. The German prisoners are given decent accommodation, in most cases with such things as hot showers and facilities for games, and sufficient clothing and food.

The question of food has aroused considerable controversy. Until recently, German and Italian prisoners undoubtedly were better off than the British civilian in that respect. They received the equivalent of the generous rations of the British Army. The German working prisoner received 42 oz. of meat, a little more than ½ lb. of bacon and about 5½ lb. of bread, as well as vegetables, cheese, cake, jam, tea and 10½ oz. of margarine a week. The Italian prisoner had rather more bread and less meat. This diet was readjusted in June as shown in the table in this page.

Money to Spend at Camp Canteen

At present the work on which prisoners are engaged is of two kinds. They are working on farms, hedging and ditching, draining and so on, as well as dealing with the different harvests; and they are being employed in increasing numbers in connexion with rebuilding, chiefly preparing sites. For the latter they are paid about three shillings for a 48-hour week, the War Office receiving a sum in respect of that labour to be credited to the Government against the cost of housing and feeding them, this being a War Office responsibility. Prisoners can spend this earned money at a camp canteen, on the purchase of cigarettes, razor blades, hair oil and such articles as NAAFI generally stocks. They are given "token money" instead of British cash, to obviate the possibility of this being used for escaping.

On the farms, only "good conduct" prisoners are used. They may be guarded by British soldiers, but generally they are reliable men and the farmer is made responsible for them during working hours. They return to the barbed-wire camp every night. They have given little difficulty and generally are very pleased to get the opportunity of earning money. The farmers report them good workers and rate one German prisoner as the equal of three Italians. In gangs the men work much better than the Italians and are managed by their own N.C.O.s. The average scale of guards is one to twenty prisoners. With the release of many searchlight and A.A. soldiers the problem of providing guards will be easier.

WEEKLY SCALES OF RATIONS FOR BRITISH CIVILIANS & NON-WORKING PRISONERS OF WAR IN BRITAIN

Commodity	Civilian (Oz. per week)	P.O.W. (Oz. per week)
Meat	Fresh meat (1/-) Canned meat (2d.)	14
Butter	2	Nil
Margarine	4	4
Cooking Fats	1	1
Bacon	3	3
Cheese	2	2
Jam	4	3
Tea	2	2
Sugar	8	6
Dried Fruit	Points	4
Oatmeal	Points	7
Bread	Unrationed	70
Flour	Unrationed	4
Offal or Sausage	Unrationed	10
Cake	Unrationed	Nil
Milk Powder	Unrationed	7
Potatoes	Unrationed	70
Fresh Vegetables	Unrationed	56
Dried Vegetables	Unrationed	8

Working prisoners receive in addition every week 56 oz. of bread, 5 oz. flour, 6 oz. oatmeal, and their potato ration is doubled. Italians receive 35 cigarettes or 1¼ oz. of tobacco free weekly, but not the Germans.

It has been definitely stated that the work done by German prisoners will not result in a single British man being out of employment. In the case of blitz rebuilding, hours and wages of the prisoners have been agreed by the trade unions. Nevertheless, there has been evidence of some opposition on the part of British workers. Some hundreds of men in the repair squads in London struck, and when the proposal was made that German prisoners should help reduce the unloading-bottleneck that was holding up fish supplies, British workers threatened to walk away. In Newcastle they volunteered to do two hours extra a day rather than have German prisoners on a job. In reply to the T.U.C., who raised the point, the Ministry of Labour has said that without the use of P.O.W. it would be impossible for certain public utility services to be properly maintained; and that had not Italians worked in our beet fields the sugar ration would have been cut long ago.

GERMAN PRISONERS levelling the site of a housing estate at Shooter's Hill, London, on May 22, 1945. Enemy troops taken by the Allies as a result of the surrender are to be known as "disarmed personnel," to distinguish them from prisoners taken during the fighting. *Photo, Topical Press*

Only a proportion of German prisoners are working. A large camp between Barnet and South Mimms, Hertfordshire, was expected to be ready before July, and it was believed further camps would be prepared there and in Kent, giving access to blitzed areas. But there will remain many thousands of officers who cannot be made to work, and perhaps some "dyed in the wool" Nazi fanatics who it may be thought unsafe to allow outside the barbed wire. The problem of these fanatics is a difficult one. There seems no doubt that in many camps they have been ruling moderate prisoners and anti-Nazis by threats, chiefly of reprisals when they return home. A short time ago three Germans in Camp No. 22 complained that they had been threatened with hanging for participating in anti-Nazi propaganda, and two were beaten-up. Three prisoners were sentenced to 168 days' detention for the first assault, which suggests the authorities are determined, with the aid of Germans of a reasonable type, to stamp this out.

'Redemption Through Labour'

It is possible work will be found for many prisoners inside their barbed wire. Many lorry loads of bricks from blitzed areas have been delivered to one camp. These will be cleaned by the prisoners and sorted ready for re-use in rebuilding. This summer the shortage of labour on the farms is likely to lead to a big increase in the prisoners employed.

Russia from the first has based her treatment of German prisoners on two fundamentals: "political re-education" and "redemption through labour." These are the principles which the U.S.S.R. has used with its own criminals. The Germans are already at work in great numbers clearing Russian towns they devastated. They are paid in accordance with the work they do. The better they work, the better the rations and privileges they receive and the better the chances—or so they hope—of release. This work is accompanied by political re-education by specially trained Russians as well as anti-Nazi Germans.

IN France and Belgium German prisoners are wanted for work, particularly in the mines. Some are engaged in clearing up war damage in the devastated towns of Normandy. In America large numbers of prisoners of war are at work. America has been called "the prisoners' paradise." This is not because of any "softness" in the treatment of the prisoners, but because the relatively high standard of living in the U.S. Army gave prisoners—entitled to the same scale—rations which would make the civilians of many other countries envious.

The problem of the prisoners taken in North-West Germany—about 2,000,000—in the final surrender is a considerable one. About 1,000,000 are being held on the west coast of the Schleswig-Holstein isthmus. The rocky island of Nordstrand has been specially reserved for fanatical S.S. and parachute troops. Another half-million will be held on the east side of the isthmus, another 500,000 will be held in the regions between the Ems, Weser and Elbe. Yet another 500,000 are estimated to be in military hospitals. The fate of this host remains to be decided.

1939-Along the Hard Road to Victory-1945

SEPTEMBER 27, 1939. Warsaw surrendered to the Germans. Four weeks after the Nazi armies crossed the Polish border without a declaration of war, the burning capital was entered.

DECEMBER 13, 1939. Battle of the Plate. Graf Spee defeated and scuttled.

MAY 14, 1940. Centre of Rotterdam laid waste by the German Air Force.

MAY 26, 1940. Last stand at Calais Citadel ends five days' siege.
From the painting by Charles M. Gere, R.A. By permission of the artist.

JUNE 4, 1940. Evacuation of Dunkirk; 335,000 withdrawn.

JUNE 14, 1940. Paris—declared an open city—entered by German armies.

AUGUST 8, 1940. Battle of Britain opens. On one day—Sept. 15—185 Nazi planes shot down.

FEB 7, 1941. Benghazi taken by Wavell in Libyan offensive.

MARCH 28, 1941. Battle of Matapan. Shells fall near H.M.S. Orion during rout of Italian fleet.

JUNE 22, 1941. Germany attacks Russia. Within two days enemy troops were in streets of Brest-Litovsk.

DECEMBER 7, Japanese: 19 U.S.

AUGUST 19, 1942. Dieppe "Reconnaissance in Force." Landing craft move in during bitter engagement in which Canadians lost 3,350.

AUGUST 22, 1942. Stalingrad besieged; defenders greet relieving troops.

OCTOBER 23, 1942. Battle of Eg Montgomery inflicts crushing defeat o

FEBRUARY 15, 1942. Singapore falls to Japanese. Gen. Percival negotiates surrender terms with Gen. Yamashita.

JUNE 21, 1942. Tobruk (Libya) captured by German assault troops supported by tanks.

Harbour bombed by
nk or badly damaged.

NOVEMBER 3, 1942. Australians drive Japanese from Kokoda. This victory proved to be a decisive turning point in the New Guinea Campaign.

JANUARY 14, 1943. Casablanca Conference. Roosevelt, Churchill, De Gaulle and Giraud meet.

h 8th Army under Gen.
Afrika Korps and Italians.

FEBRUARY 10, 1943. Guadalcanal in Solomons cleared by U.S. Marines after six months' struggle.

JUNE 13, 1944. The Flying Bomb—V1—opens its eighty-day attack on the population of London and Southern England

AUGUST 25, 1944. Liberation of Paris: vast crowds in Place de l'Opera.

SEPTEMBER 17, 1944. Allied airborne troops at Arnhem and Nijmegen (Holland).

JANUARY 9, 1945. General MacArthur returns—after three years—to Luzon in the Philippines.

MARCH 6, 1945. Cologne captured by Gen. Hodges' U.S. 1st Army.

MARCH 20, 1945. British and Indian columns march triumphantly into Fort Dufferin, citadel of Mandalay.

MARCH 23, 1945. British, Canadian and U.S. forces of 21st Army Group cross the Rhine.

APRIL 13, 1945. Victorious Red Army enter Vienna after their fighting advance from Volga to Danube.

May 7, 1945. British meet Russians in Germany. Montgomery greets Rokossovsky at Wismar.

MAY 8, 1945. Unconditional surrender signed by Germans at Soviet H.Q. in Berlin.

VIEWS & REVIEWS Of Vital War Books

by Hamilton Fyfe

WHAT I am wondering just now is whether the Armies of Occupation in Germany will be up against the same dangers and difficulties that beset the German troops while they occupied France. I do not think they will. For one thing the circumstances will not be the same. The French Resistance forces fought against an invader insolent, nervous, haughty, cruel when thwarted. The British, American, Russian and French soldiers in Germany will not be there to hold the country down but to keep order and protect the temporary rulers. For another thing, I doubt whether many Germans have any fight left in them.

They are always most at ease when they are told what to do; they are trained to obey, whereas the French are trained, one might almost say, to rebel. Still, it is impossible to predict what will happen during the next few years. If there should be anything in Germany comparable with the Resistance Movement in France, you can guess what it will be like by reading George Millar's book entitled Maquis (Heinemann, 10s. 6d.), which gives by far the most vivid and informative account I have seen yet of the way in which the F.F.I. harassed the enemy, made his nerves jumpy, prevented him from ever settling down and feeling secure.

Running Head-on Into Danger

The author was a newspaperman who joined the Army and received a commission. Early last summer he was asked if he would like to be dropped by parachute in France to work with the men of the Maquis. He said "Yes!" and was immediately put through a course of intensive training. He acquires a new name and tries to fit a new personality on to it. He is a Frenchman who went at an early age to Australia, so his French is not perfect. He is employed by an insurance company and has to travel about. His papers are, of course, in order. He gets the story of his life by heart, and that, as a matter of fact, was the last he ever did with it. In the district round Besançon, where he worked, he was known as Emile, and he adopted any number of disguises, but never that one which had been so elaborately prepared for him in London.

They were a queer crowd, the resisters he found waiting for him. At first he despaired of being able to do anything with them. Those who were active and ready for desperate efforts, lived in appalling squalor, and were slack in taking necessary precautions. "There's no risk!" they would assert cheerfully, when they were running head-on into danger. The Maquis who had the virtues of cleanliness and order were too mild and unenterprising. "They were of the clerk type. They looked like a benevolent society or a ramblers' club." These latter Capt. Millar avoided; with most of the others he got on very well indeed. But he knew it was wise not to have too much money with him. "The men come from all sorts of miliex," he was told. Here and there ruffians used the Resistance Movement as a screen for banditry and crimes of the worst kind. One such scoundrel terrorized a countryside and had to be shot by his fellow-resisters.

THEN there was the difficulty of persuading the right sort to keep their mouths shut, and the danger of the wrong sort giving secrets away either for German money or, if they were captured, under stress of torture. At one time cigarettes were so scarce that tobacco shops were raided. Capt. Millar was not able to find excuses for their carelessness with the weapons and explosives which were dropped to them by British and American aircraft at great risk to the crews. A dump of such material was in a very bad state, having been exposed to the weather for months. "Rage consumed me as I handled rusty grenades and explosives soggy with moisture. Everything was in such a wet condition that in England it would have been unconditionally scrapped." He had to conceal his fury, however, for the relationship among the Maquis was not that of officer and men, but of comrades equal in every way. At the same time natural leadership or expert knowledge was readily recognized. The inexperienced were glad to be told what to do. Orders tactfully given were carried out.

A Briton's Adventures with the Patriots of France

WHAT Capt. Millar was chiefly concerned with were attacks on railway lines, stations and trains. Of the French local police some were friendly, some hostile. Even more hated and feared than the Boches were the French militiamen, who collaborated with the enemy under orders from Vichy. But almost all the peasants and small-town folk and country-house owners were inclined to help "la resistance" if they could do so without getting into trouble. Some willingly took the chance of that. There was Gustave, for example, a village mechanic whom the Germans had beaten for setting up an illicit oil-press to supply the villagers with cooking oil. "He will never forget that beating. He will take it out on every German he meets for the rest of his life!" Another was an aristocratic old lady living in a château, who was mayor of the hamlet close by and sheltered any refugees or escaped prisoners of war, including many Russians. "Stalingrad and Leningrad cured my old-fashioned ideas about Communists," she said. Then there was the Mother Superior of a convent, where the author and other F.F.I. leaders lay in hiding for a time.

Capt. GEORGE MILLAR, D.S.O., M.C., British Army officer and former Fleet Street journalist, was dropped by parachute near Dijon in France on the night of June 1, 1944, to become a Maquisard and keep radio contact with H.Q. in London. A review of his book is given here. *Photo, Daily Express*

There are unforgettable portraits in the book of men with whom Capt. Millar worked. One was a Frenchman who spoke English with a London accent and a lot of slang. He had lived at Ealing for many years and liked it: had left to go back to France only because he found his son was speaking French with an English accent! "My mind was instantly made up. At great sacrifice I closed down or sold my businesses in England. I left the town and country I had learned to love." Comfortable as his life had been, he took to the woods as if he had always been a brigand, accustomed to sleeping in holes scooped out of the soil and seldom enjoying a square meal. As a contrast to this genuine Patriot we have the former French officer who was in the pay of the Gestapo and whirled about the district on a motor-cycle, feared by all, but unmolested until a Resistance leader, whose exploits belied his gentle appearance, soft, purring voice, and fluffy hair and side-whiskers, stopped him one day, marched him into a wood, made him write out a confession of his infamies, and then shot him.

Midnight Visitation Minus Boots

The Gestapo had a good many Frenchmen in their service and naturally brought their own thugs from Germany. "They looked solidly respectable, these Gestapo men, like successful stockbrokers or bookmakers, who had toned themselves to a look of easy opulence. It struck me that they looked happy, too. As though their life were good and as though it were permanent." Well, they were wrong there! They seem to have failed utterly to terrorize the population. When a lad of nineteen was killed on his way to take part in blowing up a train loaded with petrol, he was given a funeral, "the biggest ever seen in these parts. There were more than 3,000 mourners, and every village sent its contingent. There was a guard of honour of Maquisards dressed in their khaki uniforms and carrying Sten guns." A funeral oration was pronounced by a retired army colonel. He was afterwards compelled to go into hiding, and the grave was despoiled of its wreaths and banners by German troops. But it is astonishing to read of such a ceremony taking place openly in daylight in an occupied area.

Of the many exciting incidents skilfully described by Capt. Millar the one I shall remember longest, was when the author and a comrade were in a little town where they slept in a house opposite the hotel. In the night they happened to be awake and opened the window. They saw a truck filled with soldiers drive in silently. "The driver must have squeezed gently on his brakes, for the heavy vehicle came so gradually to a stop that not a stone crunched beneath its tires." Out of it jumped silently a load of soldiers, without their boots. This was most unusual. "They were the first Germans I had seen who made no noise with their feet." Without a sound they took up positions with machine-guns and automatic weapons. Another truck followed as silently.

THEN a car arrived with two officers. They went up the hotel steps. The door was opened to their knocking. The two men watching could see that the rooms were being searched. When this was over, the officers came out, saying good-night civilly to the proprietress. They drove noisily away with the two trucks. But the stocking-feet soldiers remained at their posts. Evidently the idea was that someone they wanted and had failed to find would come out, thinking they had all cleared off. There they stayed until it began to get light. Then they marched away. It must have been an eerie, nerve-racking scene.

Japan May Be Seared Out of the War by Fire

Fifty-one square miles of Tokyo had been destroyed in Super-Fortress attacks, it was announced on May 29, 1945. And Japan's other target-cities are being subjected to an ordeal by fire without parallel. Latest types of Allied incendiary bombs, for similar distribution, include "Hirohito's Hotfoot" and the "Goop," whose violent behaviour is described by MARK PRIESTLEY.

AIR RAIDS will knock Tokyo completely out of the war said conservative experts after they had scanned photographs of the fire-damage already inflicted upon Japanese military might, and had watched a demonstration of the new Allied fire-bomb, the M.69. The raid by 450 Fortresses on Osaka on June 1, when 3,275 tons of incendiaries added to destruction wrought on March 14, when eight square miles of the city's centre had been burned out, further indicated the trend the Far Eastern war is taking.

Hirohito's Hotfoot, as airmen have nicknamed one of their latest types of fire-bomb, is fast proving that successful incendiary bombing can be five times as devastating as high-explosive bombs of equal weight. Imagine a thin, six-sided steel pipe, 19 inches long, flattened at the ends and packed with gluey, incendiary petrol jelly, net weight 6½ lb. Two thousand comprise a comfortable plane-load, and the bomb cannot be smothered with sandbags or quelled with a stirrup-pump. On crashing through a roof, the M.69 lies still for five seconds. Then, with tremendous violence, it explodes.

Simultaneously it throws out a burning jelly-stuffed cheese-cloth bag which is liable to rocket for 100 yards or so in the blast, spraying puddings of flaming glue in its wake. Whether the bag bursts at the end of its run or hits an obstruction, the result is the same. Gobbets of adhesive fire are splashed over an area of 60 square yards. Ravenous flame adheres to walls, floors, ceilings, stock-piles and machinery. The effect is not unlike that of a flame-thrower. Every inflammable object in the path of the fire-shower instantaneously combusts: the heat can be so intense that metal melts and brick and plaster rapidly crumble.

AN efficient fire brigade, if on the spot almost immediately, might hope at best to limit the conflagration caused by a single bomb. Precise pattern bombing of selected industrial areas, however, presents the enemy with an insoluble problem. The authorities first made certain of this in test and counter-test in America, where the National Defence Research Council made an exhaustive study of the building construction of 16 enemy cities. Specifications were drawn up identical with the real thing in all the important physical properties, and on the salt-flats of Utah the Army then co-operated by building a series of mock Japanese cities.

They were perfect in detail down to the position of machinery and the arrangement of halls and partitions. At the same time the finest fire-fighting services were assigned to protect the "targets," just as the Japanese might be expected to do. When the earliest prototypes of the M.69 were used, the fires were swiftly put out. The research workers made changes in the weight and size of the bombs, as well as the oil-jelly charges, while a fire-fighting department did everything possible to improve counter-skill and equipment. In raid after raid the odds proved to be equal, until the firemen were standing-to in asbestos suits for "surprise raids." Eventually, an oil-jelly bomb was devised that defeated the Americans, defeated British N.F.S. teams at a research station, and was used with success against Germany. The M.69 had arrived.

Oil and Magnesium Block-Burner

In one demonstration, the standard pattern (now obsolete) magnesium bomb was used in a parallel test with the Hotfoot. The magnesium treated the observers to sparks and sparkle, fireworks and brilliance, but in 20 minutes merely burned a hole through the floor of a sample building. The jelly bomb, in less time, burned its building to the ground.

Today the M.69 has a big sister, a 500-lb. block-burner known unofficially as the "Goop," formally listed as the M.76. (The intervening serial figures are believed to represent types discarded under test.) It is known to contain a mixture of jellied oil and powdered magnesium, and its destructive power is tremendous.

IN mid-April 1945 an appalling mixture of 500,000 of these types drenched the Germans in the Gironde pocket during the closing phase of the war in Europe and may well have heralded the final Nazi collapse on all fronts. When the Germans tried to burn out London with a magnesium bomb triggered with thermite, the Japs could not have foreseen that a fire-bomb in the hands of the Allies would prove the final answer to aggressive war.

In the same way, the jet-propelled flying bombs now under manufacture in ten mighty American war plants will put into the shade anything ever encountered in Britain. The American type has a total length of 27 feet, as compared with the German 25-footer, and the additional two feet packs an extra charge of high explosive. The time seems to be approaching when it will be possible to "buzz-bomb" Japan from the Chinese coast or adjacent islands.

A rocket bomb, travelling faster than sound and exploding after deep penetration, was also used in the last stage of the war in the European theatre. It was employed with special success in smashing the E-boat pens at Ijmuiden, Holland. Striking its target at a speed of more than 1,100 ft. per second, the Anglo-American rocket bomb is a special type for a special task, and one of its more obvious purposes could be the smashing of Japanese coastal naval facilities.

READY FOR RAIDS on enemy occupied Malaya, giant bombs are lined up for loading into a Super-Fortress. Latest types of incendiaries include the one seen (top right) being secured in position for dropping; it is filled with a gelatinous substance which, when burning, generates heat up to 1,400 degrees Fahr. and is practically impossible to extinguish. *Photos, U.S. Official*

With the use of airfields on Okinawa the Allies are no farther from the Japanese mainland than the Ruhr is from East Anglia. The Iwojima bases, too, are within Liberator and Lancaster distance of such great centres of the Japanese aircraft industry as Osaka and Kobé. The release of flying crews from the European theatre menaces Japan with nightly raids, with monthly tonnages of 50,000 and more. Eastern Air Command has thought nothing in the past of round trips of 2,000 miles and farther, and the capture of the Ryukyus is bound to bring the 10-tonner to Tokyo's door. When President Truman declared that unconditional surrender would not mean the destruction of the Japanese people, the consequences of refusal to surrender were implicit!

'Fate of Jap Empire Hinges on This Battle'

OKINAWA, only 325 miles from the Jap mainland, is so vital to the enemy that Admiral Toyoda, C.-in-C. Japanese Combined Fleet, told the Nippon Navy on May 6, 1945, that "the rise or fall of our Empire hinges on this battle." On April 1 over 100,000 U.S. troops had effected a landing on this island key to the Sea of Japan in the greatest invasion operation of the Pacific. Landing craft are seen (1) nosing ashore. By May 30 the toll of enemy dead was 61,519, with 1,353 prisoners. Representative of oppressed natives liberated are this young islander and her baby (2).

Support was given by 1,400 ships of Admiral Chester Nimitz's U.S. Pacific Fleet, the biggest sea force ever mustered by the U.S. Navy; covering the landings a battleship blazed a broadside (3). *Photos, Planet News, Paul Popper. Map by courtesy of The Evening Standard*

Nemesis Trails More Infamous Nazi Ex-Leaders

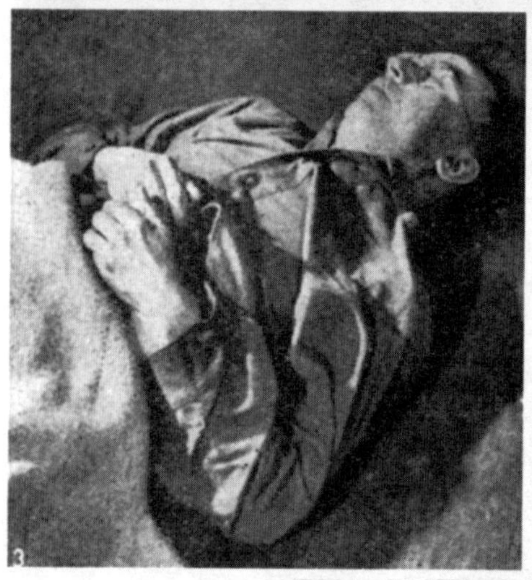

COVERED by a British Bren-gunner (1) are three members of the self-styled German "Government" at Flensburg—Albert Speer (Armaments Minister), Admiral Dönitz, and General Jodl—after their arrest, with three hundred of their officials, on May 23, 1945. Some of the Germans were still half-clothed when lined up, hands-on-head, in a corridor of their H.Q. (2).

Heinrich Himmler, Gestapo and S.S. chief, lay dead (3) at British 2nd Army H.Q. at Luneburg on May 23, less than 30 hours after being detained at Bremervoerde by our Field Security Police; he had swallowed a capsule of cyanide of potassium. See also illus. page 84.

Last hut of the Belsen concentration camp (see illus. page 50) went up in flames on May 21, by Allied orders (4).

Photos, British Official, British Newspaper Pool, Associated Press

London Bus-Driver Runs 'Local' in Luneburg

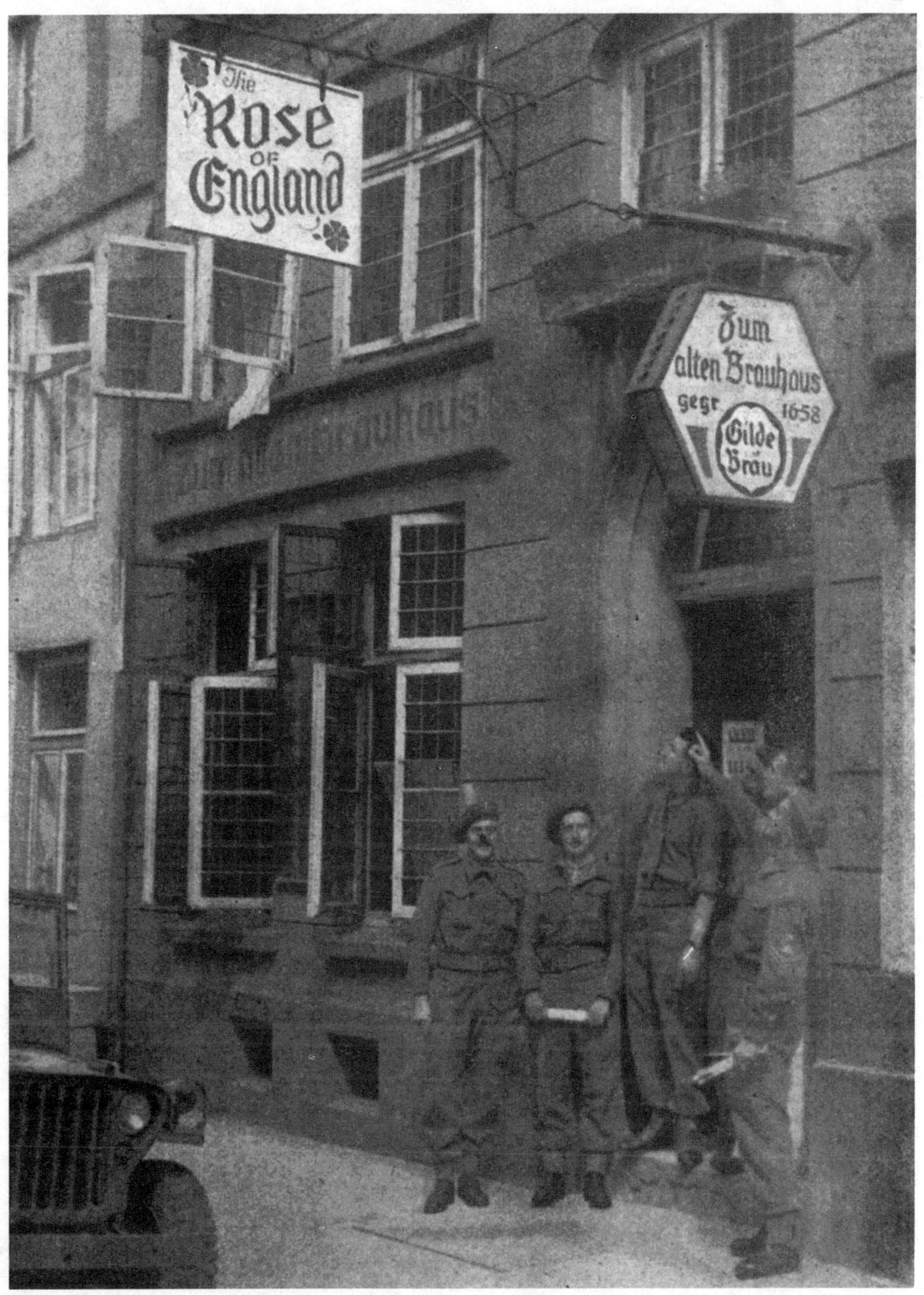

MINE HOST OF THIS OLD GERMAN TAVERN, now under British management serving beer, tea, cakes and rolls to the 1114 Heavy A.A. Regiment, Royal Artillery, is Sgt. W. H. Ellis, who in civilian life drove a London bus. Near to the scene of the Unconditional Surrender, as a club-house with rooms for reading and writing it is an unqualified success. And the N.C.O. artist (right) is justifiably proud of the new signboard to which he is pointing and which is his own inspired handiwork.

Photo, British Newspaper Pool

Now It Can Be Told : 'Operation Pluto'

ONE OF THE GREATEST supply stories of the war was released on May 23, 1945, when the existence of an oil pipeline system across the bed of the Channel to the Continent was revealed. This all-British triumph of engineering and seamanship, known officially as Operation Pluto, solved one of the master problems of the whole war, enabling 1,000,000 gallons of petrol to be pumped daily, from a few weeks after D-Day, through the submarine pipe-way into France and later deep into Germany, supplying the entire petrol requirements of Montgomery's Armies. By V Day over 120,000,000 gallons had thus been transported.

From tankers discharging at our ports the petrol was conveyed across Britain, through a network of pipelines, to cleverly concealed coastal high-pressure pumping stations, staffed by R.A.S.C. personnel, whence it was received by the submarine pipes. The latter, of 3-in. steel tubing, were laid under the supervision of the Royal Navy, ships of all sizes, comprising "Force Pluto," manned by Merchant Navy seamen, being engaged.

For paying-out, the tubing was wound on floating drums each 40 ft. in diameter, 60 ft. long, carrying 70 miles of it, and weighing 1,600 tons. Many of the various laying operations were completed under adverse weather conditions and against strong tides ; 500 miles of this pipeline were laid between Dungeness and Boulogne, to name only two points. The title "Pluto" is made up of the initial letters of Pipe Line Under The Ocean.

TWO HUNDRED MILES OF PIPELINE in three-quarter-mile sections (1) stowed on the English coast, ready for welding into continuous lengths of 30 miles or more, then to be wound on floating drums or "Conuns" (H.M.S. Conundrums), one of which, laying its line as it goes, is seen (2) being towed across Channel. Cable used in the operation was developed by Mr. A. C. Hartley (3). Force Pluto was under Capt. J. F. Hutchings, C.B.E., D.S.O., R.N. (5). H.M.S. Latimer (4) was one of the ships engaged.

Photos, British Official, G.P.U., News Chronicle

I WAS THERE! Eye Witness Stories of the War

How Germany's Vaunted Underwater Navy Died

First U-boat to come to London in the Second Great War was the U 776. Escorted by a Navy sloop, the dark grey shape that our merchant seamen know so well was in the Thames on May 22, 1945, heading (as told by Rosemary Hirst of The Evening Standard) for the spot where she was to tie up at Westminster Pier. See also illus. page 102.

I WENT to meet the submarine in the cutter which was taking the river pilot aboard. It was a grey morning, with fine rain hanging over the quiet basin. The river was "sleepy" after the Whitsun holiday. As the pilot cutter left Royal Terrace Pier crews from tugs and merchant ships were coming out on deck, rubbing their hair and yawning ; other men on the wharves were smoking and talking. All were soon peering down river for the first sign of U 776.

Her escort, who had brought her round during the night from Weymouth Bay, slowed down beyond the Fort, gave a parting salute and departed. U 776 came up river alone, looking the evil thing she was—fast and heavily armed for so small a vessel. She has been left just as surrendered for us to see.

She was a minelayer. On her fore-deck, rendered harmless, are the dozen acoustic "oyster" mines she hoped to lay for our shipping off the south-west coast of Ireland. She was a sink-at-sight destroyer. Aft is still her gun, pointed in menace. Three anti-aircraft guns she has abaft her conning tower. It is fitting that London should see her, for U 776, a comparatively new 500-tonner, was commissioned while Hitler hoped to head the R.A.F. off his U-boat nests with V1.

She surrendered to a naval sloop off Weymouth before she had time to do any harm. It is fitting, too, that Captain E. R. Ferguson, a Gravesend man, should be the lucky river pilot to bring her in. He has been a waterman for 22 years. His father was a Trinity House pilot. Captain Ferguson was piloting river traffic safely to the docks all through the blitz. He never spent a night away from the river. He was in the Merchant Navy in the last war ; was torpedoed in the Bristol Channel and shelled in the Mediterranean by German submarines.

STRANDED IN THAMES MUD at low tide, the U 776 heeled over to port a few hours after her arrival at Westminster Pier.
Photo, The Daily Herald

"This is the greatest pleasure I have had in my life," he said, as our cutter drew nearer. We could see clearly now the White Ensign she was flying, and on her bridge the cap of the young officer who commanded her. She had slowed down to four knots to pick us up, but we were going down-tide, and her slim lines gave her a greyhound speed.

The cutter circled round and drew alongside, both vessels keeping speed and station. The young commander jumped down on the submarine's fore-deck, looking pink and smiling after his all-night trip. "Morning, pilot !" he called cheerily. The grey U-boat, small as she is, looked huge and slim by our side. Captain Ferguson leapt nine feet from our deck, catching the chains on her deck side to steady himself, and scrambled briskly up to the bridge.

"Have you a sea pilot to come off, sir ?" we called. "No fear—came up ourselves," called the commander, and with a wave he, too, disappeared to the bridge. As we drew away she rang down for more speed; and, fast as was our launch, she left us, as it seemed, all standing. As she gathered speed for her 30-mile trip up to Westminster, I saw the silent crowd gathered thickly on the river banks.

Lieut.-Cmdr. P. B. MARRIOTT, D.S.O., R.N., in the control-room of the surrendered U 776 which he brought from Weymouth to London, as narrated here. *Photo, Kingstone*

Ships' crews, too, were silent. Not a cheer, not a siren. It was too great a day for every man on the river for much speech. The submarine's engines, powerful and silent, carried U 776 swiftly up the river. *In such simple scenes as these the German navy dies.*

We Found a U-Boat Nest in Bergen Harbour

The secrets of a practically invulnerable concrete U-boat pen in Bergen Harbour, Norway, which after the liberation of France became Dönitz's main advance U-boat base, were being unearthed on May 23, 1945, by Capt. D. B. Nicholson, R.N.V.R., head of the Allied Naval Control Commission in Bergen, as told by W. E. Mundy, of The Daily Telegraph.

WITH British naval members of the Commission, I have just been taken through this huge concrete bunker on the first Allied visit of inspection. We drove up to the German guardhouse outside the gate of Bergen Harbour, where the U-boat pens are situated. Inside the car were Lt. A. J. Sumption, R.N.V.R., who has commanded submarines throughout this war, and an armed Royal Naval escort of one petty officer and a submarine rating.

A young German guard refused to open the gate and stared at us truculently. Lt. Sumption remained in the car and quietly said : "Open the gate immediately, and then fetch your superior officer to me." The German hesitated, but Lt. Sumption stared him down and the German obeyed.

We drove through down a long narrow drive to the entrance of the pens, where we stopped the car and got out. The drive was completely walled in with concrete from six to ten feet thick as protection against lateral blast. The Bergen bunker is built up above water level on the dockside and is not cut into the sides of the fjord. The whole bunker is about the height of a three to four-storeyed building. It is made of concrete into the shape of a solid rectangular box.

Already the solid concrete roof is at least 18 feet thick, and up to the time of the surrender work was still in progress on the top of the bunker. If the Germans were able to refit nearly a dozen U-boats at a time in practical safety under the heaviest air attack, then the Bergen bunker is something for our naval and air experts to examine !

Inside, the bunker is divided into seven pens. All the U-boats had been moved out into the open harbour before our arrival. Powerful flood lighting turned the darkness almost into day. Some bunkers had a sliding crane in the roof capable of lifting out the heaviest machinery and torpedoes. Three were single pens for one U-boat, but three others could hold two U-boats each.

One pen was fitted as a dry dock and others only needed water-tight doors to transform them into dry docks. In short, at least nine, or probably 11, U-boats could be serviced in the pens. Master switches could immediately black-out the whole bunker during an air alarm, but I noticed that huge black-out curtains could be draped over the entrances to enable work to proceed during the night.

Mobile power lines could carry current direct to the U-boats for welding repairs. If Lt. Sumption asked something to which the German would not or could not answer, the German had the stock answer : "I do not know. I am a U-boat commander, not a landsman." Dönitz provided every comfort for U-boat crews. They had at least fourteen days leave after each patrol, and once they docked they were taken to rest hotels, in the mountains above Bergen, established in peacetime for winter sports.

R.A.F. Lancasters and Halifaxes made a heavy attack on Bergen harbour last October, and a German U-boat engineer told me that bomb damage to the harbour installations halted the operational use of the pens "for some time." The U-boats, later widely dispersed under camouflage hoods along the fjord, were difficult to observe from the air.

I COULD see only one direct penetration of the Bergen U-boat bunkers. This was in one pen and measured about three feet by nine feet, but is now filled in. Outside the bunker lies a scene of devastation, mostly the result of the R.A.F. raids, but some undoubtedly was caused by the explosion of a German ammunition ship in Bergen harbour last year.

All the harbour buildings are smashed flat by air attack, except for some new concrete buildings, with walls 15 feet thick, which appear undamaged. Some U-boats lie crippled, with bomb hits, and have been left where they lie. The dry dock is half submerged, with a submarine lying inside. Four U-boats are tied up in a bunch, under repairs. They had been hit where they lie.

As we walked through the harbour it was a desolate sight. Rain poured down. German naval personnel, most of them youths, armed to the teeth, stood around watching us.

In Bergen town the Royal Navy members of the Allied Submarine Disarmament Commission are installed in the offices of the S.S. chief, who must have left in a hurry. One of my happiest moments in the last five years was to watch a young British submarine rating writing a letter to his girl on German notepaper headed: "Der Höhere S.S. und Polizeiführer Bergen." I typed this story on similar paper.

U-BOAT NEST AT TRONDHEIM, Norway, with solid concrete roof. A visit to Dönitz's main advance U-boat base in Norway is described in story commencing in page 121. *Photo, British Official*

Blasted for Hours Off the Coast of Japan

How Japanese bombs struck the 27,000-tons aircraft-carrier U.S.S. Franklin on March 19, about 60 miles off the southern coast of Japan, causing one of the most appalling losses of American lives in naval history, is narrated by Pacific War Correspondent Alvin S. McCoy, by arrangement with I.N.S. The carrier's own bombs and a vast quantity of octane gas oil blasted her near to complete destruction. See also illus. page 125.

I WAS the only war correspondent aboard, a dazed survivor of the holocaust only because I was below decks at breakfast in the unhit area. The rescue of the crippled carrier, towed flaming and smoking from the very shores of Japan, and the saving of more than 800 men fished from the sea by protecting cruisers and destroyers, will be an epic of naval warfare.

Heads bobbed in the water for miles behind the carrier. Men floated on rafts or swam about in the bitterly cold water to seize lifelines from the rescue ships and be hauled aboard. The official loss of life will be announced by the Navy Department in Washington. Unofficial figures at the time showed 949 dead, more than 221 wounded.

Scenes of indescribable horror swept the ship. Men were blown off the flight deck into the sea. Some were burned to cinders in the searing white-hot flash of flame that swept the hangar deck. Others were trapped in the compartments below and suffocated by smoke. Scores were drowned, and others torn by exploding shells and bombs.

Countless deeds of heroism and superb seamanship saved the carrier and about two-thirds of the ship's complement of more than 2,500. The tenacity of the Franklin's skipper, Captain L. E. Gehres, who refused to abandon the ship and accept the aid of protecting ships and planes, virtually snatched the carrier from Japanese waters to be repaired so that she can fight again.

Fire and damage control parties who stuck with the ship performed valiantly. The carrier was all but abandoned, although the "abandon ship" order was never given. An air group and about 1,500 of the crew were sent to the U.S.S. Santa Fé. A skeleton crew of some 690 remained aboard to try to save the ship as it listed nearly twenty degrees. The Franklin's aircraft which were airborne landed safely on other carriers.

3,000-Miles Crawl to Pearl Harbour

Navy officials said the Franklin took more punishment than any other ship has ever taken and yet remained afloat. It was her own highly destructive bombs and rockets that created the havoc. A Japanese plane launched its bombs at the precise moment when it would cause most destruction.

The tragedy took place during the early hours of March 19 when the Franklin was about sixty miles off Japan. Combat patrol planes and fighters had been launched long before dawn. A powerful striking force of planes loaded with all the munitions they could possibly carry began launching about seven o'clock. The sky was dull and overcast. Eight Corsair fighters and eight or nine Hell-diver bombers had already roared off the decks. Other planes were massed aft and loaded with bombs and rockets. It was at this moment that Japanese planes flew in undetected and discharged their bombs.

Reuters correspondent at Pearl Harbour continues the story:

When the Franklin steamed in here—a mass of twisted, blackened steel hardly recognizable as a ship of war—the dead were still being dug out of the tangled ironwork. Having survived five more dive-bombing attacks she had crawled the 3,000-odd miles to Pearl Harbour under her own steam. And, still under her own steam, she left next day for a U.S. mainland naval yard.

FLAMES WREATHED THE GUN TURRETS OF THE U.S. CARRIER FRANKLIN after she had been set ablaze (left) by a Japanese dive-bomber when a task force of Vice-Admiral Mark Mitscher's Pacific Fleet struck at Tokyo. Surviving the explosion of 200,000 lb. of her own bombs, shells, bullets and petrol, and suffering over 1,000 casualties, including 832 dead or missing, she listed badly (right) on her 3,000-mile voyage to Pearl Harbour under her own steam. See story above and illus. page 125. *Photos, U.S. Navy*

We Sent a Jap 'Island' to the Bed of the Sea

British submarines engaged in Far Eastern waters regard curious episodes as the rule rather than the exception. Lieut. A. C. Chandler, R.N.R., tells of the phenomenon encountered during a patrol on which the submarine of which he is the commanding officer destroyed 20 Japanese coastal craft and set shore installations ablaze with gunfire. Commander A.R. Hezlet, D.S.O., D.S.C., R.N., relates another surprising story.

Lieut.-Cmdr. A. R. HEZLET, D.S.O., D.S.C., R.N., commanding officer of a British submarine, relates here remarkable experiences of undersea warfare. *Photo, British Official*

I WAS called to the periscope by the officer of the watch to look at something which he described as "queer," and I saw what appeared to be an island, with two palm trees and hibiscus and other foliage entwining them. The "island" was moving rapidly about a mile from us. After I had been studying this phenomenon for a little while, a number of heads became visible among the foliage, and I knew then that it was a Japanese landing craft of large size.

It was loaded with stores and crowded with at least 100 Japanese troops. We surfaced about a thousand yards on the starboard quarter of this "Coconut Grove," and opened fire with our 4-in. gun and Oerlikon. On sighting me the enemy turned hard to port, but the second round of 4-in. hit him right aft. With a terrific explosion the stern blew off, and up went stores and Japanese in a great column of flame.

Japanese troops left in the forward half of the vessel hastily put on their life-jackets and jumped overboard. By this time, after continuous pounding by our gun, there was nothing left of the craft, but a sheet of flame over a large area sent up a wide column of smoke 100 feet high. It was obvious that the draft had been carrying a quantity of petrol besides other stores and troops. Even if survivors had been willing to be picked up it was almost impossible to get near them owing to the flames that were leaping up savagely around the wreckage.

GUN CREW AND AMMUNITION PARTY of a British submarine which tried to rescue survivors of a sunk Japanese ship, only to see them deliberately attempt to drown themselves. It was announced on June 1, 1945, that Allied naval losses—excluding those of the U.S.—from Sept. 1939 to May 1945 included 77 submarines. *Photo, British Official*

Deliberately gulping mouthfuls of water and flinging up their arms in an effort to drown, scores of Japanese sailors committed suicide when their ship was sunk, as told by the Commanding Officer of the submarine which tried to pick them up—Commander Hezlet, D.S.O., D.S.C., R.N.:

It was one of the most fantastic sights I have ever seen. We had sighted a Japanese submarine-chaser on the point of entering harbour, and we surfaced and engaged her by gunfire. With our fifth round, at just over a mile, we scored a hit on her bridge, probably killing the captain. For twenty-five minutes we manoeuvred around the chaser, exchanging shots at close range, until she became completely out of control and nearly collided with us. In the end she turned over and slid into the sea, bows first.

The survivors made no attempt to save themselves when we stood by to pick them up. We threw a line to one sailor who was wounded and who didn't appear to be trying to drown himself like the rest. He grasped it, but one of his "chums" tried to wrest it out of his hands. We succeeded in pulling him inboard, however, while the other chap threw up his arms, took in mouthfuls of water and sank. The Japanese prisoner, thinking he was going to be executed, was terrified at first, but when treatment was given to his wounds, he actually smiled. Later, we put him to work polishing brass in the engine-room.

On another occasion recently Commander Hezlet's submarine sighted through the periscope a convoy of coasters, escorted by two motor torpedo boats and a twin-engined bomber:

We remained submerged, and attacked with torpedoes. After one of the M.T.B.' had passed overhead, we fired. A minute or so later there was a dull explosion. But we were in only 12 fathoms and we lost depth immediately after firing. We grounded for'ard with only sufficient water above us to cover the hull. A quick observation through the periscope showed me that one of the coasters had been hit and that her bridge was awash. By bumping along the sea-bed we eventually got into deeper water.

OUR DIARY OF THE WAR

MAY 23, Wednesday *1,263rd day of War against Japan*

Germany.—Himmler committed suicide after capture. Members of Dönitz's "acting government" and German High Command arrested in Flensburg.

Japan.—550 Super-Fortresses attacked Tokyo with fire-bombs.

Home Front.—Mr. Churchill tendered resignation to the King and was invited to form a new administration in place of Coalition.

MAY 24, Thursday *1,264th day*

Austria.—Field - Marshal Alexander issued proclamation of military government in part of Austria occupied by 8th Army.

Ryukyu Islands.—At night Japanese made "suicide assault" with planes carrying troops, on U.S. airfields and shipping in Okinawa area.

Burma.—14th Army troops reached inland port of Bassein.

MAY 25, Friday *1,265th day*

France.—In Paris, Field-Marshal Montgomery received Grand Cross of Legion of Honour from General de Gaulle.

Japan.—500 Super-Fortresses dropped another 4,000 tons of incendiaries on Tokyo.

MAY 26, Saturday *1,266th day*

Germany.—Gen. Eisenhower moved his H.Q. from Rheims to Frankfort-on-Main.

Norway.—Vidkun Quisling appeared in Oslo court for preliminary investigation.

U.S.A.—Announced that Gen. Doolittle would lead U.S. 8th Air Force in Pacific.

MAY 27, Sunday *1,267th day*

China.—Chinese troops entered Nanning, capital of Kwansi province.

MAY 28, Monday *1,268th day*

Japan.—Seaport of Yokohama attacked for first time by Super-Fortresses.

Pacific.—Vice-Admiral Rawlings, with units of British Pacific Fleet, arrived at Apra Harbour, Guam.

Home Front.—Ministry of Labour order relaxed control of engagement of labour.

Germany.—William Joyce ("Lord Haw-Haw") captured by British 2nd Army.

MAY 29, Tuesday *1,269th day*

Levant.—Fighting broke out in Damascus and other towns between French and Syrians.

MAY 30, Wednesday *1,270th day*

Germany.—Marshal Zhukov appointed Soviet representative on Allied Control Commission.

Ryukyu Islands.—On Okinawa, U.S. Marines captured Shuri Castle.

Levant.—Truce arranged in Damascus for evacuation of British and American civilians.

Persia.—Persian Foreign Minister demanded withdrawal of British, U.S. and Russian troops from Persia.

MAY 31, Thursday *1,271st day*

Levant.—"Cease fire" in Syria after intervention of British Government.

Burma.—U.S. Air Force units withdrawn from Eastern Air Command.

JUNE 1, Friday *1,272nd day*

Germany.—Berlin radio broadcast warning of reprisals for attacks on Soviet soldiers or officials.

Japan.—Osaka heavily attacked by Super-Fortresses with incendiaries.

Burma.—Announced that new British Army, 12th, formed under Lieut.-Gen. Sir Montagu Stopford.

JUNE 2, Saturday *1,273rd day*

Ryukyu Islands.—U.S. troops captured Shikiya town on Okinawa.

JUNE 3, Sunday *1,274th day*

Levant.—French troops in Damascus escorted from city by British.

Japan.—U.S. carrier-aircraft attacked "suicide plane" bases on Kyushu.

JUNE 4, Monday *1,275th day*

Japan.—Kobé attacked by 450 Super-Fortresses with incendiary bombs.

Pacific.—U.S. Navy Dept. announced loss of two destroyers off Okinawa.

JUNE 5, Tuesday *1,276th day*

Germany.—Eisenhower, Montgomery, Zhukov and Lattre de Tassigny signed in Berlin declaration of assumption of supreme authority in Germany by governments of their countries.

Sea.—Mr. Churchill disclosed transfer of British warships to Russian fleet

Flash-backs

1940

May 28. *Belgians capitulated.*

June 4. *Evacuation of 335,000 troops from Dunkirk completed.*

June 5. *Opening of Battle of France on lines of Somme and Aisne.*

1941

May 24. *H.M.S. Hood sunk off Greenland, engaging Bismarck.*

May 27. *Bismarck sunk.*

June 1. *Clothes rationing came into effect in United Kingdom.*

1942

May 26. *Twenty-year Anglo-Soviet Treaty signed in London.*

May 30. *First R.A.F. 1,000-bomber raid made on Cologne.*

June 4. *Battle of Midway Island began; ended in Japanese defeat.*

1943

May 29. *Organized Japanese resistance ended on Attu, Aleutians.*

June 1. *Heavy naval and air bombardment of Pantelleria began.*

1944

May 25. *5th Army in Italy joined up with Anzio beach-head patrols.*

June 4. *Allies entered Rome.*

With Our Airmen Today

By CAPT.
NORMAN MACMILLAN
M.C., A.F.C.

JAPAN'S air position is like that of Germany about a year ago. British and American aircraft, both carrier-borne and land-based, are smashing Japanese home airfields and pounding Japanese aircraft factories. Britain's contribution to this campaign has so far been made by the Fleet Air Arm, but no doubt British heavy land-based bombers will soon join in. They are the only aircraft so far available to carry the 5½ and 10-ton bombs, developed for the R.A.F., which played such a notable part in the final destruction of German heavy warships, submarine pens, viaducts, canals and industry.

Although the Lancasters that attacked the Tirpitz made a round flight of about 2,000 miles, the striking ranges in the Pacific have hitherto been rather too stretched for the special features of British heavy bombers to be advantageously employed. For them to maintain a steady pounding of Japanese targets it would certainly be better to be able to operate at shorter range. From Okinawa (see illus. page 117) they could be used with great efficiency. That opportunity should be not far distant now, and the R.A.F.'s heavy bombs would accelerate the downfall of Japan as surely and spectacularly as they aided the downfall of Germany.

HALIFAX BOMBER CARRIES FREIGHT in its bomb bay and eleven passengers in the fuselage as part of the Handley Page contribution to civil air transport. With a load of 12,000 lb. it has a range of 1,850 miles ; the bomb bay, redesigned as a freight boat, is seen in lowered position. See also page 534, Vol. 6 *Photo, C. E. Brown*

DISINTEGRATION of Japan's Air Strength is Proceeding Briskly

The figures of U.S. naval aircraft losses and those inflicted on the Japanese by American naval aviation indicate plainly that in the Far East the process of disintegration of Japan's air strength has proceeded along the road to its final demise. By April 1, 1945, the total U.S. Navy and Marine Corps aircraft losses for the Pacific war were 2,070 against a Japanese total of 11,601. In the first quarter of 1945 Japanese aircraft losses were 1,782 to the U.S. naval 188. From the beginning of the U.S. Navy's air offensive against the Japanese air forces the ratio of loss inflicted on the Japanese has risen from 3 to 1 to 9·4 to 1. (These figures do not include the losses inflicted and sustained by other Allied air formations.) In April the Japanese air force was estimated to have been reduced by 13 per cent ; over 2,500 Jap aircraft were destroyed that month.

President Truman stated on June 1, 1945, that the Japanese " air force still comprises over 3,000 combat (i.e. first-line) planes." (That was about the Luftwaffe's strength after the break-through in Normandy nearly 12 months ago.) President Truman also said in his message to Congress, " We are cutting heavily into Japanese aircraft production through our Super-Fortress raids, but Japan remains capable of producing planes at the rate of 1,250 to 1,500 a month."

IN April, 20 U.S. air bombardment groups received orders to move from Europe via the U.S.A. to the Far East. At the beginning of June the Eighth Air Force (now being strengthened by the addition of Super-Fortresses), the U.S.A. 20th Bomber Command from India, and the U.S. Army air units of the British-American Eastern Air Command, were moving nearer to Japan. Eastern Air Command became a R.A.F. formation when Major-General George E. Stratemeyer, its former U.S. commander, was succeeded on May 31, 1945, by Air Marshal W. A. Coryton, his former assistant. General Stratemeyer said on leaving, " With the fall of Rangoon our mission in Burma is accomplished and our joint task fulfilled." He has been promoted to Lieut.-General.

The American Army Air Force did fine work in Burma. Both tactical and transport squadrons of the U.S.A. 10th A.F. played a decisive part in repulsing the Japanese from the North Burma-China border and in re-opening the overland route to China. A captured Japanese officer attributed the defeat of the Japanese army in Burma to the Allies' superior mobility. This mobility was due almost entirely to air supply, wherein the Allied Air Forces reached a new Burma record by exceeding a lift of 2,900 tons a day in April.

The end of the war in Europe and the change from the Allied Military Government of Germany to the Allied Control Commission (which will have an air formation not subject to the attrition of war with A. C. M. Sir Sholto Douglas as A.O.C.-in-C. British Air Forces in Germany) will enable large formations of the R.A.F. to be moved East to operate against the Japanese invaders of the Malayan peninsula and the Netherlands East Indies. It is not now a matter of sending three squadrons of medium bombers from the Middle East, as was the case at the end of 1941 ; huge air forces with powerful aircraft are available. Probably the greatest need is the creation of new airfields, so there should be more work than ever for airfield construction companies.

While desperate fighting continues for the possession of all Okinawa, British carrier aircraft continue to bomb airfields in the Sakashima group, while U.S. carrier aircraft attack airfields in Kyushu, both to neutralize the Japanese counter-air offensive against the American forces fighting on Okinawa. The Japanese suicide airmen flying their Kamikaze aircraft right on to the decks of aircraft carriers have attempted to prevent this Allied intervention (see facing page). They have been reported to be using 500-lb. bombs in their suicide attacks. These would not be deadly against the big British Fleet carriers (the Indefatigable, Indomitable, Victorious and Illustrious have been named as serving in the Pacific Task Force), for these ships have armoured flight decks. On May 25 ships of the U.S. Fleet shot down 111 Jap planes off Okinawa. Two hundred carrier planes were over South Japan on June 2.

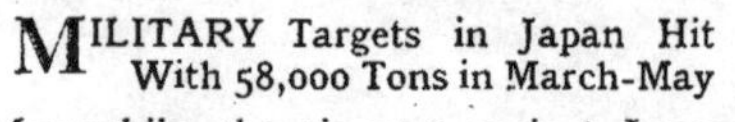

MILITARY Targets in Japan Hit With 58,000 Tons in March-May

Meanwhile, the air war against Japanese industry goes on from the Marianas and Iwojima. Attacks have been stepped up to sorties of 450 to 500 Super-Fortress bombers carrying greater weights of bombs than the 2,500 tons dropped by the R.A.F. on February 15, 1945, in Berlin's biggest raid. On May 16 Tokyo was attacked by a force from Iwojima. On May 16-17 500 Super-Forts dropped a million 6-lb. petrol-jelly bombs on Nagoya. Tokyo was the main target on May 19, but over 300 Super-Forts bombed Hamamatsu the same day ; here, 30 miles south-east of Nagoya, were four airfields, a railway centre, textile and war industries. On May 23 and 25 Tokyo was attacked by 500 Super-Forts ; on the first day 4,500 tons and on the second 4,000 tons of incendiaries fell.

On May 28 Yokohama was the target ; 500 Super-Forts dropped 3,200 tons following neutralizing attacks against the Jap defence fighters by Iwojima-based Mustangs ; 60,000 houses were destroyed and 250,000 persons rendered homeless. On June 1 Osaka received 3,275 tons of a new incendiary bomb called the M.74 containing a mixture of magnesium powder, phosphorus, and asphalt-thickened petrol jelly (see page 116) ; 150 fighters accompanied the 450 Super-Forts that made the raid ; and 86 square miles of the city were reduced to ashes. Nearby Sakai was also burning. Over 58,000 tons of bombs were dropped on Japanese military targets in the three months March to May, and at least 43 of Japan's biggest war factories were hit. The Japanese aircraft industry has been ordered to disperse still more and increase fighter production. Fifty-one square miles of Tokyo and about half Yokohama are destroyed.

THE airman's worst enemy, ground fog, has been defeated by the war development of petrol burner apparatus around airfield runways. Known as FIDO, from its war-time code name of Fog Investigation Disposal Operation, the apparatus uses 70,000 gallons of fuel an hour to clear fog by heat. First successful experiment was on November 4, 1942. First experimental fog landing was on July 17, 1943. Since then more than 2,500 Allied aircraft have been safely landed in fog. This British-developed apparatus helped to foil Rundstedt's offensive, which was launched in fog.

The first R.C.A.F. squadron to return home (15 Lancasters) left Britain on June 4.

Death-Plunge Tactics in Hot Pacific Battles

ATTEMPTING A SPECTACULAR SUICIDE DIVE on a U.S. task-force carrier, a Japanese twin-engined bomber was hit by Ack-Ack gunners on an Essex-type carrier nearby and disintegrated (1). The bomber is seen (2) in its last nose-dive. Driven forward by heat and flame, the crew of the U.S. carrier Franklin (see story in page 122) clustered on the listing flight-deck (3), after the vessel had been set ablaze on March 19, 1945. The cruiser Santa Fé (left) came alongside to help fight the fires and remove the wounded.

Photos, L.N.A., Central Press

Editor's Postscript

For nearly five years many simple pleasures were forbidden for complicated but only too obvious reasons. I mean such utterly innocuous, inexpensive and unobtrusive delights as sitting on the beach at Brighton, Eastbourne and other seaside resorts—or walking through Richmond Park. And now, every week-end, people are taking these pleasures again, a little warily, a little guiltily, as though the fruit were still forbidden, trying with varying success, amid the fragments of barbed wire, to accustom themselves to the attractions of a new freedom. Richmond Park was reopened to the public in good time for the rhododendrons, after some years as an Army camp and a centre for experiments in bomb disposal. Over Whitsuntide there must have been many who made a first tentative pilgrimage thither, anxious to discover the worst that had happened to their favourite walks in this most beautiful and generous of London's royal parks. Most of the old tracks are still recognizable, though roughened and a trifle overgrown. Army lorries and Bren-gun carriers have not left too marked an impression. Many acres are at present under cultivation, railed off, with apposite notices saying: "This crop is YOUR FOOD." Nobody will object to that, especially as the wonderful vistas for which the park is famous are all the richer by reason of the brilliant green of the crops. The Pen Ponds have been drained, presumably as too useful a guide for the Luftwaffe. White Lodge, where the Duke of Windsor was born, and the present King and Queen began their married life, has taken a bad knock. But you can still see the dome of St. Paul's from the brow of the hill by Richmond Gate, and that is something no man could be sure of when the gates were sealed in 1940.

After the Crystal Palace, the Alexandra Palace is now also planning to get itself rebuilt and revivified. Months ago I wrote (page 511, Vol. 8) what I thought of schemes for a new Crystal Palace, and any proposal to perpetuate the life of its even uglier half-sister on London's northern horizon leaves me equally unenthusiastic. R. L. Stevenson once bracketed the two together in one sentence as symbols of London's utmost limits: "Behold! from one end to another of the city . . . from the Alexandra to the Crystal Palace, there is light!". I can claim a particular interest in the Alexandra Palace, for at one period of my life I was condemned to see it every time I looked out of my bedroom window, and, during the First Great War, to listen to the band playing there for the delectation of the German internees who peopled it! Just as the monster of Sydenham Hill commemorated the Great Exhibition of 1851, so the monster of Muswell Hill was reconstructed from the buildings that housed the International Exhibition of 1862. It had its big fire very early in its history, the first building being gutted a fortnight after its opening, in 1873. As a suburban musical and amusements centre it had its little heyday, but it never recovered from its treatment during the last war when it was occupied first by a crowd of German prisoners, then by an even bigger crowd of Civil servants.

Since then it has fallen into shabby neglect, and has long been just a great sprawl of ornamented nothingness, an off-white elephant of a place. The Grand Hall, when I last visited it, reminded me of an enormous provincial railway station without any railway in it. There was a sprinkling of ancient automatic machines and advertisements, and a few pieces of dusty and decaying plaster statuary. Then in 1936 whatever virtue of symmetry the exterior of the Alexandra Palace had possessed was destroyed by the B.B.C.'s giant television mast, shooting upwards from one of the corner towers, as disproportionate to the rest of the building as the building itself is to the rest of the landscape. Nevertheless, this was a sign of vitality. Television belongs to the future; the rest of the Palace belongs only too obviously to a not very glorious past. Might it not be the best hope for "Ally Pally," as the B.B.C. people call it, if it were given over entirely to the development of television and rebuilt to that purpose?

It is recorded that when the young Queen Victoria returned to Buckingham Palace after all the pomp and ceremony of her coronation and all the acclamation of loyal citizens in the streets, the first thing she did was to put off her magnificent robes and bath her favourite dog, Dash. Another "royal" dog figured in a tailpiece—or should it be tail-wagging piece?—to the recent Victory celebrations in London. Again the scene was Buckingham Palace, the exterior this time. It was just after midnight at the end of V Day plus one. Their Majesties had acknowledged the greetings of their cheering subjects for the last time, the floodlights had been switched off, the crowds were quickly dispersing. But a few groups of people still lingered by the railings, vaguely disinclined, even in the face of the sudden blackness, to sever too abruptly those ties which seemed to bind the Londoner with peculiar intimacy to the persons of his King and Queen. They were rewarded. For presently a door opened and a servant appeared in the forecourt with a dog. It was Crackers, the Queen's Corgi, out for his nightly airing, probably somewhat impatient that it had been delayed so long. On this exceptional occasion Crackers was introduced to the people through the railings and was held up so that his handsome proportions could be generally admired. Then he was led back to bed. "Where does he sleep?" an over-inquisitive woman asked, and was courteously rebuked with, "I wouldn't like to tell you that, madam." Those who took part in this informal encounter with an important and privileged member of the Royal household found it a happy little anti-climax to all the tumult and the shouting.

MR. HERBERT MORRISON, Home Secretary since October 1940, leaving the Home Office on May 28, 1945, after he and the other Labour Ministers in the Cabinet had handed back their seals of office to H.M. the King. This followed Mr. Churchill's resignation five days earlier. *Photo, Keystone*

That persistent superstition which discourages three smokers from sharing one match was unknown before the 1914–18 war. It had a common-sense basis, for sad experience in the trenches of France proved that the extra split-second required for the lighting of a third cigarette was just long enough for an enemy sniper to get his sights trained on the spot. Has this war seen as firm a rooting of any new superstition, I wonder. Not so far as my inquiries go. The Navy has stuck to its traditional ones. The R.A.F., most likely source of new inventions in this line, seems content to cherish its beloved gremlins, which are devised to cover broadly every occasion of good or ill luck. Again, this war seems to have produced no myths or legends so circumstantial or so widely believed as those of the Angels of Mons or the thousands of Russian reinforcements "with snow on their boots" who were supposed to have been rushed through Great Britain in September 1914, or the theory that an undrowned Lord Kitchener would turn up at the war's end after completing a highly dangerous and complicated mission. Against these colourful credulities of 1914–18 we can set only a few promissory signs in the sky and an insistence that the full truth has not yet been revealed about that September night in 1940 when the church bells rang their warnings all over the West of England. But what need is there for legend, indeed, in a war that has been so generous with extravagant facts? What could be more pleasantly incredible than the mad flight of Rudolf Hess?

The much-abused race of statisticians have, it appears, contrived a new yard-stick. It is called the "Net Reproduction Rate," and is now the accepted device for representing trends of population. Calculation of the figure is intricate, but it has one supreme advantage: it tells at a glance whether a nation's population is growing. The method employed takes into account births, expectation of life, age and sex distribution, and deaths. Briefly, a net reproduction rate of 1·0 indicates that the mothers in the nation are giving birth to the same number of potential mothers within a generation. That is to say, a net rate of 1·0 means that a community is just managing to reproduce itself and no more. If the figure is over 1·0 the population is growing; if less than 1·0 it is decreasing. The net Reproduction Rate of England and Wales in 1931–32, for instance, was ·81. This meant that the following generation would be a little over four-fifths of the 1931–32 generation. By the Net Reproduction Rate, therefore, we can compare one nation's population trend with another's. I glean these facts from a highly topical (and disturbing) sixpenny pamphlet by Mr. L. J. Cadbury, entitled This Question of Populations: Europe in 1970, which the News Chronicle has put out. Mr. Cadbury's population forecast of the Europe of 25 years hence is intimately bound up with any effective European settlement we may achieve—especially if we recall that from 1918–38 the populations of Southern and Eastern Europe alone increased by 20,000,000 and were virtually hemmed in. Fascism of any kind must not be allowed to provide the answer this time. Mr. Cadbury's solution would seem to be that of increasing industrialization.

North Pole to London With Our Roving Camera

PROTECTING SCAPA FLOW, famous naval base in the Orkneys, against U-boats, barrier roadways had been laid across the neighbouring straits. One of the roadways formally opened to traffic by Mr. A. V. Alexander, early in May 1945.

NEW RAIL COACHES, seen being painted, were the first to be built by the L.M.S. in five years. A switch-over from war-production, they formed part of better travel facilities, providing seats for 33,000 passengers on this line.

AFTER HER TRANS-POLAR FLIGHT, the R.A.F. Lancaster research plane Aries touched down at the Empire Air Navigation School at Shawbury, Shropshire, on May 26. She had flown non-stop from the Yukon over the N. magnetic and geographical poles.

IN WESTMINSTER ABBEY, workmen in late May began removing the 80,000 sandbags which had successfully protected the historic monuments against air-raid damage (below).

GRATEFUL FOR W.V.S. HELP IN SEWING on badges and chevrons, these British ex-P.O.W. had been freed by the Red Army. Scheme for sending home 30,000 from Russian-held territory came into operation on May 23, 1945.

Photos, British Official, G.P.U., Planet News, Fox.

Riverside Respite for Our Men in Germany

BY THE SHADY BANKS OF THE RIVER ELBE men of the British 2nd Army relaxed during the heat-wave which spread over Germany immediately after the enemy's unconditional surrender. It was at the mouth of the Elbe, only a few days before, that—with the fall of Lübeck and Wismar on May 2, 1945, and of Hamburg twenty-four hours later—the whole northern German defence system collapsed under the crushing weight of Field-Marshal Montgomery's armies. See also illus. page 64.
Photo, British Newspaper Pool

Printed in England and published every alternate Friday by the Proprietors, THE AMALGAMATED PRESS, LTD., The Fleetway House, Farringdon Street, London, E.C.4. Registered for transmission by Canadian Magazine Post. Sole Agents for Australia and New Zealand: Messrs. Gordon & Gotch, Ltd.; and for South Africa: Central News Agency, Ltd.—June 22nd, 1945. S.S. *Editorial Address:* JOHN CARPENTER HOUSE, WHITEFRIARS, LONDON, E.C.4.

Vol 9 **The War Illustrated** No 210

SIXPENCE Edited by Sir John Hammerton JULY 6, 1945

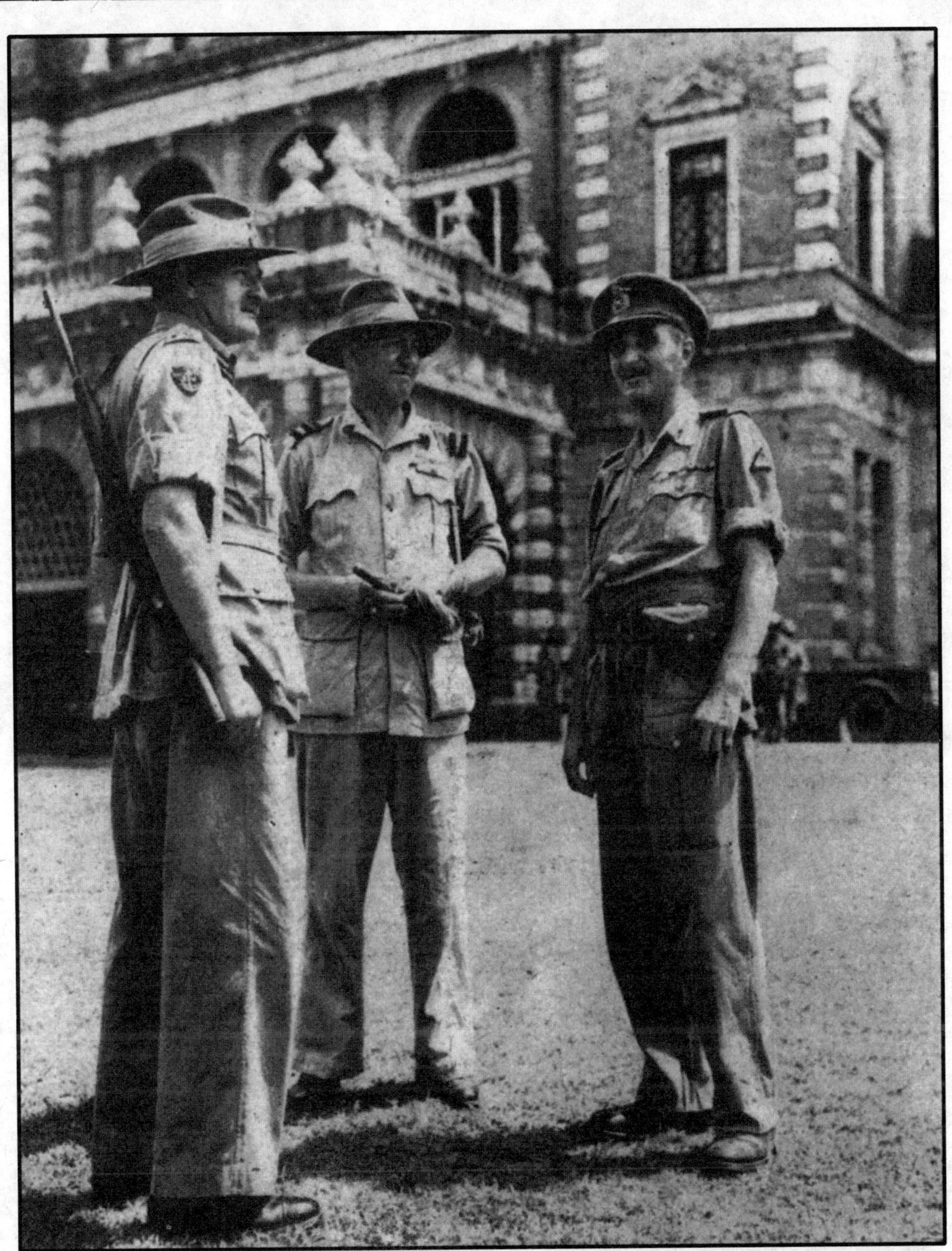

LEADERS IN THE BURMA CAMPAIGN met in Rangoon after the city's fall on May 3, 1945. They are (left to right) Lt.-Gen. Sir William Slim, G.O.C.-in-C. the 14th Army; Air Marshal S. F. Vincent, A.O.C. 221st Group, R.A.F.; and Maj.-Gen. H. M. Chambers, commanding the 26th Division which occupied Rangoon. British forces were carrying the full weight of the Burma fighting, it was declared on June 9, following the transfer of the U.S. Mars Task Force to China, and the withdrawal of the U.S. air forces from S.E.A.C. Formation of a new Army—the 12th—under Lt.-Gen. Sir Montagu Stopford, was announced on May 31. *Photo, British Official*

NO. 211 WILL BE PUBLISHED FRIDAY, **JULY 20**

Island Gateway to Rich Oilfields of Borneo

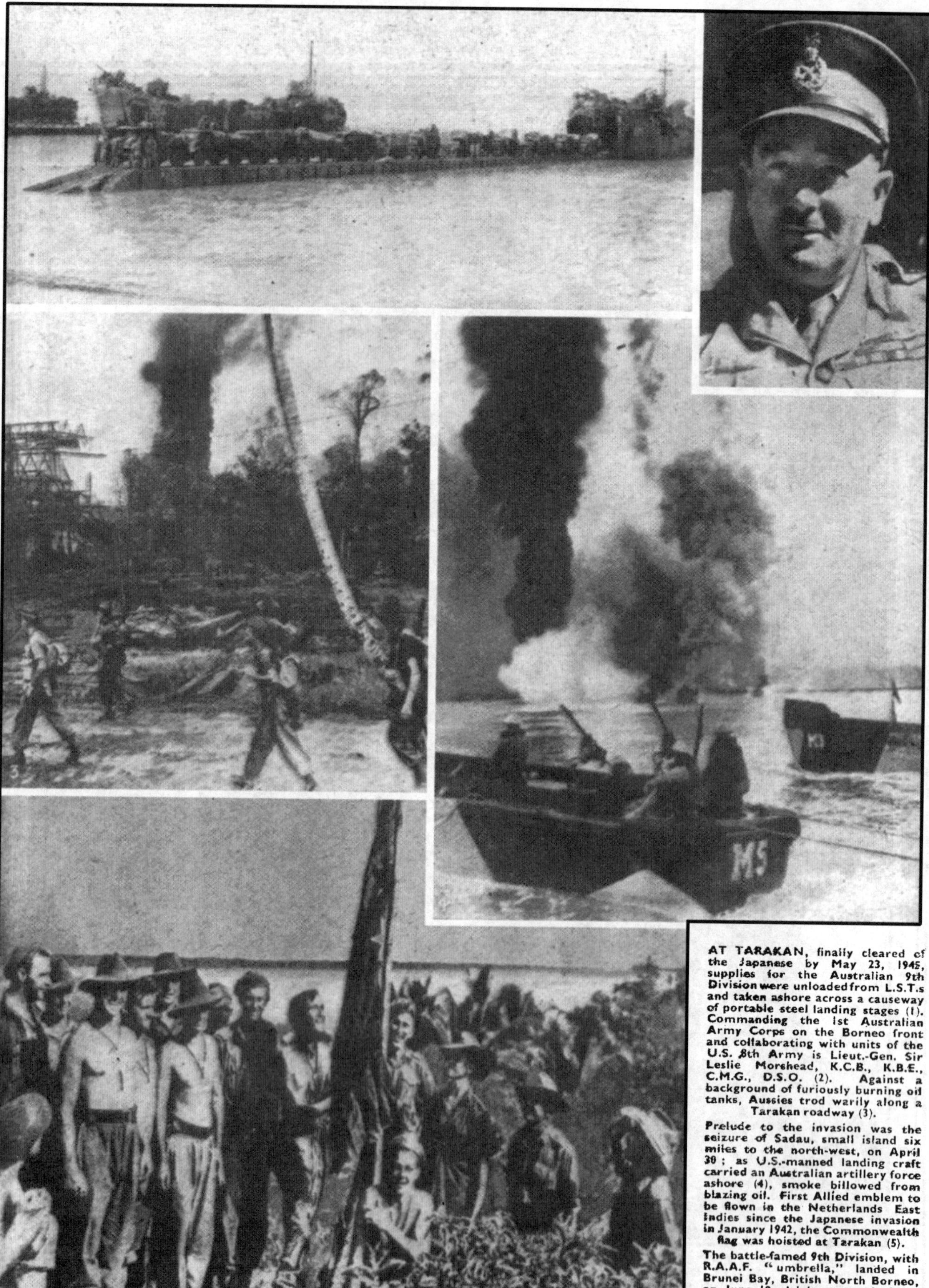

AT TARAKAN, finally cleared of the Japanese by May 23, 1945, supplies for the Australian 9th Division were unloaded from L.S.T.s and taken ashore across a causeway of portable steel landing stages (1). Commanding the 1st Australian Army Corps on the Borneo front and collaborating with units of the U.S. 8th Army is Lieut.-Gen. Sir Leslie Morshead, K.C.B., K.B.E., C.M.G., D.S.O. (2). Against a background of furiously burning oil tanks, Aussies trod warily along a Tarakan roadway (3).

Prelude to the invasion was the seizure of Sadau, small island six miles to the north-west, on April 30; as U.S.-manned landing craft carried an Australian artillery force ashore (4), smoke billowed from blazing oil. First Allied emblem to be flown in the Netherlands East Indies since the Japanese invasion in January 1942, the Commonwealth flag was hoisted at Tarakan (5).

The battle-famed 9th Division, with R.A.A.F. "umbrella," landed in Brunei Bay, British North Borneo, on June 10, driving towards Sarawak. See facing page, also page 100.

Photos, Australian Official, Central Press, Associated Press, Keystone

With Our Armies Today

By MAJ.-GENERAL
SIR CHARLES GWYNN
K.C.B., D.S.O.

It may seem to many that the task of establishing order in the chaos created by the surrender of the German armies and the liberation of millions of prisoners of war and slave labourers is proceeding slowly. It is, of course, impossible from a distance to realize fully the complexities of the task or the necessity of some of the expedients that have been adopted. We are apt to give undue weight to views expressed by those who, on the spot, have strictly limited interests and few opportunities of becoming acquainted with all the aspects of the problem involved.

Yet it does not require much exercise of the imagination to realize the number of problems that have to be dealt with and their scale, and in forming our opinions I suggest that it is better to rely on our common sense than individual criticism.

There is one point especially which excites general interest, that is the attitude that should be adopted by the Armies of Occupation towards the German people. We all, I think, agree that while operations were in progress and in the early days after the German surrender, strict orders forbidding fraternization were necessary, not only to prevent leakage of information and to maintain the vigilance of the troops but also to impress on the German people that they cannot escape their responsibility for the war and for atrocities committed. There is no doubt, however, that as the Armies of Occupation settle down these orders will become increasingly irksome to the troops to a degree that would almost certainly lead to their evasion. That, of course, would be exceedingly bad for discipline.

I feel sure, therefore, that in due course the orders will be modified or cancelled, and will perhaps be replaced by advice and instructions in general terms as to the attitude the troops should adopt and with which they will be expected to comply for the credit of their respective units. It is often better and easier to establish a tradition of behaviour than to attempt to enforce rigorous orders which are easy to evade. Many regimental and Army traditions are based on well-recognized rules of conduct rather than on orders. Certain things are "done" or "not done."

General Eisenhower's relaxation of orders in respect to children is clearly a concession to the uncontrollable instincts of his men, and Field-Marshal Montgomery's broadcast to the German people also explains to his troops the reasons for the attitude he has ordered them to adopt. Once those reasons are clearly grasped much, I think, may be left to the good sense of the men themselves. In the first instance, however, it could hardly be left to the individual judgement of the men to define "fraternization" or to decide on a standard of behaviour.

Brunei Bay a Base for Tighter Grip on Jap Sea Communications

The very successful landing of Australian troops in British North Borneo is an interesting development. Once again it has been proved that Australia not only still produces fighting men of outstanding quality but also possesses generals of exceptional ability. Lieut.-Gen. Sir Leslie Morshead, who has conducted the operations in Borneo, is a notable example. In the last war he served with great distinction as a regimental officer, and in this war his defence of Tobruk will never be forgotten. Since then he has shown time and again equal skill in offensive operations under most difficult conditions.

Clearly, Brunei Bay will provide a valuable base from which to exercise a tighter stranglehold on Japanese sea communications in the East Indies. It brings the Indo-China coast and the eastern entrance to the Straits of Malacca within comparatively close range for air and naval operations. It may also provide a stepping-stone for the acquisition of bases still nearer to Singapore. I do not think, however, that the landing implies any immediate intention of recovering the whole of Borneo, for it is evident that the Allies are still engaged in the battle for bases prior to launching their main offensive. The strategic purpose of the Brunei operation is easier to see than that on Tarakan.

Both deprive the Japanese of valuable sources of oil supply, and both give a tighter control over sea communication, but Brunei much more clearly suggests a stepping-stone operation. It is possible that Tarakan may have been intended to some degree to be a diversionary operation or a preliminary one to deprive the enemy of airfields from which he could attack shipping at Brunei. It will be interesting to see whether the Japanese possess in the East Indies an air force of effective strength. At Okinawa, from their bases in Japan and Formosa, they have been able to make formidable attacks on American shipping, but it seems improbable that in the East Indies they will have sufficient resources to exploit similar tactics.

The comparative ease with which the landings at Tarakan and Brunei have been effected prove conclusively, though it might have been expected, that the Japanese garrisons in the islands, large as their total strength probably is, are quite inadequate to protect the immense length of coastline. No doubt local garrisons may be able to withdraw into the interior or to offer prolonged resistance in positions favourable to defence, but that can have little effect on the strategic development of the Allied campaign. The decisive factor is that the Japanese by losing control of sea communications have lost strategic mobility, whereas the Allies, as they develop new bases, steadily acquire it over a constantly widening area. However successfully Allied strategy develops, it is certain that at the more vital centres there will be tactical operations demanding great sacrifices; unless, as seems improbable, the Japanese Government agrees to surrender and its outlying forces obey orders to lay down their arms.

In the case of Japan herself it is obviously inconceivable that if she was determined to prolong a fanatical struggle we should embark on a war of extermination such as is in progress on Okinawa. We should presumably be content to capture and occupy points which would render her impotent.

Problems of Japanese Outlying Detachments in Cut-Off Islands

The policy to be adopted as regards her outlying detachments may, however, involve more difficult decisions. Large areas will have to be recovered and native populations liberated. On small islands of strategic importance extermination may be necessary even at heavy cost; but in the larger islands that might prove an interminable process involving prohibitive exertions, even if carried out piecemeal.

Assuming, as seems possible, that there will be no formal surrender or withdrawal of troops we may be compelled to suspend military operations except in as far as they might be necessary to re-establish control over the greater part of the territories involved, and to accept the existence of colonies of Japanese in certain areas which might eventually be assimilated. Such colonies might for a period be capable of defending small areas, but without means of communication or contacts with their home islands they could not exercise control outside them, because for defence they would be compelled to concentrate. No doubt a considerable mixed population would develop, but the numbers of pure-blooded Japanese would be bound to decrease. Apart from the cost involved, the danger of continuing active operations beyond what was necessary for recovery of control would be that the Japanese remnants might become bandits, preying on the country, rather than recognized colonists.

It is quite clear that Japan realizes the danger she is in and that she would be prepared to make peace on face-saving terms, but though I am optimistic enough to believe that she may eventually accept unconditional surrender, that cannot be counted on implicitly. Japanese fanaticism is of a different order from German fanaticism, and there are many military and other factors which make it unsafe to count too confidently on the complete abandonment of a suicidal policy. It is well, therefore, that we should be prepared for such a possibility and to form a clear idea of our commitments and essential and practicable aims.

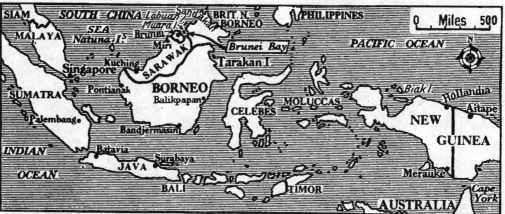

NETHERLANDS EAST INDIES, which include Sumatra, Java and Celebes, besides large portions of Borneo and New Guinea—to an extent of almost 750,000 square miles—was the scene of much heavy fighting in May and June 1945, in which combined naval, land and air forces of Britain, the U.S. and Australia took part. Brunei Bay, North Borneo, was invaded by the Australian 9th Division on June 10. *By courtesy of News Chronicle*

Our Relief Programme for Hun-Wrecked Holland

FLOODS RELEASED by the retreating Germans gravely imperilled Holland. Almost totally submerged was the village of Wieringerwerf (1), April 16, 1945. A Dutch housewife could not take her eyes off Allied relief food at a distribution centre in Utrecht (2). Officers and men of the 2nd Battalion Princess Louise's Regiment of the 49th Division (the "Kensingtons"), who had fought all through the Dutch campaign, subscribed £1,100 for the Netherlands Red Cross; Princess Juliana received the cheque at Nijmegen on June 6, when she chatted with Maj.-Gen. Rawlings, G.O.C. the 49th Division (3, left) and Lieut.-Col. Glover, commanding the battalion. Members of a British road patrol (4) interrogated a Dutch family (with belongings) trying to enter a built-up area without a pass and thus interfere with the relief programme.

Photos, British Official, Planet News

From War to Occupation Duties 'Over There'

THE GUARDS' Armoured Division said good-bye to their tanks, after five years of mechanized warfare, at a parade on June 9, 1945, at Rothenburg, Germany, where the farewell salute was taken by Field-Marshal Montgomery standing in a jeep (1, left centre background); they are to become an infantry division once more. The casino in Blankenberghe, peacetime Belgian seaside resort, was re-opened by NAAFI as a club for our Forces (2). Alsatians (3) were German police-dogs; taken into the British 2nd Army for guarding military property, they are being groomed by men of the Veterinary and Remount Corps. With our army near Kiel, troops of the Seaforth Highlanders (4) off duty go to "the pictures" in the town by landing craft manned by a German crew. A.T.S. girls of the 137th mixed heavy A.A. Regiment arrived on June 5 by air for service at Hamburg; they are seen (5) leaving their aircraft at Luneburg.

Photos, British Official, Newspaper Pool

With Our Navies Today

By

FRANCIS E. McMURTRIE

It has taken three months to conquer the island of Okinawa (see illus. page 117), in spite of the fact that the initial landing after a series of bombardments by the U.S. Fifth Fleet under Admiral Spruance met with only light opposition. Apparently the Japanese had based their preparations on the belief that the American forces, marines and soldiers, would be landed in the south-eastern sector of the 60-mile long island. Instead, they came ashore near its centre, on the west coast.

Though the Yontan airfield was occupied with trifling loss, an immensely strong line of defences was encountered to the north of Naha, the capital, and it took weeks of the hardest fighting, with heavy casualties, to overcome the resistance that developed thenceforward. It became a matter of entirely wiping out the Japanese garrison, together with a considerable number of civilians who had been drawn into the defensive organization. As at Iwojima, caves and underground galleries formed part of the scheme of defence; and in some areas high cliffs honeycombed with these workings had to be scaled by the Americans.

All this time the Fifth Fleet was protecting the anchorages in which lay the transports, landing craft and supply vessels maintaining the invading forces. No longer able to muster sufficient sea strength to intervene effectively, the Japanese have for some time past devoted their energies to "suicide" attacks, using both aircraft and flying bombs directed towards their targets by pilots prepared to sacrifice their lives to this end. Though great numbers have been shot down by Allied planes and A.A. guns, some of these attacks have had a certain degree of success, as evidenced by the casualties officially reported by the Navy Department.

OKINAWA Operations Rank With Those for Normandy Invasion

These casualties included loss of 11 destroyers, the U.S.S. Bush, Colhoun, Drexler, Emmons, Halligan, Little, Longshaw, Luce, Mannert L. Abele, Morrison and Pringle. All are fine modern vessels designed for operating in the Pacific; the Mannert L. Abele, indeed, was one of the 2,200-ton ships of the Allen M. Sumner class, considered by their builders to be the last word in destroyer design. With the exception of the Emmons, which is a 1,700-ton destroyer adapted for minesweeping duties, the others all belong to the 2,100-ton Fletcher class. Two fleet minesweepers of 700 tons, the Skylark and Swallow, together with two destroyers converted into transports, the Dickerson and Bates, have also been lost, as well as a number of supply vessels, landing craft and other auxiliaries. Various other warships of different categories have received damage of a more or less serious nature.

PRINZ EUGEN'S officers lined up on deck when the 10,000-tons German cruiser was handed over to Royal Navy authorities at the Port of Copenhagen on May 22, 1945. See also page 103. *Photo, Associated Press*

It is clear, therefore, that even regarded from a purely naval standpoint the Okinawa operations deserve to rank with those for the invasion of Normandy; for though the actual number of ships employed may have been less, they had to operate from bases far more distant. Once the troops were put ashore, the protecting warships had to depend for supplies on their own resources in the way of depot and repair ships, as the nearest base able to deal with a fleet's immediate needs was Guam, 1,500 miles away.

With Okinawa in U.S. hands, a fresh base will doubtless be established there, simplifying problems of supply and opening the way to future attacks upon enemy installations in the other islands of the Ryukyu group, in Formosa and in Japan itself. Its excellent harbour facilities were undoubtedly one of the main reasons for the choice of Okinawa as an objective.

If it has taken a quarter of a year to overcome the resistance of the Okinawa garrison, how long will it be before the main Japanese forces—hardly tapped up to the present so far as armies are concerned—are defeated? The United States Secretary of the Navy, Mr. James Forrestal, recently stated: "I expect that the Japanese will fight with increasing tenacity and fury as our power begins to concentrate on their homeland. We have seen evidences of that fury at Iwojima and Okinawa. It will take the full power of the tremendous war potential that we have mustered in the past four years if we are to secure complete, unequivocal and unconditional surrender of Japanese militarism." From this it may be assumed that we shall be lucky if we see the end of the war in the Pacific in 1946.

ENORMOUS Concentration of Naval Power Building-up in Pacific

For the subjection of Japan there is now being assembled in the Pacific the largest concentration of naval power the world has ever seen. In addition to the fleets provided by the United States Navy, which is now nearing the peak of its strength, this country is dispatching additional ships and personnel to the Far East as fast as they can be provided. It may be assumed that in the course of a few months there will be left in European waters only such forces of the Royal Navy as may be considered sufficient to deal with any local difficulties that may emerge from the aftermath of a great war. Ships so employed will be mainly the older units, with those more suitable for service in home waters and the Mediterranean, such as the smaller cruisers and destroyers of the escort type.

Two instances of the ingenious methods used by the Germans to facilitate the operations of their U-boats have recently come to light. One was a compact little handbook, Die Handelsflotten der Welt (Merchant Fleets of the World), containing particulars of every merchant vessel in existence. As in the case of Lloyd's Register, from which the details would appear to have been copied, these are listed in two sections, the first comprising ships of 1,000 tons gross and upwards, the other smaller craft. A most ingenious code enabled the user of the book to refer to a series of outline drawings showing the appearance of each ship, so that the identification of every type was a simple matter.

In the introduction there is an elaborate key to this code, with examples of how it should be used. It consists of letters and figures denoting the number and arrangement of masts, funnels and deck erections, and reflects credit on the author of the book, Dr. Erich Gröner. Before the war Dr. Gröner was well known as the illustrations editor of the German naval annual, Taschenbuch der Kriegsflotten. There is no doubt his mercantile fleet handbook proved of considerably greater value to the German Navy than the publication with which he was first connected. Other sections of the book contain lists of shipowners all over the world, with the ships controlled or managed by each, and the names of the principal shipbuilders in each country. U-boat captains must have relied extensively on this handy little volume.

Another instance is equally interesting. In spite of precautions taken since the war began, tide tables of the estuary of the St. Lawrence, the great river of Eastern Canada, were found in U-boats that surrendered. These tables had also been regarded as confidential since 1939, but it is not easy to keep inviolate data of this kind, which from its very nature have to be communicated to numbers of people. Possibly when enemy records come to be examined the channels by which such information travelled may be exposed.

H.M.S. KING GEORGE V ARRIVED AT GUAM, it was announced on May 31, 1945, heading a British Pacific Fleet task force operating with the U.S. Pacific Fleet. Flagship of Vice-Admiral Sir Bernard Rawlings, she was escorted by the destroyers Troubridge, Tenacious and Termagant, with whom she went into action off the Sakishima group on March 27. See also facing page and illus. in page 141. *Photo, Associated Press*

Quarter-Deck Greetings to Our Men in the Pacific

ADMIRAL CHESTER L. NIMITZ, C.-in-C. OF THE U.S. PACIFIC FLEET and commander of all Allied Pacific naval operations, standing beneath the 14-in. guns of the British battleship King George V, as she docked in Guam harbour after being in action off the Sakishima group, hailed Royal Naval co-operation in the Japanese theatre of war, it was announced on May 31, 1945. Addressing the ship's company from the quarter-deck he declared, "From the very beginning we have welcomed your coming and we will continue to welcome your help!" British Pacific Fleet units pounded Truk atoll (Carolines) on June 15-16. See also facing page, and page 141 *Photo, Keystone*

Along the Terrible Trail that Led to Wewak

Last Japanese-held port on the mainland of British New Guinea, Wewak fell to the 6th Australian Division on May 19, 1945. Two-thirds of the 30,000 enemy troops defending it perished. The remainder had but one escape route to the west—along the disease-ridden Sepik River. The Allied path to victory is specially described for "The War Illustrated" by ROY MACARTNEY.

NEW GUINEA is liberally besprinkled with sleepy mission towns and tiny trading ports which sprang overnight into the headlines when engulfed by the Japanese drive of 1942. One by one they have returned to the keeping of Australia, each with its mangled planes, bomb-blasted stores, rusting hulks, shattered bungalows and splintered palms as record of the swift rise and decline of Japan in the fluctuating fortunes of the Pacific War.

Wewak, formerly administrative centre of the Sepik River district, is such a town. Standing on a raised headland, it boasts perhaps a dozen buildings. Its narrow bay provides a rather poor shelter for sea-going craft, a large coral reef near the shore nullifying what few natural advantages it possesses. Prospectors before the war discovered rich alluvial gold at Maprik, 45 miles westwards from Wewak in the rugged Torricelli Mountains, and the sleepy little port was the main supply base for the goldfields. Copra was practically the only other commercial interest, neat coconut plantations flanking numerous missions along the flat coastal plain. There were several traces of oil found in the Sepik area, but although many bores were put down it was not located in any paying quantities.

Following their conquest in 1942, the Japanese quickly turned Wewak into their major air base on the northern New Guinea littoral. They enlarged the existing field at Wewak, constructed another at Boram, five miles to the south-east, and hacked two more out of the jungle at But, 27 miles, and Dagua 20 miles to the north-west.

Wewak was a busy base, lying as it did in the lifeline of airfields the Japanese constructed to their outposts at Rabaul and Salamaua. From its fields large numbers of bombers took off daily to hammer the last Allied toeholds in New Guinea at Port Moresby and Milne Bay, but Japan's early aerial superiority quickly slipped from her hands and by August 1943 the scales were ready to tip in favour of the Allies.

Mighty Punch to be Delivered

Australian and American aircraft by that time were operating from bases as far north as Dobadura, outside Buna, but Wewak was still out of their fighter range. While heavy bombers maintained a sporadic bombardment of the base, American engineers prepared a surprise knock-out blow for the once omnipotent Japanese New Guinea air force. They were secretly flown into a small flat at Tsili Tsili, in the upper Watut Valley, beyond Wau, early in June 1943. By mid-August they had completed a formidable fighter base, and the Fifth Air Force was ready to deliver its mighty punch.

Early on the morning of August 16, 100 Mitchells, escorted by the same number of Lightnings, skimmed in low over the coconut palms at Wewak and took the Japanese completely by surprise. They had no fighters in the air, Ack-Ack guns were not manned, and at Boram 60 enemy bombers and fighters were lined up ready for a raid on one of our bases. Within the space of a few minutes Allied planes had accounted for nearly 170 grounded enemy planes and added another word to their vocabulary. Thereafter, to "Wewak" an objective was to blast it out of existence.

By January 1944 Wewak was well within the field of land operations as Australians drove along the northern coast beyond Finschhafen and the Americans broke clear of the Vitiaz straits with landings on New Britain and in the Admiralties.

It was clear the Japanese expected the next Allied amphibious blow to fall upon Wewak. With what small craft they could still smuggle through, they rushed reinforcements to the area; and at the same time withdrew to strongly prepared positions behind the Sepik what remained of the formations the Australians had mauled on the Huon Peninsula.

When General MacArthur struck, he by-passed Wewak, landing instead at Hollandia and Aitape, 100 miles to the west; within 24 hours of the American seizure of Aitape, Australian engineers had whipped the nearby strip of Tadji into operational condition and Australian fighters were patrolling the sky over the vitally important objective of Hollandia.

Aitape fitted into the American strategy only as a staging point along the road to the Philippines and Tokyo, and as with all such bases General MacArthur was content to build up a perimeter defence to cover the airfields and leave the by-passed Japanese to their own ends. Despite the constant pounding given them by Australian Beaufighters and Beauforts operating from the Tadji strip, by July the Japanese had been able to move up sufficient men and material from Wewak under cover of darkness to stage what the Americans describe as a "reaction."

They furiously counter-attacked the eastern approaches of the 20 mile perimeter held by two American divisions with the support of an attached Cavalry Regiment. Savage hand-to-hand fighting went on for days, the fanatical Japanese discounting the losses they suffered at the hands of the Americans and from low-flying Australian bombers.

LATE last year the American divisions were wanted for the Philippines operation, and the 6th Australian Division relieved the American force, which was twice its size. Its role was not just to hold the airfield but to drive a hundred miles down the coast to Wewak and liquidate the Japanese still remaining in the area.

Australian Intelligence successfully contrived to convince the numerically superior Japanese that they were opposed not only by the 6th Australian Division but also by an additional full division. Small as was the Australian force detailed for the operation, its prowess and battle experience were in marked inverse proportion to its size. Of all Australian Divisions, the 6th is perhaps the most famous. Formed in 1939, it was composed of the first Australian volunteers in this war. It opened its account with the storming of Bardia and Tobruk, followed with the gallant struggles of Greece, Crete and Syria, and, returning to the Pacific, spearheaded the drive across the Kokoda trail, and other arduous early New Guinea campaigns.

EARLY spectacular results were not possible when the Australians took over last November. First, it was necessary to stem the steady stream of Japanese who were by-passing Aitape to the south through the Torricelli Mountains and making their way westward. Veterans of the 17th Brigade drove inland into the razor-edged mountains. Struggling over terrible terrain, they hacked and wended their way over a series of heart-breaking ridges, closing one escape track after another in the face of sporadic but desperate Japanese resistance. When they captured Maprik, former gold centre, their arduous task was completed.

Meanwhile, the 16th Brigade had driven forward from the holding line the Americans had established east of Aitape and were rolling up the Japanese along the flat, swampy coastal strip leading to Wewak. The numerically superior enemy stubbornly contested every yard of the way, sowing numerous mines and taking every advantage of the terrain. Between Aitape and Wewak, Australian engineers constructed no less than 80 bridges: a grand achievement.

N.E. NEW GUINEA, showing Aitape and the important enemy-held base of Wewak which finally collapsed on May 19, 1945. Division of the island into Netherlands possessions, Australian-mandated territory and the Australian-owned Territory of Papua is shown (inset).

Eighty miles lay behind the Australians early in April 1945 when they increased the tempo of their advance and took But and Dagua airfields at the point of the bayonet in irresistible charges. The fresh 19th Brigade, which early in the war had marched and fought 29 miles in the opening day of the break-through inside the Tobruk perimeter, took the ball from the feet of the 16th Brigade.

H.M.S. Newfoundland, H.M.A.S. Hobart, supporting destroyers and Australian and American bombers, delivered a tremendous bombardment to pave the way for the final assault late in May. Headed by tanks the 19th swept across the base of the Wewak peninsula, then moved in to stamp out the 800 Japanese who had remained to make a last stand. Using flame-throwers, explosives and grenades, they liquidated the enemy one by one in their foxholes, caves and tunnels. Where the caves were too deep for flame-throwers to reach the fanatical defenders the Australians sealed the entrances with dynamite, thus entombing them.

An amphibious force landed ten miles east of Wewak, astride the main track leading to the Sepik escape route; and when it linked up with the main Australian force moving along the coast the rout of the enemy was complete. With Australians hot in pursuit, the shattered Japanese remnants were fleeing into the forbidding Torricellis.

SO ends the story of Wewak, so costly for Japan. The fate of the luckless survivors of the garrison is certain. They will probably try to make their way up the terrible Sepik to the no more hospitable territory of Dutch New Guinea. Divorced from their last supply dumps they will have to live off the country, which will mean death by starvation for many of them.

Through Dense Grass and Jungle in New Guinea

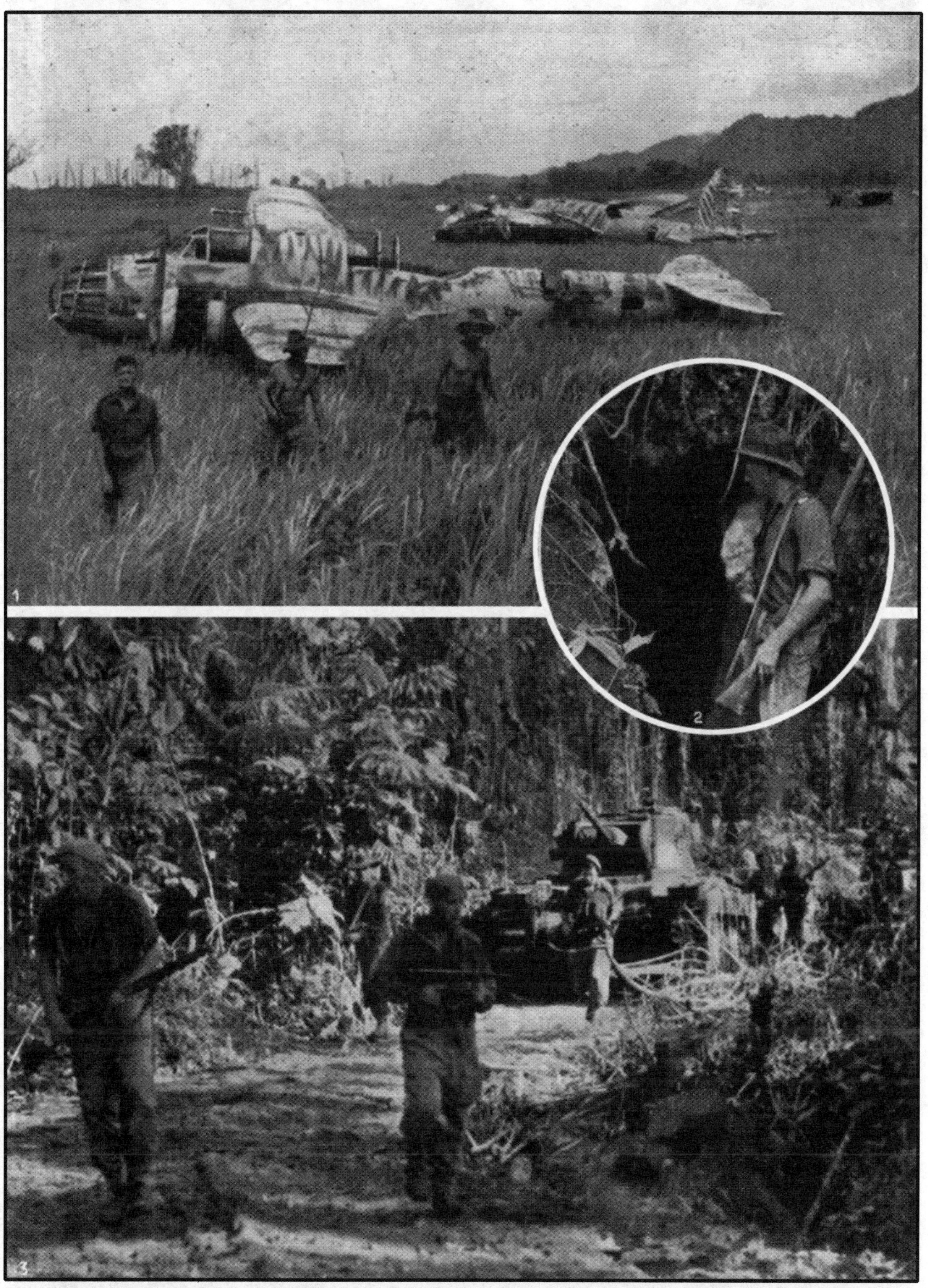

JAPANESE BOMBERS CAUGHT ON THE GROUND BY THE R.A.A.F. at Dagua in the Aitape sector of New Guinea were joyfully inspected by Australian infantrymen, seen (1) plunging through tall grass after seizing the vital airstrip on March 25, 1945. Near Wewak (see facing page) an Aussie private carefully scrutinized an enemy foxhole (2) whose occupants he had liquidated. Armour of the 6th Division, with protecting infantry screen, moved up to attack in the same area along a hacked-out jungle track. See also page 97.

Photos, Australian Official

FIRST FULL-DRESS RED ARMY PARADE IN BERLIN was held late in May 1945, when Col.-Gen. Berzarin, Soviet Military Commandant of the City (killed in a motor-cycle accident on June 17), addressed his troops (top) in the Tiergarten. The occasion was the return to Moscow of the Banner of Victory—the first red flag (extreme right) to be flown over the Reichstag. Badly blasted was Berlin's most famous hotel, the Adlon (bottom left). Some of the 2,000,000 German civilians who remained in the capital helped to clear this rubble-blocked street (right) by order. On June 5 military representatives of Britain, the U.S., the U.S.S.R., and France announced from the Reich capital the joint occupation of the "Greater Berlin" area by forces of each of the four Powers (see facing page).

Photos, U.S. Official, Pictorial Press

Men of Destiny Who Govern Occupied Germany

At Marshal Zhukov's headquarters on the outskirts of Berlin on June 5, 1945, there was signed by the four Allied commanders-in-chief an historic agreement for the future government of every phase of German life, in four zones of occupation. How these tasks, of enormous complexity are being pursued is told by JOHN ALLEN GRAYDON. See also illus. pages 148 and 149.

STRIPPED of her ill-gotten conquests, Germany has had her frontiers provisionally fixed as those existing on December 31, 1937. And in the absence of a central government or authority in Germany capable of accepting responsibility for the maintenance of order, the administration of the country and compliance with the requirements of the victorious Powers, the Governments of the U.K., the U.S.A., the U.S.S.R., and the Provisional Government of the French Republic formally assumed that authority on June 5, 1945.

This was signalized by the signing of an agreement by the four Allied commanders-in-chief: Field-Marshal Montgomery, General Eisenhower, Marshal Zhukov and General de Lattre de Tassigny. As governors of post-war Germany, their zones of occupation and authority were for the time being fixed as Eastern Germany for the Russians, North-Western for the British, Southern for the U.S., and extreme South-Western for France.

THE first meeting was too brief for these points to be settled, but within a few hours Russia made it known that she wished to occupy about 50 per cent of the Reich's total area. If this were agreed upon, it would necessitate a withdrawal by the Americans of over 150 miles to the west from parts of Saxony and Thuringia, and of about 60 miles in Central Germany. A comparatively small British withdrawal would be mainly from the Wismar area, where our 2nd Army met the Russians; Lübeck, Hamburg and the Kiel Canal would remain under British control.

The Governments of the Four Powers announced it to be their intention to consult with the Governments of other United Nations in connexion with the exercise of this authority; and if smaller Allies assisted in the occupation by sending contingents of troops these would be under the control of the C.-in-C. of the zone.

Administration of the Greater Berlin area is to operate under the general direction of a Control Council consisting of the four Commandants, each to serve in rotation as Chief Commandant. In these tasks each is assisted by a highly qualified staff.

Offices of Grave Responsibility

To ensure that all German authorities and the German people shall carry out unconditionally the requirements of the Allied representatives, the Control Council has under it a permanent co-ordinating committee, composed of one representative of each of the four Commanders-in-Chief, and a control staff organized in the following divisions: military; naval; air; transport; political; economic; finance; reparation, deliveries, and restitution; internal affairs and communications; legal; prisoners of war and displaced persons; manpower. There are four heads of each of these divisions, one designated by each Power.

These are offices of grave and tremendous responsibility, and as adviser on political matters Field-Marshal Montgomery has the services of Sir William Strang, K.C.M.G., C.B., M.B.E., whose experience in this sphere marked him as pre-eminently fitted for the position. As head of the Central Department in the Foreign Office, he went to Moscow in June 1939 for negotiations (which, unhappily, proved abortive) in connexion with a Mutual Assistance Pact with the Soviet Union. In October 1943 he accompanied Mr. Eden to a conference of Foreign Secretaries in the U.K., U.S.A. and the Soviet Union in Moscow. And in November 1943 he was appointed U.K. representative on the European Advisory Commission and given his knighthood.

Head of the British economic division is Sir Percy H. Mills, whose efforts are directed at seeing that Germany never again has the opportunity of harnessing her industrial machine to the purposes of war. He knows German industry well, and is considered to be one of Britain's greatest experts on machine tools. In normal times managing director of a big Birmingham engineering firm, W. and T. Avery Ltd., he is performing his present onerous duties without payment.

Sir Percy Mills has had a striking career. He went to a council school at Stockton-on-Tees, won a scholarship and went to a local central school, then at 16 was apprenticed to a local engineering firm. Five years later he moved to the Midlands and concentrated on high-precision engineering. Early in the war, when there was threat of a serious bottle-neck in the vital machine tools industry, he was called in to put matters right. He broke the bottle-neck, and within a year was Director-General of Machine Tools and was knighted for his great services. His team of experts includes men skilled in the various fields of industry—who know all there is to know of mining, food, agriculture and other activities of German industrial life.

ALLIED OCCUPATION OF GERMANY as fixed before D Day, showing the line to which the British and U.S. armies had advanced when the Germans surrendered. Following the announcement by Moscow on June 6, 1945, of an extension to the Soviet zone, adjustments will need to be made in the British and U.S. areas. *By courtesy of The Observer*

FIELD-MARSHAL MONTGOMERY'S chief representative for control problems is Lieut.-General Sir Ronald Weeks. He served in the First Great War, and in the Second Great War as Director-General of Army Equipment and, since 1942, as Deputy Chief of the Imperial General Staff—the first Territorial Army officer ever to receive a Staff appointment. Many were surprised when a Territorial—a non-professional soldier—was given such an important post, but it should be remembered that Gen. Weeks was a "Terrier" as long ago as 1912 (he is now 54 years of age). A lover of hard work, he was at his post at the War Office at 9 o'clock every morning and invariably remained there until 8 in the evening. Even then his day was not complete, for he took home papers to be studied at his flat.

Son of a mining engineer, Sir Ronald Weeks wanted to follow that occupation, and for nearly a year he worked below ground, then began training as a research chemist with a firm of glass manufacturers, later becoming a director of the firm. Now the destiny of Europe is partly in his hands.

Sir Ronald Ian Campbell, K.C.M.G., C.B., an Assistant Under-Secretary of State in the Foreign Office, also is on the European Advisory Commission, with the rank of ambassador. Entering the Foreign Office in 1914, he has served in Washington, Paris, Brussels, Cairo and Belgrade.

MONTGOMERY TO THE GERMANS

AS British Representative on the Allied Control Commission (Marshal Zhukov representing Russia; Gen. Eisenhower the U.S.; Gen. de Lattre de Tassigny, France), Field-Marshal Sir Bernard Montgomery, C.-in-C. of the British area in Germany, issued on May 30, 1945, the following proclamation to the population.

1.—I have been appointed by the British Government to command and control the area occupied by the British Army. This area will be governed for the present by Military Government under my orders.

2.—My immediate object is to establish a simple and orderly life for the whole community. The first step will be to see that the population has (a) food, (b) housing, (c) freedom from disease. The harvest must be gathered in. The means of transportation must be re-established. The postal services must be restarted. Certain industries must be got going again. All this will mean much hard work for everyone.

3.—Those who have committed war crimes according to international law will be dealt with in proper fashion. The German people will work under my orders to provide the necessities of life for the community, and to restore the economic life of the country.

4.—There are in the British area a very large number of German soldiers, sailors and airmen, and all these are now being assembled in certain localities. The German Wehrmacht, and other armed forces, will be disarmed and disbanded. All German soldiers, sailors and airmen are being sorted out by trades and occupations. In a few days they will start to be discharged from the armed forces so that they can get on with the work. The most urgent need is the harvest, therefore workers on the land are going first: men of other occupations and trades will be discharged to work as soon as it can be arranged.

5.—I will see to it that all German soldiers and civilians are kept informed by radio and newspapers of how the work is going on. The population will be told what to do. I shall expect it to be done willingly and efficiently.

Now It Can Be Told!

'OPERATION FIDO': BEATING AIRFIELD FOG

Within about 15 minutes of the light-up order being given, a fog-enshrouded airfield can be completely cleared of this greatest natural enemy of the airman. The miracle is performed by "Fido," another astonishing all-British achievement just recently revealed. Pre-war experiments in fog dispersal were inconclusive. Now it is a matter of routine, and from exclusive R.A.F. use it is passing to civil aviation; a super-installation, the biggest and most up to date so far, is being installed at the new aerodrome at Heath Row, Middlesex.

It is another chapter in the story of the Battle of Oil. In the early days of wartime experiment, when the experts prophesied failure, the code name "Fido" was derived from the initial letters of "Fog Investigation Dispersal Operations." When the apparatus proved a brilliant success, the R.A.F. retained the code name and fitted it to "Fog Intensive Dispersal Of."

The first success was gained with it on Nov. 4, 1942, when in Hampshire a dense fog of 50 yards' visibility was cleared by petroleum burners in an area about 200 yards square to a height of 80 feet. By Jan. 1943 large-scale runways had been constructed for further experiments. These were on the same scale as actual operational runways and had the advantage of being available for experiments by day and night.

On Nov. 19, 1943, Fido first came into operational use, when four Halifaxes landed successfully after a bombing expedition to the Ruhr, though the surrounding visibility was only 100 yards; ten minutes after Fido had been lit the visibility on the runway increased to the equivalent of from two to four miles. Since that day more than 2,500 Allied aircraft have been safely landed—many of them in dense fog—with their crews of over 10,000 airmen.

Rundstedt's Ardennes offensive at Christmas—the last German major offensive of the war, which was launched at a time when fog covered Europe—was halted at a critical period largely by the weight of Allied air attack because bombers were able to take off and land with the assistance of Fido.

FIDO PUMPING MACHINERY feeds the fuel pipes along the airfield runways in the fog-clearance "miracle" described here. *Photo, British Official*

This installation for dispersing fog in bulk by artificial heating of the air consists of three main portions, (a) burner lines, (b) pumping and distribution, (c) storage, and its crew consists of a sergeant, three corporals, 17 aircraftmen. Pipes through which the petrol is pumped enclose the airfield in a rectangle, and through small holes at intervals in the pipes blazing petrol vapour is forced under great pressure, billowing two feet high. An aerodrome so equipped may use 70,000 gallons of fuel in an hour. So far the total of petrol consumed is 30,000,000 gallons.

DOWN A LANE LINED BY FLAMING FUEL a Lancaster takes off in conditions of perfect visibility from an airfield which a few minutes before had been completely fogbound. *Photo, British Official*

The apparatus frequently clears the air to a height of several hundred feet, with the result that sky and stars are visible over the runway. The glow of the burners on an aerodrome has been seen by air crews over the North Sea, and from the Dutch coast.

WAR FACTORY UNDER HOUSES OF PARLIAMENT

When doodle-bugs were falling thick and fast on London, a secret factory beneath the Houses of Parliament—in the vaults made famous by Guy Fawkes—was busy turning out weapons to counteract the flying bombs. They were new instruments, urgently needed at the coastal gun-sites, and when the order was given to the Palace of Westminster's Munition Unit (the factory's official title) there was no dallying. In a matter of hours the weapons were delivered and in action.

Flying bombs now figure only in evil dreams, but the factory still hums with great activity. For the 150 men and women have heard the call for a secret "something" designed to hasten the end of the war with Japan.

During the war with Germany there were 1,224 Alerts at the Palace of Westminster, and Parliament was hit by bombs on 12 occasions. Two of our own shells struck the building, one damaging Big Ben, the other exploding in the Royal Court. A shell crashed into the library of the House of Commons but did not explode. Total casualties were three killed and 15 wounded. And still the work went on in the factory.

INSIDE THE SECRET WORKSHOP where men and women workers turned out anti-flying bomb weapons. Today "something" for use in the Far East is being manufactured.

Three hundred square yards it covers, comprising a large vault and several passages, and for two and a half years it has been in operation with few outside of those immediately concerned aware of its existence. Honour for its inception goes to three M.P.s, and when the idea was cautiously made known amongst those most likely to accept employment, there was no lack of response. Mostly voluntary part-time workers, the 80 men and 70 women engaged inspected and assembled 2,000,000 shell fuse parts in the first 18 months of their labours.

At one time eight different war contracts were being skilfully handled by these policemen, Cabinet Ministers' wives, mothers and daughters, Parliamentary counsel, firemen, Civil Servants, retired Army officers, young men awaiting their call-up, and others who constituted the factory's capable "hands." The ages of these workers in the vault have

H.M.S. KING GEORGE V, 35,000-TON BATTLESHIP, it was revealed on May 23, 1945, collided off the Irish coast with H.M. destroyer Punjabi in May 1942, cutting her in two; only a few of the destroyer's crew survived. The battleship (above) in an Icelandic fjord after the collision, and (right) her damaged bow. See also page 135, and illus. in page 678 Vol. 8. *Photos, British Official*

ranged between 17 and 70 and, not to be outdone by youth and advanced age, Houses of Parliament postal, telephonist and kitchen staff personnel have joined in, as extra demand has fallen on the establishment. Hard work demands reasonable living, and so a factory canteen was established to serve 150 two-course meals per day.

It has been no case of " All work and no play," for on occasion a grand piano and a R.A.F. dance band have been introduced into the Grand Committee Room of Westminster Hall. And in the early days of this year the first act of " Love in Idleness " was played before the workers: this making history in that never before had a theatrical performance been staged within the area of ancient Westminster Hall.

SECRETS OF LONDON'S MYSTERY CITADEL

MANY thousands of people stared in wonderment during the last four years at an enormous, fortress-like building erected at the back of the Admiralty in London, with walls eight feet thick and guarded by A.A. guns. Here is the first description of a visit to this mystery building, known as "The Citadel." It was the Admiralty's wartime home. (See illus. in page 450, Vol. 8).

Through the vast Admiralty buildings in Whitehall, winding round a labyrinth of passages, I was halted by my guide in front of two massive steel doors—rather like a ship's watertight compartments, with controlling wheels by which they are closed. "This is the Citadel," he explained, as an armed policeman came forward. We were "vetted," for even high Admiralty officials cannot wander through those secret rooms and passages willy-nilly.

Thirty seconds later I was in that "hide-out"—the building specially constructed so that adequate protection from air raids and other forms of enemy activity could be given to vital Admiralty departments, so that if the main buildings were rendered useless the work of directing the operations of the Fleet could be carried on.

WE went down through the air-locks to a cool, air-conditioned atmosphere. There was a clatter of teletypes, the buzz of conversation in the biggest telephone exchange I have ever seen; the glimpse of gold braid on the sleeves of high officers. But although my guide told me that 700 people, many of them girls, worked the clock round in three shifts, I could not realize that I was in the most important building in London—if not the whole Empire.

In the 156 rooms housing all those people were many of the Admiralty's secrets. I saw dozens of people handling messages to all ports of the world. "There is no place we cannot contact," said a senior member of the Admiralty staff. "We use from this hitherto secret place every known method of communication—teleprinter, radio, voice frequency, and for the not too secret messages the telephone."

Up in the top of the building great dynamos have stood ready for five years to take over the task of giving life-blood to the Admiralty's radio, by which any ship on the high seas of the world can be contacted. They stood yesterday grim and silent. They have never been needed.

Every 24 hours 8,000 messages go out through the Admiralty's signals communication branch. "Not only do we see that these thousands of messages are correctly received or transmitted, but we see that they are properly delivered, and that often means 100,000 copies a day, using a ton of paper every 24 hours," it was explained.

In other rooms teletypes chattered to all parts of the world, giving out thousands of words to the Fleet and the shore establishments. Then I was shown the true "holy of holies," the secret Fleet Information Room, where the movements of every craft are plotted, and where the Naval Chiefs of Staff confer when they want an over-all picture of what is going on.

The Duty Captain showed me round the whitewashed walls transformed into maps, with plots of movements of hundreds of craft—no matter where a naval action is pending this room knows all about it. And deeper still is the Radio Room, in touch minute by minute with the outposts of the Empire.—*R. G. Grant, in Sunday Dispatch*

HOW BRITAIN'S GOLD WAS SHIPPED ABROAD

THE greatest gamble the world has ever known was brought off under the noses of the Germans when, in 1940, Britain's entire gold reserve was moved out of this country. It was totally mobilized for total war, and the vaults of the Bank of England were scraped almost bare. In bars, ingots and coin it went—to America, to pay for war supplies. Story of this modern gold rush was released in June 1945.

Our proud liners the Queen Mary and the Queen Elizabeth carried vast quantities of it. Rusty "tramps," whose cargoes had formerly been of the very humblest, shared with warships the task of ferrying more of it away. Such was the haste of this transatlantic adventure, and such the activity of the ships, that at one moment there were on the High Seas consignments totalling more than £150,000,000 of gold.

From ports all over Britain the bullion ships set sail, taking in their cargoes from motor vans escorted to the docks under armed guard. Gold reserves and current production in the overseas countries of the Empire were "conscripted," too, for the Empire's benefit, and this was concentrated at naval bases all over the world, at points where its presence was most desired.

Some of the ships went unescorted. But in spite of U-boat packs and lone hunters, commerce-raiders and enemy aircraft, the loss was almost insignificant: only £500,000 out of shipments exceeding £1,000,000,000 handled for the Treasury by the Bank of England. Masterly salvage work kept the figure thus low, as in the case of the Niagara, whose sinking represented the biggest single loss. The Niagara went down in 420 feet of water, with its £2,000,000 cargo. And from that depth an Australian salvage team recovered most of it—all but £80,000 or £90,000 worth.

No insurance company in peacetime would have undertaken the risk of "covering" some of these cargoes. In war it was a case of take a chance and hope for the best. The sheer impudence of the undertaking carried them successfully through. After the start of the Japanese war the risk was increased. It was necessary to move bullion to America across the Indian Ocean and the Pacific, and this was done, in open defiance of the odds piled heavily against the accomplishment. It was on this run that the Niagara was sunk; an old steamer which used to ply regularly between Auckland, Sydney, and Vancouver, she finished her plucky career in the Tasman Sea, off New Zealand.

Eisenhower: the Man Behind the Name

One year ago this great American led that mighty Allied venture, the seal on which was set with the Unconditional Surrender of Germany. In command of 5,000,000 troops, he has achieved almost overwhelming fame and popularity. "He has walked right into the history books," says RALPH McCARTHY, who in this appreciation reveals something of the man himself.

JUNE 6 is for ever bright in the story of Britain. One year ago on that day—D Day—the Allied armies stormed on to the shores of Normandy, and the people of this land held their breath.

Do you remember that morning? How men in buses and trains called out: "Have you heard? It's started!" How people exchanged the latest news, queued up for newspapers, hastened to the radio. How the sun seemed to shine with a peculiar brilliance. How silent it seemed here in Britain, despite the squadrons of planes incessantly in the sky. How the thoughts of all were across the strip of Channel, with the men daring the barricades of the beaches.

It was for British people the greatest day of the war, Dunkirk was avenged. And it had been avenged from Britain. From the shores of the homeland the Allied troops had set sail to Normandy on their way to Germany. Should there be any question of a Memorial Day for the Second Great War, as November 11 was chosen for the First Great War, the people of Britain would choose, not May 8, V Day, but June 6, D Day, as the day of memory.

He Conceals His Own Greatness

How well that expedition fared can be judged today. Before a year had passed the last battle had been won and Europe wrenched from the Nazi grasp. But though this is Britain's day, the British people know that it was an Allied venture, that American troops fought and died on June 6, that the army of liberation were really brothers-in-arms, that they came from Pasadena as well as Paisley, from Nebraska as well as Norfolk.

And on this day it is fitting to pay tribute to the one man who more than any other individual made that success possible—one of the really great men of the war—one who, because of his own avowed policy of hiding his greatness, has not received the credit which he deserves: to General Dwight D. Eisenhower, Supreme Commander of the Allied Expeditionary Force.

Now that it is all over we can step back and look at him and his achievements. Really they are remarkable. He has walked right into the history books, and his place is permanent. Because, too, his task of winning battles is done we can disobey his request and tell something about him, something that reveals Eisenhower the man. There are two stories that I particularly like.

THE first one happened a few weeks after the Allied landings in North Africa. The fighting was hard and bitter. The American Army was in battle for the first time. Back in the United States the newspapers and radio networks told flamboyant stories of American achievement, until one day Eisenhower sent for the U.S. war correspondents.

"Listen, boys, you're making a mistake. Most of the fighting is being done by the British. Give them the credit. Our troops are new to this war. They'll learn—as the British had to learn."

The result was that U.S. newspapers, while naturally continuing to give considerable space to the actions of their own men, did tell their readers of the feats of British troops. Later events justified Eisenhower's faith in his men; America will remember Bastogne with Bunker Hill.

THE second story is more recent. Before the war a woman, who is British, married in Southern France a stateless Russian. On the collapse of France she escaped home to London; her husband remained. He fought with the Maquis and, in the liberation battles, fought in American uniform with the U.S. troops. He was badly wounded. He was taken to an American hospital, but he had no identity tab, no papers; officially he did not exist. His young wife made every effort to get him to Britain, but all failed. Finally she wrote to Eisenhower.

A few days later she had a reply; the letter expressed sympathy, told her that investigation was being made and, if the facts were true, action would be taken. It was signed "Dwight D. Eisenhower." The next day her phone rang; a pleasant American voice said: "I'm speaking for General Eisenhower. Gen. Eisenhower wants you not to worry. Just that, not to worry." The husband is now in a hospital in Britain.

What is remarkable about that story is not the big-heartedness of the man, but the fact that Eisenhower, in command of 5,000,000 troops, is surrounded by no barrier of officialdom. His system allows him to see everything, listen to everyone. Other facts about Eisenhower are already known; he is 54, one of six sons of hard-working parents. He is descended from a family which left Germany in the seventeenth century as a protest against religious persecution.

Personal Reply to a Grievance

His army career has been achieved without influence; in 1941 he was a colonel with a reputation as a "brain" and military organizer. He is unconventional and direct; he swears; in peacetime he plays golf and bridge. He is married and has one son. But there is something else; he avoids publicity. He is one of the few men who really mean it when he says he wants to be ignored.

When American troops flooded into Britain in preparation for the invasion, a British citizen who thought he had a grievance wrote to the U.S. authorities. The reply was a charming letter rectifying matters signed "Dwight D. Eisenhower." A Fleet Street editor wanted to publish the correspondence to clear the atmosphere of this island, overcrowded with British and American troops. Again Eisenhower wrote, "Please, my policy is no personal publicity."

Instead he has turned the limelight on his brilliant lieutenants—on Montgomery, beloved by Britain, on Bradley, on Patton and, especially, on his troops in the ranks, the Tommies and the G.I. Joes. But never on himself. This is wrong. For long the talk has been: "Of course, Eisenhower is good, but he's not a fighting man. He is the super-managing director of the world's biggest enterprise." That is untrue.

Not until the war had almost ended did we learn how good a soldier he was, of the important part he played in the strategy of the battles of victory. Indeed, the astonishing manoeuvre which surrounded and broke up the whole Ruhr defence area has been revealed to have been Eisenhower's own plan.

In all ways he is a big man. Today the people of Britain honour him. They recall with gratitude that it was he who decided on June 6 as D Day; it was he who led the liberating armies on to victory.

GENERAL EISENHOWER "CAPTURED" LONDON on June 12, 1945, when, accompanied by Air Chief Marshal Sir Arthur Tedder, he drove to Guildhall to be made a Freeman of the City. Outside the Royal Exchange (in background) one of the biggest crowds within memory cheered him on his way from Guildhall to the Mansion House. Later that day he was invested by H.M. the King with the Order of Merit—the first U.S. soldier to be so honoured. The article in this page appears by arrangement with the News Chronicle. *Photo, Central Press*

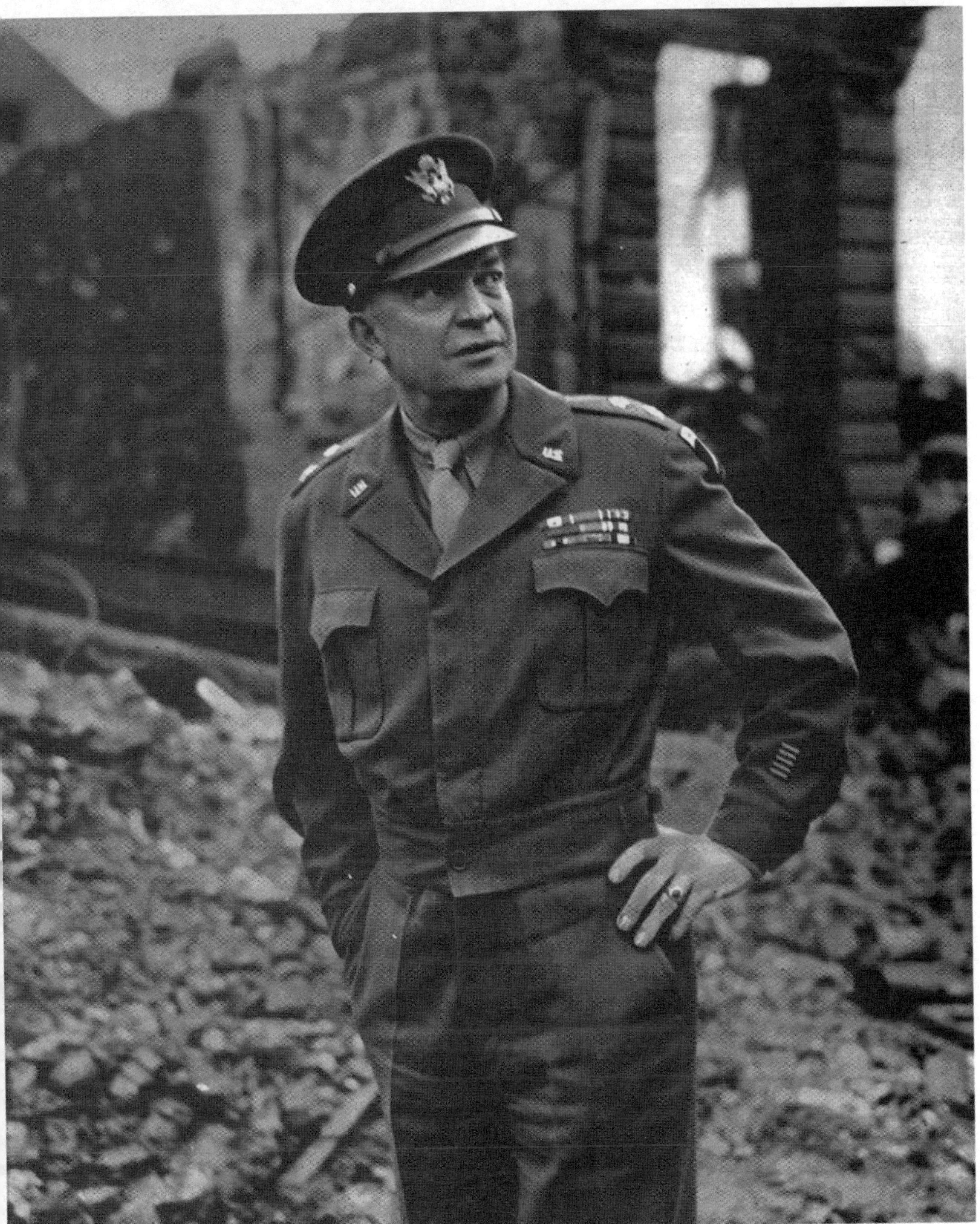

Photo, U.S. Official

He Led Our Liberating Armies to Victory

Following his great reception in the City of London on June 12, 1945, General of the Army Dwight D. Eisenhower, Supreme Commander of the Allied Expeditionary Force, left Germany for the United States on June 16 for an indefinite period. A hero's welcome awaited him at La Guardia Airport, where he would arrive from Washington after seeing President Truman: then a two-hour triumphal ride through New York to the City Hall to receive a special gold medal.

On the Normandy Beaches Were Remembered—

Photos, B[illegible] Keysto[illegible]

First anniversary—June 6, 1945—of the D-Day assault on the coast of France saw the deep scars of war being softened by Nature or slowly effaced by man's hand. A beach the British assailed (1), with the houses of Arromanches in the background. Outside Caen a farmer's team plodded by the grave of one of our fallen (2). Probably the most completely destroyed city of France, St. Lo (3) is being cleared for rebuilding. Omaha Beach (4), near Bayeux, where the Americans landed.

er Pool,
nicle

—Those Who Had Fallen on That Fateful Day

Tribute was paid at Arromanches by 600 British troops, Allied diplomats and thousands of French men and women at an impressive D-Day service (5): the centre-piece a wooden altar, in the distance a crumbling line of blockships that had formed the breakwater for " Mulberry B " (see pages 430–434, Vol. 8). A British naval guard of honour presented arms, eleven Mosquitoes dipped their wings in salute, and Royal Marine buglers sounded the Last Post.

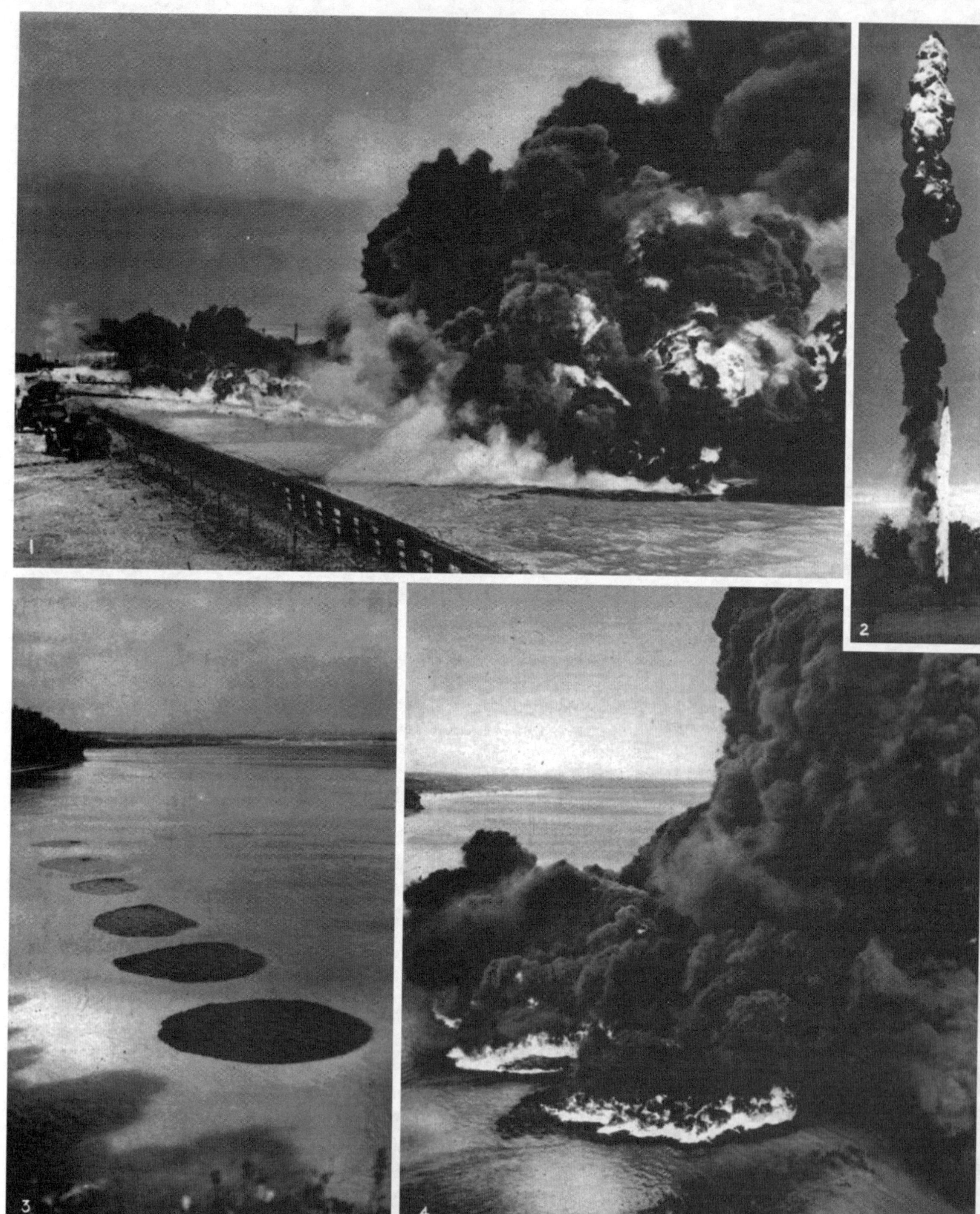

Nazi Invaders Would Have Been Roasted on the Sea

Photos, British Official

A terrifying reception was ready for any German seaborne force attempting to land on Britain. Among recently revealed devices of the Petroleum Warfare Dept. were heavy flame-throwers installed for the defence of the Channel Ports in 1940 (1), and a vertical type which hurled blazing fluid against low-flying aircraft (2). Yet more deadly to any landing craft was a means of setting the Channel ablaze by projecting oil into the sea from shore pipes (3), and igniting it by chemical means (4).

VIEWS & REVIEWS Of Vital War Books

by Hamilton Fyfe

A BOOK by Brigadier J. G. Smyth, V.C., M.C., demands, by reason of his qualifications, careful study, and it is certain that nobody who reads Defence Is Our Business (Hutchinson, 10s. 6d.) is likely to feel that time has been wasted upon it. The writer deals with the future more than the past. He draws conclusions from experience (his own including service in Burma, where he commanded a division, and the skilful handling of a brigade at Dunkirk). He discusses the qualities of the leaders who beat the German armies decisively and beyond all doubt. But the main purpose of his book is to sketch a plan for the solution of our military problem when the Japanese as well as the Nazis have been soundly defeated. It is to a great extent, he says, a business proposition.

> It is a question of balancing what we ought to have with what we can afford. If our defence force is too weak, we shall become a second-class power. If it is too strong it will adversely affect our trade, our prosperity and our standard of living.

We cannot safely "leave it to the experts. That would be a grave mistake, which landed us in trouble before." Blame for our weakness in the face of German rearmament "has generally been placed on the shoulders of our politicians, but they were really only the mouthpieces of the British people," who "took very little interest in the whole business of defence in the period between the wars." That must not happen again, urges General Smyth. "It is the British public which should dictate the quality and quantity of our peacetime defence forces." His aim is to help the British public to do that.

They Defied Treasury Orders

As an illustration of what he wants the public to do he cites the obstacles which the Treasury put in the way of our making ourselves secure.

> In the years between wars the Treasury had been insistent that we should not embark on any construction of heavy tanks. No notice was taken of the many warnings given as to the numbers and performance of the German tanks which were being turned out in increasing numbers. Had it not been for a small number of tank experts and enthusiasts at the War Office who, in spite of orders to the contrary, continued to study and design heavier tank models, we should have taken even longer than we did to evolve any tanks at all.

As it was, "the British Army went to war, practically speaking, without the most effective weapon of the last war, which they themselves had invented."

NOW, it seems to me that to blame the public for this is to ignore the conditions of our political life. Neither a nation nor an individual can reach decisions about anything unless they have the facts. If the facts are concealed from them (as in this case they were), it is impossible even to begin making up their minds as to what course should be taken. The public were told they could trust the War Office and the Treasury to take care of their interests. Ministers in the House of Commons read out answers, prepared for them by their permanent officials, assuring M.P.s who asked questions that everything in the garden was lovely. Baldwin kept on saying there was no need to be afraid of Germany. How could the public know what the truth really was?

The public does not know, never has known, what the Treasury is, what decides its actions, who prompts its interference with such matters as the building of tanks. Now and then a little corner of the veil is lifted, as when Mr. Churchill admitted he had made a mistake in returning to the Gold Standard when he was Chancellor of the Exchequer and head of the Treasury, and explained that he had been misled by the leading financial authorities in the City of London. It has never been made plain to the public that it was those same financial authorities who played their own game by forbidding the expenditure of large sums on the armaments required to enable us to stand up to German Nazis and Italian Fascists and make them understand it would not pay them to make war.

In the Years Between Wars

General Smyth's conception of democracy is too simple. He thinks the masses can settle matters as they choose. He does not allow for their abysmal ignorance, due to their being kept in the dark about everything that matters by those who ought to be their instructors—the politicians, high and low. Democracy can never work well unless clear issues are presented to the electors by honest men and women who are desirous only of the public good. It works well during war because there is then a perfectly clear issue—are we prepared to submit to the enemy or are we determined to win? The people know the facts—not all of them, but enough on which to form judgement.

Misled About German Rearmament

If they had known the facts in the 1930's, had been told of the stupidity of the generals who did not believe in tanks and longed to go back to the days of cavalry, had been kept informed correctly about German rearmament, had realized how weak our Air Force was in numbers compared with Germany's, had been given such books as this to enlighten them, they would, I am certain, have voted overwhelmingly for a change both of methods and of men. But you cannot blame anyone for not knowing the right road to take if you have closely bandaged his eyes and thoroughly plugged his ears with cotton-wool.

Brigadier J. G. SMYTH, V.C., M.C., who commanded a brigade at Dunkirk and a division in Burma, is the author of the book on defence problems reviewed here. *Photo, G.P.U.*

General Smyth's plan includes Navy and Air Force as well as the Army. He wants a Defence Ministry to manage all three together, with the assistance of a strong Defence Council. This would be far better than having Ministries and separate management for each. It would do away with a great deal of waste. If the Treasury had looked into this and made recommendations to prevent money being thrown away, many millions could have been saved yearly. By "adopting the principle that there are not three Services but one Service," says the author, we could "produce a better article at a reduced price."

WHETHER we shall continue conscription for defence or not it is impossible to say. General Smyth does not think we shall, because he cannot imagine any Government being bold enough to propose it, though he believes that "Britain would be ready to accept it after the experience we have had of what unpreparedness means." It would "simplify and cheapen our defence problem enormously and would ensure that every man and woman for a small part of his or her life would bear a share in the national defence." He holds that if everyone between 18 and 19½ were put through physical training, lessons in citizenship, some general education and special training for the service they would give in case of need, "it would raise the physical standard of the nation considerably, greatly benefit those undergoing it, and make for better citizenship." Few who have studied human nature or have thought at all would disagree with that.

Office Work in the Services

General Smyth would like us to get into line with the Russians by abolishing "that very expensive institution—the peacetime Officers' Mess." He says that "the good old days (how most subalterns used to hate them!) of shining mess silver, gay mess kit, long tables, port wine and long dinners are as dead as the dodo." There should be, he suggests, in every Service station an eating-place for all three Services run on the principle of an ordinary restaurant where meals could be obtained at moderate prices.

> The officer wants his private life just as any other citizen does. He has seen his fellow-officers all day; in the evening—in peacetime, of course—he wants to be able to get out of his uniform and become a private individual and dine where and when he likes. It was fancy uniforms, expensive messes and entertaining which made life so expensive for the young Army officer.

Another reform the general would be glad to see is in office work. When he was a staff officer and when he commanded a brigade, he secured a firm of business organizers to overhaul his office arrangements. This made the work go through more quickly and easily and it gave staff officers more time to go out and about to visit the troops. He hoped other brigades and divisions would follow the example set, but he was disappointed, and he warns us that "office work in the Services will lapse again to its pre-war depths if we do not insist on a high standard." There is far too much of signing forms in triplicate, and issuing in hundreds of circulars orders that could be given verbally, printing all sorts of instructions that need not be printed at all. Annual consumption of paper by the War Office alone is truly terrific.

GENERAL SMYTH does not pretend to believe war is going to be abolished. He hopes so, but evidently thinks it unlikely. He insists that we must be ready to meet invasion. "We have proved that on a large scale amphibious operations are possible. What we have done to others, others may do to us. The English Channel is a good ditch, but no longer an insuperable obstacle." Flying bombs and rockets, poison gas and germ-spreaders may be on the largest scale. Well, we have been warned!

Conjuring Sanity Out of Nazi Chaos After—

DEMOBBED FROM THE BEATEN WEHRMACHT, German ex-soldiers were questioned by the C.O. of No. 1 Disbandment Control Unit in the British 2nd Army zone (1) after being directed to farm work. This German teacher at Aix-la-Chapelle (2) held her first lesson in re-educating Nazi youth, under Allied supervision. At Hamburg, church bells (3) plundered from occupied countries for smelting will ring again. Inhabitants of Brestinfurt were obliged to attend prison-camp horror films (4).

Photos, British Official, British Newspaper Pool, Associated Press

—Four Allies Assume Joint Authority in Germany

SOVIET GUARD OF HONOUR FOR FIELD-MARSHAL MONTGOMERY lined up at the Templehof airport, Berlin (1), when he arrived on June 5, 1945, to sign—with General Eisenhower, Marshal Zhukov and General de Lattre de Tassigny—the historic four-Power agreement assuming supreme authority in Germany and dividing the country into four occupation zones. Marshal Zhukov (2, left) enjoyed a joke with Monty and Eisenhower. Before signing, the delegates assembled at Zhukov's H.Q. (3). See also page 139.

Photos, British Newspaper Pool, Associated Press

Facts Behind the Syria-and-Lebanon Dispute

With the cease fire order to French troops there ended on May 31, 1945, a grave situation in Syria and the Lebanon involving heavy casualties and damage to property, and including the shelling by a French warship of the ancient capital of Damascus. The intricate background of the dispute between France and the Levant Republics is dealt with in this article, specially written for "The War Illustrated" by SYED EDRIS ALI SHAH.

TOWARDS the end of May 1945, while negotiations between France—the mandatory Power—and Syria and the Lebanon were taking place, it was learned that severe disturbances had followed the landing of French reinforcements in the Levant. Conversations ceased immediately, and skirmishes took place between the Arabs and the French and Senegalese forces. Syrian and Lebanese soldiers deserted their French officers and joined their compatriots fighting in Damascus, Homs, Aleppo, and the Jebel Druse. Damascus, age-old capital of Syria, was bombed and shelled by the French forces.

Repercussions were soon felt not only throughout the Arab world but among the Great Powers. Arab solidarity, reinforced by the bonds of the recently created Arab League (see page 398, Vol. 8), which aims at federation of all Arab States, quickly manifested itself in protest. Egypt complained to those countries to which she has accredited diplomats; a strike was proclaimed in Palestine; while the Council of the Arab League was summoned for the first week in June. The Iraq oil pipeline was cut, for the first time since the outbreak of the European war, and the leader of the hundred million Muslims of India registered his protest.

ACTION to end the bloodshed, it was felt, must be immediate. Good will of the Arab peoples to the United Nations was at stake; French commercial interests in Egypt were threatened, and the whole world of Islam—numbering over 300,000,000 people—began closely watching the affair as a possible test-case of Western policy towards Islam. There was the further possibility that the many millions professing the Muslim faith in South-East Asia, as well as those in China under Japanese occupation, might fall a prey to enemy propaganda.

Attitude of Our Foreign Office

While fighting continued, and the Levantines called for volunteers for a national army, an official statement was issued from the Foreign Office in London on May 26:

> His Majesty's Government are aware of the serious situation which has developed in the last few days in Syria and the Lebanon, but especially in Syria. They regret that the improved atmosphere should have been disturbed by the dispatch of certain reinforcements, and that this should have been the occasion for breaking off negotiations between the Levant States and the French Government for a general settlement. His Majesty's Government are in constant consultation with the United States Government, and in constant contact with the parties concerned, regarding these developments.

The Syrian and Lebanese Ministers in London in a statement said:

> If France does not recognize the facts which she has been trying to ignore for the last twenty-five years, namely the desire and determination of Syria and the Lebanon to be completely independent States, and to exercise their legitimate rights as such, this crisis is bound to increase in intensity, and to become less amenable to settlement.

The diplomats were not mistaken. The revolt spread, increasing in violence, until the British Government, with the approval of the Government of the United States, decided to intervene. Mr. Eden read in the House of Commons on May 31 a communication addressed to General de Gaulle, requesting the French forces to cease fire and return to barracks. There was a further suggestion that a conference of the interested parties might be held in London. The cease fire was sounded, and the affair, from being merely an isolated event in France's colonial history, became an international dispute.

BRITISH ARMOUR AT DAMASCUS was cheered by the Syrians as it entered the capital on June 2, 1945, to act as escort for the 3,000 French troops forming the garrison who were evacuated by night to a concentration area at Mezze, five miles from the city. France's dispute with the Levant Republic is explained in this page.
Photo, British Official

To trace the development of the situation it is not necessary to examine closely the evidence as to when the cease fire was ordered, or other minor points that do not in any way affect the fundamental issues; though these have been given a great deal of prominence.

ON June 2, 1945, General de Gaulle, at a Press Conference in Paris, asked that the Middle East problem should be viewed as a whole and settlement sought by a conference of all the powers interested: Russia and the U.S. as well as Britain and France, the Arab States as well as their neighbours—on the assumption (maintained by the Arab League) that the Arab world is one unit, politically, economically and historically. Two days later the Council of the Arab League—after condemning the precipitate action of General Oliva Roget, the French commander in Southern Syria, since removed by De Gaulle—announced their agreement with the General that discussion of all Arab questions should be reopened. Thus the affair had vastly outgrown its original proportions.

Mr. Churchill, in the House of Commons on June 5, while willing to discuss these subjects, pointed out that if all the Great Powers were to be invited it might considerably delay the settlement of a matter that should not be left long in abeyance.

The Main Trend of Happenings

Before detailing the points at issue between the Levant Republics and France, it would be advisable to recapitulate briefly the main trend of happenings in the history of French interest in the Levant. In accordance with the Anglo-French Convention of 1919, Great Britain withdrew from the Levant in favour of France. The Mandate was granted to France in 1920 by the Supreme Council of the Allied Powers, and ratified by the League of Nations Council in 1922. This area, with a combined population of something under four millions, is vital strategically, being not so far from Suez in the south, within striking distance of the Middle Eastern oilfields, and communicating with the Persian Gulf to the east. Although these Arab peoples are mixed (including Druses, Alawites, Christians and Muslims) there is no friction or disagreement, particularly on the issue of independence.

After the First Great War the Sykes-Picot agreement had recognized France's "special position" in Syria and the Lebanon. (General Gouraud succeeded Georges Picot as High Commissioner at Beirut in November 1919.) This treaty had provided for an independent Arab kingdom embracing Damascus, Aleppo, Homs and Hama; and the Emir Faisal, son of the King of the Hejaz, ascended the throne in March 1920. In July, the Syrian National Congress unanimously adopted a democratic constitution, by which Syria was declared to be united on a basis of decentralization.

THE French High Commissioner, who had been confined to the small area of the Lebanon, issued an ultimatum to Faisal. After a brush with the Arab army, French forces entered Damascus. That same year General Gouraud, French High Commissioner at Beirut, issued a Declaration of the Independence of Lebanon—a marked constitutional advance. Five years later, however, revolt broke out among the Druses when their delegation to the French authorities was imprisoned. At last, in 1936, the French offered the Syrians rights equal to those obtained from Britain by Iraq. But in September 1938 the French refused to ratify their 1936 treaty, in which they had guaranteed independence within three years; trouble in the Levant followed, and the High Commissioner declared that no one should have any illusions as to the "permanence of French rule in Syria." After the French and British announcement of the independence of the Levant in 1941 and 1943, its independence was recognized unconditionally by nine Great Powers and it was able to accredit diplomatic representatives to countries abroad where Levantine interests existed.

The present French demands are for bases in the war against Japan, troops to maintain order, and proposals for negotiations by the Syrians and Lebanese. These are resisted by the Levant Republics on the ground that they are internationally recognized as independent and sovereign; therefore, they say, they are at liberty to behave as such, and to grant no rights if they so desire—particularly for the Japanese war, when there are, they say, better and nearer bases open to the French.

Strange Royal Naval Contrasts in the Aegean

FORMERLY A SYRIAN TRADING SCHOONER, H.M.S. RAGEA, of 275 tons, acted as a supply ship for Allied coastal forces in the tricky waters of the Aegean ; she is seen off the Greek coast unloading a torpedo on to the deck of a M.T.B. of the Royal Navy. Retaining all her old rigging and fittings from the placid days when she sailed with wine, oil, and fruit between Syrian ports and the Central Mediterranean, she was commanded on her war-time duties by Lieut. O. L. Hooker R N.Z.N.V.R., of Auckland, peacetime sign-writer and yachting enthusiast. *Photo, British Official*

U.N.R.R.A. Now Busy in Stricken Yugoslavia

DELIVERY OF 500,000 TONS OF SUPPLIES FOR THE BALKANS was discussed at this conference (1) between representatives of the British Army, U.N.R.R.A. (United Nations Relief and Rehabilitation Administration), and the Yugoslav State Commission at Split, in hunger-stricken Yugoslavia, just before U.N.R.R.A.—as announced on June 2, 1945—took over relief work from the Allied military authorities; British Military Liaison Officer, Brigadier C. F. Forestier-Walker (centre), presided. Consignments range from British-made farm tractors (2) to Red Cross supplies (3), seen being unloaded at Split. See also pages 46 and 659, Vol. 8.

Photos, British Official

I Was There! Eye Witness Stories of the War

Today Where Our Invasion of Europe Began

Early in June, Stanley Baron, News Chronicle War Correspondent, flew over the Normandy landing-sites where a year ago Britons and Americans gave new glory to the world. Here he describes the desert-like scenery and the remains of our magnificent Mulberry Harbour. See also illus. pages 144, 145.

I FLEW yesterday afternoon over the D Day beaches. The sea, dully gleaming like a pewter dish, lapped on the edges of an empty shore. In 50 miles from the entrance to the channels leading into Carentan and Isigny to the Rade de Caen, a handful of American soldiers were the only living creatures to be seen on the sands, and what they were doing I do not know. The scene of the most titanic enterprise of Western Europe's military history which began a year ago today has become a desert.

Rainwater gleams in the open shell and bomb holes. Where a patient farmer has filled them in poppies redden and fill in the outlines. Mulberry Harbour, amazingly durable, though partially dismantled, glows with rich yellows, orange, reds and soft lichenous greens. Rust has painted it thus. Oil still leaking from the half-sunken ships so skilfully laid bow to stern to form the breakwaters makes its pretty pattern of mother-of-pearl on the slow swell.

Nothing is as it was in this perishing memorial to the Britons and Americans who gave new glory to the world a year ago. I flew out from an airfield hard by Chalgrove Field in Oxfordshire, in a two-engined plane piloted by Lt. Otis Taylor, of Paragould, Arkansas. It was hard, so much has happened between, to put the mind back these 12 months. Even the wind, which looked as if it was going to reproduce last year's conditions, had abated.

THE mind's eye peopled the water with thousands of ships of that other June, but yesterday there was nothing. Not until we had made our landfall over Pointe de Barfleur, taken by the American First Army before Cherbourg fell, and flown down over the beaches first at 1,000 feet, then at treetop height, did we see so much as a sail.

Now we could peer into the ruins of the houses. Now we could see the first of the actual landing beaches. One above all which no American will ever forget. They called it Omaha. In nine months with the great American First Army I have learned to know and love Americans. This was the place at which they came ashore, most of them seeing Europe for the first time. Here many died. They were buried in the sands. The sea has washed over their resting-places.

The rusting hulks of landing barges and ducks and here and there a merchant ship which has been blown ashore are their only memorials. Their comrades went on, and many of them were friends of mine. I looked down on the beach and inland towards St. Lo, where the First Army cracking the German defences began the great run which was not to stop until Germany was reached.

Remembering the breaking of the Siegfried Line, the capture of Aachen, the drive to the Rhine and the taking of Cologne, the triumph of Remagen bridge and the great break-out which brought the men of this army to the Elbe, it seemed as though all these scenes were telescoped into one, and that for ever memorable.

Mingled Skeletons of Landing-Craft

The plane swung lower still, edging over the Normandy hedges of ill-fame and down again to the beach level. Now we were flying below the rim of ochreous cliffs against which winter storms had flung the wrecks of three and four thousand tonners, mingling them with the skeletons of landing-craft of every size.

We saw the German defences, the pill-boxes smashed and powdered, some with the tatters of camouflage netting draping them yet. Here we were in the British sector. We flipped over a village. "Arromanches," said the pilot—a dead place now with no one in the streets and the shot-up houses on the front still unrepaired. In a tight half-circle the plane bent out to sea, nearly grazing a line of huge concrete caissons, all but one still in place, the caissons of Mulberry Harbour.

Red rust streaked their sides. The huge girders which had carried men and materials in such vast quantities in to shore have now been wholly dismantled. Down the sands and under the sea only to be seen from the air runs the steel trackway which was the lifeline up which the troops, tanks and vehicles of Britain had poured. How magnificent was this job! Mulberry Harbour could be used still. The seas of many, many winters will batter vainly around it before it is entirely destroyed. It should be a place of pilgrimage for thousands who would understand how great was the blow which was struck for liberty.

OUT to sea lie merchant ships which were sunk by mine or bombing. Others lie broken on the beaches. We flew down low over one named Yewdale. The men who sailed in her will like to know she is in superficially good shape still, apart from her smashed stern wedged at right-angles amidships of another vessel of the same size.

At the mouth of the River Orne we thought we would vary our pilgrimage by flying up the canal to Caen. Three times we circled over the city, for one flight is not enough to appreciate the price paid by France in those days of suffering and splendour. There were more people here in a single street than we had seen on the whole of the beaches. How they are living in this desolation of grey dust it is difficult to tell Green weeds are spreading among the ruins of the Gothic and classical glories. Yet some survive, a challenge, surely, to build and create again.

I Saw Norway in the Hour of Her Greatest Joy

Welcome which the people of Oslo gave to King Haakon when he arrived home from exile on June 7, 1945, came as a climax to four weeks of non-stop celebrations. These impressions of Norway during the Liberation were recorded by Sgt. A. J. Wilson, R.A.F., specially for "The War Illustrated."

I FLEW to Oslo in a Sunderland flying boat of the Royal Norwegian Air Force, the crew of which were on their way home for the first time in five years. As the rugged coastline of their native land thrust itself through the blue of the North Sea, the Norwegian airmen exchanged congratulations and later, over the little fishing villages which hug the shelter of the mountains in creeks and fiords, the pilot waggled his wings in greeting to his countrymen. Below us, the shadow of the great flying boat leaped the fiords and flitted triumphantly over field and mountain, bringing children and old folks running out to wave.

After a perfect landing on the shimmering water of Oslo Fiord we drove through the gaily beflagged streets of the city where thousands had gathered outside the Royal Palace to welcome Crown Prince Olaf, who had arrived by cruiser a few hours earlier (see illus. p. 76). British airborne troops and a few R.A.F. men were mingling with the crowds and everywhere they were being given a tremendous reception.

For several days the Norwegians in Oslo did little work. They thronged the streets and missed no opportunity for celebration. Allied troops were besieged by children for autographs, and wherever a crowd gathered they sang their national anthem and traditional songs. Just when things were

THE BREAKWATER FOR "MULBERRY B" REMAINS, whilst the noise and fury of battle that broke on the Normandy Beaches are but year-old memories. These sturdy blockships—as seen on June 4, 1945—half-sunken bow to stern, battered by winter storm, scorched by summer sun, shield still the gigantic prefabricated harbour which was towed in sections from Britain to its site off Arromanches. Harbour and blockships crumble with the passage of Time, but, as told in the anniversary story above, their dissolution is not yet. *Photo, News Chronicle*

KING HAAKON OF NORWAY and the Crown Princess Martha acknowledged their people's cheers when they drove through Oslo on June 7, 1945, the day of His Majesty's return after exactly five years in exile.
Photo, Associated Press

beginning to return to normal, new events, such as Constitution Day on May 17, the Whitsun Bank Holiday, and the arrival by sea and air of notable Norwegian and Allied personalities, brought rejoicing crowds into the streets again.

Unfortunately, it will probably be some time before all Germans are out of Norway. The towns were cleared in the first few days after the liberation and the Germans have been collected—or have collected themselves—in reservation camps where they will await complete disarmament, when there are sufficient Allied troops to supervise the job.

The roads leading out of Oslo have been packed with German convoys, nearly all of them unescorted by our troops but all flying the white flag of surrender. For the most part the Germans are docile and ready to co-operate. Later will come the problem of transport—when the Allied authorities in Germany signal that evacuation can start. Meanwhile, the last of the quislings are being enthusiastically hunted down by members of the Norwegian Home Front. Norway's Resistance Movement is now revealed as one of the best in Europe. It had many branches and its work was always well co-ordinated.

The R.A.F. Kept Them Supplied

I asked a Norwegian army officer, who had been sent home to organize a Resistance group, what would have happened if the Germans in Norway had decided to hold out. He smiled and said that such an eventuality had been foreseen and that everything had been taken care of. Everyone in the Resistance knew exactly what his job was to be ; in every street of every town and village things were organized down to the last detail. As long as the R.A.F. kept them supplied and they had some airborne help, they would have beaten the Germans.

The Home Front in Norway was 50,000 strong and there would have been many more members but for the fact that for two years recruiting was stopped so that there should be no German infiltration into the Movement. Most colourful of the patriots are the big, blonde young men who took to the mountains to wage active warfare against the Germans with arms dropped to them by British supply planes. They ambushed convoys, made road-blocks and often fought pitched battles with the Germans.

Those who carried on the underground work in the cities and towns lived even more dangerously. Under the noses of the Gestapo they smuggled men out of the country to fight in the armies overseas and organized acts of sabotage. If they were caught they were "grilled" by the Gestapo and most of them disappeared for ever.

In the first fortnight after the liberation in Oslo every German building, every street and every office block was guarded by the patriots. When darkness fell they brought their Sten guns down to the ready and unslung their rifles. Going home after midnight, their Stens would follow you with every step ; you would never be out of sight —or out of range—of a Resistance man.

"You must forgive us if we seem too warlike," one of their leaders told me, "but we cannot take chances as long as there are quislings and Germans still about. The boys have been forced to fight underground for so long that it is strange to be able to come out into the open in their uniforms and armbands!"

All over Oslo there is evidence of the patriots' work of sabotage. Blocks of offices which housed German military and civil administration officials were blown sky-high. In one day last year no fewer than 30 explosions kept Nazi fire tenders and rescue squads dashing all over the city.

Many Norwegians still wear their concentration camp numbers on their civilian clothes. It was almost a matter of pride to be "concentrated," despite the bad conditions which prevailed in the camps. I heard of one old woman of 70, who was a regular "customer" for repeatedly defying the Germans. She was serving her fifth term of imprisonment when freed by the Resistance on Liberation Day.

If there are any doubts about how the Norwegians feel towards their British and American liberators they can be quickly dispelled by the readiness of thousands of Norwegians to volunteer for the war against Japan. One patriot, just released from a German prison, asked me how soon it would be before he and his colleagues could be shipped to the Far East. I asked him why he was so anxious to fight the Japs—had he not had enough of war and suffering ? He replied : "Are we not Allies ? We should be failing in our duty if we did not go !"

Sgt. A. J. WILSON, R.A.F. (right), who tells the story commencing in page 153, talks with a Norwegian patriot guarding an important building in Oslo and who a few weeks previously had been fighting the Nazis in the hills.

We Blockaded the Japs Escaping from Ramree

Screaming "Hullo ! Help me !" from the darkness of a channel near the Burma coast, a Jap officer was taken prisoner by a motor launch of the Burma R.I.N.V.R. blockading the enemy escape route from the island of Ramree. The story is told by the M.L.'s commanding officer.

When he was certain he had been detected, the Jap screamed at the top of his voice, using the little English he knew in a bid to save his life. We lowered the dinghy and caught him before he could reach the opposite bank. The prisoner turned out to be a very scared officer, convinced that he was going to be executed. But when we treated him as an officer, allowing him the use of the wardroom, he appeared to regain his confidence. He was a well-educated man, with a university degree, and he had been employed in an official capacity in Tokyo.

He agreed to appeal over our loud-hailer system to his comrades to give themselves up. Unable to escape by sea, they had been wandering in the mangroves for days without food or water. But probably because of the denseness of the mangroves preventing those more than a few yards inland from hearing his appeals, the attempt was abortive. Later he was handed over to the authorities on shore, and placed temporarily in a hut. I was amazed to learn that here he turned to his guard, pulled open his shirt, and said, "Now shoot me !" The astonished guard called an officer, and it transpired that, unconvinced by our correct and humane treatment he still thought he was to be executed !

Those Japanese who attempted to escape and refused to surrender when challenged received short shrift. One small boat, camouflaged with bushes, shot out of a creek, paddled furiously by a party of Japs. We opened fire and soon reduced the boat to wreckage. On ceasing fire, we shouted to any possible survivors to surrender. There was no reply. But at least one swimmer continued on his course to the other bank, so we re-opened fire until there were no survivors left. We finally brought the remains of the boat alongside, and found it contained one dead Jap and an officer's sword, which now hangs in our wardroom. I think we accounted for six to ten of the enemy on that occasion. Landing craft and other M.L.s added to the bag. The channel proved a death-trap for the blockade-runners, and enemy bodies were floating past for days.

BURMESE RATINGS OF THE R.I.N.V.R., who took part in blockading the Japanese escape route from Ramree Island, as narrated here, examine a ceremonial sword taken from a captured enemy officer. See also page 648, Vol. 8.
Photo, British Official

In the early part of the campaign M.L.s of the Burma R.I.N.V.R. were engaged on convoy work, patrol operations and bombardments. They also took part in the landings at Akyab, Mayebon, Mkauk Pyu and Cheduba, towing and escorting landing craft, leading assault waves into the beaches and giving covering fire.

Our first actual contact with the enemy was on the first night after the Myebon landing. With other M.L.s we pushed up a very narrow stream. On arrival at a junction we heard the chug-chug of engines coming down from the north. Although we had no charts, we went in pursuit. Eventually we turned our searchlight full on—to reveal a motor supply craft, containing five to seven Japanese. Giving them everything we had, the craft quickly disintergrated.

Two nights later we met three more armed motor supply craft. The one we tackled blew up immediately. Of those who jumped into the water we rescued six press-ganged Burman labourers, and captured a Japanese army corporal in charge of one of the boats. We claimed that he was the first Japanese prisoner to be captured by the Navy since the start of the big offensive.

At dawn the next day we again penetrated the chaung to finish off an armed supply craft which had been previously shot up and had gone ashore on a sandy spit (said the First Lieutenant of one of the M.L.s). I went in the dinghy with some Burman ratings towards the Japanese craft. Suddenly the captain, warned by an M.L. of another flotilla that the enemy had been spotted ashore, withdrew stern-first, towing the dinghy, under covering fire from the M.L.s. I saw the Japanese in the mangrove swamp and we opened fire from the dinghy with a Tommy gun and a Lanchester carbine. By the time we were hoisted inboard, the M.L. had been carried up the creek.

We decided to investigate this reach, and soon discovered a suspected camouflaged boat in the mangroves. We opened fire, and when the camouflage fell away a heavily armed Japanese gunboat was disclosed. Pumping her with shells, we started a fire in her magazine. She blew up, her ammunition exploding in all directions.

Tail of a Fantastic Procession in Germany

There are no lifts for the Germans who have taken to the highways. They trudge, and keep on trudging. Or men and women take turns between the shafts of a cart when no horse is available; nothing on wheels has been written off as useless, says John Gilbert, correspondent of The Star.

You can drive along Germany's great highways hour after hour without seeing a car. Private motoring is now only a memory. All German cars, except, perhaps, those still hidden, have gone into the Allied pool, reserved mainly for essential civilian work in the towns. Doctors are provided for. Public officials who must travel may also draw on the pool.

There have been long spells during a 200-mile run when my jeep has had the road entirely to itself. A convoy of Army lorries lumbers past, and then again we are alone till we catch up with straggling horse or ox wagons taking land workers to the fields, transporting families to homes from which they have fled, or packed with Hitler's slaves, who again know the meaning of freedom.

The mass movement of German civilians who were swept forward by the retreating Nazis has ended. Today we are seeing the tail of a fantastic procession. Nothing on wheels has been written off as worthless. Where it has been impossible to find horse or oxen, men and women take turns between the shafts. For others it is a footslogging business all the way—men with pack on back and a bundle in each hand, women pushing overloaded prams, with a child or two trailing behind; whole families on the move, with mounds of luggage piled on the strangest collection of handcarts I have ever seen.

Hitch-hiking would provide relief for those with blistered feet on the roads of England. There are no lifts for Germans who take to the highways. "It's tough on the kids," my driver says, thinking of his own family in California, "but it was tougher on the kids in Russia, Poland, France, Belgium and other places, where the Germans plastered the roads with bombs and cannon fire."

He obviously does not find non-fraternization easy when he looks into the smiling, appealing eyes of children. With him, as with so many more, it is an eternal conflict between heart and reason. Men and women deported by the German armies, and forced to toil on farms and factories, no longer swarm on the roads. They have been persuaded to remain in the camps set up for them, and await their turn to be sent home in comparative comfort. Trains leave the concentration points daily, with German crews working under the direction of Allied officers.

Sometimes the waiting brings romance. In one town through which I passed, German women interrupted their shopping to line the street as a bridal party passed along in two carriages, each drawn by a pair of prancing horses. The bride, a Pole, and her bridesmaids were in white. The bridegroom, too, came from Poland. A military policeman, who halted me at the cross-roads, grinned and said, "A swell little wedding! I guess I've got just such a date when I collect enough points to land me back in the States!"

HOMEWARD TREK of German civilians presents strange spectacles, such as this worn-out column of Bavarian ox-carts resting by the roadside near Pilsen. Their peasant-owners had sought refuge in the Czechoslovakian mountains. *Photo, British Combine*

OUR DIARY OF THE WAR

JUNE 6, Wednesday
1,277th day of War against Japan
Ryukyu Islands.—U.S. Marines captured whole of Naha airfield, Okinawa.
Brazil.—State of war between Brazil and Japan announced.

JUNE 7, Thursday — 1,278th day
Channel Isles.—King George VI and Queen Elizabeth in Jersey and Guernsey.
Norway.—King Haakon returned to Oslo after exactly five years.
Japan.—Osaka attacked by Super-Fortresses with H.E. and incendiaries.
New Guinea.—First Allied cargo ship for three years entered Wewak harbour.
Home Front.—Fleet carrier H.M.S. Leviathan launched by Duchess of Kent.

JUNE 8, Friday — 1,279th day
U.S.A.—Agreement reached at San Francisco between the five Great Powers on scope of veto in Security Council.
France.—Wreckage of aircraft found on June 4 near Grenoble definitely identified as that of plane which was carrying Air Chief Marshal Sir T. Leigh-Mallory to S.E. Asia.

JUNE 9, Saturday — 1,280th day
Germany.—At Rothenburg, Field-Marshal Montgomery took last salute of Guards' Armoured Division as tank formation.
Trieste.—Agreement between British, U.S., and Yugoslav Governments signed in Belgrade.
Japan.—Large forces of Super-Fortresses raided Naruo, Nagoya and Akashi.
Ryukyu Islands.—New Allied landings on Okinawa, south of Oruku.

JUNE 10, Sunday — 1,281st day
Germany.—Marshal Zhukov decorated Field-Marshal Montgomery and Gen. Eisenhower with Soviet Order of Victory.
Japan.—Diet granted Premier Suzuki full powers as dictator. Super-Fortresses from Marianas attacked island of Honshu.

JUNE 11, Monday — 1,282nd day
Home Front.—Official date of end of European War announced as May 9.
Ryukyu Islands.—U.S. forces launched frontal attack on remaining Japanese garrison on Okinawa.

JUNE 12, Tuesday — 1,283rd day
Home Front.—General Eisenhower received Freedom of City of London and O.M. from H.M. the King.
Russia.—London Poles invited to attend Moscow talks.
Borneo.—Australians advanced on Labuan.

JUNE 13, Wednesday — 1,284th day
Japan.—U.S. aircraft attacked air bases on Kyushu Island.
Home Front.—H.M. the King awarded G.C.B. to Marshal Zhukov.

Flash-backs

1940
June 10. *Mussolini declared war against Britain and France.*
June 14. *Germans entered Paris.*
June 17. *Marshal Pétain asked Germany for an armistice.*
June 18. *De Gaulle appealed from London to French to fight on.*

1941
June 8. *British and Free French troops entered Vichy-held Syria.*

1942
June 10. *Prague announced Lidice massacre for killing of Heydrich.*
June 13. *Japanese landed on Attu Island in the Aleutians.*

1943
June 7. *French Committee for Nat. Liberation formed in Algiers.*
June 11. *Island of Pantelleria occupied by Allied Forces.*

1944
June 6. *D-Day. Allied landings on coast of Normandy.*
June 13. *First flying-bombs came over Southern England.*
June 15. *U.S. troops landed on Saipan Island in the Marianas.*

JUNE 14, Thursday — 1,285th day
France.—General Eisenhower awarded Cross of Liberation by General de Gaulle.
Caroline Islands.—British Pacific Fleet heavily attacked Truk.
Borneo.—Australians captured Brunei.
China.—U.S. aircraft bombed Hong Kong.

JUNE 15, Friday — 1,286th day
Japan.—Over 500 Super-Fortresses bombed Osaka.
Burma.—Lord Louis Mountbatten addressed Victory Parade in Rangoon.
Home Front.—Dissolution of Parliament which had been elected in 1935.

JUNE 16, Saturday — 1,287th day
Borneo.—Australians "cut off Japan entirely from all her stolen property," declared General MacArthur.
Home Front.—William Joyce, flown from Brussels, lodged in cell at Bow Street.

JUNE 17, Sunday — 1,288th day
Russia.—Polish talks began at Moscow.
Italy.—Signor Bonomi resigned; Signor Parri accepted as Premier-designate.
Burma.—General Raymond Wheeler succeeded General Sultan as commanding general of U.S. forces.

JUNE 18, Monday — 1,299th day
U.S.A.—General Eisenhower arrived in Washington.
Germany.—Death announced in accident of Colonel-General Berzarin, Soviet military commander of Berlin.

JUNE 19, Tuesday — 1,290th day
Japan.—"Very large" forces of U.S. 21st Bomber Command struck at Honshu and Kyushu Islands.

With Our Airmen Today

By CAPTAIN
NORMAN MACMILLAN
M.C., A.F.C.

FOUR new types of British aircraft are now available for use against the Japanese. Three are fighters and one a bomber. It is certain that in speed and hitting power Japanese army and navy aircraft will be outclassed by them. The special feature of Japanese aircraft construction has been light structure weight and small fuselage cross-section; the first of these qualities has given Japanese aircraft a fast rate of climb and good manoeuvrability; the second has produced a good turn of speed for the engine power employed. Their defects have been absence of armour protection for the air crew, and relatively light armament.

The most powerful Japanese aero-engine so far reported is the Nakajima Homare, an 18-cylinder air-cooled radial of 2,000 h.p., which by means of water injection can produce in emergency a still greater power output. Japanese engineers have succeeded in squeezing this power from an engine 46½ inches in diameter, against the 52 inches of the Bristol Hercules of 1,650 h.p. Their intention is obviously to keep their fuselages slim so that they will gain the utmost speed value from the aeroplane using the Homare engine, thereby profiting from the small stature of the average Japanese.

Two aircraft are known to be powered with this engine, the Nakajima Myrt, a reconnaissance plane with a speed of over 390 m.p.h., and the Frank, an Army single-seater fighter, also made by Nakajima, having a speed of about 420 m.p.h. and armed with two cannon-guns and two half-inch machine-guns. It was possibly a Frank that was encountered by the U.S. naval pilot on June 3 during a carrier-plane raid on Kyushu. This pilot reported being unable to keep up with the Japanese aircraft, but two days later it was denied in Washington that the Japanese had aircraft superior in performance to the Americans. Probably it all depends which aircraft met which.

FASTEST Aeroplane in the World Today is the 500 m.p.h. Vampire

The three new British fighters are all superior to the Frank. The De Havilland Vampire, a single-engined gas-turbine fighter, was the first aircraft in the world to fly at more than 500 m.p.h., and is claimed to be today the fastest aeroplane in service in the world. The De Havilland Hornet is a scaled-down version of the Mosquito, redesigned throughout for fighter duty; it has two Rolls-Royce Merlin engines and a top speed of over 470 m.p.h. Vickers-Armstrongs have produced the Spiteful, a single-seater fighter, with a Rolls-Royce Griffon engine and a speed of more than 460 m.p.h. The Hornet is the fastest propeller-driven aircraft in the world, and it combines this speed with long range, a quality necessary for the Pacific war. The Hornet was drawn, built and began its first test flights in exactly twelve months.

THE new bomber is the Avro Lincoln, a development of the Lancaster, carrying the heaviest bombs over a greater range and at a faster speed than the Lancaster. It is fitted with four Rolls-Royce Merlin engines, and is being made in the United Kingdom, Canada and Australia. When these aircraft "get cracking" in the Pacific they will add still more punch to the blows being inflicted on the enemy.

TORPEDO-CARRYING AVENGER of the Royal Naval Air Arm (formerly Fleet Air Arm) was skilfully "landed" on the sea after its engine failed on taking-off from a British Pacific Fleet carrier during a strike in late March 1945 against the Sakishima group, the object of which was to screen Admiral Nimitz's invasion of Okinawa on April 1. It was announced a month later that Okinawa was to become a R.A.F. base. See also page 117. *Photo, British Official*

BALLOON-BOMBS Released by Japs Cause First Casualties Within U.S.

Near Lakeview, Oregon, about 300 miles from the west coast of the United States, a child picked up a bomb and while playing with it the bomb exploded and killed the child, the mother, and four more of her six children. The father and one child survived. The bomb was one of those attached to balloons released by the Japanese which are allowed to drift across the ocean towards America. These were the first casualties within America from enemy action.

Regrettable as such incidents are, America is fortunate compared with the United Kingdom. Details have just been revealed of the damage done to the Merseyside docks during the air raids of early May 1941. The German bombers damaged 60 per cent of the docks, and put many out of action. (Yet within three months the port was again in full operation, an indication of the fact that air bombardment derives its power from continuity.) Forty vessels were hit in the docks and most were sunk. Others were sunk in the river. (I have heard it said that at one time nearly 250 vessels were affected.)

THE worst incident was that of the Malakand, laden with 450 tons of ammunition for the Middle East. She was hit, but the damage was controlled, and everything appeared to be safe until overhead a barrage balloon caught fire and fell blazing on to the ship. There was a terrific explosion as the Malakand blew up. Afterwards I saw the dock where she lay and it was a horrifying spectacle, the graveyard of a dead ship, its twisted frame lying in a huge hole that was unrecognizable as a dock. During the London blitz the traffic of the Port of London was reduced to 15 per cent of its pre-war volume. One ship was sunk by an air-laid mine at The Pool, just below Tower Bridge. But by 1944 the Port was again handling 90 per cent of its pre-war traffic.

FIGHTERS Directed via Radio Phone by R.A.F. Controller

Details of the radar night interception of enemy aircraft have also come out. The radar ground equipment enabled each R.A.F. controller to direct his fighters by radio telephone, giving them the course and height to fly. When each aircraft was close enough to enable the pilot to use the radar fitted in his aircraft he changed from G.C.I. (ground control of interception) to A.I. (air interception). But it should not be forgotten that the aircraft plots in the operations rooms were all the time flowing in from the posts of the Observer Corps, with 32,000 observers manning the whole area of the country. Fighter interception after the installation of radar in the planes became more deadly, because it enabled the pilot to overcome his difficulty of lack of vision in the dark.

The difference between the air war in Europe and in the Far East is revealed in the figures of Bomber Command for the whole war. Out of a total of 955,040 tons of bombs dropped, 196,355 tons were incendiaries; against Japan the U.S.A. 21st A.F. drops scarcely any high explosive and concentrates on incendiary warfare.

Kobe, sixth city of Japan, was attacked on June 5 by 450-500 Super-Fortresses with incendiary bombs; eight Super-Forts were lost. On June 7 the undamaged part of Osaka got 2,500 tons from over 450 Super-Forts. On June 10, towns in Honshu—Chiba, Tomioka, Hamahatsu, Kasimagaura, Tachikawa and Sukagawa—were attacked by 150-200 Super-Forts with 150 Mustangs as escort. Like the Germans, the Japanese are unable to prevent the bomber from getting through to its target. The Japanese themselves announced that Lancasters bombed Hong Kong on June 13.

THE Japanese have produced a small glider bomb which, released from an aeroplane, is steered to contact with its target by a suicide pilot. How long the Japanese air training scheme can stand the loss rate of one pilot per aircraft per raid remains to be seen. No Western Power could supply the manpower and training speed involved in such methods.

Aircraft combined with surface units in a 72-hours' beach defence bombardment in British North Borneo before the Australian 9th Division went ashore in Brunei Bay and on Labuan Island at dawn on June 10. The airfield on Labuan Island was quickly captured. (See illus. page 130.)

Air Chief Marshal Sir Trafford Leigh-Mallory's aircraft was found on June 4 crashed in the Alps 30 miles east of Grenoble. It was missing since Nov. 17, 1944, whilst flying to the East.

Carriers of Death Over the Heart of Japan

SUPER-FORTRESSES FLEW OVER FUJIYAMA, Japan's 13,000-feet "sacred" mountain sixty miles south-west of Tokyo, on one of their many raids on the enemy capital. Also Tokyo-bound were another flight of these giant bombers (bottom), winging their way through billowing clouds. It was disclosed on June 20, 1945, that Tokyo had experienced no fewer than 23 raids by Super-Fortresses between November 24, 1944, and May 30, 1945, mostly by aircraft based on the Marianas, midway between Japan and New Guinea.

Photos, Keystone

Editor's Postscript

SOMEWHERE in the lumber-room of my mind there has lain for many a year the recollection of what I had considered a fine example of the skill with which the Muse of History sometimes dramatizes her story. In the far-off days when the Greek city states were often at war with each other, or in temporary league against the Persians, the Medes, or the Asiatic Greeks, the galleys of the Athenian navy, on returning to the Piraeus after an engagement in which they had suffered reverse, would hoist black sails to warn the crowds, waiting by the "long walls" to welcome them, that they came with bad news. At least that was what I seemed to remember from youthful reading, and I thought of this when, in very different circumstances, the U-boats arrived at British ports flying black flags. I have failed, however, to verify my reference to this ancient use of the black flag, but I repudiate the suggestion of a scholarly friend that I may have dreamt it. An ingenious dream it would have been! It may be, as my friend also suggests, that I am merely confusing it with the myth of Theseus and the Minotaur. Returning from Crete, where he had slain the Minotaur and escaped from the Labyrinth, so runs the legend, Theseus was to carry a white sail on his ship as token of his success; but he forgot to change the black sail with which the fatal ship set out, and his father Aegeus, King of Athens, seeing the black sail on the approaching vessel, threw himself from the Acropolis hill in his despair. In my vain research I have at least discovered that Tamerlane, some twenty centuries later than the Heroic Age of Greece, showed black flags to any city he was besieging if it had held out too long for his liking, as a warning that he was no longer willing to be merciful to its defenders, but would put them all to the sword. In other words, "You have been warned!"

I WAS just a shade disappointed to find that the name "Pluto," given to one of the greatest contributions to victory of British inventive genius and enterprise (see illus. page 120), was not arbitrarily chosen but, on the contrary, actually stood for "Pipe Line Under The Ocean." For a moment I suspected similar ingenious acrostics hidden in other famous code names of the war, like Mulberry, and Dynamo (the Navy's official name, you remember, for the operation that most people call the miracle of Dunkirk). The invention of code words and passwords, for innumerable exercises no less than for actual operations, seems to be one of a war's minor relaxations; and the essential charm of such words lies in their sheer Itma-like inconsequentiality. There is reason for this too: the more unlikely the word, the more unrelated to any hint of the reality for which it stands, the greater the security. Members of the Home Guard and Civil Defence who took part in a certain extensive week-end exercise over the London area will remember (and so will their wives) the telephone call or police call that roused them from their beds at 4 a.m. with the words "Gadfly swat gadfly"—words ridiculous in themselves but enough to send men stumbling hurriedly out into the darkness to their appointed posts without any breakfast. There were other equally foolish-sounding code words known to every Home Guard, which fortunately never had to be uttered. A historic example of this code nomenclature was established in September 1916, with the first use of an entirely new weapon of war—a British invention, let it never be forgotten! The official communiqués originally spoke of "heavily armoured vehicles of a new type," but in factories, assembly shops, and testing grounds they had been called, for reasons of security, tanks. When the secret was out the soldiers insisted on adopting this word.

A PILOT officer, who received his training at an R.A.F. cadet school in Arizona, passed me a copy of a small-town paper, the Arizona Contact, published in Phoenix, Arizona. An entire page is given to the announcement of a Rugger match which the R.A.F. cadets were staging among themselves for the benefit of war charities. "British Cadets Collide Saturday Night in Union Stadium Feature," the headline runs; and the introductory paragraph enlarges on the theme in words that could have been put together only in the U.S.A.:

> Rugby football, a game more gruelling than that played on the American gridiron, goes on display for the disportment of Salt River Valley fandom one week from tomorrow night.

The writer is anxious to impress upon his American readers that in this strange "action-packed" game the rules recognize no substitutes, no "time out," and no protective padding. He also stresses the fact that there is a "lone referee." In a huge advertisement covering the rest of the page, leading local advertisers combine in a salute to the British players. "We whose signatures appear below, as ardent boosters of wholesome sport, a characteristic long common to our two peoples, wish to take this means to salute you." There is no doubt that our R.A.F. boys are great ambassadors, and that the good citizens of Phoenix, Arizona, have taken them to their hearts.

ONLY the dimmest hint of the Isolationist campaign now in full swing in the Hearst and McCormick Press of the United States has been suggested over here—in the belief, presumably, that least said's soonest mended. Which is a poor tribute to the sensible-thinking people of the two great English-speaking nations, each of whom can surely afford to inspect the other's warts at close quarters and—if necessary—tactfully hint at a remedy. As an editor I consider it my duty to let my readers at home know what their American cousins (or some of them) are thinking about them—even if it is not always palatable and is often hopelessly wide of the mark. A friend has just sent me, for instance, some recent issues of the Hearst-controlled Chicago Herald-American with a remarkable outburst from San Francisco by one Samuel Crowther, described as "noted author and economist." Writing just before V Day, this noted author frankly declared, "The question is not what Russia wants, or what Britain wants, or what this or that country wants. The great question is what the United States wants!" He went on to say, "When the day of victory comes it will be an American victory. That is not mere breast-beating (*sic*), but a plain statement of fact. Our men and armour, both on the battle and the home fronts, kept Germany and Japan from overrunning the earth. No one fought for us. We have been alone in the Pacific, and since we invaded Italy and France we have been nearly alone in Europe." Again, "The military situation is such that we can finish the job entirely alone. Indeed we might be stronger, and certainly we should have fewer cares, if we cut off Lend-Lease." To all of which one might reasonably add, "As long as we know—we know!" Not for the first time since 1939 has Mr. Hearst sadly underestimated the intelligence of his vast numbers of readers, I feel.

Vice-Admiral D. W. BOYD, C.B., C.B.E., D.S.C., former Fifth Sea Lord, the announcement of whose appointment as Admiral (Air)—the first of its kind in the Royal Navy—was made on June 12, 1945. He will control the 50 Naval air stations and training establishments in the British Isles and the groups of aircraft carriers used for training.

Photo, British Official

I HAVE frequently mentioned in these Postscripts of mine attempts to combat wartime outbreaks of pilfering in high and unlikely places. Here are two more. The other day a friend astonished me with the news that at his Club—one of the oldest and staidest in Pall Mall—the Committee had found it necessary to provide a locked glass-case for their newest library books. The Librarian holds the key, and new books are now issued only against a member's signature in a book kept for that purpose. To which, by way of comment, I can only add that we aren't so far removed from the days of chained books and Bibles as we used to imagine! At another famous London club I know they have been obliged to chain the nail and clothes brushes. No doubt the Committee at this club have discussed ways and means of chaining the soap. All, however, is not so austere in this war-toughened country of ours as these instances would lead the foreigner to imagine. The other day in the country I lunched at a moderately-priced hotel where not only were fresh towels, soap and even brilliantine provided, but an ample supply of luxurious and heavily-embossed notepaper crammed the racks on the writing-tables in the lounge. Which is something I have not seen, exposed to public view, for a very long time.

THE Dublin newspaper, Irish Press—of which Mr. de Valera is "Controlling Editor"—has been good enough to send me in pamphlet form the full text of the Eire Premier's broadcast reply to Mr. Churchill's recent reference to him, in the hope (presumably) that this Irish propaganda will receive wide attention in the English Press. After reading those portions of it in English I personally have not the slightest inclination to extend its circulation, but I give the opening paragraph in "Dev's" adopted language:

> Go mbeannaí Dia dhídh, a cháirde Gael. Is libhse a Ghaelgeóirí is ceart dom an chéad fhocal a rá. Tá an cogadh san Eoraip caite. Ba é deonú Dé, as méid A mhór-thrócaire, sinn a shábháil ar an troid agus ar an dóirteadh fola agus sinn chaomhnadh ar an bhfulang atá ag céasadh furmhór tíortha na hEorpa le cúig bhliana anuas.

To this extent am I happy to meet the wishes of the Editor of The Irish Press.

In Britain Now: Back to the Ways of Peace

EVACUEE children and mothers from London—over 400 of them—returned home from Leicester on June 4, 1945, by the first L.M.S. "Homeward Special." Although their stay in the Midlands had been happy, they were all smiles on arrival at St. Pancras station (left).

GERMAN PRISONERS, all ex-miners, filed on board a Royal Navy landing craft at Tilbury (below) in mid-June, en route for the Ruhr, where they had been detailed to work in the coalfields under Allied military supervision. It was announced on May 26 that German prisoners of war captured on the Elbe would be brought here as farm labourers and over 20,000 were to be employed in the building trades.

OUR C.D. AND ALLIED SERVICES were inspected by their Majesties, accompanied by Princess Elizabeth, at a farewell parade in Hyde Park, London, on June 10. Nursing detachments marched past the saluting base. Three days earlier the King and Queen visited the Channel Islands for the first time since the Liberation: at Candie Park, Guernsey (below, right).

LAST OF THE SHELTER BUNKS was removed from this London Tube station on May 31 after 4½ years. Eighty stations had between them accommodated over 7,600 three-tier bunks for air-raid shelterers.

Photos, Fox, Planet News, The Daily Mirror, P.N.A.

This Battle For Britain Is Not Yet Ended

CLEARING OUR BEACHES OF MINES, a task which has been going on since August 1943, had so far cost the Royal Engineers 98 officers and men killed and 26 wounded or blinded, it was announced on May 31, 1945. An ejector pump, costing about £3,500 (seen above on the beach at Great Yarmouth), is one of the devices used; slung from a crane, it turns over the sand with water jets and reveals the mine. The sapper in control is protected by a screen of heavy armour plating. See also page 424, Vol. 8.

Photo, Keystone

Printed in England and published every alternate Friday by the Proprietors, THE AMALGAMATED PRESS, LTD., The Fleetway House, Farringdon Street, London, E.C.4. Registered for transmission by Canadian Magazine Post. Sole Agents for Australia and New Zealand: Messrs. Gordon & Gotch, Ltd.; and for South Africa: Central News Agency, Ltd.—July 6, 1945. S.S. *Editorial Address:* JOHN CARPENTER HOUSE WHITEFRIARS, LONDON, E.C.4.

Vol 9 The War Illustrated No 211

SIXPENCE Edited by Sir John Hammerton JULY 20, 1945

R.A.F. MOSQUITOES IN BURMA contributed in large measure to the 14th Army's reconquest of that country. Maintenance of aircraft was conducted often in conditions of extreme difficulty, and of necessity in great haste: this one is being worked upon in the Arakan—coastal sector turning-point in the Burma campaign. Activities of Mosquitoes of Eastern Air Command during 18-months' operations included harrying Japanese forces and supplies, and photographic reconnaissance. *Photo, British Official.*

NO. 212 WILL BE PUBLISHED FRIDAY, AUGUST 3

Beginning of the End of the Japs on Labuan

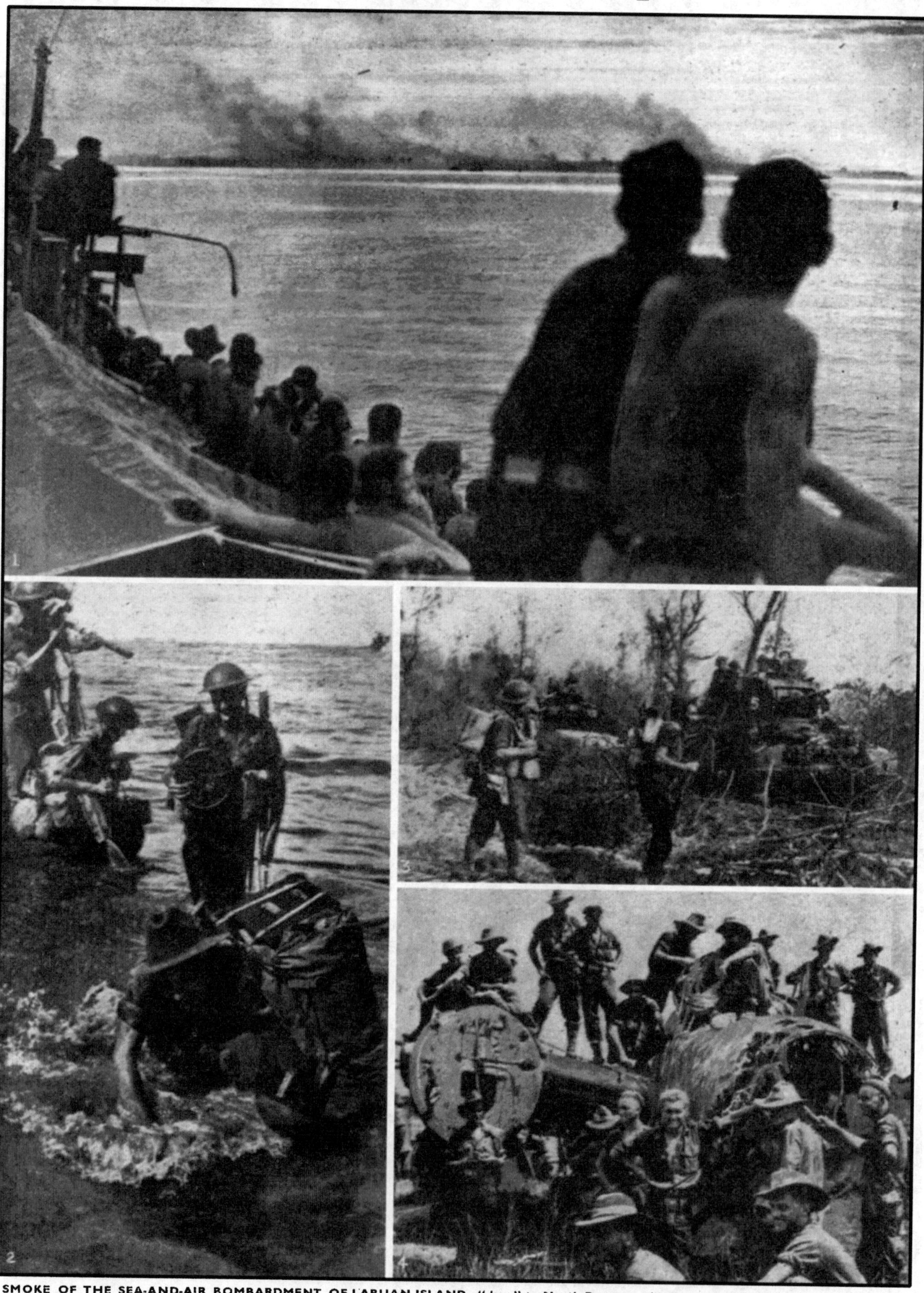

SMOKE OF THE SEA-AND-AIR BOMBARDMENT OF LABUAN ISLAND—"key" to North Borneo—still obscured the coastline (1) as transports carrying men of the Australian 9th Division moved inshore on June 10, 1945. Landing was effected without a fatal casualty. Wading waist deep, Aussies unloaded their signal equipment (2). Matilda tanks nosed forward (3) to flatten the jungle. On the captured airstrip, these troops exultantly clambered over a wrecked Japanese bomber (4). The island was cleared by June 23. See map in page 131. *Photos, L.N.A.*

With Our Armies Today

By MAJ.-GENERAL SIR CHARLES GWYNN K.C.B., D.S.O.

General Sir William Slim's very interesting broadcast and his statement to the Press fully confirm the belief that the Burmese campaign has been conducted with exceptional ability, and that the troops displayed immense dash and energy under most trying conditions (see illus. page 129). Clearly, the experience and training gained in Burma will be of the utmost value in the campaigns that have still to be fought. In new theatres it may not be possible again to use armour as effectively as was done in the final advance on Rangoon, but it seems certain that air transport will be developed still further, and that it will greatly accelerate the pace at which operations can be conducted.

Air transport will be an effective instrument should the Japanese adopt evasive tactics and withdraw into regions where lack of roads would slow down the movements of large forces of heavily armed troops, and where supply problems limit the action of lightly-armed infiltrating parties. General Wingate's great experiment, originally designed, I gather, to attack the communications of the enemy's main forces and to cause confusion in their rear can, I believe, be adapted to deal with an enemy who adopts guerilla tactics. Guerillas in all their offensive operations rely on surprise ; but they themselves are particularly vulnerable to surprise, for even when they can evade destruction by dispersal they can seldom save their munition and supply reserves. Obviously, if troops can be landed and supplied in an unexpected quarter, surprise is much easier to achieve than when the hunt is carried out by the deliberate advance of slow-moving columns.

General Slim has, however, given us fair warning that even heavier tasks than those in Burma lie ahead, and there are undoubtedly places where the Japanese will stand to fight in strength in skilfully prepared positions ; and in such cases their determination to fight to the death, as Okinawa has proved, will demand heavy sacrifices on our part. We may, in fact, have to conduct two forms of warfare : what amounts to trench warfare against an enemy who can only be disposed of by practically complete extermination, and guerilla warfare in which mobility will have to be developed by every means in a country where the obstacles to mobility are exceptionally great.

STEREOTYPED Doctrines of Warfare Giving Place to Original Thought

This applies to the task of dealing with Japan's outlying detachments, which, presumably, will be the chief share the Empire will take in land operations. But if and when Japan's home islands are invaded operations may be of an entirely different order, possibly involving mobile operations of great armies similar to those conducted in the war with Germany. Much, however, would depend on the strategic aims the Allies set themselves and on the reliance they placed on the effects of devastating air attack. It is conceivable that the Allies would be content to aim at seizing certain limited areas and holding them against attacks the Japanese would be bound to deliver, at the same time developing to the utmost the devastating effects of air power.

One thing seems certain—that in all theatres there is little likelihood that the war will be conducted on stereotyped lines, and there will be ample scope for original and imaginative thinking. It is, perhaps, fortunate that the war presents problems of an unprecedented character and therefore stimulates original thought. So far since the Allied counter-offensive started, there are encouraging signs that commanders have risen to the occasion and have not been tied to stereotyped doctrines. But it should, I think, be realized that success achieved has been mainly strategic. The initiative has been

CHINESE TROOPS listen to a talk by their commanding officer before going into action. On June 26, 1945, Chinese forces were reported 65 miles north-east of Wenchow.
Photo, U.S. Official

recovered and Japan has been forced everywhere on to the defensive, and communication with her outlying detachments has been cut. Valuable strategic points have also been secured, providing bases for further operations; and the enemy is kept guessing where the next blow will fall.

ALTOGETHER Unprecedented Problem Presented by Japanese Fanaticism

It is true that a number of tactical successes have also been gained, but on land they have only locally been decisive, and not in every case completely decisive even locally. The main tactical battles are still to come, and undoubtedly it is in the tactical struggle that Japanese fanaticism presents an altogether unprecedented problem. How hard it is to crush fanaticism in defence, Okinawa, and numerous other encounters involving the use of tremendous weight of metal in the attack, have clearly proved. On the other hand, fanaticism in the open or where it spurs on the enemy to attack defensive positions, can accomplish little against modern weapons and leads to immense and disproportionate losses. In the Philippines and in Burma this probably accounts for a ratio of death of over ten to one. Where it is impossible to get the Japanese to fight in the open and to outmanoeuvre them, it might sometimes be possible to play on their fanaticism by deliberately standing on the defensive in positions which fanaticism would induce them to attack. Possession of the strategic initiative often gives opportunities of exploiting such tactics, which are after all as old as warfare itself.

They were, for instance, in a modified form adopted by the Russians in the battle of the Kursk salient, and in a very different setting by Kitchener at Omdurman—two battles which produced exceptionally decisive results. Stalingrad might seem to be of the same character, but I do not quote it, for there the German disaster arose from the misuse of the strategic initiative and there was no question of deliberately inviting attack To stand on the defensive at certain points does not necessarily imply the abandonment of strategic initiative but only the temporary loss of tactical initiative, which is of less importance. It may actually confer advantages by providing better opportunities for the effective use of modern weapons, and in this case it might be a method for making Japanese fanaticism a source of weakness instead of being a military asset—and that, surely, must be one of the aims of the Allied commanders.

SPEED-UP in Chinese Operations Producing Encouraging Results

The completion of the Okinawa battle and the liberation of Luzon obviously releases a large force of American troops for further operations, but presumably a pause for regrouping must be expected before the next major operation is undertaken. Meantime, the Chinese operations in Kwangsi and Chekiang are producing interesting and encouraging results. It is not yet clear how far the success that has been achieved is due to a deliberate withdrawal of the Japanese northwards, in order to shorten lines of communication, difficult to proteet, and to secure greater concentration. In Kwangsi the Japanese can hardly have willingly abandoned their land-line of communication to French Indo-China, and they offer stubborn resistance at the railway centre at Liuchow.

They also counter-attacked with some success from the direction of the Indo-China frontier, apparently in hopes of re-establishing the line of communication that had been cut. The breach is, however, so wide that the prospects of closing it must be small. The obstinate defence of Liuchow, if a general withdrawal northwards is contemplated, may either be a delaying or face-saving fight. Part of the Chinese force engaged has evidently by-passed Liuchow and is approaching Kweilin, where the U.S. Air Force in China had, till it was lost, one of its chief bases.

The progress of the Chinese force which in the middle of May recaptured the large port of Foochow, opposite Formosa, has been even more remarkable. After defeating an evidently weak counter-attack by the Japanese it has advanced northwards from Fukien into Chekiang and now controls some 150 miles of coast line, including the considerable port of Wenchow. Presumably the reason for the weakness of the opposition is that in the coastal regions the Japanese have relied on sea communications which can no longer be effectively maintained in face of air attacks. There is no railway line serving the areas through which the advance has been made, and it should be realized that Japanese permanent occupation exists only in the neighbourhood of railways or steamer communications. In northern Chekiang a railway, however, runs south-west inland from Hangchow, and on it much stronger opposition will probably be met.

BATTLE ZONE IN CHINA, showing Formosa's proximity to the mainland, also Hong Kong and the approaches from the South and East China Seas.

B.L.A. at Work and Play Across the Channel

BRITISH TRANSIT-CAMP at Calais, through which, up to mid-June 1945 over 1,000,000 of our leave men had passed, features a gift-shop (1). B.L.A. troops, homeward bound, paused to look at the attractive wooden cut-out toys, whose prices, however, were in some cases as much as 800 per cent above pre-war level.

Guarded by a Canadian infantryman, Col.-General Blaskowitz (2), once commander of the German 25th Army, in captivity at Appledoorn, Holland. First dance at Belsen camp (see also illus. in page 118) after its partial demolition on May 21 was an open-air affair (3); our men's partners were Yugoslav girls awaiting repatriation.

At Hilden, near Düsseldorf in Prussia, on June 16, at the handing-over of the zone previously occupied by the U.S. 22nd Corps to the 53rd British Division (G.O.C., Maj.-Gen. R. K. Ross, C.B.E., D.S.O., M.C.), the Union Jack floated gaily at the masthead (4).

Photos, British Official, Topical, Keystone, New York Times Photos

8th Army Activities Under Italy's Blue Skies

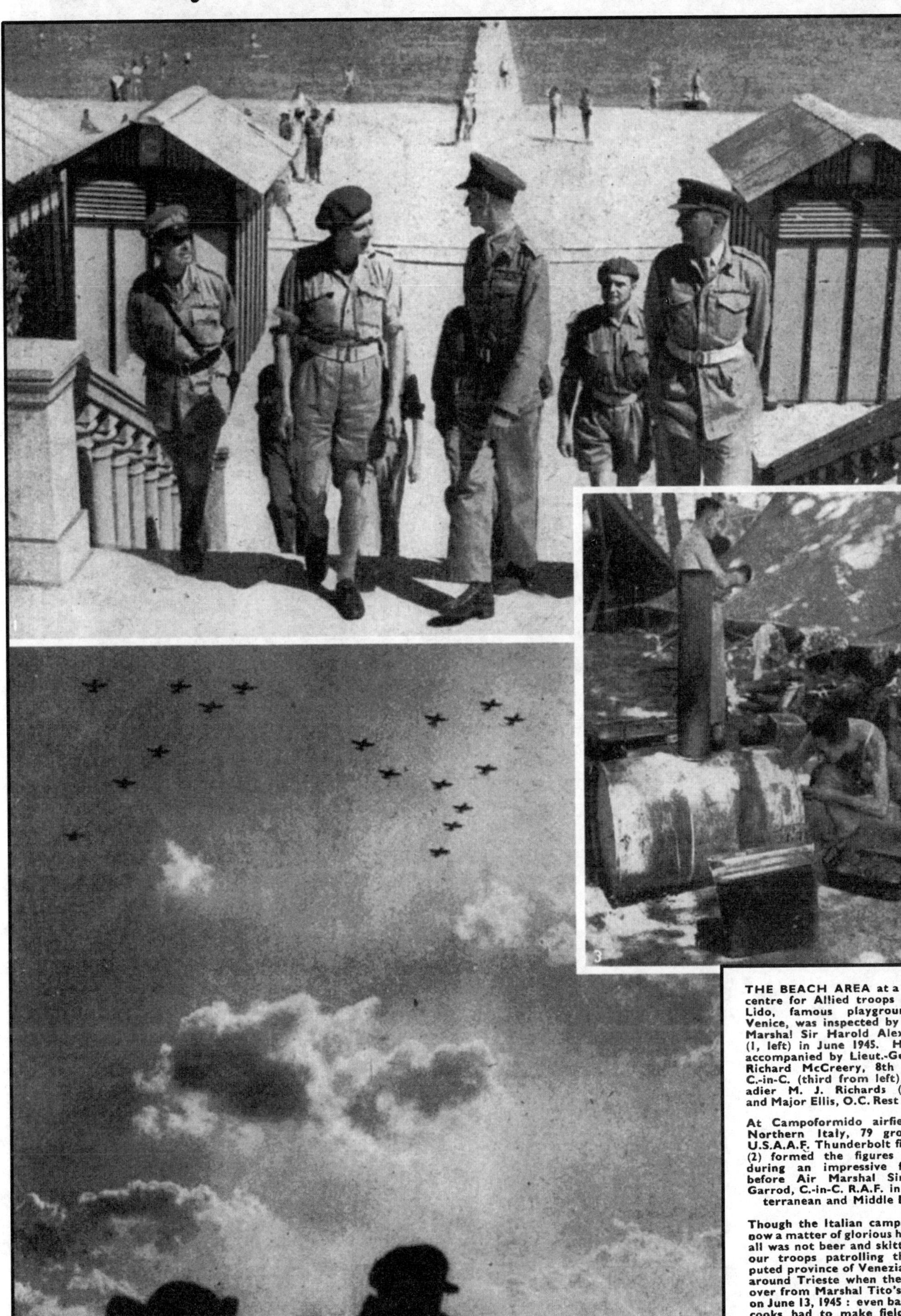

THE BEACH AREA at a leave-centre for Allied troops at the Lido, famous playground of Venice, was inspected by Field-Marshal Sir Harold Alexander (1, left) in June 1945. He was accompanied by Lieut.-Gen. Sir Richard McCreery, 8th Army C.-in-C. (third from left), Brigadier M. J. Richards (right), and Major Ellis, O.C. Rest Camp.

At Campoformido airfield, in Northern Italy, 79 group of U.S.A.A.F. Thunderbolt fighters (2) formed the figures "79" during an impressive fly-past before Air Marshal Sir Guy Garrod, C.-in-C. R.A.F. in Mediterranean and Middle East.

Though the Italian campaign is now a matter of glorious history, all was not beer and skittles for our troops patrolling the disputed province of Venezia Gulia around Trieste when they took over from Marshal Tito's forces on June 13, 1945 : even battalion cooks had to make field-ovens from old oil barrels (3).

 Photos, British Official

HOME FROM THEIR LAST VOYAGE IN CONVOY, a big fleet of British merchant shipping lies peacefully at anchor off Gourock, on the Clyde, after safe return from the United States. The official end of the war at sea anywhere this side of the Indian Ocean or the Pacific coast of the American Continent—and with it the convoy system in those waters—was announced by the Admiralty on May 29, 1945, when the burning of navigation lights "at full brilliancy" was sanctioned. Outstanding is the liner Queen Mary (left centre), whose wartime adventures are described in page 168. British merchant shipping losses since 1939 were: 1,360 ships (7,620,000 tons) by U-boats; 340 ships (830,000 tons) mined; 970,000 tons sunk by surface raiders; 1,590,000 tons destroyed by aircraft; 370,000 tons by other enemy action. *Photo, J. Hall, Gourock*

With Our Navies Today

By

FRANCIS E. McMURTRIE

On the first of July 1945 the most famous ship in the Royal Australian Navy arrived at Devonport to undergo a complete refit. H.M.A.S. Australia is a cruiser of 10,000 tons, with a main armament of eight 8-in. guns, and was launched on the Clyde in 1927. Since the outbreak of war in 1939 she has seen service in many seas. After some preliminary convoy work in the waters around the Australian Commonwealth she proceeded to the Atlantic in the spring of 1940, and took part in the attack on Dakar in the following July. In March 1941 she returned to Sydney to hoist the flag of Rear-Admiral J. G. Crace, under whom she served in a mixed Australian and American naval force based on New Caledonia from December of the same year.

The Australia took part in the Battle of the Coral Sea, the first check given to the tide of Japanese conquest, in May 1942. She was also present at the landings at Tulagi and in Guadalcanal in the month of August, when her sister ship, H.M.A.S. Canberra, was lost. Under Rear-Admiral Crutchley she participated in various amphibious operations in the South-West Pacific, including the landings in Dutch New Guinea in 1943.

In 1944, wearing the broad pennant of Commodore J. A. Collins, R.A.N., she was attached to the Seventh U.S. Fleet under Vice-Admiral Kinkaid, which covered the landings in Leyte. In the fierce struggle for that island she played an active part, and in October 1944 was hit by a Japanese plane which crashed on to her bridge. Nineteen officers and men were killed and 54 wounded, including the Commodore, who was temporarily invalided from his command as a result.

Commodore H. B. Farncomb, R.A.N., succeeded to the command of the Australian Squadron, and hoisted his broad pennant in the Australia shortly afterwards. Three months later the ship was again severely damaged by Japanese air attack while she was covering the landing of American troops in Lingayen Gulf, Luzon, three officers and 41 ratings being killed and one officer and 68 ratings wounded. Though temporary repairs were executed, it has since been decided that the ship shall be thoroughly overhauled, refitted and modernized. Captain J. M. Armstrong, D.S.O., R.A.N., is now in command of the cruiser. Like Commodore Farncomb, he was one of the first entry of Commonwealth naval cadets when the Royal Australian Naval College was opened in 1913. He and his officers and ship's company have received a warm welcome in this country. Greeted on arrival by an appreciative signal from the Board of Admiralty, they have since been entertained by the City of London.

As the result of investigations by Allied experts, more is now known of the naval developments which the Germans were planning. Though designs for very large battleships are believed to have been prepared these never got beyond the paper stage, all energies being concentrated on submarine construction. One of the improvements which enemy inventors were trying to perfect was a torpedo with a possible range of 80 miles and an acoustic device in its nose which would enable it to find its target. Experiments had also been carried out with controlled torpedoes, intended to overcome the baffling effect of ships zigzagging. Another ingenious contrivance which it was hoped to bring into operation was a glider, to be released from an aircraft and directed towards a fleet or convoy. As it neared its objective it would drop a torpedo—another example of the German tendency to produce automatic weapons in which no personnel was risked.

Secrets of U-boats Building at Time of the Great Surrender

Jet propulsion for submarines was also proposed. It was hoped by this means to increase under-water speeds to about 25 knots, as compared with the normal maximum of eight or nine knots when submerged. As an instalment, there were U-boats under construction which were expected to be capable of 15 knots under water. This speed is not unprecedented, as towards the end of the last war it was actually attained in submerged condition by the British submarines of the "R" class. These were specially designed with the object of stalking U-boats beneath the surface, for which purpose they were given this very high submerged speed, obtained by a special type of electric motor. In the case of the German vessels, fuel of a novel kind is understood to have been the main factor.

It may be assumed that all results so far obtained by the Germans in these experiments will be placed at the disposal of British naval constructors for their guidance in designing our future ships and weapons. In this war British scientists, when confronted with novel problems by the enemy have invariably proved themselves equal to finding antidotes, notably in the case of the magnetic and acoustic mines and the many complicated variations of these unpleasant inventions. Moreover, we have improved on them by devices of our own which have baffled the enemy. For the Germans the war is by no means over while there remain large numbers of British mines of the most diverse description to be swept from the channels around the ports on the Baltic and North Sea coasts. Inevitably there will be casualties amongst the German minesweepers engaged in this work, whose personnel are probably wishing heartily that Hitler's first secret weapon, the magnetic mine, had never been devised (see story in page 124, Vol. 7). Since the foregoing was written, news has been received that a German minesweeper engaged in clearing a minefield off the coast of Norway had been blown up with the loss of most if not all of those on board.

It was recently disclosed that the U.S.S. Bunker Hill, a sister ship of the Franklin (see page 122), had, like the latter, an extremely narrow escape from destruction by Japanese suicide aircraft on May 11. An aircraft carrier of 27,100 tons, the Bunker Hill was the flagship of Vice-Admiral Mark A. Mitscher, in control of the fast task force which has operated repeatedly within close range of the Japanese coast. Within half a minute two enemy planes crashed into the ship in quick succession. One of them struck the island superstructure, where control of the ship is centred, killing three officers and 11 ratings within 20 feet of where the admiral was standing. Previously the other aircraft had dropped a 500-lb. bomb through the flight deck ; this luckily passed out through the side of the ship and exploded in the air. The plane itself skidded over the side into the sea. But a bomb from the second aircraft penetrated to the gallery deck of the carrier, where it exploded, starting a terrific fire.

A cruiser and three destroyers drew close alongside the blazing ship, taking off many of the injured and helping to fight the fires. The admiral himself remained on board until the flames were under control. This was not achieved until the captain ordered the ship to make a sharp turn under full helm. This caused the great vessel to list heavily, with the effect of sliding overboard masses of burning debris and tons of water. Even so, it was many hours before the ship could be considered out of danger from burning petrol and exploding ammunition. By that time there were 392 dead and 264 injured. After temporary repairs had been executed, the Bunker Hill was ordered to Puget Sound Navy Yard for refit. She is the third U.S. fleet aircraft carrier that has been saved by a slender margin from destruction as the result of Japanese suicide attacks recently. (See also page 180.)

SURRENDERED U-BOATS moored at Lisnahilly, near Londonderry, Northern Ireland, totalled over fifty ; they included nine of the "21" class (1,600 tons, carrying 23 torpedoes); four of "9" class, and 39 of "7" class (each of 500 tons).

Photo, British Official

How Two Sea-Queens Ran the Gauntlet of War

Ferry-boats for millionaires, Britain's two greatest liners were pitched by the war on to the troubled waters of the world with thousands of fighting-men and tons of stores cramming decks and holds. Something of the meaning of this mighty change is conveyed in this account of the wartime careers of the Queen Mary and the Queen Elizabeth, by Capt. FRANK H. SHAW.

Few who saw the stately Queen Mary start her maiden record-breaking Atlantic voyage would have visualized the mighty ship as one of the most potent factors-to-be in world-victory. She was the acme of luxury, a ferry-boat for millionaires; the biggest, fastest, most superb ship afloat. And when she pulled out from Southampton one received the impression that half the seaport was leaving its moorings and heading for the Atlantic.

When the war came she was stripped of her elaborate trimmings and converted to national service. Her sleek black paint was overlaid with battleship grey; 6-in. guns were mounted on her afterpart; high-angled artillery pointed skywards from every salient angle. Her swimming baths became ammunition magazines; her children's playgrounds quarters for expeditionary troops. Because of her high speed she was qualified to hurry through the worst danger zones. Her enormous capacity made her ideal for transporting vast numbers of men and masses of war material to whichever quarter of the embattled world was most in need of such reinforcements. Similarly with her sister ship, the Queen Elizabeth, whose construction on the Clyde was arrested through industrial depression in the pre-war years.

September 1939 found the Queen Mary outward bound from Southampton with 2,332 passengers. The Atlantic swarmed with U-boats, but she gained port unmolested. She stayed tied up in New York, partly because she was too valuable to be risked in open sea. For the enemy to have claimed her sinking would have been reckoned as a major victory. There was a question of converting her into an armed merchant cruiser, but fortunately this was vetoed. For armed merchant cruisers were, even in 1939, anachronisms. They were too vulnerable, because of their enormous freeboard, their comparatively slow speed and their inability to carry guns of big enough calibre to engage such ships as the so-called German pocket battleships and 8-in. gun cruisers on anything approaching an equality.

The Queen Elizabeth was not completed when war began; and she was a source of great anxiety to the Admiralty, for the Clyde was wide open to enemy air attack. When she was fit for sea, in February 1940, she was at once dispatched to the security of New York harbour. A month later the Queen Mary was sent to Sydney, going through Panama; and there she was stripped and made ready for service as a gigantic transport. She packed 5,000 Australian troops into her hull and having landed these in England, she collected an equal number of British troops and sailed with them for the Middle East.

Major Mishap off Donegal Coast

That meant the long way round—via the Cape of Good Hope—for the Mediterranean was by then a danger zone alive with enemy submarines, and under persistent threat of air attack by a seemingly invincible Luftwaffe and Regia Aeronautica. Having nearly twice the speed of the average Far East liner, the Queen Mary devoured distance greedily. At full speed she would have outdistanced almost any escort, and had a range exceeding that of most warships.

She had one major mishap, off the coast of Donegal, on Oct. 2, 1942, though this was not disclosed by the Admiralty until May 1945. With 15,000 American troops on board the Queen Mary was travelling all-out for the Clyde with an escort of two cruisers, one of which was H.M.S. Curacoa. The Queen Mary's look-out raised an alarm—a suspected U-boat had been sighted. The liner immediately wheeled and, travelling at nearly 30 knots, crashed full-tilt into the Curacoa which, cut in half, sank in five minutes. Although rescue measures were promptly taken, 338 men and officers of the Curacoa were lost. The Queen Mary arrived at the Clyde with a great dent in her bow. Temporary repairs were carried out at Greenock, and when she returned to New York a new bow was fitted.

Meantime the Queen Elizabeth went from New York to Singapore, where she was converted from luxury liner to utilitarian trooper. By removing her bulkheads, alleyways, panelling and the ornate furnishings of peacetime employment, her carrying capacity was more than trebled. Intended to set the world on fire as the last word in sea travel, the Queen Elizabeth performed her first passenger trip as a grey, crowded trooper; her decks crammed with men and her holds with warlike stores. Carrying from 5,000 to 6,000 men at a time, by the end of 1941 the two great ships had transported at least 80,000 soldiers to zones where their services were urgently needed.

THE QUEEN ELIZABETH'S CAPTAIN in the wheelhouse during a recent voyage to New York. On June 24 the great liner took aboard nearly 15,000 American airmen for transport home from Scotland. See also facing page, and page 141. *Photo, British Official*

Improvisations were made to adapt these Atlantic ships for tropical and sub-tropical work. Heat was the main enemy, especially in vessels crowded to capacity; but this was overcome with the usual resourcefulness of the Merchant Navy, to which the leviathans continued to belong. Although under Admiralty and War Office direction, their care and upkeep were in the hands of the Ministry of War Transport, skilled in such matters.

Hard, tireless work compelled overhauls; these were completing when Japan hit at Pearl Harbour. That meant added activity for the two great liners. A certain amount of improvisation enabled them to load some 8,000 U.S. fighting men aboard, and at top speed, with Japanese submarines and aircraft-carriers a steady menace, they bore these urgent reinforcements to Sydney, for the defence of Australia. Here again their speed saved them. Going all-out they could outpace most surface-craft, and careful navigation took them clear of air-attack zones.

The U.S.A. being now in the war to the hilt, the value of the two ships as transports for helping to convey a U.S. Expeditionary Force to the European war theatre was evident. They were returned to New York, via the Panama Canal, whose locks had recently been enlarged to permit the transit of the mightiest vessels; and, once again laden very heavily, they tackled the ever-menacing problem of the North Atlantic. Here the German U-boat campaign was brewing up to its climax. There were big surface ships still threatening forays; the Luftwaffe was far from being licked.

What a bag either would have been had she been hit! By virtue of still greater economies of space, the "Queens" could carry a matter of 15,000 troops apiece. Fifteen thousand men—a whole division transported at a time to whichever area of war stood most in need of them. Mussolini's action in closing the Mediterranean hardly mattered. By way of Freetown and Simonstown to Suez, the great Cunarders made distance a laughing-stock, and were able to reinforce the Desert Army so as to permit it to inflict that shattering defeat at El Alamein.

They Scented Victory from Afar

With Alexander and Montgomery supplied, the "Queens" resumed a shuttle service across the Atlantic. Come hell or high water, they flashed east and west; and each westward trip brought into Europe the eager young legions who scented victory from afar. By 1944's stormy end they had conveyed but few short of a million men—80 per cent of them American. More than once each ship carried as many as 20,000 men. Hitler learnt of their activities. Maybe his intuition told him that such colossal craft threatened him, and he offered fabulous rewards to such U-boat commanders as could destroy them. But 33-knot speed laughed disdain at the best the Fuehrer could do.

Nevertheless the Queen Elizabeth had a narrow escape from heavy damage, when in April 1945, two days out from New York, an enormous wave almost overwhelmed her. Thousands of tons of water cascaded on to her decks, and for one terrible second the 85,000-ton liner almost disappeared. Miraculously she righted herself, and there was not a single casualty, though a great deal of material damage had been done.

Each westward trip these great liners crammed their holds with prisoners of war, dispatched to the United States for safer keeping. Three times during the war did the Queen Mary carry our Prime Minister and his Staff to the U.S.A. for consultation with America's leaders. Throughout this arduous service the ships have valiantly maintained the Cunard Line's proud record of safety. They have, between them, established a record never before approached, never likely to be surpassed.

They were originally designed to serve in emergency as Armed Merchant Cruisers. Their record is prouder by far than if they had been so employed. Thus it was, that between the spring of 1940 and May 1945, the Mary and the Elizabeth steamed over 950,000 miles—equivalent to 38 journeys round the world—to bring safely across the oceans 1,250,000 fighting men of the Allied Nations. Now, with that other famous British liner the Aquitania, they are to run a shuttle service between Britain and the U.S., taking home thousands of American troops.

Hitler Put a Price on the Two Queens' Heads

QUEEN ELIZABETH, 85,000 tons, world's biggest and fastest liner, and her sister ship the Queen Mary (80,000 tons), since the spring of 1940 between them steamed over 95,000 miles to bring safely across the oceans 1,250,000 troops of the United Nations, it was disclosed on May 19, 1945. U.S. wounded attended a mid-Atlantic religious service held in the Queen Elizabeth's Officers' Lounge (left). Defensively armed against likely attack—her wartime transport missions took her from the Mediterranean to the Atlantic and westwards to the Pacific—her forward gun-turrets (below) were always manned: the massive anchor-cable is seen in the foreground. Her fastest Atlantic war-time crossing took under five days.

QUEEN MARY, holder of the Atlantic Blue Riband, badly dented her bows (above) when she collided with H.M.S. Curacoa (story in facing page). On three occasions she carried Mr. Churchill and the Chiefs of Staff to the United States for important war conferences. She is seen (right) dead ahead from the bridge of the British cruiser Scylla as, with the Premier and his party aboard, bound for Washington, the Queen Mary sped across the Atlantic in May 1943. So vital were the Queen Mary's and the Queen Elizabeth's war-transport work that Hitler offered the equivalent of £50,000 and the highest State honours to any U-boat which sank either of them.

Photos, British Official, Keystone

Eyrie Where Hitler Planned World Conquest

FUEHRER'S "EAGLE'S NEST," ON A 6,000-ft. MOUNTAIN TOP above his famous retreat at Berchtesgaden, is now a show place for U.S. troops. It is entered through a vast bronze doorway (1) at ground-level, leading to a passage tunnelled through the rock to the lift (2). A superb view of the Austrian Alps (3) is had from the all-stone house (4) which miraculously survived the bombing of April 25, 1945 (see page 58). Predominant feature of the living-room (5) is a solid oak table 15 ft. in diameter. The all-electric kitchen (6).

 Photos, Keystone

Vast Floating Dockyards in the Pacific War

FIRST PHOTOGRAPHS OF ADVANCED BASE SECTIONAL DOCKS (ABSDs) of the U.S. Navy reveal the staggering nature of these floating workshops in size and conception. Constructed in separate units, these are towed as near as possible to the combat zone and there speedily assembled. The largest (top), with capacity up to 100,000 tons, accommodates two ships at once. In the 10-section dock (below) a battleship stands high and dry for repairs. See also pages 666 and 743, Vol. 8.

Photos, Associated Press, New York Times Photos

Now It Can Be Told!

PHANTOM PATROLS: G.H.Q. LIAISON REGIMENT

BEATING the speed of normal communications by hours, patrols of the Phantom Regiment (officially, G.H.Q. Liaison Regiment) did their "recce" work up with, and sometimes in advance of, our front-line troops, keeping Army, Army Group and Base H.Q. informed almost minute-by-minute of all that was happening. In no other way could such complete and speedy "pictures" of the progress of operations have been presented to those immediately responsible.

COMMANDED by Lieut.-Col. A. H. McIntosh, this remarkable organization founded by Maj.-Gen. Hopkinson (killed while commanding the 1st Airborne Division in Italy) began secret operations early in 1940, in France, and its existence was not revealed until May 1945. How the 150 officers and 1,250 other ranks gathered and swiftly passed back vital information throughout the war in Europe and elsewhere is told here.

Messages were sent from under the noses of the enemy by means of very small and special wireless sets, invented for the purpose by Captain Peter Astbury. These "scrambled" the coded messages, in which condition —if intercepted by the enemy or any other unauthorized person—they were, of course, quite unintelligible. Transformation to sense came at the other end. During the eleven months of fighting on the Western Front, Lieut.-Col. McIntosh's "Phantoms" sent more than 70,000 of these messages from the battle areas to the headquarters of the 12th and 21st Army Groups.

When circumstances required it, men were dropped by parachute—sometimes behind the enemy lines at night—with their very small wireless sets. And if either operators or codes fell into enemy hands the enemy would be left none the wiser. Codes were changed daily, the men being kept informed of the changes in a highly ingenious manner.

WHEN the secret regiment came back from Dunkirk, and other places, after the fall of France, sections were deployed around the coasts of England where invasion was most probable. They were to speed the news of any attempted landing, and their headquarters were in very innocent-looking surroundings in St. James's Park, London. Here were the base wireless sets to which the Phantoms worked, information being passed therefrom to the G.H.Q. Home Forces and what ultimately became the 21st Army Group. The headquarters in St. James's Park comprised also some pigeon lofts containing carrier-pigeons which supplemented the Regiment's wireless. "There," said Lieut.-Col. McIntosh, "we had an engine which would run a lighting set and wireless sets if the main current of London were cut off by bombing, and an air raid shelter in which the work could be done."

Towards the end of 1940 a squadron of the Regiment left this country for Greece, and until almost the whole squadron was made prisoner they were in wireless contact with London. Adopting a commando role, a squadron joined the raid on Dieppe, and suffered rather severe casualties; one patrol failed to return and nothing since has been heard of them. In November 1942 two squadrons went with the 1st Army to North Africa and operated throughout the campaign, finally joining up with the 8th Army.

There they listened-in to the wireless "talk" of the tanks, gleaning every scrap that was of interest and weaving this into a running commentary, so that out of the fog of confused battle there was presented to headquarters a clear outline of positions, casualties and strengths.

EARLY in 1944 a squadron was trained for parachute work. This was the squadron which had been in action at Dieppe, and special volunteers were called for. After the parachute training they joined the S.A.S. (Special Air Service—see page 350, Vol. 8) as their "communications," and finally dropped with the S.A.S. parties behind enemy lines. Then in June 1944 came the greatest test and ordeal of the organization.

Some of the Phantoms were parachuted into France before D-Day, others went in with the assault troops. First news of the Normandy landings were sent back by them. By July the complete Regiment was in France, deployed with the British, Canadian and American Armies. How Phantom, "one of the brains trust units of the British Army," as it has been called, became a Lend-Lease service from Britain to the U.S.A. in military operations in north-west Europe was revealed in June 1945. In the early stages of the assault on the Normany beaches General Eisenhower, Supreme Commander of the Allied Expeditionary Forces, visited the British 2nd Army H.Q., then located near Portsmouth, and was considerably impressed by the complete picture of operations which was available.

He asked how it was done. The answer was, "Phantom patrol." It was explained to him how the organization flashed back by wireless to England the positions of brigades and battalions in the beach-head battles. Gen. Eisenhower immediately asked if he could have a Phantom unit for work with the U.S. formations.

"There was a Phantom squadron in Scotland," said Capt. K. W. Salter, commander of a Phantom patrol in the 2nd Army, "and that squadron, within 24 hours, was brought south and sent across the Channel, complete with officers, other ranks, vehicles and equipment to join formations of the U.S. Army. Throughout the campaign those patrols worked with the American divisions and corps and did a great deal to give a full picture of the battles to the higher commands." The Americans had planned to build up their own U.S. Phantom organization, modelled on the British, but the campaign was won before they had an opportunity to put their own Phantoms in the field.

The map-room of General Crerar (1st Canadian Army) secured a substantial proportion of its information from the Regiment,

MAJ.-GEN. HOPKINSON, O.B.E., M.C. (right), founder of the Phantom Patrols ("one of the brains trust of the British Army"), and Capt. P. Fletcher. *Photo, British Official*

General Patton (U.S. 3rd Army) acknowledged a very great deal of assistance, and our own 2nd Army was also greatly benefited. They were with the parachute troops at Arnhem, patrols went with the assault parties across the Rhine and into Germany, and "due to us," said the Commanding Officer of the Regiment, "nearly everybody knew exactly where all the leading troops of all the Armies had got to and a firm grip on the situation was kept."

HOUR by hour during the Ardennes breakthrough every move of German armour was reported by these men who wear a small "P" on the right shoulder. The closing of the Falaise Gap became news through their efforts. They made known the first details of the German concentration camps and prisoner of war camps. The last spectacular event was the link-up with the Russians; a Phantom patrol was directed by the U.S. 1st Army to a certain point where the link-up was expected to take place, and the moment it became an accomplished fact the news was put through.

Now the patrols are in Hamburg, Bremen, Copenhagen. They flew to Norway, Rotterdam, Amsterdam, The Hague. And the curtain is now waiting to go up on what will be the final scene of all.

PIGEON LOFTS IN ST. JAMES'S PARK held their secret throughout the war with Germany. They housed carrier pigeons which supplemented the G.H.Q. Liaison Regiment's wireless, as told in this page. Here also were base wireless sets to which the Phantoms would have worked had necessity arisen during the invasion-scare days of 1940. *Photo, Keystone*

Military Ports Were Built Secretly in Scotland

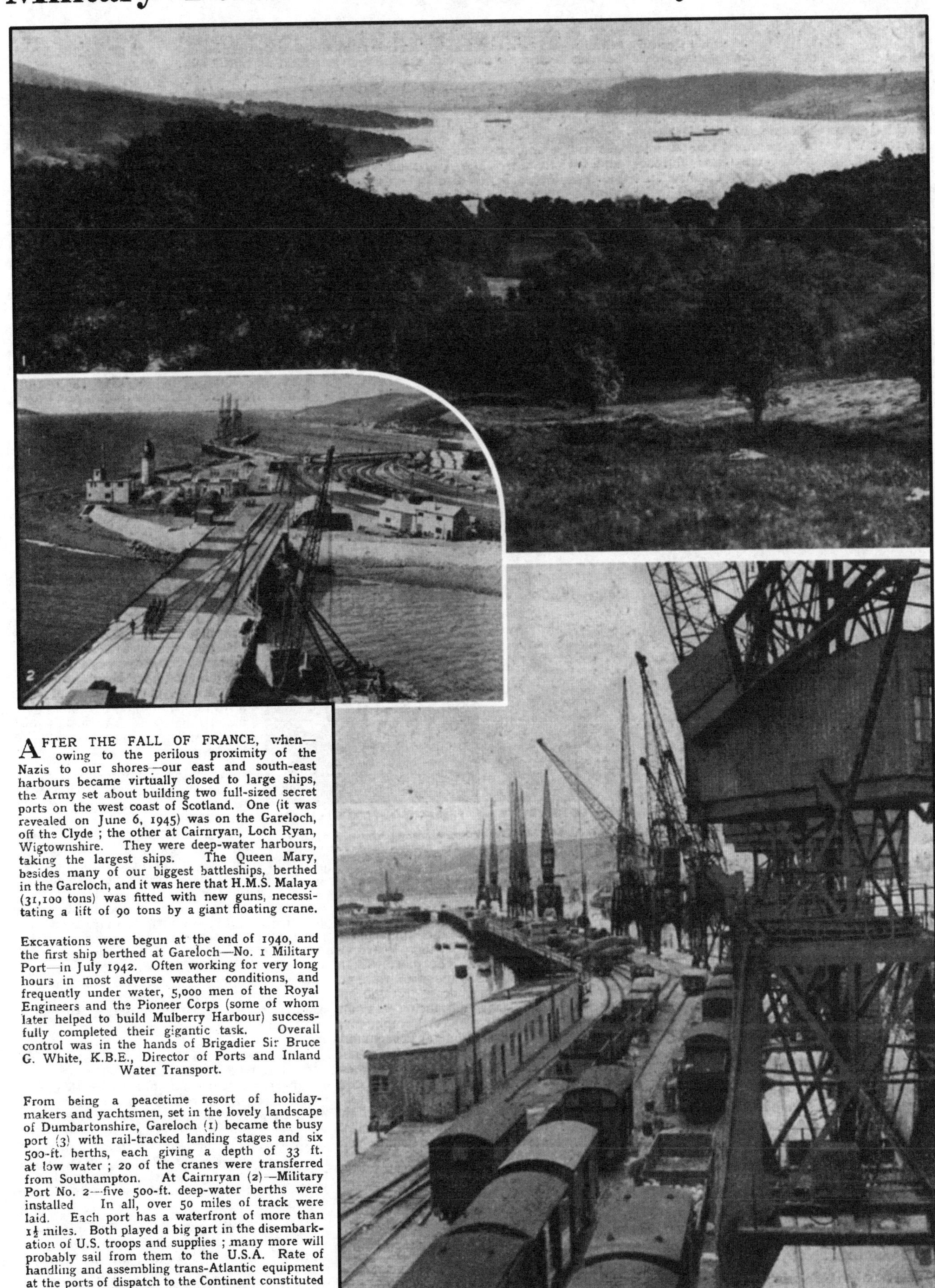

AFTER THE FALL OF FRANCE, when—owing to the perilous proximity of the Nazis to our shores—our east and south-east harbours became virtually closed to large ships, the Army set about building two full-sized secret ports on the west coast of Scotland. One (it was revealed on June 6, 1945) was on the Gareloch, off the Clyde ; the other at Cairnryan, Loch Ryan, Wigtownshire. They were deep-water harbours, taking the largest ships. The Queen Mary, besides many of our biggest battleships, berthed in the Gareloch, and it was here that H.M.S. Malaya (31,100 tons) was fitted with new guns, necessitating a lift of 90 tons by a giant floating crane.

Excavations were begun at the end of 1940, and the first ship berthed at Gareloch—No. 1 Military Port—in July 1942. Often working for very long hours in most adverse weather conditions, and frequently under water, 5,000 men of the Royal Engineers and the Pioneer Corps (some of whom later helped to build Mulberry Harbour) successfully completed their gigantic task. Overall control was in the hands of Brigadier Sir Bruce G. White, K.B.E., Director of Ports and Inland Water Transport.

From being a peacetime resort of holiday-makers and yachtsmen, set in the lovely landscape of Dumbartonshire, Gareloch (1) became the busy port (3) with rail-tracked landing stages and six 500-ft. berths, each giving a depth of 33 ft. at low water ; 20 of the cranes were transferred from Southampton. At Cairnryan (2)—Military Port No. 2—five 500-ft. deep-water berths were installed. In all, over 50 miles of track were laid. Each port has a waterfront of more than 1½ miles. Both played a big part in the disembarkation of U.S. troops and supplies ; many more will probably sail from them to the U.S.A. Rate of handling and assembling trans-Atlantic equipment at the ports of dispatch to the Continent constituted a world-record. See also page 190.

Photos, T. R. Aman, British Official

Secret Service Agents Helped to Win the War

The suggestion recently made in the U.S.A. that they should endeavour to build up an Intelligence Service on the British model is a compliment even greater than that paid to us after the 1914-18 war by the Germans, when the latter declared that the superiority of our espionage system undoubtedly had proved disastrous to them. Striking facts are here revealed by PETER LEIGHTON.

"A V2 storage depot between two hospitals was one of the targets of Spitfire bomber pilots when they attacked rocket launching sites in Holland yesterday . . . Several trains loaded with supplies for the front were found and destroyed outside Deutz near Cologne . . . Shortage of raw materials is believed to be the explanation of the fact that several large plants at the Leuna Works of the I.G. Farben were idle for four days last week . . ." Common enough were these reports during the war with Germany.

How was that storage depot discovered? How was it known that certain vitally loaded trains would pass the station of Deutz at a given time? How did it become known that the Leuna Works were idle? Photographic reconnaissance can, of course, work wonders (see illus. page 733, Vol. 8), but we have yet to get a camera that sees inside buildings and looks up time-tables.

The answer to the question how these typical pieces of vital knowledge were obtained can be given in one word—"Intelligence." That covers many things, involving hundreds, possibly thousands, of men and women who are willing to risk their lives in obtaining information. You can call them spies, if you like, but only a few of the Secret Agents are traitors to their own country, ready to sell information to anyone. The most valuable information comes from men and women to whom fame and monetary reward are secondary. These who take their lives in their hands to ferret out the enemy's secrets get no medals. For obvious reasons their names and stories seldom appear in the newspapers.

But over 40 names of people appeared in headlines of German papers last year as having been executed for "intelligence with the enemy." No details were given as to what they did or how they were caught. It is possible some of them were not Agents at all. The Gestapo would rather execute ten innocent people than allow one spy to slip through the net. Reading the names, one wonders what stories may eventually be told in full. There was the elderly Flora Tropfer, mother of five children, for instance. She was executed "as a British spy" in Mulhouse under German occupation. And Arno von Wedekind, described as a Swiss student, devoted to the study of philosophy in the University of Goettingen.

Germans Revealed Luftwaffe Secret

The typical spy is not a Carl Lody, a Sidney Reilly or a Mata Hari. In spite of Hollywood films, the success of an Agent must depend upon his being so very ordinary, having regular work and a normal background. There are very few super-spies these days. The really big men in Intelligence do not go to enemy territory. Their task is to weld together a score or a thousand separate reports, often of the most prosaic and apparently unimportant kind, sent by the Agents who actually do the "spying."

The days when blue-prints of secret weapons or other documents might be stolen in trains (if, indeed, those days ever existed) are over. But occasionally valuable information may be picked up by the sheerest luck. Air Vice-Marshal C. E. H. Medhurst, the Intelligence Service expert, early in the war, told how an Englishman making a journey in Italy got into a compartment with two Germans and an Italian. The Germans swapped stories and then, gently chaffed by the Italian, blurted out why the Luftwaffe kept flying to the Shetlands but never dropped bombs there. The Englishman, whose name of course may not be revealed, reported the conversation. It meant nothing to him. But to our technical experts it was the clue to a line of radio research that the Nazis were pursuing, of which our authorities had no previous inkling. To say that this information led to the saving of the lives of hundreds of our merchant seamen would be no exaggeration.

One of the most effective pieces of intelligence work was at Peenemunde (see pages 510, 617, Vol. 8; also p. 253, Vol. 7). Reconnaissance planes may have given us clues to the importance of the place, but where the Nazis thought that we obtained our information was obvious immediately after the great raid which set their V-weapon campaign back a year. The place was at once swamped with Gestapo men who put every civilian within miles "through the hoop." What staggered them was our exact information that at a certain time on a certain day a certain building at Peenemunde would be filled with scientists, technicians and high officers of the Luftwaffe; 5,000 of them were reported to have been killed in the raid, including Germany's "V-weapon genius," General von Chamier-Glisczensky, and the Luftwaffe's chief of staff General Jeschonnek. There were medals for the R.A.F. men who carried out the raid. There were no medals for the spies! Possibly they themselves perished in the raid.

Months before D-Day and up to the end of the war in Europe hundreds of men and women were dropped by parachute on enemy-held territory, including two British girls, who played small but vital parts in our preparations for invasion. One revealed that she was twice searched by the Germans, but had always written anything vital on toilet paper, which her searchers rapidly passed over in embarrassment. (See photographs in this page.) "Carpetbagging" was the code word for these dropping operations. A fortnight before V Day, Liberators flew by night from bases in Dijon, France, with Agents who parachuted down in Southern Germany and sent by radio to London urgent reports of enemy movements. Crews on this and other expeditions were all sworn to secrecy, the most stringent security arrangements were enforced at the base aerodromes, none but the station commander and crew were allowed contact with the Agents who were to be their passengers: and that meeting was only an hour or two before the take-off.

Section-Officer SONIA BUTT Flight-Officer M. O'SULLIVAN

YOUNG W.A.A.F. AGENTS, they were among those dropped by parachute before D-Day; to contact the Maquis and render other valuable help to the Allies. Maureen O'Sullivan crawled through hedges and ditches to watch German troop movements, sending and receiving coded messages to and from London through the medium of her portable wireless set. *Photos, British Official, News Chronicle*

Often Extremely Dull Routine Work

In the year of Munich (1939), Parliament voted the modest sum of £180,000 for our Secret Service. During the war years Parliament has, for obvious reasons, given a blank cheque. But the sum spent is not vast. Many of our agents are patriots who want no more than enough to keep up the pretence that is vital to them. Many are engaged on extremely dull routine work. One may have nothing to do but watch trains going by on a particular stretch of line that can be seen from his window. Maybe he has to pretend to be an invalid and lie up, naturally with the bed drawn near to the window. Nothing happens for weeks, perhaps months. Then one day the rhythm of the traffic is changed. Passenger trains are held up while a heavy goods train is shunted on to a branch line. Next day it is the same . . . And later the R.A.F. drop 1,000 ton of bombs on a new factory that the Germans thought was completely concealed and unknown to us.

Parachute and portable wireless have revolutionized intelligence work. It is interesting to recall that it was five French parachutists, dropped behind the German lines in 1918, who solved the mystery of the shells falling on Paris and revealed the existence of the Big Bertha gun. It was the brilliant work of Lieut. N. L. A. Jewell, R.N., in his submarine that paved the way for the Anglo-American landings in North Africa in November 1942 (see article p. 398 and portrait p. 635, Vol. 6). This episode, and others prior to D-Day on the beaches of Normandy, as well as in Sicily and Italy, resulted in the coining of the phrase "Undersea Secret Service."

Mr. Churchill in the House of Commons has paid tribute to the work of our Intelligence Agents and told how the many reports, often apparently of no importance, have frequently enabled a picture of what was happening to be pieced together. It was no accident that Mr. Churchill was able to give Marshal Stalin warning of the impending German attack on Russia in June 1941, and to tell him by how many divisions it would be made.

We have no elaborate schools for espionage such as the Germans had at Sonnhofen, and on the outskirts of Hamburg, with its laboratories for the faking of official papers. But the war has proved that our Intelligence is one of the best organized in the world. Hitler's V-weapons, as further instance, were known to our experts before they appeared over here.

Photos, British Official, Pictorial Press

Through Mud and Rock to Flay the Japs in Burma

Beaches of Rangoon river were awash with mud when the R.A.F. Regiment landed Ack-Ack guns (1) on May 2, 1945; 14th Army units entered the capital the following day. On June 16, Gen. Chambers' 26th Indian Division marched in a victory parade through the captured city (2). Chatham Island, Jap base in the Andamans joined by a quarter-mile causeway to Port Blair, was bombed on May 17 by R.A.F. Liberators (3). Blasting the last rock separating constructional teams from North and South, U.S. engineers (4) helped to complete the vital Ledo Road (see also page 719, Vol. 8).

Suicide Pilots Plunge to Death in the Pacific—

"The war in this area is now going faster than anyone thought," declared Admiral Sir Bruce Fraser, C.-in-C. British Pacific Fleet, on June 24, 1945. Smearing a death-trail, a Jap bomber (1) caught by gunfire from a U.S. carrier off Kyushu is about to finish up in the sea. Tense moment as a Jap suicide pilot tries to manoeuvre his Zero on to the deck of a U.S. warship (2). Seven have crashed on British ships: firefighters on one of our carriers after one such attack (3).

Photos, U… Popper, …

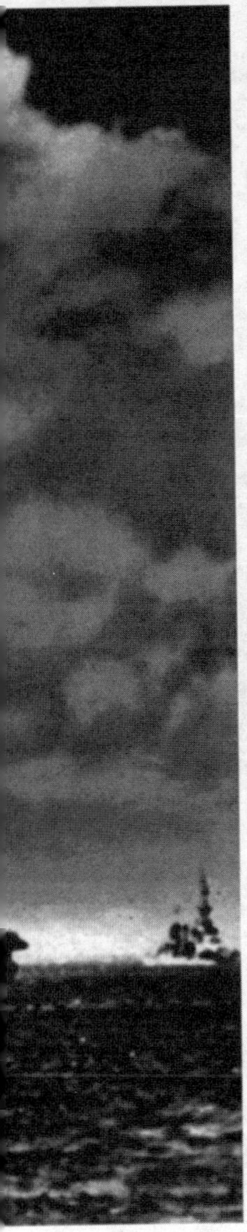

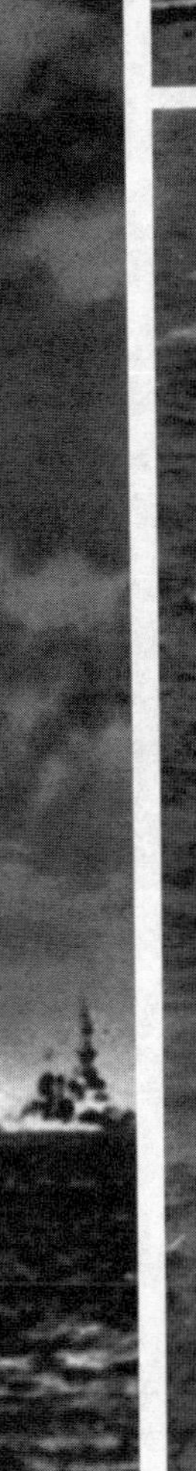

ficial, Paul
ork Times
s

— *Whilst Flat-Tops Scourge the Enemy in the Sky*

After hot action, escort carriers of the U.S. Pacific Fleet, with full loads of fighter and bomber aircraft, return to a forward base (4) to refuel and take on supplies for the resumption of battle; extreme right of the anchored five is a heavy cruiser. Close-massed on the flight deck of this Essex class carrier steaming at full speed in enemy-infested waters (5), swarms of Grumman Hellcats and Curtiss Helldivers are ready at a moment's notice to take to the sky.

Behind the Scenes on Battle-Torn Okinawa

Photos, Keystone, L.N.A. Associated Press

A costly victory for the Americans, Okinawa has been hell for the natives: aged Okinawans rest on the way to safety under guidance of a U.S. Marine (1). Cleverly camouflaged with foliage, Jap coastal luggers feel the weight of air attack: in background, a direct hit (2). Marines examine an enemy "Baka" bomb (3) found on Yontan airfield; rocket-propelled, it is launched from an aircraft and, guided by its suicide pilot, is thrown into a dive to explode on contact. See also page 117.

VIEWS & REVIEWS Of Vital War Books

by Hamilton Fyfe

I HAVE often heard the question asked, as a rule rather petulantly, "What do all these young women in uniform do?" I have often heard people, usually other women, comment on the elaborately dressed hair of W.A.A.F. or W.R.N.S. or A.T.S., their carmined lips, their darkened eyelashes; and add the scornful comment: "How could they do any real work when they're got up like that?" I have always known this was nonsense. I have seen for myself how useful the girls make themselves in all sorts of ways. And now, whenever I hear such ill-informed remarks, I shall recommend the persons who make them to obtain a book called Wrens in Camera (Hollis & Carter, 8s. 6d.) which has told me a great deal about the varied duties the members of this auxiliary naval service perform.

The book consists chiefly of photographs by Lee Miller, but the text by Miss K. Palmer is a valuable part of it. Her studies of Wrens at work are delightful to look at, as well as informative. "Beautiful," they are called by Mrs. Laughton Mathews, Director of the Women's Naval Service.

In her introduction, Mrs. Mathews tells how the Admiralty at the beginning of the War intended to employ women "only on duties which convention had marked as their sphere." There were not more than about half-a-dozen different sorts of job from which they could choose. In the course of five years the number grew to nearly a hundred. One reason for this was that there were not enough men to go round. Another was "the remarkable success of women in the roles allotted to them." It was discovered that they "could not only do the jobs expected of women, but all kinds of technical and mechanical work; they could run boats in the black-out and when it was blowing half a gale; they were calm and cheerful under bombing and shelling."

AT Portsmouth in one of the early blitzes an Order of the Day commended "the manner in which they conducted themselves" as "worthy of the highest praise." About the same time the Flag Officer at Dover, which was under almost continuous fire, wrote, "In spite of all, I still see your Wrens grinning all about the place."

It was on D-Day that the value of their efforts reached its peak. They were employed as Signal Officers and Duty Officers, they operated the wireless, they kept in fighting trim ships and aircraft, guns and torpedoes. "They saw that Jack received his mail, that his pay was in order and that he left shore well-fed; they took supplies of medical stores and ammunition to the ships. They repaired, by electrical and oxy-acetylene welding the landing-craft that by one means or another got home for the impatient repairs so that they could return to the Normandy beaches." To the success of that marvellous combined operation Wrens contributed their full share.

WREN BOARDING OFFICER'S duties require a sound nautical knowledge as well as much tact. This member of the W.R.N.S. is climbing the swaying ladder of a Merchant Navy vessel lying offshore. See also illus. in page 514, Vol. 7. *Photo, British Official*

ONE aspect of their work is that a lot of it fits them for highly skilled jobs when they go back to civil life. The decision to train them to look after machines was taken without any great confidence in their making good. "It could do no harm and it might do a great deal of good" was the attitude at the Admiralty. But very quickly that attitude altered. It was seen that the Wrens who were picked for skilled technical training were keen and easily disciplined as well as intelligent. "Once these pioneers were drafted, they proved themselves so good there was ever-growing demand for them at Naval Ports and Naval Air Arm Stations."

Young Women in Naval Uniform

They were able to take on "maintenance" work, which means work enabling motor-torpedo-boats, motor-gun-boats and other small craft, which return battle-scarred and splintered to their bases, to put to sea again. "Alongside the men of the Navy, dressed in serviceable dungarees, they worked against time to get their little ships repaired so as to be afloat again in the shortest possible time." They cleaned and greased the guns, and they cleaned the ammunition. That sounds a strange operation, but it is a necessity. Both get dirty when seas run high and break green over these small warships. "Up to their elbows in grease," Wrens worked in the torpedo-sheds. In the blacksmith's shop they swung hammers, made new links for chains, straightened out bent davits. As wood-workers they were equally useful, could "replank a stove-in dinghy, and cut up wood accurately for the Naval shipwrights."

Many will find employment as radio mechanics when they put away uniform, thanks to what they have been taught at Naval Air Arm Stations. A photograph shows one of them testing radio equipment in flight, which requires "apart from her trained knowledge, powers of concentration and a steady nerve." Some have learned to be cinema operators, know all about projection, film cutting and servicing, and will no doubt make use of their knowledge in civil life. Those who have been engaged on engines—"making adjustments to the carburettors of a Barracuda," for example, will be able to keep their own cars in running order and, if they want to earn a living that way, to run a garage or find work in a motor-car factory.

"Casting gears in a submarine repair depot" looks dangerous; there is a lot of molten metal about, running in a white-hot stream. "The specialist in charge of a milling machine in a repair and maintenance shop" handles a complicated mechanism with ease and evidently has the "exceptional

WREN HOISTING TORPEDOES from a naval M.T.B. for storage at a British port—just one of the manifold wartime duties the W.R.N.S. have performed, as outlined in the book reviewed here. *Photo, Fox*

ability and skill" which are needed for her work. Another concentrates her mind on a torpedo engine. A Wren electrician is seen carrying out repairs on a M.T.B. A maintenance Wren tests pressure gauges for submarines. A safety equipment worker goes over a rubber dinghy looking for defects in joints or punctures. That may mean the difference between death and safety to an airman shot down into "the drink."

Very often Wrens are disinclined to take commissions because the work of officers is mostly on shore and at desks. They do not care to cut loose from going down to the sea in ships. Their chance to be boarding officers solved this difficulty. "Once again they can feel the live movement of a deck beneath their feet and taste the salty tang of the flying spindrift as they answer the call of a ship from the convoy."

Up the Swaying Jacob's Ladder

Many Wrens have been employed as boarding officers to give instructions to ships or convoys of ships as to where they must go. Miss Palmer pictures a number of vessels that have crossed the Atlantic and lie, deeply laden with cargo, off the shores of Britain, waiting for their confidential orders to proceed.

> Signals have been picked up and acknowledged and presently a drifter runs alongside. Incredulous hands, peering over the merchantman's side, hardly believe their eyes when the swaying Jacob's ladder is caught by a young W.R.N.S. officer, who proceeds to climb aboard. But sure enough this is the Boarding Officer of modern warfare. Man-power was scarce, so she stepped into the breach and proved her ability to pass the necessary examinations after an eight weeks' course in Naval Control Service work. In addition to her mental prowess she proved that physically she was also master of the situation, for the Boarding Officer must be a good sailor, as her duties are liable to take her some miles out to sea in a drifter or launch in all weathers; and to climb from the deck of a bucking drifter up the swaying ladder, to the deck of a merchantman pitching and rolling in a winter's sea is not for the faint-hearted.

What influence will the Wrens' wartime tasks have on their future lives? Some, as already indicated, will be fitted for employments they could never have aspired to before. Mrs. Laughton Mathews in her Introduction foresees a wide extension of "the potentialities of woman-power and the full co-operation of women in public life." She wants women to lay stress on "the things of the spirit," and to work as co-partners with men for "a society based on spiritual values." I wonder if women in uniform have been spiritually uplifted by their experiences. I am afraid I rather doubt it.

What Significance has Bornholm to Russia ?

Entered by Russian forces whose business it was to rid this small Danish Island in the Baltic Sea of its occupying German garrison, the strategic value of Bornholm is considerable. How the position is viewed through Russian—and other—eyes is explained in detail by HENRY BAERLEIN.

When the German commander in the Danish island of Bornholm refused to obey his chiefs and submit, as they did, to unconditional surrender, it became necessary for one of the Allies to dislodge him and his troops. This duty fell to the Russians who were already occupying German territory to the west of Bornholm; and it has been suggested that the Russians may intend to remain in Bornholm permanently, since the possession of that large island would serve them exceedingly well.

The Finnish radio on May 14 of this year declared that "the occupation of Bornholm by the Red Army, even if they withdraw after having completed their task, has settled the Russian rule over the Baltic. There is no question that anybody else will be permitted to have a share in this, and the matter must therefore be considered from the realistic point of view and taken as closed."

It is quite true that Bornholm's geographical position at the entrance to the Baltic and to the Gulf of Bothnia makes it a valuable advance post for Russia in the event of a clash between that country and other Powers. Similarly, in the event of other Powers contemplating hostile action against Russia it is obvious that Bornholm would in their hands play a considerable rôle. Swift vessels have in this Second Great War run the gauntlet from Lysekil (north of Gothenburg) to Britain and have returned to that Swedish port. But with Bornholm in German hands it has not been possible to attempt any surface traffic between Britain and Russia except via the north of Norway and the White Sea, a much more perilous and longer journey. Russia would thus have sufficient inducement for converting her temporary stay in Bornholm into permanent possession.

What do we find? While her troops were engaged in ejecting the Germans it was unavoidable that damage should be done to a good many of the small houses at Rönne, the island capital; and also at Nexö, the next largest town, because the Germans had sited their guns in the midst of these built-up areas. But the Russians had given timely notice of their intention so that the authorities could evacuate the civilians, less than ten of whom lost their lives. Bornholm airfield, in use for civil aviation, had to be enlarged by the Russians, so that their speediest military aircraft could land there. Not one act on the part of the Russians justified the Finnish radio comment previously quoted.

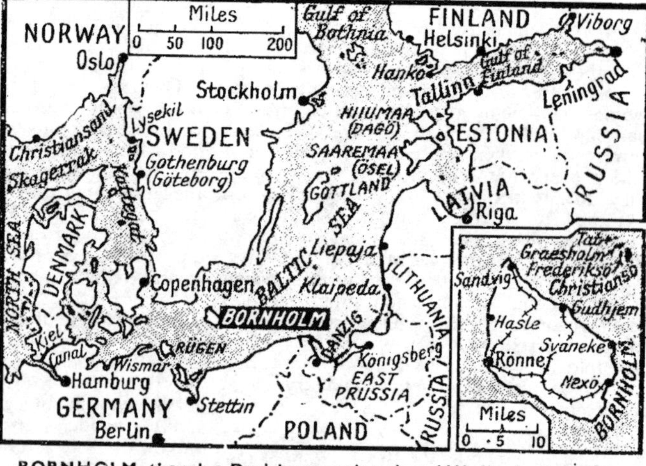

BORNHOLM, though a Danish possession since 1660, lies in the Baltic some 100 miles beyond Copenhagen. Strategically situated as it is between Sweden and Germany this large island has possibilities of development as a submarine and air base.

Naturally the Russians could not be otherwise than uneasy if Bornholm were to be allowed to remain in the future—as in the past—wholly in the hands of a weak Power, so that, if Germany should ever rise again, it would once more be possible for her to seize the island. The other countries that use the Baltic—Sweden, Poland and Czechoslovakia—would view such a contingency with equal concern. And, of course, if there is to be any occupation of Bornholm other than Danish, those three would prefer it to be of an international character.

An international airfield in Bornholm would probably be the best solution of a number of problems. It would give the Russians security against any hostile use of the island, while it would allay any nervousness on the part of other Baltic countries with regard to Russia's intentions. For the control of northern Germany this aerodrome would also be most useful.

'The Malta of the Baltic'

When we are considering what Bornholm means to the Russians we must obviously have regard to the harbours. The most extensive one is at Rönne, and when I saw four or five Danish destroyers anchored there it was somewhat inconveniently full. Gudhjem's harbour on the east coast has been increased in size; but even so it is scarcely larger than that of Svaneke, whose normal occupant is the daily motor-boat from Christiansö. It is said that Nelson called the little Christiansö group of islands, which lie some miles to the north-east of Bornholm, the Malta of the Baltic. But that was a slight exaggeration, because the harbour can scarcely be compared with Malta's Grand Harbour, consisting as it does of the few dozen yards that separate the two small islands of Christiansö and Frederiksö.

Its capacity is so limited that no country is likely to cast covetous eyes upon that group, while the venerable cannons which have been there for so long will not be superseded. Nor will they ever be fired again. The sole occasion when they went into action coincided with the descent of Nelson's fleet upon Copenhagen. Various British warships attacked Christiansö, standing so far out to sea that no reply seemed possible; and when one of the cannons was at last fired it was fortunate enough, when it burst, only to wound one of the garrison.

One may confidently hope that an equally pacific future is in store for Bornholm. On May 26 a party of Danish journalists visited the island and they unanimously reported that not the least friction had arisen between the inhabitants and the Russians, the former being very grateful for the manner in which the Germans had been driven out. And at the beginning of June, General Koratkov, the Soviet commander, eleven other high ranking Russian officers and Governor Stenman of Bornholm proceeded to Copenhagen to take part in Allied celebrations.

It is a fact, as we have pointed out, that Bornholm's harbours offer very slight accommodation for a modern navy; but in the north of the island there is a region of formidable granite rocks, with wet and dry caverns already formed. By lowering the sea bottom of the wet caves ideal submarine pens would be created. The international air force in Bornholm might be supplemented by an international fleet of submarines based on these pens.

There are some who assert that if Russia, alone of the Allies, uses Bornholm, even as she occupied the Finnish port of Hankö, the conditions will be as drastic for Denmark as for Finland. That is not the case, because Hankö being at the south-western extremity of Finland any approach to that country can be prevented by the Russians. Denmark with her west coast on the North Sea is in a very different position.

In our consideration of the strategic value of Bornholm, we have assumed that Denmark would not object to some degree of Allied control of that area. There have been cases in the past of small neutral countries refusing to permit any operations on their territory to which any other country might take umbrage. But it is known that Mr. Christmas Moeller, the Danish Foreign Minister, who for so long during the war was a prominent member of the Danish Council in London, maintains that his country should accept any responsibility which the Allies regard as necessary; and that is believed to be the view of the vast majority of Danes.

DANISH ARMED PATRIOTS AT NEXO, Bornholm's second port, examined the wreckage of German naval vessels sunk by Russian bombers before the Soviet forces—with Danish patriot assistance—finally cleared the island of enemy resistance on May 16, 1945. See also facing page. *Photo, Black Star*

Soviet Occupation of Strategic Baltic Isle

RÖNNE, CAPITAL OF THE DANISH ISLAND OF BORNHOLM (top), where 25,000 Nazis refused to surrender after the general capitulation, was invaded by Red Army forces on May 11, 1945. Soviet officers chatted on the quayside (bottom) as supplies were unloaded after the enemy garrison had been rounded up in a whirlwind five-days' campaign. On May 25 the Russians announced that their occupation of the island was only temporary—" until questions pending in Germany in connexion with the war have been solved." See facing page. *Photos, Black Star*

What the Wavell Plan Means to India

A new chapter in Indo-British relations was opened on June 15, 1945, with the publication of the "Wavell Plan." What these proposals—and the momentous conference between the Viceroy and 21 Indian leaders, opened at Simla ten days later—may augur for India's future is examined in this article specially written for "The War Illustrated" by EDWIN HAWARD.

THE momentous conference of Indian political leaders with the Viceroy (Lord Wavell) in Simla arouses hopes of securing full Indian co-operation in the war against Japan and in important measures of economic and social reconstruction. As a military campaigner Lord Wavell was noted for the care and patience of his planning. The same qualities stand him—and India—in good stead now. Indian leaders themselves need time for readjustment of ideas; some of them come to the Conference from a long detention; most have been in the political wilderness for many months. Indeed, it is a great achievement to have brought the leaders together. Mr. Gandhi's tribute to the Viceroy's handling of the preliminary stage was heartening.

What is the issue? Lord Wavell seeks to obtain active assistance for making his own Executive Council (a virtual Cabinet) more truly representative of Indian opinion, so as to clear the way effectively for the transfer of power from British to Indian hands when the time comes after the war with Japan is ended. As a corollary to this change, he hopes to bring about the complete restoration of ministerial and, consequently, Parliamentary government in the eleven provinces of British India.

DESPITE the unfortunate controversy which, at the instance of the Executive of the Congress Party, produced the resignation of the ministries composed of members of that party in eight of the eleven provinces in November 1939, there have been important changes in the administration to keep step with British intentions on India's behalf. Until 1941, the Viceroy's Executive Council had, for many years, been composed of five British (including the Viceroy and Commander-in-Chief) and three Indian members (i.e. Ministers). Now it consists of five British and eleven Indian members.

In the discussions with Sir Stafford Cripps in 1942, it was made clear that, whatever might be British intentions regarding India's status after the War, Indian political leaders, especially those of the Congress Party, strongly desired an immediate "Indianization," to use convenient jargon, of the Viceroy's Council. It also seemed that, however much we British were convinced of the sincerity of our own Government's offer, Indians were inclined, or at any rate professed, to be sceptical in that regard. As the stalemate subsequently developed, there arose a desire for a further British move to end what was described as the "deadlock," with proposals which, as far as practicable, gave a definite earnest of our determination to see India become a Dominion as defined by Lord Wavell in February 1944 when conferring the "solemn pledge of His Majesty's Government that India shall have full control of her own destiny among the nations of the Commonwealth and the world."

IT may be objected that the magnitude of India's war effort in the field on many fronts and in factory and workshop showed a general confidence in British policy. That, happily, is true. Yet since, in the long run, the good will of Indian political leaders was necessary to the smooth transfer of power from British to Indian hands, failure to harness that good will presently to the country's service must, if possible, be repaired.

How do Lord Wavell's proposals fit into this picture? They begin with making the Viceroy's Council entirely Indian in composition, with the exception of the Viceroy himself and Sir Claude Auchinleck who, enjoying Indian confidence and affection in an especial degree, is to retain the War portfolio as Commander-in-Chief. Then, the British Government has empowered the Viceroy to announce that, with the appointment of Indians to hold charge of External Affairs (hitherto in the hands of the Viceroy personally), India is to have Indian diplomats to represent her Government in other countries in addition to the U.S.A. and China.

This enables Indian leadership effectually to prepare the ground for the post-war status of Dominionship (or Independence). That new regime is to be further anticipated immediately by the appointment in India of a High Commissioner for the United Kingdom on the same lines as already given such British representation in the self-governing Dominions. This meets Indian objections to the present system in which the Viceroy combines with his headship of the Government the duty of protecting British interests in India.

APPOINTMENTS to the Viceroy's Council are to be as nearly as possible on a popular basis, short of complete adoption of a full Parliamentary system—which cannot come until the responsibility of the Council to Parliament at Westminster is transferred to the yet-to-be-created Dominion Legislature at Delhi. The plan must be regarded as transitional, to tide over the period which must elapse until, after the war, Indians in conference (perhaps a constituent assembly) have succeeded in agreeing on the form of constitution to be adopted in future when the transfer of power can be effected. The proposals, for the time being, relate only to the eleven provinces of British India (9/16ths of the country with a population of 296 million) and do not directly concern the Indian States (7/16ths of the country, comprising 562 States with an aggregate population of approximately 94 million).

Spirit of "Forgive and Forget"

The restoration of ministerial government in the provinces of British India will entail the holding of elections (total electorate about 30 million). It is suggested that stability will be best secured by forming such provincial ministries on a coalition basis. To that, the success of the Punjab Ministry in maintaining an uninterrupted parliamentary system since 1937 with a Muslim-Hindu-Sikh coalition under a Muslim Premier, points.

These far-reaching proposals are commended by the Viceroy in the spirit of "forgive and forget." He seeks to clear the air and so avert recrimination over the past—an arid but unfortunately all too-human tendency not only in India. Responses to the appeal have been good. The leaders are meeting round a table—an experience they could not face when Sir Stafford Cripps made his offer three years ago. This has brought them at once face to face with difficulties which can be overcome only by a readiness to compromise for the common weal.

LORD WAVELL has suggested that the Congress Party and the Muslim League should have an equal number of representatives in his Council, in addition to such representation as is agreed upon for the Sikhs, Depressed Classes and others. The Congress Party, although, as Mr. Gandhi puts it, overwhelmingly Hindu, does not confine itself to any one community. Its present President is a Muslim, and some Muslims are with him in the Party. The Muslim League, led by Mr. M. A. Jinnah, claims exclusive rights to represent Muslims. That is not fully accepted either by all the Muslims of the Punjab or by Congress.

Hopefulness must not blind us to the reality of the difficulties confronting the Conference delegates. Nor should it make us impatient of delay. We cannot be impatient if we bear in mind recent international conclaves this side of Suez. The decisions which these Indian leaders make must profoundly affect the pattern of India's political destiny in determining the shape of things to come.

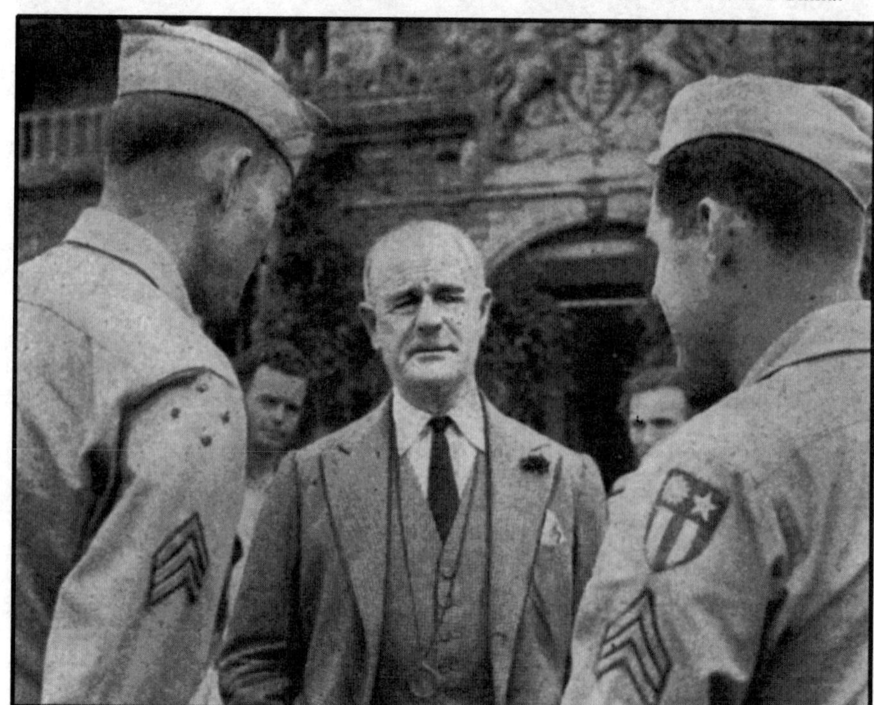

LORD WAVELL, INDIA'S VICEROY, chatted with two U.S. soldiers at Viceregal Lodge, Simla; occasion was the opening of the "Elephant and Palm" resort for Allied troops on leave. Both Lord and Lady Wavell have devoted much time to studying the welfare of the Forces. The Viceroy's plan for India is explained in this page. *Photo, British Official*

Very Gallant Gentlemen Honoured by the King

DECORATED WITH THE V.C. BY H.M. THE KING at Buckingham Palace on June 22, 1945, were four ex-prisoners of war and a legless Canadian Army officer. Left to right: Lieut. Basil Place, D.S.C., R.N., commanded a midget submarine which in Sept. 1943 attacked the Tirpitz (see page 649, Vol. 7). Lieut.-Cmdr. Stephen Beattie, R.N., in charge of H.M.S. Campbeltown at St. Nazaire in March 1942 (page 669, Vol. 5). L.-Cpl. Harry Nicholls, Grenadier Guards, awarded the V.C. "posthumously" in 1940 (page 139, Vol. 3). Lieut. Donald Cameron, R.N.R., in the Tirpitz raid (page 649, Vol. 7). Major Frederick Tilston, Essex Scottish Regiment, Canadian Army, suffered the loss of both legs in a desperate action in the Hochwald Forest, Germany, March 1, 1945.

Photo, Sport & General

Czechoslovakia Remembers the Horror of Lidice

PEACEFUL SCENE OF ONE OF THE NAZIS' VILEST CRIMES, the little Czech mining village of Lidice (1) before it was blasted out of existence, its menfolk butchered, its women and children deported, on June 10, 1942—on suspicion of harbouring the killers of the notorious S.S. leader Reinhard Heydrich. The village in flames (2), a photograph only recently available. Three years later Soviet soldiers acted as guard of honour at the memorial (3) unveiled by President Benes. All that now remains of Lidice (4).

Photos, British Official, Sport & General, Keystone

I Was There! Eye Witness Stories of the War

It's Hard Not to Fraternize Now Out There

The officer-son of a well-known London journalist expresses himself candidly here on this most human problem of non-fraternization with a conquered people. It is one of the most difficult that all ranks have to contend with today in Germany. The youngsters made it harder still.

On V Day my batman-driver, who is a very good chap, said to me, "I suppose it's all right to fraternize with these girls now, sir?"

"Good heavens, no!" I said. "What do you think your friends in Holland and Belgium would think if they knew you wanted to get friendly with Germans?"

"Oh well," he replied, "the war's over, and they're only girls, anyway. *They* didn't commit any atrocities, and they couldn't have stopped them being committed even if they knew about them."

In Schleswig-Holstein particularly, an area which has suffered relatively little from war damage of any kind, the young girls, generally speaking, are only too ready to be friendly with our troops, more especially now that the German soldiers have been cleared away into small concentration areas. And it cannot be denied that of the four countries that the Expeditionary Force has passed through in the last twelve months, Germany has by far the most attractive young girls.

For one thing, they haven't been half starved for years, as have the French, the Belgians and the Dutch, and for another, it is evident that the intensive physical culture that Germany has imposed on her young people during the past ten or fifteen years is having its effect, in that the girls up to the age of 25 or 30 are extremely well developed, and carry themselves gracefully; in fact, are fine physical specimens. Add to this the fact that blonde, blue-eyed types predominate, and you get an idea of the temptation.

You see the way my batman-driver's mind works. His attitude is typical of many soldiers, and while as officers we do our best to jump on any signs of fraternization, it really is almost impossible to stop it completely. Fellows do it secretly; sometimes they're caught, and then there's a court martial. But when you've got hundreds of attractive girls only too ready to be intimate with British soldiers, and when you've got soldiers who get leave only about once in six months—well, what do you expect?

It would be so much easier if the girls didn't adopt such a friendly attitude; there are, of course, girls who resolutely refuse to have anything to do with the British, who look in the opposite direction when a soldier comes anywhere near them. That's the type of girl for whom I have a bit of respect, because it's how I should have expected English girls to behave if the Boche had landed in England in 1940 and overrun the country. But girls of that type are scarce.

Personally, while admiring the physique and beauty of the German girls, I have little desire to fraternize with them. I have very good friends in France, Belgium and Holland, and I have only to remind myself of the fearful privations and misery they have suffered at the hands of the Boche during the last five years. Furthermore, I strongly suspect that inside these attractive blonde heads there is very little intelligence or culture; after so many years of being filled with Nazi ideology, I don't see that there can be much room for anything else.

The children made the fraternization problem harder still. When a sweet little golden-haired five-year-old girl comes up to you, all smiles, and asks what your dog is called—well, as Syd Walker used to say, what would you do, chums? Strictly speaking, we should ignore the child, look very stern, and so forth. In actual fact, an Englishman smiles back at the child, tells her the name of the dog, and pats her on the head.

When a toddler comes up and puts his hand in yours before you've realized what's happened, well, it doesn't come naturally to fling the hand away as though it were a scorpion and tell the infant to get to hell out of it. Now, fortunately, non-fraternization orders have been relaxed to the extent of allowing British and American forces in Germany to speak or play with little children.

FRATERNIZATION between Allied troops and German children was sanctioned by Field-Marshal Montgomery and Gen. Eisenhower in June 1945. *Photo, Associated Press*

Courage That Won Even the Enemy's Praise

LIEUT.-COL. AUGUSTUS NEWMAN, THE ST. NAZAIRE V.C., ex-P.O.W., happily reunited with his wife and daughters at their Buckinghamshire home near Woburn Sands. It was not until they read the citation of the award that the children learned how their father led the famous attack and brilliantly supervised operations. *Photo, Planet News*

The man who led the St. Nazaire raid (see page 669, Vol. 5) has been awarded the V.C. three years and three months after the daring action that made him a hero to all Britain. He is Lt.-Col. Augustus ("Gus") Newman, Essex Regiment, who was captured after leading the raid in March 1942. When he and other St. Nazaire men were repatriated a few weeks ago, the War Office heard the full story of the raid for the first time. One result of the Colonel's own report was the award of a posthumous V.C., also announced on June 19, 1945, to Sergeant Tom Durrant, whose courage won even the enemy's praise. Both awards are dated March 27, 1942.

You could have knocked me over with a feather when I heard of my award, said Lt.-Col. Newman. I have a jolly big family at home, but an even bigger in the Commandos. There are not many left. The last of my lot, about 50 of them, sailed from North Italy today (June 19), and I am meeting them at the port. It will be a grand moment. My group was 550 strong in 1940. At St. Nazaire they were torn to ribbons, and only 150 were captured with me. They were cut up again at Salerno and in landings in the Adriatic.

This is what the Colonel said of Sgt. Durrant at the meeting of his men's relatives:

He was in a little motor launch which came alongside a German destroyer and engaged her. Durrant manned a gun and for mile after mile blazed away at the enemy vessel. He was riddled, but kept on firing at point-blank range, with 25 wounds. He was well-nigh dead when the Germans eventually captured the launch. His great courage was commended by the Germans, who said that his action was deserving of the greatest praise. Durrant was a grand chap and a tough nut.

—Published by arrangement with News Chronicle

Sergeant TOM DURRANT, V.C.

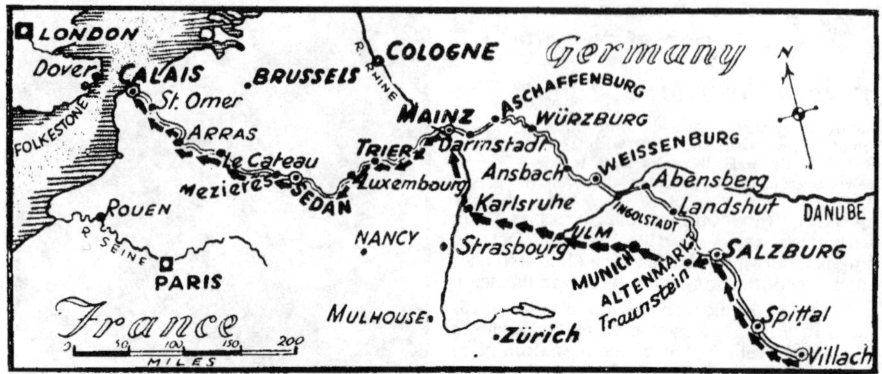

THE ROUTE THEY FOLLOWED. Three hundred 8th Army men, homeward bound on leave, journeyed in lorries from Austria to the French coast in five days. They went by way of Salzburg, Munich, Ulm, Karlsruhe and Darmstadt, into France near Sedan, and so through Arras and St. Omer to Calais, as described below. *By courtesy of The Daily Sketch*

On the Road Home With 8th Army Leave Party

"This is a great day. You are travelling by the overland route home on leave. This leave has been richly earned by you all as victorious veterans of the African and Italian campaigns. Good luck, and a happy time with your families." Every man going on leave from the 8th Army receives that message from the Army Commander. Maurice Watts, The Daily Sketch correspondent who came home with the first party, describes the journey.

Six days ago eighteen men leapt out of a three-ton truck as it threatened to stall on the Katschberg Pass between Villach and Salzburg, in Austria—a pass which is reputed to be one of the steepest in all Europe. "We're going to get this truck to Calais if we have to push it all the way," they shouted. Next minute they were aboard again, roaring with laughter at my own misfortunes and difficulties in the commandeered German car in which a fellow correspondent and I were also making the journey to Calais.

We all made it. At ten o'clock yesterday morning, with 300 Eighth Army men—fifteen officers and 285 other ranks—I stepped on to English soil once again. It was the first time most of the men had been home for nearly four years. And for the Eighth Army it was the climax of the great march towards home which began at Alamein in November 1942.

Our convoy left Villach in Austria on June 15, 1945. We moved in daily 200-mile stages, a triumphant procession greeted with cheery smiles everywhere en route by British and American, French and Polish troops. Behind us, day by day, and now stretching right across Europe, similar convoys have left for Calais, each bringing 300 men home.

A Spring Bed for Every Man

Only five days after the final approval of the overland leave scheme the first convoy left Villach. Ahead of the convoy had gone parties to set up transit camps which must all be self-contained and self-supporting. The work these parties did was little short of superhuman. Never in my life have I seen men work so hard and so unselfishly or lavish so much kindness and thought and attention on their fellow-men. For example, at the first camp at Traunstein, run by the 56th Division, they begged, borrowed or otherwise acquired a spring bed for every man.

After 200 miles over the pass, fighting their way through the decrepit vehicles of a German Panzer Division on the move, bounding and bumping on the not over-luxurious seating in the three-tonners, the men gave the 56th Division transit camp party full marks for that. This bit of the journey had taken us through Salzburg and close to Berchtesgaden, but unfortunately it was not possible to turn from the route to see Hitler's eyrie.

Next day was luxury travel along the famous Reichsautobahn to Ulm. Here we began to see what the war had meant to Germany. For miles along the wide, double concrete highway the Luftwaffe had parked its jet fighters, its night fighters, its light bombers among the pines which stretch back for miles. The highway had been their runway. The woods were their funeral pyre. All were wrecked. So it was in Munich. It is ten thousand times worse than London. I did not see a single building or house undamaged. Munich, Mainz, Mannheim, Stuttgart have to be seen to be believed.

Not one of us could say with assurance he remembered Ulm being bombed. Yet when we pulled in to that town on the second night the devastation was breathtaking. Apart from some residential property on the outskirts, where the 6th Armoured Division had set up transit camp, the only building standing in the centre of the town is the lovely Gothic cathedral with its tracery spire soaring up above the ruins around. Hardened as they were to destruction in Italy, not a man of our party had ever seen anything like that.

All this is American Army territory, and we felt that those Americans who had been standing, stony-faced, amid equally stony-faced Germans, were delighted to see the 8th Army Leave Party bowling along and have a chance to smile at friends and comrades.

That night we stayed with the 78th Division—at Centuripe Transit Camp. None of the other transit camps must be offended when I say that everyone gave Centuripe full marks. In five days the party had cleared up a German barracks and given the men a dining-hall with bowls of flowers and cherries and pink tablecloths and shining cutlery which recalled pre-war hotels. There was a canteen and we had beer and a sing-song after dinner.

Next day, after eleven hours of bumping and bouncing over the road to Sedan, everyone was really whacked, dusty, tired, worn. Then, as we turned the last corner or so, the band of the 46th Division Concert Party were waiting in a lorry and struck up cheery music as they led us up the hill to the transit camp. Maybe it sounds odd, that touch. Believe me, it did wonders. It was yet another of those warm, friendly touches of soldier to soldier.

And then the last drive to Calais through the battlefields of the last war—Bethune, Arras, Le Cateau—battles fought when many of these returning warriors were unborn—a drive through industrial France which looks tired, poor and wan, a land where still one sees few men in the fields except oldsters, where people glowered at my German car until they saw its Union Jack, and then gave the V sign and a wave.

"Queue Up Here for Sand!"

Then in Calais a sense of wonderment among the B.L.A. men as the Eighth Army convoys, covered with humorous banter about B.L.A.—"Britain's Leave Army"—rolled in. "Queue up here, B.L.A., for sand." "Get your knees brown." "D-Day Dodgers? We've had thousands of 'em," and so on. Everyone in high spirits. The vast machinery of the B.L.A. transit camp swallowed up the Eighth Army men. This is a place where they handle 7,000 men in and out each day and they do it so smoothly no one knows how it is done.

Reveille at 4.30 a.m.—how we shall sleep tonight—the march down to the S.S. Biarritz, veteran of Dunkirk and D-Day as well as a boat of pre-war memory—and then the White Cliffs of Dover . . . Well, here we are home. None of us was expected. My own wife had the shock of her life when I rang her up. Imagine the thrill in the 300 other homes where the home-comer has not been home for four years!

"ENGLAND AT LAST!" SHOUTED THESE 8th ARMY VETERANS who had come 850 miles from Austria to Calais by lorry, as their cross-Channel leave-ship docked at Dover. Their highly unorthodox overland trip, crossing both the Danube and the Rhine, is described here by a British war correspondent who accompanied them. *Photo Topical*

I Flew to Truk with First Wave of Avengers

From dawn on June 15, 1945, to late evening of June 16, Seafires, Fireflies and Avengers from British Pacific Fleet aircraft carriers pounded the Jap bases in the Truk islands. Story is told by Arthur la Bern, Evening Standard reporter with the Pacific Fleet. **See also illus. in page 192.**

My pilot was a 23-year-old Londoner, Sub-lieutenant Walter Davis, R.N.V.R., of Northcote Road, S.W.11. The tail-gunner was Petty-Officer "Shorty" Elliott, of Romford. I was in the observer's seat. Pilot Wally Davis and Air Gunner Shorty Elliott helped me buckle on my parachute harness and Mae West. Shorty showed me how to work the Browning machine-gun in case of emergency. We climbed into the airplane, and it seemed an eternity while we sat there waiting our turn to take off.

Suddenly, the pilot's voice came over the inter-com: "Hell, the Boss is in the Oggin!" In Fleet Air Arm (now Naval Air Arm) slang this meant that the commander of our flight, his crew and airplane had fallen in the sea. I looked down and saw three heads and a yellow dinghy bobbing up and down in the rain pitted blue of the Pacific.

Their Avenger was sinking some yards away. Their engine had cut out just as they were taking off, and although the pilot put the brake on, it was too late, and they slithered into the sea. All three were picked up, but we had no time to watch the rescue. We were next off, and got away to a clean start. The only thing dirty was the weather.

Our target in the Truk group was the important airfield at Moen. As we approached Truk the sun began to break through the clouds. I looked down and saw huge coral and basaltic reefs circling the lagoon in which we had to pinpoint our target. When we did spot the target I was disappointed. Ten thousand feet below us it looked not more than a heart-shape clot of green jungle. The inter-com whistled and Wally Davis said: "Bomb doors open!"

We were diving down now and bumping with every thousand feet drop. I got the sensation that the target was rushing up at us at something over 300 m.p.h. Every second it seemed to swell in size, and then it seemed to be tilted up at us at an angle of 30 degrees. Then, on the fringe of the steaming mangrove swamps, I saw the air-strip and four parked aircraft like motionless ants. As we dived down there was no sign of life on the target.

We did not see the flak coming up at us, because the Japs were not using tracers. How accurate it was we were in no position to judge. We just could not see it. Even crews of aircraft that got back to the carrier with holes in the wings and fuselage reported that they did not see flak. One pilot did not realize there was any until he got back and found a piece embedded in his Mae West.

We were flying in close formation. I saw the first two Avengers peel off and bomb, and then we bombed at 1,500 ft. The airplane jumped as the bombs were released. We kept going down, while Shorty blazed away in the gun turret. We went down so low that a 300 ft. hill was towering above when we began to climb up again. Then, for the first time in my life, I was violently air-sick. Wally Davis happened to glance round just as I put my head down, and his voice came urgently over the inter-com. "Shorty, has La Bern been hit?" "No, just being sick as a dog," said Shorty.

Throughout the whole strike of two days and nights, the Japs put up no fighter opposition, much to the disappointment of the Naval Air Arm boys. One aircraft was lost by enemy action; others were damaged taking off and landing on the carrier, a factor always to be reckoned with in this type of warfare. Whenever an aircraft went down "in the Oggin," to use Naval Air Arm slang, destroyers were on the scene in a matter of minutes to pick up the crews.

In a later flight I took off in another Avenger. We flew into more dirty tropical weather and for ninety minutes were completely lost in a raging Pacific rainstorm. As the Naval Air Arm boys might say, it was touch and go whether this story went down in the Oggin.

FAIREY-FIREFLY PILOTS AND OBSERVERS operating with the British Pacific Fleet and seen on the flight-deck of H.M.S. Indefatigable, between them destroyed four out of five Japanese planes which attacked them while they were escorting a U.S. Navy flying-boat engaged in rescuing "ditched" crews during the Fleet's attack on the Sakishimas on March 27, 1945. *Photo, British Official*

OUR DIARY OF THE WAR

JUNE 20, Wednesday
1,291st day of War against Japan

Borneo.—Australians landed at Lutang in Sarawak.

U.S.A.—Liner Queen Mary arrived at New York with 14,000 U.S. troops.

Trieste.—British-Yugoslav agreement on zones of occupation signed.

JUNE 21, Thursday *1,292nd day*

Ryukyu Islands.—Organized Japanese resistance ended on Okinawa after 82 days' fighting. Jap aircraft began heavy attacks on U.S. shipping.

Pacific.—Lt.-Gen. Stilwell appointed by Gen. MacArthur to command U.S. Tenth Army.

JUNE 22, Friday *1,293rd day*

Japan.—400 Super-Fortresses from the Marianas attacked naval arsenal at Kure and industrial plants on Honshu.

Ryukyu Islands.—Japanese C.-in-C. on Okinawa and his Chief of Staff committed suicide.

JUNE 23, Saturday *1,294th day*

Poland.—Poles from Lublin and London agreed in Moscow on formation of New Provisional Government.

Philippines.—Glider-borne U.S. troops landed in North Luzon and made contact with guerillas.

JUNE 24, Sunday *1,295th day*

Borneo.—Australians ended Japanese resistance in Tarakan, cleared Labuan island, and captured Seria oilfield.

Russia.—In Red Square, Moscow, the Red Army held a victory parade.

JUNE 25, Monday *1,296th day*

Borneo.—Australians captured Miri town and oilfield.

Japan.—Super-Fortresses from Marianas again attacked aircraft and munition factories at Nagoya, Osaka, and other towns in Honshu.

Pacific.—Jap aircraft made torpedo attacks against Allied warships in Macassar Strait.

JUNE 26, Tuesday *1,297th day*

Japan. — Super-Fortresses attacked Yokkaichi, S.W. of Nagoya.

General.—World Security Charter, approved by fifty nations, signed at San Francisco.

JUNE 27, Wednesday *1,298th day*

France.—Gen. Leclerc appointed to command French Far East expeditionary force to serve in Pacific.

Russia.—Marshal Stalin promoted to new rank of Generalissimo of the Soviet Union.

JUNE 28, Thursday *1,299th day*

Japan.—Heavy attack by Super-Fortresses on seaports in Kyushu and industrial centre of Okayama on Honshu.

Poland.—Formation of new Polish Government of National Unity, including Mr. Mikolajczyk, announced from Warsaw.

Pacific.—Story released of Jap suicide aircraft attack on U.S. aircraft carrier Bunker Hill near Okinawa.

JUNE 29, Friday *1,300th day*

Japan.—Super-Fortresses bombed Kudamatsu oil refinery in Honshu.

China.—Chinese troops captured Liuchow airfield.

Czechoslovakia. — Ruthenia transferred to Soviet Union by agreement between Soviet and Czech governments.

Poland.—French and Swedish Governments recognized new Polish Govt.

JUNE 30, Saturday *1,301st day*

Pacific.—U.S. occupation of Kume island, west of Okinawa, announced by Admiral Nimitz.

JULY 1, Sunday *1,302nd day*

Borneo.—Australian forces under Gen. MacArthur landed at Balikpapan.

Japan.—Nearly 600 Super-Fortresses dropped 4,000 tons of incendiaries on Kure, Shimonoseki, Ube and Kumamoto.

Germany.—Red Army troops took over Magdeburg from British.

JULY 2, Monday *1,303rd day*

Japan.—Super-Fortresses attacked oil refinery at Shimotsu, S.W. of Osaka.

Solomon Is.—Australians on Bougainville secured Mivo River line.

JULY 3, Tuesday *1,304th day*

Japan.—About 500 Super-Fortresses bombed Himeji on Honshu, and Tokushima, Takamatsu and Kochi on Shikoku.

Germany.—First United States occupation troops arrived in Berlin.

Flash-backs

1940

June 21. *French received German armistice terms at Compiegne.*

July 1. *Pétain's French Government established at Vichy.*

July 3. *British Navy attacked French warships at Oran.*

1941

June 21. *Damascus (Syria) occupied by Free French forces.*

June 22. *Germans invaded Russia.*

1942

June 21. *Rommel captured Tobruk.*

July 1. *Germans took Sebastopol. Rommel's troops in Egypt reached El Alamein and were held there.*

1943

June 20. *Friedrichshafen attacked by R.A.F. Lancasters, which flew on to North Africa.*

June 30. *U.S. forces landed on Rendova island, New Georgia.*

1944

June 26. *Cherbourg fell to Allies. Mogaung, Burma, captured by Chinese and Chindit troops.*

June 28. *Russians captured Mogilev and forced the Dnieper.*

TROOPING BY AIR TO INDIA scheme was inaugurated by R.A.F. Transport Command in May 1945. By autumn it is expected 10,000 troops will be flown each way every month, the journey between a West of England airport and Poona occupying about seven days. There are six staging posts between the termini, and two 48-hour rest periods en route enable the men to arrive fresh and well and give them a chance to become acclimatized. British Army units boarding a Dakota (left), and in their seats (right) ready for the take-off. *Photos, British Official*

With Our Airmen Today

By CAPTAIN NORMAN MACMILLAN M.C., A.F.C.

THE capture of Okinawa (completed on June 21, 1945, after 82-days' battle) gave the Americans ten airfields some 350 miles from the southernmost main island of Japan. This should ease the strain on the carrier-borne aircraft which have had to bear the brunt of the tactical operations around Okinawa and Sakashima, with strikes into the area of Kyushu and the Inland Sea, for shore-based tactical aircraft can now operate from the Okinawa airfields. It was considered that existing facilities would enable 1,000 first-line aircraft to be deployed from Okinawa, and with American genius for quick airfield construction there is little doubt but that the number of airfields can be increased if necessary.

There is evidence that the aircraft carriers have had a rough passage during their concentration around Okinawa. The Japanese suicide pilots have done what the Italians once threatened to do if the Royal Navy intervened at the time of the Abyssinian crisis; but the Italians never did it when their country's entry into the Second Great War brought about the conditions which gave the Regia Aeronautica the opportunity to crash their bomb-laden aircraft into ships. (See illus. pages 176-178.)

FIRES Swept the Flight Deck and Made the Hangar Almost White-hot

The story of the Bunker Hill, U.S.N. aircraft carrier, indicates what may be done for a relatively small expenditure of life and material if men are willing to take off and fly to certain death, as the Kamikaze pilots do. The Bunker Hill was Vice-Admiral Marc Mitscher's flagship. Thirty-four U.S. planes were lined up with full tanks ready to take off from her flight deck, and more were below in the hangar, when two Japanese suicide pilots each dropped one 500-lb. bomb among the concentration of aircraft, and then crashed their own planes on to the ship. A third Kamikaze was shot into the sea by the guns of a destroyer. For the loss of these three aircraft and their pilots the Bunker Hill was wrecked (although she succeeded in steaming back to Puget Sound Navy Yard, near Seattle, under her own power), about 70 aircraft destroyed, 392 killed and 264 members of the crew wounded.

But that is not the only side to the story, for the Bunker Hill had been in the Pacific since the autumn of 1943 and had played a part in every principal strike. Her pilots had sunk or damaged almost 1,000,000 tons of Japanese shipping and had shot down 475 Japanese aircraft, so that even if this ship had been lost she would still have had a credit balance sheet. Most of the damage to the ship appears to have been caused by the fires from the aircraft fuel which swept her flight deck and made the hangar almost white hot. This is one feature of aircraft carriers which makes fire a particularly dangerous hazard.

SPECIAL precautions are taken against fire in peacetime. On one occasion when a British aircraft carrier was on her way home from the Mediterranean an aircraft-hand working on an aircraft in the hangar dropped his mechanical cigarette-lighter out of his pocket into the metal drip-tray beneath the aircraft's engine. The lighter was of the kind that sparks automatically when a spring catch releases the top which turns the steel as its spring makes it fly up. The lighter set fire to the mixture of petrol and oil in the tray, and in a matter of moments the hangar was in a blaze. The safety-curtains came down and the sprinklers began to play on the blaze. This fire was controlled, but not before several aircraft were badly damaged. The carrying of matches about an aircraft carrier had previously been prohibited. That incident resulted in the prohibition of lighters too.

It is probably fortunate that the Japanese suicide pilots use comparatively light bombs. If they had the bombs that the R.A.F. have used against ships, the Bunker Hill would have gone to the bottom Even so, the accounts of the attack indicate that one of these relatively small bombs penetrated the flight deck at an angle and exploded in the hangar below. This is consistent with American practice of saving weight by using thin plate flight decks, sometimes reinforced on top with wood. It will be interesting to see if the Americans will revise this policy as a result of their experience.

BEFORE the final fall of Okinawa, U.S. carrier aircraft combined with land-based aircraft flying from Okinawan airfields in an attack during the week-end June 16-17 against airfields, barracks, radio stations and harbour installations on the Amami group of islands 150 miles north of Okinawa and about 200 miles from Kyushu.

Before dawn on June 17, between 400 and 450 Super Fortresses flying in four formations attacked Omuta and Kagoshima on Kyushu, and Hamamatsu and Yokkaichi on Honshu, all towns of fewer than 200,000 population, dropping a total of 3,000 tons of incendiary bombs upon them, thereby beginning attacks against the secondary group of Japanese industrial towns.

On June 18, General H. H. Arnold stated in Manila that "the Air Force alone can completely wipe out Japan by the end of 1946, if the Japanese are capable of fighting until then." He said that British bombers would soon join in the attack on Japan's mainland, and that in six months' time the joint air forces would be capable of dropping 2,100,000 tons of bombs on Japan in one year, three times the concentration of bombs dropped on Germany in the heaviest year of bombing. Japan's oil position was becoming like Germany's before the latter's collapse.

ISOLATING Japs in Japan from Japs on the Asiatic Mainland

The general's figures showed that when Germany's oil supplies were estimated to have been reduced to 14 per cent, they were in fact down to 7 per cent. In March 1945, German oil production was at zero, although the Allied calculation allowed them 5 per cent. Oil is now the biggest Japanese problem. The fall of Tarakan on June 24 adds to its gravity.

In the Tsushima Strait between Japan and Korea, American aircraft sank 50 supply ships in 49 days and damaged 64 more, thus beginning the isolation of the Japanese in Japan from the Japanese on the Asiatic mainland. Truk, garrisoned by about 40,000 Japanese, was attacked by a British cruiser and carrier force. For two days and nights from dawn on June 16, Avenger bombers, with Seafire and Firefly fighters in support, bombed airfield runways, batteries and other targets with 500-lb. bombs. Then Seafires spotted for the ships' guns.

On June 19, Fukuoka, Shizuoka and Toyohashi were fire-bombed by 450 Super Fortresses. On June 22, the targets were the Kure naval arsenal, the Mitsubishi and Kawasaki aircraft plants north of Nagoya, and aircraft plants at Himeji, Akashi and Tamashima, all on Honshu. On June 24, Mustangs flew 1,645 miles from Iwojima and back to attack Hyakurigahara and Shimodate airfields north of Tokyo, where they destroyed 32 and damaged 37 aircraft, for the loss of three Mustangs. On June 26 ten big factories on Honshu received 3,000 tons of bombs from 450 to 500 Super Fortresses escorted by 150 Mustangs; two days later a similar force attacked Sasebo, Moji, Nebeoka seaports, and Orayama, industrial centre.

'Grand Slam' Taken for a Ride by a Lancaster

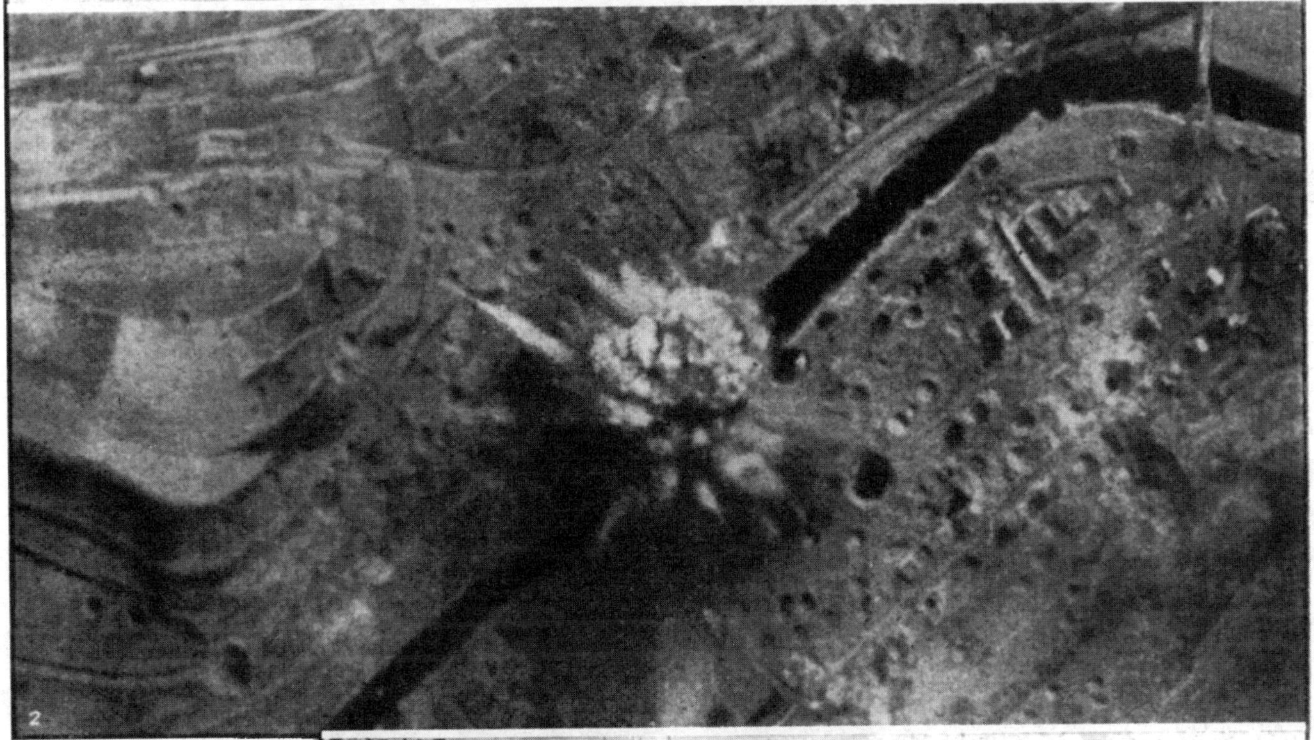

22,000-lb. BOMB OF THE R.A.F. lives right up to its nickname "Grand Slam." One is seen leaving a Lancaster (1) during an attack on the famous viaduct at Arnsberg, south-east of Hamm, on March 29, 1945, and another crashing on that target (2). Devastating effect at the moment of impact is tremendous. They are not lightly handled when drawn from the bomb-dump: hoisting a Grand Slam at a R.A.F. bomber station in Britain (3).

Twenty-five feet five inches in length, with a tail-unit approximately 13½ feet long, diameter 3 feet 10 inches, it is a mightily scaled-up version of the 6-tonner. Able to shatter almost any building or fortification, its primary role is against underground structures and precision targets requiring deep penetration. It was specially effective against thick-roofed U-boat pens. First use of these enormous missiles, on March 14 (see illus. in page 764, Vol. 8), took the enemy completely by surprise, so well kept was the secret of its production.

Photos, British Official

Editor's Postscript

THE blast-defying brickwork that has defaced so many façades in our city streets is gradually disappearing, and people are now able to enter police stations and post offices without feeling furtive about it. The street shelters will go next, I suppose. But there is another residuum of the nightmare we have endured with which I am more reluctant to part. I refer to those pocket fortresses, strong-points, or look-outs which sprang up in a thousand strategic spots in towns and villages all over the country in the brave summer of 1940, at street corners and rural cross-roads, by bridges, on seaside promenades, sometimes even in cottage and villa gardens, often cunningly camouflaged or garbed with a cloak of innocent pre-occupation—like the fake bookstall in Parliament Square, which thousands passed every day without recognizing its real nature. Wherever these things are a nuisance, of course, they must go. There is one just round the corner from this office, for example, at the corner by Blackfriars Bridge, which people are for ever bumping against. But many might well be left where they are and as they are, to remind us not so much of what war meant to us as of what it might have meant, and of the grand, grim spirit in which this country was determined to meet it. Most of them are not unsightly. At least they are far less so than the rusty tanks which were distributed over the public parks and recreation grounds of Great Britain after the last war. So let them mellow through the years like the Martello towers of Napoleonic times, like Hadrian's wall or those earthworks of an even older day which remain to delight the antiquary. Let them add their firm impress to the rich palimpsest of our island. We have lost all too much history in brick and stone through the vandalism of an enemy. What could be a more appropriate foundation for the new history that future generations will build than these simple memorials of our finest hour ?

WHAT I may call the Baconian Fifth Column which so long has been trying to pull down William Shakespeare and stick up Francis Bacon in his place, has been quite active during the War Years, despite the scarcity of paper. In one way I don't object to their activities nor to the co-operation of those Americans who carry on the bad work which was first taken up with vigour "over there," for it is an evil out of which good may come by attracting new readers to the plays : the facts of Shakespeare's authorship are well enough established to withstand the slings and arrows of these misguided assailants ; but I don't like to see foreigners chipping in. I have been reading an article on "Le Cas Bacon-Shakespeare" in the June number of La France Libre, wherein Matila Ghyka (whoever she or he may be) is allowed to fill five large pages of good paper (provided by our Government) to rehearse the moth-eaten stuff which the Baconians have been plugging for years to the discredit of our greatest genius. Why should we furnish the means for any foreigner to attack our national poet, the supreme genius of the English renascence ? This French article almost amounts to an insult to us and ought not to have been printed in a magazine which exists under sanction of the British Government as an organ of Anglo-French friendship.

ALL that Matila Ghyka seems to have done is to dish up once more the nonsense of our Baconians. Shakespeare's acknowledged prosperity is explained by his having been a moneylender ! That a "butcher's boy from Stratford" could go to London and acquire wealth as a moneylender seems to me almost as great a wonder as a man of native genius arising during the English renascence. Yet that is the gravamen of Ghyka's case against Shakespeare. That the occasion of this ridiculous article is attributed to the fact that "le doyen des critiques dramatiques de Londres" has been persuaded to believe in the Baconian heresy leaves me frigid. Ghyka may not have heard of the other anti-Shakespeare movement which would credit the brilliant Edward de Vere, 17th Earl of Oxford, with the Shakespearean laurels. This reminds me of the philosopher who persuaded himself that life as we know it had originated in some other planet and had somehow been transferred to Earth, thus merely shifting the problem of its origin to another sphere. Why should the 17th Earl of Oxford be more liable to be a genius than William Shakespeare of Stratford ?

WHILE selecting the illustrations for the "Now It Can Be Told" pages in this issue I was reminded of a family association with the Gareloch, where the old quiet beauty of green hills and shining loch has been sadly discounted by the construction of Britain's Military Port No. 1 (see page 173). Many a happy summer have I spent there at Rhu, Shandon and Garelochhead as a boy—dream days in a Golden Age, to telescope two of Kenneth Grahame's best-loved titles. Among the hills on the east shore is a little old rambling graveyard, where, not so very long ago, one of my own relatives was buried in what one might have reasonably supposed to be an everlasting resting-place. Reasonably—that's to say—in a world which had not yet thought up the bull-dozer. For it was here, at the foot of this very old world graveyard, that the Royal Engineers and Pioneer Corps laid the railroad track linking the newly-built military port with Scotland's railway system. That little cemetery among the hills has now more than one "unquiet grave," and it is not too comforting to know that Military Port No. 1 is to have a short-lived career, being already in process of dismantling. Most of us have painful memories of the rusty trail of half-demolished buildings and constructions left behind to rot and decay after the last war, on what had once been fair plots of England's green and pleasant land. Nor am I likely to forget a sight I once saw on Gareloch itself : some forty once-proud ships of our Merchant Navy visibly decaying at anchor during the shipping "slump" of twenty years ago !

Maj.-Gen. ALAN J. K. PIGGOTT, Director of Recruiting and Demobilization, who is in charge of the vast release scheme for the British Army which came into operation on June 18, 1945 (see facing page.)

Photo, The Daily Express

MANY of my non-musical readers must have been amazed the other evening when they listened-in to the ovation given in the Albert Hall to Pau Casals, the great Catalan 'cellist, on his first appearance here since the war. What the precision-minded programme-planners at the B.B.C. must have thought of it I can hardly imagine, and for once they were helpless. Casals finished playing the Elgar concerto dead on time, leaving the requisite twenty minutes for the Brahms St. Anthony Variations which led up to the Nine o'clock News. But, alas ! for the programme-planners, the excited audience would not let Casals go. For three—five—seven minutes they applauded and cheered him—until the Unforgivable Sin (according to the B.B.C.) was committed and he returned once more to the platform to give an encore. Nothing like this has ever happened before in British broadcasting : B.B.C. officials with whom I have discussed it are all agreed that not even Nellie Melba on her (positively) final farewell received such an ovation. Nor can any of them recall any public figure within living memory being applauded at such length and so vociferously—on the air. That such a thing should have happened to a jewel-bedecked *prima donna*—or to a film-star—is conceivable, declare my musical friends. That it should have happened to a 'cellist, and a little bald-headed, bespectacled, tubby-shaped man of over middle age seems to them to prove that the English are not only a musical race, but are probably the most *discriminating* musical public in the world today.

I WAS interested, if not altogether surprised, the other day to read the opinion of an Allied scientific authority that one of the causes contributing to the Nazis' defeat in the field was the inferiority of their medical services which in many instances were computed as being as much as twenty years behind the times. Just how far ahead of the times were our own medical services has now been underlined in an attractively produced half-crown pamphlet written by that very able journalist, John Langdon-Davies, and published by the Pilot Press under the title British Achievement in the Art of Healing. Indeed, I would go so far as to recommend it as the best possible nervous stimulant to relatives of our men still fighting on the battlefields of the Far East. The author has, naturally, much to say of plastic surgery and blood transfusion ; of "the world's first perfect antiseptic," penicillin, discovered by Sir Alexander Fleming ; of M & B 693, "the drug invented at Dagenham" and first tried out—at Bart's Hospital—early in 1939 (It may not be generally known that M & B takes its name from the fact that it was invented in the May and Baker laboratory after 692 not-so-successful experiments). Personally, I was interested most of all in Mr. Langdon-Davies's description of the work done by Forces psychiatrists in tackling what in the last war was misnamed "shell shock" and mistakenly treated as if "some incurable physical damage" had been done to the neurons of the unhappy patient's central nervous system by high explosive blast. As Mr. Langdon-Davies points out, "If we are wise we shall be able to use for the building of a better world the psychological lessons of war."

In Britain Now: Demobilization Commences

UNWINDING OF BRITAIN'S MIGHTY WAR MACHINE began on June 18, 1945, with the first demobilization of men and women of the Services. Troops disembarked at Dover from Ostend (above, left). At the Regent's Park centre others (above, right) inspected a useful signboard. To his Surrey home came ex-P.O.W. Mr. (L/Cpl.) Alfred Blake (left centre), just demobbed.

EVERYTHING went without a hitch on "Demob Day No. I." The Directorate of Demobilization had laid its plans as long ago as March 1943, so that men from India, Burma and the Middle East were brought back to England to be released with their group at the same time as those stationed at home or with the B.L.A. At Chatham W.R.N.S. handed in their uniforms (above). At Plymouth, Admiral Sir Ralph Leatham, C.-in-C., said farewell (right) to men of the Royal Navy, who stood smartly to attention in their new civvies.

SIX R.A.F. demobilization centres (there were nine for the Army) passed out 5,000 airmen on the first day. At one reception section three candidates for release waited their turn (left) as a W.A.A.F. called on the microphone, "Next, please!" By mid-August, aircrews in the first eight age groups will have been released.

Photos, Planet, New York Times Photos, G.P.U., Central Press, Sport & General

Indomitable's Brood in Far Eastern Waters

HER 75-ft. FLIGHT DECK lined with Corsair fighters and Barracuda dive-bombers, H.M.S. *Indomitable*, 23,000 tons, is one of the most up-to date carriers of the Illustrious class, with an approximate complement of 1,600 officers and men. She took part in the attack by the British Pacific Fleet on the Sakishima group on March 27, 1945, preceding the U.S. invasion of Okinawa. Admiral R. A. Spruance, commanding the U.S. 5th Fleet, described the achievement of this task force as " typical of the great traditions of the Royal Navy."

Photo, British Official

Printed in England and published every alternate Friday by the Proprietors, THE AMALGAMATED PRESS, LTD., The Fleetway House, Farringdon Street, London, E.C.4. Registered for transmission by Canadian Magazine Post. Sole Agents for Australia and New Zealand: Messrs. Gordon & Gotch, Ltd.; and for South Africa: Central News Agency, Ltd.—July 20, 1945. S.S. *Editorial Address:* JOHN CARPENTER HOUSE, WHITEFRIARS, LONDON, E.C.4.

Vol 9 The War Illustrated N° 212

SIXPENCE Edited by Sir John Hammerton AUGUST 3, 1945

FAMOUS DRUM OF THE 5TH BATTALION GORDON HIGHLANDERS, which fell into Nazi hands at St. Valéry-en-Caux in May 1940, and was recovered by an American officer in Germany almost five years later, was handed over to Brigadier J. R. Sinclair, D.S.O., commanding the 153rd Brigade, by General Wade Haislip, the U.S. 7th Army's new commander, at an impressive ceremony in the Koenigsplatz, Munich, on June 7, 1945. Relic of the First Great War, it was proudly carried by Corporal Willie Simm (above) at the parade which followed the presentation ceremony. *Photo, U.S. Official*

The Monsoon Delays Our Final Blow in Burma

IN RANGOON, after its fall on May 3, 1945, British troops inspected the "New Law Courts," built by the Japanese for special Allied prisoners; closely examined were these insanitary wooden cells (1). On the Mawchi Road, serpentine jungle highway running east into the Shan hills from Toungoo, the going was sticky for this mud-encumbered Sherman tank (2) caught in the monsoon in mid-June 1945.

A signaller of the 14th Army at work (3); laying cable, often under fire, these men kept communications going through the whole of the 950-miles advance from Assam to Rangoon. In one year up to April 1945 the headquarters signals of the 33rd Indian Corps alone laid 10,000 miles of cable and transmitted 300,000 messages.

Commander of Allied land forces, South East Asia, General Sir Oliver Leese (4, left) discussed operations with staff officers at Brigade H.Q. in Burma.

Photos, British and Indian Official

With Our Armies Today

By MAJ.-GENERAL
SIR CHARLES GWYNN
K.C.B., D.S.O.

Our Army of Occupation in Germany appears now to have taken up its positions, and troops should be in process of settling down with some prospect of making themselves reasonably comfortable before winter sets in. It is satisfactory that this time the Union Jack flies in Berlin, and few, I think, will quarrel with the composition of the British contingent there. The honour has been well earned and those inclined to be envious may take consolation from the fact that Berlin in its devastated condition is not likely to be a particularly attractive station. As I suggested was probable, the ban on fraternization has now been partially lifted, and this should improve matters. The degree to which it can be further eased may, however, depend on whether when nights are longer there are any signs of Werewolf activity. It is too early to assume that the Werewolf idea is dead.

It is to be hoped, too, that relations with our Russian allies will by degrees be on a more friendly footing. In the meantime I think it is a mistake to attach too much importance to the atmosphere of suspicion that is reported to exist. Relations with senior Russian officers are said to be excellent and that is certain to have good effects and lead to greater uniformity in the attitude of the occupying armies towards the Germans and towards each other.

The language difficulty is, of course, a handicap in dealing with the Russians, and I doubt if the diversities of race and background to be met with in the Russian Army are fully appreciated. Furthermore, I think it should be recognized that for years it has been taught in Russian schools, not without some justification, that the Western nations are hostile to Soviet ideology, and the effects of early teaching are not easily eliminated. It is generally agreed, too, that while standards of living in Russia have greatly improved they are still much lower than in the West. Possibly, therefore, the Soviet authorities may think that close contact with Western standards might give rise to discontent. On these and similar grounds it would seem to be wise to exercise patience and to allow such contacts as are bound to occur to improve relations gradually and without fuss.

BURMA In Burma the Japanese seem to be taking advantage of the concentration of their forces behind the lower Sittang to adopt a more offensive policy. They succeeded in establishing a bridge-head on the west bank of the river and isolated a Gurkha battalion, which was only withdrawn after some sharp fighting. They may be aiming at the recapture of Pegu, but more probably they would be content to open an escape route for their troops still marooned in the Pegu Yomas, west of the main road to Mandalay. Presumably, under monsoon conditions, the number of our troops deployed in forward positions is kept to a minimum, and local Japanese successes must be expected for a time if they consider it worth while to face the cost, which is likely to be disproportionately high.

BORNEO The landing at Balikpapan in Borneo which the Japanese expected has been made very successfully by Australian and Netherlands troops after preparatory bombardment. Once again, although elaborate defences had been prepared, the Japanese offered practically no resistance to the landings which were made at a number of places. The town and three airstrips have been captured, but the Japanese having withdrawn inland, presumably partly to escape the devastating fire of ships' guns, are now offering determined resistance in positions covering the oilfields. It would seem to be their policy to avoid dissipating their strength in attempts to hold ports which are no longer of use to them, and to concentrate on denying the Allies the oil supplies which might relieve the strain on shipping.

Although the oil is now of no value to the Japanese it is clearly to their advantage to delay the restoration of the fields as long as possible. Meanwhile, the Allies have secured a valuable asset by acquiring the use of the harbour and airstrips at Balikpapan. The Brunei operations are also proceeding steadily and all the Sarawak oilfields have been recovered, although in a badly damaged condition. Specialist personnel was required to deal with the wells that were on fire as the troops were unable to extinguish them (See map in page 131.)

PACIFIC The air attack on Japan from the Marianas and from Okinawa airfields is steadily increasing, and Admiral Nimitz's carriers, acting with the utmost boldness and in great strength, have carried out even more devastating attacks, which not only took the defence by surprise but were more prolonged and concentrated than attacks delivered from the island bases have so far been. A great measure of air superiority had undoubtedly been established, and the carrier force met with practically no opposition in the air. It is probable, however, that the Japanese are husbanding their reserves for the time when they would be used against the transports of an invading force. If and when landings are attempted suicide attacks even more determined than those at Okinawa must certainly be expected.

Although the Allied offensive is far in advance of schedule and the Japanese believe that invasion is imminent, it seems improbable that preparations for such a great undertaking can as yet be complete. Softening up processes are well advanced, but I am afraid that some recent statements made by a senior American officer as regards the ease with which Japan can be invaded and finally crushed may prove misleadingly optimistic. At this stage it would be best to be content with the very remarkable progress of current operations.

The Japanese are undoubtedly, and justifiably, alarmed, but there is little evidence of loss of morale. It is possible they may lose their heads and become confused, but I doubt if that will affect their willingness to fight to the death or to counter-attack fiercely. Until we see Japanese troops surrendering or deserting in large numbers it is safer to conclude that the end of the war in the Far East is not yet in sight.

That Japanese pilots now rarely accept combat should not, I think, be taken as an indication of lowered morale, for that is the normal policy of the weaker side desirous of husbanding its resources. On the other hand, few cases have been reported of flinching in suicide attacks, although there is some evidence of lack of training in the delivery of the attacks. Without assuming that all Japanese pilots are ready to undertake suicide missions the possibility that large numbers of those in reserve are undergoing specialized training has to be considered.

That Admiral Nimitz has now with impunity been able to bring the guns of his fleet into action on a maximum scale against shore targets is, however, clear proof of the extent to which the enemy's naval and air defences have broken down. It has been no mere hit-and-run attack but a deliberate bombardment of places where strong resistance might have been expected.

CHINA There are increasing signs that the Japanese are withdrawing from south China to the line of the Yangtse, and possibly a further withdrawal to the Yellow River is envisaged. War industries have long since been established in north China and Manchuria, and they evidently are being expanded. Raw material which the Japanese islands lack is obtainable in these areas, and Japanese man-power is sufficient to provide large forces for the defence of the northern zone. Meanwhile, the Chinese operations in the south are proceeding favourably. A number of airfields have been recaptured and Chinese troops have advanced southwards up to the Indo-China frontier. The difficulty of maintaining adequate supplies of war material still, however, remains a limiting factor to the number of troops that can be employed and to the use that can be made of airfields. There is, therefore, not much prospect that the withdrawal of the Japanese will be hustled to any great extent.

The future course of events is on the whole unpredictable, and above all it is impossible to foretell how long Japan's will to maintain a ruinous struggle may last. Her capacity to continue resistance if she is willing to face the sacrifices involved should not be underestimated, and has not yet been reduced to the same degree as was Germany's when she surrendered.

VOTING in the General Election held few difficulties for most of our troops abroad. At Hamburg a voting section was set up in the Army P.O. (top); while near Cairo a R.A. officer dropped his ballot-paper into the special container (below). See also page 221.

Photos, British Official

These Ingenious Nazi Weapons Arrived Too Late

A 54-cm. **SELF-PROPELLED MORTAR**, weighing 120 tons (1), was among the monstrous weapons devised by the Germans, but never used against us; it is capable of firing a 1-ton projectile 14,000 yds. With a reputed range of 80 miles, these 400-ft. long pipe-like "projectors" (2), were found sited in the French cliffs and trained directly on London. They were intended to fire a fin-stabilized shell 92 ins. long. An Allied officer examines a round-the-corner rifle (3), fitted with special sights but more tricky than accurate. A rocket-propelled guided missile (4); in the experimental stage, it is 100 ins. long, with a wing-span of almost 36 ins. On July 12, 1945, Lord Brabazon, former Minister of Aircraft Production, declared that on the day the first V2 was launched against Britain, every other form of war weapon was rendered obsolescent.

Photos, Keystone

Hitler's Worst Nightmare Was Never Like This

FROM THE BALCONY OF THE REICH CHANCELLERY Hitler was wont to harangue his followers (1). "The Nazi State will survive for 1,000 years!" he thundered on May 4, 1941. Four years later his favourite balcony had other occupants (2)—British soldiers who gazed down curiously on the shattered remains of the Fuehrer's capital. Within the Chancellery itself the great main hall was a desolation open to the sky (3). Half-a-mile away, on the pillared facade of the gutted Reichstag, men of the Red Army had left their mark (4).

Photos, Keystone, G.P.U., Daily Mirror

With Our Navies Today

By

FRANCIS E. McMURTRIE

DISTANT though V Day may already seem, repercussions of the naval war in Europe continue to be felt. In the Atlantic the danger from drifting mines is likely to continue for a long time. Several are reported to have been washed up on seaside beaches in this country recently; and one was responsible for the loss off the Lizard of H.M. trawler Kurd, with 15 out of the 26 officers and men on board, on July 10. It has been stated that this was the first naval vessel to be lost through enemy action since V Day, but that is not correct. On May 12 a British motor gunboat was sunk through striking a floating mine in the middle of the North Sea.

For a time it was imagined that the destruction of the Brazilian cruiser Baia off St. Paul's Rocks, 100 miles from Pernambuco, was also due to a mine; but the ship is now thought to have been lost through one of her magazines exploding. She was a vessel of 3,150 tons, built on the Tyne in 1909, and modernized about 20 years ago. Of her complement of about 400, all seem to have been lost except 33 picked up by the Lamport and Holt liner Balfe, and 45 who reached the island of Fernando Noronha on a raft. This is the third ship of the Brazilian Navy to become a total casualty since that force became involved in war against the Axis. About a year ago the surveying vessel Vital de Oliveira was torpedoed by a German submarine; and almost at the same time the minelayer Camaqua foundered in heavy weather while on escort duty.

THERE was a tendency at first, when it was supposed that a mine had sunk the Baia, to connect the occurrence with the unexpected arrival shortly afterwards at Mar del Plata, the Argentine naval base, of the German submarine U530. She is reported to be a submarine of the 700-ton type, with a total complement of 54. According to statements by her captain, a lieutenant whose name is given variously as Wermhutt or Wemoutt, this U-boat had been on patrol for four months. If this is true, it is obvious that she must have been obtaining supplies from somewhere, or was concealed in some harbour for part of the time. Since the foregoing was written, the presence in Argentine waters of a second U-boat has been reported.

It is tempting to speculate whether, in fact, U530 may not have made her escape from a German port immediately prior to the surrender, in order to facilitate the escape of war criminals. It may be assumed that the United Nations will insist on the submarine and everyone belonging to her being given up, in order that a strict inquiry may be made into all the circumstances of the case. Failing some such action, there would very soon be a whispering campaign set on foot in Germany to the effect that the Fuehrer was taken to safety in her, to return in due course and re-establish Nazi domination. In the Far East, one of the last remaining cruisers of the Japanese Navy, the 10,000-ton Asigara, has been torpedoed and sunk by H.M. submarine Trenchant in the Java Sea. She was launched in 1928 and mounted ten 8-in. guns as her main armament. During the Coronation Review at Spithead in May 1937 the Asigara represented Japan, and gave an elaborate reception. Tea was taken on the quarterdeck; those who cared for it being invited below to drink saki in the wardroom. A display of wrestling by a picked team of athletes from Tokyo was the outstanding item in the entertainment.

Otherwise there has been no fresh sign of activity on the part of the Japanese fleet, surviving units of which are now mostly in the naval ports of Yokosaka, on Tokio Bay, and Kure, in the Inland Sea, repairing damage or being used as anti-aircraft batteries. Nor have the "suicide" planes which gave trouble to Allied naval forces during the reduction of Okinawa been so much in evidence in recent weeks. It is now known that three of H.M. aircraft carriers received some damage from attacks of this kind.

According to the account given to the Press by the commanding officer of one of them, the Illustrious, Captain C. E. Lambe, C.B., C.V.O., R.N., a suicide aircraft crashed on the flight deck of the carrier just by the island superstructure, producing a spurt of flame as the petrol tank exploded. Fortunately the fire was overcome before it could spread, and in 20 minutes the ship's own machines were landing on the flight deck again. In another similar attempt a Japanese plane made a forty-degree power dive which occupied just 11 seconds before it crashed into the sea, heavily hit by the anti-aircraft fire of the carrier. This time the aircraft just missed the island superstructure and passed ahead of the bridge as it descended. One or two of the aircraft on the flight deck were damaged by the huge splash caused by the enemy's dive into the sea. For some obscure reason most of these suicide planes appear to carry a rubber dinghy as part of their equipment. So far not a single British carrier has been put out of action for more than a few hours.

JAPANESE CARGO SUBMARINE, 137 ft. long, rests aboard the U.S. landing ship (dock) which transported it from the Pacific to the port of San Francisco to be repaired and put on public display. It was found abandoned by the enemy in Lingayen Gulf in the Philippines, scene of heavy fighting in the early months of 1945. *Photo, Associated Press*

WITH Okinawa and some smaller adjacent islands firmly in Allied hands, the bombing of Japanese cities and factories is being intensified. On July 14 a task force of the United States Navy under Rear-Admiral J. F. Shafroth, comprising the 35,000-ton battleships Indiana, Massachusetts and South Dakota, the heavy cruisers Chicago and Quincy, and sundry other vessels, approached closely to the main island of Japan (Honshu) to bombard the port of Kamaishi. This lies on the east coast, between Miyako and Sendai, and about 275 miles to the north-eastward of Tokyo Bay. Its importance lies in its steel foundries, blast furnaces and coke ovens which, owing to the devastation wrought in other centres farther south, were playing an essential part in maintaining Japanese war production. No opposition whatever was encountered; if there were any shore batteries they do not seem to have opened fire, and not a single aircraft appeared. For two hours the bombardment continued, leaving the town covered by a pall of dense smoke, rising thousands of feet into the air.

Subsequently, Hakodate and Muroran, in the northern island of Hokkaido, and the Hitachi copper-smelting area and other objectives nearer Tokyo, were the targets for similar attacks by British and U.S. naval forces.

Another operation which goes to show Japanese impotence at sea was the close approach recently made to Karafuto, the southern portion of the island of Sakhalin, by an American task force under Vice-Admiral F. J. Fletcher, which entered the Sea of Okhotsk, inside the chain of islands known as the Kuriles. The northern half of Sakhalin belongs to Russia, and the southern part to Japan.

JAPANESE Fishing Fleet Driven from Waters Round Sakhalin

It is probable that one of the objects of the attack on Karafuto was to interfere with the shipment of coal to Hokkaido, the northernmost of the Japanese main islands, where there is considerable industrial activity. An enemy convoy of six ships was wiped out, and the fishing fleet which supplies so large a proportion of Japan's meals was driven from these waters.

Vice-Admiral Marc A. Mitscher, U.S.N., whose name has been prominently in the news during his command of the task force which has carried out so many air raids on Japan, has been selected for the post of Deputy-Chief of Naval Operations (Air) in the Navy Department at Washington, where his experience should be of the utmost value.

Afloat and Ashore with Our Pacific Fleet

OPERATING OFF THE RYUKYUS in April and May 1945 an Australian destroyer with the British Pacific Fleet transferred mails to a Canadian cruiser seen (top) refuelling in rough seas from the same oiler as the British battleship in the foreground. Warwick Farm (bottom), famous race-course near Sydney, New South Wales, was transformed into a Royal Naval barracks and British Pacific Fleet transit camp. Known as H.M.S. Golden Hind, it is magnificently appointed, the grandstand being now a spacious canteen ; there is also an open-air concert platform. See pages 135, 192, and page 423, Vol. 8.

Photos, British Official

The Men from Alamein Came to Journey's End—

GUARDING H.Q., BRITISH TROOPS IN BERLIN, when our advance units moved in on July 3, 1945, was this N.C.O. of the Corps of Military Police (1). Present at the flag-breaking ceremony at the Victory monument were (2, left to right): Lt.-Gen. Sir Ronald Weeks (representing F.-M. Montgomery); Maj.-Gen. F. L. Parks (U.S.); Maj.-Gen. Baranov (U.S.S.R.); Gen. V. de Beauchesnes (France); and Maj.-Gen. L. O. Lyne (British C.-in-C., Berlin). The 11th Armoured Brigade (3) led the way into the German capital, as Gen. Lyne took the salute.

—When the Union Jack Flew Over Dead Berlin

THE BRITISH FLAG WAS FLOWN in the heart of the Reich for the first time on July 6, 1945—at the base of Berlin's 1870 Victory Memorial in the Koenigs-Platz. After the brisk ten-minute ceremony the British troops—led down the Sieges Allee by pipers of the Argyll and Sutherland Highlanders of Canada, first of our soldiers to enter Holland—returned to their posts. The march past was taken by Maj.-Gen. Louis O. Lyne, O.C. British troops, Berlin area, in the presence of U.S., Soviet and French military representatives. See also pages 197, 217 and 222 *Photo, Keystone*

82 Days that Lost the War for Japan

Springboard for the final assault on the Nippon mainland, Okinawa fell to American forces on June 21, 1945, after a fanatical defence which cost the United States the highest price she has yet paid for any island in the Pacific. This authoritative survey of the bitter 82-days campaign was written expressly for "The War Illustrated."

THE American victory at Okinawa—the bloodiest and toughest yet wrested from the Pacific—ended one phase of the Far East war and set the stage for the closing act. This small island, of about 485 square miles, has a significance in the fighting picture out of all proportion to its size. It constitutes the last island stepping-stone on the Allied road to the enemy's mainland and its conquest is the death-blow to any Japanese hopes of final victory.

With the occupation of Okinawa, Tokyo has been virtually defeated at sea and in the air, and the final clash between Allied land forces and the bulk of the Japanese armies is now tensely awaited by the enemy. With Okinawa, island-hopping in the Pacific is practically over, and the Japs themselves realize invasion is inevitable.

To the enemy the Okinawa conquest means an early and terrible intensification of the air raids which have already inflicted serious damage upon Japan's industrial cities, her ports, her shipping, and her aerodromes. Up to now these wounds have been dealt by squadrons of long-range aircraft operating at first from southern China and more recently from bases in the Mariana Islands, more than 1,300 miles from the nearest targets in Japan. The airfields of Okinawa are less than a third of that distance away.

EXPERTS have calculated that airstrips constructed on the island by the Japs in the vain hope of protecting this fortification and thus fending off the full violence of amphibious invasion from their mainland, together with those which American engineers are now rapidly preparing, can accommodate at least 1,000 planes of the most powerful types. In addition to aircraft based on Okinawa, the Allied air potential for striking Japanese home cities includes the squadrons operating from more distant bases, and the carrier-borne planes, fighters, light and medium bombers, and fighter-bombers, which have been increasingly active over Japan since the defeat and virtual blockade of the Japanese battle fleet.

In less than two weeks after organized resistance on the island came to an end, American B-25 Mitchell bombers, operating for the first time from the newly won base, hammered enemy suicide plane bases on Kyushu, marking a beginning of the increasing air blows which are being launched against Japan proper from these airfields.

Base for Land and Sea Attacks

Okinawa, in addition to its strategic position as an airbase, affords a base near Japan for the assembling of hundreds of thousands of troops which can be deployed for an invasion of the enemy homeland. From the naval standpoint, the island boasts at least three protected anchorages—Hagushi Bay on the west, where the Americans landed, and on the other side, Chimu Bay and Nakagusuku Bay, well sheltered from typhoons, and with accommodation for a large modern fleet which will simplify problems of supply in future attacks on the Japanese home islands.

The Okinawa operations presented, in one campaign, all the problems of Far Eastern fighting with which the Allies have had to contend in various phases of Pacific warfare since 1941 as well as new hazards never before encountered in Pacific landings. During the campaign American troops had to cope with the problem of a large civilian population which had hampered operations in the Philippines and Burma. The U.S. forces underwent simultaneous attacks by land, sea and air power as they had done before at Iwojima. Caves and other hidden positions gave the Japanese superb artillery sites and equally good "spotting" posts for directing their guns. Skilfully employing their weapons against the invading forces, the Japs made especially clever use of their new giant mortars which throw 1,000-pound projectiles. Seeking to gain only a few yards of ground, the Americans sometimes had to face automatic fire from five different points.

The Japanese used suicide forces as a defence measure as well as a battle tactic. The "Kamikaze," Jap pilots who dived their planes and bombloads squarely into naval and merchant vessels, were used in other campaigns but never with such frequency as at Okinawa. A new type of "Kamikaze" personnel emerged from the campaign. The island had been a training base for suicide swimmers and boatmen. The suicide boats, abandoned by the swimmers at the final moment of attack, carry in their bows explosives and rockets which fire upon impact. The Japs also experimented with a new type of flying bomb. A more accurate weapon than the German one, the bomb was piloted by a suicide flyer (see illus. p. 178).

OKINAWA, 60-mile-long island in the Ryukyus, cost the Japanese 113,351 casualties in just under twelve weeks' fighting; U.S. 10th Army casualties totalled 46,319. **See page 117.**
By courtesy of The Daily Herald

THE 82-day campaign was launched on Easter Sunday, April 1, when the 10th U.S. Army, under the command of the late Lieut.-Gen. Simon D. Buckner, Jr., invaded the island. (Gen. Buckner was killed by a shell on June 17, his command being temporarily taken over by Maj.-Gen. Roy S. Geiger and on June 21 by Gen. Joseph Stilwell). The 10th Army making the landing comprised one corps of four U.S. Army divisions, and one corps of two U.S. Marine divisions (the 3rd Marine Amphibious Corps, under Maj.-Gen. Geiger). The opposition to the initial landings was so slight that it gave no indication of the grim struggle ahead.

Turning southward the Army divisions ran against the main Jap forces and prepared defences, and the advance slowed into an artillery and infantry slogging match. The Japs dug themselves into caves and along high ridges and the southern front became a series of hand-to-hand encounters supplemented by use, where possible, of flame-throwing tanks. American troops had to fight over and through hills honeycombed with caves and tunnels and the most elaborate system of concealed fortifications they had encountered in the Pacific war.

The defence was as skilful as it was determined, and the strong, well-prepared and well-equipped enemy of around 120,000 men had orders to hold out to the end. Japanese losses were fantastic, totalling more than 1,000 a day. There was no relenting. Every Jap pillbox had to be taken individually and destroyed by demolition charges.

Heavy Toll of U.S. Ships

During the vital stage of the Okinawa fighting the Allied naval forces, under the general Navy command of Adm. Chester Nimitz, sustained high casualties and lost more ships than in any other single Pacific engagement. The Japanese Navy took this heavy toll despite the fact that its battle fleet was virtually destroyed before the campaign even opened. It turned almost its entire remaining fleet air arm, together with small surface units such as torpedo-boats, into one great terrible suicide force.

The protracted and critical battle gradually subsided in violence as the American troops and Marines smashed their way through to the southern cliffs of the island and divided the enemy into shattered remnants, and on June 21, organized Jap resistance ceased. But during the 12-week battle the United States paid dearly to win their springboard for an attack on the Chinese or Japanese coasts. The American casualty figure of 46,319, of which 11,897 were killed or taken prisoner and 34,422 wounded, shocked the nation and drew fierce criticism from some military commentators.

Assessing the price paid by America for the island, however, Mr. Robert P. Patterson, U.S. Under-Secretary of War, said: "Considering the airfields and ports we have won on Okinawa, the size of the enemy force we have overcome and the damage done to enemy aeroplanes, airfields, warships and industrial war-making ability in the homeland in these last three months, the cost to us has not been heavy."

COSTLY as the operations were to the United States, Japanese losses were far higher. The enemy lost 113,351 men, of which 9,498 were taken prisoner, and suffered destruction of 3,776 planes at a cost of 650 American planes shot down.

If Okinawa cost the Americans more than they had reckoned, the same thing was most certainly true of the Japanese. The enemy spent a large part of his dwindling naval and army air forces against the Okinawa armada. The Japanese garrison on the island probably did not amount to much in the over-all total of Japan's fighting forces, but the aircraft and other naval units, cut down like flies off Okinawa, belonged to the last-ditch defences of the homeland itself.

The campaign on Okinawa, small when compared to the later actions that must be fought, was a vivid illustration of the time it takes to subdue a beaten enemy, and proved that final surrender will be bought only by a high price in life, blood and money.

Okinawa—Island of Bitter Battles—is Purged

AFTER 82 DAYS OF THE TOUGHEST FIGHTING IN THE PACIFIC, Okinawa fell to the U.S. 10th Army on June 21, 1945. Marines warily entered minestrewn Naha, the capital (1) on May 27; others boldly dashed across the open (2) in the final stages of the campaign. Watching the end at Naha were Maj.-Gen. Lemuel C. Shepherd (3, left), commanding U.S. 6th Marine Division, and (right) Lieut.-Gen. Simon Bolivar Buckner, commander of U.S. 10th Army (killed in action on June 17). A landing net (4) used to scale a stronghold. *Photos, U.S. Official, Associated Press, Keystone*

Now It Can Be Told!

How We Won the Battle of the Sea-Mines

To destroy our shipping faster than new construction could replace it, to dislocate vital traffic and make our ports and channels unserviceable, was Germany's great mine-laying objective. To defeat it, British minesweepers and scientists played brilliant parts, as revealed in the following facts officially released in June 1945.

The acute shortage of tennis balls during the war with Germany has now been explained. They assisted the Royal Navy to achieve victory in the first technical battle of the war: the battle of the magnetic mine. It is part of one chapter in the great and yet-to-be-told history of the triumphs of British minesweepers and scientists who so brilliantly countered Germany's determined efforts to block our ports and destroy our shipping by mining.

Heavy, and for a time unexplained, shipping casualties in the early days of the war were traced to the enemy's magnetic mine (see story in page 124, Vol. 7). Competition was keen among technical and scientific experts to discover the antidote to this mine; finally there emerged the one completely successful method, which proved so effective that this particular mine menace never again reached dimensions comparable with those of the first year of the war.

This method was the double longitudinal sweep, which comprises two minesweeping ships each towing a long tail of self-buoyant electric cable. The current is generated in the ships, stored momentarily in batteries and passed through both cables as a large "surge." The current goes into the sea, and by this means ten or more acres of the sea bottom can be subjected to a magnetic field of sufficient strength and duration to explode all the magnetic mines therein. The ships towing the sweep proceed on their parallel courses and make a second "surge" of magnetic field, and in this way a continuous line of sea bottom is cleared, providing a safe channel through which ships can pass.

The main advantages of the double longitudinal are that the sweep is easy to tow and to handle, and it does not foul wrecks and buoys. It is not damaged by the explosion of the mines and it will sweep a large area with 100 per cent effectiveness. The original double longitudinal sweep was constructed on the shore of the Isle of Grain near Sheerness, and towed behind a tug. It was made from cable used for charging submarine batteries, and floated on logs originally intended to make masts for ships.

On a day in late December 1939 two tugs, filled with motor-car batteries and each towing one of these "giant snakes," left Sheerness Harbour for the first full-scale trial. This trial confirmed the

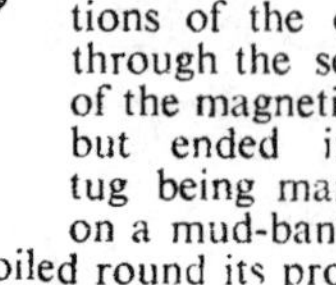

scientists' calculations of the current through the sea and of the magnetic field, but ended in one tug being marooned on a mud-bank with its "giant snake" coiled round its propeller. However, the answer was there, and that same evening orders went out from the Admiralty for the final modifications to the big programme of production, fitting out of ships, training of men, and so on, which had all been provisionally arranged in anticipation of success. The logs gave way to self-buoyant cable produced by two of the leading British cable manufacturers, and the menace of the magnetic mine had been overcome.

Those self-buoyant cables—that's where the tennis balls came in. One of the cable manufacturers said to himself, "We make both cables and tennis balls. So why not combine the two? Why not carry the heavy electric wires on cables made of tennis balls? Not just a ball here and there, for that would not give enough buoyancy; but tennis balls compressed and packed tightly one after the other to form one long, self-buoyant cable." And so 23 million balls went to make hundreds of buoyant sets involving over 1 million yards of cable.

Seas Cleared of 20,429 Mines

At the outbreak of war the minesweeping service of the Royal Navy consisted of about 36 fleet minesweepers and 40 trawlers, with a sea-going personnel of about 2,000. This was at first a polyglot fleet of fishing trawlers and drifters, paddle steamers, whale-catchers, tugs, yachts, mud-hoppers and dhows, assisted by a handful of fleet minesweepers. At the end of the war with Germany we had 1,350 minesweepers manned by about 50,000 officers and men.

Up to June 13, 1945, a total of 20,429 mines had been swept by British, Dominion and Allied sweepers, and German minesweepers operating under Allied control, that total being exclusive of operations carried out by sweepers of the U.S. Navy. Naturally the cost to the minesweepers has been heavy—237 lost: 99 by mining, 68 by aircraft attack, 70 by other causes.

In foreign waters our sweepers have done magnificent work; at home, credit was given in May 1945 to the achievements of the Liverpool minesweeping trawlers and motor minesweepers in clearing Liverpool Bay and the Mersey. So far, two sweeping flotillas and two trawler groups had steamed nearly 2 million miles and cleared 500 square miles from Holyhead to Cumberland.

Throughout the Liverpool air raids the sweeping continued, enabling the docks to deal with as near a normal flow of traffic as circumstances would permit. "We were at it day and night," said Lieut.-Cmdr. Matthews, D.S.C., M.M., R.N.V.R., of H.M.S. Hornbeam, "not only clearing and destroying mines but firing at the enemy aircraft and the mines as they came down by parachute. We used to be out five days at a time, dash back to harbour to restore, and then get out again. We came in one night to tie up at Wallasey, and got a frantic message to get out again as quickly as possible as we were 'sitting' on two mines!"

This mine-laying business was by no means one-sided, of course. We guarded ourselves with mines intended to protect our coastal shipping, and we hit back with offensive mining in enemy waters. It is revealed now that well over 250,000 sea-mines were laid by the Royal Navy, the Naval Air Arm and the R.A.F. during the War; and it is estimated that more than 1,000 enemy vessels were sunk or damaged by them. The number of mines laid by Britain alone exceeds by 14,000 the total number laid by *all* nations in the last war!

MINESWEEPING SECRETS of the war at sea divulged in this page, included "L.Ls," or double longitudinal sweeps, in which H.M. minesweepers towed long tails of "live" electric cable tightly packed with tennis balls to keep them afloat. After the day's work, Naval ratings (left) hauled in the magnetic "sweep" wires, two of which are seen (below) as they trailed from the stern of the operating craft at anchor.

Photos, British Official

Our "Met" Men Fought Germans In the Arctic

THE ARCTIC WASTES of Spitsbergen were in 1942 the scene of a great Allied adventure—it was disclosed on June 9, 1945—when a small meteorological party, established there to obtain vital weather information for the North Russian Convoy system, waged a five-months' "war" against Nazi meteorologists carrying out a similar task in a neighbouring fjord. For months they carried on, using a disused coalmine as shelter against ceaseless enemy air attack; while R.A.F. Coastal Command flying-boats kept them alive by dropping frequent supplies and evacuating wounded, as well as themselves carrying out valuable meteorological flights. Eventually, the enemy left the area, and the Allied scientists secured the all-important data.

The "Met" force arrive at Barentsburg, in Ice Fjord, on May 13, 1942—under the enemy's noses. The following day, while they were breaking the ice in Green Harbour, their ships were viciously attacked by four Focke-Wulf 200s. Only two of the 40 men sheltering behind tiny hummocks on the ice were, hit, however; although heavier casualties were sustained on the ships. Food, arms and clothing were lost, but the party managed to make do with old padded jerkins left behind by former Russian mineralogists, with dentists' white coats and bed-linen from the same source as camouflage.

ON RESCUE MISSION to a secret Allied "Met" station in the Arctic archipelago of Spitsbergen, 360 miles north of Norway, in 1942—details of which have just been released—the crew of a R.A.F. Coastal Command flying-boat (1) fended off drift-ice as they lay at anchor. The wireless station in Advent Bay (2) under the shadow of towering snow-clad mountains was close to a similar "Met" organization operated by the Nazis. Allied scientists' H.Q. (3) at Sveagruya, showing buildings and radio masts.

Photos, British Official

New Zealand's Fighting Ships and Men at War

A recent official message expressing appreciation of the very valuable services rendered by the R.N.Z.N. contained the passage : "The Board of Admiralty and the officers and men of the Royal Navy and Royal Marines look forward to the continued co-operation of the Royal New Zealand Navy in bringing about the early defeat of Japan." Outstanding actions of the R.N.Z.N. are here recalled by FRANCIS E. McMURTRIE.

THE Royal New Zealand Navy was granted that title as recently as September 1941, but its actual existence began in 1913. In that year the New Zealand Division of the Royal Navy was formed, with a Captain, R.N., as Senior Officer. It was composed of three small cruisers, the Philomel, Psyche and Pyramus, and a sloop, the Torch, partly manned by ratings recruited in the Dominion.

All four of these ships took part in the First Great War. They escorted convoys across the Indian Ocean, patrolled the East African coast and the Persian Gulf, and shared in the occupation of German territory in Samoa and New Britain. After a time the Psyche was transferred to the Royal Australian Navy, while the Philomel was made over entirely to New Zealand for use as a training ship. In May 1920, with the return of peace conditions, the New Zealand Division was reconstituted. The Philomel was joined by H.M.S. Chatham, a cruiser of 5,400 tons, which was presented to the Government of the Dominion by the Admiralty. Captain A. G. Hotham, R.N., was appointed to her with the rank of Commodore, second class, for command of the N.Z. Division.

WITHIN a year the New Zealand Naval Board was constituted. It was modelled on the lines of the Admiralty, with the Commodore as the First Naval Member. This arrangement has stood the test of time, and holds good today. In the years between the two wars the strength of the force gradually increased. By 1939 it included the cruisers Achilles and Leander, of 7,030 and 7,270 tons respectively, both maintained at the charge of the New Zealand Government. A couple of sloops attached to the station remained the responsibility of the Admiralty.

There were besides certain local units which were entirely New Zealand property ; these were the veteran training ship Philomel, built as long ago as 1890, the trawler Wakakura and the fleet tug Toia. To these have since been added five corvettes—one of which has been lost—and 18 additional trawlers. The latter are mostly organized in flotillas for minesweeping. Most recent and important of the war additions is the fine new cruiser Gambia, of 8,000 tons.

IN the Battle of the River Plate (see pages 303-306, Vol. 2), one of the three cruisers which drove the Admiral Graf Spee into Montevideo, a beaten ship, was the Achilles. She was largely manned by New Zealanders, who were highly commended by their commanding officer, Captain W. E. Parry, in his report after the action. Though no less hotly engaged than her consorts, the Achilles was more fortunate in that she received damage of a less severe nature. All eight of her 6-in. guns continued to fire throughout the action. In the final phase she was assigned the task of shadowing the Admiral Graf Spee right up the estuary of the Plate until it was certain she was entering the port of Montevideo. Of the other two ships, H.M.S. Ajax had taken a course to the southward of the large sandbank which lies in the mouth of the estuary, in case the enemy ship should try to double back around it ; and H.M.S. Exeter, which had been badly knocked about early in the day, had been obliged to break off the action to repair damages.

A Great Ovation for the Achilles

Rear-Admiral Sir Henry Harwood in his dispatch records "the honour and pleasure I had in taking one of His Majesty's ships of the New Zealand Division into action," and declared that "New Zealand has every reason to be proud of her seamen during their baptism of fire." As may be imagined, the Achilles and her officers and men received a great ovation when the ship returned to New Zealand waters a few months later.

Her sister ship, the Leander, saw a good deal of service in the Mediterranean and the Indian Ocean. In March 1941 she intercepted the Italian armed merchant cruiser Ramb I, an ex-banana carrier, in the latter area, and sank her by gunfire. Two months later, while cruising in company with H.M.A.S. Canberra, she was responsible for rounding up the German merchant vessel Coburg, which had been acting as a supply ship to enemy raiders, as well as a Norwegian tanker which had been captured.

In June 1941 the Leander was one of a squadron operating against French naval forces under the orders of the Vichy Government off the Syrian coast. Later she returned to the Pacific, and in company with the Achilles and certain ships of the Royal Australian Navy, was attached to the task force of the United States Navy operating in the Solomon Islands area. More than once she was in action with Japanese cruisers and destroyers, and is understood to have sustained some damage.

Amongst the first war-built ships of the R.N.Z.N. to come into service were the three corvettes Kiwi, Moa and Tui. All three were built at Leith, the order for their construction having been placed before the war. On the night of January 29-30, 1943, the Kiwi and Moa, while on patrol to the northward of the island of Guadalcanal, in the Solomons, detected the presence of a Japanese submarine of 1,600 tons. Depth charges were at once dropped, and the enemy was forced to the surface. A brisk gun duel ensued between the submarine, which mounted a 5·5-in. gun, firing an 80-lb. shell, and the Kiwi. The latter carried a single 4-in., whose projectile weighs only 31 lb. Several hits were scored on the enemy, which was also rammed three times by the Kiwi. In attempting to escape the submarine ultimately ran into shallow water and struck a reef, on which she was completely wrecked.

ON April 7, 1943, the gallant little Moa was lost. She fell a victim to a cluster of bombs dropped by Japanese aircraft during an attack on the U.S. positions at Tulagi. H.M.N.Z.S. Tui, the third of the trio of corvettes, was in action with another Japanese submarine in the Solomons area. She was supported by aircraft of the United States Navy, and the submarine was ultimately destroyed. It is believed to have been one of the largest type, with a displacement of 2,563 tons, and was probably carrying supplies to some isolated Japanese garrison.

These are merely the outstanding incidents in a series of active patrols carried out by these ships in hostile waters. When the full story of their achievements is released, it will be possible to fill in the gaps in this narrative. Many officers and men of the Royal New Zealand Navy are serving in ships of the Royal Navy and with the Naval Air Arm.

They have specially distinguished themselves in Coastal Forces, both in Home waters and in the Mediterranean. In the official report of a smart action in the North Sea on the night of March 21-22 last, when German motor torpedo boats were driven off with loss in an attempt to strike at a convoy, it was mentioned that H.M. corvette Puffin was commanded by a lieutenant-commander of the R.N.Z.N.V.R.

IN SERVICE WITH THE R.N.Z.N., whose history is related in this page, is the 8,000-ton cruiser Gambia (top) which, completed in 1942 for the Royal Navy, has recently been in action with Admiral Sir Bruce Fraser's British Pacific Fleet, manned by New Zealand personnel. Scots-built corvette Kiwi (below) saw gallant service in the Solomons. *Photos, British Official*

Our King & Queen Through the War Years

SEPTEMBER 3, 1939. On the day Britain declared war on Germany, King George broadcasts to the Empire.

DECEMBER 1939. Visit to units of the Royal Navy at Plymouth.

DECEMBER 1939. With the R.A.F. in France: entering an ack-ack post.

MARCH 1940. Inspecting the first magnetic mine to be salvaged.

JUNE 1940. Queen Elizabeth converses with wounded evacuated from Dunkirk.

FEBRUARY 1940. Viewing the assembly line at an aircraft factory during a tour of military and civil defence centres in the West Country.

JUNE 1940. While visiting an arms factory, the King makes himself acquainted with the working of a Bren gun.

JULY 1940. Dockyard workers loudly cheer King George during a visit to a famous naval port in Britain, where he inspected personnel of the Royal Navy and the Fleet Air Arm.

JULY 1940. At a Government Training Centre, the King, accompanied by Mr. Ernest Bevin, examines the mechanism of fuse and shell gauges.

AUGUST 1940. With a schoolboy harvester on a Southern England farm.

SEPTEMBER 1940. The Queen sy pathizes with bombed-out Londoners.

FEBRUARY 1941. Inspecting units of his Indian troops stationed at a coast town in south-west England.

MAY 1941. Firing a tommy gun for the first time, while visiting Southern Command.

SEPTEMBER 1941. Inspection of Canadian Forestry Corps at Balmoral.

MAY 1942. King George takes the salute at a drive-past by tanks of the Guards' Armoured Division.

JUNE 1942. During their visit to Northern Ireland, Their Majesties spend a day with United States troops, inspecting men and equipment and watching manoeuvres.

OCTOBE during

NOVEMBER 1940. The day after the merciless air attack on Coventry, he sees for himself the ruined Cathedral.

MBER 1940. After their own London home has been damaged by a nb Their Majesties talk with Buckingham Palace Civil Defence staff.

OCTOBER 1941. Boarding a landing craft during preliminary invasion exercises with the Scottish Command.

APRIL 1942. At Grenadier Guards' parade in honour of Princess Elizabeth's 16th birthday.

onoured guest of Their Majesties ,ondon: Mrs. Eleanor Roosevelt.

MAY 1943. Examining photographs of Ruhr Valley dams after their bombing by the late Wing-Cmdr. G. P. Gibson, V.C. (on the King's right).

MAY 1943. At St. Paul's for the Thanksgiving Service after the African victory.

JUNE 1943. In Tunisia, cheering British troops line the route when the King inspects the 1st and 8th Armies at the victorious conclusion of the two-and-a-half years North African campaign.

JULY 1943. A warm handshake extended to Air Chief Marshal Sir Arthur Tedder, at Malta, G.C.

MAY 1944. During the Empire Conference in London; with Mr. Churchill and Dominion premiers.

JULY 1944. With F.-M. Alexander in Italy, visiting 8th Army.

JULY 1944. Conferring accolade of knighthood on Gen. Sir Oliver Leese on the Italian battlefield.

OCTOBER 1944. Studying the campaign on the spot: with Field-Marshal Montgomery in Normandy.

OCTOBER 1944. With Eisenhower and U.S. generals in France.

MAY 8, 1945. On V Day, triumphal celebration of victory in Europe. the Royal Family acknowledge cheers from Buckingham Palace.

VIEWS & REVIEWS Of Vital War Books

by Hamilton Fyfe

I TAKE a family interest in submarines. My brother, Herbert C. Fyfe, wrote the first book about them. That was just before the end of last century, when most people either guessed little of their possibilities or dismissed the idea of under-water boats as "ridiculous Jules Verne stuff." Even now, says the writer of a Stationery Office booklet prepared by the Ministry of Information for the Board of Admiralty and called His Majesty's Submarines (price 9d.), "to the layman even now the submarine is still a novelty, strange and little understood"; this branch of the Navy is still "cloaked in mystery." Well, if that is so, this account of its doings in the European war will go far to dissipate the fog of ignorance. It will also spread more widely the admiration and gratitude felt by those who have been able to follow those doings closely, for the men who have shown such pluck and dogged endurance and, as the booklet puts it, "high-hearted determination," and contributed so mightily to the defeat of the German enemy.

What the crews of a submarine endure can be fully realized only by those who have served in one under war conditions. To begin with, there is very little room to move about or even to sit or lie still. The ship is "closely packed with a bewildering mass of pipes, valves, gauges, instruments, electric cables." The air becomes thick and sleepifying while you are submerged during the daylight hours. It is an immense relief when in the dark the vessel rises to the surface and the engines are started.

> Instead of the silence there are engine noises and the sound of the sea. The boat lurches into a roll, and men can move and breathe freely. A draught of fresh night air is sucked through. There comes the welcome order: Carry on smoking. Somebody begins a song. Breakfast will soon be ready. "Midday" dinner is at midnight, and supper just before dawn.

Soon after that the crew settle down with a sigh to another period of tedium, doing nothing for the most part, relieving their dry throats with boiled sweets, which are served out to them as a regular ration, and longing for the dark hours again.

Complicated and Deadly Instrument

But most of those who serve in submarines will agree that life in them has its compensations.

> In that small dim world below the sea there is a unique companionship. A submarine is a self-supporting unit and the members of her company must have confidence in each other. There is discipline, but with it a democratic spirit which compensates for much of the hardship. It is a rare comradeship shared by all, from the commanding officer to the youngest member of the crew.

Above all is it necessary that the captain should be trusted by his crew. He looks through the periscope, he alone knows what is happening above in sea and sky, he must decide swiftly what is to be done and he must decide correctly, for the slightest error, an inaccurate estimate of distance, or a few seconds' delay may cause not only the failure of an attack, but the destruction of the ship and the whole company.

"The most complicated and deadly instrument of war," the submarine is styled. The description is exact so far as it goes. We might add that it is among the most expensive. Not in itself only, but in the ammunition with which it does its deadly work. Each torpedo discharged costs £2,500, and is for its size as complicated a piece of mechanism as the submarine. Small submarines carry four, large ones eleven, ready to be fired; also some spares. The "human torpedo" (see illus. p. 775, Vol. 7) is for use against ships in harbour or at anchor which cannot be drawn into the open for a battle at sea. Two men wearing diving-suits sit astride it. They drive it slowly by its electric batteries towards the target, under which they dive. A charge like that of a torpedo is then detached and fixed to the hull of the enemy ship. A fuse is set and the "human torpedo" gets away as quickly as possible so as to be out of range when the explosion occurs.

His Majesty's Submarines

There are also midget submarines for use in much the same conditions. They did a fine job when they entered the Norwegian fjord where the German battleship Tirpitz lay and damaged her badly. Of this exploit, the full story has not yet been released, but what they did was to navigate first of all a thousand miles of rough sea, then to pass through the enemy minefield and go up the long, narrow fjord where "every conceivable device which could ensure their destruction" was known to be in use. They slid past listening posts, nets, gun defences. They actually reached the nets only two hundred yards from the Tirpitz, designed to protect it against such attacks as theirs. From there they launched their missiles. These caused an immense explosion. The battleship was lifted several feet into the air. One submarine was seen from the Tirpitz's deck and fired at with rifles. Guns were trained on their supposed positions, depth-charges were dropped. They could not make their way back out of the nets. Two were scuttled by their crews, who were then taken prisoner. The third was never heard of again. (See illus. page 183; also page 649, Vol. 7).

This operation "for daring and endurance is unique even in the annals of the Royal Navy."

"GONE NATIVE" for the occasion, these R.N. submarine officers enjoyed a brief respite in Far Eastern waters after destroying over 30 enemy coastal craft. Life in these undersea craft is vividly described in this page. *Photo, British Official*

The effect of depth-charges bursting round a submarine is a severe test for the nerves.

> You hear faintly at first and then louder the "chuffle-chuffle" of a destroyer's screws. Then it comes—a great metallic clang, the "tonk" they call it. The boat shudders; the corking, a special form of paint used to prevent metal surfaces from sweating, falls in a white shower; depth gauges are put out of action; glass is broken. It comes again, a second terrible crash, followed by another, and the boat lurches and shudders. There is a pause and you wait for the next blow.

This might go on for as long as the best part of an hour. One captain, recording an attack which lasted forty minutes, said he was much impressed by the bearing of all hands during this unpleasant time, "but particularly so with that of J. V. Crosby, Acting Leading Telegraphist, who, knowing full well when an attack was developing, calmly continued giving the information for the records as though it was merely a peacetime exercise that was in progress." The sea-pressure on a submerged submarine is an added anxiety to its commander when a depth-charge attack is on. Its weight is some 130 pounds to the square inch, and it has been known to bend a steel pillar four inches thick.

FOUL air is another worry. This is sometimes so bad that it makes the engines difficult to start. Its effect on human beings can be imagined. In one engagement the Tetrarch was under water for 42 hours and 40 minutes. When she came to the surface and fresh air could be breathed again, most of the crew were dizzy, many violently sick. The harder you work, the more you exhaust the wholesome atmosphere, because you breathe more quickly. So the men in submarines have to spend as much time as possible, while they are submerged, lying still or at any rate doing as little as possible. This is the time when the boiled sweets come in useful—may even be life-savers. A bag of peppermint bull's-eyes has been known to revive a working party when they were literally gasping for air.

Bomb Disposal Under Difficulties

This was during the long ordeal undergone by the Spearfish when she was trapped in shallow water off Norway. Depth-charges exploded round her about every two minutes. Were the crew rattled? Listen!

> A sixpenny sweepstake was started among them on the time of the next explosion, the stake to be settled on the next pay-day. No words were spoken. A seaman moved softly through the boat, booking the bets, which were agreed to by signs.

Depth-charges were bad enough. Bombs from the air were worse. They could be avoided by submerging, but this was, to say the least of it, inconvenient. Highly dangerous was the situation of the Thrasher when it was discovered that two unexploded aircraft bombs lay on the forward casing. The discovery was made at night. The submarine lay on the surface, but the enemy patrols were not far off; at any moment she might have to submerge. Two of the crew, Lieut. Roberts and Petty-Officer Gould, volunteered to remove the bombs. They were exposed to two risks. The bombs might explode, the ship might have to go under suddenly, in which case they would almost certainly be dragged down and drowned. (See illus. page 59, Vol. 6).

They went about the operation with quiet confidence. It took fifty minutes, and they had only faint torchlight to work by. They had to lie on their stomachs, one pushing, one pulling, till they manœuvred the bombs overboard. Their task was not made easier by the second of the two missiles giving off a loud twanging sound every time it was moved, "which added nothing to their peace of mind," as the official report put it. They both received the award of the Victoria Cross, and well they deserved it.

Learning to Beat the Japanese--in Britain

IN A HOME-MADE "JUNGLE" IN DERBYSHIRE, at Rowsley, between Chatsworth and Haddon Hall, our experts back from Burma and the Pacific train troops for the final defeat of Japan. Favourite exercise is a mock-ambush of a "Japanese" patrol by a British Sten gunner (1). Having just "killed" an officer, this "Jap" (2) shammed death in a tree. Demonstration of an enemy fox-hole (3) complete with sniper, and identification of enemy badges (4): The British tommy in tropical war-kit carries a Mark V Sten gun and a short bayonet for jungle warfare. *Photos, G.P.U.*

Lord Wavell Outlined His Plan at Simla

TALKS BETWEEN THE VICEROY AND INDIA'S LEADERS opened at Simla on June 25, 1945, only to break down on July 14. Before they began Lord Wavell (1) chatted with Dr. Maulana Abul Kalem Azad, President of Congress. The 21 Indian delegates included (2, left to right): Master Tara Singh, head of the Akali Sikhs; Malik Khisr Hyat Khan, Premier of the Punjab; Mr. M. A. Jinnah, President of the Moslem League; and Iman Hussain, leader of the Moslem League Party in the Council of State. Mr. Gandhi arrived by rickshaw (3). *Photos exclusive to* THE WAR ILLUSTRATED

Non-Fighting Heroes at the Front in China—

Sharing the Quaker view on war, these conscientious objectors have chosen the relief of suffering among the fighting-men and stricken civilians as alternative to combatant service. The work of one group of the Friends' Ambulance Unit, comprising 60 British, 15 American, a Canadian, an East Indian and 38 Chinese, is described here by SENYUNG CHOW.

ENGAGED in almost world-wide activity, the Friends' Ambulance Unit has done medical, relief, and transport work in England, Italy, France, Belgium, Holland, Greece, Albania, North Africa, the Dodecanese, Yugoslavia, Syria, Ethiopia, India and China. The origin of the society dates back to 1660, when a "Declaration from the Innocent and Harmless People of God, called Quakers" was made to King Charles II of England to "deny all outward wars and strife and fightings with outward weapons for any end, or under any pretence whatever."

However, the Unit as now constituted was not founded until the 1914-18 war, when a group of the members of the Society of Friends organized a team to do ambulance work with the Allied armies in France. In 1939, at the outbreak of the present war, the Unit was again brought into being. In China, it is supported financially by the American United China Relief, the British Government, and the Canadian War Relief Fund. A yearly contribution comes from the American United China Relief and a subsidy from the British Government.

IT is staffed with men and women from all walks of life and most of the foreigners speak good practical Chinese. There are Oxford and Harvard graduates driving trucks, school teachers supervising mechanical workshops, former college students cleaning charcoal filters and changing tires. The whole group ranges from civil servants and businessmen to lawyers, farmers, clerks and schoolboys. And all the members are living on the same financial basis. According to a voluntary rule, no personal money is allowed to be brought into China. Provided with board and lodging, each member draws from the Unit monthly pay in Chinese currency, equivalent to about 12s. 6d. That is his total income.

There is no limit of work. In August 1944, with two doctors, the rate of work in one team averaged 12 operations a day, including Sundays. In September, with an additional doctor, it rose to 18. The main part of the medical work is now concentrated in south-west China. There are four medical teams stationed in Paoshan and Tengchung, western Yunnan, and in other areas where Chinese troops are fighting. They are of two types: a more stationary one with hospital equipment remains a little behind the front to receive wounded soldiers, while a mobile one follows the troops to the front line and treats cases on the spot.

In Remote Villages in Yunnan

In addition, these teams set up delousing stations, give inoculations to civilians and soldiers, fight epidemics and generally prevalent diseases. In some remote villages in Yunnan which have never before seen modern medical service, the teams are doing medical relief and rehabilitation work at the same time. When they move forward with the army they leave the hospitals behind to the local government for the continuation of the work.

They have many medical achievements to their credit. In the Tengchung area one of the Unit's doctors was summoned by an emergency wireless message to investigate and confirm an outbreak of bubonic plague. He made two visits. On the first he found only convalescent plague, but on the second he discovered specimens of P. Pestis from a dead rat's spleen. The epidemic was detected at its outset and countless lives were saved.

Medical work in the rugged and waste terrain in south-west China taxes both the spiritual and physical stamina of Unit members to the extreme. When marching with the troops teams have to carry their equipment over mountain trails, travelling mostly on foot when no mules are available. The food usually consists of handfuls of fried rice and water, the same as for Chinese soldiers on the march. Night operations are performed with the aid of crude oil lamps hung from rafters or perched on the edge of the table. Despite these rough conditions, five English and six Chinese girl nurses have pulled their weight as thoroughly as the men.

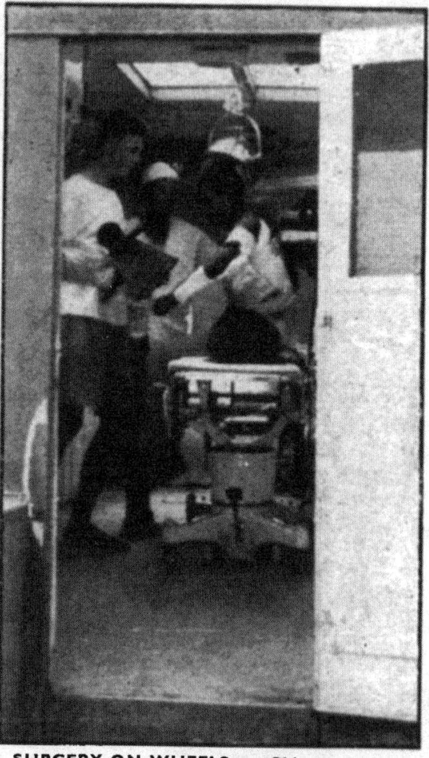

SURGERY ON WHEELS: a Chinese soldier being X-rayed in a mobile operating theatre of the Friends' Ambulance Unit. The eighth anniversary of the Sino-Japanese war in July 1945 found the Chinese again on the offensive in Kwangsi and Fukien.

Illustrative of the general conditions is this extract from the diary of Philip Egerton, member of the Friends' Ambulance Unit Mobile Medical and Surgical Teams on the Yunnan front:

Wakened early by sound of distant gunfire over mountain ridges—the attack had begun. My mule and driver had deserted in night. Found two coolies to carry supplies and set off for ferry. The road was narrow all the way, so steep and muddy it was almost impossible to keep one's feet. As we came over the mountain ridges we heard the rattle of machine-guns, the explosion of shells and the "plump" of mortar fire.

This had been going on all afternoon; along the pathway to the river horses carrying ammunition were halted under trees, stretcher-bearers with camouflaged hats were waiting by the hundreds, heavy gun crews, half-naked, were ramming off round after round to some direction on the other side of the river. As I came nearer the river it was possible to see the explosions of mortar shells and groups of men about a mile away up river apparently doing nothing except walk about or dodge under bushes.

The ferry was apparently safe, so we walked over to the small shack under some trees by the river, and here I found the girls and John surrounded by stretchers of wounded men. They fixed each case calmly and systematically as it was brought up. Every man was given hot water to drink and had his blanket tucked round him, fractures cleaned up and splinted and loose flesh cut away—all seemed to be done in such a matter-of-fact sort of way it was almost like London over again. There was no initial muffing that one finds often under conditions such as these. Towards dusk more and more wounded were brought over, and the mules and bearers that I had seen along the trail began to come down. Long after dark we finished off the last casualty and tried to sleep—the row continued all night, so we spent the night trying to sleep!

Being the only relief organization in China engaged in the transport of donated medical supplies, the service of the Friends' Ambulance Unit has proved very valuable to various Chinese and foreign relief organizations such as the National Health Administration, the International Relief Committee, the Emergency Purchasing Committee, the International Peace Hospitals, the Ministry of Education, the American Red Cross, and other bodies.

"Cannibalizing" Supply Trucks

Behind these great relief efforts lie stories of adventure, pertinacity and courage, for the roads the trucks run on are mostly precipitous, narrow, full of hairpin turns and insecure edges. On one occasion a truck rolled over an almost sheer cliff where the road made a sharp turn. The driver jumped out of the cab just in time, the truck bounced over the top of him and came to rest against a tree 25 yards below. The truck was finally taken apart and hauled back to the road piece by piece to be reassembled. The bottom of the gorge into which the truck had plunged was over 1,500 feet below the road surface.

Since December 1941 the Unit in China had been cut off from the supply of new trucks and replacements. As a result a number of makeshifts and methods of tinkering have been devised. A Hercules Diesel engine may be found on a Ford chassis. The process of "cannibalizing" has been resorted to, to convert worn-out trucks into serviceable ones. By both experience and mechanical skill, the members have in the last three years learned to keep old engines running and make replacements, ranging from springs and bodies to rods and tools.

With the supply of petrol dwindling after the closing down of the Burma Road, the Unit designed its own type of charcoal truck for the main haulage of medical supplies. It has proved to be much superior to other charcoal models in operation in China. The Chevrolet trucks which are rated by the manufacturers at one and a half tons now carry two and a half tons with the charcoal system. When technical experts from the American Foreign Economic Administration made a survey of transport in China, they found the Unit needed less than one-third the men required by other organizations to maintain its transport system.

BUT the switch from petrol to charcoal imposes an acid test on the driver's patience. Over the long, desolate route which usually takes a month to cover, he has to nurse, coax, goad, and urge his charcoal truck whenever it stages a no-go strike. Usually the engines are taken apart about every 2,000 miles, rings replaced, bearings refitted, everything checked over. The driver considers he is lucky if he does not have to park his truck high up on a long hill for the night when his engine "packs up." Ever the charcoal trucks need some petrol to start them off or to help them up too steep grades. To fetch the requisite quantity of petrol, twice a year the Unit had to send three of its Dodge trucks over a 2,000-mile journey to Suchow, in north-west Kansu

—Battle for the Lives of Nippon's Victims

MEDICAL AND RELIEF SUPPLIES FOR WAR-STRICKEN CHINA administered by the Friends' Ambulance Unit (see facing page) were contained in these lorries (1) parked outside a many-storeyed pagoda in Kunming. Two members of the Unit kindle charcoal blocks (2) for the charcoal-driven trucks of a type specially designed by the Unit for main haulage. A Chinese member injects a child with cholera vaccine (3). British and U.S. members prove their prowess with chopsticks at a wayside eating-house (4).

Photos by courtesy of the Friends' Ambulance Unit

Sea, Land and Air Heroes Win the V.C.

Lieut.-Cmdr. G. B. ROOPE, R.N.
He was commanding officer of H.M. destroyer Glowworm which—it was only recently revealed—rammed the German cruiser Hipper in northern waters on April 8, 1940. After fighting off a superior force of enemy destroyers, he engaged the cruiser "against overwhelming odds," finally ramming it. He was not among the survivors, all of whom were taken prisoner.

Havildar UMRAO SINGH
In the Haladan Valley, Burma, in December 1944 the havildar was in charge of a gun with his battery of the Indian Artillery when fiercely attacked. With ammunition expended and all his detachment killed or wounded except two he engaged the enemy hand - to - hand, killing ten fanatical Japanese and saving his gun.

Lieut. G. A. KNOWLAND
On January 31, 1945, near Kangow, Burma, this lieutenant of the Royal Norfolk Regiment (attached Commandos) held a vital hill-position against vicious enemy fire, evacuating casualties and encouraging his men till—after twelve hours—he was mortally wounded. His heroism saved the position at a critical hour.

Capt. EDWIN SWALES, D.F.C.
The only member of the S. African Air Force to have flown with the Pathfinders, Capt. Swales was master-bomber during a raid on Pforzheim, Germany, on Feb. 23, 1945. His aircraft crippled, he remained above the target till the attack was over, being found dead on landing.

Pte. JAMES STOKES
During the attack on Kervenheim, Holland, on March 1, 1945, Pte. Stokes, of the King's Shropshire Light Infantry, single-handed captured two enemy posts, with 17 prisoners in all, sustaining serious wounds. Attacking—again single-handed—a third objective, he fell, mortally wounded. His self-sacrifice and determination saved his company many casualties.

Sepoy NAMDEO JADHAO
On the Senio River, Italy, on April 9, 1945, company runner Jadhao, of the 5th Mahratta Light Infantry, carrying wounded to safety under fire, determined to silence the enemy machine-gun posts—which he did, though wounded and alone. His bravery, enabling the battalion to deepen its bridge-head, spared many lives.

Lieut. I. O. LIDDELL
In almost full view of the enemy and under heavy fire, Lieut. Liddell, of the Coldstream Guards (right), captured intact a bridge over the River Ems, near Lingen, on April 3, 1945. Unprotected yet unmindful of danger, he neutralized the enemy's demolition charges. He subsequently died of wounds received in action elsewhere.

Rifleman THOMAN GURUNG
This rifleman of the 5th Royal Gurkha Rifles (left), helped materially in the capture of Monte San Bartolo, N. Italy, in mid-November 1944. Attacking enemy posts alone, he braved certain death, throwing grenades and discharging his tommy-gun into slit-trenches, finally being killed.

Photos, British and Indian Official, G.P.U., Topical, News Chronicle, Evening Standard

I Was There! Eye Witness Stories of the War

Cossacks Welcomed Us as We Entered Berlin

Prelude to Potsdam, the historic entry of the first advance units of British and U.S. occupation troops into Berlin on July 3, 1945, is indelibly recorded in this dispatch from Edwin Tetlow his first message to The Daily Mail from inside Berlin since August 25, 1939. See also illus. page 200.

Cossack horsemen, cavorting in the early morning drizzle and shouting their traditional war cries, gave us a rousing welcome today on our way into Berlin. We met them soon after our convoy of British and U.S. troops, with 200 war correspondents, crossed the Elbe. They were exercising their horses, sending great clods of earth into the air as they performed their unrivalled tricks of horsemanship.

We entered Berlin with warm hearts after a journey which began at dawn. In a few hours now the full occupation of the silent capital by the victorious Powers will have begun, and the stage will have been set for the meeting of the Big Three at Potsdam.

The first phases of the entry today were full of novelty and colour. One extraordinary thing about it was that, despite the many preliminary announcements of its imminence, it came as a surprise to Russian troops and German civilians alike.

The Russians reacted with beaming smiles and the smartest of salutes. Some Germans in the outskirts of Potsdam and in the Zehlendorf suburb half-smiled as they watched the convoys go through, and some even waved. But I saw two young women shake their fists and scowl as they stood on the roadside and saw us speeding on through the April-like showers this morning.

It was just light enough to see the gaunt outlines of the bomb-wrecked buildings in Halle when we set out on the last lap of our journey—light enough, too, to see the white cloth banners which were displayed over the roads, bearing the blood-red words in German: "We greet the Red Army."

Our way was leading through an area into which the Red Army is now moving fast. Very soon we saw it coming in. We passed small columns of infantrymen and gunners hauling their cannon behind them as they sped westwards along the autobahn. They looked across at us in bewilderment at first, and then, recognizing us, they waved and smiled a welcome.

And now we are in Berlin, where a bemused and hang-dog populace awaits the next moves of its conquerors. When I stopped in the Kaiserallee, more than a score of people came out and eagerly asked how long we were staying, what areas we were to take over, and whether there would soon be more food. They even began asking for cigarettes.

BRITISH TROOPS IN BERLIN, where our advance units arrived on July 3, chatting to a Russian soldier near the Brandenburg Gate, with a Polish civilian as interpreter. *Photo, British Official*

I Visit Lübbecke—Germany's New 'Capital'

A sleepy old market town of 5,000 people—Lübbecke in Westphalia—on July 1, 1945, became the temporary capital of British Occupied Germany. Writing from the town on June 21, Daily Herald correspondent Peter Stursberg described the preparations then going forward for transforming this single-track town with no telephone-exchange into one of the most important centres in the occupied Reich.

All the carpenters in this part of Westphalia are hammering and sawing away to prepare Lübbecke's gabled houses as offices and quarters for the British Control Commission. The first members of the Commission have already arrived, and so have the first trucks, causing an immediate traffic jam in the narrow cobblestoned streets.

You won't find Lübbecke on any large-scale map, so I had better tell you where it is. It is near Minden, and Minden lies between Osnabruck and Hanover. We drove along a country lane through the pleasant rolling Westphalian farmland to reach it, and then we fell in love with its little rose gardens pouring blossoms on to the pavement, and its cool tree-shaded square, with the 500-year-old church in the leafy background.

As my Army driver said: "It's really quaint." And as the capital of a third of Germany with 23 million population, it's quaint in more than one way.

It is not on a main railway line, and the only railway which reaches it is a single track branch line. It is not a road junction of any importance and the roads that lead to it end in bottlenecks. Its communication facilities are poor; it has no telephone exchange.

When I mentioned these matters to the Colonel who was in charge of the Commission's advance party, he said: "The single track railway line doesn't worry us. We wish there was a telephone exchange, but the Army Signals will put one in for us. We chose this town because it is conveniently

GUARDS VETERAN of Dunkirk, C.S.M. Eric Cole, broke the Union Jack at the historic ceremony in Berlin on July 6, 1945 (see page 201), while the band of the 2nd Battalion of the Devonshire Regiment played the National Anthem. The flag—which is to fly permanently—was struck at the base of the gilded 1870 Victory monument overlooking the Sieges Allée—in full view of thousands of silent Berliners. In the centre of the dais is Lieut.-Gen. Sir Ronald Weeks, Chief of Staff to the British Control Commission. *Photo, G.P.U.*

placed to run the British zone. We shall have to work in close co-operation with the Occupation Forces and we are only fifteen miles as the crow flies from the headquarters of 21st Army Group."

Of course, Lübbecke is only the temporary capital. The full Commission personnel of more than 8,000 would never fit into it. The displaced townsfolk are being quartered near by in an old Nazi labour camp which has been cleaned up to receive them. I am told they are quite happy about leaving their homes, because they have been promised that it will be for only three months.

The permanent headquarters of the British Commission and capital of our occupation zone will probably be in Bielefeld, a somewhat larger town on the main route between the Ruhr and Hamburg. Until the Commission moves into its permanent headquarters, a tax collector's office on the edge of Lübbecke will become the nerve-centre of a large part of Germany, because that is where it is going to set up its main office for the time being.

Nothing like this has happened to this sleepy little place since Charlemagne invaded Saxony and granted an obscure little fortress among the hills the right to become a market town. Sir William Strang, Foreign Office advisor to the Commission, will have a house in the town. A castle belonging to a German Baron a few miles outside has been requisitioned for Lieut.-General Sir Ronald Weeks, Deputy High Commissioner. Field-Marshal Montgomery is High Commissioner, but he will stay at 21st Army Group Headquarters, which is in the little spa town of Bad Oeynhausen.

The soldiers and civilians on the Commission are going to like Lübbecke. They are going to find it picturesque and they are going to be pleased about the fact that they can buy beer for thirty pfennigs, or 1½d., a bottle of gin for four marks, or 2s. a bottle. A brewery and distillery are working for us.

We Lay on the Sea-Bed—All Lights Out

After successfully torpedoing an escorted Japanese supply vessel, a submarine of the Royal Netherlands Navy, patrolling in Far Eastern waters, was heavily depth-charged and lay on the sea-bed with all lights shattered, deadly carbon dioxide leaking into her engine-room. How she miraculously survived is here described by her Dutch Commanding Officer.

FIRST a hail of electric light bulbs came down and we were in complete darkness. Water poured into the forward battery compartment, the gyro-compass went mad, and a short circuit burnt itself out in the control-room. But in the engine-room the conditions were more serious. The air-conditioning plant started leaking carbon dioxide into the boat, and nothing could be done to prevent it.

We evacuated the stern compartment and the engine-room, and closed all watertight doors. But the fumes leaked steadily into the control-room, and we soon had to start breathing through special containers supplied for such an emergency. The air pressure in the boat had risen most noticeably.

After about an hour those of us who had been shut in the control-room evacuated it for the compartment above, in the conning tower, and there conditions were more tolerable. The carbon dioxide, being heavier than air, remained below us. But there was no communication between us and the rest of the crew in the forward torpedo compartment. Telephones were out of action, and the over-pressure prevented the communicating door from being opened.

Seven hours after our first sighting of the enemy we managed to surface slowly. It was a pitch dark night and I made out two black shapes, which were either two ships close together about 1,500 yards away or the funnel and bridge of one vessel much nearer. It was probably the escort picking up survivors of the ship we attacked, but I took no chances. We dived again to the bottom. I then decided that we should make a determined effort to get to the engine-room without delay, and to try to get the engines ready to make a dash away at the first opportunity. Meanwhile, in case of further accidents, I made all secret books and papers ready for destruction.

AFTER an effort three E.R.A.s opened the engine-room watertight door, and found the compartment full of deadly fumes and flooded up to the deck plates. They worked furiously to get all outboard valves closed and they had to take off their safety apparatus to get at some of them. At last they got the engines ready, and then one man was dragged out unconscious by the other two, both of whom nearly collapsed when the effort was over. The unconscious man revived, and five minutes later was back in the engine-room again.

When both engines were reported ready I surfaced again, as quietly as possible, and it was an immense relief to find nothing in sight. Then we proceeded at full speed on both engines. But our troubles were not over. Two days later, on our passage back to base, we suddenly felt a strange vibration in the stern. We found that the starboard hydroplane—one of the horizontal rudders which determine the angle of the dive when a submarine submerges—had disappeared. So further diving was out of the question, but we got back all right.

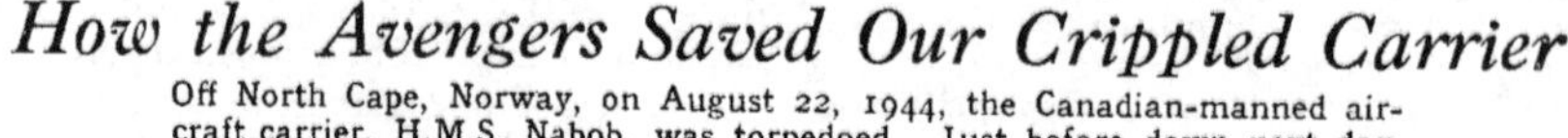

How the Avengers Saved Our Crippled Carrier

Off North Cape, Norway, on August 22, 1944, the Canadian-manned aircraft carrier, H.M.S. Nabob, was torpedoed. Just before dawn next day, two Avenger bomber-pilots were precariously catapulted from her tilting deck to chase off the U-boat that had trailed her all night, and so saved the crippled carrier. The story is here told by the Nabob's Commander (Flying) Lieutenant-Commander R. J. H. Stephens, R.N.

THIS DUTCH SUBMARINE—under the command of Lieut.-Cmdr. Van Dulm, D.S.O. and bar, Royal Netherlands Navy—recently returned to a British port after 19 months' duty in Far Eastern waters. The amazing escape of another Netherlands submarine is told here. *Photo, Royal Netherlands Navy*

WE had hoped we wouldn't hear any more of the submarine that had crippled us, but I think most of us guessed we would. "Yes," said Chief Yeoman Jarvis. "He's following us, sir. He'll have a look at us at dawn and then put us down." The Chief Yeoman had spent all his life in submarines and he spoke with assurance and almost, it seemed, with pride for the branch of the service he belongs to. You could see he could picture himself on the bridge of that U-boat, doing the follow-up himself.

But that didn't help us any ; we had to get rid of the U-boat. But how? We must just put a couple of Avengers over him and swat him. That's our job. But somehow it did not look just then as though old Nabob could put any Avengers anywhere that night except perhaps to the bottom of the Arctic Ocean. However, I thought, let's try it. You never know what you can do, and anything is better than folding the hands and waiting to get knocked on the head. So about one o'clock I piped "Flying Station !" This is what the picture looked like.

The ship was steaming about nine knots and somewhere near into the wind. That was good, as we would not have to turn her to get her into the wind to get the aircraft off, but there was plenty that was not so good. The flight deck was about thirty feet lower aft than it was forward. That does not sound very much in a ship more than four hundred feet long, but it seemed a lot. The normal runway of an airfield is allowed to slope one foot in two hundred, and we had a slope of one foot in eighteen. However, I thought it was just possible that someone might be able to take off up it, and land back again.

The after aircraft elevator was up and could not be moved, but the forward one had been on its way down when we were hit, and had stopped half-way when the power came off. I sent a man to see whether it would move, and it certainly was a surprise to find it come up as though nothing had happened to us.

Catapult ? "Yes," said Lt. (E.) Edmund Ward ("Gus") Airey, R.C.N.V.R., of London, Ontario, the catapult officer. He felt it should work. He had sent a petty officer down to blow the air-pressure after the torpedo had hit us, but by some great good luck some one had given that man another job of work and he had never carried out the order. So we had our power all right. Very good, then, spot one Avenger for catapulting, I decided. It wasn't too easy moving aircraft around on that deck in the dark, but I'm lucky in this ship. I have some wonderful men under me. Most of the aircraft handling party are farmers, miners and lumberjacks, and they all have heads on their shoulders. In charge of them is a lad named Ray Warnock from Vancouver, a petty officer at the age of twenty. And he did a wonderful job that night. No fuss. No shouting. Just "Come on lads !" and the aircraft moved around that deck and into the right place as though we were drilling on a quiet afternoon in harbour. I don't say it couldn't have been done as well in other carriers, but . . . well, I doubt it.

The report came through, "One Avenger

H.M.S. NABOB, CANADIAN-MANNED ESCORT CARRIER, carried out a remarkable feat of seamanship (related in this and the facing page) after being torpedoed in August 1944 while operating with the British Home Fleet off North Norway. Although flooded, listing badly, 16 ft. down at the stern and carrying 50,000 gallons of high-test petrol, she was brought safely to port through 1,100 miles of rough seas, under her own steam, by her commander, Capt. Horatio Nelson Lay, O.B.E., R.C.N. (inset), who obstinately refused to acknowledge defeat. *Photos, Royal Canadian Navy*

aircrew in readiness!" I didn't say I wanted the squadron commander to fly himself. He decides in this ship which aircrews are used, but of course I expected him and I wasn't surprised when Lt.-Cdr. R. E. ("Bob") Bradshaw of Oxford came up to the flying control position with his helmet on. We stood together there and weighed up the chances. We had no figures, on how the catapult would take the load of hurling an aircraft up a slope like that, but I thought it might be all right, and so did he.

I'd almost forgotten to tell you about the bombs. We keep some on deck usually, ready for use, but all these had been thrown into the sea to lighten the ship's after end and the rest were in the magazine now twenty feet under water. For a time it looked as though even if we got an aircraft off it would not be armed and that wouldn't be much good with that U-boat closing us all the time. He might be fooled into diving, but he might not. However, about this time the air gunnery officer reported he had found some bombs in the hangar. It was all very wrong, of course. There is no greater sin you can commit in an aircraft carrier than to leave explosives around among the aircraft. But we certainly blessed the careless fool who had left them lying around.

All was ready then. It was just after half-past two and the aircrew manned the Avenger. The Arctic dawn was just breaking and it was a depressing-looking morning, low clouds, rain squalls and a visibility of about one mile. Lt.-Cdr. Bradshaw tried his engine twice and didn't get a kick out of it. We hadn't many minutes to spare now, and still the engine wouldn't start. Bradshaw tried twice more and then, thank God, it picked up. He ran it right up from cold, which is a shocking thing to do to an engine. It would probably give Mr. Wright a fit, but it took it all right. The control officer circled his flag, dropped it and off she went. The launch was normal, perhaps the most normal thing that crazy morning, and the aircraft disappeared into the gloom astern.

I think that that submarine captain coming in on the surface for his kill must have had the surprise of his life. Bradshaw put him down and he stayed down. To make sure, Sub-Lt. Don Jupp, R.N.V.R., of Gloucestershire, was catapulted off after Bradshaw. The two carried on a patrol, the ship's captain ordered an alteration of course, and when the submarine was next heard from she was miles off on our original course.

The Avengers came back, first Jupp with his, and then Bradshaw. The fog was dense, and how they made the flight deck is amazing. They could scarcely see it, and it was rising and falling in a sickening fashion. Yet Jupp's landing was so perfect that for some reason we all laughed. Then Bradshaw came in. He fouled the barrier, cracked into a couple of aircraft lashed up forward, but neither he nor any of his crew was injured. We saw no more of the U-boat. Perhaps he was telling them in Germany that we had given him the slip—or perhaps he wasn't as honest as all that about it. Anyway, the German news came out next day with the information that they had sunk us!

OUR DIARY OF THE WAR

JULY 4, Wednesday *1,305th day of War against Japan*
Germany.—Main body of British occupation troops arrived in Berlin.
Philippines.—Gen. MacArthur announced liberation of whole of Philippine islands.
Pacific.—Korea attacked by U.S. navy privateers.
Burma.—Japanese launched attacks on British positions on Sittang.

JULY 5, Thursday *1,306th day*
Borneo.—Centre of Balikpapan captured by Australians.
Japan.—Nagasaki and airfields at Tokyo attacked by U.S. aircraft.
Australia.—Death of Rt. Hon. John Curtin, Prime Minister of Australia.
Poland.—Polish Provisional Government at Warsaw recognized by Britain and U.S.A.
Home Front.—Polling took place for General Election.

JULY 6, Friday *1,307th day*
Belgium.—R.A.F. held farewell parade in Brussels.
Japan.—Super-Fortresses from Marianas attacked oil refinery near Osaka and four cities on Honshu.

JULY 7, Saturday *1,308th day*
Germany.—Troops of French 1st Army entered Saarbruecken.
Pacific.—British East Indies Fleet attacked Nicobar Islands.

JULY 8, Sunday *1,309th day*
Japan.—U.S. aircraft from Okinawa attacked Kyushu and airfields in Formosa.
Borneo.—Australian troops crossed Balikpapan Bay and landed at Penajam.
Pacific.—Announced that three British aircraft carriers had been damaged by Japanese suicide aircraft.

JULY 9, Monday *1,310th day*
Japan.—More than 1,000 carrier-borne aircraft of U.S. 3rd Fleet struck at Tokyo after night attack on four cities on Honshu by large force of Super-Fortresses.

JULY 10, Tuesday *1,311th day*
Sea.—German submarine entered Mar del Plata harbour, Argentina, and surrendered to authorities.
Borneo.—Japanese used barriers of flaming petrol to halt Australians east of Balikpapan.

JULY 11, Wednesday *1,312th day*
Germany.—British and U.S. authorities in Berlin took over control of their zones of occupation.
Pacific.—British carrier aircraft attacked airfields in Sumatra.

JULY 12, Thursday *1,313th day*
Germany.—Field-Marshal Montgomery in Berlin invested Marshals Zhukov and Rokossovsky with British decorations.
Japan. — More than 500 Super-Fortresses attacked cities in Shikoku and Honshu with 3,000 tons of bombs.

JULY 13, Friday *1,314th day*
Germany.—March-past by British garrison in Berlin before Allied commanders.

JULY 14, Saturday *1,315th day*
Germany.—Fraternization ban lifted in British and American zones of occupation in Germany and Austria.
Japan.—U.S. fleet bombarded industrial city of Kamaishi, while 1,000 carrier aircraft attacked Hokkaido.
General. — Supreme Headquarters, Allied Expeditionary Force (Shaef) dissolved at midnight.

JULY 15, Sunday *1,316th day*
Germany.—President Truman and Mr. Churchill arrived in Potsdam for Big Three Conference.
Japan.—U.S. 3rd Fleet and aircraft bombarded steel-centre of Muroran on Hokkaido.
Borneo.—Australians captured Mount Batochampar, north of Balikpapan.

JULY 16, Monday *1,317th day*
Japan.—British fleet task force joined U.S. 3rd Fleet in air attacks against Tokyo area.
China.—Chinese troops recaptured Liukiangshien, on Kweilin-Liuchow railway.

JULY 17, Tuesday *1,318th day*
Germany.—First Big Three meeting in Potsdam presided over by Pres. Truman.
Japan.—U.S. and British battleships shelled Hitachi area of Honshu; carrier aircraft continued to attack Tokyo area.
Indo-China.—Chinese troops occupied port of Moncar, near Kwantung frontier.
Home Front.—The King, Queen and Princess Elizabeth flew to Northern Ireland.

★ *Flash-backs* ★

1940

July 15. *Pétain Govt. broke off diplomatic relations with Britain.*
July 14. *British garrison of Moyale (Kenya) withdrew after prolonged resistance to Italians.*

1941

July 12. *Anglo-Soviet agreement signed in Moscow for mutual assistance against Germany.*

1942

July 12. *Germans began drive towards Stalingrad following failure to capture Voronezh*

1943

July 5. *In Russia, Germans launched abortive offensive in the Kursk salient.*
July 9-10. *Allied airborne and seaborne forces landed in Sicily.*
July 15. *Russians launched offensive in direction of Orel.*

1944

July 9. *Main part of Caen captured by British and Canadians.*
July 13. *Russians took Vilna.*
July 16. *8th Army entered Arezzo.*

THE METEOR, BRITAIN'S JET-PROPELLED SINGLE-SEATER FIGHTER, seen in flight, was removed from the secret list on July 11, 1945, when it was revealed that it first flew in 1943 and was used against the flying bombs the following year. Powered with two gas jet turbine engines, its dimensions include: span, 43 ft.; length, 41 ft.; height, 13 ft.; and wing area, 374 square ft. It is a low wing monoplane of all-metal construction, with tricycle landing gear and is built of separate units. The high tailplane, necessitated by the jets from the propelling nozzles, splits the rudder into two parts. Armament consists of four 20-mm. Hispano guns, with a camera gun mounted in the nose. It was developed by the Gloster Aircraft Company from the E 28/39, first jet-propelled aircraft in this country and possibly the world. *Photo, British Official*

With Our Airmen Today

By CAPTAIN NORMAN MACMILLAN M.C., A.F.C.

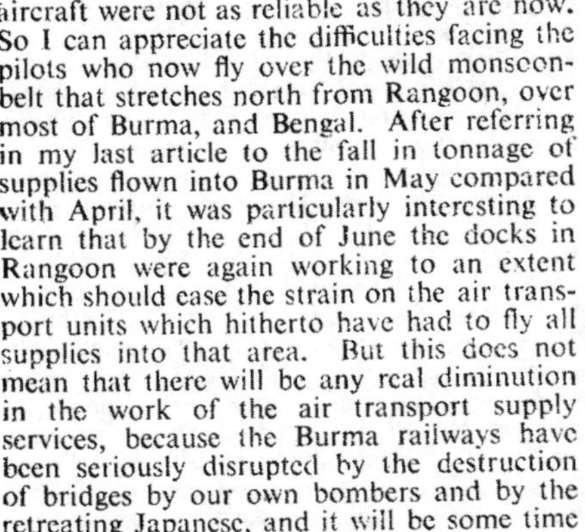

It happened that I was the first pilot to fly across India in the monsoon, in days when aircraft were not as reliable as they are now. So I can appreciate the difficulties facing the pilots who now fly over the wild monsoon-belt that stretches north from Rangoon, over most of Burma, and Bengal. After referring in my last article to the fall in tonnage of supplies flown into Burma in May compared with April, it was particularly interesting to learn that by the end of June the docks in Rangoon were again working to an extent which should ease the strain on the air transport units which hitherto have had to fly all supplies into that area. But this does not mean that there will be any real diminution in the work of the air transport supply services, because the Burma railways have been seriously disrupted by the destruction of bridges by our own bombers and by the retreating Japanese, and it will be some time before surface transport services are able to carry normal traffic inland from Rangoon.

Thus the capture of Rangoon has not affected the importance of the India base. China has still to be supplied from Calcutta. Air transports still fly the "hump," and four-engined aircraft now make the trip non-stop from the neighbourhood of the Calcutta docks. It must not be thought that the monsoon does not affect this traverse of the Himalayan spur. Even much farther to the north-west, Everest climbing expeditions have encountered the monsoon raging over the peaks around Everest and breaking a plume from the topmost pyramid of that great mountain. Moreover, as height increases, the tempest speeds faster, for the air has to find a passage through narrowing valleys, and is pushed more swiftly through them, just as airflow accelerates through a carburettor where the neck of the venturi restricts its passage. In such conditions flying can be extremely unpleasant, and even dangerous, while the effort called from the pilot to stabilize his plunging craft demands physical stamina of a high order.

PAPER BALLOONS, 33 ft. in diameter, carrying Japanese incendiary bombs, were reported over the U.S. and Western Canada in June 1945, causing casualties. They were said to have floated some 6,000 miles eastward through the stratosphere. *Photo, New York Times Photos*

AMERICAN Super-Forts Now Bomb Industrial Targets in Manchuria

Smaller aircraft still fly the hump, using an air staging post in North-Eastern India to which both aircraft and the Bengal-Assam Railway carry supplies from the Calcutta base. This enables each air transport crossing the hump to carry a heavier load of cargo. The operation of the oil pipeline from Calcutta to China has eased the demand for aircraft to transport fuel, and they are now able to ferry alternative loads. It is probably this factor, combined with the renewed use of the Ledo road and the Burma road to Kunming, that has made it possible for the Chinese troops to make their recent successful drive against the Japanese and recapture the airfield at Liuchow.

From that airfield the U.S.A. 20th A.F. Super-Fortress bombers opened their attack on Japan. But, even more important, from there and other airfields around it, they bombed targets in Manchuria. Now that the Japanese have announced a definite programme of evacuation of industry from the Japanese main islands to Manchuria, the airfields in China assume a new importance.

The tightening of the air and sea blockade of Japan must mean that it will be increasingly difficult for Japanese island industry to supply forces outside the homeland zone, and the Manchurian industries will form the bases from which supplies will be forthcoming for the Japanese forces operating on the Asiatic mainland. It is also known that Japanese industry has been dispersed within Japan itself. Thus it is to be presumed that there will be two main defensive zones within which the Japanese can be expected to offer resistance, one in Japan itself and the other on the mainland of Asia. As the Allied air and surface forces are disposed at the moment it would appear that the Allied assault is more likely to fall first upon Japan proper, although it must be remembered that in war such a situation may sometimes be engineered to fool the enemy into a false estimation of intentions. But from Japan the Japanese are evacuating the aged, the very young, and expectant mothers; in the Far East the trek away from the bombing has begun on a large scale. Within the islands of the Japanese mainland the remaining civilian population has been regimented into a volunteer corps to assist the army; this probably amounts to a form of total mobilization.

Eight classes of civilians deal with communications, transport, distribution of essential goods, labour, farming, medical, civil defence, and observer corps duties. The Japanese observers and war correspondents who were attached to the Allied side before the Japanese entry into the war have no doubt made good use of the facilities granted to them to copy defence measures taken in Europe against the once-powerful Luftwaffe.

I was very pleased to see that that fine pilot, Group Captain R. N. Bateson, D.S.O., D.F.C., had received a Bar to his D.S.O. He won his first D.S.O. for leadership as a Wing Commander, with special mention of his success when leading a formation of Mosquitoes against the "House in The Hague." At that time there was quite a lot of misunderstanding about these low-level attacks, and Bomber Command (which made the attacks against the Gestapo H.Q. in Oslo and against Berlin when Goering was due to broadcast) received credit in many minds for the pin-point attack against the House in The Hague, simply because many persons did not realize that there were three Mosquito Wings in 2nd T.A.F.

I met Group Captain Bateson when he was commanding No. 140 Wing in France. In addition to British decorations he wore the ribbon of the Dutch Flight Cross with which Prince Bernhard had invested him after The Hague attack. His headquarters was on an aerodrome in the Somme Department, and it was a grand sensation to fly over the old battlefields of the First Great War where Camels and Fokkers had waged battle at 100 miles an hour in a Mosquito that swept through the skies at three-and-a-half times that speed.

The Wing Mess was in the Chateau de Goyencourt, home of the Marquise de Montpoisier, a pleasant place with ample stabling for the enjoyment of more peaceful sports. Among the officers of one of the jolliest R.A.F. wings I have happened across for many a long day was Squadron Leader E. B. Sismore, D.S.O., D.F.C. and Bar, of Kettering, who had been Wing Commander R. W. Reynold's observer. His D.F.C. was gained for the Goering speech attack, the Bar for the Aarhus show, and the D.S.O. after an attack on the Zeiss factory at Jena, but Sismore was far too modest to say a word about all these adventures.

GROUP-Capt. Bateson's War Record More Fascinating Than Any Film

Bateson had had an exciting time after Japan entered the war. His Blenheim squadron flew to Singapore from the Middle East, then was directed to Palembang, where it used Dutch bombs, thence to Java, whence they had to take ship to Australia. The ship stranded and they finally got away in a river boat navigated by a Flying Officer who happened to be a Master Mariner. From Australia, Group Captain Bateson was posted to Ceylon. There, his brother, also in the R.A.F., whom he believed to be thousands of miles away, suddenly walked in to see him. And there, too, he met the lady who is now his wife. His was a story more thrilling and fascinating than any film of adventure I have ever seen.

BALLOT PAPERS—forty tons of them—for Forces serving overseas were dispatched (and returned) by aircraft of R.A.F. Transport Command, so that our serving men and women abroad might vote in the General Election. **See page 223.** *Photo, British Official*

Editor's Postscript

TURNING on the six o'clock news the other night I had the pleasure of listening to the concluding words of the Broadcast for Schools. "There they go," a cultured voice was saying to a boy, "leaving you and I to do the work." Of late I have everywhere noticed a tendency to ungrammatical speech and writing: the daily press abounds with errors of syntax and many of the persons "brought to the microphone" to enlighten the listeners stand in need of a few lessons in English before being permitted to address these millions, many of whom will probably find confirmation for their own errors of speech in what they hear on the air. "Leaving you and I" is as good an instance as I might quote of these solecisms; scores of similar offences against English usage and pronunciation might easily be compiled by anyone with the time and the patience to listen to the B.B.C. emissions for a week or two. "Between you and I" is an abomination which seems to have a peculiar attraction for some broadcasters and for a great many moderately well-educated persons.

I HAVE been reading with bemused bewilderment of a young woman who is engaged on what must be one of Britain's strangest jobs. In the bedroom of the 500-year-old Borthwick Castle, near Edinburgh, where Mary Queen of Scots and Bothwell spent their honeymoon, she is looking for—Mormons! Employed by the Genealogical Society of Utah, she is methodically searching 3,500 volumes of Scottish parish registers in an effort to trace the ancestors of present-day Mormons in the United States so that they (the ancestors!) can be baptized into the Mormon faith. As each ancestor is docketed—and many have been dead upwards of 300 years—details are forwarded to Utah where he is incorporated in the Mormon church—even though he may have been an Anglican, a Presbyterian or a member of the "Wee Free." Mormon ancestor-hunting would obviously appear to be a labour of love as I read that the genealogist—her name is Miss Katherine Horner—has been collecting Mormon ancestors for five years at a cost to Utah, apart from other incidentals, of £1 for every ten days she is at work! The Church has already made over 1,000 of these posthumous "converts." When I was a boy in Scotland the mother of an unruly child had only to whisper the word "Mormons" to scare her offspring into obedience. I am sure she could not do so today though whether it is that Mormonism has lost its terrors or small boys are more self-possessed I would not attempt to hazard.

AT the outset of the war many good people were genuinely concerned about its probable effects on the minds and nerves of children. They need not have worried. Tragedies there have been, of course, and every tragedy is one too many; but on the whole children confounded the prophets by taking the worst facts of war in their stride at least as imperturbably as their elders, if not more so. They may feel more acutely, but they forget more easily, and are mercifully protected by a limited understanding. In the air raids, for example, they seem to have found less of terror than of excitement—and even of beauty, if one may accept the evidence of the wartime drawings by children of all nationalities lately on view near Piccadilly Circus. I saw some of the little refugees when they arrived from Holland. Their wan faces and famished bodies, above all, their look of extreme loneliness, caught at the heart. But I am certain that after a few good meals most of them were ripe for mischief again, such is the natural resilience of their years. The most enviable of all children is Master Nicholas Panton, born behind barbed wire in an internment camp in Denmark and repatriated at the age of four. The outside world, which others of this age have had to assimilate so gradually, burst upon him all at once—streets, houses, shops, buses, cars, trains, boats, trees, fields, rivers, and the sea, with a thousand other wonders. He may well cry with the innocent Miranda: "O brave new world!" and mean it just as fervently.

AN American journalist friend revisiting London for the first time since 1941 tells me something about Londoners I hadn't, I must confess, noticed. Whereas in the days of the blitz he found us communicative almost to the point of garrulousness, expanding almost embarrassingly in railway carriages, pubs and places where they queue, today he observes, as he puts it, that we have resumed our "deep primeval silence." The odd thing is that he likes it better that way. "When the Londoner opened up in those bad old days," he writes, "and let you into the secrets of his private life and maybe brought out a snap of the wife and kids, it made me uneasy—as if the actors in a play had changed parts in mid-act. It was out of character; somehow you didn't feel you were among Londoners at all and would catch yourself looking over your shoulder—just to make sure. Today, wherever you meet him, the Londoner has gone back to his clam-shell. He gives you a granite glint if you try to catch his eye and shifts to the other end of the bar before you have had time to open up with a weather-gambit." And he comments, "That's how it should be, how it always has been, and I don't suppose that, deep down, any honest American would have it otherwise." The Englishman has been praised and blamed for many qualities, and not always with justification. The next thing I expect to hear is a visiting Frenchman praise the old-fashioned British Sunday.

Maj.-Gen. LOUIS OWEN LYNE, D.S.O., Commander of the 7th Armoured Division (Desert Rats) and O.C. British occupation troops in Berlin, took the salute at the march past in the Reich capital on July 6, 1945. Rising from subaltern to Major-General in ten years, Maj.-Gen. Lyne in December 1944 gave outstanding evidence of his leadership in the Ardennes. He is only 44 years old. **See also pages 200 and 201.** *Photo, Fox*

DRIVING through the outer London suburbs the other day I found myself, as often before, speculating on the improbable names with which many householders burden their homes. There were, of course, the inevitable The Firs, The Pines, Mon Repos, and so forth, all with a faintly Edwardian flavour. There were the Vimy Ridges, Malines, St. Quentins, and others dating from the last war and half-obliterated. Then I began to notice names which had made but recent history. There was Falaise, there was Colmar, there was Remagen. Not so far off I passed Duren, Malmedy, Venlo and, least likely of all, Bratislava. About to exclaim to my companion "Quick work!", it dawned on me that these name-plates were at least as pre-war as the others, and that far from being attempts to keep up with the march of time they were probably merely echoes of long-ago honeymoons and holidays abroad—of people most likely dead. There must be hundreds of thousands of such houses scattered over England, each with its impalpable link with present-day battlefields. One wonders whether the occupant of Remagen felt a superior thrill as he opened his newspaper in the train one morning last March and read the banner headlines "Remagen Bridge falls to U.S. Troops without a Shot," and whether his neighbour from Falaise didn't feel just a little bit out of date—just as the man from Remagen must be feeling now.

I STRONGLY suspect that prices in the horticultural industry are running so high that they may curtail the charm of English gardens for some time to come. I write from personal experience, quoting two cases which may or may not be typical. Having decided to plant a few water lilies in a little pond, I ordered a dozen of a quite common variety, and was astounded when the bill arrived to find that they had cost me £9. I might have been prepared for this, as a week or two before I had ordered 200 dwarf lavender plants. They did not seem a very vigorous lot; indeed, some fifty of them were not deemed worth while planting by my gardener. Even so, my bill for them was £7 10s. I make no further comment except to point out that anyone who is thinking of laying out a small garden just now is going to encounter costs which will greatly curb his choice of flowers and plants.

"POST-WAR reconstruction" is a high-sounding phrase that can be called upon to cover a multitude of sins of commission. It is put forward as the reason for the coming demolition of a house on the fringe of Regent's Park that was for twelve years the home of Charles Dickens, the house in which David Copperfield was written. No doubt many ardent lovers of that great novelist and all that appertains to him will be grieved, but they have several other shrines at which to worship. The birthplace of Dickens in Portsmouth escaped the bombs; Gadshill Place, near Rochester, the house in which he died, still stands; the house in Doughty Street, where he wrote Pickwick, is in the safe keeping of the Dickens Fellowship. And, anyway, Dickens explicitly stated in his will that he desired no memorial other than his books. What is far more regrettable is that any handsome old London house that is redolent of its period should come under the axe, whether it was the home of Charles Dickens or of Tom Noddy. No such destruction should ever be permitted without full assurance that any replacement will be at least as satisfactory a sample of present-day architecture as the demolished building was of the architecture of its own time

In Britain Now: Choosing a New Government

AIR-RAID SHELTER was used as a polling station in East Smithfield, London, where first votes were cast by two crossing-sweepers (1). Polling Day for the first General Election for nearly ten years was on July 5, 1945, when over 1,500 candidates contested 640 seats—apart from 24 constituencies in the North and Midlands which polled on July 12 and July 19 and three returning their M.P. unopposed. Familiar sight since polling-day at a Wiltshire airfield of Transport Command was the unloading of ballot papers completed by our forces overseas (2). At eve-of-the-poll election meeting at Leamington (3), Mr. Churchill roused the crowds in Pump Room Gardens on behalf of Mr. Anthony Eden.

SAPPERS at work in Oxford Street (left) in early July 1945 grew tired of being mistaken for enemy prisoners-of-war by passers-by: building a Bailey bridge across a bomb-site for a forthcoming Services exhibition, they chalked up the announcement: "We are not Germans or Italian. We are Royal Engineers." The Ministry of Health declared on June 24 that a big step-up was being taken in the employment of the 185,000 German prisoners held in this country: over 1,250 were already on site-clearing jobs.

HERO AT HOME—Field-Marshal Sir Harold Alexander, G.C.B., C.S.I., D.S.O., M.C., enjoyed a quiet hour with his wife, Lady Margaret Alexander and small son in the garden of their Windsor Forest home (right) during a brief visit to this country in early July 1945. Victor of the North African and Italian campaigns, the Field-Marshal was presented with his baton (announced November 26, 1944) by the King on July 8, 1945.

Photos, British Official, Keystone, G.P.U., Planet News

As Our Troops Took Over the Heart of Berlin

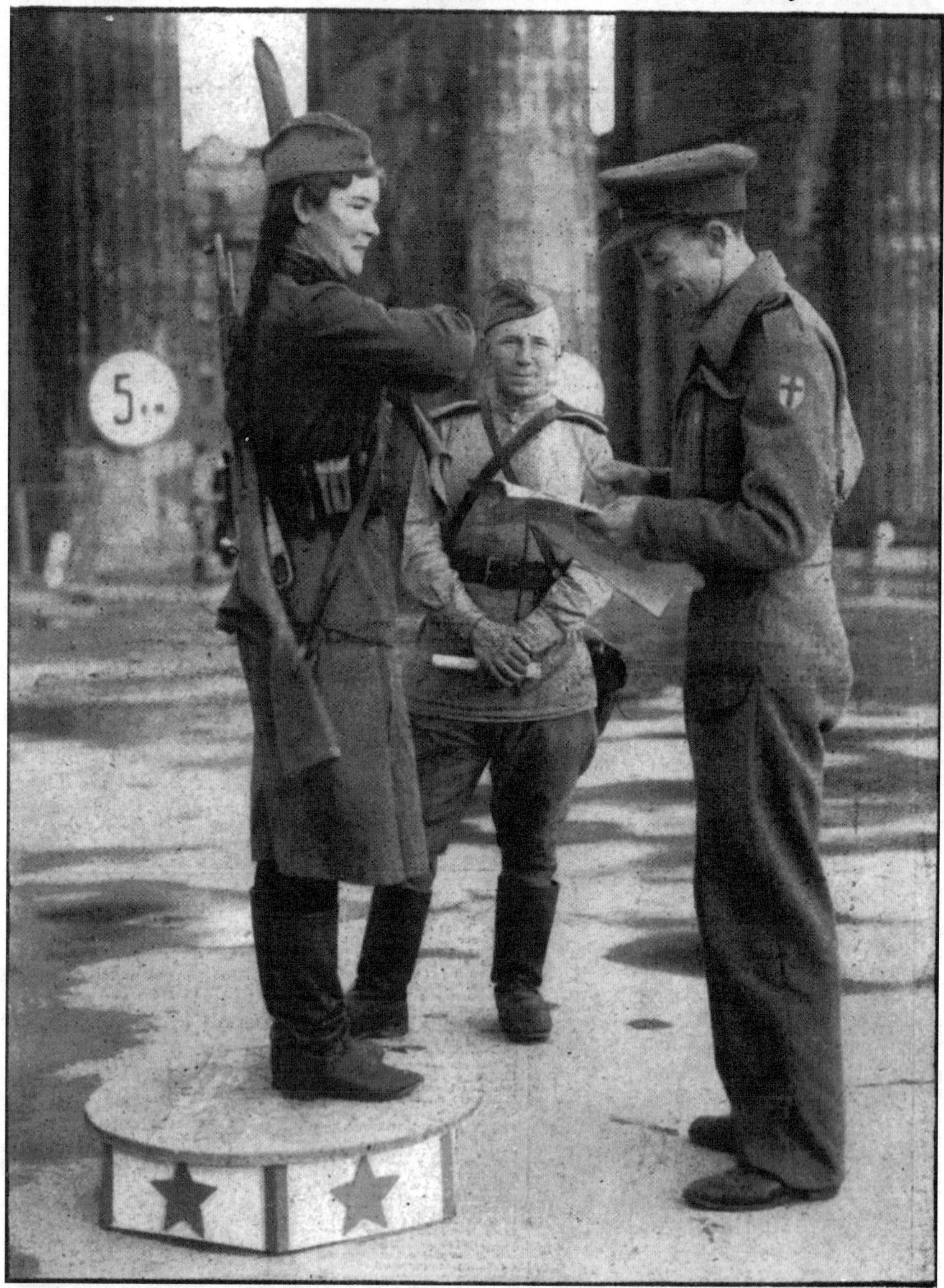

IN THE ALLIED-OCCUPIED CAPITAL OF THE REICH, a British war correspondent chatted with a Russian girl, Feodora Bondenko, on point-duty at the Brandenburg Gate. On July 4, 1945, the main body of the British occupational force, headed by a squadron of the 11th Hussars from the 7th Armoured Division and including troops of the Grenadier Guards, the Devonshire Regiment, and other famous British units besides a Canadian composite battalion, entered the German capital to take up their allotted zones. *Photo, G.P.U.*

Printed in England and published every alternate Friday by the Proprietors, THE AMALGAMATED PRESS, LTD., The Fleetway House, Farringdon Street, London, E.C.4. Registered for transmission by Canadian Magazine Post. Sole Agents for Australia and New Zealand : Messrs. Gordon & Gotch, Ltd. and for South Africa : Central News Agency; Ltd.—August 3, 1945. S.S. *Editorial Offices:* JOHN CARPENTER HOUSE WHITEFRIARS, LONDON, E C 4.

Vol 9 The War Illustrated No 213

SIXPENCE Edited by Sir John Hammerton AUGUST 17, 1945

WARM HANDSHAKE BETWEEN PREMIER AND PRESIDENT as Mr. Winston Churchill called on President Truman at the latter's headquarters on the eve of the Big Three conference which opened at Potsdam on July 17, 1945. It was their first meeting since Mr. Truman succeeded Mr. Roosevelt as President of the United States. When the conference opened Mr. Truman was invited to preside over the meetings; preliminary discussions had been held between the British, U.S. and Soviet Chiefs of Staff. *Photo, British Official*

NO. 214 WILL BE PUBLISHED FRIDAY, AUGUST 31

Here Life and Death are Divided by a Hairbreadth

SMOKE AND BLINDING FLAME burst from a British Pacific Fleet carrier (1) hit by Jap suicide planes; but within three hours she was made operational again. Petrol tank of his Corsair was ablaze as Naval Air Arm pilot Cmdr. F. Charlton landed on another carrier (2); by a miracle both he and his aircraft were saved. A Walrus amphibian swooped under fire from Jap coastal batteries to rescue the shot-down pilot of an Avenger: the fortunate airman is seen (3) being helped out of the Walrus on the deck of his carrier.

Photos, British Official

With Our Armies Today

By MAJ.-GENERAL
SIR CHARLES GWYNN
K.C.B., D.S.O.

THE Japanese who crossed to the west bank of the lower Sittang River, in Burma, and threatened an offensive on a considerable scale, retain their bridge-head positions but have made no further progress. No co-ordinated offensive, in fact, has been attempted, although local attacks in some strength have been made, especially at night. During a temporary break in the monsoon, in the course of which floods subsided, our troops resumed the offensive on a limited scale and recovered some points which had been evacuated, chiefly owing to the difficulty of maintaining supplies.

Since then, a recurrence of monsoon rains has brought operations to a standstill. It now seems that the object of the Japanese was to cause a diversion which would induce us to concentrate in this area and thus afford their troops marooned in the Pegu Yomas (now believed to have numbered 10,000) a better chance of breaking through our thinly-held line of posts along the Mandalay railway farther north, rather than to open a corridor for their escape. Although our dispositions have not been modified materially the attempt to break through or filter through the railway cordon has in fact been made, and some 5,000 Japanese appear to have penetrated our line of posts in the neighbourhood of Pyu. A few may have reached and crossed the Sittang on rafts; but the majority are trapped between the railway and the river, where they are still under fire of guns and air attack as they seek shelter in villages or on ground above water level.

THE crossing of the Sittang, in flood and flowing at 15 miles an hour, is very difficult and probably impossible as an organized operation, even though the Japanese on the east bank have the advantage of observation from higher ground. The condition of the Japanese attempting to escape is very bad; they have little ammunition or food and are suffering from malaria and hunger. The number that finally escapes across the river is therefore likely to be small and of little importance. On the whole the attempt, clearly made in desperation, has only hastened the end of the trapped force, for over 5,000 have been killed either after breaking through or trying to pass the cordon.

Progress in Borneo has been steady, although not very rapid. One of the smaller oilfields in the Balikpapan area has been captured, but the Japanese still hold the main fields. From the latest reports it appears that the Australians on Bougainville are in a fair way to complete their laborious and difficult task. The main Japanese force has been driven into its base at Buin at the south end of the island, against which the Australians will have opportunities of employing the more powerful weapons they now possess.

ROOM for Deployment for Major Invasion Is Not Yet Available

Air and naval attacks on the Japanese home islands and on their sea communications increase in intensity, and part of the air force employed in Europe has come into action in the east. It is doubtful, however, whether sufficient bases for the whole force which will become available have as yet been secured. It is certain that sufficient room for the deployment of the land forces required for a major invasion is not yet available, nor have jumping-off points for an invading armada near enough to the probable objectives of a large scale operation yet been obtained. Unless a prolonged period of calm weather could be relied on—and that will not be the case until the winter—a shorter passage for landing would appear to be essential.

The Japanese policy of non-resistance to mounting air and naval attacks continues to be a surprising feature of the war, and must be taken as a sign that Japan's hopes are centred on being able to repel actual invasion or to make it prohibitively costly. There is certainly no indication as yet that she is contemplating unconditional surrender, however anxious she may be to come to more acceptable terms.

With the war in Europe over and with the practical certainty that the San Francisco Charter will be ratified, it is not surprising that already the future strength and organization of our fighting Services is becoming a subject for speculation. It is, of course, obvious that fundamental changes in our outlook will be necessary, and that it will not suffice to revert to our pre-war organization, merely increasing the numerical strength of its components and arming them up to modern standards in order to prevent a recurrence of the condition we were in six years ago. It would be rash and premature to attempt as yet to form definite conclusions as to our requirements and the shape they should take, for we are far from knowing our future commitments.

WE must still be inclined to judge our requirements by wartime rather than peacetime conditions, and there is perhaps more danger of our embarking on over-ambitious security plans, which might become so burdensome as to lead to reaction, than of our setting standards too low in the first instance. It will not be easy to balance our commitments and security measures against the financial and service burdens we are willing to accept. It is perhaps fortunate that this time there will be no sudden transition from war to peace; for so long as the Japanese war may drag on and we have to maintain a considerable army in occupation in Europe, normal peace conditions will not be established.

In 1919 the change-over was sudden; our Army of Occupation soon became little more than a token force, and certain commitments accepted in the aftermath period were dealt with by *ad hoc* expedients. We and the French soon settled down to thinking in terms purely of defence. Our Expeditionary Force practically ceased to exist and the French produced the Maginot Line for security. We have to some extent learnt our lesson; the occupation of Germany is real and at San Francisco the necessity of providing offensive forces to deal with aggression has been recognized. The existence of such an organization as was outlined at San Francisco would, of course, act as a powerful deterrent, but I have a feeling, though I may be wrong, that the conference intended that the organization should be brought into action only in case of overt aggression, rather than in preventive action.

DEFENCE Against Surprise Use of Enemy's Secret Weapons

The greater may be thought to include the less and that preventive action is not ruled out; but I think there is a distinction between the two conceptions which would affect the strength and composition and state of readiness of an international police force. The new weapons which German inventive genius has devised have obviously made prompt preventive action much more necessary than formerly, and prevention rather than capacity to punish aggression should be the aim.

U.S. MARINES INVADING THEYA SHIMA collected a cartload of young goats, which was being drawn by a sturdy bullock, after the island had fallen without opposition from the Japs. Theya Shima is 15 miles from Okinawa, which is the largest of the Ryukyu Islands and—far from falling easily to the Americans—was the scene of the bloodiest Pacific fighting **(see pages 202-203.)**

There is a school of thought which believes that air power should be the main constituent in an international force, and no doubt the possibility of being attacked from the air would be a powerful deterrent to aggression. But air power is not a suitable instrument for preventive action. Unless used in very great strength it, as far as experience goes, cannot decisively interrupt preparations for war. Moreover, there would probably be hesitation in using an instrument which causes great losses to non-combatants.

ON the other hand, an army promptly used to occupy enemy territory might effect its preventive object without firing a shot, although in case of resistance it would have to be supported by every means available. Clearly, occupation of territory affords the most effective way of breaking up preparations for war and, incidentally, of providing defence against the surprise use of the enemy's secret weapons. This does not mean that the air and naval components of the International Force should be neglected, but that armies are most suitable for preventive action, and should be in a state of readiness.

Defeats Pile Up Steadily for Mikado's Myrmidons

MORTAR BOMBS, from which these Australian troops (1) are taking cover, were used extensively in the Japanese defence of Borneo. By mid-July 1945, with all primary objectives in their hands, the 9th Australian Division had begun to clear the enemy from the productive hinterland of the north-east.

On Tarakan Island, off Borneo, this Japanese 7·5-cm. coastal gun (2) was captured. Although a Krupp product of 1913, it could still throw a shell, and its captors proceeded to use it, with excellent effect. See also page 130 and map in page 131.

Clearing up in the Tarakan area after the month's campaign which ended Japanese resistance there in June 1945, troops seized this abandoned dump (3) of enemy naval equipment, consisting of a small type of paravane and spherical mines.

Photos, Australian Official and Paul Popper

DURING THE LANDINGS on Labuan (see page 162) Australian artillerymen took equipment ashore from landing-craft (4) in readiness to support advancing infantry with their famous 25-pounders, which in duels have proved too much for Japanese guns. The magnificent harbour of Brunei Bay is now in Australian hands.

Our 'Scissors' Bridging-Tank at Work in Burma

HELD UP BY GULLIES, watercourses or cratered roads, our armour during operations on the Continent proved the tremendous time-and-life-saving value of bridge-laying tanks, which until June 1945 were on the Secret List. They can be carried in landing craft, to go into action with the assault wave, enabling other tanks to deploy and fight quickly.

Among them, now operating on the Burma fronts—and demonstrating to the Japanese that the reliance they hitherto placed on natural ground defences is largely nullified—is the scissors type: so-called because the bridge is carried folded on the top of the tank which lays it. Mechanism within the tank unfolds the bridge and lowers it across the gap.

A Sherman tank halted by a steep-banked watercourse (1) radios back for a scissors bridge. The bridging-tank sets off at speed in answer to the call (2). Arriving at the obstacle, the crew set in motion the apparatus which proceeds to "throw" the bridge (3). The two halves are opening out (4), "feeling" for the opposite bank. The operation completed (5), the Sherman continues its pursuit of the enemy; the bridging tank has departed for its base to pick up another bridge in readiness for the next urgent call. See also illus. in page 237.

Photos, Indian Official

HOSPITAL FOR INVASION BARGES is a floating dock, part of which is here being towed to a new berth at Southampton. Equipped with workshops it repairs damaged craft, which enter when the dock is lowered in the water by the process of pumping its ballast tanks full ; door in the stern is then closed, tanks emptied, and the barges rest on the dry " floor." At left background is the troopship Capetown Castle, about to be reconverted to a peacetime liner, its long and honourable war service now ended.
Photo, Planet News

With Our Navies Today

By
FRANCIS E. McMURTRIE

How long can Japan stand the strain of incessant bombing, supplemented by naval bombardments of vital points ? In some quarters it is thought that the end of resistance is near ; but there is at least as much support for the view that the war is likely to drag on into 1946. It is possible that Japan's rulers will wait to see whether the Soviet Government will add its weight to the forces arrayed against them. This might provide an excuse for surrendering without " losing face," as the odds would thereby have been increased.

At present the Japanese possess large resources in men, munitions and supplies in China, Manchuria and Korea, so far virtually unaffected. All these would be jeopardized by a Russian declaration of war. Yet there is something to be said for the wisdom of giving in while none of these resources has been dissipated. It is improbable, however, that the Oriental mind would see the situation in that light.

JAPAN'S Most Powerful Battleship Heavily Hit in the Superstructure

In attacks by carrier-borne aircraft of the Allied Fleets, the enemy naval bases at Kure and Yokosuka have suffered severely. The latter port, which is in Tokyo Bay, below Yokohama, was heavily bombed on July 18. The battleship Nagato, of 32,720 tons, the most powerful remaining unit of the Japanese fleet, received a heavy hit in the superstructure. A destroyer, seven motor torpedo boats, a cable-laying vessel and three small cargo ships were sunk, and two destroyers were damaged.

Kure was attacked by British and American aircraft of the Third Fleet on July 24. The battleship Hyuga, of 29,990 tons, which has been partially reconstructed with a flight deck aft, was damaged, as were the new aircraft carrier Amagi, two cruisers and a destroyer. Less serious damage was inflicted on the battleships Haruna, 29,330 tons, and Ise (sister ship of the Hyuga), the fleet aircraft carrier Katuragi, the escort carrier Kaiyo, the training carrier Hosyo, the heavy cruiser Aoba, a light cruiser, a coast defence ship, three destroyers, a gunboat and a midget submarine. In addition, an escort aircraft carrier is believed to have been sunk.

At this rate it would seem as though complete extermination of the Japanese fleet will not be long delayed. It will be recalled that similar reports were coming in concerning the surviving German warships shortly before the surrender of Dönitz. While it does not follow that the Japanese will imitate the Germans in this respect, it is obvious that their defences are becoming very weak, or it would not have been possible to cause such havoc in a big naval base like Kure, situated in a well-protected position in the Inland Sea. Most of the bombardments which the Allied Fleets have so far carried out have been undertaken at night. In such circumstances it is not possible to ensure hitting every target ; but by smothering an area with hundreds of shells, very great destruction can be done, as seems to have been the case at Kamaishi and Muroran, both important steel production centres, and in the Hitachi area, where copper is smelted. Large fires were caused and plant left in ruins.

Battleships of the King George V class, mounting 14-in. guns, (including that ship herself, which wears the flag of Vice-Admiral Sir Bernard Rawlings) and of the U.S. Iowa and South Dakota classes, mounting 16-in. guns, were the principal units taking part in these bombardments. Little or no opposition appears to have been offered by the enemy, either from shore batteries, aircraft or submarines. It has not been reported whether or not minefields were encountered, but it may be assumed that minesweepers swept the bombardment area as a precaution.

MINORITY of Allied Escort Vessels Will be Needed Now in the Pacific

Now that the Battle of the Atlantic is a thing of the past, many of the escort vessels which played an important part in winning it have become redundant. Moreover, as demobilization proceeds, there will not be enough personnel to man them all ; and only a minority will be needed in the Pacific, where Japanese submarines have failed to operate against Allied shipping with any effect. Already it is reported that the Royal Canadian Navy has placed some 70 of its 112 corvettes on the disposal list. Probably a majority of the older corvettes of the Royal Navy, particularly those of the early " Flower " type, which bore the brunt of the work in 1940–42, will soon be joining them. Obsolete ships of designs dating from the last war, such as V and W class destroyers, and the remaining flush deck destroyers taken over from the United States Navy in September 1940, will also be paid off and prepared for scrapping in the near future.

There are also a certain number of larger ships which, in the normal course, would have been discarded by this time had not war intervened. These include the old battleships Revenge, Resolution and Ramillies, of 29,150 tons, the cruisers Frobisher, Hawkins, Dauntless, Delhi, Despatch, Diomede, Ceres, Cardiff, Caradoc, Carlisle, Colombo, Caledon and Capetown ; and the repair ship Vindictive, formerly a cruiser. Though some of these may still be used, for a time, for subsidiary purposes, such as training, all must ultimately be consigned to the scrapheap, since it is uneconomical to spend large sums every year on the upkeep of obsolete vessels, to say nothing of the folly of locking up personnel in ships which could not be expected to fight effectively under modern conditions. Another ship which will not be kept in service much longer is the Furious, our first fleet aircraft carrier. Quite recently Mr. A. V. Alexander disclosed that this ship had been removed from the effective list.

RESPECTABLE-SIZED Fleet to be on the Sale List Before Long

There must be fully 70 of the old destroyers already mentioned, a dozen or more submarines, and a number of small craft of all descriptions, which may be expected to come on to the sale list before long. Thus quite a respectable little fleet, superior to the navies of some minor Powers, will be in the market, though doubtless on condition that the purchasers break the ships up and do not use them for war purposes.

H.M.S. Renown, in which the King met President Truman at Plymouth, might also come into the above category were it not for the fact that she was completely rebuilt a short time before the outbreak of the war. Originally she was to have been a battleship of the same type as the Revenge, but plans were recast and she was completed in 1916 as a battle cruiser of high speed with a displacement of 32,000 tons. She saw comparatively little service in the last war, as her protection was considered inadequate, causing her to be sent into dockyard hands for additional armour to be fitted.

In 1920 she took the Prince of Wales to the U.S., Australia and New Zealand. A year later she was called upon to convey H.R.H. to India and Japan. Yet another honour was bestowed on the ship when she carried our present King and Queen (then the Duke and Duchess of York) to Australia in 1927. Some anxiety was caused while crossing the Indian Ocean by the outbreak of an oil fuel fire, but this was subdued before it could spread.

In the present war the Renown has taken part in the hunting of the Admiral Graf Spee, in 1939, and of the Bismarck, in 1941. She was in action with the Scharnhorst and Gneisenau off the coast of Norway and with the Italian fleet off Sardinia. Last year she was operating with the Eastern Fleet.

Long Overdue U-Boat Takes Secret to Argentina

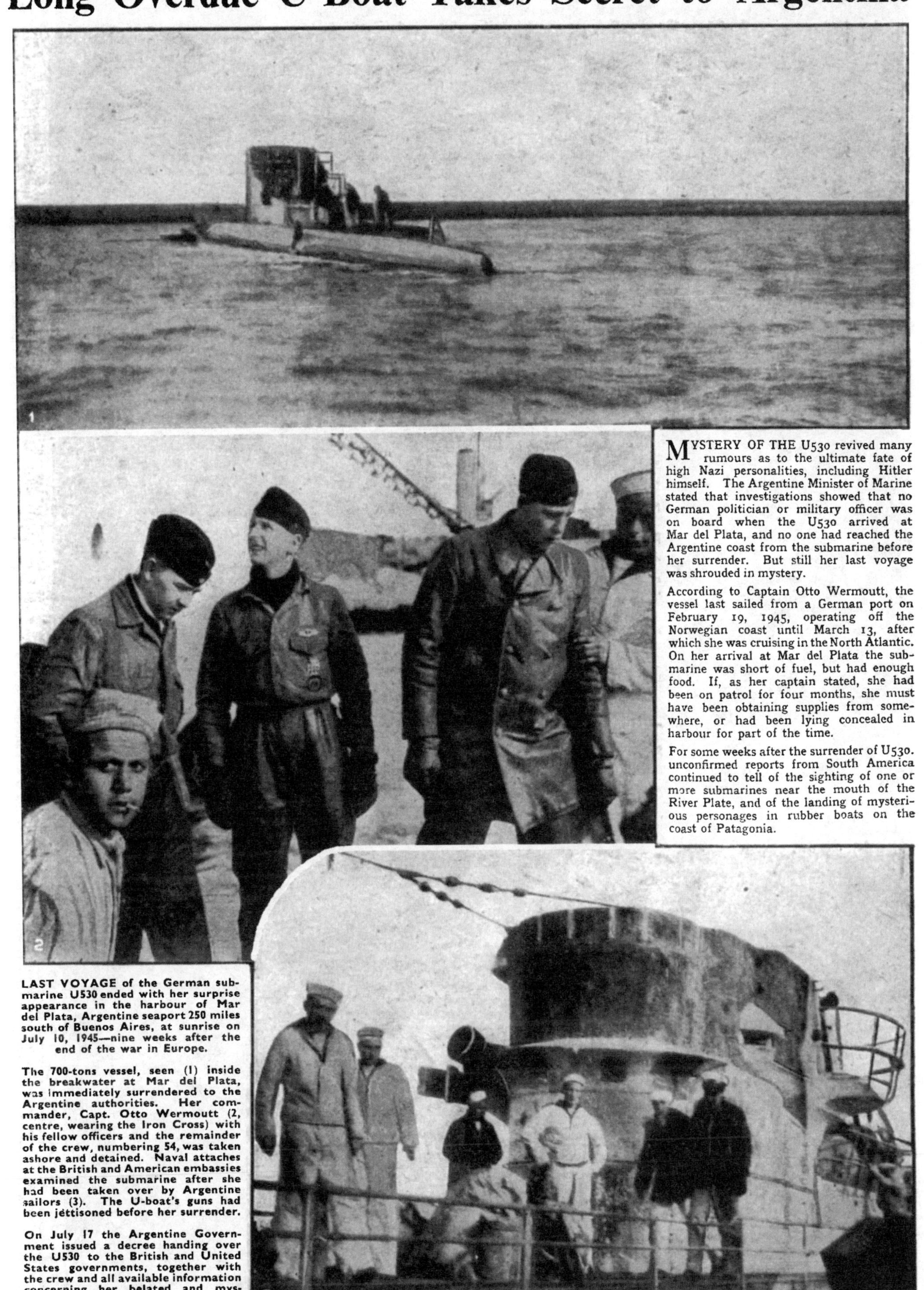

MYSTERY OF THE U530 revived many rumours as to the ultimate fate of high Nazi personalities, including Hitler himself. The Argentine Minister of Marine stated that investigations showed that no German politician or military officer was on board when the U530 arrived at Mar del Plata, and no one had reached the Argentine coast from the submarine before her surrender. But still her last voyage was shrouded in mystery.

According to Captain Otto Wermoutt, the vessel last sailed from a German port on February 19, 1945, operating off the Norwegian coast until March 13, after which she was cruising in the North Atlantic. On her arrival at Mar del Plata the submarine was short of fuel, but had enough food. If, as her captain stated, she had been on patrol for four months, she must have been obtaining supplies from somewhere, or had been lying concealed in harbour for part of the time.

For some weeks after the surrender of U530. unconfirmed reports from South America continued to tell of the sighting of one or more submarines near the mouth of the River Plate, and of the landing of mysterious personages in rubber boats on the coast of Patagonia.

LAST VOYAGE of the German submarine U530 ended with her surprise appearance in the harbour of Mar del Plata, Argentine seaport 250 miles south of Buenos Aires, at sunrise on July 10, 1945—nine weeks after the end of the war in Europe.

The 700-tons vessel, seen (1) inside the breakwater at Mar del Plata, was immediately surrendered to the Argentine authorities. Her commander, Capt. Otto Wermoutt (2, centre, wearing the Iron Cross) with his fellow officers and the remainder of the crew, numbering 54, was taken ashore and detained. Naval attaches at the British and American embassies examined the submarine after she had been taken over by Argentine sailors (3). The U-boat's guns had been jettisoned before her surrender.

On July 17 the Argentine Government issued a decree handing over the U530 to the British and United States governments, together with the crew and all available information concerning her belated and mysterious surrender.

 Photos, Associated Press

FIRST AIR PHOTOGRAPH OF THE CITY OF LONDON SINCE 1939 (taken in April 1945) shows what a tremendous undertaking the rebuilding of the capital's blitzed areas will be. Unharmed St. Paul's dominates the scene: in the left middle distance stands the G.P.O. Telephone exchange also miraculously untouched by bombing. In July 1945, Mr. W. S. Morrison, Minister of Town and Country Planning, rejected the rebuilding scheme drawn up by the City's Town Planning Committee. "The City of London," he said, "possesses buildings and remains of the greatest architectural and historical interest, and is the workplace of more than half-a-million persons . . . A great opportunity was lost in 1666 of laying it out afresh . . . an even greater opportunity has now occurred." Compare with illus. page 242. *Photo, British Official*

The Royal Navy's Big Debt to the 'Wavy Navy'

More than 80 per cent of Naval personnel today are R.N.V.R. men—without whose aid the White Ensign service could never have kept the seas in the way it has done. It is about the prowess of these "enthusiastic amateurs," who have struck dread to the hearts of the enemy's seamen, and whose officers bear rank-insignia of wavy gold lace, that Capt. FRANK H. SHAW writes here.

THE Senior Service prefers to catch its man-power young, the younger the better, and mould it into its own peculiar shape. But war renders many preconceived ideas obsolete. When hundreds of thousands of efficients were suddenly required to crew our expanding Navy, when a multitude of small craft were commissioned to sweep mines, when the flotillas of motor torpedo boats and motor gunboats came into being, there was an alarming scarcity of officers and men capable of handling them under wartime conditions. The intake of Royal Naval Reservists was insufficient to supply the pressing need; in any case, as the majority of R.N.R. men were sorely needed by the savagely attacked Merchant Navy, new entries could not be spared.

The difference between R.N.R. and R.N.V.R. (Royal Naval Volunteer Reserve) should be understood. The R.N.R. is recruited from professional seamen employed in merchant ships. In peacetime, all personnel holding an R.N.R. appointment were required to perform a stated number of drills aboard a warship or in a naval depot—they corresponded to the Special Reserve or Militia of the Army. Being trained seamen they required only a slight Navy polish to make them efficient officers and crews of warships, from the largest to the smallest. They were paid an annual retainer, on condition they remained qualified by regular training-courses.

THE R.N.V.R. was different. It corresponded more to the original Territorial Force, in that it was mainly recruited from amateurs; though some of its senior officers —notably the Duke of Montrose, now retired—had qualified as seagoing yachtsmen. All around our coasts abounded, prior to the war, thousands of enthusiasts who devoted most of their leisure to a variety of small craft: racing yachts, motor-cruisers, catboats, dinghies—anything, indeed, that would float. Here was priceless raw material! Several cities had training centres, where these enthusiasts learned the work of war.

H.M.S. President, lying alongside the Thames Embankment, was the headquarters of the London Division of the R.N.V.R., established in 1903; and passers-by grew familiar with the sight of men practising boatwork, signalling, or undergoing other instruction required to qualify in the R.N.V.R. Men working in offices found this form of national service a healthy outlet for their energies; and when the 1914-18 war came, hundreds of them were given seagoing appointments. The R.N.V.R. acquitted itself well under war conditions. It freed regular naval personnel for manning the more powerful fighting ships. It displayed exceptional dash and daring in its work; distinctions were won, casualties were suffered.

IT has required the rigours of the present war to prove to the full the invaluable aid the R.N.V.R. has been able to give to the Senior Service. During the peace-years the force was whittled down wellnigh to vanishing point, though in 1918 it had risen to a strength of 38,000. But its peacetime establishment was always amply filled, with long waiting-lists. A great number of surgeons were commissioned even before the war came. Budding airmen, too, were granted commissions in the R.N.V.R. Officers were granted opportunities to go to sea on training cruises, to study navigation, gunnery, seamanship, and generally to equip themselves for such active service as the future might hold.

R.N.V.R. Had to Fill the Gaps

On the outbreak of war R.N.V.R. trained men were immediately drafted to responsible positions in such ships as had been kept on a "care and maintenance" basis with only skeleton crews. A new and immediate intake of recruits was required; and to the recruiting depots a stream of the prime of the nation's manhood flocked eagerly. Many had no more knowledge of salt water than that acquired during brief summer cruises.

"Hostilities only" recruits came under the aegis of the R.N.V.R. To secure a naval appointment, as midshipman or sub-lieutenant, service on the lower deck was deemed necessary. The vastly-expanded Fleet Air Arm—the Navy of the Clouds—was greedy for personnel. Since few regular naval officers and ratings could be spared for this vital branch of the Navy the R.N.V.R. had to fill the gaps—and right nobly they filled them, as the Honours and Casualty Lists only too plainly tell. "Sub-Lieutenant (A) R.N.V.R." is one of the commonest entries in the casualty returns of the Senior Service.

The most remarkable feature is the aptitude the R.N.V.R. displayed from the outset for regular seagoing service. Many a destroyer was manned, as to her lower deck, almost completely with R.N.V.R. ratings, and carried a large proportion of officers from the same volunteer service. Not only were the Wavy Navy officers—the distinguishing rank-insignia of the R.N.V.R are of wavy gold lace, not intertwined as in the case of the R.N.R.—appointed as watchkeepers in seagoing ships but also as navigating officers.

With the enormous increase in our light coastal craft, the Admiralty were hard-set to find responsible personnel with which to commission these waspish craft; but it was found by experience that the R.N.V.R. were ideally adapted for this purpose. They were dashing, venturesome, hardy, and not hidebound by convention. Some of the most outstanding successes of the war have been achieved by light coastal forces, operating not only with single units under R.N.V.R. command but with entire flotillas so commanded. When the German magnetic mine first announced its deadly presence, it was the R.N.V.R.'s response that enabled hundreds of wooden drifters to take the seas, as an emergency measure, until the de-Gaussing of our ships was completed.

One complaint of the R.N.V.R. in the last war was that the Admiralty gave promotion only tardily, and that advancement to senior rank was almost unknown, but now a much more liberal attitude is shown. Promotion by seniority has to a great extent been abolished, promotion by merit being the usual thing. So that we now see numerous lieutenant-commanders, commanders, and even captains, R.N.V.R., figuring in the Navy List; both in the executive, or deck, department and in the Special Service branches.

A GREAT number of honours and awards have been won in the light coastal forces, whose tireless, indomitable work can never sufficiently be praised; many more have resulted from conspicuous gallantry in the Fleet Air Arm. But officers and men of the R.N.V.R. can be found today serving not only in M.T.B.s, destroyers, corvettes and frigates, cruisers and battleships, but in submarines—for long the Regular Navy's special preserve. Destroyers, submarines, frigates and sloops are commanded by R.N.V.R. officers in some cases.

STALWARTS of the MERCHANT NAVY

Capt. THOMAS J. LACEY Master of the S.S. Defender, he was awarded the O.B.E. on June 26, 1945, for "indomitable spirit, leadership and organization" during enemy attacks in the Mediterranean—typical hero of the Merchant Navy.

Chief Officer JOHN ALLERTON When his ship, the S.S. Sampa, was mined while returning from Antwerp he organized a rescue party for the wounded, going round the entire ship, though badly injured and temporarily stunned. Awarded the M.B.E.

Second Officer G. R. HUGHES Awarded the M.B.E. for his conduct and courage when the motor-vessel Harpagus was mined off the Normandy beaches. The Master killed and Chief Officer wounded, Hughes took command of the ship, safely landing the cargo.

HARRY M. FORTUNE Apprentice in the S.S. Ascot, torpedoed by a Japanese submarine in the Indian Ocean. He was awarded the B.E.M. for his bravery in assisting the wounded while under enemy fire.

Photos, L.N.A

Where Hitler's Vaunted Legions Used to Stamp

BRITISH VICTORY PARADE OF 10,000 MEN passed before Mr. Churchill in Berlin's Charlottenburger Chaussee on July 21, 1945 : at the saluting base (1) before the march past stand Field-Marshals Maitland Wilson and Montgomery on the Premier's right ; on his left, Field-Marshal Alexander, Mr. Eden and Maj.-Gen. Lyne. Salute of 192 rounds was fired by the R.H.A. at the parade entrance (2). Armour passing the base included self-propelled 25-pounders (3) of the immortal "Desert Rats."

Photos, Planet News, Central Press

Big Three Tackle Europe's Knotty Problems

POTSDAM CONFERENCE, which opened on July 17, 1945, differed in some vital respects from previous meetings of the heads of Government of the U.K., U.S., and the Soviet Union. First, the site itself—Potsdam, cradle of Prussian militarism—signified that the main purpose of the earlier conferences at Teheran (November 1943) and Yalta (February 1945) had been fulfilled with the overthrow of Germany. Second, the chief representative of the U.S. was no longer President Roosevelt but President Truman.

In addition to Chiefs of Staff and representatives of the armed forces of the Three Powers (including Admiral Lord Louis Mountbatten, C.-in-C. South East Asia), there were in attendance the British Minister of War Transport and the head of the U.S. Maritime Commission; for distribution of fuel and food in the liberated countries and in conquered Germany was a priority subject for discussion.

Result of the General Election (see p. 255) brought changes in the British representation at the Conference, Mr. Attlee and Mr. Bevin replacing Mr. Churchill and Mr. Eden.

ROUND THE CONFERENCE TABLE in Potsdam (1), Mr. Churchill faced the camera; Generalissimo Stalin (with cigarette) towards the right; President Truman's party, to the left, included the new U.S. Secretary of State, Mr. James Byrnes (2). Mr. Eden chatted with Mr. Molotov (4) and Mr. Gusev (left), Soviet Ambassador to Great Britain. Dinner guests of Mr. Churchill at "No. 10 Downing Street, Potsdam," on July 23 were Truman and Stalin (5); the latter saluted the Guard of Honour of Scots Guards (3).

Photos, British Official, (2) Karsh, Ottawa

Now It Can Be Told!

PLAQUE FROM THE ADMIRAL HIPPER recording the death "for his Fatherland" of Gunner Josef Ritter during the fight with H.M.S. Glowworm, described here. *Photo, British Official*

BRITISH MAQUIS WERE READY FOR INVADERS

ONE of the most interesting chapters in our anti-invasion plans of 1940-41, recently disclosed, is that describing the organization of an underground movement—a British counterpart of the Maquis!

The organization was divided into two distinct branches—each with quite separate duties—one part an elaborate set-up of guerillas, armed with automatic weapons, explosives, knives, and so on, the other equipped with secret wireless sets, forming an intelligence system, and provided with all the paraphernalia for espionage behind the enemy lines. Both of these branches of the "Maquis" were controlled by a central secret military headquarters which trained civilian personnel and devised methods whereby they could do most harm to the Germans.

The "guerilla" branch comprised several hundreds of teams of seven men, each team being housed in a camouflaged dug-out (of which there are many today spread round our coasts), armed with automatic weapons for self-protection, but with their main weapon—explosives—for offensive use. Their task was to emerge from this dug-out at night, ambush German transport, blow up aircraft on landing grounds, destroy enemy dumps, and generally create havoc and confusion among the advancing enemy. The personnel were enrolled in special battalions of the Home Guard, and much speculation about them was aroused since they did not parade, wore different sleeve signs, and followed a separate course of training.

The other branch of the organization's activities was known as "Special Duties," and this follows more closely the lines of a "thriller" in the manner of its working, in the type of person employed in it, and in the high degree of secrecy which of necessity surrounded it. Special Duties had thousands of members in our coastal counties, all prepared as civilians to report on enemy movements and activities by their radios, communicating with senior military headquarters.

Of the great numbers employed in the organization, few knew their neighbour members, and probably are entirely unaware even today that the farmer up the lane, or the postman in the village, was also a "Special Duties" man. Women, land owners, business men and labourers attained a high proficiency of wireless skill, including the use of codes.

LAST GLORIOUS FIGHT OF THE GLOWWORM

IN one of the most daring and courageous sea-battles of the war, the British destroyer H.M.S. Glowworm, of 1,345 tons, fought a single-handed duel at point-blank range with the 10,000-ton German cruiser Hipper; then, battered and burning, she turned in a last superb gesture of defiance and rammed the giant enemy towering above her. On July 10, 1945, it was announced that Lieut.-Cmdr. G. B. Roope, R.N., the Glowworm's heroic commander, had been awarded the V.C. (See illus. p. 216.)

Only then, with the repatriation of the Glowworm's one surviving officer, 27-years old Lieutenant Robert Ramsay, R.N., did the story of this epic fight come to light. All that was known previously was that the Glowworm had been sunk by a heavy enemy vessel in the North Sea on April 8, 1940. This is what happened: The Glowworm was escorting the battle cruiser Renown when a man was washed overboard in heavy seas. In her efforts to find him, the destroyer lost touch with the main British force, and as the weather worsened she had to reduce speed to less than ten knots. Her gyro-compass failed, and she had to steer by magnetic compass. At daybreak on April 8, 1940, she was trying to rendezvous with another British force, when she sighted an unidentified destroyer.

SHELLBURST within a cable's length of the Glowworm during the action in which, heroically, she rammed the 10,000-ton Nazi cruiser Admiral Hipper. Taken from the German vessel, the photograph shows the Glowworm laying a dense smoke-screen as she cuts across the enemy's bows. Story was released on July 7, 1945, with the repatriation of the one surviving officer, Lieut. R. Ramsay, R.N. He was awarded the D.S.O. three days later, when the posthumous award of the V.C. to the Glowworm's Captain, Lieut.-Cmdr. G. B. Roope, R.N., was also announced (see page 216). *Photo, Planet News*

"We immediately challenged her," said Lieut. Ramsay, "and she replied that she was Swedish—then she opened fire." A few moments later another destroyer was sighted, and the Glowworm began her gallant fight—against odds from the start.

The battle developed into a slamming match, with the destroyers manoeuvring at full speed and firing with all guns. "Very soon our Director Control Tower was flooded out by heavy seas," continued Lieut. Ramsay. "The ship was being thrown about and rolling very heavily. We lost two men overboard and several were injured by the roll of the ship, but we scored a hit on the leading enemy destroyer. They didn't hit us. Shortly afterwards they broke off the action and were obviously trying to lead us on to something more powerful."

ALTHOUGH the Glowworm's Commanding Officer, Lieut.-Cmdr. Gerald Roope, R.N., knew what the enemy was trying to do, he decided to follow with the idea of finding out what big ships the Germans had at sea. He hoped to shadow them and report their movements. A few minutes later, the Hipper hove in sight—the Hipper armed with eight 8-in., twelve 4·1-in. and twelve 37-mm. guns against the destroyer's four 4·7-in. guns. Weather conditions made shadowing impossible, and from then on the Glowworm knew her fate was sealed.

The sole purpose of Lieut.-Cmdr. Roope was to inflict as much damage as possible on the enemy before being sunk, and the heroic battle began.

Long before the Glowworm's guns were within range, the Hipper was pouring 8-in. shells at the destroyer and hitting her mercilessly. "We made smoke," said Lieut. Ramsay, "and began to close the enemy cruiser. When we got within range, I fired our torpedoes."

The Sirens Screeched Unheeded

Meanwhile, the Glowworm was rapidly becoming a blazing inferno. One of her four guns was out of action. Her range-finder was hit. The upper yard of her mast collapsed across the siren wires and her sirens were screeching unheeded in the blaze of battle and stink of cordite and black smoke. Then it was that Lieut.-Cmdr. Roope decided to ram the Hipper. Going in under a storm of fire from 8-in., 4-in. and machine-gun fire, he steered for the enemy's starboard side.

There was a grinding crunch as the destroyer's bows crumpled against the cruiser's armoured plating. Men fell to the deck in a welter of blood and sea water, fire and smoke. Those who could, picked themselves up again.

"As we drew away we opened fire once more," Lieut. Ramsay said. "We scored one hit at 400 yards. Our bows were badly stove in. A shell had passed through the wheelhouse. Another had burst in the Transmitting Station, killing most of the crew and all the staff of the Wireless Office. A third entered the ship under the after-torpedo-tubes, crossed the ship and burst against the forward bulkhead of the Captain's cabin. The cabin was being used as a first-aid station and the explosion turned it into a shambles. This shell also made a huge hole in the ship's side abreast the engine-room, and another completely wrecked the after superstructure.

"The Captain was so far unhurt, and as the ship heeled over to starboard he gave the order to abandon ship. He sent me down from the bridge, and I tried to get as much timber and other floating material over the side as possible. There seemed to be very few unwounded, but all that could be done was done to put lifebelts on the injured men in the hope that they would float.

"The Captain, who was the only other survivor on the bridge besides myself, then came down. E. R. A. Gregg reported he had gone down to the boiler room and let off steam to avoid an explosion as the ship sank. Then shortly afterwards—about 10 o'clock—the Glowworm capsized. After floating bottom-up for a few moments, she sank.

"The Hipper stopped and picked up survivors. Our Captain was not among them, though he was seen in the water. I was taken before the Hipper's Captain, who told me our torpedoes had missed his ship by only a few yards. The ramming had damaged one set of her torpedo tubes, flooded two compartments, and put her fresh water system out of action. She took us to Trondheim, but later she had to go to Germany to be docked for repairs."

SPECIAL BRIDGING DEVICE KNOWN AS THE ARK, which helped us defeat Germany and is being used in Burma, can now be revealed as a tank on which are mounted two ramps for dropping down at front and rear. Here, two of these ingenious bridging-tanks are ditched one on top of the other, and the ramps have been lowered, enabling British armour to cross a shellhole in Germany. See also illus. page 229. *Photo, British Official*

We Ferried Invasion Trains to France

While planning the invasion of the Continent it was realized that as soon as we were established on the far shore railway communications behind our lines would be of major importance and that locomotives and rolling stock captured would be in no condition to satisfy our needs. Thus a large programme was arranged for the manufacture of additional supplies of locomotives, wagons, ambulance trains and railway mobile workshops. Over 1,000 locomotives were specially built in Britain alone.

It devolved on the Transportation Service, War Office, to arrange for suitable vessels for shipping locomotives and rolling stock from the United Kingdom to France. For since 1940 all existing train ferry vessels had been converted to other uses and plans had to be made for their return to normal use.

The main factors governing the re-establishment of the pre-war train ferry service were, first that we could not expect to find the original terminal works on the French side left intact by the enemy, and second, that the location of the French and Home Terminals did not suit invasion plans. It was decided, therefore, to equip the ships with special gear so that locomotives and rolling stock could be picked up and landed at any quay which was rail-served or which could be quickly linked up with any nearby railway system.

Designs for special gantry cranes, to handle locomotives and other heavy lifts up to 84 tons for the Southern Railway's Twickenham Ferry class steamers and for special loading ramps for the ex-L.N.E.R. vessels, were put in hand in late 1942, the fabrication of the structural steelwork and crane machinery proceeding during 1943. It is of interest that the ships could not be fitted out with their new gear as it became ready, but had to remain in service until the last moment on urgent operational work.

But these ferries were not enough, and it was decided to convert British and American L.S.T.s (landing ships, tank), so as to carry railway wagons or tanks. The work on the former was done by Naval Dockyard personnel and on the latter by U.S. technicians. The scheme was successful and some 50 craft were fitted out; these in due course transported upwards of 30,000 wagons and coaches to the Continent.

Concurrent with the need for modifying the ferry vessels was the necessity for new terminal facilities to be built at suitable locations on the South Coast which would not interfere with other shipping facilities. The War Office carried out the necessary reconnaissances and prepared designs for three sites. Construction work on these terminals was carried out by Port Construction and Repair Companies R.E., supplemented by Pioneer Corps Troops and Railway Construction Troops as needed.

Terminal arrangements required for the L.S.T.s were simple. It was only necessary to lay rails into the "hards" which had been constructed for the loading of tanks, and connect to new holding sidings for the wagons, and provide rail-mounted ramps to run up and down the hards with the tides. (See illus.) In the case of the "far shore" terminals nothing much could be done on the planning side, but the experience gained in this country enabled certain basic requirements to be determined which greatly expedited work when it came to be done at Cherbourg and elsewhere. Cherbourg was captured on June 26, 1944, and on July 29 the "Twickenham Ferry" delivered her first cargo of locomotives. As the tide of war swept eastwards, further terminals were successfully developed at Dieppe and Calais.

LOCOMOTIVE FROM THE U.K. LEAVING A L.S.T. for its journey via French quay-rails to an Allied base, during operations on the Continent. How special ships and gear were devised to enable locos, rolling stock and tanks to be transported across the Channel just when the need was greatest is revealed in this page. *Photo, British Official*

'Home Is the Sailor, Home From Sea'

The Merchant Navyman afloat not uncommonly visualizes himself as one day with a garden to cultivate and hens as a profitable hobby. Mostly this paradise ashore remains a dream. But it, and more, is becoming happy reality for seamen no longer able to serve because of age or partial disability, as explained by STANTON HOPE specially for "The War Illustrated."

THE novel idea of a community centre for seamen in a country setting was conceived after the South African Navy War Fund had donated £50,000 in practical appreciation of the Merchant Navy's immense war services to the Empire. This generous gift was placed at the disposal of the National Union of Seamen; and the secretary, Charles Jarman, and his colleagues were prompt to use it for a welfare scheme more ambitious than anything formerly attempted.

During the London blitz it became advisable to transfer the N.U.S. headquarters from town to a mansion known as Sachel Court, at Alford, Surrey. The commodious house, set in an estate of 100 acres, will become available as a community centre for selected seamen according to the agreed plan; and some of the surrounding farms, comprising another 200 acres, will be purchased, if possible, for cultivation and special development by them in other directions.

When negotiations and constructional work are completed, Springbok Village will exist in the rustic peace of Surrey as a permanent and practical memorial to the wartime heroism and self-sacrifice of British seafarers. A third of those accepted for residence will be aged seamen and their wives, but Springbok will have no melancholy atmosphere of the "eventide homes" such as are sponsored by some well-meaning charitable organizations.

A HULK may rust at its last moorings, and times were when an old sailor was allowed to rust in idleness despite willingness and capability to undertake light employment. At Springbok he will have the satisfaction of proving himself a useful member of the community, sharing for his own interest in such light duties as he can perform.

Disabled seamen and their womenfolk will form the majority of the new community, acceptable applicants being discharged men whose disability does not require constant medical care or that precludes them from doing work of some kind for the common good. Unfit to continue a seagoing career, they will be rehabilitated in civil life by training under an expert staff for cultivation of the land, tending horses and cattle, maintenance and repair of mechanical plant and vehicles, and for other employments. When the whole Springbok estate becomes established, at least 150 seamen will be launched on new careers in this Surrey haven.

Sachel Court itself will be the hub of the community. This will house the administrative and domestic staff, and provide for the offices, a meeting-room, lounge, library and a large dining-hall where the residents may foregather for the principal meals. Bungalows and maisonettes, each with a bathroom, will be constructed on the estate for accommodation of married couples, and dormitories will be available for the single men. Electrical power from the grid will supply lighting and heating, and hot water will be on tap throughout for domestic use.

A nursery school for children of the younger married seamen is included in the plan; this to be supervised by the local educational authorities, who are taking keen interest in the project. Numbers of amenities exist already at Sachel Court, such as garages and stables, which are to be extended, several fine greenhouses, rock and rose gardens and tennis courts. Future plans include the construction of bowling greens, a putting course and an open-air swimming pool. Presumably, too, the community will not be without its own welcoming "Dog and Duck," where the salts, young and old, can relive experiences.

Recreational facilities would not be complete without radio and cinema, and provision of these has not been neglected. A special feature will be an *al fresco* theatre with compact covered theatre adjoining. To provide these, Doris Hare, hostess of the popular B.B.C. "Shipmates Ashore" programme, has raised a substantial fund. The prospect is attractive, and Springbok Village bids fair to become a "one-night stand" where many a professional touring company may well be proud to perform.

IN popular conception, the sailor in his off-watch hours at sea, especially in foul Western Ocean weather, is peculiarly apt to think with affection of his native soil. But this does not necessarily imply that when it comes down to brass tacks he would enjoy tilling that soil more than the average landsman. Sailors have gravitated to the land after "swallowing the anchor" and have become farmers, smallholders and poultry-keepers with more or less success. But many of the new breed of Merchant Navymen, as the chiefs of the Seamen's Union are fully aware, are mechanically minded through familiarity with machinery in modern steamships and motor-ships. For which reason Charles Jarman and his colleagues are determined that such men who become resident in the new community of Springbok Village shall have adequate opportunity to follow their natural bent.

The main plan, therefore, includes the erection of a factory for some light industrial enterprise to give employment to a proportion of the seamen; and, where necessary, machinery will be adapted to suit those men who otherwise would be handicapped by disability of an arm or leg. Training will be given in plumbing, oxy-acetylene welding, carpentering and other pursuits, and workshops built where these trades can be followed profitably on attaining proficiency.

Those seamen who prefer the farmer's life will find healthful employment on the many fertile acres of the Surrey Utopia, cultivating crops, fruit and vegetables, and tending livestock. Beside model dairies and piggeries, the plan provides for an up-to-date cannery and packing sheds. Not only will the community be self-supporting so far as food is concerned, but there should be a large surplus for marketing.

The executives of the National Union of Seamen have had useful experience in sponsoring the Merchant Navy Convalescent Home at Limpsfield, Surrey, and other communities of seafarers. One thing they have learnt is that an extraordinary number of sailors of all ages frequent the carpenter's shops and hobby rooms to make model boats and mechanical toys.

THIS tendency has been encouraged at a welfare centre at Kendal with the result that it is hoped to extend the market for these products for the mutual benefit of the seamen and the public. The N.U.S. officials intend, as further funds become available, to construct an additional workshop at Springbok Village for the pleasant trade of toy-making, convinced that the products of disabled Merchant Navymen would compare favourably with any foreign toys.

The handsome sum placed at the disposal of the Seamen's Union by the South African Navy War Fund will be sufficient to purchase the Surrey farms to add to the Sachel Court estate, and to get the main plan in operation. Shipping companies and other interested bodies are coming forward with financial aid, but further funds are needed to transform a wonderful dream into lasting reality.

Behind the project is the dynamic personality of Charles Jarman and that of his energetic colleagues. They have roughed-it themselves on stormy seas in the past, and their hearts are attuned to the needs of lower-deck seamen whom they now serve. The odour of charity is abhorrent to them, and whatever is done by Governments or the public for Merchant Navymen they regard only as part payment for vital services rendered. Their own reward will come when they see in full glory the Springbok haven to which they have set their course.

SACHEL COURT, set in fertile Surrey acres, at Alford, is to be the hub of Springbok Village: immensely useful and permanent "Memorial" to the heroism and self-sacrifice of British merchant-seamen. Training for civil life, under an expert staff, will be directed from this commodious mansion. *Photo,* THE WAR ILLUSTRATED

This Was Hitler's Legacy to Berlin!

Photos, British Combine, Associated Press

AT the Brandenburg Gate, marking the boundary between British and Russian zones in Berlin (top), Field-Marshal Montgomery on July 12, 1945, invested Marshal Zhukov, Deputy Supreme Commander of the Red Army (on Montgomery's right), with the insignia of an honorary Knight Grand Cross of the Order of the Bath, and bestowed the K.C.B. on Marshal Rokossovsky (on the Field-Marshal's left); the ceremony was followed by a march past of Grenadier Guards. The next day 10,000 British troops and over 560 vehicles paraded: looking down the Charlottenburger Chaussee (bottom) as the parade began. Spearheaded by tanks, every British unit in the German capital was represented and every arm of Britain's Forces. The column, with marching and lorried infantry, took more than half an hour to pass the saluting base.

Phot
C

'Bitterest Foe of Nazism, Best-hated in Germany'

The day after his arrival for the Big Three Conference at Potsdam, the Premier, in khaki drill uniform of a colonel of the 4th Hussars, on July 16 made a tour of the centre of blasted Berlin: outside the shattered Reichstag (1), with Mr. Eden. To the amazement of Berliners, Mr. Churchill, leaving his jeep, walked through the streets with only a couple of detectives and a handful of military police to guard him (2). Comments of crowds included, "So that's supposed to be a tyrant!"

Mr. Churchill in a Jeep Tours the German Capital

The grandiose Chancellery was also visited, in company with his A.T.S. daughter Mary: on leaving the building, Mr. Churchill gave the famous V-sign to British soldiers and sailors (3). At the imposing entrance to the Chancellery (4), on the Wilhelmstrasse, the Whitehall of Berlin, which lies in the Red Army sector of occupation, with his Russian guide who had fought in the taking of the building on May 2, 1945. Red Army officers also accompanied the party.

At the End of the Fuehrer's Trail

Photos, L.N.A.

Once the most famous building in Berlin, the Reichstag (top) as the airman now sees it. The original structure was burned out on February 27, 1933, a month after Hitler became Chancellor, the fire being the signal for Nazi Party terrorism and their assumption of power. A mile south of the Reichstag lies the ruin that was Anhalter Station (bottom). Comparing these photographs with that of London on page 232, it should be noted that little clearance has been done in Berlin.

VIEWS & REVIEWS Of Vital War Books

by Hamilton Fyfe

In Australia they call the Japanese "the Nips." But that doesn't mean they like the people of Nippon any more than we do. For they lived during several months under threat of invasion.

They have not forgotten those months; they never will. They were spurred to efforts unexampled anywhere else, allowing for the smallness of their population. A nation of seven millions has put into the field vast armies; has achieved an immense production of war material including aircraft and tanks; has built and manned ships; has almost stopped manufacture for civilian requirements. In addition to armed forces numbering not far short of a million, they have rounded up into Civilian Construction Corps (see pages 584-585, Vol. 7) men too old for soldiering, but able-bodied enough to make the roads and airfields and camps which the soldiers need.

One of the tasks carried out triumphantly by these men between 35 and 60 is described by Mr. George H. Johnston in his new book, Pacific Partner (Gollancz, 7s. 6d.). A very large airfield was urgently required. It was to be at "a tiny little town on the edge of the scrub, sleeping in the dust and heat of the sun-browned plains." A labour force of 2,500 went there, and in three months laid 49 miles of concrete roadway, put up 450 permanent buildings, and moved some 30,000 tons of earth. Within little more than twelve weeks from the start of the job thousands of men of the Australian and American Air Forces were established on the new field, and planes were taking off to bomb enemy positions and communications.

Provocative and Infuriating

This was just after the Americans arrived to help the Australians protect themselves against the Japanese. They also helped them to defeat procrastinators and red-tape officialism. Nothing was allowed to stand in the way of swift and effective solution of problems, often very difficult ones.

The regimentation of civilian labour was an action altogether opposite to the basic principles of labour in Australia. The conscription of labour gangs was something which violated the worker's code on which so much of Australian life had been based for decades. But Australia had accepted the spontaneous assistance of the United States in the hour of danger. And it was Australia's duty to discharge her reciprocal obligation, to prepare, if necessary, every square inch of the entire continent as one vast base for the United Nations in the fight against Japan.

"Work, Fight or Perish!" was the slogan adopted throughout the country, and they saved themselves from perishing by fighting and working with a tight-lipped intensity which has few parallels in history. Naturally they feel admiring, even affectionate, gratitude to the Americans who in their dark hour went to their aid. When Mr. Johnston's publisher put on the jacket of his book the warning that it would "provoke and infuriate some," he was thinking no doubt of the emphasis laid on that new tie of friendship and mutual esteem. It was drawn all the more tightly because for a time we were unpopular and were angrily blamed for the sudden and alarming change in Australia's position. "A common accusation in the streets of every town and city was 'Britain let us down.'" And Britain remained the scapegoat until Australian soldiers began to return.

These men corrected misconceptions quickly. They had fought shoulder to shoulder with the British Tommy. They had seen the humble London householder standing up to the fury of the blitz. They had been able to escape from Greece only because of the iron resolution of the British armoured brigade that fought the rearguard action until it was almost annihilated. They had seen the magnificent work of the Royal Navy. The wave of anti-British sentiment that had surged through the Empire's refractory dominion was stilled.

All the same, it seems to have left a backwash of feeling that the Old Country must expect more criticism than it had in the past and that relations between Australia and the U.S. will become closer than they have been before. If, says Mr. Johnston, the Atlantic Charter is to be more than a form of soothing words, Australia must "throw away its tariffs and its dependence on others," must be "less tied by tradition to questions of Empire preference," while "Britain must end the period of exploitation of subject peoples in Asia." That, we know, is how Mr. Curtin felt; his successor, we must suppose, feels the same.

How Australia Went to War

If there is a touch of self-righteousness in the charge of "exploitation," its source must be looked for in Mr. Johnston's justifiable pride in the handling by Australians of their only colony, Papua, where the native people have shown their appreciation of all that was done for them by the loyal devotion of their behaviour during the war. "Papua for the Papuans" was the watchword adopted by Australia.

The slogan of independence came not from the subject people, but from the ruling people. The Papuans have no more idea of the meaning of independence than the man in the moon. But they do have a deep-seated sense of justice and humanity, and they are prepared to make untold sacrifices to express gratitude for just and humane treatment. There must be lessons in that for other countries and for the people who will shape the destinies of colonies in years to come.

STRETCHER-BEARERS IN PAPUA earned from the Australians the name "Fuzzy-Wuzzy Angels" for their skill and care in transporting Allied casualties through mountainous jungle country. Tribute to the New Guinea natives is paid in the book reviewed here. *Photo, Australian Official*

The Papuans have acted as guides in swamp and jungle, across river-mouths, over mountain ranges. They have helped Allied troops to move from island to island for fresh offensives. They have rescued American flying crews, forced down in forests, under the very noses of the Nips. "Thousands of them—many coast natives unaccustomed to the terrible mountain trails and the chilling alpine mists—slaved for months carrying great loads of ammunition and food along the world's worst military supply road. And then they came back with the wounded on their shoulders, often taking weeks to carry one man from the battlefront to the safety of a rear hospital. They marched by day through dank swamps and steaming jungles and always the face of the wounded man was shielded from the burning tropic sun by a great green leaf. During the night-rains they took turns sitting up with the patient, washing his wounds with the tenderness of skilled nurses. They did it not for gain but because of friendship and gratitude."

The Other Fellow's Viewpoint

That sidelight on Australian sentiment—and good sense—will be new, I think, to most British readers, who are inclined to think of our fellow-citizens "down under" as rather hard and lacking in tolerance for "the other fellow's point of view." They are certainly an odd mixture. It is hard to believe sometimes that the people of Sydney and of Melbourne, for instance, can be of the same stock—especially on a Sunday. Nowhere else in the world, I should imagine, is Sabbatarianism kept up so rigidly as it is in the capital of Victoria. No hotels, no entertainments, no newspapers, no shops open in Melbourne, very few eating-houses, very few street-cars—"apparently on the theory that there is no place to go and therefore nobody should need transport to go there." But all the same Americans like Melbourne because they found refuge and friendship in private homes.

Many of them have seen more of Australia than the Australians themselves. Few of the latter have been, either on pleasure or business, to Darwin, the little port in the extreme north of the continent. It is not quite so hot there as it is at Wodgina, where temperatures rise to 130 degrees in the shade and for six months at a time the thermometer never registers less than a hundred. But it is hot enough to make you risk swimming in crocodile-infested rivers and in the sea where sharks abound. Into this dreary little township, with its "endless swarms of flies and mosquitoes," poured more white men than had ever been in this part of the country before. The Northern Territory, half a million square miles, had fewer than 4,000 white inhabitants, some 1,600 Chinese, and 17,000 aborigines. "War brought tens of thousands of soldiers to this barren, cruel land." They laid out airfields, made roads, built camps.

Mr. Johnston is very amusing about the railway to Darwin, on which there was before the war one train a week. Now there is one a day, but the service is still regarded as something of a joke. Trains are liable to get "lost"—that is to say, to defeat the efforts of officials to locate them for an hour or two. It used not to run after dark. "The custom was to pull up at a convenient hotel at nightfall and resume the journey next morning. The main reason was that the engine was not fitted with a headlight and there was a grave risk of charging into a wild buffalo. On this line was thrown the task of carrying armies and their supplies. Somehow it did it, and that is an example of the way Australia went to war.

Desert Rats Hoist Their Proud Sign in Berlin

FIRST BRITISH OCCUPATION TROOPS to settle in Berlin were accompanied by a N.A.A.F.I. mobile canteen (1) under the charge of Cpl. Harvey, who has followed the 7th Armoured Division (" Desert Rats ") to final victory. The sign (2) reminds all who pass how long that historic journey was. Whilst British and Americans queue for dinner, German children wait expectantly for tit-bits (3). Some of the first A.T.S. in the capital go sightseeing (4) in intervals of their duties at the Potsdam Conference.

Photos, British Official, Planet News, Associated Press

Pétain—Marshal of France—on Trial for His Life

AT THE PALAIS DE JUSTICE IN PARIS, on July 23, 1945, Marshal Philippe Pétain—erstwhile leader of Vichy France—was brought to trial by the State on a charge of treason. First witness was M. Paul Reynaud, Prime Minister of France in the spring of 1940, giving evidence (1, left) while the 89-year-old Marshal listens with ear cupped in hand. A stormy scene between the Public Prosecutor, M. Andre Mornet (2), and the defence counsel led to the court being cleared by police, seen (3) entering the Palais. Petain stares into the future (4).

Photos, Associated Press, Fox

Holland Now Faces Vast Task of Rebuilding---

Their liberation complete, the people of the Netherlands have begun a new struggle, this time to restore their devastated country. All their determination and courage will be needed for what is perhaps the greatest engineering task of the century. This article by E. H. COOKRIDGE sets out clearly some of the tremendous problems now facing Holland's Government and people.

HOLLAND is free again, but since the liberation the Dutch are waging another struggle, not less daring, determined and courageous than that which the Dutch Resistance Movement led during five years of Nazi oppression. No other country in Europe has been so ravaged and devastated by the Germans. Because of its smallness, practically no area, no town or village has escaped. Almost a third of the country was flooded when the Nazis destroyed the dykes and put large areas under water. The Gestapo deported many thousands of men, women and even children to Germany, thousands perished in the concentration camps of Buchenwald, Belsen and Dachau, and in the slave camps for foreign workers. Most of the national wealth, machinery, tools, rolling-stock, raw materials, live-stock, art treasures were looted. In July 1945 the Netherlands Central Bureau for Statistics estimated the total war damage inflicted by the Germans on the Dutch at about £2,000,000,000.

The Dutch are now shouldering the Herculean task of restoring their country and draining the sea from their lands, which have been spoiled for agriculture by the salt water for many years to come. It is the greatest engineering task of the century on which this small nation is now embarking.

THE food shortage is still appalling, in spite of every possible help the Dutch are receiving from Britain, the U.S.A. and other of the United Nations. They voluntarily imposed semi-starvation upon themselves during the last phase of German occupation by the gallant railway strike that speeded the German defeat (see page 54). But because of that strike, the last ounce of food reserves, not looted by the Germans, was exhausted long before the country was liberated.

The new Dutch Government, headed by one of the most active leaders of the Resistance Movement, Professor W. Schermerhorn, has just announced its plans for the reconstruction. For the first phase an "Emergency Plan, 1945," has been drawn up, to deal with the various urgent needs of the nation. It will be followed by a "Reconstruction Plan, 1946-1948," which will comprise a bold rebuilding and rehousing scheme and provide for a revival of Dutch agriculture, industry and communications.

35-Miles Journey Takes Six Hours

The plans foresee the nationalization of important industries. Plans have been prepared to transfer—after the mining industry and the Netherlands Bank—various branches of the economic life into public or semi-public ownership. The State will also control the confiscated property of Germans or Dutch quislings, who during the Nazi occupation acquired land and industrial concerns taken away from the legitimate owners. A state-controlled financial corporation, the "National Reconstruction Financing Company," has been established to provide credits with which private banks are unable to cope.

The transport difficulties are tremendous. At the beginning of July the first few train services between Amsterdam, and Rotterdam, Amsterdam and Alkmaar, and Amsterdam and Utrecht had been put into operation again, but there is only one train daily on each of these lines and the journey from Amsterdam to Rotterdam—a distance of only about 35 miles—takes more than six hours. Very shortly, seven spans of the old London Waterloo Bridge will arrive from Britain to rebuild railway bridges, most of which the Nazis had blown up. Of the 850 modern railway engines there remain 165, of the 30.000 goods trucks there are little more than 500 left, of the 2,000 passenger coaches 284 remain, and of 300 modern coaches for electrified trains only five remain usable.

All the rest of the rolling stock of the Dutch Railways has simply vanished, stolen by the Nazis and carried away to Germany. Britain and America have now lent 235 railway engines and 3,000 freight wagons, which, however, are needed almost exclusively for food transport. The emaciation of the population is indescribable. Although food supplies are now reaching Holland regularly, there are still hundreds of people dying in hospitals and emergency centres from the results of prolonged starvation. Although there is now food for them, they cannot eat and it is the most tragic experience to see people—including children—perishing from cachexy because the food came too late. Dutch doctors and nurses, often themselves ill and weak from hunger, have made superhuman efforts to help.

ONE of the great problems of the immediate future is the revival of the once-flourishing agriculture and market gardening, which before the war provided an important part of the export. We, in Britain, were good customers for Dutch dairy products and vegetables. Dutch tulips were once the pride of our front gardens. This year large districts of Holland will bear little or no harvest. This grim situation may prevail for another year or two before the land is once again fit for successful cultivation. Tens of thousands of people have been already mobilized for this work. The British and Americans are assisting by giving to the Dutch army bulldozers and other equipment. Canada is sending agricultural machinery.

DUTCH CABINET FORMATION was announced on June 25, 1945, when members included (left to right) Prof. P. Lieftinck (Finance); Mr. H. Vos (Industry and Commerce); Prof. W. Schermerhorn (Premier and leader of the Popular Party); Mr. H. A. M. T. van Kolfschoten (Justice); Mr. Drees (Social Affairs). *Photo, Pictorial Press*

There is a great need for clothing and shoes. The Dutch are literally barefooted. Some 500,000 pairs of shoes have been bought in America and the Allied Supreme Command has promised to provide about three million pairs of reconditioned army boots, which may be worn by men and women alike. Belgium will supply some millions of pairs of wooden clogs. Dutch babies are without napkins. There are people who have worn the same shirt, the only one they possess, for 15 months.

Lack of Power Mutes Radio Sets

The authorities are facing staggering problems, but the Dutch, these industrious, determined, gallant people, are clenching their teeth to solve them. They hope to rebuild their lives, though the task seems sometimes too big for human power and endeavour. Much help is needed and is being given by the Allies, though it is limited because of the shortages all nations are suffering themselves. Holland will be, of course, entitled to a large share in those reparations in kind which are going to be extracted from Germany. But the progress of the negotiations about these is necessarily slow. It will be probably many months before the Allied Reparations Commission, now in session in Moscow, can commence to attend to the various claims.

Therefore, Holland is looking for help in the first instance to Britain and America. Here, apart from the shortages we have to deal with ourselves, the problem of shipping is one of the greatest handicaps. The Dutch Merchant fleet, which fought so gallantly on our side, suffered great losses. Dutch ports have been partly destroyed by the Germans. One of the piers of the Hook of Holland was blown up, causing the river mouth to silt up, the Germans stole or destroyed Rotterdam's famous elevators and cranes, all dredging equipment has been destroyed or taken to Hamburg, Kiel or Luebeck. But already thousands are working on the rebuilding of the ports and it may be hoped that Dutch shipbuilding yards will be working again before long, turning out new ships. Supply of power, however, is still the paramount problem. Rotterdam's supply of electric current was resumed only on June 27, but the ration is so small that it will do little more than light a single room for a couple of hours. Even radio sets cannot be used and a score of large towns and many great rural districts have no current at all. Now plans have been completed to "import" current from Germany by long-cable system, and in rural districts windmills are used to generate electricity. (See illus. in facing page.)

MANY Dutchmen to whom I spoke told me that Holland feels that she is indebted to the British for ever, as it was they who liberated the country under the most difficult conditions and suffered great sacrifices, as at Arnhem or on Walcheren, in an endeavour to bring rescue as quickly as possible. A pleasing token of this gratitude is the recently given promise by the Royal Netherlands Navy to provide the gardens of the Royal Naval Colleges at Dartmouth and Greenwich and the Royal Naval Barracks at Devonport, Portsmouth and Chatham, with Dutch flowers every spring in remembrance of the hospitality and friendship experienced during the war.

There is today a strong trend among many Dutch people to see their country more closely linked with Britain. Although, of course, there is no intention to limit the Netherlands' ancient independence and sovereignty, bound so intimately with the beloved Orange dynasty, many Dutchmen hope that economic and cultural bonds with Britain will be far closer than they were before the war

—A Country Paralyzed by German Devilry

WINDMILLS GENERATE ELECTRICITY for rural areas in Holland (1); this particular district near The Hague was a launching centre for V2s and the crater made by one of the many misfires can be seen in the foreground. Unloading Allied food supplies for the Dutch at Rotterdam (2). Works of art were removed by German order from the Rijksmuseum, Amsterdam, to massive strong-rooms specially built at Paasloo, near Steenwijk (3). Clothes from Britain are cherished by Netherlands youngsters (4). Scheveningen (5), fashionable seaside resort, was regarded by the Nazis as a likely invasion point and was defended by them with anti-tank obstacles.

Photos, British Official, Planet News

Their Majesties in the Isle of Man and Ulster

ANCIENT TYNWALD HILL in the Isle of Man, where every year public proclamation is made of Acts passed by the Manx Parliament, saw new history made on July 5, 1945, when for the first time a King of England directed the traditional rite. King George and Queen Elizabeth, preceded by sword-bearer, walked from St. John's Chapel (1) to the Hill.

Continuing the royal victory tour, a fortnight later, Their Majesties, accompanied this time by Princess Elizabeth, flew to Northern Ireland. After opening the new Parliament at Stormont, Belfast, on July 18, the King held an investiture in the Great Hall of the Parliament Buildings (2). On the dais behind the Queen and Princess Elizabeth were the Duke and Duchess of Abercorn; the former soon to be succeeded as Governor of Northern Ireland by Lord Granville, brother-in-law to the Queen. Seated on the city walls of Londonderry (3) happy youngsters waved Union Jacks as the royal party passed by; the King was accompanied by the Mayor and the Bishop of Derry.

Photos, Topical, New York Times Photos

I Was There! Eye Witness Stories of the War

Winged 'King's Messengers' Go Home Again

Even the pigeons are being demobilized—the 300 civilian-owned pigeons that flew from the battlefronts to Britain through barrage and storm, carrying vital messages and precious reconnaissance photographs. Adventures of these birds-of-war are here related by an Evening Standard reporter who visited their London lofts, in Piccadilly.

I HAVE just visited the war pigeons' lofts 80 ft. above the traffic, after climbing an iron staircase. There are more than 300 of these birds belonging to people all over the country. They are now on furlough and will soon be going back to their original homes. Officially the birds have no name. A ring on a leg is their only identity. Some of the best birds were engaged carrying messages from the underground fighters of France and Belgium, who came over here to collect baskets of pigeons.

One bird brought to England the depressing news that the raid on Dieppe was unsuccessful. They now call him Dieppe Blue. He is a beautiful bird of dark blue plumage. He will go back to his original home with the reputation of a hero.

Captain Caiger, in civilian life a pigeon breeder, has been in charge of the lofts at Piccadilly since the war began. He is a case of a square peg in a square hole. He pointed out Dieppe Blue to me and explained how the bird had been dropped in the Dieppe area by parachute, afterwards to be sent back home with the story of the raid.

"These birds," he said, "were lent to the Government for the national pigeon service. We lost very few of them, and many of them have gone right through the war. A lot of youngsters have been hatched and they will go back to the people who loaned the pair of birds. If the owners do not want all the birds some may be given to demobilized Servicemen who would like to begin to breed pigeons."

The experience gained by these war pigeons has resulted in an increase of speed and stamina. Some of them took part in a race between Fraserburgh and London for £1,000 worth of prizes. Captain Caiger told me that they returned to London having flown the 430 miles of air-line in 10 hours, a speed of 43 miles an hour, faster than a racehorse or a greyhound.

Captain Caiger, who has lofts at Bognor Regis and Tottenham, told me of a scheme which he put up to the War Office for using pigeons for blowing up enemy searchlights. "In 1943," he said, "I made the suggestion that pigeons should fly to the searchlights carrying on their backs a charge of high explosive weighing 2 oz. The authorities turned the idea down because they considered there was danger in carrying the birds by bomber. Experiments, however, were carried out."

During the war the suggestion was made that it would be useful if pigeons could be induced to call at an intermediate station to deliver their messages before flying home to their lofts in Piccadilly. This problem was overcome in a neat way. The pigeons were taken to the station on several occasions and fed there until they acquired the habit of calling at that station for food before flying home. These birds were afterwards called two-way pigeons.

Different kinds of receptacles for carrying messages were used. One large cylinder, about two inches long and an inch in diameter, was used for films. It was fixed to the pigeon's neck with elastic. Another was a small cylinder of metal, about three-quarters of an inch long and a quarter of an inch in diameter.

WILLIAM OF ORANGE, dropped at Arnhem by parachute with airborne troops on Sept. 17, 1944, flew 260 miles back to Britain in just over four hours. *Photo, Associated Press*

ARMY PIGEONS BEING DEMOBILIZED include some who flew for 21st Army Group throughout the fighting in Europe; they are released (1) for their final flight from Berlin to Britain. Birds of the Mobile Section in portable lofts (2), which weigh two cwt. complete with 30 pigeons and can be carried by air or in a small truck. Capt. Caiger (story in this page) offers a tit-bit to one of the war pigeons wearing on its back a specially designed carrier (3). *Photos, 1, British Combine; 2 and 3, exclusive to THE WAR ILLUSTRATED*

H.M.S. VENUS, the destroyer of the East Indies Fleet whose notable action against a Japanese cruiser in the Malacca Straits is narrated here. *Photo, British Official*

We Settled a Jap Cruiser in Malacca Straits

Early in the morning of May 16, 1945, a destroyer flotilla of the East Indies Fleet intercepted a Japanese cruiser in the Malacca Straits and sank her after a spirited engagement. Story of the action is told by Commander H. G. de Chair, D.S.O., R.N., of H.M.S. Venus, the destroyer which delivered the knock-out blow.

We had practised the plan many times. Luck was with us, and our plan and practice achieved success. We first made contact with the enemy shortly after midnight. It was some time later, after a dash through heavy rain squalls, that I could see the Jap cruiser from the bridge through binoculars. She was silhouetted by vivid flashes of tropical lightning.

She turned sharply to the southward to avoid the torpedoes fired by H.M.S. Saumarez, but in vain. There was a bright flash from her stern as they found their mark, and immediately we opened fire with starshell and commenced hitting her with all our guns. We then made our successful torpedo attack. Seven minutes later we received the order "Finish her off!" from Captain Power in the Saumarez. We fired our remaining torpedoes, which reached their target, and the cruiser sank almost immediately.

Searchlights from the Venus were switched on to the blazing hulk of the cruiser as she sank. A pinnace had been lowered, full of what were probably high-ranking Japanese officers. The sea was full of survivors, but owing to the likely proximity of enemy aircraft from nearby airfields it was impossible for survivors to be picked up.

The Venus's Chief Engineer Officer, Lieut. (E.) J. W. Galer, R.N., said:

In the dash to catch up with the cruiser, our bearings reached a temperature of over 600 degrees. At one time during the action I heard a whirring noise above the roar of the engines. Puzzled, I turned to the Engine Room Artificer on the starboard throttle and shouted through the din:

"What do you make of that peculiar noise?"

"That, sir, is a torpedo passing alongside from one of the destroyers on its way to the Jap!" he replied.

A few seconds later a second whirring denoted another "tin-fish"—passing close to the ship's side. Offering a cigarette to Chief Engine Room Artificer Perrett, I noticed that my hand was shaking.

"I think I must be getting nerves, Chief," I said.

"That's not nerves, sir—just excitement!" he replied, calmly.

At the Receiving End of the Jungle Supplies

Of immense importance throughout the Burma campaign, airborne supplies of all kinds were nowhere so essential as in the sustaining of Wingate's Chindit operations behind the Japanese lines. How anxiously awaited food, ammunition and mail were collected by the men in the jungle is told by Cpl. L. J. Wells, specially for "The War Illustrated."

The dark, dank jungle seems charged with an air of expectancy. Only the drip of rain on fallen teak leaves disturbs the silence. Here, deep in enemy occupied country, history is in the making. Wingate's Chindits have returned to harass the Jap where he will feel it most, to quote Wingate—"in his guts."

SUPPLIES DROPPED FROM THE AIR to the 7th Division of the 14th Army on the Arakan front, when the Division was cut off in February 1944, were eagerly collected by (among others) Private John Bache and Sergeant W. Meadows. How our jungle-fighters react to such aid is described in the accompanying story. *Photo, Indian Official*

On this night our column has no wish to meet any of the Sons of Nippon. For the column is receiving its five-day supply drop of food and ammunition, and for the next few hours it is essential that its location be unknown to the enemy. The supply planes are due in half an hour. Everything is in readiness for their arrival. Great piles of dead wood have been collected and placed in the shape of a giant letter "L" which, when lit, will guide the planes in on their dropping runs.

Our nerves are taut. Through all our minds are running two questions. Will the planes come? Will the Japs come? As the expected time of arrival draws near, our ears are strained to catch the first dull throb of the distant aircraft. The keenest ears pick up the sound. A low murmur goes around as the word is passed to stand by. Precious dry paper is produced from packs and pockets and held ready to ignite the wooden "L." The R.A.F. officer stands ready with his Aldis lamp to flash out our prearranged recognition signal to the leading Dakota plane.

Now the first plane is roaring overhead, its powerful engines making the jungle vibrate. "Light the fires!" comes the order, and almost immediately orange flames leap up, casting weird shadows across the jungle clearing. The Aldis throws out its signal and is answered by the plane. The "Signals" have also contacted the aircraft and receive word that the latter are about to commence dropping. As the first Dakota begins its run-in, slouch-hatted figures silhouetted against the marking fires prepare to collect the supplies as soon as these land; not a moment can be wasted. The quicker the column moves from the area the less likely the Jap is to find it

With engines booming and exhausts red against the dark sky, the first plane comes in low over the trees. Out come the bundles: six of them, their statichutes (small parachutes) billowing behind, grey-white in the darkness. Hard on the heels of the first aircraft comes the second. Before it commences its drops, men have picked up the first containers and delivered them to the column administrative officer.

Everyone is working at top speed: R.E.s feeding the fires, infantry platoons picking up supplies, "Q"-bloke and Rear Column H.Q. sorting the stores ready for issue. Others are spotting and counting bundles as they leave the planes, watching for 'chutes that fall outside the dropping zone. If there is time these will be searched for after the remainder of the supplies have been collected,

Far out in the surrounding jungle the remainder of the infantry lie in defensive positions, on the alert for enemy patrols who know only too well that somewhere in the jungle beneath the widely circling planes are British troops receiving much-needed supplies. It is during supply drops that columns most fear attack and at these times every precaution is taken to prevent enemy action.

Instinctive Prayer of Thanks!

There are four planes now doing a follow-my-leader act, up above in the darkness, each loaded with precious food, ammunition, maps and other vital supplies. Those of us on the ground instinctively offer a prayer of thanks for their safe arrival. As we sweat at the task of collecting the containers we cannot help but think of those in the planes above. Not so much of the pilot and crew as of the men who are employed in the important job so aptly termed "chucking out." These men are our pals from the same regiment, graded chaps who had not reached the high standard of fitness so essential for the gruelling work of long-range penetration.

Many a dirt-begrimed Chindit remarked through his beard, "You lucky people!" as the planes flew over, for were they not soon returning to their base, with their charpoys (beds) and good grub instead of the damp earth and "K" rations? Far be it from me, however, to belittle the work of the supply-dropping crews. Their job is an important one, and hazardous. Flying conditions over this theatre of war are seldom good and the Dakota is an easy prey for lurking Zeros.

Time and time again the mighty planes swoop over, round and around. Steadily the piles of stores grow higher, and the piles of wood beside each marking fire diminish as smoke-begrimed men stoke the flames. Excitedly the word is passed, "The mail's O.K. Number 2 Section has found it!" The special 'chute that always holds the container of mail is one of the most important items that comes on supply drops. There is always the fear that it will be lost. Mail to jungle warriors cut off from the outside world by hundreds of miles of Jap-occupied territory is the best morale builder there can ever be. It is possible it will not be distributed for 12 or 24 hours, but we are happy in the knowledge that it is there.

At last the planes are empty, and with one last swoop over the column they turn their noses west and head for home. The jungle is silent again, except for the tramp of feet as men complete the gathering of containers and commence to draw their rations. It has been a good drop. Only a few 'chutes have been lost. Each man receives a full five days' "K" rations plus a few extras, such as fruit, onions and cigarettes. Ammunition is distributed to replace that used in a previous action. A new wireless set has arrived for the "Signals." The operators are soon making a quick examination by torch light for any defects caused through landing. A small supply of bread has come to earth in a nearby chaung (river). Fished out, it is a sodden mash; but it will make good duff tomorrow. A mule, as if knowing what is going on, tries to voice her opinion. She will soon discover that mule fodder was among the supplies dropped.

Everything has gone smoothly; the column commander has every reason to be pleased. He decides to allow us time to brew-up before moving. At once "crash cans" (these are any large, empty tins suitable for heating water to make tea) are filled, section fires made, and with the skill born of long practice tea is soon ready. And it will have a dash of newly-arrived rum in it.

Soon, in the first grey light of dawn, a watcher would observe a ghostly column, backs bowed beneath bulging packs, move across the clearing to disappear into dense undergrowth, deeper into the jungle, deeper into enemy territory. Ghostly in appearance but hard of body, tough as nails—Wingate's wonderful Chindits!

PLANE LAND HERE NOW was the ground-signal formed with parachutes which had brought down supplies to Wingate's Chindits. On the jungle track are men of that special force which penetrated 200 miles into Jap-held territory in Burma and was dependent on airborne food, ammunition, medical and other stores.

Photo, Associated Press

OUR DIARY OF THE WAR

JULY 18, Wednesday
1,319th day of War against Japan

Japan.—British and U.S. warships and aircraft again struck at Yokosuka and other targets near Tokyo.

Borneo.—Australian troops entered town and oilfield of Samboja.

China.—Lt.-Gen. Stratemeyer assumed command of U.S. air forces.

JULY 19, Thursday *1,320th day*

Burma.—Japanese broke out from Pegu Yoma Mts. in attempt to escape east.

Borneo.—Australians occupied town of Marudi.

JULY 20, Friday *1,321st day*

Japan.—More than 600 Super-Forts made record attack on Choshi, Hitachi, Fukui, Okazaki and oil refinery on island of Honshu.

Germany.—President Truman presided over hoisting of Stars and Stripes in Berlin.

Home Front.—Ministry of Health empowered local authorities to requisition empty houses.

JULY 21, Saturday *1,322nd day*

Germany.—Parade of 10,000 British troops in Berlin before Mr. Churchill.

Pacific.—Liberators from Aleutians bombed Matsuwa airfield, and warships bombarded coast of Paramushir, in Kurile Islands.

JULY 22, Sunday *1,323rd day*

Japan.—Super-Forts attacked Ube coal plant on Honshu with demolition bombs; at night U.S. destroyers penetrated Tokyo Bay and torpedoed ships.

Borneo.—Australian troops moved up headwaters of Balikpapan Bay and landed at Tempadeong

JULY 23, Monday *1,324th day*

France.—Trial of Marshal Pétain on charge of treason opened in Paris.

China.—Shanghai area attacked by Allied aircraft.

Japan.—U.S. and British destroyers swept close inshore in Sagami Bay, Honshu; carrier aircraft attacked Kure.

JULY 24, Tuesday *1,325th day*

Japan.—British and U.S. carrier aircraft attacked Japanese navy in Kure; Allied naval force bombarded military targets on tip of Honshu; big force of Super-Forts hit Osaka and Nagoya.

China.—Airfield at Shanghai again bombed by Allied aircraft.

Austria.—British troops entering Graz were enthusiastically welcomed.

JULY 25, Wednesday *1,326th day*

Japan.—British and U.S. fleet aircraft renewed attacks on Japanese warships near Kure and Kobe. Super-Fortresses bombed oil refineries at Kawasaki near Tokyo.

Far East.—British East Indies Fleet engaged in mine sweeping off west coast of Malay isthmus, near Puket Island.

JULY 26, Thursday *1,327th day*

Japan.—Proclamation issued from Potsdam in name of U.S., British and Chinese Govts. gave Japan choice between unconditional surrender and "prompt and utter destruction."

Home Front.—Labour Party obtained large majority in General Election. Churchill resigned; Attlee to form Govt.

JULY 27, Friday *1,328th day*

Japan.—Warning leaflets dropped on 11 towns on list for fire-bombing by Super-Fortresses.

JULY 28, Saturday *1,329th day*

Japan.—Carrier-aircraft again hit ports and airfields on Inland Sea.

Germany.—Mr. Attlee and Mr. Bevin arrived at Potsdam to resume Conference.

JULY 29, Sunday *1,330th day*

Japan.—Six of 11 towns warned of air attacks bombed by Super-Forts. Allied fleet bombarded Hammamatsu.

China.—Kweilin airfield recaptured by Chinese troops.

General.—Eighth Army disbanded.

JULY 30, Monday *1,331st day*

Japan.—Carrier aircraft struck at airfields near Nagoya.

JULY 31, Tuesday *1,332nd day*

Japan.—Allied destroyers of 3rd Fleet entered Suruga Gulf, southern Honshu, and bombarded Shimizu. Super-Forts. dropped warning leaflets on 12 cities.

France.—Laval flew from Spain to Austria and was handed over to French.

General.—F.-M. Sir Harold Alexander to become Governor-General of Canada.

★ *Flash-backs* ★

1941

July 28. *Japanese troops landed in French Indo-China, following cession of bases by Vichy.*

1942

July 27. *Russians announced loss of Rostov and Novocherkassk.*

1943

July 19. *Rome marshalling yards bombed by American aircraft.*

July 22. *Palermo, capital of Sicily, captured by Allied forces.*

July 25. *Resignation of Mussolini; Badoglio became Premier.*

1944

July 19. *In Italy troops of the 5th Army captured Leghorn.*

July 20. *Attempt on Hitler's life by group of Reichswehr officers. U.S. troops landed on Guam.*

July 25. *Polish National Committee formed at Kholm, Poland.*

July 27. *Russians captured Lvov.*

July 28. *U.S. troops captured Coutances. Russians took Brest-Litovsk and Przemysl.*

July 31. *Avranches and Granville entered by American armour.*

With Our Airmen Today

By CAPTAIN
NORMAN MACMILLAN
M.C., A.F.C.

In the south-west Pacific, General Carl Spaatz has been appointed commander of the strategic bombing force operating against Japan. Within this Command is the U.S.A. 20th Air Force, which has led the heavy bomber attack against Japan proper and is now commanded by Lt.-Gen. Nathan F. Twining; and the 8th Air Force, which was the American opposite number of R.A.F. Bomber Command, and is now transferring to the Pacific under its last commander in Europe, General J. H. Doolittle, who was reported to have reached Okinawa in July.

Not all the 8th Air Force has been transferred from Europe, but the main force redeploying to the Pacific is to be strengthened by the addition of Super-Fortress bombers. The U.S.A. 8th A.F., which possessed 300,000 personnel and about 2,400 first-line heavy bombers and 1,200 fighters, is now split into three. Its main force of heavy bombers began to leave Valley, Anglesea, and Prestwick, Scotland, to fly to the U.S.A. on May 19, and 2,118 Fortress and Liberator bombers had gone by July 9. It was a striking tribute to the efficiency of this Air Force that more than 40,000 men flew the Atlantic in this fleet with the loss of only a fractional number of aircraft. The former great adventure of the Atlantic flight has today become almost a routine journey.

Seven heavy bombardment groups of the 8th A.F. have been allocated for service on the continent of Europe. These have 72 aircraft each. Some fighter Groups were already on the Continent in July, but others were still in the U.K. Fighter Groups have 85 aircraft each. Altogether 4,802 U.S. aircraft had been redeployed from the U.K., France and Italy to the Pacific by July 22, 1945.

In China, Lieut.-General Stratemeyer has taken over the 14th Air Force from General Claire Chennault. General Stratemeyer was previously in command of the air forces in Burma. Now that air and land routes from Burma into China are both wide open after the defeat of the Japanese by the forces under Lord Louis Mountbatten, the U.S.A.A.F. in China is being heavily reinforced. This is possible because the earlier handicap of very limited supplies has been lifted, and a larger number of aircraft can therefore be made fully operational.

The strengthening of Kunming, the U.S.A.A.F. main base in China, with additional material, indicates that powerful bombing operations are not far off. These should be capable of aiding an Allied landing on the China coast or of smashing the Japanese war factories in Manchuria, according to the strategic requirements. It is significant that General Chennault stated recently that Japanese air strength in Manchuria and Korea has been substantially reinforced, and it is to be expected that there will be stubborn ground and air fighting in these areas before the Japanese are defeated. This may also be a pointer to Japanese fear of Soviet pressure; for if the Soviet were to enter the war against Japan, the Japanese would of necessity have to attempt to gain control of the Russian Maritime Provinces or face the bleak prospect of bomber aircraft being based there for action against the Japanese main islands, already so heavily bombarded from the other side.

That R.A.F. heavy bombers will soon join the American heavy bombers in the assault against Japan is indicated by a series of conferences in Guam attended by Air Marshal Sir Hugh Lloyd, who gained his knighthood for his command of the air defences of Malta. The subject of his talks in Guam was the Pacific deployment of British heavy bombers.

Strafing the Ancestral Homeland at Will Against Feeble Opposition

July 1945 will be remembered by the Japanese as the month of increasing air attacks on the ancestral homeland. Not only did the Super-Fortress bombers maintain their devastating raids on the cities, but American and British fleets with aircraft carriers cruised up and down the east coast of Honshu, and bombed, machine-gunned, cannon-gunned and rocket-attacked at will, while the ships shelled targets with their bigger guns. From early on July 9 until late in the evening of the same day aircraft carriers of the U.S. Third Fleet assaulted the Tokyo area with more than 1,000 aircraft.

Within this zone lie operational, training and experimental airfields. Avenger, Corsair, Hellcat and Helldiver aircraft strafed the Kanto Plain against feeble opposition; 342 Japanese aircraft were destroyed or damaged and only 10 American aircraft were lost. At times 700 American aircraft were simultaneously over Tokyo. Later that week the same Fleet again appeared off Japan, this time farther north. Targets in Northern Honshu and Hokkaido were bombed and shelled, including the towns of Kamaishi and Muroran.

Meanwhile, on the night of July 9, 550 Super-Fortresses bombed five large Japanese towns (Sendai 190 miles north of Tokyo, Gufu, Sakai, Wakayama and Yokaichi) with 3,500 tons of H.E. and incendiary bombs. On July 12 another 3,000 tons fell on the munitions-making centres of Ichinomiya, Kawasaki, Tsuruga and Uwajima. On July 17 between 450 and 500 Super-Fortress bombers, making the first attack under General Spaatz' command, dropped 2,500 tons on Oita, Hiratsuka, Kuwana and Numazu 50 miles south-west of Tokyo. Early on July 20 more than 600 Super-Fortresses flying in the biggest formation seen over Japan to that date, dropped 3,500 tons on Hitachi, Chosi, Okazaki, and Fukui, all situated around Tokyo at distances varying from 50 to 200 miles. At midnight on July 22 between 75 and 100 Super-Forts stoked up the Ube Coal Liquefaction Co.'s synthetic oil plant with 500 tons of bombs.

Throughout the second half of July, American and British fleets cruised off the eastern shores of Honshu. Aircraft from their carriers bombed and shot up targets around Tokyo almost at will, while the ships steamed under the shore guns of Tokyo Bay, shelling radar and other shore installations.

After a fortnight's action, Admiral Halsey's Third Fleet claimed the destruction of 596 Japanese aircraft and 791 vessels. What is happening off Japan is exactly what has happened off every South Pacific island prior to invasion. But in the case of Nippon it may be expected to take longer than in the case of the "outpost" islands. On July 24, after a respite of six days, more than 1,000 carrier-aircraft of the Third Fleet attacked the Kure naval base area. They began to attack from dawn. At noon 600 Super-Fortresses dropped bombs weighing from 500 to 4,000 lb., by radar instruments through cloud, on five targets in the Nagoya area—the industrial areas of Kuwana and Tsu, the Aichi and Nakajima aircraft and the Toya bearing factories. Visual bombing was possible on the Sumitomo light metal plant and the Kawanishi aircraft factory at Osaka. British carrier-borne aircraft took part in these combined Navy and Army air operations.

On July 25 more than 100 Super-Forts dropped 450 tons on two oil refineries (one the biggest in Japan) and an oil storage installation, all at Kawasaki, 10 miles south of Tokyo. Lieut.-General Kenney, commanding the U.S. Far East Air Forces, stated that the Allied air forces will have 7,500 aircraft to use against Japan before any are redeployed from Europe.

BRUNEI AFTER ATTACK BY R.A.A.F. Beaufighters and Liberators which have given invaluable support both before and during landings in British North Borneo by Australian troops. The important town of Brunei ***(see map in page 131)*** **was captured by the Australian 9th Division on June 14, 1945, four days after landing.** *Photo, British Official*

Scourges of Germany Are Ready to Strike Japan

FLYING FORTRESSES PARKED WING-TO-WING at a replacement depot near Munich in the U.S.-occupied zone of Germany wait to go East. From Okinawa on July 22, Lt.-Gen. James H. Doolittle, of the U.S. A. 8th Air Force, declared that Super-Forts of his command would be attacking Japanese targets by August. Another American air chief in Europe, Lt.-Gen. Nathan Twining (formerly of the U.S. A. 15th Air Force), was on July 24 appointed to command the 20th Air Force of Marianas-based Super-Forts. *Photo, Associated Press*

Editor's Postscript

THE announcement that the Air Ministry have granted to ex-officers of the W.A.A.F. permission to retain their service ranks in civilian life must have posed a question in the minds of many of my readers. After the First Great War "Captains" were two-a-penny. One met them, alas ! in all sorts of queer trades, eking out precarious livings on a frayed reputation and dressed, many of them, in even more frayed attire. (J. B. Priestley immortalized the type in his early play, Cornelius.) This time, with so many of our young soldiers achieving the rank of major at twenty-one or twenty-two, they will more likely be four-a-penny. It is rather early to make a definite assertion, but I am prepared to wager that few of our young ex-officers under and including the rank of colonel will care to retain their ranks on settling down into private life. It is not as if (like the Germans) we were a military race and made soldiering a lifelong profession. We are content to take war—and warmongers—in our stride, and get on with our jobs as civilians as soon as the fighting is done with. The Air Ministry is on a perfectly safe wicket with the W.A.A.F. How many of our young women would willingly go through life with the handle "Section Officer" or (worse) "Assistant Section Officer" prefixed to their names ? Even "Squadron Officer" is a mouthful—especially if you happen to have a lisp !

LONDON'S many bridges have been more remarkable for the historic associations of their predecessors than for themselves, I found myself reflecting as I strolled along the Embankment on a recent fine day. But no sooner had I begun to probe the generalization when a shaft of sunlight cut across London River, revealing in all its elegance of masonry and cambering Sir Giles Scott's new Waterloo Bridge. At that moment, as if to point the argument, I was stopped by a young U.S. officer, complete with the inevitable camera. "Can you tell me the name of that bridge ?" he inquired, pointing to somewhere between Somerset House and the Savoy. I told him—the new Waterloo Bridge, I explained, which for five weary and (sometimes) despairing years of war Londoners had gone on building in the hopes of a better world to come, in assurance of ultimate victory over the powers of darkness. It was only after he had gone his way that I began to realize the full truth of the words I had spoken. For if ever there was a symbol of London's undimmed faith in her future it is Waterloo Bridge. What other city in the world would have expressed her confidence in herself so boldly, so unmistakably and at a time when her very existence seemed no more than a matter of weeks ? I am afraid I am unrepentant when it comes to comparing the new bridge with the old : unrepentantly a modernist, I mean. Rennie's famous structure had a certain early 19th century grace which many professed to admire, often, I have thought, in excess of its real qualities. Apart from its weakening structure it was utterly unable to cope with modern traffic and would have been only a means of bottle-necking the Aldwych round-about which our London-planners have long had in mind for easing congestion in the Strand and giving ampler access to Waterloo Station and the south side of the river.

A MODERN author with the familiar-sounding name of Richard Jefferies—though not, need I say, the author of Bevis or Wild Life in a Southern County—has just produced a highly stimulating book about Wood in which he makes the most vigorous plea I have yet read for the development of our home-grown resources (Entitled The Wood from the Trees, it is published by the Pilot Press at nine-and-sixpence). Forestry enthusiasts have always seemed to me somewhat cranky individuals, I must confess—grinders of axes which they would die rather than use. For that reason Mr. Jefferies' matter-of-fact outlook is all the more welcome. He is content to leave us chewing over such facts as that there are at least 2,000,000 acres in this country which could be afforestated ; that Europe has still to import part of her timber from North America, even with the vast production of the U.S.S.R. ; and that, with the exception of a few Crown forests, there was no such thing as State Forestry in this country before the First Great War. As Mr. Jefferies is careful to point out, forestry is a slow-yielding form of investment which often takes as long as eighty or a hundred years to produce a return of capital ; which explains a lot. Two of his facts, new to me, will probably come as a surprise to most readers. Much as I have respected the inventive genius of the ancient Egyptians, I had not credited them with the manufacture of plywood over 4,000 years ago. Nor do I recall having read that Britain's first Forestry Commission was appointed in 1786 to secure the planting of sufficient oak-trees for increasing the Royal Navy—which they did to the extent of 100,000 acres.

A FRIEND in Eire sends me an unusually interesting copy of Letter from America, latest and last of the propaganda news-sheets issued and distributed free in the "distressful country" for the past three years by the American authorities in Dublin. As a parting shot it is most effective, for it contains a detailed account (with photographs) of the German plans to invade Eire, unearthed in Brussels and heavily marked "Geheim" ("Secret"). The Nazis—as we frequently found to our cost—did things thoroughly, and here is one of them. Most thorough, as might be imagined, were their analyses of Irish communications, maps of which indicated almost the veriest cart-tracks through the most desolate districts. I doubt, however, whether Mr. de Valera's more ardent supporters, who are always boasting of their country's mineral and industrial resources, while doing little or nothing to develop them, will find much to their liking in the Nazi survey. They must have been considerably dismayed, for instance, at the reflection : "Relatively little material can be expected in Ireland except building-stone and turf." One striking fact which may or may not console An Taoiseach (as "Dev" is known officially) is that the Nazis do not seem to have counted on native Irish support for their proposed invasion. Not quite so thorough—I am assured—was the Irish-German glossary compiled for use by invading units of the Wehrmacht. Some of these synonyma produced broad smiles on the even broader faces of the Gaelic speakers when retailed in the Irish capital recently. We may comfort ourselves with the thought that in Ireland few things are so destructive to a "cause" as ironical laughter.

Rt. Hon. CLEMENT R. ATTLEE, C.H., P.C., M.P., as Leader of the Labour Party was invited by The King to form a new Government on July 26, 1945, after the defeat of Mr. Churchill's Coalition. Sixty-two years of age, educated at Haileybury and Oxford, he served in the Army throughout the First Great War, and has been Labour member for Limehouse since 1922. See also facing page. *Photo, Topical*

COMMON current complaint is against the tameness of the B.B.C. news-bulletins and the newspapers in general. Certainly, the popular "National" dailies—surfeited on a five-years daily diet of screamer-headlines—have been hard put to it to sustain their readers' interest in the backwaters of European "peace." Only the General Election and reports (various) of ex-Corporal Hitler's suicide and/or immolation seem to have sustained the news-editors, though even in the latter instance public interest would appear to have drooped somewhat. Last time, as far as I recall the events immediately following the Armistice, things were different ; even if they were not very different the "popular" newspapers' problem was considerably eased by the fact that they had not yet gone all-American in the matter of headlines and tabloid lay-out, were not (as Oscar Wilde remarked of Hall Caine) writing at the top of their voice. Today the only papers not finding themselves a trifle hoarse (so to say) are the more reserved, like The Times, The Glasgow Herald and The Manchester Guardian, and The Daily Telegraph, which during the war indulged in banner-headlines only with the highest of high spots.

GLITTERING plans for a complete overhaul of Britain's rolling-stock have recently appeared in the Press, with details of buffet-cars and observation-coaches in the American style. To which I can only say "Amen," for if ever anyone deserved a little luxury it is the British railway traveller who, after five years of war, had reached a state of numbness beggaring adequate description. I have, however, one reservation to make. It concerns the proposed abolition of the photographs which have long adorned our railway compartments—slightly faded pictures of watering-places, panoramas of the British countryside, aerial (and other) views of our great cities. Doubtless these offend the aesthetics of modern interior decorators, but let them be warned. These pictures, originally intended as part of the decorative scheme as well, of course, as publicity for the holiday-resorts depicted, have long since assumed a deeper significance in the minds of travellers—especially those of an earlier generation. To us they bring back thoughts of a happy past, of holidays almost forgotten—a sort of family-album nostalgia delightful to indulge in when our eyes have wearied of the newspapers, books and magazines we had planned to read *en voyage*. Who knows what memories have been recalled to elderly travellers by a railway-coach picture of the promenade at Rhyl, the beach at Grange-over-Sands, or even a distant prospect of Middlesbrough ?

In Britain Now: How the Great Count Went

ELECTION CANDIDATES and their agents with returning officers' staffs sworn to secrecy had a preview of the great count. Purpose of the check-up was to ensure that no soldier, sailor or airman overseas had voted twice. Mr. T. Hall, assistant to the Returning Officer at Holborn Town Hall, sealed a Forces ballot box after checking (1). Counting votes at St. Pancras, London, on July 26, 1945 (2). Mr. Churchill was elected Conservative M.P. for Woodford, Essex (a new constituency), in a straight fight with Mr. A. Hancock, who polled 10,488 votes to Mr. Churchill's 27,688 : Mr. T. Binks, the Town Clerk, held up the board carrying the figures (3) on the steps of the Woodford Borough Council offices. **See also facing page, and page 223.**

NEW GOVERNMENT CHOSEN

STATE of the Parties after the polling on July 5, 1945, and subsequently, was as follows : Two results remained to be announced. Labour registered a large majority over all other parties.

Conservative	200
National	2
Liberal National	13
Liberal	1

The foregoing represented the Nation's vote for the Government : total, 216.

Labour	393
Liberal	11
I.L.P.	3
Communist	2
Irish Nationalist	2
Common Wealth	1
Independent	8

Total for the Opposition, 420.

Gains and losses, as declared on July 26, were : Labour, 215 gains, 4 losses ; Conservative, 7 gains, 183 losses ; Liberals, 3 gains, 11 losses. Thirty-two members of the Caretaker Government lost their seats. Of the Labour M.P.s 119 were trade unionists, half of them under 40, and 126 had come straight from the Services. Total of votes (which, all told, represented more than 75 per cent of the electorate) registered for Mr. Churchill's Government (July 26) was 10,075,283 ; against, 14,874,951.

BELGIAN GIRL, one of the first 250 who volunteered for domestic work in British hospitals, and recently arrived in this country, is issued with her British Identity Card before being posted. On her right is an Interpreter.

HOUSE OF COMMONS CHAMBER (right), destroyed by German bombs, is to be restored in its old style, with improvements in lighting and accommodation. Clearance of thousands of tons of rubble is a preliminary.

Photos, Planet, Fox, Topical

Polling Day in the Shadow of the Pyramids

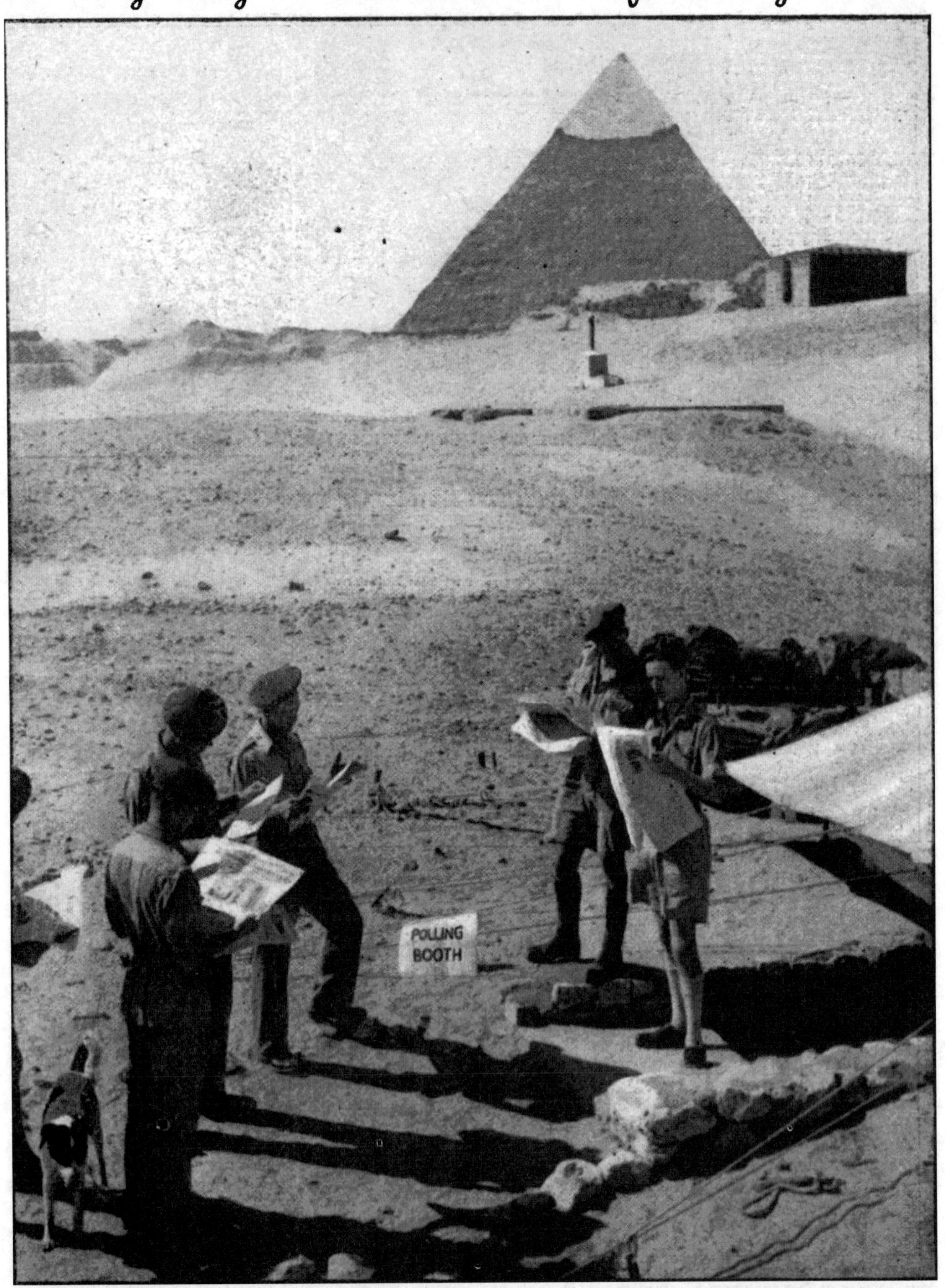

SERVING IN THE MIDDLE EAST, men of a Royal Signals unit recorded their votes in the General Election, in July 1945, in this historic setting : their polling booth a tent. To every front line and rear base unit where British Forces are stationed ballot papers were flown by the R.A.F. Though many polling booths were of necessity improvised, arrangements for secrecy of voting received special attention. Further unconventional touches included the use, at some booths, of German ammunition containers as ballot boxes. See also pages 195, 221, 223, 255. *Photo, British Official*

Printed in England and published every alternate Friday by the Proprietors, THE AMALGAMATED PRESS, LTD., The Fleetway House, Farringdon Street, London. E.C.4. Registered for transmission by Canadian Magazine Post. Sole Agents for Australia and New Zealand: Messrs. Gordon & Gotch, Ltd.; and for South Africa: Central News Agency, Ltd.—August 17, 1945. S.S. *Editorial Offices:* JOHN CARPENTER HOUSE, WHITEFRIARS, LONDON, E.C.4.

Vol 9 **The War Illustrated** Nº 214

SIXPENCE — Edited by Sir John Hammerton — AUGUST 31, 1945.

SYMBOL OF CHINA'S RESURGENCE is this sentry at Kunming, capital of the Chinese border province of Yunnan, where the Burma Road from Lashio joins the highway to Chungking. Following the building of the Ledo Road and the re-opening of the Burma Road, the first convoy reached Kunming on February 1, 1945. Since then the famous roadway has streamed with supplies for Generalissimo Chiang Kai-shek's armies, reported on August 19, five days after Japan's surrender, to have entered Canton, chief commercial city (after Hong Kong) of southern China. *Photo, Pictorial Press*

Russia Smashes In to End the War With Japan

SOVIET Russia declared war on Japan on August 8, 1945, when Mr. Molotov, Russian Foreign Commissar, informed Mr. Sato, the Japanese Ambassador to Moscow, that the declaration would come into operation the following day. Mr. Molotov's words were terse. Indicating that after the rout and capitulation of Hitlerite Germany Japan remained "the only great Power insisting on the continuation of the war," he declared that since the Nippon Government had refused the Allies' unconditional surrender terms issued from Potsdam on July 26 (see page 264), the U.S.S.R. had accepted the Allied proposal that they (the Soviets) should declare war on Japan. "The Soviet Government," said Mr. Molotov, "considers that such a policy on its part is the only means capable of bringing peace nearer, freeing the people from further sacrifices and sufferings, and giving the Japanese people the opportunity to avoid those dangers and destructions which have been suffered by Germany after her refusal to capitulate unconditionally." Japan's fate was sealed.

NOATAKE SATO, Japanese Ambassador to Moscow, to whom Mr. Molotov handed the U.S.S.R.'s declaration of war. *Photo, Associated Press*

THUS ended the uneasy truce between Russia and Japan as set forth in the Soviet-Japanese Pact of April 1941 and denounced by the Russians in April 1945 when Mr. Molotov stated that Japan had been helping Germany and was, moreover, at war with Russia's British and U.S. Allies. In his declaration of war, Mr. Molotov revealed that the Japanese had sought Russian mediation in the middle of June this year—in the form of a personal message from the Emperor, the text of which was made known to the British and U.S. leaders at Potsdam.

THE Russians lost no time in executing their declaration. On the evening of August 9—exactly 24 hours after Mr. Molotov had seen the Japanese Ambassador in Moscow—Generalissimo Stalin issued his first official communiqué on the progress of the war. It stated that the Manchurian frontier had been crossed in many places, the River Amur forced, and several places, including the important railway town of Manchuli, captured; advances up to 14 miles were being made on a front of over 1,000 miles. Three days later was announced the Soviets' capture of the Korean port of Rashin. It was then reported from Moscow that the enemy had already lost Northern Manchuria from a strategic point of view and in many areas was completely disorganized.

IN a broadcast from Tokyo on August 10—four days after the fall of the first atomic bomb (see page 278)—the Japanese Government announced their readiness to accept the Allied ultimatum of July 26 on the understanding that it did not "prejudice the prerogatives of the Emperor." Next day the Big Four (Britain, the U.S., Russia and China) replied with the demand that the Emperor's authority to rule Japan should be subject to an Allied Supreme Commander, while the Emperor would be required to authorize the surrender terms needed to carry out the Potsdam ultimatum. On August 14 the Japanese finally surrendered.

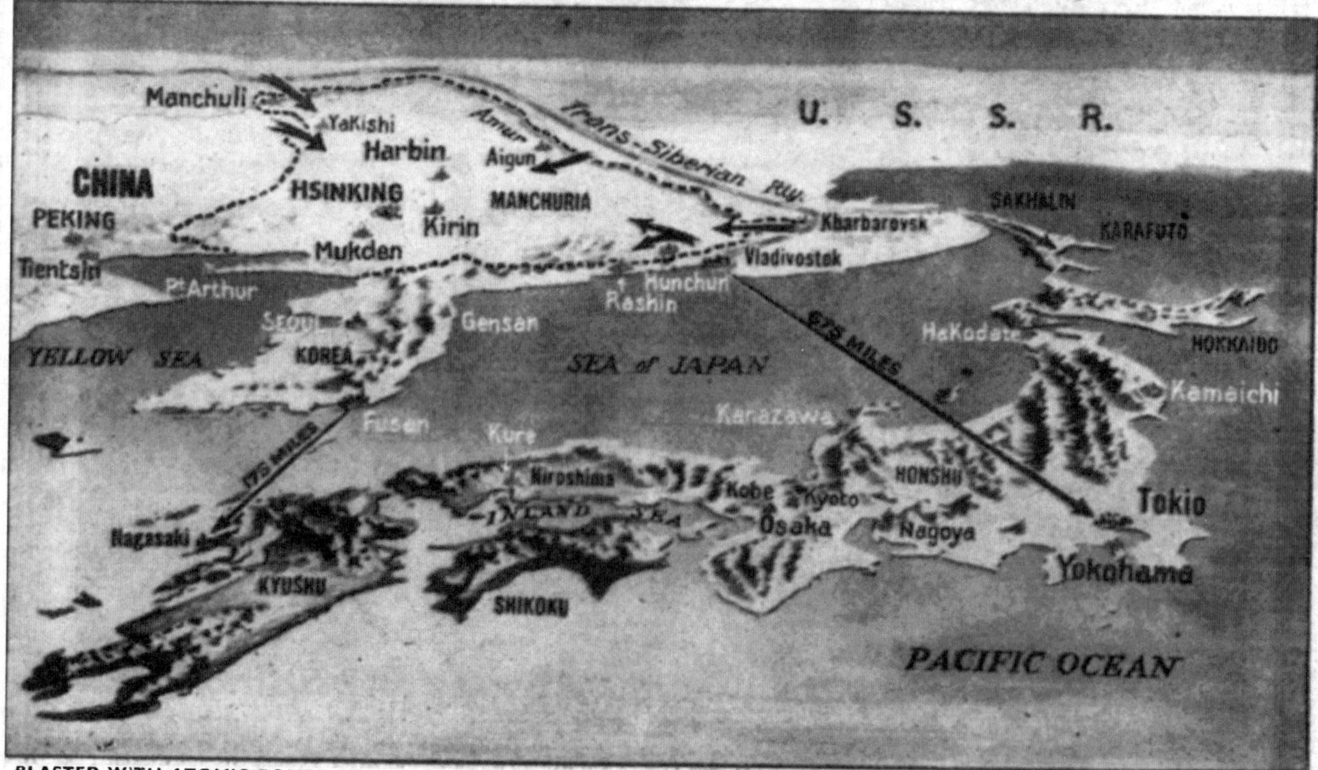

BLASTED WITH ATOMIC BOMBS, held in powerful pincers gripped by the Soviets to the west and British and U.S. air and naval units to the south, the Japanese homeland (top) was faced with certain destruction when Russia declared war. As the perspective drawing (bottom) shows, only 675 air miles separate the Russian port of Vladivostok from the Japanese capital; while Japan's inland sea lay at the mercy of the Allied fleets. Black arrows indicate direction of Soviet thrusts.

Maps by courtesy of The Daily Express and The News Chronicle

Lt.-Gen. Sir Alan **CUNNINGHAM** *(November 16, 1941).*

Maj.-Gen. Neil M. **RITCHIE** *(November 26, 1941).*

General Sir Claude **AUCHINLECK** *(June 25, 1942).*

Lt.-Gen. Bernard **MONTGOMERY** *(August 13, 1942).*

Lt.-Gen. Sir Oliver **LEESE** *(December 30, 1943).*

Lt.-Gen. Sir Richard **McCREERY** *(November 3, 1944).*

With Our Armies Today

By MAJ.-GENERAL SIR CHARLES GWYNN K.C.B., D.S.O.

As was most right and proper the passing of the 8th Army did not escape general notice, in spite of the fact that the great achievements of the 2nd and 14th Armies had for a considerable time occupied a more conspicuous place in the limelight. While it would be invidious to compare the remarkable accomplishments of any of our armies, it is, however, fair to say that the 8th Army for the first time made the general public realize that an army could possess an individuality and develop an esprit de corps that deserved recognition.

That the 8th Army acquired those qualities to an unprecedented extent was probably due partly to the strange nature of the terrain in which it initially operated, and partly also to the fact that it was for a long period fighting as an independent force and was the sole Empire army in active employment at the time against the Axis. Its individuality was therefore a natural growth, though undoubtedly it was fostered by Field-Marshal Montgomery when he took command and deliberately invited public interest. His methods did not escape criticism, but it is now admitted even by the most critical that they produced valuable results, not only in his own army but by exciting a spirit of emulation in others.

OUR Special Debt of Gratitude to Wavell's Army of the Nile

The record of the 8th Army's achievements is too well known to need recapitulation, but I should like to draw attention to the special debt of gratitude we owe to it and to Wavell's Army of the Nile which began the good work. Incidentally, I prefer to look on the latter army as the child which grew up to be the 8th Army rather than as its parent, which is the relationship assigned to it in the brochure on the 8th Army's independent campaign issued by the Ministry of Information. Some troops fought in both armies, and the experience they gained of desert fighting and of the terrain in Cyrenaica in the earlier campaign was of immense value in later operations. Moreover, there was an obvious continuity in the development of the war in Libya. The primary task allotted to both armies was the defence of Alexandria and the Suez Canal—the core of our position in the Middle East—and in both cases offensive defence was adopted with success in spite of temporary reverses : one on a disastrous scale.

THE special debt we owe to the Army of the Nile is that despite appalling weakness in numbers and equipment it not only saved Egypt, but so completely and swiftly destroyed Graziani's Army that German intervention came too late to effect more than a partial restoration of the situation. The Italians were rushed off their feet and their morale shattered beyond recovery by a bold and brilliant offensive. The feeling of relief and encouragement inspired by Wavell's victories at a time when it was sorely needed should never be forgotten, and it should be realized that the ulcer had been started which, as it spread, cost the Axis a limb and materially weakened the whole frame of the monster. Wavell had neither the men nor transport required for the exploitation of success beyond Cyrenaica, and, weakened by the diversion of troops to Greece, withdrawal to the frontier was inevitable when Rommel took the offensive. But Tobruk stood blocking his lines of communication and the defence had not broken down.

When the 8th Army was formed on November 16, 1941, the defence of Egypt remained to be carried out by an offensive intended to remove finally the threat of Rommel's Afrika Korps. A substantial victory was gained after heavy fighting, and Tobruk was relieved. But although reinforced and re-equipped the Army was not yet strong enough to achieve its object decisively. Rommel again emerged from El Agheila and recovered much ground. For a time the opponents stood facing each other at El Gazala, each steadily preparing to resume the offensive.

8th ARMY FLASH

ROMMEL struck first, and after a swaying battle his weight of metal told. The disaster that resulted was the more serious because of the desperate situation on the Russian front ; but Auchinleck's exhausted and depleted army, aided by reinforcements, notably the magnificent New Zealand Division, rallied after its long retreat to cover Alexandria, and this time it was Rommel who was not strong enough to attain his main object. The 8th Army, in spite of the undeniable defeat it had suffered, staved off disaster on a scale which might have affected the final issue of the War.

Time was thus gained and reinforcements poured in, though at the expense of our forces in the Far East. America parted with some of her newest tanks to ensure that the disparity in weight of armament should be eliminated. By the time Rommel was ready to start again the 8th Army, though not yet prepared for offensive battle, had been re-organized under its new commanders, and was able to defeat him in a skilful defensive battle, which proved to be the decisive turning point. With his communications suffering from air and submarine attacks, Rommel had not fully recovered from defeat before the storm broke upon him at Alamein. Deserting his despised Italian allies and making full use of the mobility afforded by mechanical vehicles, he retreated precipitately and did not pause till he again took refuge at El Agheila. The safety of Egypt in a few days had been finally ensured, but at El Agheila the pursuit had also to pause till the port of Benghazi could be cleared sufficiently to relieve the strain on the 8th Army's long line of communication.

WHEN Rommel's Great Reputation For Invincibility Was Smashed

Before he could again be attacked in strength, when his open desert flank was threatened, Rommel resumed his retreat, using every delaying artifice. Pursuit was slowed down by this and by the ever-increasing problems of maintaining supplies, but it was maintained with a vigour which gave the enemy no chance of rallying to hold Tripoli. Tripoli was occupied, the Italians losing their last possession in Africa, and Rommel continued his retreat to join forces with General von Arnim in Tunisia.

Strictly speaking, the 8th Army's career as an independent force closed with the occupation of Tripoli ; for there it became part of Alexander's 18th Army Group. But in practice it continued to act independently until by notable victories it had driven Rommel's armies out of the formidable Mareth and Akarit positions and left them no alternative but to fall back on Von Arnim's stronghold in northern Tunisia. It is true that Rommel himself, a sick man, did not command in these battles, but by that time the bogy of his world-wide reputation for invincibility had been well and truly laid ; and that of the 8th Army and its commander had been equally well established.

For a short time the 8th Army had a hot competitor in the 1st Army, and credit may well be divided between them for the crowning victory which liquidated Rommel's and Von Arnim's combined armies. After that victory the 1st Army was dispersed before it had received the public recognition its great achievements deserved ; but the 8th Army went on to gather fresh laurels in Sicily and Italy, ending its career by being largely instrumental in bringing about the first German mass surrender in April, 1945.

IN these later campaigns the fighting was of a very different character and was often more severe and entailed even greater hardships than in the desert. Moreover, there were many changes in the Army's composition—valued divisions were transferred from it, and it absorbed elements of many nationalities. At times it was split up to take part in operations conducted by the American 5th Army, but whether operating united or divided its Army esprit de corps and individuality were never lost. Its great deeds stand on record. It had saved Egypt and played a major part in knocking out Italy and opening the Mediterranean, and not the least of its services was the development of co-operation with Air Arm and Royal Navy to a standard which was to serve as a model

'Stand Easy' at a Jungle Naval Air Station

BREAK-FOR-MUSIC at a British East Indies Fleet Air Station was made memorable to an enthusiastic audience of maintenance ratings—with a Seafire in the background—by radio singer Miss Paula Green (1). Other side of the picture of life "out there" is presented by the arrival of a wounded Jap (3) at a portable surgical hospital during our advance on Pinwe. Burmese sappers, working continuously for three days, hauled into position sections of a 174-ft. Bailey Bridge (2) across the Pegu Canal (see also illus page 271).

Photos, British Official

Union Jack Waves Beside the Flag of Austria

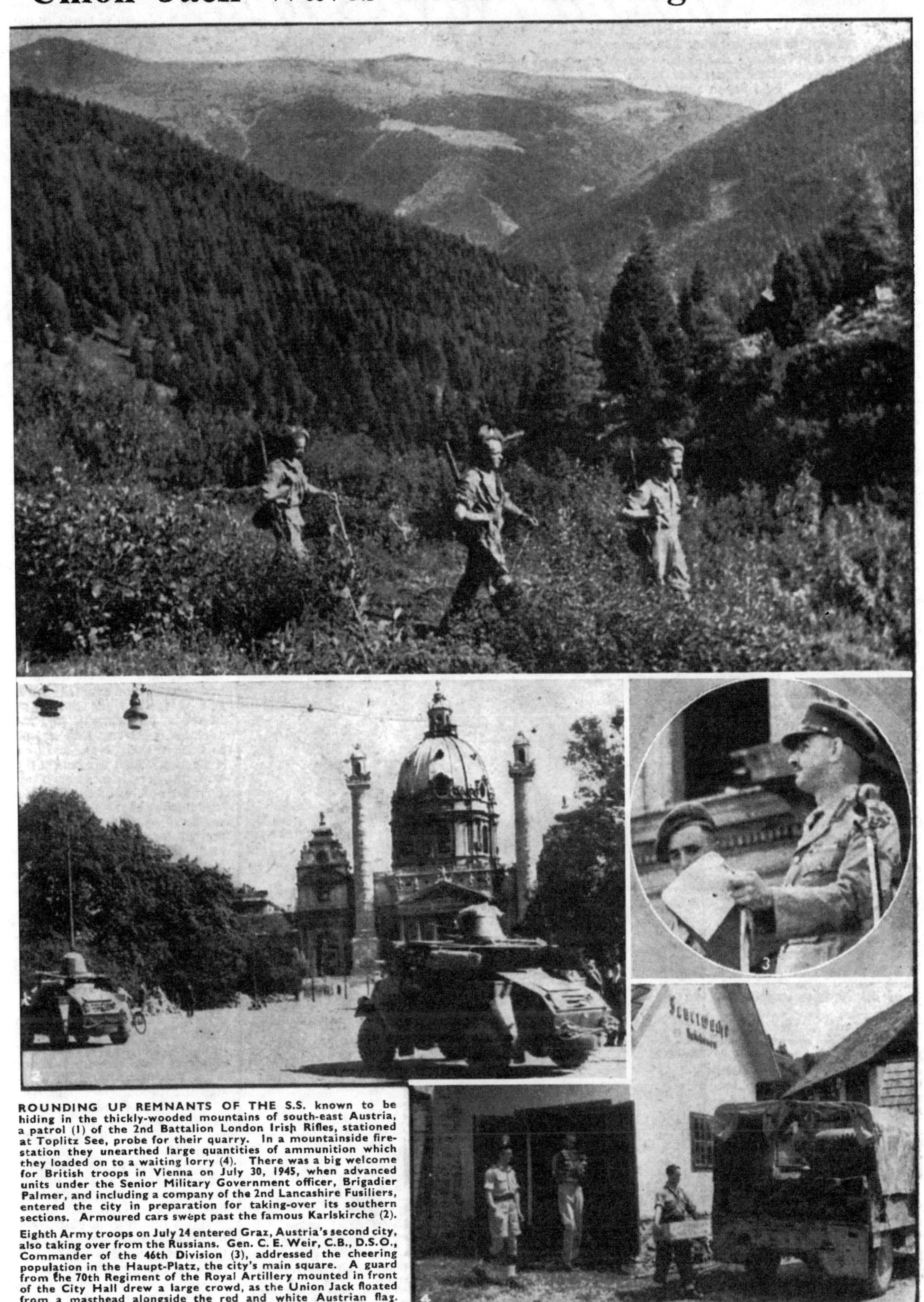

ROUNDING UP REMNANTS OF THE S.S. known to be hiding in the thickly-wooded mountains of south-east Austria, a patrol (1) of the 2nd Battalion London Irish Rifles, stationed at Toplitz See, probe for their quarry. In a mountainside fire-station they unearthed large quantities of ammunition which they loaded on to a waiting lorry (4). There was a big welcome for British troops in Vienna on July 30, 1945, when advanced units under the Senior Military Government officer, Brigadier Palmer, and including a company of the 2nd Lancashire Fusiliers, entered the city in preparation for taking-over its southern sections. Armoured cars swept past the famous Karlskirche (2).

Eighth Army troops on July 24 entered Graz, Austria's second city, also taking over from the Russians. Gen. C. E. Weir, C.B., D.S.O., Commander of the 46th Division (3), addressed the cheering population in the Haupt-Platz, the city's main square. A guard from the 70th Regiment of the Royal Artillery mounted in front of the City Hall drew a large crowd, as the Union Jack floated from a masthead alongside the red and white Austrian flag.

Photos, British Official

With Our Navies Today

By

FRANCIS E. McMURTRIE

Now that Japan has faced surrender, it is useful to survey the course of the war in the Far East. One of the most fortunate things in its incidence is that Germany and Japan never tried to synchronize their operations to an appreciable extent. Had Japan entered the conflict in 1940, when this country was in great difficulties owing to the defection of France and the simultaneous declaration of war by Italy, the situation would have been grave indeed. Nor was the United States then fully prepared, so recovery from such a disaster as Pearl Harbour would have been far more protracted.

In fact, Japan made her move too late. Moreover, her naval strategy in the Pacific was halting to a degree; which suggests that the Naval Staff in Tokyo never had a free hand. In all probability the theory that the Army had absolute control in this respect is a sound one. The long delay between the delivery of the initial blow at Pearl Harbour and the start of the combined naval and military expedition against Hawaii, which came to utter grief in the Battle of Midway, six months later, is inexplicable on any other grounds, however one regards it.

The Japanese fleet was frittered away in a series of more or less disconnected thrusts in the South-West Pacific; when at last the whole available force was assembled in a final effort in the Philippines in October 1944, the arrangements for concentration of the three fleets concerned were so faulty that each was defeated in turn, without being able to give support to the others. This miscarriage seems to bear the marks of Army inspiration, for the lessons of naval history, with which Japanese admirals profess to be well acquainted, contain ample warning against such grotesque folly.

Owing to shortage of suitable fast merchant vessels, the Japanese were forced to employ their destroyers as troop transports, a proceeding that resulted in heavy losses. Consequently in their later operations they were seriously distressed through lack of enough destroyers to provide a screen for their battleships and aircraft carriers, and to carry out the many other duties for which destroyers have become indispensable. There was an almost total neglect to make any effective use of the numerous submarines which the Japanese Navy possesses. These again were employed extensively for transporting reinforcements, supplies and ammunition to garrisons in Pacific islands which were otherwise completely cut off from succour.

This is not to belittle the magnificent recovery made by the United States Navy after the staggering shock of the Pearl Harbour onslaught, nor the brilliant strategy by which Fleet Admiral Nimitz wore down his adversaries until they were left to flounder helplessly, ignorant of where the next blow was likely to fall.

It will be interesting to see whether there are many Japanese ships of importance surviving when the formal surrender of all fighting material is made. Probably there are four or five battleships, all more or less disabled; two or three large aircraft carriers, with others building; a similar number of cruisers and a handful of destroyers, with a miscellaneous collection of coast defence ships, training vessels and small craft of all kinds. Most of these are likely to be found in the naval ports of Yokosuka, Kure and Sasebo, though some may be at Shanghai or Hongkong.

Possibility of Russian Claim to a Percentage of Jap Ships

It may be assumed that the Chinese will be able to take over some cruisers and destroyers to reconstitute their depleted fleet. The remnant of the Chinese Navy which was put out of action on the Lower Yangtse in 1937 and handed over to the quisling Government at Nankin by the Japanese, will also be restored to its rightful owners. Nor would it be surprising if the Soviet Government were to lay claim to a percentage of the Japanese vessels in compensation for the loss of the entire Russian Far Eastern fleet in the war of 1904-05. An ice-free naval base to supplement Vladivostok is another Russian ambition; it will be recalled that it was the occupation of Port Arthur for this purpose that led to the war with Japan 40 years ago. Other Soviet territorial claims that may be foreshadowed are the southern half of the island of Sakhalin and the chain of the Kurile Islands, stretching from the Kamchatka peninsula, eastern Siberia, to Hokkaido, which is Japan's northernmost island.

For a considerable time now the Allies will require to maintain a strong police force, comprising naval, military and air elements, in the Far East. Hundreds of thousands of Japanese will have to be evacuated from China, Manchuria and Korea, a process which may well take years to complete in view of the great destruction of enemy shipping which would otherwise have been available for the purpose. In any case, any merchant ships larger than coasting vessels will doubtless be taken away from Japan, so that, like Germany, she may be debarred from all ocean trade.

In pre-war days the British China Squadron was composed of a cruiser squadron, an aircraft carrier, a destroyer flotilla, a submarine flotilla and half-a-dozen sloops, together with a number of minelayers, minesweepers and gunboats of which the majority were stationed at the ports of Hongkong and Singapore. Presumably some such force will again assume responsibility of protecting British interests in the Far East when Japan has complied with the surrender requirements. It is abundantly clear that the Americans are determined to stand no nonsense about surrender. Admiral Halsey showed his hand in this connexion when on VJ day he signalled all ships: "It looks like the war is over, but if any enemy planes appear, shoot them down—in a friendly fashion."

From the illustration in the facing page it is possible to form some idea of the heavy damage sustained by H.M.S. Argonaut, a cruiser of about 5,500 tons, when she was hit by a salvo of torpedoes from a U-boat in the early part of 1943. It must have required extremely skilful seamanship to navigate her across the Atlantic with her bow and stern blown off. It is said that when she put in at Bermuda, on her way to Philadelphia, observers were unable to believe their eyes, and for some time failed to identify the ship in her truncated state. That her bulkheads should have held against the strain must be a source of pride to her builders, the Birkenhead firm of Cammell, Laird & Co. Ltd.

Though exceptional, such hazardous passages as that of the Argonaut are not unprecedented. Both in this war and the last there have been several cases of ships having their bows blown away, and reaching port without foundering. In one famous example, in 1916, H.M. destroyer Nubian lost her bow, and her sister ship Zulu her stern. The two halves were recovered and united, the single destroyer that remained being given the name of Zubian to signalize the fact. (See page 714, Vol. 8.) Quite recently a similar case occurred in the United States Navy. The destroyer escorts Holder and Menges were both damaged to the extent of requiring about 50 per cent of the structure of each to be renewed in dockyard. As in the case of the British destroyers mentioned above, the two portions were joined together, but the ship that survives in service is known as the Menges, as more of that vessel than of her consort is included in the union.

UNITS OF ADMIRAL HALSEY'S 3rd U.S. FLEET, off the Japanese coast on July 11, 1945 (top), steamed to within almost rifle range of their target and fired 16-in. and 18-in. shells. An observation plane stands ready on the deck of U.S.S. Massachusetts (bottom) as two other U.S. warships string out behind, one firing a broadside. *Photos, Sport & General*

Naval Operation Gave Argonaut New Lease of Life

EXTRACTION OF A GIGANTIC 'TOOTH' from H.M.S. Argonaut : one of the after gun-turrets being lifted out complete with turntable and the trunk leading down to the magazine. In 1943 the cruiser had bow and stern, including rudder and two propellers, blown away by torpedoes from a U-boat. Her bulkheads stood the strain—great tribute to the soundness of her construction by Cammell, Laird & Co., and skilfully she was navigated across the Atlantic, steered by the two remaining propellers. Of her total 'ength of 512 ft., 59 ft. at bow and 123 ft. at stern were replaced by the U.S. Navy Yard, Philadelphia. See also facing page.

Photo, U.S. Navy Official

Thoughts on the Peace of Potsdam

The Berlin Conference of 1945 will long be remembered as one of the red letter events in world history ; its importance outweighs that of the once celebrated Congress of Berlin (1878) as greatly as the mighty forces of this World War have surpassed the military and naval resources of what by comparison was a local affair. Our well-known contributor, HENRY BAERLEIN, who writes this article on the Conference, is a recognized authority on European politics, with intimate knowledge of the Balkans and Central European countries. See also facing page.

THE first thing that is obvious about the decisions arrived at by the Big Three at Potsdam is that they contain the beginnings of a constructive programme, instead of limiting themselves, as was done for the most part at previous conferences of these Great Powers, to a programme of destruction. Not that the destruction, root and branch, of Nazism is now neglected ; far from it. But for the first time the world is now given a positive vision of the Germany which is to emerge and survive, with freedom of political parties—certain democratic ones are indicated—and of trade unions, freedom of assembly and public discussion, freedom of Press and religion, with the re-creation, from the bottom, of freely elected authorities.

These various decisions are welcomed whole-heartedly and the Germans, apart from an irreconcilable minority, will themselves be glad enough to enjoy what the Nazi system utterly denied them. Democratic institutions have never had much of a chance in Germany. But the Germans are an intelligent people, and the plight in which their adherence to the Fuehrer principle has landed them may induce the majority to be very willing to give democracy a trial.

The Germans will recognize that the sanctions taken against them are inevitable ; they will not sulk on account of them. Thus the Potsdam decisions as regards Germany are to be applauded. Likewise the replacement of the European Advisory Commission by the Council of five Foreign Ministers with a permanent secretariat in London is admirably adapted to simplify the task of creating machinery for carrying on the work of reconstruction in our sorely tried Continent. It is a great thing that a common policy towards Germany has at last been clearly proclaimed.

IT will be noted that Britain and the United States have refrained from any official statement regarding the proposed frontiers of Poland in the west. This caution is not by any means due to a lack of generosity and a tenderness for Germany, but we and the Americans have wished to be assured that so wide an acquisition of territory as is envisaged will in fact increase Poland's strength and security. It is true that her birth-rate is higher than that of most other countries, but how will she be able to populate such extensive areas of East Prussia, Pomerania, Brandenburg and Silesia ?

Of course, Poland's own previous lands have suffered vastly from the German invasion, and if they are left, as it were, fallow for a time in order to recover, then many of the people there would be able to seek other pastures, particularly if the Government will not merely allocate so many acres to a worthy citizen but will provide the necessary assistance for him to get the land into productivity.

Most people will admit that the decision to have the new Polish western frontier on the Oder-Niesse line is excellent—for the reason that the winding, pre-war frontier with Germany will thus be shortened to about 200 miles, while the frontier with Czechoslovakia, which is linked to Poland as a member of the eastern security pact, will be lengthened. Another advantage of the new frontier for Poland is that the industrial gains will give her economy a greater balance ; hitherto she has been mainly agricultural, despite the fact that around Lodz and in upper Silesia she had a flourishing industry. The Poles are an adaptable people, and it must be the hope of all of us that they will make as much of a success of the new territories they will occupy as they did between the two wars of the port of Gdynia, which they wonderfully created out of a fishing village. It is all to the good, by the way, that the Allied Press is to enjoy full freedom to report upon developments in Poland before and after the prospective election.

France and the Potsdam Decisions

The whole future of Eastern Europe is alluded to in a somewhat vague fashion, while nothing is said of Turkey, the Straits or the Middle East. The claims of France to the west bank of the Rhine and in the Ruhr are passed over in silence—which certainly does not imply that the claims are allowed. As for the various matters on which nothing is said, one may fear that no agreement was reached between the Big Three. If that be so, then the Foreign Ministers may be able to tackle the job ; and in the meantime it will be advisable to leave these topics in abeyance.

That her claims have not, as yet, been granted is one reason for the discontent felt in France with the Potsdam decisions. She was bitterly resentful at not being invited to take part in the proceedings herself, and it is possible to sympathize with her present frame of mind, one that causes General de Gaulle to provide her with more circuses than bread. It seems to have been settled that Russia is to have 56 per cent of all goods and services taken out of Germany ; Britain and the United States each having 22 per cent. But Russia has undertaken to satisfy, or at any rate endow, Poland from her share ; and Britain and America will probably not be niggardly in the claims of other Allies.

One Government wholly enraged against the Potsdam declarations is that of General Franco, for "they feel bound," say the Big Three, "to make it clear that they would not favour any application for membership of the United Nations' Organization put forward by the present Spanish Government, which having been founded with the support of the Axis Powers does not, in view of its origins, its nature, its record and its close association with the aggressor States, possess the qualifications necessary to justify such membership." Here, indeed, is plain speech.

THIS condemnation, says General Franco, is arbitrary and unjust ; he ascribes it to the false atmosphere created by the libellous campaigns of exiled Reds and their accomplices abroad. Spain, he says, will continue at home and abroad to collaborate in the work of peace in which, by remaining neutral in two great wars, she made such a signal contribution. But the Spanish people are wondering if action of some sort will be taken against their country unless Franco yields to the storm of the Big Three. If their attitude causes him to hand over power to a Provisional Republican Government, which would at once hold elections, we would have further reason to applaud the work of the Big Three at Potsdam.

THE WORLD OF TOMORROW—BY THE BIG THREE

AT the conclusion of the Potsdam Conference (see illus. page 235) on August 2, 1945, the Big Three's decisions on the future of Germany and on European problems in general were made known to the world in a document of over 6,000 words. Imposing on the Reich rules which are stern and drastic but which allow the Germans eventually to take their place among the free peoples of the world, the momentous declaration included the following :

GERMANY.—Allied Control Council in Berlin to retain supreme authority. The Reich to be completely disarmed and demilitarized. All German war industries eliminated or controlled. No German central Government will be allowed to function for some time. Political parties permitted, but the electoral system will be developed only gradually. A beginning to be made with local elections.

REPARATIONS.—Claims of the United Kingdom, the United States and other Allies (except the U.S.S.R.) to be met by industrial removals from Germany's western zones. Russian and Polish claims will be met mainly from the Soviet zone of occupation. All removals to be completed within two years.

FRONTIER CHANGES.—Soviet claims to Königsberg and the northern triangle of East Prussia received the support of Britain and the U.S. Poland to assume administration of the rest of East Prussia besides all German territory to the east of the Oder-Neisse line. (See p. 265.)

LONDON COUNCIL.—A Five-Power Council of Foreign Ministers to be set up with headquarters in London. France and China invited to join. While London will be the permanent seat of the joint secretariat which the Council will form, meetings may be held by common consent in other Allied capitals as may be agreed upon from time to time.

TREATIES.—Peace treaties to be drawn up by the Five-Power Council will include those with Italy and ex-satellite countries in eastern Europe—as it is made possible.

WORLD ORGANIZATION.—Governments neutral during the War may join the United Nations organization—with the exception of the Franco régime in Spain.

★ ★ ★ ★

ON July 26 an ultimatum to Japan for the unconditional surrender of all her armed forces was issued from Potsdam in the names of President Truman, Mr. Churchill, and Generalissimo Chiang Kai-shek. Leaving the Japanese with "prompt and utter destruction" as the only alternative to unconditional surrender, the ultimatum was contained in 13 stinging paragraphs, admitting of no equivocation. "The following are our terms," it began. "We will not deviate from them. There are no alternatives. We shall brook no delay." Among the conditions insisted upon were complete Japanese disarmament ; the break-up of all armament industries ; the elimination "for all time" of the influence of "those who have deceived and misled the people of Japan into embarking on world conquest" ; the limiting of Japanese sovereignty to the islands of Honshu, Hokkaido, Kyushu, Shikoku "and such minor islands as we determine."

ANNOUNCING Soviet Russia's declaration of war on Japan on August 8, M. Molotov revealed that after Japan's refusal to surrender, the Allies submitted to the U.S.S.R. Government a proposal to join against Japanese aggression "and thus shorten the duration of the war, reduce the number of victims and facilitate speedy restoration of universal peace." Japanese acceptance of the Potsdam proposals (see page 258) was not finally transmitted to the Allies until late on August 14, when at midnight the British Prime Minister announced the end of the War.

They Laid the Foundations of the New Europe

THE BIG THREE AND THEIR FOREIGN MINISTERS in the gardens of the luxurious Cecilienhof Palace, Potsdam, one-time seat of Germany's ex-Crown Prince, as the momentous Conference neared its end. Front row (left to right) Mr. C. R. Attlee, President Truman, Generalissimo Stalin; behind (left to right) Admiral Leahy, U.S.N., Chief of Staff to the President, Mr. Ernest Bevin, Mr. James Byrnes, U.S. Secretary of State; and M Molotov. The Conference, which opened on July 17, 1945, held its final session on August 2. See facing page, also page 235. *Photo, Associated Press*

PROVISIONAL BOUNDARIES OF THE NEW POLAND as agreed at the Berlin Conference. Poland now secures part of Pomerania, including the great port of Stettin, Upper and Lower Silesia, besides part of East Prussia. The Western Ukraine and Western White Russia go back to the Soviet Union. The Russians also take part of East Prussia, including the important industrial centre of Königsberg, capital of the province, which had a pre-war population of almost half a million. *By courtesy of The Observer*

Potato Queues and the Black Market in Berlin

DO YOU WISH TO LEAVE YOUR BONES IN BERLIN?
IF SO, DRINK UNTREATED BERLIN WATER.
SEWER RATS CAN, DESERT RATS CANNOT!
БЕРЛИН ЦЕНТР

ONCE-LUXURIOUS ADLON HOTEL, bomb-damaged, is serving meals again—though the only room available is a bedroom, the bathroom is a pantry, a tiny hall the cloak-room. Dining at the Adlon, this girl (1) examines her coupons, without which food is unobtainable in Berlin restaurants. Potato shortage is keenly felt in the capital: British Army lorries, each loaded with 8 tons, arrive with German-grown supplies at the suburban station of Spandau (2). In the suburb of Zehlendorf, loads were dumped on the pavement (3) to be weighed and sold against coupons; the ration works out at approximately 8 lbs. per person.

Linking hands, young Berlin policemen round up vendors of suspected "Black Market" goods, for an identity check in the gardens of the blitzed Reichstag (4); 20 cigarettes are reported to fetch as much as £2:10:0 in Berlin's "Petticoat Lane," where British and U.S. soldiers are forbidden to trade. A British Army warning (5) explains itself. See also story in page 281. *Photos, Keystone, Planet News, The Daily Mirror*

Our King and U.S. President Meet for First Time

FROM THE BATTLE CRUISER H.M.S. RENOWN officers and ratings watched the U.S. cruiser Augusta (top, background) sail down Plymouth Sound on August 2, 1945, as she carried President Truman and his staff back to the United States after the Potsdam Conference. Earlier in the day the President lunched aboard the Renown as guest of H.M. the King, with whom he is seen (bottom), pacing the quarter-deck. It was their first meeting. The King later paid a return visit to the President on board the Augusta.

Photos, G.P.U.

Now It Can Be Told!

HOW ROYAL MARINES HACKED A BASE FROM JUNGLE

THE dramatic story of another secret war port was revealed by the Admiralty in July 1945. It is the story of "Port T"—a naval base with full defences—hacked out of the jungle on Addu Atoll, a collection of waterless coral islets in the Indian Ocean, 590 nautical miles from Colombo and 3,000 from Australia.

Like the Mulberry (see page 710, Vol. 8), Pluto (page 120) and Fido (page 140), "Port T" was always known by its code name. Absolute secrecy was essential, for this port was a vital link on the convoy route to Australia and for certain operations in the Indian Ocean. Now it is possible to tell how a force of Royal Marines drawn from the first Mobile Naval Base Defence Organization, working against time and tropical disease, began preparing this secret Fleet anchorage while the Japs were still planning their attack on Pearl Harbour.

The Royal Marines went ashore on Addu Atoll in September 1941. Their task was to establish coastal batteries, searchlights, signal towers, roads, camps and jetties for a naval base. The price they paid was heavy; 23 per cent of the whole force had to be evacuated in the first three months by the hospital ship Vita, as too ill to be of further service, but by the time Japan declared war the base was ready, and on January 3, 1942, the first convoy of five troopships, escorted by the cruiser H.M.S. Emerald, put in to water and refuel.

THE atoll, in the extreme south of the Maldive Islands, consisted of a rough triangle of coral islets, surrounded by a coral reef which enclosed a deep lagoon. On four of the islands—Gan, Hitadu, Midu, and Wiringili—coastal batteries and searchlights were required while Gan was developed as the main base. When the First Royal Marine Coast Regiment and the Landing and Maintenance Company of the M.N.B.D.O., under the command of Lieut.-Colonel W. B. F. Lukis (now Major-General Lukis, C.B.E.), first reached Addu Atoll they were faced with virgin jungle without roads, landing places, or the most primitive amenities. The great swells of the Indian Ocean broke in a perpetual surf on the coral reef; tall palms towered above the islands.

But the disadvantages of this apparent island paradise soon made themselves felt. The climate was hot and very damp. Flies, mosquitoes and rats were plentiful. Practically every drop of water had to be shipped to the atoll and landed across the beach. Supplies were seldom sufficient to allow for washing.

Ate the Skin From the Flesh

The Royal Marines soon found that every small scratch immediately turned septic and developed into an ulcer that refused to yield to treatment. The humid climate favoured the growth of micro-organisms that literally ate the skin from the flesh, while the diet of dry or tinned food with no green vegetables or fresh fruit reduced a man's natural resistance to such infections.

Soon a form of scrub typhus, born of the rats and their parasites, broke out. While working, a man would suddenly fall unconscious without having previously complained of sickness. A violent fever followed for fourteen days, leaving the victim weak and debilitated. Malaria also appeared in malignant form, but never became a serious menace owing to the stringent anti-malarial precautions. The rapid deterioration of tinned food caused the Quartermaster great anxiety and gave rise to occasional food poisoning.

ADDU ATOLL, group of coral islets in the Indian Ocean, 590 miles from Colombo and 3,000 from Australia, site of a secret Naval base.

But work was pushed on with relentless speed. First, landing-places had to be improved by blasting away the coral, then sites cleared in the jungle for camps. Roadways to take heavy guns and equipment had to be cut through the scrub to the battery sites before the work of gun-mounting could begin. The natives, though friendly, were timid and easily amused. For instance, they roared with laughter at the sight of the lorries landed to transport the guns. They were willing to help but could do little but aid in stripping vegetation from the sites.

SECRETS OF "PORT T" became known with the disclosure (in this page) that on disease-ridden and waterless islets of the Maldives in 1942 Royal Marines completed a base with full defences. The barrel of one of the big coastal guns being installed (right), and, later, a camouflaged gun-position (above).

Photos, British Official

The programme required the guns to be mounted in six weeks, and in six weeks to the day the batteries fired their proof rounds—but not before the Devon and Kent batteries of the R.M. Coast Regiment working on Hitadu and Midu had been reduced by sickness to less than 50 men apiece.

On Hitadu, the four-mile roadway from landing-place to battery site had to be laid across a swamp infested by giant land crabs. The major in command stripped and led his men thigh-deep into the black, foul-smelling mud to lay foundations with palm fronds lashed into bundles of ten. The running surface destined to carry 13-ton wheeled loads was made with prefabricated track and crushed coral held together with the trunks of palm trees staked down. Another road on Midu was entirely built by a corporal and six Marines continuously at work for two months. They used cord as the hard core, with a top dressing of earth and sand.

The islands were swept at regular intervals by torrential storms that washed away the road surfaces and flooded clearings and gun-sites. Unloading ships could only take place at certain stages of the tide, so that it had to continue day and night, with men working two six-hour shifts in twenty-four.

Yet by December 8, when news of Japan's entry into the war reached the islands, the anchorage was already in a state of defence ; only camouflaging, administrative installations and the completion of the war signal station remained to be done.

To improve communications a tubular bridge was built between the islands of Midu and Hera, and on Wiringili a channel was cut between the sea and a mosquito-breeding lake, so that the brackish water became tidal and the mosquito larvae were killed. Later still the islands were linked by causeways. When later in the year the Marines of the landing-party returned to Addu Atoll with a company of Royal Marine Engineers to build an aerodrome, they witnessed the most stirring sight in the history of the islands—they saw the Queen Mary herself, carrying home Australian troops from the Middle East, steam into the anchorage that they had built.

NEW LIGHTWEIGHT RIFLE, the No. 5, for S.E.A.C. troops, has an 8-in. bayonet (1) with cutting edge on both sides of blade. The rifle (2) weighs 7 lb. and serves a dual purpose—hurling grenades 250 yards. The grenade (in firing position, 3) weighs 1 lb. $4\frac{1}{2}$ oz. and penetrates 4 ins. of armour.

Photos by courtesy of Soldier Magazine

GOEBBELS TRIED TO MAKE PEACE TERMS

As the Nazi Reich lay in its death agonies, Goebbels offered to play Judas to his master, Adolf Hitler, and take over the leadership of a reorganized German Government which would conclude an armistice with the Soviet Union. This was revealed to me here tonight (Berlin, July 23, 1945) by Lt.-Gen. Peter Kosenko, Chief of Artillery in the late Col.-Gen. Nikolai Berzarin's Fifth Russian Striking Army, which played the lion's part in storming Berlin. It is the first time that any Allied correspondents have been given a complete picture of the savage battle for Hitler's capital by senior Russian officers who themselves took part in the fighting.

At midnight on April 30, with fighting for Berlin at its fiercest, a small group of Nazi officers under a flag of truce presented themselves to the Soviet H.Q. in the southern part of the local Gestapo H.Q. in Friedrichstrasse. Their senior officer said he came from General of Artillery Weidling, Commander-in-Chief of all German forces in Berlin, who had authorized him to ask for an armistice between the Russian Government and a German Government under the leadership of Dr. Goebbels.

No mention was made of what would become of Hitler, but the inference was that he had already left Berlin, was dead, or would be handed over to the Russians, alive or dead, if they agreed to this suggestion. In this connexion it is interesting to recall that Goebbels was always reckoned as the leader of the "Eastern" wing of the Nazi party, which favoured reconciliation with Russia and switching all Germany's resources against the Western Allies.

The answer of the Soviet High Command was immediate and uncompromising: "Unconditional surrender—or else . . ." The Germans returned to their lines and all that night and the next day the battle raged. During the night of May 1, Hitler's Chancellery was finally stormed after bloody hand-to-hand fighting, and with the first light of May 2, General Weidling broadcast an order to all German troops in the Berlin area to lay down their arms.

The battle for the city divides itself into two phases: the encirclement of Berlin, which took five days, and converging attacks into the centre of the city from the south, north-west and east. All organized resistance was ended by May 2, but mopping up of small groups of desperados and franc-tireurs who held out in various parts of the city, especially the suburb of Spandau, lasted until May 10.

The Germans had prepared the city thoroughly and cleverly for defence. They had two S.S. tank divisions, two Volkssturm divisions and the remnants of S.S. and Wehrmacht units withdrawn from the Oder front. These were concentrated inside the Berlin trap and they were prepared to defend each house until it fell in ruins.

Population Cowered Underground

The Russians therefore organized their forces in special small "storm groups" for street fighting, each supported with tanks and artillery both light and heavy. According to General Kosenko, everything at that time was so mixed up that some of their light artillery was firing from the outer suburbs of Berlin while heavy guns were in action over open sights. Tanks were used wherever possible, but it was predominantly an infantry and artillery battle.

During most of the battle the civilian population remained cowering underground, dying in hundreds beneath the falling ruins of their houses. Many of them, however, emerged in the Russian rear and began sniping with rifles and bazookas. These were shot out of hand by special Soviet units detailed to deal with this nuisance.

Berlin seemed to be on fire everywhere, General Kosenko said. Smoke was so thick that visibility was sometimes less than 50 yards. German corpses were piled in streets that were almost impassable mazes of debris and fallen masonry. Big explosions rocked the city and sent columns of fire forking skywards as Russian aircraft and artillery exploded ammunition dumps which the Nazis had piled in the city's centre. It was here, at the crossing of the River Spree, and during the attack on the Chancellery and Air Ministry buildings in Unter den Linden that the struggle was fiercest.

This fighting was described by Maj.-Gen. Vladimir Antonov, the man who defended and saved Grozni's Caucasian oilfields from the Germans in 1942. The battle for the Chancellery began on April 27 after the River Spree was crossed, he said. This extremely difficult operation was carried out on rafts in face of murderous German fire at close range.

The Chancellery area itself was especially well held exclusively by S.S. men armed with tanks, self-propelled guns and a new sub-machine-gun the Germans were trying out for the first time. The defenders collapsed at the last and surrendered en masse.

General Kosenko said there was no evidence whatever to prove conclusively that Hitler was in the Chancellery during the battle. He was certainly not there when Gen. Antonov's troops came in. Aircraft had been seen taking off from Charlottenburger Chaussee during the last days, but nobody could identify the type or say who were the passengers. The riddle of Hitler's fate remained unsolved.—*Ossian Goulding, condensed from The Daily Telegraph.*

EIGHT MEN TO GUARD THE KING

When this country faced invasion, after the withdrawal of the B.E.F. from France by way of Dunkirk, in 1940, prompt and serious consideration had to be given to the safety of Their Majesties and the two Princesses. How they were protected remained a secret until June 7, 1945.

A special bodyguard was formed of eight officers of the Brigade of Guards. To these fell the duty of safeguarding the Royal Family in the event of mass invasion. The chosen eight were known as the Coates Mission—after James Coates, commanding officer of the holding battalion of the Coldstream Guards—and one of their number was posthumously awarded the V.C. on the day that the secret of the Coates Mission was made public. He was Lieut. I. O. Liddell (see page 216). He had remained with the Mission until danger of invasion had passed, going back then to his regiment and taking part in the fighting in Normandy within a fortnight of D-Day. Seventeen days after the action which won him the V.C. a German sniper's bullet laid him low. He died without knowing that the greatest military award this country can bestow was his.

San Francisco Background to World-Wide Peace

At San Francisco on April 25, 1945, delegates from fifty Allied Nations undertook the task of agreeing on a framework within which the sovereign states could resolve differences without war. How this was achieved, and the Charter signed on June 26, is described for "The War Illustrated" by PETER HUME, who was present at the Conference. **See also illus. pages 52 and 272-273.**

THE heterogeneous war-swollen population of San Francisco is itself compounded of as many racial elements as were represented at the Conference, and the arrival in their midst of Ministers and senior representatives of the old countries from which they or their fathers had come stirred in San Franciscans many old bonds, half-forgotten in the melting pot of Americanism which in two or three generations had bred in their city a microcosm of the international harmony to be plotted by the Conference for all the world. Thus, though flags were tragically at half-mast for the President whose vision of a world at peace had brought the Conference into being, San Francisco stretched its traditional hospitality to the utmost for the thousands of delegates, experts and staffs of forty-six nations who at the end of April made their way by special trains and planes across America or the Pacific.

Might be "World's Last Chance"

At their first session they heard speeches from the delegation heads of the four convening nations—the great Powers which were playing the major part in bearing the burden of the war. These speakers, the Foreign Ministers of Britain, China, Russia and the United States, joined in stressing the magnitude and urgency of the task confronting the Conference. Theirs might be, as the then British Foreign Secretary, Mr. Eden, put it, "The world's last chance" of avoiding "another world conflict which this time must bring utter destruction of civilization in its train." The great Powers' Foreign Ministers were followed at a series of Plenary sessions by the heads of the smaller countries' delegations, who devoted their opening speeches to expressing their nations' attitude to the general problems before the Conference and in particular to the Dumbarton Oaks proposals, in whose drafting they had had no share and which many of them sought to modify in the preparation of the final Charter.

Thorniest of the early problems was the question of admission to the Conference of Argentina, whose Government had only very belatedly fulfilled the Yalta qualifications for membership of the United Nations. Perhaps nettled by the Conference's refusal to admit the Provisional Government of Poland pending its modification as proposed at Yalta, Russia strongly opposed the admission of Argentina, and after being outvoted in the Steering Committee (composed of all delegation heads), M. Molotov brought the issue before a plenary session by proposing that a decision be delayed. Again he was outvoted, though the predominantly anti-Soviet tone of local American opinion swung generally in the Russian favour.

SUCH clashes, combined with the increasingly unspectacular nature of the real work of the Conference following the panoply of the formal opening, awoke a slightly disappointed San Francisco to the fact that this was not, as the city had vaguely expected, a sort of super American-style convention dominated by brass bands and splendid oratory. Instead it was a serious and difficult attempt to solve by discussion a number of the most delicate problems of vital importance to the world's peace. As the Conference entered its second stage—the actual drafting of an agreed Charter by privately-meeting Commissions and their dependent committees—it receded almost into the background of the city's normal wartime life.

With this change of attitude there came also, as the Committees continued to meet through May, a certain impatience and even pessimism about the apparent failure of the Charter to take recognizable shape, and about the constant checks which held up work at first thought completed. As each clause of the Charter worked its way up the necessary chain of approval, from the original drafting committee to the Steering Committee for final presentation to the full Conference, such checks inevitably appeared —often from unexpected quarters.

MEANTIME the Nazis had gone down to their final defeat, victory pointing the urgency of the Conference's work and at the same time forcing several of the leading delegates to return to their countries to deal with the pressing problems which followed victory. Among those departing were Mr. Eden and M. Molotov, whose absence (especially in the latter case) tended to slow up the unravelling of the difficulties previously referred to. Particularly on the question of the Great Powers' right of veto of action by the organization's Security Council on disputes laid before it, the remaining Soviet delegation proved unable without reference to Moscow to agree with other delegations on the interpretation of the decision taken at Yalta. Since this question of the right of any one Great Power to block action by the world organization was obviously central to the whole construction of the organization and its Charter, this delay held up the otherwise almost completed work of the Conference.

Tattered Banners, Tired Officials

Nevertheless, after days of anxious waiting, agreement was reached between the sponsoring Powers, and a proposal laid before the Conference which, in the words of the American Secretary of State, "preserves the principle of unanimity of the five permanent members of the Council (Britain, China, France, Russia and the United States), while at the same time assuring freedom of hearing and discussion in the Council before action is taken."

The spotlight came back to San Francisco as President Truman flew across from Washington to witness on behalf of the United States the signing of the United Nations Charter. That was on June 26, and next day it was left for San Francisco and the world to ask what remained besides tattered banners and tired officials; what had the world gained which would not be taken away with the loaned typewriters from the delegates' hotels? The San Francisco Conference had not done—and had not set out to do—anything territorially specific. While its deliberations were inevitably coloured by the movements of armies across the map, its concern was with the demarcation lines of international behaviour rather than of international boundaries.

AND in this vital sphere, 50 nations, comprising more than four-fifths of all people on earth (White Russia, the Ukraine and newly-liberated Denmark as well as Argentina had joined the nations represented at the start of the Conference) had agreed over a wide range of subjects to work together rather than in a spirit of sovereign irresponsibility. In brief summary, this is how in nine weeks at San Francisco "the world's last chance" was taken.

First, the Charter establishes an international organization "based on the principle of the sovereign equality of all its members," who are (at least provisionally) those nations taking part in the Conference. These members pledge themselves to settle international disputes by peaceful means and not to threaten or use force against any other State, as well as to give the organization every assistance in any action it may take against States (whether or not they be members) who are ruled to be acting contrarily to these principles.

Kernel of the New Organization

The world organization will have—apart from its secretariat—five principal organs with functions clearly defined in the Charter. A General Assembly of all member States will discuss any subject within the scope of the Charter, including general questions of international co-operation and specific questions brought before it by any member or by the Security Council. This Council, described by the Times newspaper as "the kernel of the new organization," will consist of five permanent members representing Britain, China, France, Russia and the United States, and of representatives of six other nations chosen by the General Assembly for periods of two years each. While the Assembly will, except in special circumstances, meet only annually, the Council will "be so organized as to be able to function continuously." It is designed, in fact, as the executive committee of the organization with delegated power to take any action against threatened or actual aggression, including armed action in which use might be made of forces drawn from member States. In such cases, any State providing forces will be invited to participate in the Security Council's deliberations. An International Court of Justice (fifteen members of different nationalities) will assume the international legal authority of the old Hague Court, backed by the Security Council.

This machinery, though, by the provisions of the Charter will only be set in motion when seven members of the Security Council, including all the permanent members, vote in favour. Only in the case that one of these members was party to a dispute would this rule be waived and the member concerned abstain from voting. Otherwise Britain, China, France, Russia or the United States could individually check the working of the machinery. Just as the Assembly (providing the general base for all the organization's functions) and the Security Council are in effect strengthened developments of the old League of Nations Assembly and Council, so the other three organs set up by the San Francisco Charter serve as more virile, wider-embracing versions of the specialized sections of the League brought into tune with the new spirit that has succeeded the Second Great War.

THUS in two long documents of 171 Articles, every word of which had to be hammered out over the Conference table, the victors of the Second Great War laid down at San Francisco a framework which they could feel sure was ready to receive and hold the flesh of understanding and the breath of continuing good will in order that war might vanish. At the final session Lord Halifax, of Britain, was in the Chair, and when he called for a vote on the adoption of the Charter he asked the delegation heads to register their approval by standing in their places, because "this issue upon which we are about to vote is as important as any we shall ever vote on in our lifetime." Fifty men stood, representing fifteen hundred million seekers after peace.

Photos, British Official

Monsoon and Mud Were the Japs' Allies in Burma

Torrential rains fell, sometimes for ten hours without a break, churning the country to mud. Yet on August 1, 1945, S.E.A.C. was able to announce the closing stages in the attempt by remnants of the Japanese Imperial 28th Army to break out from the Pegu Yomas; more than 10,000 were killed. Our men on patrol (1) in local craft across a flooded paddy field, and (2) close to the Pegu Canal. On their return, Cpl. R. Kemp, of London, washes mud from his clothes (3).

Fifty Allied Nations Signed the World Charter—

United Nations Conference on International Organization (UNCIO), which opened at San Francisco on April 25, 1945 (see illus. p. 52), held its final session on June 26, when President Truman (1, standing on dais) addressed the delegates. On that date the representatives of 50 Allied nations put their names to the Charter, which was ratified on July 28 by the U.S. Senate. The President examines the bulky Charter (2). The Earl of Halifax adds his signature (3).

eneral,

—To Ensure Durable and Just Peace for the Future

As the Conference neared its triumphant close, chairmen of the delegations stood (4) to record a unanimous vote of approval of the Charter. Among the signatures recorded (5) were those of the Russian delegation (left), the British (top right) and the U.S. (bottom right). " If we had had this Charter a few years ago," said President Truman, " millions now dead would be alive. If we should falter in the future in our will to use it millions now living will surely die."

Mortar Crew in Action at Balikpapan in Borneo

Photo, Australian Official

Important oil-centre on the south-east coast of Jap-occupied Borneo, Balikpapan was regained after the Australian 7th Division landed there on July 1, 1945. This mortar crew was supporting infantry attacking a feature near Vasey Highway—specially named by the 7th Division to commemorate its former leader, the late Maj.-Gen. George Vasey. Maj.-Gen. Milford, commanding the Division, told his men that their assault would remain an outstanding achievement of this War.

VIEWS & REVIEWS Of Vital War Books

by Hamilton Fyfe

By this time everyone knows the name of Admiral Chester Nimitz, and most of us are aware that he is Commander of all naval forces in the Pacific. But very few know more than that. The sketch of him that Duncan Norton-Taylor gives in his book, I Went to See For Myself (Heinemann, 7s. 6d.), is therefore very welcome. The admiral is described as "a sunburned, apple-cheeked man with cotton-white hair and sky-blue eyes, who looks like a Texas farmer." He was born and brought up in Texas ; he is said to be of German stock ; his family were hotel-keepers.

I should have guessed they came from Russia, for "Nyaymitz" is Russian for "German." However, his origin does not matter. He is American and has been American all his life, and he is one of the most famous Americans of the War. He had no advantages to start with. His first job was driving a butcher's cart. But as soon as he managed to enter the Navy he showed that he meant to rise high in the service. He studied naval problems deeply and came to the conclusion that the usefulness of the battleship was by no means over, as many have been thinking these last thirty or forty years. He is at the same time a strong believer in the great value of the submarine. He is not quite so sure about aircraft at sea.

He told newspaper men at his headquarters (Pearl Harbour of sinister memory) that it would be a long war and that it would be decided by the Navy. His staff took the view, which seems to be his own as well, that it was "problematical"—which meant in the highest degree unlikely—that Japan could be destroyed by the bombing of her homeland.

> The Navy's theory was Clausewitz's : to defeat the enemy you have to destroy his armed forces.

That has most certainly been carried out, so far as the Japanese Navy is concerned ; so perhaps Admiral Nimitz looked on with approval at the efforts being made to reduce Japanese cities to ruins and thus shatter the morale of the people and their leaders who brought this misery upon them. He will certainly not gloat over their distress, for he is "rated as a kindly man." He "has a look of stern preoccupation," but he is no martinet, "which a lot of other, older admirals are." He is fifty-eight : that is reckoned young, and he is inclined to "act young" in the matter of etiquette and costume. He receives the Press in his shirt-sleeves. "The four stars on his collar are the only mark that sets him apart from the rest of his khaki-clad officers."

Cockroach-Ridden Colonial Port

There is no doubt as to his capacity and driving-force. He was put in charge of Noumea, New Caledonia, when the Vichy French governor was driven out, and under his control the "threadbare cockroach-ridden colonial port, with broken-down utilities scarcely adequate for the needs of the slovenly little town" became a first-class military establishment.

> Ships from Australia, New Zealand, the United States hauled timber for dock-piles, strip steel for huts, pipes for plumbing, men and machinery to do the digging and erecting and assembling ; and overnight a town of thousands of men whose business was war was superimposed upon a town of a few thousand outnumbered, bewildered colonials. The construction units had to pioneer in the mountains before they could get to work building roads, reservoirs, fuel and ammunition dumps, warehouses, repair shops, barracks and hospitals.

New Caledonia is, or was, a French possession. The American naval officers there shook their heads when asked what would become of it after the War. But we appreciate their idea on the subject from the following passage :

> Certainly if we (that is, the United States) intend to dominate the Pacific we will have to occupy the island. Apart from its importance to us as a base, New Caledonia will be then, as it is now, a place to deny the enemy. Beyond its deep, now heavily-fortified harbour lie mountains filled with minerals, nickel and chromite, which are being shipped to American war plants ; cobalt and iron. But we have no title. France will probably want back her once-neglected stepchild.

That sounds as if this French island with a British name might be a source of trouble in the not far distant future. The French used it from 1863 to 1895 as a convict settlement. They have never managed to colonize it with free people. Noumea is a wretched place, even by Pacific standards, which are not high.

America's Citizen Navy at Work

The sailors have the best of it. They live in clean, wholesome ships and have plenty of any air that happens to be about, instead of sweating on shore in smelly surroundings (Noumea has open sewers in the streets). Life at sea is infinitely preferable, most of us would say, to life on a tropic island. But soldiers have their point of view about it also. A sergeant told the author, "Sure, it's a nice life on a ship if you don't get seasick and so on. But when the shooting starts I like to have a lot of ground under my feet in case I want to go somewheres else. The trouble with a ship, mister, is you can't get off it. You got to stay and take it. By and large, when there's a war on I prefer the infantry."

One can understand this when one reads Mr. Norton-Taylor's account of the battle at sea during which he crouched on the bridge of a United States cruiser. It was the first time he had been on a big ship in action. The discharge of the fifteen 6-in. guns knocked him sideways and all over the place.

> Sight and sound were merged into one physical concussion that sent me staggering backwards. I was shocked and terrified and angry. The platform seemed to rise under me. I wanted to yell a protest. Possibly I did . . . I put my fingers up under my helmet and pressed my ears. The cotton plugs were not enough . . . I had only one sensation : passionate longing for it to cease.

That passage reveals the author and the nature of his book. He is not hard-bitten, unemotional, like most war reporters—I was like that myself, I think. He is more interested in himself and his feelings than in the events around him. He is always analysing, sentimentalizing, imagining. So he isn't anything near a typical war reporter. But he certainly can write. I have read numberless accounts of torpedoes approaching ships, but never a more vivid one than this :

> It was a thick white finger coming straight at us like a chalk line drawn across a blackboard. On this disengaged side of the bridge there was only one other man at the moment—a signalman who screamed : "Torpedo Torpedo !" But even if anyone had heard him it was too late for the ship to dodge. My eyes were fixed on the advancing track. I thought that our speed might yet carry us clear of the converging white finger. I was fascinated and leaned out over the rail to watch, and saw the wake end abruptly and squarely against our side amidships.
>
> Men in the engine-room and in repair parties below decks and in sick bays and central stations and in the control room and in the magazines and handling-rooms under dogged-down hatches heard it bump and grate along the ship's bottom and thought their time had come. They told me afterwards that I should have thrown myself flat on the deck to escape flying fragments and the possibility of being flung overboard by the concussion. It was then, thinking back, that I felt a little sick, and thankful for some Jap's error of workmanship or calculation. The torpedo was a dud.

Admiral CHESTER NIMITZ, U.S.N., whose appointment as Allied Naval C.-in-C. Pacific was announced on April 5, 1945. An unconventional study of warfare in the Pacific is reviewed in this page. *Photo, U.S. Official*

Blind Target for Bursting Shells

But the enemy did not often fail in that period. Norton-Taylor tells how the surprise attack on the Australian flagship Canberra was made with disastrous results, off the Solomon Islands on August 8, 1942. It was a dark night, with a fine rain falling. Suddenly "the whole ship and the stiff, surprised men aboard her leapt into view, illuminated by a searchlight which fell full upon them. It was one of those occasions when men had to depend on reflexes set up by long rehearsals. . . . The enemy landed some of his first salvoes on the Canberra's bridge, wounding her captain and disrupting her controls. The Canberra was like a fighter hit in the face, momentarily blinded and paralysed. Before she could recover bursting shells had transformed her into a pyre. Flames lighted her, made her a target into which the enemy continued to pour projectiles." How the Japs escaped detection by the destroyers detailed to escort her has never been explained.

The author pays warm tribute to the fighting qualities of the men he saw in action, but they had little idea of what the war was about. They supposed that life in their country would be just the same as before when they returned, and they ached to return as soon as possible. "They had no great hatred for the enemy ; if they were embarked on a crusade they did not know it. They had no ideologies which they could put into words or which anyone had put into words for them. This was just a lousy business which had to be tended to." It was a tedious business, too. They were bored beyond belief and they sought distraction in gambling, which gave them "something for their money to do." There was almost nothing they could buy with it. They acquired the habit of playing poker whenever they had any spare time. The correspondents did not play much. They were too much occupied in trying to beat one another by securing "scoops."

Burma's Civilians Retread the Peacetime Paths

IN RANGOON, freed in early May 1945, life was slowly returning to normal by midsummer after the long Japanese occupation: a start was made in demolishing blast walls outside this dignified civic building (1). On June 20, in a British warship moored in the harbour, there opened an important conference between Sir Reginald Dorman-Smith (2, left), Governor of Burma, and Burmese leaders to discuss plans for the country's future as outlined in the White Paper published in May; on Sir Reginald's left sat Lt.-Gen. F. A. M. Browning, C.B., D.S.O., hero of Arnhem and Chief of Staff to Lord Louis Mountbatten at S.E.A.C. Hdqrs.

Urgent problem is the schooling of young Burmese whose education, totally neglected by the Japanese, has had to begin again. Intent pupils attended this class (3) in the open air. Lt.-Col. Steele Perkins, Chief Administrative Officer at Maymyo (4), interviewed a native mother and her children at a refugee camp. Labourers (5) carried baskets of rice from paddy fields of the Shwebo plain for the relief, via the country's many waterways, of the starving population.

 Photos, British Official

De Gaulle Sees the Ruins That Were Brest

FRANCE'S LEADER SAW FOR HIMSELF when he paid a brief visit to the great Breton shipping and shipbuilding centre of Brest on July 28, 1945, and inspected the war-devastated streets of the once-populous town, and the arsenal. Accompanied by Naval and Army officers, he was followed by enthusiastic crowds waving the Tricolor. With a peacetime population of almost 100,000, Brest capitulated to U.S. troops under Maj.-Gen. Middleton on September 19, 1944, when General Ramcke, commanding the German garrison, hoisted the white flag. *Photo, Planet News*

Atomic Bomb: World's Most Terrifying Weapon

"It is now for Japan to realize in the glare of the first atomic bomb which has smitten her," declared Mr. Churchill in a memorandum issued from 10, Downing St., on August 6, 1945, "what the consequences will be of an indefinite continuance . . . This revelation of the secrets of Nature, long mercifully withheld from man, should arouse the most solemn reflections in the mind and conscience of every human being capable of comprehension." See also story in page 280.

THREATENING Japan with annihilation, the atomic bomb is the most staggering invention of this war. The first one was dropped by an American Super-Fortress on Hiroshima, important Japanese Army base with over 300,000 inhabitants, on August 6, 1945. "That bomb," according to a statement by President Truman, issued from the White House, "had more power than 20,000 tons of T.N.T. It had more than 2,000 times the blast power of the British 'Grand Slam' (ten-tonner), the largest bomb yet used in the history of warfare." (See illus. p. 189.) This makes the effect of a single atomic bomb approximately equivalent to a raid by 2,000 Super-Fortresses.

"One of our major worries in Europe," said Gen. Carl Spaatz, commander of the Strategic Air Forces in the Pacific, "was the fear that the Germans had perfected some secret weapon comparable to this. The Germans were actually experimenting in this direction in a huge factory at Oranienburg (on the northern edge of Berlin), but we wiped out the factory in a big raid in the spring of this year." In answer to a question as to whether the new bomb would have speeded the end of the European War, he replied, "If we had had it, it might have shortened the war by six or eight months. We might not even have had a D-Day."

IT was Japan's fate to be the testing-ground of this amazing result of British and American research carried out at a cost of £500,000,000. Work was first done mainly in the Universities of Oxford, Cambridge, London (Imperial College), Liverpool and Birmingham. At the time of the formation of the Coalition Government in 1940, responsibility for co-ordinating the work and pressing it forward lay with the Ministry of Aircraft Production, advised by a Committee of leading scientists presided over by Sir George Thomson—and there was a full interchange of ideas between these scientists and their colleagues in the United States.

In late October 1941, President Roosevelt sent to Mr. Churchill a letter suggesting that any extended efforts on this important matter might usefully be co-ordinated or even jointly conducted. Accordingly all British and American efforts were combined and a number of the British scientists concerned proceeded to the U.S. Apart from these contacts, complete secrecy guarded all these activities and no single person was informed whose work was not indispensable.

By the summer of 1942, Great Britain being overbusy with war output, it was decided to build the requisite full-scale production plants in America. And Mr. Churchill has paid tribute to Canada's co-operation: "The Canadian Government provided both indispensable raw material for the project as a whole and also necessary facilities for the work on one section which has been carried out in Canada by the three Governments in partnership."

AS part of the great co-operative effort, Canada had undertaken (it was announced by Mr. C. D. Howe, Canadian Minister of Munitions, in August 1945) to build a pilot plant for the purpose of investigating one of the methods of making material which is required for the atomic bomb. Canada also supplies uranium, which is the raw material on which this new source of power at present depends.

One of the places where the atomic bomb was made is Oak Ridge, a "secret" city in Tennessee. Extraordinary measures were taken to seal off the workers from the outside world. About 125,000 laboured there but none spoke of it. To make security possible in the first place, every worker before he was taken on had his record closely inquired into and the same attention was given to the members of his family. If a single doubt arose, the seeker of employment at Oak Ridge was turned down.

Locality and factory cost £276,500,000 to build and equip. Today Oak Ridge's houses number 10,000, and dormitory beds total 13,000. For the 11,000 children nine schools are provided and amenities include a hospital. There were other areas similarly engaged, as revealed by President Truman:

"More than 125,000 people worked to construct atomic bomb factories in the U.S., and more than 65,000 are now engaged at two great operating plants and many lesser factories. Many have worked there for two and a half years. Few know what they have been producing. They see great quantities of materials going in and they see nothing coming out of these plants. For the physical size of the exploding charge is exceedingly small. The Potsdam ultimatum (he added) was issued to spare the Japanese people from utter destruction. Their leaders promptly rejected the ultimatum. We are now prepared to obliterate more rapidly and completely every productive enterprise the Japanese have above ground in any city."

Sir Charles DARWIN — Descendant of the Victorian biologist. Director of National Physical Laboratory. A member of the British Research Committee. **Sir Edward APPLETON** — Head of Britain's Department of Scientific and Industrial Research. Authority on Astro-Physics and Wireless Telegraphy.

Photos, Topical Press, Keystone

That obliteration began at Hiroshima. After General Spaatz had issued a communiqué from Guam to the effect that reconnaissance photographs showed that 60 per cent of the city had been destroyed, Tokyo broadcast (on August 8) that "The destructive power of the bomb is beyond words. When buildings were hit every living being outside simply vanished into air because of the heat, and those indoors were killed by indescribable pressure and heat."

WHO invented the atomic bomb? In answer to that question, Sir Edward Appleton, head of Britain's Department of Scientific and Industrial Research, declared that the final result had been the product of many brains. "But everyone would agree that the starting point of this wonderful discovery was the pioneer work of the late Lord Rutherford (in 1919 Lord Rutherford for the first time made an atom explode), whose experiments on the artificial disintegration of nitrogen directed attention to the stores of energy locked up in the heart of the atom." Earlier pioneer work, however, had been done by Sir J. J. Thomson, whose son, Sir George Thomson, was head of the panel of British scientists working on the bomb.

Sir George THOMSON — One of the greatest authorities on the atom. Professor of Physics at Imperial College of Science. Scientific adviser to Air Ministry. **Prof. Niels BOHR** — Professor of Theoretical Physics at Copenhagen and Nobel Prize winner, he smuggled Nazi atom secrets to Britain in 1942.

Photos, British Official, New York Times

And so at long last we have freed the energy of the atom. Will the atom become mankind's master? Sir John Anderson, who as Lord President of the Council was appointed by Mr. Churchill to be responsible for atomic research, has said: "We have got to see to it that the colossal energy created by the atomic bomb is harnessed for the benefit of mankind . . . War purposes have been given absolute priority, but the basic investigations, the fundamentals of the whole thing, will stand when investigation is made into using the energy of the bomb for industrial development. My opinion is that it will take a long time . . . The cost of producing the essential materials is very great."

And how is the awful secret of the atomic bomb to be kept only in the hands of those well disposed to their fellow men? It is a problem of the first magnitude. "We must indeed pray," says Mr. Churchill, "that these awful agencies will be made to conduce to peace among the nations, and that instead of wreaking measureless havoc upon the entire globe they may become a perennial fountain of world prosperity."

Sir James CHADWICK — In 1932 he discovered the neutron, thereby transforming conception of the constitution of matter and making the atomic bomb possible. **Sir John ANDERSON** — As Lord President of the Council in Mr. Churchill's Government he organized a committee for research into the atomic bomb.

Photos, Walter Stoneman, Pictorial Press

Transition from Warplanes to New British Homes

PREFABRICATED HOUSES, largely made from aluminium alloy, are being built in a British aircraft factory which produced the R.A.F. Beaufighter. In the erecting shop (1) workers assemble roofs of the new houses, with Beaufighters in the background. The structure contains two bedrooms, hall, living-room, kitchen and bathroom, etc., is built in four separate units, each approximately 22 ft. 6 ins. by 7 ft. 4½ ins., ready for transport to the site. Sectional view (2), showing roof, bathroom, living-room doorway. The kitchen (3) is all-electric and is fitted with refrigerator and garbage shoot.

FIRST OF THEIR KIND, prefabricated houses of the "Howard" type are being built in a Woolwich factory. Two-storeyed, they will cost between £800-£900. A "Howard" takes shape on the site (4). Royal Marines have been busy solving the housing problem at Orpington, Kent: laying drains and, in the doorway, plastering (5).

Photos, Central Press, Planet News, Daily Mirror

I Was There! Eye Witness Stories of the War

We Dropped the First Atomic Bomb On Japan

Two men in the Super-Fort which dropped the atomic bomb on Hiroshima on August 6, 1945—Col. P. W. Tibbets, the pilot (awarded the Distinguished Flying Medal immediately he returned from the raid), and Capt. W. Parsons, a U.S. Navy Ordnance expert—gave these first accounts of the awesome effect. And the first test of the bomb is described in the Reuter message which follows their story. See also page 278.

IT was hard to believe what we saw. We dropped the bomb at exactly 9.15 a.m. Japanese time, and got out of the target area as quickly as possible to avoid the full effect of the explosion. A tremendous cloud of smoke arose which completely blotted out Hiroshima. When we felt the explosion it was like flak bursting close by. We stayed over the target area for two minutes.

The whole thing was tremendous and awe-inspiring (added Capt. Parsons). After the missile had been released I sighed, and stood back for the shock. When it came, the men aboard with me gasped " My God ! " and what had been Hiroshima was a mountain of smoke like a giant mushroom. A thousand feet above the ground was a great mass of dust, boiling, swirling, and extending over most of the city. We watched it for several minutes, and when the tip of the mushroom broke off there was evidence of fires.

The success of the mission can be gauged by the fact that the first laboratory test of the new bomb was carried out on the Alamogordo bombing range in New Mexico, on July 16, and the finished product was delivered in Japan 20 days later. The men in the Super-Fortress knew they were in on something big, but no more. They were, however, told to expect a blinding flash and were issued with black goggles. Only three of us in the plane—Col. Tibbets, Bombardier Major Ferebee, and myself—knew what type of bomb was being dropped.

The first test, at the experimental centre, was like a Wellsian drama. Gen. L. R. Groves, a key man in the project, who was in the observation post 17,000 yards from a steel tower which was entirely vaporized by the explosion, said :

Two minutes before firing time, everybody lay face down with their feet pointing towards the explosion. As the remaining time was called over the loudspeaker, there was a complete, awesome silence. Dr. Conant (President of Harvard University) said he had never imagined seconds could be so long. Most of the individuals—in accordance with orders—shielded their eyes.

First came a burst of light of a brilliance beyond comparison. We all rolled over and looked through dark glasses at the ball of fire. About 40 seconds later came the shock-wave followed by the sounds, neither of which seemed startling after our complete astonishment at the extraordinary lighting intensity. Two supplementary explosions of minor effect other than lighting occurred in the cloud—which reached the substratosphere in five minutes—just after the main explosion.

General Thomas Farrell, General Groves' deputy, said :

The scene inside the shelter was dramatic beyond words. As the time for the test shortened from minutes to seconds tension increased. Everyone knew the awful potentialities of things they thought were about to happen.

The scientists felt that their figuring must be right and the bomb had to go off. But there was in everyone's mind a strong measure of doubt:

Col. PAUL W. TIBBETS, pilot of the Super-Fortress which dropped the first atomic bomb on Japan August 6, 1945. *Photo, Keystone*

We are reaching into the unknown, growing tenser, scarcely breathing. There came this tremendous burst of light, followed by a deep growing roar. Several observers standing at the back of the shelter were knocked flat by blast. All pent-up emotions were released in those few minutes, and all seemed to sense immediately that the explosions had far exceeded the most optimistic expectations and wildest hopes. All seemed to feel that they had been present at the birth of a new age—the age of atomic energy

I Saw the Glider Pilot Survivors on Parade

Commemorating their fallen comrades, at Stedham, near Midhurst, on July 29, 1945, survivors of the Glider Pilot Regiment remembered that two out of three of the Regiment's troops were missing or dead. The memorial service was attended by Edward Denny, whose description of the moving occasion is reprinted from The Evening News.

THE inhabitants of this sleepy ancient Sussex village were very privileged spectators. As the troops came down the road behind the band, with the perfection of march discipline, they had in their gait the confident lilt that comes to men when they are sure of themselves and justifiably proud of themselves and their Regiment. It would have been difficult to find a finer or more alert body of young men. For these were the survivors of the Glider Pilot Regiment on parade.

As I watched them my thoughts went back to their beginnings—to the early days when I first saw them, a " hush-hush" unit—on that windswept hill at Tilshead in Wiltshire. Then they had nothing but enthusiasm and a couple of gliders. I remember Brigadier George Chatterton, their commander (who hand-picked his officers, rejecting 11 out of every 12 of the volunteers who came forward for this strange new form of warfare), addressing them. It was a regiment in those days without traditions, without precedents to go on. They were regarded somewhat askance by the orthodox War Office pundits.

The traditions had to be created. The glories of Sicily, Normandy, Arnhem and the Rhine were unguessed in those far-off days when Britain thought in terms of countering, rather than staging, airborne invasions. " In this regiment," said the Brigadier, " we aim at the discipline of the Guards, the toughness of Commandos, individual intelligence and initiative of the Intelligence Corps."

How well they succeeded ! For here was indeed a *corps d'élite*—officers and men (sergeants, most of the latter) trained to be not merely first-class airmen, not merely to get their loads down at the right spot and at the right moment, but, if necessary, to fight as an infantry unit or as individuals (like the officer who fought a captured gun for many hours after all his companions had been killed), to fight with any and every type of weapon, and at all times to display that energy and initiative that only come to the highly trained, intelligent individual. In those far-off days there were 1,200 of them. Today there are 400. Two out of every three of the Tilshead boys are dead or missing.

The chance of their being in camp in the neighbourhood of the Brigadier's house had

ONE CENTRE OF PRODUCTION—general view of the Hanford Engineering Works at Pasco, Washington, D.C., one of the plants which helped the U.S. to produce the atomic bomb. First test took place on July 16, 1945, on the bombing range at Alamogordo in the New Mexico desert as narrated above. *Photo, Keystone*

Brigadier G. J. S. CHATTERTON, D.S.O. (left), inspired the formation of the British Glider Pilot Regiment, a memorial service to whose fallen is described here. *Photo, Topical*

led to an invitation from that officer to make his house and grounds their own, and to attend a memorial service for the fallen in the village church. For him, as he is being invalided out, it was probably his last parade.

And now they were in the church—a strange invasion, filling every pew, making the ancient crossbeams echo with the clump and scrape of army boots, drowning the stalwarts of the village choir, the high thin voices of the children with a volume of noise which the little church can seldom have heard, as 400 voices thundered "Fight the Good Fight," "O God, Our Help in Ages Past," and finally "Abide With Me."

The thoughts, the memories evoked by that moving and extremely simple service must have been varied. The long browning-off periods between operations; the first not very successful *coup* in Sicily, when the inexperienced tugs cast off too far out at sea and most had to swim for it; Normandy, and the bloody weariness of Arnhem; the thick haze of smoke and rubble dust which made the last, most costly and most successful operation, the crossing of the Rhine, so hazardous; grim memories of the young corporal simply disappearing when caught by the German flame-thrower; humorous memories . . . all these and many others may have been in the atmosphere of that little church, highly charged with the emotion which is only evoked by simplicity.

SIMPLE, too, was the Brigadier's farewell address. I wish it could have been recorded. He spoke without histrionics, of "the things I have watched as the Commander of this Regiment—the wonderful qualities of patience, discipline, and fortitude of all concerned. I have always wanted you to have the better qualities which are given to men. By that I mean simplicity, faith, and that good courage on which you would have to fall back when the real trial came—and you had them." He recalled old memories and abiding comradeship. There was nobody in that church who was not intensely moved.

The slanting sunlight caught and gilded the memorial tablets of long-dead squires and their relicts. The Regiment's first flag, designed by the men of the Regiment and struck for the first time, so long ago it now seems, on that bare hill at Tilshead, blessed by the vicar, later to hang in the church. Last Post, Réveillé, then out in the sunshine past the grassy mounds, the ancient yews and the lavender hedge, murmurous with bees, for that final pulse-quickening march past: these are things which the spectators of that little ceremony will not soon forget. It gave one a nagging sense of dissatisfaction not to have been privileged to be of that goodly company—and a quiet pride in a country which can still produce such men.

Toil and Trouble I Saw in the 'New' Germany

Today the German people in the British zone of occupation are writing their own Kampf. Remnants of their surrendered army, released under the "Barleycorn" scheme, help with the harvest. Undisciplined Displaced Persons need considerable attention. Problems of shelter and health and schooling are in process of being solved. Of these things John Fortinbras has written an account specially for "The War Illustrated."

JUST after 5.15 a.m. I was called from my billet in Hanover. Outside, on a patch of earth intensively cultivated as allotments, laboured an elderly frau. I judged her to be past 60 years of age, and in the half-light she was tending her vegetable crops with painstaking diligence.

Her example of "early to work" is not exceptional. At the base of bombed flats in the cities (cities of ruin beneath which bodies still lie uncovered, where normally stood little patches of grass enclosed by privet hedges) are pocket-handkerchief allotments—and no privet hedges, because their roots suck dry the moisture needed so vitally for vegetables. "Defeat gardens" the American soldier calls them.

Even waste areas in the towns have been put to the spade and, where there is sufficient earth made to sprout greenstuff. "Where weeds can grow, there should food be," said a German driver to me philosophically. The country's plight is realized. In the British occupied zone, which is the worst off agriculturally of the Allied zones, no assistance can be expected from the American or Russian sectors, not a grain of wheat in fact. Normally the zone we occupy produces but 15 per cent of the total foodstuffs necessary to sustain its population. It is thought that this can be stepped up to at least 30 per cent. The Germans are being restricted by their rationing authorities to a basic ration of 1,500 calories a day, just half that previously enjoyed, but three times the basic ration allowed the citizens of Rotterdam, Amsterdam, Utrecht and other cities of Northern Holland when these were under the Nazi heel.

The corn harvest is now almost entirely stacked, thanks to the British foresight of demobilizing—under Operation 'Barleycorn'—several thousand ex-farm workers from Wehrmacht prison cages. It is an unusually good harvest, especially in Westphalia, consisting mainly of pea, wheat, barley, and rye crops. A rich potato crop is to follow. These blessings owe their being to an exceptionally favourable season.

At a pinch, the food problem may solve itself. But certain signs must be watched. Almost every town in the British area has its D.P. (Displaced Persons) problem. These non-German nationals, forced labourers under the Hitler regime, still feel something of the licence which incensed them after liberation. Then, hundreds of them looted, plundered, pillaged, burnt, killed and raped almost at will. They even dragged girls off their bicycles in the streets, and in some districts, still strive to do so, at night. Much too much time of the Military occupying forces is devoted to keeping an eye on groups of undisciplined D.P.s.

Spoils Removed in Stolen Carts

I have known of German smallholders "visited" surreptitiously at 2 a.m. by gangs intent on killing their stock without reason or provocation and leaving it cold on the floors of styes and stalls. More enterprising D.P.s take away the slaughtered pigs, and dispose of their flesh at black market prices, 40 marks or so a pound. They even purloin, on occasion, the farmer's horse and cart to remove the spoils.

In Hanover it is proposed to establish this winter five permanent camps to accommodate 25,000 Polish nationals, some of whom are now living in this part of Germany for the first time; when Russians were repatriated, the authorities receiving them thought fit to send back Poles in lieu. D.P.s, in contrast to the Germans, are rationed on German foodstuffs according to a basic scale of 2,000 calories a day. In winter, with cold sharpening the appetite, and more young German men back on the farms, clashes may occur.

THEN there are problems of shelter and health. Many people have been amazed at the high standard of health revealed by the mere physical look of German children, their mothers and elder brothers and sisters. Their open-air fetish is quite remarkable. It continues even in wet weather, when barefooted children scramble up and down the pavements, oblivious to the rain, their sodden

LANDING TARGET FOR GLIDER PILOTS is demonstrated at a briefing during training. Cream of the world's fighting men, the Glider Pilot Regiment was formed, as part of the Army Air Corps of the British Army, in March 1942. Its finest hour was at Arnhem in September 1944. **See also page 73, Vol. 6, and p. 370, Vol. 8.** *Photo, Topical*

clothing or the slimy cold slabs underfoot, enjoying themselves hugely.

On Sunday mornings it is a sight to see all these children, with their parents, using shovels and pails outside their dwellings, leveling-out bomb craters and carting rubble away to organized dumps. At present they are splendidly fit. But German doctors, who have given every co-operation to date, complain of a shortage of diphtheria immunization serum for child innoculations. The serum used (serum Behring) also gives protection against scarlet fever. There is a shortage, too, of curative serums for these infectious diseases, but every effort is being made by our own authorities to step up supplies, since winter ravages amongst civilians are no part of Military Government's plan, and may react to the detriment of our occupying forces, especially as non-fraternization prevails no longer: (the ban was lifted July 14).

Their Public Utility Services

I have received reports of a few cases of spinal meningitis due entirely to overcrowded living conditions. These cases have arisen in villages which, long before the R.A.F.'s bombing ceased, served as dormitories and hide-outs for large sections of the civilian population, and fresh influxes of refugees at the time of battle greatly intensified their problems. Most six-roomed houses, even in the remotest hamlets, accommodate today from four to five families; and most flats are shared by two families. Now, also, since civilians are at liberty to rove within 100 kilometres of their home area, there is a constantly shifting population, and in infected localities the establishment of a cordon sanitaire is a matter of real difficulty.

Each day more and more Germans are assuming an active role in the running of public utility services under Military Government's supervision. At the outset, those given positions of responsibility, selected as a rule from men who were dismissed when the Nazi party obtained power in January 1933, or former concentration camp victims, lacked confidence; they behaved, as officials, indecisively and weakly. Today they begin to appreciate that so long as they act in good faith they can count on the backing of the British Army and all the authority embodied in Military Government.

It is expected that the state burger schools and universities will open shortly, by October at the latest. The difficulty, common to each Regierungsbezirk (administrative Government district), has been lack of non-Nazi text books and teachers. A fair number of schools, some very well-equipped ones with modern gymnasiums for children aged 6–10, and classrooms well-endowed with models and specimens for lessons in anatomy, have survived the bomb raids. Meantime, the "vetting" of teachers continues. They are examined politically by the educational staff of Military Government after first being approved by the German authorities as persons of proper cultural attainments—and experience.

As I find them, the Germans are obedient, co-operative, hard-working, well-disciplined and at no time since Occupation began hostile to British forces. In fact, in most cases they are anxious to cultivate our friendship. But they are still, of course, Germans. "Wer kampft hat Recht, wer nicht kampft hat allen Recht verloren." (Who fights has right, who fights not has all right lost.) They are fighting today, hard and cheerfully, for a bare livelihood. But it must not be assumed that the taint of Nazism which this slogan embodies has vanished utterly.

"OPERATION BARLEYCORN" is the name given by the British Military Government in Germany to harvesting—by former members of the Wehrmacht: some are seen leaving their farm work in the Ruhr, accompanied by girl companions and an accordionist. There are 300,000 such workers in the British occupation zone alone. *Photo, Keystone*

We Christened Our Isle with Salts and Rum

Tristan da Cunha, world's loneliest island, was revealed by the Admiralty in July 1945 as the Royal Navy's strangest "Stone Frigate." Commissioned 18 months ago as H.M.S. Atlantic Isle, it is now an important meteorological and radio station. Surgeon Lieut.-Comdr. E. J. S. Woolley, appointed Medical Officer-in-Charge, and later Commanding Officer, tells the story.

WITH his wife and two young children, a naval chaplain and a nursing sister, the new "Governor" set sail from Liverpool on March 20, 1942. In South Africa various "hands" were added to Woolley's party. A construction party of the South African Engineering Corps and the Union Defence Volunteers, together with several members of the Meteorological Defence Volunteers, and of the Meteorological Section of the South African Air Force, had gone to the island three weeks before, taking 2,000 tons of stores and building materials, in addition to sheep and other animals to provide food.

We arrived at Tristan at the end of April, and by the end of August the construction personnel had left. By November and December 1942 the Meteorological Section could forecast all the weather for the Cape and the Indian Ocean. The islanders' homes were primitive stone cottages, mostly grouped on a small plateau with a mountain face rising steeply behind to 2,000 feet, dominated by a 6,760-ft. peak.

The naval party shared this grim plateau, building sleeping quarters, bathrooms, a galley mess and recreation rooms, store rooms, sick quarters and houses. The weather was most demoralizing. There were almost perpetual gales while the sunshine, even in summertime, was never more than four or five hours a day. At first we were known as Job Nine; then the Admiralty decided to commission the island as a ship. On January 15, 1944, we were commissioned as H.M.S. Atlantic Isle.

We chose a West African surf-boat for the naming ceremony, which was performed by my wife, using an empty champagne bottle filled with fruit salts and a dash of rum. The whole ship's company was mustered, and the Tristan da Cunha Defence Volunteers—the local Home Guard—paraded. I made a speech, my wife christened the boat—in which sat Percy the Penguin, one of our pets—and the Tristan One Man Band played Heart of Oak, the National Anthem, and other appropriate music.

This "band" was Chief Engine-Room Artificer McGee, who had to play his accordion sitting in a bullock cart as he had a broken ankle. At the end of the ceremony the Defence Volunteers smartly about-turned and fired three volleys out to sea. This was quite unexpected by the bullocks, which bolted down the beach. Out tipped McGee's crutches, the accordion followed, then finally McGee himself—unhurt.

Council of Eleven Islanders

Instructions issued to Lieut.-Comdr Woolley before he sailed suggested that he should act as "guide, philosopher and friend" to the population of over 200 islanders under their Head Man, William Repetto, and his mother, the Head Woman, Mrs. Frances Repetto, a figure of extraordinary character and influence in the little community. So in November 1942 a council of eleven islanders was formed to advise on island affairs and assist in the enforcement of order. Typical problems discussed included building a new parish hall, the control of grazing, the reduction of geese, the care of widows, the suppression of swearing, bird protection, and the "control of the improvident." Another problem was the introduction of money to the island.

When we arrived work among the islanders was paid for in kind. We paid by chits for a certain amount, to be cashed for provisions at the naval stores. This system was clumsy and we asked for some currency. Eventually

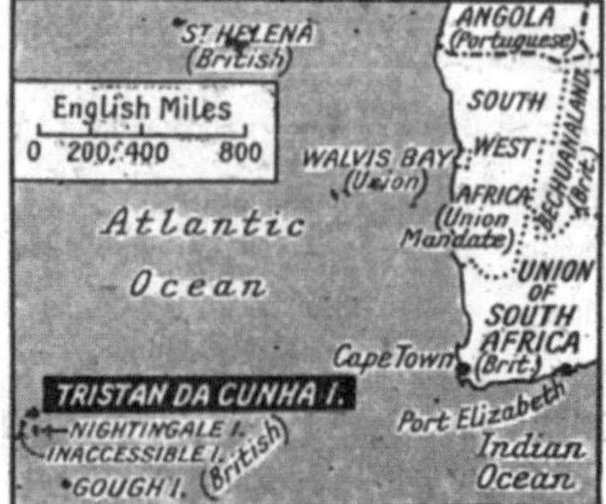

TRISTAN DA CUNHA, a 44-square-miles extinct volcano in the South Atlantic, almost midway between Cape Town and Buenos Aires, is the subject of the story here.

the money arrived—£3,000 in British and South African currency, crated in three packing-cases. I explained its use and the principles of banking through the P.O. Savings Bank to the islanders and stressed the desirability of saving for after the war. They picked up the idea very quickly and we had a most successful savings campaign conducted in simple language.

An island newspaper. The Tristan Times, was first produced in March 1943, selling for two cigarettes, three potatoes, or a halfpenny. It was sold by small boys who carried a sack for the "money." For welfare work on Tristan Lieut.-Cdr. Woolley was later awarded the O.B.E.

Western Desert Memory of the 8th Army Men

In connexion with the passing of the victorious 8th Army, which as an army exists no more (see page 259), Squadron Leader Derek Adkins, R.A.F., recaptures specially for "The War Illustrated" a memory of the khamsin, so well known to those who fought in the Desert.

I HAD been to the mess of a fighter wing at Gambut, just south of Tobruk. It was a clear night, and I drove back quickly down the coastal road to my own camp and went to bed. At three in the morning I woke up suddenly. The canvas sides and roof of the tent were lurching about in a helpless and most disconcerting fashion.

As I put on my torch the beam of light shone through the hanging sand-dust like a searchlight. Everything was covered with sand—my pillow, clothes, shoes, table and chairs. The tent poles seemed to sway as the wind billowed against the whole of one side of the tent.

I got out of bed and groped my way outside, hoping forlornly to rearrange the sand-bags that kept down the flaps at the foot of the tent walls. It was just about as much use as trying to stop the sea. The sand seeped in through every crack and vent, and the wind made the double flies of the tent flap together with a noise that was strangely unnerving.

I was alone at the time, so perhaps my isolation accentuated the feeling of utter helplessness. I wondered how long it would be before the guy ropes were uprooted. I started packing some of my more personal belongings, almost feverishly. I went back to bed and left my torch on; the light gave one a sense of companionship, and I could see where the dull flapping noise came from and watch the tent poles as they creaked and groaned. It was only the complete darkness that produced an uncanny feeling of fear and loneliness.

I must have fallen asleep again, for it was murkily light when I woke up. A layer of fine sand rested on everything. It was the same effect as you see in a garden after a heavy fall of snow. It seemed a pity to disturb the smooth pattern of it all. I looked at my pillow. The only clear patch was where my head had lain, but even there the tiny yellow grains were slipping down the creases into the impression that was left. Outside, the air was thick with sand. I lost all sense of direction as I groped my way instinctively across to the mess, with eyes half open and mouth tightly closed. After a few more experiences I became "desert worthy" and accepted sand storms and khamsins as a matter of course.

"ATLANTIC ISLE" commissioning ceremony at which Surgeon Lieut.-Comdr. E. J. S. Woolley, R.N.V.R., and his wife officiated; he is seen reading out the commissioning order. The West African surf-boat (left) was used as a "token" for the island, the ship's company was mustered and the local Home Guard paraded, as told in facing page.
Photo, British Official

OUR DIARY OF THE WAR

August 1, Wednesday ***1,333rd day of War against Japan***
Japan.—Record force of 820 Super-Forts bombed five towns on Honshu.
Pacific.—Wake Island bombed and shelled by U.S. planes and battleships.
Austria.—Advanced party of British troops began to take over Schonbrunn Palace in Vienna.

August 2, Thursday *1,334th day*
Germany.—Potsdam Conference ended.
Japan.—U.S. fighter-bombers made attacks in Osaka-Kobe area.
Home Front.—King George met President Truman on Renown at Plymouth.

August 3, Friday *1,335th day*
Pacific.—Announced that Super-Forts had mined all large ports in Japan.
France.—Battleship Strasbourg refloated after scuttling in 1942.

August 4, Saturday *1,336th day*
Japan.—Super-Forts dropped warning leaflets on 12 more cities, making 31 warned of impending air attack.
Pacific.—Announced that General MacArthur's command had been extended to include Ryukyu Islands.

August 5, Sunday *1,337th day*
Japan.—Aircraft of Far East Air Force from Okinawa bombed port of Tarumizu, southern Kyushu.

August 6, Monday *1,338th day*
Japan.—First atomic bomb dropped, on Hiroshima, Honshu, by U.S. aircraft.
Pacific.—Reported that Canadian troopships and aircraft had arrived in Guam area.

August 7, Tuesday *1,339th day*
Japan.—Rail and industrial centres in southern Kyushu again attacked by Allied bombers.
Yugoslavia.—Marshal Tito appealed in National Congress for republican form of government.
General.—Third session of council of UNRRA opened in London.

August 8, Wednesday *1,340th day*
Russia.—Soviet Union declared war on Japan from August 9.
China.—Kukiang island reoccupied by Chinese troops.
Austria.—Zones of occupation of four Allied governments announced.
Yugoslavia.—King Peter charged Tito with dictatorship and withdrew his authority from the Regents.

August 9, Thursday *1,341st day*
Japan.—Second atomic bomb dropped, on port of Nagasaki. Three million leaflets urging Japan to end the war dropped by U.S. aircraft.
Russian Front.—Soviet troops crossed Manchurian frontier, forced River Amur and captured Manchuli.

August 10, Friday *1,342nd day*
Japan.—Tokyo broadcast offer to surrender provided "prerogatives of Emperor" were not prejudiced.
Russian Front.—Red Army advanced 100 miles into Manchuria at western end of 1,000-mile front.

August 11, Saturday *1,343rd day*
Japan.—Allied reply to Japanese surrender offer demanded that Emperor should be subject to Allied Supreme Commander in giving effect to terms.
Pacific.—Off Okinawa a "major U.S. warship" was hit by Jap aerial torpedo.
Home Front.—Liner Queen Mary docked at Southampton for first time since 1939.

August 12, Sunday *1,344th day*
Japan.—Allied air forces attacked shipping off Kyushu, Honshu and northern Ryukyus.
Russian Front.—Landing parties of Soviet Pacific Fleet captured ports of Yuki and Rashin in Korea.

August 13, Monday *1,345th day*
Japan.—Carrier aircraft of British and U.S. fleet attacked Tokyo area; U.S. warships bombarded Kurile Island.
Far East.—Mongolian People's Republic (Outer Mongolia) declared war on Japan.
Germany.—French troops took over control of part of Berlin.

August 14, Tuesday *1,346th day*
Japan.—Japanese Government accepted Allied terms of surrender.
Russian Front.—Soviet troops crossed frontier on Sakhalin; Korean port of Seishin captured.
Germany.—Three non-Nazi political organizations sanctioned in British zone.
General.—Chinese-Soviet treaty of alliance signed in Moscow.

Flash-backs

1940

August 4. *Italian forces invaded British Somaliland.*
August 8. *Battle of Britain began.*

1941

August 14. *Churchill-Roosevelt meeting, and Atlantic Charter, announced by Mr. Attlee.*

1942

August 7. *U.S. troops landed on Guadalcanal in the Solomons.*
August 12. *Mr. Churchill arrived in Moscow on his first visit.*

1943

August 5. *Russians captured Orel. British entered Catania, Sicily.*

1944

August 1. *Poles in Warsaw began fighting Germans openly.*
August 4. *Myitkyina, Burma, fell finally to Allied troops.*
August 9. *U.S. forces reached St. Malo and took Le Mans.*
August 10. *Organized resistance ended on Guam in the Marianas.*
August 12. *Troops of the 8th Army entered Florence.*

With Our Airmen Today

By CAPTAIN
NORMAN MACMILLAN
M.C., A.F.C.

BOMBING reached a new and terrifying point of development on August 6, 1945, by the employment in war for the first time of a bomb utilizing atomic energy as its explosive. One bomb of this kind was dropped on Hiroshima that day at 8.20 a.m. Japanese time (shortly after midnight B.S.T.). This target was doubtless chosen because Hiroshima was a supply depot for the Japanese army, with shipbuilding yards, cotton mills, and war industries as additional factors in the still considerable Japanese war potential (see pages 278 and 280).

The first test firing of this bomb took place in a remote area of New Mexico at 5.30 a.m. on July 16, 1945. Heavy pressure waves knocked down two men outside the control tower, which was 10,000 yards from the explosion. The coloured cloud formed by the explosion boiled to 40,000 feet. The steel tower from which the bomb was suspended (this indicates that it was a blast bomb) disappeared, entirely vaporized. A man standing six miles away and who disregarded the order not to look in the direction of the explosion was blinded.

THE U.S. War Department stated that the first atomic bomb to leave the United States was in the care of Brig.-General Thomas Farrell, who departed with it only nine days before it fell on Hiroshima. Major-General Leslie Groves commanded the atomic bomb project, and co-ordinated final preparations for the launching of this extremely technical mechanism from a tiny Pacific coral island.

The atomic bomb was dropped on Hiroshima by parachute from a Super-Fortress bomber. It exploded before reaching the ground. Its weight was in the order of 400 lb. Reconnaissance photographs showed that this one bomb destroyed 4·1 square miles of Hiroshima's built-up area of 6·9 square miles, or nearly 60 per cent of the city.

Colonel Tibbets, of the U.S. Army A.F., who led the first atomic bomb attack, had trained for this task for some time. With him in the aircraft was Captain William Parsons, U.S. Navy ordnance expert, who said that the great cloud that covered Hiroshima after the explosion consisted of "boiling dust."

THE aircraft was about ten miles away when the bomb exploded, yet it was thrown about violently by the air waves. Below, in the doomed city, the tremendous electrical discharge seared the buildings with flame and disintegrated them by blast. Reconnaissance photographs taken in sunlight after the dust and smoke cleared disclosed only a few shadows indicative of vertical structures left standing within the wrecked area of the city. Over most of that area there were no recognisable features. Tokyo stated that the "impact of the bomb was so terrific that practically all living things—human and animal—were literally seared to death by the tremendous heat and pressure engendered by the blast. All the dead and injured were burned beyond recognition. . . . One cannot distinguish between men and women killed by fire. The corpses are too numerous to be counted."

The dropping of the atomic bomb was additional to the almost continuous pounding of the Japanese main islands with increasingly powerful forces of aircraft carrying ordinary bombs, of both high explosive and incendiary types, from land bases in the Marianas and Okinawa, and repeated strikes by carrier-aircraft of the Third Fleet in which British ships and aircraft formed an important element. On July 24 Admiral Halsey's attacks on remnants of the Japanese fleet at Kure included about 250 British carrier-planes, and about 1,000 American. On July 30 more than a thousand U.S. and British carrier-planes attacked military targets in the Tokyo-Nogoya areas; their original targets—airfields—were blotted out by fog, so they were switched to targets of opportunity. The Japanese estimate for that day was that 1,600 aircraft had attacked the Japanese main islands up to 6 p.m.

FIRST BRITISH SEAFIRE OVER JAPAN, this aircraft (top) operated from a British Pacific Fleet carrier. Details of the Seafire XV, fastest naval interceptor fighter built in Britain, were released on August 10, 1945. Speed is approximately 400 m.p.h.; span, 36 feet 10 inches; length 31 feet 10 inches; armament two 20 mm. cannon, four ·303 machine guns, and one 500 lb. bomb. It is powered with one 1,890 h.p. Rolls-Royce Griffon VI engine. *Photo, Associated Press*

MORE Than 1,000 Planes on a Two-Day Strike at Honshu

At the end of July it was announced that at least 1,230 Japanese ships and 1,257 aircraft had been destroyed or damaged during the preceding 22 days by the Third Fleet. On August 9 and 10 the same Fleet sent more than a thousand planes on a two-day strike against targets in Northern Honshu. The British aircraft struck at targets around Sendai Bay area, the naval base 180 miles north-east of Tokyo, attacking power stations and dock-yards, hangars, barracks, workshops, dispersed aircraft, airfields, shipping, gliders and tugs. Several enemy aircraft attacked the Fleet as it withdrew, without doing damage, and a small force of enemy torpedo planes was completely wiped out.

ON July 26 a proclamation signed by President Truman and Mr. Churchill at Potsdam was delivered in the form of an ultimatum to the Japs, after its approval by Chiang Kai-shek by radio. Clause 8 read: "The terms of the Cairo declaration shall be carried out and Japanese sovereignty shall be limited to the islands of Honshu, Hokkaido, Kyushu, Shikoku and such minor islands as we shall determine." Failure to accept this ultimatum as a signal to surrender was to be followed by a war of annihilation upon Japan. The Japanese elder statesmen rejected the warning.

ON July 27, Super-Fortresses of the 20th A.F. dropped leaflets warning people to flee from *Aomori*, Nishinomiya, *Ogaki*, *Ichinomiya*, Nagaoka, Koriyama, *Ujiyamada*, *Tsu*, Kurume, *Uwajima*, and Hakodate. Two days later the six cities in italics and the Shimotsu oil refinery were bombed with more than 3,500 tons of bombs from 550-600 Super-Fortresses. Five were left in ashes and the sixth badly burned. In the night of July 31, twelve Japanese cities were similarly warned: *Mito*, *Hachioji*, Mayebashi, *Toyama*, *Nagaoka*, Nishinomiua - Mikage, Maizaru, Otsu, Fukuyama, Navona, Kurume, Hakodate. The four cities in italics were among the targets of the record force of 800 bombers which dropped the record load of 6,000 tons during the first day of August.

On August 5, twelve cities were again warned: Miyakonojo, Saga, Yawata, Hachinoje, Akita, Fukushima, Urawa, Tottori, Iwakuni, Takayama, Otaru, Imbari, and next day 580 Super-Forts bombed Mayebashi, Nishonomiya, Ube, and Saga. On August 7, Toyokawa naval base received 880 tons from 125 Super-Forts, and next day Yawata (Japan's Sheffield) was set ablaze with 1,500 tons of H.E. from about 225 Super-Forts.

BY then the Japanese armies in China and Manchuria were virtually isolated from the home islands. Japan's seaborne commerce was paralysed by the mine-laying of Super-Forts, which since March 27 had sunk or damaged more than half of Japan's shipping. Generals MacArthur and Spaatz were drafting plans for 7,000-ton raids against Japan. There were almost daily strikes from medium and heavy bombers and fighters from Okinawa. On August 8, the Soviet Union declared war on Japan as from midnight that night. Next day her bombers swept out from bases to smash at Manchuli, Harbin, Changchun, Kirin, and the ports of Seishin and Rashin. Five hundred tons of demolition bombs fell on Amagasaki, chief refinery for aviation petrol. On August 9, a second atomic bomb fell—on Nagasaki.

No nation could withstand such strokes, and on the following day President Truman announced that Japan was in communication with the U.S.A., U.K., U.S.S.R. and China with a surrender offer. The bomber had beaten Japan without an invasion.

Flying Boat Base for War on Japs and Locusts

A 2,400 H.P. CATALINA IS HAULED UP THE SLIPWAY for a maintenance check at Korangi Creek, Karachi, one of India's largest R.A.F. flying boat bases (1). From there (2) Catalinas and Sunderlands arriving from the United Kingdom are "routed" on to their forward destinations. Besides normal operational duties and the ferrying of casualties, Catalinas carry out anti-locust patrols, checking these pests in their Baluchistan breeding-grounds. Sunderlands have destroyed much enemy coastal shipping in the Gulf of Siam. Air Vice Marshal C. E. N. Guest, C.B.E. (in circle) commands R.A.F. Transport Command Group operating in India and Burma.

Photos, British Official

Editor's Postscript

SOME time ago (see page 158) I was urging my readers never to forget that the tank was a British invention. Since then Lieut.-Gen. Sir Giffard Le Q. Martel, who knows as much about tanks as any man living (he was the first commander of the Royal Armoured Corps) has reminded me that the British inventors beat the French only by a short head. Each of the two Allies had been working in secret along the same lines. Early in 1916 there was a joint demonstration at which the secrets were exchanged, the existing new weapons of each country being paraded before the eyes of the other. In armour and armament there was little to choose. The all-important difference was that the British looked upon their tanks primarily as a means of breaking out of the trench system, and had therefore evolved that essential feature of tank construction, the caterpillar track; whereas the French were still gambling on the power of artillery to destroy the stalemate of the trenches. Their "assault cars," lighter and speedier than the tanks, were designed only for use *after* a breakthrough, as a sort of bullet-proof cavalry. This was the rôle assigned in the closing stages of the Second Great War to our own cruiser tanks, which owed much of their lightness and mobility to that French assault-car conception of 1916.

MOTORISTS enjoying their basic petrol ration will have noticed how nearly all our signposts are back again. Yet the other day I passed a village 1914–18 war memorial still worded: "To the memory of the men of——", the blank being an ugly strip of matchboard tacked across the name of the village. There seems little excuse for such dilatoriness. Anyway, I have often wondered sceptically just how far any German parachutists would have been hindered by the extensive anonymity that cloaked the British countryside. One supposes they would have had excellent maps and a knowledge of how to use them. Still, the principle that even if we were not able to hinder them we need not go out of our way to help them was sound enough; and the thoroughness with which the idea was carried out was justified at the time as a stimulant to morale. Incidentally, how many remember that the man responsible for getting the signposts removed was Lord Reith, who was Minister of Transport for a brief period in 1940? It was an appropriate task for one who had been already renowned in his B.B.C. days for an insistent belief in the virtues of anonymity.

CHRONICLERS of the Second Great War, like their predecessors in other wars, must be heartily sick of History's recurring capacity for repeating itself. One of the least known and most romantic of these historical repetitions is disclosed by Charles Graves in his lively two-shilling pamphlet, Drive for Freedom, which Hodder and Stoughton have sent me. It concerns the Battle of Britain and a decision taken some years *before* the War by a firm of British motor manufacturers to build up a real British watch industry—and so perfect our Hurricanes and Spitfires! The story switches back to the 18th century when London craftsmen were pre-eminent in watch-making. (There were no fewer than 3,000 watchmakers in Clerkenwell alone.) Their mutual jealousies, alas! enabled an enterprising Swiss named Ingold to acquire their secrets and return with them to his native country, where he established an industry which soon completely eclipsed that of the Londoners. A century later—in the 1930's—three Swiss professors and twenty-five skilled operatives were imported to revive the ancient English industry. As Mr. Graves points out, these twenty-eight men had, perhaps, as much to do with the defeat of the Luftwaffe as anyone in Great Britain—with the exception of the actual fighter pilots concerned. For by their assistance Britain was able for the first time to make her own all-British lever escapement, the nerve-centre of a watch, which hitherto had been imported from Switzerland. Without this device it is impossible to make any of the time-fuse mechanism necessary for the caps of shells and sea-mines, quite apart from any clock or watch-equipment so essential to high-precision flying.

ONLY the incurably sentimental among our diners-out, I imagine, will regret the proposal of the Réunion des Gastronomes (an influential body in the catering trade) to abolish the traditional attire of the British waiter. Instead of the soup-stained dickey and shiny tails, after the cut of the late Billy Bennett, the waiter of tomorrow is to wear "washable white jackets, with interchangeable shoulder-straps or epaulets"—as worn by all waiters in Hollywood films as well as by most in smart resorts abroad before the war. The old-fashioned waiters' clothes provided much shaggy humour for music-hall comedians, and the publishers of picture-postcards, yet I doubt if one diner out in a thousand ever reflected, between courses, that this highly soilable *tenue de soir*, with its almost daily change of cuffs, dickey and collar—often made of paper, it's true—had to be provided and maintained by the waiter himself, often at considerable expense. Any new garb that combines cleanliness and smartness of appearance with cheapness and ease in laundering will be a blessing all round. I make only one reservation: that in future revivals of G.B.S.'s still delightful play You Never Can Tell, the philosopher-waiter continues to dress in his old and familiar pea-souper. Shavian philosophy and washable white jackets, I somehow feel, would not go hand-in-hand.

Air Chief Marshal Sir W. SHOLTO DOUGLAS, K.C.B., M.C., D.F.C., appointed Commander-in-Chief British Air Forces of Occupation in Germany as from July 15, 1945. He is also responsible for disarming the Luftwaffe in Denmark, Belgium and Holland. *Photo, British Official*

MANY a motor-bus has travelled far from its accustomed beat in the last few years. It began with the blitz, and the hundreds of provincial buses that were rushed up to help London through the bad autumn of 1940. Do you remember when you could ride down the Strand on a bright blue bus from Hull and make the return trip on a dark blue one from Bradford or Birmingham, or possibly a muddy orange one from Glasgow? Later on, the proud vermilion of London Transport was to be seen in the streets of Coventry and similarly stricken towns. Altogether 283 London buses were lent to the provinces. And now there are men serving in the Army of Occupation, coming from Maidstone, Northampton, and other districts, who rub their eyes at the strange but gratifying sight of their home town buses scudding across Germany, in the process of transporting those tragic thousands officially known as Displaced Persons. Of course, buses went far afield on war work between 1914 and 1918, too. A battalion shifting from one part of France to another would often find a fleet of them waiting at the railhead; and though the buses were all disguised in a uniform of drab grey, Londoners at least could never mistake the peculiar topheavy tilt of the old B-type vehicles, and always hailed them as old friends. The oddest encounter of this kind, however, concerns a steam roller. It happened out in Iraq, a year or so ago. A lad in the Royal Engineers, who had formerly worked in the highways department of the local council office at Barnes, saw the great lumbering thing at work on a new military road. Something about the cut of its jib struck a familiar chord, and he went up for a closer look. Sure enough, he found the inscription "Barnes Borough Council" He said he could have hugged it!

"AS a potential agent of world peace broadcasting stands supreme." I quote from a recent newspaper article. The words strike a familiar chord. Was not the original motto of our B.B.C. the pseudo-Scriptural "Nation shall speak peace unto nation"? It was a motto well suited to the somewhat woolly idealism of B.B.C. aspirations at that period. The actual words are to be found nowhere in the Bible, the nearest approach being in Isaiah ii, 4: "Nation shall not lift up sword against nation." However, soon after the emergence of Hitler this motto was dropped, at whose instigation I know not, in exchange for the innocuous "Quaecunque," meaning (roughly) "Whatsoever things." The B.B.C.'s three journals were instructed at the time to make no comment on the change. In the event, the B.B.C. proved far more successful as an agent of war than ever it had promised to be of peace. A series of circumstances totally unexpected by the B.B.C. even after the war had begun enabled it to become a rallying-point, almost the only one, for the scattered and trampled forces of freedom in Europe. You and I may not have thought much of the Home Service and Forces programmes at times; but hundreds of thousands of men and women in the occupied countries of Europe will always remember the voice of the B.B.C. gratefully as the one perpetually glowing spark in a world of darkness, a stimulus to resistance, and a constant assurance of final victory.

In Britain Now: Members of the New Cabinet

HERBERT MORRISON
Lord President of the Council

ERNEST BEVIN
Foreign Secretary

ARTHUR GREENWOOD
Lord Privy Seal

HUGH DALTON
Chancellor of the Exchequer

SIR STAFFORD CRIPPS
President of Board of Trade

A. V. ALEXANDER
First Lord of Admiralty

LORD JOWITT
Lord Chancellor

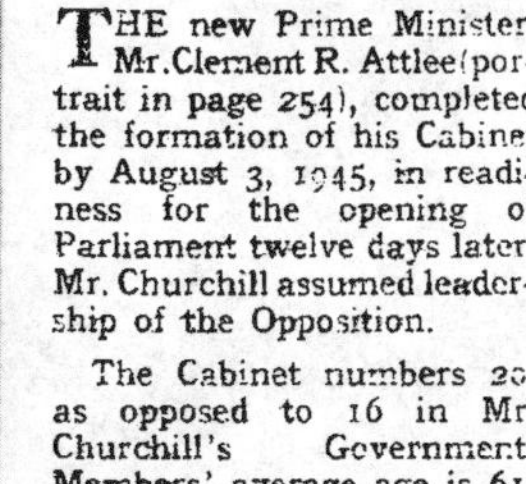

THE new Prime Minister, Mr. Clement R. Attlee (portrait in page 254), completed the formation of his Cabinet by August 3, 1945, in readiness for the opening of Parliament twelve days later. Mr. Churchill assumed leadership of the Opposition.

The Cabinet numbers 20, as opposed to 16 in Mr. Churchill's Government. Members' average age is 61, compared with 56 for the late Cabinet. Average age of M.P.s was lowered substantially by the election; that of Labour members dropped, it is calculated, from 56 to 43, while that of Conservative members is given as 47. See also page 255.

J. CHUTER EDE
Home Secretary

VISCOUNT ADDISON
Dominions Secretary

LORD PETHICK-LAWRENCE
Sec. of State for India

G. H. HALL
Colonial Secretary

J. J. LAWSON
Minister of War

VISCOUNT STANSGATE
Minister for Air

JOSEPH WESTWOOD
Secretary for Scotland

GEORGE A. ISAACS
Minister of Labour

EMANUEL SHINWELL
Minister of Fuel

ELLEN WILKINSON
Minister of Education

ANEURIN BEVAN
Minister of Health

TOM WILLIAMS
Minister of Agriculture

Brussels Says 'Thank You!' to the Guards

TROOPS OF THE GUARDS ARMOURED DIVISION—seen marching along the Rue de la Régence towards the Palais de Justice—were honoured by Brussels on July 28, 1945, when the Burgomaster presented them with plaques and standards recording the citizens' gratitude for their liberation eleven months previously. (On September 3, 1944, advanced elements of the Division entered the Belgian capital after a 206-mile thrust in six days; see page 313, Vol. 8.) Collected from all over Germany and headed by Maj.-Gen. Sir Allan Adair, G.O.C. the Guards Division, 3,500 men took part in the ceremony. Next day our troops presented Brussels' famous "Mannikin" statue with a Guards' uniform—made to measure. *Photo, G.P.U.*

Printed in England and published every alternate Friday by the Proprietors, THE AMALGAMATED PRESS, LTD., The Fleetway House, Farringdon Street, London, E.C.4. Registered for transmission by Canadian Magazine Post. Sole Agents for Australia and New Zealand: Messrs. Gordon & Gotch, Ltd.; and for South Africa: Central News Agency, Ltd.—August 31, 1945. S.S. *Editorial Address:* JOHN CARPENTER HOUSE, WHITEFRIARS, LONDON E C 4

Vol 9 The War Illustrated No 215

SIXPENCE Edited by Sir John Hammerton SEPTEMBER 14, 1945

OUR KING AND QUEEN, WITH THE TWO PRINCESSES, entered St. Paul's Cathedral to a fanfare from trumpeters of the Household Cavalry when they attended a special afternoon service there on August 19, 1945, to commemorate the conclusion of the War. The Prime Minister and his Cabinet, Mr. Churchill, distinguished representatives of all the United Nations and the Dominions, and heads of the Services and civil departments were among a large congregation. *Photo, P.N.A.*

No. 216 WILL BE PUBLISHED FRIDAY, SEPTEMBER 28

The Day for Which the World Had Waited

CELEBRATING THE JAPANESE SURRENDER, Generalissimo Chiang Kai-shek (1) broadcast, on August 15, 1945, from Chungking. In Paris, U.S. troops (2) sold newspapers in aid of the Red Cross. New York's famous Times Square (3) was packed. In Cairo, British Service men and women (4) scanned the latest editions. In Rangoon our troops heard the news from the S.E.A.C. radio-car (5). Seven days previously, Filipinos in Manila (6) had hailed Russia's war declaration.

Photos, British Official, Associated Press, New York Times Photos, Keystone, Fox

Is This The End Of War?

By The Editor

ALTHOUGH I have on various occasions expressed my opinion that the Japanese, for all their preposterous boasting, would not be able to prolong the War for any considerable stretch of time after the complete collapse of Germany, and I have never expected them to endure many months beyond that happy event, I readily confess that one could not easily have submitted a good case for that belief, which was more in the nature of a "hunch" than a conviction based upon reason. That Russia would soon or later attack Japan was fairly obvious, for the Soviets regard themselves as the heirs of "Mother Russia" along the vast and still indeterminate borderlands of Manchuria and Mongolia, where for generations the competing interests of Russia and Japan have been awaiting final solution. One could, of course, argue that the tremendous bombing which the war plants and industrial centres of Japan had been receiving for months past was "softening up" the island empire preparatory to mass invasion and naval attack, which would quickly precipitate the early collapse of the far-scattered Japanese forces, as these had been robbed of all naval support by the almost total destruction of the Mikado's sea power; but it was a mere handful of men in America and Great Britain who knew about that greatest of all secret weapons, the atomic bomb.

"A Bomb to End Bombs"

Without that stupendous instrument of offensive war, to which by comparison the most diabolical of Hitler's V weapons was only a medium of terrorism, war against Japan might still have been going on, even though its end would have been clearly in sight. The fact that no more than two of these bombs were required to reduce the fire-eating race of greedy and envious Nipponese to submission, is the best proof of the value of this great discovery, in which both British and American scientists have shared. A quick-witted humorist has described it as "a bomb to end bombs." And quite seriously that may prove a truer description than "a war to end wars" which, for a time, so many of us hoped the First World War might prove.

We can restrain our tears for the large destruction of two populous cities of a people who have shown themselves to be as cruel and barbarous as the Western Huns and even more treacherous. These bombs, produced at such fabulous cost —five-eighths of the total national debt of Great Britain at the end of the Napoleonic Wars—may yet be looked upon as cheap at the price, and there can be little doubt that they have saved at least a million lives of the Allied armies by bringing the Mikado and his war-mongers to their knees when confronted with their impending fate. Moreover, they have quite probably saved far more Japanese lives than they have taken. And it is pretty evident that from the first the atom bomb was devised as an awful warning rather than a weapon to be used at large; for the two peoples whose men of genius solved this tremendous problem of unleashing on earth that primal force which exists at the core of the Sun itself and is the very mainspring of our solar system, are foremost among the peace-minded nations.

Had Hun or Jap First Used the Atom!

We must realize that had the Germans or the Japanese been the first to solve this problem which has long occupied their men of science, neither of these ruthless races would have troubled to warn us what they were about to do with it. They would have used it to the full: two bombs would not have sufficed to slake their thirst for destruction. Indeed, it may yet be said that the Anglo-American powers that first secured command of this mightiest force of nature showed an extreme of human consideration in the use they made of it.

But is it then the end of war that has thus been achieved at one blow, so to speak? Provided an international body controlled the use of the weapon and that its secrets might remain known only to the few, that would seem to be a possibility. For unlike every other instrument of aggressive war, with the possible exception of the V2 rocket bomb, there would seem hardly any chance of inventing an opposing weapon which would effectively counteract its destructiveness. Also, there is the prohibitive cost of its fabrication. That, for the present at least, its secrets rest with the scientists of the two great world powers for peace is our best assurance for the future.

Atomic Power Applied to Peace

The pictures that have been painted by excited writers, of humanity immolating itself on the altar of the atom, or even bringing chaos to the universe by projecting atomic bombs into those regions where the morning stars still sing together in blissful harmony, need not greatly disturb us. We should rather contemplate the vast possibilities which, by this invention, are opened to the mind of Man who is now in possession of one of the greatest of nature's secrets, and if its first and easiest use would appear to be destructive, it may be that it is so only in the sense that the surgeon destroys a lesser part of the human anatomy in order to save a major part, much as forest fires are fought by burning large tracts of country in their course: the "scorched earth" policy wherewith Stalin saved Russia.

THE thanksgiving services and natural rejoicings with which the submission of the barbaric God-King of the Japanese was marked throughout the world, and especially in those countries which have borne the burden of the war against the oriental aggressors, were not immoderate, having regard to those long years of suffering which had been endured. It is, however, regrettable that certain prelates assumed the right, not merely to ignore this occasion for rejoicing, but refused to allow any form of thanksgiving in their churches because of the means whereby the superior intelligence of the West has overwhelmed its imitators in the East. Those who have wrested this awful secret from the innermost recesses of nature will yet discover how to apply it to the good of humanity. That will take many a year of research and experiment. I remember reading in a New York journal fifty years ago the breath-taking details of the possibilities awaiting the world when science had discovered how to obtain from coal its total energy without destroying most of it in the furnace fires. A few buckets of Welsh coal were to do, by the new method of abstracting their full calorific value, what hundreds of tons were needed to produce by the methods then in use! After half a century we are still burning away in needless smoke most of the calorific content of the coal!

The Dawn of a New Era

But the human factor remains. Will those on whom we have inflicted complete defeat in the West and the East be willing to accept the verdict of this World War? It is a question to which your answer is as good as mine. All that we do know today with any certainty is the fact that we possess a weapon of offence which has never before in the history of the world been at the disposal of any group of human beings, and if we fail to use it in such a way as may prevent all predatory peoples from disturbing the world's peace we shall have proved ourselves unworthy custodians of a power in which there must reside potentialities for the good of Man no less than for his harm. On the whole, the chances that we have stifled for ever the willingness to make war are as great as the potentialities for war-making which have now been demonstrated by the use of the atomic bomb. In any event the world has entered a new, if not unforeseen era of human activity, and we must go forward in it not full of fear and trembling, but with high hope for the triumphs of the human mind.

J. A. HAMMERTON

LORD LOUIS MOUNTBATTEN, SUPREME ALLIED COMMANDER S.E.A.C., and his chiefs of staff drew up surrender terms for the Japanese in Burma. Left to right: Gen. Sir William Slim, Gen. Raymond Wheeler (commanding U.S. forces in the India-Burma theatre), Lord Louis, Admiral Sir Arthur Power, Air Marshal Sir Keith Park, and Lt.-Gen. F. M. Browning. The Jap surrender delegation, headed by Lt.-Gen. Numata, arrived in Rangoon on August 26, 1945, and a preliminary agreement was concluded the following day. See also facing page. *Photo, British Official*

With Our Armies Today

By MAJ.-GENERAL SIR CHARLES GWYNN K.C.B., D.S.O.

We are fully justified in rejoicing at Japan's surrender, even though we may wish that it had been brought about by other means. It remains to be seen whether fighting will cease even when the Emperor's orders have reached his troops. His broadcast was far from satisfactory, and had more sinister implications than a mere face-saving statement. General MacArthur may have no easy task in enforcing the adoption of a more chastened attitude even among those who have experienced the bombardment of the heart of Japan by sea and air, and who must realize the effects of the atomic bomb. Outlying troops and commanders who have not had these experiences nor been decisively defeated—in some cases they have not been engaged at all—may not consent to lay down their arms while they are in a position to continue the struggle.

POLICE Operations to Suppress Banditry by Fanatical Groups

The Russian offensive so admirably, and, as Mr. Churchill has told us, so punctually timed, has removed the most serious danger of prolonged resistance in defiance of the Emperor's orders. But it would, I think, be premature to count on the surrender of the many detachments in Malaya and in islands where evasive tactics can be employed to avoid decisive defeat. In such cases much must clearly depend on the character and fanaticism of the local commander, for the rank and file of his force would probably obey his orders. I hope I may be mistaken, but I certainly foresee the necessity of police operations perhaps on an extensive scale, even if it may only be to suppress banditry by fanatical groups. Meanwhile, everyone who has followed the Japanese war closely throughout will be pleased that the Australians, who in New Guinea were the first to defeat the Japanese on land, should on Bougainville be the first to receive the surrender of a complete detachment, still capable of resistance.

It will be interesting to learn, though we may never do so with certainty, how nearly the Japanese Government was brought to surrender by intensive bombing before the atomic bomb was used, or whether Russia's intervention would by itself have proved a decisive factor. In the event, there cannot be a shadow of doubt that the use of the atomic bomb was decisive and that it accelerated the end. That is the immediate justification for its employment, for it probably saved more lives than it destroyed.

The long-term effects of its use may be infinitely more important. It gave convincing proof that the most peace-loving nation in the world possessed this terrible weapon. If its existence had remained secret or been merely a subject for rumour, an aggressive nation might have produced it independently and, in the belief that it could spring a surprise on the world, have used it unhesitatingly. As it is, it would seem that a weapon has been devised and is in the right hands to form a deterrent against any attempt to establish world domination by aggression.

EFFECTIVENESS of Intervention Dependent on Prompt Action

It would, however, be over-optimistic to assume that a complete deterrent to war has been devised or that other forms of security armament have become obsolete. Humanity is by nature quarrelsome and only to a limited extent law-abiding. In spite of the law, stree quarrels and rioting will continue to occur and the burglar will continue to ply his trade. A well-devised legal system backed by an efficient police reduces the frequency and scope of such occurrences, and that is all we can hope for from international courts and police forces. The police must be prepared to use force, and the householder is permitted to use weapons in defence of his life and property, but neither is entitled to use more force than is necessary. International police forces will be under the same obligation, and the effectiveness of their intervention will depend rather on prompt and firm action than on its violence. It is unthinkable that the atomic bomb or even strategic air bombing on a decisive scale should be used except as a last resort, and that in itself precludes prompt action. The older types of weapons, modified as they may be by invention, obviously lend themselves to restricted and regulated use to a much greater degree, and the more that military force is designed for police purposes only the more are the old weapons likely to remain the primary form of armament.

The atomic bomb must surely be looked on as a reserve of power only to be exerted as a last resort. I am assuming that we have to consider the employment of the international police to deal not only with deliberate aggression but also for intervention in disputes of a more localized character between hot-headed States. For armies of occupation on preventive duties, motorized infantry are clearly most suitable, and it is interesting to learn that Field-Marshal Montgomery is already arming and training artillery and armoured units for employment as infantry; though that may be partly in order to allow his infantry units to have their fair share of leave and to facilitate demobilization processes without unduly depleting his infantry force of experienced men.

It is too early to come to definite conclusions regarding the use of the atomic bomb as an instrument of war, but we may be unduly alarmed at its appearance. I think there is every probability that it will never again be used. So long as it remains a unilateral weapon in the hands of a peace-loving power the limitations imposed on its use are so great as to be practically prohibitive. If, on the other hand, its secrets become widely known it is hardly conceivable that even an aggressive power would dare to make use of it.

After the 1914–18 war it was generally believed that, in spite of prohibition, gas would be a principal weapon in future wars, and every nation took precautions against it and was prepared to use it immediately in case signatures were repudiated. As we know, expectations proved wrong and gas was not used at all; not, we may be sure, because of scruples on the part of Germany, but because of dangers arising from its reprisal use. It was not a sufficiently deadly weapon to form an absolute deterrent to war or to ensure decisive victory, but it was a sufficiently formidable weapon to be a deterrent to one particular form of war—because there was no prospect of its unilateral employment. The atomic bomb is evidently an immensely more terrible weapon than gas, and provided an aggressor nation is given no opportunity to use it unilaterally it may fall into the limbo of unused weapons.

GAME of Bluff Might be Played with the Older and Normal Weapons

Perhaps the greatest danger is that should an aggressor be given the opportunity of providing himself with the weapon he might carry out his designs with normal weapons, counting on the unwillingness of other nations to initiate a form of warfare with such catastrophic potentialities. Too implicit reliance on the deterrent effect of the new weapon might, in fact, result in a game of bluff in which the side that had neglected the older weapons would probably be the loser.

We have perhaps to take into account the weapon as a threat rather than the effects produced by its actual use. But the main conclusion to be drawn is that more than ever there is a need for pacific nations to be armed and prepared to take anticipatory preventive action boldly and promptly.

Japan's Surrender Envoys Receive Their Orders

AT MANILA on August 19, 1945, in response to a command from General MacArthur, arrived the Japanese surrender delegation, numbering 16. Filing down the gangway from the U.S.A.A.F. C-54 transport plane (1), which had brought them from Ie Island, off Okinawa, they were preceded by Gen. Torashiro Kawabe, vice-chief of the Imperial Japanese staff.

General Kawabe bowed as he presented his credentials to Gen. E. Richard Sutherland, Gen. MacArthur's Chief of Staff (2). At Nichol's Field, the Manila airport (3), they were escorted off the runway by Maj.-Gen. C. A. Willoughby. Maj.-Gen. S. J. Chamberlain (4), in charge of all U.S. staff engaged in occupation plans. Map shows where Allied troops were first landed on August 26; shaded is zone to which enemy had to withdraw.

Photos, Associated Press. Map by courtesy of The Daily Mail.

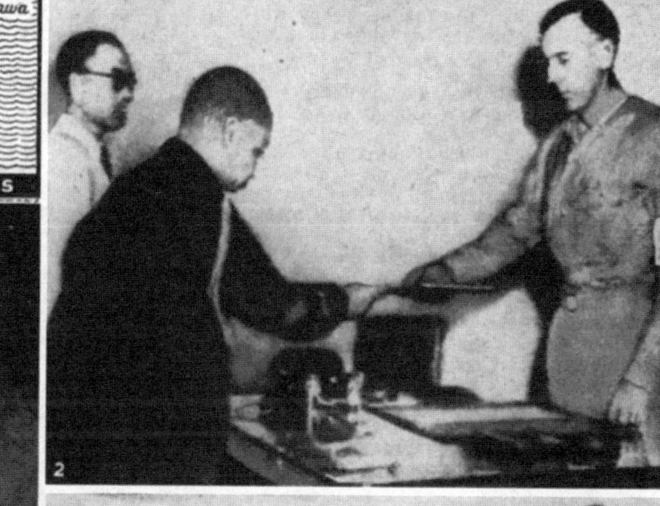

PROCLAIMING from the White House on August 14, 1945, the news of the Japanese capitulation, President Truman announced the appointment of General MacArthur as Allied Supreme Commander to receive the enemy's formal surrender. Within 24 hours the General had ordered the Japanese to cease fire and send to Manila representatives fully empowered by the Emperor. That same day (August 15) Tokyo radio announced that the Premier, Baron Suzuki (appointed on April 8), had resigned and that the 58-year-old War Minister Anami had committed suicide to "atone for his failure." Later, the Emperor himself addressed his people by radio (for the first time) to announce the surrender of the Japanese fighting forces.

Japanese radio began pleading for an extension of the time-limit to complete surrender arrangements; not until August 19 did the awaited envoys from Tokyo reach MacArthur's headquarters in Manila. There they were received by Gen. Sutherland, Chief of Staff. The C.-in-C. himself did not appear, and Admiral Nimitz was represented by his Assistant Chief of Staff, Rear-Admiral Sherman. On Bougainville, in the Solomons, enemy land and sea forces, through Lt.-Gen. Kanda, surrendered to Lt.-Gen. Savige, commanding the Australians.

ON Aug. 20, broadcasting from New Delhi, Lord Louis Mountbatten ordered F.-Marshal Count Terauchi, commanding the Japanese Southern Army, to send representatives to Rangoon. Not until the following day, however, did the enemy divulge to their people the imminent occupation. It was revealed on Aug. 23 that among Allied warships to anchor in Tokyo Bay for the signing of the instrument of surrender on board the U.S. battleship Missouri were H.M.S. Duke of York, flagship of Sir Bruce Fraser, commanding the British Pacific Fleet, and H.M.S. King George V, flagship of Vice-Admiral Sir Bernard Rawlings, commander of the British Task Force.

With Our Navies Today

By

FRANCIS E. McMURTRIE

SIMULTANEOUSLY with the VJ celebrations, an Allied Naval Exhibition and Navy Week was opened at Rotterdam by Prince Bernhard of the Netherlands. With the Prince were the Dutch Minister of Marine, Mr. J. M. de Booy ; Admiral of the Fleet Sir John Tovey, Commander-in-Chief at the Nore, who crossed the North Sea to attend the ceremony ; Admiral J. T. Furstner, Commander-in-Chief of the Royal Netherlands Navy ; and Vice-Admiral Sir Gerald Dickens, Senior British Naval Officer in the Netherlands ; Rear-Admiral R. K. Dickson, Chief of Naval Information, Admiralty ; and Rear-Admiral G. W. Stoeve, Royal Netherlands Navy.

After the opening ceremony a display was given by Royal Marine Commando troops drawn from the 4th Brigade, which stormed Walcheren. This consisted of an attack on an enemy position, in which the assault party took advantage of every inequality in the rough ground, in the blitzed area of Rotterdam. The few buildings that remain standing here, including the large store in which the exhibition was housed, echoed to the sound of thunder-flashes and the patter of machine-gun fire, while a crowd of nearly 20,000 people cheered themselves hoarse.

In the evening there was a firework display from the British and Dutch warships present. These included the cruiser Bellona, flagship of Rear-Admiral A. E. M. B. Cunninghame-Graham ; the destroyers Onslow and Garth ; the submarines Tuna (British), Dolfijn and Zeehond (both Dutch) ; two tank landing ships and two motor torpedo boats, one of which was Dutch. During the day there were opportunities for the people of Rotterdam to take passage in " ducks " to the landing ships, a highly popular diversion.

INGENIOUS Device for Training Crews of Anti-Aircraft Guns

Other features which drew crowds were Royal Marine Band performances, including the colourful ceremony of beating the retreat ; a display of close-order drill by the King's Squad, Portsmouth Division, Royal Marines ; two sailing regattas, one between local yachts sailed by British and Dutch crews, the other between service whalers ; a football match between H.M.S. Bellona and Rotterdam ; and sundry dances and other entertainments. Coinciding with the peace celebrations these events aroused tremendous enthusiasm in Rotterdam and The Hague, where people are just recovering from the long strain imposed by the German occupation. The exhibition itself included exhibits of weapons of all kinds, including torpedoes, mines, shells of various calibres, and naval aircraft. Amongst the last-named was the latest type of Seafire, with a speed of over 400 miles an hour. There were specimens of enemy weapons such as the " Biber " and " Seehund " midget submarines, a one-man human torpedo and an explosive motor boat. An exceptionally interesting exhibit was the Portobel Dome, an ingenious device for training anti-aircraft guns' crews, in which the sounds of the aircraft's engine and of the firing of the guns are realistically reproduced. Each man under training mans his gun just as he would on board a ship, and does his best to hit the enemy aircraft as it passes over in the form of a shadow on the dome. The number of shots fired and the total of hits are registered automatically.

EXCHANGES of Warships Between the Royal Navy and U.S. Navy

The Wrens produced a very effective section, in which methods of rigging and splicing and visual signalling were demonstrated. Wrens could also be seen working on radio gear for aircraft. There were a great many photographs showing the gradual progress of the war in the Atlantic, Mediterranean and Pacific. It was noticeable that the Dutch took the utmost interest in these photographs, examining them closely and reading out the captions to one another. Altogether the occasion was a tremendous success, and I returned from Rotterdam wondering how long it would be before the Admiralty is able to stage a Navy Week in this country again.

With the end of Lease-Lend, warships are starting to change hands. The first of these exchanges took place at Chatham and Harwich last month, when ten American-built frigates of the Royal Navy were turned over to the United States Navy in return for ten British-built corvettes which hoisted the American flag in 1942. All the frigates were of the Diesel-propelled type, belonging to the " Captain " class, while the corvettes were of the " Flower " design. In the former were included H.M.S. Grindall, and in the latter the U.S.S. Tenacity, which was launched as H.M.S. Candytuft. There are, of course, many more American-built British warships than there are British-built United States ships.

An official summary of the war in the Pacific was issued by the United States Navy Department on August 15. Fresh facts exposed in this statement are that the formidable Japanese expedition defeated in the Battle of Midway in June 1942, was almost certainly aimed at Hawaii, though Midway was included in its preliminary programme. This is described as " potentially the greatest threat ever poised against the United States during the war." By 1943 it was the many enemy-occupied islands with airfields, " far more than the Japanese fleet," which threatened to hamper the free movement of the United States Navy in the Central Pacific, along the most direct route to the Philippines and Japan.

A REMARKABLE instance of the cautious way the Japanese used their fleet was the engagement off the Komandirski Islands in 1943. Here a small American group comprising one heavy cruiser, two light cruisers and four destroyers succeeded in turning back a Japanese force twice its size when the latter sought to reinforce and supply garrisons in the Aleutian Islands. United States submarines are believed to have accounted for more than 146 enemy fighting ships and 1,041 merchant ships during their unceasing patrols in Japanese waters. In this way they established a highly effective blockade of the enemy's supply routes.

It is probable that the battle on June 20, 1944, in which U.S. naval aircraft attacked the Japanese fleet to the eastward of the Philippines, sinking two of its carriers, two destroyers and a tanker, would have been even more disastrous to the enemy had not the American planes been short of fuel, which obliged them to break off the action.

IN the greatest Japanese defeat, a series of three engagements between October 23 and 26, known together as the Battle for Leyte, it is now suspected that five enemy battleships may have been sunk. This appears to be borne out by the number found in port in subsequent air operations. The fifth ship may have been the old battleship Kongo. It is considered that the battleships Ise, Hyuga and Haruna, all of which were bombed at Kure in July, were so heavily damaged that they may be written off as total losses. As regards aircraft carriers, the position is somewhat more obscure, according to the latest American reports. It is thought that not more than two of the large fleet type and two of smaller size remain afloat ; but there may be one or two more in the completing stage.

" ONE OF THE MOST SENSATIONAL STORIES OF THE WAR " was how Admiral Nimitz, Allied Naval C.-in-C. in the Pacific, described the rescue of 159 British and Australian prisoners. They were survivors from the torpedoed Japanese transport Rakuyo Maru, sunk in the Marianas during July 1945, when U.S. submarines Sealion, Barb, Queenfish, Pampanito and Growler destroyed at least ten enemy ships. After five days at sea some were too weak to move (left) as the Queenfish came alongside. Others boarded the Sealion (right).

Photos, U.S. Official

After Years of Trooping the Queen Mary is Home

SOUTHAMPTON ROARED ITS DELIGHT when on August 11, 1945, the giant Queen Mary entered her peacetime berth for the first time since 1939, when she became the world's largest troopship. Crowds cheered, bands played and aircraft circled overhead as, with flags flying, the 80,000-ton luxury liner sailed up Southampton Water. As her thousand privileged passengers from the U.S. disembarked, other gangways were being hurriedly run into position for the embarkation of stores for the return trip with 15,000 U.S. soldiers six days later, when her passengers included Admiral Harold R. Stark, former Commanding Officer of U.S. Naval Forces in Europe. See also page 312. *Photo, Central Press*

Removing All the Nazi Smears from Norway

THE TASK OF EVACUATING by land and sea the 140,000 members of the Wehrmacht then in the Narvik area of Norway—at an average rate of 2,500 a day—was begun in early August 1945, by British troops transformed from Royal Artillery A.A. regiments to infantry. At the request of the Norwegian Government, 7,000 Germans were sent to Finmark (see pages 588-89 and 749, Vol. 8), to help restore life and communications to this heavily-despoiled province of northernmost Norway; vast quantities of equipment fell into British hands, for the Nazis had built up stores sufficient to maintain their forces there for at least nine months. Small arms ammunition and brass casings of all shells were salved, but large-calibre ammunition was dumped in the Narvik fjord. Metal from all seized gun-barrels, except those likely to be of use to the Allies, was scheduled as scrap. On August 4 a cemetery at Narvik, in which 85 British, French and Polish troops are buried, was handed over to Allied care by the local town council.

KING HAAKON INSPECTED 3,000 Allied troops outside the Royal Palace, Oslo, on VJ-Day; among them were men of the British 1st Airborne Division (1), withdrawn from Norway on August 27. On August 20, in the Masonic Temple, Oslo, began the sensational trial of Abraham Vidkun Quisling, former leader of the Norwegian Nazi Party, charged with treason by facilitating the German Occupation in 1940. On the opening day of the trial, as grim-faced Quisling (2, foreground) faced his accusers, his Counsel, Hr. Henrik Bergh (formerly a Resistance leader), poured him a glass of water under the supervision of a Norwegian soldier in British battle-dress.

Among the tasks allotted to our forces was that of destroying vast stacks of Nazi propaganda material; thousands of books and pamphlets were burned daily (3). Ex-members of the Wehrmacht en route for the Fatherland embarked at a Norwegian port (4).

Photos, British Official, Associated Press

Jap Resistance Flickers Out in the Sittang Bend

WAITING FOR THE ORDER TO FIRE was this mountain battery of the 14th Army (1) east of Toungoo in Burma, during the monsoon in mid-summer 1945. In the Sittang Bend, where fighting was still reported after the Japanese surrender on August 14, Gen. Sir Claude Auchinleck, C.-in-C. India, spoke with men of the Royal Tank Regt. (2). In a fox-hole a U.S. Field Service volunteer tended a wounded Gurkha (3). Hunger-weakened Japanese, supporting themselves on sticks (4), were captured while trying to escape.

Photos, British and Indian Official

Radar Helped the Army Gunners to Beat the Blitz

Among the greatest scientific achievements in the field of war was radar, details of which are now released. Its enormous value, in defeating enemy air attack, is here described specially for "The War Illustrated." It was radar, uncannily ingenious, which reinforced the skill of our A.A. gunners to such a degree that Hitler's terror-campaign of doodle-bugs failed in its purpose.

THIS phase of radar, the brain-child of Sir Robert Watson Watt, C.B., Scientific Adviser on Telecommunications to the War Cabinet, and colleague of the other radio "back-room boys," was begun for the Army in conditions of great secrecy on October 31, 1936, under the special care of two of Sir Robert Watt's scientists, Mr. H. Dewhurst and Mr. W. S. Eastwood. As their work progressed, their secret A.A. laboratory was moved to Dunkirk, near Canterbury. They were joined and reinforced by workers from the War Office, and there came into being the magic letters "G.L."—Gun and Light Laying.

Three experimental models of the first radar apparatus for automatically spotting the position of an enemy aircraft for A.A. gunners were made. And on June 20, 1939, Mr. Churchill inspected the first working G.L. radar for the A.A. This gave a bearing accuracy of about one degree on either side of the possible target in the night skies, and a pick-up range for "first warning" of about ten miles.

IN the early months of the War, residents at the edge of green spaces around London were puzzled by the sudden appearance of U.S. bulldozers, the crews of which swiftly levelled the ground. And then about two acres of wire-netting were erected on low posts as a sort of giant spider's web close to the ground. In the centre of the web was a small wooden hut. It can now be told that these webs were the centres of the G.L. system which very rapidly helped the A.A. network to beat the blitz. Mr. L. H. Bedford, a private scientist working for a firm of television manufacturers, was the first to suggest that a height-finding (or, more accurately, elevation finding) attachment could be fitted to the first G.L.s, and as it was necessary to measure the elevation angle above a smooth surface the irregularities in the ground had to be smoothed out.

Radar as at first used by the Ack-Ack crews had the disadvantage that radio echoes were being picked up from the balloon barrage. It was as though a powerful but dispersed searchlight were trained on a forest in the hope of spotting a man walking between the trees. There was another snag, in that manual controls had to be used with the first Army radar equipment to keep the invisible beam fixed on the invisible target.

Looking at An Unseen Target

But by the summer of 1940 scientists working in laboratories of the Ministry of Aircraft Production had produced a "radio-theodolite" with a very narrow beam. German aircraft could be spotted between the wires of a balloon barrage—and as though by a miracle the apparatus trained itself on the target at about 30,000 yards, and then kept the aerials fixed on the bombers no matter how they weaved through the clouds. Canadian scientists were also at work during 1940, and very soon from Canadian workshops came an independently designed version of this G.L., and it was actually in production before the English set.

Within the next 24 months amazing progress was made with the "continuous follow" device, so that G.L. radar aerials were able to keep themselves automatically in line with the enemy bombers. "It is," says one of the scientists who worked on this gear, "an impressive and at first uncanny experience to see the aerial system 'looking' at an unseen target miles away (maybe in cloud, or so far distant that it cannot be distinguished by eye) and following the evolutions of the target unerringly and automatically, its movements to keep the target in 'view' being used to inform the gun predictor, without human intervention, of the target position and velocity."

BEHIND the scenes, scientists in other M.A.P. laboratories had been striving to use tinier wavelengths, of centimetres (less than half an inch) instead of the more familiar metre-length waves of ordinary radio. These give a much narrower invisible pencil of radar waves. The truth was that we were too near the front line. Enemy bombing meant that our Ack-Ack radar posts were in use night and day. We could neither manufacture the latest stuff which scientists had invented, nor stop the war machine to fit the new parts. We had, however, sent a mission to Washington at an early stage in the war and had told the U.S. experts all we knew about radar. They copied our ideas, improved on them, brought our own aspirations to reality: and while this was a blow to national pride, when the V1 flying-bomb campaign began we had good reason to be grateful to the American enterprise.

"ELSIE"—RADAR EQUIPMENT used in conjunction with Ack-Ack searchlights which enabled the beams of the latter to be switched directly on to the target. **See also facing page, and page 320.** *Photo, Planet News*

AS the menace began, the coastline of Britain was dotted with tiny, efficient mobile American "SCR.584s"—the only visible sign of which was a huge wire-mesh basket shaped like a rose-bowl and facing towards the launching sights of the flying bombs. Immediately each bomb was launched from the Calais coast the radar vans picked up a signal, and the "wire basket" aerials turned themselves in the direction of the bomb's flight. These amazing robots could actually feed the "rates" of target movement directly into a No. 10 gun predictor.

"This combination led to our remarkable success in shooting down the flying bomb," a scientist stated, "and together with the work of fighter aircraft (which used their own airborne radar weapons) in preventing fully 80 per cent of the missiles from reaching their targets."

Before the V1 menace, scientists had been standing outside a group of huts on the south coast during the first violent raid on Christchurch (on the night of June 20, 1940), and they were anxious at the way searchlight operators had to grope ineffectively about the skies while the bombers droned overhead unseen. This night was the turning point in yet another amazing new device to help the gunners. Its official code-name was S.L.C.—searchlight control; but this did not remain for long before being changed affectionately and unofficially to "Elsie."

Contribution by Jap Inventors

"Elsie" uses five aerials. If you have been close to a large searchlight battery you may have seen the wire-mesh circles behind the little groups of sticks which suffice for aerials on the tiny wavelength of about 10 feet employed. The five aerials give a pair each for "up and down" and "left and right" direction sense, with a fifth to transmit the steady radar beam. The aerials are known as "Yagi"—this being the only material contribution Japanese inventors have made to radar.

First tests with "Elsie" were so startling that a private message was sent to Mr. Churchill. Lord Cherwell (Churchill's scientific adviser) and Watson Watt gave a report of what "Elsie" could do against the night bombers. Britain was already committed to an overwhelming radio programme, but with characteristic decision Mr. Churchill ordered that a number of sets should be produced with all speed and that "Elsie" should become a top priority job. But for "Elsie," Britain might have been bombed to surrender-point.

"Eighteen sets were produced in a few weeks," I was told, "and they were mostly made from bits and pieces of other equipment by the most intense day and night effort of men and women in the factories. Apart from a few failures the majority of sets worked well—and yet another weapon had been born, the searchlight capable of being directed on to the enemy with the certainty of illuminating him immediately the order 'Expose' was given."

"ELSIE" went into the N. African campaign, and played a big part in the Sicilian landings. We had to land on steeply shelving beaches, and some form of radar predictor for the guns was necessary to protect our armies during the critical hours immediately following the landing. The standard G.L. was too large for the purpose, so somebody at the War Office had the bright idea of sending specially adapted "Elsies" out to Sicily. This would give, they thought, sufficiently good guidance to our Ack-Ack at short range, and the portable gun-laying version of "Elsie" became known, flippantly enough, as "Baby Maggie."

As troops scaled the Sicilian shores, concealed and camouflaged "Baby Maggies" gave warning of Italian and Luftwaffe fighters overhead. The secret radar "Elsies" of the type which had shielded London from the full force of Goering's hatred, most ably protected our first invasion forces in the North African campaign. The supreme example of radar in defence (it was disclosed by Air Chief Marshal Sir Arthur Tedder on August 14, 1945) was at Malta when the available fighter defence was worn down to almost nothing.

These Were the Uncanny Secrets of A.A. Command

EQUIPMENT FOR SHOOTING DOWN FLYING BOMBS was included in a radar demonstration (1) given in Hyde Park, London, in mid-August 1945. Attached to a light A.A. gun, it transmitted range, bearing and elevation data automatically to a standard predictor controlling the gunfire. Invaluable in the operation of radar were the A.T.S.; a predictor detachment at action stations (2) gives the gunners instructions to fire (4). This Canadian-designed radar set (3) is contained in a cabin which rotates on a trailer for direction-finding; the balloon, when released, is used for checking the accuracy of the set at the closer ranges. See also facing page.

Photos, British Official, P.N.A., Keystone

Now It Can Be Told!

HOW THE NAVY'S PHANTOM FLEET HOAXED THE HUN

For nearly two years of the war the Royal Navy used a fleet of wooden warships fitted with dummy guns to hoax enemy reconnaissance aircraft and bombers. They were merchant ships with elaborate superstructures of plywood and canvas, painted to transform them into replicas of R-class battleships and an aircraft carrier.

Dummy warships had been used with success in 1914-18, and in 1939 a new force of dummy ships, known as Fleet Tenders for purposes of security, was constructed on the instructions of Mr. Winston Churchill, then First Lord of the Admiralty. Three 7,900-ton merchant ships were used: the S.S. Pakeha and S.S. Waimana being turned into the 33,500-ton battleships Revenge and Resolution, and the S.S. Mamari becoming the aircraft carrier Hermes.

They were manned by naval "runner" crews, and their holds were filled with thousands of empty barrels to give them greater buoyancy in the event of their being hit by bombs or torpedoes. Many rumours, which are known to have reached the enemy, were started by the appearance of one of these mystery ships in ports in Scotland and on the Tyne. By 1941 the dummy warships had served their purpose. S.S. Mamari (alias Hermes) had been wrecked off the Wash; the other two were handed back to their owners and still sail as merchant ships.

It was left to a real battleship, the 33-year-old H.M.S. Centurion, disarmed under the Washington Naval Treaty, to carry this imposture into foreign waters. In a fortnight in April 1941, while the Devonport dockyard was under heavy air attack, she was converted into a creditable imitation of the new battleship H.M.S. Anson. She was fitted with a dummy after-funnel, mainmast, main armament and, with a crew of 16 officers and 265 men, set out on a 20,000-mile trip round the Cape that ended at Bombay. In June 1942 she sailed in a Malta convoy that was intercepted by the Italian Fleet. She was repeatedly attacked by bombers, shot down one Stuka, and damaged at least four J.U.188s. Her greatest danger was that her wooden armament might catch fire.

Once, in a monsoon in the Indian Ocean, her dummy "A" turret was swept overboard by a heavy sea, and astonished lookouts in the convoy reported a 14-in. gun floating down the fairway! Perhaps her strangest trip was the voyage home manned by a scratch crew of naval officers and men due for repatriation. Their main armament was half-a-dozen rifles, apart from the dummy guns. When they entered the Suez Canal from the Bitter Lakes a signal was made to the ship from the Senior Naval Officer ashore. "You leave the Pyramids on your left," it said. The Centurion was finally sunk as a blockship off the Normandy coast on D-Day to form a breakwater for landing craft—part of the Mulberry project.

ROYAL NAVY'S DUMMY WARSHIPS which had foxed the Luftwaffe included a replica of the 10,850 tons carrier Hermes, seen (top) at Scapa Flow in July 1940 and (in the left background above) flanked by dummy battleships of the "R" class (38,000 tons)—all merchant vessels camouflaged with wood and canvas, as revealed in this page. *Photos, British Official*

THIS WAS HITLER'S AMAZING PLAN FOR BRITAIN

There recently fell into British hands a document which now can be regarded as grimly humorous. Entitled "The Military Administration of England," it was a close secret of the German High Command. From it we learn that Hitler had planned to complete the occupation of this country before September 9, 1940, and it was to be transformed into Germany's main war workshop.

Weapons were to be produced under Nazi direction for the Battle of Russia. To prevent sabotage Field-Marshal von Brauchitsch, then C.-in-C. of all German forces, ordered that the entire male population between 17 and 45 should be deported to the Continent and interned, as soon as possible after Britain was defeated. They were presumably to be distributed on the Continent as slave labourers, and German workers sent to this country to keep the war machine operating with the minimum interruption.

This blue-print for Britain in defeat was mapped out a year before Hitler invaded Russia by a staff of administration experts working under the direct guidance of Von Brauchitsch and General Halder, the chief of staff of the German High Command. Only 195 copies of the document were printed, 78 were distributed among high Nazi authorities and Army officers, the remainder reserved for the archives of the High Command.

Von Brauchitsch, who was relieved of his command by Hitler soon after the Stalingrad debacle, issued a directive that "the chief task of the military administration in England will be to use all the resources of the country for the German war economy." In the German idiom, "England" usually signifies Great Britain, and the document probably applied to all areas of the United Kingdom. Here are some other regulations outlined in the document:

Any person impeding the German war

effort in Britain by starting hostilities will be treated as a guerilla and shot. Hostages will be taken as a "security" measure. National laws in force before the occupation will be maintained only if they are not contrary to the purposes of the occupation. The country's state of health will be considered important only as a safeguard for the resources of the country, and non-fraternization policy for the troops will be enforced on a limited scale.

Death-Threat Hanging Over All

In conversation with the population the utmost reserve is ordered. The enemy's intelligence service will be active, and any fraternization might therefore have severe consequences. Any violence against the population, and looting, will be a Military Court offence and punishable by death. Monuments will be protected. There will be compulsory acceptance of German State banknotes and coins. The rate of exchange will be 9·6 marks to the pound (the pound would thus have been debased to a value of 13s. 7d., according to pre-war exchange rates).

All public utilities, including gas, electricity, the railways and objects of art will be under the special protection of the Army. Sabotage will include the concealment of harvest products. The concealment of firearms, including shot-guns and other hunting arms, will be punishable by death. Severe punishment will be passed by military courts on civilians who associate with prisoners of war, make slurring remarks about the German Army of Occupation or its commanders, circulate pamphlets or organize meetings.

Industrial concerns, and commercial firms, including banks, must be kept open. Closing without adequate reason will be severely punished. German soldiers can purchase what they desire. Instead of cash payment, in many cases, they can issue certificates for the value of the purchase. A military court can use its discretion in trying persons under 18, but may pass death sentence if it sees fit.

Listening to non-German radio broadcasts is a punishable offence. Excepted are non-German radio stations which have been permitted by the occupation army. The death sentence can be passed on persons retaining radio transmitters. A curfew will be imposed from sunset to sunrise.

The following commodities will be requisitioned: Agricultural products of all kinds, ores, mica, asbestos, precious and semi-precious stones, fuel, rubber, textiles, leather and timber. Farmers and dealers, including innkeepers, may only dispose of agricultural products in quantities necessary for the most urgent needs of consumers.

Britain was to be divided into districts in the charge of army commanders, who were to act as "governors." Subordinated to them were field and town units. The document finally reveals that astonishingly intricate arrangements had been completed for our economic enslavement.

"An army economic staff will function under the direct orders of the C.-in-C. of the Army," it states. "It will be installed in all harbours and industrial centres, and will have charge of transporting raw materials and completed war equipment. Immediately upon the defeat of England, administration staffs will join the Armies of Occupation. They will be made up of experts on food, agriculture and industrial production."

—A.P. Dispatch from Hamburg.

GANGSTERS FOR COMMANDOS

AMONG recruiting suggestions considered in the early days of the Commandos was whether it would be better to use real toughs or gangsters either from the United States or British cities rather than soldiers. The view taken, it is revealed in "Soldier," the British Army magazine, by Brig. Dudley W. Clarke, who recruited the first Commandos, was that the gangster was too unreliable. The idea was dropped. So, too, was a proposal from a convict who offered to form a Commando of convicts and warders!

SOUTHEND'S "PIER SHIP" was a wartime secret well-kept by the townsfolk of that famous Essex watering-place. On the outbreak of the air raids on Britain a special upper deck was superimposed on the Prince George extension of the pier and a battery of Ack-Ack guns embedded in concrete mounted on it. From here the gunners inflicted heavy toll on the Luftwaffe and the flying bomb. Pulling on their coats, the gun crews (above) raced to action stations on the approach of enemy aircraft heading for London. *Photo, Planet News*

WHITEFIELD MEMORIAL CHURCH, Tottenham Court Road, was completely destroyed on Sunday evening, March 25, 1945, by one of the last rocket bombs to fall on London. Of a congregation of 35, seven were killed. The church—as it was (above left), and (right) after being struck—was named after the famous evangelist, the Rev. George Whitefield (1714-70). Built on the site of a tabernacle he inaugurated in 1756, it was opened in 1903. Whitefield, a remarkable preacher, was credited with over 18,000 sermons.

Problem of Sudeten Germans in Czechoslovakia

A new chapter opened for Czechoslovakia with the restoration of her independence : this time the Czechs are seeing to it that they remain masters in their own country. Sternly they are evicting most of the Sudeten Germans. HENRY BAERLEIN sets out the background of this long-standing minority problem which led to the disintegration of the Republic in 1939.

It may seem surprising that the Germans, invited by the Czech rulers to settle in Bohemia in the 13th century because they were industrious artisans, should subsequently conduct themselves as if they were first-class citizens while they regarded the Czechs as very second-class. But when the Battle of the White Mountain, fought near Prague in 1620, resulted in a dire defeat of the Czechs at the hands of the Hapsburgs and a German domination which lasted for three centuries, there was every encouragement for the Germans in the country to consider themselves a Herrenvolk. The more so, seeing that after the aforesaid battle almost all the Czech Protestant noblemen were decapitated, their estates being given to German and other foreign aristocrats.

At last, in 1918, the Czechs regained the mastership of their own house. There are nations who in similar circumstances would have taken bitter vengeance on their oppressors. The German Parliament at Frankfort in 1848 marked one of the highest points in German democracy ; yet these very democrats strove to crush the last remnants of Czech political autonomy and treated the Czechs as if they were Germans—" Czech-speaking Germans." In their attitude to the Czechs there was no difference between German reactionaries and German democrats.

In 1914, Bethmann Hollweg, Chancellor of the Reich, declared that the war then opening was the struggle of the German world against Slavdom. Although the Czechs

KARL HERMANN FRANK, notorious Sudeten German and instigator of the wiping-out of Lidice (see illus. p. 184), in his prison cell in Prague in August 1945. He is among the war criminals to stand trial at Nuremberg.

avoided fighting when they could, and took every opportunity of going over to the Allies, their casualties were very great. Thousands were executed, greater numbers were imprisoned. Leading politicians were condemned to death or imprisonment. The country was ruthlessly pillaged, and it issued from the war impoverished. Yet when in October 1918 the Czechs were among the victors not a single German was molested. They lost their dominating position, remaining citizens with equal rights in all spheres of private and public life. After a few years President Masaryk gave them three portfolios in the Cabinet. It seemed as if the German citizens had been won over to friendly cooperation within the Republic.

But this hope was justified only so long as international conditions made it inopportune for the Germans to show their real intentions. With the rise of Hitler's power extreme German nationalism sprang up, which was hostile to the Czechoslovak Republic. In March 1938, immediately after the fall of Austria, both the German popular parties, the Agrarians and the Clericals, resigned from the Czech Government. The Social Democratic party continued to resist Nazi influence, and, together with the Communists, it did so for some time most courageously. But in the 1938 elections 92 per cent of the Czechoslovak Germans voted for Henlein, who had assumed the leadership.

After Hitler's arrival in Prague in March 1939—he slept for a night in the Hradshin, the castle of the old Czech monarchs—this small loyal percentage melted away, and during the years of his domination there was no visible sign of protest or disagreement among the Germans of the frontier districts, who are usually called Sudeten Germans. Indeed, throughout the War of 1939-45 they perpetrated more crimes against the Czechs than did the other Germans. They could speak Czech, they were familiar with Czech technique of resistance during the First Great War, and they were the best equipped *agents provocateurs* and tools of the regime. The real ruler of the "Protectorate" was Karl Hermann Frank (portrait in this page), the Sudeten German bookseller, who had gone bankrupt in Carlsbad and thus had a grievance against the Czechs.

Two and a Half Million to Leave

One million three hundred thousand Czechs were carried off to Germany. Tens of thousands were tortured, many of them to death, in concentration camps. The Jews were practically wiped out. There are some who try to excuse the German guilt by saying that they could not imagine what Hitler's regime would mean. But the Sudeten Germans had access to reports from all over the world, and they had a free Press. The Czechoslovak Government and the most important German newspapers, which preserved their liberal tradition to a certain extent, made no secret of what was going on in Germany. Yet, in spite of this—if not because of it—92 per cent and later 99 per cent were for Hitler.

The Czechs have decided not to return like for like, not to torture Germans in concentration camps and not to kill them ; but the majority of Germans will have to leave Czech territory. On July 21, 1945, Dr. Hubert Ripka, Czechoslovak Minister of Foreign Trade, stated in London :

> A number of Germans will be allowed to remain in the country. However, at least two and a half millions of them will have to leave Czechoslovakia. We must beg our British friends to understand the situation and to help us to solve this problem. The hatred and the distrust of the Germans is so intense that it will be better, even for the Germans themselves, to leave the country. Otherwise—I must state this quite frankly and emphatically—we do not know what may happen to the Sudeten Germans.
>
> Our Government desires to carry out the evacuation gradually and in an organized way. But we are not able to do so as long as the great Powers have not reached an agreed decision on the issue. The Soviet and the French Governments fully share our viewpoint. I have reason to believe that the British and the U.S. Governments are not opposed to it. But the expulsion of the Sudeten Germans has now been stopped because the Allied military authorities on the spot, Soviet as well as American, have received no instructions from their Governments how to act. The Soviet Commanders sympathize with our viewpoint, but the Soviet Government does not wish to force the issue before formal inter-Allied agreement has been reached.

SUDETENLAND, once more Czechoslovakian after seven years of, first, German infiltration, then Nazi military occupation.
By courtesy of News Chronicle

Under the German occupation the Czechs were officially listed as "Subjects of the Protectorate," whereas Germans in Czech territory were "Citizens of the German Reich." Let them then go home to the Reich. To enforce this would not, as some people have said, be to abandon the humanitarian traditions of which the Czechs are rightly proud. So large a number of potential enemies within the State, waiting only for another opportunity, is a threat to which the Czechs do not wish to be exposed. After a struggle of hundreds of years they would like finally to have an opportunity of sleeping in peace. The Germans will not be expelled indiscriminately. Those who fought against Hitler and persevered in the struggle will receive full protection. The Czechoslovak Government is naturally aware of the technical and economic difficulties of this transfer which might create some labour shortage in such industries as glass manufacture, the mines, and so forth. And for humanitarian reasons also it is more than likely that, as the Czechs say, the meal will not be eaten as hot as it is cooked.

Of course, a large number of Germans will depart of their own free will, their consciences not being very easy. A good many have fallen in the war and others have obtained posts in Germany. Those who stay will be given something equivalent to "first papers" in the United States, to be followed by citizenship after a certain period of satisfactory behaviour. The "Committee of the Alliance of Democratic Germans in Czechoslovakia," which was formed here in London, became the rallying point for Germans with sincere Czechoslovak sentiments. This committee has been for some time genuinely serving the interests of the Czechoslovak Germans, especially by warning them against all Pan-Germanism and systematically guiding them to democratic sentiments as loyal Czechoslovak citizens. The Czech Government counts on the cooperation of this committee in the process of re-establishing the Republic.

This will demand much effort, much self-denial and self-sacrifice, and it will also pre-suppose an entirely new conception of the problems involved, a discarding of old ideas and notions which have been rendered obsolete by the course of events, and their replacement by a new intellectual and political approach to the future. Karl Hermann Frank, handed over by the Americans to the Czechs, was lodged by them in that same prison in Prague where by his orders thousands of Czechs had been most brutally tortured.

Photo, Topical Press

'The Last of Our Enemies is Laid Low!'

Broadcasting at midnight on August 14, 1945, the Prime Minister said "Japan has today surrendered. The last of our enemies is laid low!" The next two days were proclaimed public holidays, and the spate of rejoicing that had prematurely overflowed in the welter of rumour became like a mighty torrent in the accomplished fact. This unique scene in Piccadilly symbolized the profound feeling of relief and thankfulness that swept through Britain and the Empire.

Their Majesties Drive in State to Open Parliament—

At the commencement of the two-day Victory holiday, on the morning of August 15, the King, accompanied by the Queen, drove in an open landau from Buckingham Palace (top left) for the ancient ceremony at the Palace of Westminster. Escort was provided by the Household Cavalry, and the route was lined by troops of the Brigade of Guards backed by cheering spectators. Rain falling steadily damped no-one's ardour, nor did it induce Their Majesties to raise an umbrella (top right).

Photos

—While Multitudes of Citizens Assemble to Rejoice

Around the Victoria Memorial and down the Mall vast jubilant crowds swayed and surged (bottom) : this was the remarkable scene from the roof of Buckingham Palace. All day long and far into the night the throngs, in highest good humour and orderly withal, continued to celebrate. Those able to approach the Palace clamoured again and again for sight of the King and Queen, who made their sixth and last appearance that day on the Palace balcony shortly before midnight.

Monty's Day of Triumph Down Lambeth Way

Photos, Keystone, Fox, Central Press

Lambeth held its own particular "party" on August 15, to acclaim Field-Marshal Sir Bernard Montgomery (top) as he drove like a prince in triumph through the streets to the Town Hall to receive the Freedom of the Borough, his birthplace (see also story in page 313). Many of the welcomers, still hoarse with cheering, went at night to swell the crowds that revelled in London's floodlighting: St. Paul's Cathedral (left) and the Tower of London (right) were among the spectacles.

VIEWS & REVIEWS Of Vital War Books

by Hamilton Fyfe

Never in any war before the one that has just ended have war reporters had such marvellous opportunities. When I think of the restrictions we were forced to endure between 1914 and 1918, I am consumed with envy. Yet we were considered to be highly favoured. In this war flying has been as much the reporter's routine as walking or riding in jeeps. The only army that let *me* fly was the Russian, and then I used to go up in such a crazy old Farman machine that I didn't altogether enjoy it.

This time, along with the enlarged opportunities, there have been many galling disappointments for men sent out to gather news of the far-flung battle-line. Take the case of Mr. Leonard Marsland Gander, on the staff of The Daily Telegraph, who has written a book called Long Road to Leros (Macdonald & Co., 10s. 6d.). Leros is a small island in the Aegean Sea. Mr. Gander's road to it began with a visit to Iceland, then he was ordered to Singapore at the time when "the situation in Malaya looked already desperate." He did not get there. By the date of his arrival by sea, at Mombasa, Malaya had been lost. He received a cable telling him to "proceed Rangoon earliest." But before he could get nearer to Burma than Calcutta, Rangoon had fallen too. Now his office cabled him to go immediately to Ceylon. He went: as soon as he reached there he was asked if he would like to go to sea in an aircraft carrier, which was about to join in operations of an offensive character in the Indian Ocean.

Long-Distance Naval Actions

He jumped at the chance of seeing a naval engagement, but unfortunately for him it turned out to be a "phantom battle." Although not a single shot was fired at the enemy, "the threat of our presence turned him back," and the whole incident made Mr. Gander believe that "naval actions of the future will be fought in the decisive stages between fleets which are invisible to each other, hundreds of miles apart. It will be a clash of air power, and only when one side or the other has lost its wings will the battle-fleet be able to use its strength." This would, comments the author, "be after all a logical continuation of the history of naval warfare. Once, the sailor had to get to grips by boarding; then, as the range of naval gunnery increased, so the distance at which actions could be fought extended."

It gives me a shiver to read of a future where, in the writer's opinion, war will be still one of the chief industries of mankind. How the atomic bomb would affect fighting at sea could not be taken into account for the purpose of this forecast; when Mr. Gander wrote his book nothing was known about this newest and most devastating of weapons. Until we can learn a great deal more about it and its effects, it seems to me to be useless to speculate on the manner in which human beings will destroy one another, if they persist in doing so, in years to come.

His voyage in the aircraft carrier ended, not at Colombo, where it had begun, and where Mr. Gander had left most of his baggage, but at Bombay; and there, after writing and with the greatest difficulty dispatching a message about the naval operations in which he had taken part, he received instructions to go to the Burmese Front. The story of that message is worth notice, as an illustration of the obstacles put in the way of the war reporter, even when he has been given special chances to produce good "copy." Mr. Gander asked if it could be radioed. He was told it could not, but if he would submit to Admiral Somerville's blue pencil going over it, it could go by cable. He sent it in, full of hope that it would quickly be on its way. But in three days' time he had it back. The authorities at Delhi declined to let it be cabled. They suggested "Send it by air mail." So by air mail it went. It reached the Admiralty in Whitehall but went no farther. It was quietly suppressed. That is the kind of maddening misfortune which every newspaper man has had to endure when obliged to submit what he writes to censorship. It seems to have happened with painful frequency to Mr. Gander's dispatches. Luckily he was able to send his account of an interview with Field-Marshal Wavell by Army signals wire, and it reached his office.

This happened just after he had arrived on the Burma frontier. He sketches the general "who gave Britain her first real military victory in the war, in the desert campaign" as a man with "a mastiff head and a face so lined and wrinkled that he would have seemed more than his threescore years but for his extremely vigorous manner and burly, youthful physique. His one eye, that of a highly intelligent man, roved abstractedly as he spoke. We had, I believe, interrupted him in his favourite relaxation, the solving of difficult crossword puzzles, at which he is particularly adept."

50,000 Miles With a War Reporter

Of General Alexander, as he was then, Mr. Gander says that "he has a forbidding, almost supercilious appearance, given him by his drooping upper lids, his close-clipped moustache, his prominent rounded jaw, and his Guardee style cap. There is nothing supercilious about him, however, except superficial looks, for he has the most charming, unaffected if entirely direct manner." Mr. Gander was able to give him two half-bottles of whisky, which were very welcome in the jungle, where evening meals had to be eaten in darkness because of stringent black-out and where night was "made hideous by howling hyenas, mosquitoes, croaking lizards and sweat." Again misfortune befell Mr. Gander's dispatch from the Burma border. It was sent off by naked native runner in a sealed waterproof tin. Later, when he reached the place to which it was addressed and whence it should have been sent on by wire, he was greeted by a British sergeant who said casually, "I think I've got a package for you." It contained the report sent by "those cheerful and dauntless native runners."

While he was still lamenting this blow, Mr. Gander had a cable from Fleet Street: "Can you get to Moscow quickly?" The quickest way was to go by Baghdad and Persia, but no sooner had he arrived at Teheran when he was told in another cable, "Regret Moscow off. Complete your visit and return India." Back in Delhi he ran across General Wingate and found that "anybody less like the conventional idea of the hardy bronzed soldier and man of action could hardly be conceived. He had a thin, pallid and aesthetic face" (I think Mr. Gander must have meant "ascetic") "with a long bony nose. He was a great talker and, as he talked rapidly on an immense variety of subjects, leaning earnestly forward, a rebellious lock of his thick brown hair would fall over his forehead. He did not smoke and hardly ever took strong drink. It was hard to associate this gentle, mild-mannered man with his reputation as a ruthless, resourceful jungle fighter and brilliant guerilla leader. Only when he began to dogmatize on some favourite subject could you get a glimpse of the iron will and the driving power in that frail frame."

LEONARD MARSLAND GANDER was the only war correspondent to witness the heroic British defence of the Dodecanese island of Leros in November 1943. This and other of his experiences are described in the book here reviewed. *Photo, The Daily Telegraph*

From Delhi Mr. Gander flew to Cairo in accordance with an order from his office to join the Eighth Army in the Middle East. But he was too late. The Eighth Army had left; it was concentrating for the invasion of Sicily. Then followed "weary fruitless months in which nothing happened. The 'forgotten' war correspondents in Egypt grew more and more despondent at our inactivity." However, everything comes to him who waits. In September 1943, after the Italian surrender, the Germans started attacking the islands in the Aegean known as the Dodecanese (there are twelve of them, and "dodeka" is the Greek for twelve). Mr. Gander was told by the British army authorities he could go in that direction if he "made his own arrangements." That, you can guess, was a very difficult job, but at last after encountering many obstacles, he managed to land on Leros just before the German invasion began.

Gun Barrel Became White-Hot

There was a small British force on the island and a good many Italians, who were no use at all, with a few exceptions, such as an Ack-Ack gunner who "fired with great verve and prodigality till the barrel of his gun went white hot" and did some useful, accurate shooting, too. If the attack had been made only from the sea, it would certainly have been repelled. But, in spite of the unsuitability of the rocky surface, parachutists were dropped in large numbers and gradually the defence was worn down. At last Mr. Gander had his chance, and his story of this little engagement went all over the world. He escaped before the surrender in order to send it.

He had wandered far and wide, travelled 50,000 miles at least, seen many lands, suffered many disappointments, but he struck good fortune at last. And he was collecting all the time materials for a very entertaining book.

We Helped the Dutch With Their Harvesting

AT AN AMSTERDAM LABOUR Exchange British troops offered their services as harvesters to worried Dutch farmers. A hearty welcome awaited each volunteer on arrival in the fields (right).

IN RESPONSE TO A BROADCAST APPEAL by the Netherlands Prime Minister in mid-July to the effect that "though the corn stands yellow in the fields there are not the men," British soldiers lent a hand—and Dutch newspapers carried the headline "The Tommies Help!"

HOLLAND'S GRATITUDE

At Buckingham Palace on August 19, 1945, there were delivered to Their Majesties a letter and a bunch of flowers—the simple gift of Netherlanders who had served in Britain during the war. The flowers, picked that morning from some of the fields of Holland, were brought to England by plane and, with the letter, were presented to Queen Elizabeth by the Netherlands Ambassador, His Excellency Jonkheer van Verduynen. Here is the letter :

None of us has yet had an opportunity to thank the men and women of Britain who received us in their midst, not as refugees but as guests, and who have put up with us and our thousands of fellow-exiles year after year. It is to these, our patient and generous hosts, that we now crave to say, "Thank you and thank you again."

To the Ministers of State and the Members of Parliament who threw beleaguered Britain's doors wide open to the highest and lowest of us, and thus enabled some of us to hoist again our country's flag and all of us to serve it. To the ministers of God, in whose churches many of us have found that which can raise even the most sorely tried above the fears and sorrows of exile. To the soldiers, sailors, and airmen who protected us. To the farmers who fed us, the landlords who housed us, the miners who warmed us, the drapers who clothed us, the shopkeepers who served us, the doctors who cured us. To the housewives who allowed us our place in the longest of queues, and to the publicans who allowed us our share in the shortest of stocks. To the Bobbies who told us the way, and the cabbies who helped us to get there. To the air-raid wardens with whom we wardened, and the fire-watchers with whom we fire-watched. To the telephone operators who never lost their patience at our most weird pronunciations.

Your Majesties, in leaving your people to go home, our hearts are so full that there is much else we should like to say. But rather than speak we would do something, something that tells more convincingly of our feelings than mere words can do. But what use is a commemoration plaque, or even such a modest monument or gift to charity as our mere handful could provide, to the housewives, the bus-conductors, or the farmers of Britain ? None, indeed. And so, forced to admit our inability to accompany this letter with 44,000,000 presents, we thought of something else. We thought that if we wanted to give some small pleasure to all the people of Britain there was only one way to do it, and that was to send our gift to those two persons whose joys are shared by all Britons in like measure, as all Britons' joys are shared by them. That, then, is why we decided to send these few flowers, picked from our own recovered fields, to Your Majesties, asking that you will accept them not only as a token of our gratitude, but also as an earnest of the resolve which is engraved in all our hearts in these four words :

WE SHALL NOT FORGET !

"GOOD-BYE—AND THANKS!" waved these young Netherlanders to departing Tommies who had helped to gather in the crops of 1945. Pulling flax (left) was one of the important tasks ; the soldier engaged on this back-breaking job had helped to build Bailey bridges at Arnhem and Nijmegen.

Photos, Pictorial Press

Mulberry Methods to Give Britain New Houses

"MULBERRY" HARBOUR CAISSONS were made of concrete, and similar methods of construction are now being tried in the erection of permanent houses. By building only the front of brick and the other walls of concrete 12 ins. thick a considerable saving of skilled labour is effected. The concrete is poured between the outer framework, already in place, and steel shuttering, a section of which is here being lowered into position on an experimental site in Middlesex. The brick-front is left to the last so that the concrete mixer and other equipment can be removed.

Royal Signals Have the Gloves Off in Germany

British Military Control serves out no soft treatment to German civilian workers. First perhaps to acknowledge the truth of this would be the employees of the supremely important communications system there. How these are supervised and controlled by the Royal Signals—present managers of Reich telecommunications in our zone—is explained by Capt. MARTIN THORNHILL, M.C.

THE whole German communications system in the British-occupied zone is in the charge of officers and men of the Royal Signals. This is the most important service in the country ; upon its successful operation depends the smooth running of the entire economic system. Under this rigorous supervision German workers are outshining even the sternest Nazi-run organization ; for the disciplined efficiency displayed by the Royal Signals in fighting days was a byword.

These are the men who built and maintained hundreds of miles of metallic strands and countless radio links forming the invasion army's vast communications web over beaches, mountains, through forests and rivers, tying together all units, co-ordinating the whole attack. As rapidly as areas were absorbed in the advance, Signals would go to work on the rehabilitating of existing telephone lines. Under withering sniper fire linesmen repaired damage done to overhead circuits by artillery, mortar and small arms fire ; soldering defective splices, transposing wires to clear cross-talk, replacing insulators shattered by retreating infantry, fixing new poles for those splintered by heavy guns, re-tying and re-sagging wires until reliable communication was effected.

IT was the specific mission of Royal Signals to weave and maintain this network with one hand while fighting off the foe with the other. For the swift tempo and varied needs of mechanized total war made it imperative that every man in the Corps should be fully battle-trained as well as expert in every aspect of communications. That is the measure of the training which qualifies the present managers of Reich telecommunications, and their German civilian employees have no option but to square up to the stern standard of labour and discipline which their soldier overseers expect of them.

There is another reason for this rigorous control. This is a sphere where watertight surveillance is vital. Only the strictest compliance with military orders can ensure British Army of the Rhine lines of communication, with secret circuits for messages in code. These are to enable the Army, should this prove necessary, to function with the same measure of security as it did throughout the invasion campaign. A second priority is hospitals and doctors, but no civilian can be linked up with Exchange without an Allied Military Government permit.

Staffed by German Civilians

All switchboards, including large automatic exchanges like Düsseldorf, Mülheim, Essen and München Gladbach, are, of course, staffed by German civilians. This area is controlled by the 53rd (Welsh) Division, and here again the system comes under stringent Royal Signals supervision. Line maintenance, too, is the job of German Post Office engineers. But while Royal Signals are responsible for supervision, discipline and for ensuring general maintenance up to the highest possible standard, cable work and repairs come within the sphere of British G.P.O. technicians, who form a large section of the Royal Signals and have been working with them throughout the war.

At Hamburg, where much of the damage to the city was caused by fire, underground cable systems are in a reasonably sound state. But in the industrial Ruhr, where destruction was largely due to the deep penetration of H.E. bombs, these systems are in a chaotic condition. Here German P.O. engineers are tasting the fruits of reprisals for their countrymen's handiwork in Britain, for the problem of bombed cable repairs in the Rhineland areas is on the pattern of that which (as described in the next column) once applied to the County of London, only larger.

So much larger, in fact, that German cable engineers have a task that will keep them busy for months. And, since it is so important to British occupation, speeding the work with stern rigour equal to that exacted by Royal Signals in the Exchanges, are many of those same British technicians who extricated Britain from a colossal communications catastrophe when this country itself became a battlefield. They are men who learned their lessons in the hard school of reconstruction along a 20 million-mile network of smashed wires and cables, most of it underground.

Throughout the tragic walk-over of the Battle of France these Wire Men were there, contriving extraordinary measures to maintain vital contacts between armies and units which were perpetually on the move, unable to give advance information of their next locations. When the Expeditionary Force was being evacuated under grave difficulties via Dunkirk, had it not been for the skilled feats of these Royal Signals P.O. engineers the contacts essential to the retreat and evacuation might have been irretrievably lost.

ONLY at the last moment was this little band of telecommunications men extricated from Dunkirk, to be hurled a few months later into a nightmare for which it would be difficult to find a parallel. In the London area alone, between September 1940 and September 1941—the worst phase of the Battle of Britain—1,700 separate cables were fractured by bombs, involving the rejoining of more than 500,000 wires. For a single phone cable may contain as many as 2,800 separate wires, and each must be joined to its proper partner at the other side of the break. It was work for skilled and brave men, since the job had to go on day and night, bombs or no bombs, in fair weather or foul, unhurried and unresting.

Three hundred miles of wire were laid in the devastated streets in the weeks following raids which burned out half a square mile of the City of London and scattered H.E. bombs among the flaming streets and buildings. It meant, as well, the jointing of 250,000 pairs and the soldering of 100,000 points. Under the worst blows which Britain suffered—at one period there were 92 successive days of raids on London—communications scarcely faltered. Contacts between the all-important Defence Services were uninterrupted.

"PEOPLE at home think," a Royal Signals officer told me, "that we are giving the Germans kid-glove treatment, but I can assure you that the gloves are off." And while they are off the hands of men with the backgrounds of Royal Signals and the G.P.O. engineers who serve with them, there is little cause for disbelieving his statement. The iron hand is not a rôle which falls happily on the British soldier, but there is not a man among them—and certainly not in the Royal Signals—who does not realize the urgency of ending for all time and by every fair means the ridiculous myth of "The Master Race."

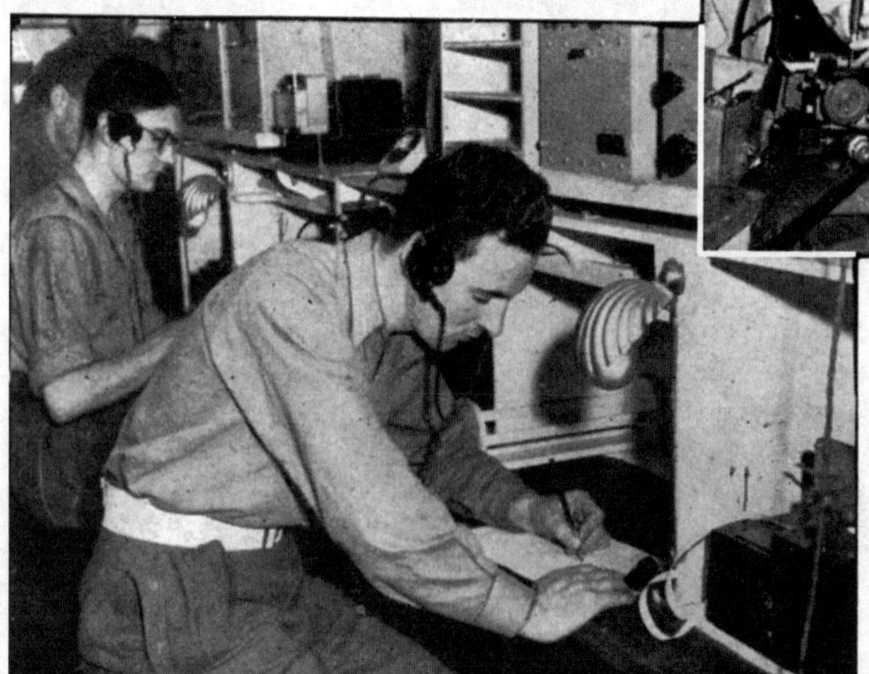

"LONDON CALLING!" Background to the Berlin Conference in July was the communications service for over a hunderd Allied Press correspondents. Working without a break, two Golden Arrow wireless sections of Royal Signals maintained a 24-hour service which reached its peak on July 20, when 40,823 words were transmitted. A Berlin operator takes down a message from London (above). Instrument mechanic at work (right). *Photo, British Official*

Cleaning-up the Rhine for Peacetime Traffic

FIVE MONTHS AFTER MONTY'S FAMOUS CROSSING of the Rhine on March 23-24, 1945 (see illus. pages 783-785, Vol. 8), U.S. Army engineers were still removing the wreckage of the river's several bridges blown up by the retreating enemy. Among these obstacles were the remains of the Hindenburg Bridge at the famous tourist centre of Rudesheim (1), near Wiesbaden. Helping to clear the river for traffic, a monster crane (2) capable of handling up to 250 tons was employed on the bridge, a large fragment of the wreckage of which (3) was made secure after the devastating explosion (4) that blasted a passage through the central spans.

Photos, U.S. Official

God-Speed to America's Homebound Warriors

ABOARD THE QUEEN MARY, 15,060 men of the U.S. 30th Infantry Division left Southampton (1) on August 17, 1945, for New York. Their task in Britain completed, 35,000 U.S. Army vehicles were by mid-August being reconditioned, sprayed with rust-preventive and packed for the voyage home. Stripped to its minimum length and height, this truck (2) was swung by mobile crane on to the base of a crate. German P.O.W. (3) helped to render rust-proof the ignition system of other trucks. Crated vehicles (4) at Ashchurch, Glos., waiting to be taken to a British seaport. *Photos, U.S. Official, Keystone*

I Was There! Eye Witness Stories of the War

We Had a Night Without Parallel in London

End-of-the-war celebrations on the night of August 15, 1945, were on a scale without precedent in the Capital's picturesque history. All previous celebrations paled by comparison. Boisterously, hundreds of thousands of revellers kept up the fun into the small hours of the following day, as told by News Chronicle reporters. See also illus. pages 303–306.

THERE was dancing round floodlit Nelson's column, and in Piccadilly Circus where a middle-aged portly man, standing nine feet above the crowd on top of the traffic lights and placidly smoking his pipe, might almost have filled the place of Eros. London's streets everywhere echoed to the noise of singing and whistling. Every now and then rockets shot up from tall buildings, and Very lights like multi-coloured butterflies lit the sky. But perhaps the most impressive of all sights was that of the cross above St. Paul's silhouetted in the beams of two searchlights.

Outside Buckingham Palace a crowd of 200,000 chanted for the King and Queen, who made several appearances on the balcony. From six o'clock onwards all roads led to Piccadilly, Trafalgar Square and Buckingham Palace. Whole families journeyed, buying paper hats and whistles and rattles on the way, from the East End, and places as far away as Barnet and Wimbledon, Mitcham and Chiswick. They came in such numbers that early in the evening, a bright cloudless evening after a day of showers, traffic was diverted. No buses passed through the Strand, Trafalgar Square and Piccadilly. Had they tried they could not have got through—the crowds were so dense.

THEY came, many of them, without suppers. Restaurants and public houses had since noon displayed their "Sold out" signs. But there were plenty of fruit barrows selling plums, pears and apples. So Londoners made an evening meal of fruit. By eight o'clock a solid mass of people jammed the area from Piccadilly, extending south and east to Trafalgar Square.

Trafalgar Square was packed with people assembled to hear the King's Speech. At nine o'clock the King's voice was heard and all singing was hushed. There were no more fireworks, no chatter. When the King had finished his message to his people there went up a cheer such as Trafalgar Square had not heard for a long time. It went on for what seemed endless minutes.

The noise and singing and pushing and the exploding of fireworks was almost entirely the work of young men who would have had to fight the Japanese war. But the songs they sang were not those of victory, but such popular and traditional favourites as In the Shade of the Old Apple Tree, Yi, Yi, Yippy, and Old Father Thames.

Mr. Attlee received a tumultuous welcome when he appeared on the balcony of the Ministry of Health building with Mr. Bevin and Mr. Herbert Morrison. "We are right to rejoice at this victory of the people, and it is right for a short time that we should relax," said Mr. Attlee.

Thousands of people packed the court of Westminster Gardens to cheer Mr. Churchill. In response to roars of "We want Churchill," Mr. Churchill made six appearances at his window. Then the crowd sang For He's a Jolly Good Fellow.

Princess Elizabeth and Princess Margaret left Buckingham Palace before 11 o'clock to mingle with the crowds. With an escort of two plain clothes officers they walked to the front of the Palace and watched the King and Queen make another appearance on the balcony. The Princesses were surrounded by cheering men and women. Police told them that the Princesses wished to be treated as private individuals and they were allowed to go on their own and see what they wished.

Just before midnight there were still many thousands of people outside the Palace fixing their eyes on the floodlit Royal Standard, cheering and calling for the King. Women outside the Palace fainted and ambulance men and policemen lifted them over the heads of the crowd and on to the stands in front of the Victoria Memorial. More than 150 people were injured in the West End by exploding fireworks. Thirty-five people had to receive hospital treatment for eye injuries, facial burns, and other mishaps. Superintendent Treneamin, of the Poplar Division, St. John Ambulance, said: "This is a million times worse than VE night!"

There were more private cars out in London than at any time since the rationing of petrol began. The Embankment, to which a lot of traffic was diverted at times was black with vehicles all crowded to capacity. The whole of South, East and North London was ablaze with hundreds of bonfires, fed with tons of debris that had lain on bombed sites as a melancholy memorial to the blitz and the V-bombs. To see characteristic Cockney rejoicing one had to go to places like The Angel at Islington, Notting Dale or Kennington.

I went to Lambeth Walk where they had a score of bonfires. "There's a good few men out in the Far East who will be wondering what's going on in the Walk tonight," an old lady said to me as she watched the broken stairs, window frames, doors, joists and flooring dragged from the bomb-wrecked buildings and built into huge stacks that were fired at nightfall.

A huge bonfire was built on the tiled bottom of the derelict Lambeth Baths and children climbed on to ruined walls to watch and cheer. The whole area was smothered with flags and bunting and fairy-lights twinkled in the windows. London firemen received more than 100 calls inside an hour and a half. They were mostly made by nervous residents alarmed by bonfires!

The Welcome We Gave to Lambeth's Own Monty

"Local boy who made good" became, with all due ceremony, a Freeman of the Borough of Lambeth on August 15, 1945. This was that Monty who 50-odd years ago sprawled and tumbled and got into fixes in the vicarage of St. Mark's, where his father was the parson. How the great Field-Marshal received the people's thanks on this day is told by John Redfern, of The Daily Express. See also illus. page 306.

LUCKY Lambethites! Frisking in the beflagged streets and cheering for victory, with the architect of their new-found fortune there, standing in a landau and saluting with a smile, while the beaming policemen and firemen leaned backwards on 30,000 people who wanted to clap him on the back.

The idea was that the Metropolitan Borough of Lambeth would admit this famous lad to the honorary Freedom. That, indeed, was duly done according to the rubrics. But it was the Joes and Alfs and their womenfolk who really made this Monty's day—for him and for themselves. It was his day all right. The crowds spilled into the Brixton Road and flooded the junction against the town hall.

He entered the borough at Westminster Bridge, this chirpy-looking little man with seven rows of ribbons and knife-edge battle-

VICTORY BONFIRE in London's West End, shortly after the midnight peace announcement was made, had its counterpart in unnumbered instances wherever inflammable material was to hand. In the delirious joy of the occasion, park seats, doors and hoardings were used to feed the flames. Darkness resounded to the din of motor-horns, bells, whistles, drums and clanging dustbin lids. Daylight in Piccadilly Circus found dustmen busy clearing up the debris (right). See story above.

Photos, Keystone, Planet News

MONTY AT LAMBETH TOWN HALL on August 15, 1945, after receiving the Freedom of the Borough. On his left, the Mayor. See also illus. page 306. *Photo, G.P.O.*

dress trousers. He was three minutes early. Typical! So the Mayor's landau wasn't ready, and he sat for a moment in his "Priority" labelled motor-car. Then someone in the throng took an observation and bawled "Oi!" They simply surged forward then, and it was a good job the Mayor's landau turned up on time. Through Kennington Road and Brixton Road Montgomery went in triumph. After the conquest of Germany here was a conquest of hearts, all done in five minutes.

"Good old Monty!" That was the rallying cry now. They took it up; from the men standing dizzily on the roofs to the squeaking children all mixed up with the sturdy policemen and the police horses, fussing and tending one and all. As the Field-Marshal walked, slowly for him, up the steps to the town hall he gave a quick look at the glaring, sultry sky.

Was he remembering? This day, 1944, thunderstorms thrashed the reeking ground about Falaise. The gap was almost closed and Montgomery waited while the rumour ran that Rommel was dead.

Then we quietened down a bit to listen to the loudspeaker versions of speeches within, while the 70 aldermen and councillors sat solemnly and the Field-Marshal fingered his battledress. Outside, the horses fidgeted and the children wriggled (those with any room), but we listened. For now Lambeth was surely speaking for England:

"I submit the motion with some confidence. Behind him is the shadow of every man and woman who has joined in these great adventures; these glorious deeds in Sicily and Italy, the waterlogged fields of Holland, and finally in triumph across the Rhine." The carefully-thought-out phrases flowed over our heads; inside, the guest of honour was thoughtful.

Memories again, Field-Marshal? This day, 1943, the Germans were running from Messina and you were planning to move your caravan headquarters from that dusty field near Lentini to the heights of Taormina, where you directed presently the assault on the Italian mainland.

They gave him the scroll in a casket, with a base of wood from the war-maimed church of St. Mark, where young Bernard said his first prayers. They wished him "Long life, good health, great happiness, and peace—all of which you richly deserve!" We crammed and jostling outsiders said "Aye!" or "Oi!" We cheered with such good heart I had my fears for the men perched on the tall roofs. The blast must have been truly terrific!

Montgomery rose, his head on one side, his voice crisp, just as though he was addressing an eve-of-the-battle conference at "Army Group." He had taken our measure. The little man knew. "I like to think that my welcome is meant as a mark of your gratitude to those wonderful fighting men who have won the final victory we enjoy today." Just that. And every mother in the crowd with a son in this war, living or dead, was still with a great pride, and every father opened his mouth to cheer the speaker—and found that somehow his voice had gone rusty; something to do with his heart.

These fighting men . . . This day, 1942, Montgomery was the new commander of the Eighth Army, and Rommel was at Mersa Matruh.

Great Eighth Army, you had a long way to travel, but on your way you slogged, inspired by this man!

Somehow Monty managed to get through the thousands to the Empress Theatre, where he spoke again to 2,500 ticket-holders. There he gave them a slogan, first used by an Eighth Army sergeant-major in Tripoli days: "We will see this thing (the task of reconstruction) through to the end." And there we gave him The Warwickshire Lad, regimental march of his old regiment, and For He's a Jolly Good Fellow.

Pulling his beret well down he went off to the crowds again, this new Freeman. These days a Freeman receives no special privileges. No free travel round the borough or anything like that. But Monty went away with the freedom of our affections; the little man we love.

Two 'Grand Old Cabs' with the Pacific Fleet

For the two months April–May 1945 the fleet maintained constant operations against the Sakishima Group, a vital link in the Formosa–Kyushu defence chain. This involved over 4,000 sorties, the destruction of over 100 Jap planes, and the hazardous task of refuelling and transferring stores at sea. This account, by Sub.-Lt. (A) D. Ash, R.N.V.R., who flew on one of the strikes, was written specially for "The War Illustrated."

After many months waiting, our crew ("Abe" the pilot, and "Fozz" the air-gunner) joined a fleet carrier. During March, as one of several reserve Avenger crews, we followed the fleet in an escort ship. Many miles from land, she had come out from operations to refuel and take on supplies. Rocket lines were fired between ships, followed by thick cables, and soon, "all hands on deck" were heaving them taut, as large canvas bags went back and forth with supplies. Abe was almost the first of these "supplies," over to a destroyer and then to the carrier. Fozz and I were luckier; we were flown over.

Next day the fleet, with battleships in the centre and carriers on each side, ringed by escort destroyers, steamed back to the operational area. Ahead, two Avengers kept an anti-sub patrol, and fighters maintained an all-day air defence against possible Kamikazes. The planes that got through did no great damage; no ships were put out of operation. The fleet's task was to bomb the island runways and prevent their use by any reinforcement aircraft coming up from the south to attack the Americans on Okinawa. Avengers and Corsairs were responsible for keeping the Japs busy night and day filling in bomb craters. Towards mid-May the Japs "threw in the towel."

This was the climax of the amazing growth of the Fleet Air Arm during the war. The Swordfish, which did such great work at Taranto—with other biplanes—has now been superseded, and the performance of modern carrier planes is not far behind those which are land-based. That is, all but two—Darby and Joan. In the 1930's, the Supermarine Walrus was the king-pin of the Fleet Air Arm, and still she chugs bravely on. Many Allied aircrews have cause to thank her for air-sea rescue; she played a valuable part in saving four out of every five American airmen who came down in the Channel. Though laughed at Darby and Joan, the two Walrus on this carrier, are viewed with affection. Two grand old cabs, we call them.

On April 19, aircraft from another ship were returning from a raid. As they passed

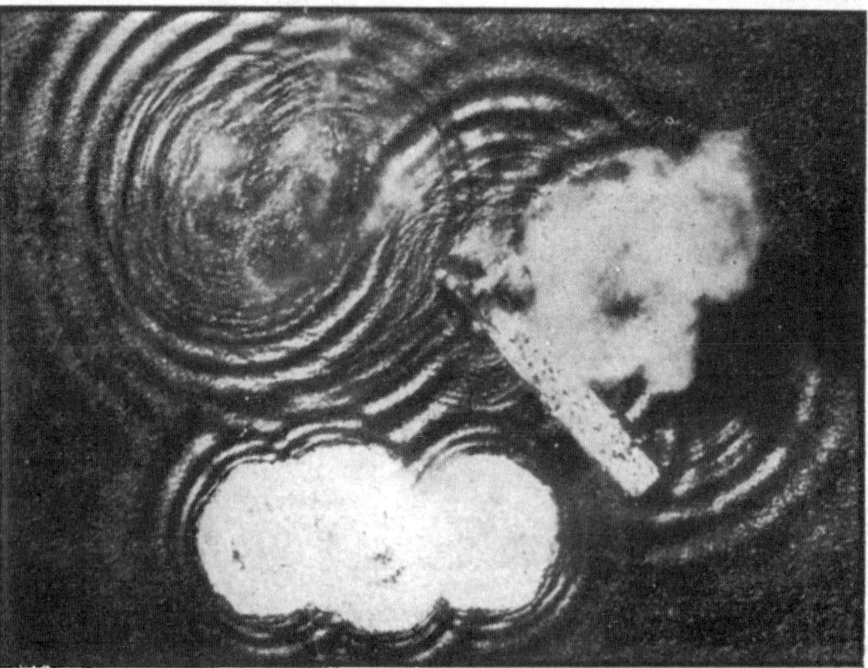

BOMBS FROM AVENGER TORPEDO-BOMBERS of the Naval Air Arm made these odd-looking patterns as they showered on a Japanese escort carrier trapped in the Shido Bay area of Northern Shididu Island in the Ryukyus (retaken in June 1945; see map, page 117). One is bursting alongside the carrier, which later received a direct hit. *Photo, Associated Press*

over the enemy coast, one shuddered and caught fire—hit underneath by Ack-Ack. Unfortunately, only the observer managed to bale out. Landing in the sea from only 500 feet, he found himself less than a mile from the coast. He had slight burns, and though his Mae West would not inflate he managed to keep afloat for nearly two hours.

In the meantime, Darby was sent to the rescue. We all turned out to watch P.-O. Bruce Ada, of the R.A.A.F., totter him down the deck and soar off the end like a prehistoric bird, racing towards the islands at 85 knots. The waiting Japs must have been amazed, probably thinking it to be a new British "suicide" weapon! Darby had to land in shallow water, quite half a mile from the survivor, and then weave slowly up to him, avoiding jagged coral beds. Sub.-Lt. (A) R. Marshall, R.N., the observer, had great difficulty hauling the survivor aboard, but the Japs encouraged him to hurry by firing their A.A. guns. Fortunately these wouldn't depress sufficiently, and shells whistled overhead. Chuggling speedily out to sea again Darby took off, and returned safely home.

Modern planes have so increased their landing speeds that it becomes very necessary to control them. Hooks, fitted to the tail of the aircraft, engage arrester-wires stretched across the deck and quickly haul the planes up. Not so Darby; as he came slowly over the stern of the ship many hands seemed to grab him and haul him safely on to the deck. This is the second time Darby had made a rescue in this way, earning himself a bouquet from the Admiral. "Understand," the Admiral had said in a signal, "Darby bombarded Japanese with his machine-guns." "No," replied Darby, "we threw coral at them instead!"

Mob Law and Gangsters in the Italy of Today

You can't walk far in Rome today without someone touching you on the elbow and asking if you have any foreign money to sell. Leave your car unguarded for a couple of minutes and you come back to find the wheels have been removed. Other startling revelations are made by Alexander Clifford, of the Daily Mail, writing from Rome on August 16, 1945.

In the back streets you can buy anything you want—any article of Allied equipment—on the Black Market. Your newspaper is full of stories of crimes and disturbances. Your pocket may be picked at any minute. Italy is going through a crime wave which recalls the less settled periods of the Middle Ages.

Robbery, with or without violence, is the favourite crime. And it revolves mainly round food, oil, petrol, tires, and motor-car spare parts. In Rome and Naples notices in English are everywhere displayed warning us to look out for every sort of thief. An old motor tire will fetch £50 or more on the Black Market. So there are organized gangs who can whip off your spare wheel while you pause to light a cigarette.

A friend of mine had his entire luggage stolen from the back of his jeep while he was sitting in front and driving. He swears it must have been done while the vehicle was actually moving. There are gangs who rush an Army lorry with a planned technique like an American football scrum; gangs who siphon the petrol out of your tank; and gangs with incredibly ingenious systems of robbing ration dumps. It is all done with violence, if necessary.

I have been sniped at between Rome and Naples, in the early dusk—a shot across the bows of the truck—and Daily Mail correspondent Jenny Nicholson got into a regular machine-gun battle when crossing the Apennines from Bari. Every day you read of the discovery of huge dumps of food and oil held back secretly for the Black Market. Large-scale rings of forgers have been rounded up in Naples, and whole factories found for making false identity cards.

One by one the laboratories for concocting bogus gin and brandy to sell to the troops are being discovered. But plenty still remain undetected. There are other sorts of crime too. There are jealousy gangs who go round cutting off the hair of girls who walk out with Allied soldiers. There are far too many out-of-hand shootings of alleged Fascists by alleged Partisans. There is a great increase of beggars, with artificial injuries. Happily a law has now been passed to prevent the hiring out of small children to beggars.

But this gang crime is the serious thing. In some places there is real danger of a minority mob rule. Already some of these gangs have so frightened law-abiding citizens that no one dares give evidence against them. The causes of it all are obvious enough. The war has swept through the country. Industry has been ruined and the army largely dissolved—so, inevitably, there is a mass of unemployed.

Now the departure of the Allies is throwing further men out of work, and thousands of displaced persons are drifting back from abroad. Many Fascists in hiding are taking inevitably to crime. In Southern Italy there is a natural propensity to brigandage. Hundreds of courts, police stations, prisons, and records have been destroyed by the war.

Italy needs a refurbished and strengthened police force. More men with a sense of responsibility must be got in, and they must be paid enough to remove the temptation of bribes. Especially the police need more transport and better means of communication. But the basic need lies in the Italian people themselves. Colonel Poletti, the American A.M.G. chief, who probably knows more about it than anyone, said publicly the other day: "The most pressing political and moral need of Italy is respect for the law." He wasn't far wrong.

ROME'S "BLACK MARKET" is a straggling alley-way, the Via di Nona. Trade is done quite openly—with sky-rocket prices.
Photo, Keystone

OUR DIARY OF THE WAR

AUGUST 15, Wednesday
Japan.—Gen. MacArthur ordered Japs to cease hostilities and send representatives to Manila.
France.—Marshal Pétain sentenced to death by French High Court.
Home Front.—First of two-days Victory celebrations. State opening of new Parliament.

AUGUST 16, Thursday
Japan.—Suzuki Cabinet resigned.
Russian Front.—Marshal Vassilevsky sent ultimatum to Japanese in Manchuria to surrender arms by August 20.
Burma.—Surrender leaflets dropped to Japanese troops.
Home Front.—Announced that basic petrol ration increased from September 1.

AUGUST 17, Friday
Japan.—New Premier ordered army to observe Emperor's proclamation to lay down arms.
France.—Gen. de Gaulle commuted death sentence on Pétain to detention for life.
Sea.—German submarine U977 arrived at Mar del Plata, Argentine.

AUGUST 18, Saturday
China.—Troops of 1st Chinese Army entered Canton.
Solomon Islands.—Japanese troops began surrendering to Australians in Bougainville.

AUGUST 19, Sunday
Japan.—Japanese representatives arrived in Manila to arrange surrender.
Home Front.—The King and Queen attended Thanksgiving Service at St. Paul's.

AUGUST 20, Monday
Burma.—Lord Louis Mountbatten broadcast surrender instructions to Japanese Southern Army.
Pacific.—Surrender overtures made by Japs in Luzon and New Guinea.
Norway.—Trial of Vidkun Quisling opened in Oslo.

AUGUST 21, Tuesday
U.S.A.—Announced that all outstanding contracts for Lend-Lease were to be cancelled.
Germany.—Field-Marshal Montgomery issued warning of drastic measures against Displaced Persons committing crimes against civil population.
Home Front.—Announced that 24 clothing coupons to last from September 1 to April 30.

AUGUST 22, Wednesday
Russian Front.—Soviet airborne troops landed at Dairen and Port Arthur. Japanese Kwantung Army surrendered at Harbin.
China.—Sino-Japanese surrender negotiations in progress at Chihkiang, Hunan.

AUGUST 23, Thursday
Russian Front.—Order of the Day issued announcing Soviet occupation of whole of Manchuria, of south Sakhalin, and of Shumshu and Paramushiro in the Kuriles.
Home Front.—Charter of United Nations approved in Parliament.

AUGUST 24, Friday
Russian Front.—Soviet troops, still advancing in Korea, occupied Ifflu.
China.—Gen. Chiang Kai-shek signed United Nations Charter in Chungking.
New Guinea.—Japanese commander ordered "cease fire."

AUGUST 25, Saturday
Germany.—British forces in northwest Europe (B.L.A.) renamed British Army of the Rhine (B.A.O.R.).

AUGUST 26, Sunday
Burma.—Jap envoys arrived in Rangoon for surrender negotiations.
China.—Chiang Kai-shek's forces entered Shanghai and Nanking.

AUGUST 27, Monday
Japan.—Carrier-aircraft dropped food to Allied prisoners in Tokyo area.
Germany.—Maj.-Gen. Nares succeeded Maj.-Gen. Lyne as British representative on Kommandatura in Berlin.

AUGUST 28th, Tuesday
Japan.—First Allied troops landed at Atsugi airfield; Allied ships entered Tokyo Bay.
Far East.—British naval forces arrived off Penang and Sabang.
Burma.—Preliminary agreement with Japanese envoys signed at Rangoon.

Flash-backs

1939
August 23. *German-Russian Pact of Non-Aggression signed.*

1940
August 15. *Croydon airport bombed; 182 German planes destroyed over Britain.*
August 24. *First German bombs fell in Central London.*

1941
August 28. *Russians announced the evacuation of Dnepropetrovsk.*

1942
August 19. *Combined Operations raid, lasting 9 hours, on Dieppe.*

1943
August 15. *Allied forces landed on Kiska, in the Aleutians.*
August 17. *Enemy resistance ended in Sicily. Allies entered Messina. First R.A.F. raid on Peenemunde experimental station.*
August 23. *Kharkov recaptured by troops of the Red Army.*

1944
August 15. *British, U.S. and French troops landed in S. France.*
August 17. *Falaise captured by British and Canadians.*
August 24. *Gen. Leclerc's armoured division entered Paris.*

With Our Airmen Today

By CAPTAIN NORMAN MACMILLAN M.C., A.F.C.

When the Japanese surrender offer was first received, Admiral Lord Louis Mountbatten was in England after having attended the Potsdam Conference. He decided to return immediately to his headquarters in Kandy, Ceylon. His York aircraft had been serviced while in England by Avro, Rolls-Royce and Air Ministry servicing and maintenance staffs, and his crew were standing-by at Stoney Cross airfield for the admiral. Sqdn.-Ldr. J. F. Matthews, A.F.C., of Iver Heath, Bucks, was the first pilot; Wing Commdr. A. E. Millson, D.S.O., D.F.C., of Tonbridge, Kent, second pilot; F/Lt. R. J. Wainright, A.F.M., of Hertford, navigator; F/Lt. H. Griffin, of Abbey Wood, London, wireless operator; and F/Lt. E. Maxwell, of Carlisle, engineer.

The York landed at Cairo 11 hours 3 minutes after taking off from Stoney Cross, and in 66 minutes the York was refuelled and checked over. Ten hours 17 minutes carried the aircraft on to Karachi, where in a fraction over an hour it was again refuelled. Seven hours 18 minutes took the York from Karachi to a South-East Asia Command airfield in Ceylon. Total flying time was 28 hours 38 minutes, an average of 222 m.p.h. for the distance of 6,345 miles. Elapsed time, including stops, was 30 hours 46 minutes, giving a travelling average of 206 m.p.h

DENMARK REMEMBERED THE R.A.F. on July 22, 1945, when Mr. Wedell-Heinen, a local government official (right), unveiled in a forest north of Copenhagen a memorial recording the help given by our airmen to the Danish Freedom movement and in particular the names of Flt.-Lt. R. H. Thomas and Flying-Officer G. J. Allin who crashed there in a Mosquito in September 1944. Wing-Commander H. M. Kerr, A.F.C., of the R.A.F. mission to Denmark, represented Britain at this ceremony of commemoration. *Photo, British Official*

At 1.5 p.m. local time (7.35 a.m. B.S.T.) on August 15 the official order from the C.-in-C. land, naval, and air forces was issued from S.E.A.C. Hqrs. to suspend operations so far as is "consistent with the safety of the Allied forces." That was VJ Day in Britain—and the day that the new Parliament opened with the King's speech—for the Japanese had accepted the Allies' demand for surrender in a reply handed to the Swiss Foreign Office at 8.10 p.m. on August 14. But that did not immediately end the war situation in South-East Asia, and on August 20, Admiral Mountbatten broadcast surrender orders to Field-Marshal Count Terauchi, the commander of the Japanese southern army. Terauchi was instructed to send representatives with full powers in no more than two specially-painted aeroplanes, easily recognizable at 500 yards, to meet the Allied Chief of Staff at Rangoon on August 23 to arrange the surrender of all Japanese forces under his command.

Meanwhile, on August 10, Spitfires had been bombing and shooting-up Japanese troop concentrations and positions on the east bank of the Sittang river, and two days later, while giving close support to the Allied ground forces east of the Sittang, Spitfires destroyed many jungle huts and buildings. On August 11, Thunderbolts and Spitfires were in action between Kyaukkyi and Boyagyi; and at Paingkyon, north-east of Moulmein, Spitfires bombed and strafed other enemy troops. Mosquitoes were in action that day south of Moulmein and north of Peinnegyaung.

During the three days Sunderlands and Liberators attacked and sank or damaged shipping and barges from the Gulf of Siam to west of the Kra Isthmus. Flying over that dangerous water area has called for intensive air-sea rescue operations, and since the beginning of 1945 no fewer than 80 airmen have been rescued by Catalinas in the Bay of Bengal. I can share the feelings of the rescued men, for many years ago I was myself adrift on an upturned seaplane in that Bay, without either food or water, in the full blaze of the tropical sun in midsummer.

Flew Without Dinghies, Relied Solely on Their Mae Wests

The record of the whole air-sea rescue service is a proud one. Having grown from the make-shift organization improvised during the Battle of Britain, when the first pilots of "the few" flew without dinghies and had to rely solely on their Mae Wests, it has become a world-wide service, equipped with many ingenious devices for saving life. Around the coasts of Britain 3,723 British and 1,998 American airmen have been rescued, while in the areas other than British waters 3,200 airmen, 4,665 soldiers sailors and civilians, have been saved. In July 1943, out of a total of 196 Fortress crews lost 139 were saved; on one day that month 78 out of 80 were rescued. During the D-Day operations 136 R.A.F. craft, many naval craft and 60 U.S. Coastal Cutters scoured the invasion areas.

On August 13 Thunderbolts and Spitfires were again in action south-west of Kyaukkyi, in the Shegyin and Mokpalin-Billin areas. All over the widely scattered terrain of South-East Asia Command it must take time for the Japanese surrender to become effective, but there is almost certain to be a time limit during which active operations will be suspended; following which, presumably, bands of enemy troops still resisting would be classified as guerillas.

Biggest Single-Day Raid Made by the Far East Air Forces

While the negotiations and discussions proceeded mysteriously within Japan, the air action against the Japanese in their home and occupied islands was maintained. On August 10, more than 500 aircraft from Okinawa dropped petrol-jelly bombs from a low altitude on Kumamoto, a military supply centre on Kyushu, in the biggest raid made in a single day by the Far East Air Forces. Oita, on north-east Kyushu, was also fire-bombed. On the same day the R.N.Z.A.F. co-operated with Australian troops and naval elements to silence the Japanese strong-points on Sohaua island guarding the Buka Passage between Bougainville and Buka Island. Australians were fighting with air support in the Wewak area of New Guinea.

On August 12, the Japanese reported an attack by Super-Fortresses against Shikoku Island to the south and east of the Inland Sea, and the north-west coastal town of Matsuyama. Next day 1,500 U.S. and U.K. carrier-aircraft of the Third Pacific Fleet bombed six airfields in the Kanto Plain around Tokyo, shooting down 21 Japanese aircraft of the interceptor force that tried to intervene. Aircraft installations and a radar manufacturing plant were among the targets.

During daylight on August 14 and early morning of August 15 (Japanese time) 800 Super-Fortresses with nearly 200 fighters as escort, flying from Tinian in the Marianas, bombed targets on Honshu: these were the naval arsenal at Hikari; the army arsenal at Osaka; the Marifu railyards south-west of Hiroshima; the Nippon Oil Company at Atika; and industrial areas of Kumagayas and Isezaki. Next day the cease fire signal was given on British warships off Tokyo at 11.15 a.m., but isolated Japanese aircraft continued to attack the Allied ships, and five were shot down around them after 11.15, according to instructions, "in a friendly way." British-flown Avengers dropped what may be this war's last British bombs on a factory near Kamohaura at dawn on Aug. 15.

There are three postscripts to these events. It is now thought that the Japanese launched thousands of paper balloons carrying explosive against the United States. On a single day during the San Francisco Conference the Navy saw hundreds off the Aleutians heading for the California coast, but none were seen to reach land. By the end of July, 230 of these ineffectual weapons, or their remnants, had been recovered.

Squadron-Leader Ian W. Bazalgette, D.F.C., has been awarded a posthumous V.C. for his bravery in action on August 4, 1944, while acting as Master Bomber of a Pathfinder Squadron detailed to mark an important target at Trossy St. Maximin for the main bomber force. Chief of the Air Staff, Marshal of the R.A.F. Sir C. F. A. Portal, was elevated to the peerage as a Baron in Mr. Churchill's farewell honours list.

This Is the Atomic Bomb in Trial and Practice

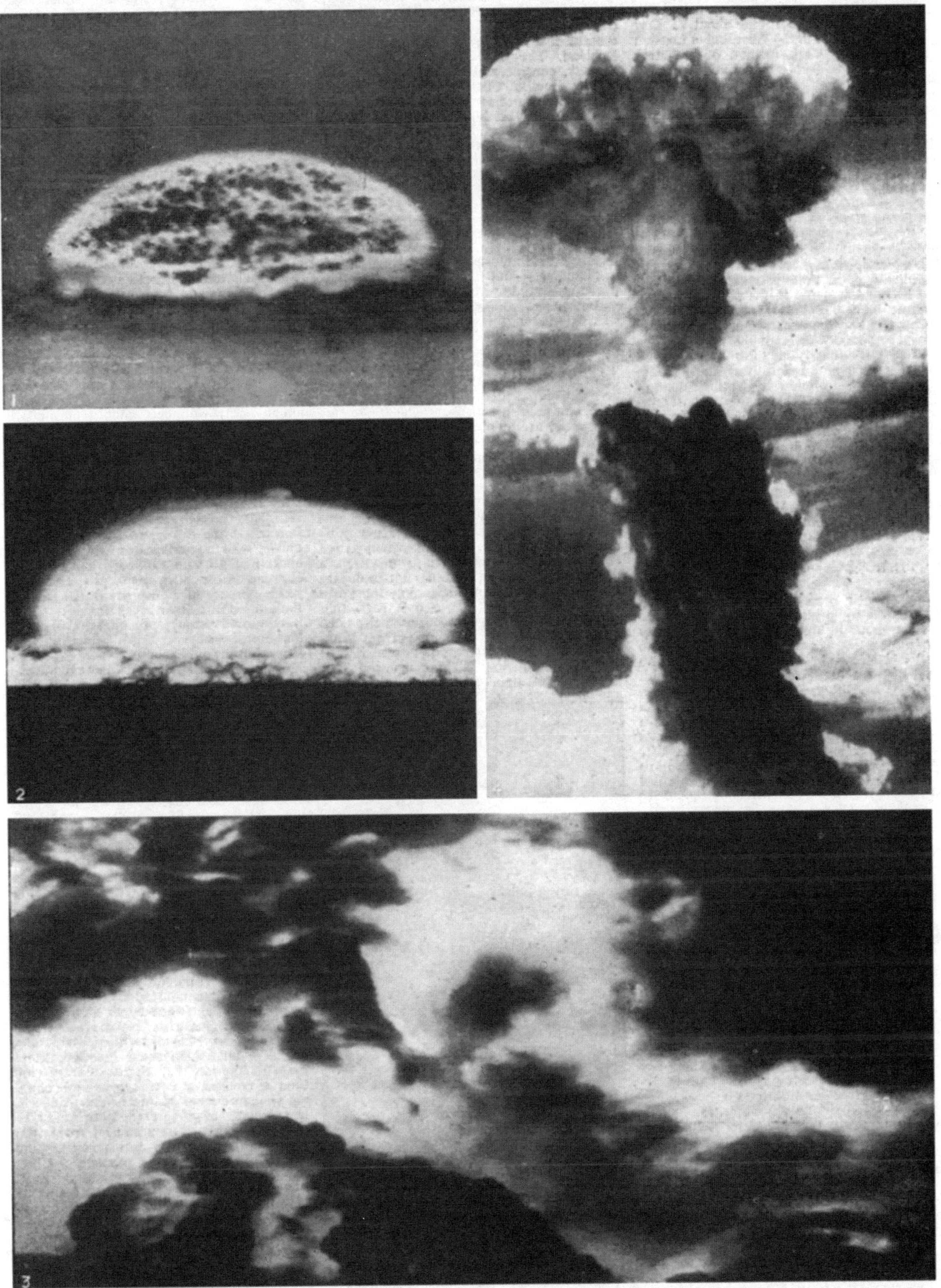

SPECIAL CAMERA FOCUSSED SIX MILES AWAY secured this remarkable picture-sequence of stages in the explosion of the atomic bomb during the test at Alamogordo, New Mexico, on July 16, 1945 (see story in page 280). Flames and smoke rose from the target like a monstrous fungus (1), giving place to a gigantic " hat " of fire (2) which developed as at (3). At Nagasaki, three minutes after an atomic bomb (the second to be dropped on Japan) had exploded on August 9, smoke had risen to over 20,000 feet (4).

Photos, Keystone, Associated Press

Editor's Postscript

Sporadic attempts round about VJ Day to introduce in the West End of London the New York method of jubilating with showers of torn paper were, I am glad to record, a miserable failure. I hope that following the snub implicit in the official request that was issued before the Royal procession to St. Paul's, we have now seen the last of it. It should be obvious enough that the custom, native to the city of sky-scrapers, depends wholly on skyscrapers for its effectiveness. The wastepaper-baskets and telephone directories of thirty office floors piled one above the other can combine with those of thirty more on the other side of the street to let loose such a white cascade as the upper floors of even Piccadilly and Regent Street can never hope to emulate. There is infinitely more paper in the air at one time, and it takes far longer to flutter to the ground if only because of the draught that plays perpetually through the long canyons of Lower Broadway and Fifth Avenue. And when ticker-tape streams from thirty floors up, it can be an impressive sight by reason of its sheer length. In other words, against such a background, paper dropped out of windows may create a picture of the spirit of carnival beyond the most riotous fancy; whereas in London it is—well, just paper dropped out of windows. There is another point. Before the war, by a mixture of blandishments, cajoleries, threats, and punishments, we as a nation had at long last just begun to be cured of the litter habit. We have slipped back since then, and any practice that encourages further retrogression is to be deplored.

The popular press gave H. G. Wells full marks for producing over 31 years ago a story about the atomic bomb. One can only hope the event will prove that he showed an equal prescience in foreseeing it as the bomb that will end bombs. One interesting point arises. Wells's story, The World Set Free, described prophetically the outbreak of a great war only a few months before such a war began in fact. But in the book the date was given as 1956. In a preface to a later edition the author apologized for making so extraordinarily wide a shot, and explained that in the matter of dates he always erred on the cautious side, partly out of consideration for his more sceptical readers. He continued as follows:

> In the particular case of The World Set Free there was, I think, another motive in holding the Great War back, and that was to allow the chemist to get well forward with his discovery of the release of atomic energy. 1956—or for that matter, 2056—may be none too late for that crowning revolution in human potentialities.

Events have still beaten his calculations by at least eleven years!

The other day I fell to thinking again, as I so often do, of that constant change in the significances and values of words which keeps our language a living force. Every war speeds up the process for a time, and this war has been no exception. I was not thinking this time of the multitude of new words that these six years have given us, so much as of the old words that can never again mean precisely what they meant before 1939, simple words like pathfinder, hedgehog, pin-point, or mulberry. Take another simple example, the verb to march, and see how it has enlarged its meaning to become the romantic synonym for a nation-wide taking of military action. This usage, indeed, was already in vogue before the war. Hitler will march, we were warned. On the eve of the war Mr. Arthur Greenwood told the House of Commons, "If we are to march, I hope we shall march in complete unity, and march with France." A year later our enemies were renewing their inspiration with the aid of a song called We March Against England. They could scarcely have meant it literally, considering the breadth and depth of the English Channel, though with the Fuehrer were not all things possible? Anyway, the odd fact is that there was never a war in which the combatants did less actual marching. Possibly the figurative sense of the word originated with Mussolini's notorious march on Rome in 1922, which was done in a railway train!

Tucked away in The Times newspaper some time ago I came on startling news of a scheme which may conceivably mean the fortune or the failure of millions of people in this country. And yet not a word of it have I seen elsewhere in any of the dozen national and other newspapers which I make it my job to study daily. "Under the auspices of the Veterinary Educational Trust," it began, prosaically enough, "three veterinary experts, including a woman, have begun research upon the Horse, particularly the thoroughbred." With a fund of over £60,000 already raised on their behalf, these equine experts, it appears, are at present studying the ways of Welsh ponies; soon they are to extend their researches to potential Derby and Grand National winners being trained at Newmarket and elsewhere. There—tantalizingly—my information ends, but not, alas, my passion for speculation. Does this simple announcement cloak an attempt by our big racehorse breeders and owners to put their highly chancey industry on such a scientific basis that in some not-so-distant future the Stud Book will assume the awful accuracy of Bradshaw or the A B C—that one may pick winners from it with the same sense of security as one chooses from Bradshaw a train to Edinburgh or Penzance? It would be agonizing to think that the Tote may finally extinguish the bookie on the racecourses of tomorrow and that the palpitating, if harmless, "flutter" of today may become as joyless and uneventful a transaction as investing one's surplus cash in Consols at 2½ per cent. Win or lose, the fun of racing, as of all gambling, is its glorious uncertainty. No one, bookie or winner, has anything but contempt for the horse that romps home odds on. So that whatever startling discoveries are made about the Horse there will, I fancy, still be bookies and "mugs" to spare on the English racecourses of the future. Your biologist turned tipster is, of course, a possibility!

The Rt. Hon. JOSEPH BENEDICT CHIFLEY, whose election as Prime Minister of Australia in succession to the late Mr. John Curtin was announced on July 12, 1945. Aged 60, he is Leader of the Australian Parliamentary Labour Party. *Photo, New York Times*

One of the first instructions given to amateur criminologists, I seem to remember, is to search out the motive of the crime. That being so, I still find myself at a loss to discover the motive for one of the most caddish (if motiveless) tricks I have heard of for many a year. The story was told me by a colleague to whose niece it happened a short while ago. This young woman had been married only a few months when her husband, an officer in the Parachute Regiment, was posted missing at Arnhem. A month or so before the German surrender she was visited by a youngish man in officer's uniform who told her that her husband was still alive, though badly wounded, and in hospital in Germany where he (the visitor) had met him. The young man assured the girl that her husband would write to her as soon as he was well enough. Before leaving he gave her his name and address in case she should wish to get in touch with him. To her horror the letter she addressed him a few days later was returned through the post marked "not known." She thereupon informed the War Office, who communicated with her to the effect that no such "officer" had ever been gazetted in any such regiment! The astonishing absence of motive lies in the fact that the scoundrel neither asked for nor received money or assistance of any kind, not even his out-of-pocket expenses which included (he said) a journey of over fifty miles. To heighten the mystery, the woman's husband has since been reported as "presumed killed."

Looking back on our six-year ordeal, I am inclined to agree with a friend who declares that the average Londoner's most outstanding memory will continue to be that of the variously-named Flying Bomb, Buzz-bomb or Doodle-bug (which no doubt had other less mentionable appellations as well) long after the blitzes have become a dimly-remembered nightmare. For those of an objective turn of mind, Mr. Frank Illingworth has produced through the Citizen Press a one-and-threepenny pamphlet, entitled Flying Bomb, in which he very vividly recounts the dread story of Southern England's eighty days of V-bombing. Those in search of background material for their private histories of the war will find much to draw on from Mr. Illingworth's tightly-packed store of facts, which range from the R.A.F. raid on the Nazis' experimental station at Peenemunde in August 1943 (when 5,000 German technicians and scientists perished, including General von Chamier-Glisezenski, chief technical adviser to the Luftwaffe), to the firing of the last V2. Statistics are a chilly kind of comfort at best (unless they come in the shape of news of income-tax relief), but it is solace of a sort to learn from Mr. Illingworth that while a million houses were damaged by V-bombs and no fewer than 33,537 people killed and wounded by them the rate of mortality was approximately one person killed per bomb. Of the 8,000 Flying bombs estimated to have been launched only 2,300 reached London—surely the best of all tributes to our R.A.F. fighters and Ack-Ack gunners, if, indeed, tribute were needed. By "launched" I take it that Mr. Illingworth means they were logged as approaching our coasts. The number actually launched may, therefore, have been considerably more than the 8,000 mentioned.

In Britain Now: Speeding Peacetime Recovery

WHALING-FACTORY SHIP, the Norhval, of 21,000 tons (left), was one of two launched at Haverton-on-Tees, Yorkshire, on July 31, 1945, for the Norwegian whaling industry in the coming winter. Negotiations between the British and Norwegian Governments have extended the whale-catching season from November 24 to March 24. Each whaling-factory is served by nine whalers. Whale-oil is used in making margarine and other foodstuffs.

REHABILITATION TREATMENT in the form of exercise for badly-wounded limbs, was provided for these two officers (above) by a treadle-lathe at Horton Emergency Hospital, Surrey. It is one of many centres throughout the country where over 30,000 patients, both Service and civilian receive special treatment.

WAR CRIMINALS' last hopes of evading justice were dashed on August 8, 1945, when an agreement was signed in London between representatives of Great Britain, the United States, the U.S.S.R. and France. At the signing ceremony (above) were (left to right) Justice Jackson (U.S.A.), Lord Jowitt (Britain), and Gen. I. T. Nikitchenko (U.S.S.R.). As a result of the agreement, a Four-Power tribunal has been established and a much greater precision than heretofore arrived at in defining international crimes and criminals. Such crimes are now categorized as follows: (1) crimes against peace; (2) war crimes; (3) crimes against humanity.

U.N.R.R.A. (United Nations' Relief and Rehabilitation Administration) held its first Council meeting outside the North American Continent on August 7, 1945, when the Council's third session opened at County Hall, Westminster (right). The delegates were welcomed by Mr. Ernest Bevin, British Foreign Secretary, and Lord Latham, leader of the L.C.C. Mr. H. Lehman, the Director-General, stated that by June 30, 1945, U. N. R. R. A. had shipped 1,250,000 tons of supplies to needy countries, but at least £375,000,000 of additional resources would be needed.

Photos, Topical, Planet, New York Times Photos

A Radar Tower that Foiled the Raiders

KNOWN AS "CHAIN HOME LOW" STATIONS, towers such as this were erected at strategic points along our Southern and Eastern coasts during the early weeks of the War, it was revealed in August 1945. With rotating aerials mounted on steel-trellis structures 185 ft. in height, these radar devices were designed to pick up echoes of low-flying enemy aircraft. Early in 1940 they were sometimes hurriedly erected by University research-workers rushed to the site with labour provided by R.A.F. ground-staff. See also pages 298-299. *Photo, British Official*

Printed in England and published every alternate Friday by the Proprietors, THE AMALGAMATED PRESS, LTD., The Fleetway House, Farringdon Street, London, E.C.4. Registered for transmission by Canadian Magazine Post. Sole Agents for Australia and New Zealand: Messrs. Gordon & Gotch, Ltd.; and for South Africa: Central News Agency, Ltd. September 14, 1945. S.S. *Editorial Address:* JOHN CARPENTER HOUSE, WHITEFRIARS LONDON E.C.4

Vol 9 The War Illustrated Nº 216

Edited by Sir John Hammerton

SIXPENCE SEPTEMBER 28, 1945

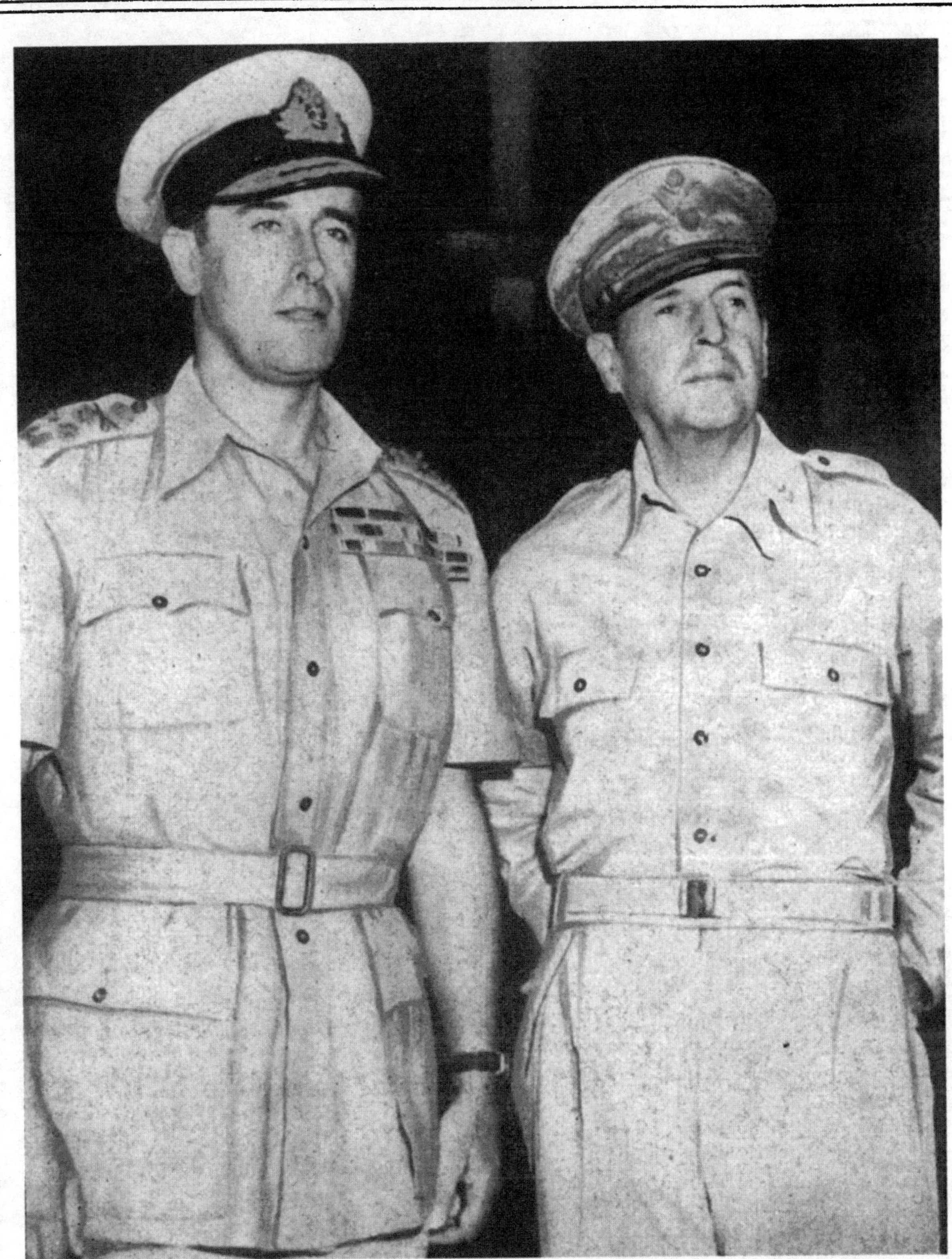

MEN WHO HELPED TO SMASH THE JAPS—Admiral Lord Louis Mountbatten, K.C.B., G.C.V.O., D.S.O., Supreme Allied Commander South-East Asia Command, and General Douglas MacArthur, Supreme Allied Commander in the Pacific—seen together when the former visited U.S. headquarters at Manila in mid-July 1945 to co-ordinate final blows. On September 4, Gen. MacArthur issued his first orders to the Japanese people: to disband their armies and cease foreign-language broadcasts. *Photo, British Official*

Bitterest Moment for the Japanese in Burma

FIRST PRISONERS and civilian internees, numbering over a hundred, were flown by R.A.F. Dakotas of Transport Command on August 28, 1945, from Bangkok, capital of Siam, to Rangoon, en route for home. Nationalities of the first batch of released men and women, some of whom are seen (right) alighting at Mingaladon, near Rangoon, included British, Australian, American and Dutch.

AT RANGOON, on August 27, 1945, was signed a "local agreement" (see page 352) between Lt.-Gen. F. A. M. Browning and Gen. Takazo Numata; their signatures to the document are reproduced below. The ceremony in the Throne Room at Government House, Rangoon (bottom), took seven minutes; facing the Allied commanders sat Gen. Numata, with Rear-Admiral Kaigye Chudo on his right and Lt.-Col. Tomura on his left. At the front table (from the back wall) sat Brigadier E. G. Gibbons, Capt. F. Habecker (U.S.N.), Maj.-Gen. Fung Yee, Maj. M. E. Dening, Rear-Admiral W. R. Patterson, Lt.-Gen. Browning, Air Marshal Saunders, and Maj.-Gen. Denning.

SOUTH EAST ASIA COMMAND HEADQUARTERS

- 3 -

Supreme Commander, Japanese Expeditionary Forces, Southern Regions, to make such translation into Japanese as he may require.

ARY FORCES,

SOUTH EAST ASIA.

1825 HRS TIME (GMT) 27 AUGUST 1945

GOVERNMENT HOUSE, RANGOON

SURRENDERING HIS CEREMONIAL SWORD to Lt.-Col. O. N. Smyth, commanding a Gurkha regiment, at Abya in the Sittang area, was the bitterest moment for Major Wako Lisanori, of the Jap 28th Army, and for his beaten hordes. Japanese officers were then sent out under British escort to contact isolated groups and inform them of the capitulation. Last shots in the Sittang bend were fired on August 16. (See also page 334. *Photos, British Official*

FRENCH TROOPS TOOK OVER IN BERLIN part of the British occupation zones of Reinickendorf and Wedding on August 13, 1945. They marched to the Wedding Platz, where the Union Jack was lowered and the Tricolour raised. With a guard of honour provided by the 2nd Battalion of the Devonshire Regiment and armoured cars of the 11th Hussars, Brigadier J. M. K. Spurling, commanding British combat units in the area, handed over to the French commandant, General de Beauchesne, in front of the ruined Dankes church. *Photo, Planet News*

With Our Armies Today

By MAJ.-GENERAL SIR CHARLES GWYNN K.C.B., D.S.O.

THE war having been brought to a successful end it is very important that we should form a correct judgement on the reasons for our initial disasters and our ultimate recovery so far as we ourselves were directly responsible. The main reason for our initial failures was, of course, our unpreparedness for war both as regards armaments and trained personnel. For that, public opinion which pinned its faith on disarmament and on a policy of collective security, which without the support of adequate armaments was bound to be meaningless, must accept responsibility.

The defence departments, without the necessary funds and authority, cannot be blamed in the main for deficiencies ; and although in matters of detail they made mistakes they were powerless materially to improve conditions. To seek scapegoats among them for the policy which public opinion supported would manifestly be unjust.

WHY the War Machine at First Was Driven at Slow Pace

Our ultimate success, we may justly flatter ourselves, was due to the courage displayed by the Nation, the quality of the fighting forces it produced and to the higher direction of the war effort under Mr. Churchill's leadership. But I think it is insufficiently realized that neither courage nor even Mr. Churchill's genius would have effected our great recovery if in some respects we had not been better prepared than ever before in our history to conduct a great war. A system had been produced, and to a large extent perfected, for Government control in war which eliminated many of the disadvantages a democratic nation is liable to labour under in waging war.

IT may be admitted the machine was, in the first instance, driven at too slow a pace in the desire that the deficiencies should be made good in an orderly manner and without danger of a breakdown through overloading. But the soundness of the machine was proved when the collapse of France and the disaster of Dunkirk not only vastly increased the load but necessitated driving at a maximum pace. We all agree as to the debt we owe Mr. Churchill for the skill and courage with which he drove the machine, but I doubt if we fully recognize the merits of the machine or the debt we owe to those who kept it in repair and improved it while it was lying comparatively idle before the war. It is, I think, indisputable that the higher direction of our war effort was admirable and markedly superior to that of Germany. There was no question of our having muddled through, though we had to effect amazing recovery.

My contention is that the system on which the higher direction operates and the machinery at its disposal provide the basic reason for our escape from defeat and our ultimate recovery. Nevertheless, the system is now coming under criticism and there are would-be reformers who wish to change it drastically. As they will have many opportunities for airing their views it is fortunate that Lord Hankey, in his booklet entitled Government Control in War, has given us a concise and clear account of the evolution of the system and how it works, together with an answer to some of the chief criticisms that have been directed against it. It is to be hoped that his book will be widely read, for we have had our warning how necessary it is that interest in defence policy should be general and well-informed. It is especially important that we should know how far we should have confidence in the directorate of the war machine, and no one from his wealth of experience is better qualified than Lord Hankey to judge if confidence is justified.

IT is impossible in a short article to give an adequate description of the system that has been evolved and has stood the test of war with such remarkable success, but there are some outstanding features that may be noted. The evolution of the system started with the establishment of the Committee of Imperial Defence in the early years of the present century. That, for the first time, brought the Government and its technical advisers together in a systematic attempt to make preparations for war. It was the work of that Committee that to a very large extent was responsible for our prompt and effective intervention in 1914. We were then admirably prepared for the war that had been envisaged, although not for the expansion of the war effort required, nor for its effective control.

AS a consequence, there was muddling through and improvisation before, towards the end of the war, under Lloyd George's dynamic leadership, the system of control began to develop fully. During the war the Committee of Imperial Defence was suspended, but its highly trained Secretariat formed an indispensable element in the development of the wartime machinery. After the war, however, it resumed its functions and it had to deal with problems of greatly increased complexity, especially with those connected with the advent of air power as a major factor. Air power provided us with a new instrument which might be used independently for offensive action, but it also implied a new menace to our security. Naval power to control sea communications was still our primary requirement, but it was clear that circumstances might arise which would necessitate the employment of the three fighting services in independent roles or, on the other hand, in the closest co-operation. It was also evident that behind the fighting services it might be necessary to develop all the resources of the Nation.

The full system of Government control developed during the 1914-18 war obviously could not be maintained under peace conditions, and the C.I.D. became the caretaking party with the duty of keeping the machinery in order and of effecting improvements necessary to meet new conditions. Perhaps the most important measure taken was the constitution of the "Chiefs of the Staffs Sub-Committee," supplemented later by combined planning and combined intelligence committees. This, after some initial teething troubles, ensured that not only should the independent roles of the three Services be kept under review but also, what was even more important, their co-operative action.

FLEXIBILITY of Our System is One of Its Greatest Virtues

The Chief of the Staffs Sub-Committee, in fact, became a super-chief of the Staff in Commission, and its members had joint as well as individual responsibility for advising the Government on war policy. The Prime Minister or his deputy sat as Chairman to the Committee, and no doubt that and the constant and systematic bringing of the heads of the three Services together did much to develop the close co-operation between the Services which war required.

IT has been argued that our system relies excessively on committees, involving the dangers of delayed decisions and weak compromises ; and that the three Services should be governed by a single Defence Ministry with a single chief of the staff. Even if it were possible, however, to find an individual qualified for the post it is certain that he would be overloaded by the complexities of his task, especially as circumstances may require each of the Services to act independently or in greatly varying degrees of co-operation. The flexibility which our system gives is one of its chief virtues and provides an admirable means of making the best use of specialized knowledge and experience. The proof of the pudding is in the eating, and we have little reason to be dissatisfied with the results. Surely a system which has dealt so successfully with the many complex circumstances of the war should be trusted to deal with the problems raised by the arrival of the atomic bomb.

In Manchuria the Russians Settle Old Scores

SOVIET 2nd FAR-EASTERN ARMY troops entered Harbin, Manchuria, strategically important junction on the Chinese Eastern Railway, on August 30, 1945, and were acclaimed by the townspeople (1). Among the enemy forces to surrender was this transport column (2). A typical Japanese roadside fort (3) in the Manchurian steppes. Ratings of the Soviet Pacific Fleet (4) displayed the Russian naval flag at at Port Arthur on September 3; the port was captured by the Japanese from Russia in 1905.

Photos, Planet News, Pictorial Press

How Allies Were Poised at the End of the War

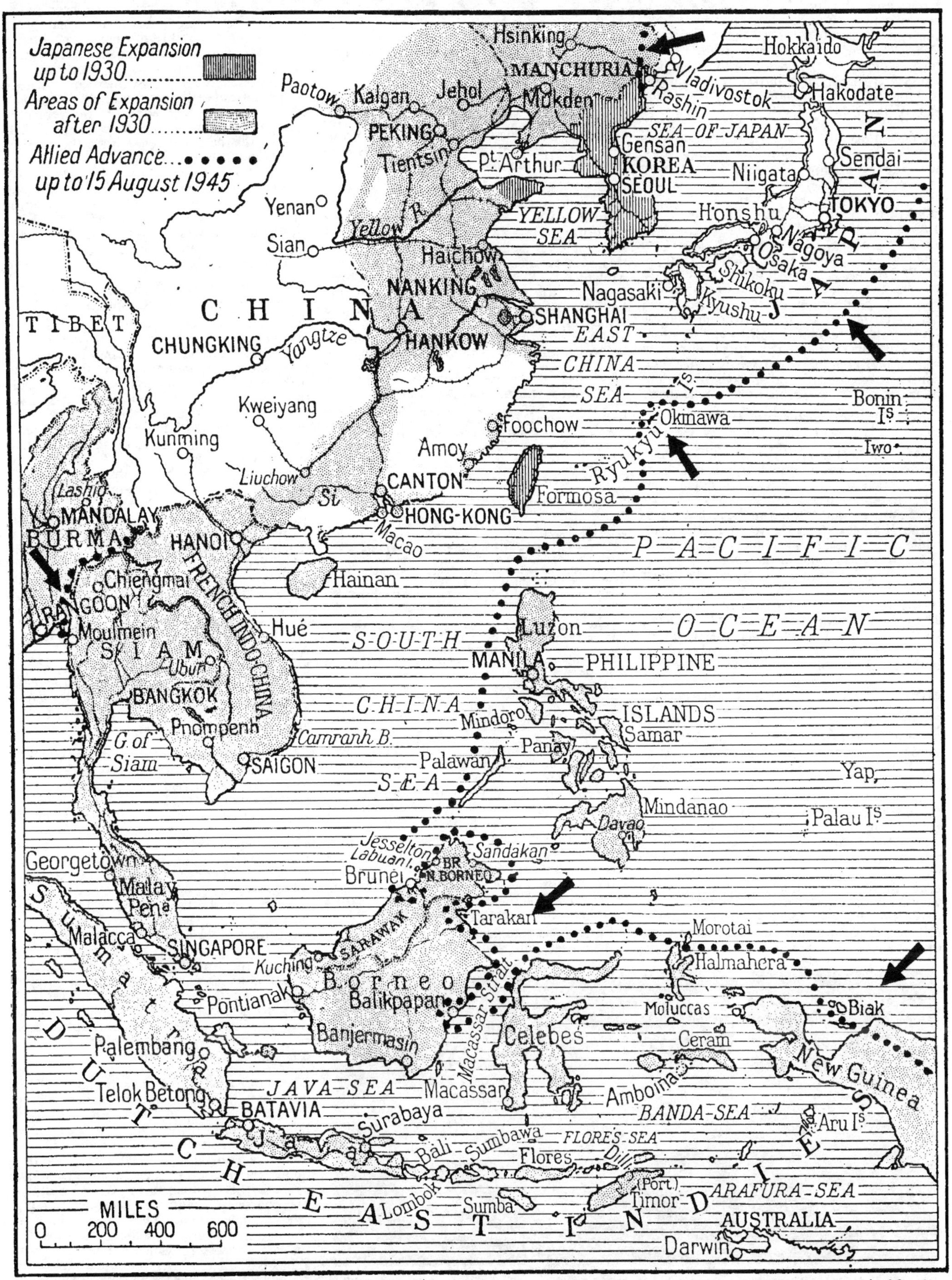

AS THE CURTAIN DESCENDED ON AUGUST 14, 1945, when the Japanese accepted unconditional surrender terms, Allied forces were poised for the kill as depicted here. To the north the Soviets, declaring war on August 8, had all but cut off Manchuria and were streaming into Korea. In Burma resistance against the 14th Army had ended except for rearguard actions in the Sittang bend. On Borneo the Australians had pincered the island between Brunei, Tarakan and Balikpapan. Less than three hundred miles south-west of the Japanese mainland, U.S. forces had firmly established themselves in the Ryukyus with the final clearance of Okinawa by June 21. Most telling blows of all were air raids on the homeland, culminating in the dropping of atomic bombs on Hiroshima and Nagasaki (see illus. page 344). *By courtesy of The Times*

With Our Navies Today

By

FRANCIS E. McMURTRIE

With the occupation of Tokyo, Horg Kong and Singapore comes news of such ships as are left to the Japanese Navy. Official estimates have been made of the losses suffered by the enemy in the past three and a half years; and all that is now needed is more information concerning the actual fate of individual vessels.

According to a statement issued from Fleet Admiral Nimitz's headquarters, few Japanese ships of importance remain in serviceable condition. Only one battleship, the Nagato, of 32,720 tons, is considered to be worth repairing. She is at Yokosuka, the naval base on Tokyo Bay. At Kure, on the Inland Sea, are the Hyuga and Ise, of 29,990 tons, and the Haruna, of 29,330 tons, all of them reduced to wrecks by Allied bombing attacks during July. A photograph of the Hyuga shows her to be resting on the bottom in shallow water, apparently gutted by fire and explosion. It is reckoned that these three ships are what a marine underwriter would call "total constructive losses," implying that it would be waste of money to attempt to refit them.

German Submarines Have Been Discovered in Japanese Waters

Only one fleet aircraft carrier appears to be seaworthy. This is the Katuragi (or Katsuragi), believed to have been converted from a battleship or heavy cruiser hull. Two or three more are understood to have been irreparably damaged, at Kure and elsewhere, while others are probably still incomplete, on the slips or fitting-out in dockyards. It is believed that four more carriers of the latest type were under construction; further information about these would be of interest. Their names have been reported as Amagi, Aso, Ikoma and Kasagi—all Japanese mountain peaks. Two heavy cruisers remain afloat, both at Singapore. These are 10,000-ton ships armed with 8-in. guns, the Takao and Myoko. They are reported to be disabled.

If there are any escort carriers left—which is doubtful—they are not in a seaworthy state; but there are two light fleet carriers, the Hosyo and Ryuko, still afloat at Kure, though damaged. Two light cruisers are said to remain serviceable, one of them being the 6,000-ton Sakawa, of the Nosiro type, built during the war, and the other the 25-year-old Kitagami. There are 26 destroyers, four of them badly damaged, and 16 submarines. Six German submarines have also been found in Japanese waters, though whether they were still manned by their original crews is not reported. Two or three Italian submarines had been taken over by the Japanese and their crews interned. Two old coast defence ships, the ex-cruisers Aduma (or Azuma) and Kasuga, have also been found at Yokosuka, and a third was sunk at Kure. These ships were in their prime during the war between Japan and Russia in 1904–05, and are now of little fighting value.

It was recently disclosed that the Japanese battleship Kongo, of 29,330 tons, was torpedoed and sunk by an American submarine off Formosa last December. Previously she had not been definitely accounted for; and this remark also applies to the Mutu (or Mutsu), of 32,720 tons, which had not been heard of for two or three years past. It had been suggested that she was sunk at the same time as the smaller battleships Hiei and Kirisima in the Battle of Guadalcanal, in November 1942. It is now known that she was destroyed by an internal explosion in the Inland Sea in July 1943.

JAPANESE NAVAL LOSSES

Of her 369 warships and destroyers Japan has lost all but 49, and the wreckage of her once-proud Navy strews the Pacific islands seaboards, Rear-Adml. Forest P. Sherman, Deputy Chief of Staff to Fleet Adml. Nimitz, stated on August 21, 1945, at Guam.

Battleships. Of 12, now **one** left, the Nagato, which is heavily damaged and without a crew in Tokyo Bay.

Aircraft Carriers. Of 9, **one** is operative, and is heavily damaged.

Light Aircraft Carriers. Of 7, only **two** heavily damaged remain.

Escort Carriers. Of 5, **none** left. These ships and another battleship were sunk in the Coral Sea, midway between the Solomons and the Philippines, and in ports where they were finally tracked down.

Heavy Cruisers. Of 19, the Japanese Navy list now carries only **two**, both at Singapore and badly damaged.

Light Cruisers. Of 24 (approx.), only **two** are left.

Destroyers. 165 (estimated) reduced to **twenty-six**, of which four are badly damaged.

Submarines. Of 140, now only **sixteen** in addition to six German U-boats.

Presumably Japanese naval records will be seized and examined, in order that all these doubtful matters may be investigated and made clear. What is to become of the surviving enemy ships? It seems likely that they will be scrapped by the Allies after thorough inspection, for their value to a Western Power is problematical. It is possible that the Soviet Navy may put in a request for one or two of the less severely damaged units, but otherwise there is going to be no great demand for them.

For a considerable time to come a strong British fleet will require to be maintained in the Far East, for until the whole of the Japanese armies overseas have been taken back to their own country the possibility of their giving further trouble cannot be overlooked. How they are to be transported is another problem. The bulk of the Japanese mercantile fleet is at the bottom of the sea, and Allied merchant ships are urgently needed for the return of our own people and for the carriage of food and merchandise to rehabilitate the ravaged countries of Europe. Thus the Japanese cannot expect their troops home quickly. Idle soldiery, especially in the East, are difficult to control; and there is good reason to suppose that many Japanese military officers are dissatisfied with the surrender terms and would gladly seize any chance to make difficulties for the Allies.

Reconstitution of Naval Stations for Peacetime Routine Duties

In other parts of the world the Royal Navy may be expected gradually to resume its peacetime routine of policing the seas so that those proceeding "on their lawful occasions" may navigate in safety. Already the fleet in the Mediterranean appears to have been reorganized as a cruiser and destroyer force, with units of types unsuitable for service in the Pacific, by reason of their size or limited fuel capacity. Presumably the Africa station will be reconstituted on pre-war lines, with a small number of cruisers, supported by sloops. Whether the America and West Indies Station will function exactly as before is more doubtful. It is possible that ships of the Royal Canadian Navy will take over the northern waters of the station, including the West Indies. This would leave to the care of the Royal Navy the South America division, which might then become a separate station, as it sometimes has been in the past. Between them the Royal Australian Navy and Royal New Zealand Navy may be trusted to police the island regions of the Pacific effectively, leaving the China and East Indies Stations to the Royal Navy. On the latter station the Royal Indian Navy will share in the work.

Even so, a number of new cruisers will be needed before the overseas duties of the Navy can be carried out efficiently. It is not generally realized how short we are of ships of this category, as the result of the unwise departure in peacetime from the establishment of 70 cruisers estimated by Earl Jellicoe to be the absolute minimum needed for the proper defence of our seaborne trade. As the result of war losses, there are in service in the fleet today, including ships of the R.A.N., R.C.N. and R.N.Z.N., no more than 62 cruisers. At least a dozen of these are obsolete and overdue for replacement; and another has been relegated to special duty as a seagoing training ship for cadets. So far as is known, there are only four cruisers completing or under construction, leaving a deficiency of 17 ships as compared with the prescribed figure of 70 as our minimum requirement.

For the time being it may be expected that the escort aircraft carriers will be utilized to fill the gap. There are 39 of these, but all are too slow to undertake the function of a cruiser satisfactorily. Moreover, 35 of them are understood to have been acquired under the Lease-Lend arrangement, so will probably be returned to the United States in due course, as a number of smaller warships already have been. Thus they cannot be counted upon in any sense as a substitute for the cruisers of which we are so short. What is wanted is a considerable number of cruisers of a standard type such as the Swiftsure, which on a displacement of between 8,000 and 9,000 tons mounts nine 6-in., eight 4-in. and numerous smaller guns, and has a reputed speed of 33 knots.

Rear-Adl. C. H. J. HARCOURT Flying his flag in H.M.S. Swiftsure, he commanded the force which entered Hong Kong on Aug. 30, 1945.

Rear-Adl. C. S. HOLLAND In charge of the British landing at Singapore on Sept. 5, 1945, when British and Indian troops went ashore uneventfully.

Vice-Adl. H. T. C. WALKER Commanding the R.N. force which entered Penang, he received the Japanese surrender aboard H.M.S. Nelson, Sept. 1.

Photos, British Official, Elliott and Fry, Walter Stoneman

Carriers Serving With the British Pacific Fleet

ROYAL NAVY'S NEW LIGHT FLEET CARRIERS were constructed under a special wartime building programme to augment the larger fleet carriers for the war in the Far East. A smaller version, their speed is 25 knots, displacement 14,000 tons, extreme length 695 ft. extreme breadth 80 ft., draught 23 ft. Each carries 33 aircraft, comprising torpedo-bombers and single-seater fighters. Armament consists of 24 two-pounder pom-poms, with a large number of 20-mm. oerlikons. Two of the new carriers are H.M.S. Glory (top) and H.M.S. Colossus (bottom). Surrender of Japanese in South-west Pacific area was signed in H.M.S. Glory, off Rabaul, New Britain, on September 6, 1945.

Photos, British Official

Tracing Millions of Europe's Lost Families

To the military authorities it is "Operation Humanity." To the Red Cross organization in Geneva it is a gigantic cross-indexing involving 30,000,000 names. To the far-distant hapless Displaced Person—the wanderer torn by Nazi tyranny from far-distant home and friends—it may be a miracle. How the task, one of the most urgent in European history, is being handled is explained by MARK PRIESTLEY. See also story in page 281.

SOME order has been achieved at last in the vast tangle of Europe's "lost." Men from the hospitals of Belsen and Dachau are being restored to their families—even though their homes have been utterly destroyed, and their wives and children moved away leaving no addresses. The "missing men" of France, Holland, Poland and other countries are being traced with efficiency and speed.

World-wide organizations are working as a team, at full pressure, in this odyssey of the lost and found. A typical centre is the Red Cross bureau in Brussels, where 2,000 cases have been satisfactorily settled in the past few months. Less than two per cent of the inquiries are listed as untraceable, and even for these there is hope. Here is a typical example. A Belsen victim was a patient from a Frenchmen's hut; he could recall nothing of his past life and could only repeat a term of endearment he had obviously used in the past. The R.A.M.C. private who tended him wrote the word down, and in due course it travelled to the Red Cross offices in Geneva. There it was discovered that no less than five families in France and Belgium who hoped for news of their loved ones had given this word as a possible clue. Volunteer workers drew blanks when they followed up the four French possibilities, but the Brussels office was able to show an inquiry from a Belgian woman whose vanished husband had been a member of the resistance movement.

Almost Hopelessly Tangled Clues

In another case, the D.P.s—as displaced persons are known to the officials—were being sorted out during adjustment of frontiers between the British and Russian zones of occupied Germany, when a woman approached one of the liaison officers. "I am registered as Czech," she explained, "because I managed to cross the border after the outbreak of war. But I am really Polish. Can you help me to find my son, who was last heard of when travelling as a business agent in Brussels?" No trace of the son was found in Brussels until reference to old shipping lists showed him to have sailed to Kenya. The Kenya authorities in turn reported that after a few months he had sailed to London. In the end, the Polish-born son was found to be serving in the British Army. He had changed his name, his mother had all but changed her nationality, but they are now in contact.

THE Hamburg area had in its 400 slave compounds about 100,000 D.P.s when the British 23rd Division took over their rehabilitation. They included nearly every European nationality, and some, in the first wild delirium of liberation, had torn up their work and ration cards, the only official proofs of identification. Others had left the camp in which they were indexed, and had turned up weeks later hundreds of miles away. Many could not agree on the subject of their nationality. Often, a long cross-examination has been the only means of deciding whether a D.P. is Polish, German, Russian, stateless, or in some other category.

Every refugee and internee, after being clothed, fed and medically cared for, pleads for help in getting in touch with his family. "Where can I find my wife?" asks a Rumanian repatriated from a Swiss internment camp. "Our home was bombed, and she was sent to armaments work in the Rhineland." Perhaps a concentration camp survivor turns his face to the wall, spiritless, hopeless, feeling he has nothing left to live for. Then a Red Cross official sympathetically questions him, reminds him of lost and broken contacts, assures him again of his safety (many of these victims still cannot believe the Nazis are broken) and undertakes to help reinstate him.

THE ex-internee is told how a message will circulate in his name, giving full details of former addresses. Often this assurance is of immense value in helping a D.P. to realize that he is once again a name, not a number: a human being, not a brute. He is buoyed to normality by the fact that a great international organization is putting the whole of its resources of investigation at his personal disposal.

DISPLACED PERSONS' RELATIVES anxiously examine the lists posted in Bloomsbury House Refugee Office, London, of survivors of Nazi concentration camps, whose whereabouts have been traced.
Photo, Topical Press

A hospital patient who had once been a leading Viennese scientist said sadly that all his relatives were dead, all sent to the gas rooms, poisoned or butchered. "All, all, all!" he reiterated brokenly. But his surname appeared in the Geneva file. It was an unusual name, shared, it seemed, by a refugee who had escaped from Austria and found sanctuary in Switzerland. The Red Cross contacted him and discovered that he was the scientist's cousin. The two men met—and wept. Now there is hope that they may meet others of their family circle.

By August 1, 1945, more than 4,000,000 had been repatriated from the British, American and French zones of occupation. The Red Cross and St. John War Organization, and a dozen other agencies, employ a check-reference to the identity and address of each individual, to help give them fresh clues to the missing. Many thousands have gone blithely home, as they thought, to their wives, to find their families vanished, and their house in ruins or in hands of strangers. For a time they try to follow-up their own trails, but all too often their appeals return to the Red Cross.

AT the Italian exits from Germany nearly 1,000,000 ex-internees are still enduring the slow and tragic march homewards. The Italian Red Cross set up a reception centre at the Milan railway station where refugees were received in the station corridor, and then in order to make room for incoming refugees they were moved on a south-bound bus to a delousing station. Old men and women, children with an expression matching the eyes of their grandparents, could not be moved on because they were ill.

Transport of D.P.s back to their homes is indeed one of the big problems of the British occupying forces. Something has been done to relieve the situation by taking English buses off their own home routes for this special duty in the British zone. Round about Paderborn the 7th Field Regiment, R.A., assumed responsibility for 25,000 D.P.s, and, said an officer of that regiment, "The people of Maidstone, Ipswich and Norfolk ought to know that their old coaches have been a real help to us in moving these former slave-workers!"

Overtaken by Freakish Fate

To add to the congestion, some of the people return, reporting that they had no homes, that their loved ones were gone. One old woman returned from her daughter's address to report that the daughter had been murdered by the Germans and her body taken away. A few days later the daughter was registered at another centre. She, in turn, had been told that her mother had been executed. That is an instance of freak Fate in action. The Oslo Red Cross bureau is proud of a case in which its detecting methods could not have been bettered. A Norwegian soldier found in a German hospital had lost his memory, could not recall rank or name. All he knew was that someone had promised to knit him another sweater similar to the one he was wearing. Investigators found that the wool and the method of knitting came from a certain district of Norway. Circularizing a description of the man, they were able to find relatives.

A young German in the British Pioneer Corps, parted from his mother over ten years ago, knew nothing but her name—one name to trace among the millions in Germany. The soldier knew they had lived in Leipzig during his boyhood, so the officials looked up the family name in a ten-year-old Leipzig directory at the British Museum, in London. Then Red Cross officials with the U.S. Army Group in the Leipzig area patiently traced the mother, year by year, from that first address to others. The trail seemed to end at last at the site of a flattened ruin, but the mother's name did not appear on local casualty lists, and the Red Cross kept up the hunt. They questioned neighbours, made inquiries in local shops, looked through military government directory files, followed up air-raid evacuation lists. There they again found the mother's name, followed it across Germany, and ran her to earth in a little village.

ANOTHER aspect of this wholesale disruption and displacement is giving the authorities serious concern. On August 21, 1945, Field-Marshal Montgomery issued a stern warning, for publication in German newspapers: "I am determined to put an end to the serious crimes committed by displaced citizens of the United Nations. This message is directed to you all. I realize that the majority of you are peace-loving people and not responsible for the outrages committed by a small minority. I warn those of you who are tempted to commit reprehensible crimes against the German population that I have ordered my troops to take drastic measures against all persons caught in the act of rape or murder or those who are committing acts of deliberate looting."

Now the Germans Wander in Their Native Land

CLEARING-HOUSES FOR GERMAN HOMELESS included a large camp at Kevelaer in the Rhineland, seen (1) from the air. Frontier-post at Schaanwald (2) in the principality of Liechtenstein, barricaded to prevent gate-crashing. Between July and August 1945, 800,000 Germans from Poland and Czechoslovakia swarmed into Berlin. Some studied the improvised time-table at the Stettiner railway-station (3). Others squatted in the blitzed street (4) to read their first newspaper for months. See facing page.

Photos, British Newspaper Pool, Keystone, Planet News

Germany's New 'Bobbies' at Work Under British

NEWLY-RECRUITED GERMAN POLICE are inspected by a British Army Officer (1) attached to the Public Safety Department of the Allied Military Government in Hanover and accompanied by a former German police-chief. Posting of proclamation dissolving the Nazi party in Hanover (2) was witnessed—in accordance with military law—by two townspeople, the Secretary and Chief of the local police, and a sergeant of the R.E.M.E. A German policeman directs cross-roads traffic (3), releasing British Military Police for other duties.

Photos, British Official

Conquerors' Flags Flutter in the Berlin Breeze

COLOURS OF THE FOUR GREAT POWERS were flown in Berlin on September 3, 1945—sixth anniversary of the outbreak of war—at the headquarters of the Allied Control Council and (top, left to right) Field-Marshal Montgomery (Great Britain), Marshal Zhukov (U.S.S.R.), Gen. Eisenhower (U.S.), and Gen. Koenig (France) stood at the salute. Formerly the Reich Supreme Court of Justice, the building contains 546 rooms, and was known as the Kammergericht. At the ceremony (bottom) a guard of honour was provided by men of the U.S. 82nd Airborne Division, heroes of D-Day and Nijmegen landings.

Photos, Associated Press

Crowning Efforts of the Australians in Borneo

One of the signatories of the Instrument of Surrender in Tokyo on Sept. 2, 1945, was Australia's General Sir Thomas Blamey. Thus was recognized Australia's place as a principal Pacific Power. The operations in Borneo, crowning efforts of the Australian Military Forces, are the subject of this article, specially written for "The War Illustrated" by ROY MACARTNEY.

When the sullen capitulation of Hirohito brought the Pacific war to a sudden and uneasy halt, troops of the veteran 7th and 9th Australian Divisions had all but completed the recapture of British and Dutch Borneo. They had driven a wedge south through the enemy-held East Indies, gaining control of the strategic Macassar Strait. Further occupation of Borneo would have followed swiftly; then from the western shores of the island, Singapore—cherished goal of all British troops since the disaster of 1942—would have been only 450 miles distant.

Japan's capitulation denied the Australians the opportunity of avenging their 8th Division, wiped out in the Malayan campaign, but in the last months of the Pacific war the enemy was given good reason to remember the 8th's sister divisions. There were six of them, operating in an arc extending over approximately 3,000 miles from Bougainville to Borneo. On no previous occasion in this war had so many Australian formations been committed simultaneously. The 3rd and 11th were fighting on Bougainville in the Solomons, the 5th besieging the enemy at the tip of north-eastern New Britain, the 6th in New Guinea had all but exterminated the Wewak garrison, and the 7th and 9th had secured domination of Borneo. It was a fitting final contribution in a war in which Australia had given so much.

Lt.-Gen. V. A. H. STURDEE, C.B.E., D.S.O., commanded the four divisions comprising the 1st Australian Army in New Guinea, where the Japanese continued to fight on after the surrender declaration. *Photo, Australian Official*

It took just over three months' campaigning to secure domination of Borneo, rich East Indies prize. Japanese militarists and industrialists had good cause for satisfaction when, early in 1942, Borneo was engulfed by their irresistible southern surge. Borneo, third largest island in the world, derives most of its economic wealth from its great rubber production and rich coal and oil deposits. Although British and Dutch engineers wrecked most of the installations of the great oilfields lying around the oil ports of Balikpapan, Miri and Tarakan, the enemy was able to repair much of the damage. By the end of 1942 Borneo was a major source of fuel oil and aviation gasoline for the Japanese Navy and Air Force.

Australia's famous 9th Division, which fought through the siege of Tobruk and at El Alamein before returning to the Pacific to plunge into the jungle struggle for New Guinea, was chosen for the initial landing on Borneo. On May 1, 1945, under cover of a devastating barrage of rockets and guns of all calibres, troops swept ashore from a fleet of assault craft to seize a bridge-head on Tarakan island. Australian Liberators moved up specially from Darwin to Morotai saturated the bridge-head area with high explosive in front of the first wave of assault troops. Other Allied aircraft provided an impenetrable air umbrella as warships steamed lazily up and down the coast, bombarding at will.

Spearheaded by tanks, the Australians cleared the Tarakan town area after four days' fierce fighting, and then overran the Pamoesian and Djoeata oilfields. Within a fortnight the 9th Division had gained control of nearly all the strategically important points on the island, although Japanese pockets of resistance held out in difficult country in the interior. Displaying their customary skill in burrowing into the earth, the Japanese had turned a succession of razor-back ridges into a series of mutually supporting fortresses. It took six weeks' relentless hand-to-hand fighting before the 9th Division infantry ferreted the last of them out of their deep and evil-smelling bunkers.

Huge Oil Fires Raged Fiercely

Within five weeks of the landing on Tarakan, Australians struck again, this time on the west coast of British North Borneo, 800 miles north-east of Singapore and 600 miles east of Indo-China. At dawn on June 11, simultaneous landings were made at Labuan Island, at Brooketon on Borneo proper, and on Muara Island lying in Brunei Bay. Although the enemy had offered stiff resistance on Tarakan, there was little encountered in the Brunei area. Australians quickly captured the Labuan airfield and drove inland from Brooketon to seize the town of Brunei.

One Australian column driving down the coast at lightning speed reached Lutong, and then made a 25-mile advance down coastal trails to the oilfield of Seria, potentially the biggest in the British Empire. Australians found destructive oil fires raging on a huge scale, the town of Seria destroyed with all buildings, the water supply and lighting equipment wrecked. Engineers, assisted by former oilfield employees who returned from hide-outs in the hills, slowly extinguished and gained control of the fires.

Meanwhile, another column had driven north-east of Brunei along the Beaufort-Jesselton railway in pursuit of the main enemy force. The Japanese retreated with such ardour that they failed to destroy railway tracks and abandoned wood-burning locomotives. The versatile Australians fitted flanged wheels to jeeps and, with the railway intact, the strange vehicles greatly eased the supply problem. "Armoured" trains protected by sandbags piled high, and armed with Vickers and Brens, patrolled the railway, protecting it from marauding Japanese.

Within a month the 9th Division had occupied its primary objectives, including two hundred miles of seaboard, the magnificent harbour and installations of Brunei Bay, airstrips of Labuan Island, Brunei and Sarawak, all the big oilfields and refineries, and much of the richest rubber producing areas of British North Borneo. They then turned to their secondary task of clearing the enemy from the narrow productive hinterland, in preparation for the return of native producers of food and raw materials.

The stage was set for the third and most telling blow on Borneo. Balikpapan, principal port of the island, awoke at dawn on July 1 to the thunder of a preliminary bombardment which had assumed tremendous proportions (see illus. page 274). Behind the protective curtain of steel and high explosive troops of the veteran 7th Australian Division swarmed ashore east of the port and quickly a mile-long beach-head fronting the strategic Macassar Strait was secured. Pushing to the east, infantry cleared the Sepinggang and Manggar airstrips while other forces drove steadily west towards Balikpapan. Three days after the initial landing they carried the town by storm.

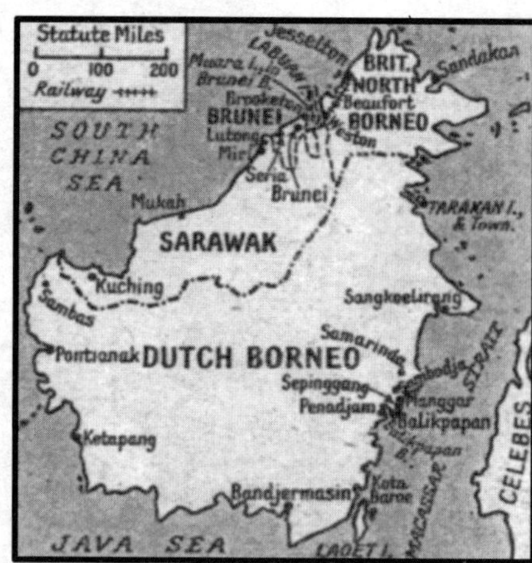

BORNEO, 284,000-square-miles East Indian Island, showing British and Netherlands possessions, also the British protectorate of Sarawak and Brunei, the Mahomedan state which is attached to the Straits Settlements.

Another amphibious force crossed Balikpapan Bay the next day and landed at Penadjam, occupying the headlands at the western entrance to the harbour. Although the 7th Division speedily swept through the area there was constant enemy sniping and desultory counter-shelling, while many pockets of stubborn resistance had to be reduced one by one. Occupation of Penadjam gave the Australians control of Balikpapan harbour. General MacArthur, who landed with the Australians, described Balikpapan as perhaps the most lucrative strategic target in the East Indies sector. Development of the existing air facilities would enable Allied aircraft to sweep the skies from Timor to eastern Sumatra. As the general commented, "It is fitting that the 7th Division, which in July three years ago met and later turned back the tide of invasion of Australia on the historic Kokoda trail, should have captured this most important objective."

Captured Airstrips Made Operative

R.A.A.F. engineers, toiling day and night, quickly made the captured airstrips operative. Australian aircraft of many types were moving in to prepare for the next big jump westward, when hostilities came to an end. 7th Division troops, having completed their primary task—the occupation of Balikpapan—had closed to within four miles of Sambodja, principal oilfield of the area, when they, too, were halted.

And so the long, hard road tramped by Australia's fighting men ended in Borneo when they were in sight of the goal they so wanted to avenge—Singapore! But should the Japanese ever boast of the success they enjoyed early in the Pacific War, the names of Milne Bay, Kokoda, Guadalcanal, Buna, Sanananda, Tarakan and Balikpapan will be a salutary reminder of how British and American fighting men in the South-West Pacific adapted themselves to the jungle and administered an historic beating.

Aussies Used 'Mixed Grill' Barrage at Tarakan

CLEARING THE BEACHES AT BALIKPAPAN, prized oil port in south-east Borneo (captured on July 4, 1945), engineers of the Australian 7th Division with mine-detectors (1) made way for the heavy armour during the landings. Infantrymen crossed the Vasey highway past shattered homesteads (2). "Mixed-grill" barrage (3) against an enemy only 600 yards away was assembled on Tarakan Island (cleared by June 24): nearest camera was a 25-pounder, next a 3·7 A.A. gun, used as field artillery, and beyond, a Matilda tank joined in. *Photos, Australian Official*

Writhings of Japan in the Last Days of Defeat

Trite but true is the saying that a war is more easy to start than to stop. Japan realized to the full the bitterness of this truth in the days following her unconditional surrender to Allied demands. How the loose ends of tangled threads of the Far Eastern War were finally caught up and disposed of is briefly outlined in this account of the final setting of the Rising Sun.

THOUGH the Japanese surrender dated from August 14, 1945, the Emperor's orders for all his forces to cease fire were not issued until August 16. It was anticipated that some delay in these orders becoming effective in China, Bougainville, New Guinea, the Philippines and other distant areas would be likely, but the Emperor's surrender broadcast made it clear that members of the Imperial family would be sent to some fronts to enforce the orders personally.

Fighting continued at a number of points, with the Russians advancing rapidly on several fronts in Manchuria (see page 258), and by August 19 they had taken prisoner more than 150,000 troops of the Japanese Kwantung Army, the strength of which was estimated at 500,000. Russian airborne troops by that date had landed in the four chief cities of Manchuria, and at one of these—Harbin—the Kwantung Army Group formally surrendered three days later; and airborne troops landed in Port Arthur and Dairen (which the Japanese had seized from the Russians in 1905) to begin the disarming of the Japanese garrisons.

IN Manila, 16 surrender envoys arrived on August 19 and were received by General MacArthur's staff officers, to arrange for Allied landings in Japan: these began at Atsugi airfield near Tokyo on August 28. The beaten army in Southern China surrendered on August 22, at Chihkiang, to a representative of Marshal Chiang Kai-shek. Formal surrender of 1,000,000 Japanese troops took place on September 9 in the walled city of Nanking, China's ancient capital, and scene of a massacre by the Japanese in 1937.

On August 19 Australian Army H.Q. announced that negotiations, affecting more then 20,000 Japanese in the Bougainville area of the Solomons, and approximately 8,000 around Wewak, in New Guinea, had begun. On September 6 the surrender of all Japanese in the South-West Pacific area (New Guinea, New Britain, and New Ireland) was signed on board H.M.S. Glory (see illus. page 327) in St. George's Channel, south-west of Rabaul. Officers, ratings and marines on the flight-deck watched Gen. Imamura, Japanese C.-in-C. South-West Pacific, hand his sword to Lieut.-Gen. V. A. H. Sturdee, commanding the 1st Australian Army (see portrait in page 332). Complete surrender of all Japanese on Bougainville and adjacent islands in the Solomons was signed at Australian H.Q. on September 8.

Quitting of "Tiger of Malaya"

In Borneo, first contacts were not made until September 4. Negotiations for surrender took place at the mouth of the Sarawak River two days later, between Gen. Yamamura and Australian representatives, and the formal surrender to Major-Gen. Wootten, commanding the Australian 9th Division was made on September 10 at Labuan.

The "Tiger of Malaya," Gen. Yamashita, surrendered the battered remnants of Japanese forces at Baguio on Luzon in the Philippines on September 3. Specially brought from Tokyo to witness the ceremony were Gen. Jonathan Wainwright, U.S. commander of Corregidor, and Lieut.-Gen. A. E. Percival, British commander at Singapore, who had both surrendered to Yamashita when Japan was at the height of her triumph. On the same day, surrenders of the Pacific islands of Truk (Carolines), Palau, the Bonins, Pagan and Rota (last remaining Japanese stronghold in the Marianas) were made aboard U.S. warships.

The position in the last major zone where things had been uncertain was cleared up on August 23, when a Japanese radio message to South-East Asia Command H.Q. announced that Field-Marshal Count Terauchi, the Imperial commander in that area, had at last ordered the Cease Fire. Referring to Admiral Lord Louis Mountbatten's broadcast instructions to the Japanese Southern Army on August 20, Terauchi said:

"We have received your message regarding occupation of coastal waters and clearing of mines. For this purpose we are prepared to send our delegates to Rangoon on August 26 so that you may carry out operations more safely in perfect mutual understanding between your command and ours. Therefore we hope that operations which your naval forces desire to carry out may be put off until complete mutual understanding can be reached between your command and ours."

JAPAN'S EMPEROR HIROHITO, "Son of Heaven," leaving a meeting of the Japanese Diet on September 4, 1945. An official bows as the Emperor hurries by. *Photo, Keystone*

THE preliminary agreement was signed at Rangoon on August 28 (see page 322), and the final S.E.A.C. surrender was signed on September 12 at Singapore, where British and Indian troops had landed on September 5—just over 3½ years after the great naval base had been taken by the enemy. In this guardian city of the gateway to the Far East were more than 30,000 prisoners, herded in 23 camps, estimated to be made up as follows: 6,700 British, 88 Americans, 5,500 Australians, 4,000 Dutch and 14,000 Italians and others unclassified.

On August 30 it was revealed that Gen. Itagaki, Japanese commander at Singapore had notified Field-Marshal Terauchi of his intention to fight on, that "the Japanese armies remained undefeated in battle." Terauchi's reply to Itagaki was to the effect that further resistance would disgrace the honour of the Japanese Army, and that continued defence of Singapore would erase all hope of retaining any Japanese army, whereas acceptance of unconditional surrender might permit the retention of a nucleus force. Itagaki thought again, and acted wisely. It was actually he who made the final surrender to Admiral Mountbatten at Singapore, Count Terauchi being too ill to attend.

Reluctant to Carry the News

An unexpected difficulty in getting surrender news to isolated Japanese forces in Burma was reported on September 4. Japanese envoys from Moulmein were reluctant to go among their own troops with the news. One of the Japanese parties entered the British lines near Waw, and was taken to an area where there were known to be Japanese forces. The envoys stated they did not like telling their compatriots the news, and suggested that pictures showing them with British officers should be taken and the pictures and leaflets sent among the units rather than that they themselves should go forward. The suggestion was not agreed to. The Commander of the Japanese forces in Burma asked that he be allowed to delay sending further envoys until the result of the first group's activities were known, as a sharp signal had been sent stating that further parties must be dispatched. A Japanese plane, flying a large white streamer, flew over one area dropping surrender leaflets.

LAST-MINUTE fighting in Burma, since the surrender, was in the village of Gyogon, which lies in the Pegu Yomas, about 35 miles north of Rangoon. Patriot Burmese forces in the village saw a party of Japanese and fired a shot into the air to indicate their presence. But the Japanese surrounded the villagers and then attempted to pass through the place. In the ensuing clash 12 Japs were killed, and the rest retreated. The following night 20 Japanese attacked the village; two were killed and the others withdrew. It was decided that the area should be visited by Japanese officers from the Burma Army Headquarters to tell any further isolated forces to surrender.

MEANTIME, British and American advance forces had landed in the Tokyo area (see story in page 345) to prepare for the main landings that were to follow the final signing of surrender terms. The actual signing of the final Instrument of Surrender took place on board the U.S.S. Missouri, in Tokyo Bay, on September 2 (see story in page 346), and two days later General Douglas MacArthur, as C.-in-C. of the Allied occupation forces, issued his first direct orders to the beaten enemy. He commanded the immediate demobilization of the Japanese Army, the clearing of mines from all harbours, and the speedy release of Allied prisoners of war (see illus. in page 343). At this time, U.S. troops were crossing the River Tama—original demarcation line between Japanese and Allied forces—outside Tokyo, in preparation for the entry into the capital itself on Sept. 8. And in the capital's House of Peers, Emperor Hirohito spoke from a golden throne:

"It is our desire that our people surmount the manifold hardships and trials attending the termination of the war, and that they make manifest the innate glory of Japan's national policy, win the confidence of the world, establish firmly a peaceful State and contribute to the progress of mankind, and be instantly directed to that end." Members left the Chamber weeping.

Photos, British Official

Changing of the Guard at British H.Q. in Vienna

At the 18th-century Schonbrunn Palace, formerly the summer residence of the Austrian Emperors, now headquarters of the British occupation troops in Vienna, the changing of the British guard took place for the first time on August 6, 1945. The new guard, provided by the 2nd Battalion Lancashire Fusiliers, presented arms (top) as they took over from the old guard (bottom), provided by 2771 Squadron R.A.F. Regiment. The band of the 4th Hussars played during the ceremony.

British Occupation Troops Parade in Austria—

Capital of the Austrian province of Styria, Graz was taken over from the Russians by 8th Army troops on July 24, 1945. They were visited on August 8 by Lieut.-Gen. Sir R. L. McCreery. In the main square he inspected men of the 70th Field Regiment Royal Artillery (top). On August 3, Air Vice-Marshal F. J. Fogarty, D.F.C., A.F.C., talked to home-bound airmen and officers (bottom) at Milan railway station—first contingent to leave there for U.K. leave under the R.A.F. scheme.

Pho

—To the Lively Strains of the Inniskillings' Pipers

Dominated by the peak of the Schlossberg, the main square of Graz echoed to the rousing sound of the splendid pipe band of the Royal Inniskilling Fusiliers, entertaining a delighted crowd before the arrival of Lieut.-Gen. McCreery (commander of British forces in Austria) to inspect the garrison troops. He was accompanied by Maj.-Gen. Weir, C.B., C.B.E., D.S.O., Commander of the 46th British Division. To the onlookers it was a stirring and memorable occasion.

'Queen Elizabeth' Takes Home 15,000 U.S. Troops

Photo, Keystone

For the first time in her chequered history the Queen Elizabeth, world's biggest and fastest liner, docked at Southampton, her home port, on August 20, 1945, and six days later sailed for New York with 15,000 American troops on board (above). She was given a great send-off by R.A.F. fighters circling over as she pulled out of the dock. Since she left the Clyde five years ago the Queen Elizabeth had sailed nearly 500,000 miles through five oceans. (See also pages 168–169).

VIEWS & REVIEWS Of Vital War Books

by Hamilton Fyfe

THE sort of battle that we see in the film of Henry the Fifth has, of course, been long out of date. Long-range weapons and rapid transport have outmoded close combat and hand-to-hand struggles. There were few encounters of the old classic type even in the 1914-18 war, though some did occur. In this War (so we shall still speak of it for some time to come) such engagements were scarcely known in Europe, and in the East they were rare. But there was one on a Pacific island which conformed to all the rules of what may be termed the chessboard battle and which will be looked back on as one of the most interesting as well as most important events of the campaign against the Japanese. The story of this is told by W. Richardson in The Epic of Tarawa (Odhams Press, 3s. 9d.), a finely illustrated volume with many maps. Although the book describes what was a purely American exploit, yet the demand for it could not be satisfied even before publication in this country.

FIRST, where is Tarawa ? It is a collection of small islands forming a coral reef around two sides of a triangular lagoon in the Gilberts group, over which there was a British protectorate from 1892 till 1942, when the Japanese seized it. They met with no opposition. The protecting Power was too busily occupied elsewhere to defend the unfortunate islanders against the brutal little yellow men who either killed them all or sent them to slave labour. It is not known which was their wretched fate. In their stead the Japs brought as slaves 400 Koreans, who were set to work to turn the island of Betio into one of the most formidable fortified places ever seen.

> They dug underground, built tunnels, and reinforced the labyrinth with steel and iron-hard palm logs and concrete. They dug caves for their men and caverns for their stores. They scooped out foxholes and trenches, and constructed pillboxes and small Maginot forts. Altogether they built 500 fortified places . . . Their blockhouses were in compartments so that they might stand against the heaviest blast and that their tenacious occupants would have to be knocked out one by one. There were 8-in. and 5-in. guns in very strong emplacements cleverly camouflaged, and any number of 3-in. guns for use against ships or planes.

Selfless Valour of Young Marines

What was the purpose of all this tremendous expenditure ? It was to protect the airfield, laid in the centre of the island. Not much of an airfield as airfields in America and Europe go : merely a strip of levelled coral sand 1,500 yards long, but of very great value to the enemy because " it controlled vast areas around it—areas limited only by the range and fuel capacity of the bombers and long-range fighters which took off from its runway."

THAT was why the High Command in Tokyo valued it so highly. That was why the American High Command decided that it must be taken and used for Allied instead of enemy aircraft. That the taking of it would be difficult and expensive in human life was recognized. But, as Admiral Stark says, " in the selfless valour of the young Marines who fought that action against such terrible odds and of the sailors who supported them, was sacrifice of which not only Americans but free men everywhere can rightly be proud."

The American Marines have traditions of which they speak with reverence. They feel that they are different from Army soldiers because they have been recruited for one purpose and one only—to fight.

> In the complexities of modern war an army needs millions of men who will never man a gun. A man may join the army to pursue his mercantile abilities in the Quartermaster Corps ; a storekeeper's qualifications may place him in the Post Exchange stores; a lawyer may enter the Judge Advocate's division ; machinists ply their trade far behind the lines . . . The Marines are a streamlined fighting force. They are formed only to the immediate end—battle.

Stark Heroism on Tarawa Atoll

The Marines who were landed on Tarawa on November 21, 1943, had therefore " an *esprit de corps* similar to the traditional pride of Britain's most famous regiments." They had something else as well which made exceptionally tough fighters. They did not, says Mr. W. Richardson, " just dislike the Japanese ; they hated and despised them. This was the enemy that had bayoneted prisoners, their faces twisted into grim psychopathic smiles while doing it. This was the enemy that would ' surrender ' in tiny groups, saunter forward with their hands up and their faces without expression, and then kill their captors with a light machine-gun lashed to the back of one of the phoney surrenderers." The Japanese had shown no mercy. The Marines would show them none.

THEY knew their foes and knew what the plan was for blasting them until they were destroyed. First, aircraft were to smash their airfield, supply dumps and gun emplacements. Then the naval big guns would silence the shore batteries. Then the Marines would move into the landing barges and make for the shore. What to do when they landed they knew by heart, but they also knew that they might be obliged to change their methods if unexpected snags were met with : they might have to act independently.

This, said the beachmaster at Tarawa, marked the superiority of the average American fighting man over the average Japanese. " It is not so much," Lieut.-Commander Grogan went on, " that the American is braver. This war has taught us that the whole human race is brave, almost incredibly brave. What makes the big difference in the Pacific is the fact that our troops have been instructed in every phase of a campaign and they know their parts. Therefore they are able to change their tactics individually to meet new circumstances. They can think things out for themselves."

As They Sped From Ship to Shore

The Japanese, on the other hand, while they understand the plan they are to carry through, often become bewildered if anything unexpected happens. However, on Tarawa the space was so restricted that movement and manoeuvre were scarcely possible. One man said it was like fighting on a billiards table without pockets. It was a fight to the death. One or other of the contending forces had to be wiped out, and at first it looked as if the Americans were destined to meet that fate. For their losses as they sped from ship to shore and when they seized footholds on the beaches were very heavy.

SCARCELY any of the leading waves of attackers reached shore. They were picked off as they sat in their barges or tried to wade to the beaches. By night, only a handful were on the island, huddled together in the shelter of a sea wall the Japanese had built. " Those alive were outnumbered ten to one by their dead comrades." It looked as if something had gone wrong, but the explanation was the skill and thoroughness of the Jap arrangements for keeping themselves safe while bombing from the air and shelling from the ships went on. Only by pouring men on to the island and pressing forward step by step when they reached there, could the enemy be shoved, yard by yard, back.

Not till the third day did the Marines reach the airfield, but by this time it was plain to the enemy that no escape from annihilation was possible. So they mustered for a suicide charge. " There was no hope of anything but death, yet the brown wave came on and on until the last man lay dead upon the coral sand." Only nine prisoners had been taken, out of the 4,000 men who held Tarawa : all the rest were exterminated. The American losses were 1,026 killed and 2,557 wounded. The figures sent a shock through the United States when they were published. But the success, though costly, was reckoned to be worth its price. It opened the way for " the series of positive and brilliant victories " that changed the face of the Pacific War.

JAPANESE H.Q. AT TARAWA, this steel-and-concrete structure was about the toughest position the U.S. Marines had to storm when they captured the collection of small Pacific islands in November 1943. During the fierce bombardment it withstood direct hits from the heavy American artillery firing from the beaches. *Photo, Keystone*

Now It Can Be Told!

CONCEALED COMPASSES FOR R.A.F. CREWS

EVERY R.A.F. man who had to bale out over enemy territory hung on to his compass to the very last—as a means of helping him to find his way across unknown country to safety. Special compasses for this purpose were issued to all air crews who might at any time find themselves in that predicament, it was recently revealed. Of necessity they had to be very tiny—smaller than a farthing—for the intention was that the compasses should be hidden on the person of the airman concerned.

Places of concealment were ingeniously chosen. A diminutive compass would be fixed to the back of a collar stud or trouser button, or hidden in the bottom of an automatic lighter, or beneath the dottle in a pipe. A photographic reconnaissance pilot who crashed in Germany and was taken prisoner owes his escape to a compass so tiny that he was able to conceal it inside his ear; there were many of this design and the lives it has saved have yet to be counted. For they were neither toys nor mascots.

SOME of the compasses were probably discovered by German intelligence officers when air crews were searched. But there was an equally ingenious standby, in the form of magnetized buttons. Sewn on battledress, to the casual eye they were indistinguishable from ordinary buttons. But the fact that they were magnetized enabled them to be used to indicate the way to freedom and home.

Removed from the battledress, the magnetized button would be mounted on another button which served as a pivot on which the first one could swing freely. In the darkness of night a luminous patch painted on the magnetized button would be clearly visible as the latter swung towards the north.

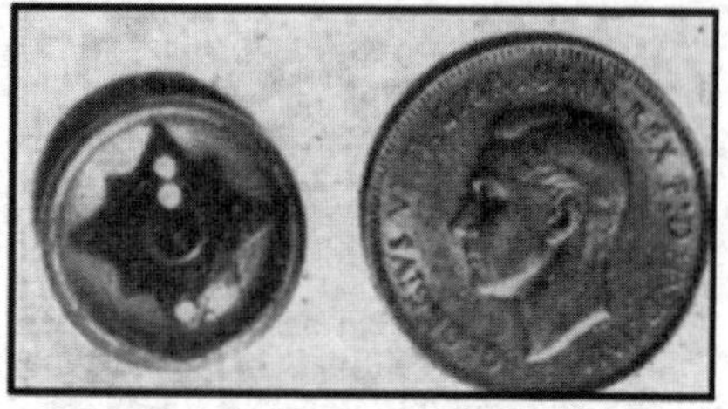

R.A.F. MAN'S COMPASS (left) concealed in a cigarette-lighter—one of the gadgets described in this page. Its size may be gauged by comparison with a farthing (enlarged). *Photo, News Chronicle*

LAST GREAT BATTLE OF THE SUBMARINE SHARK

THE full details of her epic last battle off the south-west coast of Norway in June 1940 has now been revealed by her Commanding Officer, Lieut.-Commander P. N. Buckley, R.N., back in Britain from a German prison camp. The struggle lasted more than six hours against overwhelming odds. Although it began at 10.30 p.m. the whole action took place in daylight, for in summer there is no darkness at that latitude. The Shark surfaced to recharge her batteries, and almost at once was sighted by a German seaplane, and though she dived immediately she could not escape attack. As she went down bombs began exploding close by. "Lights went out, both hydroplanes and steering failed, the starboard main motor was put out of action and a fire was started behind it. Water began coming in through a leak," said Lieut.-Cdr. Buckley. The after hydroplanes (which control the angle at which a submarine lies when dived), were jammed in the "hard-a-rise" position, and the boat rushed to the surface again.

"As soon as the bow appeared above the sea we heard a hail of machine-gun bullets on the hull, and bombs dropped around us. For a time we couldn't get her down at all, and then, when she started to dive once more, she went down rapidly, ending up 64 feet deeper aft than she was amidships. Then, for the second time, we rose to the surface. We came up at an incredible angle, and I knew that we would not be able to dive again. We discovered the rudder was jammed hard-a-port and all we could do was to go round in circles. The main aerial had been carried away, so we rigged a jury aerial and sent a signal asking for assistance, although we knew there was little chance of it reaching us in time."

FROM midnight bombing attacks were almost continuous. One bomb burst the submarine's starboard side, holed a main ballast tank and washed two men overboard. They were picked up again later in the action. The Germans used a Heinkel seaplane as a marker for their relays of bombers. It flew round the submarine, keeping up a steady fire with its cannon. "We used our 3-in. gun to keep the Heinkel at a reasonable distance, and our Lewis and rifles against aircraft which were making bombing attacks."

After three hours fighting against these tremendous odds—at 1.30 a.m.—the Shark was listing heavily to starboard. Water was rising in the engine-room. Inside, the submarine was full of smoke and fumes from the batteries.

Despite the choking atmosphere the engine-room staff kept the engines running, altering the revolutions as ordered to give some control over the boat. When it became necessary to remove all the ammunition from the magazine, the First Lieut., Lieut. D. H. B. Barrett, R.N., went down and did it personally, using a Davis escape apparatus as a gas mask, for in this part of the boat the fumes were particularly bad. But even though things were desperate the Shark's crew raised a cheer when one of her 3-in. shells exploded close under the stern of a Dornier, which made off towards the coast with sparks shooting from its tail. Then four Me.109s. appeared from the direction of Stavanger and raked the submarine's bridge and gun's crew with devastating machine-gun and cannon fire.

A Shambles of Wounded Men

"It was obvious to me that the end was now in sight," said Lieut.-Cmdr. Buckley, "although everyone stuck to his post in a magnificent manner until wounded or killed outright." After another 15 minutes of furious battle the submarine ran out of ammunition. "And having many wounded or dead—I couldn't tell which—I reluctantly decided to break off the action. I had been wounded in the head and leg and was feeling particularly shaky, so I have only a vague recollection of what happened from this time on. But I knew that the bridge was a shambles of wounded men, blood and empty cartridge cases, and that one of the seaplanes had landed close astern of us."

TWO Germans from the seaplane boarded the Shark, but as they pulled across in their dinghy, their seaplane sank; a float had been winged by the Shark's gunners. "The two Germans seemed very nervous and one kept his finger on the trigger of his pistol the whole time and they were quite content to remain on the bridge. That gave the First Lieutenant and other officers an opportunity to go below and destroy everything which might have been of interest to the enemy. Meanwhile, the wounded men were laid out on the gun platform and made as comfortable as possible." About 5 a.m. Lieut.-Cmdr. Buckley was taken off in a rubber boat and put aboard a second seaplane which had landed on the water close by.

Lieut. Barrett remained on board in command. He got the wounded and other members of the crew to safety on board trawlers, which arrived about 8.30 a.m. and then two of the trawlers began the attempt to tow the Shark away. But measures had already been taken by the submarine's crew to prevent this. No sooner had the trawlers started towing when the Shark sank. "She went down vertically, stern first," concluded Lieut.-Cmdr. Buckley, "and her last action was to damage the propeller of one of the trawlers, so that in the end it was one of the enemy's ships which was towed back to a German-held harbour and not the Shark." Casualties suffered by the Shark in this last gallant action were two killed, one died of wounds, ten wounded and eight slightly wounded.

H.M. SUBMARINE SHARK before she left on her last mission on which, in June 1940, she perished—as revealed by her Commanding Officer in this page. *Photo, British Official*

1940 SECRET WEAPON WAS A CATAPULT

IN the critical time following the fall of France, when every possible anti-invasion weapon was urgently needed, the L.M.S. Railway Company was concerned in the revival of one of the oldest engines of war, the catapult. The story is told in the L.M.S. house-journal Carry On. The Chief Mechanical Engineer was asked, at the shortest notice, to develop a type capable of throwing a two gallon can of petrol (fitted with a fuse to explode on contact) for as great a distance as possible. The minimum range was to be not less than one hundred yards. The job was carried out at the Derby Carriage and Wagon Works, all concerned making tremendous efforts.

On a Wednesday evening in July 1940 the first model was devised and made overnight. It used rubber bands for propelling the missile carriage and had a range of 25 yards. For the next model carriage springs were used, and it had a range of 50 yards. Unfortunately, though, it was very heavy.

When better elastic rubber bands were secured the range was increased to 70 yards, and finally, on the following Sunday morning, after continuous night and day work, a range of 100 yards was achieved with certainty. Ultimately this was increased to 130 yards. The accuracy was surprisingly good and the rate of fire was about one shot every two minutes.

In the final design the framework was lighter and the unit mounted on two pneumatic tires. As the weight was under half a ton it was suitable for towing or moving by hand. It had a handwheel for adjusting the elevation and two pitprop pullers for extending its eight elastic bands of 3¾ in. diameter, exerting a maximum tension of two tons.

Because the invasion never happened the catapult was never made on a production basis, but its development was of undoubted value as the potentialities of such weapons were then almost unknown and could not be determined without actual trials.

SCAPA FLOW secrets were disclosed in July 1945 with the release of photographs of the famous Naval base's wartime defence system against U-boats. The boom-defence tug Abbeville (right) towed an anti-torpedo "buffer" into position round the 23,000-ton aircraft carrier Victorious as she rode at anchor. Ratings repaired a damaged multiple-strand steel net-boom (below) effectively used against Nazi submarines.

The defences at Scapa Flow — impregnable during the First Great War—were rendered U-boat proof after the sinking of the battleship Royal Oak on October 14, 1939. (See pages 244 and 344, Vol. I).

Photos, British Official

DIVERS PREPARED WAY FOR THE D-DAY INVASION

ONE of the best-kept secrets of the war, the story of 200 men who prepared the way for the Allied invasion of the European continent was disclosed in August 1945 in a Reuter message. Six weeks before D-Day a surgeon-commander, one of Britain's leading physiologists, was sent for by the Admiralty. They told him that as well as laying mines along the French coast the Germans had constructed elaborate submarine obstacles.

"You have six weeks before D-Day," he was told. "Before then you must find out what the human body can stand in the way of submarine blast, devise a blast-proof diving suit, and train men. Mines must be cleared and obstacles blown up."

SMUGGLERS' COVES AS D-DAY BASES

OLD harbours and smugglers' coves on the south coast of England were among the United States Navy's great string of "invasion bases," the existence of which was one of the most closely guarded secrets of the War. This was disclosed in the announcement at the end of May 1945 that redeployment of U.S. Navy amphibious forces to the Pacific was in full swing and that eleven of the fifteen chief amphibious bases had been closed, or were being decommissioned. Ancient harbours and smugglers' coves in use since 1943 have been closed. From these ports 2,439 United States ships and landing craft sailed for the rendezvous off Portland Bill on the night of June 5, 1944, to join British forces for the greatest amphibious operation of all time.

The Commander began immediate experiments with volunteer "guinea-pigs," himself among them, and discovered the very important fact that an air bubble offered resistance to blast. Working day and night he devised a diving suit of sponge rubber and kapok capable of withstanding several hundred pounds pressure per square inch.

Meanwhile, concentrated training was going on of the 200 men specially selected from hundreds of volunteers for this most dangerous job. The strictest secrecy was of necessity observed.

It was necessary to carry out the vital demolition work as near to D-Day as possible. A few nights before D-Day a little fleet crept across the Channel in the darkness, stopping a few hundred yards from the Normandy coast. No sign came from the coast that the fleet had been observed, and 200 divers in their special suits, carrying apparatus for laying demolition charges slipped quietly into the sea.

Demolition machinery is usually operated from aboard ship, but for the destruction of the submarine obstacles it was essential that the divers should be very near the scene of the explosion to avoid the danger of long wires breaking. The men aboard ship waited anxiously for hours. Eventually there was a series of muffled explosions. The divers' work was done.

They clambered aboard the ships and started for home under a volley of machine-gun and rifle fire from the Germans, who, aroused at last, began firing wildly in the direction of the noise. But they were too late; the gateway to the Continent was opened, and owing to the efficiency of the diving suits not one diver was lost.

NAVAL COMMANDOS SANK SHIPS AT SINGAPORE

LED by a Scottish army officer, sixteen sailors of the Royal Australian Navy paddled canoes into Singapore harbour and sank six enemy merchant ships with limpet bombs. This daring raid deep into Japanese-dominated waters happened in September 1943, and has now been revealed by the Sydney Sunday Sun, quoted by Reuter.

Disguised as Malays, the party sailed from Fremantle, Western Australia, in a sailing vessel similar to those used by the Malays. Once a Japanese destroyer came alongside; but seeing what they believed to be only brown-skinned men dressed in sarongs, it sheered off again, blissfully ignorant of the prize it had so lightly scorned.

Hiding their little ship in the Rhio Archipelago, between Singapore and Sumatra, the raiding party embarked in canoes and paddled into Singapore under cover of darkness and of the local fishing fleet. Unobserved they drifted alongside the ships which were their targets, dived overboard, fixed their limpet bombs, with fuses attached, five feet below the water-line, and with all possible speed returned to a place of concealment ashore.

SOON violent explosions revealed that the bombs had done their work, giving rise to frantic alarm and excitement in the harbour and affording intense satisfaction to the seventeen stout-hearted adventurers. With the fall of night, they took their departure: with their hearts in their mouths, they paddled back to their hidden vessel, and sailed home to a Western Australian port after a voyage of 5,000 miles.

The officer who led the daring raid was formerly on the staff of Lieut.-General Gordon Bennett, who commanded the Australian forces in Malaya and escaped after the fall of Singapore in 1942.

In Cold Blood They Triumphed Over Nazi Mines

Lt.-Cmdr. B. H. W. FENWICK, G.M. and bar, R.N.V.R.

UNPUBLISHED until recently, two astonishing feats of the great blitz days in London are exemplified by the naval officer who saved from disaster a bridge near Charing Cross, and another who sawed a live mine in two and saved a factory. Farther afield, an Army officer effected an almost miraculous rescue from an unmapped German minefield. The stories in brief are told here.

Lt.-Cmdr. E. O. GIDDEN, G.C., O.B.E., G.M., R.N.V.R

AN unexploded parachute mine dropped on Hungerford railway bridge, Charing Cross, whilst trains and many sleepers were on fire, and the Charing Cross Hotel was burning in the background. Underground trains had to be stopped, and buildings, including the War Office, were evacuated. Lieut.-Commander (then Lieutenant) Gidden, O.B.E., G.M., R.N.V.R., found the mine shortly after dawn, lying across the live electric wire at the foot of the main signal gantry, with the bomb fuse and primer release mechanism facing downwards.

The current from the rail had melted some of the metal around the bomb fuse and primer release mechanism, to such an extent that if the fuse was to be removed at all it could only be done by drilling. But before any attempt could be made to arrest the operation of the fuse by the insertion of a "gag," a lump of molten metal had to be prised from the surface of the fuse itself.

First, the mine had to be turned to get at the fuse, and the turning was likely to detonate it, but Lieut.-Commander Gidden stood only 50 yards away while the necessary pull was being exerted from a distance. He had to stop firemen from playing water on the sleepers and trains while he got to work. But the burning wood kept giving off loud cracks, making it difficult to listen for the clockwork in the fuse.

AT last the surface of the fuse was cleared and a "gag" inserted, but melting had damaged the part in question and the gag would not fit securely. He then attempted, with hammer and chisel, to remove the remains of the ring which held the fuse in place. At the first blow the clockwork started to run. He had kept his head close to the fuse, and now made off as best he could; but as it was necessary to jump from sleeper to sleeper with a 10-ft. drop below there was little chance of escape. By sheer good luck the "gag" held. He returned with a drill and succeeded in removing the ring, but even then he found it necessary to prise the fuse out with a chisel. This exhibition of cold-blooded courage continued for six hours, until Lt.-Cdr. Gidden had rendered the mine harmless. For this he was awarded the George Cross.

Sawing a Land Mine in Two

When an unexploded mine fell on a Hackney furniture factory, Lieut-Commander B. H. W. Fenwick, R.N.V.R., twice winner of the George Medal, found that it had been badly damaged when it crashed through the concrete flooring and that it was impossible to reach the fuse without lifting and turning the mine over. This was done by means of special rigging equipment; it was then discovered that the interior mechanism of the mine had been forced forward in the casing, carrying the fuse with it. The top of the fuse had been shorn off, exposing the clockwork. To immobilize this he squeezed putty into the fuse through the narrow aperture. Then, with the help of two volunteers, A.B. Charles Halls and Driver Alwyn Ishmael Evans, of the Royal Army Service Corps, he proceeded to saw through the mine. He succeeded in removing the whole of the rear portion, then the main explosive charge from around the fuse and primer, and finally the fuse itself.

ON another occasion, during a raid on Liverpool, a parachute mine was known to have fallen on a high office building in the centre of the city, and its presence had caused the main telephone exchange to be evacuated. The building consisted of a number of small offices, storerooms and staircases which had been badly damaged during a raid on the previous night. Lt.-Cdr. Fenwick and his assistant, A.B. D. Mountford, after nearly half-an-hour's searching, located the mine on the third floor, in a room full of rubble and timber which had jammed the door shut. He had to use a long ladder to enter by a window. Inside he crawled under desks and through a mass of debris to the mine, which he succeeded in rendering safe. Had the clock in the fuse started to run there could have been no possible chance of escape

Maj. P. J. BARBARY, M.B.E., G.M.

Perilous Trail in the Dust

Trapped in the centre of a German minefield on April 26, 1945, lay a nun and two children, all seriously injured; a third child lay dead. To reach them, Major Peter John Barbary, M.B.E., of the Royal Artillery, had to make his way from the nearest road—across 150 yards of the mine-strewn ground. Bidding a party of stretcher-bearers remain on the road, the major, with a medical officer, succeeded in reaching the little group.

The equally perilous passage back to the road had now to be made. To mark a plain trail for the stretcher-bearers, Major Barbary dragged his feet heavily in the dust; if he reached the road alive they could safely go out by the same path and rescue the injured. This safely accomplished, it was then discovered that a young woman, a sister of the dead child, had run into the mined area and was wandering near the body. Major Barbary re-entered the minefield and brought her safely out. He was awarded the G.M.

ON THE MINE-INFESTED SCHELDT, two R.N.V.R. heroes whose land exploits are described in this page went searching for mines in a rubber dinghy; rowing, is Lt.-Cmdr. Fenwick; in the stern, Lt.-Cmdr. Gidden. (See also photographs at top of page.) The Royal Navy finally cleared the Scheldt by the end of November 1944, thus opening the all-essential port of Antwerp to Allied shipping.

Photos, G.P.U., Daily Mirror, Planet News, British Official

From Far-Eastern Bondage at Long Last Set Free

BRITISH AND U.S. PRISONERS FREED NEAR TOKYO, early in September 1945, cheered deliriously, waving the Union Jack and Old Glory—emblematic of the joy of Allied Servicemen and civilians to be liberated from over 150 Japanese camps in Asia and the Pacific Islands. Total number of Allied nationals in Jap hands, comprising British, Dominions, U.S., Netherlands and Indian, was on August 22 estimated by the War Office at 250,000. Of these, British Servicemen totalled 38,000, civilians 112,000.

Photo, Keystone

These Are the Husks of Hiroshima and Nagasaki

"TOO GHASTLY TO LOOK ON," declared the Japanese Premier, Prince Higashi Kuni, on September 4, 1945, describing Hiroshima (bottom) and Nagasaki (top) after their destruction by atomic bombs on August 6 and 9 respectively. Of Nagasaki's 250,000 people there were few survivors. All that remained in the blast area of Hiroshima were the gaunt shell of the Roman Catholic church (in foreground) and an unidentified building in the centre of the photograph. See story in facing page. *Photos, Sport & General, Associated Press*

I Was There! Eye Witness Stories of the War

I Visited the First City to be Atomic Bombed

Only the vultures live now in Hiroshima, writes B.U.P. correspondent James McGlincy. His is the first Allied eye-witness story from the actual ruins of "the most destroyed town in the whole of the second great world war." See also facing page and story in page 280.

THE sight that met our eyes as we entered Hiroshima was as if all the bombed towns in the world had had their devastated areas lifted out and all placed together here. There were a few Japanese picking through the ruins, and in their eyes was all the hate it was possible for a human being to muster.

Few people in Britain, even those in badly devastated areas, and no one in the United States, could have a clear idea of the vast destruction caused by one bomb unless they could see Hiroshima. The Japanese reports on the damage caused were not exaggerated. The suburbs are not too bad. They have blasted and burned-out buildings like lots of other bombed towns, but the centre of the city is a vastly different matter.

Gripped by Remembrance and Fear

I stood in what was the exact centre of Hiroshima before August 6, and looked around slowly in a circle. There was absolutely nothing for two miles in any direction. When I suddenly realized that all this complete destruction—complete is the word which best describes it—as well as the damage done to buildings miles away, had been caused by one bomb, I suddenly became very frightened.

I RODE through the city and back several times to make sure. Then I remembered that patch of ruin behind St. Paul's and behind Fleet Street in London, and offered a quick prayer of thanks that the Germans never found out how to work the atom. In this short time I had no way of checking the statements made to me by Japanese doctors still treating the wounded in Hiroshima. But this was their story:

On September 1 (the bomb was dropped on August 6) the number of dead had risen to 53,000, with another 30,000 people missing entirely. The doctors could not estimate the number of wounded. They told me that they were afraid everyone who was wounded in Hiroshima, no matter how slight the wound and even if it was only a cut, was doomed. They thought that the final total death roll would be at least 150,000.

They told me that those who were injured by the effects of the bomb found their hair falling out, their gums bleeding, their kidneys refusing to function, and, on examination of their blood, it was found they had only one-seventh of the normal number of white corpuscles. The injured grew weaker and weaker until they finally died. There were curious things—there were bridges over the river between the bombed areas that were still standing.

I saw some reinforced concrete buildings still upright. But on close inspection they proved to be of no more use than a child's set of building blocks. They were burned out, crumbling, and the steel girders in them twisted in a curious way. I believe that, from a technical point of view, they were beyond repair.

I had for a guide a young Japanese naval lieutenant who was born in California. His father still lives in California, but his mother brought him to Japan 11 years ago after he had spent 12 years of his life in the United States. I asked him: "Do the people here hate us, or do they regard all this as the fortune of war?" He replied simply and frankly: "They hate you."

General MacARTHUR wore anti-glare glasses on arrival in Tokyo with Gen. George C. Kenney (centre) and Gen. Carl Spaatz of the U.S.A.A.F. (left). *Photo, Associated Press*

How Defeat Came Home to the People of Japan

With the landing of the first waves of British and American Marines on the shores of Tokyo Bay, August 30, 1945, defeat was made absolute for Japan. News Chronicle correspondent Michael Moynihan sent this "diary of a war's end" from Yokosuka Naval Base. See also page 334.

THE diary starts aboard an assault craft half a mile from the shore. The time is 9 a.m., with the low, tree-clad hills round the bay hazy with heat. The massive pyramid of Fujiyama towers in mist. For the past hour we have been circling with other landing craft, waiting to go in. Thirty-six fully armed Marines are crowded in the body of the boat. The only shooting is being done by camera-men in a craft which has just flashed past towards the shore. Behind us the sea is congested with shipping—warships, transports, and more assault craft.

At the entrance to Yokosuka harbour lies the fire-scorched hulk of the Jap battleship Nagato, pounded by American carrier planes during the fleet's last operation off Japan. Her guns are still intact, but the hull is a mass of twisted metal. A formation of Fortresses carrying Gen. MacArthur's air-borne troops passes high overhead, a silver spearpoint aimed at Tokyo.

Carrier planes are weaving back and forth over the beaches. Now we have the signal

OCCUPATION OF THE JAPANESE MAINLAND began in earnest on September 4, 1945, when men of the 188th U.S. Parachute Infantry piled into lorries soon after arriving by transport plane at Atsugi airport, near Tokyo, en route for Yokohama. It was announced next day that by the end of the month 500,000 U.S. troops would be on Japanese soil; and enemy troops numbering 7,000,000 would be disarmed, demobilized and returned to their homes by mid-October. Gen. MacArthur abolished Jap Imperial Hqrs. on Sept 13. *Photo, Associated Press*

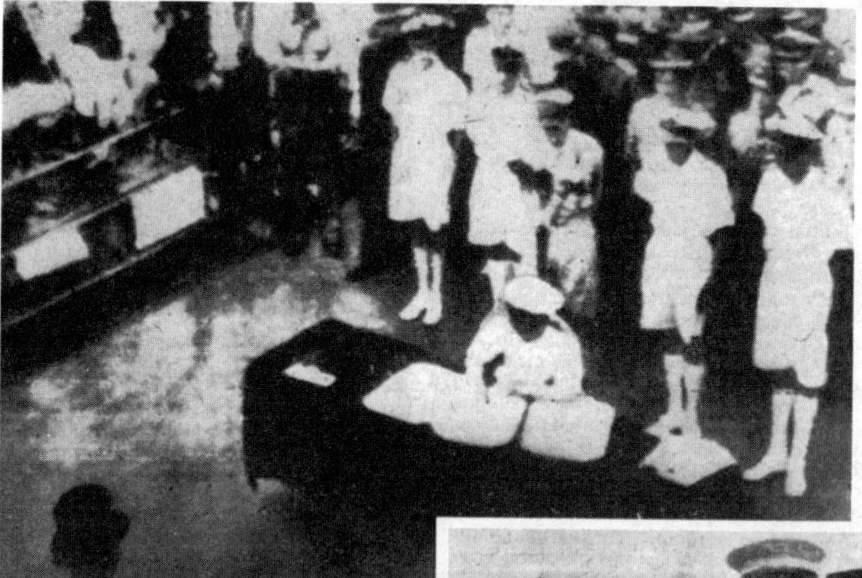

The Nagato was boarded at eight this morning by a prize crew from the American battleship South Dakota. The Japs had done a thorough job of stripping the shattered battle-wagon. There is little left but junk and a pile of mattresses, which might or might not have been for the purposes of hara-kiri. It is now 1 p.m. South of the naval air station we make our second landing at the naval base proper.

Signs of occupation are now numerous: the first bulldozers are at work. It was here that the Japanese Press were waiting to meet the Marines as they scrambled ashore. One Tokyo correspondent, in his eagerness to get in the first news of the occupation, had brought a basket of carrier pigeons. In the naval base H.Q., where I write, there is some confusion in a corner where two Jap reporters are alternately interviewing and being interviewed by American correspondents. They tell us that reports of mass suicides before the Imperial Palace have been greatly exaggerated: only a dozen or so chose hara-kiri.

ON BOARD THE U.S.S. MISSOURI IN TOKYO BAY on September 2, 1945, Admiral Sir Bruce Fraser (top) signed the surrender document on behalf of Britain, as Mamoru Shigemitsu, Japanese Foreign Minister (left foreground), looked on. Behind Gen. MacArthur (bottom) stood Lt.-Gen. J. Wainwright, U.S. defender of Corregidor, and (on Wainwright's left) Lt.-Gen. A. E. Percival, former British commander of Singapore. *Photos, Keystone, Associated Press*

to go in. The wake of the assault craft ahead of us leaps into a foam of spray.

Early this morning the first assault craft ground against the shores of Tokyo Bay. Hundreds of fully armed Marines poured across the beaches. Within three hours some 10,000 Allied troops were in full occupation of Yokosuka and the shores on the eastern side of the Straits. In defeat the Japanese have shown the reverse side of their incalculable nature. The nation whose name has become a byword for bestiality today humbled itself at the feet of its conquerors. During the negotiations of the past few days, when the processes of occupation were worked out to the last detail, Japanese co-operation has come near to farce.

On our transport ship last night instructions to the Marines dealt hardly at all with the possibilities of treachery. The danger was rather of unbending before the spectacle of a fantastic servility. There was the possibility that our troops might be met on the beaches by Japanese camera men recording the final eclipse of their homeland for the edification of the civilian populace. It was essential that the landings be kept strictly within the bounds of a military operation: for the Japanese seemed intent on furnishing it with the characteristics of comic opera.

Bataan and Corregidor Memories

Four hundred and fifty Royal Marines and Royal Navy personnel participated in the initial landings. They occupied four small islands at the entrance to Tokyo Bay between Yokosuka and Futtsu. The occupation of the naval base itself fell to the Fourth Regiment of the American Sixth Division. This was the regiment that fought and died almost to a man in the hell of Bataan and Corregidor. To the successors of the heroic dead fell the honour of leading the forces of occupation on to the mainland. In command of the landings was Brig.-Gen. William Clement who left Corregidor the day it fell.

Today he accepted the formal surrender of the Japanese admiral in command of the base. Japanese sentries at the entrances to sheds and warehouses were unarmed, their function being to allow no admittance to would-be saboteurs. Black-uniformed civilian police and khaki-clad gendarmes carried revolvers and swords to keep too curious civilians in check.

From the battered bridge of the Nagato, Tokyo Bay seems to be full of Allied shipping.

I Saw 11 Japs Hand Over Their Dead Empire

Aboard the U.S.S. Missouri, Admiral Halsey's flagship, on September 2, 1945, representatives of the Emperor of Japan, the Jap Government and People, formally signed the document of surrender to the Allies. Graham Stanford, Daily Mail correspondent, here describes the ceremony.

With a broad smile, Admiral Sir Bruce Fraser, C.-in-C. British Pacific Fleet, came aboard with other officers who have been fighting side by side with the Third Fleet. They all wore white shorts and short-sleeved tunics, in contrast with the dark Army uniform of the Russians.

In half an hour more than 100 high-ranking officers of the United States, United Kingdom, Russia, China, Australia, Canada, France, New Zealand, and the Netherlands were packed like sardines on a small veranda balcony. On the deck below the ship's band played martial music. Then—on the stroke of 8.30—the deck was cleared, leaving a bare stretch for the surrender table and a microphone. More than 100 officers and 350 war correspondents were gathered around this small "island of deck," and it was here that the 11 men from Japan would stand.

Only the whir of scores of cinema cameras broke the silence when General MacArthur came aboard and walked to Admiral Halsey's cabin. He was pale and unsmiling. A buzz of conversation died down as groups of officers stood erect. You were conscious that it was one of the world's most historic events. When he was ready General MacArthur sent a signal to a destroyer that the Japanese delegates should come alongside.

They did so, and in a strange, almost eerie silence climbed towards this little "island" on the deck of the battleship where there would be witnessed for all the world their humiliation and the funeral of all their military ambitions. His infirmity made it difficult for Mr. Shigemitsu, the Japanese Foreign Minister, to climb the ladder. He fumbled with a stick and finally reached the deck with the help of other delegates, and in his top hat and tails and yellow gloves, this old man came limping across towards the surrender table. He was halted, and he and General Umezo and nine delegates formed up and waited. Then, after five minutes, General MacArthur took up his place.

There was no expression of gloating in his eyes or in those of the Allied officers who were watching. Only his hands were trembling as he spoke. He turned from the microphone and faced the Japanese and slowly, deliberately he said : "I now invite the representatives of the Emperor of Japan and Japanese Government and Imperial General Headquarters to sign the Instrument of Surrender at the places indicated."

Across a few yards of deck the Japanese Foreign Minister limped, and, fumbling nervously, took off his top hat, put it down on the green baize, and felt for his pen. He appeared not to understand just where to sign, and was helped by a bowing younger delegate. Then General Umezo, who had been shifting nervously from foot to foot, stepped up to the table, signed, and withdrew.

A buzz ran through our ranks, and was immediately drowned as General MacArthur gripped the microphone and announced that he would sign on behalf of all the United Nations at war with Japan. He turned round, and half a smile came over his face as he said : "General Wainwright and General Percival, both of whom have just come out of prison camps, will come with me." The 11 Japanese remained standing, and it seemed that their nerves were fraying. One of them scowled darkly, and one diplomat twisted the rim of his top hat until I thought it would come apart.

Rushed Back to Their Ruined City

General MacArthur shook hands with General Wainwright and General Percival, and the tension which had gripped us all was eased. Now delegates representing all the Allied Powers stepped forward to put their names to the surrender document in this order : United States, China, United Kingdom, Russia, Australia, Canada, France, the Netherlands and New Zealand.

Admiral Fraser signed for Britain, and watching over his shoulder as boldly and quickly he wrote, stood Generals Wainwright and Percival, one American and one British, who had both fought the Japanese heroically at the beginning of the war, and had known the hardships of prison life. General MacArthur signed with two pens, and gave one each to Wainwright and Percival.

Foreign Minister Shigemitsu leaned heavily on his stick. When New Zealand had signed and the document was complete, General MacArthur stepped up to the microphone. His voice was quiet and solemn : "Let us pray," he said, "that peace be now restored to the world, and that God will preserve it always. These proceedings are closed." With General Wainwright and General Percival, he walked towards Admiral Halsey's cabin. He did not even cast a glance at the Japs.

The ceremony had taken 18 minutes. It was then that a great armada of planes roared over the ship. I watched the 11 men. They looked up at the sky, whispered among themselves, and then they were gone, the destroyer rushing them back to their ruined city. The war was over, and now all the world was at peace. But there was no cheering or laughing, and little talking, for every man felt the gravity of this occasion.

I Dropped-in on Goering and his Fellow Criminals

Eleven of the first 24 on the Allies' war criminals list were removed in August 1945 from Mondorf les Bains, Luxembourg, to Nuremberg, to await their trial before the Inter-Allied tribunal. Erika Mann, Evening Standard reporter, sent from Mondorf on August 13 this account of her meeting with some of the notorious eleven in their place of captivity.

My visit to the Big House was strange, for my family have been high on the traitors to the Third Reich list since 1933. The men looked at me in silence. I was told that I was the first woman to tour the Mondorf redoubt. Goering studied me curiously. He had converted our modest summer house at Niddeen on the Baltic Sea into a stately hunting lodge. I found the ex-Reich Marshal in bed. For some time now he has been having breakfast in bed.

Major Miller, the American physician, says Goering, creator of the blitz (German for lightning) recently had a heart attack after a mild thunderstorm. It was not serious. In fact, medical officers agree that he is in better physical shape than he has been for years. He was a morphine addict at 23, then, after being wounded in the Munich beer-hall putsch, he switched to paracodeine, relatively mild and taken by mouth, so it would not threaten his political future.

Suicide Attempts Frustrated

However, when captured he had a reserve stock of between 4,000 and 5,000 paracodeine pills, and said that his daily ration was 200, roughly equivalent to 33 grains of morphine a day. Dr. Miller, taking the air marshal's Luftwaffe figures into consideration, started him off on 40 a day. On August 8 he was down to six, August 9 to four, today none. Goering faces his trial a sober and healthy man, at least physically.

In the barber's shop were Rosenberg, Streicher, and Ley. Herr Frank, former Munich lawyer, credited with the murder of millions of Poles and Jews, and Von Ribbentrop are room-mates. This is a recent arrangement. Frank arrived at Mondorf a dying man, with four major wounds, all self-inflicted when about to be arrested. He had cut his throat, opened the veins in his left arm, sliced his left wrist and rammed a knife into his stomach. But Herr Frank still lives.

Herr Frank seems grateful—allergic to suicide. One of the hardest jobs at Mondorf is to keep some of the prisoners from attempting to commit suicide. Their window panes are Plexi glass. They have no belts, braces or neck-ties. Spoons are the only eating utensils, and eyeglasses must be deposited in the living-room where there is constant supervision. For the good influence Frank might have on Ribbentrop he was allowed to move in with him. When I visited yesterday the Butcher of Poland was reading the Bible to the ex-champagne salesman.

Down the hall was Von Kroesig Schwerin, Dönitz's Foreign Minister, who recently enchanted other inmates with a lecture on Shakespeare. The first 11 top Nazis to appear before the inter-Allied tribunal will find life even less comfortable in Nuremberg than it was up to now. The Palace Hotel at Mondorf les Bains was still a far cry from the city gaol at Nuremberg. The prisoners will now live in cells. There will be no reading room, no garden, and no terrace on which to take sun baths.

The prisoners will be guarded and commanded by the same men who ran the show in Luxembourg. Both Colonel Burton C. Andrus and Lieut.-Colonel Richard Owen, commander of the 391st American crack battalion which furnished the staff and guards, are masters of the language of stern indisputable authority.

"At first," I was told by Colonel Andrus, "these birds suffered from all kinds of hallucinations. One claimed to be a regent of something or other. Prisoner Horthy felt entitled to wear a necktie. I told him that he was nothing of the kind and that he had to obey as everyone else." By now they are all thoroughly obedient.

Our Diary of World Events

AUGUST 29, Wednesday
Germany.—First list of 24 major war criminals drawn up.
U.S.A.—Official reports into Pearl Harbour disaster made public.

AUGUST 30, Thursday
Japan.—Gen. MacArthur landed at Atsugi airfield.
China.—British naval force entered port of Hong Kong.

AUGUST 31, Friday
Japan.—U.S. troops completed occupation of Yokohama.
Germany.—Field-Marshals von Brauchitsch and Manstein arrested.

SEPTEMBER 1, Saturday
Italy.—Polish cemetery at Monte Cassino dedicated in ceremony attended by Field-Marshal Alexander.

SEPTEMBER 2, Sunday
Japan.—Allied Instrument of Unconditional Surrender signed on U.S. battleship Missouri in Tokyo Bay.
Russia.—Stalin, broadcasting on Japanese surrender, stated that Southern Sakhalin and the Kurile Islands would pass to Russia.
Far East.—Minesweeping of Malacca Strait begun by British naval units.
Netherlands.—First gap in Walcheren Island dyke sealed up.
Home Front.—Press censorship ended in Great Britain.

SEPTEMBER 3, Monday
China.—British landed at Hong Kong.
Malaya.—Royal Marines took over Penang.
Austria.—British military authorities lifted last restrictions on fraternization.
Belgium.—First anniversary of liberation of Brussels celebrated by Allied victory march.

SEPTEMBER 4, Tuesday
Pacific.—Wake Island surrendered by Japanese commander.
Spain.—Gen. Franco informed of decision of Allied conference on the re-establishment of international zone of Tangier.

SEPTEMBER 5, Wednesday
Malaya.—British and Indian troops landed at Singapore.
Germany.—Hugo Stinnes and 43 other Ruhr industrialists arrested by British authorities.

SEPTEMBER 6, Thursday
Pacific.—Surrender of Japanese in South-West Pacific area signed on H.M.S. Glory, off Rabaul.
Home Front.—Archbishop Damaskinos, Greek Regent, arrived in England.
General.—Gen. Eisenhower announced end of press censorship in Europe.

SEPTEMBER 7, Friday
Germany.—British, U.S., Russian and French troops in victory parade in Berlin.
Australia.—House of Representatives ratified United Nations Charter.

SEPTEMBER 8, Saturday
Japan.—Troops of 1st U.S. Cavalry Division entered Tokyo ; American flag raised in presence of Gen. MacArthur.
Solomon Islands.—Surrender of all Japanese on Bougainville and adjacent islands signed at Australian H.Q.

SEPTEMBER 9, Sunday
China.—Formal surrender of 1,000,000 Japanese signed in Nanking.
Korea.—Japs in Southern Korea surrendered to U.S. representatives.

SEPTEMBER 10, Monday
Japan.—Gen. MacArthur ordered dissolution of Japanese Imperial H.Q. and established press and radio censorship in Japan.
Malaya.—S.E.A.C. troops landed at Port Swettenham and Port Dickson.
Borneo.—Jap forces in North Borneo surrendered at Labuan.

SEPTEMBER 11, Tuesday
Japan.—Gen. Tojo, former Premier, made suicide attempt.
Indo-China.—Chinese entered Hanoi.
General.—Five-Power conference of Foreign Ministers opened in London.
Home Front.—Sir Arthur Tedder promoted Marshal of the Royal Air Force.

Flash-backs

1939

September 1. *War began with German invasion of Poland.*
September 3. *Britain and France declared war on Germany.*

1940

September 3. *British bases on Atlantic seaboard leased to U.S. in exchange for destroyers.*
September 7. *Opening of heavy air attacks on London.*

1943

September 3. *8th Army troops landed at Reggio, in toe of Italy.*
September 8. *Gen. Eisenhower announced surrender of Italy.*
September 9. *Allied force landed at Salerno, near Naples.*

1944

August 31. *British reached Amiens and crossed Somme.*
September 1. *Canadians in Dieppe.*
September 2. *5th Army took Pisa.*
September 3. *British entered Brussels and Tournai.*
September 8. *First V2 rocket fell in London, at Chiswick.*
September 11. *U.S. 1st Army crossed the German frontier.*

With Our Airmen Today

By CAPTAIN
NORMAN MACMILLAN
M.C., A.F.C.

Air Chief Marshal Sir Arthur Harris will relinquish command of Bomber Command in September 1945 and shortly afterwards retire from the R.A.F., the first of the great air commanders to leave the service at the end of the Second Great War. His name will be forever linked with the strategic bombing of Germany. His command was the hardest worked command in the R.A.F., and certainly the most perilous for operational crews. (Bomber Command won 16 of the 26 Air V.C.s of the Second Great War.) At one time its loss rate was so severe that the odds were against survival during one operational tour of about 25 to 30 raids.

All together, during the whole war, Bomber Command lost 9,163 aircraft, including those so badly damaged in combat that they had to be written off after landing in Allied territory. All but 1,534 were lost during the period from 1942 onwards, and it was just after the beginning of 1942 that Harris took command. But that is not the true picture. Before Harris took over, Bomber Command had dropped only some 50,000 tons of bombs and lost one aircraft for every 30 tons dropped. After he took over, the Command dropped about 940,000 tons, losing one aircraft for each 124 tons dropped.

FAMOUS R.A.F. SQUADRON No. 607 (COUNTY OF DURHAM) was disbanded in August 1945, when it carried out the last sortie over South-East Asia. Before the disbandment, Air Vice-Marshal C. A. Bouchier, commanding an R.A.F. group in Burma (left), visited fighter pilots who had fought in the Battle of Britain and been in the Far East since 1942. *Photo, British Official*

WHAT Dimmed the Glamour of the British Commanders in the Field?

It seems to me that there is a strange difference between the war leaders of the First Great War and those of the Second Great War. In the first conflict there were solitary outstanding names—Kitchener, Haig, Jellicoe, Beattie, Trenchard, with whose personality, rightly or wrongly, the public associated the winning of the war. In the Second Great War no admiral, general or air marshal appears to have attained to quite the same elevation in the public mind. (Perhaps the two who have come nearest to it are Field-Marshal Montgomery and Lord Louis Mountbatten.)

There must be a reason for this difference, for I do not believe that there were not just as colourful personalities in positions of command during the second war. There was, of course, the overriding personality of Mr. Winston Churchill, British "generalissimo" in the Second Great War, whose strategical direction of events was made manifest by modern communications enabling him to go far and wide about the world in a way that was impossible to Lloyd George, his counterpart in the first war.

But I do not believe it was simply the personality of Winston Churchill that dimmed the glamour of the British commanders in the field. The two real factors were, first, the sub-division of areas into semi-equal responsibilities. For example, Alexander counterbalanced Montgomery. In the west, Eisenhower overshadowed all the Allied commanders. In the Far East the movie-actor-like personality of MacArthur and the film-like efficiency of his great strides across the Pacific dwarfed everyone but Admirals Nimitz and Mountbatten. Yet in American eyes it must be as difficult as in British eyes to find one single hero.

Although in Russia Zhukov was the outstanding general, there were many others whose names rose to form a team. And above every national team there was the triumvirate of Roosevelt (Truman), Churchill (Attlee) and Stalin, photographed at frequent intervals in Teheran, Yalta, Potsdam, with two-personality meetings in Moscow, Casablanca, the Atlantic in warships, Ottawa, Washington. Their pictures stole the show from admirals, generals, and air marshals who stood behind them. From this emerges the thought that in total war the political strategic direction of nations transcends the military direction of navies, armies, and air forces, and that the First Great War was not quite total war while the Second Great War was.

The third factor making for the non-emergence of a great British national military figure, with the stature of Haig in the Army and Trenchard in the Air Force, is the different method of publicity used in the Second Great War. In previous conflicts the war was reported by civilian war correspondents, among whom, in the South African War, was Mr. Churchill himself. In the Second Great War a huge official publicity organization was built up. Indeed, the R.A.F. invented the idea of Public Relation Officers in uniform.

Other Ministries followed suit. As a result, in the Second Great War there were two founts of information: the official publicity department, and the professional civilian war correspondent, both, of course, subject to security and censorship restrictions. With the first organization inheriting the Services' hostility to personal publicity it was hardly possible to "build up" stories of commanders which would create in the public mind the atmosphere that surrounded the commanders of the First Great War, who were publicized by outside correspondents free to form their own judgements. No doubt the Services as organizations have been publicized as never before, with technical accuracy, but the system has not made for the endearment of commanders with the public.

HARRIS Made the 1,000-Bomber Raid Become a Real Possibility

"Bert" Harris—to give him the nickname by which his brother officer friends call him—has been built up as the ruthlessly efficient commander of a force of destruction, intent upon his object irrespective of the cost. One correspondent, commenting upon his approaching retirement, said he was known as "Butch" in the R.A.F.—short for butcher. This is not the picture of the Harris that I know. I first met him when we served in the same squadron in France in 1917, after he came out from England to command the flight I was in until he took over temporary command of the squadron.

I remember Harris saying, "You lead the formation, Mac. You have more recent experience over the line." And he was content as flight commander to follow the lead of one of his junior pilots. I have his countersignature in my pilot's logbook for the summer of 1917. One of my entries reads: "August 27, 1917, 11.40 a.m., 13,000 feet, Distant Offensive Patrol. Met some Albatross over Moorslede. Harris put one on the floor." We were flying Camels then. Harris was always cool whatever happened, his ready smile flashing across his healthy face.

In this war Harris fought for his Command and the boys who flew the bombers. He had to fight those who opposed the bombing strategy, and they were many. Under his command the 1,000-bomber raid became a possibility, instead of a dream, and Churchill, convinced of the power of the bomber, backed it, and the 4-engined bomber got man-power priority. Through his persistence new devices were developed to improve bombing accuracy, and new tactics were developed to reduce losses. When Stalin saw his Blue Book, he said, "Well, if that isn't a second front, it's the next thing to it." And Moscow propaganda about the need for an immediate second front dried up, while Mulberry Harbour was building for D-Day.

In his heart Harris mourned the loss of the gallant fellows whose lives were lost flying his bombers because Hitler and some other fools had plunged the world into war. But he knew he had to keep his thoughts to himself and guard his speech, for on his manner depended the morale of the whole Command. Some day little pig-tailed Jacqueline Harris will grow up and realize that her daddy was a great war leader. Perhaps the British public will grow up, too, and understand that Harris's policy saved countless lives in the Army and the Navy and among British civilians and that no one man contributed more to the reduction of Allied casualties in the Second Great War.

Winding-up the Defunct Luftwaffe's Affairs

COMPLETE DISARMING OF THE LUFTWAFFE is the task of thirteen Air Disarmament Wings of the British Air Forces of Occupation (formerly 2nd Tactical Air Force), which comprises some 90,000 R.A.F. pilots and crews. Once the scene of feverish activity, the airfield at Flensburg (1) is now populated with cattle grazing among surrendered JU 88s. Members of a detonation squad (2) fuse-up German bombs for destruction. At Grove, Denmark, enemy arms (3) were neatly "paraded." Up goes a dump of German bombs (4).

Photos, British Official

Editor's Postscript

THE Temple these early autumn days is filled with the encouraging, if distinctly unpleasing, sound of pneumatic drills—workmen removing temporary brickwork—such a noise as can rarely have been heard in this City oasis since the last years of the 17th century, except on those dreadful nights when the bombs came down. So far no major plan for rebuilding the Temple has been made public, though there have been many official and not-so-official deliberations on this subject which is the concern of every Londoner as well as of every visitor to London. Of the lovely 17th-century house of the Master there is not a brick left standing, or of Crown Office Row where Charles Lamb was born. Only half of Pump Court remains. The famous Temple Church—one of the very few "round" churches in England, and stiff with Crusaders' monuments—has suffered more than was at first apparent. The same may be said of the almost equally famous Middle Temple Hall where Twelfth Night had (as we say nowadays) its *première*. For the 19th-century Library, of which little remains, not many tears will be shed. In the task of rebuilding, restoration (call it what you will), the Benchers will have a supreme chance of giving a lead to the rest of the country. Whatever line they take—restoration or the creation of a new Temple—will be watched all over the country with the greatest of interest. Will "precedent"—as usual in Law—win the day? One holds one's breath and waits.

OUR old friend the Atom must by now be feeling rather like an elderly *prima donna* making a come-back. I say "come-back" though in all the recent accounts of the atom, rising out of the atomic bomb, I have seen no mention of the scientist who originally put forward the Atomic Theory. Credit is usually given to John Dalton, the English physicist, who flourished in the early years of last century. Yet the man who can justifiably claim to being the Father of the Atom was the Greek scientist Democritus, who was very much alive in the 5th century B.C. This point, I was interested to note, has been brought out by Professor Benjamin Farrington in his newly published Greek Science. What is frankly astonishing about this "wonderful anticipation of the conclusions of later experimental science" (to quote Farrington) is the fact that though inaugurated in the 5th century B.C. it was completely forgotten for well over 2,000 years. As Professor Farrington points out, "In the long series of researches that led to the enunciation by Dalton of his atomic theory in the first decade of the 19th century, the speculations of Democritus played no part." I wonder how many other instances History has to offer of a discovery of really first-rate importance being forgotten—and for so many hundreds of years?

FEW trades have worked under such difficulties in wartime as our laundries: they have received from us all—myself included—many more kicks than ha'pence. It was with considerable feelings of relief the other day, however, that I learned that the British Launderers' Research Association may soon collaborate with our textile manufacturers to work out a "code of washings," so that materials and garments can be marked according to the sort of laundry treatment that best suits them. Those who know the United States will remember that the scheme has been working there for the past eight or nine years, and from what American housewives tell me it has certainly proved a success. Under the American plan there are three types of markings—"dry clean only," "hand wash," or simply "washable," though my Scottish sense of humour suggests other, perhaps less mentionable, categories as well. The point is, and it is one with which everyone will agree, that if such a scheme were adopted over here it would put an end to many fruitless arguments between customers and laundries—besides solving the difficulty of how to treat the hundred-and-one new materials which the North Country is soon to put on the market. Hence the forthcoming link-up between the laundries and the textile manufacturers.

THREE soldiers, two on leave, the third invalided home, were talking about their experiences. One told of the miserable cold he had had to endure in Italy, icy winds sweeping down from the mountains and across barren plains. The next abused the damp climate of Holland, where water was seldom far below the surface and the air so chilly that, he declared, "it gives all the Dutch people red noses." The remaining soldier had been in Burma. His account of the tropical forests, the jungles and swamps, the malarial stagnant pools, the alternation of fierce sunshine and downpours of heavy rain, was more sensational than the conditions described by the other two, but they would not admit that it could be worse. On one thing they were all agreed: "Give them old England every time!" They had always groused about the English climate, but that was because they didn't know what other climates were like. Now that they had found out, they asked for nothing better than to stay at home in England for the rest of their lives.

THEIR whole desire was to return to the life they had led before they were caught up into the war. A lot of people seem to fancy that the men who come back will be dissatisfied with humdrum lives and will long for adventure. Those people are quite wrong. All who have opportunity to know what Servicemen are thinking say the same thing—they almost all want to pick up again the threads of life they were obliged to drop in 1939. They have had enough adventure. They long for a quiet life. That appears to be true of the great mass of men in the Forces. With the women it is different. From what I hear, they are not yearning to return to their old conditions. Most of them have had their first experience of life outside narrow limits and it has agreed with them. They don't want to go back to offices and shops and factories, doing the same thing day after day and week after week. They have tasted Adventure and they want more of it. That, at any rate, is the opinion of many observers who have the best chances of knowing what is in their minds. If there is any inclination to go to the Dominions, it will be shown by women rather than men.

Dr. T. V. SOONG, whose election as Prime Minister of China was announced from Chungking on May 31, 1945, while he was attending the San Francisco Conference. He is 54 years of age and a well-known Chinese banker and economist. *Photo, Karsh, Ottawa*

WHETHER the Red Flag is sung defiantly within the august walls of the temporary House of Commons or satirically, as I heard it recently, in the yard of the N.F.S. station adjoining this office, nothing can alter my opinion of it as the dreariest tune ever written—not even excepting Fight the Good Fight! George Bernard Shaw, likening it, in a much-quoted phrase, to the funeral march of a fried eel, added that it could only inspire people to crawl under their bedsteads. It was churned out in the House as a reply to the singing of For He's a Jolly Good Fellow. Heaven knows, the tune of the old French nursery ditty *Malbrouk s'en va-t-en guerre* is banal enough, almost as banal as the words we now customarily put to it; but at least it rises to a good shouting climax. Whereas The Red Flag can never rise above a disgruntled murmur. This is the more regrettable because when that sturdy Irish democrat Jim Connell first put together the words of the song in the train between Charing Cross and New Cross one night in 1889, the tune he had in his head was that of the Jacobite song, The White Cockade; and it was to that spirited march that The Red Flag was originally set. The present tune is of German origin. As *Der Tannenbaum* it used to be sung, with the heavy sentimentalizm that only Germans can achieve, by family parties as they clasped hands round the Christmas tree. In the 'sixties it was adopted for an American song, Maryland, My Maryland; and under that name it has also seen quite useful service as a hymn-tune.

OUR official weather-prophets have come in for some hard knocks from lay-folk since publication of their forecasts has been resumed in the daily Press. I must confess to joining in the chorus of criticism myself not a few times recently—until I met Alfred. This worthy is the middle-aged bar-tender at a well-known West End restaurant whose hobby (odd as it may sound) is Meteorology. Some thirty years ago Alfred began noticing (or so he imagined) that every time his "day off" came round, it rained. It is a reflection that must have occurred to many people, but Alfred was not content to put it down to coincidence, so he took to keeping what he proudly labels "My Meteorological Diary." Thoroughness being his motto, he also recorded weather conditions prevailing during the "days off" of his colleagues, and at the end of the year collated his entries. These revealed the astonishing fact that it had rained on less than five per cent of the "days off" aforesaid. Subsequent entries in his diary (which he still keeps) bore out his theory that it's not the good weather we remember but the bad. He advises readers of the weather forecasts to regard them as 24-hour blocks and not as covering merely the hours of daylight, and they will notice how much more accurate they seem. Try it—and see for yourself.

In Britain Now: Ministry Ends a 6-Year Task

PRESS CENSORSHIP in Britain ended at 9 a.m. on September 2, 1945, exactly six years after it began; censorship of press cables and telephone messages ended the same day. After the close-down this civilian (left) passed unchallenged into the Ministry of Information Censorship H.Q. in Malet Street, Bloomsbury, W.C.1; a few hours previously he would have been asked to produce a permit.

Highly skilled was the work of the women censors in the M.O.I.'s Photographic Division, two of whom are seen (below) handing in their rubber stamps and Defence Regulation books as the Censorship Division of the Ministry "broke up."

EX-R.A.F. MAN TURNED TOY-MAKER puts a final coat of paint on a skilfully-made model ship, all his own work. He is one of many ex-Servicemen profitably employed at the Bishopstoke Sanatorium, Eastleigh, Hants.

HOP-PICKING HOLIDAY for many Londoners began in the first week of September. A bumper crop was predicted in Kent, where almost 100,000 acres are planted with hops. A happy family party of pickers (above).

31-YEAR-OLD LINER AQUITANIA, (right) docked at her home port, Southampton, on Sept. 2, 1945, for the first time since 1939. That year she was about to be broken up, but instead was commissioned for war service.

Photos, Keystone, Associated Press, Daily Mirror

From Saigon to Rangoon the Jap Envoys Flew

JAPANESE SURRENDER DELEGATION ARRIVED AT RANGOON from Saigon two hours late on August 26, 1945. Alighting from their white-painted aircraft are Lt.-Gen. Takazo Numata, followed by Admiral Chudo. An R.A.F. officer stood by to escort them to H.Q., S.E.A.C., where Gen. Sir Montagu Stopford, G.O.C. the 12th Army, and Lt.-Gen. F. A. M. Browning, Mountbatten's Chief of Staff, received them. Agreement was signed next day at Government House, from which Ba Maw's puppet Government had declared war on Britain on August 1, 1943 *Photo, British Official*

Printed in England and published every alternate Friday by the Proprietors, THE AMALGAMATED PRESS, LTD., The Fleetway House, Farringdon Street, London, E.C.4. Registered for transmission by Canadian Magazine Post. Sole Agents for Australia and New Zealand: Messrs. Gordon & Gotch, Ltd. and for South Africa: Central News Agency, Ltd.—September 28, 1945. S.S. *Editorial Address:* JOHN CARPENTER HOUSE, WHITEFRIARS LONDON, E.C.4.

Vol 9 The War Illustrated No 217

SIXPENCE

and AFTERWARDS

OCTOBER 12, 1945

BRITISH "FROG-MAN" READY TO GO UNDER has his "fish" suit adjusted by a Petty Officer (right). Existence of these underwater Commandos, known as L.C.O.C.U. (Landing Craft Obstruction Clearance Units), was only recently disclosed. Special breathing apparatus enables them to remain under water for 1½ hours at a stretch, their "fins" giving them a speed of 60 yards a minute. On D-Day, they removed from the Normandy beaches mines and other obstructions. See also page 361. *Photo, Sport & General*

Edited by Sir John Hammerton

NO. 218 WILL BE PUBLISHED FRIDAY, OCTOBER 26

The Royal Marines Brought Freedom to Penang

BRITISH BATTLESHIP H.M.S. NELSON, flagship of Vice-Admiral H. T. C. Walker, was where the Japanese delegates headed by Rear-Admiral Uzoni (1), enemy Governor of the island, on September 1, 1945, signed documents surrendering Penang, Malaya (evacuated by our forces on December 19, 1941). Vice-Admiral Walker is on the extreme left, facing the enemy signatory. Royal Marines of the British East Indies Fleet took over the island two days later when Japanese soldiers were obliged to hold back the crowds (2) cheering the arrival of their liberators. The impressive ceremony on the quayside (3) as the Union Jack again flew over Penang.

Photos, British Official

With Our Soldiers Today

By MAJ.-GENERAL SIR CHARLES GWYNN K.C.B., D.S.O.

I HAVE always held that there is something in British mentality that makes us liable to be taken by surprise in the event of an unexpected degree of success in our undertakings. We generally make better provision for the failure or partial failure of our plans. This is a weakness I repeatedly noticed in our military planning in the last war, and I believe it has not been absent in this war. The Anzio landing was perhaps an instance.

The weakness, I believe, is largely due to the tendency there undoubtedly is to jeer at what is thought to be excessive optimism and wishful thinking, but surely it is almost as grave a fault to be caught unprepared to exploit success promptly as to be unprepared to deal with the situation arising from a disappointing reverse. How much can be gained in military operations by promptly seizing an opportunity is obvious. General Dempsey's drive which resulted in the capture of Antwerp was a case in point, and General Patton also gave us a number of notable examples. The extent of the gains must largely depend on the resources available for immediate use and that, though it may be fortuitous, is more likely to result from the possibility of the opportunity arising having been envisaged. Nevertheless, if we are to judge whether opportunities have been lost or have not been fully exploited, we should first be clear as to how far the opportunity actually existed and as to what possibilities it opened.

ELEMENT of Fairness was Essential Feature of Demobilization Plans

Now that military operations have ended the burning question of the hour is whether the Government might have envisaged the possibility of the completeness and rapidity of the German and Japanese collapse, and have been better prepared to take advantage of the apparent opportunity that opened of accelerating demobilization. That plans had been carefully made for demobilization and on a fair system is agreed, and it is admitted that it was impossible to foresee with certainty when Germany would finally collapse or the degree of sporadic resistance that might be encountered thereafter. Still less could it be anticipated that the Japanese collapse would follow so soon after.

In all these respects undoubtedly the Government was to a greater or lesser extent surprised by an unexpected measure of success. But the real question is whether, if the possibility of unexpected developments had been envisaged, better arrangements could have been made for modifying plans to meet the actual circumstances. In justice to the Governments past and present we have in fact to consider how far the opportunity to exploit the situation actually exists unless we are prepared to sacrifice the element of fairness which was an essential and widely applauded feature in the original plans.

THERE are undoubtedly men and women who could be demobilized or released without detriment to military requirements, but not without damaging the prospects of those still unavoidably retained. But we still do not know what numbers will be required for the armies of occupation in Europe or to restore normal conditions in our recovered Far Eastern possessions. It would seem highly desirable that information on that point should be given as early as possible, and as to the steps the Government proposes to take to maintain numbers at the required strength. But until it is seen how the Germans will behave under winter conditions, and until all Japanese troops in our zone of responsibility are rounded-up, it may be premature to give even approximate estimates.

Meanwhile, it should be realized how extensively the whole situation as regards demobilization has been complicated by the collapse of Japan so soon after that of Germany. It has not only greatly increased the number of our own people available for release in widely separated theatres of war, but has also meant the simultaneous demobilization of American forces on a scale that affects our plans and outlook.

IF the war with Japan had continued for a year or more after the end of war in Europe, as was expected and certainly had to be assumed, the rapid collapse of Germany would not have materially affected demobilization problems, although the absence of anticipated sporadic resistance might have called for some acceleration. But the numbers becoming available for demobilization and release would still have been limited; for reinforcement of the eastern theatre would have been required and war industries, although on a reduced scale, would have continued to operate. Moreover, American demobilization could not have begun on the scale and with the speed which undoubtedly is now inviting criticism of our own procedure. Presumably our partial demobilization would have gone according to plan, while for the invasion of Japan large American forces would have been transferred from the western to the eastern theatre. The process had actually commenced before Japan surrendered unconditionally, but when that occurred American commitments in the East were reduced to a much greater extent proportionately than our own.

The army of occupation in Japan will bear little relation to the forces that would have been needed for invasion and possibly for co-operation with Chinese and Russian armies; and since little American territory is affected no large force will be required to restore law and order. Conditions are very different for us, for although we could not have employed in our zone armies comparable in size to those the U.S.A. would have needed for the invasion of Japan, we are now confronted with the task of restoring peacetime conditions in large areas. That naturally must greatly affect the rate of demobilization. In addition to these conditions which govern the size of the forces it is necessary to keep under arms in the Far East after Japan's surrender, there is also the question of the size of the armies of occupation in Europe.

BRITAIN'S Post-War Commitments Much Greater Than America's

In the final stages of the war in the West America had deployed much larger numbers than we could produce, but for the armies of occupation our commitments are the heavier. The result has been that great numbers of American troops can be released, and it would obviously be a mistake to retain those surplus to requirements in Europe since their maintenance and the granting of leave would cause unnecessary expense and make heavy demands on shipping. The large numbers that are being shipped to America can, of course, now be demobilized, though it remains to be seen if they can be absorbed into industry as smoothly as it is hoped. Clearly, however, the problem of absorbing demobilized personnel should be simpler in America than in this country, for normal life there was less disturbed by the war. Nor does shortage of shipping bear so heavily on her demobilization processes, for she had been given priority for the removal of her surplus troops in Europe and to maintain the communications of her great Pacific armada.

IT will be seen, I think, from all this that our post-war commitments in Europe and in the Far East are proportionately much greater than those of America, and that quite apart from the desirability of adhering to a fair plan for release we have more difficulty in deciding at once what numbers we must retain to meet military requirements.

On the whole, though we may envy the speed with which American demobilization is progressing, it is fruitless and unsettling to draw comparisons since the conditions affecting the two nations are so vastly different. It is better to be content to envisage our own problems correctly. To do that it would certainly be helpful to receive fuller information from the Government. Mere statements that every effort is being made to speed up demobilization do little to relieve the natural impatience for release, especially when there are also announcements of unexplained delays in the release of certain groups. Still, it is clearly the duty of all concerned to exercise patience and to take comfort from the fact that release will come sooner than at one time could have been expected, and that a fair if perhaps over-rigid system is in operation.

"AFTERWARDS"

SO many of our readers have been coming forward with suggestions as to what we should do with "The War Illustrated," "now that the War is over," that I feel I ought to state our plans for it. The present issue bears the addition of the words "and Afterwards" on its front cover. Now "Afterwards" might mean a very long time, and lest our readers should be alarmed at the prospect of our emulating Tennyson's brook by going on for ever, let me reassure them forthwith. The fighting may be over, but "The War Illustrated" has not been a mere record of battles by land, sea and air: it has brought into its pages a vast amount of interesting and instructive matter, literary and pictorial, concerning things that happened before actual hostilities began, as well as being a comprehensive chronicle of all events in these great years of world-history.

★

YET so enormous is the unpublished pictorial material now available, and daily forthcoming, so important are the matters directly arising out of the War that our task cannot be regarded as completed until we have adequately dealt not only with the Aftermath of the War but with the elucidating of numerous censored episodes and "War secrets," and presented in more detail the achievements of our great soldiers, sailors and airmen who have given us the victory. The records of our regiments, the unrecorded exploits of our famous and unknown ships of war, the peerless prowess of the men who won for us the mastery of the air—all these call aloud for amplification.

★

AND the vast complexities of international resettlement must engage our attention until such time as we can say "Now the War is ended and the New Era begins." That is all that is implied by "Afterwards"—it is meant to indicate that we have still much that is of interest, and historically important, to give our readers in order to make the volumes of "The War Illustrated" a unique collection of the actualities of the War and the opening days of the Peace.

THE EDITOR

Hongkong Passes From the Clutches of Japan

CRUISER H.M.S. SWIFTSURE, flying the flag of Rear-Admiral C. H. J. Harcourt, C.B., C.B.E. (portrait in page 326), led the British naval task force into Victoria Harbour, Hongkong (1), on August 30, 1945, to arrange the Japanese surrender (signed on Sept. 15) of the famous Crown Colony, which they had captured on Christmas Day 1941. Guarded by Royal Marine Commandos, the enemy envoy passed along the flight deck of the carrier Indomitable (2), from which came this landing party (3). See also page 365.

Photos, British Official, Associated Press

Malayans Cheer the Flag in Liberated Singapore

AFTER THREE-AND-A-HALF YEARS of Japanese occupation Singapore was freed on September 5, 1945, when the 5th Indian Division took over without incident and crowds in fantastic ritual dress paraded the streets (1). Rescued from a P.O.W. camp was Lieut.-Gen. A. E. Percival, commander of the city when it fell in February 1942, and seen (2) in England showing his wife a pen used at the Tokyo surrender (see page 346). Malayans cheered the Union Jack (3), and greeted Gurkhas (4) driving through the streets to disarm the Japanese. *Photos, British Official, Planet News*

With Our Sailors Today

By

FRANCIS E. McMURTRIE

The United States Navy has lost no time in announcing its plans for the post-war strength of the fleet. It is proposed that it should include 18 battleships, three battle cruisers, 27 fleet aircraft carriers, 10 light fleet aircraft carriers, 79 escort carriers, 31 heavy cruisers, 48 light cruisers, 367 destroyers, 296 destroyer-escorts and 200 submarines, together with a sufficient number of minelayers, minesweepers, patrol vessels, fleet auxiliaries, landing craft, district craft, aircraft and dry docks to support the fighting ships enumerated above.

Most of the ships retained will either be comparatively new or will have undergone complete modernization. This means that older vessels, more or less worn out, will either go to the scrap-heap or be relegated to harbour duty as non-combatant units. Apparently the ships that will be discarded are to include the old battleships Arkansas, New York, Texas, Nevada, Pennsylvania and one of the New Mexico class. Presumably the 27 fleet carriers to be kept are the 24 of the Essex class and the three 42,000-ton Midways ; though it is possible that one or two of the former type may have been so extensively damaged by Japanese suicide plane attacks that they may not be considered worth the expense of refitting. However, on the assumption that all the Essex group remain in service, those scrapped will be the Enterprise, Ranger and Saratoga. Escort carriers to be retained include all those now in service with one exception ; this may be either the Long Island, or one of those damaged by suicide plane attack.

American Surplus Tonnage May Go to Allied Navies

How many cruisers are to be dispensed with is not quite so clear, but probably the Pensacola and Salt Lake City will both go, together with the nine old light cruisers of the Omaha class. No doubt cancellation of contracts for the construction of ten heavy and ten light cruisers will account for the balance.

Quite a respectable fleet could be made up from the vessels that are to be disposed of, and it is possible that some of them may not be broken up, but will be handed over to Allied navies. It has already been reported that China is to receive some surplus U.S. tonnage, together with certain British ships that are past their prime.

Another force endeavouring to fix the future strength of its material is the Royal Canadian Navy. Two new aircraft carriers of the light fleet type, the Magnificent and Warrior, are expected to be commissioned soon under the Canadian flag. Two 8,000-ton cruisers, the Ontario and Uganda, have already been transferred to the R.C.N., and eight new destroyers, the Crescent, Crusader, Crozier, Crystal, Craccher, Creole, Cretan and Crown have been earmarked for the same service. These will be the newest ships in the post-war R.C.N.

There are besides the "Tribal" type destroyers Haida, Huron, Iroquois, Micmac, Nootka, Cayuga and Athabaskan, the last four built in Canada ; and two of the British "V" type, the Algonquin and Sioux, together constituting a fine modern flotilla. Nine older destroyers, built before the war, may be discarded, as they must be nearly worn out after hard service in the Battle of the Atlantic.

This also applies to the majority of the 112 corvettes in the Canadian fleet, to many of the fleet minesweepers, and possibly to some of the 60 frigates. The latest minesweepers of the Algerine type will presumably be retained.

One of the chief problems is that of manning. In 1939 the strength of Canadian naval personnel, with reserves, was under 5,000 ; by VJ Day it was 90,000, an unexampled expansion. Since nearly all were entered for hostilities only, demobilization will reduce the total to a very low figure indeed, unless a substantial proportion can be induced to remain for a further period of service. It is hoped that a strength of from 10,000 to 15,000 can be maintained as a permanent force, sufficient to man most of the ships mentioned as likely to be retained.

In the meantime ten corvettes of the "Flower" type with three frigates of the "Loch" type and six of the "River" type have been returned to the Royal Navy, from which they were lent during the Battle of the Atlantic.

A certain amount of information has been released lately concerning new British warships. Three large fleet aircraft carriers, reported to be equal in size to the United States carriers of the Midway class, are under construction, their names being Gibraltar, Malta and New Zealand. Three others of an improved Indefatigable design, believed to displace over 30,000 tons, are to be named Ark Royal, Audacious and Eagle. Names of the first and last of these commemorate the services of two carriers sunk in the Mediterranean in 1941 and 1942, respectively.

All these ships are much larger than the light fleet carriers whose presence in the Pacific has recently been revealed. The latter are vessels of less speed and of displacements ranging from 14,000 to 17,000 tons. Names include Colossus, Glory, Ocean, Venerable and Vengeance, of the smaller size, and Albion, Bulwark, Centaur, Hercules, Leviathan, Magnificent, Majestic, Powerful, Terrible, Theseus, Triumph and Warrior, of the enlarged design. Two of these, as already mentioned, have been earmarked for the Royal Canadian Navy, provided the manning difficulty can be overcome. Four more were to have been built, but it is doubtful if they will be begun, now that the war is at an end. In fact, a certain amount of new construction is almost certain to be cancelled, just as it was in 1919.

Navy Devised Escape Apparatus for Army's Amphibious Tanks

In the success of the Army's "DD" (amphibious) tanks on D-Day the Royal Navy had a share. As these peculiar craft were very vulnerable to the lightest shell or even bullets, some method was sought of saving the crews should they sink. On the Navy being consulted, the Superintendent of Diving, Commander W. O. Shelford, R.N., devised a light and simple type of escape apparatus, with an inflated bag and an absorbent canister for disposing of foul air instead of the oxygen cylinder used in the more elaborate Davis gear. This was tried out and perfected in the Diving School at Portsmouth, and during the Normandy landings was the means of saving 95 per cent of the personnel of tanks that foundered. Thus, as in so many other successful operations in this war, the advantage of two Services working in close conjunction was demonstrated.

Another sphere in which the Navy is aiding the Army is in the return to this country of demobilized soldiers. A number of escort aircraft carriers have been equipped as transports, with troop accommodation in the hangar spaces, and will be of material assistance in bringing home men from our Armies in the East. One of these ships, H.M.S. Ranee, was recently fitted out for this purpose by Palmers Hebburn Co., Ltd., on the Tyne.

Altogether there are more than 30 escort carriers in the Royal Navy, but some of them, it is believed, may be returned to the United States, as they were built in that country and transferred to Britain under the Lend-Lease scheme.

Fleet aircraft carriers, which are much faster and roomier than the escort type, have been employed in carrying released prisoners of war from the Far East. Thus carriers are proving themselves to be remarkably versatile vessels, doing the work of transports and to some extent that of hospital ships.

"OPS" ROOM, H.Q. WESTERN APPROACHES, where the Battle of the Atlantic was planned throughout the war—at Derby House, Liverpool. The main plot is seen nearest the camera; the disks indicated restricted bombing areas for aircraft of approximately 150 miles radius, where submarines of the Allied navies were under passage. *Photo, British Official*

Piloted Torpedoes the Germans Failed to Use

SEIZED ON A DANISH ISLE were these piloted torpedoes (1) after members of the Danish Freedom Movement had discovered there (Sjaelland Island) a German trial station for secret naval weapons. In one type the pilot occupies a small enclosed "cabin" in the upper of two cylindrical hulls, the lower cylinder being the actual torpedo (4). Driven by electricity, these craft carry one or two torpedoes; the two-torpedo type has a periscope. The pilot's "cabin" (2) is fitted with instruments recording speed and depth when submerged, and controls for releasing the torpedo. Two Danish patriots examine the two-torpedo type, the "Marlen" (3); note the painted device—a Chamberlain umbrella pierced by a torpedo. These weapons were first used by the enemy in the Italian campaign in 1943, and later against our landing-forces on and after D-Day 1944. British "human torpedoes" sank the Italian cruiser Ulpio Traiano in Palermo harbour in January 1943 (see page 775, Vol. 7).

Photos, Black Star

Miracle of Mined Ship Made Seaworthy Again

THE 7,000-TON LIBERTY SHIP HORACE BINNEY, mined off Flushing on V Day, almost broken in two and with a huge hole amidships, was given up as lost—except by Capt. R. Brooks, O.B.E., Port of London Authority's Chief Salvage Officer. Thanks to his ingenuity she was beached off Deal, and supported by steel hawsers whilst P.L.A. wreck-lighters salvaged her cargo (1). After she was towed to the King George V Dock, London (2), men cleared her holds (3), and welders, watched by Capt. Brooks (4), patched her side (5).

Photos, British Official

These are Our 'Frogs' Who Won D-Day Fame

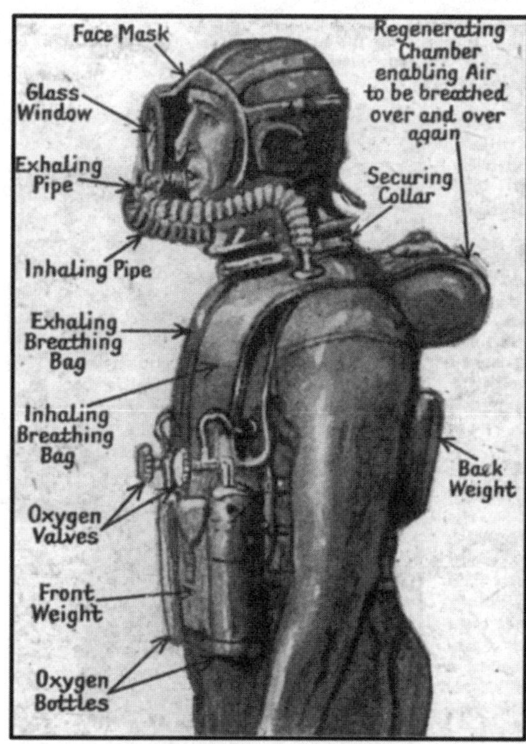

LANDING CRAFT OBSTACLE CLEARANCE UNITS—Frog-Men, for short—who blasted a hole in the Nazis' "Atlantic Wall," enabling our invasion craft to reach the Normandy beaches on D-Day, were mainly hostilities-only personnel: bank clerks, students, carpenters and engineers. Attired in their thin rubber diving suits, fitted with helmets and breathing apparatus (diagram above), and with huge rubber fins attached to their feet, they trained intensively for over five months.

Their moment came at H hour on D-Day when ten units (four Royal Navy and six Royal Marines), consisting of some 120 officers and men, went into action. Working in face of enemy shell and mortar-fire, and sniped at, in two days they cleared over 2,400 obstacles—mines, tank traps, steel barricades. Photographs taken during training in the Kingston (Surrey) Swimming Baths show a Frog Man swimming under water (1); "enemy sighted"—the men pile into the water from their dinghy (2), while one tows the boat from beneath the surface (3); rehearsing for underwater sabotage (4). See also page 353. Germany's Frog Men were illustrated on p. 551, Vol. 8.

Photos, British Official, Fox, Sport & General. Diagram by courtesy of The Illustrated London News

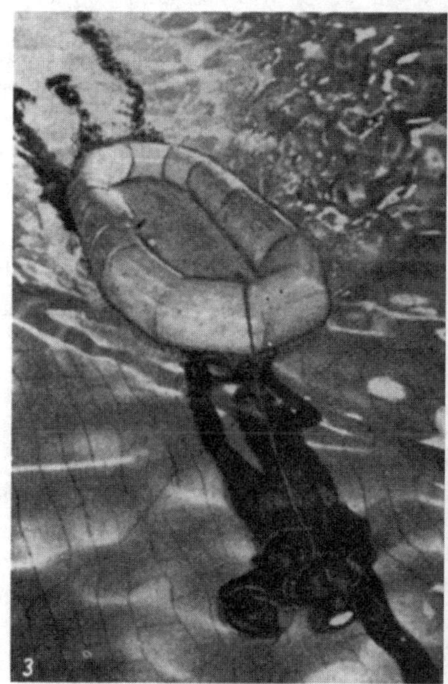

How Radar Enabled Us to Win the War at Sea

Providing the sailor with a sixth sense, radar has completely transformed the face of naval warfare. Our Naval Correspondent, FRANCIS E. McMURTRIE, explains how it works for the mariner, and reveals the giant strides that radar has made since the first practical sea experiments nearly twenty-five years ago. See also pages 298-299, 320.

In the technical sense, the most important factor in winning the war at sea for the Allies has been radar. This word, which is of American naval origin, is the equivalent of the older term radiolocation. Radar has recently been cited by President Truman as one of the three principal benefits received by the United States from this country under Reverse Lease-Lend. Practical sea experiments in radar began nearly 25 years ago, and it was in use in the Royal Navy before the War began, though in an elementary form. Echo-sounding was one of the first uses to which radar was put, it being found that sounding by this means was simpler, quicker and more reliable than by the older methods.

Since those first steps were taken radar has made giant strides. It is no exaggeration to say that it has completely transformed the face of naval warfare. Improvement after improvement has been devised by the Admiralty scientists and technical officers engaged on its study in collaboration with Army and Air Force experts. Much of the experimental work has been carried out at the Telecommunications Research Establishment at Malvern, under conditions of the utmost secrecy.

To understand how radar works, it should be appreciated that short radio waves behave similarly to light, travelling at the same speed. They can be focused in a beam in just the same way, and can be reflected by either solid or liquid surfaces. Where radar has the advantage over light is in its ability to penetrate fog, clouds or smoke, and to cover far greater distances than the human eye, which depends on light for its operation. Moreover, radio impulses are much more easily controlled than beams of light.

Radar has thus gone far to provide the sailor with a sixth sense, enabling him to "see" in the dark as well as in daylight. In simple terms, radar projects a wireless beam which, on coming in contact with an object, returns an echo which is reproduced visually on the screen. In range-finding, to take only one example, this amounts to nothing less than a revolution.

AERIAL of the Navy's metre band long range warning set used for radar transmitting and receiving. The development of this all-British invention is explained here. *Photo, Fox*

It is a curious thing that the Germans, for all their boasted scientific ability, should have failed to make any corresponding progress in this field of research. Throughout the War they seem to have been content to lag behind in radar development; and when hostilities ceased the Germans were still far short of the stage which had been reached by the Royal Navy.

Italians Surprised in Darkness

One of the first notable cases in which radar proved of inestimable service to the Allied cause was the Battle of Cape Matapan, March 28, 1941. Though the type of radar in use in the Mediterranean Fleet at that date would be regarded as crude and elementary in comparison with the highly efficient sets now in service, it enabled Sir Andrew Cunningham to locate the Italian fleet and open a deadly fire upon it out of the darkness. Three big enemy cruisers and three destroyers were sunk without being able to retaliate.

In subsequent attacks by our light forces on enemy convoys proceeding at night from Italy to Libya, equally surprising results were obtained with the help of radar. Had radar been installed in the Grand Fleet at Jutland, in 1916, the Germans would never have succeeded in extricating themselves from the battle under cover of mist and darkness, and the partial night action which ensued would have gone very differently.

By means of radar, station keeping at night or in fog is rendered comparatively simple; this has been a great boon to convoys proceeding to North Russia. It was the prime cause of the destruction of the German battleship Scharnhorst when she attacked a convoy off the North Cape in December 1943. Every time she tried to break off the action with the escorting cruisers and destroyers, her movements were followed by radar, and touch was maintained until H.M.S. Duke of York arrived on the scene. With the British battleship's gunfire accurately directed by the same means, a disabling hit was soon secured, after which the end was inevitable.

U-Boats Forced to Fight It Out

Though the fact was not disclosed at the time, radar had an important share in locating the Bismarck and bringing her to action with H.M.S. King George V and Rodney in May 1941. In the Battle of the Atlantic radar also played a prominent part. It enabled enemy submarines on the surface to be detected in time for convoys to take avoiding action, while the escort vessels closed in on them with unerring direction. Thus U-boats were forced either to dive and be exposed to depth-charge attack, or fight it out on the surface. In either contingency the convoy was able to proceed unharmed. During the Allied landings in North Africa, ships of the United States Navy fitted with radar engaged the French battleship Jean Bart at Casablanca at a range of over 20 miles. Thus she was disabled without a chance to hit back; and other French warships which offered opposition were equally unlucky.

In this way radar has proved a more efficient substitute for the human eye in gunnery fire control. It has been particularly valuable for anti-aircraft purposes. So highly developed is the type of radar now installed in H.M. ships that it is possible to locate almost anything on the surface of the sea, from a seagull to an iceberg. Though the exact shape of an object is not shown on the screen, its size can be determined. In navigation, the value of this hardly needs stressing, for shoals, buoys and other ships can be avoided with little difficulty.

PORTABLE-TYPE RADAR for navigational purposes weighs only 30 lb. It is carried by Lt. R. B. Mitchell, R.N., who used it on D-Day while leading assault landing-craft. *Photo, New York Times Photos*

Some go so far as to predict early abolition of that time-honoured friend of the mariner, the sextant. Navigating specialists are inclined to dissent, maintaining that the sextant will always be needed, if only for use in emergency. Certainly castaways in an open boat would require one to find their position in the absence of a portable radar set. Already sets small enough to be included in the equipment of aircraft are in fairly general use, and an illustration in this page shows a 30-lb. set; so it should be merely a question of time before ships' lifeboats carry something similar.

During the invasion of Normandy, radar was used as a guide to the landing craft, to ensure that they made no mistake in selecting a beach for disembarking, as well as for many other purposes. Later, when the tide of invasion had reached Antwerp, our ships were able to proceed up the Scheldt in fog at a good speed, radar picking out the varying configuration of the banks as well as every obstacle in the estuary.

A recent innovation for the benefit of navigation is a special type of buoy fitted with a device emitting radio signals in response to radar. Through this facility a ship's position in a buoy-marked channel can be exactly defined without the possibility of error. According to its exponents, radar is still far from attaining its full degree of development, so its present performances may soon be surpassed. In fact, radar is a vigorous, growing branch of science for which new uses are constantly being found.

Working of the Navy's 'Magic Eye' Explained

A RADAR-EQUIPPED CRAFT of the Royal Navy picks up a convoy of six enemy ships, which are shown as bright marks on a dark screen in the left-hand corner (1). What a gunnery radar-operator sees (2): the target is shown by the inverted "V" on the right of the upper trace; by matching with it the lower "V" the range is transmitted automatically to the guns. In a British cruiser the operator (3) alines the radar-echo with a marker and so transmits range to guns; arrow (also in 2 and 4) indicates the cathode-ray tube on which objects are reflected. Naval radio mechanic trims radar A.A. gunnery equipment (4). Diagram shows how radar works (5). Aircraft have been caught in ship's beam; plane A, not fully focused, is seen as smaller inverted "V" (in circle); plane B, in the full beam, is shown as larger inverted "V" (in circle on right). "Hump" on the left in circle is radar transmission signal. **See facing page, and pages 298-299, 320.**

Photos, British Official, Associated Press

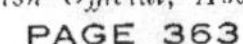

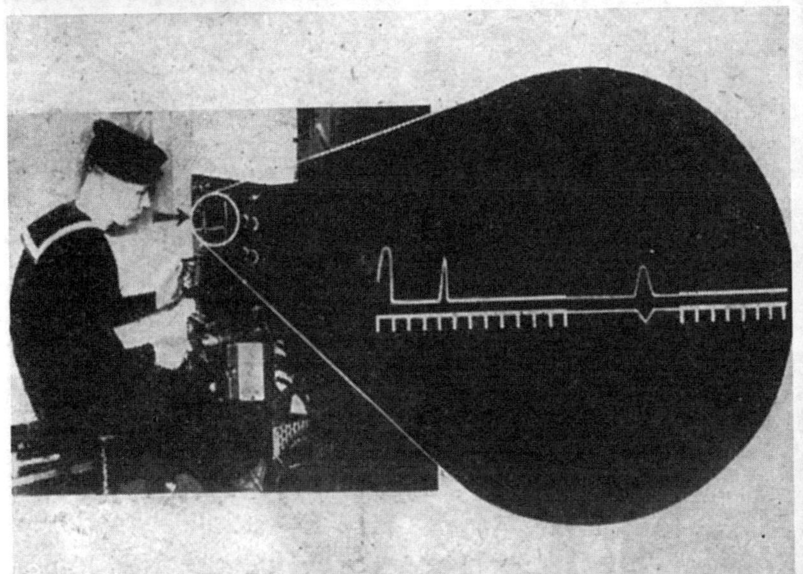

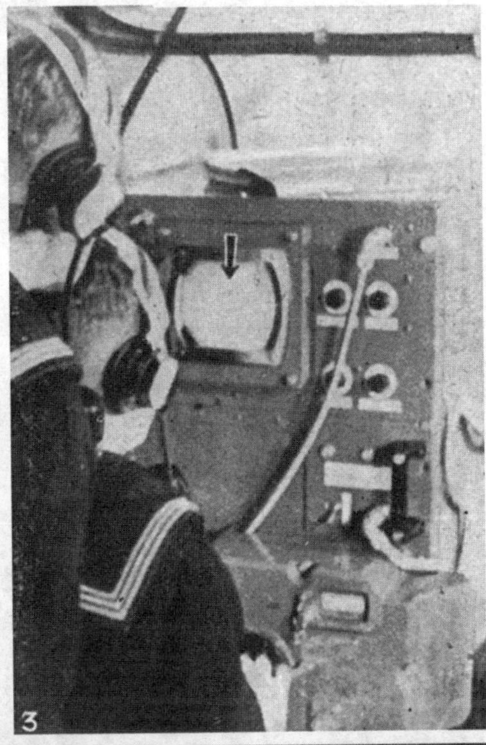

‘The China Incident’ Ends In Japan’s Humiliation

POSITIONS OF ENEMY TROOPS IN CHINA were indicated by Japanese surrender envoys when on August 21, 1945, they were interrogated by members of the Chinese command at Chihkiang, in Hunan. The Japanese officer (1, extreme right) explained the dispositions—with reservations. Arrival of the enemy delegates’ plane at Chihkiang (2), watched by U.S. troops; they were received by a junior Chinese officer and their salute to the waiting crowds was not returned. Wearing uniform of the Imperial General Staff, Gen. Takeo Imai, principal enemy envoy, affixed his seal to the surrender document (3) ; on his right his grim-faced aide-de-camp.

Photos, U.S. Official

Freed at Hongkong They Sing God Save the King

OVER 2,000 BRITISH INTERNEES IN HONGKONG sang God Save the King as the Union Jack was hoisted at Camp Stanley on August 30, 1945—the first time for almost four years. They were freed by Rear-Admiral Harcourt's force (see page 356), which included the carriers Indomitable and Venerable, carrying special medical supplies for prisoners of war. The naval task force was relieved on September 12 by the Third Commando Brigade, under Maj.-Gen. F. W. Festing (who led the 36th Division in N. Burma), newly-appointed G.O.C. China Coast. *Photo, British Official*

Must Britain Go Short to Rebuild Exports?

"The dress the mother goes without this year is helping to make sure that her children will get what they need in the years to come," said Sir Stafford Cripps, President of the Board of Trade, on September 9, 1945. Implications of this statement are clearly set out in this article specially written for "The War Illustrated" by JOHN BUCKATZSCH.

During the last few months the attention of the public has been drawn to the urgent need to increase the value of British exports. Point has been given to the many speeches and articles on the subject by the recent dramatic but long foreseen termination of the Lend-Lease arrangements. The whole problem of our export trade after the war has not arisen unexpectedly. Since a very early stage of the war, economists have been pointing out that expansion of British exports would be one of the most pressing problems of the period of transition from War to Peace.

Nevertheless, there are probably many who have asked themselves the questions: "Why this insistence on exports at a time when there are not enough goods to supply the home market? Why try to export cotton textiles at the very moment that the clothing ration is reduced?" These, and similar questions, are natural and reasonable ones to ask. They are not difficult to answer.

The fundamental reply to all of them is very simple. We must *export* in order to be able to *import*. Exports are not an end in themselves, any more than are doctors' bills, or payments for cinema tickets. It's the doctor's help we want, and the seat in the cinema. The payments are unfortunate formalities we have to go through to get them. It is the same with exports, at any rate as long as nearly every worker is employed and every factory busy. In periods of economic depression, such as that which filled the early nineteen-thirties, nations *do* desire exports almost for their own sake, as a means of "exporting unemployment."

But this policy, which is really very similar to a policy of digging holes in the ground and filling them up at once, in order to "cure unemployment," is only reasonable under those fantastic conditions of mass poverty in the midst of plenty which were allowed to develop in most countries during inter-war periods. We are entitled to hope that we have learnt how to prevent such a situation arising again, and as long as we succeed in doing so exports will be needed simply, as has been explained, to pay for imports.

Why Do We Need to Buy Imports?

In reply to this assertion, however, it is not unnatural to ask, "But why buy imports? Cannot scientific knowledge be applied so as to enable us to feed and clothe ourselves without buying as much from abroad as we used to do?" The answer is that we can certainly reduce our import requirements by making more thorough and economical use of our own resources, and in particular by increasing the efficiency of British agriculture. The possibilities of making great savings in this way are, however, limited, and their effect may well be offset by increases in our requirements at home resulting from the attempts which we hope to make to raise our national standard of living.

But the overriding consideration is that of the relative cost of imported materials and the substitutes for them which we might be able to manufacture at home. The important factor is not the absolute cost, in terms of hours of human labour and tons of raw materials of synthetic rubber, say, but the cost of the synthetic rubber in comparison with that of the goods which we might manufacture in Great Britain and exchange with the growers of natural rubber in other countries. As long as a given output of work produces enough cotton piece-goods, for example, to pay for more natural rubber than could be produced synthetically by the same amount of work, it would obviously be cheaper, more economical and more efficient to import our rubber, paying for it with exports of cotton piece-goods.

This is the fundamental principle of international trade, and explains why it is better to import even those goods which might conceivably be made at home. It is not necessary to emphasize that there are many goods, like grape-fruit and bananas, which cannot be grown commercially in Great Britain, and which must be imported or not eaten at all.

As a matter of fact, the greater part of the goods imported into Great Britain before the War consisted of essential materials, either "raw" or only partly manufactured.

FIRST BRITISH PRIVATE CAR to be exported to the U.S.A. since the war, was recently unloaded in New York. An Austin 4-door black saloon, it will be priced at 1,600 dollars including import duty. *Photo, Keystone*

At the same time it was also true that almost all the goods manufactured in Great Britain contained some material that had been imported. Even our coal was won with the aid of imported pit-props, and some of our main industries—such as cotton and wool—were far more dependent on imported raw materials. On the average, it has been estimated that about one-fifth of the goods produced annually in Great Britain was made up of imported raw materials.

After the War, for some years at any rate, a rather larger proportion of the national effort may be devoted to producing houses and other buildings than was the case before the War, and this will tend to reduce slightly the average proportion of the national output of goods consisting of imported materials, since we make all our own bricks and mortar. But the inescapable fact remains that even allowing for all the economies we can reasonably expect, the economic life of the country cannot be carried on without very large imports of all kinds. And these imports have to be paid for somehow.

How did we pay for our imports before the War? Generally speaking we raised the £866 million required to pay for our pre-war imports in four ways. In the first place we sold goods to foreigners for about £478 million. That was the value of our exports of goods. Secondly, we received about £105 million in return for carrying goods for foreigners in British ships. A further £40 million was received by British banks and insurance companies for services rendered to foreigners by the City of London.

'WE COME TO YOU AS COMRADES IN A VICTORIOUS WAR'

Extracts from a broadcast to the people of the U.S.A. on September 22, 1945, by Lord Halifax who, with Lord Keynes, headed the British Mission to Washington to discuss problems arising from the ending of Lend-Lease.

We put all our efforts, our manpower and our plants to the single purpose of victory. And now, when victory is won, our foreign investments have largely gone, our foreign trade is mostly gone, and we are still 47,000,000 people living on a small island, and only able to work or live so long as we can import.

We can only import so long as we can pay. We can only pay by means of exports or services like shipping . . . We have two courses open to us. One is to develop our trade as much as we can with what is known as the sterling area . . . that means controls, barriers and restrictions . . .

Another solution is that you and we should try to see if we cannot work out something together that will make for a freer and expanding world trade, in the belief that if we can get this, in the long run everybody will be better off.

We Are Now Heavily in Debt

Finally, about £203 million accrued as the interest owed to us by foreigners who had borrowed money from us in the past. (The remaining £40 million was obtained either by borrowing from other countries or by selling stocks and shares to foreign citizens.) Thus exports of goods were required to cover not much more than half of the total bill for the goods and services which we bought from abroad in the years just before the War.

Most of the remainder of the great sum was met from the proceeds of shipping services and earnings from investments.

If we now consider how the War has affected our ability to buy the imports we need in order to maintain our standard of living, we find a serious change for the worse. We cannot yet estimate at all exactly the effect of the War on our ability to earn money by carrying other-people's goods in British ships; but it has almost certainly gravely reduced it, and the demand for these services will not return at once to the pre-war level. On the other hand we do know that as a nation we have sold a very large part of our overseas investments, in order to raise the foreign currencies needed for buying the munitions of war abroad.

The effect of this is that we are now heavily in debt to some countries who before the War were in debt to us and were sending goods to Great Britain in payment of the interest on their debts. In particular, the British Dominions and India have extended loans amounting to about £3,000 or £4,000 *million* which have already been spent on war materials. We must now start to pay off these debts: which means exporting goods, and exporting goods which in many cases can only be manufactured with the help of imported raw materials.

The conclusion is, therefore, that we must attempt to increase our export trade enormously—some writers have suggested that an increase of one-half of the pre-war amount is necessary. The consoling fact is that we have the necessary skill, as well as the determination, and the world is in dire need of the goods which we have to offer it.

Allies Triumph Where Hitlerism Died

Photos, Planet News

First Berlin Parade of All Occupying Powers

"We are celebrating today in Berlin victory over the forces of repression in the Far East," said Marshal Zhukov when, on Sept. 7, 1945, he took the salute at a review on the Charlottenburger Chaussee of 4,000 infantrymen and 200 armoured crews representing Britain, America, Russia (bottom) and France. Men of the 5th Queen's Royal Regt. led the British column (top), followed by guns of the Royal Horse Artillery, armoured cars of the 11th Hussars, and tanks. (See page 377.)

Dreaded Are the Days to Come in a Shattered City

Even with the generous assistance of the victors, Germans are deeply apprehensive of the approach of winter. Berliners in particular find their predicament worsened by the return to the capital each day of about 8,000 refugees. Steps have been taken to hasten repairs of vital water-mains and sewers, and to clear away masses of debris. But much remains, as in the Unter den Linden (1) looking west, with the Brandenburg Gate in the background, and (2) looking east.

Women Form Human Chain to Clear Bricks Away

Bitterest reflection for the Germans is that they brought almost overwhelming hardship upon themselves. Even the women must labour now to remove the rubble from their streets (3), and in Berlin's Bismarckstrasse (5), a bare half-mile from the Unter den Linden, they salvage bricks for stacking—for the rebuilding of shops and houses. Sixteen miles from Berlin, at Potsdam, the railway station witnesses mutely to the vengeance that came by air (4); with Allied aid it may rise again.

What British Bombers Did at Bremen on the Weser

Photo, British Official

Germany's second largest port, Bremen was a prime target for attacks by the R.A.F. from May 1940 to April 22, 1945—five days before its capture by the British 2nd Army. Onslaughts included one of the early 1,000-bomber raids, on June 25, 1942. As seen in this remarkable air photograph, the result presents a mighty reconstruction problem. Sole edifice in this district to escape the fury was a massive air-raid shelter (centre). Constructed of ferro-concrete of immense thickness, this type of shelter had a minimum height of some 50 feet, and accommodated between 5,000 and 10,000 people.

VIEWS & REVIEWS Of Vital War Books

by Hamilton Fyfe

OFTEN when I see men who have been prisoners of war walking about, with their red shoulder stripes, I have wanted to ask them what were their feelings, their thoughts, their imaginations during their captivity in enemy hands. In a book by a French officer I have just come across what I have been wanting to know. The Road to Liberty (Peter Davies, 10s. 6d.) is well worth reading. Lieut. Jean Brilhac is more than a skilful story-teller; he has an analytical intellect. Here is one passage in which he describes the state of mind of the French soldiers with whom he was confined in a P.O.W. camp in Germany.

> Day after day the prisoner felt himself deteriorating mentally and physically, his knees growing heavier and heavier, his brain growing more and more clogged. It required a great deal of effort even to go on shaving every day, or to think out an idea and then to connect this idea with another one logically. "Oh, living death," the prisoner would say to himself, "you hem us in and hold us in your grip!"
>
> The bitterness he felt against mankind as a whole would poison his every thought against his will. The betrayal had bred distrust, and in the prisoner of war camps the prisoners viewed one another with suspicion even after six months. The spirit of brotherhood was for a long time restricted to a limited circle of three or four trusted friends.

Yet they went on hoping, they went on making plans for escape. They resented savagely the acquiescence of the Vichy rulers of France in their prolonged exile and misery. "Pétain's solicitude for them oozed hypocrisy. Laval spat in their faces by hoping for a German victory." But they never quite despaired. If they had, they would have committed mass suicide.

Unbelievably Violent Contempt

Perhaps it was being hungry that saved them from such a fate. Hunger drives all other thoughts from the mind. Those who were habitually half-starved "were haunted with only one obsession, i.e. how to supplement their rations." The notion that eating very little "elevates your soul" is swept away angrily by Lieut. Brilhac. "Reduced to the level of a beast, a man finds that necessity breeds primitive instincts in him, sometimes the worst instincts. Many a solid friendship based on mutual suffering has failed to stand the test of hunger." (The writer means "suffering in common.")

The food was not merely scarce; it was ill-cooked. This contributed to make the French despise as well as dislike their captors. They did not, in general, hate the Germans; they felt for them "unbelievably violent contempt." Some did feel hatred, but the prevalent feeling was one of scornful disgust. They saw that most Germans were stupid, easily deceived, not hard to overawe by bluff. They made a practice of ragging their guards, mostly peasant-soldiers, whom ridicule puzzled and worried.

A PARTY sent to a farm to lift potatoes gravely requested the sentry in charge of them—"a Prussian to the marrow, stocky, red in the face, bovine"—to lock the door at night, as they were afraid of thieves. He stammered out that he had orders to lock it, and he could not understand why they roared with laughter at him. A sly but harmless-looking Breton was told by a farmer to take a bone and a pail of milk to the dog and the calf in the stable. When he came back, the farmer asked if all was well. "Oh yes, the dog enjoyed his milk, lapped it up in three or four gulps, and the calf is busy with the bone." The German roared at him. "You fool! Aren't there any calves and dogs in your country?" The Breton answered innocently, "Yes, sir, but I have never had to feed them." The farmer accepted the excuse.

A young French officer who tried to play the simpleton to a German officer was not so lucky. He said, when asked his occupation, that he was a teacher of philosophy, which was a fact. "In Germany," said the Hun captain, "young men of your age are still students." To which the Frenchman replied, "It may be, monsieur, that in your country people are slow-witted." He was sent to hard labour on the land.

QUICK-WITTED some of the French captives in Germany most certainly were. Two of them got a small seaside resort in East Prussia completely under their control. They were sent there to help out a hotel-keeper whose manservants had been called to the colours. Their employer deferred to them. The inhabitants of the place very soon saw they had more sense and adaptability than their fellow-countrymen who sat in the seats of authority. They said and did pretty much what they pleased. One day they were asked how long they thought the war would last. One of them said, "A long time, and in the end Germany will be beaten." The hotelier offered the prediction that the end would come in September 1940, and said, "If it doesn't, I'll stand you a bottle of brandy every month until Germany wins." Every month the bottle regularly appeared until the two Frenchmen made their escape.

Life Behind Barbed Wire

Russia was the easiest country to escape into for those who, with Lieut. Brilhac, were in East Prussian camps. As many as 186 got across the frontier into the U.S.S.R. and were passed on to this country to join Gen. de Gaulle. Their state of mind before they made their decision to dash for liberty is carefully analysed. They had first to consider whether their wives and families in France would not suffer reprisals, such as having their ration books taken away. Then they knew they would be severely punished themselves if they were caught. They were told also that the Red Army soldiers would shoot any stranger at sight.

> If, in spite of all this, the prisoner was determined to escape and tried to think of a way of doing so, he was faced with a vista of worries. Before escaping he had to guard against indiscretion; afterwards he had to guard against betraying himself by his appearance. An escaped prisoner is easier to spot than an escaped gangster whose picture is posted up at every street corner. The only clothes he has are his uniform. With few exceptions he does not know the language. Finally, he could not expect any help from Germans, no matter what their political convictions. Either through fear or a sense of duty, not only would they refuse to help him but would denounce him mercilessly.
>
> He has no identity card, no compass, no money, and often no supplies of food. He does not know the exact position of the frontier, and at any step on his journey he might take the wrong road or run into someone, or find the police dog on his tracks—and it would be all up with him.

The French are brought up, both in their homes and their schools, to be cautious, to reckon up the difficulties of any course they think of taking, to look long and carefully before they leap, just as they are taught to be introspective, to analyse their feelings, to dramatize themselves and indulge in self-pity, as Lieut. Brilhac did. That makes conversation in France more interesting than it is as a rule in Britain. But there are situations in which it is better to be an unreflecting, stolid Briton, not realizing all the risks that he takes. The situation of a prisoner of war is one of these.

HORROR CAMP SURVIVORS (in prison clothes) erected at the Palais de Chaillot, Paris, on July 12, 1945, a huge wooden cross—which they are seen carrying—in memory of the countless French victims of Nazi torture methods. *Photo, Keystone*

What the Russians Feared

When they did decide to try for freedom, the French showed every kind of courage and cleverness. They dug tunnels, they got civilian clothes, they had their heads shaved in the Hun fashion. If they were challenged, they replied either with violence or bluff. Many were recaptured, and those who did get into Russia through Lithuania before Hitler attacked the Soviet Republics were put at once into prison camps again.

> On principle the Russians suspected anything that came from Germany. They expected to be involved in the war and had seen the example of the many countries where fifth columnists had done so much harm. Consequently they were afraid to send us back to Vichy in case there was a spy in our midst. Their anxiety to preserve neutrality prevented them from allowing us to join the forces of Gen. de Gaulle.

So the escaped men had to stay for a while, under fairly easy conditions, until Russia was itself at war. Then they were sent here. Lieut. Brilhac collected the stories of the 185 who had been his companions and picked out the best of them for this book.

THERE are numberless entertaining and instructive incidents in these narratives. Here is one that should please Lord Vansittart. Two of the escapers got as far as Koenigsberg and had to wait there a whole day. It was frightfully cold; they didn't know what to do with themselves, so they went into the cathedral, where they heard a Lutheran pastor tell the congregation that "if it were God's will that a hundred or even a hundred and fifty thousand young Germans should die for the greater glory of Germany, then God's will must be done." That this was the line the clergy were taking we know, but it is useful to have the knowledge confirmed by first-hand evidence of this kind.

Now It Can Be Told!

2,000 SOLDIERS HELPED TO SAVE LONDON'S WATER

ONE of the strange stories of the London blitz, recently told in The Sunday Times, was how part of the New River channel, dug originally between 1608 and 1613, in the reign of James I, had to be hastily re-excavated by 2,000 soldiers in 1940 to save a vital part of London's water supply.

Fed by the Chadwell and Amwell springs, the New River starts near Ware, in Hertfordshire, and brings in about an eighth of London's total water supply. As originally dug, more than 300 years ago, it was 40 miles long, but since then many of its meanderings have been replaced by direct pipe lines. One of these discarded river loops is in Enfield, where a mile and a half of the New River channel, known as the Enfield Loop, was replaced by a pipe line which was only half as long.

Part of the channel was filled in at Enfield Town Park, but water was left in the rest as a local amenity, and a small concrete dam was built at Southbury Road to seal off the river loop (see map).

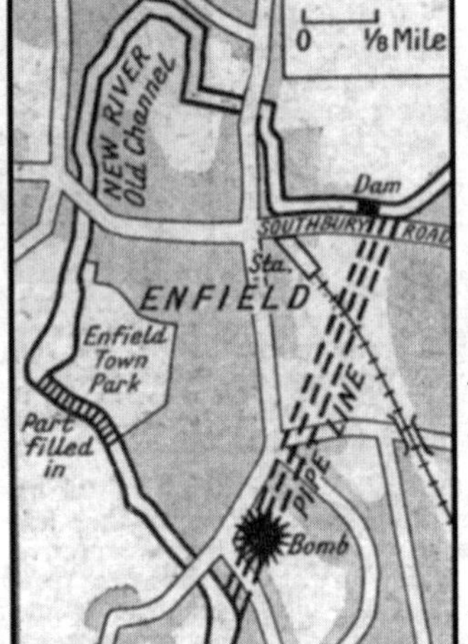

PIPE LINE AT ENFIELD, where the bomb fell on October 15, 1940 (as told here), and the course of the New River, metropolitan water-supply source.

Danger of Flooding

At 9 p.m. on October 15, 1940, a bomb scored a direct hit on the pipe line and smashed three pipes through which pass up to 46,000,000 gallons of water a day. A member of the Metropolitan Water Board's staff who lived near realized what had happened, and telephoned to the head river foreman at Hornsey for the valves at the north end of the pipe line to be closed, while he braved the blitz and collected a few workers and went to the valves at the south end. With the aid of a policeman and others they closed these valves, and the flow of water was shut off by about 9.45 p.m.—less than an hour after the bomb fell.

This ended the danger of flooding to the neighbourhood, but there was the still bigger task of ensuring that London got its water—a vital matter in those days of fire blitzes and smashed mains. The assistance of London Regional headquarters was sought in the early hours of the morning, and they arranged for military help. By 5 a.m. 2,000 soldiers, collected from various parts of London and hurried to the spot in motor transport, were digging out the filled-in part of the old channel.

The Flow Restored

At the same time N.F.S. men, summoned from a wide area, pumped water past the quarter of a mile channel where the troops were working. By 8 o'clock on the evening of October 16 the troops had dug a rough channel, and the natural flow of water was partially restored.

By the next morning when some other small dams had been broken, water was flowing at the rate of 10,000,000 gallons a day through the old James I channel, and two days later, by which time the main dam at Southbury Road had been cut through, the flow was 15,000,000 gallons—more than a third of the normal supply.

The repair of the three broken mains was a lengthier job and occupied the Metropolitan Water Board staff and the contractors until November 6.

HUDDERSFIELD GIRLS, Miss Bessie Taylor and Miss Marjorie Warwick, were given the honour of launching and naming two "X" craft constructed at this Yorkshire town.

DARING EXPLOITS OF MIDGET SUBMARINE X.24

HOW a British midget submarine twice penetrated the Norwegian harbour of Bergen—one of the most heavily defended ports under German control—and sank a 7,500-tons merchant ship, a floating dock and a smaller merchant vessel, besides damaging harbour installations, is a story delayed in the telling since April 1944. The craft which carried out these daring and hazardous missions was the X.24, a 4-man submarine carrying detachable explosive charges, and similar in type to the X-craft which damaged the Tirpitz in Alten Fjord in September 1943 (see illus. pages 327 and 649, Vol. 7).

On April 10, 1944, H.M. submarine X.24, with Lieut. M. H. Shean, R.A.N.V.R., in command, got into Bergen Harbour and laid a charge under the 7,500-ton merchant vessel Barenfels, which was berthed at a coaling jetty. The explosion sank the ship and caused considerable damage to harbour installations. The X.24 then withdrew from the harbour without being detected, and returned home safely. The Commander-in-Chief, Home Fleet, described the operation as "a magnificent achievement, ably planned and most daringly carried out." Lieut. M. H. Shean, R.A.N.V.R., was awarded the D.S.O. for this exploit.

On September 11, 1944, the same submarine—the X.24—commanded by Lieut. H. P. Westmacott, D.S.C., R.N., of Bembridge, Isle of Wight, sank a floating dock in Bergen Harbour. Having made a passage of 80 hours in extremely bad weather across open sea, the X.24 passed through 30 miles of island passages off the Norwegian coast and negotiated minefields and other defences of Bergen Harbour, to attack a target which was of particular value to the enemy at that time, namely, the floating dock.

THE craft was manoeuvred in daylight at periscope depth, among many boats and ferries, and at one time a ship was heard to pass immediately over the submarine when she was at a depth of 35 feet. During the approach to the target, Lieut. Westmacott was able to read, through the periscope, the "wreck warning" notice attached to the mainmast of the Barenfels which had been sunk five months previously. Charges were released under the floating dock, which was destroyed, as was a small merchant

OFFICERS OF SUBMARINE X.24, whose exploits are narrated here. Commanded by Lieut. M. H. Shean, D.S.O., R.A.N.V.R. (top), she sank the 7,500 tons Barenfels. Later, commanded by Lieut. H. Westmacott, D.S.O., D.S.C., R.N. (second from left), she sank a floating dock. Left, Sub-Lieut. B. J. Clarke, R.N.V.R. Second from right, Sub.-Lieut. B. H. Dening, D.S.O., R.N.V.R. Right, Engine-Room Artificer L. R. Tilley. *Photos, British Official*

vessel alongside it. The X.24 then withdrew and made her way through the fjords undetected to the open sea. Lieut. Westmacott was awarded the D.S.O. "for great gallantry in a most hazardous operation."

X-craft were also used as defence markers during the Allied landings in Northern France. They were actually the first vessels of the Royal Navy off the French shore, and they lay submerged for 48 hours before the first landing craft approached the coast.

Built Fifty Miles from the Sea

During the war midget submarines were built for the Admiralty, in conditions of great secrecy, by three inland firms—at Chesterfield, at Gainsborough, and at Huddersfield. In the latter town, of some 120,000 people, though hundreds of workers knew something of what was going on, those really in the know could be counted on the fingers of both hands. From the Huddersfield engineering works of Messrs. T. Broadbent and Sons, Ltd., a 50-miles journey to the sea faced the completed submarines, which were accompanied by their crews.

These lived in the town with their craft during the later stages of construction, and in the quiet of an early Sunday morning, before townsfolk were up and about, the journey of each completed vessel would commence. In the guise of motor-boats, the midget submarines were conveyed along the streets to the railway station, where special trains waited to take them to the Clyde and so down to the sea. Two girl employees (portraits in facing page) of the Huddersfield firm had the honour of launching and naming the craft.

The Navy's midget submarine which crippled the Tirpitz first emerged as a small wax model at the Admiralty Experimental Works at Haslar, near Portsmouth, over five years ago. Several designs and modifications were tested and improved for speed, endurance, diving and sea-keeping before the prototype was built. And there also the first full-scale midget was tested in an experimental tank, by a naval crew, before sea trials were embarked upon ; then came the specialized training and preparations for action. Here also the piloted torpedoes which the enemy had used (see illus. page 359, also pages 486 and 551, Vol. 8) were reconstructed as an accurate model, from captured fragments, and much useful information was thereby gained.

WHERE THE FIRST V2 LANDED in this country—at Staveley Road, Chiswick, London, S.W., at eleven minutes to seven on the evening of September 8, 1944. The incident was not officially disclosed until April 26, 1945, a month after the last rocket had fallen on England. Eleven houses were destroyed, three people killed and twenty injured. *Photo, News Chronicle*

Rescued After Five Months of Adventure

An episode in which the destroyer Kelvin took part at the end of 1940 makes belated news, the story being officially "released" in August 1945. Sight of the Kelvin meant the end of five months of hazardous adventures to 18 men who were standing on the rolling deck of a neutral cargo boat early in December 1940 ; after being assisted aboard, the overjoyed men "mobbed" the destroyer's crew and, between repeated thanks, told how thirteen of their number, members of the 51st Highland Division who were captured in June 1940 during the German advance on the Somme, headed by their Major, had escaped to Vichy, where they had been successful in obtaining French military uniforms.

From there they made their way to the South of France and, this time garbed in Foreign Legion uniforms and armed with forged papers, managed to reach Morocco—where luck was against them and they were interned. Again the Major organized a spectacular escape, and in due course they arrived at Casablanca, slipped aboard a small Portuguese cargo vessel in the dark, concealed themselves under cargo, and waited until they were at sea before revealing themselves to the astonished skipper. It was whilst the ship was proceeding on its journey to Portugal that she was intercepted by H.M.S. Kelvin and, after investigations, the men taken off. The rest of the 18 rescued were two Frenchmen on the way to join De Gaulle's Free French Army, two British airmen and an Austrian refugee.

REMARKABLE ESCAPE STORY of men of the 51st Highland Division captured by the Germans on the Somme in June 1940 is told above. Escaping to Vichy, they procured French uniforms, and reached Morocco, but only to be interned. Again they escaped—to Casablanca, where they secretly boarded a small Portuguese trader. The destroyer H.M.S. Kelvin intercepted her at sea and rescued the men, who are seen (left) leaving the Portuguese vessel and (right) greeting men of the Kelvin's gun-crew. *Photos, British Official*

British Justice for the Beasts of Belsen

PRESIDENT OF THE COURT at the Belsen Camp trial which opened at Luneburg, Germany, on September 17, 1945, was Maj.-Gen. H. P. M. Berney-Ficklin, C.B., M.C. (1). Chief defendants (2) were Josef Kramer the commandant—No. 1—and Fritz Klein, the doctor—No. 2. Among the Germans chosen by ballot and obliged to attend was this girl (3), being searched by a British military policeman. The court in session (4) ; on extreme left the 45 accused with (in front) defending counsel ; at far end, the witness-box ; on extreme right, the judges ; at bottom, prosecuting counsel. The court-room was formerly a gymnasium. See also pages 50 and 148.

Photos, Keystone, G.P.U.

German Atomic Bomb Research was Sabotaged

As long ago as the winter of 1941–42 the Allies had ascertained that German scientists were making alarmingly good progress in their atomic research. This account of the sabotage of the Norwegian supplies of "heavy water" which the Germans were then using in their experiments is condensed from an article by The Daily Telegraph Military Correspondent, Lieut.-Gen. H. G. MARTIN.

In the heart of the North Telemark Mountains is the Rjukan Valley. A deep, sheer-sided cleft, the valley is some 20 miles in length. At the top is the Mjoes Lake, at the bottom Lake Tin Sjoe. At Vemork, about half-way down the valley, is the great power station of the Norsk Hydro Works, which specialize in the production—from atmospheric nitrogen—of saltpetre for use in fertilizers. Beside the power station at Vemork is the high-concentration plant : it is a seven-storyed building designed by Lief Tronstad, of Trondheim, a scientist of world repute, who fortunately had made his way to England in 1940. Here it is, on the ground floor, that the heavy water is produced as a by-product of the final process. Vemork was No. 1 target, and this was its bull's-eye.

In the Rjukan Valley live the two brothers Skinnerland. The one is in charge of the sluices on the Mjoes Lake ; the other, with whom this story is concerned, is a farmer. In March 1942 this second Skinnerland made his way to England to join the Norwegian forces. At once, however, those over here who dealt with Norway realized the special value of his local knowledge : he must go back—to form a link between Vemork and London. So they gave him a couple of practice parachute-jumps, and within ten days had dropped him back again in the Northern Telemark country.

"HEAVY WATER" PLANT in the Norwegian valley of Rjukan where Nazi scientists experimented with atomic energy for warfare purposes. Elaborate pipe-system for conducting water down the mountainside for the generation of electricity is seen in the background. In 1943 the plant was wrecked by Norwegian patriots, as told here. *Photo, Keystone*

Germans Found Our Marked Maps

Throughout the next three years, till Germany's capitulation, Skinnerland was the presiding genius of the Rjukan, watching every German move, interpreting and reporting it unfailingly. Gradually the Allies' plans matured. It was decided to land about 40 men by glider, to overpower the German guard and destroy the high-concentration plant.

In October 1942 an advanced party of four Norwegians, with wireless sets, was dropped—but wide of the mark. The party joined Skinnerland only after a heartbreaking march through the mountains. About a month later Combined Operations made its attempt with two aircraft and two gliders. At the last moment the weather—always treacherous in these valleys—shut right down. One aircraft and both gliders crashed in the mountains, and in the wreckage the Germans found maps with Vemork clearly marked upon them as the objective.

The fat was in the fire. The Germans scoured the Rjukan. The advanced party had to scatter. Only Skinnerland was left, and he had to take to the mountains in the north, where, now completely efficient in all the wireless codes in use, he established his own advanced base for the rest of the war.

Men were found to succeed by guile where force had failed. On February 16, 1943, a Norwegian demolition party of four men under Lieut. Ronneberg, was dropped on the 3,500-ft. plateau about 50 miles to the north to join up with six men of the Home Front. After dark on February 24, Ronneberg and his nine men moved down to the attack. It was thawing : as they plunged down 2,000 ft. into the cleft of the Rjukan they sank to their armpits in the snow. That journey, said Ronneberg, was the hardest part of the job.

The Germans had laid minefields round the high-concentration plant ; they also employed four Norwegian watchmen. The German guard of 15 men formed an inlying picquet to the guardhouse. Ronneberg had divided his men into a demolition party of four and a covering party of six. In the darkness both parties evaded the Norwegian watchmen. The covering party surrounded the guardhouse ; the demolition party entered the high-concentration building.

So good was the intelligence—provided by Lief Tronstad over in England and also by Skinnerland—that Ronneberg knew his way about the building as though it had been his own home. Every charge slipped into its appointed place in the machinery so perfectly that he felt that he was still practising on the model Tronstad had built for him.

The object was to destroy that part of the plant—and that only—which produced the heavy water. Originally the fuses had been adjusted for three minutes' delay. Ronneberg had reasoned, however, that the Germans might arrive within three minutes, so he cut the delay to 30 seconds. When the explosion came, therefore—the explosion which told that Vemork would produce no more heavy water for the next nine months or so—the ten were all still in the compound.

At the muffled sound a German opened the guardhouse door and stood, silhouetted against the bright light within, to look around. In the darkness six Stens covered him—but no one fired. It was a tense moment. Satisfied that some stray beast must have exploded a land-mine, the German turned and closed the door. Thanks to this display of discipline and restraint, Ronneberg's party was able to make a clean getaway.

Time Bombs in the Train-Ferry

Ronneberg and his three fellow-saboteurs set off on skis to cover the 300 miles to Sweden, travelling in battle-dress, with Stens slung across their shoulders. On the 18th day, having cached their battle-dress and arms, they crossed the Swedish frontier. In due course they returned to England. Ronneberg received the D.S.O. What *we* should have received if Ronneberg had not succeeded we shall never know. From Ronneberg's blow heavy water was down but not out. Fortresses of the U.S.A. 8th A.F. struck next. Eight months later—in autumn 1943—they hit the Vemork power station, cut one of the great water-pipes and slightly damaged the high-concentration plant.

The attack made the Germans decide to cut their losses. In February 1944 Skinnerland reported they were about to quit Vemork, after they had moved all stocks of heavy water out by rail *en route* to Germany.

On that London got busy. At the time there was an expert saboteur—one Haukelid—ready to hand, about 50 miles from Vemork. He and another were told to contact Skinnerland, and "fix" that heavy water. On arrival in the Rjukan, Haukelid decided that his best chance was to try to sink the train-ferry on Lake Tin Sjoe. On Sunday mornings few Norwegians travel by the ferry. Working through the Norwegian staff of the Norsk Hydro, therefore, Haukelid arranged that the heavy water should start on the following Sunday. On the Saturday the Germans duly loaded their precious water on two trucks.

The Germans were taking no chances : that Saturday night they floodlit the siding and mounted a strong guard. "What chaps they are, to be sure ! They think of everything," said Haukelid, and off he went to board the train-ferry. He had made two time-bombs from the mechanisms of two alarm-clocks. Having calculated that the ferry would reach the deepest part of Lake Tin Sjoe by 11 next morning, he had set the mechanisms accordingly. All that now remained was to place the bombs in position.

Haukelid and his companion first thought of the engine-room—no good, the engineers were there playing cards. Next they tried the bilges. There was a look-out on deck. No quisling, he turned a blind eye, so down they went through the man-hole into the bilges.

Having placed their bombs, the pair set off that very night for Sweden. At the same time Haukelid reported to London that the ferry should sink at 11 a.m. next day. As always, Skinnerland stayed behind. In due course he, too, reported : the train-ferry—with all the trucks and all the water—had gone down in 200 fathoms at 10.45 a.m. precisely. The saga of the heavy water was ended.

Great Gallantry in Action Earned Them the V.C.

Sgt. R. R. RATTEY
Seen in Sydney being congratulated by Admiral Sir Bruce Fraser, Sgt. Rattey, of the Australian infantry, under vicious fire silenced the foe single-handed during a desperate action on Bougainville, Solomon Is., on March 22, 1945, making our advance possible.

Sepoy **ALI HAIDAR**
Completely regardless of his own safety and despite serious wounds, Sepoy Haidar, of the 13th Frontier Force Rifles, saved "an ugly situation" on the Senio River, Italy, in April 1945. He is the first Pathan V.C.

Lt. **KARAMJEET SINGH JUDGE**
This "brilliant officer" of the 15th Punjab Regiment, during an attack in Burma in March 1945 "dominated the entire battlefield by his numerous and successive acts of superb gallantry," but was mortally wounded.

Rifleman **LACHHIMAN GURUNG**
On the Irrawaddy in May 1945, Rifleman Gurung, of the 8th Gurkha Rifles, though cut off for three days, encouraged his section to smash all attacks, displaying against almost overwhelming odds "outstanding gallantry and devotion to duty."

Corporal **F. G. TOPHAM**
In bitter fighting on the Rhine on March 24, 1945, Cpl. Topham, 1st Canadian Parachute Battalion medical orderly, though in great pain, for six hours performed "a series of acts of outstanding bravery."

Corporal **E. T. CHAPMAN**
Single-handed, Cpl. Chapman, of the Monmouthshire Regiment, on April 2, 1945, though severely wounded, repulsed attacks by picked and fanatical Nazis during the struggle for a vital ridge dominating the all-important Dortmund-Ems canal.

Corporal **T. P. HUNTER**
Just before the 8th Army's final assault in Italy in April 1945, Cpl. Hunter, 43rd Marine Commandos (left), displaying "magnificent courage, leadership and cheerfulness," charged alone across open ground against intense fire from nine German Spandaus and several mortars. He was killed.

Photos, Indian, Canadian and Australian Official

I Was There! Eye Witness Stories of the War and After

Battle of Britain Pilots in the Air Again

Fifth anniversary of the peak day of the Battle of Britain was marked on September 15, 1945, by a "fly-past" over London, with survivors of the Battle in some of the 300 planes. (See illus. p. 380). These memories were recorded at famous Biggin Hill by Frank Davey in the News Chronicle.

At the controls again, over London today, Battle of Britain pilots, will you glance southwards towards the flat top of the green Kentish weald? They are harvesting in those fields beyond the charred and broken houses that surround the aerodrome you knew so well. Yesterday I saw two soldiers in battle-dress climbing up a ladder with a basket skep, trying to gather a swarm of bees from the branch of a tree.

There are no Spitfires flaring through the skies now; no Heinkels or Messerschmitts dashing over to blast craters in your runways. Only Dakotas, like buses, dropping down one every ten minutes on those very tar tracks from which you took off in such a hurry in 1940, hour after hour, day after day, to hammer Hitler's planes out of the sky.

What a changed Biggin Hill since the days of Dunkirk, when you gave fighter cover for the men driven to the last beach of Europe, while we barricaded the streets of English towns against the invasion. September 15, 1940. The score was 185 Hun planes that day, and Biggin Hill pilots got 18 of those, plus 25 "probables."

I remember a warm Sunday afternoon that year when a couple of Spitfires chased a Heinkel a hundred or two yards over the roof of my home. He dropped a bomb that split the old stone house just by Keston Church, but the Spits got him down in a field about a mile away. You'll be remembering the British, New Zealand and French squadrons round the field ready to take off instantly; the pilots living in huts near the runways; the games of chess and ludo while they waited. There's still one of those yellow bikes on which they used to rush away from the mess to reach the planes when the alarm went. No little jeeps to take them out in those days.

Today an American sentry and a R.A.F. man guard the gate. One of the Americans has scribbled on the wall of the cabin there: "*Johnnie Nicky Carioto, former Military Police with 1296 M.P. Company, now here. Been to France, Belgium, Holland, Luxembourg, Germany. Next stop New York!*"

Two land girls are cycling through the gate on their way to tend the garden. Out of the officers' mess strolls Thunder, half-Alsatian, half-greyhound, who waited in vain one night for his fighter pilot master, and refused to leave the runway for three days. He has been taken over by an American. A poster on a notice board in the passage reads: "Race Card for Release! Age and Service Groups." Another is headed: "Show Me the Way to Go Home! See Bureau of Current Affairs Circular." A Ministry of Labour booklet on careers dangles from a string. Its title is "Brewing."

Remember that celebration party at Grosvenor House for the 1,000th enemy plane scored? The taxi-drivers came and offered to drive any of you home free of charge anywhere. The old black driving wheel they gave you is hanging in the Mess Secretary's office inscribed: "From the Boys on the Cabs to the Boys in the Cabs. July 9, 1943." In the bar, those portraits hanging on the wall. Fine young faces, beautifully drawn. Flight-Lieut. "Foot and Mouth" Kingcombe, D.F.C., Wing-Cmdr. "Oxo" Oxspring, Group Capt. Rankin, Flight-Lieut. Mungo-Park, D.F.C.

That clever cartoon called "One Confirmed," with the photographed faces glued on the caricatures. "Sailor" Malan has dropped an anchor from his plane well into the enemy bomber's wing. "Al" Deere, now Wing-Commander, is lugging a helmeted German out by the legs. The gay Frenchman, René Mouchotte—since shot down on the other side—is dropping a bottle on the enemy's fuselage. Squadron-Leader Jack Charles, who helped to bring down the 1,000th plane, is doing some other nonsense. There's a bunch of dried Kentish hops hanging in the corner of the room.

Someone remembers a famous night fighter. "He crashed at Ashford . . . hit another plane head-on in broad daylight . . . they buried him in the village churchyard near here. Only two nights before he was telling me his feelings about flying in the dark . . . cold sweat down the spine when his operator told him the Hun plane was in his sector . . . complete terror till he could see him . . . then all right when the fight was on."

In the chapel today, the Book of Remembrance lies open at a name: "September 15, 1940. Pilot Officer George Louis Joseph Doutrepont, 229 Squadron." Doutrepont was, in fact, a Belgian airman, 27 years old. He flew in the Belgian Air Force from 1931 till 1940, and then came over to join the R.A.F. He was commissioned in July 1940, so he did not have very long with his British friends. "In the Shadow of Thy Wings Will I Rejoice," says the embroidered altar cloth.

Out in the sunshine, down the steps, there is fun in the bathing pool which the father of Flying Officer Bartholomew Bloom presented to the station, in memory of his son, killed in September 1941. Built into the wall of the Ace café is that stone on which was written "In Loving Memory of 10 for 6d.," when the price of cigarettes went up.

They don't need a memorial in the village. Every time a plane appears in the sunlight, the man among the stooks of corn and the woman hanging out the washing—remembers.

"HEROES' GALLERY"—a corner of the bar at Biggin Hill, near Westerham, Kent, one of the R.A.F.'s most famous fighter stations during the Battle of Britain, where the walls are lined with portraits of "The Few." (See article in this page.) Portrait on the table is of Group-Captain "Sailor" Malan; above, on the wall, may be seen Flight-Lt. Mungo-Park, D.F.C.; and at the right, on the mantelshelf, Group-Captain Rankin. *Photo, News Chronicle*

I Saw the First 4-Powers Parade in Berlin

Notable day in the history of the Allies and of conquered Germany was Sept. 7, 1945. In the capital there paraded proud representatives of Britain, U.S., Russia and France. The following account of the brilliant ceremony, which is illustrated in page 367, was specially written for "The War Illustrated" by Cpl. R. S. Ralph, R.A.S.C.

At ten o'clock this morning I was standing on the roadside in the Charlottenburger Chaussee, Berlin, opposite the saluting base, watching the hustle and bustle which preceded events of an hour later. It was a warm day, and as I looked along at the "Siegessaule"—Victory Monument of the Reich—the Angel of Victory at the top of the column was bathed in sunlight beneath the fluttering Union Jack. Military police were dashing hither and thither directing traffic and spectators—some walking, some in cars, some on cycles, all making their way to find best positions from which to see the march-past of the four Occupying Powers.

The bands of the Allies were opposite the saluting base, and the American band was playing a regimental march as I came along. By the side of the saluting base were the enclosures. I looked across at the Senior Officers' enclosure and noted the air of cordiality that seemed to prevail. French, Russian, American and British officers were mingled together, talking with each other as far as their knowledge of the respective languages would allow.

At half-past ten the first of the high-ranking officers came along with their convoys of cars and escorts. Russian officers were in American-type civilian cars with large red flags flying, French officers also were in civilian cars. Then the American officers with their fleets of cars and siren-fitted jeeps, and motor-cyclists; then the British officers in their familiar green cars with flags on the bonnets and "star" plates on the bumpers. Everything seemed so colourful, and the flags round the saluting base gave a festive air.

A murmur went round the spectators as Marshal Zukhov came along the Chaussee in his open car—a majestic figure in uniform, his breast covered with decorations and medals. He went to the saluting base, and everyone waited expectantly for Field-Marshal Montgomery—in vain.

Just after eleven o'clock, when the initial excitement had somewhat died down, a jeep came out from the base of the saluting stand and went up towards where the first contingent of infantry were waiting to move off to the march past. The band of the Russian Forces struck up, and in the distance I could see the large flags of Russia's battle honours proudly waving as the column commenced to move. The Russians came down ten abreast, smart, and every one in step. Then came the French infantry, all wearing the traditional blue beret and marching well. At the foot of the saluting base were many members of the Free French Women's Force who were unable to restrain their emotion and when the soldiers marched past almost broke through the cordon.

The "Desert Rats" Were There

Following the French came the first line of the British infantry. With battle honours flying, men of the 5th Queen's Royal Regiment, the Devon Regiment, and the Durham Light Infantry, all wearing the famous "Desert Rat" Divisional Sign, filed past the saluting base, and, to a command that could be heard all along the great roadway, eyes were turned to the right at the salute. Following these came men of the Royal Air Force Regiment, looking very smart, their light blue uniforms contrasting with the khaki all around. Last of the infantry detachments to file past were the Americans, hefty-looking men from an Airborne Division. The bandmaster of the American band turned and saluted his colours as they passed : it was the band of the Airborne Division.

After the infantry, the armour of the Allies came down the Chaussee. First the British armour—self-propelled tanks of the Royal Artillery led the British contingent, followed by "The Cherry Pickers"—the 11th Hussars in their armoured cars ; then the Comet tanks with men of the Royal Tank Regiment. The French followed with their armour, after which came the Americans. Last of all to come along were the Russians, parading tanks the like of which many of us had never seen before. Large 60-tonners these were, and all steel, with rough-cast turrets and heavy guns—I should say 5·5-in. There they were, three abreast, deadening every sound. I watched the faces of three German policemen standing near me. I wonder what they were thinking ?

The last of the tanks came by, and the combined forces of military police threw a cordon round the saluting base to keep back the amateur photographers (and official ones) who would get a photo of the Marshal. Half an hour later all had cleared—the soldiers had gone back to talk over another historic event, the few German cars and transports again rode the Chaussee, and the sun still shone on the Victory Monument.

Sea-Bed Grave for Hitler's Poison Gas

Concentrated in a big forest covering an area of four square miles is one of the greatest stocks of poison gas in Germany, wrote a Daily Telegraph special Correspondent with 21st Army Group on August 6, 1945. He tells of the fate intended for it, and of the chambers where it was housed.

I HAVE just been to see it before it disappears from the world. The deadly cargo, carried in ships manned entirely by Germans, is to be thrown into the sea. There, 200 fathoms below the surface, near the Channel Islands, it may remain intact for as many years. It is all contained in shells and three-quarter-inch steel takes a long time to corrode. Even on land the poison gas had been strictly isolated.

Dotted all over the forest which I visited were strongly built storage sheds, very commodious and all above ground. Many of them had thick concrete walls and mounds of earth with vegetation on them. Trees were growing from this protective cover to provide impenetrable camouflage. To guard against storms, each hut had a lightning conductor system of a most elaborate kind.

In each of these sheds thousands upon thousands of gas-filled shells were lying horizontally in wooden frames. There is ample evidence of Hitler's preparations to use gas. An important extension had just been completed. This was a tremendously strong structure consisting of a poison gas filling station with ten enormous containers, each capable of holding many thousands of gallons.

Brand-new shell-filling apparatus, each vital part being distinctively coloured to guard against any dangerous mistake, was ready for operation in a long well-ventilated room. The numerous vacuum filling machines, with empty shells in position below, left one in no doubt of the high speed at which the work could be done. The plant looked as if it had just failed to come into use because of the war's end.

Allied troops arrived to find a goods train ready to leave with supplies of the newest poison gas. This caused considerable excitement among our chemists. At once they probed the secret. They convinced themselves that the new gas was exactly the same as one they evolved experimentally two years ago. It had been rejected because it was inferior to kinds already in manufacture.

On My Last Strange Trail to Civvy Street

The final stretch of road that many thousands of Servicemen tread on the way back to civilian life holds unsuspected surprises and embarrassments. The eagerness to "get out" sometimes fades a little at the last moment ; or so it seemed to The Star reporter, Bernard Murphy, recently released as Flight-Lieutenant, R.A.F.

WHEN I joined the R.A.F., nearly six years ago, a red-headed corporal took one look at me and said: "This way, you dimwit, get fell in like the others." My departure from the R.A.F. a few days ago was more genteel. It was at the same depot where my dimwittedness was so promptly recognized—but the atmosphere was considerably changed.

At the gate an airman with shining white brassard saluted and with smooth automatic gesture indicated my route; at the door his counterpart repeated the motions to guide me to a luxurious waiting-room fitted with little tables around which sat 20 to 30 other officers. With delightful thoughtfulness, the highest authorities had planned this oasis where we might rest a while before beginning the long, last journey to our bowler hats.

It felt rather like being in one of those palatial but eerie half-way houses we sometimes see in films. We were alive but almost dead. Our uniforms seemed to have assumed automatically and most mysteriously a look of complete obsolescence. We smiled shyly at each other. Coffee and cakes and cheese rolls were served by N.A.A.F.I. girls. We sipped our coffee, cleared our throats.

Suddenly we seemed self-conscious in each other's presence. This was not the atmosphere of an officers' mess or a flight hut. The bold voice, cheery smile, the hearty slap on the back were instantly things of the past. I suppose subconsciously we were already practically civilians. The fat squadron leader on my right should have said, "D'you want the gen on this show, old boy ? It's a piece of cake—they just haven't got a clue ! " But instead he smiled sheepishly and mumbled some civilian gibberish that he hoped his suit would fit.

There's no denying it—for no reason at all that I can think of, getting a bowler hat is embarrassing. We were all embarrassed. We did not feel elated. For days we had been telling everyone else in the camp the great news of our release. "Lucky dog," everyone said. "Wish I was in your boots." The most self-conscious officer in the room announced: "Well, this is the best day I have ever spent in the R.A.F ! " Everyone

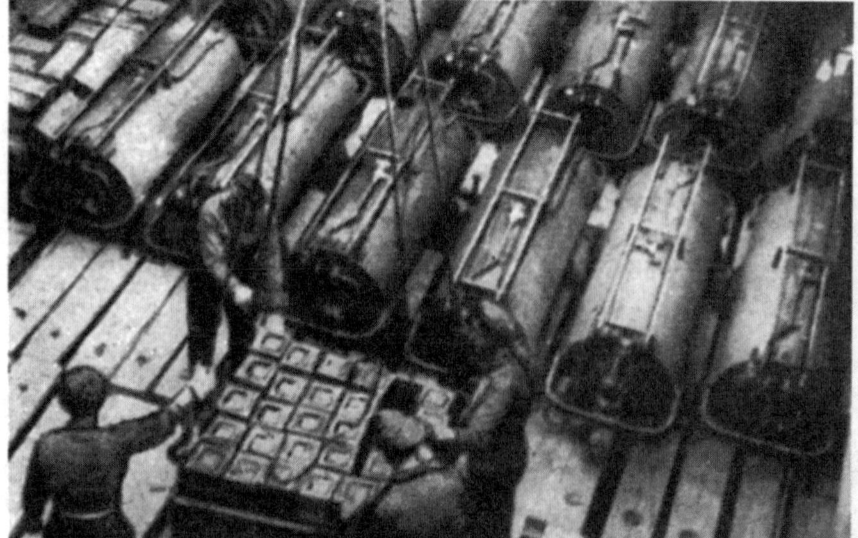

8,000 TONS OF DEADLY MUSTARD GAS, part of the store which Britain held in readiness against a German threat of chemical warfare, being loaded in the hold of the 5,690 tons merchant vessel, the SS. Empire Simba. Contained in shells and projectors—it was announced on September 7, 1945—it is to be shipped from the Scottish military harbour of Cairn Ryan, near Stranraer (see illus. in p. 173), and dumped in the Atlantic. *Photo, Daily Express*

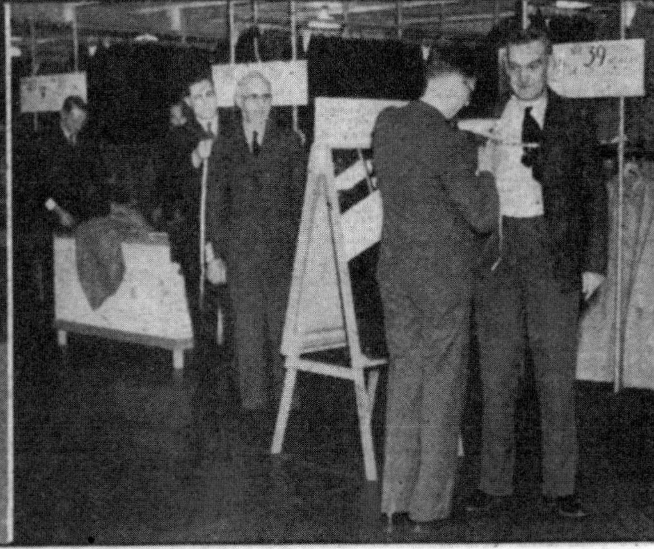

RETURN TO CIVVY STREET for thousands of Service men and women began on June 18, 1945. At a R.A.F. dispersal centre men about to be demobilized are seen (left) handing in their Service papers and receiving civilian identity cards, ration books and discharge papers. Released men (right) try on their new clothes. Each receives a suit, raincoat, hat or cap, pair of shoes, two pairs of socks, tie, shirt, two collars, collar-studs and cuff-links—or coupon value of 63. See article in this and facing page, also illus. page 191. *Photo, Sport & General*

—including himself—knew that was a lie. I looked round the room. Here we were, so many lucky dogs, getting out at last, and this was the great day !

There was not one face in that room which by any stretch of imagination could be called happy. We had been happy when we trooped in to join up, happy when they called us dimwits and gave us mountains of plates to wash and yards of floor to polish and threatened us with "jankers." But now that we were being granted our cherished freedom to cock a snook at Group Captains and above, to live where we like, say what we like, and do what we like, we were just simply depressed and a little lost. Maybe that's why the highest authorities in their great wisdom provided that refreshment-room. A cup of coffee is a great help at times. Or is it ?

Almost incessantly the loudspeaker on the wall kept announcing "Will Flight-Lieutenant J. B. Whathaveyou report to Post C immediately ?" and up would get another of us to climb the stairs. Smoothly but soullessly we passed through the machine which in half an hour or less transformed us from R.A.F. types into clearly recognizable merchants, house dwellers and men with umbrellas. An auburn-haired W.A.A.F. who has seen so many pilots file past that their appeal is less than nothing, took our little blue service and release books, removed a sheet or two, stamped something and with a bored, tired look, murmured, "Straight along on your left. Next, please." We moved on—a step nearer Civvy Street.

A DOCTOR—excuse me, a medical officer—looked at the book again, said, "Feeling all right, teeth all right; well, right you are," and passed us on. A sergeant took away some more of the book, a Ministry of Labour official, who, unlike her more R.A.F.-weary sisters of the W.A.A.F., could still summon a bright smile for us, gave us advice and an unemployment book. Someone else gave us ration cards and a coupon for two weeks' sweet ration and eight weeks' cheaper cigarettes.

Last place of call was on the welfare officer, a bright young flight-lieutenant with the D.F.C., who asked "Want any advice about civilian life, old chap ?" shook our hands warmly, and told us how we would get to Wembley for our civilian suits. We were loaded into a lorry, whisked to Wembley, and set loose in a giant hall filled with civilian clothes. We were measured swiftly by a tailor who stood by the entrance and informed us of our size number. He told me I was size 42, and from a rack so numbered I took an excellent blue flannel suit which fitted me almost perfectly.

My vanity, however, will never quite recover from the shock of beholding on the rack the completely inaccurate title, "Portly and Long." A raincoat, a pair of shoes, one shirt, two collars, "two pair of sox," cuff links, and one felt hat were given to us. There isn't a bowler hat in the place. While a wireless loudspeaker cheered us with Workers' Playtime, airmen skilfully packed our civvies into boxes labelled "High Explosive."

For the last time in our lives we visited N.A.A.F.I. for our sweets and cigarettes. Then, each with our box of clothing in hand, we walked as bravely as we could out into this strange, new, rather frightening world called Civvy Street.

DIARY OF WORLD EVENTS

SEPTEMBER 12, Wednesday

Malaya.—Surrender of Japanese forces in S.E. Asia signed at Singapore.

Siam.—First S.E.A.C. troops flown to Bangkok.

Belgium.—Field-Marshal Montgomery made "citizen of honour" of Brussels.

General.—Revealed that Field-Marshal von Busch died on July 17 in P.O.W. hospital in England.

SEPTEMBER 13, Thursday

New Guinea.—Japanese forces finally surrendered at Wewak.

Burma.—Surrender of Jap troops in Burma to British 12th Army signed at Rangoon.

Japan.—Imperial Military Headquarters formally abolished.

SEPTEMBER 14, Friday

Malaya.—Surrender of all Japanese forces in Malaya made at Kuala Lumpur.

Germany.—Right to form political parties granted to Germans in British occupation zone.

SEPTEMBER 15, Saturday

Japan.—Togo, former Foreign Minister, gave himself up to Americans.

Turkey.—H.M.S. Ajax and other British warships arrived at Istanbul on four days' visit.

Home Front.—Aircraft of Fighter Command flew over London in commemoration of greatest day in Battle of Britain.

SEPTEMBER 16, Sunday

China.—Japanese in Hongkong surrendered to British.

Home Front.—Thanksgiving celebrations throughout United Kingdom in commemoration of Battle of Britain.

SEPTEMBER 17, Monday

Germany.—Trial of 45 men and women guards at Belsen concentration camp opened at Luneburg.

Formosa.—Chinese national flag hoisted after 50 years of Jap occupation.

SEPTEMBER 18, Tuesday

Malaya.—First shipment of rubber left Singapore.

South Africa.—New graving-dock opened at Cape Town, second largest in the world.

SEPTEMBER 19, Wednesday

Home Front.—William Joyce ("Lord Haw-Haw") sentenced to death at Central Criminal Court.

Germany.—International traffic resumed on the Rhine from Duisburg to sea.

India.—Mr. Attlee and Lord Wavell broadcast on plans for self-government for India.

SEPTEMBER 20, Thursday

China.—British and American warships arrived at Shanghai.

Sea.—New British submarine Achates launched at Devonport.

SEPTEMBER 21, Friday

Czechoslovakia.—Field-Marshal Montgomery given great welcome in Prague.

SEPTEMBER 22, Saturday

Germany.—British Military Government announced that local and provincial councils of Germans were to be established immediately.

Sea.—Liner Ile de France handed back to French authorities at Southampton.

India.—Lord Wavell and Gen. Auchinleck invested with insignia of Chief Commander of U.S. Legion of Merit.

SEPTEMBER 23, Sunday

Germany.—Announced that further relaxation of non-fraternization orders would from October 1 permit British troops to enter German homes.

Denmark.—First Continental country declared free of mines, 2,000,000 having been lifted.

SEPTEMBER 24, Monday

Home Front.—Liner Mauretania berthed at Liverpool after record journey of 28,662 sea miles in 81 days 16 hours.

SEPTEMBER 25, Tuesday

Japan.—U.S. troops landed at Aomori S. terminus of rail ferry to Hokkaido.

Germany.—Proclamation to people affirmed details of subjugation to Allied control.

Home Front.—King and Queen inaugurated new Ladybower reservoir in Derbyshire.

General.—Ministry of Transport announced that ships from New Zealand and Australia to be diverted to avoid paying Panama Canal dues in dollars.

Flash-backs

1939

September 17. *Soviet troops entered Poland. H.M.S. Courageous (aircraft-carrier) torpedoed.*

1940

September 15. *Climax of Battle of Britain; 185 German aircraft shot down over S.E. England.*

1941

September 15. *Germans reached the suburbs of Leningrad.*

September 21. *Russians evacuated Kiev after 45 days' fighting.*

1942

September 16. *German troops broke into outskirts of Stalingrad.*

September 23. *Antananarivo, capital of Madagascar, captured by British troops.*

1943

September 16. *Australians captured Lae, in New Guinea.*

September 25. *Smolensk recaptured by troops of the Red Army.*

1944

September 14. *Soviet troops captured Praga, suburb of Warsaw on east bank of the Vistula.*

September 17. *1st Allied Airborne Army landed in Holland, at Eindhoven, Nijmegen and Arnhem.*

With Our Airmen Today

By CAPTAIN
NORMAN MACMILLAN
M.C., A.F.C.

September 15, 1945, was marked as a special commemoration of the victory of the Battle of Britain by the opening of R.A.F. air stations to the public for the first time since Empire Air Day of 1939. The anniversary occurred on a Saturday, and very large numbers of visitors entered the 90 aerodromes, which were open to them in England, Scotland, Wales, Northern Ireland and the Isle of Man, from 2.30 to 6 p.m. These air stations represented seven R.A.F. Commands in the following order: Flying Training 21, Transport 17, Bomber 16, Fighter 12, Technical Training 11, Coastal 10, Maintenance 3. (See illus. page 383.) That afternoon 25 squadrons of fighters and fighter-bombers of Fighter and Coastal Commands flew over London, the aircraft including Spitfires, Mustangs, Typhoons, Tempests, Beaufighters, Mosquitoes and Meteors. The fly-past was led by Group Captain Douglas Bader who commanded No. 242 Squadron, manned by Canadians and equipped with Hurricanes, during the crucial fighting over England in the summer and autumn of 1940.

Bader's Own Spirit Enabled Him to Get Back Into the Cockpit

Bader met with the accident that resulted in his amputations when flying as a young, and comparatively inexperienced, pilot in, I believe, an Armstrong-Whitworth Ajax. He pulled up in a climbing turn, the machine stalled, "fell out of his hands" and in the resulting crash something came back and crushed his feet. The outbreak of the war gave him the opportunity to get back into the R.A.F. via the Volunteer Reserve, and his own spirit enabled him to get back into the cockpit. A crash due to engine failure just after taking off during his early days on return to the Air Force would have put many a man into hospital, but in half an hour or so, after a mechanic had straightened out Bader's metal legs, the owner of them was in another cockpit again, and in the air.

On Sunday, September 16, contingents of workers from the aircraft industry, representatives of A.A. Command (including Home Guard), and of units of the Dominion and Allied Air Forces, and all Commands of the R.A.F., including men who fought in the Battle of Britain, marched from Wellington Barracks—where the famous Guards Chapel in its demolished state reminded one of the battle of the flying-bomb—through Birdcage Walk, St. George Street and Princes Street to the Service of Thanksgiving in Westminster Abbey.

New facts have been released about the Battle of Britain. In July 1940 Fighter Command had 640 aircraft available daily against which the Luftwaffe disposed in a great crescent from Brest to Amsterdam 1,200 long-range bombers, 1,100 twin and single-engined fighters, and 350 dive bombers, a total of 2,650 aircraft. British factories and repair shops provided Fighter Command with 130 aircraft a week at that time. In two weeks from August 8 nearly 300 British fighters were put out of action, 94 pilots were lost and 60 seriously wounded. From August 24 to September 6 the Command lost 103 pilots killed or missing, and 128 seriously wounded, from a total pilot strength of little more than 1,000, while 495 Hurricanes and Spitfires were lost or badly damaged. These losses exceeded the rates of replacement, and in the month of August Fighter Command received only some 250 newly-trained and untried pilots fresh from training schools to fill the gaps rent by the loss of about 300 experienced pilots killed or wounded. Many of the new men were not fit to take an immediate place in the battle.

If at that time the Luftwaffe had maintained its concentration of attack against the aerodromes of Fighter Command in South-East England, and against the aircraft factories, the outcome of the battle might have been the overwhelming of Fighter Command and the assault of sea and airborne landing craft carrying an invasion force. But, on September 7, 1940, the Luftwaffe made its first big daylight attack on the London docks, and by September 10 the phase of attack against the Fighter Command aerodromes had fully switched to the battle of London. That was the fatal mistake of the German generals—Goering, Kesselring, and Sperrle—who commanded the Air Fleets that faced Britain. Had they not switched their attack the stocks of reserve aircraft in the Aircraft Storage Units would have been depleted, and Britain's power of defence against the blows would have petered out. But after the assault switched on to London, Fighter Command began to recover, soon the fighter strength began to rise, and at the *end* of the Battle of Britain it was possible to say that Fighter Command was numerically stronger than when it entered it. So it can truly be said that the fortitude of the citizens of London was part of Britain's defence.

Fighter Command Airfields Had Improvised Ground Defences

In mid-July Fighter Command had 52 squadrons fit for operations; 25 with Hurricanes, 19 with Spitfires, six with Blenheims, and two, Nos. 141 and 264, with Defiants. Eight more squadrons were in existence, but not fit for operations. In August three more squadrons were operational, and one more was in training. No. 11 Group, protecting London, the Thames Estuary, and south-east England as far as Portsmouth and East Anglia, bore the brunt of the fighting and received reinforcements from other groups. No. 10 Group protected southern England from Portsmouth west, and South Wales. No. 12 Group protected the Midlands and East coast from Great Yarmouth to Scarborough, and No. 13 Group was responsible for the Tyne, Tees, Forth and Clyde areas and the Scottish east coast.

During the Battle of Britain Fighter Command's airfields were protected by an improvised ground defence system manned by ground gunners, who were the forerunners of the R.A.F. Regiment. Mostly they lacked training and were short of weapons. The newly-joined recruits were officered by middle-aged veterans of the First Great War. The ground defences of Eastchurch, to take one example, consisted of a few 20-mm. Hispano cannon-guns and old Lewis guns disposed to give a good arc of fire, with small sections of airmen armed with rifles in trenches to resist the airborne landings that never came. During the almost non-stop air-raid warning period these posts were manned 24 hours a day. Three thousand bombs (not including the uncountable incendiaries) fell on Eastchurch from August 1940 to March 1941, and there were frequent low-level machine-gun and cannon-gun attacks. One German bomb exploded the station's own bomb dump. The ground gunners and a few defence officers stuck to their jobs throughout, while the remainder of the personnel took cover. On another occasion enemy bomb splinters, perforating the aerodrome's siren, caused a prolonged all-clear signal while the raid continued.

Manston airfield in Kent was one of the bomber emergency fields on the east coast. Work on the runway began in June 1943, and the 3,000 yards long by 250 yards wide strip opened to traffic a few weeks before D-Day. In 1944 Manston flying control officers and staff brought in 41,865 aircraft, including 6,750 Spitfires, more than 4,000 Typhoons, Thunderbolts and Mustangs, 407 Flying Fortresses and 341 Lancasters. Radio-telephone conversations from the control tower sometimes used seven channels simultaneously. On January 13, 1945, between three and four in the afternoon, 64 Fortresses and 67 Mustangs landed safely. Part of the Arnhem force took off from Manston, and there Fido was first installed in April 1945. Altogether more than 100,000 landings were made at Manston airfield during the war.

300 R.A.F. FIGHTERS, led by Group-Capt. Douglas Bader, the legless pilot who was shot down and taken prisoner during the war, flew in faultless formation over St. Paul's during their 90-minutes "fly-past" on September 15, 1945, to commemorate the Battle of Britain. Survivors of "The Few" flew side-by-side with pilots who were still at school in the historic autumn of 1940. See story in page 377. *Photo, Keystone*

Below Decks in Britain's Aircraft Carriers

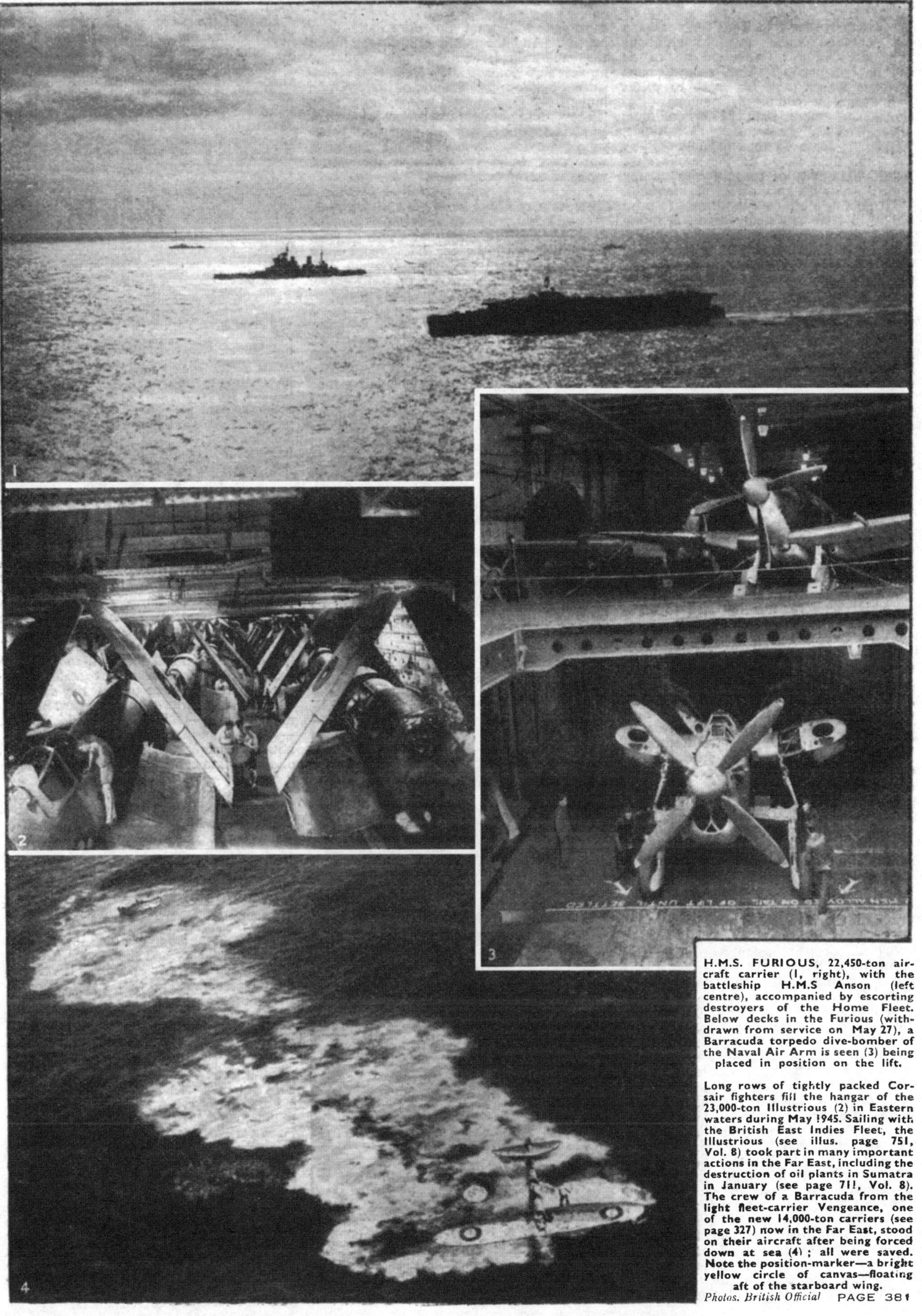

H.M.S. FURIOUS, 22,450-ton aircraft carrier (1, right), with the battleship H.M.S Anson (left centre), accompanied by escorting destroyers of the Home Fleet. Below decks in the Furious (withdrawn from service on May 27), a Barracuda torpedo dive-bomber of the Naval Air Arm is seen (3) being placed in position on the lift.

Long rows of tightly packed Corsair fighters fill the hangar of the 23,000-ton Illustrious (2) in Eastern waters during May 1945. Sailing with the British East Indies Fleet, the Illustrious (see illus. page 751, Vol. 8) took part in many important actions in the Far East, including the destruction of oil plants in Sumatra in January (see page 711, Vol. 8). The crew of a Barracuda from the light fleet-carrier Vengeance, one of the new 14,000-ton carriers (see page 327) now in the Far East, stood on their aircraft after being forced down at sea (4); all were saved. Note the position-marker—a bright yellow circle of canvas—floating aft of the starboard wing.

Photos. British Official

Editor's Postscript

A correspondent in The Times asks a question which must be bothering many of us: What are we to do with our gas-masks? That energetic and ingenious writer took his mask to pieces to find that it contained, "among other ingredients," more than 2½ oz. of pure rubber. "This," he went on to calculate, "represents some 70 tons per million," so that "the total issued to the public must contain thousands of tons of high quality rubber." Almost plaintively he inquires, "Is it nobody's business to attempt to salve this?" I have repeatedly drawn attention to the slackening-off of salvage collection since round about the middle of 1943, when the tide of war was turning in our favour. This falling-off, especially in the matter of bones and waste-paper, was largely the responsibility of housewives whose general optimism seems to have run away with them—and who, after so many years of regimentation, will blame them? But the gas-mask is another matter. Salvage in this connexion can only be inaugurated by the appropriate Government department. I for one have no fewer than five gas-masks at various places of residence and should be glad to be rid of them.

The long-standing good will between ourselves and the Norwegians, reinforced as a result of the War, is one of those things you just can't tabulate. But certain it is that the Norway of tomorrow will be even more Anglophile than ever; while we in our turn will be, if anything, more Norwegophile—if that's the word. I have long known of Norway's interest in our literature and was, therefore, not surprised to learn from The Bookseller the other day that English books were being imported into that country months before the actual liberation. Sponsored by the exiled Government in London, an agency was set up here early last autumn to buy English books on behalf of the Norwegian book trade, so that now Norway is receiving more books from us than any other country on the Continent. So delighted with their new treasures was one of Oslo's biggest booksellers that they made an elaborate window-display of them crowned with a large placard: "English Books—at last!" The stocks, calculated to last six months at pre-war rates of buying, sold out in exactly six weeks. The other day a Service reader wrote to me from near Salisbury to relate with what delight friends of his in Norway had received recent copies of The War Illustrated, first British periodicals they had seen for five years!

Coinciding, as if according to plan, with the end of the war against Japan, the Stationery Office has just published Part Two of SEAC Souvenir. Like its predecessor of a few months ago, it is edited by Major Frank Owen, one-time M.P. and well-known Fleet Street journalist who, for the past two years, has been doing a fine job for the troops in the Far East by producing Service magazines and news sheets. In Part One of this lively, well-illustrated threepenny production (in make-up deceptively like a weekly newspaper of the staider type) we had the now almost fabulous stories of Arakan and the sieges of Kohima and Imphal, of the turn of the tide when our men marched over Ledo's mountains to Myitkyina to re-open the road to China. This second part carries the battle forward across the Chindwin and the Irrawaddy to Mandalay and finally to Rangoon. Major Owen and his anonymous contributors have produced an indispensable source book (albeit of only 20 pages) on which all future historians of the Burma campaign will want to draw, and draw heavily. And the moral of it all—as far as the well-trained, well-equipped Japanese armies were concerned? Here is the considered opinion, presumably, of Major Owen himself. "They were beaten," he says. "They were beaten by better leadership, better weapons, better training and better supply services. Above all, the Japanese, who were going to dominate the world, were beaten by better men."

The ways of Officialdom grow, if anything, curiouser. The latest example to come to my knowledge concerns a member of what I had imagined to be our most-needed trade of the moment: a master builder. Of military age, this employer of considerable experience was called up with his group, as was expected, and given the job of—a member of the P.B.I. Latterly, however, things improved and he was employed on odd jobs, cleaning up bomb sites and blitzed premises. Three months ago he applied for his release, pointing out that he had a long waiting list of old clients crying out for repairs to their damaged property. But no release papers were forthcoming. Due for leave recently, he asked for and was granted a permit to carry out, by himself, repairs to his own home, part of which had been destroyed. As the job was one requiring more than a single pair of hands, a next-door neighbour and his family (also in the building trade) very obligingly offered their spare-time assistance. But here again Officialdom stepped in, this time with the order that if my builder-acquaintance accepted the services of his neighbours they must (in order to comply with "regulations") sleep under his roof and so qualify as his household!

On the obverse, as the numismatists say, I have just come across a case in which Officialdom may be credited with what certainly looks something like a brain-wave.

Maj.-Gen. E. P. NARES, C.B.E., M.C., who succeeded Gen. L. O. Lyne as Commander of the British troops in Berlin and British representative on the Allied Kommandatura on August 27, 1945. He formerly commanded the Second District in Italy. *Photo, Planet News*

The story is brief. Some months ago (I was informed) the officer in charge of Accounts at an important R.A.F. operational station was struggling with a small and overworked staff. Admittedly there had been a big "cut" in the personnel of the station, but the Accounts officer had considerable leeway to make up and still felt the need of more assistants. Unhappily, for a time—quite a time—the authorities didn't see it that way and turned down all his applications for increased staff. Then, without warning, instead of the five or six extra hands asked for there arrived a dozen or so! And the explanation? Not the usual one, I'm glad to say, for a few days later a communication was received from the Ministry explaining that it was not the intention to throw these men on the labour market as soon as the war ended but to give them as much practical experience as possible to fit them for clerical jobs in civil life when they became "demobbed."

Like countless others, I suppose, I have recently been pondering on Planning and asking myself if much of it isn't going to mean locking the stable-door after the mare has bolted. Sir Patrick Abercrombie's plan for a green-girdled London, clustered with new satellite towns, is the most ambitious scheme we have yet had, and even the most crusted of our Georgian die-hards would like to see something like it adopted. But what if the local authorities—whether because of vested interests or not—do not make full use of their powers under the Town Planning Act and allow our new (and old) towns to be defaced by ugly advertisements? The proprietors of the local cinema may obtain sanction to erect a theatre with a dignified frontage after the most approved Corinthian or Palladian models, and yet succeed in completely obscuring it with those monstrous cut-out advertisements which seem so exclusively (and needlessly garish) a feature of cinema publicity. This sort of thing, as well as ugly lettering on shop-fronts, the local authorities can veto—if they have a mind to. Not so long ago the Winchester town council requested a local shopkeeper to reduce in size the obtrusive lettering with which he had plastered his main frontage—and he did so. Electric signs—meaningless and appalling by daylight, however cheerfully they glow by night—will also need firm control.

Mr. Jack Lindsay, the poet-scholar and member of a famous Australian family which has never bothered itself overmuch about the stuffier conventions, has produced for the Pilot Press what must be the first definitive account of Britain's war-time revolution in the Arts—British Achievement in Art and Music. This is a superbly illustrated production, costing a bare half-crown, and providing for future historians a complete refutation of the theory that, apart from Poetry and the Drama, we are a thoroughly inartistic people. It is Mr. Lindsay's contention that Art in England has come to stay. "We have," he says "made an incalculable leap ahead, creating for the first time in England since folk-days a genuine mass-audience for drama, song, music . . . The British people, rising to meet the war emergency, have begun powerfully, if as yet in elementary form, to claim their cultural heritage. A cultural revolution has been initiated." I was particularly interested in Mr. Lindsay's theory that the so-called cultural revolution has been brought about, largely, because of what he describes as "a continual diffusion from the centre (C.E.M.A., now Arts Council of Great Britain, and other national or semi-national organizations) with continual spontaneous growth of local or regional activities." If we look back on our storied history we see that it has always been thus—that the Hour has not only produced the Man (as it did with Churchill) but also the rectifying circumstances.

In Britain Now: London Remembers 'The Few'

BATTLE OF BRITAIN was commemorated on September 15, 1945, by the opening to the public of 90 R.A.F. stations (see also pages 377 and 380). Among them was Hendon (above), home of British flying and wartime Transport Command station.

BRITISH P.O.W., returned by Sunderland flying-boat from the Far East (right), made their way through the cheering crowds at Poole, Dorset. Up to Sept. 22 almost 33,000 British and Indian released prisoners in S.E. Asia had sailed for home.

MERCHANT SEAMEN'S DAY, celebrated during London's Thanksgiving Week (Sept. 16-22) gave Londoners purchasing a 5s. National Savings Stamp a chance of a trip on D-Day landing craft (below). Farther up river—at Molesey Lock near Hampton Court—over 400 of the lifeboats that saved our Merchant Seamen's lives during the war, awaited disposal to private buyers (above left).

The Durhams Guard of Honour for Eisenhower

9th BATTALION DURHAM LIGHT INFANTRY provided the guard of honour for General Eisenhower when he attended the Allied Control Commission in Berlin on September 11, 1945. At present attached to the 7th Armoured Division, the Regiment saw distinguished service in many battlefields, including the Western Desert, Salerno, Burma (the sieges of Kohima and Imphal), and in the D-Day landings. They were the first Allied infantry to enter Belgium and Holland and among the first to enter the Reich. *Photo, Planet News*

Printed in England and published every alternate Friday by the Proprietors, THE AMALGAMATED PRESS, LTD., The Fleetway House, Farringdon Street, London, E.C.4. Registered for transmission by Canadian Magazine Post. Sole Agents for Australia and New Zealand: Messrs. Gordon & Gotch, Ltd.; and for South Africa: Central News Agency, Ltd.—October 12, 1945. S.S. *Editorial Address*: JOHN CARPENTER HOUSE WHITEFRIARS LONDON, E.C.4.

Vol 9 The War Illustrated No 218

SIXPENCE and AFTERWARDS OCTOBER 26, 1945

ABOARD A BRITISH MINESWEEPER the "Area Cleared" signal has been flashed, and with the sinker free of the ship's side the dan-buoy—used to mark a swept channel—is lowered from the deck. This fleet sweeper, known as a "danner," is operating in East Coast waters in the van of our fishing fleets. Both in home and in distant waters the end of the war has, if anything, intensified the hazardous work of our minesweepers and their crews, whose stupendous peacetime task is described in pages 392-393. *Photo, British Official*

Edited by Sir John Hammerton

NO. 219 WILL BE PUBLISHED FRIDAY, NOVEMBER 9

GAPS IN FLOODED WALCHEREN'S DYKES were closed by Mulberry Harbour sections, towed there from Britain in early September 1945. The panorama (1) shows the breach blasted in the original dyke at Rammekens (extreme left, middle distance) by 12,000-lb. bombs of the R.A.F. (see illus. in page 466, Vol. 8) and work in progress on the new dyke (right). Pontoon, which formed part of a Mulberry pier not required for the Normandy landings, being attached to a tug at Southampton for towing to Holland (2). Late September gales wrought havoc with the work of the Dutch engineers; at Nolle, west of Flushing, the only dyke repaired was smashed. Concrete floats—known as "beetles" in Mulberry pier-construction—were swept away by the high tides (3).

Photos, Topical Press

Are We in Japan for Long?

By MAJ.-GENERAL
SIR CHARLES GWYNN
K.C.B., D.S.O.

After her war with Russia in 1904–05 Japan's position became immensely strong, and if she had played her cards with good sense her future was assured. She had, to an exceptional degree, all the defensible advantages of an island kingdom; for the immensity of the ocean which protected her shores from invasion also ensured that her navy could always fight a hostile fleet in her home waters, where proximity to its bases would more than compensate for disparity in numerical strength. Russia was the only Power that could seriously menace her security; but she was in a position to prevent Russia developing naval strength in the Pacific, and her army with short lines of sea communication was capable of resisting any renewed attempts Russia might make to encroach on China.

Economically, Japan's position was weakened by her inability to produce food sufficient for her requirements; but, on the other hand, geographically she was better placed to develop the enormous resources of China than any other Power. Everything pointed to the expediency of cultivating friendly relations with China and giving her a lead in developing her economic potential. But Japan was in a hurry and preferred to use force; counting, presumably, on the strength of her position to defy intervention by the western world.

Britain and U.S.A. Were Not Prepared for Effort Demanded

Whether economic sanctions at the time of her occupation of Manchuria or at the beginning of the China "incident" would have brought Japan to her senses is questionable, but it is certain that armed intervention would have demanded an effort for which neither Britain nor the U.S.A. was prepared, and in which their lack of advanced bases would have been a perhaps decisive handicap. If the two great western Powers had been willing to embark on a long war in which their immense productive power could be developed, no doubt victory would eventually have been achieved. But in view of the strength of Japan's army and the favourable conditions under which her navy would operate, the magnitude of the effort required should not be underrated.

When, however, Japan forced the issue and deliberately provoked war with the western Powers her rapid initial conquests entailed the sacrifice of her strong defensive position. Her army could not be employed as a concentrated force to defend outlying strongholds, and her navy, in order to secure communications with them, was compelled to emerge from its advantageous position in home waters. Her ingenious and far-sighted development of aircraft carriers merely provoked the answer which American productive strength was able to provide. Too late, having sacrificed the greater part of her navy, Japan sought to re-establish her position in home waters, but by that time developments of sea-air warfare on which she had relied to control sea communications had turned decisively against her and enabled America to secure the bases from which air power could undermine the foundations of her former security.

Not even Germany has given such an example of a nation deliberately sacrificing an apparently unassailable position or having less prospects of ever restoring it. In the case of Germany, withdrawal of armies of occupation might obviously lead to the recovery of much of her strong position and aggressive potentialities; but with Japan the situation is very different, for sea-air power can maintain a stranglehold on her.

Prolonged or complete occupation of the country would seem therefore to be unnecessary, for sea-air power provides an instrument of control from outside both on aggressive tendencies and on the economic life of the country. Clearly Japan, however much she might develop her internal military strength or strengthen her defences against invasion, would not be able to embark on any offensive enterprises except by a seaborne operation which could have no possibility of success, particularly if America retains bases in Okinawa and other islands comparatively adjacent to Japan. Moreover, shipping on which Japan's economic future depends would equally be at the mercy of sea-air power.

Presumably it is for these reasons that General MacArthur evidently does not consider a large army of occupation or its prolonged stay in the country will be necessary. It may, of course, be advisable to maintain at least token forces in some of her large cities, and possibly to move columns of Allied troops through the more remote parts of the country in order to bring home to the people the completeness of their defeat. War criminals should be rounded up; and in that, insistence on the fullest co-operation of the Japanese Government would seem to be of primary importance.

There can be no question of a soft peace, particularly in that matter, but on the other hand a nation that has an excessive population and has lost all power of aggressive action cannot be kept in impossible economic conditions, and the case for giving her assistance may be even stronger than in Germany. There is less possibility of concessions being abused; secret or veiled war industries would lead nowhere, nor would quasi-military organizations be a danger except to Japan's internal stability.

If, as I believe from the military standpoint, Japan as a source of danger to peace has received a knock-out blow from which, under the new conditions, there is no possibility of recovery, the effects of her four years' occupation of the possessions of the western Powers appear likely to have a disturbing influence. In Burma, fortunately, the completeness of the Japanese defeat and the hardships endured by the Burmese during the occupation have combined to produce a sense of liberation, and there should be sufficient troops available to ensure a reasonably rapid restoration of good order. In a country where dacoity had so often given trouble and nationalistic sentiments are strong, the presence of large numbers of highly trained troops provide an adequate safeguard against hot-headed attempts to exploit the disturbance caused by the war. In Malaya and the Straits Settlements there is even less reason to expect trouble, whatever changes in the system of administration it may be considered advisable to carry out. The repatriation of Japanese troops and the discovery of war criminals among them are the chief immediate problems.

Minimum of Force to be Used in Carrying Out an Invidious Task

The situation in Indo-China and Indonesia is much more complicated, owing to the facts that neither French nor Dutch troops were available in sufficient force to resume occupation of their respective possessions, and that it fell to British forces to accept the Japanese surrender and to rescue prisoners of war. Unfortunately the vacuum created by the disappearance of Japanese authority could not be filled by British troops. The resentment against European control, fostered by the Japanese during the occupation, was therefore able to express itself.

Once again British and Indian troops have been compelled to intervene in the interests of law and order where they have neither political authority nor are in adequate strength to do so with immediate effect. Moreover, the situation requires us to use the minimum of force. That it should have been necessary to call on the surrendered Japanese troops to assist in the maintenance of order is a regrettable if unavoidable complication. But it shows that our forces in the Far East do not yet exceed requirements.

IN TOKYO A U.S. military policeman stood beside a Japanese, helping him to direct the capital's tramway traffic which was resumed within a few days of the Allied occupation. Heaviest damage was in the residential and factory areas, where large numbers of the population were reported to be living in improvised timber shacks.
Photo, Associated Press

Change-Over of Roles at Recaptured Singapore

RELEASED AUSTRALIAN PRISONERS watched their former gaolers filling in defence trenches (top) which the Aussies themselves had been forced to dig in sweltering sunshine during captivity. The Bishop of Singapore conducted a service for them in Changi Prison courtyard (bottom), when some 120 were confirmed. Last batch of Singapore prisoners and internees, including several hundred men of the British 18th Division—" last in " as prisoners of war—left the port aboard the Polish motor-ship Sobieski on September 27, 1945.

Photos, British Official

British Army of the Rhine where Nazis Trained

AT LUNEBURG, scene of the German surrender on May 4, 1945 (see pages 79-82), and former famous Wehrmacht training-ground, troops of the Royal Artillery with the British Army of the Rhine attended an open-air course on tactics (1) in late September. Marking the site of the surrender, a temporary wooden plaque (2) was erected, later to be replaced by a permanent monument of stone. The plaque was on Sept. 24 reported to have been defaced by local Nazis.

After the surrender hundreds of buses from all over Germany were rounded up in the area. Used by the enemy in their retreat, some are being dismantled, others employed in transporting our troops. A Cockney wit renamed the destination of this Berlin vehicle (3). On Luneburg's outskirts is a small well-tended British military cemetery (4) where lie a hundred of our brave dead.

 Photos, Keystone

C.-IN-C. OF THE BRITISH PACIFIC FLEET, Admiral Sir Bruce Fraser, G.C.B., K.B.E., (about to enter his car), leaving H.M. Australian destroyer Warramunga which, on September 10, 1945, had brought him to Yokohama from his flagship, the 35,000-ton battleship H.M.S. Duke of York, moored in Tokyo Bay. Fifteen days later—while visiting General Chiang Kai-shek at Chungking—the Admiral disclosed that Britain is to keep a small Fleet in the Far East. " Britain is a small country depending on ships and sea trade. We shall need a small Fleet out here to keep it going," he declared. At present it consists of three battleships, four carriers, nine cruisers and 32 destroyers. Our naval bases in the Pacific would not be increased beyond the present ones at Singapore, Hongkong and in Australia.

Photo, British Official

Great Deeds of Little Ships

By

FRANCIS E. McMURTRIE

In this country little has been heard of the war in the Adriatic. Yet the rapid progress of the Yugoslav armies in 1944 would not have been possible had it not been for the invaluable aid rendered by the Royal Navy. As the result of a series of small craft actions, control of the channels between the numerous islands that fringe the Dalmatian coast was wrested from the Germans. With their sea communications cut, enemy garrisons in the coastal strip were forced to surrender to the Yugoslavs.

One of the hardest-fought engagements of this half-forgotten campaign was that known locally as "the Battle of Vir," in October 1943. Lasting six hours, this night action is claimed to have exceeded in length any corresponding operation undertaken by Coastal Forces. At that time a small force of British coastal craft was using the island of Ist (Italian name, Isto), in the outer fringe of the Dalmatian archipelago, as an advanced base from which to harry enemy traffic between Fiume, Zara and smaller ports. This force comprised a motor gunboat and three motor torpedo boats.

M.G.B. 662, commanded by the senior officer of the little force (Lieut.-Commander T. J. Bligh, R.N.V.R.), was armed with a power-operated two-pounder pom-pom on the forecastle, with a pair of Vickers ·303 machine-guns on each wing of the bridge, flanked on either side by a 20-mm. Oerlikon. Amidships was mounted a pair of Oerlikons, while right aft was the biggest gun of all, a six-pounder. M.T.B. 634, 637 and 638 each carried two 18-in. torpedo tubes, six Oerlikons and four ·5 machine-guns.

OERLIKONS Blazed Away as Tracer Bullets Pierced the Dark Night

On the night of October 11–12, the four boats were lying, for the second night in succession, in wait for German convoys, which usually tried to get through under cover of darkness. They were concealed from enemy observation by the shadow of Vir Island, a useful strategical point about 15 miles north-west of Zara. The Chief Motor Mechanic of one of the m.t.bs, who was going up on deck to get some fresh air after a spell in the engine-room, described to me how he was greeted with a sudden burst of gunfire from somewhere close by. As the boat started to move, tracer bullets of various colours could be seen approaching. An enemy vessel then appeared about 100 yards away, but by that time the C.M.M. was diving down the engine-room hatch!

Overhead, the Oerlikons were blazing away, making the deck shake, and the steady thump-thump of the pom-pom could be heard amidst the din. Above all sounded the louder note of the motor gunboat's six-pounder, as the flotilla dashed to and fro firing into the convoy. Nobody in the C.M.M.'s boat was hit, but a man in the m.g.b. lost the number of his mess. In M.T.B. 634 one of the engines failed, and the other gave trouble, the engine-room being full of fumes, but those below carried on in smoke helmets and the boat continued in action. One of her torpedoes scored a hit on an enemy vessel, the other running ashore on Vir Island.

Meanwhile, the ships of the convoy had scattered, but one by one were hunted down and destroyed. Until the moon rose it was difficult to keep touch, and star shell proved an inadequate substitute. For a time all would become quiet; then a two-pounder would go off with a bang, echoing through the surrounding islands. "There they are!" someone would shout, and the chase would be resumed.

M.T.B. 637 had the task of finishing off a couple of F-lighters which had run ashore, badly damaged, one of them being on fire. The motor torpedo boat lay off the shore and neatly placed a torpedo in each, causing them to blow up with a terrific explosion, throwing up a huge column of smoke and debris. Evidently they were loaded with explosives. Ultimately no more enemy craft could be found, so the four boats returned to Ist, well satisfied with their night's work. There was a danger of German aircraft appearing with the dawn. This fear was almost realized when some Beaufighters dived on the flotilla under the impression that it was an enemy force, but they found out their mistake just in time.

As the four vessels entered harbour at the base, each was wearing a broom at the yardarm, in token of having swept the seas of the enemy for the time being. Later it was ascertained that 13 enemy vessels had been destroyed, including at least half-a-dozen of the very useful F-lighters. These were Diesel-engined vessels, 150 ft. in length, built of steel and reinforced concrete, giving good protection. Each of them mounted one 88-mm. gun, besides 40 and 20-mm. pieces. On paper, this well-armed convoy should have had the better of it, but the fine fighting spirit of the attackers carried the day, or rather night.

CRAFT'S Short Life May End in Being Scrapped or Superseded

Though exceptional in duration and for the number of enemy vessels sunk, this affair may be regarded as typical of the many actions in which Coastal Forces were concerned in the Adriatic. In somewhat different circumstances they exercised the same mastery over the situation as did the British naval forces under Hoste in 1811. In those days the French, who had occupied most of the territories of the Republic of Venice, were driven out of their foothold on the Dalmatian coast as the Germans were in 1943–44. Geography remaining the same, history is apt to follow a similar pattern.

Coastal craft have a short life. If they escape destruction in action or by accident, they soon wear out and are scrapped or superseded by improved types. Already many of those which played a brilliant part in winning the war have gone, or are being offered for sale to the public without their engines.

Some of our surplus ships are being acquired by Allied Navies. The latest to go are the destroyers Quilliam, Savage and Scorpion, all built during the war, which have been purchased by the Royal Netherland Navy. One of them has already arrived in Dutch waters, and has been renamed Piet Hein, after the celebrated admiral who captured a Spanish treasure fleet and ultimately fell in action off Dunkirk in 1629. Further transfers to the Dutch flag are expected to include a cruiser and an aircraft carrier, names of which have still to be announced.

H.M.S. Geranium, one of the numerous corvettes of the "Flower" class which proved so valuable in the early days of the Battle of the Atlantic, has arrived at Copenhagen on being taken over by the Royal Danish Navy. She has been renamed Thetis. H.M.S. Annan and Monnow, two frigates of the "River" class which were lent to the Royal Canadian Navy during the past two years, have also gone to the Danish fleet, so sadly depleted as a result of the German invasion. A corvette of the "Castle" type is expected to follow.

According to messages from Chungking, there is some prospect of the Chinese Navy's losses being made good by the transfer of ships from the British and United States Navies. Nothing appears to have been settled, but the suggestion is that a cruiser or two, with destroyers, escort vessels and minesweepers, might be acquired from the Allied surplus of tonnage.

The effect of this in practice would be to give China a completely new navy, for with the exception of a couple of small cruisers which were in the hands of the Nanking "quisling" government, the only vessels in Chinese hands were a collection of river gunboats. It is possible, moreover, that some of the smaller Japanese ships which have been surrendered may be handed over to China instead of being scrapped.

GERMAN TORPEDO-RECOVERY LAUNCHES at London's East India Docks in October 1945 with their crews. Twenty feet long, with black hulls and yellow funnels for identification purposes, they were part of the fleet of specialized vessels which the Nazis still had afloat when they surrendered. "It was a fine Navy," declared a British officer. "They had a ship for every job."

Hard-Worked British Minesweepers Still Busy—

Even after the end of hostilities our minesweepers are still gallantly engaged—now in the gigantic task of clearing the waters round the coasts of Western Europe as well as those of the Far East. What they have already accomplished and how much remains to be done, in making the seas safe for traffic, is told here. See facing page, and 385; also page 204.

THE war may be over—but not for British minesweepers; their work goes on. They are still busy—and will be for another year or more—bringing to a triumphant conclusion one of the greatest minesweeping feats of modern times—the non-stop clearance of every port in north-west Europe, from Brest to the Kattegat.

In August of this year a hundred British minesweepers made a start on clearing the vast defensive mine-barriers laid round our coasts to protect coastwise shipping. A hundred thousand moored mines were laid in these waters during the war; in addition there are hundreds of enemy ground mines—magnetic and acoustic or a combination of both—which lie outside the war channels and were not swept during hostilities. Between V Day and mid-August over 2,000 mines were swept—often at the rate of 300 to 350 a week.

The mines in these fields, which cost a total of some £25,000,000, are being cut and sunk, for they have small value as scrap. The TNT with which they are filled would be worth little more than a shilling a pound and would not repay the cost and labour of the salvage. Besides the 11 flotillas at present engaged, 22 special minesweepers have been built to operate in shallow waters, and since sweeping will be restricted during the winter months the main effort will not be made till next summer. In minesweeping operations both in home and foreign waters, 1,350 sweepers, manned by 50,000 officers and men, are employed. Of the personnel 90 per cent are temporary wartime reserve.

Instruments Still on Secret List

A word or two about the actual operation of sweeping. When an area known to be mined is swept, the sweepers adopt an echelon formation (see diagram in opposite page), so that only the leading ship, that of the Senior Officer, enters unswept waters. The others follow, each leaving a safety overlap, so that the ship herself is in water already swept by the ship ahead. Last of all comes the "danner," laying dan-buoys to mark the area. When one length has been completed, the flotilla turns and repeats the sweep in the opposite direction, the process continuing until the whole area has been cleared. The British Navy has without doubt the finest fleet of minesweepers in the world. These craft are not converted trawlers; they are vessels fitted with numerous still-secret instruments able to cope with the varied assortment of sea-mines thrown into the sea-lanes by German aircraft, U-boats and E-boats.

Much progress has been made in cleaning up the North Sea and English Channel. It is in the southern waters of the North Sea that our minesweeping patrols are encountering the most trouble, for here German minelaying aircraft, spotted by British patrols, often jettisoned their mines and swooped towards the nearest Luftwaffe base.

As regards drifting mines sighted in the English Channel, Irish Sea, Eastern Atlantic, and Denmark straits, an Admiralty statement issued on September 27, 1945, pointed out that these are British mines which are designed to become automatically harmless on breaking from their moorings. The risk to shipping of damage from drifting mines in these areas is, therefore, very small.

In home waters, incidentally, one of the most intensive (and expensive) minesweeping operations of the war was carried out in the Firth of Clyde—over an area of 1,000 square miles—in a quest for moored magnetic mines laid by the U-boat 218 on April 18, 1945. At the end of July, three out of 15 mines were still unaccounted for, despite an intensive search made by 26 minesweepers with the co-operation of the U-boat's commander.

AFTER the German surrender, full information about all minefields sown around the British Isles during the war was given to the Admiralty by German naval experts. The Germans stated that some of their latest mines could neither be swept nor recovered without exploding when moved. But British naval divers, searching the bottom of Bremen harbour in pitch darkness, working by a sense of touch alone, removed the firing mechanisms from three of them. Elsewhere, at sea, there was at first some difficulty because German sweeps are designed to surface only British mines, while our sweeps work the other way round. Modifications were made and the difficulty overcome.

One of the most thickly-mined areas in the world is the Kattegat and here British and German minesweepers, sweeping together, are clearing their respective mines from this vital stretch of water separating Denmark and Sweden. One minefield alone hereabouts—between the Skae and Swedish waters—is some 250 square miles in area. As a start, safe channels about 1,300 miles long are being cleared. Gradually these will be widened to three miles, and, as every channel has to be swept between ten and twenty times, the minesweepers engaged will have to steam approximately a quarter of a million miles. After that there will still be check sweeps to cover the whole area. In this work some 160 German minesweepers with personnel numbering over 5,000, are co-operating with a British force. They fly no ensign and receive their orders from the British Naval Mission in Copenhagen.

Although negotiations are now in progress to make minesweeping an international obligation on all maritime nations, the clearance of north-west Europe's ports fell exclusively to British minesweepers. They began their task shortly after D-Day at Cherbourg, which had been used as a dumping ground for every type of German mine. During September 1944 approaches to the River Seine, Le Havre, Calais, Dieppe and Boulogne were swept, frequently under fire from heavy coastal batteries.

Under Guns of Shore Batteries

With the capture of Antwerp on September 4, the centre of interest moved up to the Nore Command, where sweepers had already begun the task of running a channel across the southern North Sea from the South Falls to the entrance of the Scheldt. The Scheldt was forced by British minesweepers on November 2 and 3, under the noses of shore batteries; by November 26 the narrow unbuoyed waters were declared open. Nine days later the first sizable convoy of 19 big ships berthed at Antwerp (see p. 521, Vol. 8). The arduous clearance of the docks in Antwerp itself took from October 16 to December 4, under heavy bombardment by V1s and V2s.

IN Italy, U.S. naval blimps (airships) are co-operating with Royal Navy minesweepers in clearing enemy minefields in the northern Adriatic and the Gulf of Genoa. In the blimp is a British naval officer who acts as aerial mine-spotter to the minesweeping Commander. The blimps carry out reconnaissance flights and plot on the charts any mines they detect, besides dropping smoke floats above the target.

In the Far East the task of our minesweeping flotillas is far from enviable. A Senior Naval Officer, speaking at Singapore at the end of September 1945, declared that the seas of the East Indies will not be entirely safe for shipping for many years. Minesweepers of the British East Indies Fleet are opening up areas from Java to Indo-China so that a sea passage will be available for supplies and the evacuation of liberated prisoners. Known safe channels are being permanently buoyed.

In Malaya a passage has already been cleared from Port Swettenham to Singapore—a distance of 210 miles. Here as elsewhere, the sweepers' task has been complicated by the fact that the Japanese minefields appear to have been laid a long time ago, and that many mines have obviously parted from their moorings and drifted away.

WHEN EXPLODING MINES WITH HAND GRENADES, the latter are discharged from the side of the minesweeper. Preparing for action, a seaman (left) primes his Mills grenade which is projected through the horizontal tube (right); the heavy armour-plated guard attached to the taffrail provides protection should a grenade explode prematurely: a possibility by no means remote. These photographs were taken during clearance of the defensive mine-barrier laid round our East Coast from northernmost Scotland to the Thames Estuary. *Photos, Associated Press*

—Ridding the Troubled Seas of Hidden Death

LOWERING THE OROPESA FLOAT from a Fleet minesweeper (1) during a double sweep in a German-laid minefield off our East Coast. In the water (2) it is being checked to ensure its correct running. Towed by the minesweeper, it supports the wire which cuts the mooring cables of the mines.

SWEEP IN PROGRESS, illustrated diagrammatically above, showing a single Oropesa sweep to starboard, the vessels sailing in echelon formation. In the wake of the last float is the "danner," which lays dan-buoys to mark the area swept and thus opened to navigation (see page 385). The Oropesa is named after the minesweeper by which it was first tried out, in 1918. Released mines can be exploded or sunk by rifle-fire.

ACOUSTIC HAMMER being lowered (3) over the side. Highly sensitive, this mechanism is towed below the minesweeper; by means of sound vibrations set up within the hammer, acoustic mines are exploded at a safe distance.

Photos, Associated Press. Diagram, British Official

How the Captives Fared in Sumatra and Siam

REPATRIATION from South-East Asia began on August 18, 1945. It was organized by R.A.P.W.I. (Recovery of Allied Prisoners of War and Internees), which by October 10 had evacuated over 3,500 Allied nationals from Sumatra and 18,500 from Siam. At Pakan Baroe, Sumatra, British and Australian troops were found in primitive buildings (1), more than 150 to each shack. After liberation they strolled in the compound (2).

At Bangkok, Siam's capital (occupied September 12), the R.A.F. ensign was flown from the airfield control-tower (3) and saluted by (among others) two subalterns of the Siamese Air Force (in slacks) who assisted R.A.F. Transport Command in the evacuation. Here also Allied ex-P.O.W.—some on crutches—waited their turn to embark in transport planes for Rangoon.

Photos, British Official, Sport & General

Tokyo Settles Down Under Allied Occupation

AT YOKOSUKA, famous naval base in Tokyo Bay, 25 miles distant from the capital, ratings from H.M. Australian destroyers Napier and Nizam, attached to the British Landing Forces, performed guard duties: the Changing of the Guard ceremony (1). Note the Shinto shrine in the background. Tokyo woman (2) solved the problem of what to do with baby when mother goes to work—by strapping it to her back as she cleaned windows at the Azubi barracks taken over by U.S. units.

Taking no chances, American troops searched everyone they met in Tokyo streets—even two British nuns just released from internment (3). Common sight in Japan's capital, following the surrender, were hordes of downcast soldiers awaiting demobilization orders (4). Outside Hirohito's palace, subjects of the Emperor (who visited General MacArthur at the latter's H.Q. on Sept. 27) bowed in homage (5). Many Japanese are reported to have committed hara-kiri here.

Photos, Associated Press, Fox, Sport & General, L.N.A.

Now It Can Be Told!

MAN-MADE ISLANDS AND FLOATING BRIDGES

BRITISH scientists have found a way of increasing the natural surface tension of water, making it technically possible to build a mid-Atlantic aerodrome or a floating cross-channel bridge, it was disclosed by the Admiralty in September 1945. This latest discovery in engineering-on-water began when an inventor's brain-wave sent him motor-cycling at 50 m.p.h. along a tarpaulin stretched over a river ford. The new discovery has been sponsored and developed by the Royal Navy, and brings dramatic dreams within the realms of actuality.

Ordinary tension will support a needle on the water's surface. By putting a flexible synthetic surface on the sea, and by increasing the tension about 400,000 times, it has been found possible to support heavy lorries and aircraft in mid-ocean. One practical result of the discovery is the production of man-made "islands"—composed of hundreds of hexagonal buoyancy cans—"islands" which can be built to any shape or length required, and which can be easily dismantled, transported and reassembled. Another, which has already stood up to the severe practical tests of war, is the "Swiss roll," a floating pier that can be rolled up, carried on board ship and later rolled out again from ship to shore. This pier is nearly twenty times as light as a Bailey bridge of equal length, yet it will carry a nine-ton lorry.

INVENTOR of these new devices is Mr. R. M. Hamilton, of Victoria Street, London, who served at the beginning of war as a Petty Officer in the Royal Naval Patrol Service. He is an inventor by profession. Co-operating on the involved mathematical calculations required was Mr. J. S. Herbert, Housemaster at Eton College. "Further developments from the original discovery are being made," Mr. Hamilton said, "but for a time their nature must remain secret."

It was in 1944 that the first practical result was employed—the "Swiss Roll" pier, used in the Normandy invasion. In this flexible canvas-and-wood jetty, a tension of 18 to 30 tons is applied to any length stretching from ship to beach and the result is that a laden lorry can be driven ashore in safety over the sea. Some 2,700 feet of "Swiss Roll" were in continual use at the invasion harbour at Arromanches in spite of the appalling weather that, unluckily, was encountered there.

The Navy's latest experiments, only recently concluded, have been with a further development of the same fundamental principle, the "Lily" floating airstrip. Given its name because of its resemblance to a carpet of lily leaves on a pond, "Lily" is a very different proposition to "Swiss Roll." It consists of numbers of buoyancy cans with hexagonal surfaces, so linked together that they "give" in a controlled manner to the motion of the sea from any direction, yet remain sufficiently rigid to take the weight of a heavy aircraft. Whereas in "Swiss Roll" tension is applied externally, "Lily's" hexagonal surfaces, when linked together, create their own tension.

The Navy's experimental airstrip is the smallest on which practical tests could be undertaken, 520 ft. long and 60 ft. across. On this an aircraft, laden to 9,000 pounds, has been landed and has taken off again A strip of this size can be assembled by 40 men in one hour. At present the cans are only six feet across and 30 inches deep, but their size could be scaled-up to take greatly increased weight.

The whole surface of "Lily" is flexible so that it will not break up, but this flexibility is controlled by the use of underwater dampers

"With Straws in Your Hair"

The inventor claims that with the latest dampers more than three tons pressure is required to move the surface at all, and that "Lily" will remain flat in waves up to 36 ft. from crest to crest. The dream of Atlantic aerodromes has hitherto been unattainable because it has not been possible to build large enough stormproof flat-surface structures. Modern transport aircraft would need a carrier or a strip twice the length of the Queen Elizabeth, largest ship in the world. Such a floating structure has hitherto been impractical. The Navy's new "seadrome" can be transported in ships and assembled anywhere. With the present size buoyancy can, a "Lily" 2,500 feet long, could be transported in three merchant ships.

"Lily's" possibilities for bridge-building are underlined by those responsible for its development. "To mention a cross-Channel bridge immediately places you with straws in your hair," said Mr. Herbert, the mathematician, "but we can say that it would be possible to build a floating bridge 22 miles long that would not break up in a sea."

LANDING ON "LILY," the novel floating airstrip described here, a Swordfish torpedo-bomber of the Naval Air Arm has neatly touched down. *Photo, British Official*

UNROLLING THE "SWISS ROLL," the floating roadway or pier which was used so successfully at Arromanches during the landings on the Normandy beaches. Testing "Lily," the floating airstrip, in the Scottish loch of Lamlash (left), a photograph taken during the original experiments with this remarkable British invention. *Photos, British Official*

SINGAPORE RE-OCCUPATION PLANNED IN 1942

PLANS for the restoration of Singapore Naval Base, begun immediately after the surrender in February 1942 (see page 514, Vol. 5), were by September 1945 being put into operation by the Royal Navy. For over three years a secret planning staff in the Admiralty prepared rehabilitation details for the inevitable return, working out an administration blue print and the material support requirements for Rear-Admiral John Anthony Vere Morse, C.B., C.B.E., D.S.O., secretly appointed to restore, when the time came, the Naval Base (see story in page 666, Vol. 8).

Floating docks up to 50,000 tons in size were built months ago in India, ready for towing to Malaya to supplement port facilities. In case the monster King George V dry dock at Singapore, one of the world's largest, had been damaged, a complete spare caisson was put under construction.

A "Mormonster" (mobile naval radio station), complete with office equipment and a power supply, manned by more than 100 ratings and ready to land within 24 hours of occupation, was prepared.

Oil fuel tanks with floating pipelines through which tankers could discharge off-shore were also designed, and water-purification plants constructed in readiness. To maintain landing craft, a self-contained Mobile Landing Craft Defence Base, complete with every facility, including laundry, canteen, and cinema, was built up in India.

Mobile Naval Air Bases were planned, and cranes and dockyard machinery, tools, locomotives and repair stores ordered. Huts to accommodate personnel were shipped to India for the day when Singapore surrendered again. Even a mobile bakery and refrigerators for N.A.A.F.I. canteens were ordered. To provide electricity, should shore power installations be destroyed, two frigates were fitted in the U.K. as floating power stations. More than 500 special repair ratings and a battalion of Royal Marine Engineers were sent to the East Indies Station, ready to move in and restore port facilities as soon as Singapore was freed.

All rehabilitation plans were eventually co-ordinated by a specially created Admiralty Committee known as "Sefar"—Singapore Extemporized Facilities After Recapture—which acts as a liaison with requirements in Singapore. When the surrender of Singapore took place on September 4, 1945, Rear-Admiral J. A. V. Morse—now Flag Officer, Malaya—and his staff of experts in port restoration were ready to enter the city the following day (see illus. page 357).

14th ARMY'S 20 TONS OF MAIL A DAY

SIXTY field post-offices, served from special forward airstrips, daily delivered 500,000 letters and parcels, weighing 20 tons, to 14th Army troops in Burma. When the great push south began army post-offices had to revise their methods of distribution. All 14th Army mail was sent to Imphal, where it was loaded into Dakotas and carried to forward airstrips. There, field post-office representatives took delivery and handed back mail for the United Kingdom.

Whenever units because of their remote positions were unable to collect their mail from these forward airstrips it was packed in special containers and dropped to them by other aircraft. Sometimes, in the monsoon, airstrips became unserviceable. The army post then employed mules and porters to carry it along hill tracks and through jungle; small boats sailed up chaungs with it. Many of the casualties, among troops who were being evacuated by light aircraft, came out carrying a mailbag on their knees. The army post managed to maintain almost a day-to-day service from Imphal to Rangoon. Letters from the troops went daily to all parts of the world, and letters from remote English villages were delivered to forward troops in the jungle in six days.

THE NIGHT THAT LONDON'S TOWER WAS BOMBED

HITLER made the night of April 16, 1941, the most memorable in the history of the Tower of London "ceremony of the keys." Nothing has ever been permitted to stop this pageant which, since the days of the Tudors, has marched like a ghost through the centuries.

Throughout the war the ceremony of locking the gates went on night after night, sometimes with bombs falling and fires all round. "Only a direct hit would have stopped the locking of those gates," said Chief Warder Arthur Cook, Military Medallist of the First Great War, on September 4, 1945. It nearly happened on that April night.

The war had shorn the ceremony of most of its traditional colour. The escort of Guardsmen were not wearing scarlet uniforms and bearskins, but khaki and steel helmets. The chief warders and the watchman wore scarlet coats, but in place of their customary Tudor hats they had steel helmets.

The Alert sounded at 9.3 p.m. The raid was one of the worst up to then. At 9.53 the chief warder (the late Mr. A. Smoker) left the Byward Tower to join the escort waiting near the Traitors' Gate. Punctually to the second the little parade moved off.

"As the escort approached the Byward Tower, I, as watchman for the night, joined the party," said Chief Warder Cook. "When we were midway between the Byward and Middle Tower arches I heard an aircraft diving before releasing its bombs. The Guards went stolidly on.

"The guard had just presented arms to the keys when there was a crash. Something red-hot flashed straight through the escort, struck the ground in front, sending up sparks, and disappeared. Next moment we were all sprawling on the ground. I was bowled head over heels into the doorway of the Middle Tower. I got up and helped the Chief Warder to his feet. He said, to my surprise, somewhat testily, 'Where's the escort?'

"I answered, 'In just as undignified a position as you were.' 'Come on,' said he, 'get them together and let us get on with it.' Rifles were picked up, the escort fell in, the guard took up their position, and off we went on our way . . .

"The Conqueror's Tower never looked grander," concluded Cook, "than it did on that terrible night. It stood out proud and haughty and seemed to defy those unseen engines of destruction in the skies."

PLASTIC ARMOUR, a wartime innovation, details of which are still on the secret list, was successfully employed on our merchant ships against air attack. Above, it is being bolted over the well-deck of a vessel in the West India Docks, London. Gun-nests (left) on the ship's bridge were similarly reinforced.

Photos, British Official

Our Swimming Tanks Took Them by Surprise!

Only now can the story be told of the part played on D-Day, and subsequently, by the D.D. Tanks and those who crewed them. The utmost secrecy was preserved as to their existence; production was carried on behind sealed doors, trials and training were screened from public gaze. But all these elaborate precautions brought a rich reward. See also illus. pages 400–401.

WITH the full telling of the story of D-Day has been released one of the most astonishing exploits of the war—the invention of the Swimming Tank and the part it played in what at one moment seemed the most hazardous crisis in the history of warfare.

For many years scientists of all nations have striven to produce an amphibious tank. The Germans tried submersibility and when the war ended were within a few months of producing a method by which Tiger tanks could crawl along the bed of a river with air supplied to the crew and engine by long pipes. Other countries tried attaching pontoons to the sides of tanks to make them float. A variety of more fantastic and less practical methods was tried out but none with great success.

The Duplex-Drive tank was officially born in 1941 when Mr. Nicholas Straussler, the inventor, was given War Office authority to experiment with a light tank. The principle of flotation employed by him was remarkably simple. It consisted of a collapsible canvas screen fitted to the hull of a tank and raised or lowered at will. When erected, the screen completely surrounded that part of the tank above the tracks and, based on the principle of displacement, enabled the tank to float. At the touch of a lever the screen collapsed to lie like a skirt about the hull. Power came from a propeller at the rear turned by the main driving shaft.

Maj-Gen. SIR PERCY C. S. HOBART, K.B.E., C.B., D.S.O., 59-year-old tank pioneer. Though retired from the Army, he was recalled by Field-Marshal Montgomery to train special troops needed for the D.D. tanks.
Photo, British Official

STRAUSSLER's tank had two main advantages over previous amphibious inventions. It was easy to operate and could go into action as a normal tank within a few seconds of its tracks touching dry ground and the driver lowering his canvas screen. It was extraordinarily seaworthy and, contrary to original opinions, quite capable of surviving all but the highest seas.

There is always a tendency to distrust simplicity, and this, coupled with the unconventionality of the D.D. tank, caused many a heated argument in Service conferences before the invasion. To begin with, many people simply refused to believe that the thing would work. It was the C.I.G.S., Sir Alan Brooke, advised by his specialized tank experts, who gave the D.D. tank its chance. Production was started at once.

An assortment of famous regiments was selected to be trained in the operation of D.D. tanks. They were placed under the command of Maj.-Gen. Sir Percy Hobart, commander of the 79th Armoured Division in which was centralized the control and development of specialized armour and trainees in the British Army.

Monsters Moving Along Under Water

A mixed British and Canadian team of instructors was assembled and set to work in different parts of the country. Two lakes were requisitioned, which proved extremely inconvenient to the adjacent landowners, who by their co-operation made a valuable contribution to the war effort. In these lakes the preliminary training of crews was completed. Here, under the patient eyes of experienced instructors, men acquired confidence in these floating chariots. They learned that when the tank hatches were closed and they were moving along under water with only a canvas screen to save them from sinking, this apparently slender protection did indeed keep them safe and very few accidents occurred. It is a striking compliment to the instructional staff as well as to the tank itself that in more than 30,000 individual tank launches both in smooth lake water and in open seas, in good climatic conditions and in bad Channel weather, only one fatal casualty occurred during training.

A very real life-saver was the Davis Escape Apparatus used by submarine crews and specially modified by the Royal Naval Diving Establishment. A special cistern was built in which old tank hulls were sunk and every crew taught how to escape to the surface from a submerged closed-down tank. Statistics have shown furthermore that this apparatus saved many lives on the ever-memorable June 6, 1944.

AS training progressed great strides were made in technical and tactical development. During the spring of 1944, in Scottish waters as well as in the Solent, training of crews was completed on the recently produced D.D. Sherman. They learned to navigate landwards from 10,000 yards out at sea, for it was planned to launch the tanks from landing craft sufficiently far from shore to prevent observation. This would eliminate the vulnerable moment of disembarkation when tanks and craft are almost stationary and present a perfect target to coastal guns.

The greatest secrecy had been maintained throughout as to the very existence of these tanks. Production had been behind locked doors, and trials and training in areas screened from the public gaze. The words "D.D. tanks" themselves were a code name and used with the greatest care during the months of planning.

Movement to the marshalling areas went on throughout April and May 1944, and by the end of that month the assaulting troops were all in their respective camps. Five British regiments drove their D.D. tanks on to landing craft ready to sail for France. These were 4/7th Dragoon Guards, 13/18th Hussars, Nottinghamshire Yeomanry, 1st Canadian Hussars, and the Fort Garry Horse. Three U.S. battalions had also been trained and were embarked in the West Country.

On the evening of June 5, the Combined Service Commanders, Admiral Ramsay, F.-M. (then General) Montgomery and Air Marshal Leigh-Mallory made what was probably the gravest decision of the war. The weather report was bad, verging on the impossible. It had already caused a delay of 24 hours; further postponement might be fatal. Despite the possibility that seas might be too high for D.D. tanks and the lighter types of landing craft, the decision was made to invade the following day.

AMERICAN VERSION, after landing, with its canvas "walls" lowered. How this type of amphibious tank assisted in D-Day landings is told here. *Photo, Associated Press*

In the event, the D.D. tanks and their crews fully justified the confidence placed in them. One regiment, the 13/18th Hussars, launching their tanks some 5,000 yards from the shore, brought in 33 out of their total of 40. Other regiments fared less well but on the whole casualties were low and if the seas had not been exceptionally rough, would have been much lower.

Small Arms Fire Would Sink Them

It had always been hoped that the D.D. device had been kept secret and that the Germans would take the tanks for nothing more than a fleet of small boats, probably containing infantry. Everything points to this having happened. The D.D. tank is of course very vulnerable to fire, which if accurate will sink it. There was no single case reported of much small arms fire, either from land or sea, being directed at D.D. tanks. On one beach where infantry were meeting stiff opposition the German defenders held up their hands in surprised surrender the moment a number of these "monsters" emerged from the sea, shook off their skirts and opened fire.

SO it came about that the D.D. tanks together with other special assault devices landed on D-Day broke through Hitler's concrete coast defences and opened the way for penetration deep into Normandy.

Field-Marshal Montgomery had broken the accepted principle of Combined Operations by landing tanks in the van of his army. We know now how right was his decision and how well placed the confidence that he and other senior officers had in the special tanks.

Two more regiments were later trained in operating D.D. tanks. These were the Staffordshire Yeomanry, who took part in the assault on South Beveland in October 1944, and the 44th Bn. Royal Tank Regiment who, together with the Staffordshire Yeomanry, operated in the Rhine crossing. The last use of D.D. tanks in Germany was when a squadron of the Staffordshire Yeomanry successfully stormed the River Elbe on April 29, 1945. But their use has not been restricted to North-West Europe. In the final operations in Italy they were used with success, manned by the 7th Hussars, and but for the collapse of Japan would have been used in the Far East by the 25th Dragoons.

Photos, British Official

Navy at Hongkong Rounds-up Jap Suicide Crews

H.M. Destroyers Whirlwind and Quadrant braved unswept minefields and found 150 explosive Jap "suicide" motor-boats at their base in Picnic Bay, where the captured crews were assembled (bottom). The port was entered on August 30, 1945, by a British Naval force under Rear-Admiral C. H. J. Harcourt, C.B., C.B.E., who on that date was appointed C.-in-C. Hongkong. His flagship, the 30,000-ton aircraft carrier H.M.S. Indomitable (top), rode at anchor in Victoria Bay.

These Floating Chariots Meant Doom to Germany—

The astonishing story of Britain's secret amphibious tanks is told in page 398. Here they are seen afloat and ashore. On the banks of the Rhine (1) Shermans are inflated from huge bottles of compressed air; completely surrounded by its canvas screen, a tank glides into the river (2), to be driven across by its twin propellers. Stores and ammunition were towed on a floating sledge (3). A Valentine leaves the ramp of a L.C.T. and enters the sea 3,000 yards from shore (4).

— As They Carried Assault Troops Deep into Europe

During the final operations in Italy, a Sherman crosses the River Adige (5). With collapsible screens down (6), at Lauenburg, after swimming the Elbe ; the twin propellers have been raised to avoid contact with the ground. Driver Barrett, Canadian Armoured Corps (7), having his escape apparatus adjusted by an instructor before driving into the sea for a practice swim. Only one fatal casualty occurred during training, in more than 30,000 individual tank launches in all weathers.

Tokyo As It Is and As It Was

Amidst wide areas of rubble only a few modern steel structures remain intact in the industrial section of the Japanese capital, along the Sumida River (above). At the left is part of the same district of Tokyo before the Allied raids. The city's first bombing was an attack on April 18, 1942, by Mitchell bombers from the U.S. aircraft carrier Hornet, led by General Doolittle (see pages 154–155, Vol. 7). Heavy incendiary and high-explosive raids by Super-Fortresses began on November 24, 1944, rising in fury in the spring and summer of 1945. In the later stages it was increased by British and U.S. carrier-borne aircraft, continuing until the Japanese capitulation on August 14.

Photos, Keystone, Sport & General

The Fateful Road to Rome

By

HAMILTON FYFE

When you have toothache there are periods when the pain is acute, almost unbearable ; at other times you suffer just a dull, grumbling discomfort. So it is in war. While the Germans overran France, Belgium, and Holland, our ordeal was severe, and it was scarcely less so when our expeditions to Greece and Crete failed so lamentably. During the winter of 1943-44 we were afflicted by disappointment about progress in Italy which became a constant nagging ache.

What was the cause of this ? Why did we miss what Mr. Christopher Buckley in his book, Road to Rome (Hodder and Stoughton, 12s. 6d.), calls the "great opportunity" created by our swift success in Sicily, our landings in Italy, and the collapse of Italian resistance ? Why in the "race for positions," the winning of which promised "immense advantages to whichever side should be quickest to seize them," were the enemy allowed to forestall us, "to take the initiative almost everywhere," and garrison with their own troops the regions formerly controlled by Italian soldiers ?

To answer these queries fully is not yet possible. "One cannot know," Mr. Buckley says, "all the circumstances which resulted in the bright promise of the spring and summer being dissipated in the winter shambles around Ortona and Cassino." But one thing is "abundantly clear." We had not enough men for the job. We made the same mistake which Lloyd George denounced so bitterly in 1917 when he delivered his "too little and too late" oration. So "when the hour of opportunity struck, the British and Americans did not possess the necessary forces with which to exploit it."

Kept Short of Men, Ships and Guns

For this "grave strategic error," Mr. Buckley, who followed the campaign as a war reporter, declines to blame Mr. Churchill. He was forced by the pressure of his Allies to "whittle away the original grand conception of Mediterranean victory. Left to himself, he would have followed up our initial successes of the spring and summer with every man, ship and gun that was available." Instead, our commanders in Italy were kept short of men, ships and guns. The Quebec Conference had decided on the invasion of Europe through Normandy in June 1944, and the "build-up" for this was begun in autumn 1943. The consequence was, in Mr. Buckley's words, that on the Italian battlefields "too many died."

Fortunately we had enough aircraft to save the situation at Salerno, where the first landing nearly met disaster. So sure were the Germans of accomplishing another Dunkirk, by driving our troops into the sea, that they announced on their radio the start of evacuation by "demoralized" Americans. But Air Chief Marshal Tedder put everything he had into a determined effort to break up the German formations and smash the base from which they were attacking. This effort was completely successful ; the danger at Salerno was over. We had a foothold in Italy, the invasion could go ahead. It had been touch-and-go, but we went.

The other landing later on at Anzio was a failure. The idea was to put ashore a force that could raid Rome. But, instead of rushing the raiders towards the city as quickly as possible, Gen. Maitland Wilson waited to "consolidate," as military text-books advised, and prepared to meet a German counter-attack. The operation, declares Mr. Buckley, was muffed by "timidity, pusillanimity and excessive concentration upon safety-first principles." That is a heavy indictment. It is framed by a responsible man who is not only a prominent journalist but a student of war. "Routine had to be followed," he writes. Will the conduct of commanders who preferred routine to swift, imaginative action be inquired into ?

The politicians also come in for censure in this connexion. The Anzio landing was a political move, Mr. Buckley asserts, and quotes Mr. Churchill's "burst of irritable candour" in the House of Commons when he told M.P.s : "We had to attack the Germans somewhere, unless we were to sit still and watch the Russians do all the fighting." Political moves are invariably disastrous in war. The soldiers will agree with Mr. Buckley that "there were more profitable places in southern Europe in which to fight the Germans than the Italian peninsula."

Feeble-Wit Gave in to Mussolini

I don't want to leave the impression that his book consists entirely of military criticism and accounts of operations. It is full also of information about Italy and the Italians, about the way the British soldier comported himself among them, about personalities of the hour. Mr. Buckley admired intensely Field-Marshal Montgomery's "crystal clarity and simplicity" in discussing military operations with war correspondents. His three governing principles he stated in this way :

> Never act until everything is ready.
> Never give any commander or any unit a task beyond their capacity.
> Never tolerate failure.

Of King Victor Emmanuel the book takes a poor view. By all accounts he is a feeble-wit who gave in to Mussolini, as weak men always give way to bullies. Why "influential elements in Britain" supported him, as they supported the Greek king, Mr. Buckley cannot understand. Nor can he quite fathom the reasons for the arrogance shown by some sections of the Italian people after their surrender. "They felt themselves absolved by a stroke of the pen from all responsibility for having made unprovoked war upon their neighbours," and at the same time they simply seemed to forget that they had for twenty years "passively accepted tyranny, culminating in eight years' raucous support of an aggressive and belligerent foreign policy." Italian soldiers gave themselves up grinning and glad to be prisoners of war. Those who were on the beaches when our troops landed offered to assist in unloading stores and appeared to expect a tip for their services.

> I do not suppose that in the history of the world there has ever been a case of an invading army being met by its opponents on the shores of their native land with a touching of caps and requests to "Carry your bag, sir ?"

ITALIAN WELCOME for 8th Army men entering Maida, Calabria, in September 1943, was emphasized by the display of British and U.S. flags, and greetings in English. An account of the campaign is reviewed here. *Photo, British Official*

There were examples, however, of less accommodating disposition among the Italians, especially hotel-keepers. They had to be taught to behave reasonably, not to refuse rooms out of spite or greed, not to overcharge beyond a certain limit. Soldiers were robbed unmercifully by shopkeepers. In Naples especially prices soared to fantastic levels. The city was dead when our troops entered it. Scarcely a shop was open, and those which were had almost nothing to sell. But their windows soon began to be filled again, and they played an ingenious game. They kept back most of their wares until scarcity had created an eager demand for anything they had to sell. Then they added gradually to their exhibited stock and pushed up the prices.

Our Men Gave Away Their Rations

Neither the Americans nor our men bore them any resentment. They were just mad to buy something, anything, scent, stockings, wrist-watches, toys for their children, fruit and wine for themselves. The British soldiers often gave away their rations to hungry Italians. They were kindly and sympathetic in all human relations. But Mr. Buckley calls them "scientific rather than emotional" in their approach to what they must do in battle. They knew "the job had got to be cleaned up before we can go home." They felt no animosity, indulged in no heroics. "The enemy was merely 'Jerry' or 'the Ities,' regarded respectively with grudging admiration or more than half humorous contempt," and "this dispassionate quality in the British soldier was his strength." Like everyone else who has ever campaigned with them, Mr. Buckley considers our "other ranks" and those from the rest of the Commonwealth the salt of the earth.

About the officers, and in particular those of high rank, the author is less enthusiastic. He is sarcastic about our clumsiness in letting Mussolini be rescued from captivity. "The British showed their customary embarrassment when faced with the prospective custody of one of their national enemies." It seems to have been thought that the Duce did not any longer matter a hoot. That was a foolish miscalculation. When the Germans rescued him and planted him down in Northern Italy with a sham Government, Fascism acquired a fresh lease of life which prolonged the war in that theatre.

An equal lack of imagination was shown when news of Mussolini's fall from power was radioed to the Italian people. Rumours had circulated, there was an atmosphere of expectancy. The British would give them the whole story. Well, the news bulletin began twenty minutes late. It maundered on about small engagements, and places put out of bounds, then it simply stated that Mussolini had resigned and Badoglio had succeeded him.

The people, listening intently, could have been worked up to a joyful sense of relief and hopefulness. As it was, they were flattened out. And the British officer responsible could not understand why Mr. Buckley attacked him so furiously. The value of "psychological warfare" had never been taught him, and the officer had not intelligence enough to discover it for himself.

In the Low Countries Now War's Tumult is Over

ONE OF FIFTY THOUSAND church bells looted by the Nazis from occupied countries for smelting and later found by the Allies at Hamburg (see page 148), this fine Dutch specimen (1) is being admired by a British soldier.

South of The Hague, German P.O.W., ordered to clear Nazi mines, blew up the dyke "by accident"—flooding vast areas (2). During the Canadian advance from Arnhem in April 1945, Royal Engineers and Canadian engineers built two temporary bridges (3) while under heavy fire; replacing the famous old bridge (background), these were named Simonds Bridge and Foulkes Bridge after Lt.-Gen. G. G. Simonds, commanding Canadian forces in Holland, and Lt.-Gen. C. Foulkes, 1st Canadian Corps.

German P.O.W. and Dutch collaborators (4) dug up the bodies of murdered patriots buried in the sand dunes. On the Dutch frontier was this reminder (5) for our forces.

Photos, British Official, Pictorial Press

Britain's Front-Line Mayors Keep a Calais Date

CELEBRATING THE FIRST ANNIVERSARY OF CALAIS' FREEDOM, the Mayors of Britain's "Front-Line" towns of Canterbury, Dover and Folkestone, on October 2, 1945, visited the French port whence German batteries had shelled our Southern coast. A Nazi gun they inspected (1) had its barrel split: right to left, Alderman F. C. Lefevre (Canterbury); a British officer acting as guide; Councillor W. J. Pudney (Dover); Alderman A. Castle (Folkestone). The party at the Town Hall (2), and at the British cemetery (3).

Photos, Associated Press

More Bones of Contention in Central Europe!

A problem-area of Europe long before the War, Teschen—rich coalmining district between Czechoslovakia and Poland—is claimed by both Poles and Czechs. The importance of the strategic town and duchy is explained, and the background story of the tug-of-war told, specially for "The War Illustrated," by HENRY BAERLEIN, recognized authority on Central European affairs.

A GOOD deal was heard after the First Great War of Teschen, and most people heard of it then for the first time. But this ancient duchy of some 450 square miles had for centuries been an apple of discord between the Czechs and the Poles. Originally ruled by the Piast Princes of Poland, it came under Czech rule in 1292, and was finally united to the Bohemian Crown in 1335. In common with the rest of Bohemia and Moravia, this Silesian region came under the domination of Austria for three hundred years. During that time the racial struggle was between Czechs and Germans, for practically no Poles were to be found in the duchy before 1848.

After 1848 the population began to change. Polish priests and teachers coming from Galicia were supported by the Austrian authorities in their work of making Teschen to all intents Polish, for this was a good weapon against the Czechs. By the end of the 19th century the district had become highly industrialized; the mines, for instance, giving employment to large numbers of men who migrated from Galicia, and the struggle for supremacy between these Poles and the Czechs became intensified.

At the end of the war in 1918, both Poland and the liberated Czechoslovak State claimed Teschen. Strategically it is of great importance, forming as it does the eastern part of the Moravian Gap. It is also the watershed between two great river systems—those of the Polish Vistula and the Austrian Danube. It is a crossroads of railway routes from north to south, from Berlin and Prague to Bratislava and Budapest, as well as from Moscow and Kiev to Brno and Vienna. It is also on the main route from Bohemia and Moravia to Slovakia by way of the Pass of Jablunka. But perhaps the most important consideration for the liberated Czechoslovakia was the possession of the coalmines, on which the heavy industries of the newly formed Republic mainly depended.

AT the Versailles Peace Conference the question of Teschen was considered in accordance with the Austrian census of 1910. This had been based upon "language of intercourse" and not upon "mother tongue." It gave the Poles a percentage-population of 54·85 per cent, the Czechs having 27·11 per cent and the Germans 18·04 per cent. The total population now numbered 426,370. Of that total, 101,138 had no rights of citizenship, as they were more or less migrating labour of Polish nationality, whose introduction the Austrians, true to their principle of "divide and rule," had encouraged in order to control the Czechs.

If the whole duchy had been given to Poland it would have caused the Czechs to lose some 100,000 of their compatriots, while the railway route joining the western and the eastern territories of the Republic would have been cut—an alternative line through the mountains could only be constructed at vast expense—and, furthermore, the Czechs would have been deprived of the Karwina coal basin, which to them is vital. If the Poles had lost the entire duchy it would have meant the loss of some 230,000 Poles and native Silesians and the coalmines. But Poland possesses other coal areas of a similar nature and of a very much larger coal output, so that for her the Teschen mines had not the same extreme value as they had for Czechoslovakia.

Greeted by Riots and Strikes

It was decided that there should be a partition of the duchy. In the closing period of the First Great War, Masaryk and Paderewski met in the United States and endeavoured to settle the matter in amicable discussion. This method, however, did not find favour in Europe, where the Poles summoned to their Parliament representatives from the duchy, to which the Czechs replied by sending troops to occupy Oderburg, in January 1919. Thereupon the Great Powers, fearing further trouble, intervened and decided, in September 1919, to hold plebiscites under the auspices of the principal allies. When the Commission arrived in the following January it was greeted by riots and strikes, so the plebiscite method was discarded and Czechs and Poles requested arbitration by a Council of Ambassadors.

On July 28, 1920, the issue was decided, was duly ratified by both countries, and became a sacred bond between them. The greater part of the territory, including the town, went to Poland, the western portion with the coalfields and a suburb of the town going to Czechoslovakia. It is improbable that any better solution could have been achieved by international arbitration, but the Poles were not satisfied and later declared that if they had not been engaged in war with Soviet Russia they would never have accepted this settlement.

TESCHEN, central European town and duchy on the banks of the Olsa, tributary of the Oder, claimed by both Poland and Czechoslovakia.

By the Treaty of Warsaw, signed in April 1925, the conditions of the minorities left on both sides of the frontier were arranged. It must be admitted that the Poles in Czechoslovakia derived great benefit from the social legislation, land reform and other measures which made Czechoslovakia the most advanced democracy in Central Europe. But this did not cause the Polish authorities to forget their grievance; and when in 1938 it became probable that Czechoslovakia would have to make territorial concessions to Germany, the Polish Foreign Minister, Colonel Beck, thought the appropriate moment had come for an ultimatum. The demand for Teschen by Poland at the Munich Conference was a stab in the back for Czechoslovakia, made at a time when she was unable to defend herself in spite of her military preparedness. Teschen became Polish, Beck making it clear that his policy was guided by expediency. His joy lasted for a year; then his own country was ravaged by the Nazis.

THROUGHOUT the Second Great War the Czechs and the Poles fought and died as allies. Beck's reputation in his own country has suffered a final eclipse, while that of Benes was never brighter. We can therefore hope with some confidence that reason will now prevail and that the pledge of friendship made between the two exiled Governments in London in November 1940 will form the basis of a new order in Central Europe and in a settlement of the Teschen question.

When in June of this year Marshal Rola-Zymierski, C.-in-C. of the Polish Army, entered Teschen the Czechs showed admirable restraint. Their Premier, M. Fierlinger, went to Moscow, where he had been Ambassador for seven years, to enter into negotiations with the Polish Government at the request of Russia. He pointed out that the Teschen district is an indispensable part of the Czech economic system, and that without its coal the great Czechoslovak industrial centre to the south-west of it could not be maintained.

Central European politics present many difficult problems. They can be solved only by good will and the realization of the impracticibility of full satisfaction to every member of the community where historic, ethnic, geographic, economic and strategic claims are inextricably interwoven. It will be a splendid feather in Russia's cap if she can settle this problem between her two Slav kinsmen in such a manner that no sense of grievance remains on either side

CZECH PREMIER, M. ZDENEK FIERLINGER (right), and his wife, with members of the Czechoslovak Government, were greeted by M. Molotov, Soviet Commissar for Foreign Affairs, when they arrived in Moscow in June 1945 to discuss, among other problems, the future of Teschen, whose industrial importance is explained in this page. *Photo, Pictorial Press*

Our King Sees Ships that Brought Us Victory

ON HIS FIRST PEACETIME VISIT TO HIS NAVY, H.M. The King, accompanied by the Queen and Princess Margaret, inspected the Home Fleet in the Firth of Forth on September 28, 1945. The Royal party was received by Admiral Sir Henry Moore, K.C.B., Commander-in-Chief of the Home Fleet, in his flagship, the Rodney. Among the ships visited was the 9,100-ton cruiser Birmingham, on whose forecastle our photograph shows the King, with the Queen and Princess in the background. *Photo, G.P.U.*

Kirkby Explosion Heroes Awarded George Medals

Mr. M. V. ROWLING

Mr. W. J. PANTON

Mr. J. S. MURDOCH

Mr. W. E. DENNY

Fireman R. D. FORBES

Fireman W. TOPPING

AWARDS for bravery by civilian workers during explosions at the Royal Ordnance Factory at Kirkby, Nottinghamshire, during the night of September 15, 1944, were announced in the London Gazette of September 18, 1945. The first explosion occurred during the filling of highly dangerous ammunition. While bombs and ammunition continued to explode in the wreckage, girl workers who had escaped from the burning building ran back to bring out injured comrades. They ceased their rescue endeavours only when ordered to take instant shelter, which they did in the nick of time, for immediately afterwards another explosion occurred, wreaking even worse havoc and endangering still more lives.

After the assistant superintendent, Mr. W. E. Denny, had withdrawn everyone from the building, a pile of bombs, crushed in their wooden crates beneath the fallen roof, was seen to be on fire; and these were beyond reach of the firemen's hoses. The fire was gaining and, had it taken hold, the consequences would have been disastrous over a wide area. Mr. Denny entered the building alone and, having found a way of attacking the flames, explained his plan to the leading fireman, Mr. Ronald D. Forbes, and fireman William Topping. Both volunteered without hesitation, and the three contrived to extinguish the blaze ; they were awarded the George Medal. Other recipients of the award included Mr. M. V. Rowling and Mr. J. S. Murdoch, shop managers, and Mr. W. J. Panton, foreman.

The factory Superintendent, Mr. Gale, was awarded the O.B.E. ; though on leave, he at once returned and organized the salvage task without incurring a single casualty. Our photographs show the converted tank (above) with which bomb clusters were removed to safety, and (below) a view of the damaged areas showing bomb clusters under the wreckage.

Photos, British Official

I Was There! Eye Witness Stories of the War and After

We Toiled 17 Hours a Day in Siamese Jungle

Goaded by Japanese task-masters to help build the Burma-Siam railway was the fate of many who fell into enemy hands at Singapore in 1942. The Daily Mail Pacific Bureau Correspondent sent this dispatch, including the story told to him by Lieut. P. A. D. Jones, on Sept. 6, 1945.

A TALL, gaunt Australian bowed to me when I entered a prison camp near Singapore Docks today, then, recovering himself, was so embarrassed that he could not speak for a minute. "It is a little trick they taught us," he said. "It will take us some time to get rid of it." We were standing in a long room where 70 men, all Australians, were lying or sitting on low wooden bunks. Until a few days ago every time a Japanese guard or orderly entered that hut all had to stand up and bow.

Some of the men were as thin as those I saw in the Nazi horror camps, and many were suffering from beri-beri and chronic malaria. Most of them were survivors of the dreadful Siam jungle camps where the fiendish Japanese took delight in beating and humiliating our men as they toiled at building the Burma-Siam railway, toiled till they fell dead from half a dozen fearful diseases and sicknesses. From dozens of the stories I listened to in this camp today I have selected one—that of Lieut. P. A. D. Jones, of Smethwick, Staffordshire, regimental No. 98857. He said:

I was captured in Singapore the day it fell, February 15, 1942. For the first 48 hours the Japs left us to ourselves. Then they ordered us to march out to Changi, now the Jap show camp. They separated all the Indians from the whites. Of the 52,000 Indians taken here, there are now only 15,000 left. We can only guess at the fate of the rest.

At Changi, just outside Singapore, we soon settled down to camp life—a life made unbearable at the outset by Japanese cruelties. After about eight months I was moved. After many weary weeks, during which we were kicked and beaten by our guards, we arrived at Sungkrai camp in Siam. Our working hours were from dawn to dark, roughly 17 hours a day.

If three of us failed to lift a felled tree, then Japanese guards would make two men do it somehow. When an elephant got lazy and jibbed at moving a tree trunk, the Japanese would put us on to it, then laugh at us. We strained ourselves.. They called us their elephant power. Guards would often set on us for no reason and beat us with their rifles or bars of iron. During the building of a bridge over a gorge Jap guards struck at several of our unfortunate comrades until they fell off and were killed.

Several Australians took Japanese guards with them to their deaths off that bridge. Finally, we as a party were worked out. The Japanese could not get any more out of us, and work on the railway was slipping again. So they marched us all the way back to Singapore—without 500 of our comrades whom we had buried.

RICKSHAW MAN IN TOKYO tries to bargain with a U.S. war correspondent. Fares have doubled since the Occupation, and rickshaws are scarce. *Photo, British Combine*

Smiling Men of Nagoya Plan a Jap Come-Back

Third largest city in Japan, Nagoya is ready to "get going" again—largely at the expense of Allied troops. How the battered city's business men are reacting to the Occupation is described by Arthur La Bern, of The Evening Standard, in this story dispatched on October 1, 1945.

THE Kanko hotel—catering exclusively for foreigners—was empty save for an American journalist and myself. We sat alone in a large dining-room surrounded by tables gleaming with silver, cutlery, white cloths and fine glassware. There were ten little Jap waitresses in gay pantaloons waiting on our one table. When we entered the dining-room they bowed their heads, nearly touching the luxurious crimson carpet. Steaks, eggs, lobster and trout were plentiful. Fruit was served with every meal.

I was looking down on the ruins of Nagoya when four smooth-faced bespectacled Japs bowed, and presented cards. They were the President and members of the Nagoya Chamber of Commerce and Research Bureau. They smiled, showing gold and silver fillings in their teeth. They were at my service, they said. Any information I required they would gladly supply. Any questions, however frank, would be answered to the best of their ability.

I had a three-hour discussion with them and gathered that their ulterior motive was to put Nagoya back on the peacetime map. Nagoya, the third largest city in Japan, was the centre of porcelain ware, gaily coloured textiles, fans, clocks and fancy goods.

"It was such a shame that the Government converted our peaceful productions to war factories and drew bombing attacks upon us," they said. I agreed. They winced when I told them that Nagoya was the third on the list for the Atom Bomb, and the surrender just saved them. "We had had enough already," they said.

Nagoya, switching from peacetime pretty-pretty stuff to Mitsubishi war plants, produced 80 per cent of Japan's aircraft until it was razed to the ground by raids. They obviously didn't like the change of topic, but said: "Frankly we wept. We just couldn't understand the surrender. We knew nothing about the real position."

Asked what they thought of the possibilities of democratic Government in Japan, they admitted it would take a long time. The people have no political education, they said. Did they desire democratic Government? Oh, yes, they did. Did they think the Emperor shared the responsibility for the war?—Oh, no, the Emperor was hoodwinked too.

Would they go to war again if the Emperor ordered them?—Oh, they were quite sure the Emperor would do no such thing. Had not the Emperor left his sacred Palace to visit General MacArthur? "Excuse, please, but we must go now unless there is some commercial or research information," they said.

Forty thousand occupation troops of the United States Sixth Army are arriving in Nagoya this week. The landing barges will touch down at Sinmaiko pleasure beach. The troops will live in tents pitched on bomb sites. But the sleek Jap business men intend exploiting the troops' arrival. Fancy goods, lacquer work, porcelain, are already appearing in the windowless, burned-out department stores. Notices over the counter announce boldly "For Allied soldiers only."

SUMATRA RAILWAY BUILT BY P.O.W. working under Jap task-masters. The Japanese commander vowed that it would be completed even if he had to use human bodies for sleepers. Released Australian prisoners who helped to lay the track declare that it was sabotaged during construction. See Burma-Siam railway story in this page. *Photo, Australian Official*

FREED P.O.W. AT ARAIE waiting repatriation by ships of the U.S. Navy. They included British, Canadians and Americans released from the Narum Daito camp in Japan. *Photo, British Combine*

'We Thought This Day Would Never Come'

Three hundred British P.O.W. shook the dust of Japan from their weary feet on August 30, 1945, and that night slept the sweet sleep of deliverance aboard the hospital ship Benevolence in Tokyo Bay. Arthur La Bern, of The Evening Standard, tells of their dramatic arrival.

We looked down at them as the landing craft swarmed round waiting their turn to unload. No two were dressed alike. Some wore a tattered vest and ragged slacks or shorts. Some wore even less. Some had had broken limbs. Some were so weak that the effort of waving once or twice was too much for them and they collapsed back into the arms of their comrades.

Many of them had pathetic little bundles—ragged paper parcels with the contents bursting out of the torn sides. In them were cherished things which had consoled them through their three years of imprisonment—photographs of their families, dog-eared books, card packs, crumpled letters tied with string, boxes of dominoes and chess.

There was one strangely vivid note about them. Nearly all wore bright crimson or yellow scarves, a contrast to the rest of their clothing. This rather puzzled us until they explained the scarves were cut from parachutes Flying Forts had dropped with food and cigarettes. One man had used a large piece of red parachute cloth to patch his ragged khaki trousers. As they filed along the deck towards the hot shower, a meal and medical inspection, they looked like shipwrecked men who had lived for years in a jungle or desert island. Many were suffering from beri-beri or dysentery; others looked remarkably fit.

Most of them were captured in Hongkong and had been in Jap hands since Xmas 1941. They were from P.O.W. camps in Sumidagawa and Omori. A large contingent of them were men of the Royal Scots and Middlesex Regiment, and an odd thing was that these British Army men who had been in captivity three years and eight months looked fitter than many captured more recently. One of them, Private Joseph Walter Newman, of the Middlesex Regiment, explained this to me. He said: "We lived by our wits. If we had depended on food the Japs gave us we should have been dead long ago. But every time we went out on a working party we resorted to the good old army practice of scrounging. We hid rice in our boots and socks and cooked it when we got back to camp."

Sergeant F. Pigeon, Royal Artillery, said: "We played a cat-and-mouse game with the Japs all the time. We learned to become as crafty as they are. No matter what job they sent us out on, we usually managed to steal rice or soya beans, which we hid in clothes and boots. We cooked it secretly at night on a little electric stove we rigged up under the floor of our hut, using electric light power."

Aircraftman Fred Harker, who was captured in Java, said to me: "I thought this day would never dawn. It is like a dream." His wife and daughter—four-year-old Judith Valerie—live in Norbett Road, Arnold, Nottingham. He said of them: "I have not seen them since Christmas 1941 when Judith was only nine months old."

All the British P.O.W. testified to this: "Our treatment was mild compared to that dished out to the American Fortress crews. The captured American air crews were continuously assaulted, kicked, tortured and starved, and the Jap civilians, if anything, were worse than the Jap military."

I got confirmation that the Jap civilians were worse than the Japanese military from British Fleet Air Arm Sub-Lieutenant Victor Spencer, an Avenger pilot, of Edge Lane, Broad Green, Liverpool. By a coincidence I flew in the same Avenger wing in a strike from the Implacable some weeks ago.

He failed to return from a later strike on Koriyama on August 10 and I did not expect to see him again; but as I was standing on the deck of the Benevolence he walked up to me and said: "Haven't we met before?" Spencer said: "We had just bombed the dispersal areas at Koriyama when we were hit twice by flak. One hit set the engine alight and we force-landed in paddy fields. We ducked into the hills, but were caught after two days' hiding. Civilians who caught us knocked us about pretty badly, but that stopped when we got into the P.O.W. camp."

Dutch soldiers captured in Java received particularly bad treatment. Sgt. Kuipers of the Dutch Army, said to me: "We did not even get any letters, so we have no idea what happened to our wives and children in Java. The Japs stole our Red Cross parcels and we had no soap for the first eight months as prisoners. When the war ended they cut down our meagre rations by 25 per cent. When the Swedish Consul asked why, the Japs replied: 'The prisoners have stopped working, and we are afraid they will get indigestion if we give them too much food.'"

The P.O.W. were continuously moved. One of the worst camps was at Kawasaki. Here 263 men had to make meals for a day from 25 pounds of flour and a can of water. One day the same 263 men had to make a meal from one pound of meat. Prisoners working in coalyards were expected to shovel a load of 50 tons of coal per man every day. When boots or shoes wore out they were not replaced and gangs of prisoners often worked in bare feet or with rags tied round their feet even in winter with snow on the ground.

I Was a Prisoner Where Men Died Like Flies

This "last letter" of a British Secret Service Agent, who was captured in civilian clothes in France by the Germans, was smuggled home while he was awaiting death at the notorious Buchenwald Camp (see illus. page 50). He later succeeded in escaping to the American lines. Dated Sept. 14, 1944, permission has now been given for its publication.

These are "famous last words," I am afraid, but one has to face death one day or another, so I will not moan, and get down to brass tacks. I will not attempt to make a report on my journey except to say that up to the very moment of my arrest it had been a success, and I was quite pleased with things. My capture was due to one of those incidents one cannot provide for. I had so much work that I was overwhelmed, so I asked for a sure, dependable *agent de liaison*, and I was given a young chap called Guy, whom I renamed Antonin. He worked for me for a week, and then got caught; how I do not know, but he had an appointment with me at 11 a.m. on Tuesday, March 21, by the Metro Passy, and brought the Gestapo with him.

He was obviously unable to withstand bullying and very quickly gave in to questioning. I was caught coming round a corner and had not an earthly chance, being collared and handcuffed before I could say "knife." I was badly beaten up in the car on the way to Gestapo H.Q., arriving there with a twisted nose and a head about twice its normal size. I was then subjected to four days' continuous grilling, being beaten up and also being put into a bath of icy cold water, legs and arms chained, and held head downwards under water until almost drowned, then pulled out and asked if I had anything to say. This I underwent six times, but I managed to hold out and gave nothing away.

Wrist Cut to the Bone by Chains

I was interrogated for about two months, but dodged everything. I was offered freedom if I would hand over X—some hopes! I nearly lost my left arm as a result of the torture, as I got blood poisoning through my wrist being cut to the bone by chains and remaining unattended with handcuffs biting into them for about six days. Apart from that I was kept in solitary confinement for four months at Fresnes. I was very unpopular as a Britisher, and one of the German N.C.O.s was particularly glad at every opportunity of punching me or slapping my face. He gave me three weeks of "glass-house" in a darkened cell, without mattress, blankets, deprived of all means of washing, and with about half a pound of bread per day as sole food.

I was pretty weak when I came out, and had lost about 2½ stone in weight. I was sent to Compiègne on July 17. Whilst there I recuperated a bit, and had arranged an escape together with a chap well known to —— but got sent to Weimar on the eve of escaping. The other chap succeeded. Bad luck for me. The journey here was an eventful one; it took eight days. The first man I ran into when being entrained was A., and the second was B. We had various adventures, all were handcuffed the whole time, 19 men in one compartment and 18 in another. We could not move, being packed like sardines. The gates of the compartments were padlocked and we had very little air—or food.

We were given one day's rations which had to last five days; luckily some had Red Cross parcels or we would have starved. The train was bombed and machine-gunned on the way and we had a very narrow shave. Our escorts ran and left us helpless; had the train caught fire we would have burned like trapped rats. We had to stop at Saarbrücken for three days in a punishment and reprisals camp, and were beaten up on arrival. As usual I seemed to attract particular attention and got well and truly slapped and cuffed. We were confined for three days and nights, 37 of us in a hut 9 ft. by 7ft. It was Hell.

We then came on to this place, Buchenwald. On the way our escorts plundered and stole practically all our effects. Never believe a word about German honesty; they are the biggest thieves, liars, bullies and cowards I have ever met. In addition they delight in torturing people and gloat over it. Upon arrival, which took place at about midnight, we were locked up in disinfection quarters and next morning were very nearly hanged summarily, but temporarily reprieved. We were stripped, completely shorn, and dressed in prison rags, losing our few remaining belongings, and 16 of us, including B., were told to report to a certain place.

We never saw them again and found out that they were hanged without trial on the night of September 11-12. They have been cremated, so no trace remains of them. We are now awaiting our turn. There are 170 airmen (British and American), brought down and captured in France, but they are being treated as "terror fliers" and sleeping in the open, living under appalling conditions in violation of all conventions. They ought to be treated as prisoners of war. Men die like flies here.

I sent a message to you through——. I hope you received it, but I have no means of telling. The bearer of this letter will give you all details; whatever he tells you is Gospel truth and he will never be able really to do justice to the horrors perpetrated here. For God's sake see to it that our people never let themselves be softened towards the German people, or there will be another war in 15 years time, and all our lives will have been sacrificed in vain. I leave it to you and others to see that retribution is fierce. It will never be fierce enough.

SEEING THE HORRORS OF BUCHENWALD, Nazi prison camp (overrun by the U.S. 3rd Army on April 11, 1945), where thousands suffered indescribable cruelties, are these German women from the nearby city of Weimar. Under U.S. escort, they were marched through the camp to receive impressions that would not fade this side of death. *Photo, U.S. Official*

DIARY OF WORLD EVENTS

SEPTEMBER 26, Wednesday

Indo-China.—U.S. officer killed and other Allied casualties in clashes with Annamite nationalists.

Home Front.—King and Queen visited Edinburgh for Victory parade.

General.—Bar to V.C. awarded to Capt. C. H. Upham, N.Z. Army.

SEPTEMBER 27, Thursday

Japan.—Emperor Hirohito made formal call on Gen. MacArthur in Tokyo.

Germany.—Larger food rations for children 9-17 and for victims of Nazi persecution approved by Allied Kommandatura in Berlin.

General.—International agreement signed in London for establishment of European Central Inland Transport Organization.

SEPTEMBER 28, Friday

Germany.—Gen. Patton reported to Gen. Eisenhower on "denazification" programme in Bavaria.

Mediterranean.—Malta again became headquarters of British Fleet.

Home Front.—King and Queen visited ships of Home Fleet in Firth of Forth.

SEPTEMBER 29, Saturday

Germany.—Himmler's secret grave at Luneburg Heath decked with flowers.

Netherlands E. Indies.—British troops landed in Java without interference from Indonesian nationalists.

SEPTEMBER 30, Sunday

Germany.—British officials announced clothing levy to be made on Germans.

China.—U.S. Marines landed at port of Tientsin.

Home Front.—Accident to Scottish express on L.M.S. railway near Hemel Hempstead caused 39 fatal casualties.

OCTOBER 1, Monday

General.—Czechoslovakia resumed diplomatic relations with Rumania.

OCTOBER 2, Tuesday

Germany.—Gen. Patton to be replaced by Lt.-Gen. Truscott as commander of 3rd Army and of eastern half of U.S. occupation zone.

Indo-China.—"Cease-fire" agreed on between French authorities and Annamite nationalists.

General.—Meetings of Council of Foreign Ministers in London suspended.

Home Front.—First travelling Post Office train for five years left Euston for Aberdeen.

OCTOBER 3, Wednesday

Germany.—Gen. de Gaulle visited Saarbrucken in French zone.

China.—Fighting in Kunming between Chungking troops and local forces.

Indo-China.—French battleship Richelieu covered landings of Allied troops.

U.S.A.—President Truman recommended Congress to set up commission on control of atomic energy development.

OCTOBER 4, Thursday

Japan.—Allied authorities abolished secret police and demanded removal of Home Minister and release of political prisoners.

France.—Trial of Pierre Laval on charge of treason opened in Paris.

OCTOBER 5, Friday

Japan.—Japanese Prime Minister and entire Cabinet resigned.

Home Front.—Household Cavalry mounted guard in Whitehall for first time since the war.

OCTOBER 6, Saturday

Japan.—Baron Shidehara appointed to form new Cabinet.

Palestine.—Illegal immigrants on northern frontier caused clash between Transjordan Frontier Force and Jewish villagers.

OCTOBER 7, Sunday

France.—Laval and his defending lawyers withdrew from court as protest against conduct of trial.

Home Front.—First party of ex-prisoners of war from Far East arrived at Southampton.

OCTOBER 8, Monday

Germany.—Rudolf Hess flown from Britain to Germany to stand trial.

Palestine.—Orderly demonstrations by Jews protesting against British immigration policy.

OCTOBER 9, Tuesday

France.—Pierre Laval sentenced to death in his absence.

Far East.—Andaman Islands re-occupied by British.

Netherlands E. Indies.—British and Dutch officials arrested by Indonesian extremists.

Greece.—Government of Admiral Voulgaris resigned.

Flash-backs

1939

September 27. *Fall of Warsaw.*

1940

September 27. *Tripartite Pact between Germany, Italy and Japan signed in Berlin.*

October 7. *German troops entered Rumania and occupied oilfields.*

1941

October 6. *Two-pronged assault against Moscow launched by Germans under Von Bock.*

October 8. *Evacuation of Orel announced by Russian Command.*

1942

October 4. *Combined Operations raid on Sark, Channel Islands.*

October 8. *British captured at Dieppe and Sark enchained.*

1943

October 1. *5th Army took Naples.*

1944

October 3. *R.A.F. breached dyke and flooded Walcheren Island. Warsaw rising crushed by Germans after 63 days.*

October 5. *Allied troops landed on mainland of Greece.*

CLAIMED TO BE THE WORLD'S FASTEST FIGHTER is Britain's jet-propelled de Havilland Vampire (1) which first appeared over London on September 16, 1945. A single-seater, its speed is described as "handsomely in excess of 500 m.p.h." It is powered with a single gas turbine and was intended as an answer to the latest German jet-propelled aircraft. Designed for battle in the stratosphere is the Westland Welkin (2), the world's biggest single-seater fighter with a speed of 385 m.p.h. Off the secret list (September) is the Blackburn Firebrand IV (3), our Naval Air Arm's most formidable attack aircraft and fastest single-engined (2,580 h.p.) torpedo-carrying aircraft, with a speed of 350 m.p.h. Believed to be the fastest propeller-driven aircraft is the de Havilland Hornet (4), capable of over 470 m.p.h. *Photos, Charles E. Brown*

R·A·F· to Fly Them Home

By CAPTAIN
NORMAN MACMILLAN
M.C., A.F.C.

NOTHING better illustrates the greatly developed carrying capacity of the R.A.F. than the statement of Mr. George Isaacs, the Minister of Labour, when dealing with the question of demobilization, that "Between October 1945 and May 1946 the R.A.F. will transport about a million personnel and 250,000 tons of freight." Men and freight will be carried by air from all theatres of war, from Europe, the Middle East, India and the Far East. They will come not only from seaports, as with ships, but from airports situated both on the seaboard and inland.

There is no need now to send men to the Hook of Holland, Antwerp or Ostend, Alexandria, Bombay, Calcutta or Rangoon for transhipment home. They can emplane at Hanover, Berlin, Khartoum, Delhi or Mandalay, and fly direct to London. How immense the saving of transport man-power that will result, can be appreciated when one remembers the great numbers of dock and railway workers that would be needed to handle the ships and trains necessary to transport a million men. Thus a dual man-power problem will be simultaneously solved; and the use of petrol to carry these men and women will save coal for other purposes.

MR. Isaacs' statement drew attention to the huge network of military airlines that now enmesh the globe as with a spider's web. While civil aviation is obstructed by failure among the nations to agree on policy affecting the freedom of flight and carriage of passengers and freight, the R.A.F. and the U.S.A. Air Transport Commands operate with the utmost freedom and regularity services that span the world. Nothing can better punch home the moral that the world is still under military government although the war is over. In Europe alone the R.A.F. flies a route network of 114,000 miles, and due to vacant seats in the Dakotas it has been reported that the public will soon be able to book seats for travel to Europe by R.A.F. Transport Command at same fares as British Overseas Airways would charge.

If this is correct it is to be regretted that the military air transport command should usurp the function of civil air transport. One cannot see the Admiralty placing His Majesty's ships at the disposal of fare-paying passengers between Folkestone and Boulogne, and the Air Ministry might well have regard to the procedure of the senior Service with its fine respect for tradition. But perhaps this report was incorrect.

HORNET'S Great Improvement on Britain's Famous Hurricane

British aero-engine horse-powers are steadily increasing. The two Rolls-Royce Merlin engines fitted in the de Havilland Hornet fighter (which was first delivered to the R.A.F. in February 1945) give a total of 4,140 h.p. for take-off. This fighter can fly 2,500 miles non-stop when fitted with long-range tanks, a great improvement on the fighters with which Britain entered the war; for then the Hurricane had the greatest duration—about 750 miles. But to cover this distance non-stop it was necessary to fly at such a reduced speed that operationally it was of little value, and the maximum striking range of our early fighters did not exceed about 120 miles. It was the loss rate of the American Eighth Air Force heavy day bombers that brought about the urgent need of long-range escort fighters, thus making the fighter an offensive, instead of a defensive weapon, in pure air war. The Hornet is also remarkable for its rapid climb off the ground; in the first minute it can reach 4,500 feet. (See illus. in facing page.)

This rate of climb is first-class for an aircraft driven by airscrews, but it does not compare with the phenomenal rates of climb developed by rocket-driven aircraft. The latter were developed by the Germans when the R.A.F. and American and Allied air forces drove the Luftwaffe on to the defensive.

INDEED, that effect may be said to have occurred in the Battle of Britain, although the actual air offensive against Germany did not really begin until 1942. As the wearing down of German air defence grew continually stronger, the enemy concentrated ever more on interception, and the Messerschmitt 163 rocket-propelled interceptor, the Komet, was literally a flying rocket.

This pterodactyl-like aeroplane normally took off under its own power, jettisoned its wheels in the air, and landed on a skid. It climbed to 30,000 feet in just over two minutes and a half, and was capable of a level speed of 550 m.p.h. It carried the pilot, two 30-mm. guns, and was built partly of wood. A later model, the 163-C, used a special rocket unit with a second jet to give cruising economy. Its endurance under power was about 12 minutes, and its maximum speed was 590 m.p.h.

But the Komet was outclassed by a project under development in Germany when the war ended. This was the BP-20 Natter (Viper) of the Bachem company. This tiny aircraft had a wing-span of about 18 ft., about the same as the flying bomb. Its prime mover was a rocket, as in the Komet. It was to start flight vertically (like the V2), assisted by auxiliary rockets, and climb to about 37,000 ft. in the first minute and continue climbing, if need be, above that height. Its task was to destroy a bomber with its battery of rocket projectiles, and when the pilot had fired them he was to be ejected from his cockpit and descend by parachute. To save the valuable rocket-engine, the rear half of the fuselage broke off and also came down by parachute. The front half, being quickly replaceable, was left to fall where and as it might.

LIGHTWEIGHT Aircraft Rocket Unit Installed in the Messerschmitt 163

These rocket-propelled aircraft (the Natter was almost a human controlled anti-aircraft rocket) were driven by two fuels: concentrated hydrogen peroxide and a mixture of hydrazine hydrate and alcohol; each contained in a separate tank, whence they were delivered to the combustion chamber jets by turbine driven pumps. The most important aircraft rocket unit was the HWK-509 which weighed only 365 lb. It was installed in the Messerschmitt 163. It developed a maximum thrust of 3,300 lb., when the fuel consumption exceeded 1,000 lb. a minute. It could be throttled to a minimum thrust of 220 lb., but only with a big loss in fuel consumption efficiency. The HWK-509C had the separate cruising combustion chamber. Its main combustion chamber gave a thrust of 3,740 lb., and the cruising chamber 660 lb.

THE latest British war aircraft to come off the secret list is the Blackburn Firebrand (see illus. in facing page), a Fleet Air Arm strike aircraft, fitted with one Bristol 18-cylinder sleeve-valve Centaurus engine, which develops 2,580 h.p. Originally designed as a fighter, the Firebrand became a torpedo attack aircraft. It has folding wings, large slotted flaps, subsidiary split flaps in the trailing edge of the main flaps, dive brakes on the upper and lower surfaces of the main planes, and a specially developed torpedo attachment which allows the torpedo to be released at unusually high speeds. Its sea-level speed is 320 m.p.h. and it is 30 m.p.h. faster at 13,000 ft. It stalls at 75 m.p.h., and takes off in a 20-knot wind in 480 ft., which means that in the smaller carriers it must require rocket-assisted take-off.

NAVAL AIR ARM'S NEWEST WEAPONS include the all-metal Seafire Mark 45 (top), with a single 2,050 h.p. engine, and counter-rotating airscrews. Speed is about 440 m.p.h., span 36 ft. 11 ins., length 32 ft. 11 ins., armed with four 20-mm. cannon guns. Jet-propelled Vampire (see facing page), also in service: tail-end view (below). *Photos, Associated Press*

Editor's Postscript

Berkeley Square has been in the news again. For the greater part of its 247 years of existence it has been reckoned one of the most beautiful, as it certainly was one of the most exclusive, of London's backwaters, long famed in history if only because of the many famous people who have lived and died there, and variously celebrated in poetry, drama and song. Was it not at his house in Berkeley Square that Kipling's Tomlinson gave up the ghost, when the spirit came to his bedside and gripped him by the hair? In the popular play of the 1920s to which the square lent its name it was made to symbolize all that was fragrant as well as all that was malodorous about that eighteenth-century gilt-golden age to which so many romantic souls have longed to return. As for song, throughout the summer of 1940 we were assured *ad nauseam* by Eric Maschwitz, who wrote the lyric, and Manning Sherwin, who wrote the music, that a nightingale sang in Berkeley Square, though I for one found this difficult to believe. Still, there were always plenty of leafy plane trees there, and the fact that it is almost unique among London squares in being set on a recognizable hillside gave the garden at its best the effect of a miniature parkland, so possibly a solitary nightingale may have made a mistake at some time.

When I first knew Berkeley Square the houses and the garden were very much what they must have been in, say, 1774, when Lord Clive set the clubs and coffee-houses prattling by committing suicide at No. 45. There was only one shop, an old bookshop. And never were garden gates kept more jealously locked. One of the now extinct race of crossing-sweepers had his pitch by Lansdowne House to the south of the square, and he was invariably dressed in a scarlet coat. The story ran that Lord Cork kept him supplied with throw-outs from his hunting wardrobe. In short, Berkeley Square had a unique flavour compounded of equal parts of very expensive lavender and very rare old lace. In recent years this has all been changed. Today it is only for a few paces on the west side, and then only at night, that the most lively imagination could think in terms of powder and patches, buckles and brocade, linkboys and sedan chairs. Gentility has fled before the tide of commerce, and the sedate old houses have given place to modern blocks of offices and flats—magnificent, no doubt, but not Berkeley Square. The bombs came. Then those precious railings came down, and the shelters and E.W.S. tanks went up. The busy public learned to take short cuts across the open ground, and every blade of grass has vanished. Now the Westminster City Council has agreed to restore at least the garden to its former glory. Never again can it be preserved as a pleasaunce of aristocracy; but there is no reason why it should not be made an oasis to gladden the hearts of Mr. Jones and Miss Smith as they scurry past it to and from their work.

Discovery of the Gestapo's secret list of British people and British institutions marked down for liquidation served to revive for a time the ever-pertinent query: "What would have happened *if*...?" I wonder the Nazis, confident as they were in 1940 of the imminent collapse of Britain, did not make full propaganda play with the list as a trump-card in the war of nerves. After all, there were few surprises in it, very little that we could not have guessed for ourselves even then. They might have used it as they used their notorious film of the Polish campaign, Baptism of Fire, for the intimidation of hesitant neutrals. And, incidentally, the Nazis were by no means first with the idea of saying it with threatening pictures. After the defeat of the Spanish Armada an enemy ship was seen one day floundering about in Bridlington Bay. A boatload of local toughs rowed out and scuttled her, presumably killing the enemy crew. Among the loot they brought back were a dozen pictures painted on leather, showing horrifically and in unmistakable terms what the Inquisition proposed to do to all Englishmen who were not Catholics. These old propaganda paintings, after being hidden for a time lest Good Queen Bess should demand them for herself, have been preserved to this day at Howsham Hall in the East Riding.

It is twenty-one years since Imperial Airways was founded and started its daily London-Paris service. Since then the history of British civil aviation has hardly been a glorious one—largely thanks to misguided subsidies and the fact that none of our Governments since that time had the courage to go "all out" on the question. I am reminded of this by the timely publication of Tomorrow's Airliners, Airways and Airports (Pilot Press, 15s.), by Mr. S. E. Veale, which I do not hesitate to describe as the most comprehensive book on civil flying I have ever read. Mr. Veale is no mere Wellsian dreamer: his pages are spatch-cocked with odd and curious facts. Did you know, for example, that an attempt to bring international air services under a unified control was first made as far back as 1910, when delegates from eighteen countries assembled in Paris? Or that the following year (1911) a Frenchman, Captain Ferber de Rue, forecast jet-propulsion when he wrote: "In order to go higher—and man will try to go higher—another principle will have to be adopted. The principle of the rocket is indicated for this purpose, and the reaction motor will be the result"? Mr. Veale has some supremely sensible things to say about Germany's future as an air-Power, especially of the possibility of her secretly manufacturing rocket weapons. And he anticipates "a steady expansion of the world's air services, which may continue to the turn of the century," making air transportation one of the world's greatest industries. But in case you should be pondering setting up in business as an air-line proprietor be warned by this: "Assuming a useful life of five years, an airliner costing £100,000 must be written off in the operating company's books at the rate of £20,000 a year—or £55 a day, or more than £2 an hour." This takes no account of lost revenue and the company's normal overheads!

Capt. CHARLES HAZLITT UPHAM, awarded in September 1945 a bar to the V.C. he had received in 1941 (see page 281, Vol. 5), was the first soldier to be thus decorated in the Second Great War. In the New Zealanders' gallant attack on El Ruweisat Ridge, in the Western Desert, in July 1942, though badly wounded and with his arm broken he destroyed, with grenades, a truckload of Nazis, a tank and several guns, capturing the position.

Photo, New Zealand Official

An officer lately repatriated from Malaya has been telling me about Jap methods of propaganda which, he says, was somewhat subtler in its appeal than that put out by the Nazis in occupied Europe. At Singapore, it seems, the Japs made desperate efforts to stir up in the Malayans a sense of the teeming numerical superiority of the "Indies" over Britain's mere forty-and-odd millions. "Britain," ran one of the slogans, "is only a 1-24th of us; Britain itself means really nothing." Sums in simple arithmetic always appeal to the Oriental mind as possessing magical properties of a kind, and no doubt the strictly arithmetical logic implied in the equation had in many cases the effect desired by the Nippon invader. Another type of appeal—incidentally used against us by the Germans in Africa before the First Great War—was on the subject of domestic service. On the lines that Jack is as good as—which is to imply better than—his master. One of the coloured leaflets scattered about Singapore shortly after the Japs took over depicted a Malay, a Burman and an Indian (Peterborough reproduced it recently in The Daily Telegraph) bringing Mr. Churchill an early-morning cup of tea. It is an old dodge—as old as Wat Tyler. Extremists of the Congress party in India once tried to exploit it in an attempt to get servants in Bombay to "go slow" on their English masters, but without any appreciable degree of success. The psychology here would seem to be at fault, for among the better type of Indian servant to be in an Englishman's service is very often a matter of proud family tradition, many such going back over two hundred years.

A war memorial for animals may sound odd until you begin to realize—as not many do—that during the War thousands of animals and birds went on active service with the Allied forces (see page 696, Vol. 8). Among them were birds and animals lent by their owners to the Government for war work—pigeons used by crews of crashed aircraft; dogs used by fighting patrols to give warning of the presence of the enemy, for detecting mines on the battlefield; dogs attached to the Civil Defence services for locating casualties trapped under bomb debris; and—not least—the mascots. To commemorate the fine work of these animals the People's Dispensary for Sick Animals of the Poor (which began its now famous caravan service as long ago as 1923) is appealing for funds for the P.D.S.A. Allied Forces Animals' War Memorial. And what more practical form could such a memorial take than by providing a fleet of new caravan dispensaries to ease the sufferings of birds and animals in what one hopes are the more peaceful days to come? I pass on the appeal to you in the hope that you may wish to contact the Secretary, who is to be found at 14 Clifford Street, London, W.1. As a surprising example of the value placed on animal war-work I was told the other day of a "squadron" of R.A.F. "nomadic homers," as they are called, whose job and training are so heavily swathed in the folds of the Secret List that it is unlikely that they will ever be revealed. There would thus seem to be more than one reason why budgerigars weren't chosen for the task.

In Britain Now: Helping Our Ex-Servicemen

TIMELY WARNING ON THIS POSTER outside the demobilization centre at Olympia, London, is being considered by a soldier about to re-enter civilian life. He is reminded that there are sharks ashore as well as at sea, and that ex-Servicemen have to be careful to whom they entrust their gratuities. *Photo, The Evening News*

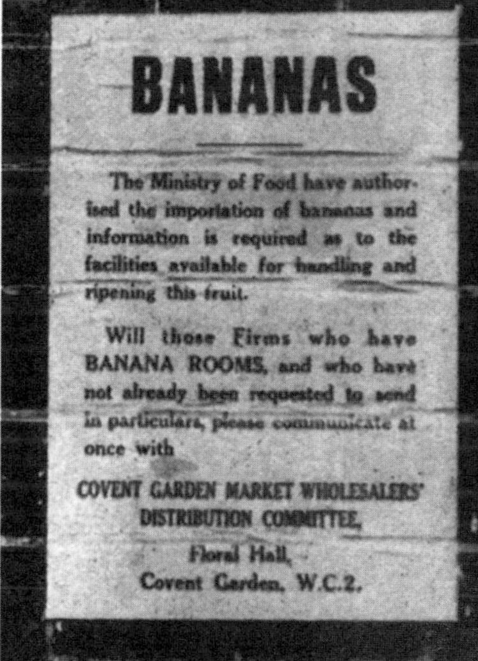

BANANAS

The Ministry of Food have authorised the importation of bananas and information is required as to the facilities available for handling and ripening this fruit.

Will those Firms who have BANANA ROOMS, and who have not already been requested to send in particulars, please communicate at once with

COVENT GARDEN MARKET WHOLESALERS' DISTRIBUTION COMMITTEE,
Floral Hall,
Covent Garden, W.C.2.

BANANAS ARE ON THE WAY if one may judge by this appeal posted in Covent Garden, London, during October 1945, for Banana Rooms, of which there are about a hundred in the market ; many lay empty during the war or were used as air-raid shelters. In these rooms green bananas just arrived from the docks are ripened in five or six days, heating being provided by gas—the only type of artificial warmth supplying the requisite humidity. On the Clyde, banana boats are being refurbished in readiness for resumption of this trade with Jamaica and the Cameroons.

LEARNING TO BUILD TOMORROW'S BRITAIN, ex-Servicemen are training at Eley's Estate, Edmonton, London, where workshops have been erected for them to study various crafts. Much use is made of models : trainees (above) are at work on a model staircase ; others (top) are perfecting themselves in bricklaying as appertaining to the construction of railway tunnels and bridges. *Photos, Keystone, The Evening Standard*

Rocket Bomb Helped to Swell London Savings

THIS V2 ARRIVED IN TRAFALGAR SQUARE BY LORRY as main attraction of London's Thanksgiving Savings Week display, September 15-22, 1945. Captured during our advance in the Low Countries, it weighs over three tons; its height of 49 ft. may be gauged in comparison with that of the workmen erecting it in its launching position. It was disclosed on September 23 that in June 1944 an unexploded V2 landed accidentally in Sweden, was handed over to our agents and dispatched to Britain by air.

Photo, Illustrated London News

Printed in England and published every alternate Friday by the Proprietors, THE AMALGAMATED PRESS, LTD., The Fleetway House, Farringdon Street, London, E.C.4. Registered for transmission by Canadian Magazine Post. Sole Agents for Australia and New Zealand: Messrs. Gordon & Gotch, Ltd. and for South Africa: Central News Agency; Ltd.—October 26, 1945. S.S. *Editorial Offices:* JOHN CARPENTER HOUSE WHITEFRIARS, LONDON, E C 4.

Vol 9 The War Illustrated No 219

SIXPENCE

NOVEMBER 9, 1945

and AFTERWARDS

HOMEWARD-BOUND AT SINGAPORE after three-and-a-half years of captivity, this British corporal was one of 40,000 Allied P.O.W. and internees evacuated from the Malayan port by the end of September 1945. On arrival at their destination—Liverpool or Southampton—each ex-P.O.W. is dispatched on leave within forty-eight hours, after a medical inspection and a combined Intelligence and Casualty interrogation. See also illus. page 434. *Photo, British Official*

Edited by Sir John Hammerton

NO. 220 WILL BE PUBLISHED FRIDAY, NOVEMBER 23

Trouble Flares Up in Java and Indo-China

AT SAIGON, capital of French Indo-China, Annamite prisoners and civil servants listened attentively to Col. W. G. Cass, a British Intelligence officer (1, standing, back to camera), after Allied capture of the prison on October 3, 1945, when he told them they must give up their arms and that order would be restored by the Gurkhas. The rebels surrendered rifles and revolvers without incident. In the city's public gardens (2) sailors from French warships helped to man hurriedly erected barricades.

INDONESIAN NATIONALISTS checked up on captured Japanese arms (3) in S. Java and inspected an armoured car taken from the Japs (4). Two days after Japan's unconditional surrender on August 14, 1945, "President" Soekarno, with Japanese support, proclaimed the "Indonesian Republican Government," and called on all workers to strike against Dutch re-occupation of the island. See also story in page 441.

 Photos, Associated Press

This Holland Needs Our Help

By GODFREY WINN

As the Dakota swung in along the coast an echo from one's pre-war consciousness suddenly returned. It is a beautiful sight, someone had reiterated, to fly low over the Dutch bulb farms in the spring. But this was the autumn, this was the aftermath of war, and staring down through the slits in the side of the aircraft it was difficult to be sure which was the sea, which the land, flooded and ravaged when, a year ago, the dykes, which normally protect the island of Walcheren, were busted wide open in three crucial places by the R.A.F.

Did human beings really live here once? Harvest their crops, give birth, grow old? Somewhere beneath that apparently solid sheet of water? And then, as I peered more closely, my angle of vision changed, and I seemed to be staring now into a vast mirror, in which was reflected, not the outline of our aircraft, but the shape of farmsteads, and whole village streets, submerged and crystallized beneath the flood.

If it makes an extraordinary picture from the air, it is equally unforgettable, though rather less spectacular, from the eye-level of the human beings who lost all their possessions last winter, and now huddle together, on the nearest dry land, refugees, within their own little island kingdom. You find them at Middelburg, the beauty of whose famous town-hall has been only partially damaged by bombing, and in Vere, where desperate efforts are now being made to stem one of the breaches in the dyke.

In Vere I talked with a farmer who had nothing left but some photographs of the considerable holding that had been in his family for generations. They invited us into their borrowed kitchen. The wife wore the traditional white cap, her husband in his dark corduroys had a face that Hals would have delighted to paint. What is it that the younger boy peers at so eagerly in his brother's hand as he lounges by the door? A cigarette. And what is it in the centre of the table that the two little girls, with the prominent eyes of the half-starved, stare at with such wonder? A tin of cocoa.

The farmer, Jacobus David Gideonse, was saying: "We do not hold any grudge against the British for the dyke. It was necessary." *It was necessary*. I heard that phrase a hundred times during my visit. Even in The Hague, where there are large wastes of damage, caused by British bombing; and again, in Arnhem, where after the avalanche suddenly descended from the skies, and this pretty, harmless town became a battlefield, they had the bitterer aftermath of seeing those of their houses which were still standing stripped and pillaged. I have been to Arnhem and seen whole roads of houses without a stick of furniture between them.

Who Will Pay for Allied Damage?

So one began to understand what Total Occupation has meant for a country whose sufferings have been too little publicized, if that is the right word to use. One began to understand why there were so many gaps between the tramlines in Amsterdam—"last winter they tore up the wood blocks for fuel and the floors of their houses, both here and in Rotterdam, even the lavatory doors"—and why, when we went to pick up a guide for a few hours, his small son clung to the car handle, and wept bitterly. The only cars the boy had known belonged to the enemy. If such a car arrived at your door and your father left with strangers, you never saw him again. But those were the only tears I witnessed. I heard no whining, no demanding, no expressions of self-pity: I saw no holding out of hands, even for cigarettes.

As a gesture of admiration for our sorely tried Dutch allies, we gladly reprint in "The War Illustrated" this brilliant article, slightly abridged, whose author generously gave all publishing rights to the Help Holland Council. We have remitted a substantial sum to their Fund in recognition of Mr. Godfrey Winn's action.—Editor.

Just over the border into Germany much of the domestic loot was taken. It is still there today. And the Dutch ask naturally: when is it to be returned? That question and one other were constantly on their lips. Who is going to pay—especially for *Allied* damage? For instance, that farmer at Vere asked, not unreasonably, from whom would he—and all the others—receive compensation? "First they said the Germans would pay; then it was the British; now no one seems to know."

Even Rusty Nails are Precious

In any case, astronomical sums in a vague future mean less—so much less—than a ploughshare in your hand this very minute. The men are coming back from incarceration in Germany to find their families in districts near the Maas living in chicken-coops. They want to start rebuilding at once, and they are helpless because in whole villages the Germans have not left a single hammer behind. (On the waterfront at Rotterdam I watched a port official, with idle time on his hands, searching among the rusty rubble for nails.) While the dearth of all agricultural instruments is so acute, film "galas" are held in aid of the peasants. Admittance is with a novel coin. A tool. A spanner. A pair of pliers even. A rake.

"Is soap, then, rationed in your country?" (Their own ration, I discovered—after three years of no soap at all—is for two months one half of what we receive each month.) I got tired of answering such questions, and exasperated, too, until I came to the realization that in the whole of Holland is not to be found a single English newspaper, review, or recently published book on sale. This, in contrast with Brussels and Paris, where the kiosks are piled high with news from England. Yet many more ordinary people in Holland speak our tongue . . . and would like to think our way still, if they only knew what way it was.

The new decree, recalling the old currency, was being received everywhere I went by all classes of the community with satisfaction, and, indeed, acclamation. The honest will have nothing to fear, while those who sought greedily to benefit by the scarcities of Occupation are struck off the pay-roll at last. It is thought that there will be many prosecutions but many more secret bonfires.

You can clean up your currency, but that does not fill your shops with goods. I walked through the square at Breda, and was almost deceived by a giant cheese—a beautiful example of modern plastic art. Only the flowers are real, the flower shops piled with outsize blooms of gladioli, and huge waxy dahlias, possessing all the colour that the pale ghosts of passers-by lack. While the final irony was that the flowers were so cheap that everywhere we drove we saw them in the windows . . . the wide windows of the workmen's dwellings, so attractively designed that you could not designate them slums, even down by the docks at Rotterdam, even in Plaretstraat, where I spent an afternoon going from house to house with a young Red Cross doctor.

One remembers the mother, just back from hospital—"starvation made their limbs swell like dropsy" my companion said—holding up her two babies to the open window and the sun. One remembers young Johan Peperzak at No. 55, dressed in a cut-down Canadian uniform, complete with three stripes on the arm (but this wasn't a children's fancy-dress party, this was his only suit); and most of all, one will remember the family that lived on the ground floor at No. 44. Today their living space is one room, because none of the other floors are left. So what will they burn this winter? What clothes will they wear when it is really cold, I thought, fascinated by the two little girls, in one corner, solemnly making dolls' clothes of the last scraps, as clean as their own cotton-thin, much-patched dresses.

As though she could sense what was in one's mind, their mother, with a rough gesture, pulled them towards her, and showed us their bare chests. "You see, no lice, no vermin," she cried with passion and anger. "But they cannot go to school because they have no shoes, no coat. And my eldest daughter cannot take a place as servant, for the same reason." In the ensuing silence my eyes went past the group to the table where, aloof and impersonal, stood yet another vase of white gladioli.

Outside in the street again, I reminded my companion of the stack of garments, collected by the Help Holland Council, that I had seen an hour before being sorted in a warehouse down by the blitzed docks. He explained that first the victims of the Allied battlefields, the refugees from the far-off flooded areas must be fitted out with *something;* and when I was not altogether convinced, he added that so far, despite all that voluntary organizations in Britain and America are doing, only ten per cent of the immediate help needed was being received.

Cabbage and Thin Soup a Luxury

Ten per cent. That is a fact, checked and counterchecked. Here are some more. Last winter one bulb grower alone in Haarlem sold 2,500 tons of bulbs, crocuses for coffee, daffodils and hyacinths for fodder, tulips for human beings. ("They taste like a sweet swede, and aren't bad if fried in fat, if there is any fat.") In Amsterdam last Sunday, at the "best" restaurant, our lunch consisted of cabbage and a little thin soup. I am sorry I cannot offer you any salt, our host said, but I haven't the coupons. Automatically one looked down for a piece of bread to crumble that wasn't there . . .

Mercifully the old city has been spared much bombing, and its serene autumn loveliness was assuaging one's stomach, when suddenly there came into view a sight that is all too common today in liberated countries. One more hotel turned into an Allied leave centre, and there in the window, guzzling away, were a frieze of happy warriors, tackling the Sunday joint, piling their plates, and spreading several pats of butter on their bread. I know now why from time to time respectable citizens long to throw a brick through the window. What must be the feelings of those who pass that way every day and always lunch off cabbage!

As you approached the Rijks, you saw them in a queue a quarter of a mile long it seemed, waiting in their shabby Sunday best for their meal. At last there is space for another batch inside, and now, too tired to stand any more, they flop down on the rows of benches in the improvised gallery, where on the walls all the Rembrandts in Holland—salvaged from their hiding-places in the sand-dunes—are gathered together today for the first time under the same roof. It is good to have that as one's final memory.

What We Escaped in 1940

By MAJ.-GENERAL SIR CHARLES GWYNN K.C.B., D.S.O.

If the Germans in the autumn of 1940 had attempted to put into operation their "Sea Lion" plan for the invasion of England, what prospects of success would it have had? There are, I think, two hypothetical situations worth consideration if we are to judge our capacity at that time to meet the threat; namely, those that would have arisen: (*a*) had the R.A.F. failed to win the Battle of Britain, (*b*) if, having lost the Battle of Britain, the Germans had still persisted in their plan—as for a time seems to have been their intention.

Our own subsequent experience of amphibious operations, to some extent at least, enables us to judge what the chances of German success in either case would have been. We must frankly admit that our land forces were quite inadequate either to repel an assault on the beaches or to deal with the enemy successfully after he had made a landing—provided he could have maintained his sea communications. We have since seen how even the strongest coast defences have failed to repel assault by determined troops, and how forces immensely more powerful than we then possessed proved incapable of dealing with invading armies that had once secured a footing.

We now know that against the 39 well-equipped and war-trained divisions the enemy intended to land on our shores we could have opposed only one fully-trained and equipped Canadian Division and another partially trained. There were, of course, also coast defence units, the Home Guard and British troops in process of training and re-equipment, but for lack of transport and equipment these would have been incapable of concentrated action or large-scale manoeuvres. There was also a complete lack of armour, whereas the Germans proposed to deploy six panzer and three motorized divisions in their first assault.

With such disparity of force it is evident that no solid resistance would have been practicable once a landing had been effected. The enemy's plans for advance inland have, therefore, little interest. The utmost the defence could have hoped to achieve would have been to cause casualties, to delay the advance and possibly to deal with airborne landings; but unfortunately there was no strategic reserve available with which to take advantage of time gained or depletion of the enemy's resources.

Cut-and-Dried Plans for Assault on Our East and South Coasts

Yet the formation of the Home Guard, and the spirit of determination displayed, combined with an element of bluff, had their effects. The enemy was induced to plan his invasion on a scale for which his shipping resources were inadequate, with the result that his invasion armadas would have been cumbersome and ill-protected, offering vulnerable targets to the Navy and R.A.F. on whom—in the absence of adequate land forces—the defence essentially relied.

Briefly, the enemy proposed to attack in two groups on a front of some 160 miles. "A" Group, composed of his 16th and 9th Armies, was assigned the 100-mile frontage between Margate and Portsmouth. The 16th Army, starting from the ports between Ostend and Boulogne inclusive, was to land between Margate and Hastings; the 9th Army starting from Dieppe, Le Havre and Caen, was to land between Brighton and Portsmouth. "B" Group, his 6th Army, starting from Cherbourg after "A" Group had gained a footing, was to land in Weymouth bay.

For the initial assault the two groups were to employ eleven infantry and two mountain divisions, together with a mobile force of

"SEA-LION" was the Nazis' secret code-name ("Seeloewe" in German) for their ill-starred plan for the invasion of our shores, disclosed on September 25, 1945. The map illustrates Sir Charles Gwynn's accompanying analysis. *By courtesy of The Daily Telegraph*

six panzer and three motorized divisions available for rapid exploitation, and there were 17 additional divisions in reserve. On the "A" Group frontage airborne troops were also to be landed, and of course it had been hoped that in the Battle of Britain air superiority would have been gained to cover the operation. If landings had been successful, the capture of airfields would naturally have greatly increased the degree of superiority achieved.

Germany's Misconception of the Problems of the Great Invasion

In view of the immense disparity between the land forces available on either side it is self-evident that the defence of Britain depended, as indeed has always been the case, on preventing the enemy reaching our coasts in force. That is to say, he had to be attacked at his ports of assembly, during the slow process of emerging from them, in passage and while attempting to disembark. It may be noted that if this had successfully broken up "A" Group it is improbable that "B" Group would ever have started.

Formidable as the German invading force obviously was, the whole plan for its employment was vitiated by a misconception of the nature of the problem. The difficulties of overcoming beach defences and of subsequent exploitation seem to have been over-estimated and the size of the force it was thought necessary to employ emphasized the difficulty of providing shipping and craft suitable both for making the passage and effecting the landing. In addition, it clearly increased the difficulties of protecting convoys and of navigating them in an orderly manner.

Comparing the successful amphibious operations of the Allies with the abortive German plan, it is clear that material resources, especially of shipping and suitable landing craft, were the governing factors. Although for defence the Axis powers relied on land forces, the strength of the land force which the Allies employed for the initial landing was kept to the minimum required to gain a substantial footing and within the limits of shipping available. Safety in passage, and as great an element of surprise as could be achieved were essential to initial success, and the later development of the strength of the striking force depended on maintaining the safety of sea communications.

Failure of the Axis defence in each case resulted not from weakness on land, but primarily, from inability to interrupt the passage of the Allied armada on its line of sea communications by air or naval attack.

Royal Navy Could Have Played Havoc With Enemy's Convoys

In the Mediterranean, the Italian Fleet failed to intervene, and the air arm, both there and in Normandy, was mainly used to interfere with landing operations. Perforce in the latter operation the German naval defence was limited to the action of U-boats and mosquito craft, but it sufficed to show the need for powerful protection of convoys. The essential difference to be noted is that whereas the Axis relied mainly on their land forces to resist an actual landing, the British problem was to defeat the invading force in passage by sea and air action.

Since the Royal Navy was never called on to intervene in the Battle of Britain, it is impossible to say definitely how far it would have done so successfully, in spite of the dislocation of its dispositions caused by the loss of French naval co-operation. The defence of Crete does, however, provide on a small scale an analogous situation. There the Navy, although without air protection, successfully broke up all attempts at seaborne landings, compelling the Germans to depend entirely on airborne invasion.

The analogy is worth examination in spite of the difference in scale: first, because the vessels the Germans employed were of much the same order as they would have been forced to employ for an invasion of Britain in 1940; and second, because it revealed the fact that though darkness might provide immunity from air attack to convoys in passage it does not provide immunity from naval attack.

In view of these considerations let us return to the chances of German success in the two hypothetical situations I suggested:

(*a*) Would failure of the R.A.F. to win the Battle of Britain have left us in a hopeless position to resist invasion? I believe it would not. We may safely presume that failure would not have entailed the complete annihilation of our air defence, but rather the withdrawal of depleted squadrons to bases out of range of the enemy's fighters and fighter-escorted bombers. From these bases they could still have attacked the enemy's shipping as it neared our coast, and during daylight have given some protection to our naval forces. Bombing of enemy embarkation ports by night could still have continued, and the Navy might have played havoc with the enemy's convoys.

(*b*) Once the Battle of Britain had been won and the Navy assured of air protection the abandonment or postponement of the German plan was inevitable. It is, however, interesting to learn from Field-Marshal von Keitel that it was fear of naval action that prompted the decision, presumably because all hope had been lost that the Luftwaffe would be able to prevent that most devastating form of attack from developing.

WHEN BRITAIN WAS HELD BY BLUFF

General McNaughton, who commanded the Canadian forces in Britain threw further light, in a speech at Detroit in October 1945, on Britain's plight during the days of threatened invasion in 1940.

"With great truth," he said, "Britain was held largely by bluff. We searched ancient manuscripts in the old Bodleian library at Oxford for the formula for Greek fire used in 1100 to rout the Russian Fleet at Constantinople.

"Even the guns, which dated back to the era preceding the South African War, which had been placed in store by the thrifty Admiralty, were taken out and pressed into use, mounted on commercial vehicles of sorts, with boiler plates for armour."

Passing the Time with Our Army of the Rhine

BERLIN'S "BLACK MARKET" in the famous Tiergarten was raided by German police and British military police on October 14, 1945, when some 2,000 arrests, including over 100 Russian officers and men, were made. A British tank (1, foreground) dominated the proceedings. A B.A.O.R. major examined the papers of Wehrmacht youths about to be demobilized at Staaken, near Berlin (2). Quiet backwater of the Ilmenau at Luneburg provided some of our men (3) with the chance of a "bite." Official notices, in English, French, German and Polish, have to be carefully studied (4) for day-to-day instructions.

Photos, Keystone, Planet News

How the Barham was Lost

By

FRANCIS E. McMURTRIE

It is practically four years since the battleship Barham was lost, yet a full official account of the disaster has still to appear. In the Admiralty account of naval operations from April 1941 to January 1943, entitled The Mediterranean Fleet, there is no more than a bare reference to "the loss of the battleship Barham, torpedoed by a U-boat on the 25th November."

Named after the Admiral who was First Lord in the year of Trafalgar, H.M.S. Barham was launched from the yard of John Brown & Co., Ltd., at Clydebank, on the last day of 1914. At the Battle of Jutland she wore the flag of Rear-Admiral Hugh Evan-Thomas, commanding the Fifth Battle Squadron, and suffered casualties amounting to 26 killed and 37 wounded.

From 1919 to 1924 she was flagship of the First Battle Squadron in the Atlantic Fleet, and was then ordered to the Mediterranean. Returning to England in 1927, she rejoined the Mediterranean Fleet a year later. In 1929 she went back to the Atlantic Fleet, from which she was paid off at Portsmouth in December 1930. During the ensuing 2½ years she underwent an extensive refit which considerably altered her appearance. Her original two funnels were replaced by a single massive uptake, but she was never completely rebuilt and modernized, as in the case of three of her sister ships, the Queen Elizabeth, Valiant and Warspite.

FORMIDABLE Fighting Unit Though Speed Reduced by Added Weight

After a couple of years in the Home Fleet the Barham was again sent to the Mediterranean in 1935. Save for two brief interludes in home waters, she continued to serve on that station until the date of her loss. In the victory of Matapan, on March 28, 1941, she played an important part (see illus. page 682, Vol. 6). A ship of 31,000 tons displacement, she was armed with eight 15-in., twelve 6-in. and eight 4-in. guns. Her original speed of 25 knots had been considerably reduced by the additional weights added in the course of 27 years, but she remained a formidable fighting unit, whose loss could ill be spared on the eve of Pearl Harbour.

On November 25, 1941, British light forces had just intercepted an Italian convoy on its passage across the Ionian Sea, bound for Libya. In case the enemy fleet might come out, the Commander-in-Chief, Admiral Sir Andrew Cunningham, deemed it wise to have his battleships at hand to support the cruisers and destroyers. Thus the Queen Elizabeth (flagship of the Commander-in-Chief), Barham (flagship of the Second-in-Command, Vice-Admiral Pridham-Wippell), and Valiant were proceeding at 18 knots through the area between Crete and Cyrenaica, with a few destroyers acting as a screen.

U-BOAT Forced to the Surface as a Result of Violent Explosion

Unfortunately, a skilful U-boat captain contrived to dive beneath the screen unobserved and fire a salvo of torpedoes at the three battleships. According to some accounts these were aimed at the Queen Elizabeth, which was narrowly missed. Three are believed to have hit the Barham simultaneously from a distance of a few hundred yards, producing an explosion so violent as to force the submarine momentarily to the surface. She passed quite close to the Valiant, which hoisted the signal "Submarine astern," but the smoke from the explosion prevented the flags being seen by any but a few.

Within four minutes the Barham sank after a second explosion, that of the after magazine. How many were on board her at the time is not precisely stated, but 859 lost their lives. Others were picked up by the destroyers nearest to the scene of the disaster. A graphic account of the rescue work is given by Lieutenant-Commander Hugh Hodgkinson, D.S.C., R.N., in his book, "Before the Tide Turned," published by Messrs. Harrap (and quoted here by kind permission of the publishers). H.M.S. Hotspur, the destroyer of which he was first-lieutenant, was the closest, so was directed to proceed to the aid of survivors :

"Already the crew were cutting the stowage lines of the rescue nets. All rafts were being man-handled to the side. The whaler was manned, and I sent down the young midshipman to cox her. The Captain had slowed down, and we were nosing into what looked like a London fog, and smelled worse. We passed into and through the thick fog, which had by now drifted to leeward, and suddenly it cleared. Dozens of heads bobbed in the water, far more than I had ever hoped for.

"The Captain steered for a large clump who were clinging to the Barham's mast. I shouted final instructions to the midshipman : 'Go for the far and solitary ones, or those in distress. Leave the rest for us.' Then I lowered the whaler to the waterline and slipped her.

"As soon as we stopped the little bobbing heads moved slowly in towards us and the men were heaved on board. At the same time all our Carley rafts were slipped, and two men from our own crew dived over the side and clambered on board each of the rafts to paddle them out to more distant groups. Each raft had a grass line paid out behind it, so that as soon as it was full we could heave it back at high speed to the ship.

"Each man as he came over the side was black with oil. Bales of cotton waste were brought up from the store to clean them. The whole upper deck became layered with oil, so that one could hardly stand. The sick bay was filling with oil-smeared wounded. The whaler came alongside with men too badly wounded to climb. Neil Robertson stretchers were lowered and the men hoisted out, groaning, by tackles slung over the torpedo davit.

ADMIRAL Holding on to Raft too Thickly Oil-Covered to Recognize

"The Captain, meanwhile, moved the ship slowly towards the group clinging to the mast. Here the oil was thickest. It was solid, and the men could hardly swim or even cling to the great spar. It touched alongside, just by our foremost net, and men started clambering up limply.

"There was a Carley raft there, too, from which men were climbing. One seemed to be in charge, and was exhorting each to make his utmost effort. He was too thickly covered with oil to recognize, and he was swimming by the raft and holding on, to give the weaker ones a chance to lie in the raft. When all were up he started too. He put up an arm to a helping hand. It seemed to be nothing but gold stripe, and I realized who it was. I never expected to receive an admiral on board in such circumstances."

It was, in fact, the Second-in-Command of the Mediterranean Fleet, now Admiral Sir Henry Pridham-Wippell. He has recently been appointed Commander-in-Chief, Plymouth, as from November 27, 1945—almost four years to the day since he was rescued in the way just described.

Within a fortnight of the loss of the Barham, the battleship Prince of Wales and the battle cruiser Repulse were both sunk by Japanese torpedo planes in the South China Sea ; and a little later the Queen Elizabeth and Valiant were disabled by a daring Italian penetration of Alexandria Harbour in a tiny craft carrying two men. Although so slender a margin of naval strength was left to us in the Mediterranean, the Italians showed no disposition to send their main fleet out to seize control of that sea. Instead, they redoubled their efforts to bomb and starve Malta into subjection ; and Rommel's armies threatened to invade the Nile valley. Tobruk fell in June 1942, but the tide turned at El Alamein in October.

SHORTLY BEFORE SHE WAS TORPEDOED off Sollum, in November 1941, Mr. Leslie Kent, R.B.A., the well-known marine artist, painted this picture of the 27-year-old British battleship H.M.S. Barham as she steamed through the wintry waters of the Aegean with the snow-capped landscape of Crete in the background. The picture is here reproduced by permission of the artist.

Four Minutes in the Life—and Death—of Barham

OUR ONLY BATTLESHIP TO BE SUNK AT SEA BY A U-BOAT during the war was the 31,000-ton H.M.S. Barham, intercepted by the U-331 while operating with the Mediterranean Fleet some 200 miles W.N.W. of Alexandria on November 25, 1941. Hit by a salvo of torpedoes, she took a heavy list to port (top). Within four minutes of being struck, between the funnel and after turrets, the after magazine blew up (above) in a thick pall of smoke, causing the deaths of 859 officers and men. See also facing page. *Photos, British Official*

The Navy's Midget Submarines at Close Quarters

AUSTRALIA'S SYDNEY HARBOUR BRIDGE is the background for a surfaced midget submarine (1), on the occasion of a visit there by her depot-ship H.M.S. Bonaventure (2). On the tiny craft neither the sub-lieutenant operating the hydroplane controls (3) nor stoker (4) has spare elbow-room. Divers from this type of submarine, operating with the Bonaventure, mined the 9,850-ton Jap cruiser Takao in Johore Strait, near Singapore, on July 31, 1943. See also story in page 372 ; and illus. page 649, Vol. 7.

Photos, British Official, Sport & General

Life Guards Again at the Old Familiar Archway

FAMOUS PRE-WAR SPECTACLE of the Life Guards at Whitehall was enjoyed again by Londoners, for the first time in six years, on October 5, 1945. In the long interval the regiment had seen service in Africa, all through the Italian campaign and in Germany. On their reappearance the men wore Service dress, in sombre contrast with previous peacetime splendour. The first contingent is approaching the archway from the Horse Guards Parade—scene of the ceremonial Changing of the Guard—with the Brigade of Guards Memorial in background. *Photo, Sport & General*

UNSERVICEABLE AIRCRAFT OF THE R.A.F. being stripped for salvage at No. 1 Metal and Produce Recovery Depot (1) set up by the Ministry of Aircraft Production at Oxford. Here, besides heavy bombers which blasted Berlin and the Ruhr, Hurricane and Spitfire veterans of the Battle of Britain are broken up for aluminium, which will later be transformed into cooking utensils for British housewives, many of whom so willingly gave up their old ones to build aircraft in the early days of the war. A crowded corner of "Bombers' Graveyard" (2) with aircraft waiting to be reduced to 28-lb. ingots of metal which are seen (3) being stacked. Between 30,000 and 40,000 tons of scrap lie at the depot, and the store is being added to at the rate of 2,000 tons a week. See also facing page.

Photos, Keystone, The Evening Standard

The Greatest Mopping-Up Operation in History

Swords into ploughshares, Mosquitoes into saucepans : these transformations and many others are now taking place hand-in-hand with the salvaging of equipment and wreckage of war. The scale of operations is vast and millions of pounds are being saved. Organization and results are explained by Capt. MARTIN THORNHILL. See also facing page, and story in page 442.

SALVAGE units which are combing the battlefields are paying huge dividends. Equipment, stores and scrap metal collected in the sweeps eastward from the Normandy fighting zone are estimated to be worth over £14,000,000. The final figure is expected to be enormous.

Before Japan's defeat the salvage picture was a rather different one ; every available ammunition expert of the Ordnance Corps, Royal Engineers and Pioneers, was busily engaged sorting and classifying captured guns and ammunition, of which special categories were oiled and stored in Hamburg for transportation to the Far East. But since the collapse of the Japs the objective has become the slightly more simplified but no less vast one of collecting virtually everything for shipment to the United Kingdom.

Metal of knocked-out tanks, guns, planes and vehicles is quickly carved up by oxy-acetylene cutters, loaded into lorries which then trek to selected Continental ports and pile their valuable cargoes aboard tank-landing craft bound for home. Much salvaged equipment is cleaned, repaired and re-issued to our own Forces, or sold to the Dutch or Belgian Governments to help in the equipping of troops to garrison frontier posts or parts of occupied territory.

SALVAGE sales in one recent month included disposal of 20,000 dry batteries, 13 tons of torpedo netting and 27 tons of unserviceable gas capes, while equipment and stores worth £410,000 were recovered and reissued. In the same month the home market benefited to the extent of over 20,000 tons of scrap metal (value £62,000), and £21,000 worth of parachute equipment which went to make silk stockings—so much in request by women at home and now on sale in the shops at controlled prices.

It must be a consoling thought to most of us that if old metal, frying pans railings and so on could be transformed into bombs and Mosquitoes, then these items can, for a great part, be conjured back into saucepans, tables, tools and steel. For months—perhaps years—to come, a large proportion of factory machinery and accommodation will be engaged in rendering-down scrap metal to its original foundations of copper, lead, brass, aluminium, to form the basic constituents of motor-chassis, machine tools, engine bearings, radio apparatus, electrical equipment, telephone cable, ships' propellers, pots, pans and a further diversity of peacetime equipment.

Loot Found in Nazi Rat-Runs

So much for the major instruments of war—or some of them. Quite apart from our own masses of material, there are hundreds of thousands of items accumulated by the German Todt organization and its various groups, which are now passing forward to a legion of valuable functions. There were, too, vast quantities of domestic materials stripped from local homes by the German military commanders to furnish comforts for the personnel of large-scale Boche defences—furniture, cutlery, glassware, stoves, bed linen, pianos, clocks, electric irons, chicken runs, even window-frames and outbuildings. For when these Nazi "rat runs" were overtaken by our men they were found to be fitted with "every modern convenience," all filched from the homes of local inhabitants. Wholesale confiscations had been made from hundreds of hospitals and institutions by regimental headquarters, by individual soldiers, by gauleiters themselves, entrusted with local government. These things have now for the most part been returned to their owners ; an intricate and laborious task.

The 1914–18 war ended with about a million tons of ammunition in hand. The expense of removing hundreds of dumps to a central disposal point proved so costly that break-up plants had to be built on the sites. In the end, converted into scrap metal, the mountains of shells and bombs brought the Government less than £1,000,000. That was better than nothing ; but nobody being able to think of any use for the explosives and propellants which had been extracted, these were prodigally piled on the beaches of France and Belgium, and burned.

GIGANTIC ELECTRO-MAGNET unloads scrap-iron from a wagon and places it in a bin for later transport to the blast furnaces. During the great salvage drive of 1940, eighty per cent of old iron recovered went to make bombs for the R.A.F. *Photo, Topical Press*

High explosive, which had cost us £100 a ton, simply went up in smoke. There will be a great deal more to dispose of this time, purchased at a higher price, and widely increased technical knowledge is combining with wartime education in salvage to separate the constituents into thousands of tons of valuable fertilizer. For the basis of all explosives is nitrogen ; some contain potash as well, and both are excellent land fertilizers.

BREAKING down of T.N.T. and amatol involves great risk to the lives of those doing it, but the value of the chemical constituents to our worked-out farms is going to prove immense ; fertility of Britain's land is likely to be immensely restored by using this means of resuscitation which lies ready to hand.

These tasks, as well as the reconditioning of thousands of vehicles and stores after collection, are all part of a brilliantly executed scheme. It has meant the retention of highly trained personnel in the R.A.O.C., R.A.S.C. and Pioneers, and none perhaps was better qualified to administer it than the soldier who was appointed to the task. For the Director of Salvage, Brigadier Charles Vere Bennett, O.B.E., R.A.S.C., a one-time high official of the Institute of Mechanical Engineers, was, between the wars, an instructor and administrative officer in Army technical schools. At the beginning of this war he became Assistant Director of Supply and Transport.

The basis of Army salvage is that everything which passes out of effective use by the Army comes within the scope of salvage. The battlefield having been divided into specific areas for ease of administration, it becomes the duty of each military unit to report surplus or waste material in its own zone. To illustrate the efficacy of this decentralizing of duty, as the result of a drive by the Third British Infantry Division for recovery of "jerricans," dumped all over the countryside during battle operations, fifty units in the British Second Army salvaged 110,060 cans in one week, thus saving nearly £50,000 of taxpayers' money. One man alone collected 4,207. (See illus. in page 532, Vol. 8).

"Sifting" the Western Desert

After sorting and classification, any salvage still militarily useful is reissued against special demand. Such other material as is repairable, or otherwise usable, finds its way to the Ministry of Supply. There is a future even for "unusable" matter, such as rusted barbed wire. Priority in this is held by the occupier of the land where it is salvaged, the remainder being sold to local inhabitants or disposed of by public auction.

While salvage operations in different areas may be varied to suit local conditions, the general scheme is the same everywhere, and the last chapter of British salvage in France and Germany will doubtless have a good deal in common with what is now taking place in North Africa. The Western Desert is a salvage area of itself, and an example of thoroughness and perfect completion. Nothing has been wasted. Tires which could not be repaired locally were shipped to Britain to be melted down into rubber. Scrap steel made new tanks and aircraft, for which hundreds of tons of magnesium alloy—worth £1,000 a ton—were recovered from old castings. Earlier, from Western Desert salvage, one smelter alone was turning out enough ingots daily to produce ten fighters.

THE Turkish Army and Civil Defence Corps had in use thousands of guns and rifles captured by Montgomery from the Italians. Linen was stripped from the backs of old maps and handed over to the medical services for use in plastic surgery. Boots unfit for repair became leather washers. Wet batteries, sparking plugs and so on were reconditioned, and old battery plates melted down for lead. Four-gallon petrol tins, too badly damaged to be used again, were turned into fly-traps, ration boxes, petrol funnels and trays. Vast quantities of medical stores were captured intact ; even the pills proved useful, rendered down to their chemical components. The sands, once thick with mines along a wide belt stretching westwards for hundreds of miles, have long since been freed of this menace. Only waste material remains in this once vast and active battle zone—and even this is still in the process of sale to Egypt and the folk of the Mediterranean seaboard.

Hundreds of other trappings of battle can be turned, and in fact are being turned, to good account by transforming them into articles of civilian use. For this is the greatest "mopping up" operation in history ; and it will go on for a long time.

Now British Scientists Fire V2s From Germany

ROCKET BOMBS were successfully test-fired from Cuxhaven, Germany, into the North Sea in October 1945 by British scientists and technicians who, during the war, had organized counter-measures against them. So satisfactory were the new guiding devices that one of the rockets fell within three miles of the target, 150 miles distant. The experiments, to test information supplied by the Germans after the surrender, were conducted by the Special Projectile Operations Group (S.P.O.G.), composed of Royal Artillery experts and technicians from the Ministry of Supply.

Although over 8,000 German rocket troops were captured during our advance in the Low Countries, together with numerous rocket parts, the Nazis had gone to great lengths to destroy equipment, and no complete rockets could be found. Some parts—as a result of R.A.F. bombing of German production centres—were made in Britain from captured blueprints.

On its six-wheeled trailer, a V2 is about to be towed (1) to the launching site specially constructed by men of the Royal Engineers, where it is seen being elevated (2) to the vertical firing position (3). Up she goes (4), well into the sky (5).

Photos, British Official

At Biggin Hill 'Where They Won the War'

On the Westerham Road, "Towerfield" lies almost midway between Bromley Common and the R.A.F. aerodrome at Biggin Hill, on the Kentish Downs. A rambling late-Victorian mansion (right), embowered in grounds well wooded with pine and larch, it is plainly the product of an age of leisure, of peace and plenty. Yet it was from here during what was probably our most critical period that the Battle of Britain (September–October 1940) was largely directed—and largely won—when, in the undying words of Winston Churchill, "Never in the field of human conflict was so much owed by so many to so few." The story is part of our history, with Trafalgar and Waterloo, and it is suggested that this Victorian mansion, now shabby and deserted, should become a national monument, preserved intact for posterity as a visible reminder of Britain's finest hour and of the imperishable glory of the R.A.F.

Inside the building, in what was once a sumptuous lounge, is the famous Fighter Command "Ops" Room (below), nerve centre of the Battle of Britain in its most critical stage; from here the defence of London was mainly conducted. Earlier in the Battle, the Luftwaffe bombers had all but wiped out Biggin Hill aerodrome, wrecking its "Ops" Room. By way of hurried stop-gap a village shop was requisitioned, then "Towerfield." Here, in the lounge, was erected the famous six-sided table shown below with its large-scale map of south-eastern England and the Continental approaches—on which counters denoting aircraft were feverishly moved backwards and forwards to indicate the positions of the enemy and those of our fighters opposing them. On the benches around the table sat the Assistant Controller with representatives of the Royal Observer Corps, the Searchlight Section of the A.A. Batteries and the Army, pooling their efforts as one magnificent team. On the dais (left), at a desk, sat the Controller, then Group Captain R. Grice, O.B.E., D.S.C., coordinating data flashed through by telephone and planning the campaign—under the Supreme Command of Sir Hugh (now Lord) Dowding, C.-in-C. of Fighter Command. As Richard Dimbleby, B.B.C. commentator, broadcasting from here on September 15, 1945, fifth anniversary of the Battle of Britain, declared, "It is one room in which you could say, 'That is where they won the war.'"

Drawings by Captain Bryan de Grineau by courtesy of The Illustrated London News

When London's Docks Visited the Clyde

One of our most astonishing and successful feats in the countering of the Nazis when Britain had her back to the wall was the partial removal, in the autumn of 1940, of the Port of London to the Clyde Estuary. Official disclosure of details of this great enterprise of "the Port in the Sea" has only recently been made: the following account is compiled from information in the October issue of the Magazine of the Port of London Authority. See also illus. page 166.

AFTER the overthrow of the Low Countries and the fall of France in the early summer of 1940 it was quickly becoming obvious that shipping could make use of London and our other south and east coast ports for very little longer. There was the Luftwaffe. There were the E-boats. There was the magnetic mine. Each and all conspiring to cut us off from world supplies.

A major diversion of shipping to our west coast ports at once suggested itself to the Ministries of Shipping and Transport (later to be combined in the Ministry of War Transport); but it was soon discovered that even working at maximum pressure these ports would be sadly unequal to the vast demands imposed by our ever-growing war-effort. The position indeed seemed grievous. And as the weeks dragged on into late summer it worsened.

Whose was the inspiration we may never know. But it was born. At once plans were put into operation establishing the Clyde Anchorages Emergency Port, a brilliantly-conceived scheme for a vast port at sea in the safely-enclosed waters of the Clyde where British and ocean-bound shipping could anchor, and, without touching land, load and discharge their cargoes overside, with protection afforded by the boom between Dunoon and the Cloch Lighthouse erected at the outbreak of war. Details were worked out with the help of the Port of London Authority's Assistant General Manager, Mr. (now Sir) Robert Letch.

THE Clyde Anchorages scheme went into operation almost immediately after the Port of London received its first heavy air attack on September 7, 1940. Within a few days the first stevedoring unit, consisting of London men and gear, proceeded north. The men were billeted in the Greenock and Gourock districts, and within a month totalled some six hundred. The administration was in the hands of Sir Robert Letch, as Executive, and a small staff loaned by the Port of London Authority.

Exactly a week after that heavy Luftwaffe raid on London's docks, the first ship discharged her cargo at "the Port in the Sea." She was the S.S. Nardana, with a general cargo from India. She was the first of the many. The date was September 14, 1940—a memorable day in the history of this island.

DISTRIBUTION of cargo to various ultimate destinations involved a highly-skilled degree of planning, for there were no quays or sheds available for housing goods pending instructions. Before each cargo rose from the ship's hold it was necessary to decide its route of consignment. As often happened, cargoes were transhipped direct from ocean vessel into coasters awaiting to hurry them to our home ports.

This scheme had many advantages, including the saving of precious time, and the risks to the cargoes were spread over a much larger number of vessels. Cargoes needed for delivery by rail or road were discharged into a special fleet of power barges, dumb barges and Dutch schuyts, and sailed ashore. Here they were unloaded at emergency wharves—some of them exclusively for passenger use in normal times—by means of small electric cranes and trucks brought all the way from London. The stevedoring was carried out by the London dockers.

In all, some 300 Thames dumb (towed) barges were dispatched to the Clyde, either towed round the coast or carried on the decks of freighters. A fleet of punts was taken by road, as far as the port of Glasgow and there launched. Under the guidance of a lighterage foreman loaned by the P.L.A., local hands from Greenock were trained in the task of handling these craft. And they did it thoroughly. Most of the powered barges were Thames Estuary auxiliary sailing barges, which were moved to the Clyde and operated there by their normal crews. Because of weather conditions they did not make use of their sails but relied on their auxiliary engines. Many of them had, earlier in the year, performed gallant service at Dunkirk.

Almost every kind of cargo was unloaded at the Clyde Anchorages. Included among them was bulk grain, and for this the Port acquired portable bucket elevators, operated by an expert P.L.A. grain machinist. When supplies from the U.S. began streaming in, large tonnages of explosives were discharged at remote anchorages in the neighbouring lochs. An even trickier task was the unloading of vast quantities of tanks, tracked and other vehicles and landing craft in sections, with the help of a powerful floating crane.

Discharging Damaged Ships

Rarely was the work of a straightforward nature. And there were always vagaries of the weather to contend with. Frequently ships which had been severely damaged by enemy action while at sea had to be discharged from flooded holds so that repairs could be effected. Of these shattered craft some were so heavily waterlogged that they arrived with too deep a draft to enter any normal port, and thus had to be discharged in deep-water anchorages.

On one occasion men and gear from the Anchorages made an overland journey of some 250 miles to render assistance to the S.S. Staffordshire which, limping badly, had managed to enter Loch Ewe, well north of the Clyde. Another ship carried a cargo of oranges, from Spain, among which Nazi agents had placed bombs timed to explode on voyage—which they did. The whole cargo, on arrival in the Clyde, had to be shot loose into barges, each case being opened on board under the supervision of bomb disposal experts. Another frequent task was the re-stowing of deck cargoes which had shifted during rough weather in the North Atlantic or on the Murmansk route to Russia.

WITH the lessening of the Luftwaffe's attacks on southern and eastern ports, British shipping slowly returned to something like normal. But the work of the Clyde Anchorages went on, as a vast terminal for the larger troopships. After America's entry into the war, five of the world's biggest passenger liners—Queen Mary, Queen Elizabeth, Aquitania, Ile de France and Nieuw Amsterdam—operated a regular ferry service between the U.S. and the Clyde Anchorages, transporting hundreds of thousands of American troops for service in Europe. These swift vessels sailed singly, and in addition smaller types of troopships continuously sailed in and out of the "Port" in convoy. The Port authorities grappled skilfully with the prodigious tasks of ferrying the troops ashore and entraining them besides refuelling and storing the ships themselves.

It was from the Clyde, too, that a large part of the fleet engaged in the North Africa landings embarked; from here, also, they sailed in large numbers for Normandy, following D-Day, with the equipment necessary for exploiting the invasion. In all, from September 1940 to its discontinuance at the end of August 1945, the Clyde Emergency Port discharged and loaded 1,885 ships. The cargo discharged and loaded amounted to 2,056,833 tons; while military equipment, stores, mails, and so on discharged and loaded numbered 6,032,872 packages.

HOW LONDON DOCKS LOOKED TO THE LUFTWAFFE, revealed in a photograph taken from a Nazi bomber during a daylight raid in the Battle of Britain; Surrey Commercial Docks and the West India and Millwall systems are enclosed in the loop of the Thames known as the Isle of Dogs. Tower Bridge is at the top left. It was the threat of heavy damage to these docks that brought into being the Clyde Anchorages Emergency Port. *Photo, British Official*

Battle to Save War-Famous Dutch Island

To flood the German gun-sites on the island of Walcheren R.A.F. bombers on October 3, 1944, at high tide, tore great gaps in the dyke that prevented the sea from submerging the low-lying land. The waters then surged over most of Walcheren, and the breach at Westkapelle was used by Royal Marine Commandos as the gateway for their attack on November 1. (See pages 463–466, Vol. 8).

Now, with the aid of British equipment, Dutch workers are rebuilding the blasted dykes; by October 3, 1945, the first of the gaps had been sealed. Filled sandbags, and faggots for foundations, are used (top left). Nearly closed (top right), with the sea on the left; flood-water on the opposite side stretches away for many miles. Through the last few yards swirls the rising tide (right), but at next low-water the sandbag barrier will be completed. When the dykes are restored, Mulberry Harbour sections will be joined together to form an outer sea-wall. (See also illus. page 386).

Where Nazi Tank Crews Trained in Norway

In August 1943 it was reported that the Germans were clearing tracts of some of Norway's finest forests at Trandum, south of the Hurdal Lake, in order to establish practice sites for artillery and tanks which were to fire at speed. In one locality German pioneers with mechanically operated saws had cut down all the timber on a front of more than 500 yards. Now a British officer, **Major Kenneth Hare-Scott**, recently stationed near those woods, 35 miles north of Oslo, has described specially for THE WAR ILLUSTRATED the peculiar methods adopted for the training of the tank crews in street-fighting tactics ; the exclusive illustrations are by **Driver Walter Bell.**

There is a sinister implication in the discovery of many graves in the immediate vicinity a discovery which resulted in Trandum becoming one of the horror-places of Norway ; for there took place frequent executions of resistance workers from Oslo, and Russians from neighbouring labour camps Erected in great secrecy by the Germans, a stone's throw from the rough graves, is the ingeniously contrived tank range shown in detail above.

Entering the first of the archways or screens (1), massively constructed of concrete and timber (shown in section at 2), tank drivers were confronted by a long vista of the semblance of a built-up area, with all its (assumed) possibilities of frequent ambushes and the concomitants of street-fighting, as indicated by the side view (3). A straight run is provided through the remaining screens (4) towards the distant target. It is presumed that the purpose of the two tunnels at the far end of the range was to confine the blast of the shells fired by each speeding tank as it neared the completion of the course.

The targets ? It is considered likely by Norwegians now in the vicini these had been provided by bodies found in the adjacent graves, a few of are seen at the extreme right (4). These each contained more than corpses, toppled in carelessly at all angles. It may be that these unfort were the only people, other than the Germans, who knew the real purpose erections. Many of the graves have now been uncovered and the bodies to Oslo for identification ; some bore no trace of wounds, and it has been i that these were buried alive—tied to the dead. The work of disinterri bodies was carried out by quislings, under compulsion, and Quisling was compelled to witness the gruesome proceedings.

OTHER places in Norway specially associated with Nazi brutality are a concentration camp to which members of the resistance movemen sent for confinement. Victoria Terrasa and Mollargaten 19 in Oslo are where the initial "grilling" of victims took place, whilst an island nea possessed a gallows and torturer's implements behind high walls, well sc from public view. Nobody quite knows what happened on this islan evidence points to it being another centre of human suffering and extermi Greni has now changed its name to Ellabu, and today houses a large n of quislings awaiting trial.

As in other countries, the Gestapo in Norway was ruthless in its me The quislings would be paid for a denunciation, and the victims selected by were invariably ordinary citizens against whom some personal grudge may

Victims Were Tumbled into Nameless Graves

d but who had committed no crime against the occupying forces. The g and torture would continue for twelve or thirteen hours, until the unate individual, completely exhausted, probably not only "confessed" ne misdeed he had not committed, but implicated friends as innocent as lf. In some cases genuine workers in the resistance movement would be d down by the Gestapo, but their bravery in maintaining silence in face of e completely baffled the efforts of the Germans to find the nerve centre of the strongest and most effective underground movements in Europe.

Norwegian woman whose husband played a leading part in the resistance and was eventually tracked down, told me (writes Major Kenneth Hare- of a visit of the Gestapo to their house. The husband had received warn- e same evening and left the country for Sweden. The Gestapo made her all his possessions into suitcases, and mounting a machine-gun at the foot parents' sleeping child's bed, they warned her that if she omitted to pack e item they would shoot the child out of hand.

vas the constant fear of detection or denunciation by a quisling which the five years of German occupation as much of a nerve-racking experience in England ever suffered through aerial bombardment. The Norwegians d to do as little work as possible during the occupation, and now they that they find it difficult to complete a full working day without feeling omething is wrong! They fed from what they could buy on the Black t—fats were scarce, they had no milk or butter at all during the last year of German occupation, and there is little doubt that had the conditions continued tuberculosis would have been rife. Farmers were compelled to supply all the needs of the invader, who admittedly paid—but with notes "wet with the printer's ink," as one farmer described it. Worthless currency flooded the country and had little or no purchasing power—for there was nothing to buy.

A GREAT area of devastation is in the extreme north—Finmark (see page 749, Vol. 8). There the Germans burned and looted everything—towns, villages, boats, forests and communications—in the belief that should the Russians advance into northern Norway, as at one time seemed likely, the Nazis would be able to pin the responsibility for the destruction upon Marshal Stalin's troops. Wisely the Russians stopped short of Finmark, and yet another German bluff failed to come off. But that in no way mitigated serious loss to the Norwegians.

Recently I attended the first trial by court-martial of a German officer accused of murdering a Russian ex-prisoner. The court, composed of American, British and Norwegian officers, sat for several days and a very able defence was put forward for the accused. He was, however, convicted and sentenced to be shot. One left the court-room (the dining-room of a hotel in Lillehamar), where scores of Norwegians had been sentenced to death on trumped-up charges after trials lasting a few minutes, with the impression that no court-martial could have been conducted more fairly or with more consideration for every aspect of the prisoner's defence and character . . . Justice has returned to a brave little country which knew only the basest injustice and inhumanities during five weary years.

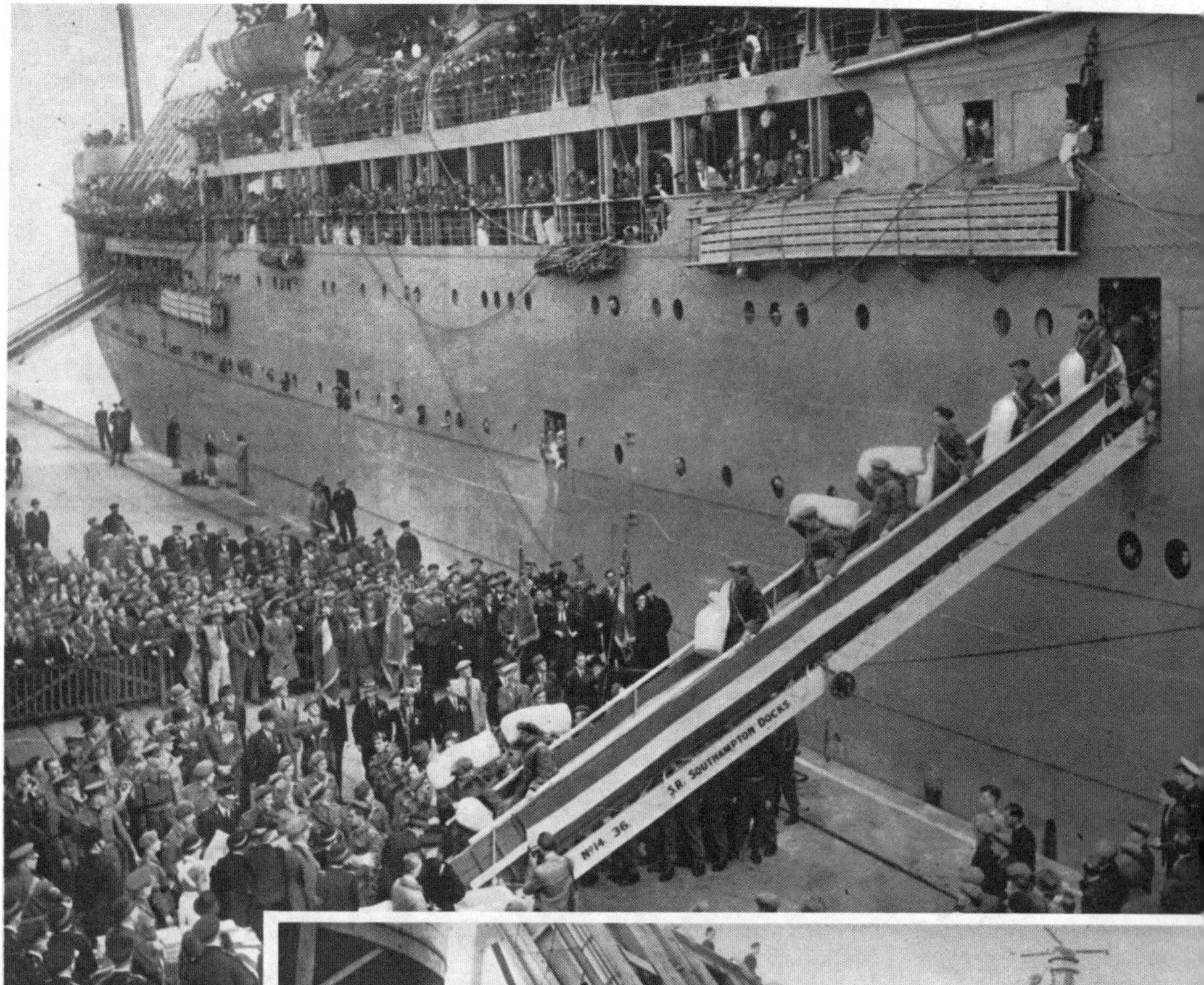

First Home by Sea from Far East

October 7, 1945, will remain a red-letter date for 1,134 ex-prisoners of war, and their friends and relatives, for on that day there docked at Southampton the P. and O. liner Corfu bringing home the first seaborne batch of P.O.W. from captivity in the Far East. General Sir Ronald Adam, Adjutant-General, went on board and read to them a message of welcome from the King and Queen; and a copy, typed on Buckingham Palace notepaper and bearing the King's signature, was given to each. Lining the rails (right), eager to step ashore, the men were prepared for a rousing reception—and were not disappointed. The scene on the quayside as they disembarked (above). Each as he left the ship was presented with cigarettes, chocolate and other gifts and a free telegram form on which to send a message home.

Our Lightships in the War

By

HAMILTON FYFE

Which of the German crimes committed during the Second Great War will be considered the most dastardly, the least forgivable? In the opinion of Sir Geoffrey Callender the attacks on lightships were "one of the world's foulest crimes, which no tears of penitence can ever wash away, no apologies ever condone." That is not altogether an unprejudiced view, for Sir Geoffrey is Director of the National Maritime Museum at Greenwich, and is specially concerned with shipping and the seamen who work the ships.

But no one is likely to disagree with his statement that when the Nazis decided, as part of their campaign against the British Merchant Navy, to bomb lightships, they proclaimed themselves "the foes of all humanity, the enemies of all who in a spirit of self-negation untiringly worked, not for profit or gain, not for prestige or promotion, but for the good of all mankind."

That is how he describes the crews of the lightships in his introduction to a book written by one who was in the service of the Trinity House—Looming Lights, by George G. Carter (Constable, 8s. 6d.)—and who had "personal experience of the atrocities committed against the lightships by the champions of the Crooked Cross." But before coming to these, let us ask and try to answer the query: Why the Trinity House?

This was a Corporation which received in 1514 a charter from King Henry VIII, who laid upon it the duty of taking care that the Thames pilots, who brought vessels up to the Port of London from the Nore, should be competent and trustworthy. Evidently they hadn't all been, or this supervision would not have been necessary.

That Dangerous Old Enemy the Nore

About a century after this institution was founded a proposal was made that it should put a light on the dangerous sandbank called the Nore, so that masters of ships should know where they were and should not attempt the passage up the Thames without taking on a pilot acquainted with all its difficulties. Why it took a hundred years for this eminently sensible plan to be carried out does not emerge. Probably it was the "can't-be-done" school which stood in the way. No vessel, it was argued, could be kept in position during storms. And that certainly was an obstacle; for when, in the 18th century, a lightship was moored at the Nore it broke away more than once and narrowly escaped being completely wrecked. However, by this time the need for a light was generally admitted and perseverance brought its reward. By the beginning of the 19th century six more had been established off our coast; now there are between forty and fifty.

Some of these have electric lights, on the same principle as those of lighthouses; others rely on vaporized oil burners. Every half-hour a clock has to be wound to keep the lantern revolving. The beams, which are level and steady, thanks to an ingenious mechanism, are all different, so that masters can tell which lightship they are near. Some "flash," that is, go on and off at regular intervals; some vary the colour of the beam. In foggy weather they give warning of danger by means of very powerful sirens.

The first time Mr. Carter heard one of these "deafening, ear-splitting" contrivances give its "hellish shriek" (as Sir Geoffrey Callender puts it) he felt it very badly. One of his shipmates noticed his distress and told him not to worry about the horn too much—"you'll get used to it."

> Here he stopped as the two blasts from the siren interrupted him. "Always let that feller have his say, you'll save a lot of breath and patience." And thus I learned to regulate my conversation to the intervals between the blasts and rarely was I interrupted, though conversation was usually cut down to a minimum when we were "blasting."

Actually he missed the "hellish" din when the weather cleared and it was no longer needed. He found the silence positively uncanny. For the first night he could not sleep, but "lay in my hammock, listening to the silence."

In the first war-winter the Nore lightship in which Mr. Carter then served was often in danger from mines that had broken loose. Some were British, some German. It was said that ours became harmless after they were adrift, but "how could one tell the difference? They all had horns projecting from them." One day a black speck was spotted through binoculars a long way ahead.

EAST DUDGEON LIGHTSHIP, whose machine-gunned lantern turret is shown here, was one of those heavily attacked by the Luftwaffe in 1940. The story is told in the book reviewed in this page. *Photo, Fox*

As it came nearer, its horns could be seen. The alarm was given. "Jump out, lads! There's a —— great mine right dead ahead and the tide is fetching it down fast!"

Very quickly all the crew were on deck with as much of their property as they could carry. The sea was running too high for a boat to be lowered. The skipper seized the huge iron tiller and shoved the helm hard over, hoping to sheer the ship away from the mine. But the current drove it under the bows and "petrified, the men waited for the blast that would tear them and their ship to atoms." Imagine their relief when it reappeared—with one of its horns badly bent—and drifted harmlessly astern.

As well as these underwater perils there were frequently planes overhead, but the old hands didn't worry about them.

> The lightships weren't touched in the last war, they said; and so we remained smugly complacent in our safety—poor fools that we were. How little we understood the Hun!

The first lightship to be attacked was the Smith's Knoll, in January 1940. Then came the assaults on the East Dudgeon. Aircraft swooped down, bombing and machine-gunning. The lantern was shattered, the rail and part of the ship's side blown away, the rigging too. Master and crew managed to scramble into the lifeboat and lay a short distance astern. When the planes had gone and they saw their ship was still afloat, they pulled back to her in a flurry of snow and climbed aboard. Scarcely had they done so when another attack developed. They jumped into the lifeboat again and made for the shore.

It was not far distant and they knew the Norfolk coast, but they were numbed by the icy wind and spray, and it was dawn before they saw land. It seemed close, but between them and the shore was a sandbank; on this the huge waves were breaking heavily. Their boat was overturned, they were flung into the breakers. Crawling slowly, painfully, in the last stages of exhaustion, they tried to reach the top of the beach. One by one they had to give up the effort. Only one survivor reached safety. He called back from time to time, but "one by one the voices ceased to answer, for the men were lying dead along the sand."

Unarmed and Prey to Any Attack

After this, the lightshipmen knew what to expect. "Lightships whose traditions of life-saving had made them inviolate through the ages were being deliberately attacked." They were too important for their lights to be allowed to go out, if this could possibly be avoided. So there the men stopped, "absolutely unarmed, prey to anything that cared to sink or board us. Many of us had visions of an E-boat dropping alongside and the whole crew of us driven aboard under the threat of a sub-machine-gun, and finally thrown into a concentration camp somewhere in Germany."

They saw any number of Stukas, "hordes of them," and hardly any of our own (they were too busy elsewhere). The Stukas were usually looking for convoys, but one day they turned their attention to the East Sand Head lightship. This was an old one and the crew had fortunately been taken out. Another, which had its crew on board, was very badly damaged—sides pierced by cannon shell and armour-piercing bullets, boats shot into a mass of splinters; but by good luck not one of the ship's company was injured.

Next came the tragedy of the South Folkestone Gate lightship. The crew were at dinner when six bombers started the attack. A rush was made for the deck. Here the Master was clearing the falls of the lifeboat, with blood running from a gash on his face. Two men who had been with him had been blown to pieces. Half the bulwarks were gone, the deck-house steel-plating was all crumpled up. Somehow the survivors manoeuvred the boat away, most of them with wounds; they were picked up by a speedboat and hurried to hospital on shore.

The North Sand lightship, to which Mr. Carter was transferred, had now become one of the only three left in the approaches to the Thames. They had narrow escapes, all of them. One day 25 Dorniers rained bombs all round the North Sand, but by what seemed a miracle she was not hit. "The bombs fell only a few feet either side of us. In fact, the only stretch of water they didn't strike was where we floated." The Master radio-ed cheerfully, "Heavily bombed, but still afloat undamaged. No casualties." He could have stayed on, but the authorities felt it was time to withdraw the crews both of North Sand and South Sand. They had been "taking it" long enough.

So the coastwise lights went out. But, wrote Mr. Carter, ending his book: "They are immortal. The hour will surely come when once again they will sweep the darkening sky, pointing, guiding, warning; symbols of hope, deliverance and justice to humanity." His prediction was right. That hour has come.

Now It Can Be Told!

'Ghost' Forts Sent to Crash on Heligoland

While the flying-bombs and rockets were crashing on London we were using an 11-ton V-weapon against the Germans. And the Germans who survived this weapon never knew how it worked. I can now reveal (writes D. Gould, in the London Evening News) that "ghost" bombers, piloted by radio control and loaded with eleven tons of bombs, were being aimed across the North Sea to crash on the heavily defended German island of Heligoland.

The Germans were mystified by the fact that they flew through the heaviest flak and crashed without anybody baling out first. The planes were old Flying Fortresses. One of them caused a scare right across England from the Wash to Liverpool when it got off course and headed west instead of east. Because the Germans were "in the dark" about it when Flying Fortress Melancholy Baby went the wrong way in September 1944 everybody in the know had to tell a story which would not give the secret away.

So the explanation was offered that "George," the automatic pilot, had become awkward, that Gremlins had taken over the control of the plane after the crew had baled out, and had piloted it safely if a little erratically across England and Eire and out over the Atlantic! Because of the death load it carried, sirens were sounded in every town and village along the plane's course.

It went from the King's Lynn area, south of the Wash, in a north-westerly direction to Derby, over Spalding and Melton Mowbray, then to Merseyside, passing over Congleton, Middlewich, Northwich and Runcorn.

It gave Liverpool its first air raid warning for 18 months, and R.A.F. officials who knew the danger were appalled to see it circle the city twice before setting off in a westerly direction again, causing an alert in Bangor as it went.

Fighters went up to pursue "Baby," who was flying perfectly at more than 250 m.p.h., and they were ready to shoot it down into the sea. At one time it looked as if it would outstrip its pursuers, and a warning was flashed to America that the bomber was heading on a course which might carry it right across the Atlantic. But finally R.A.F. fighters caught it and shot it down into the Atlantic. These "ghost" bombers were taken into the air and set on their course by two pilots who baled out while still over land.

Human Minesweepers and Divers of the R.N.

That the 50,000-ton liner Europa was recently able to make safe passage out of Bremen was largely due to the efforts of the Royal Navy's "human minesweepers," divers specially trained to find and render safe mines which could not be swept by normal methods. Since D-Day these teams of naval diving and mine-disposal experts, known as "P" Parties, often working in appalling conditions and submerged in mud, have cleared every major port from Cherbourg to Bremen.

It was at Bremen that the greatest test of their courage and skill was made. Some 60 mines had been laid by the enemy before the surrender. Their location was unknown, and the opening of this vital port was entirely dependent on these mine-clearance experts. Diving and mining history was made when a "P" Party officer, Lieut. George Gosse, R.A.N.V.R., of Adelaide, Australia, first rendered safe a little-known enemy "oyster" mine underwater at Bremen.

"I had seen bits of one before, but this was quite different from the one I had seen," Lieut. Gosse said afterwards. "The mine was resting on a body—there was plenty of rubbish and bodies in the harbour—but I didn't worry about this. It was very dark and I had to work by sense of touch in about two feet of mud. It was quite cold, too, and a little lonely. I took the primer off and brought the mine up to the surface. It was like taking a sparking plug out of a car. You can do it in the dark if you know what you are looking for!"

Birth of the "P" Parties came in the Mediterranean campaign, when charges ready for laying in deep-water berths were discovered at Bizerta. It was found that the enemy could lay mines with a delayed action of up to 80 days—an unexpected threat to port liberation which had to be overcome. It was decided that divers trained as human minesweepers were the reply to this menace.

Accordingly, the Admiralty Experimental Diving Unit of Tolworth, Surrey, under Commander W. O. Shelford, R.N., of Ryde, Isle of Wight, working with the Unit's Senior Medical Officer, Surgeon Lieut.-Cmdr. K. W. Donald, D.S.C., R.N., of London, designed a special shallow-water diving suit, based on

the Unit's previous research on human torpedoes and midget submarines. The suit embodied the first operational application of the revolutionary principle of mixture-breathing in a closed circuit, a self-contained apparatus giving a mixture of enriched air supplied from portable bottles.

Two "P" Parties, each of about 40 ratings and two officers, all volunteers, were recruited, and by D-Day were ready. Personnel were trained in mine and bomb recognition, in avoiding booby-traps, in the use of automatic weapons, in field work and in tying bends and hitches blindfold—a preparation for their hazardous underwater work.

A search technique was developed, using guiding ropes anchored in parallel patterns over the search area. By crawling along these ropes over the harbour bed divers could complete an intensive search, often relying merely on their sense of touch. Route marches, P.T. and swimming training maintained vital standards of physical fitness. The parties went into action soon after D-Day, one at Caen to clear the Caen Canal and the port, the other to open the port of Cherbourg.

Three more British parties and one Dutch party were speedily trained and were soon

ROYAL NAVY "P" PARTIES did much of their training in Brixham Harbour, where an "undersea museum" was laid down to familiarize them with enemy mines, obstacles and booby-traps. Attached to ropes, two trainees (above) enter the water; another, fully accoutred (right), is ready to go down. *Photos, The Evening Standard*

moving along the European coast hard on the heels of the liberation armies. Cherbourg, Ouistreham, Caen, Boulogne, Calais, Brest, Dieppe, Le Havre, and Rouen were all cleared and new types of ground mines, demolition charges and jettisoned enemy gear were successfully recovered.

APPALLING conditions of ice and thick mud, often over the divers' heads, were encountered; but the work, vital to speed European liberation, never stopped. The clearance of Antwerp was completed in record time, and by the end of December, Terneuzen, Zeebrugge, the south Beveland Canal and Flushing were free. By this time parties were completely mobile, with four 3-ton trucks and one 10-cwt. van. Despite the dangers of having to breathe oxygen under pressure and the continual menace of underwater explosions, strict observance of standing orders enabled the gigantic task

of "P" Parties to be completed with no lives lost through diving accidents during training, or during operations.

With the most up-to-date equipment, brought from Britain, divers started work in October 1945 on lifting the mines in Dunkirk harbour—which the Germans heavily defended against an invasion of the Continent after our evacuation from the beaches there in 1940.

ALL this in spite of the fact that German naval mine experts, questioned after the surrender, stated that some of their latest mines could neither be swept nor recovered without exploding when moved. But British naval divers, searching the bottom of the Bremen harbour in pitch darkness, working by sense of touch alone, had already removed the firing mechanisms from three of these mines and had hoisted them on to the dockside.

When a diver locates a mine he comes to the surface and reports its type. Here is an actual report: "German C-type mine, sir, about 8 ft. 6 in. long, welded in three places, parachute housing at one end. Underneath the mine a dead body. Civilian. Turn-ups to his trousers." Then it is the officer diver's turn. If the mine is clear of the dock wall he places an explosive charge against it and blows it up. If this would

PRESSURE MAGNETIC MINE, the first to be recovered at Bremen, had its clock removed by Lt. George Gosse, R.A.N.V.R., of a British naval "P" Party (see accompanying story). A mine blows up (left) after attention by our "human minesweepers." *Photos, British Official*

cause damage, he removes the firing mechanism, working under-water by sense of touch, so that the mine can be safely hoisted out of the harbour.

"Tin-openers" is the name the Royal Navy has given to its experts who open up captured ports and harbours. The story of how they cleared 19,000 mines and other obstacles at Leghorn lay behind an announcement in the London Gazette of July 2, 1945. Described officially as "crack men of a picked team," they wear a tin-opener on their vehicles as their badge. They had previously cleared and opened up the ports of Algiers and Naples. On arrival at Leghorn they discovered that the port itself was a mass of Teller mines.

THE port was blocked with sunken ships which divers had to cut up. There were numerous booby traps to be faced as well as intermittent enemy gunfire. Yet by "resolution and dauntless devotion to duty" the "tin-openers" cleared the port within ten days. When the first demolition charge was fired a mine went off sympathetically. This in turn set off an explosive charge under a lighthouse, which sent several hundred tons of masonry 300 feet into the air.

As an example of the booby traps left behind by the retreating Germans, one diver brought up a box which he had found on the sill of the dock. Inspection revealed that it was filled with 20 kilos of T.N.T. which would have exploded if the diver had trodden on it. Yet the divers considered that their most nerve-racking experience was the intermittent enemy shell-fire from 9-in. gun batteries outside the town. For if the diving boat is put out of action the diver faces the loss of his air supply, and if a shell explodes in the water even some distance away the consequences are as unpleasant as one could possibly wish for.

MONTY'S D-DAY BLUFF FOXED THE GERMANS

HITLER'S High Command were deceived over the date of D-Day—June 6, 1944—by the appearance of Field-Marshal Montgomery in the Mediterranean a few days before the invasion went in. He was received by Field-Marshal Sir Henry Maitland Wilson at Algiers with public ceremony. He visited other military headquarters. Fascist agents, by way of Spain, transmitted the news to Berlin that Monty was away from his invasion base.

BUT it was not Monty at all who flew from Britain to the Mediterranean. It was Lieutenant Clifton James of the Royal Army Pay Corps, a peacetime actor, the Field-Marshal's perfect double. Morley Richards, who met the lieutenant in a London restaurant on Oct. 4, 1945—"the likeness was so startling that until I noticed the two pips on his battledress I was certain it was the Field-Marshal"—has told the story of the great deception, in The Daily Express:

Clifton James, son of a Western Australian Chief Justice, is not permitted to tell anything about the greatest part of his career. But it is possible to piece together the story of one of the biggest bluffs of the war.

James was an entertainments officer at Leicester early last year. One night, he walked on to the stage in battledress and was loudly cheered by the troops under the impression that Monty was visiting them. The incident was reported in the Press, and a picture of James was printed.

It gave Britain's Military Intelligence an idea. Immediately before the great attack in December 1940, by Field-Marshal Lord Wavell on the Italian Army in Cyrenaica, the Italians had been fooled by the arrival by air of the British commander in Malta. If the Italians could be hoodwinked, why not the Germans?

James was sent for. He underwent special training for the part he was to play. Monty's voice, gestures, walk and distinctive salute had to be studied. The two men met, somewhere in the seclusion of the North. But there was a difficulty. Clifton James had lost a finger of his right hand on the Somme in the First Great War. That was the saluting hand, which could not be concealed. So they built a false finger for him.

A few days before D-Day, seen off by leading members of the Imperial General Staff, "Field-Marshal Montgomery" left on a tour of inspection in the Mediterranean. He was received at Algiers by Field-Marshal Wilson's aide and they drove with an American escort through streets of cheering people. There were introductions, presentations, and drinks at Field-Marshal Wilson's headquarters. Clifton James, deceived eye-witnesses say, played his part superbly. The plot had worked beautifully.

"FIELD-MARSHAL MONTGOMERY" was Lieut. Clifton James of the Royal Army Pay Corps, who made use of the resemblance to hoax the Nazis. *Photo, The Daily Express*

Will Atomic Weapons Cancel Themselves Out?

The only really revolutionary weapon produced in the War was the atomic bomb, effects of which are not yet fully known. That scientific research into atomic energy should be placed under International control, and that a general knowledge of its potentialities would tend to prevent its use in any future war, are the views of Lieut.-Col. GRAHAM SETON HUTCHISON, D.S.O., M.C.

SOME military critics suggest that the scientific discoveries associated with the transfer of matter into energy, so dramatically illustrated in the use of the atom of uranium, have completely revolutionized all military thought.

It is even asserted—I think with some cynicism—that the defence force of the future will consist of scientists, graded as Field-Marshals, Admirals, and Air Marshals, working in a laboratory set in reinforced concrete deep in the earth ; and that one airborne corporal, a pilot officer flying a jet-propelled plane, and a naval rating, as the combined force, will convey the laboratory product to the theatre of war while the supermen sit pretty and collect the honours and the medals !

THERE is much discussion as to whether secrets of the atomic bomb should be shared among the Allies at once ; and, indeed, whether the knowledge should be more widely revealed. Scientists assert that within three years, at any rate, these secrets will be the common property of the scientific world. It would seem, therefore, that all the secrets concerned with the use of atomic power should be available to the world. The results of the atomic bombing of Hiroshima and Nagasaki (see pages 344-345) are as yet not fully known ; but they are altogether terrifying, not only as affecting human life in the mass, but also the soil over a wide area, producing changes in materials at present beyond computation.

There has been grotesque speculation that man might blow up the world by means of his experiments. It is comforting to know that most of the substances of which the world is composed react as a smothering agency against atomic energy processes. It is true, also, that though an atomic energy blast heightens the radio-activity of every substance within the explosion area, the effect disappears very quickly. Nevertheless, unexpected phenomena are likely to be discovered when the bombed Japanese areas are subjected to a scientific inquest.

Energy Unequalled Even in the Sun

The blasts which levelled Hiroshima and Nagasaki on August 6 and August 9, 1945, had never occurred on earth before, nor, scientists believe, in the sun or the stars, whose heat is generated from sources working infinitely slower than does uranium. The first atomic bomb was equivalent to 20,000 tons of T.N.T. The energy released was beyond imagination, producing a wind with a velocity of millions of miles an hour, vaporizing everything within a mile of the explosion, producing temperatures comparable with that of the sun, and light visible to spectators 100 miles from Hiroshima as " brighter than the sun."

Let us come down to earth. The world must control this menace, and by mutual consent, or by sheer force. The purpose of war, as stated in our own Field Service Regulations, " is to force the enemy to abandon the purpose for which he is resorted to arms and to conclude peace on satisfactory terms." War results only after " all of the means of persuasion " have been employed, and these include " diplomacy, economic influence applied in the form of financial or commercial restrictions on its opponent or of assistance to its allies." If the world is foolish enough again to go to war, we can reflect with some satisfaction that war can be limited.

THE war of 1914–18 produced a new and horrible weapon. It was gas. It was expected in 1939 that gas would again be used. Every army was possessed of its offensive and defensive gas weapons and devices, produced also to serve entire nations. But gas was never used during the war now ended. And why ? The element of surprise is that which is effective in both strategy and tactics. Setting high hopes on gas, the Germans first used the weapon at Ypres in 1915. The first gas attack caught the British Army unprepared to meet it, but it was not sufficiently effective to accomplish our defeat ; and soon the opposing sides were both using gas shells, cylinders for the discharge of gases in a favourable wind, with gas-masks and chemicalized screens to protect dug-outs. Surprise had disappeared, and the novelty cancelled itself out by its use on both sides.

Source of An Immediate Reprisal

So gas was not used during the late war. Both sides feared to use it on account of the immediate reprisals to be expected, directed chiefly against the civil populations, though the Allies were undoubtedly also deterred by International Agreements. The war produced some surprising developments in weapons and devices. But the only really revolutionary weapon, launched with such staggering surprise, was the atomic bomb which brought about the almost immediate capitulation of Japan. In any future war, it can be assumed that weapons based on the atomic bomb, combined with developments of the V2 rocket, will be available to both sides, held in readiness, secretly positioned in remote districts and islands.

Even should one side resort to the use of such a weapon and succeed in blotting out a vast territory with all its inhabitants, somewhere within the vast perimeter controlled by one of the Great Powers there will be positioned the source of an immediate reprisal, capable of producing in the first aggressor country results equivalent to the devastation it has already wrought. In war it is futile to use means which will bring a dreadful retribution, and for this reason I believe weapons based on atomic energy will cancel themselves out. Victory must be worth while. What use is a victory when nearly all are dead and everything destroyed ?

WHEN all is said and done, the situation calls for the placing of scientific research under International control. The world has been given its lesson, and we may be thankful that it was in a land accustomed to mass slaughter and destruction through earthquakes, and where a fatalistic religious belief robs death of many of its terrors.

Germany was only a short lap behind our scientists ; and if an atomic bomb had been the explosive charge in a V2 rocket, the effect of but one successful shot at London would have been annihilating. Scientific research must therefore at once be placed under International control, with an International Inspectorate with free access to every country, so that no lunatic, or wicked group anywhere, can experiment with the object of, or at the risk of, destroying mankind.

THE CYCLOTRON AT CAMBRIDGE has revolutionized British researches into atomic energy. Principal constituent of the atom bomb is the metallic element uranium ; the world supply of this hard white metal is very small, but by means of the cyclotron our physicists have been able to endow other substances with the needed properties of uranium.

Harnessing the Atom for Peacetime Purposes

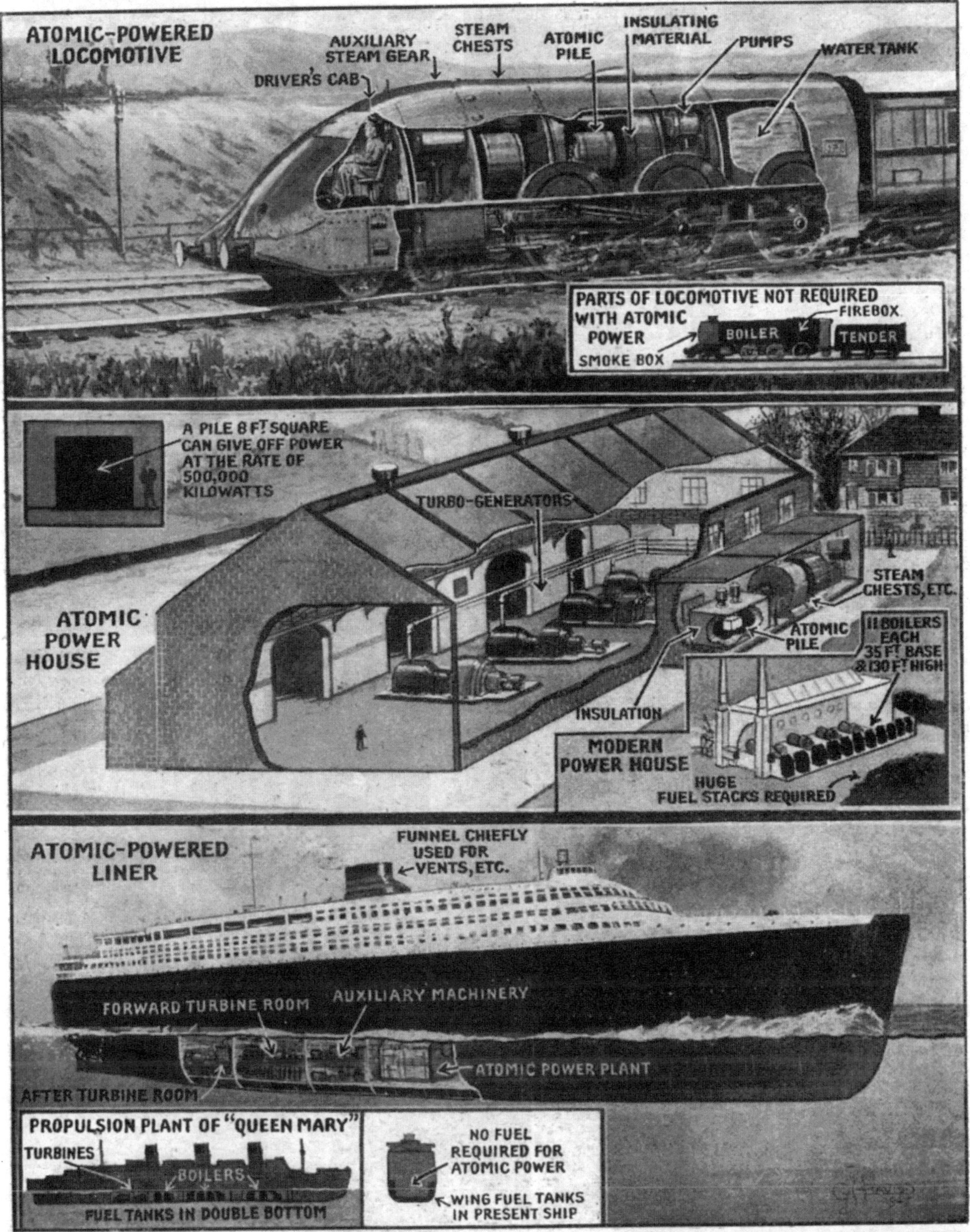

WONDERS OF THE ATOMIC AGE in the not-too-distant future—with nuclear power harnessed to the uses of peace—are shown in these diagrammatic drawings, based on the suggestions of Professor M. L. E. Oliphant, Professor of Physics at Birmingham University, who played an important part in the research work leading to the production of the atomic bomb. At the top is an atomic-powered locomotive; in the centre, an atomic power-house; at the bottom, a streamlined atomic-powered liner. In all these the motive force is derived from uranium which has been electrically disintegrated, the atoms having become energized and induced to "seethe" in tremendous movement. The natural uranium (U238) is in the shape of rods embedded in a graphite block and contained in an atomic "pile." The U238 contains small amounts of the special type of uranium (U235) used in the atomic bomb and which is particularly suited for the breaking-up of the atom. When this breaking-up is started, the turbulence caused by the colliding atoms produces heat which, by means of water-tubes surrounding the uranium rods, in turn produces superheated water under great pressure. When this pressure is lowered, the result is superheated steam which can be employed for power purposes, including the production of electricity.

The advantages of this system will obviate fuel and stoking. The doing away with masses of cumbersome machinery will obviously lead to revolutionary designs in many types of vehicles.

By courtesy of The Illustrated London News

Reconstruction in Poland's Wrecked Capital

WARSAW, FIRST ALLIED METROPOLIS TO FALL TO THE NAZIS (September 27, 1939) and later devastated by the sixty-three days' internal struggle of August–October 1944, was on the road to recovery by the autumn of 1945. New shop-fronts were being fitted (1), and among the shattered buildings workmen toiled at the mixing of mortar (2) to unite stones and bricks of the new city-to-be. Transport began to come to life again, mobile repair units erecting trolley-bus standards (3), whilst the removal of debris proceeded at speed (4).

Photos, Associated Press

I Was There! Eye Witness Stories of the War and After

I Was in Java's Semi-Beleaguered Capital

Trouble in Java in the autumn of 1945 resulted from Indonesian resentment of Western rule, Japanese propaganda and arms, and a shipping shortage delaying Allied landings after the Tokyo capitulation. This dispatch (condensed from The Daily Telegraph) was sent on October 11. See also page 418.

Last week I was besieged in Saigon. This week I am besieged in Batavia. It is a singular experience. Of course, neither city is besieged in the sense of being cut off from communication with the outside world. Contact by air has been assured in each case, and latterly by sea and river with Saigon, while Batavia has always been open by sea. But in the sense that armed and hostile bands encompass each city, and those who attempt to travel beyond the city limits do so at their own not inconsiderable risk, Batavia, like Saigon, is a beleaguered city.

With the exception of the capital itself the Indonesians appear to be in almost total control of the island. The Japanese forces in Java have handed over their own arms to them with an alacrity that suggests a prior understanding. As a result a force of Javanese of quite unknown dimensions, but almost certainly running into tens of thousands and clamorous for national independence, is now in possession of a great number of infantry weapons and a few light tanks.

While British and Australian prisoners of war have all been safely evacuated, there remain about 60,000 Dutch civilians, including a large proportion of women and children, scattered about the island—tiny European enclaves among the 70,000,000 Indonesians of Java. It is a situation that gives adequate reason for disquiet. To the traveller arriving as I did this afternoon by air this state of tension is not immediately apparent.

A report widely current in Singapore yesterday afternoon stated that the Indonesians had taken possession of the airfield of Batavia—a bare two miles from the city—and it seemed unlikely that any planes would take off for Java today. I did in fact succeed in getting a lift with a Dutch plane, and the situation on our arrival at Batavia airfield seemed normal enough. R.A.F. and Dutch personnel were in complete control and promptly gave the lie to the reputed Indonesian coup. "Do you carry a revolver?" I was asked. "It is better not to show it in the streets of the town."

Grand Display of Mural Eloquence

We clambered into a truck and drove into the town towards the Dutch Army headquarters. Everywhere one saw the red and white flag of the native Indonesians prominently displayed. Every blank wall space was painted with proclamations and slogans written for the most part in English—a significant point.

They expressed a profusion of sentiments which suggested that the works of Jean Jacques Rousseau, Jefferson, Abraham Lincoln and Gladstone had been patiently thumbed by native propagandists. Not since Mussolini's Italy have I seen such a display of mural eloquence, though in this case the sentiments are impeccably democratic.

My lorry driver, mistaking the turning, deposited me in front of a long, low building which I learned with some surprise was the headquarters of the Indonesian Nationalist movement. Half a dozen somewhat sombre-looking Javanese in European costume seated on a veranda reading newspapers, feigned an elaborate lack of interest in my lorry.

The walls were painted with slogans in Dutch and in the native vernacular. But

IN BATAVIA, capital of Java, propaganda placards urged support for the Indonesian Republican movement. *Photo, Sport & General*

INDONESIAN REPUBLICANS WHIPPED UP ENTHUSIASM as they drove through a suburb of Batavia following the outbreak of disturbances in October 1945. On October 19 it was reported that British troops driving into central Java had reached Samarang, the third largest city, where extremists were said to have seized internment camps containing 22,000 people. Two days later Brigadier N. MacDonald, British commander at Bandoeng, stated that violence in any form would be answered by death. *Photo, Sport & General*

among these I noted with surprise Mr. Churchill's "Give us the tools and we will finish the job" printed in large characters in English. A drive of less than two minutes brought us to the Dutch military headquarters barely a couple of streets away.

Hitherto, Soekarno, the Indonesian leader, has been allowed to take charge of the reins of government in default of opposition from the scanty Dutch forces at present in the island and to the obvious satisfaction of the local Japanese troops. The Indonesians do not control the capital in the sense that they control the rest of the island, but they can at present move about Batavia without hindrance where they will.

They can and do post their propaganda notices all over the town and compel Asiatic residents, whether natives or Chinese immigrants, to display the red and white flag of the movement. They can and do print and circulate leaflets inciting the British Indian soldiers to revolt against their commanders.

We are, in fact, on the eve of a showdown here. The Indonesians look as if they are bent on forcing things to a crisis. There is a slowing down in the life of the city. Today many shops were closed, their owners fearing disorders and looting. The trams have ceased running, and there has been a partial strike of hotel servants in the employ of Europeans.

A temporary discoloration of the water in the town today set up a rumour that the Indonesians had poisoned the water supply, and though this has proved unfounded it does appear that a body of 20 Japanese troops who had been guarding the reservoir have today decamped on their own initiative and without orders. More and more it would seem that Lt.-Gen. Nagano Yoshiuchi, commander of the Japanese forces in Java, has been playing a decidedly questionable part in facilitating the present state of near-crisis.

Pans and Kettles from Sky-Battle Veterans

Just twisted lumps of metal on a scrap-heap, with great days of glory behind them. And now? Further service they will render, in new guise, as told by The Evening Standard air reporter James Stuart, recording a visit to Oxford on October 4, 1945. See also pages 426-427.

WHERE, I wonder, are the crew who used to fly the white-painted Coastal Command Wellington H.Z. 574? I have just been examining this old warrior which, when Britain was close to being strangled by the blockade, used to stalk the Nazi U-boats in the Bay of Biscay. She lies, wingless and tailless, with scores of other once proud aircraft—just one item in one of the world's biggest scrapheaps.

It is the bombers' graveyard: the last resting-place of some of the aeroplanes that turned the Ruhr into the greatest scrapheap in the world. The burial ground, too, of some of the Hurricanes and Spitfires which fought off the German invaders in the Battle of Britain. Some of these aeroplanes, broken up into almost unrecognizable twisted lumps of metal, I must have seen taking off from mile-long runways to bomb Berlin or Essen.

Seeing them today, piled into great heaps spread over acres and waiting for the 700 degrees centigrade heat of the furnaces to reshape them into oblong 28-lb. ingots of alloy, I was glad that the men who flew them, who affectionately painted on their sides names and a bomb for each raid or a swastika for each Nazi aircraft shot down, were not there to see the ignoble end.

40,000 Tons of Scrap to Handle

That is the sentimental view. The more realistic Ministry of Aircraft Production, whose establishment this "graveyard" is—officially it is the No. 1 Metal and Produce Recovery Depot—are getting on with the job of turning old, unwanted aeroplanes into material to be used for peacetime products. There are between 30,000 and 40,000 tons of scrap, and it is being added to at the rate of 2,000 tons a week. An even greater recovery depot is working near Durham.

Besides the great stacks of scrap of battered fuselages, wings, old engines and gun turrets, there is a huge store of ingots, stacked in piles of 200 tons each. These are being kept for help in peacetime reconstruction. One day soon, perhaps some of those ingots may be converted into saucepans, kettles and frying-pans for use in Britain's kitchens.

I Walked Into a Junkyard and Found Green Gold

In the ruins of Tokyo's bombed mint Henry Keys of The Daily Express wandered among treasure whose value is not yet computed—much of it loot from conquered countries. In the city, homeless and starving wandered in threadbare clothes. His illuminating story is dated October 11, 1945.

IN pouring rain and biting wind I have just been tramping over millions of pounds' worth of gold, silver and platinum in the bomb-shattered ruins of Tokyo's mint. It was treasure found by the U.S. Army. I have handled small but heavy ingots of gold, shaped like chocolate bars, worth thousands of pounds apiece.

Like the silver, they had turned green and discoloured by exposure to weather. Most of the roofs and walls of the mint had been thrown to earth by bombs from Super-Forts, and the treasure left naked to the sky. Rusty riches, inextricably mingled with broken mint machinery, made it seem as though I wandered through an abandoned junkyard. Yet I was stepping upon one of the richest pieces of ground in the world.

When the army arrived, all this treasure was unguarded. Today heavily armed American sentries stand defending a hoard no part of which anyone ever attempted to steal since the mint was bombed. When I arrived the only people in the mint were 200 Japanese employees who survived the bombing. They were little more than boys and girls. Nobody had thought to tell them to cease work, so they had gone on patiently adding up accounts, patiently polishing by hand gold and silver medals struck at the mint for Japanese soldiers.

Apart from a few buildings, most of the mint was burned to the ground. Ashes of the fires have blown away, and there is little rubble. But everywhere I stumbled over masses of precious metals which looked like solidified lava. In one cell, like a blockhouse, partially melted teapots and other silverware were heaped high in a solid disordered mass. Standing on a concrete floor, all that remains of another building, were hundreds of silver ingots almost too heavy to lift, wet and slimy, without a gleam to them. In a vault under the strongroom was yet more of the vast treasure, piled in water ankle deep. In the same building little Jap boys and girls huddled round a fire to cook their rice. They had no more interest in all this wealth than the man in the moon.

Evidence that much of the treasure is loot stolen from conquered countries was found in barrels and melting pots. I saw gold and silver coins, some British, many from Indo-China and other Far Eastern countries. This stolen wealth, it is expected, will be returned to the rightful owners.

"I CAN'T understand the Japs," said an American officer. "They'll rush into the hills with a looted lathe for which they have no earthly use, or a broken sewing machine and a thousand worthless things, but here they don't seem to have touched a thing." So, as the Japs are doing no harm, and there seems to be nowhere else for them to live, Americans are allowing them to stay and sit by their fires, or play with their account books, poor and half-starving amid wealth the like of which I never expect to see again.

My outstanding impression after seven topsy-turvy weeks in Tokyo is that the Japs are pleasantly surprised. Although they are under the conqueror's heel—and no two ways about it—it is not an iron heel. And the Japs have themselves, not MacArthur or any of the occupation troops individually, to thank for it.

You see, Suzuki San (Japan's Mr. Jones), for reasons best known to himself, surrendered with such complete whole-heartedness that, far from making himself objectionable or showing any signs of hostility at any time, he has gone to the other extreme. If you ask your way Suzuki San will not be content with trying to give you directions. He will ride in your jeep with you to the place you want, and then cheerfully set out to walk several blocks—or several miles—back to the spot where you picked him up.

Thousands Fled Before the Landings

And yet Suzuki San when we first arrived was in a dangerous mood. He was sullen, and you could see hatred smouldering in his eyes. Possibly that was because he was frightened. He and his womenfolk had been given a strong propaganda injection and were expecting anything from beatings to theft, murder and rape on a grand scale.

In fact, thousands of women fled before the landings from our initial area of occupation in and around Yokosuka and Yokohama. Those who remained dressed themselves as unattractively as possible in ugly Japanese slacks or siren suits which had not apparently been washed in years. Now, seven weeks later, the population of Tokyo itself has increased by more than half a million. And the women, far from being frightened, try to flirt with any G.I. they see.

Money is desperately hard to come by. So the Japs are taking in washing, for washing is one way to earn money. Throughout Tokyo,

IN HIROSHIMA small girls in long-legged bloomers—a wartime fashion—wear masks to protect them against infection in the atomic bomb-blasted city's ruins. *Photo, Keystone*

in the back alleys, along the main roads, or in the middle of ash heaps, wherever, in fact, there are pools of water caused by broken mains, you will see women and children squatting on their haunches washing khaki clothes, without the benefit of soap, because there just isn't any in Japan.

One of the great mysteries of Tokyo is where its 3,000,000 people are living. The trains and trams are always crowded with silent men, women and children, most of them in threadbare and much-patched clothing. They appear as if from nowhere out of the vast waste of ash and rubble, wait quietly at the tram stops, travel a mile or two and get out in the midst of another waste of ashes. Then they disappear, clumping up the streets on the miniature platforms they use for shoes.

'Free to Lie Their Heads Off'

It takes time for the eye to identify in the rubble the tiny, rusted, corrugated iron shack of a single room with earth floor which represents home. Some of these wretched hovels have walls of paper and thin boards. They are scarcely waist-high for the white man, but that is the way Japan's poor are living in the capital—like rabbits in a warren, with small hope of anything better for a long, long time.

The docile patience needed for train travel is beyond imagining. The Jap arrives at the station hours ahead of departure time and then, a few hours later, risks death to push a way into the foul-smelling, filthy carriages. There he goes on standing. A heavy percentage of farmer's crops is regularly seized by the Government to make the food go round.

Certainly the farmers are paid, but they would rather have their crops. You can buy much more by barter than with money. Indeed, the farmers, who are otherwise poor, just about own most of Japan's clothing. They took it during the war in exchange for food—Western-style suits, kimonos, silks.

It is hard to tell what the Japanese really think of the occupation. Many make such outrageous statements, with polite sucking intakes of breath and careful bows, that you can be forgiven for thinking they have misinterpreted freedom of speech and think it means the people are free to lie their heads off. But we do know the Japanese as a nation were forcibly impressed by the Super-Forts.

They are glad that the war is over, but largely, I think, because they believe that Japan is on the threshold of an even brighter future, and that all that is necessary is to be good and obey General MacArthur. Then, sooner or later, they will be repaid.

FOOD QUEUES IN TOKYO grew longer following General MacArthur's order on September 25, 1945, directing the Japanese Government to stimulate production of consumer goods, meaning that Japan must henceforth feed herself. Food has been strictly rationed in the capital, only fish being plentiful. This queue includes "demobbed" soldiers. *Photo, Keystone*

R.A.F. Dinghies in Action on a Flooded Airfield

In places eleven feet deep and nearly 200 yards wide, swirling waters trapped sleeping R.A.F. men in their billets at the Baroda Airfield, India. They perched themselves on upturned beds and sent distress signals until Air-Sea Rescue equipment was brought into use. The story is told by the Commanding Officer, Wing Commander D. W. Morrish, A.F.C.

BEFORE going to bed on Sept. 22, 1945, I told the guard to watch for flooding. In the early hours, a messenger called me—the telephone had failed—to say that the water was rising at the rate of 18 ins. an hour. And some airmen's billets, the equipment section and the ration store, were islands in a great lake which had appeared as if by magic. From the billets, nearly 200 yards away, a light was flashing, and I recognized Morse signals. They told us the water was up to five feet and rising steadily.

I replied, with my torch, that we were coming to their rescue. The rain was torrential, and when one of my staff instructors, Flying Officer Wilson, tried to swim to the stranded men he had to turn back after going 100 yards because the current pulled him well off course.

THEN, probably for the first time in such circumstances, Air-Sea Rescue equipment was brought into use. Four rubber aircraft dinghies were launched, the first attempted crossing being a failure owing to the increasingly strong current. Another crossing was tried, from a point well above the billets, and with a lifeline taken from the laundry, the dinghy was paddled to the billet, now in danger of being submerged. A dinghy "ferry service" was established, and 16 men, nine of them non-swimmers, were brought safely to the road, which was still above water level.

I saw the men's kit, including tin trunks with gifts the men were taking home to England, floating away. Some of them lost their money too. Dawn had broken when the last man was paddled to safety after six hours sitting on the upturned beds. The 16 went to sick quarters, but the ordeal produced only one "casualty" in the entire camp—a cold. The ferries went on salvaging what remained.

We faced another crisis when the equipment and ration stores, containing eight tons of food, were flooded. Most of the food was destroyed, and we saved only tinned stocks. Things looked grim, because there was no sign of the rain abating during Monday (September 24). So I sent an SOS to Group Headquarters for emergency food supplies.

The airfield, partly inundated, could still be used by experienced pilots. And on the Tuesday an aircraft arrived from R.A.F. Station, Palam, near Delhi, with a maximum load of rations, followed by two more from Bombay, similarly filled. I received a frantic call on the Monday night when the lifeline broke during salvaging operations, and we had to make another rescue trip in a dinghy. Indians killed ten snakes which were carried into their billet by the water.

In 48 hours more than 20 ins. of rain fell. The camp was cut off from the city of Baroda, three miles away, for two days. And, for a time, signals communication ceased when a mast was swept away. Preparations were made to evacuate the entire living site which, it was feared, would be washed away if the lake above it, in the village of Harni, burst its banks. But the banks held. One of the aircraft from Bombay carried the British Resident in Baroda, Lt.-Col. Hancock, who made a remarkable journey from the camp.

We took him as far as possible in a truck, to which we had lashed the dinghy. When the truck had reached its limit the dinghy was launched, and the Resident, enjoying the adventure immensely, was paddled to a waiting pony-cart. This could not cross the submerged bridge, and I understand he finished his journey on an elephant!

★—*As The Years Went By—Notable Days in the War*—★

1939

October 14. *H.M.S. Royal Oak torpedoed and sunk by U-boat in Scapa Flow.*
October 16. *Cruisers Southampton and Edinburgh and destroyer Mohawk damaged in bombing raids on Firth of Forth.*
November 8. *Bomb explosion in Munich beer-cellar shortly after Hitler's departure.*

1940

October 28. *Italy launched attack on Greece.*
November 5. *H.M.S. Jervis Bay sunk by surface raider while defending convoy in Atlantic.*

1941

October 16. *Rumanian troops entered Odessa.*
October 19. *State of siege in Moscow.*
October 24. *Germans captured city of Kharkov.*

1942

October 17. *Schneider armament works at Le Creusot wrecked in daylight raid by R.A.F.*
October 23. *Opening of Battle of El Alamein.*
November 2. *Kokoda (New Guinea) recaptured by Australians from Japanese.*
November 8. *Allies landed in French N. Africa.*

1943

October 13. *Italy declared war on Germany.*
November 1. *U.S. forces landed at Bougainville.*
November 6. *Kiev recaptured by Russians.*

1944

October 14. *Athens and Piraeus liberated.*
October 20. *Aachen captured by U.S. troops.*
October 23. *Red Army broke into East Prussia.*
November 1. *Marines landed on Walcheren.*

Radar in the Air War

By CAPTAIN
NORMAN MACMILLAN
M.C., A.F.C.

By December 1935, when aircraft could be detected 40 miles from the coast and at 15,000 feet, five radar stations were set up on the English east coast. These were the beginning of what was called the Chain Home. Training of R.A.F. personnel began in 1936. By 1937 radar reached out to 100 miles, and 15 more stations were authorized to cover the whole of the east and south-east coasts of Britain. By September 1938 range reached 150 miles. When Hitler's army marched into Prague the Chain Home radar stretched from the Isle of Wight to Scotland, and a 24-hour radar watch began. At the outbreak of war the chain extended to the Pentland Firth, covering Scapa Flow.

Comparatively long wavelengths of up to ten metres were then employed. These illuminated the atmosphere as a lamp bulb illuminates a room. The ground reflected the waves, and the system did not detect low-flying aircraft. Another radar set was produced to scan the low altitudes, and by September 1940 a series of Chain Home Low stations (see illus. page 320) gave continuous cover from the Orkneys to Weymouth, with local cover for the West Country peninsula, Pembroke, Merseyside, and Clydeside. The flow of information from these two radar intelligence chains passed into Fighter Command's operations rooms, to be implemented by the information provided by the Royal Observer Corps when aircraft became visible to the eye or audible to the ear. By September 1941 the only radar gap was off the West Scottish coast covered by the naval convoy approach lane.

Radar stations observed the massing of enemy squadrons behind Cap Gris Nez when the Luftwaffe formed up for assaults in the Battle of Britain, and this advance intelligence enabled commanders to place R.A.F. fighters in position at the right time to oppose the attacks. Means were devised to assess the number of aircraft in a raiding force, and thus distinguish between German feint and main attacks.

DEPTH-CHARGE Carrying Aircraft Prevented U-Boats From Surfacing

It was a logical step from ground radar to airborne radar, and when it was discovered that ships could be detected by radar-equipped aircraft, Coastal Command received priority. By the end of 1939, Air to Surface Vessel radar Mark I (ASV—pronounced Asvic) became operational, although not very efficient. Nevertheless, a radar search by a R.A.F. Sunderland of 228 Squadron preceded the Fleet Air Arm torpedo attack on the Italian fleet in Taranto. By mid-1941 airborne radar could find submarines, and 60 aircraft were carrying ASV Mark II. A year later submarines could not safely recharge their batteries on the surface at night because of depth-charge carrying aircraft equipped with radar and the Leigh light. The Germans, however, produced a listening receiver to detect the Mark II radar, and submarines were then able to submerge before the aircraft "homing" on them by means of radar could see them.

But British scientists had already discovered how to use waves of much shorter length, and under Professor J. Randall at Birmingham University the magnetron valve, the heart of modern radar—able to emit waves down to ten centimetres in length (about 1½ inches)—was devised. These new sets produced a powerful beam which could be focused, and introduced defence problems which the enemy never solved. His U-boats could not detect the approach of aircraft using centimetric radar. In May 1942 the first submarine was sunk with its aid. Flight-Lieut. J. A. Cruikshank's V.C. submarine attack was made possible by it. (See illus. in page 376, Vol. 8.) ASV centimetric radar not only played a major part in the defeat of the U-boat but also detected German convoys at night in the Skagerrak and Kattegat.

Fighter Command received second priority for airborne radar. The first airborne interception claim was made by an experimental unit on the night of July 22-23, 1940. Ground Control of Interception radar (GCI) was developed simultaneously, so that fighters could be controlled direct from ground radar stations by day and night instead of through the group headquarters operations rooms. One GCI set used the skiatron—an upright screen like that used on a pre-war television receiver; the trace from the transmitter showed as a line across this screen, and the distance of the blip from one end of the line indicated the distance of the aircraft.

BRIGHT Spot of Light Betrayed Aircraft's Bearing and Distance

Then came the Plan Position Indicator (PPI), with a horizontal screen whereon the trace ran from the centre radially outwards. An aerial swept the whole sky on a turntable. Any aircraft's location was shown as a bright spot of light on the trace, which consequently gave both bearing and distance. A map used in combination with the PPI screen showed the complete position at a glance. By Christmas 1940 the first PPI set left for its site, mounted in a mobile lorry, and five more quickly followed. In conjunction with Beaufighters carrying airborne radar this new defence began to play havoc with German night bombers, and in May 1941 more than 100 were shot down by A.I. and other night fighters and 42 were shot down by ground defences.

Early A.I. sets used the longer wavelengths which received ground reflections, and this limited the range at which the sets could be used to a distance not exceeding the height of the aircraft. The ground controller handed over to the aircraft's observer when the night fighter was about 12,000 to 15,000 feet from the enemy bomber. The observer operating the airborne radar (called in R.A.F. slang the "box-basher") then directed his pilot by means of the intercommunication telephone until the hunted aircraft came within visual range.

From this came Fighter Direction for offence. The first offensive ground radar station became operative in Kent on December 31, 1942. This and other stations warned Allied fighters operating over the Continent of enemy aircraft, and directed them into offensive actions. The Luftwaffe was forced back deeper into France as a result of the radar-directed offensive sweeps, and offensive ground stations had to be re-equipped with higher-power transmitters and longer-range centimetric height finders. Radar watch from these stations protected aircraft engaged in bombing V1 and V2 sites, and assisted fighters to shoot down V1s launched from France. After D-Day mobile radar units went to the Continent.

Bomber Command was last to have radar assistance, but it made perhaps the greatest use of airborne radar. About March 1942 a radar set called Gee was produced which enabled navigators to know their position accurately in all visibilities, day or night, over an arc from Britain to the Elbe, Hanover, Cassel and Mannheim. This enabled the Staff to plan the first 1,000-bomber raids.

The need of accurate target marking then became apparent and the Pathfinder Force was formed. Their aircraft used another radar set named Oboe, which worked in conjunction with two ground stations, called the releasing and tracking stations, which formed the British base for a triangle whose apex was the meeting point on the Continent of the two radar beams. Through the selected target ran the segment of an imaginary circle whose centre was the releasing station. The two beams were arranged to sweep so that their crossing point moved along the imaginary segment. When the pilot of the Oboe-equipped pathfinder Mosquito first picked up the point where the beams crossed he heard a continuous note in his earphones, and signalled to his home station.

The pilot then followed the beam apex towards the target by means of the continuous note. If he deviated to right or left this note broke into dashes or dots respectively, so warning the pilot to steer back into the 17 yards wide track. Above the continuous note he heard in Morse the letter A at ten minutes flying time from the target, B at eight minutes, C at five minutes, D at three minutes. Then came five pips and on the last pip the bombs or target indicators were released, and an aiming accuracy of within 50 yards could be checked at the home stations. Gee-equipped bombers followed up to bomb by the flares.

Oboe signals could not be jammed or intercepted by the enemy because they were not subject to ordinary radio interference; they required radar reception instruments to convert them into intelligible signals. But their range was limited to about 250 miles, and so the set called H2S was devised for use irrespective of distance.

ROUGH Map of Ground Flown Over Was Shown Clearly on a Screen

This self-contained aircraft radar unit had a transmitter and receiver to send signals from the aircraft to the ground and record the echoes within the aircraft. Water, giving no response, showed blank on the cathode tube screen. Buildings, ground, bridges, ships, and other objects were visible as points of green light whose intensity varied according to the radio-reflecting value of the object. The screen thus showed a rough map of the ground flown over, unaffected by clouds, fog, smoke, camouflage, or darkness, and on which, with practice, it was possible to pick out targets and so bomb solely by instruments.

From 20,000 feet Bomber Command Oboe-controlled aircraft silenced the German guns threatening the sea lanes leading to the Normandy beaches, and with H2S sets smashed the railway yards during the strategic blows preceding the break-out from the Normandy beach-heads. Attacks on oil targets were made with the aid of Gee-H sets; these enabled the aircraft navigators themselves to work out the moment for bomb release by using special charts in co-operation with ground signals.

Two more aids for aircraft were the identification, friend or foe (IFF) device, which enabled friendly aircraft to pass unmolested through the skies, and whose absence brought hostile aircraft within the orbit of defence; and an instrument to enable air gunners to determine the presence of other aircraft near his own, and to distinguish between hostile and friendly fighters.

Airborne forces used a radar beacon called Rebecca-Eureka. At Arnhem the first forces to land erected the beacon Eureka at their point of concentration, and Rebecca, fitted in the other aircraft in the lift, homed them on to the beacon by the coded radar signal which alone made the beacon respond.

Devices That Revolutionized R.A.F. Tactics

DIRECTIONAL AERIAL SYSTEM TO AID OUR FIGHTERS is seen (1) with built-in cabin housing both transmitter and receiver. The diagram (2) shows radar equipment as installed in a R.A.F. aircraft (see article in facing page). Wellington bomber showing radar apparatus atop the fuselage and beneath the wings (3). Radar map of the south-west tip of Wales (4) as shown by night on the cathode-ray tube of the "H2S" instrument (names and coastline added). A W.A.A.F. (5) plotting the position of planes from the cathode-ray tube.

Photos, British Official

Editor's Postscript

WALKING down Fleet Street towards Ludgate Circus on The Daily Telegraph side the other day a young journalist noticed a small crowd of Lancashire folk gesticulating in the direction of St. Paul's. Being a journalist—and with time on his hands—he stopped. One of the visitors was pointing at St. Martin's-Within-Ludgate, the exquisite little Wren church halfway up Ludgate Hill, which boasts one of the loveliest of the City's spires. The journalist followed the pointing finger and saw, to his astonishment, that the spire was tilting backwards quite unmistakably towards the Old Bailey. Here, indeed, was a story to cap Canon Alexander's recent "disclosure" that St. Paul's is advancing down Ludgate Hill at a speed reliably computed at one inch in a hundred years! He looked again, and there seemed to be no doubt of it: the spire was most definitely on the bias. Hurrying to the church, the journalist sought out one of the elderly women vergers who have been looking after the building since the war. She listened—in slightly amused silence, it seemed. Then she bade him retrace his steps up Fleet Street and look at the spire again, from the other side of the road. Which, in a state of mild confusion, he did, only to discover that this time the spire seemed to be tilting towards the Thames! According to the "verger," hardly a month passes without someone rushing into the church with the announcement, "Your spire's falling—have you heard?" The whole thing, of course, is an optical illusion, emphasized by demolition of surrounding buildings damaged in the blitz.

IN the train the other morning I came upon what must surely be first-prize winner in my long list of "officialese" expressions inflicted on us by our Civil Servants since the outbreak of the War. The perpetrator of this beauty was an official whose name is not entirely unknown to the public: on looking him up in "Who's Who" I find, incidentally, that his highly distinguished academic career included a much-coveted Classical Tripos. Which all goes to prove—what? I am still wondering. It occurred at the conclusion of a long description of proceedings taken by the police who had summoned him for a black-out offence two or three years ago. "Luckily," declared the High-Up from Whitehall, "I had witnesses, and we were able to prove to the chappie on the Bench that it was actually ten minutes before non-lighting-up-time." I confess my eyebrows must have betrayed my horror at this new mutilation of our mother tongue, for the phrase was repeated at "dictation speed" for my benefit. It was with difficulty that I refrained from inquiring whether since the lifting of the black-out the hours of darkness are (officially) described as "de-non-lighting-up-time"—which they well may be, following the hideous analogy of "de-requisitioning." I commend this new monstrosity — "non-lighting-up-time" — to the attention of Mr. Ivor Brown, Sir Alan Herbert and, above all, to Lord Wavell who has suggested the formation of a National Trust for words to save our language "from inflation and deflation, type-ribbon development, and suchlike."

ONE of our best-known London booksellers has been complaining to me about his inability to cope with the demand for books about Japan. Ever since the Tokyo surrender, readers of all ages and both sexes have been demanding books on Shintoism, Japanese Art and Nippon life and landscape in general. Particularly in request—believe it or not—have been the works of Lafcadio Hearn, that strange Anglo-Irishman who lived and lectured in Japan towards the end of last century, who married a Japanese wife and whose books have been somewhat of a drug on the market for the past twenty years. Why this sudden interest in a defeated enemy thousands of miles away I can't for the life of me fathom, for if ever a nation had the gilt rubbed off its pseudo-romance it was the Japanese. On the other hand, I can well understand the new "run" on Japanese prints reported from some of the sale rooms. It is, incidentally, an odd commentary on our Occidental taste that many of the most treasured Japanese prints to be found in European collections were originally designed as travel posters—pictorial inducements to voyagers to visit Japan—after Perry had opened up the country to Westerners round about a century ago. For all I (or most people) know the Japanese lettering accompanying many of them may read "Try Fujiyama this Fall" or even "Yokohama is so Bracing!" My old friend Arthur Morrison, probably the greatest living authority on Japanese prints (his £40,000 collection is in the British Museum), tells me that some of the finest of these lovely colour blocks were originally produced for the amusement of children and to decorate the houses of the humblest of artisans.

EVEN a chicken has its good reasons for crossing a road, however much the motorist may rage. The introduction of compulsory pedestrian crossings in built-up areas will deny to human beings the proverbial right of a chicken by finally robbing them of the freedom of the highway, which nowadays means in effect the freedom to risk their own lives. The arguments in favour of the proposal seem to me overwhelming, and we may yet see the day when a man who steps off the pavement is condemned as being as much of a trespasser and as much of a fool as a man who jumps off a railway platform. Meanwhile, I shall miss the agreeable courtesy of the existing notices which say, "Please cross here," even though the ambiguous wording provoked one of Mr. Punch's incorrigible old ladies to ask, "Need I cross if I don't want to?" On the other hand, the man who wants to organize a rule of the pavement for pedestrians is barking up a quite different tree. As long ago as the autumn of 1926 an all-out attempt was made with the help of public notices and a minor press campaign to coax and cajole the pedestrians of London into walking on the left of every pavement. In less than a week the experiment was abandoned not only as hopeless but as pointless. The public blandly refused to co-operate, and nobody in authority could produce any sound reason why they should. If two pedestrians collide—and how rarely this happens, in spite of the comic papers!—no one is likely to be killed or maimed. The worst that usually happens is momentary altercation and irritation, but the encounter may just as often evoke (with a certain amount of side-stepping) those mutual beg-pardons and my-faults which express in their humble way a graciousness in public conduct we can ill afford to spare.

PIERRE LAVAL, former French Premier, executed for treason, in Paris on October 15, 1945, after he had unsuccessfully tried to poison himself. He is seen during his sensational trial, from which he was several times ejected. *Photo, Keystone*

RECENTLY—and for one day only—there appeared in The Times the following advertisement, modestly tucked away in the Personal column:

£4,000.—A BATH ROOM for Private SALE; made just prior to war from rarest marbles by eminent English craftsmen, regardless of cost; approximately 15 ft. by 10 ft.; walls of Algerian Onyx with dado of Fleur de Pêche; recessed bath and lavatory basin carved in white statuary; sponge bowls, etc., in lapis lazuli; engraved Lalique mirrors; complete sanitary and electrical fittings; all now in store; erection could be supervised by eminent designer if required.

On which we can only comment: What—no coupons?

FOR over seventy years, long before Pavlov began his famous researches into Behaviourism and Conditioned Reflexes, there has been controversial deadlock over the use of animals in scientific experiments. Neither the scientists nor the animal-lovers (of whom the bulk, incidentally, are to be found in Britain) were prepared to give way. Much to my delight, I have just heard from Major C. W. Hume, Chairman of the Universities Federation for Animal Welfare, that something rather better than a compromise has at last been reached. It consists—nothing more or less—in the publication of a handbook, compiled by the U.F.A.W., dealing with the care of laboratory animals, which is about to appear with the blessing and approval of leading men of science. The handbook (Messrs. Balliere, Tindall & Cox will publish it) gives technical instructions for keeping the various species as comfortable and contented as possible, for anaesthetizing them, and for reducing to a minimum the number of animals required for achieving a given degree of precision. There is also a chapter on the "rights" of laboratory animals. Knowing something of what has been going on behind the scenes in the matter of animal experiments, I regard the scientific approval of the new handbook as an important victory for the U.F.A.W., whose unobtrusive yet highly practical efforts have always had my support. I feel sure that the Secretary, Dr. F. Jean Winter, at 284 Regent's Park Road, N.3, would welcome anything in the way of donations to help on the good work. A tragedy of our modern democracy is that small voluntary bodies doing excellent work of this kind can rarely attract the attention they deserve.

In Britain Now: Planning the Army's Future

BRITISH ARMY POST-WAR ORGANIZATION was discussed at a meeting held at Camberley Staff College, Surrey, on October 10, 1945. Field-Marshal Lord Alanbrooke, C.I.G.S., in the chair (1); Lt.-Gen. Sir Kenneth Anderson, G.O.C.-in-C. East Africa (2); Lt.-Gen. Sir John Swayne, C.G.S. India (3); Lt.-Gen. Sir William Green, C.-in-C. Anti-Aircraft Command (4); Lt.-Gen. Sir Frank Messervy, commanding 4th Corps (5); Lt.-Gen. Sir Daril Watson, C-in-C. Western Command (6); Field-Marshal Sir Bernard Montgomery (7); Gen. Sir Thomas Riddell-Webster, Q.-M.-General to the Forces (8).

TROOPS AT THE DOCKS, many of them specially brought from Germany, helped to unload London's meat ration—threatened as a result of the dockers' strike which extended to the Metropolis on October 10, 1945. Five days later over 6,000 soldiers were assisting in this urgent task all over the country, so that food-ships could be quickly turned round.

SALVAGED STEEL from the Norwegian whale-factory ship Ole Wegger, sunk off the Normandy beaches as a block-ship during the D-Day landings, was unloaded at Southampton docks. Metal from these salvaged ships will either be melted down or reconditioned. See also pages 426-427.

Photos, Associated Press, Planet, G.P.U.

Danes Help to Gather Our Rich Sea Harvest

ONE OF MANY MANNED BY DANES, and operating under British registration, the LO 265 lay at Lancashire's famous port of Fleetwood in mid-October 1945. Known as " sailers," the Danish fishing boats are larger than the equivalent British craft and they sail in deeper waters : some have been known to fare as far as Iceland. In the foreground are two British prawners, with the lines and rigging of a racing yacht. Since early in 1944 Danish seamen have helped to operate H.M. motor minesweepers.

Photo, E. W. Tattersall

Printed in England and published every alternate Friday by the Proprietors, THE AMALGAMATED PRESS, LTD., The Fleetway House, Farringdon Street, London, E.C.4. Registered for transmission by Canadian Magazine Post. Sole Agents for Australia and New Zealand : Messrs. Gordon & Gotch, Ltd. ; and for South Africa : Central News Agency, Ltd.—November 9, 1945 S.S *Editorial Address :* JOHN CARPENTER HOUSE WHITEFRIARS LONDON E.C.4.

Vol 9 The War Illustrated No 220

SIXPENCE and AFTERWARDS NOVEMBER 23, 1945

THE LAST DAYS OF A TRAITOR—the 89-years-old ex-Marshal of France, Philippe Pétain—are spent in dishonour behind bars in the Pyrenean fortress-prison of Portalet. His death sentence pronounced on August 15, 1945, was commuted two days later. His cell is that in which he confined Georges Mandel, Minister of the Interior in the Reynaud Government in 1940 and later murdered. Pétain's only contact with the outside world is by letter to his wife. See also page 245. *Photo, Planet News*

Edited by Sir John Hammerton

NO. 221 WILL BE PUBLISHED FRIDAY DECEMBER 7

SUCCOURING GERMANY'S STARVING HOMELESS surging into the British zone of occupation from the East, is the stupendous task facing our authorities at the transit camp of Uelzen, near Luneburg in Hanover. Trains carrying German Displaced Persons, such as this (1) leaving Uelzen, are crammed from axle to roof. Daily sight is the queue for rations; D.P.s receive gruel and one "solid" meal of black bread, butter, jam and sausages per day (2). General view of the camp (3) showing the wooden huts, originally built as stables by the Nazis, where D.P.s are housed overnight, on straw, 40 to a stable. British Army lorries and troops (4) are employed at Ruhr pitheads for transporting coal to France, Holland and Denmark, the German canal system being in chaos. *Photos, British Official, Planet News, Keystone*

Aftermath in Central Europe

By HENRY BAERLEIN

OUR well-known contributor, who has extensive knowledge of the Central European lands which for years have been but beds of political unrest, gives us here the results of his recent study of the problems that still await solution there although the clutch of Nazism has been withdrawn with the death of that evil thing.

WHEN, after the First Great War, the region of Malmedy on the Belgian-German frontier was awarded to Belgium its German inhabitants became deeply depressed, not so much because of their separation from a ruined land as because they were no longer under the discipline to which they were accustomed.

Many another psychological problem will have to be faced in Central Europe in the near future; they go hand in hand with the territorial problems awaiting solution. The statesmen who will undertake this colossal task are not to be envied. Pamphlets of every kind, statistics that prove everything, and apparently unanswerable arguments (until they are triumphantly answered), will assail them from all sides. Let us consider a few questions they will be asked to solve.

The Poles, whether wisely or not, have accepted in the west what they have lost in the east. One of their urgent problems, therefore, is the replacing of much of the German population of such large towns as Breslau and Stettin by Polish nationals. From the 500,000 Poles in the British zone of Germany some 3,000 a day are going to Stettin; one doubts if many of them will stay there instead of returning to parts with which they are familiar. And though the Polish birth-rate may remain the highest in Europe, will it populate these great new areas? On the other hand, the change of sovereignty in East Prussia has solved the problem of an adequate coastline for the Poles, while at the same time definitely undermining the power of the Junkers who were for so long the root of much evil.

The Best Solution for Trieste ?

There are various parts of Central Europe in which the claims of two nations are being heard. Trieste, for instance, is demanded both by the Yugoslavs and the Italians, although it has never prospered when it and Venice have been under the same flag (see page 106). A few hundred yards outside this cosmopolitan port we come to a country almost wholly Slovene, and the suggestion that the river Isonzo should be the boundary between the two races was made both by Napoleon and Mazzini. Bearing this in mind, the best solution for Trieste itself would seem to be a Trieste-Istrian Free State, with a population equally divided between Italians and Slavs.

Of course, in the harbour of Trieste, free zones should be allotted to Czechoslovakia, thus doing away with Hamburg's semi-monopoly of Czechoslovakia's commerce, and to Austria, to guard against any raising of another " Anschluss " propaganda. Fiume should not present any problem this time, for its allocation to Yugoslavia is obviously the only just solution. Under Italy since the last war it was dying a slow death, whereas its suburb of Susak, given to the Yugoslavs, flourished exceedingly.

CZECHOSLOVAKIA, on account of her central position, is naturally exposed to many problems with her neighbours as claimants. It is to be hoped that the question of Teschen (see page 406), whose mines are so vital to Czechoslovakia's industry, while Poland has other sources, will be settled on the pre-war basis. It is unfortunate that the Poles should have raised this matter and should have acted somewhat arbitrarily against the Moravian population of Upper Silesia. Between the two wars the relations between these two Slav countries were unsatisfactory, Pilsudski and Colonel Beck refusing to discuss matters with President Benes, then Foreign Minister.

It need hardly be said that the big brother of the Slavs is faced with a problem in Rumania and Bulgaria, for the governments supported there by the Soviet do not commend themselves to Britain and the U.S. The democracies do not expect a democratic regime like their own in these countries, but a modification of those now in force appears to be necessary, both for their own well-being and for the sake of their relations with ourselves and America.

Lebensraum for Teeming Refugees

The problems which confront us in Germany are manifold. There is, for instance, the question of the Ruhr, which—in the opinion of France—should not at any rate be returned to German administration. It will be remembered that after the 1914–18 war a French attempt to set up an independent State in western Germany was unsuccessful. There is much to be said for an internationalized Ruhr, for Germany has for long been the most aggressive nation in the world—which without the Ruhr and Silesia she would cease to be. The loss of Silesia would also be a belated act of justice for its theft by Frederick the Great in 1745.

An urgent problem today is the reception in Germany of the many thousands of her compatriots expelled from Poland and the Sudeten districts of Czechoslovakia. Their conduct was such that this expulsion became unavoidable, and since German soil is capable of more intensive cultivation, even in the diminished Fatherland, there will be Lebensraum for the refugees.

That is not the greatest of the internal problems which have to be faced in Europe. Yugoslavia has a number of more or less unfriendly neighbours, but their animosity is probably less than that which agitates a good many Serbs and Croats. One had hoped that, following the example of the English and the Scots after the Act of Union in 1707, they would indulge in some years of skirmishing and then settle down. But the skirmishing not only continues but increases, nor does Marshal Tito's proposed disfranchisement of some 60 per cent of the population—all those who did not actively assist his Partisans—do anything to bring nearer an understanding.

SPAIN, Belgium and Greece are confronted with various problems that involve the principle of monarchy in those countries. Between the rival republican and monarchist claimants in Spain, Franco steers an uneasy course; and whichever climbs to power the unsuccessful party will denounce it for the sins of its predecessors. In Belgium there is the unfortunate complication of the Flemings and Walloons being divided on the question of King Leopold at a time when national unity is more than ever desirable. In Greece the monarchy problem is causing the supporters of King George to abstain from the elections. A problem for the Dutch is whether to demand for a term of years a region of north-west Germany equivalent to the area of Holland devastated by the Nazis.

It would seem that there is no end to these problems. One of the most important is that of such waterways as the Danube. Is that great river to be controlled by the various riparian states or by an international body assembled *ad hoc*? This matter will always be important, but is now particularly so in view of the state of European railways.

COMMERCIAL problems will not be the least. That this is appreciated can be seen from the fact that the Soviet has not waited to arrange with Hungary that half the products of that country are to be earmarked for Russia. The multiplicity of frontiers where commerce was halted did not assist the convalescence of Europe after the First Great War; it is to be hoped that the recent example of Rumania and Hungary will be followed. Rumanian milk is being sent to Budapest for the children, and for the first time in history relations between the two countries are quite good.

This happy condition of things, however, is exceptional. There has lately fallen into Allied hands a German secret document which states that the Fuehrer had decided to erase Leningrad from the face of the world. The world is not going to treat its problems today with any such criminal viciousness.

IN ONE OF DANZIG'S SHATTERED SQUARES German " displaced persons "—formerly resident in the Baltic seaport and now ordered to evacuate by the Russian Military Government to make room for incoming Poles—try to dispose of their chattels to the new Polish population. This represents but one of Europe's post-war problems. *Photo, Associated Press*

With Montgomery from D-Day to V-Day

21st Army Group H.Q. Flash

A Retrospect by MAJ.-GENERAL SIR CHARLES GWYNN K.C.B., D.S.O.

WHILE a campaign is in progress, the interest of the average man tends to centre on day-to-day events or on speculations as to what will follow. His memory of past happenings, except those of outstanding character, is apt consequently to become blurred, and he may have to wait long before he has an opportunity to form a picture of the campaign as a whole in correct perspective.

We should therefore be grateful to Field-Marshal Montgomery for the clear and concise account he gave in a lecture to the Royal United Service Institution on Oct. 3, 1945, of the part played by the 21st Army Group in the great Western Front offensive of 1944-45. By a characteristic gesture he has had his lecture printed for distribution within the Group ; it should therefore soon be accessible to many readers.

The Field-Marshal pays tribute to the share the Navy and Air Force took in the campaign, and emphasizes the dependence of the Army on them in all military operations ; but he describes only the land operations carried out under his command. He is able, however, to give us a complete picture of the battle of Normandy which ended with the crossing of the Seine, since he had been placed by General Eisenhower in over-all charge of the combined Allied armies in that phase of the campaign. Thereafter, when General Eisenhower assumed direct control, Field-Marshal Montgomery confines himself to the operations of the 21st Army Group, composed of the 1st Canadian and 2nd British Armies, and to those in which American Armies co-operated with the Group.

NORMANDY Objective Was Reached a Fortnight Ahead of Schedule

We can now be certain that the battle of Normandy, despite the length of the struggle and of the checks that occurred from time to time in its progress, was fought very closely on the lines of a preconceived plan. Actually the territorial objective set for D+90 days was reached a fortnight ahead of schedule and a defeat more disastrous than could have been expected was inflicted on the enemy.

The chief object after securing a footing on the beaches had been to maintain the initiative in order to prevent the enemy delivering a mass counter-stroke, and to induce him to expend his reserves piecemeal on the part of the front as far removed as possible from the point where the decisive American break-out from the bridge-head was planned to take place. The enemy danced to Montgomery's tune, and when Gen. Patton's drive (U.S. 3rd Army) isolated him from his troops in Brittany and south of the Loire his wisest course would have been to withdraw north and east, rallying north of the Seine.

BUT in a desperate effort to capture the initiative the enemy decided to launch and persist in the belated counter-stroke towards Avranches. Thereby he committed himself to fighting a decisive battle with his back to the Seine, over which all permanent bridges were broken. This was the first of the three major mistakes which Montgomery considers brought about the final German defeat. In none of the three cases could the course the enemy took have been definitely anticipated, but the Allied dispositions were so essentially sound that the enemy threats were countered without abandoning the plan in operation.

In this case the counter-stroke was held up by rapidly organized defence while Patton's original mission proceeded with the brilliant modification which swung part of his army northwards to enclose the Falaise pocket. Thus the enemy had not only exposed his army to annihilation but sacrificed all chance he had of holding the line of the Seine—and that without disturbing the development of the original Allied plans.

THE subsequent brilliant drive of 21st Army Group, north-east through the Pas de Calais and Belgium, met with no organized resistance, except where the enemy elected to leave garrisons in the Channel Ports. But by the time Antwerp was reached, lines of communication with the Normandy base had become 400 miles long and all available transport had to be used to maintain forward supplies, with a consequent depletion of reserve stocks at the base.

Back on the Seine, Eisenhower and Montgomery already had their eyes on the north German plain. Field-Marshal Montgomery implies that he thought it might be reached, and a final decision achieved by an immediate massive thrust across the lines of the Maas, Waal and Neder Rijn. General Eisenhower, however, decided that the utmost that could be safely attempted before a base was established at Antwerp—which meant clearing the Scheldt estuary—was to secure a bridge-head across the three rivers. In pursuance of that plan, while the Canadian Army was clearing the Channel Ports, the British 2nd Army continued its advance northwards and crossed the Albert Canal. But German resistance had begun to stiffen and the weather broke, with the result that in a terrain seamed with water-obstacles the advance was held up.

FIELD-MARSHAL MONTGOMERY celebrates his first great victory ; he is here seen with Mr. Churchill at the dinner held in London on October 23, 1945, to mark the third anniversary of the Battle of Alamein.
Photo, Associated Press

There followed the great airborne landing which secured the passage of the Maas and Waal but failed at Arnhem to secure the Neder Rijn crossing ; weather, lack of numbers and the rapidity of German recovery holding up the attempts of the 2nd Army to support the Arnhem troops. The enterprise also suffered from improvisation, for it had originally been intended to employ the airborne force on other operations which the speed of the Allied advance rendered unnecessary. The clearance of the Antwerp approaches, a slow and difficult business, was then undertaken. The full extent of the German recovery had become evident along the whole western front. New plans had to be made, and during the autumn there was much preparatory fighting in appalling weather before they could mature.

The new plan for the 21st Army Group was to use the Maas and Waal bridge-head as a base for a thrust into the Rhineland between the Maas and the Rhine. While regrouping with this object in view was in progress, Rundstedt's Ardennes offensive was launched in December 1944 ; and in the face of its threat the regrouping was suspended. Serious as the implications of Rundstedt's offensive were it is interesting to note that Field-Marshal Montgomery ranks it as the second fatal mistake made by the Germans. Not having secured air superiority nor possessing the necessary resources for a major counter-stroke, the enterprise was doomed to failure. "A counter-attack, yes ; a counter-offensive, no !" is how the Field-Marshal summarizes his criticism of the Rundstedt plan.

HOW Germany Missed Last Chance to Stave Off Final Catastrophe

The 21st Army Group took a notable if subordinate part in frustrating the attempt, and the subsequent offensive which cleared the northern Rhineland and effected the main crossing of the Rhine was an Anglo-American operation under Montgomery's command. It started with the Canadian Army's previously planned attack from the Nijmegen area ; but now owing to floods it had to be carried out almost as an amphibious operation, while the American attack across the Roer was held up by the threat of the release of the waters of the Roer reservoirs.

The Canadian Army—largely composed of British troops replacing the Canadian Corps sent to Italy—had desperate fighting, but it drew all German reserves from the Roer defences and opened the way for the American Armies when the Roer flood subsided. The combined offensive then developed as planned, and success was rapid and devastating. As Montgomery points out, the Germans had committed their third major mistake when, after Rundstedt's defeat, they had not retired behind the Rhine—which was their last chance of staving off for a time the final catastrophe, and they again fought with a bridgeless river behind them.

BEFORE the battle of the Rhineland was completed preparations for the crossing of the Rhine had been set on foot, and the operation was carried through with characteristic thoroughness. Once the bridge-head was established the end was inevitable, but the encirclement of the Ruhr and the swift drive to meet the Russians on the Baltic settled the issue decisively.

The operation planned on the Seine had, in fact, been carried through with few modifications or serious interruptions. The initiative throughout was maintained and, as Field-Marshal Montgomery claims, this was the result of skilful grouping and regrouping of resources which made it possible to react to enemy thrusts without abandoning the main object. At no time did resources permit the formation of a strong strategic reserve free to meet emergencies. It was a case of maintaining or rapidly restoring the balance required to meet all developments. The instinctive sense of balance which marks the first-class games player is equally the hall mark of the first-class general.

Montgomery has much of interest to say in his comments. He holds that morale of the ordinary soldier was the greatest single factor that contributed to success.

Seaforths and Japs Help to Quell Rebels in Java

Brigadier A. W. S. MALLABY, C.I.E., O.B.E., 46-years-old British Commander in Surabaya, Java, was shot dead by an Indonesian mob on October 30, 1945, while touring the Javanese naval base to see that the terms of the truce were carried out. He commanded the 49th Indian Infantry Brigade which had just landed in Java.

JAPANESE OFFICERS HELPED to quieten Batavian rioters in October 1945 ; a group (1, wearing armlets) is seen smoothing out a street disturbance. Lt.-Gen. Sir Philip Christison, K.B.E., C.B., D.S.O. (3), Allied Commander in the Netherlands East Indies, immediately after the killing of Brigadier Mallaby warned Indonesians that if the culprits did not surrender he would bring the " full weight " of his forces against them. Seaforth Highlanders landing at Batavia (2) where on November 1 they went into action against snipers.

Photos, British Official, Topical, Walter Stoneman

What of the Merchant Navy's Future?

By

FRANCIS E. McMURTRIE

It was Mr. Alfred Barnes, Minister of War Transport, who said of the Merchant Navy in the Battle of the Atlantic, "Had that lifeline been cut, nothing could have saved us. To the merchant seaman we owe our preservation and our very lives."

That the Royal Navy is in cordial agreement with this view may be judged from the following extract from a broadcast by Rear-Admiral R. K. Dickson, Chief of Naval Information at the Admiralty: "Neither the Navy nor the Coastal Command could have defeated the U-boats alone; both relied first and last on the fortitude of the Merchant Navy."

Such tributes could easily be multiplied, since no one can withhold his admiration for the magnificent record which the merchant sailor has established in the past six years. But something more enduring than mere praise is required. As the author of the latest book on the subject entitled The Merchant Service, by Lieut.-Commander L. M. Bates (published by Frederick Muller, Ltd.) observes:

> After the last war (1914-1918) we repaid similar devotion and sacrifice with callous indifference. When the next test came in 1939 we had no earthly right to expect a second mass sacrifice. But the Merchant Service stood by its traditions, as it always does, and we were given the inestimable blessing of another chance. If we fail them again after this war there may be no Merchant Service to save us if a third test comes. Blood is still the price of admiralty, and our merchant seamen have paid in full on our account. Let you and me and all the peoples of this great sea-linked empire insist upon that debt being redeemed when the world-after-the-war emerges from the present anarchy.

It is the aim of a new Merchant Shipping Bill, now being considered in detail by a special committee of the National Union of Seamen, to improve the general conditions of service in the Merchant Navy—described by its drafter, Mr. Hector Hughes, K.C., M.P., as "the Cinderella of the Services." He has severely criticized the inferior accommodation still provided for the crew in some British ships.

CONTINUITY of Employment Sought by the National Maritime Board

Even more important is the need to avoid the long spells of unemployment which dogged the officers and men of the Merchant Navy in the years between the two wars. During the worst slump cases were on record of master mariners going to sea "before the mast," i.e. as members of the crew, in default of any other sea employment. Worse still was the plight of some of the more elderly officers holding masters' certificates, who failed to get to sea at all, and were driven to take casual jobs as scene painters or sandwich-board men.

A plan to secure continuity of employment has been drawn up by the National Maritime Board, the body which regulates pay and conditions of merchant service personnel. It is proposed to set up two pools, one Government-sponsored and the other for the owners, from which every ship would draw her officers and men. Every man going to sea under this scheme would be guaranteed employment for several years, subject to his proved efficiency and fitness. Articles would continue to be signed in the usual way; but when terminated, each man would pass into one of the pools and be paid while waiting for his next ship.

REDUCTION in Payment of War Risk Money Would Have Been Involved

Until effective measures have been taken, with the approval of the organizations which guard interests of seafaring personnel, to implement such proposals no alteration is likely to be made in the conditions of employment at sea. In September the National Maritime Board rejected the shipowners' proposal, put forward two months earlier, for post-war remuneration of officers and men. This would have involved reducing the amount of extra pay drawn on account of war perils, commonly known as War Risk Money, from £10 a week to £5 a week as from October 1, 1945. Representatives of the masters and officers submitted counter-proposals for a complete revision of the basis and amount of remuneration.

Representatives of the men declined to make immediate counter-proposals; and a few days later the Secretary of the National Union of Seamen, Mr. Jarman, criticized the Minister of War Transport and the heads of other departments concerned for not giving seamen a chance to state the details of their case, and for not announcing clearly the Government policy in the matter. It was suggested that everything was being postponed until the maritime session of the International Labour Office was held in Denmark in November. As to War Risk Money, it was pointed out there were still unusual dangers to be faced at sea, notably from mines.

Some idea of the scale of risk attached to seafaring in wartime may be gathered from the figures of Merchant Navy losses: 35,279 klled and missing, 4,215 injured and 4,088 interned, giving a far higher percentage of casualties than those sustained by any of the fighting Services. Yet not only was there no sign of reluctance to continue to face such perils, but there was a notable absence of any desire to exploit the war situation by bargaining for better terms. That was left until the enemy had been defeated.

So far as conditions of officers' employment are concerned, remarkable improvement has been recorded over the past 25 years, very largely through the efforts of the Officers (Merchant Navy) Federation, under the direction of Captain W. H. Coombs, to whom his colleagues owe a great debt. Through his perseverance, all Merchant Navy officers are now united in a single body, enabling their views to be presented with greater weight than ever before. As a result, the youngster who goes to sea as an apprentice in these days has a much better prospect than in the past.

It is not only the personnel manning the Merchant Navy who await Government decisions on future policy with anxiety. Shipowners have a most complex problem to face. At the end of last year the ocean-going mercantile fleet of this country had been reduced to no more than 13,500,000 tons, as contrasted with 17,500,000 tons when war began. More serious than the actual reduction in British tonnage is the unbalanced quality of the world's existing fleets. There is a marked shortage of specialized tonnage, and a vast preponderance of tramp vessels of standardized type.

HIGH Cost of Shipbuilding at this Time is a Further Complication

If, as has been hinted in some quarters, there is an intention to dispose of a large proportion of this surplus tonnage, at present under the United States flag, to countries which will employ it in undercutting freight rates, the future is a gloomy one. It would be a far sounder move to scrap the bulk of the surplus war-built tonnage and maintain shipyards in full employment by building new vessels of more suitable designs.

A further complication is the high cost of shipbuilding at the present time. Owners who are compensated for the loss of their ships during the war at the prices originally paid for them find themselves required to pay about twice as much for new vessels.

Meanwhile, in some parts of the Empire there is gratifying evidence of practical appreciation by the public of the work of the Merchant Navy in the war. The people of South Africa have contributed a sum of £75,000 towards the foundation of a self-supporting village community for veteran and disabled seamen and their families. This plan is described in full in page 238.

AT H.M.S. DOLPHIN, famous Portsmouth refitting base of our submarines, were reassembled in November 1945 British underseas craft which in the perilous years of the war had sailed round the world and back. Alongside them lay in captivity surrendered U-boats, once their deadly foe. Seen (left to right) are H.M. submarines Trespasser, Truant and Surf, with a white-hulled U-boat between the last two. A group of landing-craft lies at anchor in the left background.

Photo, The Evening Standard

Malta Once Again H.Q. of Mediterranean Fleet

TRANSFERENCE OF ADML. SIR JOHN CUNNINGHAM'S STAFF from Caserta in Italy to the George Cross Island, announced on September 28, 1945, meant that Malta had again become our Mediterranean Fleet's headquarters for the first time since 1940. Among our ships to anchor in the Grand Harbour at Valetta, the capital, was the cruiser H.M.S. Norfolk (top). To mark the arrival of the C.-in-C. Mediterranean a band of Royal Marines from the Norfolk, Aurora and Ajax marched to Valetta's Palace Square (above).

Photos, Topical Press.

How We Blew Up the U-Boat Pens at Hamburg

LUFTWAFFE BOMBS were used by the Royal Engineers on October 21, 1945, to demolish the Finkenwarder U-boat pens at Hamburg. The gaunt-looking pens (1), with walls 12-ft. thick, were the product of four years' toil by 1,700 slave labourers. Five docks, each measuring 73 ft. by 368 ft., had capacity for ten ocean-going U-boats or 30 smaller craft. The blowing up, personally performed by Major H. E. Donnelly, Royal Engineers, was watched by official spectators from a stand overlooking the River Elbe (2). A sergeant helped to fuse the Luftwaffe 500-pound bombs (3) which did this (4) to the pens in a single explosion, leaving the roof sagging in the water.

Photos, Planet News

Mighty Spans Our Sappers Flung Across the Rhine

ONE OF THE LARGEST FLOATING BRIDGES IN THE WORLD, across the turbulent Rhine at Düsseldorf, had been almost completed by men of the Royal Engineers in early November 1945. Built as a semi-permanent structure, it is known locally as the "Freeman Bridge," after a major of the R.E.s, who was largely responsible for its erection. This "Bailey on Stilts" is half-a-mile long and can carry loads up to 40 tons. It is the work of three companies of sappers, some of whom learned their craft in Burma. See also pages 564-565, Vol. 8. *Photo, British Official*

Laurels for Dover: Chief of the Cinque Ports

Target for all forms of enemy attack, base for the final push into Germany, leave-port for our victorious troops, for over six years Dover was in the hands of our Navy and Army. Now that the harbour is beginning to resume its civilian status Capt. FRANK H. SHAW reviews scenes and outstanding personalities of its tempestuous war history.

No town on our coast has taken and stood up to such serial punishment as Dover. For the best part of five years it was the target for every big gun the Germans could bring to bear on it. Distant only a score of miles from Occupied Europe, it was required to endure a daily hate from whatever the enemy could contrive against it—because the enemy knew its vital import to our strategy, defensive and offensive.

Many a M.T.B. night patrol, returning from adventures in the misted waters towards the Flemish sands, breathed sighs of relief when the white cliffs loomed into view through the morning haze: it would not have astonished them to know that the high white ramparts had been beaten flat. But Dover stood as firmly against air attack, sea attack, land attack as the valiant town had stood against persistent assaults by French pirates of the thirteenth century.

The cliffs that had witnessed the first "combined operation" of Julius Caesar might have shed white trickles of rubble as the high explosive missiles embedded themselves harmlessly in their serene bulk; but even the savagery of a world at war could not intimidate those who lived on and behind that rampart whose looming whiteness had caused the Romans to name the indomitable island Albion.

On September 17, 1945, the Navy and Army handed back the Dover Harbour to its rightful owners—the Southern Railway Company—after a period of six years and sixteen days, during which it had been exclusively under High Command control. What an amazing amount of vital history has been packed into that slice of our national lifetime! It is something to be the outermost bastion of a prolonged, dogged defence that has won the world's admiration. Dover heard the rumble of gunfire quite early in the war, and saw the first explosions of the magnetic mines as this weapon was first brought into play (see story in page 124, Vol. 7) and ships were transformed to mangled scrap.

Just how many of the returning "mosquito-craft" which brought back the first Expeditionary Force from Dunkirk berthed in this harbour it is not possible to estimate; but if Dover had nothing else to be proud of she could exult in that magnificent spectacle on the pier when the remnants of the Guards Division—wounded, weary, at their last gasp—came to attention on the word of command and marched away to the trains as indomitably as ever in their chequered history.

With war ended, Dover automatically became the arrival port for land forces returning from Occupied Europe on leave; just as it was in the 1914–18 war, when the leave-boats ran with the precision of a clock, except for rare occasions when U-boats were reported in the narrow seas. But not all the leave-boats of today are stereotyped cross-Channel "flyers," doing the 21-mile run in well under the hour. Landing craft are recruited into the service—queer, ungainly monsters with neither bow nor stern, awkward to handle in any sort of a seaway, but fairly fast in smooth open water, and a godsend to warriors who have flocked from Italy, Greece, Germany and Austria.

Outstanding personalities seen about Dover include Capt. G. Johnson, D.S.C., who commands the Royal Daffodil—successor to the famous Merseyside ferry-boat that won distinction at Zeebrugge in 1917 when she did grand service in pushing the Vindictive alongside the Zeebrugge mole, and took bitter punishment. Under Capt. Johnson's command the present Royal Daffodil has conveyed over 1,900,000 fighting men to and from Europe. She started this work in 1939, when she helped to transport the gallant few of the first Expeditionary Force to France in the early autumn of 1939. She still carries on, risking loose mines, as she risked destruction in the war.

Captain TOM WOODS The "indomitable Manxman" who commands the S.S. Lady of Mann, famous British leave-boat which has sailed between Dover and Calais with our men in all kinds of weather.

Captain H. L. PAYNE, O.B.E. Well-known Merchant Navy skipper who undertook the great task of reopening Dover Harbour in October 1944, as told in this page. *Photos, G.P.U.*

Captain G. JOHNSON, D.S.C. Commander of the S.S. Royal Daffodil, completed just before the war, which has carried almost 2,000,000 troops across the Channel since 1939, and now transports men on leave.

Capt. Johnson has stirring stories to tell of his ship's adventures. Whilst citizens of our premier Cinque Port dared the cannon-shell, bombs and doodle-bugs, refusing to abandon their homes, the Royal Daffodil and many ships like her, plied—swift shuttles of an Empire's loom—indomitably through fog and bitter storm alike. Naturally, most of her voyages were performed by night; but exigency often demanded that she should work in broad daylight—a fair target for enemy hostility; for to sink the Daffodil would have meant cheating our fighting forces of perhaps five thousand of the very cream of the nation's manhood.

In October 1944 the retributive sweep across Europe was in full swing. Our D-Day landings had burst Hitler's Atlantic Wall wide open; and the flower of the Allied manhood was pouring towards Berlin, fighting for each foot of the way. Until this fateful month, Dover had been under daily shellfire from Cape Gris Nez, where the long-range guns were stationed. The port was actually untenable for men and material in bulk. Any moment might bring a salvo of H.E. projectiles. But by October the Gris Nez guns were out of action; our left-hook swing had given us possession of the terrain where they were mounted. Apart from occasional tip and run air raids, Dover was more or less free from deliberate attack. (See illus. in page 354, Vol. 8.)

Wrecks Dynamited Out of the Way

It was Capt. H. L. Payne, O.B.E., a veteran Merchant Navy shipmaster, who undertook the reopening of Dover Harbour. He found plenty to do—the port was littered with sunken wrecks, bombed whilst the ships lay at anchor in fancied safety. The piers were crumbling. The harbour facilities were non-existent. Captain Payne took the task in hand, and in a very short while he had a whole fleet of ships hurrying men, ammunition and supplies to the sorely-tried legions across the water.

The wrecks were dynamited out of the way, shattered piers were patched into a semblance of utility, blocked channels were cleared, guarding minefields were swept and, outwardly, Dover resumed the appearance of a busy commercial port. But her exports were no longer pleasure-seeking trippers bound for Ostend or Calais and the inland cities of the Continent; now they were engines of death and destruction, together with men who understood just how those engines might be best applied to fulfilling the great plan of Victory.

You will meet Capt. Tom Woods, indomitable Manxman, captain of the Lady of Mann leave-boat, returning from a fog-shrouded voyage where every inch of the way has been haunted by perils. The Merchant Navy has adopted Dover, and, being well versed in the usages of a port, is using it now to the best advantage. Fog hinders smooth working, but Captain Woods well knows what leave means to a fighting man or woman who has not set foot on English soil for years; and he takes his ship through weather that would have left pre-war shipmasters aghast.

Two Dictators Looked and Longed

Accustomed to seeing the flotsam of war washed up on its doorsteps, Dover welcomes the returning heroes with open arms, and puts every facility into their way for quick communication with friends, and for needed refreshments. Minesweepers still use the port as they return from their labours, but the normal activities of the Royal Navy are now reduced; there is not the same need for that minute-by-minute vigilance that kept the seas open for our ships. Napoleon stood on the Boulogne cliffs and cast longing eyes at the white ramparts. Hitler probably did the same. That, of course, is as far as the two Dictators got.

And so today, if a returning prisoner of war, long deprived of news, asks the question, as Kipling's exile asked it: "How stands the old Lord Warden? Are Dover cliffs still white?" Dover's answer is: "As it was, so it is today—Dover stands fast!"

Foremost Seaport of Kent in War and at Peace

AMONG THE SIGHTS OF DOVER (the "Soldiers' Own" Port) at war was "Winnie" (1), gun of the Royal Marine Siege Regiment, which in 1940 fired the first cross-Channel shells from England to France. Now leave-troops of the B.A.O.R. dash to the quayside kiosk (2) to telegraph home. Embarking for Germany are A.T.S. and British Red Cross Society personnel (3). Channel packet Royal Daffodil (4), bearer of a famous name is serving as troop-transport. See also facing page. *Photos, British Official, G.P.U., Topical Press, and courtesy of the General Steam Navigation Coy.*

Ignominious Exit of the Traitor Pierre Laval

THIS WAS THE END OF FRANCE'S ARCH-TRAITOR at Fresnes Prison, Paris, on October 15, 1945, when Pierre Laval, former French Premier, was executed, after a vain attempt to cheat justice by taking poison. Facing his executioners (1) Laval refused to be blindfolded. Journalists interviewed the priest (2) who had been with him to the end. Unmourned, the hearse containing Laval in his coffin left the prison (3). A newspaper man (4) was ordered by police to descend from his vantage-point on a telegraph pole.

Photos, Associated Press, Keystone

The Epic Story of Arnhem Told Afresh

By MAJOR
KENNETH HARE-SCOTT

THIS vivid reconstruction is the result of a visit to that battleground in Holland where in September 1944 our men endeavoured to force a gateway to North-West Germany. Our contributor, who was concerned with airborne supplies during those memorable days, toured the area with Maj.-General Urquhart and other officers, each of whom contributed his recollections of phases of the battle. See also pages 463-467.

An intriguing official booklet has recently been published, entitled By Air to Battle, recounting that part—and a very significant contribution it was, too—played by the British Airborne Divisions in the conquest of our enemies. Military strategists and historians of the future will find plenty of scope for discussion, and doubtless will formulate divergent opinions, upon the method of employment of the "skymen." But whatever their verdict, there can be little doubt that in a war in which surprise, science and experiment played so large a part, the development of troop transport by air weighed heavily on the side of the Allies.

I have just returned from Arnhem, where—under the guidance of our Divisional Commander, Major-Gen. R. E. Urquhart, C.B., D.S.O. and Bar, and a team of officers, each of whom described that portion of the battle in which he was immediately concerned—the pattern of events was pieced together as we moved from position to position. Space will not allow me to describe the battle with penetrating analysis, nor would it be of general interest; but I will attempt to explain the intention of the operation, the method, what actually happened, and lessons to be learned from so costly an enterprise.

Before the order was given to the Divisional Commander to prepare a plan for the capture of the bridge crossing the Rhine at Arnhem, no less than sixteen previous "Warning Orders" had been received for the 1st Airborne Division to go into action at a variety of points in France and Belgium. Some involved landing on the beaches in support of the Normandy "gateway"; some the capture of ports in Brittany; another, the raising of French patriots well behind enemy positions, and another the capture of bridges over the Seine. These plans, involving careful preparations, were, for strategic or other reasons, scrapped, and for some months the Division was in a state of "On your marks—Get set—As you were."

In September 1944, Field-Marshal Montgomery called for an airborne "carpet" to be laid for his advancing troops, by combined Allied landings at Eindhoven, at Nijmegen to capture the bridge over the Waal, and, more than ten miles farther into enemy-held territory, the bridge at Arnhem was to be secured—a role given to the 1st British Airborne Division. The Commanders of the Airborne Divisions prepared their plans. Availability of aircraft was limited, and somebody had to go short. As there was no point in the landing at Arnhem being 100 per cent successful if the other two failed, priority in aircraft availability was given to the Eindhoven and Nijmegen forces; which meant that the British Division had, of necessity, to be transported in two lifts—the first of them on September 17, the other on the following day.

Naturally this reduced considerably the force for the initial assault upon the objective, but Intelligence disclosed an estimate of light opposition, a very friendly reception by the Dutch—both factors in favour—whilst it also revealed impossible ground conditions for landing parachutists or gliders anywhere in the immediate vicinity of the bridge. This latter information led to the landings being made in an area to the north and west of Wolfhezen—a distance varying between five and eight miles from the bridge.

Not According to Expectations

The morning of September 17 was bright and clear, and many of you will remember the impressive armada of aircraft and gliders which crossed our coast for this historic operation. All went well in the initial stages. The three parachute battalions of the 1st Parachute Brigade landed without untoward incident, as did also the glider-borne infantry. Quickly the parachutists and infantry deployed and began to move in on their objective, whilst glider-borne troops of the Airlanding Brigade (battalions of the Border, K.O.S.B., and South Staffordshire Regiments) secured the landing and dropping zones for the arrival of the second lift.

Very soon, on approaching the village of Oosterbeek, the advancing troops began to meet strong German opposition, and it was then realized, with some foreboding, that all was not going quite according to expectations. The Germans had, in fact, a strong concentration, almost a corps, and much of it armoured, refitting in the neighbourhood of Arnhem. The 2nd Parachute Battalion, commanded by the legendary Lt.-Col. "Johnny" Frost, D.S.O. and Bar, M.C., of Bruneval fame (see illus. in page 629, vol. 6), managed by speed of advance and a certain amount of good luck to get through to the bridge, which they took and held, at first against quite light opposition. It was this battalion which dispatched the carrier-pigeon "William of Orange" to England with the news that the bridge had been captured (see illus. in page 249).

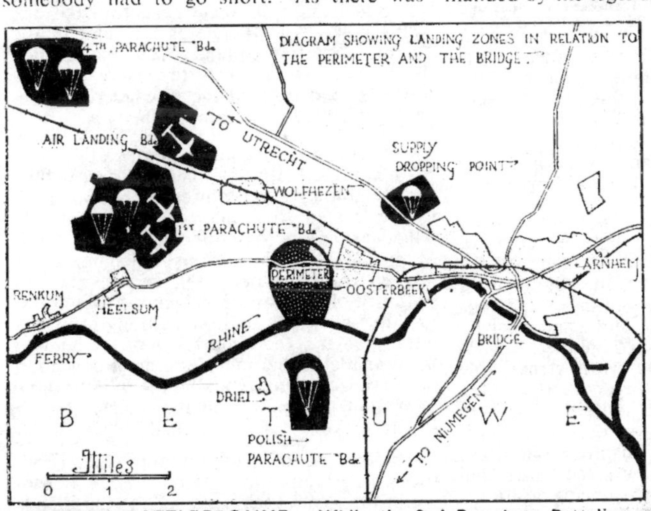

ARNHEM BATTLEGROUND. While the 2nd Parachute Battalion made desperate efforts to hold the Rhine bridge, the remainder of the 1st Brigade—and later, the 4th Brigade—strove unsuccessfully to reinforce them.

The 1st and 3rd Parachute Battalions, however, continued to be delayed in fierce fighting in and around Oosterbeek where they suffered very heavy casualties, having against them tanks, guns and numerical strength which far outweighed their own light composition. They fought heroically, but could make no progress towards a link-up with the 2nd Battalion on the bridge.

Meanwhile, in the direction of Wolfhezen and beyond, landing zones were held for the second lift. But alas! the lift was delayed through adverse flying conditions, landing at 4 p.m. on September 18 instead of at 9 a.m. as originally intended. Precious time had been lost, and they were a long way from their battle areas, nor could they push into the fight with ease, for the enemy held the only main road on the axis of advance and alternative routes led to trouble at every turn.

The second lift consisted of the 4th Parachute Brigade (the 10th, 11th and 156th Parachute Battalions), half a battalion of infantry and some elements of divisional troops. And suffice it to say that, hard as they fought, it was impossible to effect any concentration of strength sufficient, and within distance of the objective, to bring reinforcement to the men of the first lift who were still struggling to reach the 2nd Parachute Battalion on the bridge. The hours of delay in the arrival of the second lift had enabled enemy reinforcements to establish strong points.

HERO'S GRAVE in a garden in the Betuwe district, near Arnhem, being tended by a sabot-shod Dutchwoman—one of the many who will never forget. *Photo, Pictorial Press*

The Parachute Brigade was, in two days' fighting, reduced to about 250 men—one officer, Capt. L. E. Queripel of the 10th Battalion, was awarded the V.C. for supreme courage in face of the impossible odds which beset his whole formation (see illus. in page 24). Later, on September 21, a third lift, consisting of the Polish Parachute Brigade, was dropped near Driel, on the south of the river; but despite continued efforts for four consecutive nights, it was only possible to ferry 250 men across to play their part in the perimeter defence phase of the battle.

To add to the difficult situation which was developing, the "Resupply by Air" plan went adrift. The S.D.P. (Supply Dropping Point) selected for the delivery by air of food and ammunition fell early into enemy hands. My company was engaged upon resupply, and to the great distress of all no message of an alternative S.D.P. could be got back to base, and much-needed ammunition and supplies continued to fall day after day into enemy hands, and very many aircraft were shot down. Only later was it possible for a greatly limited " drop " to be made in the divisional perimeter, which comes into the story at this juncture.

THE Divisional Commander, who had shared in the heaviest close-quarter fighting in the bridge thrust, taking, as we say in the Army, " an appreciation of the situation," was faced with this picture. One battalion on the bridge was being severely mauled, and enemy pressure was increasing. The other battalions, pressing to reach the bridge, had been fought to a standstill, and their strength reduced to mere handfuls of men, dauntless in courage but facing insuperable odds, with most of their officers and N.C.O.s killed or wounded. The remaining force was scattered in a series of equally fierce engagements, with no prospect of ultimate junction with any coherent attempt to hold the bridge.

Also, his men were hungry and terribly short of ammunition. His decision, therefore, was to draw in as many men as possible and, on the old principle of Waterloo, to form a square or perimeter on the western edge of Oosterbeek, bounded on the south by the Rhine, and on the three sides by all available men. Thus a line of contact would remain open across the river with the spearhead of the advancing 2nd Army. The 2nd Battalion on the bridge had to go " into the bag," but only after resistance had reduced their number to barely a man alive and unwounded, and supplies and ammunition were exhausted. In this closing action Lieut. J. H. Grayburn earned a V.C., which he did not live to receive (see illus. in page 24).

BY skilful night movement the remainder of the Division was drawn in to form the perimeter. These comprised the remnants of the infantry battalions of the Airlanding Brigade ; the 4th Parachute Brigade ; the Independent Parachute Company (the Pathfinder Company, which lands first and lays out the D.Z. for the paratroops to follow), which is led by a remarkable wartime soldier—peacetime business man—Major " Boy " Wilson, D.S.O., M.C., over 50 years of age ; the few survivors of the 1st and 3rd Battalions and Divisional Troops ; the gunners, sappers, signallers, R.A.S.C., R.A.M.C., and the Glider Pilots, who had fought gallantly with their comrades from the moment of landing.

The R.A.M.C. had throughout the operation performed miracles. The care of the many wounded, widely dispersed, had been their concern day and night, without hope of evacuation except through enemy channels. Dressing stations and hospitals changed hands several times, and received little discrimination in the bombardment by mortar, tank and small-arms fire. The great majority —and they were great in heart and achievement—of the medical staff remained behind, to become prisoners with the wounded.

WORDS cannot describe the stubborn, offensive spirit which filled the thin line of " Red Devils " defending the perimeter ; a hedgehog which bristled and inflicted hurt at every approach of the pack of wolves. Their casualties from snipers concealed in the thick woods, and in buildings around the perimeter, and from mortar fire, never ceased ; no resupply by air of food or ammunition, except the odd pannier or container, to cheer them ; very little water and, worst of all, no news of the approach of the 2nd Army.

THEN a miracle happened. A gunner officer made wireless contact with a battery of the Medium Regiment, R.A., attached to the 43rd Division near Nijmegen. Soon afterwards the senior gunner officer of the Airborne Division attempted, and accomplished, an unprecedented feat. To gunners 21,000 yards away he was able, with remarkable precision, to indicate targets around the perimeter, and at times within it, where German infiltration had occurred. This artillery support, which inspired the tired, hungry defenders with new spirit, dislodged many of the enemy's more menacing positions.

Very careful control of food and ammunition had to be maintained within the perimeter. The enemy, in the words of Major Wilson, " usually drew stumps at 7 p.m.," after which, when night fell, it was possible to make any necessary changes in disposition. The gallant force could not hold out indefinitely, and the General sent two officers, Lieut.-Cols. Mackenzie and Myers, across the river to inform General Browning, Deputy Commander of the Allied Airborne Army, of the situation. These officers, after many adventures, fulfilled their mission, and returned with concerted plans for the withdrawal, which was now inevitable.

THE evacuation took place on the night of September 25–26, beginning at 10 p.m. Silently, with feet wrapped in bits of blanket to muffle any noise, the troops filed down to the river bank, leaving behind strategically placed rearguards, to maintain the illusion in the enemy mind that nothing unusual was afoot. The 2nd Army Artillery kept up a heavy bombardment, which the Germans believed was intended to cover a crossing of the river in strength by reinforcements. Sappers, in advance of the approaching 2nd Army, were waiting with assault craft to ferry the men across, and when daylight came over the horizon all but a few had found their way to the south bank ; and so the division, which started 10,000 strong, including the Glider Pilots, reformed in a school at Nijmegen, having lost 7,605 officers and men in killed, wounded and missing.

ONCE A FAMOUS DUTCH BEAUTY SPOT, Arnhem is today little more than ruins among which the shattered tower of the 15th-century Protestant Church, the Groote Kerk (above, in background), still stands. The tower, 305 ft. in height, formerly housed a 17th-century peal of bells famed throughout the Netherlands for its delicacy of tone. *Photo, Pictorial Press*

Braced Them for Renewed Attacks

Two more V.C.s were awarded in the perimeter fighting—to Major Robert Cain (see illus. page 478, Vol. 8) and L./Sgt. J. D. Baskeyfield (see illus. page 664, Vol. 8), both of the South Staffordshire Regiment. But every man was a hero, whilst the help given by the brave Dutch people must not be forgotten, for it included food, water, stretcher-bearing, nursing the wounded and maintaining the civil telephone system, which meant so much in the earlier days when wireless communication broke down. There was Major Lonsdale's " sermon " from the pulpit of a partially demolished church, when, reforming the remnants of the 1st and 3rd Parachute Battalions, in unprintable language he braced them for renewed attack against odds which had already killed or wounded 75 per cent of their comrades.

There were the signallers who relaid the telephone lines between Divisional H.Q. and a point 100 yards away, no less than 17 times, because the lines were as many times broken by shell and mortar fire. There was Major Cain's sergeant, who, wearing a Dutch top-hat, and within 150 yards of the enemy, ran a repair shop for weapons, " cannibalizing " different parts to make one whole gun. And there was the pilot of the Dakota aircraft, his plane ablaze, who circled the S.D.P. several times to ensure that his precious load reached the beleaguered force, before crashing to certain death.

IN conclusion, this glorious operation was no failure. It was 85 per cent successful ; for, by pinning down powerful enemy forces, it accelerated the main advance of the Allied armies across difficult country south of the Rhine. The lessons which might be learned from the operation include the importance of accurate Intelligence ; the necessity for at least divisional strength in the initial punch ; the importance of the landing being made in the immediate neighbourhood of the objective, and, finally, the infinite value of mental toughness and the offensive spirit in the make-up of the trained soldier.

The people of Arnhem and Oosterbeek today are proud of their fame. Their houses are in ruins, but their welcome for the friends of September 1944 will survive in warmth and sincerity until the battle is beyond the range of human memory.

Photos, Pictorial Press

Roofs for the Roofless in Holland

Returning citizens of Arnhem (see pages 461–462) found dwellings completely destroyed or stripped to the bricks and mortar (top) by the Germans, and no gas, electricity, telephones, lorries or building materal available. The Arnhem Council and the Netherlands Military Administration have assumed joint responsibility for restoring the town, and volunteers from all over Holland were engaged. Lacking tiles, roofs are mended or repaired with thatch (bottom).

Where Our Airborne Divisions Battled a Year Ago—

In the Betuwe (" good land ") district of Holland, between the Waal and the Lower Rhine, the once prosperous towns of Arnhem and Nijmegen present major problems. With her husband and five children this mother (1) lives in the cellars of a shattered farmhouse, and in the open prepares makeshift meals: when the rains come, and the snow—what then? Rebuilding is hindered by extreme scarcity of tools: men who must share a hammer arrange a timetable for its use (2).

—With Their Spirit Undaunted the Dutch Strive On

In a war-shattered church an emergency " house " is built (3) for one of the sadly dwindled congregation. They count themselves lucky who have shelter at all: a mother's gratitude for a home-of-sorts (4) equals her pride in the youngsters. The school has been spared (5), though bullets have scored the walls and daylight is seen through the roof. First the Germans occupied the schools, then came evacuation, so diligence in lessons to offset long idleness is imperative for Dutch children.

The Waterloo Bridge that Went to Holland!

The British Army took possession of London's temporary Waterloo Bridge when this was dismantled in 1943 (see illus. in page 311, Vol. 7). Now the spans have gone to Holland to be utilized in repairing bridges destroyed by the Germans. At Oosterbeek, near Arnhem (top), the work is already begun; "Waterloo" sections are seen in the left background. A closer view shows one span on piles ready to be erected (left), and (above) the painters at work on another section in its new setting.

Photographs exclusive to THE WAR ILLUSTRATED

"By Air to Battle"

Reviewed by
HAMILTON FYFE

THE Men in the Red Berets — how people stared after them when they were first seen in the streets! "What are they?" "They're airborne troops," was the answer.

Exactly what they did few could tell, but it was certainly something that called for nerve and courage of a high degree. Gradually the red berets became more numerous and more familiar. The nature of the duties required of their wearers was more fully known. Whether they were parachutists who dropped from aircraft in flight or passengers in gliders that floated down after being released by their "tugs," these duties evidently exposed them to dangers and difficulties of an alarming and harassing kind. Alarming, at any rate, to the civilian mind, which could not know how parachuting became after a short time as much a matter of routine as sloping arms or forming threes.

WHAT specially struck people with vivid imaginations was not so much the drop itself as the need for intense alertness and perhaps an instant plunge into battle as soon as ground was reached. One could fancy the thrill of leaving the plane, the swift fall until the parachute opened, then the swaying downward motion and the alighting on earth once more, with feet kept close together so as to avoid shock as much as possible. That would be an interesting, exciting experience—if that were the end of it, and if one could jump up and say, "Well, that's all right!" But to jump up and find yourself under fire, to know that the drop was only the prelude to hard fighting, to be obliged after a bumpy landing to collect your wits and set about dealing with an enemy who has you at a disadvantage for the moment —that is a very different sort of adventure and one that takes a lot of getting used to.

A Tough and Variegated Crowd

Clearly, therefore, the training of parachutists for war must be long and severe. A good many who started it had to be rejected, not for any fault or foolishness but because of temperamental unsuitability. In the Official Account of the British Airborne Divisions published under the title By Air to Battle (H.M. Stationery Office, 1s.) this training is described. It was beyond question the right kind, for it had the best possible results. It was altered, developed and improved as fresh experience was gained and as the "almost total lack of the equipment necessary" was overcome. In "the stony hills of Africa, the dusty olive-yards of Sicily, the green pastures of Normandy, the trim fields and ordered woods of Holland" something new was learned, some theory proved or disproved. "The result was distilled into the essence of victory and poured over the Rhine."

WHAT the training aimed at from the first was to endow the parachute soldier with "high quality both of mind and body." That this was attained his achievements unmistakably showed. He was enrolled "in that splendid company to be found in all the Services who may properly be described as the *élite* of the nation." Much of the credit for this must go to the instructors, who belonged mostly to the Physical Training Branch of the R.A.F., a tough and variegated crowd which included a number of schoolmasters, professional footballers and boxers, a road cycle champion, a circus acrobat, a "Wall of Death" rider, and a male dancer from the ballet.

Why it was not until the middle of 1940 that the formation of a parachute corps began will no doubt be inquired into. The War Office had done next to nothing in this direction until Mr. Churchill, in June of that year, wrote that "we ought to have at least five thousand" and asked for "a note from the War Office on the subject." There was no excuse for the failure to take this matter seriously. The Russians had a trained force of parachutists in 1936. Lord Wavell saw in that summer 1,200 men with 150 machine-guns and 18 light field-guns drop from the skies during manoeuvres. "If I had not witnessed the descents," he said, when he returned to Britain, "I could not have believed such an operation possible." Yet nothing was done, although it was known that in Germany also airborne forces were being organized and "great reliance placed on them to create confusion in the ranks of the enemy."

The New Arm Prepares for Action

As a consequence of the delay all sorts of experiments had to be made at first, causing many accidents. The warmest gratitude is due to the officers who in a short time managed to train and equip a fairly big force and work out a technique for the best employment of its capabilities. How little the importance of the task was at first realized is shown by the fact that a major was put in charge of the whole business. He had not previously studied it and he said "it was impossible to get any information (from the War Office) about it." Fortunately, Major (later Col.) J. F. Rock (portrait in this page) was a man of remarkable ability and vigour. By early spring of 1941 the new arm of the Service was ready for action on a small scale. An attack was made on an aqueduct in Southern Italy. This carried the main water supply to a population of some two millions in towns such as Brindisi, Taranto, and Foggia, where large numbers worked in dockyards and munition factories. It was decided to destroy a main pillar supporting the aqueduct and stop the flow of water.

This was actually done, but nevertheless the operation was a lamentable disappointment. To begin with, the damage was soon repaired. Further, one of the parties landed had to surrender because they lost their way after they had blown the pillar, while the other was dropped in the wrong place and was also captured. After this it was some twelve months before anything else was attempted. Meanwhile, the Germans showed in Crete "for the first time what a mass assault by parachutists and glider-borne troops could accomplish. True, the cost was very high. The Germans suffered enormous casualties," and if the British troops on the island could have been given air support, "there is little doubt that the airborne invasion would have failed." From its success, "many lessons of the highest importance were learned by those in command" on our side.

Col. J. F. ROCK, of the Royal Engineers, to whom was entrusted in June 1940 the task of organizing Britain's first airborne army. He was killed in action in October 1942.

Some of these were useful when, in February 1942, a village near Havre was raided with the object of capturing a radiolocation installation. This was wanted for examination by our experts, so that they might know how accurate the process of detection had become. Again one of the parties was dropped in the wrong place. It could not be said that everything went "according to plan," but plans were rapidly altered to suit events and with a loss of one killed, seven taken prisoner and seven wounded, the result was considered worth while.

WHEN North Africa was invaded in 1942 parachute troops did grand work, but after a time they were needed more in the line than in the air, so they found themselves fighting as infantry. Very well they fought and many were the tales told of individual exploits and adventures. For example, a lieutenant named Street, visiting his forward posts on a scrub-covered hillside in the half light of dawn, heard movements and voices. He called out, "Be quiet! There may be Germans near," and he was right. Next moment he had a tommy-gun pressed against his stomach and was ordered to lead a German patrol to the headquarters of his battalion. Instead, he guided them to a company strong-point, from which fire was at once opened on them. He luckily escaped being hit, and took cover in a hollow, where he had for companion the German officer in command of the patrol. He lay still for a while, then he said suddenly, "Look out, my chaps are throwing grenades at us!" The German turned his head, Street hit him, took away his weapons, and reached the strong-point.

The Relief Which Never Arrived

The contribution made by airborne troops to Allied victory in Sicily, Italy, Normandy and Holland is recounted in detail here. Especially and painfully interesting is the description of the Battle of Arnhem and the explanation of the reasons for our failure to hold that town with its bridge across the Rhine. One was that the landings had to be made at several miles distance from the town so as to be beyond reach of the enemy's guns. While the men dropped were marching to Arnhem the Germans had time to prepare for them. The other reason was that German guns commanded the only road along which relief could be sent to the hard-pressed 1st British Airborne Division. The arrangement was that this relief should arrive within forty-eight hours; it never arrived at all. No advance could be made along the causeway, raised some feet above the surrounding marshy flat country. "Large stretches of it were under observation from higher ground, and it could be shelled at will so long as that ground remained uncaptured." Thus the division which started 10,000 strong, lost three-quarters of its numbers before its retreat to Nijmegen ended. "Someone had blundered." Even this official report admits that. (See also pages 461–466.)

Gone is the Gaiety Now from Old Vienna

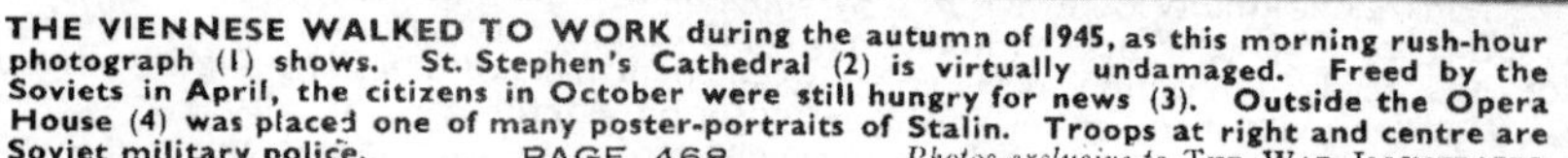

THE VIENNESE WALKED TO WORK during the autumn of 1945, as this morning rush-hour photograph (1) shows. St. Stephen's Cathedral (2) is virtually undamaged. Freed by the Soviets in April, the citizens in October were still hungry for news (3). Outside the Opera House (4) was placed one of many poster-portraits of Stalin. Troops at right and centre are Soviet military police.

Photos exclusive to THE WAR ILLUSTRATED

The Mine is Still a Peril of Our Coasts

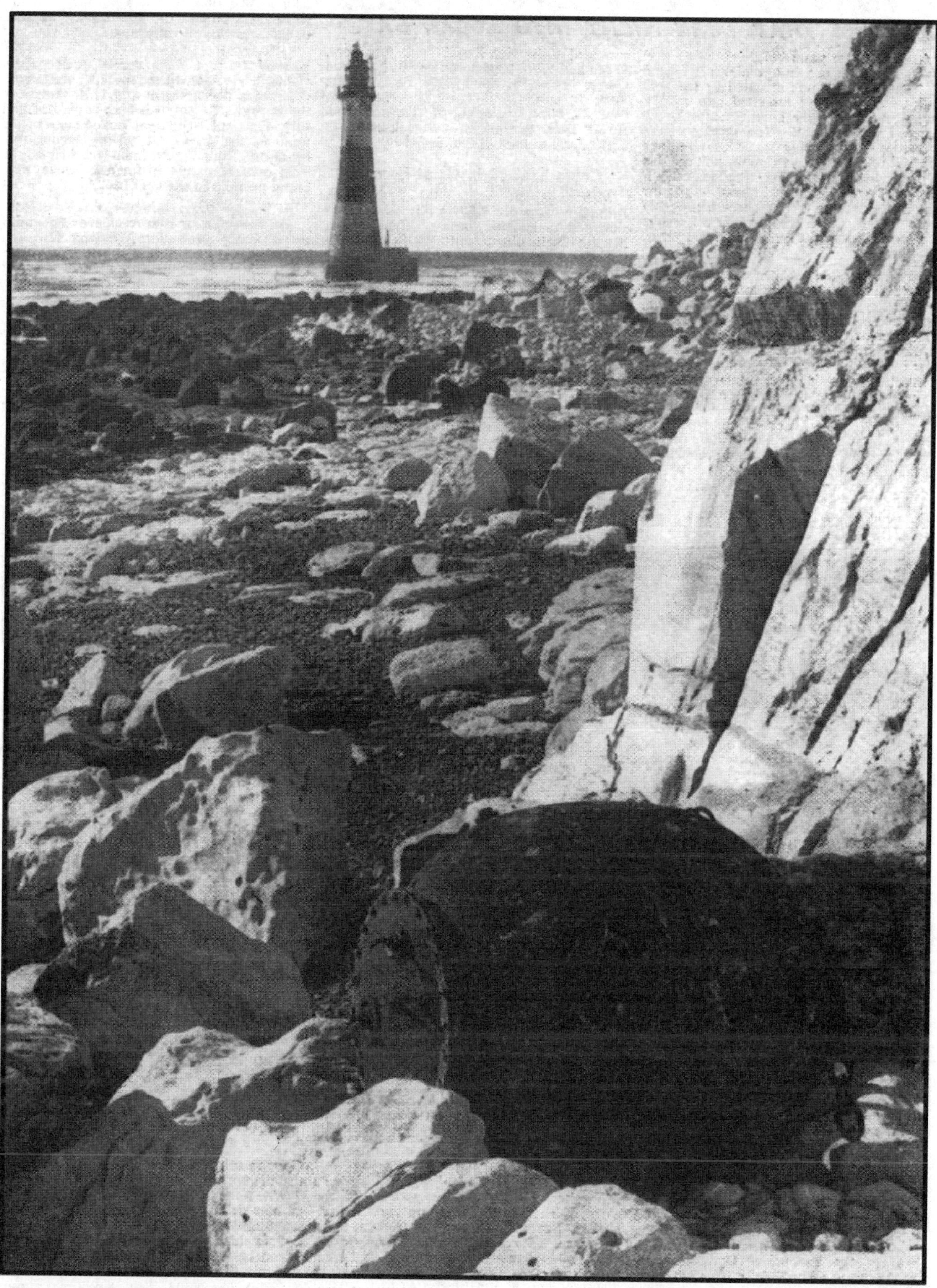

PERILOUS FLOTSAM OF THE GALES which swept Britain in late October lay this unexploded mine at the foot of Beachy Head, near Eastbourne in Sussex. It was one of hundreds which the sea flung up around our coasts, to be rendered harmless by special working-parties of the Royal Navy (see story in page 473). For a day and a night it had tossed heavily about in the wind-lashed water, endangering the famous lighthouse at the base of the rugged chalk cliffs which tower to the height of 500 feet.

Photo, Keystone

Now It Can Be Told!

TANKS THAT TURN NIGHT INTO LOCAL DAY

ABOUT three years before the war a new invention, consisting mainly of a special searchlight, was accepted by the War Office. It was later mounted into a tank turret and called, for security reasons, the Canal Defence Light. The inventors had succeeded in mounting inside the cramped confines of a tank turret a power unit capable of producing a light of several million candle-power. This was projected through a narrow slot and produced a flat beam of roughly fantail shape, which would cover a frontage of about 350 yards at a range of 1,000 yards.

The light could not be extinguished by small arms fire, although, of course, it was as vulnerable to anti-tank devices as any other tank turret. And it had flicker devices which, the inventors claimed, would dazzle onlookers and might induce temporary blindness by causing paralysis of the eye's retina. The War Office bought this invention and set up a research and training establishment in Cumberland under the command of Col. R. S. Ollington, O.B.E., who was assisted by Mr. A. V. M. Mitzakis (until recently Technical Adviser to the Ministry of Supply), and Mr. F. W. Hill, M.B.E., a specialist in searchlight construction.

Here was trained first the 11th Royal Tank Regiment and later the 35th Tank Brigade (Brig. H. T. de B. Lipscomb, R.T.R.), which consisted of the 49th Royal Tank Regiment, 152nd and 155th Regiments Royal Armoured Corps. Later, in the Middle East, the 1st Tank Brigade (Brig. T. R. Price, D.S.O., M.C., R.T.R.), consisting of 11th and 42nd Royal Tank Regiments, was converted to C.D.L. and trained in the desert.

Crews Trained in Great Secrecy

Meanwhile, at home, the 35th Tank Brigade became part of 79th Armoured Division and in isolated parts of Cumberland, Northumberland and South Wales, the training of tank crews continued, first on specially converted Matildas and Churchills, later on American Grants. The training took place under conditions of great secrecy, and it is to the credit of the School and regiments concerned and of the local inhabitants that no word of its existence reached German ears.

During the months of training before D-Day it was found that some of the earlier claims had been a little extravagant, but that C.D.L. had two definite advantages worth exploiting. When C.D.L. tanks were used to light up a wide front they could turn night into local day and thus enable the pursuit of a defeated enemy to continue throughout the 24 hours. The aimed fire-power of the tanks themselves, even if not augmented by infantry, ordinary tanks and artillery, was impressive: direction-keeping on a night advance or assault was greatly facilitated and might prove decisive against an enemy on the run. Also they provided by night an improvement on the age-old adage of warfare, namely, attack with the sun behind you and in the eyes of your opponent.

PRODUCTION of these special turrets continued in America and the U.K. American units were also trained, and both they and the 1st Tank Brigade—now consisting of the 11th, 42nd and 49th Royal Tank Regiments—went to the Continent shortly before the break-out from the Normandy bridge-head. That operation went so fast that it was not found possible to use C.D.L.

At a later stage, however, one squadron joined the ranks of 79th Armoured Division, and under the command of Major P. Gardner played a very useful role in the Rhine and Elbe crossings in protecting the bridges and ferries from floating mines and saboteurs. In the former they accounted for three enemy "Frogmen" and a considerable quantity of floating objects, including what was probably a midget submarine and a number of mines, intended to destroy the bridges over the Rhine so vital for reinforcement of our troops.

That is the story of C.D.L. to date. It has never been used in a mobile role against the enemy, although, had the special tanks been available, definite opportunities for its use presented themselves during the break-out from the bridge-head south of Caen, during the pursuit through France, the canal crossings in Holland, the fighting in the Reichswald Forest and crossings of the Rhine and Elbe.

FITTED WITH A BRITISH "CANAL DEFENCE LIGHT" TURRET a U.S. Army Grant tank (left) lightens the darkness with its millions-candle-power beam. In the background across the valley can be seen the beams of other tanks similarly equipped. A front view (right) of a Grant with a C.D.L. turret; it mounts a dummy anti-tank gun, by the side of which is the vertical slit through which the light operates. *Photos, British Official*

PSYCHOLOGICAL WARFARE DEPT. IN ACTION

ONE of the big secrets of the war was the part played by specially produced newspapers under the direction of the Psychological Warfare division of S.H.A.E.F. News for the Troops, a German newspaper designed to provide a first-class news service direct to the enemy forces in France, came into being two months before D-Day. Delivery was carried out by Lancasters, Mosquitoes, Flying Fortresses and Liberators, which took off daily from Cheddington airfield, Bucks, to fly over the German lines in France. They carried special bombs packed with newspapers which burst and scattered their contents at 1,000 feet. At first 200,000 copies came off the presses daily. On D-Day a special edition of a million copies gave the German soldier his first authentic account of the biggest military event in history.

When the Allies crossed the Rhine nine months later, News for the Troops was supplemented by Shaef, a paper brought out to help in the control of liberated prisoners, displaced persons and German civilians by giving them day-to-day information and instructions. It was printed in English, French, German, Polish and Russian, and its circulation rose to the million mark.

SECRETS OF THE CAMERA-WAR WERE REVEALED to journalists at Medmenham R.A.F. station, Bucks, on September 9, 1945. A flight-lieutenant demonstrated the photogrammetric equipment (left) which produces accurate maps from aerial photographs (" two photographs go inside, a handle is turned, and out come the maps," said the officer). Famous wartime reconnaissance pilots are now photographing Britain from the air at the request of the Ministry of Town and Country Planning. D-Day forces were " briefed " with synthetic rubber models of the Normandy coast—some 340 of them—also constructed from R.A.F. photographs and shown publicly (right) for the first time at Medmenham. *Photos, British Official*

In the Far Eastern theatre, too, the Psychological Warfare Dept. won the fight for native support by combining psychology with factual reports. The names of Fido and Pluto will be remembered for their part in the overthrow of the Nazis. Another set of initials—Felo (Far Eastern Liaison Office of Psychological Warfare)—will figure in records of the war against Japan. Felo's job was the composition and distribution of thousands of leaflets in pidgin-English for the natives of the Pacific Islands. Its propaganda. planned in conjunction with military operations, urged the natives not to work for the Japanese, to deny them food, and to assist Allied airmen shot down.

It had great successes. Leaflets used in landing operations caused at least 1,000 Japanese soldiers to surrender. And during one campaign there was a refusal of native labour to the Japanese, which forced them to use 1,000 front-line troops as carriers.

Navy's Little Ships Fought 780 Actions

At last the splendid record of the Royal Navy's M.T.B.s, M.G.B.s, and M.L.s can be revealed. During the war in Europe, Coastal Forces performed the following feats : fought 780 actions with the enemy at sea ; sank more than 500 enemy vessels ; carried out nearly double the number of individual minelaying operations carried out by all other Naval minelayers ; fired 1,169 torpedoes, scoring 301 certain or probable hits—a percentage better even than submarines ; and shot down 32 enemy aircraft.

The cost of these successes was the loss in action of 170 Coastal Force craft. This "midget" Navy—the largest M.T.B. displaces only 120 tons—expanded a hundredfold in four years. At the outbreak of war there were only two flotillas of Coastal Force craft. In 1944 it employed 3,000 officers and 22,000 ratings. Over 1,200 craft were built in the United Kingdom and over 300 in the Empire and the United States. Over 90 per cent of Coastal Force officers were R.N.V.R. and the same percentage of ratings were "Hostilities Only."

With the Germans holding the French coast, the need for these little ships became acute. Mass production and prefabrication had to be used to a considerable extent. There was so much to be done that the "utility" M.L.s originally designed for anti-submarine work in coastal waters were also used as minelayers, minesweepers, convoy escorts, gunboats, smokelayers, air-sea rescue craft and for duties with Combined Operations.

Coastal Forces started their operational career in the Dunkirk evacuation and the fall of Holland. During that tense period they evacuated the Belgian Cabinet, Admiral Keyes, General Alexander and other notabilities. In the late part of 1940 the German E-boats appeared, and then began the four-year duel. In defending our convoys, gunboats, torpedo-boats and motor launches sank 48 E-boats and mauled twice that number.

The Navy's contribution to the famous raid on St. Nazaire was exclusively from Coastal Forces, with the exception of H.M.S. Campbeltown, the destroyer which rammed and exploded at the dock gates. Of the 18 small craft that went into the attack only four came back. In the latter half of 1942, M.T.B. operations were carried for the first time into the fjords of Norway. Raids from the Shetlands entailed long sea passages in severe weather conditions and a stay of often several days hidden amongst the fjords.

In a "cat-and-mouse" campaign in the waters of the Adriatic and Aegean, M.T.B.s developed the technique of boarding enemy vessels and capturing them. During the Invasion of France, a total of 28 M.T.B. flotillas were in operation at home.

In their most successful year, 1944, Coastal Forces averaged more than one action a day over the whole twelve months, actually having 378 engagements with the enemy. In one week working with destroyers during the evacuation of Le Havre by the Germans, Coastal Forces destroyed 20 ships without loss to themselves. In the final stages of the European War, Coastal Forces had to counter midget U-boats ; of 81 midgets sunk or captured, Coastal Forces claimed 23.

Whalers That the Nazis Could Not Catch

Throughout the war in Europe the great wastes of the Antarctic ice floes were the background for one of the greatest sea hunts on record. Scandinavian captains using their skill to save their ships and vital cargoes, outwitted Nazi raiders and warships in spite of the fact that the enemy used the latest scientific location devices.

This battle of wits was carried out across thousands of miles of the coldest seas in the world. It has ended (reports an Evening Standard correspondent) with the arrival in Norway of two Norwegian whaling factory ships after years of exile in the Antarctic. The British-built 14,000-ton whale factory, Sir James Clark Ross, has berthed at Sandefjord with a cargo of 17,000 tons of whale oil. She has been followed by the Torshammer, a 12,000-ton factory.

It was in 1939 that this vessel left Sandefjord. She has since made three expeditions to the Antarctic, and three to Peru. Both these giant whalers have eluded the Nazi warships on every run. So determined were the Nazis to stop this trade that they sent out a special expedition in 1941 and eventually reached the Antarctic.

Several whale ships were taken, but the Sir James Clark Ross and the Torshammer, assisted by British intelligence code messages, eluded capture. Now peace has come in the Antarctic. The scene is changing. Two German floating factories operated by British firms will voyage south this season. There will also be two complete British expeditions working side by side with Norwegians.

GERMAN WHALE SHIP Unitas, captured at Hamburg and renamed Empire Victory, underwent a refit at Southampton. This stern view shows the opening through which the " catch " is dragged. *Photo, Planet News*

Still Mounts the War-Roll of Incomparable V.C.s

Jemadar PARKASH SINGH
Attached to the 13th Frontier Force Rifles, Jemadar Parkash Singh was, in February 1945, in command of a company in Burma. Though so severely injured that he could move only by means of his hands, he continued to rally his men to victory till he died.

Naik GIAN SINGH
In command of a leading section of the 15th Punjab Regiment in Burma, in March 1945, Naik Gian Singh by "acts of supreme gallantry" enabled his platoon to capture two vital positions, saving many lives. Though wounded, he inflicted heavy casualties on the enemy.

Major ANDERS LASSEN
In Italy in early April 1945, Major Lassen, M.C. (right) was ordered to make a dangerous diversionary night raid on the shore of Lake Comacchio. In face of overwhelming enemy superiority he achieved his object—the wiping out of three positions. He was killed by a hail of bullets.

Rfm. BHANBHAGTA GURUNG
Serving with the 2nd Gurkha Rifles in Burma in March 1945, Rifleman Bhanbhagta Gurung, showing complete disregard for his own life, cleared five enemy positions single-handed, using grenades and his kukri.

Lt. WILLIAM B. WESTON
This young officer of the Green Howards (left) won the supreme award while serving with the West Yorkshire Regiment in Burma in March 1945, when his battalion was leading the attack on Meiktila. He withdrew the pin from a grenade as he lay wounded, thus killing himself and surrounding Japanese—"an example seldom equalled."

Sqd-Ldr. I. W. BAZALGETTE, D.F.C.
The third member of the R.A.F. Pathfinder Force to win the V.C., Squadron-Leader Bazalgette met his end in a daring raid on Troissy St. Maximin, France, on August 4, 1944. Though his plane was wrapped in flames he pressed on gallantly to the target, marking and bombing it accurately

Sergeant AUBREY COSENS
At Mooshof, Holland, on February 26, 1945, this young N.C.O. of the Queen's Own Rifles of Canada was mortally wounded after killing at least twenty of the enemy and taking an equal number of prisoners, resulting in the capture of a vital position. He showed "outstanding gallantry" after his platoon commander had been killed.

W/O. NORMAN C. JACKSON
The 20th V.C. of the R.A.F., this London-born flight-engineer in a Lancaster attacking Schweinfurt, Germany, on April 26, 1945, though badly burned on face and hands, attempted to extinguish the flames of his blazing aircraft by climbing out on to the wing when travelling at 200 m.p.h.

Photos, British and Canadian Official, Topical, G.P.U., The Daily Mirror, Associated Press, Elliott and Fry

I Was There! Eye Witness Stories of the War and After

I Saw the Navy 'Killing' Washed-Up Mines

The great autumn gales that swept our shores provided dangerous work for the R.M.S. (Rendering Mines Safe) squads of the Royal Navy. This story of the men in action was sent from Hayling Island, Hampshire, on October 28, 1945, by The Daily Mail reporter Murray Edwards.

LIEUT.-COMMANDER H. E. WADSLEY, D.S.C., G.M. and Bar, leaned over a 6-cwt. canister of T.N.T. on the beach here today and said to his assistant, A.B. Leslie Blood, "Cotton waste and paraffin, please." He rammed the waste into a hole in the high explosive, saturated it with paraffin, and yelled, "Run, boys!"

I ran with them. Looking round, I saw the Commander throw a lighted match, stand calmly watching till the black smoke began to curl upwards, then stroll towards me. I know now why he got those decorations. "She may blow up and she may not," he told me when he caught up. "It's just as well to be on the safe side." He had just attended to the half-ton mine that might have crippled the Queen Mary, which lay hove-to less than a mile away for more than 48 hours until she was able to dock yesterday. Nearly half of the mine was half-inch steel, complicated electrical gear, springs and switches. The other half was raw explosive.

PEACETIME clerk in an oil company, Lieut.-Commander Wadsley, is one of the Navy's "Rendering Mines Safe" officers, the opposite number to the Army's Bomb Disposal men. Last week's gale started the war all over again for the men who call their Nissen hut headquarters H.M.S. Vernon.

Earlier, I visited the hut, in the woods behind a house called West Leigh, near Havant, and talked with the Mine Disposals Chief, Commander J. G. D. Ouvry, D.S.O., who trains the men who make the mines harmless (see story and illus. p. 124, Vol. 7). He told me that for the next 20 years moored mines which have come adrift will be a menace all round the coast of Britain.

"Since the gale started last week," he said, "we have dealt with 72 mines, 30 of them in the Brighton area, and our ground extends only from Lyme Regis to Harwich." Two of the mines were found today, one of them at Dymchurch, 10 miles west of Folkestone, and the other at Littlestone-on-Sea, a few miles farther to the west.

Blazing Mound of High Explosive

Somewhere between the British coast and Europe there are 30,000 mines of all types, and only a few thousand have been recovered. The others, moored mines that might have come adrift in rough weather and through the wire mooring rope getting "tired" and snapping, magnetic mines, and mines covered with a thin film of mud on the sea bed, will be a menace to shipping for years. If the storm which is said to be on the way breaks soon, it is certain that scores more mines will be washed up. The R.M.S. officers of H.M.S. Vernon know that they are in for a busy time.

I went yesterday with one of the Rendering Mines Safe teams to the most exposed parts of the beach here. A long way off we saw the rusty mine high up on the beach. Lieut.-Commander Wadsley, with his three pupils and two A.B.s, most of them wearing medal ribbons for bravery, lost no time in getting down to work.

For an hour I watched them twist and turn the rusty nuts holding the plug of the mine. Sometimes a stubborn one had to be knocked off with a hammer and a chisel, and I wanted to run. Then, when the plug was off at last, the Commander fiddled about inside with his head on one side. He said, "Got it!" when he withdrew his arm, and I saw that "it" was a 2-oz. gadget which works the mine.

They rolled the sinister canister nearer to the water's edge and left the steel shell for the local authorities to take away for salvage.

As he worked, the youthful Commander told me about his job and assured me that T.N.T. has to be detonated to blow up. "But it can play tricks," he said. "It is not likely to explode, so we burn it, but just in case of accident, we do the job as far away from houses as possible."

I watched the yellow mound of blazing high-explosive throwing out sparks like a giant fire-cracker. It burned fiercely for 30 minutes, then spluttered out . . . another mine gone. The A.B.s picked up the bag of tools and went away to the next "job." All the men of the R.M.S. are volunteers. They like danger. Lieut.-Commander Wadsley told me as I left, "I shall miss it all. I am to be demobbed in a month."

ROPING A LIVE MINE washed up at Hastings by an October gale to prevent its detonation against the concrete anti-invasion obstructions was all in the day's work for the Royal Navy R.M.S. squad. The Lieutenant who roped it is sprinting for the upper beach as another great wave is about to break on the shore. **See also illus. page 469.** *Photo, Sport & General*

A Commando's Farewell to His Green Beret

The disbanding of Army Commandos and the withdrawal of the famous green beret as an Army head-dress was announced on October 25, 1945. The spirit which imbued them during their five-and-a-half years' existence is the subject of this "farewell" (reprinted from The Evening Standard) by Lt.-Col. A. C. Newman, V.C., hero of St. Nazaire (see also page 185).

WE all knew the day would have to come—the day of the end of the Green Beret—and come soon after the end of hostilities. To those of us in the Army who have worn the green beret it is a sad day, but a glorious one. For we all feel that, although disbanded, we leave something behind. To hear the announcement made in the House of Commons that the lessons we learnt are to be incorporated into Regular Army training is enough.

The Commando soldier will also look back over these years of war with a much deeper feeling. I cannot put into words the high regard I; and I am certain all other commanding officers of the Commandos, feel for those officers and men who gave us such loyalty, unfailing support and friendship. The Commando meant so very much more to us than just the fighting aspect.

Far too much has been said about the Commando soldier being tough or a roughneck. From the very first day when Commandos were being organized, and the opportunity was given to collect together volunteers from the Army, the main characteristics of the force were the spirit of adventure and the spirit of the offensive. The volunteers were very ordinary young soldiers, and it was only by the build-up in training of the ideals and the spirit which afterwards meant so much to us all, that a force emerged with characteristics of its own.

Every man knew that unless he lived up to the standards required he would be returned to his unit. That was the worst punishment that any Commando could have; R.T.U. were the three most dreaded letters in the alphabet in the early days of the Commando. They soon attained by intensive training and freedom of movement and thought a new kind of fitness, physical and mental, with every man thinking for himself, self-confident, and with power to reason things out for himself.

Growing with this was a spirit of comradeship in each Commando, which soon formed into a bond of friendship between officer and man never to be broken down. Each Commando was a large family with a mutual

COMMANDOS went ashore from landing-craft on Walcheren Island, near Flushing (right) at dawn on November 1, 1944—scene of one of the major triumphs of these gallant and war-toughened troops, the announcement of whose disbandment was made on October 26, 1945

The first assault was head-on against Flushing, the greater part of which was in our hands by nightfall. Recollections of the men with the Green Beret are recorded here by Lieut.-Col. Augustus C. Newman, V.C. See also illus. page 431.

Photo, British Official

trust, firm and unshakable in any conditions. Without such a bond of friendship it would have been impossible to carry through our ideals, and overcome the obstacles subsequently met in action.

This is not the time or place to set out the various and multitudinous details of training; sufficient to say that Commando training was to a very great extent worked up by experiment and suggestions from all ranks, everyone thinking out for himself a possible way of overcoming any difficulty. Whatever the suggestion the Commando tried it out, and if it proved useful at once adopted it into the training programme.

One thing is certain; this day may be the official breaking up of Army Commandos, but the friendships gained, the mutual comradeships felt by all ranks towards each other, and the unstated but nevertheless firm resolve not to lose contact, will go on.

I would like to feel that—during these coming years when we, as a nation, are facing times as serious as those of five years ago—it must be possible to fuse into industry, business life, and all our civilian jobs, something akin to that spirit of service and determination, that closeness and mutual trust between officer and man in the Commandos. Already in industry appears that breakdown between employer and employee which is so undermining to progress.

The times that we are passing through are far too grave to permit this to happen. If it is possible in war for a body of men to understand each other and to make themselves, by understanding and determination, a force to be reckoned with, then surely it is possible to achieve the same results in peace. It is just as necessary to the welfare and safe keeping of the country.

We Brought Dido and Her Precious Gold to Egypt

With her gun-barrels red-hot from continuous firing, the British cruiser Dido evacuated thousands of pounds worth of gold coins belonging to the Bank of Greece from Crete to Egypt in May 1941. The story has now been released for publication as told to Reuters correspondent by Commander H. G. Dickinson, R.N., now commander of an aircraft carrier.

We had just taken a convoy of reinforcements to Suda Bay. It was pretty nasty and bombs were coming down all around. We received a signal—"Come inside the harbour and embark gold." We moved in, and were met by a little corvette loaded to the Plimsoll line with great heavy boxes of gold which were to be taken back to Egypt.

We decided to stow the boxes in one of the magazines forward, but just as we were opening the hatch another air-raid developed.

As Stukas screamed over the harbour, the ship's company dropped the boxes and leapt to action stations. One box went hurtling to the bottom of the magazine and burst open. The rest we stored when time and Stukas permitted. Then we forgot them.

We set sail for Egypt in company with some destroyers and a small merchant ship of some 8,000 tons carrying 400 wounded men. This little ship, captained by a Scots skipper, nearly proved our undoing. At dawn we entered the Kaso Straits, only about eight miles from the German's nearest airfield. The merchantman was having trouble with her engines and lagged behind. We signalled her and received no reply.

Then the awful thing happened: she gave up the ghost and stopped dead. We went alongside and asked the skipper through the loud hailer what was the matter. A very dour Scots voice bellowed through a megaphone, "We've broken down. I cannot be getting any reply from my engine-room!"

The sun was getting up, and any moment we knew the Stukas would be over. Our commanding officer, Capt. H. W. U. McCall, D.S.O. (now captain of H.M.S. Howe) sent a hurried signal to the merchantman: "Have all your wounded ready for disembarking immediately. If you are not away in ten minutes we propose to torpedo you."

This seemed too much for the dour Scot. Within an incredibly short time smoke was belching from the steamer's funnels and she was sprinting ahead at about 16 knots—well above her normal speed. And she still sent us no signal.

Then the Stukas came over. Screaming out of the sun, they dived down on the convoy. Our guns barked into action. One stick of bombs fell right round the merchant ship and she disappeared from view, hidden by gigantic cascades of water. We thought she'd had it and waited breathlessly. But she came steaming through placidly.

It was then we received the only signal of the entire voyage from the Scot. We spelled out one word—"Phew!" All that day we were attacked, time and again, by high level Italian bombers and Stuka dive bombers. But we weren't hit. Dido's gun crews were at continuous action stations and her gun-barrels became red-hot with firing.

It was only when we arrived in Alexandria and found lorries waiting on the quayside,

Cmdr. H. G. DICKINSON, R.N., who here relates the story of how H.M.S. Dido (illus. in facing page) successfully transported gold to Egypt in 1941. *Photo, British Official*

Capt. H. W. U. McCall, D.S.O., R.N., former commanding officer of the cruiser Dido (see accompanying story) now captain of the battleship H.M.S. Howe. *Photo, British Official*

H.M.S. DIDO, 5,450-ton British cruiser (see accompanying story), probably saw more Mediterranean action during the war than any other British cruiser, barring the Penelope. She took part in landings in Sicily in 1943 and Southern France in 1944, and formed part of our naval force which accepted the surrender of the Prinz Eugen and other units of the German fleet in Copenhagen in May 1945. *Photo, British Official*

and a regiment of battle-dressed soldiers tramping up the gangway that we remembered the valuable cargo we had been carrying. We had completely forgotten about the gold. The boxes were scattered all round the place—in the mess deck, in the canteen flat, in passages leading forward.

We checked up and found four missing. One was found in the stoker petty officers' mess, another under a side of beef in the butchers' shop, and another in the sick bay underneath an injured seaman. The fourth, I remembered, had been dropped hurriedly down a magazine hatch. I ordered a seaman to go down and sweep the contents up with a broom, and he poured the coins into an empty mailbag. We handed the whole lot over to the port accountant officer, who carefully counted the contents. There were only two pieces of gold missing !

Tricked by the Royal Navy's Invisible Ships

There were complaints during the war that the escort vessels guarding the North Atlantic convoys could not see one another. These were complaints against perfection ! Secrets of this effective camouflage were revealed to The Daily Telegraph Naval Correspondent Cmdr. Kenneth Edwards, R.N.

ADMIRALTY scientists and sailors had spent months in evolving a camouflage scheme which would render the vessels virtually invisible under the conditions of moon and visibility which the U-boats chose for their mass attacks. It emanated from the Art Gallery at Leamington Spa, at one end of which there is a shallow tank where scale models of all types of ships are tested with varying forms of camouflage.

I met there, in the middle of England, an officer who could order, " Switch on the sun," or suggest " Let's have a three-quarter moon on the starboard quarter." The day remained dull and overcast, but the conditions produced in and over the tank were those which had been called for. It was possible at will to reproduce the day and night light conditions most likely to be met with in the Western Approaches, the Mediterranean, the Indian Ocean, or the Pacific.

There were also arrangements which reproduced with great accuracy the degree of haze to be expected near the horizon at any time of the day in any latitude under normal weather conditions. The accurate reproduction of these factors has enabled the ships of the Royal Navy to be painted in accordance with a scientific and very effective scheme of camouflage.

THERE are two main principles in the camouflage of a ship at sea: to make her as invisible as possible under conditions of weather and light in which she is most likely to be in action, or look like something entirely different, or at least to disguise her course and speed. The latter system was much used in the 1914-18 war, but this time the naval experts tried to make ships invisible. They had considerable success, although the maximum of success can only be achieved after the enemy has shown the conditions under which he prefers to attack.

At Leamington I watched, as from an aircraft at about 1,700 ft., a battleship of the King George V class at a distance of 18 miles. The model was so painted that, under the usual conditions of light in the North Pacific, she was invisible through high-powered binoculars. Yet when the full and haze-free sunlight that prevails in the Mediterranean was shed on her she was obvious even at that long range.

White and Pale Blue Camouflage

Close study of the light conditions in various parts of the world, and during periods when enemy activity is most likely, led to the adoption of the almost pure white and pale blue camouflage of the convoy escorts in the Western Approaches. It was one of the most successful forms ever adopted. Lt.-Cmdr. Peter Scott, the seabird artist and Light Coastal Forces leader, had much to do with its evolution. Although invisibility under the conditions most likely to be encountered in action in a particular part of the world is the main principle on which British naval camouflage has been developed during the war, the other principle of deceiving the enemy has been by no means neglected, of course.

For instance, I found myself looking through high-powered binoculars at a model of a big fleet aircraft carrier. Haze, distance and twilight could not disguise what she was. Yet when an identical model, painted for the conditions of light obtaining, was substituted, I was quite convinced that I was looking at a Tribal class destroyer about eight miles away, instead of a carrier at fifteen miles.

Lt.-Cmdr. PETER SCOTT, R.N.V.R., artist-son of the famous Antarctic explorer, Light Coastal Forces leader and expert on Naval camouflage. See adjoining column. *Photo, British Official*

★=As The Years Went By—Notable Days in the War=★

1939

November 18. *Sinking of Dutch liner Simon Bolivar opened magnetic mine campaign.*

November 23. *Rawalpindi sunk in action with German pocket-battleship Deutschland.*

1940

November 11-12. *Fleet Air Arm made attack on Italian Navy in port of Taranto.*

November 14. *Heavy air raid on Coventry.*

1941

November 14. *H.M.S. Ark Royal sank off Gibraltar after torpedo hit on previous day.*

November 18. *Eighth Army under General Cunningham launched attack in Libya.*

November 22. *Germans entered Rostov-on-Don.*

1942

November 10. *Oran, naval station in French North Africa, captured by Allied troops.*

November 11. *Germans entered Unoccupied France in violation of armistice of 1940.*

November 19. *Russians attacked at Stalingrad.*

1943

November 20. *American troops landed on Makin and Tarawa atolls in the Gilbert Islands.*

November 22. *Cairo Conference opened between Roosevelt, Churchill and Chiang Kai-shek.*

1944

November 12. *Battleship Tirpitz sunk in Tromso Fjord by R.A.F. bombers.*

November 19. *U.S. troops entered Metz.*

How R.A.F. Learn Radar Secrets

By CAPTAIN
NORMAN MACMILLAN
M.C., A.F.C.

So that the ceaseless demand for radar for air navigation and other purposes will not be affected by demobilization, hard training continues today at the principal radar schools of the R.A.F. When the war began there was only one school for training in radar, situated at Bawdsey Manor, in Suffolk, in an area vulnerable to German air attack. It was soon moved to Yatesbury, in Wiltshire, where an aerodrome had first existed during the First Great War. There, during the remainder of the Second Great War, more than 25,000 men and women were trained in ground radar station work.

At Cranwell, in Lincolnshire, near the R.A.F. College, there was a school for training pupils in the use of airborne radar. During the high-pressure period of the war other airborne radar training schools were established at Prestwick, Ayrshire and South Kensington, London.

Air Commodore C. P. BROWN, C.B.E., D.F.C. and Bar, 47-year-old Director of Radar at the Air Ministry, was in control of one of Britain's largest secret training operations of the war.

More than half the radar mechanics who serviced the R.A.F. ground and airborne installations during the war were Canadian volunteers, and thousands of Canadian officers and men received their training at a secret radar school built at Clinton, Ontario, which was given the code-name "Problem." This school was built in a few months, with an electric-wired compound to protect the apparatus. It began work late in 1941.

Before that time all Canadian volunteers crossed the Atlantic to receive training in the United Kingdom, and Air Commodore C. P. Brown, Air Ministry Director of Radar, said in August 1945, "It would not have been possible to meet the vital and increasing demands of radar in the latter part of 1940 and the following years without the knowledge that Canada was undertaking the recruiting and training of men in thousands to help us handle this immense weapon."

The control of this great and successful effort to train men and women in the application of a new and highly scientific branch of electronics was vested in the R.A.F. Technical Training Command, with wartime H.Q. in Wantage Hall, Reading University.

While recruits with a knowledge of wireless technique were most acceptable for enlistment for radar operation, it was necessary to accept large numbers who had little or no knowledge of radio beyond switching on a receiver and tuning in to broadcasting stations. These recruits had to be given an elementary training in electricity and wireless, and learn how batteries, condensers, resistances, chokes and valves are made and what they do. For this purpose *ab initio* courses were set up in 26 well-known technical colleges in England, Scotland, and Northern Ireland, and in 15 universities in Canada.

INSTRUCTORS Wrote Own Text-Books to Keep Pace with the Developments

The schools of the Command had to take over completely many of the new radar equipments after the first course had been given by the scientists of the Ministry of Aircraft Production's Tele-Communications Research Establishment at Malvern, Worcestershire. Development was so rapid that instructors had to write their own text-books, and were often only an instructional hour or so ahead of the pupils they taught.

Different schools developed different methods of demonstrating the circuits. At one, the basic systems were wired up on "bread-boards"—flat panels which the pupils could handle. At another, large coloured plans were placed in front of the classes, with key points lighting up at the touch of the instructor's switch. And there were "synthetic" trainers, in which the green echoes of the cathode ray tubes that indicate moving aircraft were artificially simulated. Wingless "fuselages" were used for teaching pupils to handle airborne radar.

R.A.F., Dominion, and Allied pupils (including many Americans before the United States entered the war) were trained at these schools. One great difficulty was the need for strict secrecy. The ground equipment of the Oboe set used for controlling Pathfinder aircraft when marking bomber targets was housed in a special hut called "Station Type 9000" at the Yatesbury School, and only those named on a printed list outside were admitted.

All documents used in the advanced schools had to be kept locked away. Pupils could not even take their notebooks away from the classrooms to study the complicated circuits and theoretical diagrams in their spare time. During urgent periods at Yatesbury, classes were held from early morning until late at night, and even right through the night.

Women played a great part in the R.A.F.'s radar service. In November 1939 airwomen to the number of 26 were selected for this work under the classification of "special duties." At the peak of the war over 4,000 W.A.A.F. officers and airwomen were classified as radar signals officers, supervisors, mechanics and operators. In the last 18 months of the war, 22 W.A.A.F. officers became conspicuously successful interception controllers. When W.A.A.F. operators were found to have special aptitude for the task of Fighter Direction, both in control of interception and in offensive operations, it became possible to release men from home radar service for radar service overseas. W.A.A.F. ground radar operators were found to be adept also at "seeing" ships.

The growing development of British radar indicated the necessity of blinding the enemy coastal radar chain to secure the greatest advantage from our own radar and to prevent German radar interception of the seaborne forces which were later to invade Normandy. The British group of radar scientists began to investigate this problem in July 1943, and their work was regarded as so secret that only four copies of their report were made, each marked "TOP SECRET."

WHY German Radar Failed on D-Day to Pinpoint the Main Allied Force

The scientists built a dummy radar installation, and British fighter pilots used many different types of ammunition in firing trials. A German radar aerial system captured in North African operations was rushed to Britain for the experiments.

Ordinary ground-strafing by fighters was found to be an insufficiently crippling form of attack against German coastal radar stations, which were well protected by sand-bag emplacements. The scientists' final recommendations were to attack first with rocket-firing fighters to blast a breach through the protection, and second with cannon-firing fighters firing explosive shells through the breach to wreck the delicate apparatus within. For stations wholly or partially underground dive or low-level bombing was recommended.

Their recommendations were put to immediate military use. German radar defences from Brest to Heligoland became the object of effective attack, and on D-Day German radar was totally unable to pinpoint the main Allied force. How important this was in achieving maximum tactical surprise can be appreciated by all who saw the array of ships that sailed the Channel on June 5, 1944.

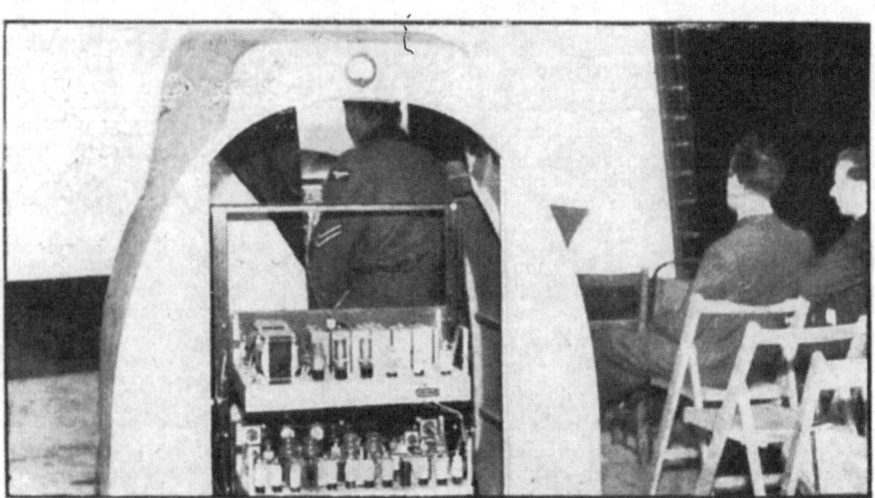

"NIGHT FIGHTER PATROL FLIGHT" was the title of this lesson in flying tactics conducted in the model cockpit in the Trainer Room at the Tele-Communications Research Establishment, the R.A.F. radar research centre. In peacetime known as Great Malvern College, here was the wartime H.Q. of distinguished scientists.

Photos, British Official, Keystone

Britain Recaptures World's Air Speed Record

TWO JET-PROPELLED METEOR IV AIRCRAFT were in October 1945 officially chosen for the British attack on the world's air speed record which stood at 469·2 m.p.h. set up in April 1939 by a Messerschmitt 109. Produced by the Gloster Aircraft Coy., these machines are each driven by two Rolls Royce Derwent V gas turbine power units. After protracted test flights "Britannia" (1) piloted by Group Captain H. J. Wilson, A F.C. (3, right) broke the record on November 7 by attaining an average speed of 606 m.p.h. flying at 250 ft. over the three-kilometre course at Herne Bay, Kent, which was marked out by balloons (2). In the hands of Mr. Eric Greenwood (4) the companion Meteor averaged 603 m.p.h.

Photos, Planet News, G.P.U.

Editor's Postscript

THE news that the Codex Sinaiticus is to be on public view again in the British Museum reminds one of my assistants of an amusing experience. It was in the early nineteen-thirties, the morning of the day on which the Museum acquired (at a cost of almost half-a-million sterling) this most perfect of all our New Testament manuscripts. The purchase had been made from Arcos—the Soviet Government's international trading house—and the Museum Director's Room was seething with erudition and Muscovite whiskers. For the first time in history a talkie-recording apparatus had been installed. The world's Press was there, in strength. Just as the precious parcel, fresh from Leningrad, was about to be handed over and the cameras were ready to click, a very young journalist in search of a "scoop" buttonholed one of the Museum's most distinguished scholars and, nodding mysteriously in the direction of the Codex, inquired in a whisper, "Has it . . . has it been translated yet?" The scholar with difficulty held his ground. Then, with just the faintest trace of a smile on his lips, he answered, in the stagiest of stage whispers, "There are two very excellent translations. One is known as the Authorized, and the other the Revised. You ought to read them—some day." And he turned again to face the camera-lights, still containing himself miraculously.

A BRITISH missionary on leave in Bombay has been describing life today among the Gonds, the "forgotten tribes" of India. Cut off from the outside world, he says, they have never heard of the war, of Hitler, Mussolini, Tojo, Churchill or Roosevelt. The only modern development of interest to them is the flight of R.A.F. transport planes over their jungles. These, they believe, carry Queen Victoria looking at their lands, for Queen Victoria is the last personality they have heard of. One wonders whether to congratulate or commiserate with the Gonds. On the whole, congratulation, I think, has it. Not to have heard of the atomic bomb—even at the expense of being a Gond—must nowadays be reckoned something of an achievement. I commend the notion to the delicate pencil of Sir Max Beerbohm.

IN Robert Federn's Peace, Prosperity, International Order (Williams & Norgate, 10s. 6d.) I seem to detect this faint glint of hope for a sadly shattered world:

> In Nature's eyes the rule of a despot is proof that something is wrong in the moral life of society . . . Sometimes it took centuries for a nation to get rid of despots, as was the case in Tzarist Russia. Compared with the duration of Tzarism in Russia the reaction of the world against Hitler and Mussolini was relatively rapid. Is that a reason for hope?

I AM wondering what the etymologists of Oxford and Cambridge, to say nothing of the Society for Pure English, will have to say of the newest word in our language—"Genocide." It occurs in Count 3 of the United Nations' indictment of the Nazi leaders due for trial at Nuremberg, and has been specially coined to describe the "systematic and purposeful" extermination of whole nations practised by the Hitler gang. The etymologists, if they run true to form, will probably object to the word on the grounds that it commits the (etymologically) unforgivable sin of combining both Greek (genos, a race or tribe) and Latin (cide, killing) in one word. And the fact that it is the work of an American—Professor Raphael Lemkin, of Duke University—will hardly make it more palatable. My own objection to the word is that its slender vowels suggest the name of a patent mouthwash rather than the vilest crime in the whole of universal history. One has only to imagine what word the ancient Greeks would have found for it, or indeed the Germans themselves, to realize how far short of the mark "Genocide" falls.

LAURENCE OLIVIER's performance in the W. B. Yeats translation of Sophocles' Oedipus, which has set the town talking, reminds me of a witticism of the type which only the Eireann capital produces. When the news that Yeats (who knew no Greek) had made the translation was announced to a famous Dublin wit, he looked up from his glass and asked, "From what into what?"

TURNING out some ageing papers the other day, I rescued an odd souvenir of that lamentable first winter of the war. It was the Ministry of Information's threepenny pamphlet, its maiden essay in that line, called Assurance of Victory, which was published at the end of November 1939. To open it was to be carried back in a flash to the exasperations and follies of the "phoney war" period; to the time when a Cabinet Minister, visiting our troops on the Belgian border, announced, "We are winning this war comfortably." In the light of subsequent events the final word in that complacent statement seems to have been the operative one. At that time we were all encouraged to feel far more comfortable than the right hon. gentleman and his colleagues had any right to allow us to feel. On the one hand they put out a rallying cry on every hoarding: Freedom is in peril—defend it with all your might! Then, as though fearing such an appeal might have over-disturbed us, they offered us this opiate in pamphlet form. Could the following phrases be beaten for Maginot-mindedness?

> "We do not have to defeat the Nazis on land, but only to prevent them from defeating us. If we can succeed in doing that, we can rely on our strength in other directions to bring them to their knees."

As Touchstone observed, there is much virtue in if!

Maj. GIDEON BRAND van ZYL, who will take up his duties as Governor-General of the Union of South Africa on January 1, 1946. He is the first Governor-General born in South Africa. *Photo, Pearl Freeman*

I AM glad I tucked this pamphlet away so securely that I never chanced upon it during, say, the autumn of 1940, or after the fall of Singapore and the retreat from Libya in 1942, when the Atlantic battle was at its grimmest stage. To have read then the jaunty claim of 1939 that the results of the Anglo-Turkish alliance were "equivalent to a first-class victory in the field," would have raised a very bitter laugh. By now, it scarcely matters. After all, we did achieve victory in the end—with the help of great allies undreamed of in 1939—so the anonymous author could plead justification. Indeed, one can now be charitable enough to admit that his pamphlet, for all its generosity in the matter of soothing syrup, did contain a great deal of wise reasoning. Here is his final paragraph:

> "The war will expose the fatal weakness of the Nazi structure; every acute crisis will bring the regime nearer to disaster. The immense staying power of democracy is the final guarantee of Allied triumph."

Well, was that true or was it not?

DR. A. J. P. TAYLOR, a Fellow of Magdalen, has managed to give a neat twist to the to-and-fro arguments about the future of Trieste. Analysing the latest Italian propagandist contention, based on population-analysis, he makes this pointed comment:

> By a similar selection of certain wards of Glasgow or Liverpool, it could be proved that Glasgow and Liverpool ought to be ceded to Eire. Yet no one doubts that Glasgow is Scottish and Liverpool English.

There is much food for thought—some of it not too easy of assimilation—in Mr. Taylor's pamphlet which the Yugoslav Information Office have just sent me, and which is published at a shilling.

THE portrait of the traitor Laval, taken during his trial, which appears in page 446, recalls the brilliant and (I believe) hitherto unrecorded motto which Sir Max Beerbohm is said to have suggested for the Vichy Government: Humilité—Servilité—Lavalité. Few Frenchmen could have put it so tersely. Or with such urbane cruelty.

ONE of the pleasanter aspects of post-war Lease-Lend in reverse is the fact that this term at Oxford 165 officers and men of the U.S. Army are attending college lectures, while waiting to be sent back home to be demobbed. It is the sort of thing that might have incalculable effects for good on Anglo-American relations twenty or thirty years hence when some of the 165 may have attained high executive position at Washington. I confess I wasn't surprised, as the academic authorities were, at the fact that the majority of these temporary students wanted to study Philosophy and that very few showed interest in the newer subjects as one must call them, I suppose. For the Americans are *au fond* an intensely serious, not to say pedantic, people—as anyone who has had to address an American women's club will tell you—and our ex-Hollywood notions of them are sadly out of focus. Had a hundred or so "Yanks" voted to remain in Oxford studying Philosophy after the First Great War (or is it my fond fancy?) we mightn't have found ourselves engaging in the present tragi-comic haggling over the "secrets" (whatever they may be) of the atomic bomb.

DEATH from strangulation—by red tape—still threatens the British Press almost two months after final victory. A member of my staff telephoning one of our most august public bodies to inquire the location of a lightship which had been attacked by the Luftwaffe in 1940, was told, "Sorry, we can't tell you over the phone, but if you care to send along a messenger we'll give him full particulars." For publication? Why, of course!

In Britain Now: London's Tribute to R.C.A.F.

NOW CALLED "CANADA WALK," the north side of Lincoln's Inn Fields, London, for over five years housed the headquarters of the Royal Canadian Air Force. On October 30, 1945, this stretch of an historic square, for 300 years known as Newman's Row, was renamed to commemorate war-time ties between the Borough of Holborn and the R.C.A.F. Unveiling one of the name plates are seen Sergeant Margaret Hillis (Canadian W.A.A.F.) and Sergeant W. C. Glendenning (both of Victoria, B.C.). To mark the occasion the Mayor of Holborn, Alderman W. E. Mullen, and Air Marshal G. O. Johnson, commanding R.C.A.F. overseas, formally walked the length of the Row.

MEN OF THE ROYAL SIGNALS in October 1945 started work in London helping the G.P.O. to handle their mammoth task of installing 70,000 new telephones for would-be subscribers who have been on the waiting-list for several years. Priority is being given to applicants connected with essential reconstruction trades, the health services, and journalism. A private of the Royal Signals is seen testing a switch-board which his unit had installed in a London office. *Photos, Central Press, Keystone*

COLOURS OF THE ROYAL DUBLIN FUSILIERS—the regiment was disbanded in 1922, following the establishment of the Irish Free State—were placed in the keeping of the Royal United Services Museum, Whitehall, on October 25, 1945. Formerly in the possession of the late Duke of Connaught, they were handed by the Chairman of the Museum, Air Marshal Sir Robert Brooke-Popham, G.C.V.O. (above), to veterans of the Fusiliers who are now spending the evening of their days as pensioners of the Royal Hospital, Chelsea.

WOMEN CADETS IN THE BRITISH ARMY assembled with instructors and male cadets on the lawns of the Army Staff College, Camberley, Surrey, for a map-reading lecture. Co-educational training was announced on October 16, 1945, when it was stated that women attending the 16-weeks' course would include an officer of the Canadian W.A.A.F., two from the Women's Transport Service of East Africa, and ten from the A.T.S. Each of these girl cadets has signed on for a further twelve months' service. *Photos, Fox, Planet News*

Carrier Formidable on Peace-Task at Sydney

WITH OVER 1,000 BRITISH AND AUSTRALIAN P.O.W. aboard, the 23,000-ton British aircraft carrier H.M.S. Formidable arrived at Sydney early in October 1945. Those well enough lined up on the 753-ft. long flight-deck with the ship's company as she prepared to enter the harbour. From Australia, Britain-bound P.O.W. are transported across the Pacific to Vancouver, whence they travel across Canada by rail to embark in the Queen Mary or Queen Elizabeth. Many carriers have been transformed to troopships.

Photo, Associated Press

Printed in England and published every alternate Friday by the Proprietors, THE AMALGAMATED PRESS, LTD., The Fleetway House, Farringdon Street, London, E.C.4. Registered for transmission by Canadian Magazine Post. Sole Agents for Australia and New Zealand: Messrs. Gordon & Gotch, Ltd. and for South Africa: Central News Agency, Ltd.—November 23, 1945. S.S. *Editorial Offices:* JOHN CARPENTER HOUSE WHITEFRIARS, LONDON, E.C.4.

Vol 9 The War Illustrated and Afterwards No 221

SIXPENCE

DECEMBER 7, 1945

TO AUSTRALIA IN TWO-AND-A-HALF DAYS, scheduled time of the British Overseas Airways Corporation service, is the regular trip of this Lancastrian, seen at Hurn airport, near Bournemouth. A Government plan to nationalize civil air services was announced on November 1, 1945. Three public bodies will operate them—the B.O.A.C. between the U.K. and the Commonwealth, the U.S. and Far East; two others between the U.K. and the Continent and the U.K. and South America respectively. *Photo, Fox*

Edited by Sir John Hammerton

NO. 222 WILL BE PUBLISHED FRIDAY, DECEMBER 21

Nazi Eclipse Perpetuated in Stone by B.A.O.R.

AT LUNEBURG, marking the site of the German surrender on May 4, 1945, our troops had by November almost completed a permanent stone memorial (1). The temporary plaque (see illus page 389) was several times uprooted. A corporal-instructor at the British Army School at Nienburg, Hanover, demonstrated a plaster mural (2) of his own design; there are over 700 pupils at this school, including Royal Engineers, who in preparation for Civvy Street learn sign-writing, plastering, carpentry and bricklaying, and R.E.M.E.s studying to be radio-mechanics, fitters and welders.

Thrill for men of the Royal Scots (3) serving with the 52nd Lowland Mountain Division, seen with a German gamekeeper, was deer-stalking and boar-hunting in Herford, in a drive to kill food for the winter larder. Enjoying a big "demob" party in a N.A.A.F.I. canteen in Berlin (4).

Photos, British Official, Keystone

Why Do We Need Dollars?

SINCE the long-foreseen but unexpectedly early termination of the Anglo-American Lease-Lend arrangements the newspapers have contained many articles on the subject of the financial relations of Great Britain and the U.S.A. Most people are aware that important negotiations have been taking place in Washington, but are deterred from attempting to understand what these are about by the apparent difficulty of the problems involved.

I will not try to pretend that they are at all simple in the form in which they have had to be solved by the negotiators in Washington, but I hope to show that the *fundamental* issues are not only of great importance to everyone in Great Britain but are also fairly easy to understand.

In the first place, all the problems are concerned directly or indirectly with the supply of dollars available to people outside the U.S.A., and in particular to people in Great Britain. Why do we in Great Britain need dollars at all? The first part of the answer is obvious—we need dollars so as to be able to make payments to American citizens who generally do not want pounds sterling because these can only be used in Great Britain.

To Pay for Current Imports

At present, most of the payments British citizens wish to make to Americans are payments for goods, particularly foodstuffs, which only America is at the moment able to supply; payments for the use of American ships; and payments of interest on sums of money lent to British citizens by Americans. Before the War, payments were also made to Americans for passages across the Atlantic in American liners, hotel services and railway tickets bought by British travellers and tourists in America. If all goes well, these additional demands for dollars will revive before very long, but at present they are negligible in comparison with the need for dollars to pay for our current imports of food and other necessary materials.

AFTER the middle of 1941, the necessity for dollars for this purpose was not a serious problem because the need for goods and services imported from America was met by the Lease-Lend arrangements. But since that particular "Weapon for Victory" has been beaten into a ploughshare, or at any rate laid aside, the continued need for American goods means an urgent requirement for dollars with which to buy them.

That is the first part of the answer to the question "Why do we need dollars?" The second is rather less easy to appreciate, but, in some of its ramifications, it is even more important. During the War, as most people realize, the Dominions, India and some other countries supplied great quantities of goods and services to Great Britain *on credit*, without current payment. That is to say, they provided the goods and services and we gave in exchange IOUs. These IOUs were expressed in pounds sterling, and together make up what are called the "Sterling Balances in London." They amount to perhaps £3,000,000,000 and represent *debts* which are owed by Great Britain to citizens of these countries.

Before long the holders of these Sterling Balances will wish to receive payment of the IOUs, and payment can only be made in three ways. Either old debts of the countries concerned to Great Britain can be set off against the new debts of Great Britain to those same countries, or the Sterling Balances can be used to buy British goods to be shipped to the creditor countries; or, finally, the Sterling Balances can be converted into foreign currencies and consequently used to buy goods in other countries.

By JOHN BUCKATZSCH

RECENT Anglo-American financial discussions in Washington have caused many people in Great Britain to be befogged by the implications of the "Almighty Dollar." Our contributor, a specialist in the monetary field, lucidly explains how the fundamental issues of the vast economic problem involved are of very real and, indeed, vital importance to everyone in this country.

The first method—offsetting of old and new debts—is of limited value. The debt owed by the Government of India to Great Britain, for example, has already been paid off, but a balance of Great Britain's debt to India still remains. The second method—the export of British goods to the creditor countries—is of much more importance, but it can only be used as and when the British goods become available, and therefore depends on the speed of the reconversion of British economy from war to peace production. The third method—conversion of the Sterling Balances into foreign currencies—means in actual practice the conversion of sterling into dollars, because America is for many purposes the only market outside Great Britain in which the owners of the Sterling Balances can buy the goods they want.

exchange rates in terms of the pound sterling). At present, though it might if necessary and at some cost be made so, the Commonwealth is not economically independent of the U.S.A.

Two final alternatives remain. We can (and must) accelerate our reconversion, of which demobilization is only the first part, and expand our exports to America; and at the same time increase the supply of British goods available to the present holders of Sterling Balances. This may, of course, mean going short ourselves. It might, too, be necessary to ration the supply of dollars (obtained by selling British goods and services to Americans) made available to the holders of Sterling Balances. In other words, we might have to persuade these creditors to spend their Sterling Balances in Great Britain, and not to ask for dollars.

Our Disagreeable Necessity

The American negotiators describe this as "discrimination" against the dollar, and its inevitability in some circumstances is not, apparently, clear to them. This procedure appears, moreover, to conflict with certain clauses of the "Master Agreements" on which Lease-Lend was based. To us in Great Britain, who have always been accustomed to being able to supply any foreign currency in

AT THE ANGLO-AMERICAN MONETARY TALKS which opened in Washington on September 11, 1945, were (left to right) Mr. Leo T. Crowley, U.S. Foreign Economic Administration head; Lord Halifax, our Ambassador; Mr. Will Clayton, U.S. Assistant Secretary of State; Lord Keynes, adviser to the British Treasury; Mr. Henry A. Wallace, U.S. Secretary of Commerce. The talks were still in progress in late November. *Photo, Topical*

In effect, therefore, the paying-off of the debts of Great Britain to the countries that accepted payment in sterling IOUs during the war really means making available *either* British goods *or* American dollars. The former method does not directly create a demand for dollars, except in so far as the manufacture of British goods requires the use of American raw material and machinery. But the second alternative obviously does create a demand for dollars which has to be added to the need for those required to pay for our own essential imports from America.

HOW can these demands be met? First, we must overhaul our list of imports from America and reduce it as far as possible by using our own equipment and home-produced material as efficiently as we can. But this will not solve the problem. In the second place, we can attempt to meet our requirements to a great extent in countries other than America, so as to avoid transactions giving rise directly to a demand for dollars. But quite evidently this will not necessarily prevent an *indirect* demand for dollars on the part of countries who are *paid* in sterling but want to exchange this sterling for dollars to be spent in America.

Besides, it is not possible to obtain all our requirements inside the so-called Sterling Area (that is, those countries prepared to accept Sterling Balances or regulate their

return for sterling on demand, such an arrangement, within a "Sterling Area," largely self-contained and based mainly on a close agreement among the members of the Commonwealth, naturally appears a makeshift, as it must also do to the other members of this hypothetical association.

But until the dollars can be made available by a great expansion of British exports to America, it would be the only choice before us—*unless* America were willing to offer "Reconstruction" Loans on acceptable terms to tide us over the transition period. As has been repeatedly emphasized, the request for such Loans is *not* a demand for Charity, but a disagreeable necessity forced on us by the completeness of our wartime mobilization, the fruits of which the U.S.A. itself is actually enjoying today.

In the short run, the supply of dollars will therefore be determined partly by the speed of our reconversion and the vigour of our export policy, and partly by the willingness of the U.S.A. to advance suitable loans. In the long run, when our economy has been reconverted and its productive efficiency increased, the supply of dollars will depend on the willingness of the U.S.A. to buy British goods. That will depend, in turn, on the American Tariff Policy, and on the avoidance, by the United States, of Great Depressions in their internal economy which would reduce the *ability* of the U.S.A. to buy imports.

Americans' S.O.S. on D-Day

By MAJ.-GENERAL
SIR CHARLES GWYNN
K.C.B., D.S.O.

It is widely realized that behind the fighting troops, and to a large extent interlocked with them, there is a great body of men carrying out ancillary services of vital importance. Few, however, can form a clear conception of the immense variety of their functions or of the problems with which they have to deal.

In the American Army these services, except so far as certain of their units form an integral part of the fighting formations, are grouped under the general title of Service of Supply (S.O.S.) and form an organization operating under its own commander and H.Q. staff. Recently, as a souvenir for the troops of this organization, the American information division has published a little book describing the role of the S.O.S. in the defeat of Germany which gives a very adequate, though necessarily incomplete, picture of the work of the rearward services of the armies.

To be frank, the weakness of the book is that it gives the impression that the American Army devised a unique organization, and it would not be surprising if it confirmed many American readers in the belief that their organizing genius alone was responsible for the victory of the Allies. Whereas, of course, each of the Allies had much the same problems to face in maintaining the service of supply and possessed similar if somewhat differently constituted organizations.

BRITISH Experience and Inventions Helped U.S. Before She Entered War

Nevertheless, the book should be welcomed as a tribute to troops whose work attracts less attention than that of those engaged in tactical operations, in spite of the fact that they have to face risks often as great and more constant. The evacuation of wounded, building or repairing bridges under fire, the lifting of mines, and the delivery of supplies and food in the combat zone, all demand qualities of cold-blooded courage quite as remarkable as courage shown in the heat of battle.

The Americans can claim with justice that their equipment was of a higher standard than in any other army, and that their troops were better fed: but that was only to be expected, for no other country, except Germany, had had more time to prepare deliberately for war, or had greater resources on which to draw. In addition to that, British experience and British inventions were freely communicated to America before she had even entered the war. She had practically no defensive problems to face, her country had suffered no damage from enemy action, and, from the first, her main problem was to prepare for D-Day in western Europe and for the developments that would follow.

The governing fact, however, is that without the closest co-operation with the British Empire she would have been unable to come to grips with her enemy either in Europe or the Far East. That was fully realized by President Roosevelt and his military advisers. As early as May 1941, observers of the U.S.A. Army arrived in London, though they could not appear in uniform till December 8. Their task was to plan the establishment of a base in Britain which would bring the U.S.A. within striking distance of Europe in case she was drawn into the war.

It is rather curious, therefore, that the establishment of this base, the first and most essential step to be taken by the American S.O.S., is dealt with only in the last two chapters of the book, and this is almost the sole acknowledgment of the share Britain took in preparing for the great amphibious operation by which alone decisive operations against Germany could be initiated.

AT CHERBOURG HARBOUR, after its delayed fall to U.S. troops on June 27, 1944 (see pages 136-137, Vol. 8), our Allies were soon landing supplies for the invading Armies hurrying towards Paris. An American engineer is seen at the controls of his towering crane as he lowered this locomotive ashore from one of our train-ferries. *Photo, U.S. Official*

Many comparisons, on the other hand, are drawn between the tasks of the S.O.S. in what the Americans call "World War 1" (W.W.1), and those in W.W.2, in order to emphasize the immense development of the S.O.S. in W.W.2. Actually the proportion of personnel in the S.O.S. organization to that of combat troops (about one-third of the total) was much the same in both wars, although the bulk and weight of material to be handled and the variety of tasks to be performed were vastly greater in the second war. The comparison is, however, vitiated by the circumstances in which the wars were fought and the advances in mechanization.

The chief changes in circumstances were that in W.W.1 the Americans could be landed straight from the U.S.A. into a country with highly developed ports and intact road and railway systems; and that once landed they could be introduced gradually into a static situation. Whereas in W.W.2 not only had the base in Britain to be prepared and the first landing on the Continent carried out as a major operation, unprecedented in character and scale, but thereafter highly mobile operations in a devastated country were immediately necessary.

The book gives a very interesting account of the landing of the American Army in Normandy, though mainly from the standpoint of the S.O.S. The point is made that the decision to commence landing at low water was taken in the interests of the rapid development of the S.O.S. rather than that of the assault troops. It was to ensure that passages should be cleared by demolition parties through the beach obstacles, to admit of the rapid reinforcement of the leading assault troops by mechanized armament and ample munitions.

How nearly the main landing came to failure is admitted, for almost nothing went according to plan; and the rising tide made matters worse. The demolition parties failed to identify landmarks and did not disembark at the appointed places. Few passages were cleared, and in the confusion those were not marked. Held up by obstacles and under heavy fire, losses were heavy; in particular, vehicles became entangled and were destroyed. When the shore was gained by the leading assault troops they therefore lacked supporting weapons, and little progress could be made inland; and only a small tonnage of supplies was landed during the day. Nothing but determined and gallant leadership of small parties prevented complete failure.

WHY Cherbourg's Capture Did Not Conform With the U.S. Timetable

Fortunately, on the smaller beach, resistance was less formidable and everything went according to plan. In consequence of the check on the main beach, however, the momentum of the first assault failed to develop, and Cherbourg, which it had been hoped would be captured within three days, did not fall till June 27. The delay in capturing Cherbourg became all the more serious when the great storm which started on June 19 broke up the attempt to construct the Mulberry "A" harbour made for the Americans' use by Britain. Thereafter the task of the S.O.S. in the build-up for further operations became immensely heavier and called for all the ingenuity and talent for improvisation that Americans possess.

The break-out from the bridge-head was certainly delayed; but when it came, it soon made up lost time by the amazing rapidity of General Patton's thrust. How greatly the speed of his thrust and the maintenance of its momentum was due to the work of the S.O.S. is told. The reckless courage shown by railway personnel in delivering the goods over a line in a "Heath Robinson" condition fully equalled that of fighting troops.

But there are limits to what even the most efficient rear services can accomplish, and though roads and bridges and railways were restored at an astonishing pace the lack of fully equipped ports and the distance over which supplies had to be hauled eventually brought the Allies to a halt. Antwerp was captured by Montgomery intact; but till the approaches to it were cleared and it became available as a base for both the Allied armies, operations on a decisive scale could not be undertaken. Throughout the story we are made increasingly to realize the dependence of the fighting army on well-established bases and good lines of communication.

An undoubted fact emerging from this is that the advantage great maritime powers have of launching amphibious attacks at unexpected points of their own selection cannot be exercised at the opening of a war.

Unless it has a continental ally who can give it well-equipped ports and space for the deployment of its armies, a maritime nation can therefore not intervene on land in a continental war with any approach to the speed with which a continental Power can launch an attack across its land frontiers against a neighbour. The success of amphibious operations in the war just over should not mislead us on this point.

Great Clean-Up in Jap Rat-Runs of Hongkong

THE SWORD OF A JAPANESE WAR CRIMINAL, Sergeant Kenichi Matsuda (1), was scrutinized by a R.N.V.R. lieutenant at Hongkong, where Matsuda's fellow-torturers were still being rounded-up in November 1945. The Crown Colony has been administered by the Royal Navy and the Civil Affairs Service since our Occupation in September. Three A.B.s try eating with chopsticks (2). In the harbour the carrier Indomitable (3), her "wings of war" folded on her flight-deck, prepared to sail for Australia with civilian ex-internees.

Photos, British Official

When Sea Mines Come Ashore

By

FRANCIS E. McMURTRIE

ALTHOUGH the war is over in Europe its after-effects are still being felt and are by no means negligible in their influence on the life of the average citizen. This has been brought home to many coast dwellers of late by the unpleasant frequency with which mines, set adrift by rough weather, have been washed ashore. Fortunately they do not often explode on stranding, but when they do so in an inhabited area damage and even casualties are to be expected.

Many are the suggestions received by the Press from readers who imagine there must be some way of averting this recurring menace. It is seldom appreciated that it is no remedy to fire at a mine when it appears on the surface inshore ; though the outer casing may be pierced and the mine water-logged and sunk, it does not then explode,

Cmdr. F. ASHE LINCOLN, R.N.V.R., head of a section in the Dept. of the Director of Torpedoes and Mining at the Admiralty, which exercises control over the business of rendering safe mines of all types.

but goes to the bottom. In deep water it would then be fairly safe ; but in the shallow seas that surround the English coasts it continues to be a perpetual menace to fishermen and divers. Thus the only course to be followed with a mine sighted drifting in a choppy sea near the beach is to wait until it has grounded without explosion, and then render harmless the mechanism by which it is detonated. In a smooth sea a floating mine can be taken in tow by a boat and sunk in deep water if an expert is available who knows how to handle it.

IN the Department of the Director of Torpedoes and Mining at the Admiralty there is a section which, in general, exercises control over the business of rendering safe mines of various types. The present head of this section is Commander F. Ashe Lincoln, R.N.V.R. (portrait above). Actual disposal of the mines washed up is mainly the responsibility of H.M.S. Vernon, the torpedo school at Portsmouth, though there are mine disposal officers also at Chatham and Devonport as well. These officers must be in readiness to proceed at a moment's notice to whatever place they may be directed, to deal with mines that have arrived on the shore.

By the average member of the public a mine is regarded vaguely as a dangerous sphere of metal, which may be found floating at sea and is assumed to be the explanation of the disappearance of ships in peacetime when no other circumstances, such as heavy weather, can be assigned as a possible cause. It is generally imagined that the high explosives contained within the sphere will detonate immediately when hit by a machine-gun bullet or other projectile fired from a ship. Although this may sometimes be true of a certain type of contact mine, there are so many other kinds of mines that this is merely to present one facet of the subject.

BASIS of the Present Technique of Rendering the Mines Harmless

In a broad sense, the business of mining and the disposal of mines may be divided under four heads. First, there is the very large field covered by the Superintendent of Mine Design, who has under him a numerous staff of scientists and highly qualified technical officers. In wartime, fresh ideas are tested and adopted, or discarded, as the case may be ; reports of enemy improvements or other novel features are investigated and made the subject of experiments ; and the recommendations received from those who have had actual experience of types recently placed in service are considered and followed where desirable.

Controlled mining is quite a specialized department. It has to do with the defence of harbours, bases and narrow channels by means of minefields controlled from the shore. Minesweeping is another important responsibility, involving sweeping clear of mines all navigable channels. This is a much longer and more tedious job than it used to be, since the great variety of mines employed by the enemy necessitates covering an area more than once to ensure the elimination of menaces of the delayed action type (see article and illustrations, pages 392-3).

THEN there is the general duty of dealing with mines of all types and rendering them innocuous when emergency demands it. Most famous of pioneers in the latter work was Lieut.-Commander J. G. D. Ouvry, D.S.O., R.N., of H.M.S. Vernon. In the early days of the war, when German aircraft began dropping mines around our coasts, especially in the busy channels of the Thames estuary, one of these mines fell in a soft spot off Shoeburyness, where it was uncovered at low water. By personally dissecting its mechanism in slow time, explaining each step as completed to his assistants in shelter close by, Commander Ouvry rendered this mine harmless, so that it could be removed and taken to pieces elsewhere (see page 124, Vol. 7,). This enabled the scientific experts, notably Commander C. F. Goodeve, O.B.E., V.D., D.Sc., F.R.S., R.N.V.R., to devise methods of rendering ships impervious to the magnetic mine danger. Similar steps were taken to guard against the acoustic mine.

It was Commander Ouvry's experience which became the basis of the present technique of rendering mines harmless, and continues to inspire those who undertake this hazardous work. However carefully it is carried out, there is always the risk of a booby trap. That methods of handling without disaster the complicated arrangements of dozens of different types of mines should thus have been perfected is a testimonial to the high standard of efficiency reached by the naval and scientific staffs of the Vernon mining departments during the late war.

BRITISH Mines Designed to Become Harmless on Breaking Adrift

Although final figures are not yet available, the number of mines laid and swept during 1939-1945 is very greatly in excess of the total for the First Great War. Not only has the work of removing mines been more difficult, but owing to the many types employed by the enemy it can never be said with safety that an area has been cleared after a single sweeping. For example, some of the mines employed by the Germans incorporated clocks set to run for lengthy periods. Not until the clock had reached the particular time for which it was set did the mine become active. Such mines laid in swept channels were apt to be a most disconcerting surprise.

Of the mines that are being deposited on beaches in the south of England today, a majority are undoubtedly German. Unlike British-laid mines, those of the enemy were not designed to become harmless on breaking adrift. Nevertheless, some which had lain submerged for long periods had become encrusted by marine growths such as seaweed and shellfish, which may indirectly have had the effect of holding up the detonating gear. Careless stripping of the encrustations might result in releasing a detonator. (See facing page, also story in page 473.)

ROLLING THE MINE INTO POSITION is one of the first tasks of the Royal Navy men engaged on the special duties of rendering these drifting lethal weapons harmless. This one is being dealt with on the shore at Littlehampton, Sussex. Subsequent operations of a Rendering Mines Safe squad are shown in the facing page. *Photo, G.P.U.*

R.M.S. Squad in Action on an English Beach

DRAWING OUT THE EXPLOSIVES-CONTAINER (1) is one of the tricky operations of a Rendering Mines Safe squad. After this mine at Littlehampton, Sussex, had been rolled into position (see illus. in facing page), the officer in charge removed the cover-plate and scrutinized the mechanism (2). Two A.B.s trundled away the case containing the charge (3)—enough explosive to wreck a street. Later, smoke-clouds billowed over the beach as the explosive was ignited to make a harmless bonfire.

Photos, G.P.U.

How Four-Footed Warriors Helped Us to Win

An astonishing variety of animals served with the troops at home and overseas, in divers capacities. Each possessed of special qualities which made them almost indispensable allies in varied conditions of warfare, they had their full share of achievements and casualties. Instances are cited here by JOHN FLEETWOOD. See also facing page, and pages 22-23, 180, 696, Vol. 8.

In the war's later years volunteer dogs from all sorts of homes were drafted to Active Service at the rate of 200 a month. They went with our men to Normandy on D-Day, and trained recruits followed continually. Although dogs had had pre-war roles as "eyes" for the blind, assisting in police work, and some had carried out a few special duties in previous wars, nobody had thought of these animals as sentries of real responsibility, as reconnaissance patrols, or as combatants on the field of battle.

The idea of their employment in such roles evolved from the training given to a number of dogs early in 1940 to act as part-sentries over ammunition stores and to watch for and tackle parachute invaders. They didn't have much opportunity to prove their worth in the second capacity, but so efficient were they at guard duty that there were soon hundreds of well-trained animals doing sentry-go at military installations, aircraft factories, and dispersed war plants. They proved a valuable aid in the detection and prevention of pilfering and unauthorized entry. By serving under a single master each group released large numbers of men for more active duties in the Forces, in this way effecting considerable economies in man-power.

These were largely home-front and base jobs. As time passed, dogs became increasingly valuable in overseas war theatres. One of the earliest recruits to the Corps of Military Police, Dog Section, was Simi. It takes a pretty strong man to battle with an 86-lb. Boxer dog and get away with it, and during his two years' service with the C.M.P this superbly trained and efficient animal made no fewer than 83 arrests at military stores and depots around the Nile Delta and in Palestine. All over this territory Simi was the terror of native gangs of thieves, who treated even his name with wholesome respect.

Dogs became indispensable on the battlefields. There was one who captured four Germans in a slit trench, standing over them snarling till an escort arrived to take his prisoners away. Another rounded up an enemy gun crew; a host of others tracked down lost soldiers as well as escaped prisoners of war. There was Henri Bachelay, a French dog who saved his struggling master from drowning off Dunkirk, seizing his clothes between his teeth and swimming to a lifeboat.

Some ships' dogs did yeoman work as aircraft spotters, sensing the approach of enemy planes long before the sound of aero engines could be heard by the vessels' crews. Many a soldier serving in the Far East was spared a mortal knife thrust by timely warning from the dog at his side. On the Burma and South-West Pacific fronts dogs served as jungle sentries to sleeping patrols, waking the men, not by barking but by tugging at a string tied to a sleeping man's wrist.

They were trained to locate Jap snipers and patrols which our men would never spot. Mongrels excelled at these tasks, living on chupattees, corned beef and rice, and apparently enjoying every minute of the life. There were Commando dogs, too—taught to attack without mercy. And Red Cross Russian Arctic orderlies, quarrelsome in off-hours, but keen enough when they were on the job, bringing back sledges of wounded across the fire-swept snows.

Red Army dogs have sacrificed their lives to destroy Nazi tanks. Carrying mines on their backs, they would bound up to enemy tanks, blowing up the tanks—and themselves. Detecting hidden mines was one of the most hazardous tasks carried out by dogs, and they were at it for years from the Western Front to Burma. Eventually there were few battle experiences denied to them. On occasions they were parachutists, equipped with outfits complete to a static line. Even that is not surprising when you contemplate the obstacle course included in the training of war dogs. You may have seen some dogs go through it: jump clean through a hole the size of a man's head, leap four 4½-ft. fences, scale a 6-ft. hoarding, finally mounting in two bounds a skeleton staircase 10-ft. high.

Cared for in Special Hospitals

Casualties were severe in the Canine Corps—kept up to strength by a stream of recruits from 16 separate breeds, many of whom made instant answer to over 100 commands—and a special blood transfusion service helped to give the injured animals a 100 per cent chance of recovery.

It is a toss-up which of the two were the more useful to the war effort—dogs or mules. The latter were cared for like humans in special hospitals. In Burma, Brigadier Wingate thought the world of mules. And no wonder. They carried all his stores, light guns, munitions, his 1,000-mile-range radio sets. Wherever the going was most difficult, there you would find mules achieving the (for all other beasts) impossible. Even mechanization has not ousted the military mule. The Romans pronounced him indispensable; he is still indispensable, tackling jobs which no machine can handle.

Thousands of mules spent the war-years carrying supplies to forward troops where the hills were so steep that men could scale them only on their hands and knees. The mules would be carrying the heaviest of loads while sinking up to their hocks in the thick mud of the monsoon, or pulling bogged tractors out of tropic swamps. The mule was a beast of burden in all circumstances where his more squeamish mare-mother and less hardy donkey-father feared to tread. During Jap infiltrations mules were enclosed in barrage "boxes" for weeks on end, shelled and mortared and bombed, existing on meagre rations. Thousands lost their lives, or were captured, or drowned in liquid mud. While climbing up and over razor-ridged mountains hundreds more of these sturdy beasts were sent hurtling to their deaths by loose boulders, landslides or bullets.

PARAPUP is the semi-official description of this U.S.-owned terrier which was parachuted from heights up to 1,500 ft. Note the special harness attachment. *Photo, U.S. Official*

Once, when Captain Norton's famous mule company were carrying rations down a jungle track, they were charged by a band of Japs mounted on elephants. That is an exceptional role for elephants, but there was little else they did not do to help the 14th Army on its way to Rangoon. They were first used in the war to evacuate the 17th Division, in 1941. Since then they have been competing on equal terms with bulldozers, whose job they took over in Burma jungles, making up the roads, building bridges, clearing heavy timber, carrying heavy guns, extracting lorries from the glutinous mud like corks from wine-bottles.

Battle-Course Tests for Bullocks

The 14th Army had an "Elephant Adviser," Lt.-Col. Williams from Cornwall. "Elephant Bill," as his colleagues called him, The Colonel knew 600 of his animals by name and recognized each one on sight. Records are kept in elephant camps as in every other military office. Name, sex, origin and brand are listed. Age, too, is important, though not unduly so, for the working span stretches from 8 to 50 years. The "old man" elephant of one camp was still to be found on the job at the age of 53.

Enemy raiders once tried to clear a path though our mine fields on the Anzio beach-head by driving a herd of cattle across them. The ruse was ingenious, though unsuccessful. The idea behind the training of a company of 15-cwt. snow-white bullocks for Burma service was both clever and productive. These well-bred beasts were highly intelligent as well as tough. They passed all their battle-course tests with full marks. Deaf to "thunder flashes," gas rattles, sirens and red rags, they swam rivers, and tight-roped brick walls, carrying even heavier loads than mules. All that remained to be done before they were packed off from the Punjab to Burma for the valuable services they afterwards rendered, was to dye the bright beasts the colour of coffee to make them invisible to prying eyes in the Burmese jungles.

Most of the "camel corps" that operated in the desert were petrol-fed—that is, motorized. But the camel still remains on the field of battle, performing feats of valour. Aircraft, car, lorry, new roads and railways have reduced the breeding of camels, but it is a long road yet to their extinction. In the mountains, in waterless bush country where aircraft cannot land, in territory where motor vehicles can be ambushed by felling trees, camels can achieve more than any M.T. unit. And so "camelry" were to be found in the forefront of the fighting, as transport of the first and second lines.

A camel doesn't panic. A sturdy, stoical, uncomplaining beast, he carries with ease a pack load the weight of four average men for most hours of the day. If necessary he will do it for several days on end, without food or drink. He will suffer a bullet wound without flinching, even travel till the day's end with lungs perforated by bullets. Which explains why so many camels were drafted for work in special regions throughout the war years.

Pulling Their Weight in Support of the Troops

ELEPHANTS MADE A NAME FOR THEMSELVES in the Burma campaigns, chiefly as transport: attached to the British 36th Division in the north, some of them are seen preparing to cross the wide Shweli River (1). Contrast in war-transport is provided at this air base (2) near Karachi, India, in an encounter between a camel-drawn vehicle and a U.S. plane. Howitzers were hauled long distances on mountainous stretches of the Burma Road by sure-footed mule-teams (3) mounted by Chinese.

Photos, British and U.S. Official

Mourning the Fallen of Two Wars We Asked—

AT THE FIELD OF REMEMBRANCE outside Westminster Abbey, on November 11, 1945, anniversary of the 1918 Armistice, the bereaved inspected the wooden crosses (1) in memory of the dead of two wars. In Whitehall, queues filed past the wreath-laden Cenotaph (2). Far from city crowds, at Shere in Surrey (3), villagers and Servicemen joined in the simple service at the memorial. In the British cemetery at Luneburg in Germany a bugler of the Duke of Cornwall's Light Infantry sounded the Last Post (4). *Photos, G.P.U., Keystone.*

—Will This be The Last Armistice Day?

AS BIG BEN BOOMED ELEVEN, thousands of Londoners and visitors to the capital, led by H.M. the King, joined in their first corporate commemoration of the dead of the two Great Wars at the Cenotaph, Whitehall. From the Home Office (left), the Queen, Queen Mary and Princess Margaret looked on. Next day it was stated in Parliament that the Government was considering, in consultation with Commonwealth Governments, the fixing of an official Day of Remembrance for both wars. See also story in page 506. *Photo, Sport & General*

Now It Can Be Told!

SHELL THAT 'THINKS' BEAT THE FLYING BOMB

THIS wartime-secret British invention not only beat the V1 but saved the British fleets in the Far East from serious loss when the Japs threw in suicide bombers. The "brain" of the shell is a fuse, a tiny radio set—transmitter, receiver and aerial all combined—in the nose of the shell (see diagram).

A heavy A.A. shell has always been fitted with a fuse intended to explode it close to the target aircraft. The clockwork fuse, used at the beginning of the war, was set before firing to go off at a given moment, when it was predicted that the shell would be close to its target. Frequently, the shell burst short or passed close to the aircraft and exploded harmlessly farther on.

The radio proximity fuse has changed all that ; if the shell passes within a certain distance of the aircraft it will explode, and that will be the end of the aircraft. The story of this device was until recently one of the most closely guarded secrets of the war.

The earliest researches were carried out in Government Experimental Establishments in the United Kingdom. Our ideas were freely passed to the United States in 1940. Development continued on both sides of the Atlantic, but the production facilities of the U.S.A. naturally enabled them to allocate far greater effort to the undertaking ; and the fuses actually used in the war were all of American design and manufacture.

THE idea of a radio proximity fuse is attributed to Mr. W. A. S. Butement (designer of the "C.H.L." radar set), whose first statement of the possibilities was discussed at a meeting at Fort Halstead in May 1940 under the chairmanship of Dr. Crow (later Sir Alwyn Crow, of Rocket fame). The idea of the true proximity fuse as it is now understood was suggested simultaneously a few days later by Butement and Mr. E. S. Shire. The original patent application is filed in the names of Butement, Shire, and A. F. H. Thomson, who (as was Shire) was one of Butement's research team at Christchurch. The driving force behind the early investigations was Professor J. D. Cockcroft, subsequently to become more famous as one of the scientists prominent in the development of the atomic bomb.

Swift Shock for the Radio Valves

Before any work could be done, it was essential to ascertain whether radio valves could be designed so that they would withstand the enormous acceleration—up to twenty times that of gravity—of a shell when fired. Experiments by Professor Cockcroft at Cambridge decided this point, and Dr. F. A. Vick, one of Cockcroft's staff, contributed much to the planning of the work. Then came the Tizard Mission to the U.S.A. in August 1940, during which radar information was passed to our American friends. The radio proximity fuse was discussed at the same time—the Americans had already been working on proximity fuses of other types—and enthusiastically taken up.

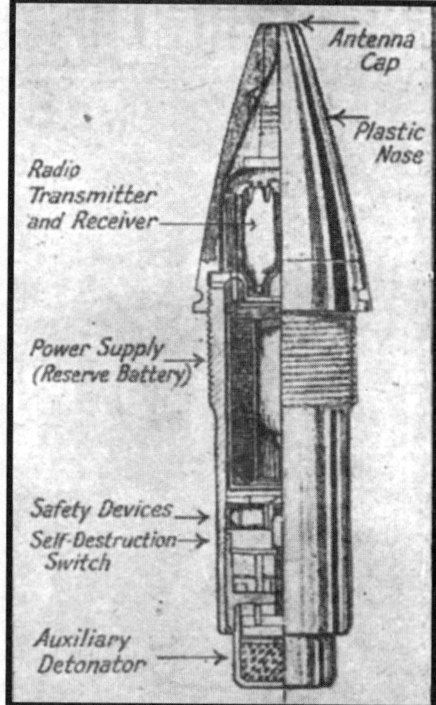

NOSE DIAGRAM of the shell that "thinks," whose secret development is now revealed in this page. *Photo, Sport & General*

Preliminary experiments in Britain continued into 1941. Serious development began in September of that year, in collaboration with certain of the great commercial radio organizations. Effort was at first devoted to a "radio operated fuse" which should be detonated from the ground, and considerable success was achieved.

However, the investigations of Professor C. D. Ellis (now Sir Charles Ellis, Scientific Adviser to the Army Council) in early 1942 showed that the gain in efficiency of the radio-operated fuse over the normal mechanical type would not be sufficient to justify its use, and all effort was concentrated on a true "proximity fuse" which should cause the shell to explode when it came within a certain distance of the target aircraft.

All this work was done at a secret Ministry of Supply Establishment (R.R.D.E., now at

BRITISH AND U.S. WARSHIPS WORKED TOGETHER on many important joint missions. From under one of the 14-in. guns of the Royal Navy's 35,000-ton battleship Duke of York are seen two of America's largest battleships—the U.S.S. South Dakota (nearer camera) and Alabama (launched 1942), both 35,000-tonners of the Washington class. The photograph was taken during an unchallenged operation in June 1943, when naval units of the two great Powers were being used as one force to patrol Northern waters and cover convoy movements, turning the tide of victory against both Luftwaffe and U-boats in the Battle of the Atlantic. *Photo, British Official*

Malvern). Certain related projects were carried on elsewhere ; a proximity fuse for rockets at the Projectile Development Establishment of the Ministry of Supply—this work was later transferred to R.R.D.E.—and a proximity fuse for bombs at the Royal Aircraft Establishment.

Meanwhile, American development was making rapid progress, and by October 1942 it seemed certain that American production would be sufficiently great to cover the immediate requirements of both America and Great Britain. It was therefore decided that the British should concentrate on certain long-term aspects of the development, and on the problems attendant on using American fuses in British shells.

THE NEPTUNE TANK rides even heavy seas (above). First news of this British tracked amphibious vehicle was disclosed in October 1945, when its specification was given as "a ship-to-shore load carrier capable of self-propulsion in any sea, able to land on a beach through heavy surf, and, having landed, to move across country." It can take a 4-ton pay-load, including the 25-pounder field gun The stern is a power-operated ramp (left), made in two hinged sections so that its height when raised is restricted. The power-unit is a 12-cylinder petrol engine.
Photos, British Official

It was agreed that first priority should go to Naval anti-aircraft applications ; and in the autumn of 1943 Thomson carried out a series of trials with American fuses under the Admiralty auspices. So successful were those trials that fuses went into operational use in the British Navy towards the end of 1943. Finally, there came the Battle of the Flying Bomb. The use of proximity fuses against such weapons was discussed by the Watson-Watt Mission to the U.S.A. in the winter of 1943, because their use by the enemy was expected, and recommendations were promptly made to the British War Office.

These recommendations were strongly supported by Gen. Sir Frederick Pile (then G.O.C.-in-C., A.A. Command), and the fuses duly arrived and were used with spectacular success. In fact, the sudden startling increase in efficiency of shooting down the flying bombs (in August 1944) was almost entirely due to the use of these fuses. The fuses were known by the Army as "Bonzo," but most of the anti-aircraft gunners had no idea of the secret weapon they were actually firing.

As already stated, the radio proximity fuse is a tiny wireless set, transmitter and receiver and aerial all combined, built into the nose of an A.A. shell. The valves are no bigger—and in some cases smaller—than the top joint of a man's little finger. There were formidable technical problems : means of providing (for land use) an overriding fuse, so that, if the shell did not pass sufficiently close to an aircraft to explode, it did not wait until nearing the ground on the return journey, with consequent danger to the civilian population ; the design of a battery which could be built into the shell and which would not deteriorate in store (this was one of the most difficult problems) ; some means of ensuring that the fuse was not so sensitive that it exploded in rain or near a cloud ; and, always, the tremendous mechanical strength needed to survive being shot from a gun.

All these were overcome, and the result has revolutionized A.A. shooting. The combination of centimetric radar, and the radio proximity fuse to ensure explosion at the right moment, has given A.A. guns a deadly precision unimagined at the beginning of the war.

Civilian Scientists Flew in Air Fighters

The scientists of R.A.F. Fighter Command's Operational Research Section, attached as technical advisers to the Commander-in-Chief, were able to do some particularly valuable work concerning the best fighter use of radar by virtue of their front line experiments.

When Britain's secret airborne interception apparatus, the miraculous radar "eyes," was first introduced in late 1940 the results were somewhat disappointing. Certain R.A.F. aces were able to achieve excellent results. But other flying crews found themselves in difficulties with the complex equipment. The civilian scientists, who had already done much experimental work leading up to the evolution of the equipment, were called in to investigate.

They accordingly took the place of Service radar operators on many operational flights, and even flew with some of the aces to observe the way they obtained results. Their experiments, a number of which brought them into actual air combat with Nazi raiders, resulted in the production of an "elementary textbook" on the use of airborne radar, which standardized procedure and increased results. They also started a school (see page 476) at which aircrews were taught the most effective use of radar equipment, and best tactics to obtain maximum results with it.

Manoeuvring for a Certain Kill

From then on, as new and improved radar sets for use in aircraft were produced, they were first handed over to civilians for air-testing under actual operational conditions. The scientists made the tests, produced their simple instruction books, and the efficiency of our night fighter force steadily increased. In another and rather similar field, Fighter Command's scientists co-operated with other scientists to man Britain's first radar "G.C.I" station, and evolve the best system for working it.

The system—"ground controlled interception"—involved a complicated plotting of our own fighters and enemy raiders, a controller manoeuvring the fighter into the best position for a kill. So well did the scientists do their job that within a very short time of their handing over the station to the R.A.F., the first enemy raider had been destroyed by this system. Numerous experimental flights were made by scientists to perfect it.

Among many other front-line tasks undertaken by them have been operational flights to observe at first-hand the effect of Nazi attempts to jam our aircrafts' radio links with base and radio navigational aids. One of the scientists lost his life on a flight of this nature, during the Arnhem operations.

Experimental flights in connexion with the laying of aerial mines and on anti-flying bomb patrols to determine whether airborne radar aids could be applied towards increasing the R.A.F.'s toll of the missiles, were among their other duties. Their work was of great value to night fighter crews, who sometimes found difficulty in estimating the speed and range of the flying bombs, purely from the deceptive light of their jets. They were also able to suggest fighter tactics for attacking the flying bombs with maximum effect and minimum damage to our aircraft.

THAMES BUOYS BAFFLED GERMANS

Radio control was used during the war to switch off flashing-light buoys in the mouth of the Thames, notes The Daily Telegraph. The equipment was used when German planes flew over at night to drop magnetic and acoustic mines in the shipping lane. This British device, operating from 15 to 20 miles away, meant that many sinkings were avoided. Miniature aerials were fitted to the buoys. Wrens at the Thames Defence H.Q., Sheerness, operated the radio signals which turned the lights on and off at the requisite times.

If Epidemics Cross the Channel this Winter

Field-Marshal Montgomery's present and greatest problem is the battle against disease on the Continent—pestilence and plague which may reach Britain and find us unprepared. For, in the words of our Minister of Health, "Our hospitals are 34,000 nurses short!" More men and women of the right kind must be attracted, without delay, to the nursing profession. How that is to be done is outlined in this article specially written for "The War Illustrated" by FRANK ILLINGWORTH partly from an interview with Mr. Aneurin Bevan.

FIFTY thousand men and women wearing the Red Cross emblem are wondering where their future lies. From El Alamein to the Elbe they dropped from the skies with stretchers and crawled from crater to crater with plasma and penicillin through the hell of battle, while all along the line through forward dressing-stations other willing hands kept the flood of wounded flowing towards the base hospitals.

Many trained in first-aid and hospital work were killed. Many more travelled the same road as those they set out to succour. But the flow of maimed and sick was maintained. In the grim school of reality these men and women fought gangrene and bubonic plague, pneumonia and all the other ills common to peace no less than to war. And now the war is over the demand for nursing staffs is more marked than at any time since 1939.

Leaning across a wide mahogany table at the Ministry of Health, Whitehall, Mr. Aneurin Bevan said to me recently, "There'll be pestilence and plague on the Continent this winter, and if the epidemics cross the Channel, well, our hospitals are 34,000 nurses short!" Mr. Bevan's slight vocal hesitation did not rob this statement of any of its significance. Thirty-four thousand nurses short, and disease on the rampage just across the water!

THE First Great War saw Serbian troops carry into what we know now as Yugoslavia a typhus epidemic that killed tens of thousands; returning troops brought dangerous diseases to Britain, and not even *our* medical services were sufficient to nip the influenza epidemic in the bud.

Conditions are infinitely more dangerous today. Field-Marshal Montgomery has made it plain that the battle against disease is his greatest problem. Already typhus, cholera, influenza, diphtheria and other diseases have a firm hold on the Continent; and returning soldiers could easily bring any of them to Britain.

"Two thousand nurses are to be released immediately from the Forces, on condition that they return to civil nursing," Mr. Bevan said. They'll help to bring into operation wards and hospitals and sanatoria which have been closed through lack of nursing staffs. But these 2,000 trained nurses will go only a little way towards answering the demand, even if this country is fortunate enough to escape serious epidemics.

Great New Charter for Nurses

We face a situation that has long been anticipated. It is part of the problem of switching from war to peace. But it will not be solved with the defeat of world epidemics. "People are more prone to go to hospital for petty ailments than before the war," Mr. Bevan declared. And more women are showing a tendency to have their babies in hospital, at a time when we want more staff to deal with disease threats and to answer the demands of the new Health schemes now being planned.

How are we to answer this demand? By making hospital work more attractive. This is exactly the aim of a new Charter for Nurses, a Charter calculated to revolutionize the nursing profession as the switch from war to peace progresses. But, it will take years for the probationers of 1946 to become trained nurses, and this is where the nursing staffs in the Forces enter the picture.

By far the greater proportion of the previously mentioned 50,000 are still hard at work in Service hospitals all over the globe. Their time for release is coming; and if many will be glad to see the end of hospital wards, be they aboard ship or on land, the reports of Service welfare officers suggest that large numbers of men and women who were mechanics or stenographers (or still at school) in 1939 have not only become proficient nurses and ward orderlies, but would like to take up civil nursing—but for the sacrifices it demands.

The new Nurses' Charter is designed partly to banish the system that saw the number of new probationers fall off year by year. Four spells in hospital during recent years have given me the opportunity of studying prevailing conditions at first hand. Many hospitals are run on the best lines. But there is no uniformity of rules—in some, junior nurses are less nurses than domestics, in many the nurses' food was appallingly bad and the hours of work fantastically long even before the war. The pay has long continued to be inadequate.

"It's not good enough to have an 'urge' to nurse," Mr. Bevan said. "You must offer good conditions of work to attract men and women to the nursing profession." To Service men and women no less than to the schoolgirl about to step into her first job, it will be good news that the switch from war to peace is based on a unanimous agreement between all the hospital and nursing organizations, local authorities and trades unions, to give the nurse a New Deal.

To Cover the Danger Period

From early in 1946 salaries are to be raised considerably. The fully trained staff nurse will begin at £120 a year and ultimately reach £180, and the ward sister will begin at £160 a year and reach £260, with board and lodging and adequate pensions on top.

Hours of duty? A ninety-six hour fortnight is the objective (including the time taken up by lectures and classes) with a minimum of one day off weekly and four weeks' annual holiday. The new Nurses' Charter banishes the convent-like rules known in some hospitals by introducing late passes and social amenities.

Health, no less than happiness, is catered for. The former includes separate bedrooms for nurses, adequate sleep, and a certain standard of food. And Nurses' Representative Councils set up in every hospital and backed by the authorities will be able to enforce the amenities agreed upon by the various nursing an allied organizations.

BUT there are more people in hospital today than in 1939 (apart from beds occupied through an increase of 170,000 births per annum since 1940), and the immediate demand born in the threat of nation-wide epidemics is such that releases from the Services must be supplemented by a part-time nursing "division."

Thirty-four thousand nurses short! To cover the danger period while this gap is being narrowed down, a National Reserve of Nurses (as distinct from the extant Civil Nursing Reserve) is to be formed from women who have given up nursing for one or another reason. The change-over from war to peace in the sphere of hospitals, sanatoria and mental institutions will be slow. With tens of thousands of wounded still to be put on their feet, the Services' demands for nursing personnel will remain marked for two or more years. But the new Charter will undoubtedly prompt many Service men and women to put their wartime hospital training to good purpose in the years of peace to come.

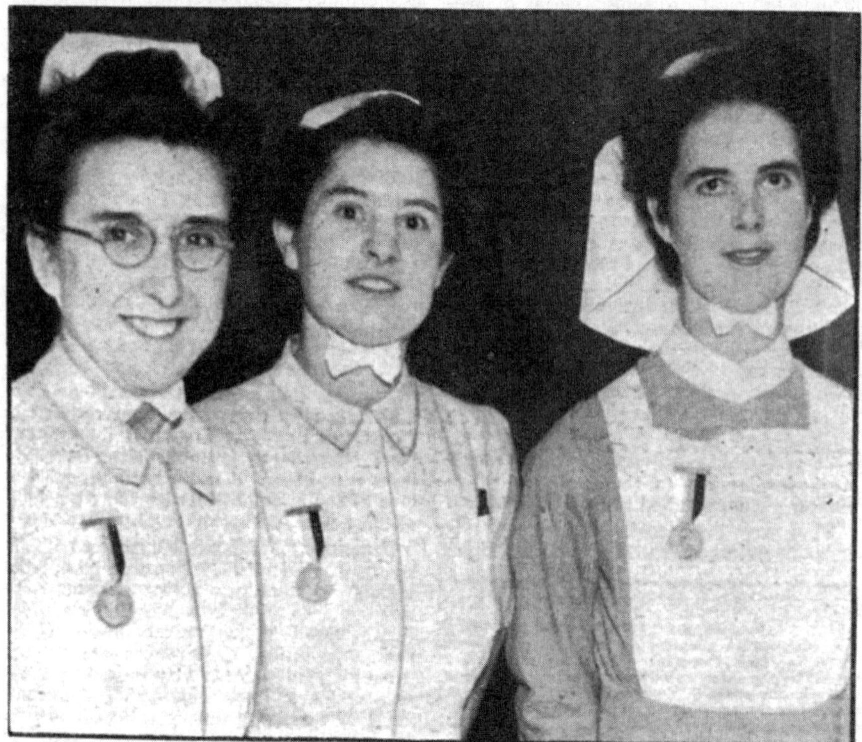

TYPICAL OF OUR HOSPITAL SERVICES, these nurses at the Middlesex Hospital, London, on November 14, 1945, were "decorated" for outstanding efficiency during the previous year. They are (left to right) Miss Marjorie Tomlinson, Miss Anne Bennett-Evans and Miss Ruth Walton—awarded the Hospital's gold, silver and bronze medal respectively.

Surcease 'twixt Prison Camp and Civvy Street

To help returned prisoners of war forget their dread experiences and fit themselves again for normal civilian life—a "jump" which many would find it difficult to take unaided—is the concern of Civil Resettlement Units. These the Army authorities, in co-operation with the Ministry of Labour and various voluntary organizations, have opened all over the country. Each establishment takes approximately 250 men at a time. Workshops are equipped for those who would revive their skill at a trade or learn the foundations of a new career. Film shows, dances, concerts, games and physical exercises provide a happy and well-filled social life.

One such unit is established at Hatfield House, Hertfordshire, built in 1610. In the magnificent banqueting hall (above) the men gather to read and talk and also to sleep; over the mantelpiece is an imposing figure of King James the First, whose home it once was. The rear entrance to Hatfield House is seen on the right.

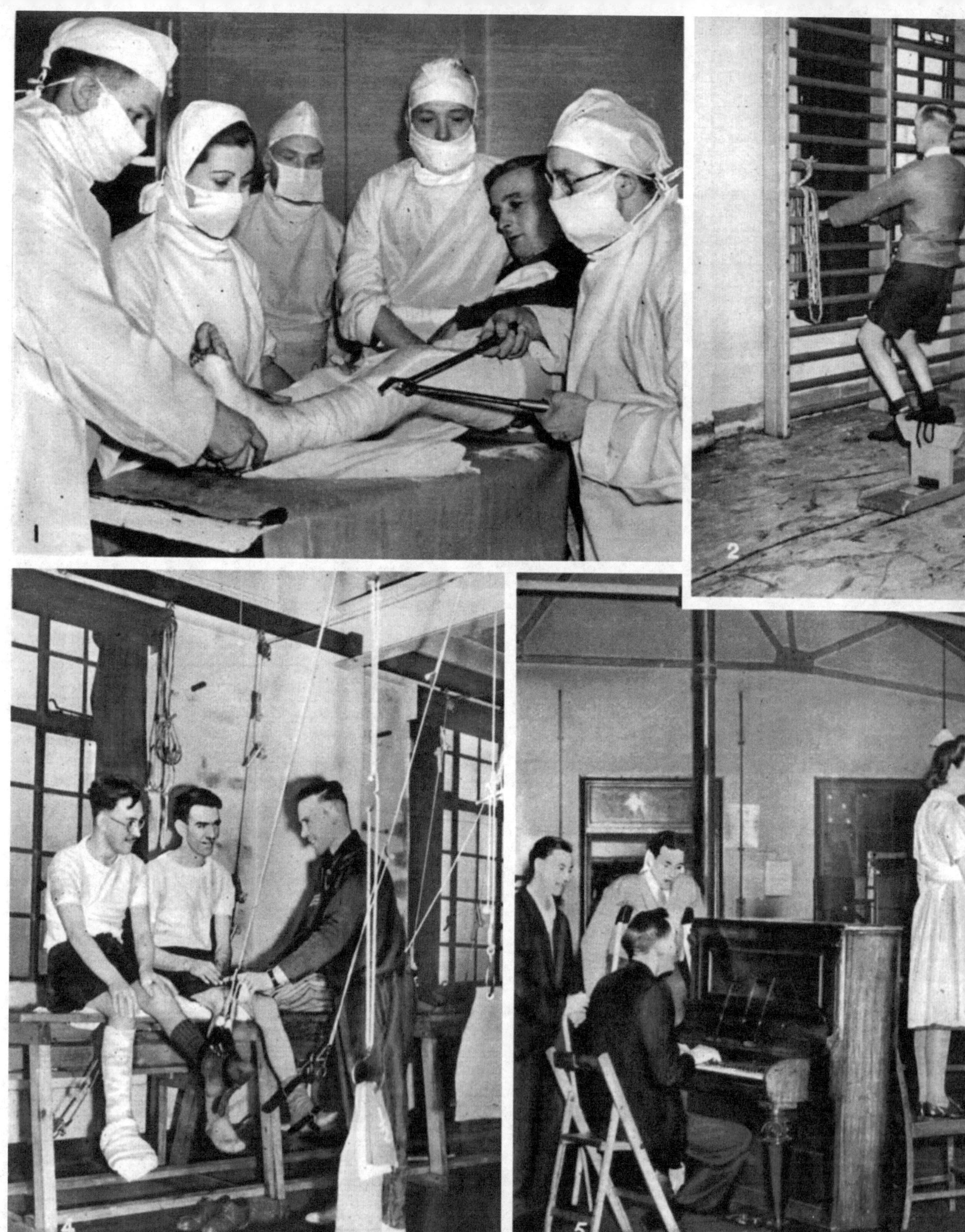

Wounded Are Helped on the Road to Recovery—

Among the most important of the Rehabilitation Units designed to assist, by occupational therapy, the speedy recovery of casualties is that at Pinder Fields Emergency Hospital, Wakefield, Yorkshire, part of the Ministry of Health service. Remedial exercises under skilled supervision restore weak muscles and stiff joints before wounds have completely healed. With a smile this patient (1) watches his plaster cast removed and his leg set free for movement. In the gymnasium (2).

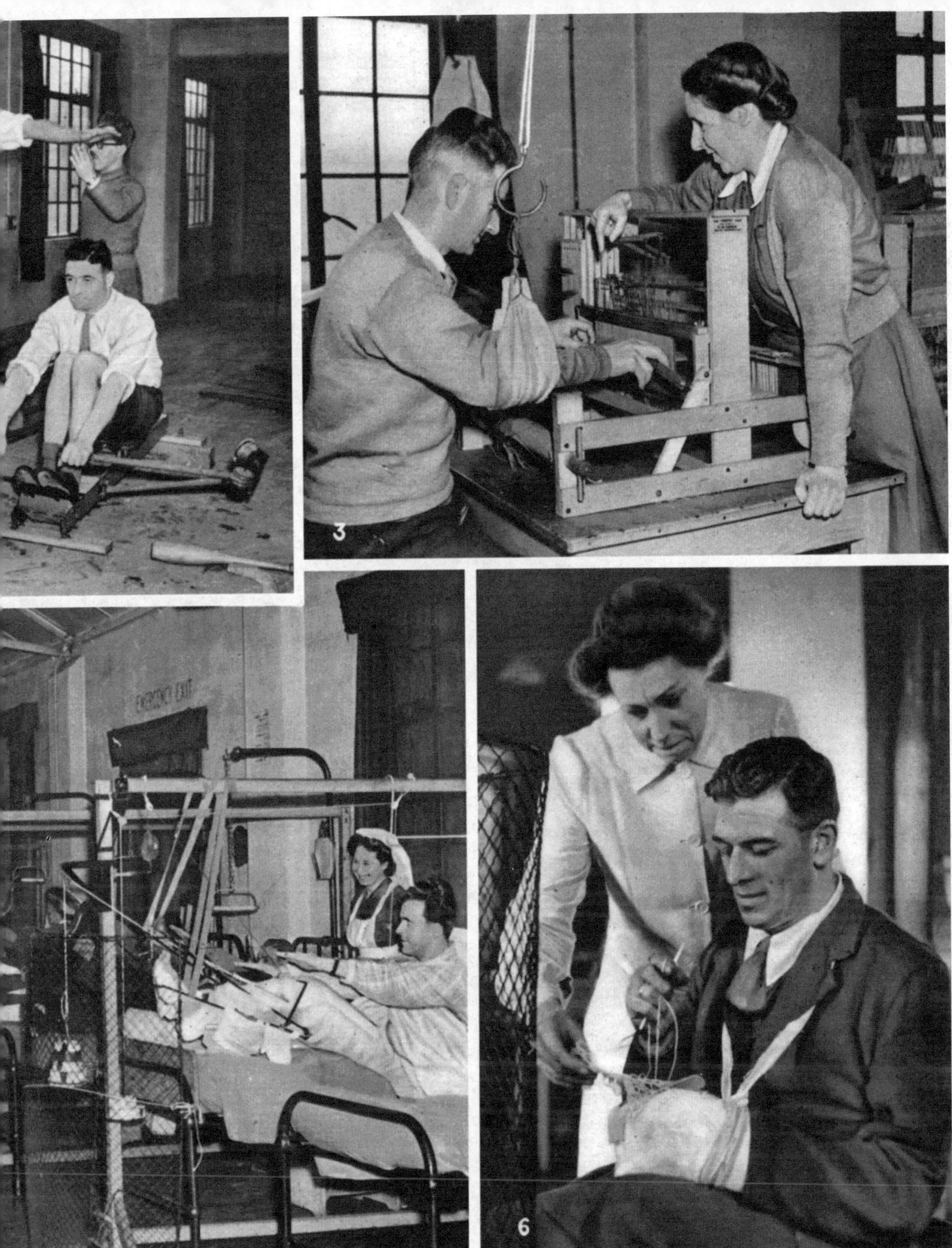

—By Curative Treatment Engaging the Mind

Use of looms to make scarfs and rugs is included in popular forms of occupational therapy. In this instance (3) the patient, with a weak right shoulder, has that arm supported in a sling. Weight and pulley exercises (4) help the thigh muscles. Here (5) they move their injured limbs to music. Muscles of his wounded arm (6) had contracted, so that he could not straighten his fingers; with the arm in a cast he is learning to make them " work," inducing the steady return of strength.

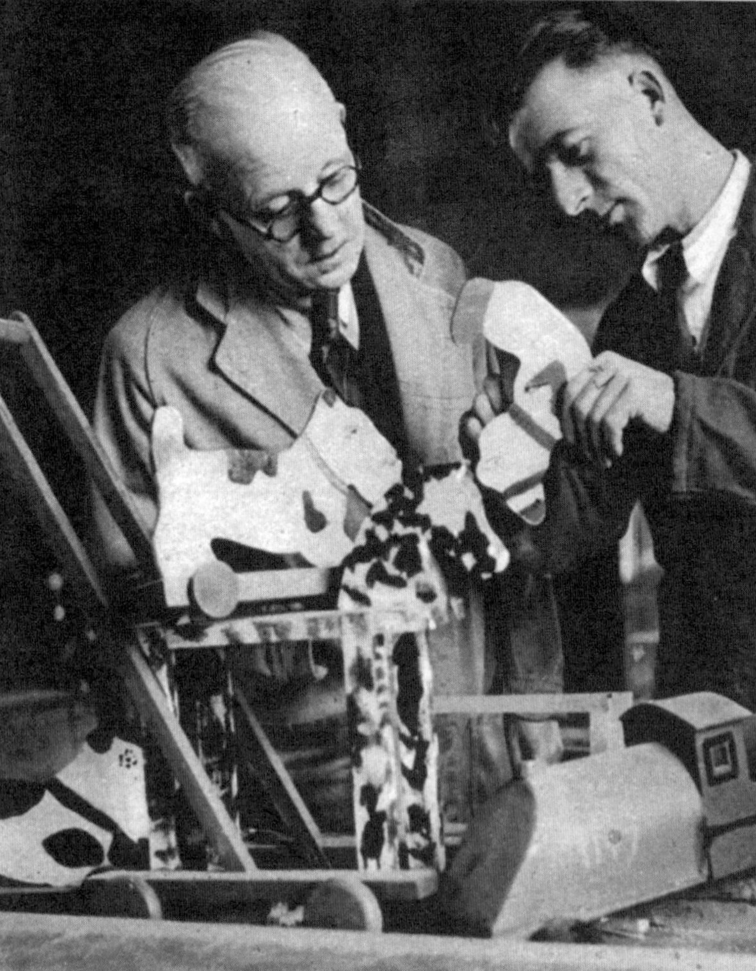

Injuries Forgotten in the Exercise of Skill

Photos exclusive to THE WAR ILLUSTRATED

Some 27,000 patients (including civilians) have been admitted to the Pinder Fields Hospital ; nearly 6,000 Service cases were received direct from the various battle-fronts. Remedial measures combined with amusement include the painting of lamp-shades (top left). A bullet wound caused paralysis in some of the right-arm muscles ; he is using and keeping in good condition the sound ones by making a rug (top right). Toy (left) and basket making (right) enter into the treatment.

Is There Any Hope for the Germans?

By HAMILTON FYFE

It is an appalling thought that nations can be changed, as the Germans were by two wars and Hitler. Or not so much changed as cowed into submission by ruffians posturing as supermen, and persuaded or forced to acquiesce dumbly to whatever brutalities and idiocies those ruffians committed. The Italians acquiesced in Mussolini's lunatic proceedings, but they were not really changed. Life went on in Italy much as it had done before Fascism took charge.

The Italians sat down under it : as they sat down under the Austrian tyranny until they were relieved of it largely by help from outside, and as they permitted politicians of all sorts to mismanage their affairs after they had become "free and democratic." They possessed none of the qualities which gained for Germans the admiration of the world during the latter part of the 19th and the early part of the 20th centuries.

I knew Germany pretty well then and, travelling about in Europe, the Americas, Mexico and the Dominions, I came across many Germans whose genuine culture and competence made them pleasant companions as well as successful business men, diplomats, farmers, manufacturers or newspaper men. At home the Germans were, up to 1914, scrupulously honest ; officials could not be bribed, they had a keen sense of public and private duty. When I went to Germany again, between the wars, I noticed a falling-off from that high standard. Hardships had made them less honest, corrupt practices had crept in ; and when Hitler raised to important positions the thugs and criminals whom other nations did their best to exterminate or keep under lock and key, the moral tone of the Germans rapidly dropped.

Masses Still Dominated by Fear

Clever scoundrels became rich and were given power. The mass of people were too terrified to make any protest, let alone try to upset Hitlerism. They must have known enough about the horrible methods of the Gestapo to denounce them, if they had dared ; now they pretend that they never heard of these abominations. Again they are dominated by fear—not of their Nazi oppressors but of their conquerors.

"They expected to be ill-treated," says Alan Moorehead in his new book, Eclipse (Hamish Hamilton, 12s. 6d.), and he adds, "they had an immense sense, not of guilt, but of defeat." I believe such an expectation was a sign that they felt guilty. They did not feel like that in 1918. They were not "mortally and utterly afraid," as Moorehead found them when he went as a correspondent into Germany with the invading force. They had no reason to feel ashamed after the First Great War. The Second made them feel they had sinned so deeply against human decency that they could not look to be treated by the victors in anything but the same savage, devilish way.

Of course they were not so treated, and now they have perked up and talk about the wicked Nazis who deceived them and perpetrated outrages about which they knew nothing. As if it were possible for what went on in internment and prisoner-of-war camps to be kept secret ! Why, the Gestapo didn't want it to be secret. They wanted everybody to be scared into more and more complete submission. It was the Gestapo, says Moorehead, which created in the Allied armies a loathing for everything German. The army had fought fairly on the whole. Our men did not hate their opposite numbers.

After the fight was over the reaction of the average soldier on seeing the prisoners was to think : "Well, the poor dumb beggars, they certainly bought it. They've had it." And he would hand out his cigarettes.

But as the atrocities of the Gestapo became known, not from hearsay but from first-hand evidence—"rooms where civilians had been tortured, the courtyards where firing squads operated, the houses looted and bodies lying about"—hatred for Germans grew.

The old feeling "We have got to fight for liberty and honour and all the rest of it" was replaced for short intervals by the more animal reaction that demanded revenge.

Wouldn't it be more accurate to say "demanded justice"? And does not justice demand that all who took part in Gestapo crimes should pay for their offences against humanity with their lives ? Most of them know what they deserve. They don't ask for mercy. Generals weep when they are compelled to surrender. Moorehead gives several instances of this. But the filthy instruments of the Secret State Police (which is what Ge-st-po stands for) brazen it out.

There is a good deal of brag and bluster still among the Hitler Youth, boys and girls of sixteen to eighteen, who "were barely coming out of the kindergarten when the Nazis got hold of them. Steadily year by year life had been represented to them merely as a preparation for battle and death for the Fuehrer. Side by side with this was a gangsterish lack of ordinary morals . . . In every French village it was accepted that the S.S. boy got drunk and smashed things."

At the same time, strangely enough, "pornography went hand in hand with a superstitious revival of religion. Many of the youths carried printed prayers and charms and lucky favours . . . They grabbed at their pleasures and then suddenly, in a fit of depression and remorse, turned to religion for support and forgiveness." Moorehead wondered what hope there could be for a nation with a rising generation like that.

Before Gestapo Became Paramount

Yet he has to admit that German efficiency was able "to persuade more than half the Continent that the Occupation might in the end turn out to be a good thing. Europe was a workable proposition under Nazi rule. That was the main thing, the thing that impressed itself on people's minds. They found they could live fairly normal, comfortable lives under Nazi rule. Up to 1942 three-quarters of the Allied propaganda about starving Europe under the Nazi boot was purest nonsense. Europe was going very well. The Germans supported the local systems of government and law. They kept the railways working and they got the food and coal distributed. They did not interfere unduly with the village life." That was before the Gestapo became paramount.

This is a view I do not remember to have seen in print before. It is probably sound, though it applies more to the countrysides than to the cities. If that efficiency can be directed into wholesome channels, it may save Germany from utter collapse. They must be told what to do—by their own people ; and they will do it. Moorehead thinks "the German soldiers were a good deal better disciplined than ours. They did not loot and destroy in the same way. With them everything was method." If they were ordered to carry out "a cruel, hard, cold, organized official beating-down of the peoples they conquered," they behaved so. When the order was "Behave decently," they did.

The book illustrates the difference between British and German methods by the story of a trout hatchery into which our men threw hand-grenades to kill the fish, while officers fired into the water with their revolvers. The German in charge had offered to net as many as they wanted, but they would not wait. For every one they pulled out they destroyed a hundred others and made them uneatable. Now, if the roles had been reversed, says Moorehead, the fish would have been carefully netted, but the manager would have been arrested, his house seized, and his family sent off methodically to labour camps.

If the discipline, the methodical habits, the devotion to duty (even when duty calls on you to act like the lowest of the low) can be used for good purposes instead of bad ones, there is hope for the Germans. For the Italians the author sees very little. "Something in their character has collapsed . . . The people cringed and whined when we arrived . . . They had no pride any more, or any dignity." They were too hungry to think that anything mattered but food. "The animal struggle for existence governed everything . . . Food at the cost of any abasement or depravity."

Never Again in Our Time a Menace

That was in Naples. "Not all Italians had fallen so far, certainly not the peasants (the peasants had not suffered hunger like the townspeople), nevertheless a rottenness ran through the country." This was due, it is suggested, to Fascism ; but ought we not to put it the other way round ? Wasn't Fascism a symptom of "something rotten"?

Italy will have to be watched. The country might fall under the domination of another Duce, perhaps a worse one than Mussolini. As for Germany, Moorehead suggests that "the Reich is ruined and exhausted beyond the recall of this or even perhaps the next generation . . . In our lifetime it can never again be a menace to us."

We have only to stick to our programme of occupation and Germany will lapse into a small agricultural state, owning no great industries, having no power to erect the vast machinery necessary for a modern war—a thing that did not happen to her last time.

However, Moorehead admits that "it might be a good thing to be vigilant in the years ahead." I don't think "might be" is nearly strong enough.

One thing the Germans ought to be taught is that Hitler was not only a dishonest scoundrel but a fool. I cannot understand Moorehead's statement that "the majority of Hitler's decisions throughout the war were remarkably sound." I should have said that Hitler made almost every mistake possible. The greatest of all was not drawing back his armies into the inner fortress—Germany itself—as soon as it was clear to his military advisers that there would be a successful invasion of Europe. We must be very thankful the conduct of the war was not left to the German generals.

Not that they were equal, man for man, to our supreme military leaders. Rommel was good, but not so good as Montgomery. The secrets of Monty's brilliance were, first, that he always insisted on superiority in numbers and armament before he struck ; and second, that he made all his soldiers feel he was "one of us." He has humour, too, which Rommel conspicuously lacked.

He can turn even blunders into assets. Once he told a brigade: "I would like to have you with me wherever I go." This caused gloomy looks. At once he added: "But you don't know where I am going. I may go home on leave." Roars of laughter and applause. He used the same trick in other speeches—with similar results.

Secrets of Britain's Wartime Nerve Centre—

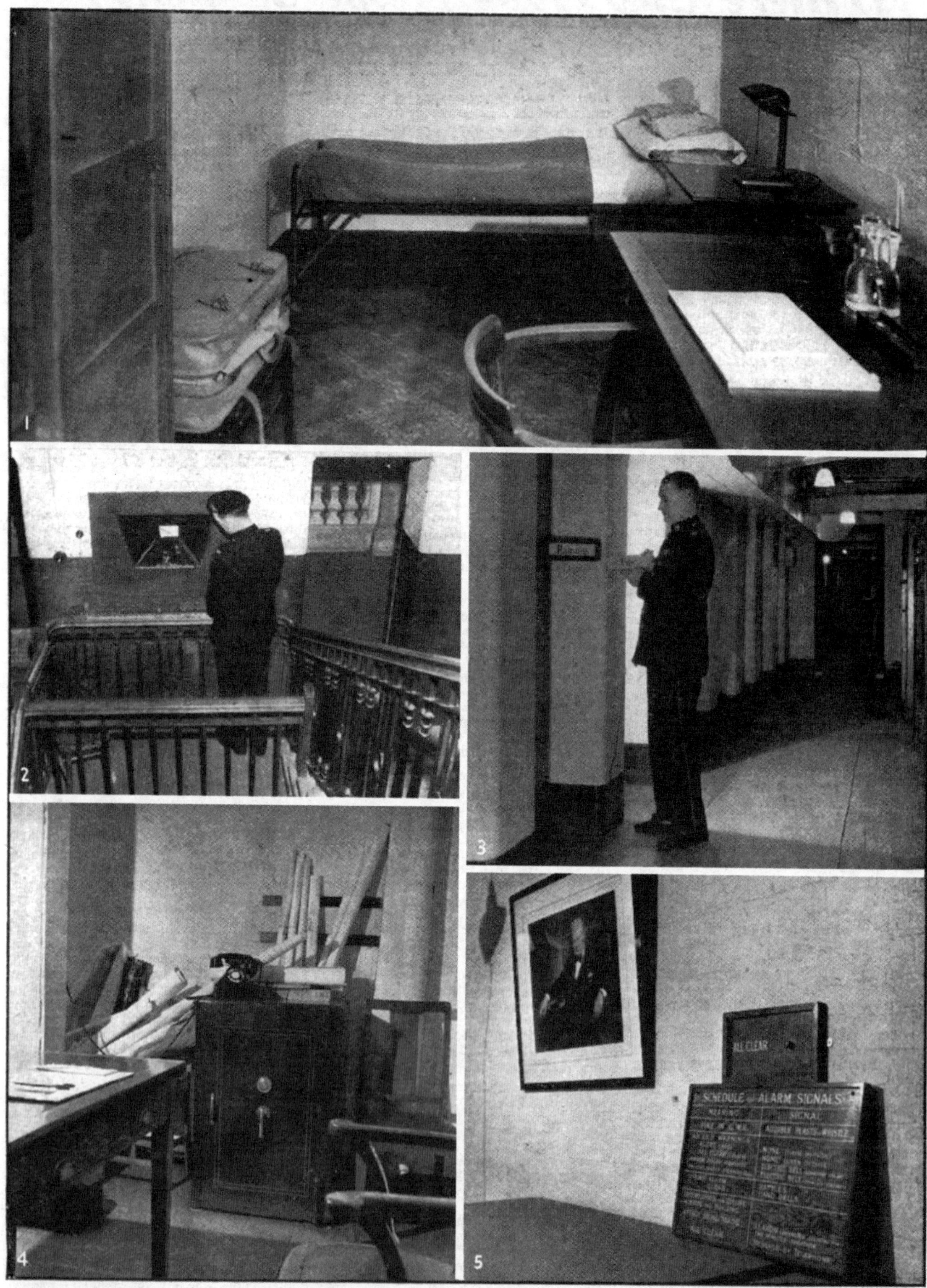

OUR WAR CABINET'S BOMB-PROOF H.Q., it was revealed in November 1945, was 70 ft. below Government buildings in Whitehall, so strongly reinforced that it is doubtful if even an atomic bomb could affect it. As Deputy Prime Minister, Mr. Attlee occupied this bedroom (1). Through a slit in the thick walls at ground-level (2) all callers were scrutinized. A notice-board (3) proclaimed the state of the weather "up above." This fireproof safe (4) housed secret documents. A schedule of alarm-signals was prominently displayed (5). *Photos by courtesy of Illustrated.*

—Where Cabinet Worked Beyond Reach of Bombs

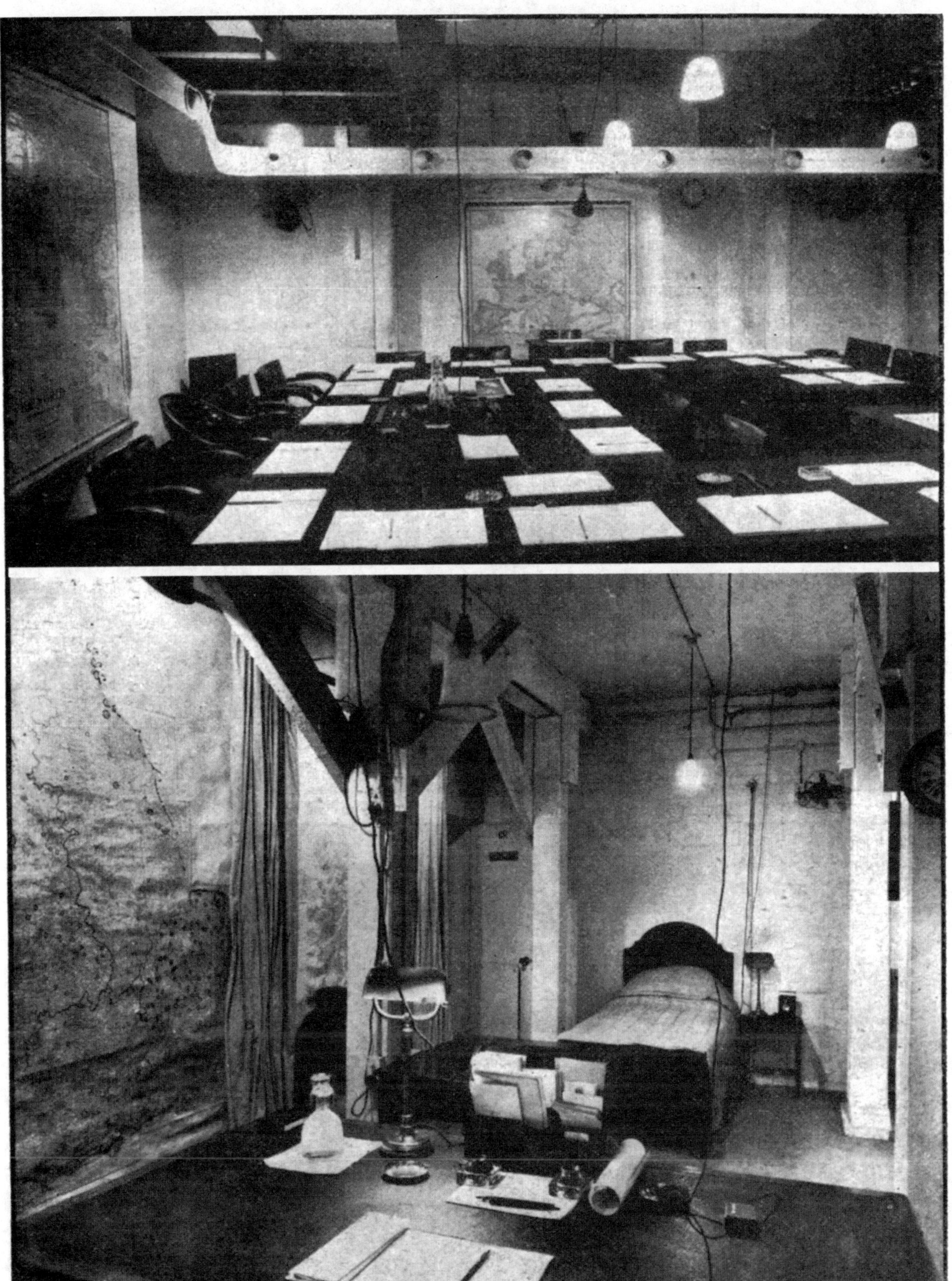

OUR CAMPAIGNS IN THREE CONTINENTS were directed from the underground Cabinet War Room (top), Britain's nerve-centre from 1939 to 1945; the round-backed chair on the left was Mr. Churchill's. Hung with wall-maps showing important changes hour by hour was the Premier's private room (bottom)—one of a suite of three occupied by him and his family—in which he worked and slept; from the big mahogany desk the Prime Minister made most of his famous war broadcasts.

Photos by courtesy of Illustrated.

R.A.F. 'Week-End' Pilots Go Back to Peace

On July 29, 1945, just before the fifth anniversary of the start of the Battle of Britain, in which the R.A.F.'s "week-end" pilots won their greatest triumph, the Air Ministry announced that squadrons of the Auxiliary Air Force were to revert to their peacetime status. Specially written for "The War Illustrated," this article recalls some of their outstanding achievements.

In the annals of the R.A.F. there are no more stirring records than those of the County and City squadrons of the Auxiliary Air Force, whose members gave up most of their spare time in the days of peace to train for the great air war they felt sure would one day break.

When the call came they exchanged their city clothes and sports jackets for flying kit and left the club-rooms of the airfields at which they had learned their craft (and where they had been in the habit of carefully arranging their take-offs and landings so as not to disturb the Sunday morning service at the local church) to fly out to do battle with Goering's professional killers.

Today the pages of their record books are rich with the chronicles of their victories. They fought over the beaches of Dunkirk; they stood firm with the rest of the Few when Britain was assailed by the mighty Luftwaffe: they helped to carry the war across the Channel to France when the sweeps began; they defended Malta; they won victory in the African skies, in Italy, and in the final battle for Europe's liberation.

First Blood to the Auxiliaries

Long before most of our regular home-based fighter squadrons had even seen a German aircraft, the Auxiliaries had opened their score by shooting down three Heinkels in the first German raid on the Firth of Forth on October 16, 1939. To the City of Edinburgh and City of Glasgow Squadrons, Air Chief Marshal Dowding, A.O.C.-in-C. Fighter Command, signalled: "Well done; first blood to the Auxiliaries." There was no stopping them after that. They continued to take a steady toll of the sneak raiders who crossed the North Sea during that first winter of war to bomb and gun defenceless fishing-boats and sow mines at British harbour mouths.

The Auxiliaries saw the first Battle of France from both sides of the Channel. A.A.F. Hurricanes had gone to the Continent to join the Air Component, and both they and their English-based comrades helped to fight off the swarms of dive-bombers which pounded the B.E.F. on their way home from Dunkirk. Then came the Battle of Britain. The Auxiliaries in the Midlands and the North moved South "for the shooting season." They did not know it then, but they carried the fate of Britain and the whole civilized world in their hands. There was no easy introduction to air combat; some of them took up their new battle stations in the morning and by the afternoon were in the thick of the fighting.

Exactly how many German bombers and fighters fell to the guns of their Spitfires and Hurricanes has not been disclosed, but it is estimated that one in every three of Goering's raiders which tumbled out of the skies was shot down by an Auxiliary airman. Squadrons increased their scores by anything up to fifteen a day; pilots became veterans in a few weeks. But they had their casualties, too—the ranks of the Auxiliaries became thinner as the desperate struggle went on into September and October.

Like their colleagues in the regular R.A.F. squadrons, the Auxiliaries fought and died anonymously. It was the policy of the Air Ministry not to build up "aces." Even today their names are little known outside the Service, except for a few like A. V. R. Johnstone (see illus. p. 559, Vol. 3), Max Aitken (see illus. p. 391, Vol. 3), George Denholm and Whitney Straight, all of whom have reached high rank in the R.A.F.

After the day battles came the struggle by night, and once again the Auxiliaries played a leading part. Londoners of Numbers 604 (County of Middlesex) and 600 (City of London) Squadrons searched the darkness in their twin-engined fighters for Heinkels and Dorniers, while cities burned beneath them. Under a succession of brilliant A.A.F. commanders, of whom Group Captain John Cunningham, D.F.C. (see illus. p. 246, Vol. 4), is the best known, the Middlesex Squadron, after many difficulties, mastered the science of fighting blind and became the acknowledged authorities on night interception. Within a few months they had 50 or more kills to their credit in this field of operation.

By this time, however, the Auxiliary squadrons—particularly the day fighter squadrons, who had suffered heavier casualties—were losing much of their "amateur" status. Regular airmen had to be drafted to fill the places of those lost in combat, and soon the little metal "A" on the lapel of a pilot's tunic was seen less frequently. However, mainly through the ground crews, the ties with City and County were retained. There are scores of non-commissioned airmen of the Auxiliary Air Force who have serviced their squadrons' aircraft for five years in many theatres of war.

Dive-Bombed the V2 Rocket Sites

Number 601 (County of London), for instance, took the winged sword of the capital to Malta in 1942 to fight in the defence of George Cross Island. The City of Edinburgh Squadron were there, too, and later operated in the Western Desert. The City of London also did a successful Mediterranean tour, and celebrated their 100th victory in Italy.

The two Scottish squadrons came together again last year and ended the war in Britain as they began it, fighting side by side. This time their targets were not Heinkels and Dorniers, which they had hunted together in the early days, but the V2 rocket installations in Holland which they dive-bombed in their Spitfires, often in face of intense anti-aircraft fire. They were defending London all over again, and the capital's ordeal would have been worse but for their skill and courage.

Most of the Auxiliary pilots who fought the early campaigns are now found in staff offices and commanding stations and sectors. Many are gold-braided, proving that their usefulness did not end with their operational flying career. In R.A.F. messes all over the world the deeds of the Auxiliary airmen were being recalled as the squadrons went back to their peacetime flying, and the Auxiliaries themselves honoured the memories of fallen comrades.

Those who flew over Kent and Sussex five years ago have probably been thinking of one man, whose combat record eclipsed all others—Archie McKellar, a Scotsman, who took part in the Forth Bridge fight and later led the County of Warwick Squadron in the life and death struggle over Southern England. He was killed in action in the last days of the Battle after shooting down no fewer than 18 raiders.

600 SQUADRON (City of London), some of whose pilots are seen (left) grouped about the tail of a Hurricane, was among the most gallant of our Auxiliary Air Force, with 10 D.F.C.s and over 100 enemy aircraft to its credit. These pre-war "week-end" pilots who trained in their spare time numbered in their ranks bank clerks, bus conductors and students.
Photo, British Official

First Raid on Britain as Seen by the Luftwaffe

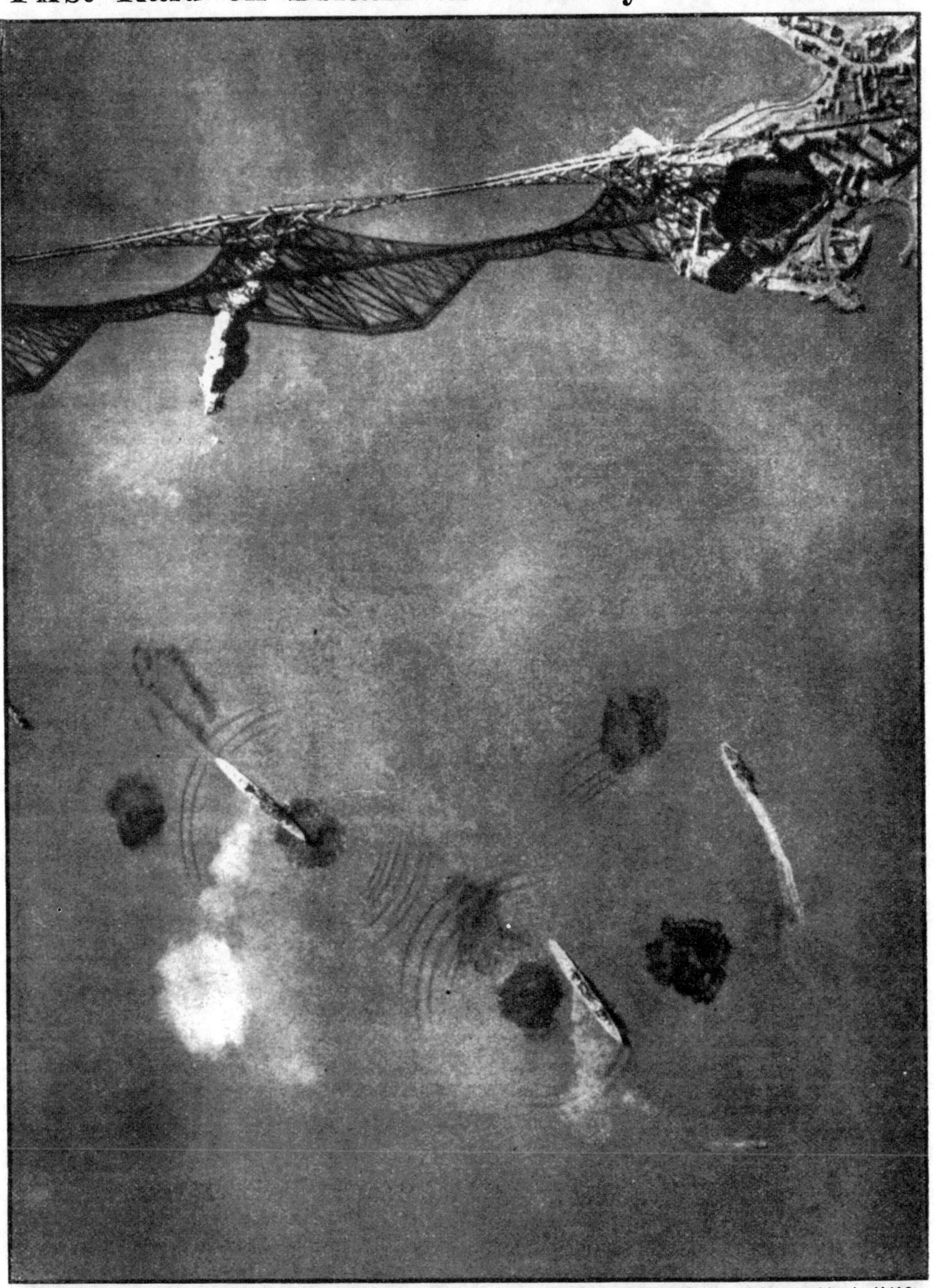

GERMAN AIRMEN SAW THE FIRTH OF FORTH LIKE THIS when they first raided Britain, on October 16, 1939, causing casualties in H.M.S. Mohawk and other warships. Dark patches in the photograph (taken from a Nazi bomber and now in R.A.F. hands) indicate where bombs fell; close to the centre pier of the famous Forth Bridge is Inch Garvie Island. Participating in the shooting-down of four of the twelve or fourteen raiders were R.A.F. Auxiliary pilots. See facing page; also illus. page 297, Vol. I. *Photo, British Official*

Now 63 Hours Only on Bournemouth-Sydney Run

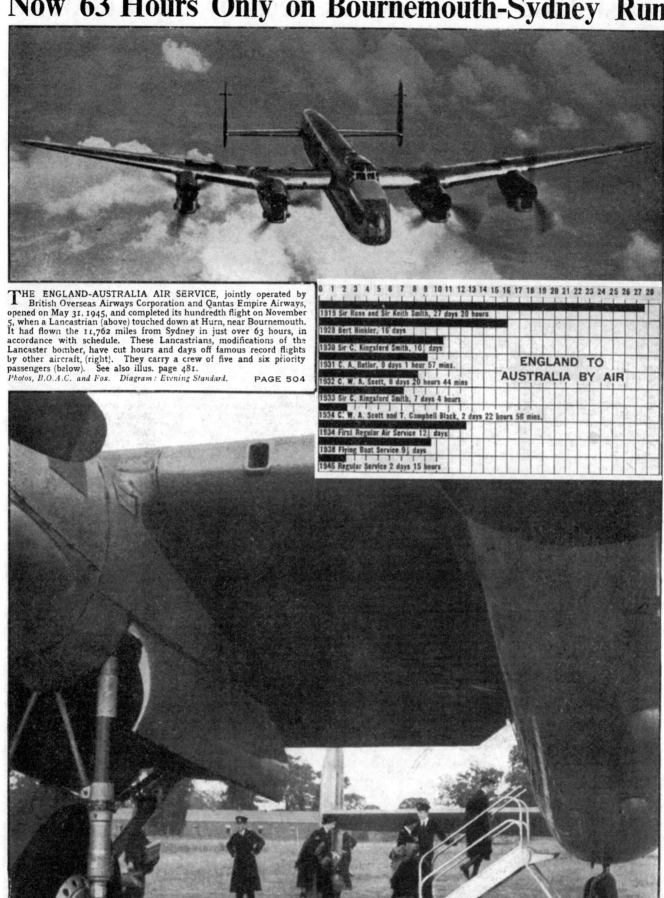

THE ENGLAND-AUSTRALIA AIR SERVICE, jointly operated by British Overseas Airways Corporation and Qantas Empire Airways, opened on May 31, 1945, and completed its hundredth flight on November 5, when a Lancastrian (above) touched down at Hurn, near Bournemouth. It had flown the 11,762 miles from Sydney in just over 63 hours, in accordance with schedule. These Lancastrians, modifications of the Lancaster bomber, have cut hours and days off famous record flights by other aircraft, (right). They carry a crew of five and six priority passengers (below). See also illus. page 481.

Photos, B.O.A.C. and Fox. Diagram: Evening Standard.

I Was There! Eye Witness Stories of the War and After

I Was in Surabaya When the Shooting Began

From the "front-line" in Java's second city came this account of the outbreak in October 1945 of hostilities between Indonesians and our troops. It was told to The Evening Standard correspondent Arthur La Bern by a British naval officer who escaped from Surabaya, minus revolver and luggage, to Singapore. See also pages 418, 441 and 453.

THIS story is pure melodrama—but it happened . . . Liberty Hotel in Surabaya was comfortable. The beer was magnificent and the food was good. We asked ourselves what all the talk was about. Why should there be trouble ? In the evening of our second day ashore the shooting started. At first it was distant, then suddenly it was outside. Our Indian guards dropped quietly behind the low wall in front of the hotel. They had a Bren gun and a two-in. mortar.

We dined to the music of occasional shots. Then we stuffed Mills bombs into our pockets, turned the pistol holster back and joined the Indian guards. In the distance grenades were exploding, Brens and Indonesian machine-guns were chattering. The whole town seemed to be fighting. Our radio was tuned to the Army transmitters, and back in an empty room a loudspeaker was telling how the battle was going on elsewhere. The news was disquieting. Isolated companies were surrounded. The Brigade H.Q. were encircled and fighting desperately.

At 7.30 next morning the Indonesians attacked us. One of our Indians was seriously wounded by fire from across the street. Two sergeants of an Army film unit took cover behind the hotel wall and began burying Dutch money in a flower bed. It meant death to be captured with these notes.

An Australian major was the senior officer. Our force consisted of 30 Indian troops, a British and two Indian Army public relations officers, and a dozen other assorted Allies. There were also four women with children. A four-hour battle started.

I remember bullets hitting the plaster. Our wounded waited patiently. Indonesians were shouting in bad English, "Come down, come down." Anton, the Indonesian kitchen manager, was crouching behind an upturned table parleying for us in an hysterical voice. Then the Australian major walked down the hotel stairs with my white handkerchief to make terms, while the crowd clamoured round to kill us.

They drove us in open trucks through turbulent streets. Rifles swung at us, mobs crowded about us at barricades with knives and spears. At Kalsosok gaol they searched us. We were locked in our cells. Educated Indonesians came to our rescue. A leader of the Antara Press Agency went to Dr. Soekarno, the Indonesians' "President," and said : "Free them. Give them police guards."

We were smuggled out in closed cars with guards on the running boards. We were driven at midnight to the palace of the Governor of East Java. He fed us and said he was sorry we had been "in trouble." We slept fitfully in an hotel with guards outside. Then at breakfast the crowd found us, and the guards lost control of the situation.

LAST R.A.F. PRISONER OF WAR left in the Bandoeing area of Java was Sergt. Tan Siong Hoon. He remained to supervise the rounding-up of Japanese. *Photo, British Official*

Only the eloquence of our Antara Press friend saved us from the mob. For two hours they crowded round us, shouting that we were Dutchmen, fingering knives, pointing rifles and machine-guns at us. Then the police arrived in strength. When we got back to the brigade they said, "Come and have a drink. We heard that you were all dead." We needed that drink !

We Cheered at London's First Peace Pageant

With all the old enthusiasm, intensified by the bleakness of later years, Londoners turned out in thousands on November 9, 1945, to greet the Lord Mayor elect, Sir Charles Davis, as he went by on his historic journey from the Guildhall to the Law Courts. Impressions of this year's Show, from The London Evening News, are by Leslie Ayre. See illus. in page 506.

TO many of us the shadow of St. Paul's seemed as good a place as any from which to watch the Show. And a magnificent procession it was—in which the young and the not-so-young all had their place—which wound its way, brave and colourful, against the background of the war-battered City. It was a nostalgic thrill for many. But to the little blonde girl, waving her streamers, and her schoolboy companion, all was new, all exciting. So it was, too, to the American and other Allied soldiers who jostled cheerily with us.

R.A.F. OFFICERS ARRIVING IN JAVA to help quell the Indonesian outbreak were formally greeted by Jap officers and aircrew on alighting from a Japanese Topsy aircraft. First R.A.F. casualties occurred on November 14, 1945, when a Mosquito crew were wounded by A.A. fire. Rebel anti-aircraft shooting was reported as highly skilled. *Photo, British Official*

Crowds of students, shouting and cheering as they marched round the side streets, helped to amuse us during the long, cold wait. Then came the joyful clamour of the bells. The cheering swelled and mingled with the clash of military bands. And round the bend into St. Paul's Churchyard came the white helmets and gleaming long bayonets of "His Majesty's Jollies"—the Royal Marines.

The American sergeant beside me was busy with his camera as they swung by. "Swell !" seemed to be the best description he could find. The blue of the Marines gave place to the khaki of the Grenadier Guards band, followed by a contingent of the regiment, this time fixing the newer short bayonets.

Then the Buffs (Royal East Kent Regiment), wearing khaki berets, with their band, and on their heels the band and a contingent of the Royal Fusiliers (City of London Regiment). And then the Honourable Artillery Company. For the first time in history we had seen a joint march through London of all the five regiments privileged to go through the City with drums beating, colours flying and bare bayonets.

But we were to see the fixed bayonets of the Royal Navy and Royal Air Force too. And now the women marched by—and none drew greater cheers. At the head of the A.T.S. Pipe Band strode their kilted, white-gloved drum major, bravely whirling her silver-topped staff. Behind them came the W.A.A.F. Band, followed by contingents of Wrens, A.T.S., and W.A.A.F.

Still more marching women, this time the Voluntary Aid Detachments of the British Red Cross and St. John Ambulance Brigade. There were grey hairs among some of these women who had played their own special part in the war years.

More stirring martial music as the Band of the Coldstream Guards swung by. Away down Ludgate Hill into Fleet Street we could see showers of "ticker-tape" and streamers cascading down on the procession. It was a merry barrage for the new Lord Mayor.

LORD MAYOR'S SHOW SEEN FROM ST. PAUL'S on November 9, 1945, was observed to have regained much of its pre-war glory as it moved in mile-long procession down badly-blitzed Cannon-street (above) to the Law Courts, headed by the band of the Royal Marines. At the Mansion House the Prime Minister, Mr. Attlee, greeted the new Lord Mayor, Sir Charles Davis (inset). Story in page 505. *Photos, Fox, Central Press*

When the Dead of Two Wars Were 'Remembered'

The Two Minutes Silence, the first Armistice Day ceremony at Whitehall since 1938, made November 11, 1945, a date specially memorable in the minds of many whose feelings were inexpressible. The thoughts of one who stood on a roof-top opposite London's Cenotaph are in this Daily Express story by James Cameron. (See also illustrations in pages 490 and 491).

It seemed for a moment at 11 a.m. that this was the first space of silence, the first relief of utter quiet our restless city had known for seven years. When the gun abruptly barked in the Horse Guards' Parade and that extraordinary, unmistakable hush spread over London like a pool, one realized how nearly one had come to forgetting what stillness meant.

The year 1938, that was the last time we had been here. Not in all that time had there been, nor could have been, all this lustrous ceremonial, bright and sombre, gay and grieving, this traditional moment which had, we must face it, become rather a wry and mocking thing by 1938.

I stood on my patch of roof opposite the Cenotaph in the biting, sunny wind, watching the thudding bands, the rhythm of moving uniform, the old-fashioned glint of silk hats held in the hand, and thought how long ago was 1938. Nothing had changed, except the world around. This, then, was the first memorial for the Twenty-Seven Years' War.

The sense of tradition, or habit, or continuity, whatever it may be, made it inevitable, I suppose, that November 11 should be the day, and that once again the ocean of people funnelling into Whitehall should be flecked with the red of poppies. Were there poppies on the fields of Arnhem, or Longstop Hill?

That was the strange telescoping of time that brought things far apart into the compass of the same moment of memory—Armentières and Alamein, the Somme and Singapore, Flanders fields and the Falaise Gap. This was not the Armistice Day of the years between, this was different; if it meant anything at all it had to mean twice as much, or all that had happened in these last years was vain and unthinkable.

Along Whitehall, past the Horse Guards, as far as it was possible to see into Trafalgar Square, the people stood jammed from kerb to kerb. There may have been more in 1919, I would not know, but I cannot imagine so. They stood so closely that they became a unified entity, as a great crowd can be.

I am no better than most people at knowing what a man a hundred yards away is thinking. But when a stooping clerk with the Mons Star stands at the side of a boy with the D.F.C.—when a woman whose light went out in 1917 stands with a girl who thinks only of Dunkirk—what in human reason can they possibly feel?

I do not believe this has happened before in quite the same way; I hope that is the answer. One may know some day. The graceful stone that Lutyens raised in memory of the war that was to end all war was gradually

PRINCESS ELIZABETH, as a Junior Commander of the A.T.S., laid a wreath at the Cenotaph for the first time. *Photo, P.N.A.*

hemmed in by all the circumstance of the day. The bands played, the troops snaked in—how extremely well is this affair produced and stage-managed!—the clergy held their flapping surplices about them.

The Cabinet gathered in their black-and-white row; Mr. Morrison spoke to Mr. Churchill and rubbed his hands together in the cold wind. The King and Princess Elizabeth and their entourage took their place; the Queen and her companions watched from a Home Office window.

One found oneself wondering irrelevantly what the other Novembers since 1938 had seen, since they had not seen this. Last year? We were storming Walcheren. The year before we were crossing the Sangro; before that we were landing in North Africa; before that again we were groping in the ruins of Coventry. All those things, when there might have been no Armistice Day for us.

Then the hour struck and the maroon cracked, and Whitehall, and London, and Britain, and who knows how much of this weary world were left in silence with whatever private thoughts seemed best. Myself, I believe I thought a little of the men not there, the statesmen tackling the atom bomb problem, whose work at that moment was probably of some particular importance to the whole sense of this day. Two minutes is not a very long time to think of the things that must be thought of.

AT THE CENOTAPH on November 11, 1945, where for the first time since 1938 Remembrance Day was observed, stood (left to right) Mr. Ernest Bevin, Foreign Secretary; Lord Jowitt, the Lord Chancellor; Mr. Winston Churchill; and Mr. Herbert Morrison, Lord President of the Council, bareheaded during the two minutes' silence. *Photo, P.N.A.*

Then the scarlet wreaths began to climb up the sides of the Cenotaph, the familiar procession of old and young, upright and limping, the ones who remember and the ones who do not yet remember, filed past the stone and became the crowd again. So we all went back and became the crowd again, out of the memory of war into what we now, rather doubtfully and desperately, call peace.

Four Nazi Flags Which Were to Fly Over London

Proof of how Nazi Germany, before ever war was declared, plotted to conquer and occupy Britain, was in evidence at the Earl's Court Exhibition on November 26, 1945, opening day of the sale by auction of the contents of the former German Embassy, Carlton House Terrace, London. An Evening Standard reporter describes what he saw there on November 12.

DRAPED round a pillar in the Exhibition's Brasserie Restaurant, where the Embassy's furniture and other goods are now stored awaiting the sale, are four Nazi flags—silver-fringed with huge black swastikas staring from white circles on red backgrounds. When I inspected these, I found that each bore an inscription in the left-hand corner in white German characters.

NAZI FLAGS, intended to be flown in London after Hitler's "occupation," were among items from the German Embassy which came up for auction, ss told here. *Photo, Fox*

Translated, these read: "North London," "South London," "West London" and "East London." The flags were those the Nazis intended to fly over the four chief centres of London, once Britain's capital was occupied. And they were hidden away in the German Embassy in the heart of London long before the war.

Hanging on one of the walls of the Brasserie I found a number of large maps of Britain. The North Sea was not the North Sea on those Nazi maps. It was the German Ocean. And Britain had been carefully divided up into a score or so of numbered areas. The Nazis were taking no chances with their private documents and papers when, with the coming of the war they had planned, they would have to vacate the Embassy.

The burning of documents by fire was not certain enough for them. So they had installed a special electrical machine which tore documents and papers into tiny, indecipherable shreds. When I looked at the machine today it was stuffed with the shreds of the last document which the Nazis destroyed before they left the Embassy for good in September 1939.

A few yards away from the pillar bearing the Nazi flags is the Embassy's enormous 25 ft. long conference table—a magnificent piece of furniture in highly polished mahogany. It was at this table that His Excellency Joachim von Ribbentrop planned with his Nazi associates.

Tucked away in a corner I found a granite head of Adolf Hitler. It must have been the German Embassy's central showpiece.

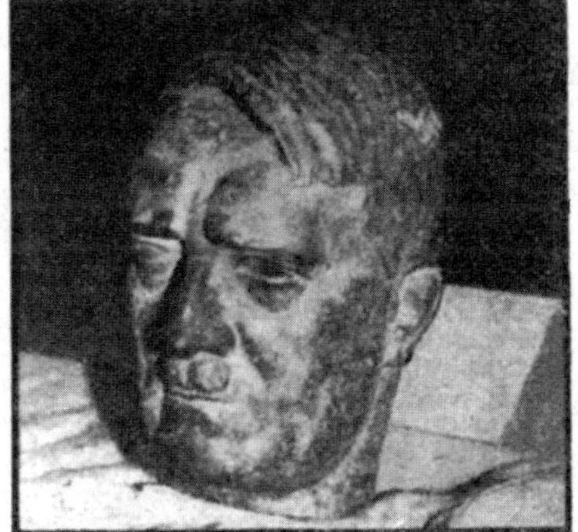

HITLER'S HEAD, in granite, weighing 5 cwt., which once adorned Ribbentrop's London Embassy, was offered publicly for sale in November 1945. *Photo, Fox*

★—As The Years Went By—Notable Days in the War—★

1939

November 30. *Russia launched land, sea and air attacks on Finland; Helsinki bombed.*

1941

November 25. *H.M.S. Barham sunk off Sollum.*
November 26. *General Ritchie replaced General Cunningham during Sidi Rezegh battle, Libya.*
November 28. *Rostov retaken by Russians.*
December 6. *On Moscow front, Red Army opened big counter-offensive against Germans. Great Britain declared to be in state of war with Finland, Hungary and Rumania.*
December 7. *Pearl Harbour bombed. Japan at war with Great Britain and United States.*

1942

November 24. *Stalingrad's defenders linked up with relieving troops north of the city.*
November 27. *Germans entered Toulon; French warships in harbour scuttled by crews.*

1943

November 28. *First meeting at Teheran (Persia) between Roosevelt Stalin and Churchill.*
December 1. *Eighth Army broke German "winter line" on Sangro River in Italy.*

1944

November 30. *Port of Antwerp declared open.*
December 3. *"Stand down" of Home Guard.*

My Flying Visit to H.M.S. Battler

By CAPTAIN NORMAN MACMILLAN M.C., A.F.C.

H.M.S. Battler's deck looked absurdly small as we curved down towards it in a left turn, the standard method of approach (to an aircraft carrier) in deck landings. I saw the deck flying control officer (called the "batsman") standing on the port side of the flight deck with one table-tennis-like bat in each hand. Pilots watch his signals, and in response hold the aircraft's nose up, lower it, turn more (or less) to left, open or close the throttle. But my pilot, Lieut. D. Wormald, R.N.V.R., "A" Branch, was no novice in his craft, and the batsman held his yellow-painted bats motionless with outstretched arms in the Steady-As-You-Go signal.

The Swordfish finished her turn central to the deck and dead into wind, and the ship vanished from my sight as the aircraft's nose blocked out all forward vision. I gripped the padded sides of the observer's cockpit. An instant later I was pushing hard with the muscles of both arms taut to prevent my body from being hurled violently forward. I know of no other sensation like this rapid deceleration after the landing hook picks up the arrester cable of the flight deck. The muscular compression builds up rapidly to a maximum, remains almost constant for a fraction of time, and then swiftly eases off. It is the quickest landing you can make except a nose-in crash, for the aircraft comes to rest in a few feet, and has to be specially strengthened to take the consequent strain.

How Arrester Cables and Crash Barriers Safeguard the Aircraft

Each transverse arrester cable is held about a foot above the deck by two hydraulic rams, one on either side of the deck. The number of cables varies in different classes of carriers. The Battler, a Carrier Escort vessel, had eight arrester cables and three crash barriers. Crash barriers are simply cables stretched across the deck up to a height which will ensure the stopping of an aircraft. They have a dual function: (1) to stop aircraft that have overshot the arrester cables from going over the bows into the sea, and (2) when aircraft are parked forward in the bigger ships to prevent aircraft failing to take off successfully from running into the parked aircraft.

Each arrester cable is free to slip off its hydraulic rams when it is picked up by the landing hook which the pilot lowers below the after half of the fuselage of the aircraft. The cable-ends are reeved through the flight deck to hydraulic braking mechanism underneath, which applies the powerful deceleration to the aircraft. Aircraft can now be landed on carriers every 25 to 35 seconds, and flown off every 15 seconds.

On the Battler's long fore-and-aft and narrow bridge on the "island" I met Captain H. Norman and Lieut.-Commander (flying) B. Sanderson. Here, too, were helmsman and signallers. From the bridge I could see the 436-ft. length of the flight-deck, overlaid with wood to reinforce the light steel plate. One fore and one aft lift conveyed aircraft to and from the single hangar, about 260 ft. long and almost the width of the ship.

Forward on the port side was a catapult track, a slotted rail flush with the deck and containing a cable. A strop connects this cable to hooks on the aircraft. The aircraft's tail is held by gear which breaks under load when the catapult takes up the strain. The aircraft is then swished into the air in about 30 ft., with a force equal to about two and a half times its own weight.

Lieut. W. M. Crichton, the Air Staff Officer, showed me over the ship. Below the bridge were the Operations Room, and working in conjunction with it, the Aircraft Direction Room which controls fighters from ship to enemy aircraft by means of radar as in the G.C.I. shore system. Aircraft Briefing and Intelligence Rooms were combined to economize space. Bomber and fighter aircrews used one Readiness Room.

An automatic beacon emitted two letter signals at 30 degrees' intervals right round the horizon; aircrews knowing the code and wavelength could pick them up to plot their course for the ship. In the Met. Office a meteorological officer prepared synoptic weather charts to provide the ship with weather information.

The captain's cabin, under the flight deck opposite the "island," where I left my flying kit, was a large, luxuriously furnished flat, more comfortable than in many a British-built warship, and comparable with the delightful admiral's flat in the Ark Royal.

The Battler, designed on merchant ship lines, was the first U.S.A. escort carrier to be handed over to the R.N. Commissioned on October 31, 1942, her executive and air operations were performed by R.N. and R.N.V.R. personnel, while engineers of the Merchant Navy with R.N.R. rank ran the machinery of the ship. The 18 knots class speed of these escort carriers is too slow for operations with the Fleet, but sufficient for their special functions of escorting convoys and serving as assault carriers. Their complement is about 400, with another 200 when fully operational with aircraft aboard. They operate Swordfish, Seafire, Hellcat and Avenger aircraft.

In the wardroom I met Lieut.-Commander J. Macdermott, a Cunard-White Star officer, with purple insignia of the engineer between his two and a half criss-cross rings of gold lace, one of six still in the ship of the original crew who took her over at Pascagoola, Missouri. He was at Salerno, where in covering the landing the Battler lost all her 24 Seafires.

The wardroom was plainly equipped with American furniture. The ante-room looked like a shore café; there was a small bar in one corner. The dining-room had long tables in parallel rows. Officers' cabins in a carrier are always rather cramped, because officer personnel is 50 to 100 per cent relatively greater than in a battleship or cruiser. The cabin I entered had two superimposed bunks, drawers for clothes, a writing-desk and a chair. To wash and shave one went along to the toilet; being an American ship, showers took the place of the British personal immersion baths.

The ratings' mess had long tables and benches, and on one side a cafeteria with American articles—Camels and Lucky Strike cigarettes, chewing gum, Ipana toothpaste, Coca-Cola and other soft drinks. I expected to find that this novelty would appeal, but one of the Petty Officers I spoke to said he would be glad to see British goods instead—perhaps nostalgic sentiment.

The galley was like a modern shore kitchen, with electric cooking, monel metal sinks and boilers. The warship atmosphere was absent between decks. No hammocks were slung in the passages. Ratings slept in beds that folded to give more room when not in use. I gathered they were not too popular, because beds are easier to fall out of when the ship rolls.

I saw the workshop with lathes, a paint-shop, carpenter's shop, boatswain's store, and laundry; a first-class operating theatre with sterilizers, X-ray, and a full, fixed operating table with operating lights; an excellently equipped surgery; and a comfortable sick bay with clean white sheets and an air of passenger comfort.

The machinery space occupied one section of the hull, wherein all the engine units were collected—the boilers, high and low pressure turbines geared to a single shaft, auxiliary plant driving dynamos, compressors and pumps. Steel ladders, catwalks and platforms, all slippery with oil, were the means by which we reached every unit in this compartment of the hull.

Asbestos-Clad Fire-Fighters in Readiness With Extinguishers

Two 4-in. high angle guns aft and two twin-Bofors guns fore and aft were the main armament. On various parts of the ship were eight twin and two single Oerlikons with gyro sights. From the aft Bofors platform I watched some Seafires coming on—looking straight up at the belly of the fuselage a few feet above my head as they crossed the stern.

From the bridge I watched some pupils ("smogs") landing on. The first Seafire made a good landing. The second was perilously near the port side. The third hit the deck aft of the first arrester cable, bounced into the air, swerved, came down, crashed the under-carriage and was saved from going over the side when his tail wheel picked up one of the forward arrester cables. A fourth crashed because its deck-landing hook broke, and it was badly damaged by running into the crash barrier; petrol swilled over the deck. Asbestos-clad fire-fighters were ready, as usual, with fire-foam extinguishers; but there was no fire, and no one was hurt.

Due to their very blind forward vision when gliding slowly, the Seafire and Corsair are regarded as two of the most difficult aircraft to land on. And a Seafire, with its finger-tip controls, is not an easy aircraft to curve semi-stalled down to the flight deck. Pilots who deck-fly them deserve admiration.

When the call came for me to man aircraft, I said good-bye to Capt. Norman, thanking him for his courtesy, and walked aft. I climbed into the radio-operator's central compartment in the Avenger whose 1,600 h.p. Cyclone engine was already ticking over, and closed the sliding roof sideways over my head. A raucous hooting sounded as Wormald moved the control to spread the wings, warning everyone to get out of the way as the wings swung forward automatically and locked into flying position. As he opened the throttle with the brakes on, another siren hooted to indicate that the under-carriage was locked down. The 14-cylinder air-cooled radial engine roared, and we were off.

The "island" flashed past in a confused blur just beyond the starboard wingtip—we spanned 54 of the ship's 80-ft. wide flight deck—and then we were over the bow and in the air. It did not seem that we rose before reaching the end of the flight deck, but I supposed that Wormald, with his experience of deck flying, did not attempt to pull up until he was well clear of the ship. There is plenty of sea room for an aircraft flying at the height of a flight deck in normal weather.

Escort Carriers: the Take-Off and the Land-On

SWORDFISH TORPEDO-BOMBER, part of the tail of which is seen in the foreground (1), has just taken off from the carrier H.M.S. Biter. The Battler (2), escort carrier visited by our Air Correspondent, is here seen from one of her aircraft. Deck Flying Control Officer (3) sometimes signals aircraft by means of handlamps. The Biter (4) as it appeared to a pilot about to land-on. See facing page.

Photos, British Official

The Editor Looks Back

As my readers know, I have maintained in "The War Illustrated" from its first number a page of personal notes on the more human interests of these six years as they have engaged my thoughts. In the earlier days of excitement and apprehension I registered especially my own reactions to the events of the moment, and at the end of 1940 a selection of these was published, called "As The Days Go By . . ." In turning over the pages of that book again I find so much in it which has assumed a new interest in the five years that have passed since it appeared, that I now offer my readers a series of extracts with a new commentary, which I hope may prove of exceptional interest now that we can all look back from the more pleasant viewpoint of "Afterwards."

HOPE REALIZED — Sept. 9, 1939

Looking at the first number of my old War Illustrated (1914–19) tonight, I find that H. G. Wells wrote in a famous contribution to that publication, "This Prussian Imperialism has been for forty years an intolerable nuisance in the earth." And we thought we had ended it in 1918 ! But like the professor who was recently attacked and pursued by the head and upper part of a venomous snake, after three-fourths of its body had been severed, the bestial thing assails us again in the form of Nazi Imperialism. Germany, Prussianized or Nazified, is indeed an intolerable nuisance on the earth, and I hope to live to see the whole foul brood of Nazi warmongers in their graves or each in that Doorn whence there is no return.

Well, that hope at least has been fulfilled and in living to witness its fulfilment I have had some reward for the six years of discomfort, anxiety and frustration which, in common with all who have not hitched their wagon to the star of Bureaucracy, I have had to endure. The "Doorn" mentioned was a reference, now obscured by the astounding course of events, to the last retreat of the abominable war-monger who plunged the world into the first world-wide conflict of 1914–18. Holland's "neutrality" from which he profited by spending his inglorious years in felling trees before he was peacefully buried, was one of the first things which his Nazi successors swept away. Alas, poor Holland !

THE BOGEY MEN — Sept. 9, 1939

"Do you think we'll win ?" I was asked last night by a young "lit'ry gent" of the true Bloomsbury blend. "If we had many of your sort, I'd not be too sure," was my ready, if rude, reply. He didn't knock me down. That's the only instance of doubt I have registered so far, and if you saw the weedy propounder of the query you would not be surprised at his trend of thought. I have, however, met again a bogey man of yore . . . famous author, too. He has written voluminously on European politics out of a plenitude of ignorance and talks always with a whispering "d'y' know ?" when unfolding his tale of terror. As nothing that he ever prophesied came to pass, I will not be so unkind to him as to mention the hair-raising horrors he foresees for those of us who carry on our jobs chiefly in central London's streaming roar . . . now reduced to the pleasant murmur of a big cathedral city.

The first of these persons unnamed has long ago redeemed himself ; by pen and voice he has done service of real value to the War effort, so that the Tennysonian line about "more faith in honest doubt" is once more vindicated. The other bogey man has been dead for years, possibly hastened to his grave by sheer pessimism, a delight in debunking, and a lack of faith in his own countrymen. Faith in victory is the first element of its achievement.

BRITISH QUALITIES — Sept. 9, 1939

Americans may be star organizers. But I conceived a new admiration for my own people when I saw how they handled scores of thousands of children and mothers evacuated to a reception area near my seaside home. And when I arrived in a childless London, passing through continuous scenes of evacuation on its fourth day, I felt that I had witnessed an absolute triumph in which care, solicitude, courage and human effort were all compact.

America's part at D-Day, 1944, gives point to my reflection at the beginning of the two years in which Britain stood alone except for those few deceptive months of "the Phoney War" when an impotent Belgium and an irresolute France were with her in arms. The British qualities I specified in my note endured all the way to V Day. And still endure !

FUTILE PROPAGANDA — Sept. 16, 1939

A few days before the fateful September 1, I collected in my club reading-room about a dozen British newspapers and periodicals with large pictorial advertisements of the scenic attractions of Germany and invitations to visit them. "Camouflage !" I remarked to the friends to whom I showed them. Camouflage they proved to be. When the treacherous rogues were lavishly pushing out these advertisements to suggest a peaceful playground for British tourists, the U-boats had already been a week or two on their way to their ocean stations with instructions to sink Allied ships at sight and "without trace" as soon as they got the word that war was "on." But at a future day Dr. Goebbels . . . if there is still a Dr. Goebbels . . . will point out these advertisements to his poor deluded countrymen as evidence that Germany was asking for British tourists when the perfidious English were scheming to go to war with their peace-loving Fuehrer. Childish, yet it might easily deceive the somewhat simple-minded German.

But there isn't a Dr. Goebbels any more, as I had half anticipated from the start, so the folly of that propaganda looks all the more foolish today when all the vast machinery of Nazi organization has crumbled in the dusty desert that was Berlin.

GOERING SCREAMS — Sept. 16, 1939

Goering has often been described as a moderating influence on the madder moods of the Fuehrer, but those who listened to his hyena-like howlings when he spoke last Saturday at the unnamed munitions factory in Berlin will agree that "moderation" can have no meaning for such a screamingly ferocious fire-eater . . . And yet in his speech, for all its bitterness against Britain, there was evidence of at least some small doubt about the issue, in the alleged willingness to discuss peace at a relatively early date. As our War Cabinet chose that same day, and almost the very hour, to state that they were contemplating a war of three years' duration, Field-Marshal Goering—famed as a *raconteur* of bawdy stories, by the by—may have many other opportunities of screaming his faithfulness to his Fuehrer, whom he pretends to revere as Germany incarnate. But a time will come when the scream no longer signifies defiance.

To which I need only add that the time has not only come, but is now long past, and the Screamer is even now appearing, with his colleagues in iniquity who still survive, before the tribunal of Justice with no scream—unless it be of mental anguish—left in him.

PROPHECY FULFILLED — Sept. 16, 1939

"Not a bomb will be dropped on London," a friend—who lives snugly in the country—assured me yesterday. He has the H. N. Brailsford notion that the Nazis will refrain from London terrorism out of fear that Berlin would quickly be made to suffer equally. Maybe, and again maybe not. But my old friend Bogey, mentioned last week, who spent a month or two studying things in Berlin shortly before the war, assures me that the total destruction of Berlin would not bother Hitler and would make no difference to the course of the war, whereas . . . Isn't it dreadful, the things they say ?

The War Cabinet's preparation for "a long war" is strictly in accord with Kitchener's prevision at the start of the 1914 struggle, when all Germans and most British expected a short, decisive trial of strength. This is a war to end Hitlerism and it will go on until Hitlerism is ended.

It has just been revealed that the ration cards issued to the deluded Germans by their villainous government at the outbreak of war were dated 1938. What say those who assured Chamberlain a year ago that he had only to "stand up" to the Hitler gangsters and they'd knuckle down ? They were clearly "all set" for war before Munich.

When this war is done, Hitler will surely be dead . . . possibly by his own hand . . . or behind prison bars . . . These may be uncertainties, but the certainty is that there will be neither a Hitler nor Hitlerism in Germany to disturb the peace of Europe for generations to come.

Comment on these last four paragraphs is hardly needed. But the reader I think will agree with me in considering them worth re-reading at this distance of time, with the reservation that we must wait a little longer to see the ultimate burial of Hitlerism as I so confidently predicted six years ago.

In Britain Now: Hail and Farewell to Heroes

S.S. STRATHMORE docked at Southampton on November 11, 1945, and was given a rousing welcome, with a regimental band playing lustily (right). The troopship carried 3,750 officers and men of the 2nd Div. of the 14th Army from the Far East for demobilization.

THE DYNAMOS, Moscow's famed soccer players, opened their whirlwind visit here on November 13, 1945, when they drew three-all with Chelsea at Stamford Bridge. They came on to the field (below) bearing posies, which they presented to their opposite numbers in the home team—a custom common at Continental sports meetings. Later they defeated Cardiff City by 10—1 and Arsenal by 4—3. The latter game (played at Tottenham, N. London, November 21) was almost obscured by dense fog.

FAREWELL PARADE OF R.A.A.F. VETERAN SQUADRON in this country took place at Mountbatten, Plymouth, on October 31, 1945, when they were addressed by Air Commodore G. H. Boyce (left foreground, back to camera) before returning to Australia on the S.S. Athlone Castle. No. 10 was the first squadron of the R.A.A.F. to go into operation in Britain, which they did early in 1940. They flew over 4,000,000 miles with Sunderland flying-boats of Coastal Command, destroying 8 enemy ships and damaging 16.

Photos, P.N.A., Central Press, G.P.U.

Smiles on Czech National Independence Day

CELEBRATED FOR THE FIRST TIME SINCE 1938, Czechoslovakia's Independence Day rejoicings went with a swing on October 28, 1945. The British Army was represented at the parade of Allied troops, held in the capital's Stadium to mark the notable occasion, by men of the 78th Division led by the pipe band of the Royal Irish Fusiliers. This Czech girl, resplendent in richly-embroidered peasant costume, tried out her few words of English on a Fusilier sergeant as they waited for the display. The Republic was founded in 1918. *Photo, British Official*

Printed in England and published every alternate Friday by the Proprietors, THE AMALGAMATED PRESS, LTD., The Fleetway House, Farringdon Street, London, E.C.4. Registered for transmission by Canadian Magazine Post. Sole Agents for Australia and New Zealand: Messrs. Gordon & Gotch, Ltd.; and for South Africa: Central News Agency, Ltd.—December 7, 1945. S.S. *Editorial Address:* JOHN CARPENTER HOUSE, WHITEFRIARS, LONDON, E.C.4.

Vol 9 The War Illustrated No 222

and AFTERWARDS

SIXPENCE DECEMBER 21, 1945

HERMANN GOERING AND RUDOLF HESS IN THE DOCK at Nuremberg were among 20 surviving leaders of the Third Reich figuring in the great trial which opened on November 20, 1945. All the accused, arraigned as major war criminals before an International Tribunal, pleaded "Not Guilty." Lord Justice Lawrence, the British president of the Tribunal, described the trial as "unique in the history of the jurisprudence of the world." See story in page 537. *Photo, Planet News*

Edited by Sir John Hammerton

NO. 223 WILL BE PUBLISHED FRIDAY JANUARY 4, 1946

Important Far Eastern Business for the R.A.F.

AIRCREWS OF THE FLYING HORSE SQUADRON of R.A.F. Transport Command in the Far East gathered round one of their aircraft (1). During November 1945 they dropped supplies to our troops in Siam, Indo-China, and Malaya, besides flying P.O.W. from Singapore. Spitfire pilots at Kowloon, near Hongkong, with "Big Wings" and "Little Wings," two Chinese boys (2) adopted by their squadron. A private of the R.A.F. Regiment (3) guards ingots of tin left behind by the Japanese at Penang, Malaya

Photos, British Official

Grasping the Palestine Nettle

By
KENNETH WILLIAMS

The setting-up of a joint Anglo-American committee of inquiry into political, economic and social conditions in Palestine as they urgently bear on the problem of Jewish immigration was announced on November 13, 1945, by Mr. Ernest Bevin and President Truman. This was a notable advance on previous attempts at settling a most thorny question, the background to which is simply explained in this article specially written for "The War Illustrated."

To judge from the very wide measure of approval which Mr. Bevin's statement in the House of Commons on November 13 won from many different sections of opinion, one might almost think that the Palestine problem had been solved. In fact, however, the Foreign Secretary's masterly analysis, in which were to be perceived alike a warm sympathy for persecuted Jewry and a belief in the Arabs' renaissance, only indicated the circumstances and the means by which such a solution might be reached.

Mr. Bevin has attempted to grasp the nettle; and he well knows how many of his predecessors have been stung by that same nettle. But boldly he has helped to disentangle the problem from the mass of misconceptions, some the result of propaganda, others of ignorance, in which the Palestine problem has lain for at least twenty-five years.

The Foreign Secretary showed, for example, that it is wrong to regard the Zionists as representing the whole of Jewry, though he omitted to confess that hitherto the British Government itself has contributed to that error by agreeing to allow the Jewish Agency to represent the Jewish people. He showed that the British Government feels itself bound to honour the pledge of helping to construct a Jewish National Home in Palestine, though he did not define what is meant by a "Home."

British Blood to Keep the Peace

Also he has pointed out that the 1917 Balfour Declaration in which that pledge was set down was a unilateral declaration, made without consultation with a people vitally concerned in its implementation, namely, the Arabs. He showed, again, that the claim that all persecuted Jews who have survived the Nazi terror wish to live in Palestine, needs, and will receive, investigation. And he showed that Palestine can never alone solve the whole Jewish problem.

This analysis was certainly an advance on all previous statements by the Mandatory Power for Palestine. But it did not add to the world's knowledge of conditions in Palestine itself. That, indeed, would scarcely be possible. For it is probable that on no problem with which the British Government has been faced since the First Great War has there been so much written and spoken. Countless books, pamphlets and articles have been published setting forth rival views; several Government Commissions have reported on their investigations; and—what to this country is most important of all in giving Britain an insight into the human questions involved—British blood has been shed in the endeavour to keep the peace.

Certainly there is no territory in the world that arouses more inflammable emotions. It touches the heart of the three great monotheistic religions—Judaism, Christianity and Islam. Thus we hear much of Jewish rights therein, much of Arab rights therein; and, amid the din of these two conflicting voices, increasingly of British rights therein.

Various motives have been attributed to Britain for assuming the Mandate for Palestine after the First Great War. Let it not be thought that she took that Mandate reluctantly, or that it was forced on her by the League of Nations, which in 1922 only ratified what was already an accomplished fact. It is sometimes overlooked that it was predominantly British arms which liberated Palestine from the Ottoman Turk: a victory without which neither Jewish nor Arab voices could have become so clamant as they are today. Now of the British motives in consenting to carry the burden of Palestine there was one more powerful than any others: the strategic motive.

It is a cardinal interest of the British Empire that there shall be peace in the lands of the Middle East that lie athwart her communications to India and the Empire beyond India. Nor is there anything unworthy in such a motive, the more particularly if, as has been indicated in the conference which the Foreign Secretary had with his Middle Eastern advisers this autumn, Britain assists the social stature of the countries that lie on either side of the Suez Canal.

But the attainment of tranquillity in Palestine has been elusive. It has proved a sore which has threatened to poison the whole Middle East. There have been periods of quiet there, during which Arab fears of being dominated by the Zionists were not so acute as they have latterly become; but those fears have been in existence ever since the Balfour Declaration was promulgated.

With the access of increasing numbers, the Zionists, more discreet in the earlier years of the Mandate, have since declared that they aim openly at the creation of a Jewish State, to be established from immigration, whether legal or illegal. It is their increasing pretensions which, in part at any rate, have furthered the establishment of the Arab League, that collection of Arab States which is sworn to defend the Arab cause in Palestine. (See page 398, Vol. 8.) Thus have international forces been posed one against the other.

No Conceivable Compromise Here

Now what, stripped of all verbiage and humbug, is the basic issue in Palestine? It is, in my view, this: Shall the Zionists—as that section of Jewry which is Nationalist and wishes to form a separate Jewish National State in Palestine is called—be allowed to impose their will on a country for which Britain holds the Mandate?

Seen thus, it is an ethical question. All other aspects, indubitably important, such as the plight of persecuted Jews in Europe, the religious aspect of Palestine, the aspirations of the Arab League, and so on, are, from the point of view of the Briton, really subsidiary. True, there are a multitude of factors, such as the safety of Imperial communications, which no Briton will overlook; but, as I say, it is fundamentally an ethical question.

From that aspect, what is called "natural right" is opposed to what is called "historical right." The Arabs of Palestine—and I call the majority of its inhabitants Arabs, whatever they be scientifically, for if not Arab by race they are, of whatever creed, Arabized—assert that they have what they term an elementary or natural right to be free, at some future time, to determine their own destiny, in a country where they have been for thirteen centuries. The Zionists, appealing to the time when they were masters of parts of Palestine (until they were conquered by the Romans in A.D. 70) assert that they are entitled to numerical superiority in a land which made their name famous throughout the world, and that they are so entitled whether the Arabs agree or not.

Between such points of view there is no conceivable compromise. Both sides claim documentary support. But the closest study of the relevant documents can lead to no conclusion which both parties are willing to accept. And so the air has become full of irrelevant cries, of which perhaps the most absurd is that the Arabs are "anti-Semitic." You can hear it said, even in Palestine, that Jews and Arabs can work peacefully together. Of course they can. That is no new phenomenon. For centuries in Arab lands Jews have been co-operating with the majority of the population; the record of the Arabs towards the Jews is, indeed, infinitely better than that of many European peoples. But to pit such a fact against the long history of Zionist-Arab strife in Palestine since 1919 is simply to miss the point that the Zionists are Jews with a difference.

If Mr. Bevin's 'Great Dream' is Realized

Again, you can hear it said with truth that the Zionists have brought great material benefits to the Arabs of Palestine. What matters is, not the truth of such assertions but their inappropriateness. The soul of a people threatened with domination is unaffected by such considerations. I say, therefore, that this question of Palestine is now a matter which can be resolved by no such side-arguments. Every individual, possessed of the fundamental data, must determine it in his own conscience, and should not allow pro-Jewish or pro-Arab sentiment to affect his conclusion.

Now, what are the prospects in Palestine? Few students of recent Palestinian history would care to prophesy with any degree of finality. Too often have hopes been deferred, and the cynical may well agree with Lord Passfield when, as Colonial Secretary, he referred to Palestine as "that recurring decimal." All that the prudent can do is to point to probabilities.

First, it seems that the idea of a Jewish State in Palestine, which was never promised and is a gloss put by Zionists on the Balfour Declaration as they have grown in strength, will never be realized, whatever be the size of the future Jewish National Home. Second, the notion of the political Zionists, that they will be enabled to enjoy a majority in Palestine, and will therefore be in a position (whatever their pretensions to the contrary) to dominate the Arabs, is chimerical. Third, the fact the Mandatory Power will at every stage consult Arab as well as Jewish opinion, appears to rule out the imposition by force of an unpopular policy on the Arabs. Fourth, the dispersal of their most cherished hopes is not likely to be taken quietly by thousands of well-armed, well-organized and well-trained Jews in Palestine.

Of this last contingency the Mandatory Power is, of course, well aware, and the Foreign Secretary has significantly stated that force will be met by force. But, if reason prevails, there may yet be fulfilled Mr. Bevin's "great dream"—and what a dream it is at present only those fully know who are intimately acquainted with present Middle Eastern conditions—of a revivified region of some 600,000,000 people stretching from the Nile valley to India.

In such a rebirth the Jews, if they wished, could play a great part, not as separatist but as integrating agents. Their genius could be of extreme value to a people awakening from a long slumber and only now trying to master Western technique. At the moment, the mood of the Zionists is opposed to any such developments; they want to be masters and the servants of none. They are politically chauvinistic. Yet this may be but a phase in the long history of the Jews.

Our Army Now Fights for Law and Order

By MAJ.-GENERAL SIR CHARLES GWYNN K.C.B., D.S.O.

When the Empire was expanding during the Victorian era the British Army was constantly engaged in what it is customary to call small wars. In some cases these wars had some of the character of police operations ; but as a rule they definitely were wars, inasmuch as they were waged against an enemy and in territory not yet included in the Empire. There was therefore no limitation to the degree of force that might legitimately be used against our opponents, although the scale of operations was generally kept to a minimum determined by financial considerations—a minimum occasionally fixed so low that it led initially to regrettable incidents and proved in the end to be false economy.

Since the enemy as a rule lacked organization and up-to-date armament, losses to our troops were, however, seldom serious, and the chief difficulties encountered were those of operating over long distances in undeveloped country. Official manuals dealt with the tactics the troops should adopt in fighting enemies with very varying characteristics, and in countries which presented conditions ranging from mountain to desert warfare ; but maintenance of supplies was, as a rule, the governing factor in dictating strategy.

From the beginning of this century, and particularly after the First Great War, the role of the army altered considerably. Although its services were as constantly required as formerly they definitely assumed the character of police duties, often as dangerous and always without the attractions of what used to rank as active service. The Army, of course, had always been, and still is, liable to be called in to aid the civil power, in which case normally the troops take such action as the civil authorities require. In India this is a frequent occurrence.

But there are occasions when either the civil Government is unable to function or the Army is required to intervene to protect British or international interests in foreign territory where the local Government is incapable or unwilling to maintain order. On these occasions operations on an extensive scale for which the military commander assumes responsibility may be necessary. In extreme cases when Martial Law is proclaimed the civil Government ceases to exercise its authority in the area affected, and its machinery is placed at the disposal of the military authorities.

Actually, Martial Law is seldom proclaimed and there is frequently a somewhat unsatisfactory division of responsibility. In practically all cases, however, there is a limiting obligation on troops to use only the minimum degree of force that the situation demands ; and this generally precludes the use of the more powerful weapons, the effects of which cannot be rigorously controlled. It is this obligation which chiefly differentiates police operations from small wars, and it is the main reason why the police duties are disliked by the Army, for it may throw on quite junior officers the responsibility for deciding what degree of force can legitimately be used.

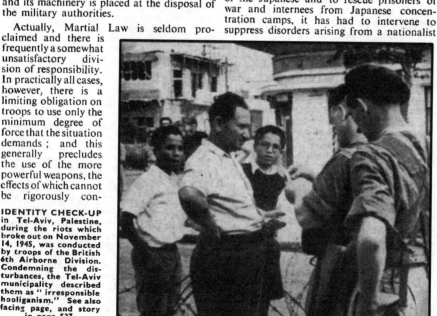

IDENTITY CHECK-UP in Tel-Aviv, Palestine, during the riots which broke out on November 14, 1945, was conducted by troops of the British 6th Airborne Division. Condemning the disturbances, the Tel-Aviv municipality described them as "irresponsible hooliganism." See also facing page, and story in page 537.
Photo, British Official

Difficult Decisions Involved in Dealing With Fanatical Elements

There are, of course, cases in which the limitation does not operate, as when organized armed bands carry on guerilla warfare. But even then difficult problems may arise when the bands are rounded up in peaceful villages, or when the attitude of the ordinary inhabitants is doubtful. It is particularly difficult to decide how much force should be used when riotous mobs have to be dealt with, for though they may include dangerous and fanatical elements the mass is probably only suffering from a form of hysteria and may include women and children caught up unwittingly in the crowd.

Another factor that differentiates modern police operations from small wars of the past is that whereas in the latter our opponents were ill-armed, in modern operations—especially during the aftermath of war—the fanatical elements of resistance often possess weapons as effective as those the troops employ. The troops may have the advantage of using armoured vehicles, but on the other hand the use of artillery or bombing by aircraft is seldom justifiable. Air co-operation is in general restricted to machine-gunning from low altitudes, and that entails considerable risks from small-arms fire.

The object of police operations is, of course, not conquest but to restore law and order without leaving a legacy of bitterness when the object is attained. This calls for a high standard of discipline and forbearance on the part of the troops, and is particularly the case when intervention in other people's quarrels draws hostility to themselves.

The Army can seldom have had a more difficult task than faces it in Netherlands India. Sent there to receive the surrender of the Japanese and to rescue prisoners of war and internees from Japanese concentration camps, it has had to intervene to suppress disorders arising from a nationalist revolt against the re-establishment of the Netherlands Government, which had ceased to exist during the Japanese Occupation. In that dispute there is no question of intervention, except so far as the British authorities are willing to provide facilities for negotiations to be opened between the disputants.

They cannot, however, allow interference with the execution of their original mission both on humanitarian grounds and owing to the necessity of disarming and repatriating Japanese forces. Nor can they avoid taking counter-action against the Indonesians who have attacked our troops and committed atrocities. The situation is complicated by the fact that Japanese arms have fallen into the hands of unauthorized persons, and Japanese troops have assisted the Indonesians. Counter-action is, however, limited by the obligation to use no more force than can be justified, an obligation all the greater owing to the large numbers of peaceful Indonesians, Chinese, and others who would suffer if force were not strictly controlled.

Japs Were Employed to Prevent Surrendered Arms Going Astray

The fact that neither the Netherlands Government nor the Indonesians have adequate disciplined forces to maintain order throws immensely greater responsibility on the British force. Owing to the nature of the outrages and the quality of the weapons in the hands of extremists more force than is usual in police operations has of necessity been used, though not nearly as much as it is in our power to employ.

In Indo-China, British troops have had a similar mission to that in Java ; but fortunately there, though firm action was needed, the situation has not developed so seriously. The Japanese surrendered their arms to proper authority and were even employed to prevent them falling into wrong hands. Moreover, the local Vichy Government had never been entirely displaced by the Japanese ; and with substantial reinforcements arriving from France, responsibility for maintaining order can be left to French troops when the British mission is completed.

In Palestine, which has been the scene of many serious police operations since Britain assumed the mandate, the situation is threatening and difficult. Between the two great wars most of the trouble arose from Arab resentment to the influx of Jews which gave rise to active hostility to the mandatory Government, and to attacks on the poorly armed Jews. But since the late war, hostility to the Government has mainly been displayed by Jewish extremists who are now well armed and organized.

Troops have been needed to assist the strong Palestine police for the protection of Government property, to quell rioting and to arrest illegal immigrants ; although operations on the scale previously employed against the Arabs have so far not been necessary. At present the Arabs are content to watch developments ; but the danger obviously exists that, should they consider too great concessions are made to Jewish claims, civil war between Jews and Arabs may break out, with both sides hostile to the mandatory power. It is not surprising, therefore, that the garrison has been reinforced.

This is far from completing the tale of the Army's recent police duties ; but it should suffice to show that they are no less important and onerous, and infinitely more distasteful, than waging small wars. Moreover, they are duties which will not be rendered unnecessary by whatever the future of the atom bomb may be—nor can air power relieve the Army of the greater part of them.

In Palestine with Our 6th Airborne Division

1

2

3

IN TEL-AVIV, a Canadian dispatch rider (1) gave latest news of the situation to a patrol of the 6th Airborne Division which had been rushed to the Palestine city on November 14, 1945, following the outbreak of serious rioting. Pathetic sidelight on the outbreak was its coincidence with the arrival from Europe of Jewish immigrants who had suffered under Hitler. As they landed at Haifa their baggage was searched for arms (2).

Lt.-Gen. Sir Alan Cunningham, K.C.B., D.S.O. (3), former G.O.C. Eastern Command, the newly-appointed High Commissioner for Palestine and Transjordan arrived in Jerusalem on November 21 without incident. G.O.C. British Troops in Palestine and Transjordan is Maj.-Gen. J. C. D'Arcy, C.B.E., M.C. (4). En route by lorry for their posts in Tel-Aviv are these cheerful parachute troops (5).

Photos, Topical, Associated Press

4

5

A Keel is Laid

By
FRANCIS E. McMURTRIE

In no British industry are post-war prospects more encouraging than in shipbuilding. From every quarter there is a demand for new ships to replace the vast tonnage lost in the war. Not only in this country, but also in Allied countries such as Norway, France and Holland there is a strong preference for the well-designed types of merchantmen for the construction of which British yards have long been famous. By the end of the September quarter the tonnage actually under construction in the United Kingdom was close on 1,500,000 tons, and this figure has been considerably increased.

Though a great many vessels were built in the war years these were of a "utility" type, turned out rapidly by mass production methods to serve the needs of the emergency. For peacetime trading they would be unsatisfactory. Thus their existence does little to meet the shortage, beyond possibly providing a stop-gap in some directions while orders for new tonnage are being executed.

On signing a contract for a large ship, such as the 30,000-ton Cunard-White Star liner ordered from Messrs. John Brown & Co., Ltd., of Clydebank, there is a good deal of preparatory work which must be got through before actual construction starts. If the design is an entirely new one and not the repeat of a previous order, tests with paraffin wax models will be carried out in the experimental tanks of the National Physical Laboratory at Teddington. Once the hull form is approved, its contour must be drawn on a flat surface while calculations are made of the amount of steel and other materials required and of the labour which will be needed for the job.

Plans are then laid out in what is known as the moulding loft, a vast, low-roofed structure with a smooth black floor, well lighted from above. Here full-sized drawings of the various parts of the vessel's main structure are sketched in chalk. From these drawings the necessary curves are taken off with wooden battens, which serve as patterns for the vessel's framework. Wooden moulds are constructed for the heavy plates, the position of every rivet hole and the contours of each curve and twist being exactly determined.

Various departments of the shipyard are thus enabled to begin their operations. Panelling and furnishings are ordered. Steel from the foundries is prepared for rolling and forging into the necessary shapes, and finished off to form a skeleton framing. All metal so used must pass tests which will satisfy the surveyors of the Board of Trade and of Lloyd's Register. Quantities have to be calculated with absolute accuracy, so that the weight may not be excessive while at the same time maintaining the necessary strength in the hull.

Electric Cranes Place Each Rib of the Vessel's Skeleton in Position

Usually a building berth is available in the yard, unless the ship is of exceptional size and requires a new one to be prepared or an old one enlarged. On a slope known as a slipway are placed a number of large wooden keel blocks. On these blocks are laid the horizontal steel plates forming the keel (see facing page). At right-angles to these plates, in the centreline of the ship, is secured the vertical keel; a huge steel girder which may be compared to the backbone of the ship. Attached to it by angle-bars are the "floors," vertical steel plates running out to the ship's side from the centreline keel. From this foundation rise the ribs of the framing, surrounded by wooden scaffolding. Each rib is placed in position by electric cranes with a delicate touch which is eloquent of the efficiency and skill of the experienced workers in charge of the operation. Ultimately the structure is riveted or welded together, ready to be clothed in steel plates.

Teams of shipyard workers are engaged in the business of fixing in position the side framing, starting amidships and gradually extending in either direction towards stem and stern. Ultimately the ship becomes a fully proportioned skeleton, upon which the shell-plating can be placed as flesh rests upon bones. Before this can be done, enormous beams that span the ship's interior have to be worked into place as supports for the various decks, the number of which in a large liner may approach a dozen. One of the principal finishing touches in the main construction is the erection of the massive stem and stern frames. These are of solid cast steel; the weight of the stern frame and brackets that support the propeller shafts is likely to exceed 100 tons in the case of so large a ship as the big new Cunard-White Star liner at Clydebank. Like a smaller ship building there for the same owners, the 13,500-ton liner "629," she will be known by a yard number until she receives her name on launching.

It is understood that she is likely to be of somewhat similar type to the existing Mauretania (second big liner to bear that name), which was delivered in 1939. With a gross tonnage of 35,677, this passenger liner is over 771 ft. in extreme length, with a beam (or breadth amidships) of just under 90 ft. She is propelled by six steam turbines geared to two propeller shafts, and is capable of a sea speed of 23 knots. Though overshadowed in size and speed by the giant liners Queen Elizabeth and Queen Mary, she is nevertheless a very large ship and is understood to have proved remarkably successful in service.

She is merely one of the various specialized types of ships now on order or under construction in British yards. Out of 387 ships on order at the end of September last no fewer than 51 were tankers, and fresh orders for such ships continue to be received. Most of them are motor vessels. This is not surprising in view of the important part that oil plays in modern civilization, and of the fact that tanker fleets suffered particularly heavily from U-boat attacks.

Holds With Refrigerating Plant to Transport Chilled Meat Cargoes

One highly specialized type of merchantman much in request is the refrigerated ship. Chilled meat comes in these vessels from such distant climes as New Zealand and Argentina. They have special holds fitted with refrigerating plant, run by expert personnel whose duty it is to ensure that the cargo arrives in first-class condition. Other holds take green fruit, which is kept sound by the skilful employment of carbon dioxide. Butter, bacon and eggs are also carried in different holds. Bananas from the West Indies and Central America constitute a different class of cargo, for which fast vessels of a particular design are employed.

Recent orders include a 13,000-ton passenger liner with much refrigerated space for the Shaw, Savill & Albion Company; half a dozen refrigerated cargo liners of 11,000 tons for the Federal Steam Navigation Co., and two of the same type for the New Zealand Shipping Co., an allied concern; and two refrigerated motorships of 8,500 tons for the Donaldson Line. Large passenger ships include two liners, of 29,000 and 23,000 tons respectively, for the P. & O. Company, and one of the former tonnage for the Orient Line; two 27,000-ton passenger ships for the Union Castle Line; a 9,200-ton passenger and cargo vessel for the Bibby Line; and a pair of passenger and cargo ships for the Elder Dempster Lines. Cargo liners for such well-known concerns as the Canadian Pacific Company, the British India Company, and the Anchor Line, besides vessels of the humbler "tramp" type are being built in very considerable numbers, and there appears to be no immediate prospect of the flow of orders slackening.

NOTE.—*In the article "What of the Merchant Navy's Future?" in page 454, the author wishes to point out that, through an oversight, the rate of war risk money was described as weekly instead of monthly. It will now be appreciated that the amount of the extra pay granted on this account to Merchant Navy personnel was even less than appeared.*

PIPED ABOARD H.M.S. BERMUDA at Tsingtao on September 24, 1945, was Admiral Sheh, of the Chinese Navy; he was greeted by Captain J. Bethell, C.B.E., R.N. The cruiser Bermuda and the destroyer Tuscan had put into the North China port with supplies for 1,800 British, U.S. and Russian internees stranded there. *Photo, British Official*

At Clydebank a New Liner Begins to Grow Up

TO REPLACE THE 'UTILITY' SHIPS of wartime building, British shipyards are clangorous with the noise of new merchant vessels coming into existence. At John Brown's Clydebank yards, Number 629 (she will be properly named on launching as a 13,500-ton Cunard-White Star liner) was cradled in November 1945. Preparing the keel for swinging into position (1). The "rise" is checked by a foreman shipwright (2). Bolting the keel-plates together (3). Assembly on the slipway blocks (4). See also facing page.

Photos, L.N.A.

They Clear Our Harbours of Death-Trap Ships

WRECK-BUOY MARKING THE GRAVE OF A SHIP (1), one of thousands round our coasts ; there are 17 at the sea-approaches to Liverpool alone. Not worth salvaging, the sunken vessels are a constant danger to shipping till blown up by divers. About to inspect the wreckage of the S.S. Innisfallen, sixty feet below the Mersey, the diver has his helmet adjusted (2). After locating the wreck he resurfaces (3) for the explosive. The boat's crew (4) wait for the detonation—at a safe distance.

Photos, Keystone

To the Glory of the 161st Brigade at Kohima

SCENE OF BURMA'S FIERCEST SIEGE, where in April 1944 the Japanese advance was halted, two men of the Royal West Kent Regiment inspect the 161st Indian Infantry Brigade Group's memorial at Kohima. It was here, for fourteen days and nights, that the garrison, just over 3,000 men, held the bridge-head to India in one of the war's most stirring engagements. On December 1, 1945, the 14th Army—for ever linked with victory in Burma—was formally disbanded. See also page 526. Vol. 8.

Photo, British Official

Has the World Quite Finished With Hitler?

Masses of conflicting evidence have been collected: the Russians are reported even to have sifted the rubble of the ruined Chancellery in Berlin in the hope of finding identifiable remains of the ex-Fuehrer. Nothing entirely conclusive has yet come to light, but the British official report, on which the following article is based, may well prove to be the "last word."

ADOLF HITLER shot himself, and Eva Braun—his wedded wife for a day—poisoned herself in the Berlin Chancellery on April 30, 1945. That is the considered conclusion of British Intelligence experts attached to the Allied Control Council in the Reich capital, propounded in a dramatic document made public on November 1.

The death of the erstwhile Fuehrer is thus presumed—at least as far as Britain and the U.S. are concerned. Russia and France, it is reported, have not yet accepted these findings as final; a fact which is said to be causing serious complications in the framing of documents concerning all Germany.

The statement describing the Fuehrer's suicide is entitled (officially) "The Last Days of Hitler and Eva Braun," and it is based largely on eye witness accounts of those last hours in what had once been a proud capital, smashed by Allied bombers and the Red Army's heavy artillery.

It appears that Hitler's original intention had been to make his escape, by air, to Berchtesgaden on April 22 and from there to continue the struggle, surrounded by his "Werewolves" and the remaining Nazi chiefs. When that day came he cancelled his departure, deciding to meet his end in the doomed capital. At about 4.30 in the afternoon he held a staff conference in the Chancellery when he at once made it evident to his advisers that he considered the war lost and that he intended to remain in Berlin to the last in defence of the city. If Berlin fell, he declared, he would die there.

Decision to Remain in Berlin

"It is clear," says the statement, "that Hitler at that time suffered from an attack of nervous prostration during which he blamed everyone but himself for the failure of Germany to win the war." His advisers, both military and civil, tried to persuade their leader to change his mind and leave Berlin, but to no avail. The Fuehrer's influence over this immediate circle of his followers was still paramount, however, for Goebbels took the same decision, and he with Martin Bormann—later to be tried at Nuremberg in his absence—Dr. Ludwig Stumpfegger, Hitler's surgeon, and other members of the personal staff, remained behind to the end.

"Hitler's breakdown on April 22," continues the statement, "was the beginning of the end. From that time he never left the bunker, surrounded no longer by soldiers but by his 'family circle,' those officers responsible directly to him for the defence of Berlin. His state of mind was reported by all who saw him to have been very much calmer after the crisis on April 22. He even gained confidence as to the outcome of the battle of Berlin."

But Hitler's regained confidence was only spasmodic. Every now and then his calm was interrupted by "tantrums" when he recalled old treacheries "and found new ones." His physical health, on the contrary, was poor. The nervous strain, the unhealthy living conditions and his eccentric hours, all told heavily on him. And yet "apart from the reported trembling of the hands, from which he had suffered for some time, and his general decrepitude, he was as 'normal' as ever in his mind."

DISSENSION had long shown itself in the Nazi hierarchy. Even Goering had fallen into complete disfavour by his endeavours to take over control from Hitler a few days earlier. On the evening of April 26, Field-Marshal Ritter von Greim reported to Hitler's bunker to receive his commission as Commander-in-Chief of the Luftwaffe—as Goering's successor. Hitler informed Greim that he had made all arrangements for the destruction of his body and that of Eva Braun "so that they would not fall into enemy hands." He gave Greim poison capsules, with which the Field-Marshal was later to kill himself. Such capsules he had already issued to all occupants of the bunker.

On April 28, news filtered through to the bunker that Himmler was trying to negotiate peace with the Allies through Count Bernadotte, head of the Swedish Red Cross. This intelligence was received with a mixture of disgust and incredulity. "During the previous three days the battle of Berlin had been drawing nearer the centre of the city," the statement goes on. "Shells were falling round the bunker, and in the early hours of April 29 it was reported that Russian tanks had broken into the Potsdamer Platz," a few hundred yards away to the south-west.

In desperation, Hitler ordered von Greim to mount a Luftwaffe attack in support of the German 12th Army, which was supposed (erroneously) to be within shelling distance of the Potsdamer Platz. Von Greim took off from the Charlottenburger Chaussee in a Luftwaffe aircraft which had been flown in to collect him. But this last slender hope was soon to be abandoned: effective relief of Berlin was beyond all human possibility.

Last Hours of Hitler and Eva Braun

On the evening of April 29 Hitler married Eva Braun, "the ceremony being performed by an official from the Propaganda Ministry in a small conference room in the bunker." The marriage may have been suggested by Eva Braun, for she had apparently always wished for "the peculiar glory" of dying with Hitler and had used her influence to persuade him to die in Berlin. The report goes on: "After the ceremony the newly-married couple shook hands with all present in the bunker and retired to their suite, with Hitler's secretary, for a marriage feast. According to her, the conversation, which had been confined to suicide, was so oppressive that she had to leave."

The last scene of all is described with grim vividness. "At about 2.30 a.m. on April 30," declares the statement, "Hitler said good-bye to about twenty people, about ten of them women, whom he had summoned from the other bunkers in the new and old Chancelleries. He shook hands with the women and spoke to most of them. On that same day, at about 2.30 p.m. orders were sent to the Transport Office, requiring the immediate dispatch to the bunker of 200 litres of petrol. Between 160 and 180 litres of petrol were collected and deposited in the garden just outside the emergency exit of the bunker.

"At about the same time, Hitler and Eva Braun made their last appearance alive. They went round the bunker and shook hands with their immediate entourage and retired to their own apartments, where they both committed suicide, Hitler by shooting himself, apparently through the mouth, Eva Braun apparently by taking poison, though she was supplied with a revolver."

AFTER the suicide, the bodies were taken into the garden outside the bunker by Goebbels, Bormann, perhaps Stumpfegger and one or two others, Hitler wrapped in a blanket, "presumably because he was bloody." The bodies were placed side by side in the garden about three yards from the emergency exit of the bunker, "and drenched with petrol."

Because of the Soviet shelling the party withdrew under the shelter of the emergency exit and "a petrol-soaked and lighted rag was thrown on the bodies, which at once caught fire. The party then stood to attention, gave the Hitler salute and retired." How often the bodies were resoaked or how long they burned is not known. One witness was informed that they burned until nothing was left; more probably they were charred until they were unrecognizable, and the bodies broken up and probably buried.

Have we finished with Hitler? "The evidence," avers the British Intelligence report, "is not complete, but it is positive, circumstantial, consistent and independent. There is no evidence whatever to support any of the theories which have been circulated, and which presuppose that Hitler is still alive. All such stories which have been reported have been investigated, and have been found to be baseless."

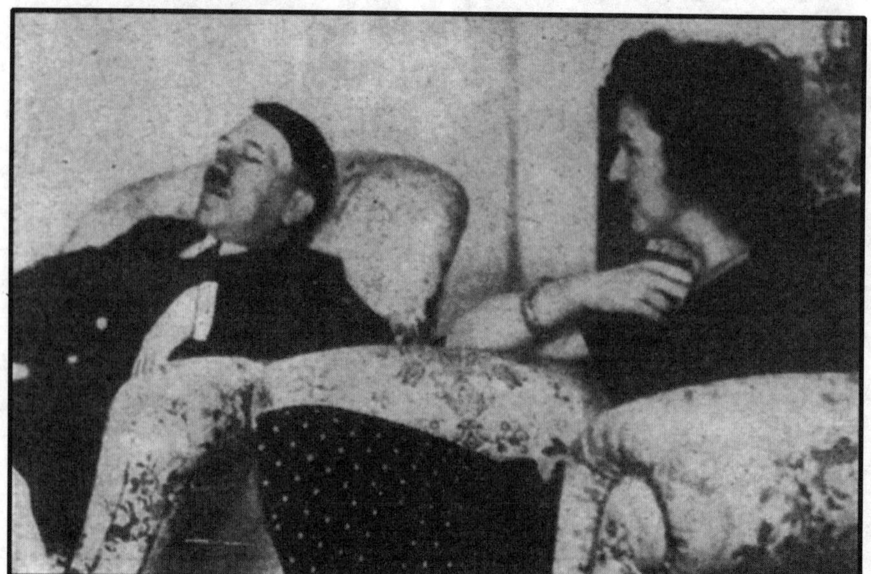

EVA BRAUN, HITLER'S WIFE FOR A DAY, seen with the Fuehrer, who seems to be taking an afternoon nap. This was one of the many photographs in her album, now in the possession of U.S Intelligence experts (see facing page). The story of her tragic marriage and of the couple's suicide is told here. *Photo, Associated Press*

Souvenirs of the Fuehrer's Private Life

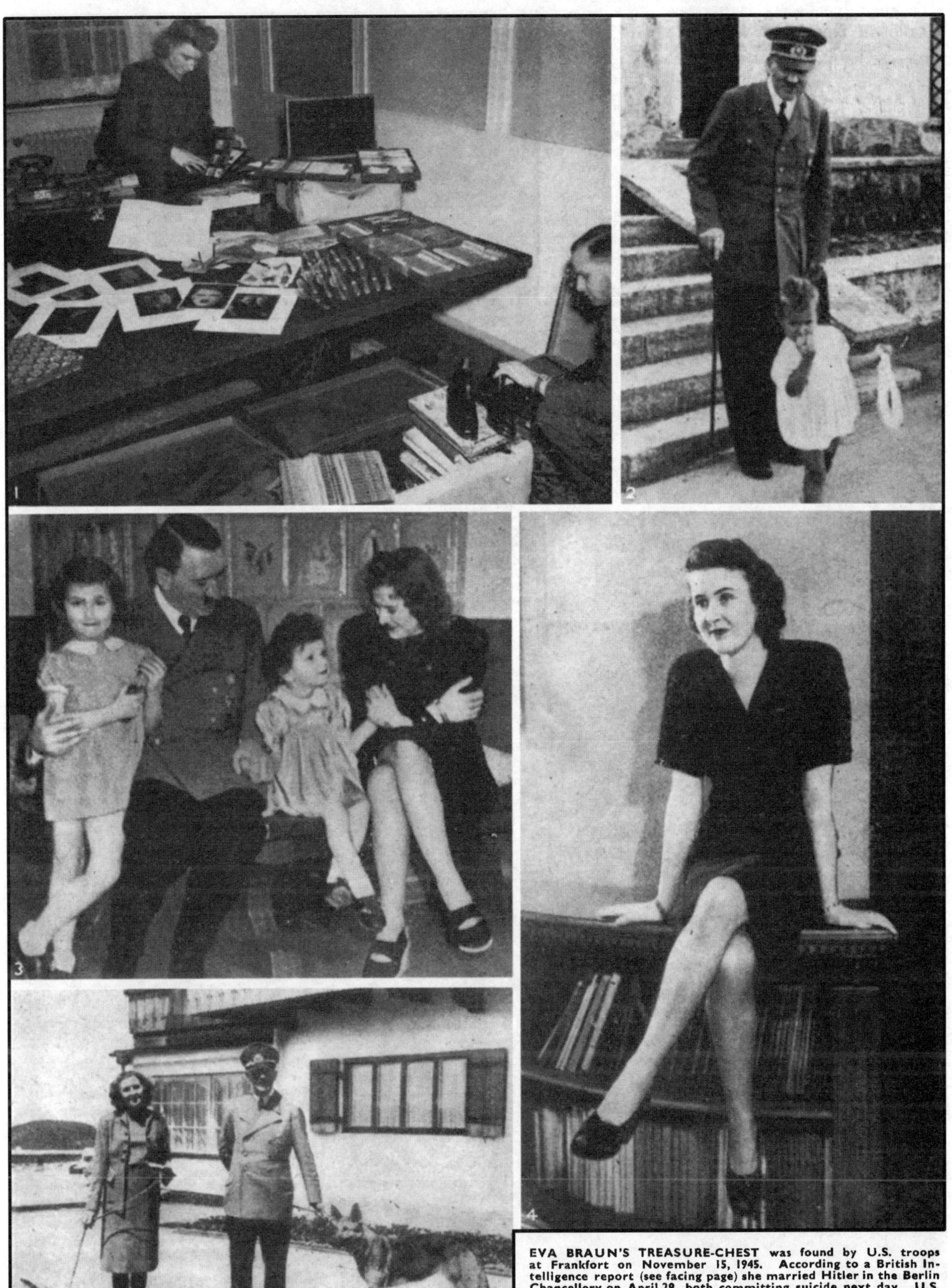

EVA BRAUN'S TREASURE-CHEST was found by U.S. troops at Frankfort on November 15, 1945. According to a British Intelligence report (see facing page) she married Hitler in the Berlin Chancellery on April 29, both committing suicide next day. U.S. officials catalogued items (1), which included British and U.S. money, jewelry and valuable postage-stamps. Among her photographs was one of Hitler and "Uschi" (2), one of two children, thought to be those of Eva's sister Gretel. Others show the children with Eva and Hitler (3); Eva herself (4); and Hitler and Eva at Berchtesgaden (5).

Photos, Associated Press Keystone

Empire Troops to Quell Strife in Batavia

ALTHOUGH INDONESIAN RESISTANCE was stiffening, Mr. Sutan A. Sjahrir, the new self-styled Premier of the "Indonesian Republic," declared on December 4, 1945, that his party would abide by any decision on the future of Indonesia taken by the United Nations in discussions between Lord Alanbrooke, Admiral Lord Louis Mountbatten and Dr. Van Mook held at Singapore on December 6. (Peace parleys held in Batavia on November 17 had broken down). The Singapore conference empowered the Allied Commander in Java to restore and maintain law and order as far as his military resources would permit.

Lt.-Gen. Sir Philip Christison, Allied C.-in-C. in Java, ordered all Netherlands and Netherlands East Indies troops to quit Batavia on November 21. The following day Gen. Sir Miles Dempsey, S.E.A.C., Land Commander, arrived in Surabaya, where a mopping-up drive had been launched by the Fifth Indian Division against Indonesians numbering close on 20,000. On November 29 it was announced that, following naval bombardment and the dropping of forty 500-lb. bombs by the R.A.F., the occupation of Surabaya was complete and a local administration set up under British control.

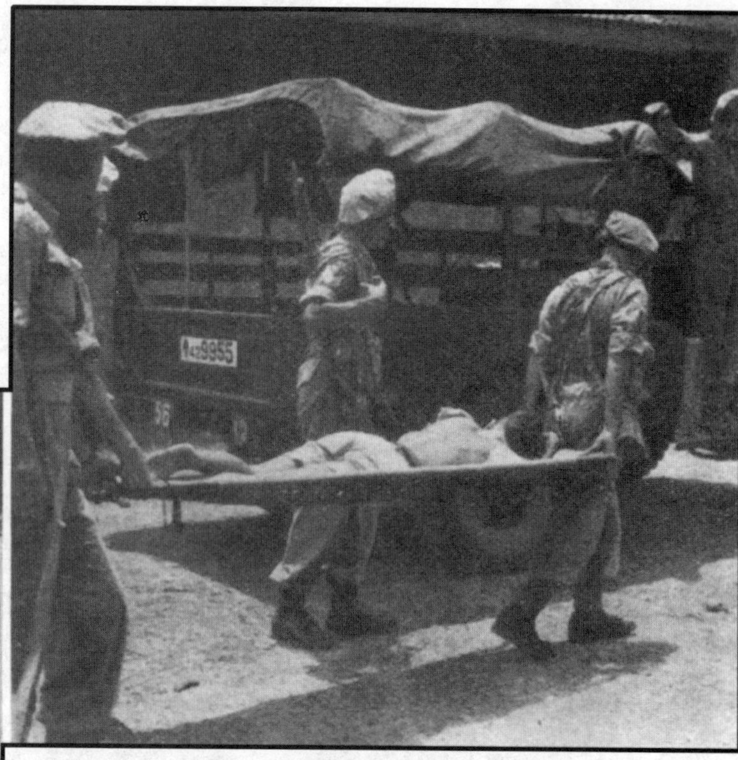

AFTER AN OUTBREAK OF RIOTING a wounded Indonesian was brought in by British Indian troops, nearly 1,000 of whom were landed at Tanjong Priok, Batavia's port, on Nov. 29, 1945, to strengthen Maj.-Gen. Hawthorn's 23rd Indian Division.

PEACE PARLEYS BROKE DOWN in Batavia on November 17, 1945, after less than four hours. Those present included (top, left to right) Lt.-Gen. Sir Philip Christison ; Mr Sutan A. Sjahrir, self-styled Indonesian Premier ; Dr. H. J. Van Mook, Lieut.-Governor-General of the Netherlands East Indies. In Surabaya (cleared of rebels by Nov. 29) Gurkhas of the 5th Indian Division patrolled past the Courts of Justice (bottom) which, with many other buildings, had been wrecked in the struggle. See also facing page.

Photos, Associated Press, Planet News

Modern Ark of Refuge From Indonesian Storm

ROYAL NAVY WENT TO THE RESCUE of Dutch women and children fleeing from Indonesian mobs : 3,000 were brought away from Surabaya in L.S.Ts. (Landing ship, tanks) such as this, in mid-November 1945. Most of the refugees had suffered cruelties and privations for four years at the hands of the Japanese, whilst some had been wounded on their way to the port in ambush attacks by Indonesian nationalists. On November 28 the Australian Government announced their willingness to receive and care for 10,000 refugees in the Commonwealth.

Photo, Planet News

British Brains and Pluck Against German Cunning

Cold-blooded courage of the highest order was demanded of the men who tackled unexploded bombs and mines. They pitted their wits against devilish devices which to them might easily have meant instant death—with always imprinted on their minds the grim warning, "Your first mistake will be your last!" Capt. MARTIN THORNHILL gives striking instances of their truly heroic work—entailing skill as well as courage. See also page 342.

At the height of the London blitz a German parachute mine came to rest with its tail propped against the side of a signal-box outside London Bridge Station. Had it exploded, one of the many consequences would have been a serious disruption of railway traffic on the Southern Railway in Cannon Street, Charing Cross and London Bridge stations.

To the scene came Lieut.-Commander John B. P. Miller, R.N.V.R., mine disposal expert, in response to an urgent call to the Admiralty. Any attempt to pull out the mine for easier working would almost certainly have set it off, but there was just room between the mine and the wall of the signal-box to give the Commander awkward access to the fuse underneath. Three times Miller tried to fit a safety gag to it. Twice the fuse-clock began its ominous ticking, then stopped. Miller made a desperate decision. Regardless of personal danger, he removed the fuse without a gag. Later it was found that the fuse was leaking, and in consequence the mine had been in an extremely dangerous condition throughout the whole of this operation.

It was, in fact, to a few Naval personnel that fell the task of making first close acquaintance with this class of Hun-born menace. Following disclosure by a prisoner of war that the enemy were employing a new secret weapon which might paralyse merchant navy traffic, Lieut.-Commander Ouvry, R.N., received an urgent summons to the Admiralty. Observers had reported parachutes bearing queer objects falling into the Thames and other river estuaries at night. In the early hours of that grey November morning in 1939 began the grim task of Commanders Ouvry, Lewis and their men to examine and de-activate the new magnetic mine (see story in page 124, Vol. 7).

R.A.F. BEACH SQUADRON members trained in mine disposal examine a German shoe mine on a Normandy invasion beach. *Photo, British Official*

All this, of course, was work for which these men had been trained—jobs which they had been long expecting. They knew the risks they ran, for there was no means of knowing beforehand what new devilries might cause the bomb to detonate at the first—or, as the enemy afterwards contrived—later stages of attempts to dismantle it. Very little of this quiet, stoical gallantry received official recognition in the shape of awards, for, as we have said, it was all in the day's work. True, there *has* been some recognition, but to the way of thinking of most of us it is quite disproportionate both to the degree of courage and its recurrent character.

Lieut.-Commander Miller, again, once tackled a mine in a dark passage of a London warehouse. Nobody knew exactly where the mine was, so Miller groped about until he found it, lying half-buried in the ground and wrapped in some lead roofing. On this occasion he worked single-handed, but subsequently he was in charge of a party which tackled fifteen mines one after another. For these and other perilous tasks Miller received the George Cross—second only to the V.C. as an award for valour—as did Able Seaman John Tuckwell who worked with him.

J. B. P. MILLER, G.C. S. J. TUCKWELL, G.C. Lieut.-Cmdr. J. B. P. Miller was decorated in 1941 for dismantling enemy mines, gallantly aided by the A.B. (right) as told here. *Crown Copyright*

Right up to D-Day, men of the Navy and Royal Marines had been lifting and immunizing thousands of mines. In the few days following the invasion of Normandy they disposed of hundreds more on the beaches there, and the terse comment of the "Bomb Safety Officer" who conducted these operations: "It has been a cakewalk," did nothing to minimize the dogged courage that lay behind the work.

Not to Explode Until Touched

Happily, it is now possible to tell the stories of *all* those who fought and conquered the menace of the unexploded bombs dropped on Britain. It would, however, be an almost endless tale, an epic of epics. Many of these bombs were not meant to explode until they were touched. Many did so only after a delay of hours or even days, unless approached and made safe in the meantime. It may well be that thousands of lives and millions of pounds' worth of property were saved by those who worked ceaselessly, and without much comment, on their hazardous tasks for the best part of six years.

After the first few months the work was shared by men of the Navy, Army and Air Force, often aided by some of the most highly skilled scientists in the land. Each Service branch was responsible within its own sphere of control, but it was on the Bomb Disposal Units of the Royal Engineers that fell the onus of clearing our towns, railways, factories and countryside. The magnitude of the task can be assessed from the fact that the R.E.s alone have disposed of over 45,000 unexploded H.E. bombs, and this figure does not include incendiary and other small missiles.

Every bomb that failed to explode had to be tackled, whether lying on the surface or buried 30 or 40 ft., when deep excavations had to be made to get at it. Then B.D. sappers would work unceasingly for days until it was reached, all the time unaware whether it might prove to be a time bomb or some newer device which could explode at any moment—a task that tested the stoutest heart and strongest nerve. The Bomb Disposal Squads toiled steadily on, undeterred by the risks they were running. To them the "Raiders Past" signal brought no respite, no relaxation of effort to protect the people and property of Britain, resulting in the deaths of 235 officers and men of the organization.

When excavations at last exposed the bomb, lying at the bottom of a hole in almost pitch-black gloom, probably with the delicate fuse mechanism in an inaccessible position, the more desperately dangerous work would begin. If the fuse was of a known pattern the Bomb Disposal Officer would know what to do; and, working alone—just in case he did make a mistake—he would ensure that one more menace to life and property was removed.

If, however, he had reason to suppose the fuse to be of a new type, then every possible detail would be rushed back to the Technical Staff, whose duty it then became to get at that fuse, somehow, without setting off the bomb. Thereafter, day and night, soldiers and scientists worked together, British brains against German cunning, to devise a means of dealing successfully with all similar fuses. An unparalleled form of courage was this persistent pluck of the R.E.s in Bomb Disposal Units—not that courage born of the excitement of battle, but grim determination to work quickly but patiently on toward an ever-developing peril.

True, this spirit had near parallel in the pluck of hundreds of students who passed daily through the mine schools. Here the main charge of every instructional mine was removed, but the igniter sets were left "alive," and they contained enough explosive to blow off the hand or foot of any student who might make one small mistake. On July 18, 1941, the chief field research and experimental officer, Directorate of

BURIED GERMAN BOMB at Greenwich was extricated by R.E.s in November 1945—five years after it had been dropped. It made a hole 26 ft. deep. *Photo, The Evening Standard*

Scientific Research, Ministry of Supply, was killed by a bomb, with seven other men who were examining it. Another fatal casualty was his secretary, who used to accompany him on his dangerous missions to take down his notes, which were often dictated while he was actually at work on the bombs.

The secrecy which so long has veiled the work of B.D. may never, for long-term security reasons, be fully uncovered. R.E. Disposal Squads are still searching for "souvenirs" of German raids, and there is still valuable information to be gleaned and applied (such are the needs and the duties of the General Staff in peace as well as war). Thus, this task still sports its maxim: "Your first mistake will be your last!"

More of the Nation's War Paintings

"TAKE OFF" Dame Laura Knight, D.B.E., R.A.

STRETCHER-PARTY MEN AT WORK IN GAS CLOTHING

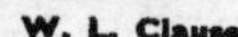

W. L. Clause

SHIPWRECKED

HOW well t
ductive
the War Artis
visory Comm
"an artistic
of the war in
aspects"—ha
fulfilled has
exemplified
casion in "T
Illustrated"
545–548, V
pages 322–32
4; pages 15–
719–722, Vol
these two pa
page 527 we
duce a final se
from origina
played (with
ception of
kirk Beaches
which—as als
wrecked—is
work of an e

DUNKIRK BEACHES, 1940

Richard Eurich, A.R.A.

MULBERRY

mond Coxon

at the Royal
my of Arts,
n, in the au-
of 1945. That
should have
what they
d was insisted
as far as pos-
by the Com-
; and the re-
bly effective
r in which
'tackled un-
r subjects
unfavourable
stances" is
l praise. Two
eir lives, in-
Eric Ravi-
whose Coastal
es is shown
and who was
while flying
r Iceland.

ight

OPERATIONS ROOM

A. Olivier

phen Bone

COASTAL DEFENCES

Eric Ravilious

Spitfires of the Fleet after Night Battle

"DRUMMED up the Channel as Drake drummed them long ago" was the lot of the enemy's ships by autumn 1944. But, as Lieut.-Cmdr. Peter Scott's foreword to his book (reviewed in the facing page, and from which these illustrations—reproduced from paintings by the author—are taken) goes on to remark, "The battle went on in the North Sea until the end came on May 8, 1945." With pen and brush Peter Scott presents the parts played in the bitter struggles, more particularly in North Sea and Channel, by our motor torpedo boats, motor gunboats and motor launches—aptly nicknamed Spitfires of the Fleet—whose chief purposes were to keep open our convoy routes and to deny to the Germans the use of the Channel ports.

WELL has he captured and enshrined "the strange and dreadful beauty" of many a modern seafight. And the brooding atmosphere that is neighbour to the climax of night battle or hazardous patrol can be sensed in his picture titled Returning at Dawn (above). The eeriness of it all is focused in Attack Completed—One Hit (left) . . . as the starshells burst overhead and float down on their parachutes they leave a trail of brightly illuminated smoke above them. And in the rear, a burning wreck.

From The Battle of the Narrow Seas, by Lieut.-Cmdr. Peter Scott, M.B.E., D.S.C. and Bar, R.N.V.R., by permission of Country Life Ltd.

"Battle of the Narrow Seas"

Reviewed by HAMILTON FYFE

"HE SERVED in the spirit of the greatest sailor of all." That was the epitaph written for a naval lieutenant who lost his life in an engagement with German E-boats off the Netherlands coast. It might be applied to every one of the young men who gallantly carried on The Battle of the Narrow Seas, as Lieut.-Cmdr. Peter Scott calls his History of the Light Coastal Forces in the Channel and North Sea, 1939-1945 (Country Life, Ltd., 15s.). They were a magnificent body of officers, and their crews caught the Nelson spirit from them. That explained why the British Navy kept the initiative in the waters between Britain and the Continent all through those six years.

They were aggressive, daring, undaunted by superior numbers, resolute in pushing their attacks home. Nelson himself wrote: "No captain can do very wrong if he places his ship alongside that of an enemy." In that tradition the Coastal Forces acted; and Peter Scott, son of the famous Antarctic explorer, has paid a very fine tribute to their splendid achievements.

He has illustrated his book himself, and his drawings of the men whose skill and courage he celebrates are both beautiful in themselves and also help us to understand what manner of men they were. In their faces we can read acceptance of great responsibility, for, although their ships were small, they were in sole command of them: their safety and the lives of all on board depended on the skipper's perception of the right thing to do and his quick decision in giving orders to do it. They may, as was said of Lieut. Leaf, whose epitaph I have quoted above, have "reduced caution to an irreducible minimum," but they never threw it to the winds.

'Crowded Hours of Glorious Life'

Nothing could be more exciting than to sight the enemy—perhaps an escorted convoy, or it might be an E-boat pack, or possibly a submarine; to manoeuvre into position so that torpedoes might be launched; to be discovered and to have the night made day by starshells; to bring guns into action, and then to make a successful get-away. But in between these "crowded hours of glorious life" came long periods of tedium. There was strain, discomfort and boredom.

> Most of the work of the coastal forces was done at night and most of it was uneventful. Normally for every action there are many nights of a fruitless patrol. Battles were only the exceptions which came occasionally to break the monotony of long nights patrolling, lying perhaps stopped and rolling helplessly in the trough of a short swell, or cruising at speed and drenched through with rain and spray.

Hard to keep continually on the alert under these conditions, through "long periods of uneventful steaming in waters where no contact with the enemy is likely."

> There may be moments of concern, a patch of fog, a rising wind a breakdown in one of the boats on patrol. Should they go on or turn back? The Senior Officer's decision must perhaps be made quickly. He may hear the high-pitched note of a wireless signal being received by the telegraphist below. Various possibilities may be passing through his mind. But probably the signal is a routine one. Will this be another of the fruitless nights? Will it drag slowly through until the faintest glow above the eastern horizon ends another dull patrol? Cocoa at midnight—and sandwiches, perhaps. There may be nothing on the sea for miles around.

Or, on the other hand, there may be enemy vessels not more than half a mile away. If there are, it is often very difficult to identify them. "Even size is often impossible to judge because the distance, and therefore the scale, is so deceptive."

Even in daylight it is not always easy to decide the question: Friend or Foe? When the three German cruisers Scharnhorst, Gneisenau and Prinz Eugen went through the Channel in February 1942 and were followed by M.T.B.s vainly trying to approach near enough for a torpedo attack, one of the British officers reported the Prinz Eugen leading, but it appeared later from statements by prisoners of war who had been on board that this ship was third in line.

ANOTHER incident noted here occurred during the Dieppe raid. One of our small ships approached to within half a mile of two larger enemy ships and fired torpedoes at them. "That he was able to approach to within 900 yards under the continuous glare of starshell can only be attributed to misidentification. The Germans must have thought he was one of them."

Usually the first warning of enemy ships near came to ears rather than to eyes. The slightest sounds had to be listened for. What was that? The noise of a motor, the roar of a turbine, the threshing of a screw? This was not at all easy when the sea ran high. On a calm moonlight night slight sounds came from a long way off, but then the moonlight was a danger in itself. "I must own," Peter Scott wrote after an action, "to a sinking feeling on sighting the enemy. The moon was so bloody bright."

Sometimes the phosphorescence on the water prevented our boats from creeping in unseen. The bow wave and the wake of moving vessels "shone with pale-green luminosity, so bright that the phosphorescence, even at slow speeds, could be seen at far greater distances than the dark lump of the vessel itself."

Mishaps in motor boats seem to be more frequent than in ships driven by steam, whether with coal or oil, and many of the former are so small that they cannot carry more than one engine. When the motor mechanic of M.T.B. 87 reported that the clutch would not engage, the chances of the boat surviving were small. Four E-boats were attacking her. All preparations for abandoning ship were made. Luckily a sudden fog came over and blotted out the combatants. When the First Lieutenant went down to see what efforts were being made to remedy the clutch trouble, "all I saw was the stoker sitting on the starboard engine and supporting himself by gripping a pipe. I jumped down, seething with rage, to find that, although badly wounded in the arm, he was holding a rag over the fuel pipe which had been pierced by a shell. He remained in that position for many hours."

Lt.-Cmdr. PETER SCOTT, M.B.E., D.S.C. and Bar, R.N.V.R., vividly portrays the exploits of our Light Coastal Forces in the book reviewed here. See also facing page.

Photo, The Evening News

In another of the coastal craft, an M.G.B. (Motor Gunboat) this time, the motor mechanic crawled up to the lieutenant in command after an engagement with E-boats had been going on at full throttle for half an hour, and said: "For God's sake, stop, sir!" The lieutenant was "extremely incensed" and asked why. The mechanic said: "You have been running your engines on full throttle for so long that all the dynamos are on fire. Give me two minutes and I will pull the leads out." That he did "without turning a hair" and "the party continued," for another half-hour, when one of the Browning guns became white hot.

To Commemorate Those Who Died

Yet another kind of accident was due to trouble with the exhaust-pipe. On one M.T.B. during a patrol the leading stoker "lurched his way up to the bridge as if he were very drunk indeed. His report was alarming. The exhaust-pipe junctions had worked loose and the engine-room was filled with poisonous gases. The seamen dashed below and fished out the other two who, not having Clarke's extremely robust constitution, were already unconscious. All three were laid out on the upper deck and gradually they came round, with splitting headaches and violent nausea." Had there been an enemy near by that boat would have been a "sitter" as a target.

Not always can the result of torpedo attack be observed. When it is watched, the observer sees something like this:

> I fired my fish at a medium-sized merchant vessel. At first I thought I had missed him—it always seems ages before your torpedoes get there—but then suddenly a glow like a bonfire started on his waterline, no enormous flash, no huge column of water, nothing dramatic at all. And then slowly he seemed to disintegrate, puffing out steam like a puff-ball puffs out dust when you tread on it. Maybe disintegrate is the wrong word—he seemed to deflate more than anything.

If you think about it impersonally, logically, it is a horrible business, this stalking and sinking of merchant ships, taking them unawares, sending the crews to their deaths "with all their imperfections on their heads." It is the sort of thing that has gone on ever since we have any record of Man's activities—with varying types of weapon, and sometimes with more, sometimes with less, ruthlessness. Warfare has become neither crueller nor kinder since the days of Sargon and the earliest Egyptian dynasties. Man's inhumanity to man has been a constant factor in life on our planet since Man began. But it is clear that Peter Scott sees at times that war is "a horrible business."

He declares truly in his Foreword, addressed to young men, that "there is no glory to be had out of war that cannot be had out of some greater and more creative enterprise," and that the best way to commemorate the men who died is to find a complete and lasting peace. But at the end he is less hopeful. We must have a strong navy, he says, and in it there must be a place for Coastal Forces—"so long as armed force continues to play a part in the affairs of men." From that attitude of mind wars have always resulted.

United Nations Organization Prepares for Action

AT CHURCH HOUSE, WESTMINSTER, on November 24, 1945, the Preparatory Commission of the United Nations Organization—product of the San Francisco Conference (see page 270)—met in readiness for the Assembly in London early in 1946. Chairman was Dr. Eduardo Z. Angel, of Colombia (1). Delegates included Mr. P. Noel Baker, Minister of State, Great Britain (2); the Emir Feisal of Saudi Arabia (3). The Commission (4) sat in the chamber used by the House of Commons after the bombing of their "home" in May 1941.

Great Pluto Has Piped Its Last Pint of Petrol

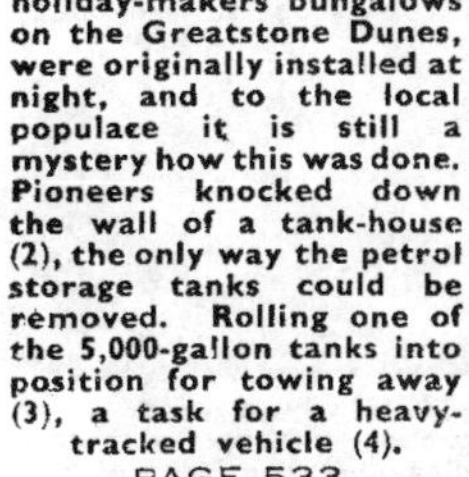

AT DUNGENESS, Kent, the Pluto pipeline system which conveyed millions of gallons of petrol across the bed of the Channel to the Allied armies on the Continent (see page 120) was being dismantled by men of the R.A.S.C. and the Pioneer Corps in November 1945. Some thirty miles of pipeline are to be left under the Channel, its removal not being considered worth while.

Pioneers carry away a 10-ft. section (1). Storage tanks, housed in former holiday-makers' bungalows on the Greatstone Dunes, were originally installed at night, and to the local populace it is still a mystery how this was done. Pioneers knocked down the wall of a tank-house (2), the only way the petrol storage tanks could be removed. Rolling one of the 5,000-gallon tanks into position for towing away (3), a task for a heavy-tracked vehicle (4).

Now It Can Be Told!

REINHARD HEYDRICH, whose death at the hands of Czech avengers from Britain is revealed below. See also page 206, Vol. 5.
Photo, Associated Press

NAIL GUN SPEEDS UNDERWATER SALVAGE

HOLED below the water-line, a wreck must be patched before it can be salvaged. How to fix the patch most expeditiously over that yawning hole? Engineering ingenuity indicated how this task could be accomplished under the sea, and also produced the means. This wartime device, no longer secret, consists of a "gun" whose charge of explosive is powerful enough to drive inch-and-a-half steel nails through two half-inch steel plates so that these are held together in the closest possible contact, almost as effectively as though riveted in the ordinary way.

The salvaging of ships sunk in Antwerp approaches has been expedited in this manner. A steel plate patch with sufficiently large overlap is lowered into position and held temporarily to the ship's hull, sometimes by means of a magnet. Around the edge of the plate the nail guns are fixed at intervals, and when the explosive charge is touched off the skittle-shaped nails are driven home violently through the plate and into the vessel's hull.

The great heat which is generated at the moment of impact serves to reinforce the join between the plate-edges and the hull, and there can be no question of the patch shifting or developing a leak. Owing to its peculiar nature the nail gun is essentially an underwater tool, but peacetime requirements may lead to even more useful developments in the manner and nature of its employment.

HOW 'HANGMAN' HEYDRICH MET HIS END

CZECH parachutists, flown from Britain, killed Reinhard Heydrich, notorious Nazi "hangman," it was learned on November 1, 1945, when the full story of the assassination of the Gauleiter of Bohemia and Moravia was told by an eye witness. The details of the assassination (as revealed here by Associated Press) were disclosed by a young Czech liaison officer attached to the War Crimes Commission at Wiesbaden, formerly a policeman in Prague, who worked with the Underground Movement.

A special mission of parachutists, armed with British weapons, was assigned to the task of hunting down Heydrich. They were led by Lieutenant Jan Opletal (aged 30), who was well known in Czech circles in London during the war. All three members of the special unit, with four companions, killed themselves when they were trapped in a church after carrying out their mission.

They were dropped in Bohemia in December 1941, and fot five months waited their chance. Heydrich was known to take the same route every day from his country house to his Prague headquarters. On the morning of May 27, 1942, he was riding with his S.S. chauffeur. One of the Czechs, stationed at a corner a little distance away, signalled to his companions with a mirror. A tram coming from the opposite direction forced Heydrich's car to turn in near the kerbstone, and that was the patriots' opportunity.

One of the parachutists started firing at the hangman's car with a Bren gun, but it jammed. Then another of the agents threw a British bomb underneath the car from a few yards distance. Heydrich tried to draw his revolver, but he collapsed before he could fire. Twelve days later he died.

Heydrich's assailants escaped by fleeing in different directions. The Nazis launched a reign of terror, and an intensive house-to-house search was begun. A cordon was thrown around the city. The three Czech parachutists, with four companions who had been dropped earlier to make preparations, hid in the Prague church of Karel Boromejsky, where they were fed by clergymen. The Nazis offered a reward for clues, and threatened reprisals against the whole population unless the killers were found by June 18.

The parachutists' hide-out was given away by another Czech parachutist, who turned traitor at the last moment when taken prisoner by the Gestapo. For ten hours the seven Czech patriots in the church held off the Nazis who had surrounded them—three of them firing from the tower and the other four from the basement. Finally, when the Gestapo threatened to set fire to the building, the trapped men inside killed themselves.

LONDON'S PETROL WAS A LUFTWAFFE TARGET

DURING the critical months before D-Day the German Air Force planned and carried out an operation on a Thames target comparable with the famous "dam-busting" raid of the R.A.F. And they achieved some measure of success. This is revealed in the November issue of the Magazine of the Port of London Authority.

In the early hours of February 19, 1944, a lone enemy bomber made a carefully planned attack on Richmond lock and weir. Three bombs were dropped, one making a direct hit on the lock, destroying the lock gates at the up-river end and causing some blast damage to the weir.

The second bomb penetrated the tow-path within a few feet of the Surrey-side river bank, just missing the downstream lock gates. Fortunately, this bomb did not explode, but it necessitated the immediate evacuation of the lock keeper and his family from the adjoining lock residence. Traffic had to be diverted from the towpath and confined to the Middlesex side of the river for at least a month, whilst the bomb disposal people got to work and eventually succeeded in extracting this unexploded bomb. The third bomb fell harmlessly in the adjoining fields at the side of the lock premises.

THE lock was put out of action completely. From then onward river traffic to and from the upper reaches was rendered more difficult. At all times traffic throughout the tideway of the Thames is considerable and important. Why was Richmond lock and weir a special target for the Luftwaffe? The answer is concerned with that commodity vital throughout the war—oil.

Normally, London's enormous petrol requirements are drawn from the great importing and storage installations at Thames Haven, Shell Haven, and elsewhere in the lower reaches, and distributed by tank barges to depots on the riverside. These installations being within very short flying time from the Continent became extremely vulnerable when war broke out, and an alternative means of supplying London had to be found.

This had been foreseen by the authorities, and a pipe-line had been laid from a point in the Severn Estuary to Walton-on-Thames. The oil pumped through this pipe-line was received into tank barges which were brought

RICHMOND LOCK AND WEIR before being bombed by the Luftwaffe on February 19, 1944. This partially successful attack (see story in this page) was aimed at disrupting London's petrol supplies which in wartime came by pipe-line from the Severn Estuary to Walton-on-Thames and thence by special tank barges.
By courtesy of the Port of London Authority

to the Thames, most of the craft usually employed being too big for the narrower and shallower upper reaches. Thus London's flow of oil was completely reversed—instead of from east to west it was west to east. The German intention was to disrupt this channel of supply, and the attack on the lock and weir at Richmond did slow down the flow of oil to some extent.

Priority permission was obtained to reconstruct Richmond lock, and work was commenced in June 1944. It has been pressed forward with all speed, and it is expected the lock will be in commission again by the end of 1945. Apart from local residents, few of London's millions even heard of the attack upon this vital river target, and perhaps none fully comprehended its significance.

Passed From High to Low Level

The locks and weirs on the Thames were built primarily to hold up the water in the upper reaches on a falling tide, to permit navigation over a longer period. This condition is secured at Richmond by means of three "undershot" weir gates and a lock. The former are movable, i.e. can be raised or lowered. On an ebb tide, when the water has fallen to roughly half tide level, the weir sluices are lowered, thus holding up the water above the weirs, the level of water being controlled by allowing surplus land water to flow beneath the weir gates by raising them. To enable navigation to be continued up and down river when the sluices are down, vessels are passed from the higher or maintained water level to the lower or tidal water and vice versa by means of the lock.

The weir structure is built in the form of a twin footbridge, the footways being 6 ft. wide and 16 ft. apart, the central space between being occupied by the weir gates and operating machinery. There are five spans, the three centre ones 66 ft. wide in the clear, with two 50-ft. spans over a slipway for small boats and lock respectively. Each weir gate weighs 32 tons, and is suspended by flexible steel wires passing round trunnions fixed at the neutral axis of the gate, the free ends of the wires passing over wheels with their ends connected to cast-iron weights of 8 tons each—two at each end of each weir gate. The balance weights rise and fall in watertight wells, to keep their weight constant whatever the level of the water in the river. The lock is 250 ft. long and 37 ft. wide for two-thirds of its length, narrowing to 26 ft. wide at the lock gates.

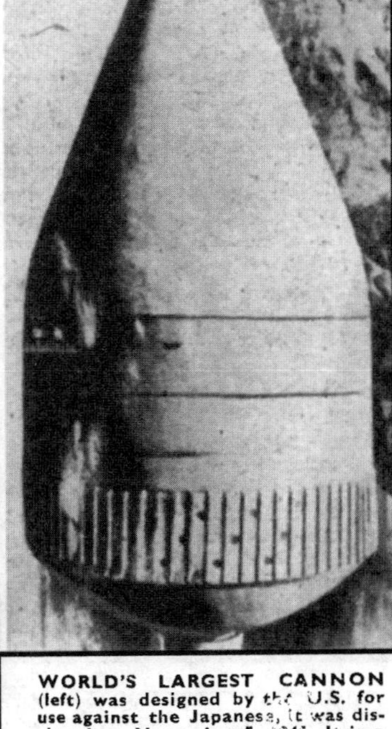

WORLD'S LARGEST CANNON (left) was designed by the U.S. for use against the Japanese, it was disclosed on November 5, 1945. It is a 38-ft. mortar with a range of 8 miles. Specially constructed projectile is a 2-ton shell (above) reputed to be capable of piercing 10-ft. thickness of reinforced concrete. *Photos, Keystone*

NAVAL DIVERS CUT JAP TELEPHONE CABLES

Working with oxygen apparatus in depths which had shortly before caused the deaths of two other divers, two British naval divers cut the Saigon-Singapore and the Saigon-Hongkong undersea telephone cables in one of the last midget submarine operations of the war. They were Sub-Lieut. K. M. Briggs, R.A.N.V.R., and Sub-Lieut. A. K. Bergius, R.N.V.R., who were carried in the midget submarine XE4, commanded by Lieut. M. H. Shean, D.S.O., R.A.N.V.R.

The craft was towed into the Japanese-controlled Saigon River area by the submarine Spearhead. She slipped her tow at 9.20 p.m. on July 30 and was away from the parent ship until the early hours of August 1. Towing a grapnel and chain weighing about 80 lb. along the bottom, she made a number of runs before she was brought up suddenly as the grapnel caught the Singapore cable. Briggs returned inboard with the short length of the cable as evidence of a job well done.

About an hour later Lieut. Shean found the Hongkong cable. Bergius had to go out twice to complete the cutting operation, because of mechanical trouble with his cutter. He brought back a foot of cable core. The divers were specially commended for working in much deeper, and therefore more dangerous, water than anticipated.

Lieut. Shean, 27, was awarded the D.S.O. in April 1944 for "outstanding skill, courage and determination in a most hazardous enterprise in one of H.M. midget submarines." Sub-Lieut. Briggs, 22, of New South Wales, joined the Navy as an Ordinary Seaman in May 1941. Sub-Lieut. Bergius, 20, of Argyllshire, also served as a rating.

Lieut. M. H. SHEAN, D.S.O., R.A.N.V.R., Commander of the Midget submarine XE4, took part in the Far Eastern exploit described here. *Photo, British Official*

COMBINED OPS HAD 6-LB. MACHINE-CARBINE

Every Saturday morning, between early March and early June, in 1944, a small Army van, almost unnoticed, visited the Dagenham factory of the Sterling Engineering Company. The van (said an Evening Standard reporter in September 1945) was on a Combined Operations assignment, to pick up the week's production of the new Patchett machine-carbine automatic rifle.

The Patchett machine-carbine was invented in 1942 by George Patchett, an English engineer and armament inventor who had worked in a Belgian armament factory and in one of the Skoda factories in Pilsen.

The complete gun weighed 6 lb. Its stock was a metal frame which folded back against the barrel, and in addition to a button-controlled bayonet it had a safety device, a little switch on the hand rest which could be set for single shot, automatic or no shot action, all by simple thumb movements. But the Army had the Sten gun in mass production then.

Early last year a senior Combined Operations officer heard of the Patchett machine-carbine. He investigated it. Although the Imperial General Staff had not given the gun its "O.K." Combined Operations ordered the Sterling Company to get into production. That service would take all it could get.

Production was slow. It was a difficult period to obtain tools and labour. But the Sterling men managed to make about 150 of the guns in all. Every week until after D-Day the little Combined Operations van called at the Dagenham factory to pick up the four or five guns manfactured there that week.

On September 21, 1945, I was able to get the story of the Patchett machine-carbine, only because a War Office spokesman said the invention was not now on the "secret list." But Mr. Patchett's communications with the War Office show it has been. The gun fires 600 rounds of 9-mm. ammunition. It is effective up to 600 yards.

Service Men and Women Train for Civil Life

OPENED AT LUTON HOO, Bedfordshire, by the Rt. Hon. J. J. Lawson, Secretary of State for War, on November 19, 1945, the first formation college in connexion with the Army Education Scheme to be set up in this country is one of eight planned to assist the Service man or woman in the adoption of a civilian career. The site is a country mansion, formerly the H.Q. of Eastern Command. Other colleges will be attached to Scottish, Southern, Northern and Western Commands; and, overseas, will serve the B.A.O.R., C.M.F. and M.E.F. For 300 vacancies for the first 4-weeks' session at Luton Hoo over 1,300 applications were made.

An officer, a house-decorator in peacetime, instructs a class in a special type of plaster ornamentation (1) executed with a cake-icer. Women students (2) learn the knack of pastry-making. R.E.M.E. lance-corporal (3) proved apt at sign-writing. Among the 50 subjects taught in this Army "university" is motor-repairing (4).

 Photos, L.N.A., Associated Press

I Was There! Eye Witness Stories of the War and After

Palestine Police are the Bravest Men I Know

How unenviable is the task of British police and troops in keeping order, in most difficult and dangerous conditions in turbulent Palestine, is made clear by Henry Longhurst in this story (here slightly abridged) from The London Evening News dated Nov. 27, 1945. See also pages 515, 517.

Last week I was in Palestine, the holy land which is at the moment so particularly unholy. There are two bodies of men in Palestine today to whose efforts the most inadequate justice is being done—the Palestine Police (who are British) and the British soldiers.

I do not believe that any country in the world except Britain, with its centuries-old tradition of tolerance, could have produced these men. If ever anyone had excuse for Hitler's " My patience is exhausted," it must be our men in Palestine. It may be said that any man who joins the Palestine Police knows what he is going to be let in for sooner or later. That is true, but it does not affect the merit of their present performance.

I would not have their job for quadruple their pay. They live in an atmosphere of propaganda, lies, intrigue, assault and sudden death. They are armed—but so hamstrung by restrictions issued from London that there is hardly any occasion on which they are permitted to use their arms. And when things go wrong they can generally reckon to get the blame.

I was not in Tel-Aviv for the principal riot, when the Jews burnt down most of the British buildings, hurled bricks and home-made grenades, and set light to a lorry in the main street ; but I was there early next morning. The rubble on the pavements and the gutted buildings, so reminiscent of the " morning after " in blitz days, made the scene easy enough to reconstruct.

Every man in our police and military forces was armed, some with pistols or rifles, or with automatic weapons. The average sub-machine-gun fires at the rate of, say, 400 rounds per minute ; in other words, press the trigger for one second and you will fire seven rounds.

In one night in Tel-Aviv our police and Army patrols, assaulted with bricks collected beforehand and flung savagely from the security of first-floor windows, and attacked by mobs numbering several hundreds, fired how many shots—bearing in mind that one man's finger on the trigger for one second meant seven ? Between the whole lot of them they fired exactly 16 rounds !

And even then the Jewish authorities, while commending their forbearance, blamed them for not preventing the rioting before it got out of hand. One can name a good many countries whose police and soldiers would have fired not 16 rounds but 16,000. Neither the police nor the soldiers have any great inducement to be good-tempered in Palestine. Police officers and men have been ambushed, shot in the back on their way to the office, blown up by bombs secreted under the door-mat of their own homes.

One of the bravest men I know is a Palestine Police officer, who has been No. 1 on the Jewish terrorists' list. They warned him that he will not leave the country alive. Every time he enters or leaves a building, particularly at night, he knows that this may be the moment they have chosen.

As for the soldiers, risking your life for your own country is a far different thing from risking it to preserve order among a minority in another man's. Some of the troops in Palestine today are new and raw, but the men of the Sixth Airborne Division are far from raw. About a third of them are veterans of Arnhem, and all have received the toughest form of war training, which tends to make a man shoot first and ask questions afterwards.

Furthermore, they are living in conditions of discomfort that can rarely have been exceeded in peacetime. They are all under canvas. With the sun shining mellowly as in an English August, Palestine can be most attractive and life in a tent not too unpleasant. But last week the weather broke, and now it will be raining for three weeks. One unit I visited a few days ago had spent a fortnight on nothing but drain-digging.

MORTAR-SHELL, of a type employed by terrorists, found in the Jerusalem area during November 1945, is being examined by members of the Palestine Police. *Photo, Associated Press*

After one day's rain their camp was in the nature of a shambles.

Tents were blown down ; the cookhouse was awash ; the officers' mess was more like a stable ; men floundered through the lines with mud above their anklets ; and wellingtons were worth their weight in gold. All after one day's rain.

Despite all this, the Palestine Police, immaculately turned out in khaki battle-dress and black cap, retain the impassive patience we associate with constables patrolling our own peaceful streets ; and the soldiers, ignorant for the most part of the background behind the eternal " Palestine problem " and looking forward only to their release, know that they have a job to do, and get on with the business of doing it. A visit to Palestine may make you pro-Arab or it may make you pro-Jew. The one thing it must assuredly make you is pro-British.

POLICE DOG IN JERUSALEM, one of 25 used on frontier patrol, learns to pick up a scent from a belt worn by his trainer at the Palestine Police Training School. *Photo, Associated Press*

I Watched at the Palace of Justice at Nuremberg

In this dispatch, slightly abridged, from the scene of the trial of 20 major Nazi war criminals, James A. Jones, of The London Evening News, presents the unforgettable background as it appeared to him on the second day. There the accused sat—to answer for murders innumerable and tortures unspeakable and treacheries beyond words. See also illus. page 513.

It still amazes me. I still blink at what seems to London eyes to be the topsy-turvey order of things. In our courts at home the magistrate comes on to the Bench first and the prisoner is then led into his presence. Here at the Palace of Justice, after showing a pass to armed guards at every corner of unchartable corridors and being " frisked " at the doorway of the court-room, I walk in and see the twenty men waiting in the dock for something to happen. The Bench is untenanted.

Early comers in the stalls and gallery are adjusting earphones on their heads. But there in the dock are the twenty waiting for us like a sort of reception committee. They have the air of having been waiting for us for a long time. Today I had the feeling that Goering, who is obviously playing to the gallery as a stout good fellow, would have been glad to shake hands with us if the guards had permitted. He turns affably to his fellows on the two rows of wooden seats and talks over good old times. At least, I assume he does. I don't know. Only the Nazis who are within earshot of him know.

And it may disconcert him inwardly though it does not alter his pink, good-natured, healthy face, that Ribbentrop treats him with faint grey politeness ; Keitel stares at him in a cold harsh military way, and Hess hardly seems to know he's there. But he's not rebuffed. He is photogenic in an ample light grey uniform and he knows it. He is aware of his appearance. His bluff good humour is well set off by the cadaverous figure of Hess beside him—with eyes sunken into sockets and claw-like hands clutching a book.

Hess to Goering is like a skeleton to Falstaff. Goering throws a kindly word to him and then looks casually round for our admiration. He does not get it. We are beginning to take him and the rest of the gang for granted. Then the Judges enter and he seems to feel the competition in interest. He shrinks to less than his 16 stone. But he never stops trying. He has scores of artful gestures. He tries anything to catch our eyes and win our sympathies. He leans wearily

AMAZING RAMIFICATIONS OF THE NAZI PARTY were explained step by step on November 22, 1945, at the Nuremberg trial of major war criminals, by the U.S. prosecution with the aid of a large chart displayed at the end of the Court Room and at which the German defendants gazed with intent interest. Its purpose was to prove the responsibility of the Leadership Corps of the Party, one of the Nazi organizations charged in the lengthy indictment. Goering, Hess and Ribbentrop are in the dock on the extreme left, behind the defending counsel. *Photo, Keystone*

forward on the front of the dock and puts his head on his arms like a nice, pink, fat boy.

He wriggles on his seat to show how hard it is. He yawns occasionally, as though calling on us to realize how dull it is for a kind-hearted man to listen to tiresome tales of massacres in places with unpronounceable names In short, he seems to be saying it is very boring to be cooped up like this with a set of stiff-necked men like Keitel and Jodl and Schacht and the rest of them, and couldn't we kindly do something about it. He is not the only claimant for attention, however. He has rivals who, though not immediately as dramatic, do their best.

Hans Frank, round-faced little S.S. general, listens through earphones in pained attention, and his lips move in unheard protests. Schacht, the banker, plays the part of an honest, grey-haired financier who simply cannot believe all this is really anything to do with him. He puffs his lips as though wishing the Tribunal would come to something more businesslike. He strokes his crisp, grey moustache wearily. He studies the interpreters who are stationed in the glass case next to him. He does everything short of consulting his wrist watch.

This Recital of the Unbelievable

But I was talking about things that amazed me. In London we make quite a fuss about one murder. Here speeches tell of millions of murders and the words "killed" and "torture" run like a scarlet thread through hours of speeches. One man murdered horrifies us at home. Here I see the counsel for the defence stifling yawns. In London we sit on hard wooden seats and listen intently. Here we listen intently but sit in seats so soft and comfortable it is like hearing a running commentary to some abnormally long news reel.

We write with neat little boards on our knees—boards specially provided for us—and what we write is taken by stalwart Scots Guardsmen to wireless transmission which is our one means of reaching the outside world from this dreary city where dead still lie beneath tumbled buildings. It is almost hopeless to try to describe this nightmare trial, this recital of the unbelievable, in unbelievable surroundings.

Outside the Palace of Justice a small German child sidles up to a sentry and the sentry swings his white truncheon playfully towards it. Inside the palace is a queue of uniformed girls waiting to buy handbags made from German officers' gorgeous uniforms. Inside the court-room the statistics of deaths, disfigurements and enslavements are as cold as the unimpassioned figures in a chartered accountant's ledger.

When a real live witness walks to the microphone and talks of murders long ago, these proceedings will leap suddenly into lurid light. But meanwhile, Goering picks up his earphones and listens casually for a moment, puts them down again and shifts with elaborate discomfort on the form. Meanwhile, you can switch a dial on your own earphone and hear statistics in English or French or Russian or German. They are too gigantic in any language to bring home the truth.

But at the moment Schacht frowns wearily, Rosenberg rubs his nose in a nervous manner, Doenitz remains palely impassive, Hess keeps up an attitude of a spectre at a feast, and Goering is plumply, boyishly determined to convince us it is all a natural but rather absurd mistake to make so much of these trifles.

Training with the B.A.O.R. at a Luxury Camp

As long as the British Army of the Rhine remains in Germany its military efficiency will be kept at the peak by the huge self-contained training centre set up at Bad Lippspringe, near Paderborn, whence this description comes from Edmund Townshend, The Daily Telegraph Special Correspondent.

THE Germans used this great training camp, covering 66 square miles, for toughening up their spearhead troops. Two and a half divisions of S.S. troops at a time were drawn from the fighting fronts for specialized training in the classroom and on the many firing ranges.

Now British troops are living in the splendid barracks and applying their own modifications and improvements to the accommodation and training installations. The officers in charge are determined to make the B.A.O.R. training centre here the finest establishment of its kind in the world. It will be the most luxurious training centre many soldiers have ever seen. Special effort is being made to raise the standard of amenities to the highest level.

Already the centre is more like a military college than a barracks. Elegant furnishings have been turned out by local factories. Rooms have been cleaned and redecorated. Bowls of flowers stand among the immaculate cutlery on white tablecloths in the dining-rooms. German servants wait at table.

The centre has sports grounds, welfare institutions and an E.N.S.A. hostel, and its own airstrip. A museum is being built up representing every type of German weapon, tank and vehicle. Throughout the centre the aim is to get away from the discomfort and boredom which have so often handicapped the work of training establishments, and to stimulate the keenest efficiency.

Men who pass through the centre are nearly all instructors, who return to units of the B.A.O.R. or of Allied armies. Courses for Allied troops are being given high priority, and military missions from Belgium, Denmark, France, Holland, Czechoslovakia and Poland come to watch the work.

The object of the nine schools of the training centre is to give short, intensive courses in a wide variety of subjects to meet the demands of our military commitments. Many technical courses are designed to replace specialists as they are lost to the Army by demobilization.

The high proportion of early discharges in technical units such as the R.A.S.C. and R.E.M.E. means a heavy demand for replacements who need more advanced training than they can get in their own units. In the last few months 3,000 pupils have passed through. By next spring the centre will be instructing more than 7,000 men at a time, passing them out at the rate of 1,300 every ten days.

British administrative staff has been reduced to the minimum by carefully planned centralization, and Germans or Poles are used as batmen, waiters, cleaners and fatigue men.

The ratio of students to British staff is four to one, showing a staff saving on the normal training centre ratio of 1·1 to one.

The nine schools give courses in infantry soldiering, offensive air support, administration, military intelligence, technical work, physical training and recreation, and the work of the Pioneer Corps, Military Police and R.A.S.C. units.

A target factory used by the German army has been taken over, together with its 100 German civilian employees, who are kept at work turning out the same products and maintaining the ranges. Khaki-painted wooden figures used as targets by the enemy are being repainted German field-grey for practice by our men. A miniature mobile tank firing harmless wooden bullets to simulate hostile fire is now also a target for our marksmen. Germans under British supervision work in the camouflage workshops on research and development, producing new designs for models and targets to be made in the target factory.

I saw an ingenious new type of miniature landscape range, with moving figures and tanks, which is used for teaching fire control and quick identification of targets. A war dogs' school, newly opened in December, will train 100 handlers and dogs a month, to save man-power in British troops guarding dumps.

Lessons learned in the war will be closely applied at the school of instruction in offensive air support. Two types of course will be run for air liaison officers. One will teach staff officers and picked commanding officers the principles and organization of air support. The other will teach regimental officers its practical application in the field.

BOXING AT A B.A.O.R. TRAINING CAMP near Neuhaus, as taught and demonstrated by amateur pugilist C.S.M.-Instructor E. D. Shakleton (right). *Photo, British Official*

Even the High-Ups in Japan Must Scrounge to Eat

Japan has "gone on the black" on a grand scale. The necessity for Black Marketing has been admitted by the managements of big departmental stores in Tokyo and other major cities; and Lachie McDonald, writing from the mountain resort of Karuizawa on November 26, 1945, has told this behind-the-scenes story in The Daily Mail.

A smart dog-cart labelled "Imperial Household" has just been bowed into the grounds of the rambling country house which Emperor Hirohito's mother, the Empress-Dowager Sadako, occupies in this mountain resort about 90 miles north-west of Tokyo. The dog-cart, behind a fast-stepping horse, contains a clue to the real importance of the extraordinary session of the Japanese Diet opening formally in Tokyo today.

The dog-cart was full of food—farm produce. Sadako's dog-cart, with its top-hatted driver and groom, makes a daily sortie into the countryside for vegetables, eggs, meat, and any other food they can wheedle the farmers into selling. The ordinary Japanese must do their own scrounging. You see them on railways stations and along country roads, with great rucksacks on their backs. Rationing throughout Japan is so muddled and distribution so erratic that people claim they cannot live adequately if they depend on official food allowances.

Casual Food Sales to be Outlawed

The necessity for Black Marketing has even been admitted by big department stores in Tokyo, Osaka, and other major Japanese cities. The managers appointed their own Black Marketeers when they found their workpeople were losing an average of two working days a week while they hunted for extra food for their families. It was cheaper for the managements to "go on the black," as the Japanese say, in a big way.

The Shidehara Government's main contribution so far to the undercurrent of discontent over food has been a hint that, unless farmers sell their produce at official rates, which are far below the prices obtainable on their doorsteps, then the Government will outlaw casual food sales to eager callers from the cities. The ordinary Japanese is hoping this 18-day session of Japan's House of Commons will give them a true picture of the conditions which are to be expected in Japan this winter.

Colonel Ray Kramer, chief of MacArthur's economic section, blames poor distribution for the present food shortages, and says the Japanese today are far better off than millions of Europeans. Kramer said, "Some wheat from surplus Army stocks in the Philippines and some salt from Korea have been allowed into Japan since the Allied occupation. Undoubtedly some other foodstuffs will be imported, but just how much food and where it will come from must be decided in Washington by Allied authorities who are familiar with the food situation throughout the world."

Immediate Allied interest in the forthcoming Diet centres on official reaction to new directives revealing MacArthur's plan for stripping war profiteers of their wealth, and his determination to kill what Kramer described as the "insidious and vicious" system of military pensions. About 12,000,000 Japanese will have lost their pensions by February 1. About 15 per cent of the coming year's Government revenue would have been swallowed up by pensions. Many Japanese soldiers served as little as three and four years to earn pensions for life.

The Allies favour a scheme providing relief for all widows, orphans, the aged, and needy rather than merely for families of men favoured by the military clique. The Allied attack on war profiteers aims to smash the power of the Zaibatsu—the wealthy families and combines which geared Japan for war. Like the pensions cut, it will help to curb inflation. Colonel Kramer considers that the banning of Government subsidies is the most important step yet taken in reshaping the Japanese way of life.

FOOD SHORTAGE IN TOKYO was the subject of this open-air demonstration in the capital's Hibiya Park, near the Imperial Palace, on November 1, 1945. British officials in Tokyo announced on November 13 that first troops of the 40,000 Empire forces to help police Japan will arrive on January 1, 1946, and may stay till 1971. *Photo, Keystone*

★—As The Years Went By—Notable Days in the War—★

1939

December 13. *Battle of River Plate between Graf Spee and the Exeter, Ajax and Achilles.*

1940

December 9. *Wavell opened victorious offensive against the Italians in the Western Desert.*

1941

December 8. *Japanese landed in N. Malaya. Tobruk relieved after 8-months' siege.*
December 9. *Japanese landed on Luzon.*
December 10. *Prince of Wales and Repulse sunk by Japanese aircraft off Malaya.*
December 11. *Governments of Germany and Italy declared war on the United States.*
December 19. *Hitler took over personal command of army from Von Brauchitsch.*

1942

December 16. *Russians opened offensive in Middle Don area on front of over 60 miles.*
December 13. *Retreat of Rommel's forces from El Agheila position began.*

1943

December 12. *Rommel appointed Commander-in-Chief of the "European fortress."*
December 15. *United States troops landed at Cape Markus, on New Britain.*
December 21. *8th Army entered Ortona, Italy.*

1944

December 10. *Fighting in Athens between British troops and Greek partisans (E.L.A.S.).*
December 16. *Rundstedt launched strong counter-attack on U.S. front in the Ardennes.*

MERCHANT AIRCRAFT, CARRIERS are described in the facing page by our Air Correspondent. Longitudinal-section of a 7,930-tons Mac-ship (for short) shows (1) the hangar, fuel-tanks, deck-accommodation, etc. Up to six aircraft can be stowed in the hangar ; four on the grain ships. The Empire Macrae is seen (2) returning to Liverpool after a successful convoy trip. Take-off of Swordfish from Mac-ships had to be rocket boosted in similar fashion to this Seafire of the Naval Air Arm (3). Ratings attach the rockets, filled with cordite, in readiness for the take-off (4). See also illus. pages 476, 615, 732, Vol. 8. *Photos, British Official*

Britain's Biggest Air Squadron

By CAPTAIN
NORMAN MACMILLAN
M.C., A.F.C.

"CAN you climb a rope ladder?" asked Lieut.-Commander Brooker, R.N.V.R., staff officer dealing with MAC-ships as the motor-boat manoeuvred alongside the motor-vessel Empire Macrae.

"Yes," I replied, "although I have not done so for years." One after another our little party seized the ropes as the whale-boat lifted on the gentle waves of the Firth of Clyde, and climbed up the wooden slats that hung vertically on their ropes over the side of the ship.

M.V. Empire Macrae was a Merchant Aircraft Carrier, MAC-ship for short, one of the six grain-carrying vessels that were specially laid down to become Britain's convoy escorts. Their armament was originally two Bofors guns, four Oerlikons, and one 4-in. quick-firing gun. And their real job was to carry aircraft so that the convoys would never be without protection from above against the U-boat that stalked them on their ocean crossings. (See illustration page 615, Vol. 8).

THERE have been reports that the duty of these aircraft was to seal the gap that existed in mid-ocean, within the area that could not be covered by land-based aircraft until the Azores base enabled this to be done. But, in fact, MAC-ship aircraft flew not only in the gap but all the way along the ocean route from Halifax to Liverpool or the Clyde, and during one serious U-boat threat they flew right through the Irish Sea up to the Liverpool Bar Light. The convoys averaged from 7½ to 9½ knots, and the journey took anything from 10 to 23 days.

No. 836 Squadron of the Fleet Air Arm supplied the aircraft and aircrews to all the Merchant Aircraft Carriers, both grain ships and tankers. This was the biggest squadron in the Fleet Air Arm and, indeed, in the British air services. It had 60 aircraft and was entitled to 80 aircrews. The British base was May Down air station, near Londonderry, whence the aircraft flew to and from their ships before and after they berthed.

FLIGHT Deck as Lid Above Holds Carrying 7,500 Tons of Grain

The aircraft were Fairey Swordfish, equipped with Asvic radar (see page 444) and carrying various combinations of depth charges and rocket projectiles, according to the conditions. The grain ships carried four aircraft and had a hangar aft with a lift to the flight deck. The tanker ships had no hangar and carried three aircraft, lashed to the deck and protected by manually fitted wind brakes when not in operation. The Merchant Carrier complement was about 110, including approximately 30 Fleet Air Arm officers and ratings for specified duties.

Now come on board the Empire Macrae with me. She was a Diesel-engined ship, with the normal speed of the average merchant vessel of her size, and flew the Red Ensign of the Merchant Navy at her mast. In her holds she could carry about 7,500 tons of grain which could be loaded and unloaded only by pneumatic elevator machinery, owing to the lid which the permanent flight deck closed over her holds. Her flight deck carried 4 arrester wires, and was 24 ft. above the water.

Her ship's crew were Merchant Navymen, her aircrews were R.N. Volunteer Reservists, and these made a happy combination. The MAC-ship pilots I met were among the cheeriest and happiest men I encountered throughout the whole war—a confraternity bound together in a common cause by a tie more silken and yet more binding than that formed of the strictest discipline.

Captain Collings was on the bridge with Lieut.-Commander J. P. Foster, the Air Staff Officer, and we went up to be introduced. It was the strangest bridge I have ever stepped on. For two persons to pass comfortably it was necessary to turn sideways; it was so narrow as to remind me of a slit trench. Timber and glass wind-shields protected one from the wind and rain. Above us rose the mast with its radio and radar antennae. Some Swordfish were exercising with rocket assisters, and a M.L. escorted us as a destroyer escorts the bigger naval cruisers.

BELCHING Twin Spumes of Flame in Most Fantastic Upward Leap

"Cover your ears," someone said, as the ship straightened into the wind. I noticed how gentle the air speed was compared with the half-gale that blows over the big Fleet carriers when their aircraft are flying off. The first Swordfish opened up at the take-off signal. A green flag was displayed from the bridge by the air-staff officer as a signal to the deck flying control officer (the batsman) to give the pilot the all clear. A negative signal was given by a red flag waved by hand. And there was also radio telephone communication between the bridge and the aircraft's pilot, both when the aircraft was on the flight deck and in the air.

The Swordfish accelerated, apparently too slowly to take off in the 410-ft. length of the flight deck, until it reached the flag on the port side of the flight deck, opposite the island bridge. That was the signal for the pilot to switch on his rockets. There was a terrific bang and a rushing roar like that of a gale lashing a forest. Flame and sparks swept from under each wing of the Swordfish, spurting downwards and rearwards towards the steel deck. And in an instant the aircraft was climbing steeply, so that it crossed the bow of the ship about level with the bridge.

It was a fantastic sight and sound while it lasted, this upward leap into the air of an aircraft belching two spumes of flame. Then, after four seconds, the rockets expended, a silence descended upon the scene until one's eardrums became accustomed to their altered tension, and for that fraction of time an apparently silent Swordfish continued to climb at a more leisurely angle up and away, her turning airscrew belying the illusion that her engine had died. Thus the aircrews took off in mid-ocean with their depth-charges, from a pocket-handkerchief flight-deck on a slow-moving ship, and countered the machinations of Admirals Raeder and Doenitz against the safety of the British Realm.

WHILE the flying continued some mugs of steaming hot tea were brought to the bridge; and very welcome they were, for the air was cold. Then, when flying ceased, we looked over the ship. We left the bridge with its gyro compass, telephone and earphones, and helmsman, and went below to the engine-room which, like all Diesel engine-rooms, was very hot. The big six-cylinder engine plugged steadily, sending a tremor throughout the ship.

In the hangar there was just room to stow the four Swordfish with their wings folded, and to carry a few spares. Each aircraft had to be struck down into the hangar when it landed on, because there was no wind brake or crash barrier on the flight deck. At one time these carriers had a complete aircraft engine as a spare, but this practice was discontinued, and servicing on board was confined to changing of main planes, replacement of an undercarriage, or the substitution of another cylinder on the 9-cylinder Bristol Pegasus aircooled radial engine. The R.N. and M.N. officers messed together in a comfortable dining-saloon and smoke-room, similar to those one might find in any merchant ship carrying about a dozen passengers. But the R.N. and M.N. crews messed separately because Union rules on hours of work made combined messing difficult. The ratings' quarters were fitted with bunks, and their mess had cushion-covered benches and wooden tables.

There were two chart-rooms, one for the ship and another for the aircraft. The M.N. radio control officer had to commuter all the time the bridge was in radio telephone communication with aircraft. A Merchant Service safety-watch was kept day and night on the radio safety wavelength. There was Very High Frequency (V.H.F.) radio direction finding for aircraft navigational assistance, and the ship carried radar.

The sick bay had three beds and a simple operating theatre combined in one room. The operating table was not fixed, for if it had been screwed to the floor it would have been necessary to remove one bed to get around it. As he showed us his pharmacy—a wall-cupboard stocked with "poisons"—the doctor mournfully said he never had anything to do. But there were some busy times. During the war three appendixes were removed at sea, and on more than one occasion a doctor was flown from one merchant carrier to another to provide two doctors at an operation.

INTIMATE With the Spirit of the Men Who Beat the Nazi U-Boats

All together there were 19 MAC-ships. The ten specially-built ships carried the prefix "Empire" before the name. The converted ships bore only a single name. The first MAC-ship went into operation in June 1943. This was a grain ship. Grain was loaded through hatches in the hangar deck. The ships sailed west in water ballast. The first aircraft to arrive on a MAC-ship had the words Royal Navy painted out and Merchant Navy painted in. This was soon discontinued, for what was the difference between the guns and naval gunners on a defensively equipped merchant ship and aircraft and aircrews on a MAC-ship? Their purpose was the same. Two MAC-ships normally escorted a convoy; but sometimes there was only one, occasionally three, and once four.

The oil tanker MAC-ships had longer flight decks, measuring 480 ft. overall. Two of them belonged to the Dutch section of the Anglo-Saxon Oil Company, a branch of Shell; these ships carried Dutch naval air personnel of the Royal Netherlands Navy. In September 1944, four of the 13 tanker MAC-ships were taken off operational work to ferry aircraft from the United States to Britain for the U.S. air forces.

Four of these tanker MAC-ships were specially laid down for the job, but the others were converted from existing ships. Not all the ships were identical to look at. In some the bridge was farther forward or farther aft, but the general principles of their construction were common to all.

While we waited for the M.L. to come alongside to take us ashore we went below to the captain's cabin. It was the comfortable, homely cabin of a typical Merchant Navy cargo vessel; and from what Captain Collings said there, we knew that he loved his ship and liked his work, and we came to know more intimately the spirit of the men who beat the German U-boats. Next day he was sailing his ship west again with another convoy for another ship-load of grain.

The Editor Looks Back

WAR HELPS MEDIOCRITY

Sept. 23, 1939

One of the minor evils of war is that it provides the lesser gifted members of the community with the chance of jumping into positions of official importance. In the social confusion that ensues the less successful in the professions somehow contrive to push themselves into official jobs, and armed with a little brief authority, to lord it over their abler fellows who have "made good" in the honest competition of peaceful times. I saw a lot of that in 1914-18. I'm hoping to see less of it in 1939. A man I knew who had never been able to do more than scrabble along as a fairly good literary hack suddenly became a well-paid official of the Censorship in 1914 with a staff of eight "assistants." After 1918 he reverted to the harder task of earning his living and died not long ago a forgotten denizen of Grub Street.

VAIN hope! The tremendous increases of ministries; the anxiety of every man or woman who snatched a good job to fortify his or her importance by multiplying "assistants" soon became an accepted routine; thousands of employable typists were torn from their commercial posts to spend much of their official time making tea or filing innumerable and mainly useless forms that helped to intensify the paper famine. Even now they are being held at this "official work" to the detriment of serious industrial concerns. No, the Second Great War left the First far behind as a time for Bureaucracy to spread, to flourish and dig itself into the body politic of the nation. We taxpayers shall have to bear the burden for years more.

THE CENSORSHIP

Sept. 23, 1939

There must be hasty and regrettable decisions in hurriedly selecting "ministries" of this and that, which accounts for the "not-to-be-published" rubber stamps that disfigure interesting and quite innocuous photographs submitted to the Censorship and returned after two days of earnest consideration by persons whose real walk in life may have been far removed from their new duties. Which reminds me that another friend of my youth had a big job in the Censorship of 1914 for which he had qualified by years of writing football notes in a provincial sporting paper.

Yesterday, I had fifteen photographs of which, to my knowledge, six or seven appeared in widely circulated journals this week, returned by the Censor disfigured with the aforesaid rubber stamp—photographs that it would have cheered British readers to contemplate as reminders of the strength of their Navy, the Navy which is their own peculiar property, but which some automaton official acting on his printed "Secret" instructions had condemned. The futility of it! The photos in question exist in thousands of copies in Germany and have long been in the hands of every Nazi spy in the British Isles, but they are not to be seen by my readers . . . A week later, on further consideration, they were released!

NOT until Mr. Brendan Bracken took command of the M.O.I. did a little common sense seep into it from the criticism with which it was daily drenched. And even he could not rid it entirely of the rule-of-thumb procedure which still contrived at times to make it do ridiculous things. A Censor's job is to censor, and if the juniors who were plentifully supplied with blue pencils didn't wear their points down for resharpening several times a day they felt they weren't earning their salaries. But, on the whole, the record of the British Censorship, as one looks back, will compare not unfavourably with that of the U.S.S.R. and the U.S.A. The M.O.I. can still do useful work, but it probably employs half a dozen assistants to do what one would accomplish in a commercial office. And all business offices are still being starved for assistants.

THE BLACKOUT

Sept. 23, 1939

The Government did right, I think, in imposing the most complete restriction straight away—even the excessive blackout. For it is easier to relax than to increase. To have begun in a piecemeal way, adding new restrictive regulations every day or two, would have led to greater dissatisfaction and irritation. The joy of getting our gloom lightened by the wise modification of the blackout as regards motor traffic and the use of torches made a welcome change in the night life of London of which I have had evidence tonight—also the partial re-opening of theatres and cinemas in the West End and the suburbs.

LOOKING back after six years to those dread nights of the early blackout, now that the lights o' London shine again, is one of the things that make us thankful to have survived. And then along come the unsocial strikes of the dockers and the gas-workers to remind us how few of our fellow-men are needed to plunge the whole community into misery by refusing to do their jobs of manual labour in a public service because their employers do not immediately agree to their wage demands. All very confusing to the non-party citizen, who sees a Labour Government in power and the strike instrument being wielded so ruthlessly.

NO PROFITEERING?

Sept. 23, 1939

"No profiteering this time!" is a brave, vain cry. In the Great War we saw certain classes, or rather numerous fellow-citizens—for all "classes" profiteered to the limit of possibility—growing rich from selling goods at unconscionable prices simply because of their rarity or the difficulty of transport. We shall see the same again . . . are seeing it now. But increase of prices is not only inevitable, it is reasonable. When supplies are unlimited any increase of price to the purchaser is stark profiteering, but where supplies are restricted and diminishing, some compensation to the seller for inability to restock seems only fair. After all, if diamonds were as common as coal they would not command fancy prices. But I do feel that our rulers are going after the profiteer today more vigorously than in 1914-18.

YES, and still prices have soared enormously. But the circumstances differ totally. There is no doubt that coupons and rationing have saved the country from inflation at least in its worst form. The idea of utility production was a good one and, having regard to all the difficulties, it has been wisely carried out. Of course, there has been some "profiteering," but not in the essentials of life; we have all been brought to one level of resource in these, thanks to our ration books. Some writer started an article on a visit to Soviet Russia the other day by remarking that it was difficult to explain a "class-divided society like that of the Soviets to a classless country like Great Britain." Quaint; but, in this matter of the essentials of life, true!

ILLUSORY SAFETY

Sept. 30, 1939

The air-raid shelters in the St. James's district are many and reassuring. A few yards from my flat is one for seven hundred persons in a magnificent seven-storey building which has just recently been completed and is still untenanted. Nothing but direct hit would disturb those sheltering in its concrete depths. On the other hand, the cellars of my own building were condemned months ago by the Westminster surveyor as unsuitable for shelter. Imagine my surprise this morning to find an official notice posted on the wall announcing that they are now available for eight persons! Nothing whatever has been done to improve them as shelters, and if the large sewer or the water main—both close by—were to be cracked, the cellars would be flooded out before you'd have time to say "von Ribbentrop."

ACTUALLY bombs fell in very considerable numbers all round about that seven-storey building in St. James's Square and much damage was done, little of which has been repaired so far. I had to quit my flat when its ceilings came down and all its windows were blasted. A very costly shelter was constructed in the basement late in 1940 but was never used, I believe. I suppose it is beyond the power of human computation to estimate the millions that must have been spent on building shelters throughout the country that served no useful purpose beyond providing an illusory sense of safety in a time of fear.

Postscript

"OH, that England may learn hatred! Hatred and fierceness and pitilessness—that we may all learn God-like hardship and simplicity and sternness with our children. At present they are taught to make money—not serve either their country or their God." That quotation, my young highbrow readers will be aghast to learn, comes not from Kipling but from the journal kept by Katherine Bradley and Edith Cooper, those two remarkable Victorian women aesthetes whose exquisite-frail lyrics appeared under the joint signature of "Michael Field." The date—significantly—is 1900.

I MUST confess to receiving quite a shock when I read in my evening paper the other night the headline: "Famous Figurehead to Leave Whitehall." But it wasn't as drastic as I'd expected. Instead of a clearance-out at the Treasury or the Duchy of Lancaster, it was merely (alas!) our old friend the massive wooden figurehead of H.M.S. Orion which has stood for many years at the entrance to the Royal United Services Museum and is now to be transported to Chatham for necessary repairs.

AT a court-martial in Germany a German witness found himself unable to identify the prisoner. For, said he, "to me all English soldiers look alike." I found this amusing until I recollected dining years ago with a Chinese diplomat who made precisely the same confession. Is it a case of the Inscrutable West? "All coons look alike to me" was long ago a popular Yankee lyric.

THE Government's proposal to enforce the carrying of identity-cards till the end of 1947 has had an unfortunately bad "Press." I say "unfortunately" since it is no secret that for the past ten years England has been a haven of rest for quite a few international undesirables who have somehow managed to maintain their pose as harmless "refugees." Identity cards without photographs may be little better than Christmas-cards—but even that little counts.

In Britain Now: A.T.A. Flag Flies for Last Time

INSIDE ST. PAUL'S in November 1945 workmen were removing 14-in. anti-blast walls from famous monuments, including Stevens's memorial to Wellington (above). The cathedral was hit by two 500-pounders and 16 incendiaries; a one-ton bomb and a land-mine fell in the churchyard.

H.M.S. NELSON, 33,950-ton battleship (right), ended her distinguished war service when she docked at Portsmouth on November 16, 1945, after a 8,076-miles voyage from Singapore. Besides her complement of 1,361 officers and ratings, she brought home 600 Service "Repats."

AIR TRANSPORT AUXILIARY closed down officially on Nov. 30, 1945, when a W.A.A.F. officer (above) hauled down the A.T.A. flag at White Waltham airfield, Berks. Since Sept. 1939 the A.T.A. delivered over 300,000 aircraft from factory and maintenance depots to R.A.F. and Naval Air Arm stations.

TIN HATS—WHO'LL BUY? The Southern Railway in November 1945 were calling in A.R.P. equipment which had been distributed among their staff (right). At a goods yard in Battersea over 64,000 tin hats were piled, awaiting sale—but there were no bidders.

Photos, Fox, Sport & General, The Evening Standard, Topical Press

Red Army Victories Enshrined in Berlin

IN THE HEART OF GERMANY'S CAPITAL, in the famous Tiergarten this impressive memorial, surmounted by a Red Army man in bronze, commemorates Russia's victory over the Third Reich and the memory of Soviet forces who perished. British, U.S. and French troops took part in the unveiling ceremony by Marshal Zhukov on November 11, 1945, when the 2nd Battalion of the Devonshire Regiment mounted a guard of honour. The Russians worked hard, often by lamplight, to finish the memorial in time.

Photo, Associated Press

Printed in England and published every alternate Friday by the Proprietors, THE AMALGAMATED PRESS, LTD., The Fleetway House, Farringdon Street, London, E.C.4. Registered for transmission by Canadian Magazine Post. Sole Agents for Australia and New Zealand: Messrs. Gordon & Gotch, Ltd.; and for South Africa: Central News Agency, Ltd.—December 21, 1945. S.S. *Editorial Address:* JOHN CARPENTER HOUSE, WHITEFRIARS, LONDON, E.C.4.

Vol 9 The War Illustrated and AFTERWARDS N° 223

SIXPENCE JANUARY 4, 1946

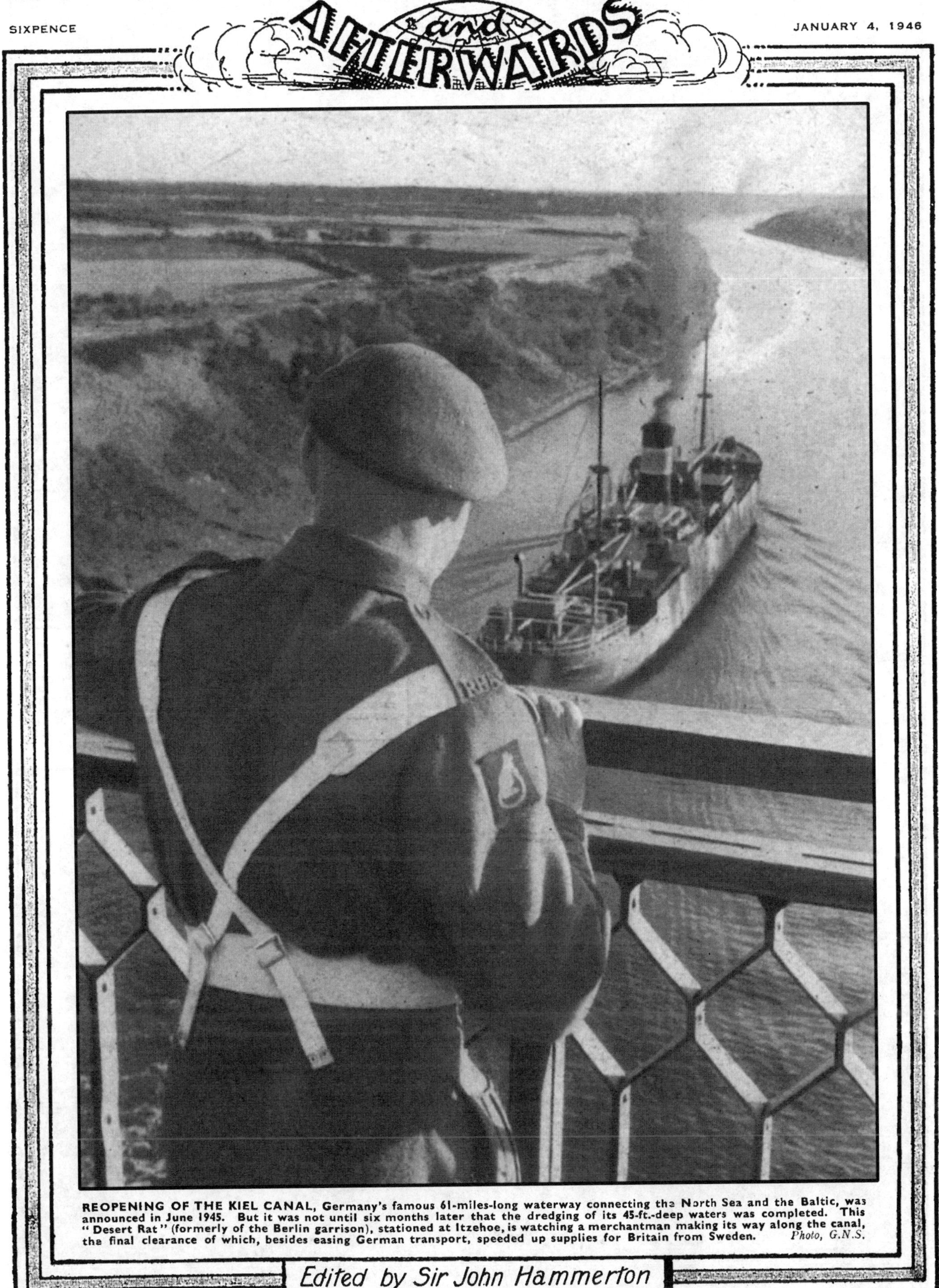

REOPENING OF THE KIEL CANAL, Germany's famous 61-miles-long waterway connecting the North Sea and the Baltic, was announced in June 1945. But it was not until six months later that the dredging of its 45-ft.-deep waters was completed. This "Desert Rat" (formerly of the Berlin garrison), stationed at Itzehoe, is watching a merchantman making its way along the canal, the final clearance of which, besides easing German transport, speeded up supplies for Britain from Sweden. *Photo, G.N.S.*

Edited by Sir John Hammerton

NO. 224 WILL BE PUBLISHED FRIDAY, JANUARY 18

Our Thankless Task in Turbulent Palestine

IN THE SHARON VALLEY DISTRICT during a clash with insurgents on Nov. 25, 1945, in which eight Jewish settlers were killed and several wounded, a patrol of the 6th Airborne Division checked this civilian's identity card (1). Insurgents opposed entry of our troops and of members of the Palestine Police to the Rishpon Valley, having previously attacked nearby coastguard stations. Armed with pick helves and metal shields, the Police are on parade (2). Another detachment piles into a patrol-lorry (3) on the order "Mount!" See also pages 515, 517, 537. *Photos, Central Press, G.P.U.*

What the Loan Means to Britain

By

JOHN BUCKATZSCH

To most people the complexities and uncertainties of the Anglo-American Loan Agreement constitute a major headache. The purpose of the immense sum involved, the terms of the loan and conditions attached, how it is likely to affect our trading relations with the Dominions, the influence it will have on the lives of us all for years to come: these and other points are made clear in this exposition specially written for "The War Illustrated."

IN the House of Commons on August 24, 1945, Mr. Attlee announced the termination by the Americans of the Lend-Lease arrangements which had been in operation since March 11, 1941, and stated that Lord Halifax, British Ambassador to the United States, and Lord Keynes, adviser to the Treasury, were proceeding to Washington to discuss the resulting situation with representatives of the U.S. Administration. Talks opened on September 11, but it was not until December 6 that the Prime Minister was able to announce that a financial agreement putting almost £1,100,000,000 at the disposal of Great Britain had been signed.

Details of the final proposals arrived at have now been presented to the House of Commons and to the British public. They have aroused little enthusiasm and some opposition, but they were accepted by the House of Commons on December 13, and by the House of Lords five days later. If, as seems likely, the U.S. Congress ratifies the agreement, the foundation of the economic life of the post-war world will have been laid. Why has the "Financial Agreement between the Governments of the United States and the United Kingdom" been accepted with such reluctance in Great Britain?

Annual Repayment Over 50 Years

A loan equivalent to about £1,100,000,000 is offered by the U.S.A. to Great Britain. Of this sum about £162,000,000 is to be used to pay for the goods dispatched to Great Britain under the terms of the Lend-Lease arrangements but not actually received when those arrangements were terminated. The remainder is available in dollars to be drawn upon at any time between ratification of the agreement and the end of 1951. The loan and the interest are to be repaid in annual sums of about £35,000,000 (except in certain circumstances), over a period of fifty years, beginning in 1951.

In previous articles—see pages 366 and 483—I tried to show why a loan of U.S. dollars is necessary. Briefly, we require dollars to pay for goods and services which we have to buy in America, and to be able to offer dollars to some of the nations to whom we owe pounds sterling, but who want to make payments to the U.S.A. (This is what is meant by "making the Sterling Balances convertible" into dollars.) In the long run, these dollars must be obtained by exporting British goods and services to the U.S.A.

UNFORTUNATELY, our ability to do this at the present time is limited by factors directly connected with the war. For example, we had to sell a large proportion of the securities on which we used to receive interest payments in dollars in order to pay for American aircraft before the days of Lend-Lease. About half our pre-war tonnage of merchant ships, which used to earn an income in foreign currency, has been sunk during the war. Above all, labour and machinery were directed from making goods for export to making munitions or filling the ranks of the armed forces.

The revival of the flow of dollars and other foreign currencies with which to buy imports will depend on the revival of the export trade, and that in turn will depend on the rate of "Reconversion." By "Reconversion" we mean not only bringing the Waafs back to the cotton mills and turning tank factories back into motor works, but also making good great arrears of maintenance work in those factories which *did* continue to make civilian goods during the war. The task is formidable, for our export trade, which fell during the war to about *one third* of its 1938 value, must be raised about three-quarters *above* that level if our essential post-war imports are to be paid for.

Even though the process of reconversion is going ahead faster than many people suppose (probably faster than the reverse process did in 1939-41), and even though the home market continues to be starved of the goods which have been enjoyed by our American Allies throughout the war, some years must elapse before this export target is achieved.

The alternative to obtaining the necessary American goods in return for British exports would be to obtain American goods on credit. It was originally hoped that the United States would see their way to making a grant-in-aid—a sort of peace-time Lease-Lend—in recognition of the terrific burden borne by this country during the war. This proposition being unacceptable, the only remaining possibility is a loan on orthodox terms; and this, broadly speaking, is what the British negotiators have received.

From one point of view, the securing of a loan is a source of satisfaction. For it will mitigate to some extent the great hardships that would otherwise have had to be endured during the next few years, and will enable us to meet some of the requests of our Sterling creditors for payments in American dollars. But, unfortunately, certain conditions are attached to the granting of the loan which can only cause very grave misgivings to many people in Great Britain.

If a Major Slump Occurs in U.S.A.

What are these conditions? In the first place, obviously the acceptance of the Loan imposes a burden of annual payments amounting to about £35,000,000 over a period of fifty years. This is not a large sum in itself, but clearly does nothing to lighten the existing heavy burden on our Balance of Payments. This sum must, of course, be paid out of the proceeds of additional British exports to America (except in so far as it is paid in gold bought from other countries). Thus the ability of Great Britain to repay the Loan depends on the willingness of Americans to buy British goods. Experience of the conditions prevailing in the inter-war period has shown that this willingness is likely to vary considerably from time to time.

In particular, if a major slump should occur in the U.S.A., the American National Income will fall, and with it the ability of American citizens to buy British goods. Under these conditions the American government will almost certainly attempt to encourage American exports, though it may be difficult for it to persuade the U.S.A. to admit imports of British goods. Now, it is true that the Loan agreement provides for the "waiving" if the annual repayments of the British Balance of Payments can be shown to be in such a state as not to permit the necessary transfer of dollars to be made. But it may still prove difficult to invoke this waiver clause.

A MORE serious cause of misgiving in Great Britain is the manner in which the offer of the Loan is tied to the acceptance by Great Britain of what is called "free multilateral trade." Essentially this means that we forgo the right to make specific trading agreements with other nations, in particular with the Dominions. We agree to make any future sterling balances freely convertible into dollars. By this undertaking a powerful inducement to other countries to buy from us because we buy from them is removed. At the same time we have undertaken that any portion of the vast existing sterling balances that are released for spending shall be made available in *either* sterling *or* dollars, as their owners choose.

Regarded as an Economic Dunkirk

Moreover, the Agreement limits the power of Great Britain to grant Imperial Preference. For we have agreed to curtail imports from Empire countries in the same proportion as we may at any future time curtail imports from the U.S.A. The effect which this provision may have on the economic structure of the British Commonwealth cannot yet be predicted.

But it is clear that we must be prepared to abandon the picture we had formed of the members of the Commonwealth establishing, if necessary, a large group of nations maintaining full employment at home and insulated from the possible international economic fluctuations generated by variations in the American willingness to buy imports.

Provided such fluctuations do not occur, all may be well; but we cannot feel justified in assuming that the American people have learned the great lesson of the inter-war period—that employment must be stabilized at a high level by systematic planning on the lines which were laid down in the British Coalition Government White Paper on Employment Policy.

The Loan Agreement, in fact, has two serious implications. In the first place, we are forced to lay aside some of the most powerful weapons by which we could hope to achieve the enormous task of rebuilding our export trade—mainly controls over our overseas trade. In the second place, we are drawn once more into a world of international economic relationships in which *all* depends on the willingness of creditor nations (to all intents and purposes the U.S.A.) to accept imports. Both these are implied by the "convertibility" undertakings and by the abandonment of Imperial Preference.

ALL, we repeat, may be well, but it is impossible to feel any confidence that it will be so. The Loan could not be rejected, but we should regard it as an economic Dunkirk, providing a breathing space which may enable us to set about the gigantic tasks of national recovery from a situation into which we were thrown by the completeness of our war effort, and hope that the U.S.A. will recognize the duty of creditor nations to accept payment in goods of the debts owed to them. This means a complete revision of American tariff-policy and a refusal to rely on the disastrous expedients of the nineteen-thirties by which nations sought to export their unemployment.

'OUT OF TUNE WITH REALITIES'

"I SHALL never as long as I live cease to regret that this is not an interest-free loan," said Lord Keynes, speaking in the House of Lords on December 18, 1945. "The charging of interest is out of tune with the underlying realities. It is based on a false analogy.

"Other conditions of the loan indicate clearly that our case has been recognized as being a special one. The Americans, one would have thought, might have emphasized the special character still further by forgoing interest.

"The amount of money at stake cannot be important to the United States, and what a difference it would have made to our feelings and our response. But there it is," he added resignedly.

New Zealanders with a Fine War Record

By MAJ.-GENERAL
SIR CHARLES GWYNN
K.C.B., D.S.O.

In the First Great War the New Zealand Expeditionary Force established a reputation second to none as a gallant and efficient fighting unit. It is, I think, well known that the reputation of the 2nd N.Z.E.F. stands as high, and that it has displayed the same qualities as those of its predecessors. In addition, it has had opportunities of acquiring a versatility denied to the first N.Z.E.F. which, like other troops, had to suffer the restrictions of trench warfare. Now that a connected account of the exploits of the Force is available (though not in general circulation in this country), a picture can be given of the part played by its 2nd Division in Greece and North Africa, where this Division's characteristics were developed and its reputation established before it took part in the campaign in Italy.

When the Second Great War started it was intended that the N.Z. 2nd Div. should assemble and complete its training and final organization in the Middle East. The first contingent arrived in Egypt in February 1940, but the second was diverted to England when the threat of invasion developed. The third contingent later joined the first in Egypt, but this left the Division insufficiently organized and trained to take its full part in Wavell's victorious Libyan campaign. Its engineers, signals and transport, however, were used and rendered service of immense importance. The transport carried to their assembly areas the infantry which stormed Graziani's Sidi Barrani defences—in one phase of the battle they debussed their passengers within a hundred yards of the Italian positions, and the drivers left their vehicles to join in the assault. Later the transport in its more normal role gained an outstanding reputation for delivering food and water punctually, whatever the conditions. The other ancillary units also rendered notable service.

They Were the First to Join Hands With Garrison of Besieged Tobruk

But perhaps the greatest tribute paid to the adaptability and toughness of New Zealanders was their selection to provide personnel for the Long-Range Desert Group formed on the initiative of Major Bagnold, and under his command, when Italy entered the war. The Group explored immense stretches of waterless unmapped desert and harassed the enemy's outlying detachments and communications. The selection of New Zealanders for the experiment was all the more curious because they had less experience of desert conditions than any of the other troops available (see page 19).

If the Division were disappointed at losing a chance of chasing Italians they soon had an opportunity of proving their metal against a more formidable antagonist. Brought up to establishment by the arrival of the 5th Brigade from England, the Division constituted a large part of the army sent to fulfil our promises to Greece. There opportunities for offensive action were denied it, but troops entering battle for the first time have seldom experienced more testing conditions—defence against greatly superior forces, which turned into a long retreat followed by a difficult evacuation, with the enemy possessing vastly superior armour and complete command of the air. The battle in Crete, where the New Zealanders fought hard for the Maleme aerodrome, was a variant of the same experiences, with the enemy still holding all the trumps.

Reassembled and reorganized in Egypt, the Division played an important part in Auchinleck's 1941 offensive. In the whirlpool battle of Sidi Rezegh the Division became split up into Brigade groups, alternately fighting offensively or on the defensive in desperate situations. It had the satisfaction of being the first to join hands with the garrison of Tobruk, and it developed a technique for retrieving apparently hopeless situations by bayonet attacks at night, in which Maoris frequently showed special aptitude. But casualties were heavy, and when Rommel was compelled at last to retreat to his El Agheila stronghold the Division was withdrawn to Syria to reorganize and to absorb reinforcements.

In the summer of 1942, an urgent call came for the Division to cover the retreat of the 8th Army after its loss of the swaying battle of Gazala and Tobruk. Covering 900 miles in five days, a wonderful feat on the part of the staff and lorry drivers, the Division took up a position of readiness south of Matruh in Wavell's old defence line. The intention was to threaten the flank of Rommel's pursuit rather than to hold a defensive rallying line for the 8th Army, which continued to retreat to El Alamein. Here at Mingar Quaim, Rommel attempted to surround the Division, and nearly succeeded, but an astonishing night assault by the 4th Brigade cut a way out ; the Germans being surprised by what they complained had been an attack by "thousands of drunken New Zealanders."

This action checked the momentum of Rommel's pursuit, and when he arrived at Alamein he was unable to break through the rallying position there. During the summer the Division took a leading part in defensive and counter-offensive actions, and when Rommel at the end of August made his last great effort to break into the Nile Delta the Division was on the southern side of the trap which Alexander and Montgomery, now in charge, had laid, and came in for heavy fighting during Rommel's attack and withdrawal.

Lt.-Gen. Sir BERNARD FREYBERG, V.C., K.C.B., K.B.E.
From the portrait painted in the Western Desert by Capt. Peter McIntyre

In the final Alamein battle two brigades of the Division (the third having been withdrawn to be equipped and organized as an armoured brigade) took a leading part in making the breach through which the Armoured Corps broke out. It had, however, been earmarked to form a mobile pursuing force. No sooner had the armour passed through than trucks for the two brigades came up into line and the Division came under the command of the Armoured Corps for the pursuit. A freak storm which halted the pursuit for a day enabled Rommel to escape utter disaster, and with the advantage of a metalled road he had little difficulty in reaching his El Agheila stronghold.

Before he could be attacked there, Montgomery had to pause to close up and to consolidate his communications. But he now had in the mobile force of which the N.Z. Division was the substantial nucleus (the whole under General Freyberg's command) an instrument with which to carry out his left-hooks round the enemy's open desert flank. During the pause, the force was organized at Bardia as a self-contained formation carrying water and food for twelve days and petrol for 350 miles. Then, when all was ready for the frontal attack, the force was brought forward and dispatched on a 250-mile desert march to come in on the rear of Rommel's "impregnable" fortress.

Astonishing Left-Hook Brought Off by Freyberg's Hard-Fighting Force

It was an amazing effort which only failed to achieve complete success because Rommel had taken alarm, and because the heavily armed tanks forming his rearguard succeeded in breaking through Freyberg's force, for which only a small number of heavy tanks had been available. Nevertheless, it was a great achievement to have manoeuvred the enemy out of an immensely strong position.

Similar manoeuvres deterred Rommel from making a determined attempt to cover Tripoli in the strong positions available, and his retreat continued to the Mareth line on the Tunisian frontier. Here it seemed that he intended to stand while looking for opportunities to strike back at the armies closing in on him. Though he failed in such attempts to achieve his full object he was still confident in the strength of his position. But again Freyberg's force brought off an astonishing left-hook which, after a hard fight, opened the way to the rear of the position and, when Montgomery sent reinforcements to exploit the success, rendered it untenable. Having suffered heavy defeat in the Mareth line and in the Akarit position, Rommel (or rather Messe, now in command) had no alternative but a rapid retreat to join Von Arnim in the north.

In the final battle the N.Z. 2nd Div. made gallant attacks on the practically impregnable Enfidaville position which misled Von Arnim as to the real danger point, but robbed the Division of the chance of playing its usual leading part in the decisive attack. In the Italian campaign the Division continued to give notable service. "The part of the New Zealand Division," said Lt.-Gen. Sir Oliver Leese, "has been as prominent as its reputation and quality deserved . . . their people at home may justly be as proud of their part in the Italian campaign as they were of their previous exploits." But undoubtedly it is as masters of desert warfare and as troops that could be relied on to cope with the most difficult conditions that the 2nd N.Z.E.F. will always be famous.

On Four Fronts They Gained Their High Renown

GREAT STORY OF NEW ZEALAND'S famous 2nd Division was worked out in a diversity of lands and conditions. Greeted by peasants in Greece (above) in April 1941. In the Western Desert campaign of 1940-42, Capt. C. H. Upham, V.C., and bar (top right, in foreground) snatches a hasty meal ; see also portrait in page 414. Highlight of this campaign was the relief of Tobruk on Dec. 8, 1941 ; N.Z. sappers are seen (centre) laying the Tobruk railway. In Italy, at Cassino, Feb.-May 1944, the New Zealanders excelled in street fighting (below) ; in white winter camouflage (bottom right).

Hunting a U-Boat to Death

By

FRANCIS E. McMURTRIE

ON March 8, 1944, the Greek steamer Peleus, under charter to the Ministry of War Transport, sailed from Freetown, Sierra Leone, for South America. She was an ex-British ship of 4,628 tons gross, built at West Hartlepool in 1928. Five days later, at about six in the afternoon, the tracks of two torpedoes were observed on the port bow; both hit the Peleus, and she sank in a couple of minutes, leaving most of the crew struggling in the water or clinging to rafts or floating wreckage. They included not only Greeks but British, Chinese, Polish and Chilean seamen.

The German submarine, U 852, which had sunk the ship, appeared on the surface and interrogated the third officer, who was summoned on board. After his lifebelt had been taken from him he was placed on a raft. Fire was then opened on the survivors from machine-guns, while some of the submarine's crew amused themselves by flinging hand-grenades at them. Most of the unfortunate men were killed outright, or soon died of their wounds; one poor wretch lingered for 25 days before expiring on a raft. This left three, who after dreadful privations were picked up by a Portuguese steamer; one of these survivors was British.

TRIAL OF U-BOAT WAR CRIMINALS opened in Hamburg on October 17, 1945, when members of the crew of the U 852 were charged with murdering British and Allied seamen after sinking the Greek ship Peleus in the Atlantic on March 13, 1944. During the hearing one of the defence counsel—a German—shook hands with Lieut. Heinz Eck, the U-boat captain later sentenced to death with two of his officers. *Photo, Keystone*

HOW the U 852 Met her End and the Capture of her Captain and Crew

News of this atrocity caused an intensive search for the enemy submarine, H.M. ships Butser, Duncton and Kelt (anti-submarine trawlers patrolling in the S. Atlantic) carrying out a sweep in the area where the U-boat was believed to be operating. She was next heard of farther east, where she was hunted by a frigate off Durban. Ultimately she was disabled by aircraft attack near Aden, in October 1944. Her commanding officer beached his sinking vessel on a sandbank and ordered her to be abandoned. He and his officers and men were made prisoners.

According to Press reports, papers found in the submarine established the fact that three other U-boats were operating in East African waters, with the result that all were in turn hunted down and destroyed. On inquiry at the Admiralty, however, I am informed that there is no basis for the belief that information obtained on board U 852 had anything to do with subsequent sinkings of enemy submarines.

Had this been true, it would not have been the first time that the destruction of an enemy submarine had led to the snaring of others. In July 1918, UB 110, after being rammed by H.M. destroyer Garry was finally sunk by depth charges from ML 263, off Roker, near Sunderland. As the water was comparatively shallow at this point, the submarine was salved and her log examined. It provided most valuable guidance concerning the routes followed by U-boats outward and homeward, and so materially assisted those engaged in hunting them.

IN October 1945, a year after the loss of his submarine, the captain of U 852, Lieut. Heinz Eck, was brought to trial at Hamburg before a court of British and Greek officers. With him were arraigned a number of his officers and men, together accused of murdering seven British, two Greek and two Chinese seamen. In presenting the case for the prosecution, Colonel Halse mentioned that the log of the submarine contained an entry recording the sinking of a ship in the position in which the Peleus was lost.

Lieutenant Eck pleaded operational necessity as an excuse for firing on the survivors, as aircraft might have sighted the floating wreckage and thus have set pursuit on his track. He also alleged that he had orders to behave harshly to mercantile personnel. Dealing with this plea, the Deputy Judge Advocate observed: "To kill survivors of a torpedoed ship is a grave breach of the law of nations. The Court has simply to judge whether, in the words of the charge, the men were concerned in killing the survivors. Duty to obey is limited to the observance of orders that are lawful."

LIEUT. Hans Richard Lenz, giving evidence in his own favour, stated that his captain had ordered the elimination of all trace of the Peleus by opening fire on the survivors. When Lenz protested, he was told that it was essential to leave no evidence of the sinking. He saw a leading seaman named Schwender, also under trial, using a machine-gun to fire at the wreckage; he admitted himself taking over this gun, but declared in self-vindication that he fired it only in the general direction of the target.

After a four-day trial the accused were found guilty. Lieutenant Eck, Surgeon Lieutenant-Commander Walter Weispehnnig and Sub-Lieutenant August Hoffmann were sentenced to death, and have since been shot. Lenz was ordered to be imprisoned for life, and Schwender for 15 years. It is to be hoped that this will not be the last of such trials, for there is no doubt this is merely one of a number of cases in which the survivors of sunken ships have been brutally murdered. Moreover, there is nothing new in this abominable method of waging war, a deliberate policy first instituted in the war of 1914-18, and then expressed cynically by a German diplomat in the infamous phrase "*spurlos versenken*"—to sink without trace.

One of the most notorious criminals of the U-boat war in 1914-18 was W. Werner, of U 55. After sinking the S.S. Torrington, 150 miles S.E. of the Scillies, in April 1917, he deliberately submerged with 20 of her survivors on the upper deck. Four days later he murdered most of the crew of the Toro in precisely the same way; he was also responsible for attacks on hospital ships After the First Great War, trials of U-boat criminals by German courts proved to be a travesty of justice. Prominent offenders were given every chance to disappear, witnesses were intimidated, and acquittals became the rule rather than the exception.

TORPEDOED Survivors Fired on In Their Lifeboat by the Japanese

So many U-boats have themselves been eliminated with all on board that it is improbable that the world will ever know the full extent of their crimes. It is to be hoped that no effort will be spared to gather every scrap of evidence that can be found against enemy submarine personnel now in custody as prisoners of war. This extends to the Japanese as well as the Germans, the former having proved themselves apt pupils in this as in other matters.

Here is a case in point, as reported in a recent issue of the Norges Handels og Sjöfartstidende (Norwegian Trade and Shipping Gazette): Arne Karlsen, master of the Norwegian motor tanker Alcides, has just arrived back in Norway from a Japanese prison camp. He states that the Alcides sailed from Bandar Abbas, in the Persian Gulf, on July 15, 1943, in convoy for Australia with a cargo of oil. On July 23, some days after parting from the convoy, the vessel was torpedoed by a Japanese submarine. Two torpedoes struck the tanker amidships, and she sank in a minute and a half. A few of the crew managed to get into a lifeboat, while the submarine surfaced and took on board as prisoners the master, mate and wireless officer. They afterwards heard rifle and machine-gun fire, and assumed that the Japanese were firing on their unfortunate shipmates in the lifeboat.

THIS is but one of several cases in which the Japanese have behaved with most callous cruelty. In certain instances they have amused themselves by torturing their unfortunate victims. It is some consolation to know that, out of a possible total of about 175 submarines, Japan lost at least 125, most of them with all hands. It is to be hoped that rigid measures will be taken to examine the personnel belonging to those that remain, in order that none of the perpetrators of atrocities may escape. Not only is it highly desirable for abstract reasons that justice should be satisfied, but the knowledge that salutary punishment has been inflicted on war criminals will be a warning to future generations of our enemies

Attack on Malta Convoy as Nazi Bombers Saw It

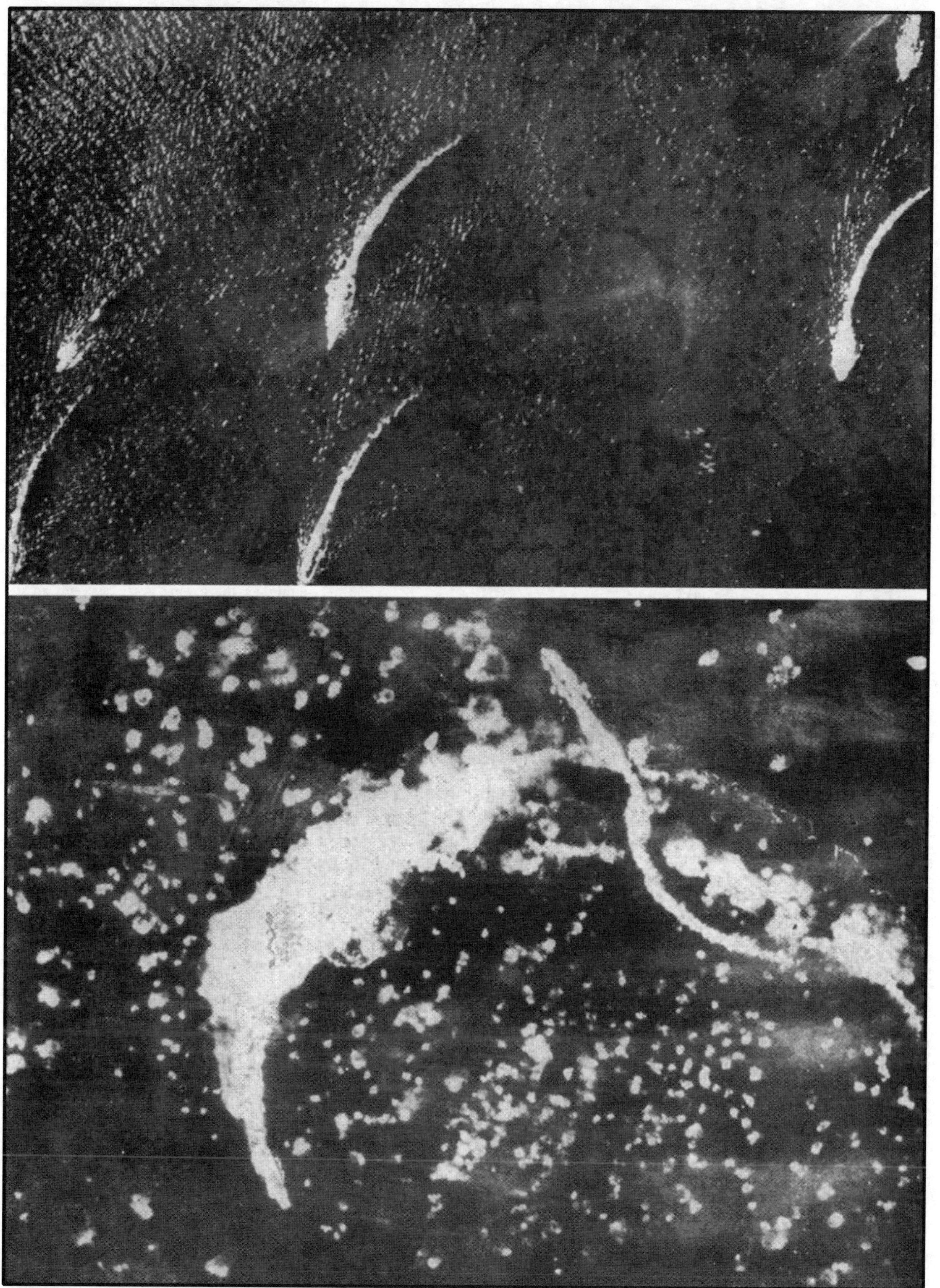

SEIZED ENEMY PHOTOGRAPHS of a Malta convoy attack during August 11-12, 1942, released for publication in December 1945, revealed the intensity of our A.A. defences. This important and continuously-blitzed convoy—known as "Operation Pedestal"—was a gallant venture in which only seven of the fourteen merchantmen got through. The battleships H.M.S. Nelson and Rodney are seen (top, centre) with merchantmen to port. Bomb-bursts close to one of the escorting carriers (bottom), which included the Indomitable and the Victorious. *Photos, British Official*

Operation Deadlight: Sinking the U-boat Fleet

Germany's submarines are putting to sea for the last time: we are scuttling them in the Western Approaches, where so many merchant ships were attacked and sent to the bottom by them during the war. Witnessing these operations in the Atlantic, GORDON HOLMAN has written this account specially for "The War Illustrated." See also facing page and 576.

THE final chapter of the story of the longest battle of the war is entitled "Operation Deadlight." It is being written now, eight months after the end of the war with Germany, in the grey bleakness of the North Atlantic where most of the story was unfolded over five and a half long years. "Operation Deadlight," which began on November 25, 1945, puts into effect the plan for the destruction of all surplus U-boats. It is a plan which has received the approval of the major Allied powers.

A large proportion of the German underwater fleet which carried on unrestricted warfare against our shipping from the time of the sinking of the Athenia on the night of September 3, 1939, until the end of hostilities had been assembled in two British ports. Some of the U-boats had been brought straight in from sea after surrendering to British surface forces. Others had made the passage from German ports, following closely the course of the German fleet that had straggled into Scapa Flow twenty-six years earlier. The fate of the U-boats was to be the same as that of the surface ships after the previous war—but now the scuttling was to be done for them.

Loch Ryan, in south-west-Scotland, with Stranraer at its head, was the main point of assembly for the U-boats. Eighty-six of them were lying there when I arrived in the Polish destroyer Blyskawica. They were in little groups of five and six, which made the fleet appear deceptively small until one got among the craft. Twenty-four other U-boats were at Lisahally, on the northern Irish coast. These two collections made up the total of 110 surplus U-boats.

TO move among the larger force of submarines in Loch Ryan was a strange experience. Here was three-quarters of what remained of a fleet that had menaced our very existence as an island people. These craft, and others like them already sunk, had imposed a never-to-be-forgotten toll on the Allied navies and merchant navies. But for the unfailing devotion to duty that we have come to expect from our seamen, they might have snatched victory for Hitler even when he had little to hope for in other directions.

In Loch Ryan, in the autumn of the same year that many of them had been on active operations against us, they looked fairly harmless, although one felt there was a lot to be said for putting them where they would remain harmless for all time. To almost anybody who has sailed the seas in times of war, a submarine has sinister suggestions. There was little need to extend the imagination in this direction when passing among clusters of them, many with their "U" markings still on their conning towers.

An American-built Captain class frigate acted as guard ship, but most of the U-boats were unmanned. A crew of about 40 men had been permitted to remain on the centre boat in each cluster. They not only looked after their own craft but supplied working parties to carry out necessary maintenance on the vessels alongside them. At the appointed time, the U-boats would move slowly down the loch under their own power until they were finally abandoned by their crews and taken in tow for the "burial ground" in the Atlantic.

Each cluster of U-boats had one White Ensign flying over it and two signal pennants which were identification numerals. There was no uniformity in the way the submarines had been brought together. U 313, a big transport craft with a flat deck the size of a Thames pleasure boat, almost hid U 2335 and U 2329, two of the Mark 23 submarines with which the Germans made their final desperate inshore attacks on our shipping.

A rusty square radar installation stood out above the conning tower of U 170, another big boat—probably of 1,500 tons. U 360 had an odd, mottled appearance where large splashes of red lead had been slapped across her hull. One trot (the Navy's name

for these clusters of craft) was impressive because five large U-boats of the same pattern were all lying side by side.

Many of the larger boats had double gun platforms but the guns were missing. One wondered what grim actions had been fought against the R.A.F. or Fleet Air Arm from these gun positions. The little U-boats, with their hulls hardly showing above the still waters of the Loch, had no gun platforms at all. Their defence was their smallness and the readiness with which they could be taken down and, with the aid of their "Schnorkel" air tubes, kept down (see pages 680-681, Vol. 8).

Symbol of End of Nazi Sea Power

Along the single wire rigging running fore and aft from the conning towers, the last of the German crews had hung their washing. Few of the men who would remain to see their boats towed away to final destruction were on deck. One small party was busy, however, with a welding apparatus. They were preparing for the last tow. As we drew away from the fleet of U-boats and their grey hulls became merged in the background of Scottish hills, the blue welding flame stood out vividly. Suddenly it flickered and was gone—a strange symbol of the end of German sea power.

On November 25 the first towing operation began. In command of the group of ships taking part was Captain St. J. A. Micklethwait, holder of three D.S.O.s, who was a prisoner in the hands of the Germans for three years. He was captured after his ship, H.M.S. Sikh, had been sunk in the Mediterranean (see pages 285-286, Vol. 6). Now, in command of the famous destroyer Onslow, he led the U-boat funeral procession.

From the bridge on which Captain R. St. V. Sherbrooke fought on to win the V.C. after he had been badly wounded (see page 544, Vol. 6), Captain Micklethwait gave his orders for the disposal of the U-boats. Onslow led the destroyers which, on the last day of 1942, in the Arctic twilight, four times placed themselves between the convoy they were guarding and a greatly superior force of enemy ships. For Operation Deadlight, Onslow still bore her proud motto, "Festina Lente"—"Hasten Slowly," or, as the sailors invariably translate it, "On Slow." Other ships in this first towing were the Polish destroyer Blyskawica (British-built before the war), the Hunt class destroyer Southdown, the British-built frigate Loch Shin, the American-built frigate H.M.S. Cubitt and four tugs.

The U-boats going out to be scuttled, six of the small Mark 23 type craft, were brought down to the towing ships by skeleton crews provided by the Royal Navy, with four Germans in addition. As each boat was taken in tow, it was allowed to run out until the strain was on the tow, and then the crew was taken off. There was no ceremony of farewell for the Germans. They were taken ashore at once and probably did not see their craft slowly head out to sea.

Heavy Strain on the Towing Gear

The chosen scuttling-ground was where the Atlantic bed shelves away sharply about a hundred miles north-west of Lough Swilly and 80 miles north-west of the Bloody Foreland in Donegal (see map). Here there is a depth of about a thousand fathoms and it was felt that there was no chance of any part of the submarines, or such fuel and oil as remained on board, coming to the surface or otherwise interfering with fishing.

Progress to this area was necessarily slow. The unmanned submarines placed a heavy strain on the towing gear, especially in the long swell encountered in the open Atlantic. Proceeding at four knots, the force arrived early on the morning of the second day after leaving Loch Ryan. An hour or so before this, H.M.S. Cubitt reported to the Onslow that the U-boat she was towing had disappeared; she had foundered.

Number one plan for the destruction of the U-boats called for the firing of three high explosive charges already fitted into the U-boats. In order to carry the electric impulse to these charges it was necessary to pick up a line trailing from each U-boat. The destroying ships were H.M.S. Onslow and the Blyskawica.

A fairly heavy sea was running, but by fine seamanship the Onslow was able to get close to U 2361 and pick up the line. In a matter of minutes a connexion had been made, and the Onslow went astern until she was about 1,000 feet from the doomed U-boat. Then a plunger was pressed home and, in a triple explosion, both ends of the submarine were blown out and debris flung high in the air from the conning tower. When the smoke cleared the U-boat had vanished.

Meantime, Blyskawica, putting into effect the second method of destruction, had opened fire on the first of her victims, U 2321. A few rounds accounted for this craft; and the Polish gunners had even more spectacular success with their second U-boat, sinking it with four quick rounds.

ONSLOW then sank her second U-boat by gunfire, and this was quickly followed by a third disposed of in the same way by the Poles. Shells screamed into the submarines at close range, tearing conning towers wide open and penetrating the hulls. By midday the first batch of U-boats had settled down in the burial ground and the Onslow was leading the "destroyers" back for more at a steady twenty knots. Before dark signals were exchanged with the Onslow's sister ship, H.M.S. Onslaught, heading a second group of ships with their sleek tows to the sinking ground.

Last Scenes Enacted in Deep Atlantic Waters

FINAL GATHERING OF THE DOOMED U-BOATS was at Loch Ryan (1) Wigtownshire, Scotland, in late November 1945, before being towed to destruction under "Operation Deadlight" (see facing page). The U 2335 received a direct hit by shell-fire (2) from the destroyer Onslaught and sank a thousand fathoms deep. Some were blown up; on board the U 2321, which sank a British ship in January 1945, a youthful German petty officer (3, left) helped to adjust the fuses which subsequently were ignited by an electric impulse carried from the destroyer by line. A destroyer (4) takes up a U-boat's tow-line. See also illus. page 576.

Photos, Sport & General, Keystone, Associated Press

Transformation to Peace at Woolwich Arsenal

FIVE OF OUR LARGEST ROYAL ORDNANCE FACTORIES—at Woolwich, Cardiff, Hayes (Middlesex), Nottingham and Patricroft, near Manchester—in the early winter of 1945 received Government orders to switch some of their space from gun and tank manufacture to peacetime production. At the Royal Gun and Carriage Factory, Woolwich, which has 2,000 employees, mechanics assembled motor-lorries for shipment to Europe as the last 6-pounder anti-tank gun left the shop (1). Here, also, thousands of railway wagons, some over 40 years old, were being reconditioned (3) for service abroad, while workmen cleared away the ammunition boxes and gun-barrel cases. At a Walthamstow, London, aircraft factory finishing touches were given to a Mosquito as cabinet-makers assembled Utility-type wardrobes (2). See also page 558.

Photos 1 and 3 Exclusive to THE WAR ILLUSTRATED ; 2, *Associated Press*

Hitler's Proud Legions are Reduced to This

LINED UP IN BERLIN in early December 1945, pitiful in defeat, German soldiers awaited transport to their homes. Replying to a Soviet charge that large German forces were still mobilized in the British-occupied zone, it was officially stated on December 11 that up to date we had disbanded in our area a total of 2,000,000 members of the former Wehrmacht, leaving about 500,000 retained as essential workers or for eventual transfer to Russian or French zones. See also story in page 569.

Photo, Keystone

Now It Can Be Told!

CERAMIC'S THREE-YEAR MYSTERY CLEARED UP

SAPPER ERIC ALFRED MUNDAY, aged 24, back in his home at Foulsham Road, Thornton Heath, Surrey, brought with him the first full story of a three-year-old war mystery—the sinking of the British liner Ceramic in the Atlantic. The 18,750-ton Ceramic, former luxury ship on the Australian run, set out for Capetown from Britain on November 26, 1942, with 656 men, women and children on board.

She went down off the Azores. For ten months relatives of the passengers heard nothing. Then the loss of the ship was admitted in Capetown. In the House of Commons, the First Lord of the Admiralty said she was not in convoy, but was a "fast, independent ship." That was all.

Sapper Munday was the only survivor of the Ceramic. He told the story of her last voyage to a Daily Express reporter on October 14, 1945. Captain H. C. Elford had taken the ship through the Atlantic before. He knew what the dangers were in that winter of 1942. And he protested to the authorities against taking women and children on board. But 155, including 50 British nurses, were in the ship when she left Britain.

ON the night of December 6–7 three torpedoes hit her. She remained afloat for three hours. Everyone on board was put into boats or rafts. At dawn a storm broke. The boats were scattered. Many sank. Munday's boat, with 40 in it, capsized. He and six other soldiers clung to it. The rest were carried away. Four hours later the U-boat surfaced near them. A rope was thrown to them, but the boat was swept by a heavy sea. Only Munday was able to grab the rope, and he was hauled aboard the submarine.

"I pleaded with the U-boat commander, Captain Henke, to save the other six men who were still clinging to the overturned lifeboat," said Munday. "He refused." The U-boat submerged. Munday saw no more survivors of the Ceramic. The next two and a half years he spent in a prison camp in Germany.

THE NAVY LANDED 'CLOAK AND DAGGER' MEN

HIDING, camouflaged, in remote island creeks by day and sailing at night on privateering raids against enemy shipping and shore installations, seven 70-ft. Naval launches sapped Germany's hold on the strategic Mediterranean islands of the Dodecanese. Their part in clearing the Mediterranean was not revealed until September 1945.

Although they knew they were always somewhere near, the Germans never caught any of these small raiding ships, the smallest and slowest vessels in Britain's Coastal Forces. These 14-knot Harbour Defence Motor Launches—originally intended only for anti-submarine patrol in sheltered waters—also ran a "Raiders Ferry Service" for British Commandos and men of the famous Greek Sacred Regiment, whose "cloak and dagger" tactics smashed enemy strong points and communications and kept enemy garrisons in a state of terror.

The German headache started in February 1944, when Captain H. C. Legge, D.S.C., R.N., who between the wars worked as a London stockbroker, established his Naval H.Q. on the tiny island of Castellorizo, a few miles from the Turkish coast and the only island in the group not under German domination. With a strategy all their own the Navy and the raiders so completely surprised the enemy that the neighbouring islands of Piskopi and Nisero also soon fell into our hands.

From these striking bases the raids continued. While British destroyers patrolled the outer seas, the H.D.M.L.s maintained ceaseless vigil in the island approaches. Only in sheer desperation did an occasional German schooner, caique or lighter attempt the hazard of a passage by night. Pouncing from hiding-places in remote creeks where, almost under the noses of the enemy, they lay by day concealed under camouflage nets, the H.D.M.L.s with their 40-mm. Bofors and 20-mm. Oerlikons played havoc with the blockade-runners.

After one such engagement Intelligence revealed that the German Chief of Naval Staff for the occupied islands and several important military personages had been sent to the bottom. Not all the German vessels intercepted were sunk. Said Leading Seaman T. Roberts, of Llanelly, Caernarvonshire, coxswain of H.D.M.L 1252, commanded by Lieut. C. A. G. Dyer, R.N.V.R., of Tiverton, Devon: "After we had opened fire on one schooner, her German crew jumped overboard and we captured the vessel intact, complete with cargo of ammunition and mines. We also rescued the Germans out of the sea and took them back to Symi as prisoners of war."

IN April of 1945 alone the "little ships" landed 45 raiding parties on the various islands. The campaign was not without its humours. Provocative messages were frequently exchanged between Royal Navy signallers and the German look-out posts as the H.D.M.L.s nightly plied between the islands. A German signaller at Cos used to flash, "Why don't you come closer?" to which the Navy's signallers replied, "Why don't you pack up? You've had it!" The inevitable triumphant end to the campaign, which had been carried on for more than a year, came on May 9, 1945, when General Wagner, with his staff officers, was brought to Symi in the British destroyer H.M.S. Active to sign the surrender terms.

WHITEHALL'S WIRELESS LINK WITH THE WAR

THE story of a remarkable British wireless set was released by the War Office in November 1945. It was used by Royal Signals soon after D-Day and throughout the campaign in Western Europe, and enabled Field-Marshal Montgomery in Luneburg to speak directly to Mr. Churchill in Whitehall with all the security of a closed telephone line. And the Germans never knew we had it.

The Field-Marshal called it his "No. 10 thing," its official and unromantic name being "Wireless Set No. 10." It provided the only speech communication across the River Maas and the Rhine for several weeks, and Montgomery's Tactical H.Q. was never out of touch for more than one hour with the whole of 21 Army Group and the War Office up to the surrender at Luneburg.

Incidentally, all speech communication to General Eisenhower after the crossing of the Rhine was maintained by the "No. 10 Set" to Brussels and thence by line. It is interesting in this connexion that the Surrender was signed on Hill 71 because the Set works best on high ground; this fact continually governed the choice of sites for Tactical H.Q. The advantage which the British Army had in possessing this Set was enormous when it is realized that a land line say of 20 miles involves the erection of 700 telegraph poles and is very vulnerable to enemy action.

The Set was designed by scientists of the Ministry of Supply, and the credit for this must go chiefly to four men: Mr. W. A. S. Butement, already well-known for his work in connexion with radar and the radio proximity fuse (see page 492), Mr. A. J. Oxford, Mr. E. W. Anderson and Mr. J. G. MacMillan, who was later seconded to Royal Signals and was responsible for the field development of the Set. Butement in 1941 was the first to draw attention to the advantages of using centimetre waves for communication equipment, and the "centimetric" side was worked out by Anderson; Oxford first suggested the eight-pulse "multi-channel" system which was worked out by Butement and Oxford.

IT looks like an Army radar equipment, a 4-wheeled trailer with a pair of the now familiar circular mirrors mounted on top. In fact, the set is technically far more closely allied to a radar equipment than to any wireless set as generally understood. It operates at centimetre waves—the first time that these have been harnessed to the work of transmitting speech—and transmits its radio beam in the form of short pulses.

The sets are used in pairs, Set No. 1 sending out its pulses of centimetre waves (on

S.S. CERAMIC, 18,750-ton passenger liner, which in peacetime sailed between this country and Australia, was torpedoed off the Azores in December 1942, and provided a three-year mystery. The sole survivor—held in a German prison-camp throughout the remainder of the war—has now revealed the facts (see top of page). *Photo, by courtesy of Shaw, Savill & Albion Co., Ltd.*

which have been impressed the speech modulation), Set No. 2 picking them up ; but since Set No. 1 sends out its pulses not singly but in groups of eight, and since Set No. 2 is fully competent to sort these out into eight separate lines, no less than eight separate conversations can be relayed simultaneously between one pair of sets.

THIS alone would not give it security ; but the great advantage of centimetre waves is that they make possible the use of a very narrow beam, scarcely wider than that of a searchlight. This beam is stopped only by any fair-sized solid obstruction ; which means that any pair of "10 Sets" can only operate over a clear unobstructed path, usually of about 20 miles and sometimes well over 50 miles. This has necessitated the careful selection of sites, and the sets (or at least their aerials) have often been mounted on towers, or on the roofs of tall buildings, to obtain the clear "line of sight" essential for successful operation.

THE "HEDGEHOG," A BRITISH ROCKET DEVICE, came off the secret list on November 11, 1945. Technically known as the "Mark 10 Anti-Submarine Projector," it is a battery of 24 projectile units, each weighing 58 lb., mounted in the bows of a destroyer (top). The range is 200 yards. The U-boat (bottom) was one of 300 victims claimed. *Photos, British Official, Keystone*

How Eavesdroppers Were Foiled

This might appear to be a disadvantage : in reality it was a great advantage from the security aspect. For, just as the narrow beam implied that it could not be intercepted or even detected unless the eavesdropper was actually in the beam, so the clear line of sight implied normally that there was no means of getting into the beam short of hovering in mid-air with a quantity of heavy equipment. And although the Germans later claimed to have intercepted our wireless transmission with ease, careful interrogation showed not only that they had never intercepted a "10 Set" transmission, but also its very existence was entirely unsuspected.

The details of the disposition of these 20-mile "radio links" is a matter for military historians ; and the history would make interesting reading. It would tell of how, at the end of 1942, the first experimental two-stage link was set up between a building in Horsham and the roof of Berkeley Court in London ; of the link between Ventnor, Isle of Wight, and Beachy Head ; of the first operational link, between Ventnor and Cherbourg (the most difficult of all, because the distance is inconveniently great, and the necessary sight line could only be obtained by raising the aerials several hundred feet.) ; and, finally, of the chain of ten "10 Set links" from Luneburg to Brussels, whence a normal land line connected it to Whitehall.

It would also tell of how the "10 Set" chain was able, because of the mobility of the set and of its specially designed transportable 60-ft. towers, to follow close behind the advancing front in a way that telephone lines could never have done. It might also tell of how the "10 Set" crew once arrived even earlier than usual and proudly captured a German official, resplendent in the ornate and glittering uniform of a Chief Air Raid Warden—under the entirely excusable impression that such magnificence must surely imply high military rank. Information was passed to the U.S.A. ; and the Americans promptly set to work to design a set on the same lines.

Our Mighty Switch from Tanks to Peacetime Cars

There is no simple way of stepping across the frontier separating war and peace—of getting industry into its peacetime stride again: and the British Motor Industry, with its magnificent record of wartime production, is now experiencing tricky problems of its own. The nature of these is made clear in this recent interview (exclusive to "The War Illustrated") by Frank Illingworth with the Vice-Chairman of the Nuffield Organization, Sir MILES THOMAS.

NOWHERE else, perhaps, is the changeover from war to peace so marked as in the motor industry—war weapons at one end of an assembly line and saloon cars at the other, with the goods of war relegated to transitory parking places while the goods of peace flow on towards the factory railway siding and the consumer.

Five long and weary years saw the motor industry turning out weapons ranging from heavy tanks to light guns, from aircraft to submarine parts. Today it is crossing the production frontier between war and peace; and a slowly mounting flood of sleek cars inch along the assembly lines.

The British motor industry could fulfil a large part of the overseas demand for £500,000,000 worth of cars if the materials and the labour were available, and subject to modifications in taxation. As it is, the aim is to export £30,000,000 worth of cars in the next 12 months. One firm has agreed to fulfil orders for 10,000 cars almost immediately. Another firm has exported well over 2,000 cars since the war ended, and has contracted to fulfil orders worth £5,000,000 towards the close of 1946.

I am certain that the late unlamented Hitler under-estimated the real productive potential of the British motor industry, thereby making one of his major mistakes. It played a primary part in winning the war. Indeed, way back in 1938, when the Government refused to think about war, one firm of motor manufacturers began to build tanks at its own expense, and to Anglicize the measurements and metallurgy on the original Swedish plans of the Bofors gun—in readiness for things to come. The result was that when war came the motor industry had already laid the foundations. And then, under the stress of war, the brains, ingenuity and craftsmanship of the industry solved engineering problems which had once baffled it.

HASTE! Haste! Give us tanks to stem the Panzers! Give us guns and aircraft to meet the Luftwaffe! Haste! The industry answered the call. Hurriedly, men with brushes painted over hundreds of acres of glass roofs, blackout curtains fell across the windows, and beneath blue lamps grimy men, and then men and women, translated into steel designs born in the drawing offices.

In the North, the blast furnaces roared through the day and into the night, and the rolling mills hammered out the rough shape of war. At Hartlepool the air was heavy with the fumes of synthetic rubber. Over Billingham hung the choking reek of nitrate manufacture. From Birmingham came the vital links in the chain of armour, and at Coventry and Cowley, Luton and London, motor manufacturers married the products of a dozen related industries to the blueprints of war weapons.

Tanks! Aircraft! Guns! More men and women went to work beneath the blue lamps and the blacked-out factory roofs until the motor industry employed twice the 1939 figure. The switch from cars and lorries to tanks and guns was slow. "The first year, nothing at all," Mr. Churchill said in 1941. "Second year, very little; third year quite a lot: fourth year, all you want."

One Car to Every Five Persons?

So it proved. One firm alone turned out 12,000,000 shells; 3,210 Tiger Moth aircraft; 1,625 military gliders; 4,000 light and heavy tanks; hundreds of Bren gun carriers, ambulances, canteens, and Bofors guns that went into action on every battlefield from Mandalay to Hamburg. It made amphibious tanks for the Normandy landings, marine engines for lifeboats, torpedoes, mines, and 13,000 of the engines that carried the great bombers over Berlin. And while one section turned out a flood of weapons, others repaired 80,000 battle-damaged aircraft and tanks.

This gives some idea of the versatility of the British motor industry. And if it swung quickly from peace to war, it is switching just as quickly from war to peace. Furthermore, the demand for cars is as marked now as was that for tanks in 1939. Lack of transport is the foremost factor in the rehabilitation of Europe; even countries that have been spared war are crying out for new transport vehicles; and, starved of cars for six years, this country is in sore need of new wheels.

Before the war the British motor industry—the third largest in the country—employed one and a half million workers. My firm alone turned out one car a minute throughout the working day. But we've got to improve on that to meet the demand of the next five years—and that means employing more workers than before the war. The industry is looking forward to the day when instead of the 1939 figure of one car to every twenty-five of the population we approach the American ratio of one in five. Think what that would mean in increased employment! But first the industry must vault the hurdles on the course between war and peace—heavy taxation, shortage of materials and labour.

One of the great problems is the rehabilitation of Servicemen returning to the motor industry. In the background is the task of preventing two factions from forming in the factories—the men who fought in uniform, and the factory hands who earned good wages even if it sometimes meant standing up to bombing. And in the foreground are the tasks of finding houses for the "returnees," combating emotional strain born in the sudden switch from service to civil life, finding jobs for employees who joined up as office boys and return with a major's crown.

There can be no hard-and-fast rule in the allocation of jobs. Six years of engineering experience in the Services has immeasurably increased the value of some of the motor industry's returning employees. Others, six years older but lacking in six years' industrial experience, will be a charge on the motor industry until they have been trained to hold down jobs at twice the pay they earned on going into uniform.

Then there is the question of lost skill; and even men who passed from Civil engineering to Service workshops will have acquired an engineering skill unsuited to the peculiar requirements of the motor industry. They, no less than the war-wounded returning to their old firms, and employees new to motor manufacture, will have to be trained.

All the big firms have established training centres. The Service Welfare departments and the Ministry of Labour Resettlement Advice Service are also playing their part in getting industry into its peacetime stride.

SHORTAGE of materials is another hurdle on the route from war to peace. The tire factories must accomplish the turn-over, the electric equipment plants and a dozen other industries, faced with a sudden, colossal demand, must reorganize themselves before the motor industry can answer the demand for cars. The price of steel, too, is alarmingly high; and until it comes down competition with America will be difficult.

British motor manufacturers are receiving orders in every language, and from countries which have never bought British cars in bulk before. The total pre-war production was 400,000 cars a year worth £60,000,000. All being well, by late in 1946 the industry will have exported cars worth £30,000,000. This trade will help to set the home market—the foundation of the export trade—on its peacetime feet. When that is accomplished prices may be due for revision, and a demand for yet more cars will see up to a million more workers employed in the industry. We will, in short, have cast aside the caterpillar tractors of war in favour of the soft rubber tires and easy suspension of peace.

THE TANKS HAVE HAD THEIR DAY: now it is the turn of the private cars. Assembly lines at the Morris works that were busy with the war vehicles (left) but a short time ago are now concerned with cars (right), which in increasing numbers reach the packing sheds, en route for the railway sidings, the docks and ships that will deliver them all over the world to build up Britain's depleted reserves of foreign exchange. By October 1945 the production lines were more than 50 per cent concentrated on cars for export

Photos by courtesy of Morris Motors Ltd.

The Greatest Crime Trial in World History

Beginning of the End for 20 Nazis

"THE trial which is now about to begin . . . is of supreme importance to millions of people all over the globe," said Lord Justice Lawrence (above), the British President of the International Tribunal, on November 20, 1945, when Germany's major war criminals entered on their public trial at Nuremberg. It opened with the reading of the indictment in four languages, by prosecuting counsel of Great Britain, U.S.A., Russia and France. On November 30 the U.S. prosecution put forward the first oral witness, Gen. Erwin Lahousen (top), formerly of German military intelligence. Sir Hartley Shawcross (right), Attorney-General, opened the British case on December 4, under Count 2 of the Indictment: "Crimes against Peace, the planning, preparation, initiation and waging of wars of aggression, in violation of international agreements."

‘Gangsters, Empty Frauds, Common Thieves—

Twenty Nazi war lords in the dock (top and left) heard Sir Hartley Shawcross describe them in the words quoted above. Russian judges Maj.-Gen. Nikitchenko and M. Volchov are seen at (A). British judges Sir Norman Birkett (B) and Lord Justice Lawrence (C). U.S. prosecuting counsel Major Wallis (D). The 20 criminals are (E) Goering, Luftwaffe C.-in-C. and successor-designate to Hitler. (F) Hess, Hitler's former deputy. (G) Ribbentrop, Foreign Minister. (H) Keitel, Chief of High Command. (I) Rosenberg, chief of Nazi racial ideologists. (J) Frank, Governor-General of Poland.

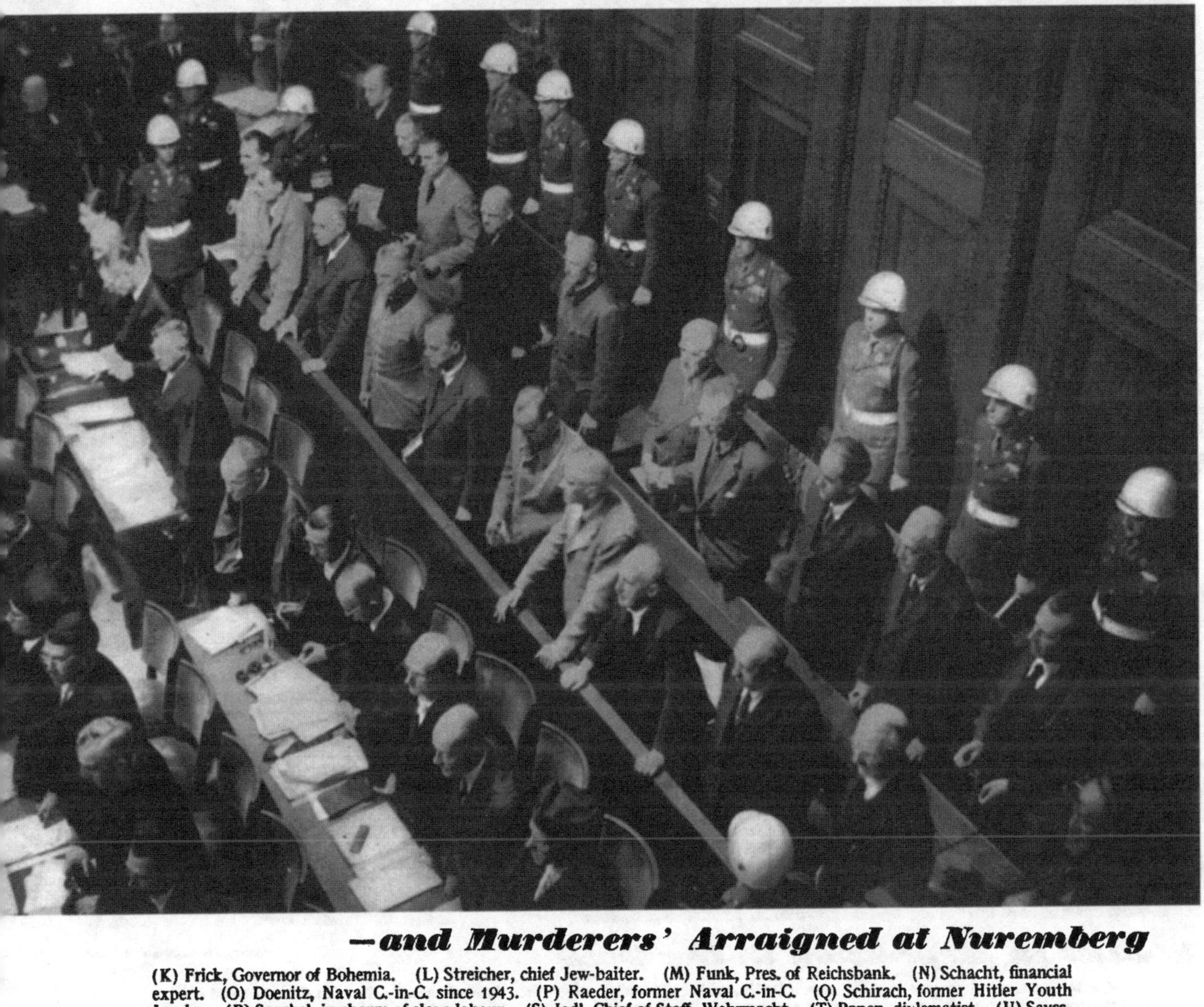

—and Murderers' Arraigned at Nuremberg

(K) Frick, Governor of Bohemia. (L) Streicher, chief Jew-baiter. (M) Funk, Pres. of Reichsbank. (N) Schacht, financial expert. (O) Doenitz, Naval C.-in-C. since 1943. (P) Raeder, former Naval C.-in-C. (Q) Schirach, former Hitler Youth Leader. (R) Sauckel, in charge of slave labour. (S) Jodl, Chief of Staff, Wehrmacht. (T) Papen, diplomatist. (U) Seyss-Inquart, Reichscommissar in Netherlands. (V) Speer, Armaments Minister, head of Todt organization. (W) Neurath former Protector of Bohemia. (X) Fritzsche, radio propagandist. As the judges enter the accused stand (above).

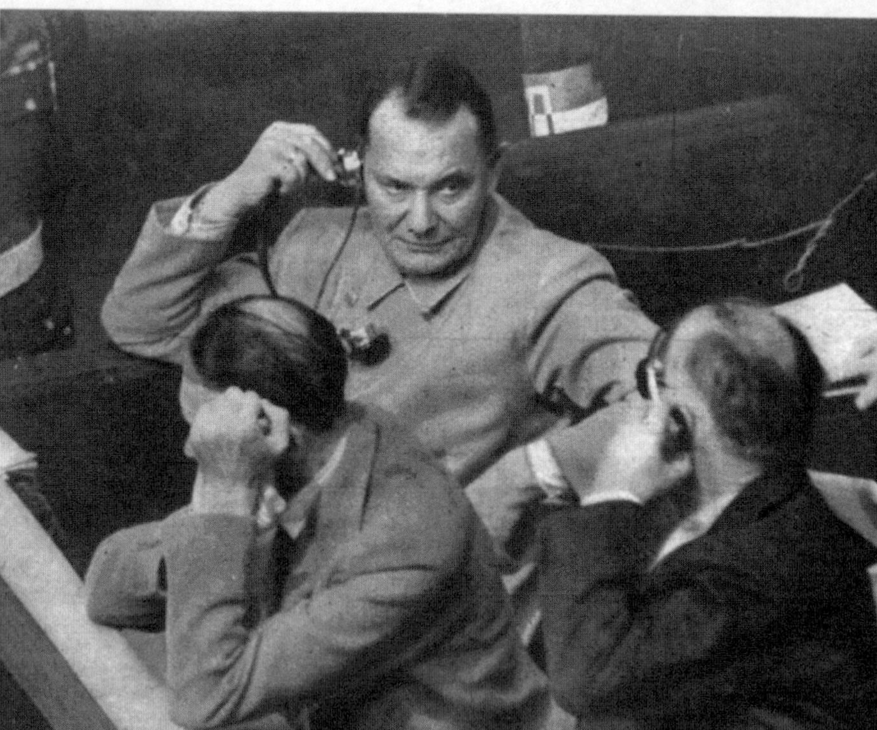

Studies in Expression in the Dock

Photos, Planet News, Associated Press

Mostly the accused sit quietly and listen intently, with set faces, through their headphones, to the recital of the flood of evidence brought against them. Goering confers with Ribbentrop (top right) behind the back of Hess; as the Court rises for lunch he stands (top left). Uneasy laughter breaks out occasionally (below) at some quip which stirs them from their usual gravity. Front row, left to right, Goering, Hess, Ribbentrop, Keitel. Back row, Doenitz, Raeder, Schirach, Sauckel.

"War Below Zero"

Reviewed by HAMILTON FYFE

I SUPPOSE I have kept up with the flow of war books as closely as anyone, yet I have just come across a description of one phase in the struggle against Nazism about which I knew almost nothing. One heard vaguely that weather reports were being sent from Greenland, occasional stories of adventure among the ice-floes filtered through the British and American censorships, rumours of new air routes from New York to London, from San Francisco to Russia and India, went round among the few people interested in such matters.

Now that I have read War Below Zero (Allen and Unwin, 7s. 6d.) I am filled with admiration for the courage and almost superhuman endurance with which American flyers and soldiers battled for what Gen. Arnold, commanding U.S. Army Air Forces, calls in his foreword "the vital far North-east." Why was it "vital"? First, because Europe's weather could be predicted from Greenland with some degree of certainty and it was immensely important to know what conditions would prevail when bombing raids were to take place and when military operations were started. The success of the invasion on D-Day may have been due, say the authors, Col. Balchen, Major Corey Ford and Major Oliver La Forge, to the fact that the Allies and not the Germans were in control of the Arctic.

Had No Idea of the Ordeals Ahead

Also, this campaign was important for the reason that Greenland was a springboard necessary to the Nazis if they decided to attack the American continent, and "a logical stop-over point in ferrying fighter planes and bombers to the U.S. Army 8th Air Force in Britain." If there were to be the thousand-plane raids on Berlin, of which there was talk already in 1941, adequate bases and landing strips in the Arctic would be essential, as well as weather stations. So it was in the summer of that year, before Pearl Harbour, six months previous to America's declaration of war, that President Roosevelt, looking ahead and feeling sure that his country must come in some time or other, sent an expedition with secret orders to establish the northernmost American air base.

A few of those who composed that small force were men who had been in the Arctic. Mostly they had never seen snow and could form no idea of what they would have to go through. They fancied Greenland was as big as Long Island or the Isle of Wight instead of being the largest island there is, almost half as wide as the United States. Even the officers in command "had little or no knowledge of what problems they would face in erecting docks, how close they could get to the site of the landing-field before unloading their construction gear, how many miles of road would have to be built."

EVERYTHING they required, literally *every thing*, had to come from the U.S., and no ships could land stores after the winter closed down. That made the men in charge serious, but the rank and file, of whom numbers came from the Southern States where winter didn't mean a thing, thought their war was going to be "a sort of Errol Flynn movie of polar bears and walrus and Northern Lights, with demure Eskimo maids in fur parkas driving teams of reindeer across the ice in the light of the Midnight Sun."

They found out their error as soon as they landed, but the authors doubt whether "the full realization of how utterly isolated we were was borne in on the men until the last ship sailed back to the States; there would not be another until next summer. Standing on the beach and watching it disappear around the bend of the fjord was worse than leaving home; it was like seeing home leave them."

Now they could "hear the silence." Now they saw the thermometer drop a few more notches every day, and had to fight down a rising panic. "It couldn't get any colder; they couldn't survive if it got any colder."

> And still the thermometer went down, the shadows lengthened, the silence drew closer, like a tightening noose.

When they went outside their quarters their rubber-lined trench coats froze stiff as a board before they could shut the door behind them. They felt their faces "wither in a matter of seconds as though they had been seared by a flame. A white dot on the forehead foretold a week of agony; a deep breath might shrivel the lungs. A little snow sifting down carelessly inside the boot-tops might mean a couple of amputated toes."

At first the men put on several woollen shirts, but they found this cut off circulation and finally came down to one, worn with "one-piece union suits of long under-wear," windproof gabardine jackets, and ski-ing trousers fastened at the ankles to keep out wind. They learned, too, what food could keep them warm. They devoured with relish codfish liver and roe, seal-meat, reindeer, ptarmigan, Arctic hare. They cooked fish Eskimo-fashion, cutting it into chunks and boiling it in sea water. The diet agreed with them. They kept fit and put on weight.

ON GREENLAND'S ICY FRONT a reconnaissance patrol of U.S. coastguards set up camp—as portrayed by the official American naval artist Norman Thomas. Duties of these patrols included the "spotting" of hostile ships and aircraft.

But all day and every day they had to fight against the merciless Arctic. The climate of the ice-cap of Greenland is the worst known anywhere. Gales rage with appalling ferocity—up to 170 miles an hour. The surface of the cap is neither solid nor flat. Here it is deeply furrowed, there lakes form on it, at any moment a crevasse may open under your feet. Two planes, with their pilots, were lost in them. One day three of the Americans were just going to take a ride in a motor sledge. One knelt down to take off his snowshoes. Another took the wheel, the third was waiting to give the sledge a shove when the engine started; suddenly he went through the surface. He clutched at the sledge for a moment, trying to secure a grip with his mittened hands, then he disappeared. It happened as quickly as you have read this account of it. For two hours the other two waited, hoping against certainty. He had gone beyond recall.

FOR nearly six months the party of which these men were members was marooned on the ice-cap. They were the crew of an aircraft which had crashed and broken in half. No story-teller, not even the creator of Robinson Crusoe, has invented fiction more improbable or more interesting than the account of the way these comrades in misfortune lived through their ordeal. They had supplies dropped to them, but not regularly because of the weather. Sometimes they had plenty to eat and smoke, sometimes almost nothing. What kept them going were the letters from their homes which floated down in the parachute packages of supplies, and the knowledge that plans for their rescue were being prepared.

> The stranded men understood better than anybody what their rescuers were up against, but disappointed as they might be, as one attempt after another failed, they always learned that new ones were being made. They knew that the people on the outside would not give up trying, and they could even tell that the interest in their safety was not merely local but must reach back to headquarters and to high authority.

Every day Washington was informed of what had or had not been done to extricate them, for "they belonged to the armies of that half of the world which believes that all men are valuable and even a single human being is important. It is hardly probable that in the full tide of war any of the Axis nations would have so joined their forces for the saving of a few lives." Nor does it seem likely to me that many groups of a few men cooped up together for so long a time, would have "never ceased liking one another" and, when they came out of their exile, "still enjoyed each other's company."

One worry the nine men at headquarters had to contend with was not knowing whether their meteorological reports went through. It was "heart-breakingly difficult."

> As soon as they repaired their instruments after one devastating storm another blizzard would strike, knocking down the vanes and blowing the anemometer (wind-measuring) cups to a frozen Kingdom Come.

"Strained and empty" their life became as the months passed; it was mostly waiting and they had very little to help them through it. When a Norwegian-American colonel who knew the Arctic was sent to inspect them, he took one look at them and radioed back a message of six words: Get these guys out of here

They were rescued, and as soon as they lined up before their C.O. at base headquarters their misgivings about "the whole nine months having been a total flop" were blown away. Their weather reports had been received regularly every day. "I tell you this, fellows," said the C.O., "you got weather for me which no one else has ever been able to get." He thanked them, too, for what they had learned, learned in "the hard way," about cold-weather equipment, about Arctic tents, clothing, machinery; this would "make it a lot easier for all American soldiers stationed in northern regions."

Remembering Roosevelt: at Hyde Park, U.S.A.

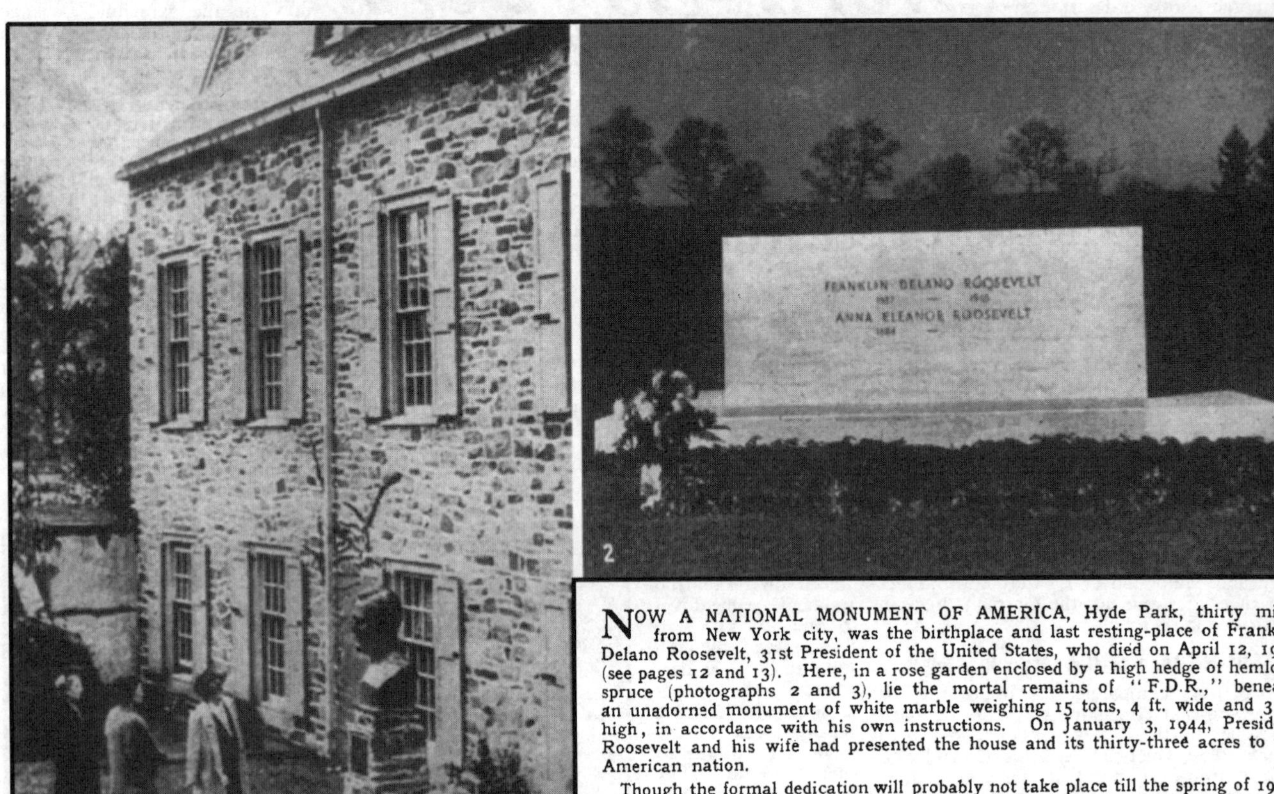

NOW A NATIONAL MONUMENT OF AMERICA, Hyde Park, thirty miles from New York city, was the birthplace and last resting-place of Franklin Delano Roosevelt, 31st President of the United States, who died on April 12, 1945 (see pages 12 and 13). Here, in a rose garden enclosed by a high hedge of hemlock spruce (photographs 2 and 3), lie the mortal remains of "F.D.R.," beneath an unadorned monument of white marble weighing 15 tons, 4 ft. wide and 3 ft. high, in accordance with his own instructions. On January 3, 1944, President Roosevelt and his wife had presented the house and its thirty-three acres to the American nation.

Though the formal dedication will probably not take place till the spring of 1946, visitors can inspect the Memorial Library in front of which stands Walter Russell's striking bronze bust of the dead President (1). One room in the Library is not for show—that in which Roosevelt used to work, surrounded by his souvenirs and ship-models, at a desk which once was President Wilson's. In this room, too, "F.D.R." was accustomed to relax before a blazing log fire, smoking his cigarette in the long holder. Among many famous visitors to Hyde Park in the past have been King George VI and Queen Elizabeth, Mr. Churchill, Mr. Mackenzie King and Mme. Chiang Kai-shek.

Photos, New York Times Photos

200 Days' Tussle With Croydon's Giant Bomb

" HERMANN," THE 4,000-lb. LUFTWAFFE BOMB, which buried itself over 40 ft. deep in a Croydon, Surrey, timber yard on January 11, 1941, was finally rendered harmless and removed on December 17, 1945. A bomb disposal squad of 26 sappers of the Royal Engineers completed the task in 200 days, earlier efforts being hampered by an underground stream. During the last stages over a hundred local residents were evacuated. At the bottom of the shaft sunk to find it, two of the sappers are here digging around the bomb. Inset is part of the fuse. *Photos, Associated Press*

How Much Has U.N.R.R.A. Actually Achieved?

This brief summing-up, exclusive to "The War Illustrated," of the work of the United Nations Relief and Rehabilitation Administration (to the end of 1945) reveals that though the task in Europe is still tremendous much has been accomplished. Our Correspondent also indicates the work awaiting attention in the Far East. See facing page and pages 46, 659, Vol. 8.

When war ended, more than sixty million people all over the world were left completely stranded—miles from their original homes, without money, resources or sufficient clothing, many with no shelter of any kind, most of them suffering from various diseases caused in part by malnutrition.

Homeless slave labourers and concentration camp victims in Germany numbered 11,000,000. In other European countries 7,500,000 displaced persons were wandering about. The situation in the Far East is still more appalling: at least 43,000,000 terrorized men, women and children left their homes in the Chinese coastal towns and fled from the Japanese to lead a nomadic, hand-to-mouth existence.

Supplies of food, clothing and medicine, when the war ended, were so scarce in all countries where fighting had taken place that thousands were dying daily. This was the stark aftermath which everywhere confronted the victorious Allies. What could they do about it? The 44 members of the United Nations acted promptly, effectively, and in a staggeringly big way. November 9, 1945, was the second anniversary of the establishment of a kind of world bank whose assets are chiefly a gigantic pool of goods and facilities. It is staffed by what is, in effect, an international civil service now employing 2,300 people, the majority of whom, by the way, do not wear uniform.

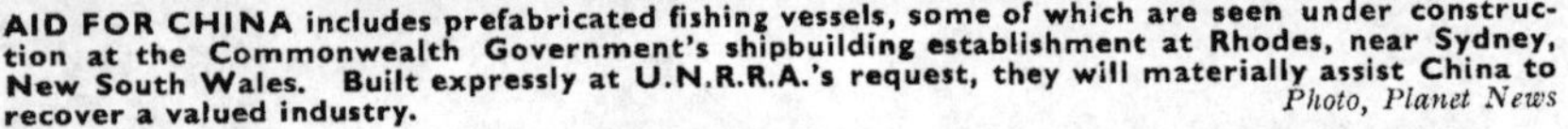

AID FOR CHINA includes prefabricated fishing vessels, some of which are seen under construction at the Commonwealth Government's shipbuilding establishment at Rhodes, near Sydney, New South Wales. Built expressly at U.N.R.R.A.'s request, they will materially assist China to recover a valued industry. *Photo, Planet News*

Headquarters of this vast organization, called the United Nations Relief and Rehabilitation Administration—U.N.R.R.A. for short—is in Washington, with Director-General Herbert H. Lehman at its head (see portrait, page 46, Vol. 8). His right-hand man is an Australian, Commander Jackson, who was in charge of supplies at Malta during the darkest days of that plucky island. U.N.R.R.A. has regional offices in London, Cairo, Sydney and Chungking.

Apart from caring for displaced persons and controlling epidemics, U.N.R.R.A. does not operate in ex-enemy countries. The relief and internal reorganization of those countries is a responsibility of the occupying military authorities.

This leaves Greece, Yugoslavia, Czechoslovakia, Albania and Poland as the main territories for U.N.R.R.A.'s attention and into which about 4,000,000 tons of urgently needed supplies, to the value of about £250,000,000, had been poured by the end of the year 1945. Italy, although an ex-enemy country, has been treated as a special case, and U.N.R.R.A. is providing there a £12,000,000 programme of help specifically for mothers and children. By the end of 1945 supplies worth £61,000,000 had gone to Greece, £62,000,000 to Yugoslavia (see page 152) and £68,000,000 to Poland.

British Rations are Not Affected

At nearly every European port in non-enemy countries the U.N.R.R.A. army can be seen busily at work. Typical, for instance, was the scene at the Dalmatian ports in October 1945. In the first 20 days of the month 18 U.N.R.R.A. ships delivered 2,000 mules purchased from British and U.S.A. armies, 262 tractors, 2,720 tons of clothes and footwear, and large quantities of petrol and fertilizers. Except in a few instances, U.N.R.R.A. does not distribute the supplies thus imported. That job is generally undertaken by the countries receiving aid.

Does the feeding and clothing of these impoverished countries mean that our rations in Britain suffer in consequence? The answer is No. Only a negligibly small part of the food sent to Europe comes from Britain. The bulk of it is sent direct from the United States, Canada, Brazil, Peru, Australia, New Zealand and South Africa. All the clothing supplied is second-hand.

It should not be thought that the United Nations intend to equip and supply these devastated countries on a permanent basis. U.N.R.R.A.'s object is to put them on their feet and to promote self-help. About nine-tenths of these countries' requirements are coming from local resources or are being imported by them without outside help. France, Norway, Belgium, Luxembourg and Holland are able to manage their own relief affairs without U.N.R.R.A.'s assistance.

In the House of Commons on November 16, Mr. Noel Baker stated that roughly 65 per cent of U.N.R.R.A.'s resources was spent on relief and 35 per cent on rehabilitation, but in 1946 rehabilitation would account for rather more than half. In view of the fact that the organization had less financial resources than were required for its vast task—a task incomparably greater in difficulty and scale than anything attempted or discussed before—Mr. Noel Baker said that the Government intended to ask Parliament to increase the British contribution by a second 1 per cent of a year's national income.

U.N.R.R.A.'s most troublesome problem has been, and still is, the huge number of displaced persons in Europe. How to sort out, care for and repatriate all these homeless people has been solved by the creation of nearly 400 teams of special workers in Germany. A team is usually formed of thirteen people, consisting of a director who is British or American, a doctor, nurse, welfare officer and other helpers. British and other recruits for this work were given intensive training at a school at Reading (see illus. page 659, Vol. 8). These D.P. teams in Germany comprise nearly 6,000 trained and untrained workers. It was estimated that by the end of 1945 some £28,000,000 would have been spent on this branch of U.N.R.R.A. services.

All over the British, U.S. and French zones in Germany the teams have established camps for dealing with displaced persons. Old Nazi army barracks are being widely used as premises; here the refugees are temporarily housed, properly clothed, deloused if necessary, fed and given any medical attention required until transportation arrangements can be made for return to their own countries. Any who are seriously ill are sent to the numerous U.N.R.R.A. hospitals. One of the most famous of these, which contains 550 beds and deals with all kinds of medical, surgical, maternity, T.B. and infectious diseases, was set up at Belsen by Brigadier Glyn Hughes, the first Allied doctor to reach this black spot of Nazidom in the spring of 1945.

Rescue of the Destitute Children

Most praiseworthy and most heartrending of U.N.R.R.A.'s manifold activities is the rescue and care of the millions of destitute children in Europe. It is estimated, for example, that in Poland alone there are more than 7,000,000 children all suffering from varying degrees of malnutrition, and many of whom not only have lost their parents but cannot remember ever having a proper home. Thousands of these starving orphans have passed through U.N.R.R.A.'s special depot at Warsaw. More than 10,000 have been sent to recuperate at centres in Sweden. Here is the account of an eye witness of the scene at the Warsaw depot:

> Two rooms were piled high with clothes brought in by U.N.R.R.A. from the West, and here the children exchanged their tattered filthy rags for decent apparel. The children were undressed in a very short time, for they had little to remove—perhaps a worn-out dress or remnants of a pair of trousers. The dressing took longer, as they had to be fitted up with clothes that would withstand the winter's cold. The whole operation had a noisy gaiety, for the arrival of U.N.R.R.A. supplies and clothes seemed like the coming of Father Christmas.

Officials of U.N.R.R.A. consider that the most formidable task still awaiting their attention is in the Far East, where at present emergency work only is being done. The widespread hunger and devastation throughout China, Borneo, French Indo-China, Netherlands India and the Philippines baffle description. At a recent meeting in Australia of the U.N.R.R.A. Far Eastern committee, an extensive programme of help was decided upon—China alone is to have some £150,000,000 worth and the first vital supplies are arriving.

Starvation Threat Staved Off in Southern Italy

AT AN U.N.R.R.A. CAMP at Santa Maria di Leuca (top) in southern Italy, refugees of various races, including Greeks, Yugoslavs, and Albanians—besides the Italians themselves—were being saved from starvation in late 1945. In the hospital (above), doctors and nurses make a thorough examination of sick child-refugees. On October 22, 1945, U.N.R.R.A. estimated that £250,000 000 would be needed to feed and supply Italy during 1946, of which £112,000,000 would be handled by U.N.R.R.A. See also facing page.

Official U.N.R.R.A. photograph by G. D. Boria

Mussolini's Shame Still Haunts Rome's Byways

IN WHAT WAS ONCE CASSINO'S MAIN THOROUGHFARE traders had begun selling their wares in the open (1) towards the end of 1945, a broken-down Nazi tank in their midst. Most of the rubble had been cleared and a housing area erected a short distance from the shattered town (see illus. page 727, Vol. 8). Striking examples of Italy's ignominy were ragged P.O.W. returned from Russia (2), formerly the flower of Mussolini's vaunted cohorts. Wearing an old army tunic a beggar in Rome (3) shares a meagre meal with his children.

Photos, Keystone

I Was There!

Eye Witness Stories of the War and After

Hitler's Ex-Soldiers Cold-Shouldered in Berlin

The pitiful condition of the men who fought for Germany evokes no scrap of sympathy from the civilians, writes Stanley Nash in The Star. He has recently returned from a visit to one of the centres in Berlin where the British tend these broken men before sending them home (see also page 555).

THE attitude of the Berlin people, particularly the women, to the crippled, ailing and ill-nourished German soldiers now streaming from the East is puzzling British soldiers. Many of these white-faced men struggling along on crutches or dragging weary feet wrapped in sacking must have left this city with good wishes showered on them by civilian friends.

How bitter has been their disillusionment on returning. No German hand is extended to them in friendship, no kindly glance cast at them by their fellow countrymen. Girls wrapped in their thick coats avert their faces when they pass these human wrecks on the pavement. This studied indifference to the sufferings of the menfolk who fought for them is so obvious that all visitors notice it.

I have just been to one of the collection centres in Berlin where the British house, feed and give medical attention to these broken men before dispersing them to their homes. It was not a pretty sight. Many of the men are dying when they reach the centre. They just shamble in, bent and spiritless, with faces from which suffering has wiped every expression but that of hopeless misery. German girl clerks take particulars of each man with indifference.

Standing at the gate of this camp were two frauleins, aged about twenty. Both were fairly well dressed, and they appeared to be directing their charm on busy, unresponsive British soldiers in the barbed wire compound. I did not see them bestow one sympathetic glance on the men in field-grey uniform.

Some of the men are as bad as the women. I saw one well-dressed fellow deliberately turn his back on a crippled German soldier who had merely asked him for directions. "Personally," said a British officer to me, "I have no use for Hitler's ex-soldiers, but one must admit that most of them fought very hard for Germany, and it is odd that they should be accorded this treatment by their own civilians."

It may be that civilians have wished to impress the Allies by cold-shouldering the men who fought for Hitler. If so it is an inhuman method of currying favour. Or it may be that the Berliners, short of food and fuel, can think only of themselves.

MEDICAL EXAMINATION of German ex-soldiers homeward-bound through British control-points is thorough. Many have foot and leg complaints, having tramped great distances. *Photo, The Daily Mirror*

I Escaped from the Terror of a Java Jungle

A grimly fantastic adventure of the Java campaign concerns three Englishmen, who were on an errand of mercy to inspect hospitals and stores at Benkolen. Only one survived—with ten wounds, after a terrible ordeal. Here is the dramatic story by Capt. J. W. Smith, R.A., as told to Lady Louis Mountbatten, Superintendent-in-Chief of St. John Ambulance.

WE ran into a large road block, with about 100 natives gathered round it. I pulled up, and Mr. Treveroe stepped out to talk to the natives. Captain Mockler opened his door and left the car. Then he turned back, presumably to pick up cigarettes. The first indication I had that anything was wrong was when the doctor suddenly yelled, "Oh, gee!"

I saw him turn away from the car. A spear was stuck in his back! As I grabbed my gun I felt a searing pain. A knife had cut my thumb to the bone. I dropped my gun. I fought my way through the spears and left the car by the nearside door. As I left the car the doctor went down—the natives still stabbing him. He was dead. I fought my way round to the front of the car, where Treveroe was making a gallant stand. By the time I reached him he, too, was dead.

I was completely ringed with spears. It was ironical. I was close to the natives, but their bristling spears and knives were so densely packed they were useless. Desperation gave me strength. I hit out where I could and, in the confusion, managed to break through.

Ahead of me was the sea—my sanctuary. I splashed into it for about 70 yards, until the water came up to my chin. The water swayed me—comfortingly. The natives gathered menacingly on the shore and little fountains plopped around me as bullets spurted into the water. The natives were using my head as a target for my gun. For ten hectic minutes I remained there—undecided whether to swim to Benkolen or return in case the doctor was still alive. By now the natives seemed calmer, so I risked coming out.

I WAS at once seized. My arms were bound, I was stripped of all personal goods, and led up the road to where the fighting had broken out. The bodies of Captain Mockler and Mr. Treveroe lay huddled, naked. Once more I was ringed by threatening spears. Excited chattering subsided to a hush as the leader advanced. With his ugly face an inch or so from mine, he shouted, "Nica!" (Netherlands Indies Civil Administration). This was a sign for the rest to howl in chorus.

A car approached from the direction of Benkolen. A native, who seemed to have some authority, approached me. I asked him to free my hands and take me back to

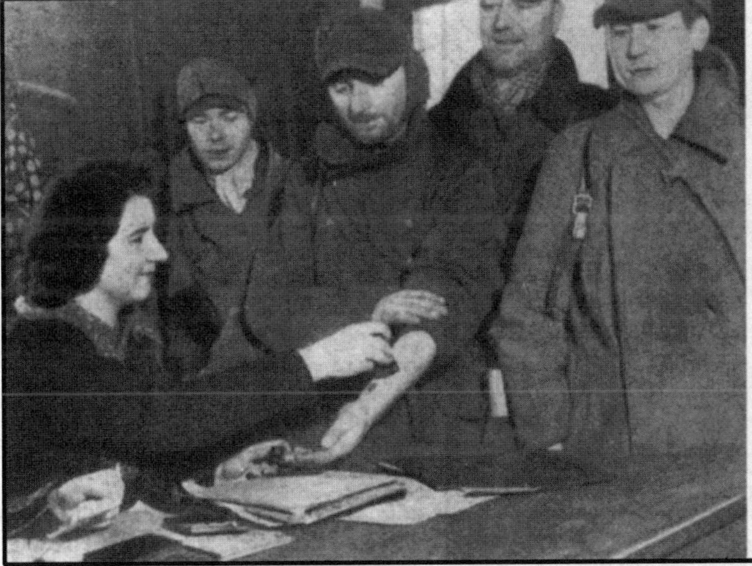

RUBBER-STAMPING GERMAN SOLDIERS returning home through a British control point in Berlin is performed (left) by a German girl conscripted for the purpose. On entering, each is closely scrutinized if his papers are in order, he is stamped on the wrist so that at the next control point only a glance from the examining officer is required. All are deloused, fed, accommodated while awaiting transport home, and (right) given a loaf for the journey. See also illus page 555. *Photo, Keystone, The Daily Mirror*

Benkolen to the so-called Indonesian Resident Tjaija. He gave no reply, but walked on to where the leader of the gang was standing.

He pointed to the bodies and then to me, then came back. I again asked him to release me. His reply was to point to the bodies and say: "This must be kept quiet." I answered: "You are a bigger fool than you look!" He went. The gang then led me back to the beach, and the remainder of the rope tying my hands, 20 ft. long, was wrapped several times round me to ensure that I was securely bound. Luckily they bound only the upper part of my body, and by straining against the ropes I managed to keep it reasonably slack.

To my horror, others began to dig a hole. It was to be my grave. Then a native tightened his grip on a vicious-looking sword and walked stealthily towards me. For the second time within an hour it was a case of now or never. So I bowled the native holding the rope into the nearest spearman, and dashed into the sea. This time I did not hesitate, but freed of rope and clothes, started swimming to Benkolen, two miles away.

Almost halfway I noticed an outrigger coming in my direction. I swam under water for as long as possible three times, and the last time I surfaced I came up under the bows of a second boat, of whose approach I was unaware. In it were two Indonesian policemen, who invited me on board.

I was dubious of their intentions and insisted on hanging on to the outrigging only. They seemed harmless on closer inspection, and eventually I climbed on to the stern of the boat. They invited me to the middle, but I refused. I insisted they should take me to Benkolen, which they agreed to do. I was handed over to the Indonesian Commissioner of Police, and was found to have no fewer than ten wounds. They dressed them and made me comfortable—at last.

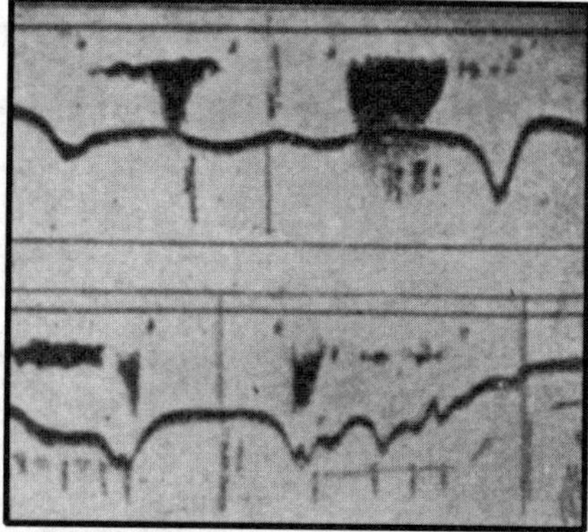

HERRING AHOY! Dark patches on the graph—above the contour of the sea bed—indicate herring shoals as detected by the Asdic apparatus. See story below.
Photo, The News Chronicle

I Met 'Pistol Packin' Momma' at Nuremberg

Highly unconventional in our eyes are the ways of Russian men and women in attendance at the great trial of Nazi war criminals. Sidelights on the courthouse scene and about the Palace of Justice are presented by Bernard Murphy in this pen-picture from The Star. See also illus. pages 559-562.

FROM plush-covered seat No. 164 I have watched the trial of the 20 Nazi leaders since it started. There is so much to see—the court is so big that you need opera glasses—so many sensational revelations to hear as they come in the tense breathless voice of a girl interpreter to your earphones that after a day at Nuremberg you feel worn out.

In front of me sits Natasha. I tried to talk to her during the luncheon recess today, but Natasha only knows one word of English—"No!" Natasha is very beautiful and I find her much more interesting to watch than fidgeting Hess or note-scribbling Hermann. She is a Russian girl soldier with fair hair and big blue eyes, and somehow she gives the impression of packing an awful wallop.

On the breast of her grey smock-like tunic is a medal ribbon from which hangs a big silver decoration for valour. Below her neat blue skirt, silk stockinged legs disappear abruptly into black top boots. Olga, another Russian girl, frightens me even more. From her belt hangs a large size automatic pistol. We have given her the nickname of "Pistol Packin' Momma."

The Russians have been rather reluctant to part with their guns. When they arrived here all the men carried pistols at their waist. In the cloakroom adjoining their sleeping quarters in an American mess, an orderly discovered rows of loaded tommy guns. Their hosts have now explained that guns are not the thing in the dining-room and they now park them on social occasions.

After a morning listening to the daily race of words I rub my ears, crushed by the earphones, put down the three-ply wooden board on which I write and stagger off to join the yards-long queue which is forming at the luncheon cafeteria.

Here a loudspeaker vibrates with the accents of Coney Island as some swoon crooner attacks our already over-sensitive ears with a torch song. As we shuffle forward to collect our tin trays of meat, sweet corn, potatoes, ice cream and jam my neighbour in the queue sums things thus: "To think it's Goering who's supposed to be on trial!"

Chasing Fish With the Navy's Underwater 'Ear'

Scientists are experimenting with the Asdic set (which helped to defeat the U-boats) with the object of simplifying the search for herring shoals. Success may revolutionize fishing. This account, from The News Chronicle, is by Vernon Brown, who went with the research trawler H.M.S. Veleta.

NIGHT in the North Sea. Two duffle-coated figures stand in the wheelhouse. Both wear earphones. A R.N.V.R. lieutenant fiddles with a knob on top of a metal box. It is cold, dreary and monotonous. Like hunting U-boats in the old days. Then, suddenly, there is a change in the atmosphere.

Ping—ping—ping. The sound comes in increasing volume into the earphones. The young lieutenant gives an order to the coxswain. Slowly the big trawler swings on a new course, forges on towards its quarry. This time it is not a U-boat. We are chasing the herring shoals under the sea. Someone crosses to a second shining metal box abaft the helm. Through a small glass square he looks at a needle making an automatic graph on a moving ribbon of paper.

At a sign from his uplifted hand the throb of the trawler's engines stops. The ship is over the herring shoal. The men in duffle-coats take off their headphones and congratulate themselves. They are scientists of the Ministry of Agriculture and Fisheries—Dr. C. W. Hodgson, chief of the Fisheries laboratory staff at Lowestoft, and Dr. H. Wood, of Aberdeen, representative of the Scottish Home Department.

THEIR earphones had been attached to an Asdic set—the Navy's underwater "ear," victor of the U-boats; the box behind the wheel was an echo-sounder depth recorder used in navigation. Between these inventions they are developing a new technique in the search for the elusive herring. The Asdic—still on the secret list—had given them the direction. Steaming to its echo they had reached the centre of the shoal. The depth recorder, sending down sound impulses, had revealed the depth and density of the herrings.

Look-outs on deck, experienced in the ways of the fish, checked the result by visual observation. The little drama in the wheelhouse has been played out on board this research trawler several times during the week.

LISTENING FOR HERRING in the wheelhouse of the specially equipped Fisheries Research trawler H.M.S. Veleta, in December 1945, was the unusual task of Dr. C. W. Hodgson (left) and Dr. H. Wood, two British Government scientists, as told on the right. The new radio-technique for tracing shoals of fish is in process of development.
Photo, The News Chronicle

The experiments are still in their initial stages, and final conclusions must be awaited.

Despite this, however, there are good hopes that before long, when the herring harvest moon is up and the silver shoals make their phosphorescent glow, British fishermen may be able to make the biggest catches in the history of the industry. Fishing in the form we have known it for centuries may be scrapped. Fishermen's "hunches" will become a thing of the past. Special instrument ships will guide the drifters to the shoals.

"The results, so far, have been encouraging," Dr. Hodgson told me, "but it will be some time before we shall be able to make a definite statement. Our first task is to make certain that the Asdic can be relied upon in a variety of circumstances, including changes in sea temperature, to detect the shoals. All danger of coincidence must be ruled out."

There have been impressive incidents in the first few tests. The Veleta went to sea with the drifter fleet and, as a beginning, the Asdic was ranged along the drift nets. The pings told the scientists where the biggest catches had been made. Fishermen and scientists waited with some anxiety for the nets to be drawn in to see whether the instruments were right. They were.

"If this new technique develops," one Lowestoft skipper told me, "it will change the whole order of fishing. Location of shoals by Asdic would cut out wasted days and might mean cheaper fish."

The Vampire Screamed Over Our Flight Deck

When Lieut.-Cmdr. Eric Melrose Brown, chief Naval test pilot, landed the 540 m.p.h. jet aircraft Vampire aboard the aircraft carrier H.M.S. Ocean, on Dec. 4, 1945, he added another chapter to the history of flying. This dispatch is from the official Naval reporter aboard the Ocean. See also page 573.

THIS is the first time that a purely jet-propelled aircraft has been landed on a carrier. The Ocean was steaming off the Isle of Wight, rolling and pitching in a heavy ground swell, when a loudspeaker announcement was made that the pilot had been ordered to remain at Ford airfield, Sussex, until conditions were more favourable.

A minute later the Vampire screamed over the flight deck, made a roll and streaked away to circle the ship. The carrier's decks were immediately cleared and she turned into the wind. Brown brought his plane directly astern and came in at 95 miles an hour to make a perfect landing, picking up the first arrester wire and stopping in 100 ft. Taking off, the pilot was airborne in half the length of the flight deck. He completed three more faultless landings and take-offs.

One of the first to congratulate Brown was Vice-Admiral Sir Denis Boyd, Admiral (Air), who said that the landing of the Vampire is a natural development of the firm intention of the Royal Navy to arm itself with the finest aircraft in the world, capable of meeting on equal terms any shore-based planes. Mr. A. Woodburn, Parliamentary Secretary to the Ministry of Aircraft Production, arrived aboard the carrier in a Firefly aircraft and saw the trials. A De Havilland team of experts, headed by the chief designer, Mr. R. E. Bishop, were also on board.

Lieut.-Cmdr. Brown—"Winkle" to his Naval Air Arm friends—is 24, and a native of Edinburgh. Having some experience as a pilot, he joined the service in December 1939 as a leading airman, and now has 3,000 flying hours to his credit. He won his D.S.C. in 1942 "for bravery and skill in action against enemy aircraft and in the protection of a convoy against heavy and sustained enemy attacks." In May 1944 he was awarded the M.B.E. for being the first pilot to land a high-performance twin-engined aircraft on the deck of a carrier. The machine was a Mosquito. Later he became the first pilot to land the high-speed Hornet on an aircraft carrier. He has been on flying duties at the Royal Aircraft Establishment, Farnborough, Hants, since 1944.

The prototype Vampire used for these trials is powered by a Goblin II jet unit rated at 3,000 lb. static thrust, which gives her a top speed of 540 miles an hour at 20,000 ft. She is claimed to be the fastest operational fighter in the world. Her landing approach speed is 95 m.p.h. and her rate of climb 4,700 ft. per minute.

THE machine that made today's attempt carried 200 gallons of fuel, giving her a range at economical cruising speed of about 500 miles. Ceiling is given as 48,000 ft. The Vampire has a wing span of 40 ft. There are two air intakes, one each side of the short streamlined fuselage. The exhaust is at the far end of the fuselage, leaving a fair clearance between the outlet and the tail assembly across the two booms.

She has a squat appearance—her height is only just over nine ft. The tricycle undercarriage is formed by two wheels under the wings and one beneath the projecting nose of the fuselage. The 14,000-ton light carrier H.M.S. Ocean is one of the newest additions to the Fleet, having been completed only a few months ago; she has a speed of 20 knots and is 695 ft long.

"BATTING-IN" the first jet-propelled aircraft to land on a carrier (as told here) was the task of Lt. J. T. Pratt, R.N.V.R.
Photo, Charles E. Brown

We Stoked an Escape Ship from Singapore

With an A.C.2 at the helm, 50 R.A.F. men stoked the coaster Ipoh, of 1,200 tons, carrying 500 passengers, from Singapore to Java during the evacuation of 1942, after her side had been badly holed by bomb splinters. The story, only recently told, is by Aircraftman Victor Mansell, the Ipoh's quartermaster on the memorable trip.

SHE wasn't seaworthy, and couldn't carry any ballast because she would have settled in the water below the damage to the sides. But there wasn't time to worry about that. I met six sailors waiting by the ship. There was a great mountain of coal to be loaded. And they said that when she bunkered we would be able to sail. We got that organized. There were two ex-skippers aboard who looked after the navigation. And the second engineer of the Singapore gasworks showed the boys how to stoke.

Of the 500 airmen aboard, between 40 and 50 went into the stokehold, and the rest carried on with their job on the ship. The cooks went into the galley. Medical orderlies looked after the hygiene. And the rest tried to clean the ship up after the coaling. The airmen stokers worked energetically. But on account of their inexperience the Ipoh was only making four and a half knots for the first twenty-four hours. Later on, when they learned the knack under the guidance of an old hand, they sent her along at ten and half knots, with steam to spare.

Every quarter of an hour throughout the trip the Captain had to move the passengers from one side of the ship to the other in order to right her. After we'd been at sea for two days, we caught up with four tankers and a coaster. Then a British cruiser came up, looked us over, and went on her way. Right after that, the Japs sighted us and began to bomb. I kept zig-zagging sharply.

She steered beautifully, but every time we heeled over we had to shout to the passengers "all to port," and a few minutes later "all to starboard," because she was top-heavy and we had to be careful to keep her above her bomb-damage line. The Japs made three low-level attacks on us. And the only thing we got was a near miss, which nearly lifted us clean out of the water.

When the Japs sheered off, we stood by to pick up survivors from another cargo vessel. We scoured our own ship for medical supplies to treat the injured, and found aboard a Red Cross ambulance probably meant for Sumatra. We fixed the wounded up and got back on our course, reaching Java three and a half days after putting out from Singapore.

The troops disembarked at Java. Mansell himself went to Sourabaya and was taken prisoner in Garoet.

★ *As The Years Went By—Notable Days in the War* ★

1940

December 29. *Fire raid on City of London; Guildhall and other famous buildings damaged.*

1941

December 22. *Japanese launched major attack on Philippines; landings in Lingayen Gulf.*

December 24. *Japanese captured Wake Island. Troops of Eighth Army entered Benghazi.*

December 25. *Garrison of Hongkong, short of water, surrendered to Japanese.*

December 26. *Mr. Churchill, on visit to Washington, addressed United States Congress.*

December 27. *Combined Operations raid on Norwegian islands of Vaagso and Maalnoy.*

December 30. *Kaluga, industrial centre on Moscow front, recaptured by Red Army.*

1942

January 2. *Manila and naval base of Cavite, in the Philippines, occupied by Japanese.*

December 24. *Admiral Darlan assassinated.*

1943

January 1. *Veliki Luki, Nazi defence bastion on central front, retaken by Russians.*

December 24. *General Eisenhower appointed Supreme Cmdr. Allied Expeditionary Force.*

December 26. *German battleship Scharnhorst sunk off North Cape by units of Home Fleet.*

1944

December 25. *Mr. Churchill and Mr. Eden flew to Athens to call meeting of Greek parties.*

December 31. *Polish Lublin Committee assumed the title of "Provisional Government."*

Will the Atom Bomb Bring Peace?

By CAPTAIN NORMAN MACMILLAN M.C., A.F.C.

EVERYONE knows that the use of two atomic bombs against two Japanese cities abruptly brought Japanese militarism to its knees. And everyone believes that it is the intention of the United Nations to prevent the resurrection of German and Japanese militarism which might enable these two Powers to wreak destruction again upon the world.

But the catastrophic properties of atomic bomb warfare, whether the atomic bomb be dropped by aircraft or propelled by rocket, are so great that it will be necessary to be assured that neither of these peoples succeed in making atomic bombs of any form in secret. Such assurance will be difficult to obtain unless the territories of Germany and Japan are occupied by police forces belonging to the outside world.

It would be quite possible to carry atomic bombs in aircraft belonging to a civil airline. Thus it would be possible for any nation desirous of springing an aggressive surprise upon a chosen enemy to do so by the employment of civil transport aircraft, and the first intimation of the attack would be the destruction of great areas of population and the death of many hundreds of thousands of innocent victims. It therefore appears to be essential for an indefinite term of years that both Germany and Japan should be prohibited from possessing or operating any civil aircraft of any kind.

BAN on German and Jap Aircrews Until World Security is Assured?

Such air services as are necessary for the maintenance of the air communications of the world to and through the territories of these two peoples must be owned and operated by the United Nations, either as a United Nations Air Transport Corporation, or by the national airline operators of the appropriate sovereign members of the United Nations Organization. And I would suggest that until world security is assured by the organization, no German or Japanese national should be employed in the capacity of air-crew in any aircraft flying to and from their own national territory. Although I would not necessarily prohibit the employment of Germans or Japanese by any U.N.A.T.C., for too drastic curtailment of the development of peoples results in eventual insurrection.

It is a less straightforward matter to prevent the manufacture and storage of atomic weapons other than aircraft-carried bombs. The weight of the bomb that dropped on Hiroshima was less than a quarter of the weight of the explosive contained in the war-heads of the flying bombs and rocket bombs that fell on Britain during 1944-45. It is therefore easier (at least in theory) to make longer range and infinitely more deadly weapons of a similar nature. And human-operated rockets, developed from the German Viper anti-aircraft design, able to attack distant areas with accuracy, are already feasible today.

PROBABLY the only way the prevention of the development and storage of such weapons by Germany and Japan is possible is by the maintenance of a great scientific bureau by the United Nations, which will ensure that the rest of the world is kept ahead of all developments of atomic power. This should enable the United Nations to know what range of materials is necessary for the manufacture of all kinds of atomic weapons, and, armed with that knowledge, to prevent either Germany or Japan from having access to the essential raw materials by the prevention of imports or the compulsory exportation of home-produced materials.

If such agreement is possible. among the nations other than Germany and Japan, the possession by a world security organization of atomic power and weapons would make it impossible for either Germany or Japan to attempt to make war again, for they would be faced with the atomic potential in the hands of the police powers.

Atomic weapons can therefore ensure peace provided the nations forming the United Nations Organization can agree among themselves. From within their ranks must come the answer to whether the nations of the world are to be faced with peace or mutual destruction, and in their case there is no question of any police provision such as can be applied to Germany and Japan. The answer in their case depends upon their willingness to relinquish a great part of that sovereignty which has been the prerogative of the governments of communities ever since man learned to form himself into ethnographic groups. They must therefore agree to work together and to accept the rule of a committee of the combined nations as greater than the rule of their own governments.

IF they come to U.N.O. with the spirit which animated statesmen of the post-First Great War period they will succeed no more than did their predecessors. They must do what every committee member knows he must do, no matter how humble the form of the committee upon which he serves, and that is to accept the ruling of the majority as having priority over the desire of the minority. They must be prepared to give, not to get. If ever U.N.O. is allowed to become a hunting ground for politicians to seize advantages for their own section of the world there can be no hope of banishing the atomic bomb from the field of arbitrament.

Soldiers naturally want the most powerful weapons they can have. And they want to keep them secret from the soldiers of other nations. This curse of official secrecy about weapons has been a part of the flux that has previously brought the world to the melting point of war. That is why I welcome the idea of the sharing of the atomic bomb secret on a basis of reciprocity. But it is not the sharing of the secret of the atomic bomb, but the genuineness of the reciprocal disclosures that is important. If that can be achieved, we may dislodge the soldiers from their past ways of secrecy, espionage and counter-espionage, and if we do this it is possible that committee rule may succeed in the world.

THE Sharing of Military Secrets on a Basis of True Reciprocity

How would your local committee succeed if all its members attended the discussion armed and each prepared to back up his point of view by force? Yet that was what the League of Nations virtually did. The atomic bomb appears to offer the only material possibility that the United Nations Organization may commence its labours in a somewhat different spirit. For if agreement can be reached among the three first Powers forming that organization that they can share their military secrets upon a basis of true reciprocity, there is a chance that all may be able to accept committee rule. If not——?

In my opinion the atomic bomb will not bring peace through the soldiers, whose task it is to obtain the most efficient weapons their compatriots can produce; they look upon the problem from an angle different from that of the civilian.

THE atomic bomb can bring peace only if the world's statesmen decide that they can disregard their military advisers' love of secrecy and agree to pool their weapon secrets, internationalize atomic power, and prohibit atomic weapons. It is not an easy problem to solve, for how are the various members to assure themselves that one member is not stealing a march upon the others? Frankly, I do not believe there is any method of supervision which will ensure certainty in this aspect. The only real way to ensure honesty is to give more power into the hands of the committee than could be possessed by any one member, however powerful.

That means world committee government. The alternative must surely be a struggle for supremacy, and the rule of force to achieve world autarchy, a process which will attain the same eventual end, but by a third destruction of man's worldly possessions on a still greater scale. Without the emergence of the atomic bomb, the second method might have been impossible to prevent: 1946 is the crucial year. It will decide the relative value of national sovereignty and thereby disclose whether the atomic bomb will bring peace.

JAPANESE ATOM-SPLITTING DEVICE, discovered in a research laboratory near Tokyo, was closely examined by U.S. Army technicians before they wrecked it on December 4, 1945, to prevent possible attempts at atomic weapons—an action denounced in the U.S. Senate as "vandalous." Known as a cyclotron (see illus. page 438) it is essential to advanced atom-research.

First Jet Plane to Land on an Aircraft Carrier

FLYING HISTORY WAS MADE BY THE NAVAL AIR ARM off the Isle of Wight on December 4, 1945, when a 540 m.p.h. jet-propelled aircraft, the Vampire, took off from and landed on the aircraft carrier H.M.S. Ocean. Directed by the Deck Flying Control Officer's "bats," the Vampire touched down on the flight deck at 95 m.p.h. (1) to be stopped by the arrester wires in a hundred feet. The pilot was Lt.-Cmdr. Eric M. Brown, M.B.E., D.S.C., R.N.V.R., seen (2) in the cockpit. The Vampire taking-off (3). See also story in page 571. *Photos, Charles E. Brown, British Officia.*

The Editor Looks Back

SECRET WEAPONS Oct. 7, 1939

When one reads the ravings of his foulness the Fuehrer one's inability immediately to "get back" at the liar leaves a paralysing sense of impotence. Only continued struggle and endless patience against all that his vile creed and evil energy have brought upon us will make him bite the dust some day—but knowing the abysmal falsity of the fellow we need not be too terrified about his "new arm to which there is no defence." Aerial attack on all our seaports—which I have envisaged from the first—is Mr. Lloyd George's idea of this mysterious and dreadful "new arm." I think he may be right. We'll know better *when the war begins.*

WRITTEN in the "phoney" period of the War that paragraph reads oddly today. Those of us who survive know well enough that "his foulness" did have in mind several secret weapons, and quite recently we have seen samples of them on exhibition in Trafalgar Square. But in September of '39 I never guessed that I should live to see scores of flying bombs passing over my country home and nearly two score of them being shot down in the Weald of Sussex. But time has shown that the Allies too had secret weapons and were able to use them at the right moment, with no preliminary shouting about them.

EARLY BROADCASTING Oct. 7, 1939

Just been listening to Winston Churchill's broadcast—masterly ! No overstatement ; clear, concise, penetrating. His slight inclination to raise his voice at the end of a sentence, rather in the "Methody" manner, is of small account weighed against the fine seriousness of his tone and the simple effectiveness of his words. Contrasted with the mouthings and bellowings . . . of a speech by Hitler, Goering, or Goebbels, it makes one proud to be British when listening to Winston Churchill. But the B.B.C. shows small sign of improving. Its dud programmes have led to a great falling-off in listening. I hear on all hands from friends and acquaintances that they have practically stopped plugging in for the drivel that is dished out between the news bulletins of noon and nine —and God knows these are hardly worth straining a tympanum to hear. A noteworthy example of ineptitude preceded Mr. Churchill's most welcome speech. It was the reading of a news item from the German communiqué which asserted that *ten* British planes had been destroyed to *two* Nazi planes. Not one word of contradiction or confirmation was vouchsafed. If the German statement is true, heaven help us when the war starts. If it isn't, why aren't we told ?

I AM glad to recall the improvement that eventually took place in the B.B.C. broadcasts as the War dragged its slow length along, and the genuine triumph it achieved from D-Day to the end. But alas, there are no more of those heart-stirring speeches by our Old Man Eloquent to listen to. I may be wrong, yet I fancy somehow that the falling-off in the number of listeners must now be reckoned in millions daily ; though how their numbers can be guessed at all is something of a mystery to me.

RETURN OF THE HORSE Oct. 14, 1939

Sorry to see the old horses coming back to London. My satisfaction in the mechanization of the Army was mainly due to the feeling that there would be fewer horses to be mangled on the battlefield, and I fear that when London really feels the weight of air raids many of the thousands of horses that have returned to the metropolis as substitutes for motors are all too likely to be helpless sufferers in the bombing. The unhappy devotion of the Poles to cavalry added a distressing amount of animal suffering to the heroic martyrdom of their people.

HOW little one could foresee things in those early days. The horrible destruction of horses that took place after Germany turned her Armies against the Soviets, and the martyrdom of mules in the Burma War, were dreadful but inevitable. I am sure the Russian Cossacks were as fond of their horses as any animal-lovers among us and sorrowed no less at their sufferings, which, however, did not exceed those of the unfortunate men, women and children who were doomed to perish by the hundreds of thousands in prison camps when the Nazis began their organized attempts to extinguish whole populations. The true horrors of the War to come were little in our minds in those exciting but almost happy days of its first autumn.

BELGIUM PRE-INVADED Oct. 14, 1939

One of the most significant things I have noticed in the news from Belgium is the fact that no fewer than fifty Nazi journalists—each of whom is merely a lying propagandist expelled from Paris—are now resident in Brussels. They have all somehow been accommodated as "press attachés" of the Nazi Embassy there. Moreover, although all the French private residents in Belgium have now returned to France, none of the German residents there have gone back to Germany. This looks like the Nazis' "fifth column" in Belgium ready for the invasion.

IT was ! And how very stupid it all seems today. No one was being deceived by those obvious tactics ; yet the web of internal cross purposes was so closely meshed that there would seem to have been no way out, no means of forcing the hand, calling the bluff, of the intending invader.

ROLE OF THE TANK Oct. 14, 1939

To me one of the most noteworthy facts of the war so far has been the conquest of Poland, not by any "secret arm," but by an arm invented by an Englishman—the Tank. Despite all the braggadocio of Hitler, the most formidable thing on wheels came out of the brains of Englishmen in the Great War, and I have little doubt that the British invention which was used with such deadly effect against Poland will yet be used effectively against Germany, for it is seldom that an original invention is beaten by imitations.

WELL, I think that, though it took four to five years to do it, the place of the tank in the victorious march of the 8th Army from El Alamein to Berlin and, later, the lightning thrusts of Allied armour through France and Belgium to the Siegfried Line and beyond fully justified my comment.

NAZI CASUALTIES Oct. 21, 1939

A letter in The Times recently, from an obviously well-informed correspondent, pointed out that the official German history of the Great War put all German casualties at 33⅓ per cent higher than the figures admitted in the bulletins issued during the War. So when Hitler states that his casualties in the murder of Poland totalled 45,000 killed and wounded, we can figure 60,000 as the minimum—"and then some." For the Prussian liars of 1914-18 were the veriest amateurs compared with their Nazi successors.

I HAVE not seen a British official record of the German losses, but according to the "Arbeiter Zeitung" of Zurich, which claimed to have access to German War Ministry statistics, the Nazi dead numbered 91,278, seriously wounded 63,417, and the slightly wounded 84,938. Until our official historians have examined all the secret records of the Nazi losses the truth about their own casualties in the rape of Poland can be no more than guess work. The only thing certain is that here again Hitler was lying ; indeed, no evidence has at any time been forthcoming of his ever having spoken the truth on any subject, even by accident.

Postscript

TWO of our leading legal lights—Mr. Justice McNaghten and Sir Hartley Shawcross, the Attorney-General—in the King's Bench Division the other day would seem to have antagonized in the course of one single case the whole regiment of hard-working housewives. The learned judge refused to acknowledge a housewife's activities in the home as "work within the meaning of the Act," while the Attorney-General apostrophized them as a "labour of love." And yet, as far as I've seen, not one single protest has been raised !

ACCORDING to a recent inquiry by one of our main railway systems, men who want "Ladies only" compartments provided on all trains outnumber women by more than two to one. What no one seems to have had the courage to suggest is the introduction of a "Men only" coach—which is what these men want. Or think they do.

MR. E. A. HAMILTON-PEARSON, who rejoices in the title of "Psychiatric Medical Inspector" of the Home Office, declares that the great increase in petty thieving, bad manners, discourtesy, irritability and selfishness may be due to our diet. Those who know their Pickwick will hardly find anything new here, for was it not all anticipated over a century ago by Mr. Snodgrass who so adroitly blamed the salmon of the night before for his morning "hangover" ?

RE-READING that totally neglected classic, John Forster's Life of Walter Savage Landor, the other day, I came upon this shrewd diagnosis of a modern tendency: "the desire to read without the trouble of thinking, which railways have largely encouraged and to which many modern reputations are due." That was written seventy-seven years ago, and the years between have only served to point its truth and throw into deeper relief the awfulness of its implications. What the pessimistic Forster would have said of Reading Habits in the Atomic Age hardly bears contemplation !

THE "peace," no less than the war, continues, happily, to enlarge our knowledge of American ways—and means. Yet there must have been many people in Britain who learnt with surprise from President Truman the other day that the U.S. is till without a national health insurance scheme. Which is something that this country has boasted for well over thirty years.

THOSE who dash into print with attacks on the work of the British Council in spreading abroad a fuller knowledge of our cultural heritage should read the Council's last annual report. Here they will read that of 2,000 students in Turkey wishing to be sent overseas, over half gave Britain as their first choice. For this the Council very properly claims its share of credit.

In Britain Now: C.D. Equipment Goes Home

LONDON'S NEW WATERLOO BRIDGE, designed by Sir Giles Scott to replace Rennie's famous structure completed in 1817, was formally opened on December 10, 1945, by the Rt. Hon. Herbert Morrison, Lord President of the Council. It had been used by pedestrians for nearly three years and was fully open for traffic since November 21, 1944. See also illus. page 466.

C. D. EQUIPMENT BARGAINS were soon disposed of on December 4, 1945, when they came up for sale in Fulham, London. They included blankets, beds, mackintoshes, kitchenware. Housewife-purchasers (right) had to produce identity cards to establish proof of permanent residence in the borough.

TRIBUTE TO THE W.L.A. was paid by Her Majesty the Queen (above) in the Mansion House, London, on December 7, 1945, when she presented armlets to 750 of the women of the Land Army with six years' service. "You have gained a great reputation," she declared.

CLEARING LONDON of its wartime protective brickwork — blockhouses, pillboxes, anti-blast walls—proceeded apace as 1945 drew to its close. These workmen (right) removed a strong-point outside the Air Ministry offices in Kingsway; Bush House in back-ground.

 Photos, Topical, Sport & General, New York Times Photos

A U-Boat is Towed to Its Atlantic Grave

ON ITS LAST JOURNEY, ONE OF 110 SURRENDERED U-BOATS is towed by a British naval craft up the waters of Lough Foyle, near Londonderry, to be scuttled in "Operation Deadlight" (see pages 552-553) in the North Atlantic. The submarines were sunk with engines and gear intact. Many were of the Mark 23 type, of 250 tons, specially designed for use against Allied shipping in the Thames estuary. Five squadrons of U-boat-killers of R.A.F. Coastal Command took part in the Operation.
Photo, Keystone

Printed in England and published every alternate Friday by the Proprietors, THE AMALGAMATED PRESS, LTD., The Fleetway House, Farringdon Street, London, E.C.4. Registered for transmission by Canadian Magazine Post. Sole Agents for Australia and New Zealand: Messrs. Gordon & Gotch, Ltd. and for South Africa: Central News Agency; Ltd.—January 4, 1946. S.S. *Editorial Offices:* JOHN CARPENTER HOUSE WHITEFRIARS, LONDON, E C 4.

Vol 9 The War Illustrated and AFTERWARDS No 224

SIXPENCE JANUARY 18, 1946

HOME FROM SEA at the turn of the year came thousands of eager men of the Royal Navy. This leading seaman, native of East London, set foot ashore at Chatham with an enormous " hand " of bananas supplementing his personal goods and chattels. The frigate H.M.S. Dovey, of whose company he was a member, arrived from West Africa on December 19, completing two and a half years' foreign service. See also pages 591-594. *Photo, Keystone*

Edited by Sir John Hammerton

NO. 225 WILL BE PUBLISHED FRIDAY, FEBRUARY 1

Winter with the Occupation Armies in Germany

GENERAL GEORGE S. PATTON'S LAST JOURNEY—to the U.S. military cemetery at Hamm, Luxemburg, on December 24, 1945. The General, who died at Heidelberg following a motoring accident near Mannheim on December 9, was sixty years of age and led the U.S. 3rd Army in its swift advance through France into Germany in 1944. Nicknamed "Old Blood and Guts," he was in charge of the American attack on Casablanca in November 1942, and commanded the U.S. 7th Army in Sicily. Another American war-leader, Lt.-Gen. Alexander M. Patch, who commanded the U.S. 7th Army in S. France in 1944, died of pneumonia in Texas on November 21, 1945.

KIPPERS IN BERLIN were being served to our men from December 1945 onwards. Heralding their arrival, an A.T.S. corporal (1) pinned up the "Corporal Kipper" poster in the Winston Club. In the snow two R.A.F. police made friends (2) with young Berliners. Members of the A.T.S. in December were obliged to be accompanied by armed escort if venturing forth after dark (3). Display at Bonneberg of "Volkswagen" (4). These "People's Cars" were promised by Hitler but never delivered—though thousands had paid instalments on them. Under British direction the first cars were being produced early in December for use by the British Army.

Photos, L.N.A., Keystone

What is Happening in Java?

By JOSEPH TAGGART

To countless people it came as a shock that British troops should again be engaged in warfare so soon after the defeat of Germany and Japan, when all our hopes were set upon the consummation of world-wide Peace. That our efforts should be, apparently, solely on behalf of the Dutch increased the general mystification. All is made clear in this article written by an expert specially for "The War Illustrated."

SINCE late September 1945 British troops have been fighting a sporadic, small-scale, most unpleasant war in the Netherlands East Indies islands, known collectively as Indonesia. British people are asking why. Why must men who have battled with the Germans and the Japanese now take up this jungle struggle to reinstate the Dutch in Java and Sumatra ?

There is a widespread notion that an unwelcome task was incontinently thrust upon Admiral Lord Louis Mountbatten and the men of his command at the behest of Washington. The facts are neither so simple nor so uncomplimentary to the Americans.

If there is a villain in the piece it appears to have been the atomic bomb. The sudden collapse of Japan after Nagasaki left a number of military vacuums in the Far East, of which Indonesia was by far the largest.

This was the sequence of events—so far as it is known. Some time after the end of the war in Europe, London and Washington agreed to the transfer of a large part of General MacArthur's scattered command to S.E.A.C. This addition to British responsibilities was very great. It included all Indonesia, with a population of over 50,000,000 Indonesians and Chinese ; 50,000 Japanese troops, and 25,000 Japanese civilians. It covered 55,000 square miles of territory.

Interval's Fatal Consequences

The transfer officially took place on August 12, 1945. It then existed only on paper. The Allied leaders had planned "future but not immediate" amphibious operations on the largest scale to free these rich and thickly populated islands. Obviously the task of assembling troops, shipping, naval squadrons and air power for the main offensive would have taken many months.

At that moment, when there was a plan but nothing more in readiness, Japan surrendered. So great was the sudden strain thrown upon Mountbatten's resources, in order to round-up and disarm the surrendering Japanese over an enormous area, that we could not land at all in Java until nearly six weeks had passed. The interval had fatal consequences. In Mr. Bevin's words in the House of Commons on November 23, we were driven to "the expedients of placing responsibility on Japanese commanders (in Indonesia) for the maintenance of law and order and for the safety of prisoners of war and internees."

If the Indonesian Nationalists saw a golden opportunity to rise, the Japs were not slow to exploit it. There is no doubt now that they allowed the Indonesians to seize vast quantities of arms, even including light tanks, armoured cars and anti-aircraft guns.

BUT for prolonged military punctilio over the main surrender to MacArthur in Tokyo Bay on Sept. 2, we might have reached Batavia in force before the Nationalists were ready for open war. But under that unlucky transfer of command on August 15—just one week after the Japanese had announced "Indonesian independence"—it was the British who had to go in and clear up the mess.

It is worth while dwelling in a little more detail upon what happened inside the islands before the first British troops—2,000 Seaforth Highlanders and 250 Royal Marines—reached Batavia on September 29.

On August 17 a proclamation signed by the Indonesian leaders, Dr. Soekarno and Dr. Hatta, stated, quaintly but succinctly : "We people of Indonesia who framed the independence of Indonesia ; matters concerning transmission of authorities and so on will be executed accurately and in the shortest time." An "Indonesian Independence Preparatory Committee" had been at work.

The next day it announced (1) Legalization of the Constitution of the Republic of Indonesia ; (2) Appointment of Dr. Soekarno as President, and Dr. Mohammed Hatta (the brains behind the whole rising), as Vice-President ; (3) Establishment of a National Committee.

On the same day, August 18, another Presidential Proclamation reiterated the existence of the independent Republic of Indonesia, and concluded : "We expect the whole Indonesian nation to be calm, quiet, prepared, well-disciplined and good." So they were ready for trouble if it came. This ukase was also signed by Dr. Jakarta.

During the long interval before the Allied vanguard reached the islands the more militant Nationalists put in a little battle practice on their fallen conquerors and Japanese officers were murdered.

On September 24, Dr. Soekarno decided to make his own position clear against the day when there might be a reckoning with the quislings. He declared that his collaboration with the Japanese during the occupation had been unwilling. Indonesians under his leadership had accepted the Tokyo offer of political freedom in order to "consolidate their position."

Their aspiration was complete independence, but there would be no racial discrimination, and all traders (even Dutch ?) would be welcomed.

Efforts to Avoid Bloodshed

On September 25, Brisbane dockers refused to load six ships for the Netherlands East Indies, and The Times correspondent reported from Batavia that Japanese officers were to be seen sporting Indonesian Republic flags. On the same day, too, it was announced that British reinforcements were on their way to Batavia to deal with what the Japanese secret police called "possible disturbances." It is scarcely surprising that all Dr. Soekarno's best efforts to avoid bloodshed were doomed to failure.

Then on September 30, the British commander, Lieut.-General Sir Philip Christison, arrived in Java. Before leaving Singapore he had said that in Java and Sumatra the British would employ the Japanese as police until the Dutch could take over. That time has not yet come. On reaching Batavia, General Christison said : "The Dutch must make a statement on the status of the Netherlands East Indies, and something must happen at once." He added that he intended to see the Nationalist leaders, with whom the Dutch refused to have any dealings. But General Christison and other Allied military leaders had a number of talks with Soekarno.

The "President of Indonesia" did his best. He issued orders that all Indonesians should co-operate with the Allies. But he added that they would fight any attempt to restore Dutch sovereignty. By October 4 the Republicans had seized Surabaya and Bandoeng from the Japs. On that day Dr. H. J. Van Mook, Lieut.-Governor-General of the Netherlands East Indies, arrived at Batavia and immediately began preparing for a joint conference of Dutch and Indonesians. Unfortunately, the attitude of The Hague Government nullified all his pacific efforts.

From the second week in October the situation in Java worsened. Largely beyond the control of their own chosen leaders, bands of hot-blooded young Indonesians sniped, ambushed and murdered small groups of Allied troops in many parts of the island.

On October 30, Brigadier H. W. S. Mallaby arranged a verbal truce, on very liberal terms, with Dr. Soekarno. The next day he was killed while engaged in an informal roadside conference with some of the Indonesian leaders. (See illus. page 453). Thereafter, naturally, the British adopted stronger measures, and fighting became bitter.

Japan's Part in the Business

Three months too late to avert all this needless bloodshed and political enmity, a solution seems at last in sight. On December 27, discussions were held between Mr. Attlee and Mr. Noel Baker, Minister of State, on behalf of Britain, and Professor Schermerhorn, Netherlands Prime Minister, and Dr. Van Mook, representing the Netherlands, as to the most effective line of action to be taken to restore law and order in Java. The British Government subsequently reaffirmed their obligation to their Dutch allies to establish without delay conditions of security in which it would be possible for the Government of the Netherlands East Indies to continue negotiations with representative Indonesians.

Though there is dissension among the Indonesians themselves the demand for some form of home rule is very strong. To be realistic the Dutch must offer something more generous than in the past, and this was foreshadowed in a New Year's message from Professor Schermerhorn.

Meanwhile, here are some facts about Japan's part in the business, given by an Indonesian. The Indonesian People's Party, called POETRA, was launched in March 1943. From the beginning its leaders included Soekarno, Hatta, and others in the present Indonesian "Government," such as Kihadjar Dewantoro, the Minister of Education, and Kijahi Hadji Mansoer, Religion Leader. Eurasians and Chinese joined in.

The Japanese encouraged efforts at economic expansion, which included a Five Years Plan for increasing rice production by thousands of acres more paddy fields. Many new villages were built. Great attention was paid to modern farming methods, including the use of artificial fertilizers. The Japanese cultivated in every way the idea that they would concede autonomy after the war.

THE game was simple. Today the politically immature masses of Indonesia say that the Japs gave them far more liberty and encouragement to emancipate themselves than they are ever likely to get from their old masters the Dutch It was that carefully stimulated surge of patriotism that fanned the flame of opposition to our troops, whom rebel Indonesians saw merely as storm troopers for the Dutch.

Many authorities now believe that if we could have landed two divisions at the end of August the whole rising might have missed fire, and order have been established with the minimum of loss on both sides. It is no use complaining that we have been unlucky in landing a dirty job that strictly belonged to someone else. But we are entitled to draw the attention of critics to these words of our Foreign Minister, Mr. Bevin : "Let not people always accuse the British of being the only villains in the piece. Our business was a rescue work and nothing else. We were not there for any other purpose but to carry out the task and get out of it again as soon as we could."

The Never-to-be-Forgotten Army

By MAJ.-GENERAL
SIR CHARLES GWYNN
K.C.B., D.S.O.

On December 1, 1945, two years after its formation, the 14th Army was disbanded. In that period its record was one of achievements which secure for it the highest rank in the history of warfare. Not only was it by far the largest single army ever put in the field by the Empire; it was the largest single army in any theatre of the Second Great War. Numbering approximately one million men, of whom one half at least were combat troops, at times it was deployed in widely separated groups on a frontage of some 700 miles.

In its ranks men of fifty nationalities found a place; yet in spite of that it developed an esprit de corps and an individuality comparable to that of the 8th Army. British, Indian and Gurkha units formed the main combat force—at one time or another two British and nine Indian Divisions were engaged (the latter, as usual, being one-third British in composition)—the remainder being composed of two West African Divisions and one East African Division led by British officers and N.C.O.s, as well as important Chinese and American contingents and valuable levies from among the Burmese natives.

ACCOMPLISHED All Tasks Successfully and Killed More than 120,000 Japs

The tasks given to the 14th Army were (1) to protect the air route to China, (2) to reopen the Burma road, (3) to destroy the Japanese Army in Burma.

The first seemed to present no great difficulties. The second, however, evidently would involve hard fighting to prevent the Japanese interfering with General Stilwell's scheme for driving a new road from Ledo in Assam to link up with the old Burma road. The third seemed likely to remain a mere aspiration until such time as a full-scale amphibious operation could be staged. For the practically roadless mountains and jungles of the Indo-Burma frontier region, coupled with the phenomenally wet and prolonged monsoon season, apparently prohibited a far-reaching invasion of Burma by large forces from the north, for these involved difficulties of supply, a short favourable campaigning season, and risk of many losses among the troops from malaria and other tropical diseases.

Yet the 14th Army accomplished all its tasks successfully without undertaking large-scale amphibious operations. It killed over 120,000 Japanese; over 40 per cent of their total losses in the war, and seven times as many as its own dead. Moreover, in the ten months of its main offensive the Army advanced 1,000 miles and liberated practically the whole of Burma.

How were these almost miraculous results obtained? Primarily by bold and far-sighted substitution of air transport for normal road supply methods, and in general the close co-ordination of air and surface power to an unprecedented extent. The supply problem having been solved, skilful and bold leadership and the amazing endurance and fighting qualities of the troops were given full play. Actually, in 1944, it was intended only to undertake the second task—because the 14th Army was not yet at full strength and much of the equipment intended for it had been diverted to the European theatre. But the organization and provision of air transport on a scale to meet future requirements was put in hand.

General Wingate's first Chindit experiment had proved the possibility of penetrating behind the Japanese lines and disorganizing their dispositions and lines of communication, and it was decided to exploit the same idea on a much larger scale with a view to attacking the communications of the Japanese Division opposing General Stilwell's force. This time a whole division was used, and it was to be conveyed by air to the scene of its operations and thereafter to be supplied and maintained from the air.

General SIR WILLIAM SLIM, G.B.E., K.C.B., D.S.O., former Commander of the 14th Army, whose appointment as Commandant of the Imperial Defence College was announced on Dec. 4, 1945, arrived from Burma on Dec. 25. He is seen (right) with Lady Slim saying goodbye to Capt. J. A. Macdonald, of the S.S. Georgic, in which he sailed.

The Division landed in March 1944, and with its co-operation General Stilwell's American and Chinese troops reached Myitkyina, at the head of the railway from Mandalay, in May. It had also been decided indirectly to support Stilwell's operations by taking the offensive in Arakan and by limited operations on the Chindwin front, in order to cause dispersion of the Japanese forces. The former provoked a strong Japanese counter-stroke which was finally defeated decisively, but troops preparing for the latter were withdrawn when the Japanese Manipur offensive developed.

MEDICAL Service Achieved Miracles Throughout the Entire Campaign

Stilwell's communications were for a time in danger; but the defence of Imphal and Kohima, followed by a decisive counter-offensive, not only fulfilled the 14th Army's first and second missions, but by inflicting a crushing defeat on the Japanese went far towards achieving the third. The Japanese offensive, dangerous as it at one time seemed, actually played into General Slim's hand, for it gave him the opportunity of engaging them at the end of inadequate and vulnerable lines of communication.

The decision to exploit success by maintaining the counter-offensive during the monsoon in terribly difficult country was taken, despite all previous beliefs that it would prove impracticable. Undoubtedly it imposed a desperate test on the toughness of the troops, but with the medical service achieving miracles—as indeed it did throughout the whole campaign—and the Air Force continuing to operate in spite of appalling conditions, the decision fully justified itself.

By December 1944 the 14th Army was across the Chindwin and had made contact with Stilwell's force south of Myitkyina. The dry season was now ahead for the prosecution of the main offensive, and it developed rapidly. Before the end of January 1945 the jungle and hilly districts of north Burma were passed and the Army emerged into a more open and dry region where armour could operate freely. The Japanese made determined attempts to hold the line of the Irrawaddy and to cover Mandalay, but before the end of March the river had been crossed and the city captured. Moreover, by a wide outflanking movement which took the enemy by surprise, General Slim had at Meiktila established a strong force in the rear of the Japanese main forces, barring their retreat to the south. After a month's hard fighting, by early April the victory was complete and the greater part of the enemy dispersed into the hills to the east.

RESPONDED With Amazing Speed to the Call for a Supreme Effort

But there was still a great problem to be faced. How was the 14th Army to be supplied during the coming monsoon? Supply by road from Assam on a sufficient scale was quite impracticable, and as the Army had advanced, the base for air supply had, in order to shorten the flight, been transferred from Imphal first to Chittagong and afterwards to Akyab and other islands on the Arakan coast captured by the 15th Corps and Navy in a series of minor amphibious operations. These vital operations secured airfields at progressively shorter ranges to the Army; but even at shorter ranges air supply could not be ensured during the monsoon.

The capture of Rangoon, the only port available, was therefore essential, but it lay 300 miles south of Meiktila. Could it be captured before the monsoon broke in May? The 14th Army was called on to make a supreme effort to provide the answer. With what amazing speed and determination it responded to the call we know, and though it fell to the 15th Corps, by yet another admirably timed amphibious operation, to enter the port first, yet it was the bold thrust southwards from Meiktila that completely disorganized all Japanese attempts to hold the port, the capture of which ensured the complete reconquest of Burma.

The Burma campaign was an undoubted masterpiece of skilful planning and bold execution, and in particular reliance on air transport was a daring experiment. But even greater credit must be given to the troops. Earlier beliefs that the Japanese would prove invincible in jungle fighting and be rendered almost unconquerable by their fanatical determination to die fighting were completely shattered. India especially should be proud of the 14th Army, for although the Gurkhas remained pre-eminent as jungle and mountain fighters, yet the war proved that other Indian races besides those reputedly martial could produce gallant men, for the great expansion of the Indian Army had spread the recruiting net more and more widely.

Moreover, all doubts as to the ability of India to supply competent and brave officers were allayed. The policy of Indianizing the officer cadre, though immensely accelerated, fully justified itself and the test could hardly have been higher. British troops displayed once again their capacity to develop their great qualities under the most unfavourable climatic conditions, though they would be the first to admit the debt they owed in this case to the medical service and science.

Recalling Great Memories of Burma's Green Hell

VETERANS OF THE NEVER-TO-BE-FORGOTTEN ARMY—the mighty 14th—congratulated by Lt.-Gen. Sir Oliver Leese (1), C.-in-C. Allied Land Forces, Burma, on their part in the campaign. This private (2) snatched a moment for needle-threading, preparatory to sock-darning—necessary precaution against foot trouble. R.A.F. pilots of L-5 ambulance planes (3) transported wounded direct from the front line. Airborne supply played a decisive part in the Burma victory: collecting parachuted material near Mandalay (4).

Photos, British and Indian Official

Most Decisive Sea Battle of the War

By
FRANCIS E. McMURTRIE

IN a general knowledge test, how many could name offhand the most decisive naval victory of the Second Great War? It is surprising that so little should be known about this, especially as the action was fought less than fifteen months ago. During the Battle of Leyte Gulf the forces engaged were larger than in any naval action since Jutland, while enemy losses considerably exceeded those of May 31, 1916. Indeed, the Japanese fleet was so hard hit in those crucial days of October 24-26, 1944, that its organization as a fighting force received a fatal blow, rendering inevitable the surrender of 1945.

Undoubtedly, the absence of any full and clear account of the battle has helped to obscure its importance to the average Briton. In view of further details which reached me recently, it seemed worth trying to remedy this omission so far as readers of THE WAR ILLUSTRATED are concerned. In October 1944 the Japanese, relying on reports that exaggerated the effect of their air attacks on the U.S. Pacific Fleet, determined to strike with full force at the American Seventh Fleet covering the landing on the island of Leyte, in the Eastern Philippines.

TWO Fleets to Deliver Converging Attacks

It seems evident that the enemy plan was to deliver converging attacks by two fleets. One, comprising nearly 20 units (including battleships, cruisers and destroyers) was to approach from the south, through Surigao Strait. Simultaneously the second force, of somewhat greater strength, was to proceed from the westward towards the Leyte Gulf anchorage by way of San Bernardino Strait. It was apparently hoped to produce confusion and dismay by successive attacks from two quarters; while the two Japanese fleets, advancing on lines at right angles to one another, would each enjoy a clear field of fire.

A third enemy force, of 17 ships, including at least four aircraft carriers, was meanwhile approaching the Philippines from some point to the northward of Luzon. Whether this was intended purely as a diversionary operation, or was designed to provide for "mopping up" the U.S. fleet after it had been defeated and scattered by the earlier attacks, is uncertain.

As a diversion it had some slight effect, for though warning had been received by October 22 of the approach of Japanese forces from the southward and westward, it was not until the afternoon of the 24th that the third tentacle of the attack was detected. Admiral Halsey, senior naval officer in the Leyte area, at once concentrated a number of carrier task groups and proceeded northward at high speed with the Third Fleet to meet this new threat. He left Vice-Admiral Kinkaid with the 7th Fleet (including six of the older battleships) to deal with the other two forces.

TO protect the south entrance of Leyte Gulf, Rear-Admiral J. B. Oldendorf, senior officer on the spot, stationed a strong force of destroyers and motor torpedo boats at the narrowest portion of Surigao Strait. These sighted the enemy about midnight, when the m.t.b.s attacked. At 1.30 a.m. on the 25th the enemy entered the Strait in two columns, one about four miles astern of the other. A second torpedo attack by the Americans was delivered an hour later.

At 3 a.m. the main fleet action began with the launching of torpedo attacks by U.S. destroyers, which reduced the speed of the enemy advance from 20 to 12 knots. In less than half an hour the American battleships and cruisers opened fire, and within 40 minutes the Japanese column, finding the American strength greater than expected, turned and began to retire. At this stage the range was down to 11,000 yards, and the enemy were punished heavily.

In the course of the pursuit through Surigao Strait the Japanese battleship Fuso, the heavy cruiser Mogami and a destroyer were sunk. A second battleship, the Yamasiro, after being badly damaged, was finished off by torpedoes from destroyers. By the evening of the 25th only six out of 15 or 16 enemy ships which had entered Surigao Strait remained afloat.

While this was happening, Admiral Halsey had struck heavily with his aircraft at the northern enemy force. Taken by surprise as it approached the coast of Luzon from the north-east, this force had only a few planes available, the remainder having flown to fields in the Philippines to refuel. When they returned it was too late, and 21 of them were shot down by the American fighters. Meantime, three of the enemy carriers, the 30,000-ton Zuikaku and the smaller Titose and Zuiho, had been destroyed by air attack, while a fourth carrier, the Tiyoda, after being crippled by aircraft, was sunk by Admiral Halsey's surface vessels. A cruiser, the Tama, was torpedoed and sunk by the U.S. submarine Jallao; and a destroyer was also sent to the bottom.

DURING the night the Japanese western force passed through San Bernardino Strait into the Pacific. News of its presence off Samar caused Admiral Halsey to return southward. While searching for the American transports and landing craft the Japanese fleet encountered a force of U.S. escort carriers under Rear-Admiral Sprague. These did their best to avoid an unequal action, smoke screens being laid by two destroyers and a destroyer escort to aid their retreat. Torpedo attacks were also delivered on the enemy by these three gallant ships, which were all sunk by the enemy fire—the Hoel, Johnston and Samuel B. Roberts. In this phase of the action the U.S. escort carriers Gambier Bay and St. Lo were also lost, the former being sunk by gunfire and the latter by bombing.

Already under attack from Seventh Fleet aircraft, the Japanese now had to face fresh onslaughts as Admiral Halsey's planes came into action. One heavy cruiser, the Suzuya, was sunk, and a second, the Tikuma, had to be left behind, completely disabled, as her consorts retired through the San Bernardino Strait under cover of darkness. Ships of the Third Fleet sank the helpless Tikuma by gunfire at 2 a.m. on October 26.

JAP Navy Accomplished Its Own Destruction

Throughout that day American aircraft continued to harass the enemy fleet as it retreated across the Sibuyan Sea. During this phase of the action Japan's newest battleship, the 45,000-ton Musasi, was destroyed, together with three cruisers, the Abukuma, Kinu and Nosiro. Two more cruisers were so seriously damaged that they got no farther than Manila Bay, where in due course they succumbed to persistent air attacks, the Nati being sunk on November 5 and the Kiso on November 13. Yet another cruiser, the Kumano, which was discovered sheltering in Dasol Bay, farther to the north-westward, met a similar fate a few days later.

An important part was played by American submarines, which shadowed the enemy for days beforehand, reporting all movements by wireless. As the Japanese fleet was passing through the Palawan Passage on October 23, two of its heavy cruisers, the Atago and Maya, were torpedoed and sunk by these watching submarines.

A noteworthy feature of the battle is that most of the fighting was at night, enabling the Americans to reap the full advantage of radar. The Japanese relied on searchlights and star shell, which proved less effective.

Thus the Japanese Navy had virtually accomplished its own destruction by assuming the initiative too late in the conflict. Seldom has an attacking force been more badly surprised by the strength of the resistance offered to it. (See illus. page 487, Vol. 8.)

THE PHILIPPINES COMMONWEALTH, a group of 7,000 islands in the northern part of the East Indies, under U.S. protection. It was in the surrounding waters during October 1944 that the U.S. Pacific Fleet achieved a decisive victory over the Japanese.

Guns of the Royal Navy Bark at Surabaya

FLEEING TO THE BRITISH LINES, Chinese (top) sought refuge after H.M.S. Caesar, Cavalier and Carron, of the 6th Flotilla, had shelled Indonesian positions in November 1945. A 4·5-in. gun is fired (below), and gunnery officer and chief yeoman of signals (inset) check the results. These ships had been operating off Surabaya since November 1, evacuating refugees and later bombarding the coast in support of the Army. On December 15, 7th Airborne Division units were landed. See also pages 524–525 and 579.

Photos, British Official

A Thousand Fathoms Deep Lies the U-Boat Fleet

AN ENORMOUS SEA-BED CAVITY over 6,000 ft. below the surface of the Atlantic, known as Rockall Deep, 100 miles to the north-west of the northern Irish land-shelf, is the specially selected scuttling site for the surrendered submarines of Germany (see pages 552-553 and 576). From Malin Head, north of Londonderry, a comparatively shallow ledge (see diagram below) stretches out to the Vidal Bank, at the northern end of which stands St. Kilda, most westernly of the Outer Hebrides. From here, towards the north-west, soundings run steeply to Rockall Deep, one of the great hollows of the North Atlantic. Rockall itself is a bird-haunted granite islet, little known even among sailors, being well off the Atlantic shipping route. Situated near the centre of the 60-mile Rockall Bank, some 200 miles to the west of North Uist in the Hebrides, it has a circumference of little more than a hundred yards and a height of about 70 ft. Our North Atlantic naval and air patrols frequently used it as a wartime landfall. The drawing above shows a line of destroyers steaming past it during the Battle of the Atlantic—a route for long kept secret. The first U-boats sunk in the Deep, during "Operation Deadlight," were sent down by gunfire from destroyers.

By courtesy of The Sphere.

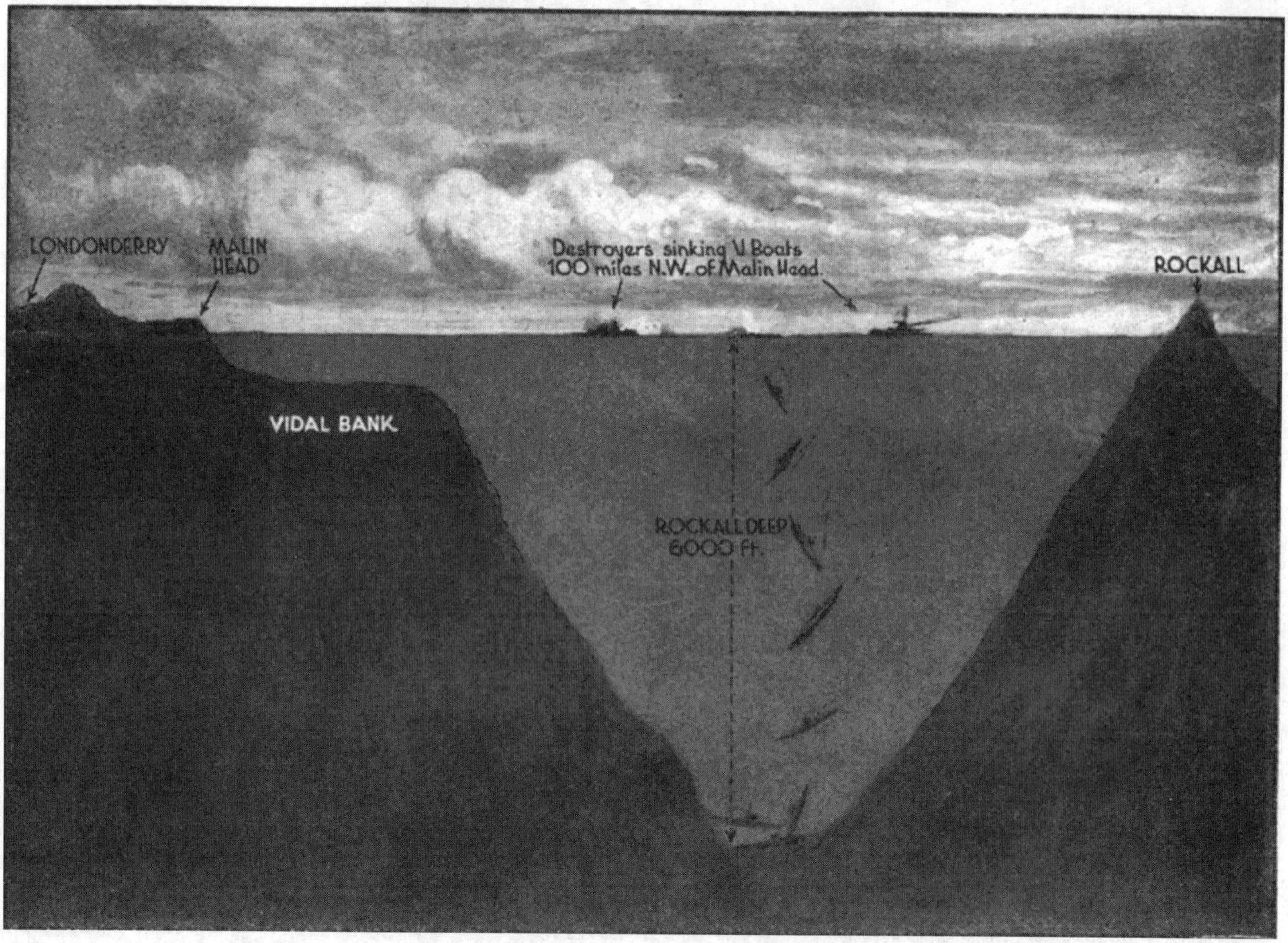

First W.A.A.F. for S.E. Asia Air Command H.Q.

COMING ASHORE AT SINGAPORE from the troopship Devonshire in December 1945 were these members of the W.A.A.F. after a six-days' crossing from Ceylon. Attached to the first draft to be sent on service east of India, they were previously stationed at Bombay, Delhi and Ceylon. Having volunteered for the transfer farther east they will work at the H.Q. of South-East Asia Air Command under the direction of the A.O.C., Air Marshal Sir William A. Coryton, K.B.E., C.B., M.V.O., D.F.C. *Photo, British Official*

In Search of Elusive Saboteurs in Palestine

BRITISH TROOPS AND PALESTINE POLICE probed a wide area in the Valley of Sharon, following attacks on near-by coastguard stations on November 25, 1945 (see page 546). Man-hunt in the village of Rishpon (1) called for the use of mine-detectors. Women of the Jewish Red Shield ambulance organization (2) assisted casualties to a clinic. Burnt-out coastguard installation at Sidna Ali (3). Troops of our 6th Airborne Division guarded Jewish settlers at Shifayim (4) while comrades searched the village. See also story in page 537. *Photos, British Official*

Where the War-Dogs Await Their Demobilization

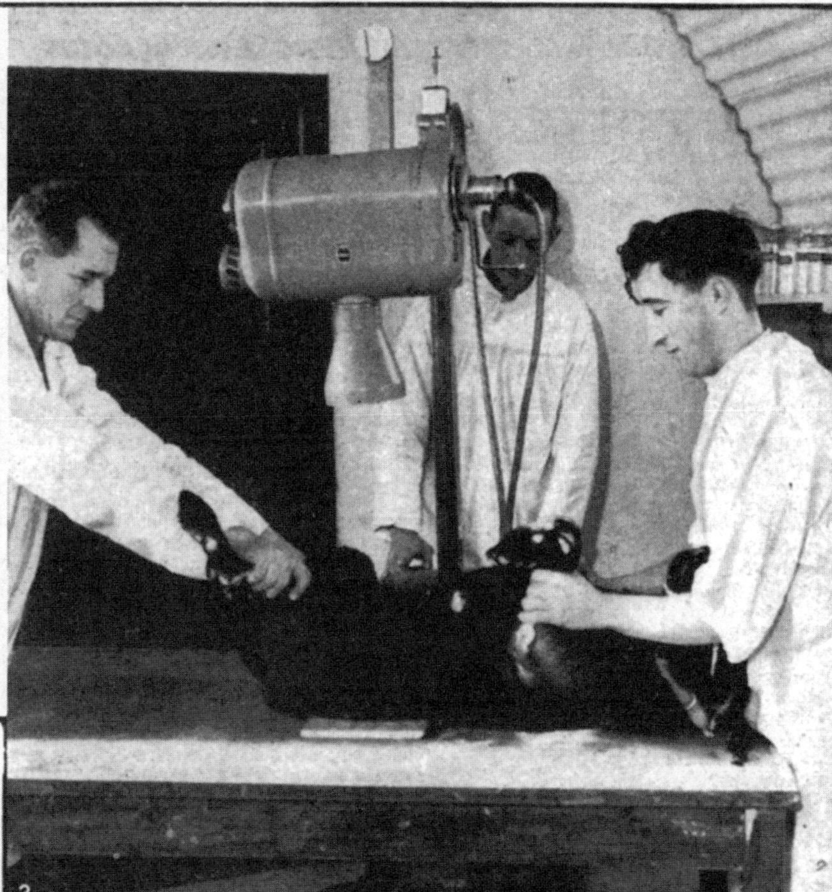

AT STOCKBRIDGE, HAMPSHIRE, is a dogs' demobilization centre. Here, while undergoing the regulation six-months quarantine, are housed Service animals (see page 488) and pets brought home by men from overseas. Among "residents" which had seen service abroad were Mac (1), an Airedale dropped by parachute in Normandy on D-Day to detect mines, and owned by Mrs. H. Paton, of Glasgow; and Lyal, a black Labrador (owner, Mr. D. Millar, of Fife) seen (2) about to be X-rayed.

IN THE QUARANTINE QUARTERS at Stockbridge the animals are exercised for two hours each day while awaiting release. As a safeguard against rabies infection no dogs are allowed to meet. Bruce (3), a black Labrador with a fine record in mine-detection, owned by Capt. Miskin, of Richmond, is seen being given a run in the kennels yard. Preparing meals, consisting of meat and biscuits mixed, receives the care and attention which the inmates deserve : scrupulous cleanliness is observed.

Photos Exclusive to THE WAR ILLUSTRATED

Now It Can Be Told!

BRITISH NAVAL OFFICER WHO LED MAQUIS

IN October 1940, Jean Henri Coleman, 32-years-old native of Paris, son of an English father and French mother and as patriotic an Englishman as any, was trudging the streets of London, almost penniless after his escape from France—trying to join the Royal Navy. In June 1945, as Lieutenant J. H. Coleman, M.B.E., R.N.V.R., he was to attend Buckingham Palace to receive his decoration from the King, for his services in France for the period of a year with the Maquis. He is the only British Naval officer to have served with this unique resistance organization.

The citation for his award states: "This officer was dropped into France by parachute in September 1943, as assistant to a resistance organizer in Lyons. He was given the task of finding grounds where arms could be dropped by parachute, reconnoitring the targets allotted to the circuit, and finding safe houses. He carried out his duties ably and devotedly. When, a few weeks before D-Day, his chief was caught by the Gestapo, Coleman took over the command of the circuit, and carried it through a difficult period until his chief escaped soon after the invasion. Coleman ensured the execution of the concerted attacks on railway and telecommunications targets on and after D-Day. He showed high qualities of leadership and devotion to duty."

BEFORE embarking on his Maquis adventure, a complete, unbreakable "cover story" had to be learned. Lieutenant Coleman took over the "life" of a French friend in London. False papers were given him in the friend's name and he studied every possible detail of the past life of the Frenchman to make his alibi, if possible, foolproof.

"He was a pretty brainy type of engineer," said Lieut. Coleman, "and although my adoption of his past never gave me much trouble, I was sometimes embarrassed by people in France asking me highly technical engineering questions, which I had to pass over lightly or change the subject. It was also a little tricky sometimes to avoid being introduced to fellows who had been at school or college with the man whose life I was leading! Otherwise my story was watertight, even down to a duplicate birth certificate—and I think I was the only one who retained the same story throughout the time I was in France."

Six Touching Farewells to Face

Then, after the parachute course, came the period of waiting for the final departure. He spent part of the time in getting married—"a move," he says, "which would normally have caused a lot of trouble, and might have disqualified me for the job, if my wife hadn't also been working for Military Intelligence. As it was, she had the embarrassment of going around London with a new husband dressed like a nondescript sort of French commercial traveller, because I had to 'wear-in' the suits I was to use in France. These were made to look as French as possible, and every item of our kit was stamped 'Fabrication Française,' even the razor blades."

Lieutenant Coleman had six touching farewells to face before eventually landing in France. On six occasions he was fitted at the airport into his cumbersome parachute equipment, with all its accessories, and he and the containers carrying supplies to his future comrades were loaded into the plane. Each time, after dodging "flak valley" and circling over the area of the Loire valley, which was his allotted territory, he stood over the parachute hatch waiting to drop—but there was no flashed signal from the ground, and the aircraft had to return.

"If I hadn't dropped on the seventh occasion," he says, "I don't think I could ever have done it. I believe I made a good landing in the bright moonlight. I went into my roll and somersaulted properly—and then passed right out. When I recovered I found I had rolled straight into a heap of stones and knocked myself cold. But luckily I had not been found, so I quickly ripped off my parachute and harness and the flying suit, rolled them up and hid them, cocked my ·45 and started to look for my collaborators.

Lt. JEAN HENRI COLEMAN, R.N.V.R., escaped from France in 1940 and returned in 1943 as an organizer of the Maquis, as told here.
Photo, British Official

Under Scrutiny by the Enemy

"In the next field I saw a crowd of men loading the containers (dropped from my plane) into a lorry. They were members of the French Resistance—although by no means the people who were expecting me so eagerly. I was able to organize their clumsy efforts, and later contacted my partner, and got down to the real job of organizing safe houses, contacts, etc." Thus the year's work was started, a year of constant vigilance against capture, in which it grew almost instinctive to smell out the houses and fields which were "burnt"—in other words under suspicious scrutiny by the enemy. Sabotage was their main job—in particular, the blowing of railway lines and bridges.

Daily the little band of saboteurs was in radio contact with London. Their sets, conveyed in broad daylight to five houses over a wide area, were operated by a daring young French operator (now a commissioned officer), who, according to Coleman, spent almost all his daylight hours in trains (as no one house was used twice running), and all his nights speaking to London in an intricate system of codes and wavelengths. Between their sabotage jobs, Coleman and his partner, another Frenchman, "flashed in" the supply planes in isolated fields and collected the dropped containers.

ALL the time he was living the life of a travelling Parisian engineer. One of his most anxious moments was when a bright official discovered he had not registered for the compulsory work of guarding vital points in Vichy France. But Coleman promptly registered, and his first job was that of guarding a railway bridge! "We didn't blow that actual bridge," he said, "but the Jerries would have been considerably surprised if they'd known what a grand opportunity it gave me of studying the railway system, with full authorization from them. Especially as the French linesmen were some of our grandest helpers."

He enjoyed bridge-blowing, particularly because it seldom involved French lives. For

RADIO VANS were employed by British railways (as was disclosed in December 1945) to enable rail services to be carried on during the height of the blitz. They consisted of mobile short-wave transmitters, as frequently used by the B.B.C. in short distance "links." An operator (left) sits at the transmitting desk of one of the network of 16 similar fixed or mobile vans used by the G.W.R. In this way the company was enabled to keep in touch with every part of the system when normal communications were disrupted by enemy action.
Photo, Associated Press

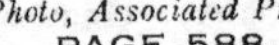

some time he spent an hour every day innocently bathing in a river—in full sight of a railway bridge, studying its construction in detail. At last he was able to operate on it almost blindfold, and he describes it as "his most satisfactory job."

Lyons, which was the headquarters of the team, was one of the "hottest" towns in France, and Coleman reckons there were 90,000 plain clothes Gestapo men after them there. Once one of their houses was burgled and, suspecting a trap, they left it, with its radio set, severely alone for months: once again they established their house, next door to the local gendarmerie; again, while two of them were loading explosive charges on to a bicycle for the night's job, a fast convoy of staff cars and dispatch riders passed by, escorting no less important a personage than Marshal Pétain.

Just before D-Day they had orders to store supplies—and so conveyed them in 12 trucks in broad daylight from their hide-out in the hills right into the heart of Lyons, a distance of 80 miles, storing them in a disused dye works next door to Gestapo headquarters.

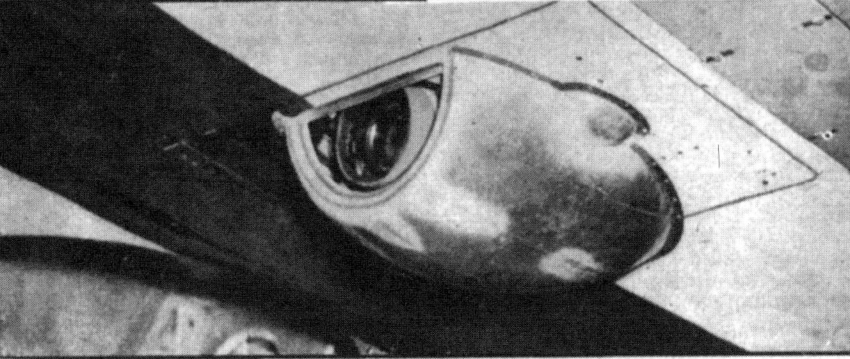

GERMAN USE OF RADAR was revealed by R.A.F. reconnaissance photographs of the Cap de la Hogue, Normandy, in November 1940. Daring low-flying tactics were called for and two attempts had to be made before identification was established. The top picture was obtained on the second attempt. A forward-facing oblique camera (above), fitted to the port wing of a Spitfire was used for low-level "shots." *Photos, British Official*

NINE MEN KEPT SIX-YEAR VIGIL

IN a feudal castle on an escarpment overlooking the Eskdale valley nine men kept one of the longest and loneliest vigils of the war. It began on August 24, 1939, when three railway coaches coupled to an ordinary passenger train left London filled with packing-cases containing famous paintings from the Tate Gallery collection. Guarded by L.M.S. police and Tate Gallery staff they were taken to Muncaster Castle, Cumberland—home of Sir John and Lady Ramsden—and with them went also the art treasures of India House.

Villagers who helped with the unloading at Muncaster had no idea that the cases contained such world-famed treasures as Constable's "Valley Farm" and Millais' "Christ in His Parents' House." They did guess that the cases held pictures, and the nine Tate Gallery men, who remained at Muncaster Castle became known as "the picture men." For more than six years "the picture men" maintained a "round-the-clock" patro of the chambers containing the famous canvases.

They cooked their own meals, washed and mended their own clothes, and even cut each other's hair. "In our spare time we did painting, toy-making, white-washing—anything to relieve boredom," Mr. W. J. Jefcut, who was in charge, told a News Chronicle reporter.

OUR MOST EFFECTIVE UNDERWATER EXPLOSIVE

FULL details of a new and powerful explosive known as Torpex, which played a large part in enabling the Allies to win the Battle of the Atlantic, have now been revealed. Officially described as "the most effective underwater explosive used during the war," the use of Torpex, in place of T.N.T., in underwater munitions resulted in an increase of the distance at which a depth-charge could kill a submarine. It also greatly enhanced the destructive effect of mines and torpedoes.

Torpex thus enabled the Allies to sink a larger number of enemy craft than would have been possible by the use of the earlier types of explosives. This new explosive was investigated and developed to the production stage in the Research Department at Woolwich Arsenal. The name Torpex denotes the explosive obtained by mixing together T.N.T., R.D.X., and aluminium powder.

R.D.X. (Research Department Formula X)—probably the only constituent unfamiliar to the public—was previously known, under the name of Cyclonite, to be a powerful high explosive, but the difficulty was to make it on anything like a useful scale, until the Research Department at Woolwich Arsenal discovered the process a few years before the war started. Safe methods of use and handling the explosive were also evolved. R.D.X. is also used in other military explosives, such as in the "Plastic Explosive" which can be moulded to fit any complex-shaped structure it is desired to destroy.

Another novel explosive which was used with outstanding success during the later stages of the war was Tritonal. This explosive consists of a mixture of T.N.T. and aluminium powder. Bombs filled with it produced much greater structural damage than similar bombs filled with T.N.T. alone, due to the resultant effects of the aluminium powder. Many of the "block-busters" dropped by the R.A.F., and other bombs dropped by the U.S.A.A.F., were filled with Tritonal, and bomb-scarred Germany shows ample evidence of its destructive power.

'LOST' JU 88 HELD VITAL RADAR SECRETS

SOME of the most vital and well-guarded secrets of German radar night fighter defences fell into British hands through a simple error of navigation. A well-disciplined and experienced young Luftwaffe pilot handed them to our scientists undamaged when he landed on a British emergency landing field at Woodbridge on the East Coast under the mistaken impression that he had touched down at Venlo in Holland. He was met by an N.C.O. of the R.A.F.

He was the pilot of a JU 88 equipped with the very types of radar that the Germans had been at such pains to keep secret. This meeting between an astonished R.A.F. Flight Sergeant and the startled German crew, which took place on a July morning five weeks after D-Day, was to save the lives of hundreds of Allied bomber crews engaged in smashing German communications and industrial installations.

The German night fighter, one of eight that had been ordered to patrol between the Dutch Coast and East Anglia to keep an eye on Bomber Command's activities, was at first mistaken for a Mosquito at Woodbridge, when at 4.30 the aircraft, having circled, was given a "green" from the watch office and made a normal landing. It taxied to the end of the runway, the engines were switched off, and the pilot had jumped out just as a tender drew up alongside.

IN a matter of minutes an armed guard stood sentry before the Junkers, which still had 40 engine hours in hand since its last major inspection, and which held the key to troublesome German radar equipment like "Naxos" and "Flensburg," known to be connected with night fighting, but whose purpose could only be conjectured. In fact, the aircraft was equipped with SN2 and "Flensburg," a homing device, and the crew revealed that "Naxos" was also used in connexion with homing.

Day and night research to produce counter-measures was conducted with such speed that 10 days later when, on the night of July 23-24, 1944, Kiel was raided by a force of 578 aircraft of Bomber Command, only four were lost. On the two following nights Stuttgart was attacked, and there is no doubt that the enemy would have scored much more heavily had he had unrestricted use of his aircraft interception equipment. The British counter-measure was a modified form of Window which remained a potent factor in neutralizing SN2 till the end.

There is No Peace for Britain's Lifeboats

In the six months following the end of the war with Germany (June-November 1945) our lifeboats responded to 232 calls and saved 295 lives, 100 of these during the week of October gales: 87 more than in the same period in 1944. Typical incidents in the noble wartime story of the Royal National Lifeboat Institution are recorded here by Capt. FRANK H. SHAW.

BETWEEN September 3, 1939, and May 8, 1945, the big red, white and blue boats of the Royal National Lifeboat Institution went out 3,760 times to the assistance of ships and aircraft in distress. This averages about two missions per day throughout the war. A good sound record for a Service that really knows no peace; for when human enemies are conquered, the chief enemy—the sea—remains defiant and aggressive. Lives to the total of 6,376 were saved in this period, averaging 21 per week.

Nineteen of the boats took part in the Dunkirk evacuation in May 1940. Thousands of our hard-beset Expeditionary Force were saved from death or captivity, and in performing this outstanding service eighteen boats were more or less seriously damaged; one was lost completely. The coxswains of the Ramsgate and Margate boats did such signal service that they were awarded the Distinguished Service Medal—immediate awards. Daring enemy bombs, they took their craft inshore and snatched men from destruction. Then the lifeboats resumed their normal task.

The East and South coasts naturally were the stage for their greatest activities, because the enemy determined to starve us into surrender by sinking the merchant ships on which our subsistence depended to so great an extent. The development of the magnetic mine provided abundant work for the R.N.L.I. They were ready for it—hard-bitten men trained to duty in the face of almost insurmountable odds. Their motor-boats were powerful, and roomy—very different from the old-fashioned "pulling-and-sailing" craft in which the reputation of the Institution had been built-up. They were capable of going almost anywhere and doing almost anything. Though the boats had altered, the spirit of the crews remained unchanged.

AN instance occurred in December 1944, when a Canadian frigate was torpedoed in mid-Atlantic, over a thousand miles from land. With her pumps going hard, and collision mats over the side, she was valiantly towed to the Bristol Channel, where she anchored off Swansea, and appeared to be a successful item of salvage. But a furious gale brewed up with the suddenness characteristic of those waters. In a few minutes the frigate was helpless in a boiling surf.

Seeing her distress signals, The Mumbles Head lifeboat was immediately launched—the people of that neighbourhood have an outstanding record of courage—and roared off at full speed through the darkness and the smother of the storm. Forty-two officers and men comprised the frigate's crew; forty-two officers and men were rescued. An officer who fell when jumping from the frigate to the lifeboat—which was swung hither and thither like a frenzied chip—was miraculously saved, thanks to the conspicuous gallantry and skill of Coxswain Gammon, in charge of the boat. (In places where the R.N.L.I. have established their invaluable stations, the Boat is always spoken of as if spelt with a capital B.)

Heroic Deeds in Dover Straits

The lifeboat was out for ten hours on that frigid December night, with the gale attaining hurricane force. The average age of its crew was 55—two men were over 70, two were in their 60's. The Senior Naval Officer at Swansea said the service was magnificent—and the Navy is not too swift to praise!

That was about the last rescue so far as the Royal Navy was concerned. One of the earliest happened off Dover on the morning of November 26, 1939, when H.M. Trawler Blackburn Rovers was on anti-submarine patrol in Dover Straits, guarding the many anchored ships in the Downs. A gale was snarling from the south-west and the Straits were ravaged by mountainous seas. A mile south of the South Sands beacon a wire fouled the trawler's propeller. Turns of the screw jammed the hawser so fast that it was impossible to free it; the little ship became immediately helpless. Anchors were dropped—but they failed to hold; and the furious wind was fast driving the hapless craft on to our own protective minefields.

It took an hour and a quarter's hard going on the part of the Dover boat, the Sir William Hillary, to reach the Blackburn Rovers, and the Sir William was like a half-tide rock all that time swept clean fore and aft. The trawler was in a precarious plight. She was actually on the edge of a deep minefield; the evil things hemmed her in. It wasn't so much that the ship couldn't negotiate the field with a prospect of safety; the trouble was that her dragging cables were likely to foul and explode one or more of the mines.

Having sensed the peril, the Dover boat had enlisted the help of Dover's Assistant King's Harbourmaster, who had brought a chart of the minefield aboard and accompanied the craft on her risky trip.

Ranging alongside the trawler the King's Harbourmaster instructed her skipper to pass over all secret papers and gear, and then, having salved his crew, to scuttle his command so that the remaining secret gear might not fall into enemy hands. Notwithstanding the fact that huge waves constantly broke over her, the lifeboat ranged close alongside, with live mines everywhere in the vicinity, and was held there in position, though she rolled so savagely that her mechanics could not stay at the engine controls.

The trawler rolled over on the lifeboat and damaged her. Any moment might bring the crash of an exploding mine, which would destroy both vessels. The work went on. All secret gear that was movable was transshipped. The crew of the trawler were hauled to safety. Although having a speed of 17 knots, the lifeboat could make only six on her homeward way. Constantly awash, rolling her rails under, the boat fought for three hours to reach Dover. The coxswain, newly recovered from a grave illness, felt the strain, surrendered the wheel to his assistant; the boat went on. No wonder Coxswain Bryant was awarded the Institution's Silver Medal!

THE Southend boat was associated with a different kind of work a year later. On December 6, 1940, she was launched at 9.45 a.m. to help a distressed barge in the estuary. The usual sou'west gale blew hard, the sea was vicious. The crew did not realize it, but they were booked for 36 hours' continuous service. During this spell of work, the crews of six other barges and the crew of a steamer were salved or aided; 12 men were rescued, two barges were towed into port. The day prior to this had been spent in a six-hour job in saving the barge Nelson and her crew.

Over a thousand of the R.N.L.I.'s launches in the war went to the succour of airmen, shot down or crashed, in the open sea or among thick minefields. The U.S.A.A.F. considers its debt to the lifeboats almost irredeemable, so often did they pull spent American aviators from the "ditch."

For some time before D-Day 1944, the Institution's boats were actively engaged in aiding the landing-craft specially built for the landings, and which were constantly in difficulties. Inclement was the June of 1944. Over 80 men were saved during these launchings. After D-Day the lifeboats went out to the assistance of those giant sections of the Mulberry Harbours which encountered difficulties on their way across to Normandy. As an example, the Appledore boat chased a caisson that had got adrift for fully 30 miles, in hard weather, and rescued its crew.

The fact that our merchant craft were established in convoys did not ease the lifeboat's work, and not once during the whole bleak six years of war did a distress call go unanswered. When young men of the crews were called up for combatant service, old men promptly took their places.

HEROES OF OUR LIFEBOAT SERVICE were honoured on Oct. 25, 1945, when H.R.H. the Duchess of Kent, President of the R.N.L.I., presented them with the Institution's gold medals for outstanding gallantry during the war. They are, left to right, Robert Cross, G.M., The Humber; H. G. Bloggs, G.C., B.E.M., Cromer; Lt. W. H. Dennison, C.G.M., R.N.V.R., Hartlepool; J. B. McLean, Peterhead, Aberdeenshire; W. J. Gammon, The Mumbles; P. Murphy, Newcastle, Co. Down; J. Boyle, Arranmore, Co. Donegal. *Photo, Fox*

The Ships and the Men Come Home

Greatest Adventure of All?

From battle in the Pacific to the peace of Home: the return of our seafarers bridges the tremendous gap and constitutes for them perhaps the greatest adventure of all. Among arrivals in late 1945 was the cruiser H.M.S. Devonshire (above) which docked—to the accompaniment of much excitement aboard and ashore—at Plymouth on November 30. On the quarter-deck (right) was Vice-Admiral Sir H. Bernard Rawlings, K.C.B., O.B.E., until late October second-in-command of the Pacific Fleet; he led the task force which bombarded the Japanese mainland in the spring and summer of 1945. On his left is his Chief-of-Staff, Acting Commodore J. P. L. Reid. Maybe their expressions relaxed as they watched the men stream ashore with turkeys and bananas and other good things from the East—for Christmas celebrations in their own homes.

Photos, P.A., Reuter

Nelson, Maidstone, Indomitable: Honoured Names—

On the long run from Singapore H.M.S. Nelson ploughs majestically through the Suez Canal (1), to enter Portsmouth Harbour (2) in November 1945 with close on 2,000 souls aboard (see also illus. in page 543). Formal surrender of the Italian Navy was signed in the Nelson, at Malta, on Sept. 29, 1943; at Penang, Jap envoys boarded her to negotiate the surrender of Singapore on Sept. 1, 1945. After five years' absence H.M.S. Maidstone (3) docked at Portsmouth on Dec. 11, 1945.

3

5

—Share the Joys of Homecoming Long Deferred

Many of the released P.O.W. whom the Maidstone carried were survivors of H.M.S. Exeter, of Battle of the Plate fame, which was sunk off Java on March 1, 1942. Enthusiastic receptions awaited all. Stoker P.O. Mulgrave (4) received his from Michael, who was only eight days old when father last saw him. Music by the Royal Marines Band in the after lift well of H.M.S. Indomitable (5) as she left Australia for the U.K. regaled the ship's company and passengers.

Brother Submariners Return With Their Commands

Photos, G.P.U.

The fortunes of war smiled on the commanders of H.M. Submarines Sleuth (above, right) and Solent seen together at Portsmouth in November 1945. Lieut.-Cmdr. K. H. Martin, of the Sleuth, boarded the Solent to greet his brother, Lieut.-Cmdr. J. D. Martin—home again after a year together in the Pacific. Ashore (bottom), welcomed by their wives, who are sisters: left to right, Mrs. K. H. Martin, Mrs. J. D. Martin with baby Richard, Lieut.-Cmdr. J. D., and his brother with baby Ben.

The Greatness of Dunkirk Revealed

A Review by HAMILTON FYFE

On May 24, 1940, London and the other big cities of Britain went about their business and their pleasure much as usual. The crowds in the streets did not look depressed or apprehensive. No one could possibly have guessed that their country was on the verge of a disaster unexampled in its history. They did not know of it themselves.

But if you had been allowed to listen to what was being said in the War Office and at the Admiralty, if you could have seen Prime Minister Winston Churchill's gloomy face when the latest news from France wa taken to him, you would have realized that the tidings must have been very bad indeed. And Mr. Churchill would have told you, had he discussed the situation of the British forces on the Continent, that still worse must be expected during the next few days. All he could hope for was that twenty or thirty thousand men might be brought back to England out of the 400,000 sent across the Channel to support the French. That was the view most of the naval and military authorities took on May 24, 1940.

Defeat Into Glorious Episode

Yet within a week more than three-quarters of the B.E.F. had been landed on English soil; only a rearguard remained on the other side of the Channel and there was every likelihood that this would be saved too (as it was). The miracle of Dunkirk had happened. Defeat had been turned, not into victory but into a glorious episode that will shine for ever in the history of war operations.

"Operation Dynamo" it was called, and the power which was generated by that tremendous effort of the human spirit not only rescued those hundreds of thousands of men who had retreated fighting to the Dunkirk beaches; it also put a new soul into the British nation. There was a "resurgence"—as A. D. Divine puts it in his stirring account of the whole affair, entitled Dunkirk (Faber, 15s.)—of national pride and national determination, a stiffening of will, a refusal to believe that we could possibly be beaten in the end. Mr. Divine seems to think that the miserable collapse of the French contributed to this result. We saw "the great and warlike tradition of that people buried in a deep and bitter dust." We knew that "the French High Command had demonstrated an inelasticity of mind that in itself was the death-warrant of France." We had heard the "fine phrases" in which French soldiers and statesmen proclaimed their unalterable resolve to stand firm, while many of them were actually preparing to scuttle the ship of State, making the best getaway for themselves that was possible and leaving us in the lurch.

All through the book Mr. Divine speaks severely, bitterly, of our former Allies. He records many incidents to show how at Dunkirk they made things more difficult. Their High Command persisted in its "strange refusal to consider realities" and could come to no decision about evacuating what remained of their northern armies. At the most critical moments Marshal Weygand sent messages to the British commander which were "empty and meaningless," with nothing in them but the love of a wordy flourish. French ships were not sent in any number to assist in clearing those beaches, almost ten miles of them "black from sand dunes to waterline with tens of thousands of men, standing in places up to their knees and waists in water, waiting for their turn to get into the pitiably few boats."

Even in those grim queues trouble was caused by French soldiers failing, in panic, to realize that boats overloaded capsize. One such crazy lot rushed an open motor-boat filled with British soldiers and then, instead of keeping very still and trimming the boat, moved about and sank it; all but the one man who told the story were drowned.

How patient and self-controlled men on the beaches were as a whole this book testifies on almost every page. It is a detailed description of what went on, day by day, from the time when the call went out for "anything that can float and propel itself" until the task for which they were summoned had been carried out. Nothing could be more convincing than the method Mr. Divine has adopted. He had the great advantage of being placed in possession by Mr. J. D. Casswell, K.C., of a large quantity of reports made by small-boat owners which at first it was intended to publish by themselves. Now we have something much more valuable, a comprehensive account of the rescue told as far as possible in their own words (taken from logs and official statements) by naval officers and skippers of all kinds of ships.

Mr. Divine says modestly that "the full story will never be told." Some of the records were lost when ships went down—the losses were heavy. Many records were never begun, since "men worked in the small ships in those days under the spur of a most desperate disaster. They worked, some of them, until they fell exhausted. They brought their ships home and collapsed in sleep. They had not time, they had not opportunity, they had not place in which to write."

The outstanding feature of the reports which are printed is their unimpassioned, purely matter-of-fact character. There is no suggestion that the writers were doing anything out of the common. Here is an example:

> I joined the Mona's Queen (as master) on May 28. I received orders to carry fresh water to Dunkirk and return with troops. Everything was uneventful until we reached to within about half a mile of Dunkirk, when the ship was mined and sank within two minutes, the survivors being rescued by the destroyer Vanquisher.

That vessel was a passenger steamer, like St. Seiriol, which carried peacetime trippers and holiday-makers to Llandudno, Colwyn Bay and Bangor. She went to Dunkirk with many of her regular crew. She worked under heavy bombing and in darkness on a strange and dangerous coast. She did boat work for which her men had not been specially trained on difficult and tricky beaches. From the captain's report you might think she was still plying from Liverpool down the Welsh coast.

> I got alongside the Mole in a very short time and embarked 600 soldiers and left the Mole about midnight. I went back to look for my lifeboats, but as they were being used to convey troops from the beach to other craft, I proceeded to Dover via the Calais route, as ordered by a destroyer. During the voyage I was again attacked by aircraft but got away without being hit.

The mention of water being taken to Dunkirk, in the former of these logs, shows how pitiful the plight of the men on the beaches had become. The waterworks of the town had been bombed. The troops had nothing to drink. They had been on half rations for many days, but thirst was worse than hunger. As for the Mole, to which the St. Seiriol had been moored, this was the only part of the fine harbour of Dunkirk which had been left usable by the Luftwaffe. The docks were "a mass of battered metal and broken walls; the basins were open to the tide; the gates wrecked and jammed; the cranes stood weakly on three legs or lay like stricken birds along the quays." With these intact, we could have embarked the B.E.F. without delay or difficulty. With only the Mole in service, "a narrow pile plankway barely wide enough for three men to walk abreast, which had not been designed for ships to berth against," the perils and postponements were hard indeed to overcome.

To Carry On Freedom's Fight

They would have been worse if the weather had been against us. It did not exactly favour us, but it might have been less favourable. "One great gale at the height of the beach work would have cost us 30,000 men." But even a little wind, which would not have bothered a swimmer, was "little short of disaster to men handling water-logged craft over-weighted with exhausted soldiers, and to men rowing heavy ships' boats for the first time or handling long sweeps without previous experience."

As the days passed, signs of unbearable strain began to appear in a good many ships. Yet the great mass of the rescuers stood up to their job magnificently. Especially grim was the ordeal of the engine-room men.

> They worked deep in the ships, at the bottom of long, frail ladders that had a tendency to jar off or smash when bombs hit. They worked in absolute blindness, for all the brilliance of their electric light, feeling only the shaking of the ship, the concussion of the bombs outside, the thud and clang of the splinters against the plating . . . Throughout the operation the self-sacrifice and devotion of engineers and stokers is beyond praise, as it is beyond description.

An equal tribute must be paid to all who took part in saving the 337,000 men who were taken off the beaches and brought back "to carry on the fight for freedom." It was a combined effort, a pull-hard-all-together struggle, in which large numbers of the civil population joined with the Navy, the Army and Air Force to cheat a very clever and energetic enemy of the decisive result he expected from his swift over-running of France, Belgium and Holland.

Not only expected, but was foolish enough to announce. "The B.E.F. is trapped, annihilated," boasted the German radio. Mr. Divine's book shows how that fate was averted and the B.E.F. saved.

Mr. ARTHUR DURHAM DIVINE, author of the book reviewed here. At Dunkirk he won the D.S.M. for his part in assisting the evacuation of the B.E.F.

Nuremberg Where Nazi War Lords are Arraigned

SCENE OF HITLER'S PARTY RALLIES, and once the loveliest of Bavaria's medieval cities. Nuremberg now stands a desolate memorial to shattered German aspirations of world domination. On January 2, 1945, it was heavily pounded in a 20-minute "cascade raid" by the R.A.F. Ruins at "Hangman's Bridge" (1, left), spanning the Pegnitz. On the moated outskirts of the old city is this tower and half-ruined gate (2). St. Lorenz Church (3), begun in 1274. A homeless Nuremberger (4) salvages scrap with which to rebuild his house. See also pages 512, 559-562.

Photos, Planet News

Hermann-Goering Salvage for the Melting Pot

AT THE EXTENSIVE HERMANN-GOERING WORKS near Brunswick operations by No. 34 Field Salvage Unit are in full swing. Here a German 12-ton gun is about to be hoisted by overhead crane for breaking up. In the British zone material already salved ranges from bullets to 20-ton tanks, from old clothes to aero-engines. The main problem is to reduce the metal to sizes suitable for transport abroad, thousands of tons of steel being shipped to Britain each week. *Photo, British Official*

Teapot Revolution Maintained the Troops' Morale

"Half the Army lives on tea" was an opinion expressed by Field-Marshal Sir Henry Maitland Wilson when G.O.C.-in-C. in Egypt. In recognition of which—and of many complaints—experts were called in during the war to raise the standard of its making. This sidelight on one factor which helped to achieve victory is by FRANK HUNTLY.

WHEN the Tipperary Club in Cairo closed its doors for the last time in the autumn of 1945, it had served nearly 8,000,000 cups of tea to the troops in five-and-a-half years. Its fame had spread throughout the Middle East and to England, where returning troops advised newcomers to the Middle East to call at "The Tip" for a good cup of tea.

This, be it noted, was *tea*—not the brew that for years had masqueraded under the name, the butt of music-hall comedians, the soldier's favourite grouse, a joke and a bad one at that. Tea-making for the Army had, indeed, come to such a pass that something really had to be done about it. It was not fitting that the national beverage should be inferior for the troops. The Empire Tea Bureau thought along these lines and placed some constructive proposals before the Y.M.C.A. at the beginning of the war.

Soon several mobile canteens, with expert staffs and up-to-date equipment, were functioning so effectively under the wing of the Y.M.C.A. that within months 1,700 "mobiles" were making regular calls on isolated gun posts and barrage balloon sites. A fine little concentration of these superbly fitted shops on wheels followed the B.E.F. into France in 1939, carrying cakes, chocolate, cigarettes, boot polish, free notepaper. On each canteen was a posting-box; there was a clothes repair service and unlimited cups of the best tea the Army had ever tasted.

When evacuation became inevitable, the staffs of these mobiles, with their ingenious insulated urns ("Multipots"), fed and tea-ed the troops all the way to Dunkirk, tea-ed them on the beaches; then burned their canteens, crossed to Dover and served tea to the soldiers as they disembarked on this side. They expected to cater for a few thousand men; on the first day they serviced 2,000; on the second 62,000. Within a few days they had cared for over 330,000 British, French and Belgian troops. It meant requisitioning the town hall, the services of all the bakers on the Kent coast and every woman in Dover.

Hitherto, mobiles had been the more urgent need; now Empire Tea Bureau-trained tea-makers were asked to apply their art to the static Y.M.C.A. canteens. Soon the difference between the Y.M.C.A. brews and those in the canteens of N.A.A.F.I. (largest tea dispensers in the world) became the subject of fresh complaint from soldiers who sampled both. The War Office, appreciating the situation, were willing that the experiment which had succeeded with the one should be tried in the other. Representatives were appointed to every Command; they inspected the canteens, gave advice, lectures and demonstrations. Within three years they had visited over 3,000 N.A.A.F.I. establishments and instructed nearly 40,000 manageresses and charge hands.

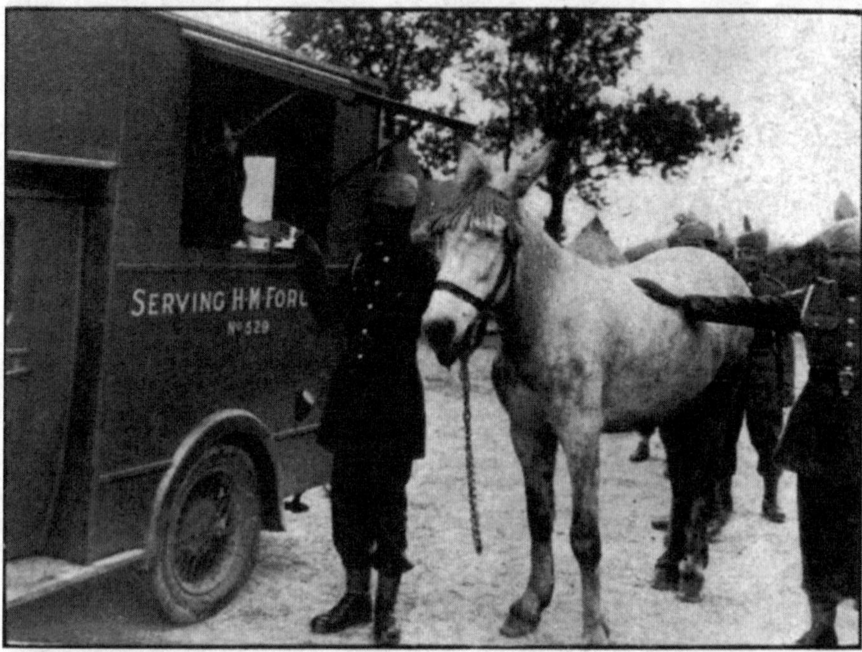

EVERYTHING STOPS FOR TEA—*even the mule—as shown by this photograph of an Indian soldier serving with a mule company of the Royal Indian Army Service Corps, at a Y.M.C.A. tea-car. How the Empire Tea Bureau and the War Office contrived an astonishing transformation in the beverage is told here. See also facing page.* *Photo, Current Affairs*

Complaints of N.A.A.F.I. tea dwindled to nil, for district meetings and constant inspection by N.A.A.F.I.'s official tea advisers insured that training in tea consciousness, once given, remained. What, in brief, did this training amount to?

AS in most matters, its basis was pains and common sense, yet these needed the organizing hand of the expert before they were adequately mobilized. Good tea may depend mainly on the tea-maker, but it needs also the right equipment, scrupulous cleanliness and correct storage. The Chinese, first tea-drinkers in the world, discovered that freshly drawn, fiercely boiling water was the first fundamental of good tea—a simple but golden rule, seldom by us obeyed to the letter. Half the justifiable complaints of N.A.A.F.I. tea were traced to under-boiled water. Maintenance is equally important—furring-up retards boiling, and urns have a habit of imparting a distasteful metallic tang to the brew if they are not drained thoroughly dry when not in use.

"One day the tea is good, another awful." This was a common complaint. One tea-maker would do the job conscientiously, another would pile tea, sugar and milk into the urn, repeatedly adding more water till the stewed liquor was no longer bearable—if it ever had been! Adding new tea to old was another habit, with horrid effects on flavour. The rule "warm the pot" applies to urns as much as to teapots; boiling water striking a cold lining loses heat and will not produce proper infusion. Milk must be added at the last possible moment before service. If it has to be tinned milk, then it should be remembered that its flavour is unduly accentuated by under-infusion; an extra fifteen minutes makes all the difference. Tea is a sensitive plant. Susceptible to damp, the leaf quickly absorbs moisture and, with it, any odours from strong-smelling commodities stored near by. Thus storage needs careful planning.

N.A.A.F.I.'s 14,000,000 Cups a Day

From Iceland to Australia these and a few more precious precepts in good tea-making were painstakingly planted in Services canteens, bringing a new-born significance to "a good old English cup of tea." The same axioms are behind the augmented and strengthened buffet service which supplies the brews in every B.A.O.R. leave train, behind the pints poured into every P.O.W. as he steps ashore from the repatriation ship. The repatriated soldier who used to curse the browned-off brew that the Institutes of old palmed off on him, now blesses the generous "Naffy" which hands out free cake, sandwiches, chocolate, cigarettes, newspaper, and piping hot mugs of A1 tea.

It has been no path of roses, this joint enterprise to insure that N.A.A.F.I. tea shall be good and recognized as such by the fighting forces. Bureau representatives have made thousands of visits of inspection to Institutes throughout Britain. Action following the issue of detailed questionnaires to Naffy's six or seven thousand canteens has entailed also thousands of lectures, demonstrations, personal and individual instructions; an immense amount of travel and office administration.

THE chief concern has been quality, but it is not hard to imagine what a problem is the consistent quality-inoculation of N.A.A.F.I.'s 14,000,000 cups of tea a day. There is a wealth of delicacy involved in such oft-occurring duties as telling some Dowager Duchess, voluntary helper at So-and-So Y.M.C.A. canteen, that she is making the tea the wrong—the old—way. Disappointments crop up, too, as when G.I.s, given their favourite coffee, thanked the canteen manageress for a nice cup of tea!

Eisenhower Pulled the Strings

Britons normally put away well over half of India and Ceylon's total annual production of more than 300,000 tons of tea. Thus, to the average Englishman, tea is of greater importance than it might have seemed to General Eisenhower when he was told of some little discontent at his advance command post: the British boys who maintained the signals communications at the camp were not getting their tea. The American Army rations, excellent as they were, provided only coffee. General Eisenhower, with characteristic attention to detail, promptly pressed a few buttons, pulled a few strings, and soon the British troops were dipping their noses into steaming beakers of good tea with their meals. And now, lifted from its old-time low to the high plane which helped to keep the Forces' morale at victory level, the better brew should find its way to civvy street—to railways, factories, offices, homes.

They Also Served Who Brewed the Perfect 'Cup'

THROUGHOUT THE WORLD the British fighting men's cup of tea stimulated them to final victory. As told in the facing page, never before had the distribution (and brew) of our national beverage been so well organized. Urns on their heads, native "boys" (1) set off to deliver it piping hot to forces stationed in jungle clearings in West Africa. At home, mobile canteens were ready to serve naval ratings (2) just ashore from patrol, as well as bombing crews about to take off (3).

Photos, Current Affairs, Associated Press

Foreign Ministers in Agreement at Moscow

MR. JAMES F. BYRNES, U.S. SECRETARY OF STATE, TOASTED MR. ERNEST BEVIN, Britain's Foreign Minister (left), while Mr. V. M. Molotov, Soviet Commissar for Foreign Affairs, looked on, as the Moscow Conference, from December 16-26, 1945, drew to its satisfactory close. The Foreign Ministers of the Three Great Powers had met in accordance with the decision of the Crimea Conference (see pages 682-683, Vol. 8), confirmed at Potsdam, that there should be periodic consultation between them. Their far-reaching decisions are outlined below. *Photo, L.N.A.*

OUTSTANDING among the agreements reached by the Foreign Ministers in Moscow—announced on December 28, 1945—was that relating to the future use of atomic energy. This vital subject had produced strong reactions in the Soviet Press and threatened to become a cause of misunderstanding between Russia and her western Allies. As a result of the discussions, Russia accepted the Washington proposals to set up under the United Nations Organization a Commission to control atomic energy.

The General Assembly of the United Nations, meeting in London in January 1946, was invited to establish this Commission which would have as its main tasks (1) To make proposals for eliminating from national armaments all atomic weapons and all other major weapons adaptable to mass destruction; (2) to make recommendations, "with the utmost dispatch," for the exchange for peaceful ends of basic scientific information between the United Nations; (3) to make proposals for effective safeguards, by way of inspection and other means, to protect complying States against the hazards of violations and evasions; and (4) to make proposals for controlling atomic energy to the extent necessary to ensure its use only for peaceful purposes.

The Commission is to be composed of one representative from each of those States represented on the Security Council and Canada when that State is not a member of the Security Council.

Far Eastern Commission

WITH the full agreement of China a Far Eastern Commission is to be set up, replacing the Far Eastern Advisory Commission. The new body will have its headquarters in Washington and will be composed of representatives of Britain, the United States, Russia, China, France, the Netherlands, Canada, Australia, New Zealand, India, and the Philippines Commonwealth. The Commission will not make recommendations with regard to the conduct of military operations nor with regard to territorial adjustments. It will respect existing control machinery in Japan, including the chain of command from the United States Government to the Supreme Commander (General MacArthur) and the Supreme Commander's command of occupation forces. Its main task will be to formulate the policies, principles and standards by which the fulfilment by Japan of its obligations under the terms of surrender may be accomplished.

Allied Council For Japan

WITH the Supreme Commander as chairman and U.S. representative, an Allied Council for Japan is to be established. It will be composed, in addition, of one representative of Russia, one of China, and a member representing jointly the United Kingdom, Australia, New Zealand and India. The Council will consult with and advise the Supreme Commander in the carrying out of the terms of surrender and the occupation and control of Japanese territory.

The Council, with headquarters at Tokyo, will meet "not less often than once every two weeks." The Supreme Commander shall issue all orders for the implementation of the terms of surrender, the occupation and control of Japan, and directives supplementary thereto, and will be the sole executive authority for the Allied Powers in Japan.

Korea as an Independent State

WITH a view to the re-establishment of Korea as an independent State, and creation of conditions for developing the country on democratic principles, there shall be set up a provisional Korean Democratic Government "which shall take all the necessary steps for developing the industry, transport and agriculture of Korea and the national culture of the Korean people." To assist in this task there shall be established a joint commission consisting of representatives of the United States Command in Southern Korea and the Soviet Command in Northern Korea.

The Future of China

THE Foreign Ministers agreed on the need for a united and democratic China under the National Government. At the request of the Chinese Government, withdrawal of Soviet forces has been postponed until February 1946. American forces are to be withdrawn "as soon as the terms of the Japanese surrender have been carried out." The Foreign Ministers reaffirmed their adherence to the policy of non-interference in the internal affairs of China.

Rumania and Bulgaria

IN south-eastern Europe important agreements were also reached. With regard to Rumania, the three Allied Governments are to advise King Michael on the "broadening" of the Rumanian Government, and when it has been "satisfactorily broadened" it will be recognized by Britain and the United States. The King has been advised that one member of the National Peasant Party and one member of the Liberal party should be included in the Government. Thus reconstituted, the Government is to declare that free and unfettered elections will be held as soon as possible on the basis of universal and secret ballot, and proclaim freedom of the Press, speech, religion and association. As regards Bulgaria, the Soviet is to give "friendly advice" to the Government for broadening the "Government of the Fatherland" now being formed. As soon as Britain and the United States are convinced that this advice has been accepted they will recognize the Bulgarian Government.

Treaties with Axis and Satellite Powers

IT was agreed that the treaty with Italy should be drawn up by the British, U.S., Soviet and French deputies; the treaties with Rumania, Bulgaria and Hungary by the American, British and Soviet deputies; and the treaty with Finland by the British and Soviet deputies. These draft treaties are to be submitted to a "peace conference" consisting of the Big Five and other United Nations "which actively waged war with substantial forces" against the European ex-enemy States. This conference will be called not later than May 1, 1946.

I Was There! Eye Witness Stories of the War and After

How Two V.C.s Were Won Under a Jap Cruiser

Lieut. Ian E. Fraser, R.N.R., of Farnham Common, Bucks., and Leading Seaman James J. Magennis, of Belfast, were each awarded the V.C. for the parts they played in a midget submarine attack on the Japanese cruiser Takao in the Johore Strait, Singapore, in July 1944. They returned to England in December 1945, and this is Lieut. Fraser's story.

We started out to attack the cruiser off Borneo, 450 miles from Singapore. Our midget submarine was towed by another submarine, and what is known as a "passage crew" manned the craft until we were getting close to the area. When we changed crews, the operational crew was passed across in a rubber dinghy and the passage crew went back to the escorting submarine. The tow was slipped and we set off on a 35-mile trip before going up the Johore Strait. We knew there were mines and a listening post—and we went into the minefields rather than chance coming within range of the listening post.

We were approaching the boom on the surface in the darkness when we came on a Japanese ship escorted by a small vessel that passed so close to us that we were forced to dive. Continuing under water we found, when daylight came, that we had been sitting on a Japanese controlled minefield for more than an hour!

At 10.30 a.m. we passed the "gate"—an old vessel on which I could see Japs running about, although they did not suspect our presence. Ten miles above the boom vessel we sighted the Takao. She was very well camouflaged if one looked at her against the background of the land, and she was very close inshore.

We started our first attack, but it was a failure as the cruiser was in such shallow water that we ran bang up against her side and could not get under her hull. Amidships, there was a hole that registered 24 ft., and out of which it was very difficult to get.

A boat full of Jap sailors going ashore passed within 25 yards of us, but we were not detected. Our craft scraped along the bottom, and Leading Seaman Magennis went out and placed in position six limpets (small mines carrying a hundred pounds of explosives) in half an hour. All the time he was at work his oxygen bag was leaking and sending up a stream of bubbles, which was very disturbing. The water was so clear that I am sure we could have been seen if any Jap sailor had looked over the side. Leading Seaman Magennis returned to the craft, having had to scrape away a lot of seaweed in order to fix his limpets. He was fairly exhausted, but when we had trouble with our mine carrier he went out again to free it in 14 ft. of water.

When we were clear, we broke surface about a mile from the cruiser. Later, submerged, we successfully passed the "gate" again. We found our towing submarine without any trouble. There were two other members of the crew, Sub.-Lieut. J. L. Smith, R.N.Z.N.V.R., who sat on the hydroplanes for 17½ hours, and Engine-room Artificer Reid, of Portsmouth, who was steering the boat for 30 hours. Smith received the D.S.O. and Reid the C.G.M.

The charges went up when we were about fifteen miles from the cruiser. We know that a hole sixty ft. long was torn in the bottom of the Takao. After Singapore was retaken I went on board the cruiser and met some of the Japs who were in her when the explosion took place. They would not tell us how many casualties there were.

To his Commanding Officer's story Magennis, who was one of the crews in the midget submarine attack on the Tirpitz, added:

"What was in my mind all the time I was doing the job was. 'At last, after all the preparation, I have my hands on an enemy hull!'"

AMONG WARSAW'S RUINS a flower-seller manages to erect a booth for her wares and give colour to the drab wreckage. **See story, below, of Poland in 1945.**

CONGRATULATIONS FOR TWO NAVAL V.C.s on their arrival from Australia in December 1945 included a handshake from Lieut. the Hon. Frederick Shore, D.S.C., R.N.R., leader of a division of M.T.B.s. The V.C.s, whose story is told above, are Lt. Ian E. Fraser, R.N.R. (left), and Leading Seaman James J. Magennis. *Photo, Central Press*

In Poland I Saw a Grim Battle for Life

Returned from Warsaw, and other towns and villages of Poland, in December 1945, where he investigated the prevailing conditions on behalf of the Friends' Service Council—who plan to send out a Relief Unit—Frederick Tritton gives below the thought-provoking impressions of his visit.

Trays of boiled potatoes to be eaten on the spot, offered by street vendors shivering in cold drizzle, is the first thing we notice as we drive in a shaky lorry into Warsaw. There is little buying and selling in the orthodox meaning of the word. Much of the daily business is done by barter.

The cost of the meal we were given at the Hotel Polonia, which is the centre for most foreign visitors in Warsaw, was not less than 300 zloty—"the equivalent of my salary for three days!" explained the woman doctor who accompanied us.

As we were passing through street after street of ruins I asked our doctor-companion, "How far is it to the inhabited part of Warsaw?" She replied, "We are in the inhabited part! In fact, this is its main street, Marszalkowska. And below these ruins, in the damp cellars and dark basements, are living the people of Warsaw!"

I discovered that many people were, quite literally, living in caves, without bed-linen or proper clothing. The doctor herself had no change of underwear. In such conditions T.B., typhus, V.D. and dysentery spread quickly. Epidemics are raging. Twenty-five per cent of the students are suffering from T.B. and many of the children are diseased. I saw youngsters, dressed in rags, scratching themselves incessantly to ease the intolerable irritation of lice. Medical supplies, of American origin, cannot be distributed because of inadequate communications. There are few ambulances, and in any case most of the roads in autumn are almost impassable by any form of traffic.

Many of the villages and small towns are replicas of Warsaw. We clambered over the ruins of what had been a pleasant country town and found that in one cellar two families of seven people had to crowd for sleeping. The cooking was done outside. A woman came out who was expecting a baby. With tears in her eyes she complained bitterly of the damp which had brought on rheumatism.

RUINS OF WARSAW'S ROYAL CASTLE stand forlornly amidst unrecognizable wreckage. Poland still suffers—as described in the accompanying story—and at the close of 1945 Warsaw was described by its Mayor as "a capital in a city which no longer exists." On the Vistula's west bank only eighteen per cent of the buildings were left undamaged.

Her family, like all the others there, lived on potatoes and water. They have no bread, because the corn was not harvested during the fighting. Her husband's hand was injured; the fingers had been torn away when he, with other peasants, had been trying to remove mines from the fields. So many of them were injured that they had to give up the attempt. No medical help of any sort was available in this locality.

Everything in Poland seems to be improvised. Goods-trains carry passengers, and owing to the lack of locomotives one sees horse-drawn single carriages along the tracks. Personal belongings are very scarce. The whole of the Lublin University has to rely on one clock; none of the students or professors has a watch. More serious is the need for bandages and medical dressings—which are made of rags. Sanitation and water supply depend upon absolutely primitive improvisation. Lorries, used instead of buses, are supplied by the Soviet Union.

So with housing. Russia is supplying prefabricated wooden houses and has offered to pay half the cost of rebuilding Warsaw. The first trolley-buses which are expected are of Russian origin. And although the Russians are giving so much material help to Poland I saw no signs of any interference in the day-to-day administration of the country. As we travelled, we dealt only with Polish authorities. If our lorry was stopped, it was always a Polish policeman (often a girl with a rifle slung over her shoulder) who examined our passes, and not a Red Army man. All public offices appear to be in Polish hands. We were left quite free to go wherever we chose, and to look at anything we wished to see.

Nightfall in Poland does not bring rest for her suffering people. To them it only means that another day of hunger and cold is approaching. And darkness brings out gangs of bandits and looters. The Red Army garrisons help in the rounding up of these gangs. It seems that all these conditions have produced two reactions among the people. Some have become apathetic and despondent and can see no farther than the terrible present. Others feel that the existing difficulties are a challenge to them to build a new Poland in which life will be better than it ever was before.

At the End of the World's Longest Ocean Hop

War correspondent Alan Moorehead "dropped in" on Sydney, in mid-December 1945, and found it to be a place which to the average Englishman might represent the ultimate bliss on earth. He found there also an echo of the universal unrest. His cable is reprinted from The Daily Express.

When you first arrive in Australia by air you come down on the north-eastern corner at a place called Learmonth, and it is exactly like the Western Desert where the Eighth Army fought. We had been flying for hours and hours—actually 15½—over the open sea from Colombo. It is the longest ocean hop in the world, and as you sit there in that awful immensity of space, you cannot stop yourself from listening desperately to the rhythm of the motors.

The sun comes up like a drunkard's bloodshot eye over Colombo, and there you will sit all day flying over the Equator with absolutely nothing but sea and sky around you for 3,000 miles. You read, you eat, and you peer out of the window at nothing. Then the tropic sunset comes down with a theatrical wallop and everything turns jet black. This one lighted tin box goes on through the night until at last, with enormous pleasure, you see the beam of a lighthouse

SIDELIGHT ON LIFE IN SYDNEY during the strike (see story) is provided by these "tellers" in the Neutral Bay by-election counting votes by the aid of hurricane lamps and candles. The New South Wales Electoral Commissioner managed to round up sixty lamps and half a hundred-weight of candles for the occasion. *Photo, Associated Press*

stabbing out from the Australian coast. Every time we tried to land on the flare path a sharp cross-wind flung us aside, and in the end we were forced to cruise round for two hours waiting for dawn. Now here we sit in the blistering desert, and it is Alamein and Tobruk all over again ; the escarpment, the rose-coloured rocky sand, the scuttling lizards, the warm listless sea, the timbered huts, the flies, and the airmen walking about in khaki shorts.

Now at first sight this does not make any sense, and it might even make you angry. Here is a place which, to the average Englishman (let alone a Frenchman or a German), might represent the ultimate bliss on earth. Steak for dinner, as much as you want. Fresh pineapples, 8d. each. Eggs, 1s.10d. a dozen. Lavish American cars all over the town—and it is a lovely town. Shoes and clothing galore in the shops, and unbelievably cheap. Sunshine and yellow sandy beaches only a quarter of an hour away from the town. A basic wage of nearly £5 a week and employment for everybody.

Civilization Nearing Standstill

Now, suddenly this week the people take hold of this delectable way of living and smash it to bits. The country goes out on strike. Result: Practically no gas to cook with so you eat cold meals. The electricity rapidly giving out so you eat by dingy candlelight, and the trams running on half schedule may stop altogether next week.

There are frantic crowds trying to get on the inter-State trains. Hundreds of thousands of men out of work. Shops and factories are shutting. All civilization is running down to a standstill, and unless something is done soon, Australians will just have to go native. Nothing as bad as this ever hit them in the war. I trudged gloomily round the city looking (a) for a drink, (b) for a packet of cigarettes, and (c) for a meal.

Failing in all three I took a ferry across the harbour to the local Blackpool or Coney Island. Had a certain amount of mordant pleasure at one of the booths hurling wooden balls at a target. Each time you hit the bullseye a show-girl, sitting on a trap door in a bathing dress, was plunged into a tank of water. Had to walk to my bed in a friend's flat—no money on earth will get you an hotel room in Sydney. Must try to find out what the strike is about tomorrow . . .

Well, here it is—and I can only ask you to believe it. A worker known as a valveman in one of the foundries was ordered by the foreman to become a lidman, which is an inferior status. The valveman refused and his union went on strike. Then the miners went on strike in sympathy. Union after union joined in, and now it is pretty well a general strike all over Australia.

That is the official story. One man started it all and nine-tenths of the Australians have not the slightest idea of what a valveman or a lidman is. Clearly this one suddenly notorious man is no more than the spark of the strike—the real tinder of the trouble lies deeper. This is not a strike for better conditions. The Australian worker enjoys conditions such as are still undreamed of in England.

Apart from his cheap butter and eggs and fixed rentals, he has a fortnight's paid holidays, high rates of pay, and a relatively short working week, which may soon be reduced to 40 hours. The real reason of the strike is this—the Communist Party, already very strong in Australia, has decided to try its power against the Government and the more conservative political groups. I lunched today with one of the Communist organizers and he saw the issue in an even stronger light. "This," he said, "is a show-down between Communism and Fascism."

FOOD FOR BRITAIN left Sydney Town Hall (above) by lorry for the docks, where it was loaded by Naval ratings (left) on board H.M.S. Nepal. This was part of the city's campaign on behalf of the Mother Country, inaugurated in November 1945. *Photos, Planet News*

I protested that there was not much outward evidence of Fascism in this workers' country, but he seemed to find dictators practically peeping out from under the plush chairs from which we were eating our oysters, roast beef and fruit salad. On one point I did agree with him. "Because conditions are so much better in Australia than in England that is no reason why we should not still go on trying to improve them here." On the following day I flew to Melbourne, which is equally gripped by the strike. The thing that maddens people most is the slightly unfair story in the papers that many of the miners and other strikers have already gone off in their cars to their Christmas camps by the sea and the lakes. These camps are alleged to be lavish affairs fitted with cinemas, ice-boxes and sports grounds, and the strikers have declared they have no intention of going back to work before the New Year, whether the strike is finished or not. The Right wing makes one other point: only a small minority of the unions turned up at the meetings which voted for the strike.

Engrossed in Its Local Problems

Further researches reveal these points—there is a thriving black market in Australia, especially in cigarettes, which are practically unobtainable. Beer is extremely hard to get, gin relatively easy. There is some wine. The pubs close by law at 6 p.m., which has the deplorable and maddening effect on the population of making them drink as much and as quickly as possible each evening before it is too late. As a promoter of drunkenness this law has no equal.

Everywhere I find sympathy and kindness towards Britain. Every State has its "Food for Britain" campaign. But this is an isolated nation, engrossed in its own local problems. I am surrounded by the most beautiful and fertile country, which is almost empty. It could support British immigrants in a life they have never dreamed of. Maybe immigration is the answer to the whole thing—strikes and all.

★=As The Years Went By—Notable Days in the War=★

1940

January 8. *Food rationing (sugar, bacon and butter only) introduced in Britain.*

January 13. *R.A.F. in longest reconnaissance raid to date dropped leaflets on Vienna and Prague.*

1941

January 5. *Bardia surrendered to Wavell's troops; 30,000 Italians taken prisoner.*

January 10. *Cruiser Southampton lost, aircraft carrier Illustrious damaged, in Axis air attacks in the Sicilian Channel.*

January 18. *Dive-bombing of Malta began.*

1942

January 10. *Japanese invaded Celebes Islands.*

1943

January 12. *Conquest of Fezzan completed by Free French from Chad under Gen. Leclerc.*

January 14. *Roosevelt and Churchill met at Casablanca, French Morocco, to plan the "unconditional surrender" of the enemy.*

1944

January 11. *Ciano and other ex-members of Fascist Grand Council who were responsible for Mussolini's fall executed at Verona.*

1945

January 9. *U.S. troops landed in Lingayen Gulf, on island of Luzon in the Philippines.*

January 17. *Russians occupied Warsaw.*

From Rotterdam to Hiroshima

The Marvellous Development of Bombing Power

By CAPTAIN
NORMAN MACMILLAN
M.C., A.F.C.

We know now from the documents captured in Germany and produced at Nuremberg that Hitler ordered merciless measures to ensure the swift conquest of Western Europe. No doubt can possibly exist that these orders were applied against Holland. And most particularly against Rotterdam. I do not forget the bombardment of Warsaw in the previous year: but, we must remember, that bombardment accompanied the forward sweep of fast-moving ground forces and was therefore a part of a military plan of action, even if we agree that that plan was pitiless, barbaric and unforgivable.

There are three outstanding air attacks upon towns which are in a category entirely unique because all bear the same stamp of savage destruction for the purpose of quenching the fighting spirit of a people, not by attacks upon their fighting forces, nor upon the bases upon which those fighting forces immediately depended, but upon open towns wherein unarmed civilians, including men, women and children, all died. The first of these attacks was made by the Condor Legion of the Luftwaffe under Sperrle—the commander of one of the Air Fleets that later bombed Britain—against the Basque town of Guernica during the Spanish "civil" war. The second was the bombardment of Rotterdam. The third was the atomic bombardment of Hiroshima. These three attacks have one common feature: that there was virtually no defence against them.

THE Use of Atomic Bombs Followed Decision at Potsdam Conference

So far as I can observe from the reports of the evidence presented at Nuremberg, the bombardment of open cities from the air is not listed as one of the major war crimes, although Goering, the titular head of the Luftwaffe at the time of Guernica and Rotterdam, is one of the defendants. I suppose it might be difficult to list such incidents in a vast war trial, when it is known that the use of atomic bombs followed a decision taken at the Potsdam Conference, and that the Japanese disasters of Hiroshima and Nagasaki followed.

There may be some who will say why pick out these three cases when the British and American air forces smashed cities all over Germany; why not list Berlin, Hamburg, Cologne and other places? The answer is that the bombing of those places was conducted in accordance with a pre-determined military plan to reduce the fighting potential of the Wehrmacht. They were not, or at least very few could be called (even by the Germans) terror attacks. These places, like Warsaw, were military targets within the new and distasteful turn that modern war has developed. Although we should never forget that the burning and sacking of cities is a belligerent act almost as old as war itself; the bomber has merely brought it up to date.

But there is a difference between air attacks on towns which constitute definite targets within a given military plan to reduce the enemy armies' ability to fight, and terror attacks against civilian populations to force a shuddering nation to accept defeat. Bearing this in mind it is wise to have some regard to the "progress" that has been made in this form of attack in recent years.

On April 26, 1937, a relative handful of German bombers attacked Guernica. First, small bombs were used to drive the Guernicians to cover. Then demolition bombs destroyed their homes within which they sheltered. Refugees were machine-gunned. Incendiary bombs completed the destruction of the little Basque town by fire. A thousand people died Here is what Baedeker, the German guide-book house, said of the place: "A small town of 3,250 inhabitants, splendidly situated on the Mundaca, was the seat of the diet of Vizcaya until the abolition of the fueros. The deputies met every two years in front of the *Casa de Juntas*, under an oak-tree. The song of the tree of Guernica (*Guernikako Arbola*), by Iparraguirri, has become the national anthem of the Basques." Later, Germany was to make other Baedeker raids—against Canterbury, Exeter, York, Norwich and Bath. Can we doubt that the Germans knew what they were doing when they attacked Guernica? Or that the Basques had no defence?

By nightfall on May 13, 1940, the last one of ten aircraft, all that remained by then of the 248 aircraft possessed by the Royal Netherlands Air Forces on the morning of May 10, 1940, was destroyed in a suicidal attack upon the German forces occupying the Waalhaven civil aerodrome on the outskirts of Rotterdam. But on the morning of May 14 the city of Rotterdam still held out. The Luftwaffe was called into action against this city, lying defenceless against aerial attack. Groups of 27 bombers flew over the centre of Rotterdam and bombed it mercilessly, with heavy high explosive and incendiary bombs. Not one house within the city centre stood intact, and 30,000 persons perished in half an hour. There was scarcely a soldier among them.

High over Hiroshima on August 6, 1945, flew a single Super-Fortress carrying a new type of bomb containing the isotope of the element uranium, and presumably using heavy water as a moderator. The bomb had been prepared on a coral atoll after having been brought from the United States. What was to happen was known to the "big three" —Truman, Stalin and Churchill—and to Attlee, who accompanied the then British Prime Minister to the opening of that Conference at Potsdam where the decision to use atomic power was taken, and, presumably, to Chiang Kai-shek.

SCIENTISTS Have Become Alarmed at the Power They Have Produced

A handful of men elsewhere among the militarists and scientists also knew the secret. The multitudes of the public among the United Nations on whose behalf this new power was to be unleashed did not know anything about it, because it was *not in the public interest* that they should know such things, to echo the ridiculous *cliché* which is used to justify secret diplomacy and secret weapons.

One 400-lb. atomic bomb fell from a great height, at least 25,000 feet, and its parachute opened in delay action when the bomber that had borne it was about ten miles away. From 70,000 to 120,000 persons died then and later from the fission of the uranium-235 content of that one bomb. Is it to be wondered that the scientists have become alarmed at the power they have produced and placed in the hands of the politicians?

Let us look at the rate of progress that has been made in this method of waging war. In 1937 a village of about a quarter square mile was destroyed. In 1940 the centre of a city extending over more than one square mile was destroyed by an increased number of aircraft. In 1945 about four square miles of a city were completely destroyed by one bomber. In each case the proportion of destroyed area increases four times over the preceding case, but in the third case 16 times as much damage was achieved as in the first, with only one aircraft employed instead of two or three squadrons.

The loss of life increases in greater proportion than the material destruction from Case One to Case Two, but not between Case Two and Case Three, but would this be so if the aircraft used in the third case had been proportionate to those used in the second case? If the number of aircraft and weight of bombs dropped had been equal in cases two and three, there can be no doubt that the proportionate loss of life would have been incalculably greater in case three.

OUTLAWING the Air Bombardment of Cities With Any Kinds of Bombs

Where is this going to end? We find in the Nuremberg trial that the defendants are charged, not with killing civilians by air bombardment, but for breaches of the rules of war and breaches of treaties signed by them. Their offences are offences against already recognized codes of law or instruments legalized between nations under treaty. If, therefore, this bombing of open cities is to become penal in the future, it is necessary for the United Nations to draw up an instrument of agreement, which all nations will be required to sign, outlawing the air bombardment of cities with any kinds of bombs, whether carried by aircraft or in self-propelling missiles. Then those who resort to this form of warfare in future will become liable to war criminal charges.

But, someone will exclaim, all cities are arsenals. If they are not attacked, war will be prolonged. That, too, I say, should be the subject of international treaty. It should be prohibited to make arms in cities; where they are found to be so made the proscription against attacking such cities should be waived by ultimatum. But at the end of a war those found guilty of having so used cities should be charged with breach of treaty. In fact, what I say is that even if we cannot control the development of the atomic bomb as a weapon, we can limit its use by defining targets against which it must not be employed under penalty of breach of treaty and subsequent indictment for war guilt.

General Marshall has informed the world of new bombers transporting 100,000 lb. of lethal weapons to any target and returning to their operational bases, and rocket projectiles steering to their intended targets by electronic devices.

January 1, 1946, produced two significant items of news. Our Royal Navy is rushing plans to revolutionize the fleet to resist atomic warfare. A special committee to be appointed by the Admiralty Commissioners is to report in March on every branch of the Navy from recruitment and training to battle tactics; modification in the design of future warships will also be considered. Our Home Office has circularized local authorities that careful study is being made of the effects of the most recent forms of attack; advice on shelters and defence organization may be given later; associations of former C.D. workers as development centres for new-type civil defence are to be encouraged.

Such things were not heard when the First Great War's end ushered in a peace that lasted uneasily, with many minor wars, for 21 years. Do current statements (remember these are usually based on accepted hypotheses) indicate the preparation of defence against an already visualized war? Has man learned nothing from the fates of Rotterdam and Hiroshima? Must he still pursue his age-old curse of Cain to the bitter end of self-extermination?

Bombers' Progress in Five Years of the War

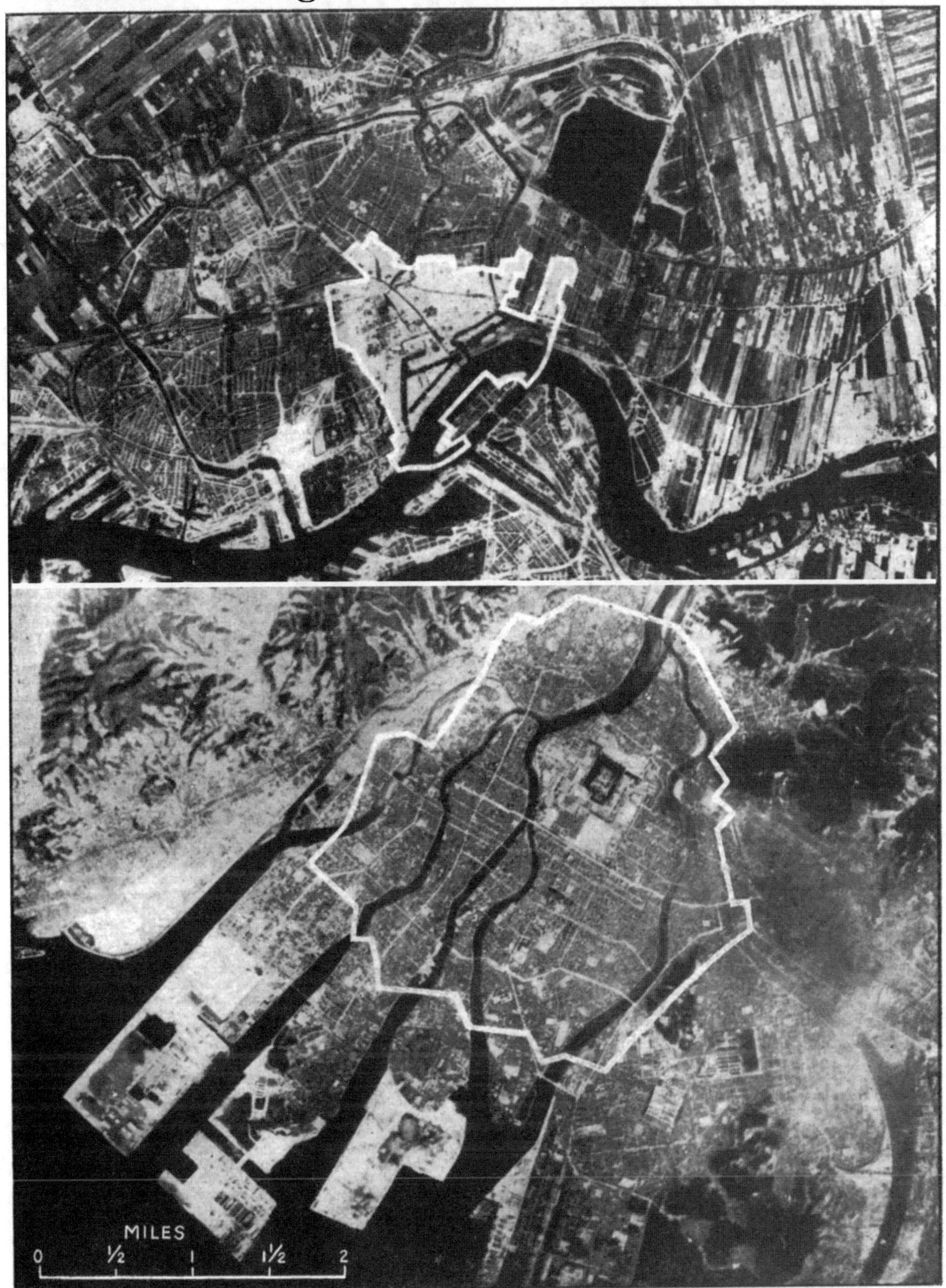

TERRIFYING DEVELOPMENT OF DESTRUCTION FROM THE AIR is forcefully illustrated in these photographs of the cities of Rotterdam (top) and Hiroshima reproduced on the same scale. Damage at Rotterdam (enclosed by white line) was caused on May 14, 1940, by two German squadrons of 27 bombers each, dropping incendiaries and 1,000-lb. H.E.s in a half-hour raid which killed 30,000. At Hiroshima, on August 6, 1945, a single 400-lb atomic bomb razed everything within the zone here demarcated (almost four times the Rotterdam area), and killed 70,000–120,000. See also facing page and pages 278 344 ; also pages 74–75, Vol. 3.

Photos, British Official, British Combine

The Editor Looks Back

THOSE 'COLUMNISTS' Oct. 28, 1939

I see that Mr. Walter Lippman, the very able author of A Preface to Morals, is described by one of his countrymen as a "columnist," which strikes me as derogatory. Yet the context of the paragraph would make Mr. Lippman seem more of a columnist than a serious student of world affairs, for he is alleged to contemplate the possibility of Britain having to surrender her fleet to Germany as an occasion for the U.S.A. to take up arms against the Dictator ! Might I suggest that a far likelier event than that would be the United States surrendering their fleet to Japan ? The trouble about these "columnists" is that they must write something when they fill their fountain pens—just as Hyde Park orators must say something when they open their mouths.

THE vogue of the "columnists" in American journalism has become almost a world menace. They are certainly a source of continual danger to the Anglo-American Alliance, for they are allowed to write with a freedom which is far beyond liberty, and the less they curb their foolhardy utterances the more they seem to be successful in tickling the ears of America's sensation-loving public. I do not class Walter Lippman, who is a writer of distinction and a serious student of international relationships, with the numerous columnists who think of nothing beyond finding a new sensation for each day, but I should like to know if his face is red when he re-reads, after a lapse of six incredible years, the stuff I pilloried in the above note. British readers who do not have the opportunity of seeing the columnar nonsense that gets printed in the American press (where there isn't a paper shortage) can have no idea of the extent to which all things British are misrepresented and burlesqued. It is fortunate that the leading American statesmen are little influenced by these irresponsible and ill-informed critics, and that there is a substantial number of fair-minded American newspapers who do their best to discount such misleading stuff.

ATLANTIC FLYERS Oct. 28, 1939

Because a young man had the good luck to make the first solo flight across the Atlantic—fifty-five had flown across before him, but not alone—is no reason for regarding that lucky young man as an authority on international politics, else we ought to hear what "Wrong-Way" Corrigan thinks of Hitler and world affairs. I regard Lindbergh's pronouncement on the war as a piece of gratuitous impertinence (a well-worn but appropriate phrase). And I think his fellow-countrymen, with few exceptions, will be ready to tell the presumptuous "Colonel" where he gets off. I wonder if he composed his anti-British broadcast entirely without prompting or advice ? One of the most grossly over-publicised personalities of our age, he expects too much if he thinks his words must carry weight just because he once flew the Atlantic, which is today no more remarkable than swimming the Channel.

IT is worth while recalling this note if only to point out how time has erased much, if not indeed the whole, of that quick and cheap reputation for greatness which came all-too-easily to Lindbergh. His name is now more a subject for laughter than for serious consideration.

THE 'PHONEY' DAYS Nov. 4, 1939

This funny war ! . . . day after day, week by week, the peoples of the world are gasping for news of it, and all that is vouchsafed to them—apart from a plentiful crop of fantastic rumour—is a daily addition or subtraction to the credit and debit of the U-boat warfare. That, and some pleasant paragraphs from the Legion of War Correspondents in France telling us that the British soldiers are having a delightful time with sing-songs in little French cabarets somewhere behind the Maginot Line, somewhere in France.

WE have learned so much more about modern war since I wrote that paragraph, that it needs a considerable effort of memory to recall the strange atmosphere of incredulity which prevailed in those early months when the iron clamp of Censorship made us uncertain what to believe and what to doubt, while rumour had a thousand tongues. Mr. Hore Belisha may some day give to the world certain information which the future historians of the War will require in their efforts to explain the "phoney" period through which we were then passing. He could have a tale unfolded of incompetence in high commands when he ceased to be War Minister, but he had to remain silent in the interests of the State. The unhappy facts are known to many, but the time has not come even now for open avowal.

GALLIC WIT Nov. 4, 1939

These Gallic wits have a way of saying a thing that eludes translation. Even so, I quote the following from Choc, the brilliant weekly edited by Mme. G. K. Guillaume, whose pages are always severely censored. "Mr. Roosevelt has spoken, in his recent discourse to Congress, of the duration of the war : 'It will be painful and of indeterminate duration' . . . We are warned. Let's arm ourselves therefore with patience and determination" It doesn't sound half so biting in English, but in French the barb strikes home.

BUT Mme. Guillaume knew no better than the world at large how inferior was the French Army as a consequence of the political rottenness of her country, and some six months later her wit had lost its point, or rather the barb had caught the thrower.

LITERARY TASTE Nov. 11, 1939

I may be wrong, but I have a fixed idea that war destroys literary taste—modern mechanical war. Thucydides could fight and write, even Socrates who, by the way, never wrote a book, was a soldier. But in those remote days war was a picnic, the Anabasis an excursion. All I can say is that I somehow don't seem to care very much today what Hazlitt thought of Shakespeare. That may be because I read everything that Hazlitt wrote so long ago. Whether I shall be eager to recapture my old literary interests after the War I just cannot guess. Meanwhile, they seem at best quite small beer compared with the clamant interests of the moment.

THAT was a mood that lasted for a very brief period. I was soon reading Shakespeare more diligently than ever and Hazlitt also, and in the six years that followed, in common with an ever-widening book-reading public, I had more delight out of literature than at any time I can remember. It is to be hoped that the unpredecented demand for books to read which was manifested during the last three or four years of the War may continue. From what the booksellers tell me, their waiting-lists for serious and scholarly books, such as Trevelyan's Social History, are getting longer every day.

MR. BUREAUCRAT Nov. 18, 1939

At the risk of seeming to harp on the subject of the thriving Bureaucracy of Britain, I must set down the information I have had from an eminent hotel proprietor. His fine establishment contains a great many bedrooms, spacious suites and splendid public rooms, and quite a number of elderly persons have made their homes there for twenty or thirty years. Enter one afternoon not long ago, Mr. British Bureaucrat. His advisory letter hadn't arrived owing to postal delay.

"I want to see the Manager," he says peremptorily. The Manager is summoned so that he may be seen. "I want you to start clearing out in fifteen minutes as I am taking over," was his greeting to that perplexed person who somewhat timidly protested, until he was informed by the bumptious official that he was evidently not aware that the hotel was required to house Government employees, who, to the extent of some thousands, were soon to invade the town. Mr. B. B. graciously extended the time for clearing out, to next morning, and one can judge of the flurry that ensued.

BELIEVE it or not, that hotel stood empty for some months before the bonnie bureaucrats came swarming into it, and it is only now in the process of derequisitioning. It had a very narrow escape in one heavy raid which destroyed other hotels in the town.

POSTSCRIPT

TURNING over the late Maurice Baring's delightful anthology, Have You Anything to Declare ? the other day, I came on this astonishing quotation from Tolstoi :

> In 1799 General Tamac received a proposal from Napoleon, who wished to enter the Russian service, but they were unable to agree, as Napoleon demanded the rank of Major.

What an "If" of History that conjures up ! But surely Baring (or Tolstoi) slipped up on his dates, for 1799 was the year in which Bonaparte (at the age of thirty) became First Consul. Make it 1789 and the story comes alive with speculation. But what a pity Baring did not document his quotation ! There must be twenty volumes in the Collected Tolstoi, and much as I'd like to follow the story to its source I find the allotted span a trifle short.

AN interesting reason has been given for the failure of a play at one of our West End theatres—that even fashionable audiences have not yet settled down to pre-war "after-dinner" hours. No doubt lack of late transport was a contributory cause of the play's failure, though I for one fail to see anything immutable about the pre-war convention of ringing up the curtain at eight-fifteen. How many of our West End theatre managers and restaurateurs are aware that seventy years ago the fashionable hour for dinner was six o'clock in the evening, and that ninety years ago our grandparents were dining at four in the afternoon ?

A CURIOUS concidence befell me the other day. Over lunch at the club a noted bore thought to regale me with the newest tale "straight from the Stock Exchange," as he put it. An hour later, turning over a volume of Pope to verify a quotation, I came on the same story almost word for word. I can only say that it probably sounded funnier in Pope's day—over two centuries ago.

THOUGHT for Our Times : "Sir, your levellers wish to level down as far as themselves, but they cannot bear levelling up to themselves." As usual, Dr. Johnson said it first. It was a way of his.

In Britain Now: Worship Again Where a V1 Fell

THE GUARDS' CHAPEL, Wellington Barracks, London, all but demolished by a flying-bomb in June 1944 (see page 334, Vol. 8), has been temporarily restored, a large metal hut, capable of accommodating a congregation of up to 700, having been erected on the site of the former nave. The first service to be held there was on Christmas Day 1945, at which Lt.-Gen. Sir Charles Loyd, commanding the London district, read the lessons.

UNLOADING PILCHARDS AT LOOE, Cornish beauty spot, in support of a big drive to revive the industry, organized in late 1945 by a local ex-Serviceman, Mr. L. E. Middleton. He has constructed tankage for at least 300 lasts (a last is a measure of 10,000 pilchards), and thousands of fish are being packed for the Ministry of Food to be disposed of by U.N.R.R.A. among the starving people of Europe (see also page 566).

UNDER-SECRETARY FOR HOUSING, at a salary of £1,825 a year, is the appointment specially created by the Minister of Health for Miss Evelyn Sharp (above), as announced on December 21, 1945. Forty-two years of age, Miss Sharp was the first woman to become a principal assistant secretary at the Treasury—a post she held from 1941-1945. At the Ministry of Health, to which she was appointed in 1945, she held the position of principal assistant secretary—again the first woman to do so.

 Photos, G.P.U., Keystone, Topical

Sappers Win the Last Round With 'Hermann'

THE KNOCK-OUT GIVEN after 200 days and nights, Croydon's 4,000-lb. German bomb, known to the local Surrey folk as "Hermann," was hoisted from its deep hole on December 17, 1945. Overall length approximately 18 ft., it had contained over 2,000 lb. of high explosive, which had been sterilized by steam-heating for 10 hours. Only sappers of the Royal Engineers, and police and Government officials, were admitted to the site, the steam-heating apparatus being still on the secret list. See also illus. page 565. *Photo, Topical Press*

Printed in England and published every alternate Friday by the Proprietors, THE AMALGAMATED PRESS, LTD., The Fleetway House, Farringdon Street, London, E.C.4. Registered for transmission by Canadian Magazine Post. Sole Agents for Australia and New Zealand: Messrs. Gordon & Gotch, Ltd.; and for South Africa: Central News Agency, Ltd.—January 18, 1946. S.S *Editorial Address:* JOHN CARPENTER HOUSE WHITEFRIARS LONDON E.C.4.

Vol 9 The War Illustrated Nº 225

SIXPENCE and AFTERWARDS FEBRUARY 1, 1946

BLACK BOAR OF THE 30th CORPS, famous " flash " sign of these renowned fighting-men, has been rendered permanent in bronze at Nienburg, centre of British-controlled Germany. It was unveiled on December 15, 1945, by Lt.-Gen. Sir Brian Horrocks, K.C.B., D.S.O., M.C. This was his last duty as the Corps Commander. The statue, mounted on a stone pedestal designed and executed by three members of the Corps and bearing the battle honours, was inspected by troops after the ceremony.

Edited by Sir John Hammerton

In the Far East Our Forces Are Still Busy

AT SAIGON, CAPITAL OF INDO-CHINA, Royal Navy ratings formed a dignified guard when, on November 24, 1945, Japanese ceremoniously laid down their arms (1). Boon to our men in Singapore is the well-stocked Services Amenities Stores in which (2) a soldier inspects a purchase. R.A.F. police (3, centre foreground), mixed with crowds in Singapore's bazaars in their war against the Black Market. Lord Alanbrooke, Chief of Imperial General Staff, inspected 5th Parachute Brigade troops at Johore (4) on December 6. *Photos, British Official*

What of the Mediterranean's Future?

By
HENRY BAERLEIN

THE almost landlocked "Middle Sea," which washes the shores of Europe, Asia and Africa, is the heritage of a number of States. Freedom of passage through its waters and the future ownership of its many strategic ports and islands are problems which will exercise to the full the wits of statesmen charged with their solving, as our well-known contributor shows in this article specially written for "The War Illustrated."

THE downfall of Hitler and Mussolini has put a stop to a couple of dreams: that of the "Drang nach Osten" (Thrust towards the East) and the "Mare Nostrum" (Our Sea), both of which would have been, if realized, most perilous to the interests of other Mediterranean Powers. It is not generally remembered that the countries surrounding the Middle Sea have, along its shores, 24 cities with over 100,000 inhabitants in each of them. These countries, great and small, now stand liberated from a certain peril, but with uncertainty on many points that demand a settlement.

The "Drang nach Osten" has been replaced by a "Drang nach Westen," for while Russia on the mainland of Europe has extended her frontiers in a westerly direction by absorbing a part of East Prussia, including Koenigsberg, its capital, re-annexing the three Baltic States and moving the eastern boundary of Poland a good deal nearer Warsaw, she has not abandoned her age-old desire with regard to the Dardanelles, though willing, for the sake of the substance, to forgo the shadow of Istanbul.

The Russians cannot be charged with overweening Imperialism if they ask that their Black Sea should no longer have at its exit a gate in alien possession. The best solution would be no gate at all, an unfortified Dardanelles with free access in and out for everyone. It is less easy to sympathize with a Russian claim to a port on the Libyan coast; but that is perhaps a bargaining counter which will be gracefully conceded.

Libya and the Arab League

The future of Libya, as yet undecided, is being watched by the newly-created Arab League, which likewise has its "Drang nach Westen." There are many Italians who have no wish to have Libya, with its Moslem background, remain on their hands; but as the fertile portions of the land have on them Italian settlers, mostly of very recent years, they would probably agree to be transferred —with adequate compensation. With the Arabs in Libya, and thus all around the eastern basin of the Mediterranean, there might be no need for them to object to Palestine being left chiefly to the Jews. The extension of the Arab world might indeed reawaken the glory of their Spanish days, before Ferdinand and Isabella drove them out in the 15th century, much to the detriment of Andalusia. Architects, poets and philosophers were the Moslems of Spain; in their centuries of exile they have handed down from father to son the unwieldy keys of many a house in Seville. Instead of seeking for what no longer exists they will, it is to be hoped, in their enlarged African home turn, as did their ancestors, the keys of the door of knowledge.

MENTION of Spain recalls the Balearic Islands, one of the Mediterranean problems we have before us. When the Catalans, like the Basques and the Galicians, achieve their long-desired autonomy after the end of the Franco regime, the Balearics, despite their ancient Moslem links, will gladly share the fortunes of Catalonia. The sole question remaining is that of the port of Mahon in Minorca.

It was this excellent harbour and not the whole island which Britain possessed for some years in the 18th century, and there seems to be no reason why a friendly arrangement for the renewal of that state of things should not be made. The people of Minorca would assuredly urge the central government to carry out such a plan, so greatly to the local financial advantage. Let us remember how the communications between France and North Africa were imperilled in the early days of the recent war by the midway Balearics, and with the best will in the world it may again be impossible for Spain to prevent these harbours being misused by some anti-democratic power.

There is another island, Pantelleria, which caused us a good deal of trouble in the war, since it made the passage to Malta far more dangerous. Mussolini had heavily fortified it and, though it has no port of any size and is incapable of sheltering more than one or two destroyers, the airfields were well developed. The administration of this small island has been temporarily given to the Italians again, but in the final settlement of the Mediterranean it should at any rate be leased to Britain. Very possibly its inhabitants, if consulted, would vote for definite inclusion in the Empire, as was the expressed wish of the Sicilians in the days of Nelson, Duke of Bronté. To be sure there are Sicilians today whose devotion to the rest of Italy is not the strongest of their sentiments, but they will not receive encouragement from this country. The Separatist movement remains so powerful that when towards the end of December 1945 the carabinieri attacked a stronghold of theirs near Catania no less than 80 Separatists are said to have been killed.

In the eastern Mediterranean the fate of the islands of the Dodecanese is not in doubt; for Turkey, off whose shores they lie, has stated that she has no objection to the hoisting of the Greek flag over islands whose people are so entirely Hellenic. Here again Russia has said a word or two, but probably not very seriously. When the Italians seized these islands in 1912 in the course of their war against the Turks, they made promises of autonomy and of evacuation which they did not fulfil. Britain, years before that, promised to evacuate Cyprus if Russia would do the same with regard to Batoum, of which there is not the remotest likelihood.

For a long time Cyprus suffered neglect, but in recent times has been so much in the eye of the Colonial Office that it is probably not mere propaganda to say that disgruntled politicians and a few churchmen are the only Cypriots who are unwilling to continue under the Union Jack. However, if, as in the case of the Ionian Islands, Cyprus is given to Greece at some future date, the port of Famagusta should be retained. With the expenditure of a comparatively small sum it can be made into a most useful harbour for our warships.

Free Passage Must Be Assured

In the Adriatic it will be for the general well-being if no obstruction is offered to any sailing on their lawful occasions. And when the Italians laid hands in 1914 on the Albanian island of Saseno, just off the southern coast, fortified it strongly and prohibited the Albanians from access to it, they were not only infringing the sovereignty of that people but were injuriously affecting a number of others; for at the narrowest part of the Adriatic they held both shores and could—theoretically, at all events—close that sea to the north of the Saseno line.

Yugoslavia would thus have been inaccessible to her friends by sea, while the great port of Trieste, serving Czechoslovakia, Austria and the rest of Central Europe, would have been denied free access to the lands beyond the Adriatic. Saseno must therefore, without any subterfuge, be wholly restored to the Albanians, with the proviso that if they are ever tempted for the sake of a loan—and their finances are not their strongest suit—to waive their sovereignty over Saseno it must be to an international body.

IT will be seen that many questions as to the Middle Sea, the Sea of Destiny, which has played so great a part in the history of our civilization, remain to be solved. There was a time, somewhat lost in the mists of antiquity, when this area of something over a million square miles was divided into two parts by the land which stretched from Africa to Europe, so that sweet water lay to the east and salt water to the west of the line in which Malta was probably a hill.

The Mediterranean is now not divided; it is the inheritance of a number of States. Freedom of passage through its waters must be assured to them; they must not exercise intolerable control in any part under their jurisdiction. In fact, the statesmen who will make the Mediterranean their problem to be solved will often find themselves sailing between the Scylla and Charybdis of that sea. And it is to be hoped they will refuse to listen to the songs of any evilly-disposed Siren.

MEDITERRANEAN ISLANDS AND PORTS, certain of which have for centuries provoked national rivalries, today present an enigma no less complex. The future of Italian possessions such as Pantelleria, the Dodecanese, and the African colony of Libya is of vital importance in a final settlement of the European problem. *Specially drawn for* THE WAR ILLUSTRATED

America's Debt to Britain and Russia

MAJ.-GENERAL SIR CHARLES GWYNN K.C.B., D.S.O., on the *Report of the Chief of Staff of the U.S. Army to the Secretary of War. July 1, 1943—June 30, 1945*

In October 1945 the U.S. Information Service issued excerpts from the biennial report dealing with the last two years of the War, which General George Marshall, the Chief of Staff of the U.S. Army, had presented to the U.S. Secretary of War. These excerpts, though extensively quoted by the Press, were not available to the general public ; the reprint of General Marshall's full report, by H.M. Stationery Office, at 2s. 6d. should therefore be welcomed, for it deserves to be carefully read and retained for future reference.

Of the 123 pages of the report 82 are devoted to a very clear, condensed account of the operations in Europe, beginning with the invasion of Sicily, and of those in the Far East beginning with the project for reopening communications with China. This record is of great historical interest, chiefly because it describes how and when the Allied strategical plans were formulated and how they had to be modified to meet actual conditions, in particular the shortage of shipping. Naturally, in describing the execution of the plans the narrative is devoted mainly to the part played by American forces, but sight is not lost of the contribution made by British and other Allied troops.

No one is better qualified than General Marshall to explain the strategical problems the Allies had to solve. He throws, for instance, much light on the factors affecting the prosecution of the War in Italy, where heavy sacrifices had to be accepted in the interests of the main offensive in western France, and to provide the force for the subsidiary southern landing. Although it has long been known that such sacrifices were necessary, I doubt if their extent is fully realized, nor do I think it is generally known that the Allied forces in Italy were outnumbered by the Germans throughout.

WHY the Landing in Southern France Had to Be Postponed

General Marshall constantly emphasizes how shortage of shipping and landing craft affected the development of Allied plans. For that reason D-Day was postponed for a month, and the landing in southern France, originally intended to synchronize with it, was held back till landing craft used in Normandy could be transferred to the Mediterranean. These and many other points are cleared up by General Marshall's authoritative narrative.

His account of the Far Eastern operations deals mainly with the American offensive in the Pacific and with General Stilwell's share in the Burma campaign, but it is none the less of interest to British readers because it demonstrates the potentialities of sea-air power and how they can be exploited. Since the operations took place in an unfamiliar geographical setting, a clear account of them is all the more to be welcomed.

BRITISH and Russian Peoples Gave U.S. Time to Arm Herself

The story of how a rapid decision was made to land on Leyte instead of on Mindanao, as had been planned, is of particular interest, for it shows that when the team is working well together and mutual confidence is established decisions can be given as quickly by a committee as by a single over-all commander. The proposal was first made to the joint Chiefs of Staff during the Quebec Conference by Admiral Halsey as a result of his reconnaisance operations, and it was immediately referred to General MacArthur in order to ascertain if he agreed and was in a position to change his plans.

MacArthur's reply was received two days later, while the Chiefs of Staff were attending an official dinner. Yet within ninety minutes MacArthur had received instructions to proceed with the new plan, and his acknowledgment reached General Marshall as he was returning to his quarters from the dinner. The execution of the new plan, which most successfully caught the Japanese on the wrong foot, was equally prompt.

Interesting and valuable as an historical record as General Marshall's account of the evolution of Allied strategy is, the parts of his report which deal with America's unpreparedness for war, with the measures taken to mobilize her potential resources, his forecast of the dangers that threaten her future security and his recommendation for the organization of defence to meet them, are for British readers of even more outstanding interest. Under all these headings American records and defence problems bear a close similarity to our own. America can no longer rely implicitly on the protection afforded by the wide stretches of the Atlantic and Pacific, any more than we can on the narrow waters of the Channel.

In commenting on American unpreparedness for war General Marshall frankly admits that "the refusal of the British and Russian peoples to accept what appeared to be inevitable defeat was the great factor in the salvage of our civilization" coupled with "the failure of the enemy to make the most of the situation." It was those factors and not the Atlantic "moat" that gave America time to arm herself.

To emphasize the risks America ran, General Marshall in his introduction gives a synopsis of German and Japanese strategic plans and the causes of their failure, quoting the evidence of high-ranking German officers obtained since the surrender. This is very interesting, but even more interesting are General Marshall's comments on it. He writes, "There can be no doubt that the greed and mistakes of the war-making nations as well as the heroic stands of the British and Soviet peoples saved the United States a war on her own soil. The crisis had come and passed at Stalingrad and El Alamein before the nation was able to gather sufficient resources to participate in the fight in a determining manner."

RATHER Terrifying Possibility Admitted by General Marshall

In another section dealing with the complete mobilization of American man-power, General Marshall records that to give General Eisenhower the impetus for final destruction of the German Army the last two combat divisions in the United States were dispatched to him, and his comment is "even with two-thirds of the German Army engaged by Russia it took every man the nation saw fit to mobilize to do our part of the job in Europe and at the same time keep the Japanese enemy under control in the Pacific. What would have been the result had the Red Army been defeated and the British islands invaded we can only guess. The possibility is rather terrifying."

So much for the dangers escaped in the past at so great a price and by so narrow a margin ; but General Marshall is more concerned as to how the dangers of the future to America can be met—dangers to which these islands are even more exposed. He accepts the view that with the continued development of modern weapons and technique already in existence, New York and other American cities might be subject to annihilation in a matter of hours, and that the only defence in that kind of warfare is ability and immediate readiness *to attack* which pre-supposes the necessity of maintaining and developing similar weapons.

But he warns us that power of attack does not rest on machine power only. There must be men not only to produce and operate new weapons of all types, but also to close with the enemy and "tear his operating bases and productive establishments away from him before the war can end." He quotes as proof that the Battle of Britain and the amazing later development of anti-aircraft defences did not relieve Britain from air attack. Not until we had physical possession of the launching sites and factories that produced the V weapons did the attacks cease.

For these reasons he advocates universal military training which will provide a source from which (a) the regular Services available for immediate action would be filled by voluntary recruitment, and (b) from which trained men would be directed by selection to such war duties as an emergency situation required. The training establishments, he suggests, should, however, normally be kept distinct from and form no part of the regular Services. This organization, he considers, would provide for rapid partial mobilization and complete mobilization within one year. Should not we be prepared to accept universal service on much the same lines?

OVER 3,500,000 AMERICAN TROOPS besides countless tons of material from U.S. passed through Southampton Docks on their way to European theatres of war. To commemorate this achievement, Col. S. L. Kiser (right), commanding the U.S. 14th Port Army, unveiled a bronze plaque at the entrance to New Docks on January 4, 1946. Mr. R. P. Biddle, Docks Manager, stands second from the left of the photograph.. *Photo, Keystone*

Siam's Youthful Monarch Returns to His Capital

KING ANANDA MAHIDOL, who went back to his country on October 5, 1945, is seen with his entourage on the steps of the Emerald Buddha's temple at Bangkok (top). He left Siam in 1938 and spent seven years in study in Switzerland. Owing to repeated Indonesian attacks in Java, some 2,500 Dutch women and children were evacuated to Bangkok and other parts of Siam on December 20 ; the British landing craft L.270 (bottom) which carried them to safety arrives at the Klongtoi docks, Bangkok, where the travellers disembarked.

Photos, British Official

H.M.S. HOWE arrived at Portsmouth from the Far East on January 9, 1946, flying the flag of Vice-Admiral Sir Arthur J. Power, K.C.B., C.V.O., formerly C.-in-C. East Indies Fleet and appointed Second Sea Lord on December 12, 1945. She was the first ship of her tonnage to navigate the Suez Canal; first of the British Pacific Fleet to shoot down a Japanese suicide plane; and the first of her class to enter Portsmouth. *Photo, G.P.U.*

Prize Money: The Great Share-Out

PRIZE money is one of the oldest of naval institutions; it can be traced back to the thirteenth century, when King John granted a moiety of their takings to those who manned his galleys in 1205. At that date, of course, the forms and rules by which the proceeds of prizes were divided had not been systematized; but in the "Black Book of the Admiralty," a treatise in Norman French compiled prior to 1351, it is laid down that two shares out of the moiety due to the ship's company should go to the admiral if present at the capture, or one share if absent. An inquiry into doubtful points of maritime law, held at Queenborough in 1375, decided that after the admiral had taken his share, "as the master has greater charge and is of higher rank than any other in the ship," he should have twice as much as any mariner. This view was duly embodied in an ordinance.

In 1642 Parliament assigned to the officers and men of a ship, in addition to their pay, one-third of the value of the prizes taken by them. Seven years later this was altered, one-half being awarded to the captors, and the other half to a fund for the relief of the wounded, widows and orphans. April 1744 was the date of an order that all prizes taken should become the property of the officers and men of the ships that captured them, any shares not claimed within three years to go to Greenwich Hospital.

IT can be understood, therefore, what an important part prize money played in the hard life of the underpaid seamen of the eighteenth century. On occasions the amounts taken were immense; but the Navy did not always get its fair share. Thus, at the taking of Manila, in the Philippines, by Admiral Cornish in 1761, the victors were promised 4,000,000 dollars in silver to save the city from pillage. Only half this sum could be collected, and most of it went to the East India Company. Fortunately, H.M.S. Panther and Argo captured the galleon Santisima Trinidad with treasure worth 3,000,000 dollars. This was probably one of the ships dispatched annually to Manila from Acapulco, in Mexico. That redoubtable leader, Commodore Anson, in the famous Centurion, took the 1743 Acapulco galleon with treasure valued at £400,000.

When Havana, capital of Cuba, fell to the British in 1762, the booty was worth over £3,000,000. Of this, £736,000 was divided as prize money between the naval and military forces. The share of the admiral, Sir George Pocock, was £122,697; that of a captain came to £1,600; of a petty officer, £17 5s. 3d.; and of a seaman or marine, £3 14s. 9½d. To Captain the Hon. Augustus Hervey and those serving under him in H.M.S. Dragon came an extra windfall, for on the passage home with dispatches a French ship worth £30,000 was taken.

In 1781 Admiral (afterwards Lord) Rodney captured the Dutch island of St. Eustatius, in the West Indies, with 150 merchantmen and produce valued at over £3,000,000. Another rich Dutch prize came with the occupation of the islands of Amboina and Banda Neira, in the East Indies, in 1796. On that occasion a captain's share of the prize money amounted to £15,000.

STRANGE and Profitable Dream of the Alcmene's 'Silver Captain'

A famous case was the taking in the Bay of Biscay by four British frigates of the Spanish frigates Santa Brigida and Thetis, with treasure from Mexico worth £600,000. This yielded in prize money £40,730 to each captain, £5,091 to each lieutenant, £2,468 to each warrant officer, £791 to each midshipman and £182 4s. 9½d. to each seaman and marine in the four British ships.

A traditional story is told of Captain Digby of H.M.S. Alcmene, whose arrival at a critical moment prevented the Santa Brigida from escaping. During the previous night he had come on deck to alter his course from S.S.W. to north as the result of a vivid dream in which he was earnestly enjoined to do so. This strange episode won for Digby—an ancestor of the present Lord Digby, and afterwards an admiral—the nickname of "the Silver Captain."

It will be observed from the foregoing that the most valuable prizes in British naval history have been Spanish. For over three centuries Spain derived her chief revenues from the gold, silver and precious stones brought across the sea from Mexico and Peru. Usually the ships carrying this treasure assembled at Havana, whence they were accustomed to sail once a year. It therefore became a settled policy for this country, when at war with Spain, to endeavour to intercept this treasure fleet—known as the *flota*—in order that the enemy might become financially embarrassed in the prosecution of the conflict.

This was the object with which Admiral Blake in 1656 attacked the Port of Santa Cruz de Tenerife (later unsuccessfully assailed by Nelson), in which the *flota* had sought refuge. Led by his second-in-command, Captain Stayner, the vanguard of Blake's fleet succeeded in taking three out of four treasure ships; two were destroyed by fire, but the survivor yielded some £600,000.

In 1708 Commodore Wager (whose name is now borne by a destroyer) fell in with the *flota* in the West Indies; he sank one treasure ship and captured another, thus becoming a rich man.

On May, 21, 1762, two British frigates, the Active and Favourite, took the Spanish treasure ship Hermione off Cadiz in half an hour. As the total value of the prize was £544,648, each captain received £65,000, each lieutenant £13,000 and each seaman £485. The Vice-Admiral and Commodore on the station, though not present at the capture, shared £65,000.

In 1914, when Mr. Churchill was First Lord of the Admiralty, a general Prize Fund was instituted, to be distributed throughout the Navy instead of being confined to those taking part in captures. Under this arrangement nearly £15,000,000 was ultimately shared amongst naval personnel in the proportions of £3,000 to an admiral, £500 to a captain, £120 to a lieutenant, £20 to £25 to a rating and £15 to a boy.

IT was generally imagined that a similar division would be made of the 1939–1945 Prize Fund, estimated to amount to nearly £10,000,000; but last autumn it was reported that the Treasury desired to appropriate this money "for the relief of taxation." So strong was the feeling in the Navy that this proposal was not carried into effect; and on December 19, 1945, the First Lord stated that the Prize Fund would be divided as before, but with less wide variations in the shares to different ranks, and with a proportion allocated to the R.A.F., presumably Coastal Command personnel. He hinted that in future wars the distribution of prize money was not to be expected.

Few will be found to disagree with the naval view of the question as crystallized in a recent letter to the Press. By surrendering the money in the Prize Fund to the Treasury, the most that could have been gained by reduction in taxes would be under £1 a head; this would scarcely be felt.

On the other hand, it would constitute a grave injustice to the sailor, who has had to fight as never before to beat the enemy and regards the sum accruing to him from the Prize Fund as something to which he is justly entitled, even though it may be no more than £20 or £30 for the lowest paid ratings.

New Guinea Heroes Homeward Bound for Sydney

FROM JUNGLE BATTLEFIELD THAT WAS WEWAK, these men of the Sixth Australian Division and R.A.A.F.—all veterans of the New Guinea campaign—cheered as they sailed up Sydney Harbour, assembled on the flight deck of one of our largest aircraft carriers. Cleared of their war-time equipment, with beds crammed into every available space, these big carriers have brought home many thousands of P.O.W. from the Far East. Largest number was 3,500—on the Implacable, our greatest carrier. See also illus. page 480. *Photo, Planet News*

How Shall We Use War Inventions for Peace?

Out of evil comes forth good: from the ruins of the Second Great War emerge new ways and means of "making" a more satisfactory—if not happier—world for us all. This knowledgeable summary of the great possibilities that lie in the present and immediately ahead has been specially written for "The War Illustrated" by JOHN LANGDON-DAVIES. See also facing page.

THE necessities of war have forced mankind to crowd into the space of five years a century or more of normal scientific advance. Most of us do not realize the revolution in our daily lives that this makes possible, and it would be well to illustrate it by selecting six fields in which the scientist has entirely altered possibilities and made 1939 look almost as out of date as the world before the steam engine.

I shall say nothing about the atomic bomb except that we hope it is already a thing of the past, while the use of atomic energy in industry is still a thing of the future. There is, however, one by-product of the making of the notorious bomb which will have immediate effect. In 1939 the total world supply of radium in doctors' hands for the treatment of cancer and other diseases was not more than thirty pounds; and hospitals considered themselves lucky if a rich benefactor gave them one-twentieth of an ounce. The "pile" which makes plutonium for the atomic bomb (see illus. page 439) produces as a by-product in a very few hours something like 1,500 lb. of radio-active substances, most of which can be turned over to the doctors. This will not only revolutionize the treatment of cancer but make possible rapid strides in the understanding of how the human body works.

WHILE it will certainly be a long time before atomic energy is used for propulsion of aircraft, aeronautical engineers have plenty to do perfecting jet propulsion and gas-turbine engines. These wartime gifts to aviation make possible air travel in the stratosphere and thus give an economic payload. But at present the gas-turbine has only a ten per cent efficiency, so that much work remains to be done. Prophecies of jet-propelled motor-cars had better be regarded with caution. Imagine getting into a traffic block just behind a jet-propelled vehicle of any sort!

The third great wartime invention, radar, may in time lead to the use of wireless telephones, but its immediate peacetime uses are likely to be confined to fighting the dangers of fog and darkness in air and sea travel (see illus. in this page). Radar has opened up whole new chapters in electron engineering, because it led to our finding out how to use ultra-short wireless waves which will come in very useful in all sorts of telecommunications. The once secret magnetron valve will one day become the delight of every wireless-minded schoolboy.

A fourth great advance with peacetime applications has been the discovery of new synthetic substances to take the place of raw materials which war put out of our reach. Let us consider five of these, every one of them of outstanding importance.

Making Sugar From Wood-Pulp

First, artificial rubber can now be produced more cheaply than natural rubber and of a quality better than natural rubber for most uses. For some time to come so much rubber will be wanted that there will be plenty of markets for plantations in Malaya and elsewhere, but the inevitable result in ten years' time will be that nations will find it more convenient to employ skilled labour at home making artificial rubber than cheap labour half-way across the world on the plantations.

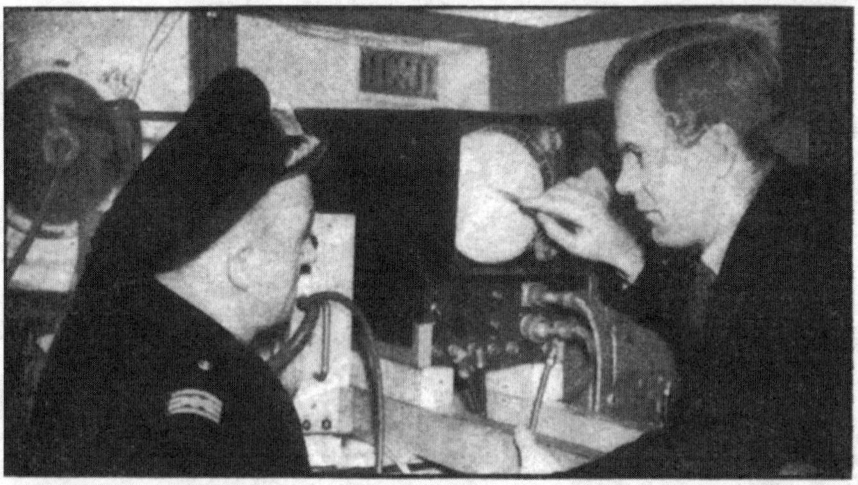

NAVIGATION BY RADAR was demonstrated to Capt. Edward Griffiths on board his ship Atlantic Coast by Mr. Fleming Williams, the radar expert. The apparatus, which gives warning of approaching vessels, icebergs, submerged rocks, and even a man floating on a raft, has proved so successful that 120 Coast Line ships are being equipped with it. *Photo, G.P.U.*

Second, in Sweden they have had to find a use for huge stores of wood and wood-pulp which they could not export owing to the war. This has led to the development of ways of manufacturing both motor fuel and sugar from forest trees. This motor fuel will make us less dependent on petrol, and in the long run the sugar from wood pulp may bring about a major revolution by taking the place of sugar from both cane and beet.

Third, in Germany a kind of butter has been produced from coal. This may sound fantastic, but it is a symbol of the way in which coal is becoming the raw material for so many valuable synthetic productions that it may one day become a crime to use it merely as fuel.

Fourth, in England and Germany it has been found possible to produce first-class protein by cultivating a kind of yeast plant. This protein costs only sixpence a pound to create, which is far less expensive than protein from beef or mutton. If we developed food yeast as rapidly and on as large a scale as we have developed penicillin, for example, the world meat shortage would disappear. We could feed starving Europe without thinking of tightening our belts, and we could raise the standard of living of millions of people in Asia and Africa.

Fifth, the announcement by I.C.I. recently of paludrine, a very cheap drug capable of preventing and curing malaria, means that the world is no longer dependent upon the Dutch island of Java for its weapons against this disease. This may seem of minor importance to the British reader, but we should remember that millions die every year in India alone from malaria, and that there has never been enough quinine available at a cheap enough price even to begin to attack the Indian malaria problem.

These five examples of how the chemist is taking over from nature the supply of raw materials, foods, drugs, fuels, should remind us that science has not only produced destruction during the last five years.

Another important scientific advance is the development of plastics; that is, of a whole range of synthetic substances which can be easily moulded into almost any shape. Let us take but one example: one of the great objects of the modern industrial scientist is the elimination of weight. That is why aluminium has taken the place of steel for so many purposes, especially in aviation. I have seen a plastic made of glass-fibre and synthetic resin which has all the mechanical properties of aluminium and which is far more easily moulded, weighing only two-thirds as much as the light metal.

Victory Over Deadly Diseases

Nobody is going to change from metal to plastics for mere variety, and a great deal of nonsense is talked of the all-plastic automobile; but plastic chemistry has provided us with a whole series of new substances which have a future because they are able to give better service in a dozen different ways than any previously known substance.

Some plastics will be substituted for glass; others for china and pottery; yet others will be successful rivals of wood and metals. Of course, none of these substances will be entirely superseded: plastics will only be used when their special qualities make it worth while. One of the great advantages of plastics, especially from our point of view in Britain, is that they can be made out of raw materials which do not have to be imported, and there is no need to emphasize the importance of that fact at this time.

NO survey of scientific advance, however brief, can exclude certain revolutionary advances in medicine. D.D.T. and possibly gammexane, one Swiss and the other British, can free the world of typhus; paludrine may destroy malaria once and for all; penicillin offers complete victory over several deadly diseases, including that cause of untold suffering, gonorrhea. The "sulpha" drugs save tens of thousands of lives; blood transfusion is reducing infant mortality and making surgical operations, which would once have been quite hopeless, successful.

The medical profession hopes to have, very shortly, a really powerful cure for tuberculosis. And the comparatively new science of psychiatry, having well used the opportunities which war has afforded it, stands ready to help us with the thousand peacetime problems of unhappy, ill-adjusted, unbalanced minds.

It would be a very good thing if those people who, terrified by the atomic bomb, think of science as a destructive force and scientists as trouble-makers, realized the creative gifts which have come from recent scientific achievement. Scientists, it is true, cannot make a peaceful world; that is the business of statesmen. But if the statesmen do their work properly, scientists can make a peacetime world far more satisfactory for its inhabitants to live in.

New Gifts of the Scientists to All Mankind

PLASTIC MATERIALS can be moulded into almost any shape, as household or car fittings, furniture, wireless-sets. Only three ingredients are needed—synthetic resin (the basis); the "filler," to mix in for the required texture and strength; and powdered dye. Manufacture is equally simple: the mixture is put into moulds of the objects desired, and pressure and heat applied.

Other new substances include nylon, samples from each roll of which are strenuously tested in the laboratory (1), and D.D.T., (2) being used to delouse a child at Coblenz. A plastics wardrobe with aluminium fittings (3). Plastic "dough" (4) is mixed before being moulded into knife-handles, fountain-pen cases, toothbrushes. See also facing page.
Photos, British Nylon Spinners, Associated Press, Keystone, Topical

Brussels' Hospitality to Our Men on Leave

VICTORY HOUSE, in the Place Eugene Flagey, is the latest of twenty hostels for British troops on leave in Brussels, run by the Princesse de Ligne's Organization, founded in gratitude to the liberating forces. Accommodating over 900, it numbers among its amenities a spacious reading-room (1), a resident photographer (2), and Victory Inn (3), a fully-licensed modern bar. Soldiers just arrived from Germany (4) check in; others enjoy the quiet of the writing-room (5).

Exclusive to THE WAR ILLUSTRATED

From B.A.O.R. to Civvy Street in Five Days

SERVICEMEN ARE RETURNING to civilian life at the rate of 12,000 a day. This first-hand pictorial record by **WAR ILLUSTRATED** artist Haworth shows the various stages of a soldier's five-day journey home from his unit with the British Army of the Rhine. He waves farewell to his comrades as the lorry moves off (1). Along the highway he passes familiar signs and traffic for the last time (2), and draws up for a welcome cup of tea at the local Naafi (3) before reaching the Regimental Holding Unit, where a bed awaits him (4)

AT THE R.H.U. the draft of men to be demobilized is assembled for England. Reveille at 5.30 a.m. is followed by roll-call outside the building which bears the familiar word Blighty (5)—reminiscent of the First Great War. Our soldier observes a notice-board displaying a warning of heavy penalties for attempting to smuggle enemy arms into England (6). Eventually the "Blighty Special" pulls out of bomb-blasted Hanover station (7), leaving behind a typical group of woebegone D.Ps. (Displaced Persons).

MANY HISTORIC LANDMARKS of the war are noted during the train journey through Germany; one of the most significant moments is the crossing of the Rhine (8), stormed by Allied troops in March 1945. Germany fades from view, and at Tournai German marks are changed for Belgian francs (9), which are subsequently exchanged for sterling. The number of the actual release centre in England for which each man is bound is entered in his pay-book (10). A Mickey Mouse film offers relaxation at the camp canteen (11).

AT THE CALAIS TRANSIT CAMP (12) a halt is made for dinner, with anticipation and excitement running high. The "draft" feel they are almost civilians again. It is the fourth day of the journey. "Tomorrow," they tell one another, "we shall be there." Impatiently they peer from the deck of the cross-Channel steamer (13) for first glimpse of the white cliffs of old England. Landed safely, our soldier goes cheerfully through the bustle of handing in equipment (14) before proceeding on the journey.

AT THE RELEASE CENTRE in London (15) "paper work" is completed and demobilization books (16) handed over. Then the short journey to Olympia, for the free issue of civilian clothing—suit, shirt, underclothes, shoes, socks, tie, hat; no rushing things here (17), for every man must be satisfied with fit and cut before he departs on this momentous day which once seemed almost incredibly remote. Comes the last stage of all: departure with kitbag and clothing-parcel and (18) up the garden path for the great welcome Home.

Now It Can Be Told!

D-DAY REHEARSAL AT CAMBRIDGE UNIVERSITY

One of the best-kept secrets of the war was revealed by an appeal launched for help in the restoration of the Union Society's premises, damage to which was caused by bombs in July 1942. Here, in this academic centre, the Debating Hall of the Society was, for a week, in March 1944, one of the most closely guarded places in the British Isles, it was reported by a Sunday Times correspondent at Cambridge, in December 1945.

It was here during that week that rehearsals for the D-Day assault in the following June were carried out. These rehearsals were attended by Gen. Eisenhower and Gen.—now Field-Marshal—Montgomery and their high Staff officers. To maintain secrecy, the whole of the civilian staff were sent away on a week's leave. The proposal to use the Union Society for the rehearsals emanated from the Regional Commissioner, Sir Will Spens, Master of Corpus Christi.

During the Easter vacation, Mr. Curzon, the Chief Clerk, was astonished one day to be visited by high Staff officers of the Security Department. They instructed him to send the staff away, and the Union building was entirely taken over by the Army. A squad of soldiers arrived on the scene, all doors leading to the basement were securely fastened, and sentries with Bren guns were posted round the building.

Conferences in the Model Room

Models, including, it is believed, some of the Mulberry harbour, were delivered during the hours of darkness and not a civilian in Cambridge knew the secrets which the building held. At the conclusion of the rehearsals the models were removed with equal secrecy, after which the building was restored to its normal condition, so that no trace remained of the unorthodox purpose to which it had been put.

Though Gen. Eisenhower and Field-Marshal Montgomery visited the model room, they did not stay in Cambridge, but Staff officers were lodged in Trinity College, and they held conferences in the model room each day. A military guard was placed round the college, and a couple of A.A. guns were installed at Midsummer Common, a large space within a short distance of the Union Society building.

SECRET MINE 'BRAIN' MADE BY A WREN TEAM

Many of them schoolgirls at the outbreak of the War, a secret team of 50 Wrens assembled the "brains" of the Navy's top-secret mines which harassed the enemy for more than three war years. They have recently been disbanded from the assembly staff of MX, highly specialized branch of H.M.S. Vernon, Naval Torpedo and Mining Establishment. Strict security guarded their vital secrets—questioners were casually told that they were "messing around with electrical circuits."

Constant changing of these circuits in British magnetic and acoustic ground mines kept the enemy guessing. The ground mine, with a normal firing mechanism, had been in use for some time when, toward the end of 1942, the expedient of varying the firing method was evolved as a special measure against enemy submarines using French coastal ports, and to counter enemy mine-sweeping operations.

The mines were mostly dropped from aircraft; some were laid by Coastal Forces. As soon as reconnaissance showed the enemy were dealing successfully with one circuit, a new circuit, varying detonation methods, was designed by the Superintendent of Mine Designs Department and assembled and tested by MX. Results proved the perplexity this game of "how, when and where?" caused the Germans.

A special organization of naval officers, ratings and Wrens under the captain H.M.S. Vernon (Mining) maintained necessary production changes to keep pace with design variations. Wrens were selected from qualified torpedo ratings. Once in MX, they remained. Their workshop was a former machine shop repaired after early bomb damage, and a start was made in January 1943, with only 13 Wrens. Original monthly output was 200 units. The establishment later expanded to total 63 Wrens, including two petty officers, with a male staff of three electrical officers, three chief petty officers and one petty officer.

An output of 500 firing units a month was eventually achieved. Technical control of the workshop was by a temporary electrical lieutenant R.N.V.R., former electrical engineer. He ensured technical perfection of mine firing circuits and that the complete mine dispatched by the Mine Depot was safe to handle. Wrens tested components and assembled units before these went to Mine Depots to be fitted to charged mines.

MX Wrens prepared 7,658 firing units during the War, and more than 50 variations of circuit were designed and assembled, as well as special assemblies intended for operations against the German battleship Tirpitz. MX Branch also prepared the successful blocking of the Kiel Canal just before D-Day. There was no time for full trials of the assembled mine before and after dropping, and a small party, consisting of one officer, a torpedo gunner's mate and six Wrens, accompanied assembled units to the aerodrome where Mosquitoes, and the mines they were to carry, were waiting.

Firing Units Swiftly Assembled

Another trial of the department's speed and flexibility was the assembly of firing units for a mixed assortment of 50 time mines, designed to obstruct salvage work on a vessel sunk across the entrance of an enemy harbour in Western France. The order was received on a Saturday morning; by Tuesday completed units were leaving the workshops. Trials of new firing assemblies in charged mines took place usually at the main depot at Frater, near Fareham, west of Portsmouth. Drop trials from aircraft were afterwards held at Weston-super-Mare.

Two MX Branch Wrens still working in H.M.S. Vernon, Petty Officer Wren Betty Forbes, of Edinburgh, and Leading Wren Doreen Jones, of Rhyl, described the occasional trip to Weston as a pleasant break in a hard and monotonous job. "There we were able to see something of what happened to the units we had to build up," they said. "Otherwise all we knew of the results of our work was from occasional talks from senior officers, who frequently told us of the sinking of submarines or minesweepers by our units. The only other variation was the periodical changing of the circuits, and we were usually very glad indeed when this came along."

SECRET TEAM of W.R.N.S. at work in one of the laboratories at H.M.S. Vernon, Royal Naval Torpedo and Mining Establishment, where (as disclosed here) they were employed in connexion with our magnetic and acoustic ground mines. It was a highly delicate task, requiring the nimbleness and sensitiveness of a woman's touch. The W.R.N.S. are seen here assembling secret firing-units which were used in special operations.
Photo, British Official

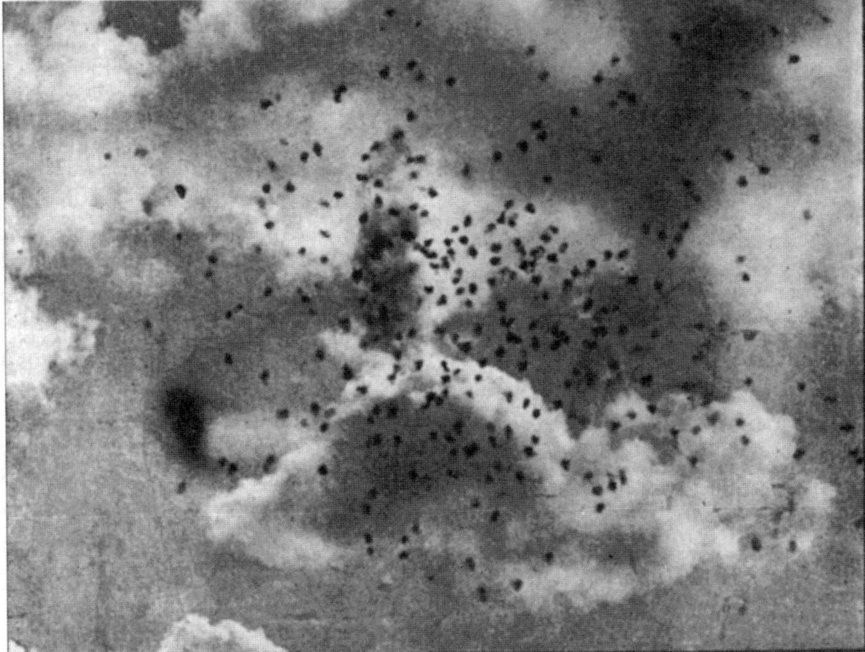

"TONSIL," ROCKET-BATTERY AGAINST V1s, consisting of units of ten projectors, was assembled on lorries between Hythe and Dymchurch, on the Kent coast, within four days of the order being given on July 15, 1944. By the end of the month the battery had scored 8½ "kills." When units were later enlarged to 20 projectors, it could fire 400 rockets at once. The battery in action (top), and the "pattern" made by the exploding rockets (bottom).

How H.M.S. Exeter Fought Her Last Battle

The full story of H.M.S. Exeter's gallant end (see illus. page 626), fighting against impossible odds off the coast of Java, reached the Admiralty in December 1945. The cruiser, famous for her part in the glorious battle against the Admiral Graf Spee off the River Plate (see page 505, Vol. 1), was sunk on March 1, 1942.

She had already been damaged in the Battle of the Java Seas two days previously; but, with her escorting destroyers H.M.S. Encounter and U.S.S. Pope, she went down fighting four Japanese heavy cruisers and five destroyers. Her commanding officer, Captain O. L. Gordon, M.V.O., R.N., brought the official story of this action back with him from a prisoner of war camp; he made complete records while a prisoner and kept them from the Japs by hiding them in a tube of shaving cream.

On February 27, 1942, she was at sea as part of an Allied force of five cruisers and nine destroyers. In the afternoon, an enemy force of four cruisers and twelve destroyers was encountered and engaged. Later the enemy was reinforced by several more cruisers. A series of actions developed in which the Exeter was damaged and two Allied destroyers and two cruisers sunk. An enemy cruiser was sunk, one probably sunk and one damaged and three enemy destroyers were seriously damaged.

H.M.S. Exeter returned to Surabaya. There was no time for proper repairs to her damaged boiler-room, and on February 28 she sailed at dark with six of her eight boilers out of action. She was accompanied by H.M.S. Encounter and U.S.S. Pope. At the time it was known that very powerful Japanese naval forces were in or near the Java Sea, but it was hoped to avoid them.

At first H.M.S. Exeter could only limp along at 15 knots, but superb work by the engineering staff got two more boilers going and speed was increased at midnight to 23 knots. During the night the Exeter and her little company met an enemy force but managed to elude it. In the morning another enemy force was seen, and the Exeter doubled in her tracks, hoping she had not been seen. But two enemy cruisers began to bear down on the already crippled cruiser and her two destroyers. A little later a large enemy destroyer appeared ahead and almost immediately afterwards two other cruisers and more destroyers came into view.

All Power on the Ship Failed

The engineering staff at the last minute managed to repair one more boiler, and at 26 knots Exeter, with the two destroyers in station either side of her, steamed into action. She had only 20 per cent of her main armament ammunition remaining after the previous battle. The fight began at 09.35. The destroyers tried to ward the enemy off by firing torpedoes and to screen the Exeter by making smoke. One enemy cruiser was hit by torpedoes from the U.S.S. Pope. Several other ships were hit by gunfire from all three Allied vessels. But the end was not far off. As Captain Gordon reported, "A review of the situation at about 11.00 was not encouraging."

At 11.20 the Exeter received a vital hit in "A" boiler room. Main engines stopped and all power on the ship failed. She was being straddled and hit by the enemy cruisers now, and orders were given to sink her and abandon ship. She sank at about 11.50. Shortly afterwards H.M.S. Encounter was also sunk. U.S.S. Pope remained at hand to the end, and then managed to escape in a rain squall, only to be sunk an hour later following an attack by Japanese bombers.

RADAR REPORTED 'INVADERS' NEAR—THEY WERE GEESE!

On a dark November night in 1941, invasion alarms and sirens sounded along the Norfolk coast between Yarmouth and Sheringham as radar sets reported approaching enemy ships and planes. But the crews of our patrol vessels and defence guns heard only the honk of flocks of geese on their way to the feeding grounds in the Humber Estuary. It was a false alarm. As told in The Daily Express in November 1945, the geese had reflected the radar beams, and to operators watching the tell-tale screens they seemed like ships and planes.

Later, flocks of gannets and starlings caused several E-boat scares. By 1943, with the introduction of higher-powered transmitters, bird echoes became a menace to our radar operations. At long range the echo from a bird flying full in the radar beam can be as strong as a ship's echo. So Major J. A. Ramsay, of the Coast and A.A. Experimental Establishment, began experiments. He suspended dead gulls from captive balloons. Radar operators soon learned to distinguish birds from aircraft or ships.

Now, in America, scientists are planning to use radar for the study of bird migration. A special set is being built on a mountain in West Virginia. It was on an R.A.F. radar set that the longest timed track of a bird so far was made. A pink-footed goose was plotted for 57 miles flying at 35 miles an hour.

Roger Keyes: The Passing of a Great Sailor

Admiral of the Fleet Lord Keyes, G.C.B., K.C.V.O., C.M.G., D.S.O., a great fighting leader, died peacefully in his sleep at his home in Buckingham, at the age of 73, on Dec. 26, 1945. After the funeral service at Westminster Abbey he was buried at Dover Cemetery, on Jan. 4, 1946. The following appreciation of this national hero was specially written for "The War Illustrated" by a personal friend of the late Admiral—Major KENNETH HARE-SCOTT.

SON of a distinguished soldier (a general who was twice recommended for the V.C.) Roger Keyes joined the Royal Navy as a cadet in 1885. His first taste of active service was in the Boxer rebellion in China in 1900, when he displayed exceptional courage in defiance of great danger, winning him promotion to Commander at the age of 28. The fighting was not confined to naval engagements, but included shore raids, providing Keyes with experience in the conception and execution of amphibious operations which, with Combined Operations of later years, were to characterize so many of his greater actions.

To Roger Keyes life was full of adventure—rattling through the midst of a hostile Chinese army, on a solitary railway engine and with the driver at the point of his revolver, to bear a vital message to his admiral; diving into a fast-flowing river in China to rescue a brother-officer; seeing for himself the performance of Naval aircraft in the Mediterranean when he was C.-in-C., not from the bridge of his ship but from a plane—which, incidentally, crashed into the sea and nearly cost him his life.

His name will for ever be associated with one of the most spirited actions of the First Great War—the storming of the mole at Zeebrugge in 1918. Early in that war he had actively directed at sea Britain's submarine warfare, with conspicuous success.

Only One Parallel in History

In 1915, as Chief of Staff in the Dardanelles, he was principal author of a plan for the naval penetration of the Straits. This was rejected by the Admiralty, greatly to Keyes' disappointment, although it won the support of Winston Churchill and strengthened the lifelong friendship of these two great fighters. After a period as Director of Plans at the Admiralty, Keyes (now Rear-Admiral) was appointed to the Dover Command, a vital responsibility in our Naval strategy.

His active patrolling of the Straits culminated in his glorious leadership of the St. George's Day (April 23) attack on Zeebrugge. His signal "St. George for England!" (to which Capt. A. F. B. Carpenter, V.C., of H.M.S. Vindictive, replied, "May we give the dragon's tail a damned good twist!") has only one parallel in history—Nelson's Trafalgar signal; and the result of the action, the temporary blocking of one of the principal enemy submarine bases, had a heartening effect upon the Allied land forces who were then so sorely pressed.

KEYES commanded the Battle Cruiser Squadron from 1919 to 1921, when he became Vice-Admiral. Then followed periods as Commander-in-Chief in the Mediterranean (1925) and at Portsmouth, where he was promoted Admiral of the Fleet in 1930. In the early thirties Keyes shared the anxiety of many in the Services and throughout the country at the crippling effects of the London Naval Treaty upon Britain's security. As an active sailor he could not criticize, and so, in 1934, he chose another course and entered Parliament as Member for North Portsmouth. Although no great orator, he strengthened the small band of M.P.s (one of them being Winston Churchill) who at every opportunity voiced their condemnation of disarmament and appeasement in the face of growing peril.

On the outbreak of the Second Great War he strained at the leash for some form of active employment—which came to him in May 1940, when he was attached to King Leopold of the Belgians as Liaison Officer between the King and our Government. With the fall of Belgium (May 27) he returned to England, contesting strongly the criticism of King Leopold's conduct throughout our national press. I have a letter written immediately after his return in which he states that when the full facts of the King's loyalty are revealed, the King's name will stand as high in public estimation as that of his father King Albert. He also described the remarkable courage of the Belgian Queen Mother, Queen Elizabeth. When I saw Keyes recently—just before his death—he was still hopeful of vindicating the name of King Leopold.

Admiral of the Fleet BARON KEYES of Zeebrugge and of Dover, G.C.B., K.C.V.O., C.M.G., D.S.O. *Photo, Karsh, Ottawa*

A month before going to Belgium, Keyes had vigorously backed a plan for the combined Naval and Military occupation of Trondheim, a possible base for sustaining an Allied Expeditionary Force in Norway. The plan was only partially carried out, in an attempt by ground forces to capture Trondheim, for German Naval craft in the fjord, which could so easily have been eliminated by Naval bombardment, dislocated the attack and finally German superiority in the air terminated the fruitless effort (see pages 526-527, Vol. 2).

Keyes, who had volunteered himself to lead—in any old battleship that could be spared—a Naval attack in support of the land operations, was furious that what he regarded as timidity on the part of the powers-that-be should have reduced a potentially successful plan to create a serious distraction for Hitler in Norway to another withdrawal.

CHAMBERLAIN went, and Churchill assumed direction of our besieged island (May 10). Keyes was appointed, in July, first Director of Combined Operations, and although in the fifteen months of his holding the office only one major raid, that on the Lofoten Islands (March 4, 1941), was permitted in home waters, he laid the foundations upon which our Airborne Army and Commandos were built to a degree of perfection unequalled in the world. One of his proudest memories of his days in creating the striking force which was to deal a mortal blow to Hitler's defences was the association of his son, Geoffrey, with the best and bravest of our fighting men (portrait in page 257, Vol. 5). Geoffrey Keyes had, as a Commando, won a Military Cross in forcing the crossing of the Litani River in Syria (June 11, 1941) when fighting with the Australians.

My last letter from Roger Keyes contained a copy of a tribute to Geoffrey which he had just received from an Australian corporal, who enclosed a photograph he had treasured for some years. The corporal wrote, "I never at any time looked upon the photo as a souvenir, but with a sense of awe and thankfulness that I belonged to an Empire which breeds such men as he and those he commanded." The story of Geoffrey Keyes' raid on Rommel's Headquarters in North Africa in November 1941 is well known. His courage, not only in leading personally a mission with the most slender hopes of survival, but in calmly planning the attack in such a way as to ensure success regardless of fatal consequences, won him a posthumous V.C. and a remarkable tribute from the man against whose life he had plotted.

His Last Naval Battle off Leyte

At Geoffrey's funeral, Rommel is reported to have laid his own Iron Cross on the body of the hero. Roger Keyes valued his son's Victoria Cross more than all the treasured possessions gathered in his own lifetime, and when I last visited him the decoration lay in a case beside Geoffrey's M.C., with the Admiral's own many decorations swept to one side. Hanging on the wall was a full-length oil painting of his son, which his brother officers in the Commandos had presented to a proud father and mother.

RAISED to the peerage in 1943 as first Baron Keyes of Zeebrugge and of Dover, Keyes, who had handed over the post of Chief of Combined Operations (as it was now designated) to Lord Louis Mountbatten, devoted himself to a series of fighting speeches, until the summer of 1944, when he flew with Lady Keyes to Australia and New Zealand, and in October witnessed his last Naval battle—off Leyte, in the Pacific. Here he accompanied one of the ships of the American amphibious command in an action which he described as "a most daring and enterprising effort 1,500 miles beyond any shore-based air cover—about 1,000 vessels landing a large force well within reach of powerful enemy air forces and Naval squadrons, but having cover of between 2,000 and 3,000 *seaborne* Naval aircraft."

He went on to say, "I was very unlucky. During a heavy Jap air attack a cruiser was torpedoed close to us, and my Admiral threw up a terrific smoke-screen, some of which was toxic. It knocked me out, and nearly everyone on the upper deck. We were badly gassed, and I was very sick for three or four days. I was warned not to fly high without oxygen, as it strained my heart a bit. I flew back over New Guinea, 15,000 feet, with oxygen, with no ill-effects. But while flying in an old boat across the Tasman Sea, with no oxygen on board, the pilot went up to 13,000 feet, with the result that I had to lay up in Australia. They told me that I would have to come back in a hospital ship, but I got well so quickly we flew home in five flying days."

It is sad indeed that one with so much energy and zest for life should so suddenly become broken in health by these experiences. But I do not think that for any consideration would Roger Keyes have missed being in that last great naval engagement of the Second Great War.

Cockle Commandos of the Royal Marines

SPECIALLY trained Royal Marine volunteers who paddled in two-man canoes—code name "cockle"—fifty miles up the Gironde River to sink enemy shipping at Bordeaux, accomplished what is officially described as one of the most daring "individual" attacks of the War. Using limpet mines, they attacked six ships suspected of being blockade runners. At least three, probably five, of the ships were holed. Ten Marines, in five cockles, were launched at night from H.M. Submarine Tuna at the entrance to the Gironde, on December 7, 1942, when Germany held the whole of the French coastline.

The crew of one cockle only—Maj. H. G. Haslar, O.B.E. (Force Commander) and Mne. W. E. Sparks—came back; of the rest of the party Mne. Moffat was drowned and Lt. Mackinnon, Sgt. Wallace, Cpl. Laver, and Mnes. Mills, Conway and Ewart—who attempted to escape into Spain—were arrested and shot on March 23, 1943, by decree of Hitler. The two cockles that reached their objective covered 91 miles in five nights, their crews hiding on land by day. On the first night of this heroic exploit, the cockles Catfish, Coalfish, Conger, Cuttlefish and Crayfish were launched in calm weather from the Tuna in the manner shown above. For 1½ hours they paddled, then ran into a tide-race. Coalfish was lost, leaving no trace. Shortly afterwards, in another tide-race, Conger capsized; the crew were towed in life-jackets inshore and left to land.

IN negotiating a narrow passage between anchored vessels and the mole at Le Verdon, Cuttlefish lost formation and was not seen again. The remaining two cockles beached at daylight on a small sandy promontory, and the crews concealed them. Shortly afterwards, a number of French fishermen landed from small boats and, joined by women from the shore, made breakfast on the beach. Further concealment being impossible, Major Haslar spoke to them and, fortunately, found them friendly.

On the second night, the cockles were manhandled across three-quarters of a mile of sand and mud for launching, impeded by outlying sandbanks, and water freezing on the cockpit covers. They hid-up in a field during the day, and early on the third night a start was made to catch the flood tide. Under way again, they took cover among thick reeds inshore as the channel narrowed. When they landed they found an A.A. battery only fifty yards away and were not able to discover another suitable spot until 7.30 a.m. Again they were compelled to lie up, in a field of long grass, all day, unnoticed by a man and a dog who passed within 100 yards.

On the fourth night, the craft reached a pontoon pier opposite the South Basin at Bordeaux and, passing it safely, found a gap in some reeds through which they could force their way. Daylight revealed two good-sized cargo ships lying alongside, immediately opposite, about 800 yards away. The crews spent the evening in setting fuses to their limpet mines. In the darkness of the fifth night, Catfish safely passed the entrance to the basins on the west bank of the river, in spite of lights on the lock gates. Eight mines were planted by her crew—three on a cargo ship of 7,000 tons, two on the engine room of a small transport, one on the stern of a tanker.

WHILE turning near the transport to go downstream, Catfish was seen by the sentry on deck, who shone his torch on her. Major Haslar succeeded in pulling the cockle into the shelter of the ship and let her drift silently with the tide. The sentry, puzzled, followed the Catfish with his torch until it passed from his sight. Meanwhile, Crayfish had reached the east bank at Bordeaux without finding any targets, so returned to deal with the two cargo ships lying near the South Basin. Five mines were placed on the larger ship, three on the smaller. The mission accomplished, both cockles sped away downstream. At 6.0 a.m. they separated, and ran ashore about a quarter-mile apart. Crayfish vanished; nothing more was heard of her or her crew. Major Haslar and Marine Sparks, of Catfish, returned safely to England, and Major Haslar was awarded the D.S.O. and Marine Sparks the D.S.M., on Sept. 28, 1943.

Specially drawn for THE WAR ILLUSTRATED *by S. Harrop*

In the Salle d'Entrée at St. James's Palace—

At a State banquet on January 9, 1946, His Majesty welcomed guests from 51 nations—delegates to the General Assembly of the United Nations Organization. The King said, " It gives me particular pleasure that the first meeting of this great Assembly should be held in London . . . You will carry on your deliberations within sight of our Parliament of Westminster . . . . It is in your hands to make or mar the happiness of millions of your fellowmen, and of millions yet unborn."

—H.M. The King Entertains Delegates to U.N.O.

In the Service uniform of an Admiral of the Fleet, His Majesty (on right of fireplace) has on his right Dr. Eduardo Zuleta Angel (Colombia), Lord Jowitt (the Lord Chancellor), Senhor de Souza-Dantas (Brazil), Mr. Peter Fraser (Prime Minister of New Zealand). On his left, M. Spaak (Belgium), Mr. Attlee (the Prime Minister), Mr. Byrnes (U.S. Secretary of State), Mr. Greenwood (Lord Privy Seal), Dr. Wellington Koo (Chinese Ambassador). See also illus. pages 532, 629, 639.

With White Ensign Still Flying H.M.S. Exeter Goes Down

Drawn by C. E. Turner. By courtesy of The Illustrated London News

Already battle-damaged and with only a fifth of her main armament ammunition left, the cruiser Exeter, of Battle of the Plate fame, engaged in her last fight most sorely handicapped (see page 621). On March 1, 1942, off the coast of Java, the end came. Her main engines stopped by a hit, there was danger of her being captured, and as salvos from the Japanese ships poured into her the order was given to sink and abandon ship. This impression of the cruiser's last moments is based on a sketch and account by Commander Drake, who had served in the Exeter for three years previously. "To sink her," he has written, "after all those years endeavouring to keep the seawater out of her went very much against the grain . . . She was certainly lucky to have come through so much previous bombing without a hit." In the last moments Exeter rolled over amidst bursting shells from 8-in. guns of Japanese cruisers (two of which are seen astern) and from 5-in. guns of destroyers, while survivors watched from Carley floats and rafts.

The Best of "Yank"

A Review by HAMILTON FYFE

Never before has there been such an output of soldier and sailor journalism as there was during the latter years of the Second Great War. I don't mean journalism *for* soldiers and sailors but papers and magazines produced *by* them for the amusement of each other. These have contained a vast amount of good writing, humorous writing, savagely satirical writing, verse of varied quality and illustrations that reveal an immense store of talent with pen and pencil. While the War did not stimulate professional authors to any efforts much beyond the ordinary (although many war reporters gave us books of rare merit), it released in large numbers of fighting men some gift of expression that had not been brought to the surface before.

This is exemplified in a recently-published American anthology, The Best from Yank (World Publishing Co., Cleveland, Ohio, U.S.A., $3.50). The American army life described in these stories, photographs and drawings, covers the period of the War between the summer of 1942 (when Yank, the Army Weekly, began publication) and the autumn of 1944; geographically it covers almost every part of the world where U.S. soldiers were stationed, both combat and non-combat areas.

How National 'Fancies' Differ

The material in the book comes from two sources: from Yank's own soldier staff correspondents (many of them experienced writers and artists in peacetime) and from enlisted men all over the world. As the editors say in their introduction to the volume: "Yank depends heavily on the unsolicited contributions it receives from the riflemen, mechanics, truck-drivers, message centre clerks, radio operators, supply sergeants, military policemen . . who spent their valuable and limited free time writing or making sketches for their army weekly, and received no reward for their efforts except the dubious pleasure of seeing their stuff in print . . . Most of the cartoons and all the fiction and poetry in this book came from such contributors."

It has interested me to study the differences between the journals produced by men belonging to different branches of the English-speaking nations. The British (I mean those born in Britain) alternate between gravity and a brand of unsmiling humour which can almost be called "dour" or "pawky," to use words that are usually applied to Scots wit. The Canadians are mostly inclined to be serious, though they break out now and then into fun of the knockabout order. The Australians go to the other extreme and are wildly comic in mockery and exaggeration. The Americans (as shown in the Yank anthology) go in for a good deal of straight description mixed with cynical, slightly acid humour, such as the meditations of a private in a training camp on Christmas Day far from home.

He recalls the late hour at which he used to finish his work in a grocery store on Christmas Eve; he is thankful not to be working there now. He wakes fresh and rested—instead of being still weary from a long, hard day, with a few drinks at the end of it, arguments with his father and mother as to where to put the Christmas tree, and hunting-out, in the attic, the bulbs and trimmings for the tree. He has a leisurely breakfast, frying his eggs and bacon and remembering how "his mother used to chase him out of the kitchen because he was in her way while she was fixing the turkey." He enjoys later on "a fine big turkey dinner with beer and cigars," and without being annoyed by badly-behaved children or by aunts who "put on crying acts" because Christmas reminds them of their poor dead relatives. It was, "all in all, the merriest Christmas he had ever experienced."

Another entertaining piece is a fashion article by Corporal Hyman Goldberg who investigated how the Fifth-avenue dress designers are "placing all the emphasis on sex," as a newspaper dress expert put it. He saw all sorts of fur coats, "made of high-class animals like mink (in the wild and bottle-fed state), leopards and Persian lambs. A little way off Fifth-avenue I am told it is possible to get less costly furs such as alley cat and Shetland ponies." But the Avenue prices run from £400 up.

Mr. Goldberg also learned that Fifth-avenue regards it as essential that "women should wear one dress in the morning, another in the late afternoon, and still another dress for dinner. And any woman who doesn't, she's a dope." If that were to be called "revolutionary propaganda," the customers of those shops in New York would look genuinely astonished. But that is the sort of thing that prepared the way for the French Revolution 150 years ago, and it is one of the chief causes of the strikes for higher wages that now threaten to paralyse American industry.

With a more sentimental note in them, Pte. John Behm's verses "A Stranger and Alone" seem to me to touch the springs of sympathy. He pictures the arrival of American troops in Britain:

> The slim, coloured boys send our heavy trucks
> Screaming along your narrow roads.
> The big tanks rip up the pavings
> Of your ancient towns . . .
> The countryside rings
> With the blare and whirl of our machines.
>
> We are loud and fast and wild and lusty.
> We are drunken, proud, hard and potent.
> We could drink your island dry if you would let us.
> We are, I'm afraid,
> Just a trifle bestial
> For your highly tempered tastes.

But, he goes on, England must try to understand us.

> Though we sneer and boast in the pubs,
> Consuming your beer and belittling your glory,
> We tremble and are afraid in the streets
> Behind the blind audience of closed doors.
> We are young men whose roots
> Have been left far behind.
> We are bewildered and weary,
> Lonely to the point of madness . . .
> We are looking for a way to go home.

That, to my mind, is the real stuff of poetry—emotional and rhythmic. It rings tragically true. But tragically false seems to me the tale which won the Yank short story competition for Pte. Joseph Dever. A soldier returns to find that his girl has become a nun. He visits the convent where she is known, not any longer as Jane but as Sister Felicitas. She has asked him to go; she is glad to see him. She "squeezes both his hands until they sting." Her dress consists of "endless and oppressive reams of black cloth, with a tremendous white starched collar and a black veil over her head." They sit on "straight-backed wooden chairs, cold, unyielding symbols of poverty, chastity, obedience." Then they go into the chapel, they both kneel and pray; then he goes out, leaving her there. I call that a dreary little anecdote. I strongly suspect the author of being in holy orders. It is well written all the same, and it throws light on one aspect of American life.

Many other aspects are glanced at in the letters which serving men sent to their paper. One most instructive correspondence raged over an objection raised by a member of a Women's Club Federation in Texas to inviting soldiers to homes where there were young girls. The writer protested against the appeal to the women of Texas "to place their daughters on the altar of sacrifice to the evil that will come." She asked mothers to consider that they would be responsible for the virtue of many girls who would lose their purity." And she went on:

> We just can't do this. Do not let us sell our daughters to such a racket. Maybe a few would meet life companions, but think of the misery and sorrow and sin we would be leading the numberless ones into.

A meeting had been held in the district where the writer lived, and "the decision almost wholly was that we fathers and mothers will not stand for this." It was felt that "the class of boys whom the girls would meet were the ones who deliberately wanted to meet strange girls, and they were not the best class. Many were filled with uncontrolled passion and lust, and many were married."

A Black Corporal Wants to Know

This aroused fury. One reply stigmatized the letter as "the most disgusting piece of writing I ever had the misfortune to read." Another accused the writer of being undemocratic. A third blamed her "nasty inconsiderate attitude," and added: "Any girl that has to have a chaperon along on a date to remain pure and clean is not the type of girl that a soldier would like to be seen in public with." A sergeant, however, writing from Attu in the Aleutians, said, "we want our gals as we left them and we don't want them on the altar of sacrifice."

Another storm of correspondence was provoked by a letter from a black corporal who described an incident at a railway station in Louisiana. A number of coloured men in uniform had to change trains there and were not allowed into any of the lunch-rooms in the town. They went at last into the refreshment room at the station to buy cups of coffee, but even there were only permitted to sit in the kitchen. And that was not all.

> About two dozen German prisoners of war with two American guards came to the station. They entered the lunch-room, sat at the tables, had their meals served, talked, smoked, in fact had quite a swell time. I stood on the outside, looking in, and I could not help but ask myself—what is the Negro soldier fighting for?

Why were Germans—enemies of the United States, taught to hate and destroy all democratic governments—treated better than American soldiers? Why did the Government allow such things to go on?

This time the comments were unanimous in condemning the raw deal of which the coloured soldiers complained. A Southerner called it "a disgrace to a democratic nation such as ours is supposed to be" and wondered "what the 'Aryan Supermen,' thought when they got this first-hand glance at our racial discrimination." A group of men wrote from Burma saying "the Negro outfits were doing more than their part to win the war in the jungles" and thought it a disgrace that "while we are away from home doing our part to help, some people back home are knocking down everything that we are fighting for." A staff-sergeant inquired, "Has it occurred to anyone that those Boche prisoners of war must be still laughing at us?"

In both these instances Yank showed commendable courage in printing letters of protest. Far better drag such topics out into the open instead of trying to hide them. Publication of the Negro corporal's letter in Yank led to its being widely quoted in the Press; the incident was also dramatized on the radio and made the basis of a short story.

R.A.F. Returns her Aluminium to the Housewife

FIVE YEARS AFTER BRITAIN'S APPEAL to housewives to surrender their saucepans for conversion into aircraft parts (see page 384, Vol. 3), aircraft parts were being reconverted into saucepans. At a London factory in January 1946 a 30-cwt. tilting furnace (1) was being used for melting down R.A.F. airscrews. Ingots, remelted, are being poured into moulds (2) from which the finished lids (3) are removed. This polisher (4) wears a protective mask. Pans are carefully scrutinized (5) before being assembled (6).

Britain's Premier Welcomes the United Nations

BENEATH THE GOLD INSIGNIA OF THE UNITED NATIONS, Mr. Clement Attlee delivered the inaugural speech in Central Hall, Westminster, at the first plenary meeting on January 10, 1946, of the General Assembly of the United Nations Organization. Behind the Premier sat Dr. E. Zuleta Angel (Colombia), acting Chairman, with Mr. H. M. G. Jebb, Executive Secretary of the Preparatory Commission, on his right, and Mr. A. Cordier, Chief of the General Assembly section of the U.N. Secretariat, on his left. See also illus. pages 624-625, 639. *Photo, Planet News*

Allied Front-Line Planes That Flew Unarmed

AIR-SEA RESCUE services were busier during the Arnhem operation than on D-Day, and no fewer than 181 airborne troops were then rescued from wrecked Hamilcar and Horsa gliders. In the Mediterranean zone, A.S.R. rescued 1,114 American airmen. The highlight of this service was the tale of Sergeant Cohen, who landed his Fairey Swordfish on Lampedusa during a heavy Allied air bombardment, ordering the Italian garrison to refuel his tanks, and then taking off to report the island's surrender.

These and other stories of the Air-Sea Rescue service are told in Volume 6 of Aircraft of the Fighting Powers (Harborough Publishing Co., Ltd., 31s. 6d. net) which continues the description, with many photographs and scale drawings, of the aircraft used by all nations who fought in the Second Great War. The complexity of this task is indicated by the announcement that this valuable air-war reference book cannot be completed until December 1946, when Volume 7 will appear with details of hitherto secret aircraft.

THE current volume gives particulars of 26 British, 22 American, 15 Japanese, and nine German aircraft. Of special interest to the ordinary reader is the historical section accompanying the description of each aircraft.

Those who have seen that fine British war film, Burma Victory, will pause at pages 48–49, depicting the Sentinel light aeroplane which the film showed operating over and amid the Burmese jungle. This "Grasshopper" class of light liaison aircraft came into service with the U.S A.A.F. in 1941. About a dozen types of high-wing monoplanes (all much like our own Auster) were produced. Eventually, two were selected for basic production. These were the Piper Cub and the Stinson Sentinel, known respectively as the L-4 or L-14, and the L-5, the letter "L" standing for "liaison" (illustrations in this page).

Nicknamed "Jungle Angels," unarmed Sentinel ambulances (L-5Bs) of the Allied Eastern Air Command carried out food and blood plasma, mail, messages, ammunition and medical supplies, and brought back sick and wounded. They acted as artillery spotters, observed Japanese troop movements, became "flying jeeps" for staff officers and technicians between bases and fronts. They rescued aircraft crews and salvaged valuable equipment—guns, instruments, and radio—from jungle-wrecked aircraft. At night, headlamps of jeeps illuminated jungle airstrips for liaison pilots to fly in and off.

Such feats by light aeroplanes fitted with six-cylinder, air-cooled engines of 175 h.p. seem remarkable until we recall that most of the fighting and reconnaissance of the First Great War was carried out in aircraft of about equal or even lower power and lighter weight. This leads to the realization that the lordly monarchs of the skies, with 2,000-plus h.p. motors, and landing speeds of plus-100 m.p.h., also illustrated in Volume 6 of Aircraft of the Fighting Powers, cannot do everything in the air, either in war or peace, and that the light aeroplane, like the family car, will have its place in the flying world.

NORMAN MACMILLAN

PIPER CUB, U.S. MARINE OBSERVATION PLANE, flew in low over Naha, Okinawa's capital, before the American landings in April 1945. Known officially as the L-4 or L-14, a three-seat light monoplane powered with a single 75 h.p. four-cylinder air-cooled engine, its wing-span is 35 ft., length 22 ft. 6 in. Maximum speed, 95 m.p.h., range 320 miles. *Photo, U.S. Official*

FROM A L-5 AMBULANCE MONOPLANE IN BURMA a walking West African casualty is being helped to hospital. These U.S. mercy-service aircraft flew wounded from front line to casualty clearing-station, normally saving many days' road journey—and thousands of lives. Unarmed, with a speed of 120 m.p.h. and powered by a single 175 h.p. six-cylinder engine, they carried food, ammunition, medical supplies on the outward trip, also acted as artillery spotters in Burma and, later, in Italy and on the Western Front. *Photo, British Official*

Awaiting Transformation to Peacetime Needs

GIGANTIC SALVAGE TASKS confronted the U.S.A.A.F. in late 1945 with the breaking-up for scrap of unwanted or unserviceable aircraft from various theatres of war. At Walnut Ridge, Arkansas (top), hundreds of B-17 four-engined bombers, lined up in take-off formation, were earmarked as scrap-metal for home industries. On Guam, U.S. base in the Marianas from which Tokyo was bombed, wreckage of Super-Fortresses and naval torpedo bombers (below) awaited the same use. See also pages 426–427. *Photos, Associated Press, New York Times Photos*

Hitler Hoped to Bomb New York by Rocket

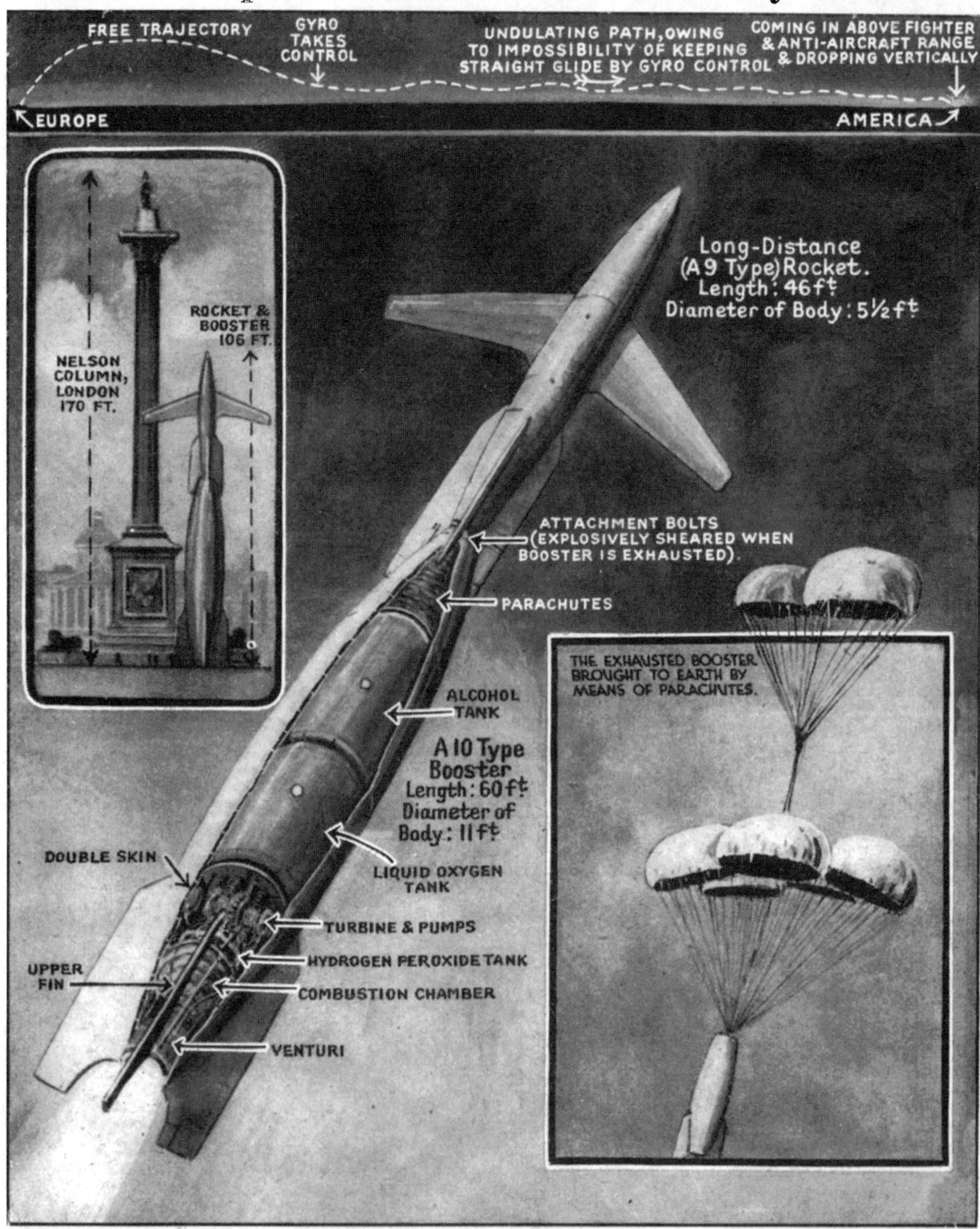

NAZI PLANS TO ROCKET-BOMB AMERICA were described to the Royal Aeronautical Society in December 1945 by Mr. W. G. A. Perring, F.R.Ae.S., of the Royal Aircraft Establishment, Farnborough, Hants. From the V2 (called in Germany the A4), with average range of 180-190 miles and total time of flight of five minutes, the Germans had begun, by the end of the War, to develop rockets with wings, whose take-off was assisted by "boosters." These projected long-range winged rockets were called A9, and their boosters A10. Intended to be hurtled across the Atlantic, the method envisaged was to control their undulating glide from a great height by means of gyroscopic instruments and for their exhausted boosters to be brought to earth, on fulfilling their function, by means of parachutes. The speed of such a rocket would be enormous. Flung from its discharge point to a height of some 200 miles, it would describe a curve and fall at a speed of something like 3,000 m.p.h. When—in its downward trajectory—it reached a point about 30 miles above the earth, the gyroscope would come into operation, pulling up the nose and putting the missile into its long glide across the Atlantic till, coming in well above fighter aircraft and A.A. range, it would drop vertically on its target. The development of winged rockets with human control, which could fly from Europe to the U.S. in three-quarters of an hour, is no mere Wellsian fancy but a forecast based on cold, scientific facts. Nearing its destination, the pilot would jettison the rocket's pointed nose, sight his landing-ground, lower his under-carriage, and touch down at approximately 80 m.p.h. Travelling beyond the effective pull of gravity during part of his voyage, the pilot—if unprotected—would at such time have no "weight" and would float inside his cabin. To obviate this, he would be obliged to wear an anti-pressure suit and be strapped prone.

 Drawn by G. H. Davis, By courtesy of The Illustrated London News

I Was There!

Eye Witness Stories of the War and After

Our Welcome Home to Nazi-Ravaged Alderney

The first hundred men and women returned in December 1945 to the Channel Island home they had left in June 1940. David Bernard, who accompanied them, likens the Alderney of today to "a lovely garden that had been ravaged by swine." His story is from The Evening Standard.

ALDERNEY lies 26 miles west of Cherbourg; it is a small island—3½ miles long by 1½ miles broad. It has many drawbacks. The sea passage is as rough as you'll find anywhere around these coasts. There are few trees, dangerous cliffs, no theatres, and morning papers only a few days a week. But in spite of this, or perhaps because of it, life there in the days before the war was extraordinarily pleasant.

There were enough inns, and whisky was 6s. a bottle, a cinema show twice a week and a dance on Saturdays, wherever you walked you were always in sight of the sea, there was a great friendliness among the islanders, they lent their horses, labour and machinery to each other for ploughing or harvesting, without expecting anything in return. That was Alderney in 1939.

The Alderney that we returned to a few days ago was like a lovely garden that had been ravaged by swine. From the ship, heaving in the race that runs round the island, it looked almost the same. The church tower stood out on the skyline, but there were new landmarks—high, black, ugly watch-towers broke the smooth, curved, silhouette of the cliffs, we could see gun-emplacements, trenches, hutted camps.

WHEN we docked we could see a huge sign, "Welcome Home," in white letters on a red background hanging on the ruin of what used to be the building that housed a stone-crushing machine. There was the usual civic reception that marks such occasions, and a band played. No one paid much attention to either. The women made their way to their houses; the men, up the hill to the plateau and their land.

Out of the 514 houses on the island, 100 are uninhabitable; most of the others had been stripped by the Germans of woodwork, doors, window-frames and floors. When our troops landed seven months ago it was almost decided to abandon the island as unfit for occupation; but the people were so eager to return that a start was made to clear up the filth and ruin of houses and fields. Even now, after the great work that has been done, most families will be living in the one room of each house that has been sufficiently repaired.

The small holdings have been pooled to form one collective farm. So have the cattle imported by the Germans—the Alderney herd was sent to Guernsey when the island was evacuated. Gradually they are being brought back. The farmers of Alderney have a passion that amounts almost to fanaticism for the small piece of rich land that has been handed down through generations.

In the chill wind of the morning when they got back, I saw them walking over what is now a 100-acre field, looking for the square stones that used to mark the holdings. But the stones have gone, and so has the independence of the farmers. They will work as labourers on the communal farm at £3 a week until the island is on its feet again.

Perhaps it is a good thing—probably the land will be farmed more scientifically, the cows will be milked by electricity in one dairy, and no doubt the profits will be greater. But, according to the men I spoke to, men who have worked hard all their lives, but have lived a full life in the true sense, this does not weigh much against working for no master and the personal pride of one's own soil. Backward? In a way; yet these people are glad to work as a community, submerging personal interests for a time in order that they can return to the way of life they knew and liked.

AS more return—in a month 1,000 will be in Alderney—more shops will open. The tobacconist is already open, so is the butcher. The innkeepers expect the local government to renew their licences this week; stocks have been taken over by boat (whisky will cost 14s. 6d. a bottle). The rough field that served as an airfield now has three good runways, and an inter-island service starts soon.

No, the picture is by no means black. In fact, many islanders have benefited by the occupation. The harbour-master, for instance. He had a small cottage; the Germans used it as an officers' mess, enlarged it to twice the size, furnished it beautifully, and left it intact. Electricity, water and drainage systems were all improved. But the main thing is the spirit of the people in volunteering to return, and, by working together, to recreate the island.

I Met British Detectives in Khaki in Berlin

Helping to maintain law and order in the British zone of the German capital are men from Scotland Yard and pre-war C.I.D. men from our provincial towns and cities. Their methods, which are notably successful, are explained in this dispatch from Richard McMillan to The Evening Standard.

IS your idea of shattered Berlin a city seething with crime and vice and violence, a second Chicago with gangsterism rampant, and with the night a riot of murder? That is not quite the right picture. That is one of the surprises that await you when you come back to the capital again, for while it may not be a model of law and order it most certainly is not the worst in the world.

In fact, crime statistics are dropping month by month. So far as the British sector is concerned there is notable success in the battle against the underworld. It is a victory for the British police methods. Men from Scotland Yard and detectives who in peace-time served in the Criminal Investigation Department in big provincial towns, are operating today as the Army's crack sleuths here.

ALDERNEY'S GREETING TO REPATRIATED ISLANDERS who returned in December 1945, after an absence of over five years, marked one of the happiest days in the island's history. After the prolonged German occupation only the barest necessities were available, but, as told in this page, homecomers who had not seen their island since June 1940 stepped ashore to a warm welcome. The quay where they disembarked had been designed (in the days of the Nazi triumph) for the purpose of a German landing at Brighton.

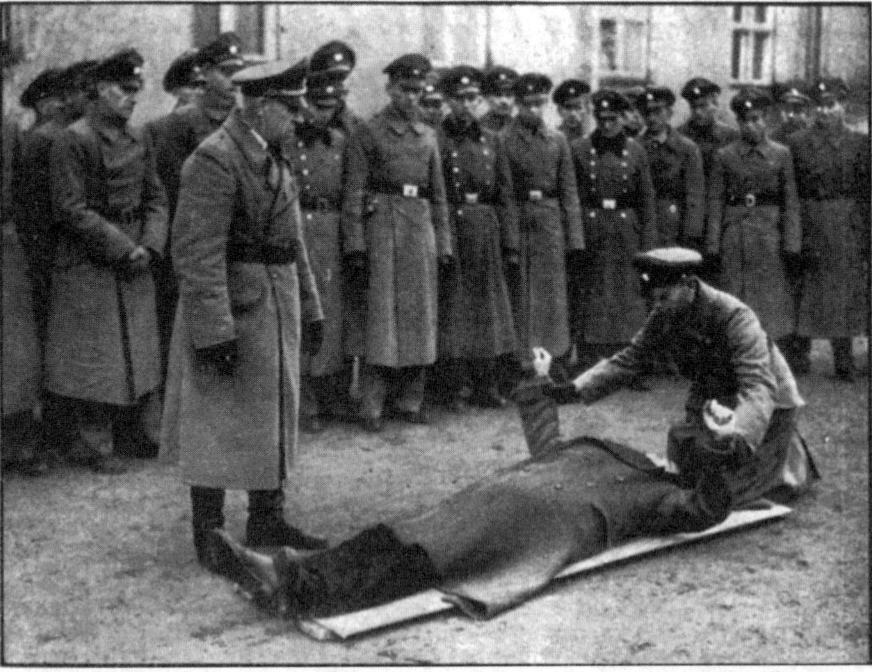

TRAINING THE NEW GERMAN POLICE is one of the important tasks of our authorities in the occupied Reich. To replenish the ranks of the de-Nazified police an increasing number of recruits are required. Suitable candidates are given a special course, including instruction in artificial respiration, here being demonstrated. *Photo, Keystone*

I met one of the chiefs of this band of British detectives in khaki—the Army's Sherlock Holmes—Colonel T. Holmes, who before he joined up was a detective-superintendent in Durham County. His job takes him into all sectors of Berlin, but principally he is concerned with helping to organize and run the German police.

As the Russians dismissed all the Nazi-tainted Berlin police, we have had to build up and train a new force. They are being trained on British lines. Our methods have been so successful in keeping the crime-wave down that the British sector is regarded as the model of police work in Berlin.

Our C.I.D. experts are teaching the Germans not only to fight murder, but blackmail, housebreaking, black market rackets and vice. Although some irresponsible elements from Allied forces, such as deserters, and roving nighthawks from among displaced people, engage occasionally in gangster-like duels this is by no means a regular thing.

Blackmail a Problem in Berlin

Colonel Holmes told me it was the custom to raid suspected houses and cafés from time to time. "That is how we are able to rope in small black market traders who traffic largely in British Army foodstuffs," he said. During such raids the German police also round up hundreds of suspected women at night clubs for interrogation.

"The murder rate is falling," added the colonel. "In November there were fifteen murders in the British sector, but in December only one. The German civilian is not the gangster type when he goes in for crime. He is more likely to be a housebreaker or robber. He knows the penalty for being caught with a pistol. But blackmail is still a problem in Berlin. Whereas it used to deal with the secrets of a person's morals, now it is usually based on a threat to betray the victim by denouncing him as a former active Nazi. We find that there is not much tendency to shield the Nazi gangs. The Berliner, in defeat, seems to hold a grudge against the Nazi leaders."

The black market in British cigarettes is decreasing. As the crime wave has died down so much, the 11 p.m. curfew has been abolished, but the midnight "off the streets" order continues in operation for American soldiers and civilians in the American zone. Berlin by night is beginning to look more gay, if there can be such a thing as gaiety among so much destruction, misery, hunger and apathy.

Lights still burn around the prisoner of war camps where the Nazi S.S. men are corralled each evening, until it is time for them to go out again in the morning to work to restore some order out of chaos. Lights blaze along the boulevards, too, as the homeless cluster around braziers to keep warm. Walking along Berlin's Piccadilly, Kurfurstendamm, at midnight, you might hear shots in the dark.

"Probably some troops having a little horseplay," a military policeman will tell you. "You know what soldiers are." Otherwise all will be quiet. Yes, Sherlock Holmes in British uniform can well be proud of a job well done in keeping down the German thug and political conspirator.

Sappers' Great Battle of the Rhine Bridges

The Corps of Royal Engineers is tackling operations which, when completed, will take a place in engineering history. Temporary structures thrown up by the Army in battle conditions are being replaced by sappers, whose manner of working was witnessed, in Dec. 1945, by H. D. Ziman, The Daily Telegraph correspondent. His account is here slightly condensed.

At Wesel a few days ago I watched the first permanent bridge across the Rhine being built over its wide waters. It was raining hard, and the rain changed to snow, but the Corps of Royal Engineers undertakes jobs which no civil contractor would attempt in winter. After dark the sappers continue by "artificial moonlight," with searchlights floodlighting their work.

Seven days a week they are putting in on Wesel Bridge. For if they have not got the bridge finished early in January, ice may sweep away the present temporary Rhine bridges and the Army of Occupation would thus be cut off from all but ferry communication with the west.

So, rain or snow, daylight or dark, the sappers are pressing on to complete a double carriageway across the Rhine. Farther up the river, at Cologne, another R.E. unit is building a similar but shorter bridge, which is to be ready later next month. These two giant bridges, involving 8,000 to 10,000 tons of concrete apiece, and roughly 2,000 tons of steel, are only a small part of the bridging on which the R.E. are engaged in this dismal region of Germany.

The bridges the Army built in a few hours in battle conditions were not meant to last more than a few months. Their design could pay no attention to the barge traffic of Continental waterways. The coal which is now piled up inaccessible at Ruhr pitheads lies there not merely because Germany's railway system is battered, but because during the battle our engineers could not pause to unblock canals or to build bridges sufficiently raised above the water-level to allow coal-barges to pass beneath them.

Before visiting Wesel I saw some of the new bridges already made and others now in their final stages. In a few instances it was possible to jack up a concrete bridge built by the Germans and put in a kind of reinforced concrete "patch" either end.

In the main, however, it has been a matter of breaking up and removing the old German bridge, building a new approach and carrying across the canal, river or road a new construction in double or triple-storey Bailey spans, with approach spans laid on steel joists.

Bailey bridges are of extremely light thin steel, and in a year or so they would rust away beyond the safety margin, but given paint and a few spanners they are not difficult to maintain, and they should last the Germans 10 or 20 years, while their foundations will stay good for permanent civilian bridging.

In general the bridging programme was completely to time before the beginning of December 1945. Sometimes two months' work was needed for a single operation; for instance, the bridging of the 110-ft. span at Hiltrup. The men who built this and many other bridges were an old Territorial unit from Kent originally trained to operate searchlights on the Medway, later used for oil demolitions at the time of Dunkirk, and in 1944 as general assault engineers. The officer in charge was a mining engineer in civil life. But searchlights, oil demolitions, tunnelling or bridge building—it is all one; the R.E. will turn their hand to anything.

One unit of three companies has cleared 20 bridges with an average span of 300 ft. from the Ruhr waterways, built the Herne bridge with 230 ft. of dual carriageway and tramways, and then turned to opening up the autobahn from Berlin to Duisburg.

Another R.E. company, having built three semi-permanent autobahn bridges, has turned to maintaining the main British traffic route into Germany, employing for the improvement of the autobahn and the supply route 13 civilian German firms. The British Pioneer Corps, which used to do much of this rough work during the campaign, has been relieved of this duty in Germany, and the sappers employ either German civilian labour or Wehrmacht parties awaiting discharge.

On the Wesel Bridge one skilled German Army steel construction company, one unskilled labour unit of the Wehrmacht and a number of German contractors with civilian labourers are employed, working under the direction of XII Corps Troops Royal Engineers, whose commanding officer is Lt.-Col. L. F. Heard, R.E.

Work started on October 1, and when finished it will probably go down in engineering history not merely as an example of rapidity of construction but as a major bridging operation carried out on entirely unorthodox lines. The bridge, 2,032 ft. long, is to carry two roadways side by side with a cycle-track between them and a foot-walk at the side.

Most of the material is standard double-storey or triple-storey Bailey, designed to get as long a span as possible, the two centre navigational spans being each 240 ft. long. It is supported on seven piers, each consisting of 70 ft. long steel tubes 22 ins. across and filled with reinforced concrete. The central pier contains a trestle of 24 of these tubes and the remaining piers 18 tubes apiece.

The designer of the bridge, Major Ralph Freeman, R.E., decided to make use in the first stages of the wooden trestle bridge built on this site by the United States Army. Above this "Roosevelt Bridge" a false or temporary Bailey 15 ft. high has been built, and above this the real bridge is to be built, with the central section run across on rollers.

Once the first main roadway is across it will be jacked slowly to one side on to the concrete bases which await it at the top of the steel trestles. Then the central spans of the second and parallel roadway will be drawn across to take the position from which the first roadway has been edged. The Army will complete in a little over three months a job which would normally take a large civil engineering contractor the best part of a year.

Meanwhile, the channel of the Rhine is clear, and I saw processions of Dutch barges being towed up and down under the half-complete new Wesel Bridge. For the present the tugs going downstream have to turn and back their barges down, but when the temporary wooden trestles are removed the passage will be less obstructed, and the battle of German coal move faster.

BAILEY BRIDGE ACROSS THE RHINE near Rees, just above the site of the assault crossings, was built by 936 Royal Engineers Port Construction and Repair Company in exactly four weeks. Work was started on April 18, 1945, and the last section swung into position on May 16. This was part of the great task of rehabilitating Germany's wrecked transport system. *Photo, British Official*

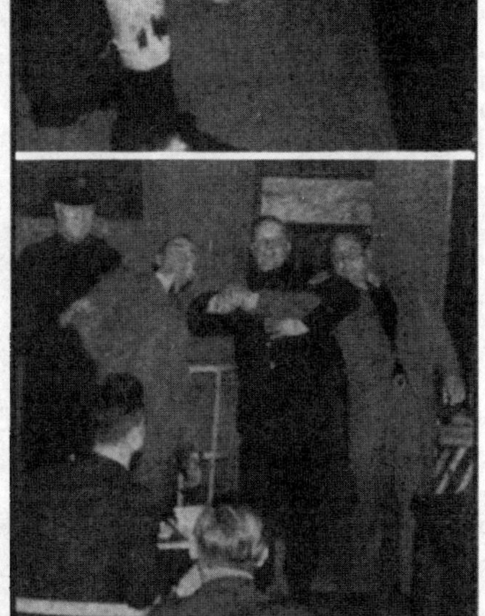

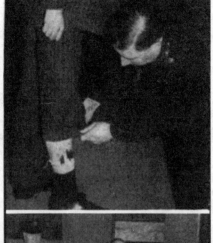

P.L.A. POLICEMEN engaged in the anti-smuggling "drive" are instructed how to search suspects (top), and (bottom) how to handle awkward offenders. *Photos, Fox*

They Teach Them All the Smugglers' Tricks

Ex-Commandos and other demobbed men are learning to be Port of London policemen—learning the multiple wiles of the modern smuggler, in order to be able to defeat him. An Evening Standard reporter looked in at their classroom, furnished with exhibits from the Port of London Authority's crime museum, and this is his story.

At the new training school within the Albert Dock, I saw the first batch of post-war recruits, 30 tall, brawny men, aged between 26 and 33, seated at their desks like schoolboys, while Divisional Inspector S. S. Cox, Director of Studies, showed them how to search a suspected smuggler, and the meaning of the peculiar collection of criminals' gadgets on the table before him. Each gadget was an exhibit in a true detective story, from the crime museum of the P.L.A. police.

There was a Chinese seaman's grubby shirt with pockets still stained with smuggled opium. And a "screw-driver" that unscrewed at the metal end and disclosed the handle as a hollow receptacle for £10 worth of cocaine. And a padlocked hinge of which the metal core on which it turned had been made removable by an upward shove of a pencil and then replaceable after the case had been robbed. Also an innocent-looking length of wood that proved when the concealed stopper in one end was removed to be bored with a tube filled with valuable essential oils, worth up to £10 an oz. It still reeked fragrantly.

Chief P.L.A. Police Officer W. H. Simmons was looking on. He praised highly the type of his recruits. Some had been commissioned officers in the Forces. All had seen rough war service in many parts of the world. He told me more of the tricks of the contraband trade they will have to get wise to.

I heard of the man with 36 pairs of stockings hung on a "line" round his chest and 12 more pairs draped round his legs. Of men whose pants tied round the ankles prove to be full of tea. Of the cases that arrived at their Bombay destination stuffed with bricks, their original content of safety razors having been stolen by black marketeers en route. Of men with rubber hot-water bottles, filled with wine or spirits, secreted in the small of their backs.

He showed me the pride of the museum—the drug chest. It contained samples of all the contraband drugs—opium, cocaine, hashish, morphia. There was a wicked-looking hashish pipe, too. The recruits will handle these dangerous drugs. Smuggling in drugs is still troublesome. Quite recently two big "stops" of opium (7 lb. and 8 lb.) were made by the P.L.A. police.

★ As The Years Went By—Notable Days in the War ★

1941

January 22. *Australians under Gen. Wavell entered Tobruk, capturing 25,000 Italians.*
January 24. *British invaded Italian Somaliland.*

1942

January 22. *Japs landed at Rabaul, New Britain.*
January 25. *Japanese landed at Lae, New Guinea.*
January 26. *U.S. troops arrived in N. Ireland.*

1943

January 23. *Eighth Army entered Tripoli.*
January 27. *U.S. heavy bombers made first raid on Germany, attacking Wilhelmshaven.*
January 31. *Field-Marshal Paulus and fifteen German generals surrendered at Stalingrad.*

1944

January 22. *Fifth Army troops landed south of Rome, near Anzio and Nettuno.*
January 27. *Leningrad completely liberated.*
January 31. *U.S. forces launched amphibious attack on Kwajalein, in the Marshall Islands.*

1945

January 19. *Lodz and Cracow taken by Red Army.*
January 23. *Russian troops reached the Oder.*
January 26. *Ardennes bulge cleared of Germans.*
January 27. *Capture of Memel by Russian troops cleared all Lithuania of Germans.*
January 28. *First convoy reached China by way of the newly-built Stilwell-Burma Highway.*

THREE OF THE WORLD'S FINEST AIRPORTS will play a part in the development of Britain's expanding air traffic. Prestwick, Ayrshire (1), has been eastern terminal for all North Atlantic flights since 1941, enjoying a reputation second to none for clear-weather conditions. From here the flight to New York is 250 miles shorter than by the more southerly routes. Mosquitoes of the R.A.F. line the well-laid-out Seletar airfield at Singapore (2), thoroughly restored since it was freed on September 5, 1945. Home terminal for the new Britain-South America service, of which the pioneer flight began on January 1, 1946 (see page 640), is at Heath Row (3), 14 miles from London. Begun in 1941 for the R.A.F., costing £25,000,000, and covering 1,500 acres, its main runway is 3,000 yards long. *No. 1 by courtesy of The Sphere*

The R.A.F. in War and Peace

By CAPTAIN NORMAN MACMILLAN M.C., A.F.C.

TODAY the R.A.F. is like a cistern, with demobilized officers and men flowing through the outlet, and volunteers and recruits directed under the National Service Act passing through the inlet. So far, no Government pronouncement has been made about the post-war strength of the R.A.F. Possibly a statement may be made when the Air Estimates are presented in March or April.

During the war years, in common with all the Services, the Air Estimates were presented as a token sum of £100. It is to be presumed that 1946 will see the first true estimate since 1939. Until the post-war strength is fixed it is impossible to form any judgement on the sufficiency of the present inlet flow into the R.A.F. compared with the fixed outlet under the demobilization scheme.

It is noticeable, however, that the R.A.F. is sending recruiting officers to country towns to interview and advise volunteers for the R.A.F. and W.A.A.F., and this leads one to suppose that without additional stimulus, the recruiting rate may be insufficient to maintain the R.A.F. at the strength required to meet current commitments throughout the world. Although bullets, rockets, cannon shells and bombs no longer engage the aircraft of the R.A.F., except on a fortunately small scale in Indonesia, the work of the Air Service is still large-scale.

R.A.F. GROUND CREW IN BATAVIA services a Thunderbolt at Kemajoran airfield, in readiness for operations against Indonesian extremists in Sourabaya—necessitated by attacks such as those of December 9, 1945, when a British convoy was ambushed, and of January 13, 1946, when a British column suffered a similar fate. *Photo, British Official*

Transport Command alone operates a large fleet of aircraft on continuous duty. There are the British Air Forces of Occupation in Germany, now commanded by a Marshal of the R.A.F. since the elevation of Sir Sholto Douglas to that rank. The other new Marshal of the R.A.F. is Sir Arthur Harris, on sick leave after treatment in Princess Mary's R.A.F. Hospital at Halton, Bucks.

During the War large numbers of Canadians entered the R.A.F. for war service. Fully half of the staff of the radar section was manned by Canadians. Some Canadians may desire to remain in the R.A.F., but many will doubtless be keen to go home. It is likely that the R.A.F. in the near future will revert to its between-the-wars personnel position of being mainly recruited from the United Kingdom. Pay increases make it a more attractive service than before.

THE demobilization position is today very different from that of 1919. Then there were only the R.A.F. and W.R.A.F to consider. The W.R.A.F. was quickly reduced in size, and on August 15, 1919, orders were issued for its total disbandment, and by March 31, 1920, the W.R.A.F. was completely demobilized. The R.A.F. was then a Service instituted in war. None of its officers had permanent R.A.F. commissions. Indeed, it was not known while the war continued if the R.A.F. had come to stay as a separate Service, and everyone connected with it knows how hard Lord Trenchard had to fight for the continuance of the R.A.F. as a separate Service, when first peacetime Chief of the Air Staff.

AUXILIARY Air Force Lost Its Distinctive Territorial Character

In consequence of the wartime status of the R.A.F. in the First Great War every officer serving in the R.A.F. had to apply for a permanent commission after the war was over if he wanted to remain in it. I well remember attending the first engineering course at Halton for permanent officers, in 1919, although I decided later to leave the R.A.F. and enter civil aviation as a test pilot. One or two officers who attended that course have done well in the R.A.F., and rose to high air rank during the recent War. In 1919 officers who did not remain in the R.A.F. permanently retired, retaining their rank, or were transferred to what was called the Unemployed List. The Unemployed List was discontinued when demobilization was complete and the permanent R.A.F. was formed. There was then no R.A.F. Reserve. In the coal strike of 1921 volunteers were called for to augment the diminutive air force, and when these volunteers returned to civil life the first Reserve of Air Force Officers was formed, which they were invited to enter. The volunteers among the other ranks were almost all N.C.O.s.; one unit had only one corporal and no aircraftmen; all the others were sergeants.

Then Lord Trenchard started his short service scheme to produce a trained reserve. It applied to commissioned and non-commissioned ranks, and gradually the regular reserve was built up behind the small regular air force. The Auxiliary Air Force began in 1925 in a small way. It grew to 16 squadrons by the beginning of the Second Great War.

About two years before the recent War began the R.A.F. Volunteer Reserve was formed, and the R.A.F. Reserve was then open only to those who had served in the regular formations. With the outbreak of the War in 1939 the R.A.F. College at Cranwell was closed, and all entrants into the air service were admitted into the Volunteer Reserve. That explains why the A.A.F. did not grow in size during the War, and why A.A.F. squadrons could not keep the distinctive territorial character which they possessed in peacetime, but after the Battle of Britain became as hybrid as any squadron of the R.A.F. with regular, reserve, auxiliary and volunteer reserve personnel serving wherever they were posted.

I believe the highest V.R. rank was reached by Air Vice-Marshal Donald C. T. Bennett, who has now returned to civil aviation and commanded Star Light on her exploratory journey from Heath Row airfield on January 1, 1946, to Buenos Aires for British South American Air Lines (see illus. page 640). Among A.A.F. members, Lord Willoughby de Broke became an Air Commodore as Air Ministry Director of Public Relations, and Whitney Straight reached the same rank.

Today it is a more straightforward matter than in 1919 to convert the wartime air force into the peacetime air force. The nucleus already exists in the full-time permanent officers and men who have survived. I have no guide to the number of pre-war regular R.A.F. who were killed in the war, but I should say that the greatest number of casualties occurred among short service, A.A.F., Reserve, and V.R. personnel, with incomparably the greatest number among V.R.s.

ESTABLISHMENT of a New R.A.F. Reserve Command With 6 Regions

In the War it was always possible to distinguish the A.A.F. by their " A " insignia. It was never possible to distinguish between the permanent, short-service, and reserve personnel by their uniform, but the V.R. section was segregated by the wearing of these initials by all ranks until an advanced period of the War. When these initials were discontinued it became impossible to tell one branch of the R.A.F. from another, with the exception of the now small A.A.F., and the medical, dental, educational and chaplain branches, who wore special insignia.

To demobilize the R.A.F. quickly it would be necessary only to disembody the R.A.F.V.R. Merely the skeleton of the wartime R.A.F. would then be left. Obviously that cannot be done, owing to Air Force requirements. Already the A.A.F. has reverted to its pre-war status, but this force was relatively so small as to have little effect upon the force required today.

Meanwhile, a new R.A.F. Reserve Command has been established with six Group regions in the United Kingdom and Northern Ireland. This will administer the A.A.F., R.A.F.V.R., and the Air Training Corps, and soon it should become possible for volunteers to enter these reserve formations of the Air Force for part-time duties, under this new organization. This indicates that the peacetime regular Air Force will comprise the staff formations of permanent and short service members and that the regular reserve created from them may be administered direct by the Air Ministry.

THE size of this regular Air Force, when fixed, will determine career prospects for those who wish to join the R.A.F. for permanent or short-term service. In that opening, together with those of the Royal Navy Air Branch, and Civil Aviation, lie the opportunities for air operational careers for the young men of today. Through the new R.A.F. Reserve Command, those who are engaged on other work in normal hours, can find the joy of part-time Air Force activity.

Elsewhere, the aircraft industry, although shrinking from its wartime size, has opportunities for the skilful and courageous among our youth.

The Editor Looks Back

FUNNY BUSINESS — Nov. 25, 1939

Indeed this war grows "curiouser and curiouser," and it certainly has many characteristics in common with the adventures of Alice. One of the curious points that I have registered was in listening last night to the broadcast of the brilliant entertainment given "somewhere in France." Even the most imperative prohibitions imposed upon editors were light-heartedly ignored by the announcer. He described a theatrical building, arranged "somewhat in the form of an opera house" with numerous boxes and tiers of seats, reaching to an imposing height and capable of containing a very large audience. And in the middle of the first row of the dress circle he informed us that Viscount Gort, the British C.-in-C., together with many others of the high command, both French and English, were seated. The whole mass of auditors being clothed in British khaki and French horizon-blue gave an extraordinary colour effect.

As I never underestimate the intelligence of our enemies any more than I should be tempted to underestimate their villainy, it struck me, on hearing this, that the information given could have left hardly any doubt as to where some German bombers might fly in order to have a rich drop of casualties with a possible chance of wiping out a large part of the High Command, for it requires no particular astuteness to guess at the locality of the building so vividly described by the very able announcer. The entertainment was first-class, however, so all was well that ended well.

THE theatre was that of Arras, as the Huns must surely have known—the compère's description of the interior was so exact—and one can only suppose they were merely codding the Anglo-French innocents by not displaying their knowledge with a few tons of bombs when Noel Coward and Maurice Chevalier and other entertainers were making fun for the crowded audience of Allied soldiers.

GERMANS OR HITLER? — Dec. 2, 1939

Thanks, Captain Balfour! Although you speak only as an Under-Secretary at present, it is a pleasure to hear one official voice that does not conform to the formula: denounce Hitler, but spare the Germans. "No Germans, no Hitler," is my answer to that. (Thanks also to Field-Marshal Lord Milne for his "plain, blunt man" speech on the same subject.) Let's admit that aggressiveness and arrogance are Prussian characteristics and we'll not be far wrong. The typical member of that square-headed, insolent-eyed race believes in aggression and conquest, and has small use for the humane virtues. Pre-war Prussia had a population of more than forty million, and over half of these were racially pure Prussians. Among the Bavarians, Saxons and Austrians there are millions of decent Germans . . . in Bavaria until Hitler corrupted them from his Munich focal centre . . . and with these it might be possible to live on terms of equality. But there will be no peace in Europe unless and until we have settled accounts not only with Hitler and Hitlerism, but with the Prussians and Prussianism.

FROM the very start I had opposed the silly effort of the British propaganda to distinguish between the Nazis and the Germans. But how wonderful it is to be alive while the effort to "re-educate" these Barbaric people is being seriously attempted! Even now they must not be trusted very far, as all observers are agreed that the general feeling of the Germans is not sorrow for the crimes of the Nazi regime, but regret that Hitler's crusade of terrorism ended in failure.

SEEN AND HEARD — Dec. 9, 1939

"This war has been checked by prayer" is the authoritative statement of a religious contemporary. I was wondering what had "checked" it.

Dec. 30, 1939

"I just can't realize there's a war on" was a phrase to which I overheard a husky young man give utterance as he walked along in the sparkling sunshine on the Eastbourne parade with a family group of pleasure-seekers during the Christmas season. That is a dreadful attitude of mind and if it were to become general it would augur badly for our victorious issue from the present conflict. Who is to blame? Nobody but the Press Censorship and the Ministry of Information, which are daily doing their damnedest to encourage this illusion in the common mind.

Jan. 6, 1940

Apropos an earlier Jotting . . "The Fool hath said in his Folly 'there's no War on.'" If he will but attempt a walk from Ludgate Circus to Piccadilly any evening during black-out . . and preferably without a torch . . . he will realize that there's something very extraordinary "on." Bombs and bullets are not the only methods of death and disablement. The black-out hath its victories not less renowned than the bomb!

PRICE OF CIGARS — Jan. 6, 1940

Talking about rising prices, my wife today purchased a refill for my pocket torch and had to pay three shillings and sixpence for it, the same as one which she bought early in the war at a shilling. And last night, after dinner at a well-known restaurant in the West End, I was charged four shillings for a cigar which would have cost at most half-a-crown before the war. These may be exceptional cases, but I am not too sure of that, as I have heard of various other instances within the experience of my friends. Anyway, it is clear that in most classes of purchasable goods profiteering is going on, despite the valiant efforts of the innumerable controllers to prevent it.

THERE was actually less reason for these prices in January 1940 than in January 1946, when a genuine Havana cigar may cost a guinea and a smokable Jamaican, which once sold for a shilling, can now command four times that! A well-known maître d' hotel told me the other day of his "disgust" at seeing visitors from starving countries "with bunches of pound notes in their hands" readily paying a guinea for a Havana cigar! So far as I can judge, the Peace is at present as "phoney" as the War appeared to be in its opening phases.

IT STILL STANDS — Jan. 13, 1940

Whichever of London's familiar monuments may be doomed to suffer damage in the air raids that are threatened . . . if Goering has by accident stumbled into truth lately . . . let's be sure the Albert Memorial will escape. Simply because so many would be glad to see it demolished. One of these is Professor R. G. Collingwood, who, in his newly-published Autobiography, says of it: "Everything about it was visibly misshapen, corrupt, crawling, verminous," and goes on, "for a time I could not bear to look at it and passed with averted eyes." I've never felt its hideous presence so keenly as all that; but then I can look even at a crocodile or the terminus of a mandrill without endangering the metabolism of my lunch in the slightest. Guess I haven't got the artistic temperament awful bad, so to speak.

BUT the Albert Memorial had a narrow squeak when in July 1944 a flying bomb, which took heavy toll of human life, fell some 400 yards away on Kensington Palace Mansions. So completely were several of the victims destroyed that no vestige of them was ever found.

WHY NO GAS? — Jan. 13, 1940

An anti-Nazi German of my acquaintance, who quite uncomplainingly had to suffer some seven or eight weeks of detention in one of our internment camps at the outbreak of the war, told me yesterday that he had met a German friend, like himself strongly opposed to the Nazi regime, who had been in "the Fatherland" more recently than he, and this friend gave him a word of advice, "Always carry your gas mask." I understand that he did not provide any reason for the advice other than a knowing look. Personally, I doubt the probability of our experiencing gas attacks, not from the slightest compunction on the part of a ruthless, inhuman enemy, but because of the difficulty of carrying them out effectively.

ACCORDING to recent information the Nazis had discovered a poison gas against which none of the millions of gas masks, which were issued to us at tremendous cost, would have been of the slightest use. Why have not those millions of masks been called in? It might be thought they were worth gathering for the rubber they would yield; but perhaps the cost of reclaiming that would not prove economic. The only use mine was ever put to was for entering a pantry where the mechanism of a refrigerator had broken down and filled the place with dense and otherwise impenetrable fumes! It would be interesting to know how many of these masks have been mislaid.

POSTSCRIPT

THE formation is announced of "The London Flower-Lovers' League," the members of which are pledged to beautify the city by growing plants and flowers. Next summer, certificates will be awarded to those window-box gardeners and others who have led the way in brightening the drabber places among London's ruins. As a garden-enthusiast, I can think of few small efforts likely to produce such large and lasting results.

IN the same week recently there came from the publishers two long and learned books dealing with The Human Face and The Psychology of Gesture respectively. Neither, it seems, proved anything very conclusively, but they set me wondering as to what has happened to a very remarkable London "character" who scorned all forms of publicity and of address other than "Jock" and who before the war numbered half the British aristocracy among his "patients." By merely squinting at the soles and heels of your shoes he could diagnose—with alarming accuracy—the most minute details regarding your health and way of living.

MAJOR-GENERAL LAHOUSEN, former deputy chief of the German Intelligence and a prosecution witness at Nuremberg, has disclosed that in the opinion of those who fought against him General Eisenhower was the greatest general of the war—with ten times the authority of any German general. The trouble with the Germans was that this particular piece of Intelligence should have taken so long to dawn on them!

In Britain Now: Where the U.N.O. Assembles

PREPARING FOR THE UNITED NATIONS ORGANIZATION Assembly, which opened in the Central Hall, Westminster, on January 10, 1946, Col. N. E. Marriott, of the Royal Marines, officer in charge of the public gallery, explained their duties to his men, whom he is facing (above). They check passes, scrutinize visitors, and conduct delegates to their places. See also illus. pages 624-625, 629.

COMBATING LONDON'S CRIME WAVE, a police officer (above) at Scotland Yard plots, on a specially-devised large-scale map, the position of each patrol car in the London area. On receiving an emergency call he is able, by means of radio, to direct to the scene of the crime the patrol car nearest to it.

BOMB IN ST. JAMES'S PARK, dropped by the Luftwaffe in 1941, four hundred yards from Buckingham Palace, came in for attention from men of No. 2 Bomb Disposal Company, Royal Engineers (right), on January 7, 1946. It made a deep hole in the concrete bed of the lake, almost under the footbridge; the same day the bridge was closed to the public and the lake drained.

Photos, Fox, Associated Press, P.A.-Reuter Photos

At Britain's New Atlantic Air Terminal

GIANT LANDING WHEEL OF THE LANCASTRIAN 'STAR LIGHT' was inspected by little Mary Margaret Moore and mother (wife of one of the crew) at Heath Row, new Atlantic air terminal near Staines, Middlesex, on January 1, 1946 (see also page 636). Captained by Air Vice-Marshal D. C. T. Bennett, former ace of the Pathfinders, Star Light was making the first survey flight for the British South American Airways service to Buenos Aires. She set up a record of 28 hours 18 minutes for the flight to Rio de Janeiro, returning on January 15. *Photo, Central Press*

Printed in England and published every alternate Friday by the Proprietors, THE AMALGAMATED PRESS, LTD., The Fleetway House, Farringdon Street, London, E.C.4. Registered for transmission by Canadian Magazine Post. Sole Agents for Australia and New Zealand: Messrs. Gordon & Gotch, Ltd.; and for South Africa: Central News Agency, Ltd. February 1, 1946. S.S. *Editorial Address:* JOHN CARPENTER HOUSE, WHITEFRIARS LONDON, E.C.4.

Vol 9 The War Illustrated No 226

SIXPENCE and AFTERWARDS FEBRUARY 15, 1946

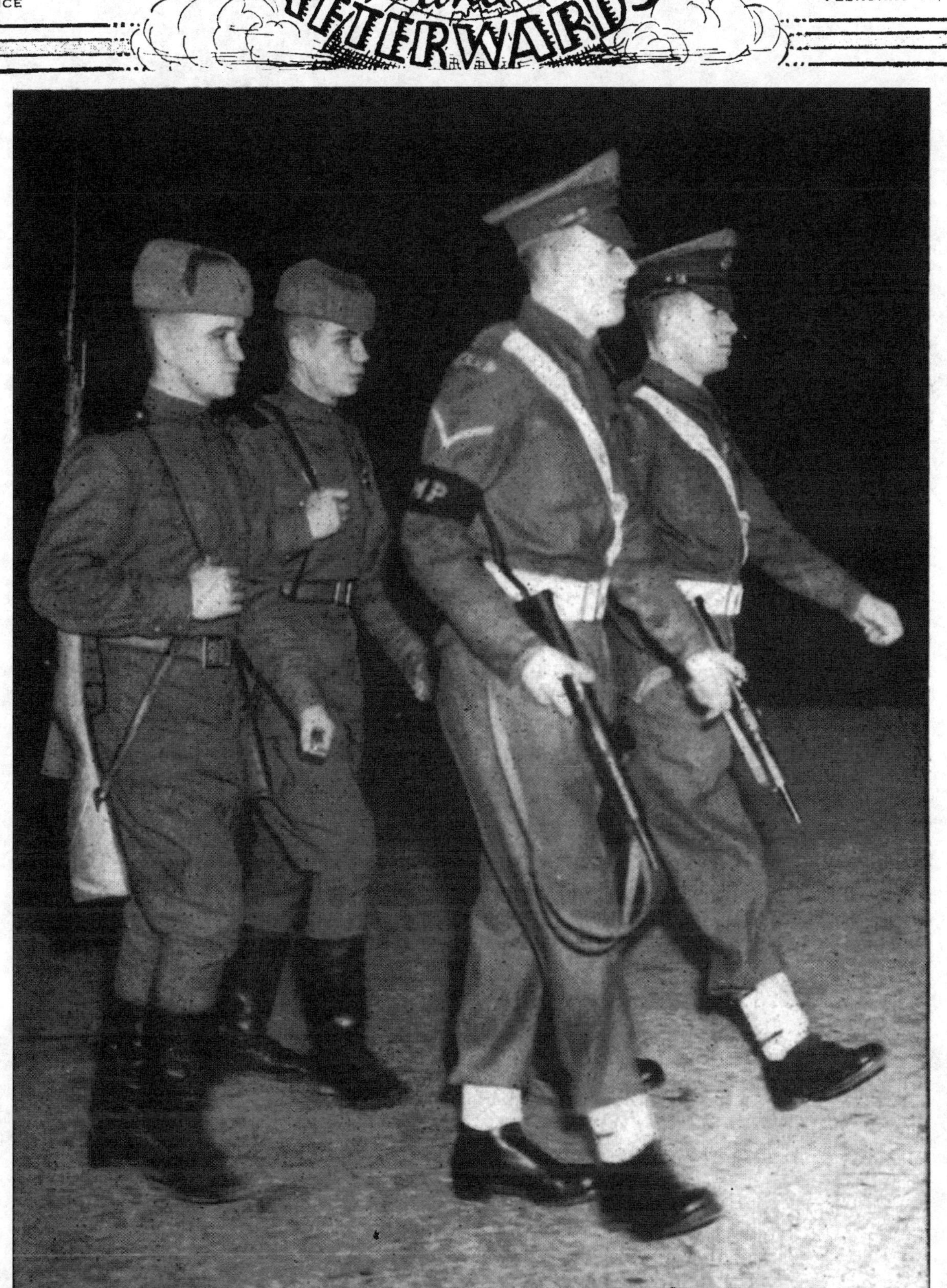

PATROLLING THE STREETS OF BERLIN BY NIGHT, British and Russian Military Police jointly undertake the maintenance of good order in the British sector of the devastated German capital. This arrangement came into force on December 30, 1945, the object being to avoid recurrence of incidents which have occasionally occurred through misunderstandings—and the language difficulty in the event of the arrest of a Russian in our zone. The co-operation is creating closer relationship between the two Allies.

Edited by Sir John Hammerton

NO. 227 WILL BE PUBLISHED FRIDAY, MARCH 1, 1946

The Daily Round in Our Zone of Germany

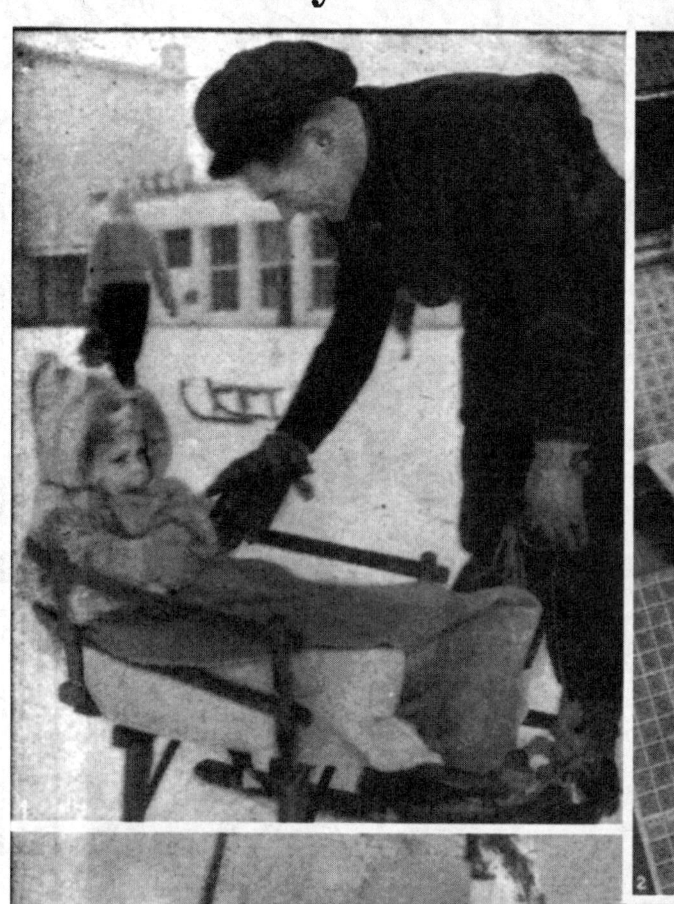

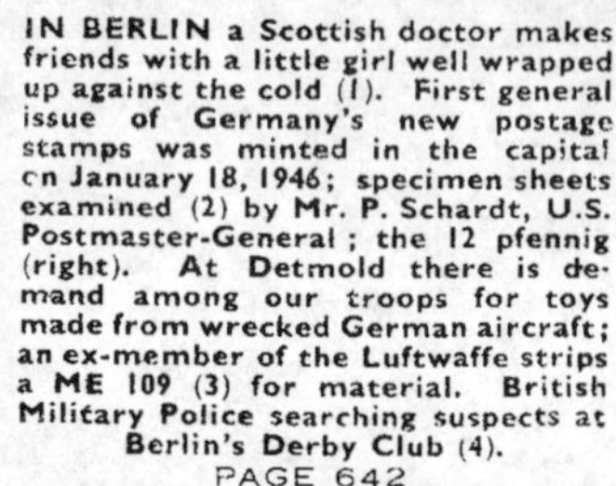

IN BERLIN a Scottish doctor makes friends with a little girl well wrapped up against the cold (1). First general issue of Germany's new postage stamps was minted in the capital on January 18, 1946; specimen sheets examined (2) by Mr. P. Schardt, U.S. Postmaster-General; the 12 pfennig (right). At Detmold there is demand among our troops for toys made from wrecked German aircraft; an ex-member of the Luftwaffe strips a ME 109 (3) for material. British Military Police searching suspects at Berlin's Derby Club (4).

Great Deeds of the Army Commandos

By Lt.-Col.
A. C. NEWMAN, V.C.

RAISED as an offensive Force in the dark days of 1940, the Army Commandos—their work magnificently done—were disbanded in 1945. Battle honours in many fields they gained between those years, imbued with a spirit of comradeship and mutual endeavour never excelled by any body of men. Founding, training and achievements of wearers of the Green Beret are described in this article, specially written by the Commando leader of St. Nazaire fame for " The War Illustrated."

IN June 1940 Britain was called upon to face a situation which was not very much to her liking. We had come out of Norway, we had come out of France, and we were confronted with the grim task of preparing to defend our shores from a possible enemy invasion ; and, if that did not materialize, the building-up of a new army that could carry the war into the enemy's territory once again. Starting from scratch, this obviously would take a considerable time, during which we could not afford to allow our enemy to hold all the initiative.

Within a few days of Dunkirk, Mr. Churchill, the Prime Minister, called for the formation of a force whose special job would be to carry out offensive operations against the enemy. At this time, some 6,000 men were to have as their role the launching of raids on the long enemy-held coastline.

As a skilful boxer worries his opponent by a series of jabs with his left hand, preparing for the knock-out blow with his right, so was this force to carry out a series of jabs until Britain was ready to put in her right, which was to drive the enemy out of Africa, then Italy, and finally through France to Berlin.

On July 17, 1940, Admiral of the Fleet Sir Roger Keyes was made Director of Combined Operations (see page 622), and the Commandos came into being. In the initial build-up, the Commando commanders had the opportunity of gathering together their men from all branches and regiments of the Army. All were volunteers, all had to be in first-rate physical condition. The majority of the men chosen had already seen action in either France or Norway, and were possessed of the spirit of adventure and the keen desire to be on the offensive again. The training was hard and intense, but because all the men were enthusiastically taking part in the moulding of a new type of unit there was born within each Commando a fervent desire to make himself as efficient as possible. And there developed between all ranks a spirit of comradeship that was later to become one of the great attributes of the Commando.

Hard Schooling for Recruits

To make the men efficient for their future tasks many unusual types of training had to be introduced. It was essential that they should be just as confident to act alone, or in twos and threes, as when fighting as a complete Commando. They must be accustomed to the sea, immune to sea-sickness, efficient in the rudiments of seamanship. Training in handling explosives and quick but effective demolitions formed part of their course. Cliff and mountain climbing had to be mastered by all ranks. A high degree of night sense and night confidence had to be attained, and complete control of street-fighting and close-quarter work in built-up areas.

Training centres were not long in taking shape ; the West Coast of Scotland became the schooling ground for the Commando recruit. Landing exercises were carried out in mid-winter from base ships—pre-war passenger-carrying vessels converted to provide for a Commando living aboard, and carrying landing craft. Very soon the Commando soldier was " at home " aboard and learning his navigation, training hard in landings by night and by day on all types of beaches and in all kinds of weather.

He was schooled to realize that as all offensive operations against the enemy's long line must come from the sea, his own natural home and hunting ground must *be* the sea. Trips in submarines and destroyers also formed a very close link with the Royal Navy and he came to know his ship by other terms than the sharp end and the blunt end !

At the same time, schools of mountain warfare assault and demolition courses all had to be passed through ; and such spare time as came to him in Scotland was likely to be spent in deer stalking and mountain climbing. Throughout the War, all subsequent Commandos went through similar training, growing in numbers, extending their spheres of operations throughout the European and Far Eastern fighting, finally becoming a force of such dimensions as was never visualized in those grim days of 1940.

Succeeding Directors of Combined Operations added their strength, and left their mark on the Commandos. Admiral Lord Louis Mountbatten followed Sir Roger Keyes in October 1941 and directed the operations until appointed to S.E.A.C. in August 1943. Major-General " Bob " Laycock, himself a Commando Commander, succeeded Lord Louis in October 1943 and remained the Commando chief until the end.

Historic 'Warming-Up' Raids

In October 1945 came the statement in Parliament that the Commandos were to be disbanded, and the lessons learnt were to be incorporated into Regular Army training. So at the end of their five-year life it is fitting to look back and see what battle honours they have gained, and what part they played in the beating of our enemies.

On March 4, 1941, a small force of Commandos and Royal Navy raided the Lofoten Islands in Northern Norway. The enemy were surprised, and the raiders returned to England without casualty, bringing with them 215 German prisoners and ten quislings. They also brought back to England all they could carry of a number of loyal Norwegians, some 300 men, who were willing to come here to join the Norwegian Free Forces. They left behind them many completely destroyed fish oil factories that had been producing valuable goods for Germany ; eleven German ships were sunk, totalling 18,000 tons, and food and clothes were left with the Norwegian population. (See pages 286 and 287, Vol. 4).

THEN on Dec. 27, 1941, the Lofoten Isles were again visited, and damage was again done to wireless installations, German oil storage units and shipping. At the same time as this second Lofoten raid, another Combined Operation was in progress a few hundred miles farther south, at Vaagso. There the Commandos, with Royal Naval and Royal Air Force support, destroyed the German garrison, killing 120 of them and bringing back 95 prisoners, together with some more Norwegian quislings. Enemy shipping was sunk and coastal defence guns destroyed. (See pages 430 and 431, Vol. 5).

Three months later, on March 27-28, 1942, the Commandos were again on the offensive, this time on the West Coast of France, in the memorable attack on St. Nazaire, where the large dry dock capable of housing the German battleship Tirpitz was destroyed. (See pages 627 and 669, Vol. 5). On August 19 came the historic raid on Dieppe, where Canadians joined forces with the Commandos to pierce the strong German defences. Against almost overwhelming odds, the German heavy batteries were smashed, many of the Luftwaffe's aircraft were brought down, and severe casualties were inflicted on the enemy in this " reconnaissance in force " from which such valuable information was obtained as to make possible the final blow on the now strong enemy coastal defences. (See pages 196-199, Vol. 6).

In the Mediterranean the Commandos were carrying the war into the enemy's territory. On Crete, in May 1941, they played their part in the tragic fighting. A month later on the Litani River in Syria a very gallant Commando landed behind the enemy lines to draw their fire whilst the main forces crossed the river. Losses were high, but their action made it possible for the advance to go on.

THE raid on Bardia (Libya), made in darkness in April 1941, produced valuable information ; large enemy dumps were blown up ; an important bridge in the Axis line of communications was destroyed, and a coastal defence battery put out of action. In November of the same year, on the eve of General Auchinleck's attack in Libya, a daring raid by some 30 Commando men on Rommel's H.Q. was carried out from submarines, the landing being many miles behind the enemy front line. A Commando played an important part in the occupation of Madagascar (May–November 1942), though the operation was mainly carried out by the Royal Navy and the Army.

These are only a few of the Commando actions in that difficult period when Britain was fast fitting herself for the whole of her armies to go over to the offensive again.

In November 1942 came the Anglo-American landings in North Africa. Commandos were there, and as the tempo of the war in the Mediterranean increased the fighting in Sicily and Italy saw many Green Beret actions. Salerno (September 1943) can be claimed by the Commandos as one of their battle honours—it was probably one of their finest actions in the war. Fighting for eleven days, holding on against terrible artillery fire, a Commando made it possible for the main forces to consolidate and maintain their slender positions ashore and thus secure the landing. In all the subsequent Italian fighting the Commandos were used, finally finishing up with Marshal Tito in Yugoslavia.

Many visits were made across the Channel in preparation for the D-Day landing, and here the Commandos were in their element, landing in twos and threes on the coast of France to gather vital information.

Bitter and Costly Actions

At long last, on June 6, 1944, the big day arrived, and the Allies put in their strong right-hand blow. Walcheren Island (November 1944) and the Rhine crossings (March 1945) will go down in the history of the Commandos—both very bitter and costly actions but invaluable in their aid to the main Allied advance towards Berlin.

Commando history cannot be completed without recording their part in the Far East. In the Burma jungle a Commando Brigade saw perhaps the toughest and most desperate fighting in the whole War, calling for endurance of the highest order.

Almost from the beginning our enemies realized the Commandos' potential, and feared them. An order was given by the German High Command in 1942 that all Commandos were to be shot if captured. Too many very gallant men paid this price at the hands of the Gestapo.

Raised, as they were, in the dark days of 1940, they were given a role to play—and play it they did. Their casualties were high, their actions costly in men and materials ; but their part in the long years of the War will not be forgotten.

Last Moments at Singapore

By MAJ.-GENERAL
SIR CHARLES GWYNN
K.C.B., D.S.O.

THE inquiry into the circumstances of the escape of Lieutenant-General Gordon Bennett, C.B., D.S.O., C.-in-C. of the Australian Forces, from Singapore in February 1942 revives memories of what, at the time, to many seemed an incomprehensible and humiliating disaster. Incidentally, the evidence given at the inquiry brings out how bitterly the troops felt the inevitability of surrender. There can be little doubt that if any good purpose would have been served and they had been called on to do so they would willingly have fought to the last man.

Units, exhausted and depleted in a long fighting retreat, continued to resist stubbornly when the situation had become hopeless. The Australians who met the initial landing in the mangrove swamps at the north-west corner of the island though compelled to fall back never lost their cohesion. Despite continuous air attack the conduct of the troops in the final stages was in general satisfactory; and discipline was well maintained. There can be no doubt that it was not through fear that the troops would crack that Lieutenant-General A. E. Percival, C.B., D.S.O., M.C., G.O.C. Malaya, decided to surrender, but rather to avoid what had evidently become useless bloodshed, and in consideration for the desperate plight of the civil population owing to water shortage.

MEMORIAL SERVICE for officers and men of the 2nd Battalion the Gordon Highlanders who fell in Malaya and Singapore, 1941-42, was conducted by the Rt. Rev. R. L. Wilson, Bishop of Singapore, on September 26, 1945. The service was held at the grave of three British soldiers who lost their lives in a slit trench—now dedicated to the dead of the 2nd Battalion. *Photo, British Official*

SURRENDER of the Fortress Came as Desperate Shock to the Nation

That recriminations and criticisms, some probably justified, should have been provoked by the surrender of so important a place and of so many men was to be expected. But now that we have recovered from the shock, sympathy for the commander who had to make the decision and for the troops whose efforts had proved in vain is surely more fitting. Perhaps those who most deserve sympathy are the troops who were landed as reinforcements at the last moment, only to find themselves committed to the miseries of Japanese prisoner-of-war camps without having had an opportunity to prove their metal.

Whether these last-minute reinforcements should have been landed when the situation had become so hopeless may be open to question. Landed after a long sea voyage into totally strange surroundings they could in any case have been of little immediate value. Possibly the need to release shipping in which to evacuate women and children was the reason for a measure which only added to the scale of the disaster. The surrender came as a desperate shock to the nation all the more because it was popularly believed that Singapore had been made into an impregnable fortress.

It was known that what for peacetime were very large sums had been expended on it, but I am afraid very few concerned themselves to inquire what they had received for their money. It has frequently been explained that it was never intended nor practicable to create a fortress in the full sense but only a first-class, strongly armed naval base. Actually, we learned in the course of the War that no fortress can be made impregnable when subjected to attack by the full power of modern weapons.

The fall of Singapore should mainly be attributed to the inability of the Royal Navy and our field army in Malaya to prevent the enemy closing on to it and not to the lack of fortifications on the land side. However strong those defences might have been made they would have served only to delay and not to avert the final disaster in the strategic conditions that had arisen as a consequence of the war with Germany. In view of those conditions it is very doubtful whether from the outset of the war with Japan it would have been practicable to avert the disaster unless Japan had displayed an ineptitude and weakness which we had no right to expect. As misapprehensions still prevail it may be worth while to review, with special reference to Singapore, the strategic aspects of our imperial defence problems.

Obviously our resources in peace, and even when our armed forces are expanded in war, are insufficient permanently to provide adequate forces for the defence of our outlying possessions and interests. We depend primarily on the Royal Navy retaining control of sea communications to admit of the reinforcement of threatened points, and secondly on reserves held at suitable points for reinforcement.

WITH the rise of Japan as a powerful and potentially hostile naval power equilibrium in Eastern waters demanded the presence of a powerful British fleet. But a modern powerful fleet cannot operate or be maintained without a first-class base, hence the Singapore base. But the main British fleet had for a number of reasons to be stationed in the West, and for financial and political reasons was not maintained at sufficient strength to provide a detachment of really adequate size permanently in the Far East. It had therefore to be assumed that in times of crisis a large part of the Fleet would be dispatched to the East, arriving there in about 56 days. During that period the Japanese, in temporary command of the sea, might attempt to destroy the installations of the base by bombardment or by raiding-parties landed on the island. Powerful coast artillery guns were therefore mounted to keep hostile ships at a distance, and a small infantry garrison was maintained to deal with raids. A small R.A.F. detachment also was stationed at the base. It was realized that during the 56-day period the enemy might also land a force on the mainland of the peninsula, but owing to the time factor it was assumed that the landing would not be in great strength or be effected at any great distance from the base.

WHY Japan Was Able to Exploit Fully Her Superior Air Power

It was, however, essential to prevent such a force advancing to within artillery range of the naval dockyard or establishing airfields from which it could be bombed. For this, a mobile field force was required to be formed from reinforcements provided by India. To have constructed an elaborate defence works on the landward side of the island would have given no protection to the dockyard, and a Maginot Line on the mainland at a sufficient distance would have not only been very costly but would have tied a large force to immobile defence. Moreover, it would not have eliminated air attack.

Such were the premises on which the defence scheme of Singapore was based, and they were falsified by the collapse of France. The main Fleet could not leave western waters, and the belated dispatch of H.M.S. Prince of Wales and the Repulse was probably only intended to be a deterrent measure, taking account of the strained relations between the U.S.A. and Japan. After the Pearl Harbour disaster their strategic value was immensely reduced. Reinforcements were sent from India and Australia, but since both these countries had already sent contingents to the Middle East they could not contribute a force strong enough to meet the new situation. For Japan, having established herself in Indo-China and Siam, could now invade Malaya by land and sea. With no prospect of a British fleet arriving she was not hampered by the time factor, and she could fully exploit her superior air power.

IN these circumstances the newly-formed British field army had to be deployed on the Siamese frontier and to cover a probable landing. Numerically, the force available was too small for the task and the troops were not trained in jungle fighting, nor was their equipment up to required standards. Manoeuvred out of one position after another, tactically in jungle fighting and strategically by landings in their rear, retreat was unavoidable. How serious the situation was from the outset may not have been fully realized, for it had been expected that the jungle would favour defence. The general public, buoyed up by belief in the impregnability of Singapore, and perhaps misled by over-sanguine communiqués, had certainly little warning of the approaching catastrophe which neither the most forceful leadership nor the strongest defences on the island could have for long averted.

Mr. Churchill at the time wisely refused to set up a Commission of Inquiry into the Singapore disaster; but his speech delivered in secret session of Parliament nine weeks after the event had unmistakable implications. Its publication would seem to demand an inquiry now, not to search for scapegoats but in justice to many brave men and for public enlightenment in strategic matters.

Navy and R.A.F. Comings and Goings Out East

MEN OF FORCE W, the naval force whose plans to make assault landings in the Port Swettenham and Port Dickson areas of Malaya became inoperative by reason of the surrender of Japanese forces in S.E. Asia on September 12, 1945, were inspected at Singapore by Lord Louis Mountbatten, Supreme Allied Commander S.E. Asia, at a recent farewell parade (top), when some 2,500 officers and men were assembled. From Britain, R.A.F. personnel recently arrived at Hongkong (below) to replace others due for demobilization.

Photos, British Official

How the "Royal Oak" Was Sunk

By
FRANCIS E. McMURTRIE

On October 14, 1939, at 1.30 a.m. H.M.S. Royal Oak, a battleship of 29,150 tons, wearing the flag of Rear-Admiral H. E. C. Blagrove, was sunk in Scapa Flow with the loss of two-thirds of her officers and men. It afterwards proved that she had been torpedoed by a German submarine which had contrived to enter the sheltered anchorage, supposed to be impenetrable. Not only was this the first British capital ship to be lost in the Second Great War, but the circumstances of the disaster enabled the enemy to exploit its propaganda value to the fullest extent. (See pages 244, 251, 344, Vol. 1.)

No clear official explanation has ever been furnished of the circumstances in which the U-boat was able to reach the spot undetected and to escape again. As described in Parliament four days later by Mr. Churchill (then First Lord of the Admiralty), a good deal of mystery appeared to surround the operation. When the first explosion occurred, in the forward part of the ship, the idea of a torpedo being responsible was never entertained. Instead, it was imagined that defective ammunition must have detonated, this having been responsible for the destruction of the battleship Vanguard in Scapa Flow on July 9, 1917. Steps were at once taken to flood all magazines in the vicinity, while the captain, accompanied by Rear-Admiral Blagrove and other officers, proceeded forward to investigate the cause of the trouble.

It was now, 20 minutes after the first muffled explosion, that the submarine fired a second salvo of torpedoes, three or four of which hit. The Royal Oak capsized and sank almost immediately, and the loss of life was increased by the spreading around of oil fuel, which smothered swimmers. Out of some 1,200 on board only 414 were saved, the admiral being one of those lost.

To quote Mr. Churchill's words, " When we consider that during the whole course of the last War (1914-18), the anchorage was found to be immune from such attacks on account of the obstacles imposed by the currents and the net barrages, this entry by a U-boat must be considered as a remarkable exploit of professional skill and daring.''

He added that a court of inquiry was being held into the whole matter.

Simultaneously with the First Lord's announcement came a German account of the affair. It stated that a submarine commanded by Kapitänleutnant (Lieutenant) Prien had returned to her base after entering Scapa Flow and torpedoing two British ships. As Prien would have had only hurried glimpses of the scene this belief may well have been a genuine one, though his suggestion that the other ship was H.M.S. Repulse was probably an official embroidery of his report. His own broadcast story said :

" It was quite a job to smuggle ourselves into Scapa Flow through all the British defences. I saw two British warships to the north of me, and discharged torpedoes at them twice. I then turned and left the harbour, as I did not want to be captured. As I was leaving I heard explosions and saw a column of water rising by the British ship farthest to the northward.'' (This would correspond to the position of the Royal Oak.)

SHIPS OF THE 2nd BATTLE SQUADRON are seen beyond the 15-in. guns of the ill-fated Royal Oak, whose story is recounted here. Mr. Winston Churchill described the action of the U-boat concerned in her sinking in Scapa Flow as " a remarkable exploit of professional skill and daring." See also pages 244, 251, 344, Vol. I. *Photo, Charles E. Brown*

Lieutenant Prien was sent by air to Berlin, where he was received by Hitler and decorated with the Iron Cross. At a later date he appears to have been advanced to the rank of Korvettenkapitän (lieutenant-commander).

How the Enterprising Lieutenant Gained Scapa Flow's Open Water

He ultimately lost his life in a U-boat which failed to return from patrol. His exploit, as a legitimate act of war, may be contrasted with the foul deeds of so many U-boat captains, who, as shown clearly by documents produced at the Nuremberg trials, did their utmost to ensure that there should be no survivors from merchant ships torpedoed without warning.

Naturally the Germans allowed no indication to be given of the route taken by Prien's submarine in entering and leaving Scapa Flow. It was almost certain that it could not have been through any of the three main entrances, Hoxa and Switha Sound on the south, Hoy Sound on the west. All three of these entrances were not only well patrolled but closed by nets, with gates which were opened only when required to permit ships to enter or leave.

This left only the narrow, shallow and tortuous entrances on the eastern side of the Flow to be considered. One alone of these was in any sense a practical possibility ; this was Holm Sound, to the northward of the island of Burray. Across it lie two smaller islands, between which during the First Great War were sunk a number of merchant ships so arranged as to make the passage impervious to a submarine.

After 1919 these blockships were raised and sold for scrap, but it was understood that arrangements had been made for them to be replaced in emergency. It is not known when this was done, and no official announcement has ever been made on the subject. It seems highly probable, however, that the work of blocking the channels had not been completed on October 14, 1939, so that the enterprising Lieutenant Prien was able to nose his way through Holm Sound and emerge unobserved in the open water of Scapa Flow. He cannot have had an easy passage, for the currents in Holm Sound are very strong, and the most careful navigation must have been required to get through without running aground. This view agrees with that which has been expressed by experienced British submarine officers.

Electrically Exploded Mines Blew the Submarine UB 116 to Pieces

In 1914 there was no such unanimity on the subject of the possibility of entering ; on October 17 of that year—25 years prior to the loss of the Royal Oak—a general alarm was sounded following a report that an enemy submarine had been spotted inside the Flow. Guns were fired, destroyers zigzagged around at high speed, and the entire Grand Fleet put to sea in haste in case the report might be well-founded. There could hardly have been a more complete contrast with the perplexity of everyone on board the Royal Oak when the first torpedo struck.

Actually no U-boat ever got into Scapa Flow during 1914-18. Only one desperate attempt was made to penetrate the defences, and the issue of that enterprise tended to strengthen the belief that they were impregnable. This incident occurred on October 28, 1918, when the greater part of the German Fleet was already in a state of mutiny prior to the Armistice.

UB 116, with a volunteer complement of officers, set off from Wilhelmshaven with the object of carrying out a last attack on the Grand Fleet, which it was supposed lay in Scapa Flow, though actually it was in the Firth of Forth. Unlike Prien, the captain of UB 116 (Emsmann) regarded Holm Sound as too difficult to attempt, and made his approach by the widest and most direct route through Hoxa Sound. The submarine was duly located on the screen connected with the controlled minefield forming part of the Hoxa defences, and as soon as she was well over the mines they were electrically exploded and the submarine was blown to pieces.

Now that the War is over there seems no reason why a full official account of the circumstances in which the Royal Oak was sunk should not be published. If, as seems probable, there was needless delay in placing blockships in Holm Sound, thus allowing the U-boat to get through, it is time this fact was admitted. It may be assumed that any who may have been adjudged to blame in the matter have long ago been dealt with suitably, and the fact could be stated without names being mentioned.

Unicorn Home With Food-Gifts From Australia

AIRCRAFT CARRIER AND REPAIR SHIP, the 14,500-ton H.M.S. Unicorn recently arrived at Devonport with 5,515 cases of food for Britain—the largest single consignment yet brought from the Commonwealth by the Royal Navy. Members of the ship's company here unload these generous gifts from the people of Sydney and Hobart. The Unicorn also brought home from the Pacific 570 Naval personnel. It was announced in late January 1946 that a further £12,000-worth of gift-food from Australia would arrive here in the battleship King George V. *Photo, G.P.U.*

V-Force Acted as the Fourteenth Army's Eyes

Many Burmese tribesmen had never seen a white man, yet in their thousands they flocked as volunteers to V-Force to fight the Japs—an enemy they had never seen. The dramatic story of this Force, which remained secret until December 1945, is told in this article specially written for "The War Illustrated" by one of its leaders, ANTHONY IRWIN, author of "Burmese Outpost."

"V-FORCE! What on earth's that?" I can't begin to count the number of times that question has been put to me. "V Force! What was it?" In short, it was a private Army formed in April 1942 when the Jap seemed certain to push, from his newly-conquered possessions in Burma, over the Indo-Burma frontier into India proper. Its name is derived from the Roman figure V (five).

It was a partisan force, led by British Army officers and local planters, policemen, forest officers or the like. The rank and file were all Burmese. Many tribes were represented, for the country in which this Force operated stretched from the China border down to the Bay of Bengal, 800 miles as the crow flies. Though some of those tribesmen are known to a few Englishmen, others have never been heard of.

We had Nagas from east of Assam, Karens from just east of the Yoma country, Lushais and Chins, Kachins and Mughs, Maraughs and Khumis, Musselman Arakanese from east of Bengal; too many to enumerate in full. There were tens of tribes and tens of thousands of volunteers. Many of these people had never seen a white man, some had never heard of one, few had ever seen a modern rifle or thought possible the existence of the aeroplane. Yet, when we called upon them to turn out from their homes and fight an enemy they had never seen, they came willingly and fought with skill and daring.

Spy Service in Dense Jungles

The original plan for this Force was that in the event of an invasion of India from Burma, parties of patriots should stay in the hills with their white officers and harry the Japs until fresh forces from overseas could drive the invaders back the way they had come. Fortunately, the Jap failed to cross the vast jungle frontier that separates India and Burma, in any strength, and so other work was found for us.

One of the most important of these tasks was to act as eyes to the 14th Army. In that thick jungle country a man cannot see more than ten yards; tracks are strange to him; maps are faulty; the aircraft cannot pick out the hiding enemy as it can in the West; for both sides movement behind the lines is made secret by the very thickness of the jungle. A commander cannot fight his troops efficiently unless he has full knowledge of the movements and dispositions of his enemy. That was where we came in. With our partisans we would pin-point Jap positions, note his movements and inform our Army Commanders.

To do this we had what really boiled down to a glorified spy service: thousands of agents spread over the whole vast area occupied by the enemy. They lived in his villages, even in his camps, acting as his coolies or contractors, some filling important posts for him, such as magistrates or police chiefs or headmen of townships. These agents would send back their information to their British commander, who lived on some lonely hill in the wild jungle ahead of our Army and often behind the enemy's lines. These messages would come to us by hundreds of queer routes. Sometimes a man would walk into a camp and throw a bamboo stick through the doorway of my hut and pass on without a word.

When that stick was broken open a message would be found. Sometimes messages came wrapped up in a cigarette, or inside a melon. One over zealous runner brought one to me in his mouth. He had travelled many miles over impossible country and was so dead beat when he arrived that in his excitement he swallowed the message as he staggered into my hut. He returned to his agent that night, and within 48 hours was back with a copy of the message.

Risks these agents and messengers ran was enormous. If the Jap caught one he received short shrift. And short shrift from a Jap is indeed an unpleasant experience. One of my agents, a man of sixty, was caught, transfixed to the ground with bayonets and, in front of all his village, skinned alive. Eighteen scouts were captured by a large patrol of Japs in 1943. They had been waiting for their officer, who had swum across the Chindwin to try to find the whereabouts of the Jap Corps H.Q. When he returned he found that the Japs had tied each to a tree and castrated them. To a man they bled to death, a longish business.

BURMESE SCOUT U AUNG, whose tribe, the Khumi, lives to the north of Arakan. He had six Japanese to his credit while serving with V-Force. **See also facing page.**

Yes, the risks were indeed great and the results of being caught unmentionable. The promises of reward were slim. We officers used often to protect ourselves against capture by strapping a grenade on to the backs of our belts. Then, if the worst came to the worst, a sharp tug, the locking-pin dropped from the grenade, and we were safe from immediate hell.

For you to realize fully the loyalty of our men, here is something about the people I knew best. I worked with two tribes, the Musselman Arakanese and the Khumis. The latter come from the northern reaches of the Kaladan River and the former live in Arakan, that country which lies south and east of Bengal and is cut off from Burma proper by the Yomas, a great chain of mountains stretching from India down to Rangoon. These Musselmen are an insular people who live a hand-to-mouth existence. They came into the country 200 years ago, at the time of the decline of the Arakan Empire. They are traders and cultivators. They come under the jurisdiction of the Burma Government and are ruled by the District Officers through their own appointed headmen.

When the War came to them they knew nothing about guns or bombs and very little about real national hate. They had not had a particularly fair deal from the Burma Government, being tucked away in a corner of territory geographically more in India than in Burma. Yet when the Jap invaded Arakan they flocked to join us.

Once in, they stood by us through every disaster. They watched two British offensives fail, and they twice saw the Jap plundering their homes. They hated the Jap, hated him far more than they loved us, and it was on account of that hate that they joined us and fought. After a time they came to respect and befriend us, until at the end I firmly believe they would have followed us anywhere. They were not given the chance: as the Army left their country and went on into Burma the Musselman Arakanese remained behind, and today I wonder whether they are forgotten.

Big Price on Officers' Heads

The best way to understand this extraordinary loyalty is to realize that most of the officers were "wanted" by the Jap. So much were they wanted that the Jap put a big price on our heads, money enough to keep a man and his family secure for many years. Although this was known throughout the length and breadth of Arakan, only three men to my knowledge tried to earn that reward; and it was the three men's own villagers who caught them and brought them to us and insisted on their execution. Times without number we had to put ourselves completely in the hands of villagers, trusting implicitly in their loyalty.

It was not uncommon for an officer, accompanied only by half a dozen unarmed scouts (perhaps, in some cases, they may have had one rifle and a couple of 12-bore shot guns between them) to walk into a Jap-occupied township in broad daylight, go to the headman's house, call a conference of the elders of the village, stay the night, sleeping peacefully, kill a couple of Jap sentries before breakfast and then start off home again. Every man and woman, and even the children, would know of the officer's presence, but not one would consider walking the few yards necessary to tell the Japs about it and earn the large reward.

Such was their loyalty, and their courage and endurance kept pace with it. For three long years they faced dangers new and terrible; their homes were destroyed because they fought with us, and we did not build them again; their country became the home of disease because an Army had passed that way, and though the Army brought doctors and medicine both moved on with the Army and only the disease remained.

Now that the War is finished and we talk glibly of Freedom, we must all remember that Burma is a vast country comprised of many different tribes. If freedom is given to Burma it is given to the largest tribe; that will not bring freedom to the millions who make up those other smaller and varied sections of the community who live amongst the tattered war-torn hills of the Indo-Burma frontier . . . and those were the people who stood by us and succoured us and, by their fortitude, saved many thousands of British lives. We must never forget this.

From Burma Villages Loyal Tribesmen Rallied

VOLUNTEERS FROM THE INDIAN AND BURMESE BORDERS, trained under British officers, proved invaluable in guiding patrols and in guerilla fighting during the Burma Campaign of 1942-45. Musselman Arakanese scouts (1) led by Col. Gretton Foster, M.C. (right background) were armed with 80-year-old rifles. A Naga guards his Japanese prisoner (2). Another Naga who acted as interpreter (3). Anthony Irwin (4, extreme left) with his Arakanese scouts at V-force H.Q. at Taung Bazar.

2 and 3 from drawings by Capt. R. J. M. Dupont, SEAC war artist

Victory and Defeat in Moscow's Hall of Banners

IN THE RED ARMY MUSEUM AT MOSCOW the standards of victorious Soviet units stand erect (1), and in a central place of honour is draped the bullet-riddled Banner of Victory—the U.S.S.R. flag which flew from the German Reichstag on April 30, 1945. (See illus. pages 41 and 138). Hitler's personal standard (2) lies at the base of the pedestal on which the Banner of Victory is exhibited, and standards of vanquished German regiments are heaped upon the floor (3). *Photos, Pictorial Press*

Aid from Britain to Set Greece on Her Feet

THROUGH THE PIRAEUS, port of Athens (1), flow urgently needed supplies from Britain. Indian troops provide necessary guards (2). The village of Karpenision is being rebuilt, and at the field hospital, installed by U.N.R.R.A., Greek nurses attend the patients (3). On Jan. 25, 1946, an Anglo-Greek agreement was signed by Mr. Bevin, British Foreign Secretary (4, right), and M. Tsouderos, Vice-President of the Greek Council of Ministers, whereby Britain provides credit of £10,000,000 for the stabilization of Greek currency. *Photos, A. P., British Official, Keystone*

Now It Can Be Told!

JAP PRAISE FOR THE GALLANT 'STRONGHOLD'

A BRITISH naval officer lately returned to England after spending nearly four years in a Japanese prisoner of war camp has told for the first time the full story of how H.M. destroyer Stronghold was sunk in a desperate action against a Japanese cruiser and two other warships. The 23-years-old destroyer was sailing from Java to Australia with passengers who had escaped from Singapore, when she was engaged by all three enemy ships. Although almost crippled by gunfire from the cruiser Maya, the destroyer closed for a torpedo attack,

Under a hail of fire she got within 5,000 yards of the cruiser. The forward tubes were out of action ; but, wallowing and out of control after her battering, the Stronghold fired her stern tubes. Both torpedoes missed their target. Then the Commanding Officer (Lieutenant-Commander Preyton Pinney, R.N.), a retired officer recalled for the War, collapsed from a thigh wound received earlier in the action and the First Lieutenant (Lieut. W. S. McFarlane, R.N.R.) took over.

Lieutenant McFarlane gave the order to abandon ship when the sinking destroyer had been stopped and was still being shelled heavily. A few minutes later she blew up and disappeared. As Lieutenant I. D. Forbes, R.N., senior surviving officer, stepped aboard the Japanese cruiser the enemy Commander praised the Stronghold for "a very gallant action, worthy of the Royal Navy ! "

The action was for Lieutenant Forbes the culmination of a series of grim adventures. As First Lieutenant of a Chinese river gun-boat, Grasshopper, evacuating a mixed battalion of Royal Marines and Argyll and Sutherland Highlanders from Singapore, he had fought back at waves of attacking Japanese bombers. He saw the Dragonfly, a sister ship, sunk and the Grasshopper, a blazing wreck, beached on an uninhabited island.

Eventually he reached Sumatra. Chief Petty Officer Verrion was his invaluable companion on the journey. Lieutenant Forbes last saw Verrion aboard the Stronghold taking charge of a gun and "by his calm and efficient manner during a particularly gory and hopeless battle" setting a fine example.

THIS IS HOW AMERICA CAME INTO THE WAR

A THREE-WORD sentence radioed from Tokyo on Dec. 5—" Climb Mount Niitaka "—launched the Japanese attack on Pearl Harbour on Dec. 7, 1941. Information of the exact signal which brought the United States into the war was received at Washington on Nov. 16, 1945, from Gen. MacArthur, Allied Supreme Commander, a Daily Telegraph correspondent reported.

From captured documents and the questioning of the Japanese High Command the United States now possess a fairly comprehensive picture of Japanese preparations for the attack.

While the Japanese Fleet was waiting to strike, about 1,000 miles from Hawaii, it was kept informed of the movement of all ships in and out of Pearl Harbour through coded messages broadcast openly over Honolulu's commercial station.

The success of the attack exceeded Japan's wildest expectations. They were prepared to lose one-third of their task force, which included two battleships, two heavy cruisers, six aircraft carriers, 16 destroyers, four light cruisers, 20 first-class submarines and five midget submarines. Actual Japanese losses were no more than 27 planes and five midget submarines.

H.M.S. STRONGHOLD, whose desperate fight with the Japanese cruiser Maya and two other warships early in 1942 is described in this page. Completed in 1919, she had a displacement of 905 tons and carried a complement of 98. *Photo, Wright and Logan*

GRAND WORK OF ALLIED OFFICERS IN SIAM

THE Siamese Resistance Movement owed much to British officers who were first sent into Siam secretly early in 1945. Siamese officers of the British Army had arrived in the previous year, for the Free Siamese in the United States and Britain had declared their allegiance to the Allies as soon as the Japanese occupied their country in the opening attack in December 1941.

The Resistance Movement risked their lives continually in order to organize, arm and train their forces for the day when they hoped they would be able to strike at the Japanese. That day never came, for Japan surrendered first. The Siamese had not risen earlier because they received orders from outside that they were not to strike except in co-ordination with the general Allied strategic plan.

The British, American and Siamese officers, who went into Siam to organize the Resistance army and distribute arms, were often on the run or hiding in the jungle, for the Japanese never slackened their efforts to hunt down the Resistance leaders. Yet thousands joined the movement. It would become known in a village or country town that a certain patriot was enrolling recruits. Men would approach him secretly and be instructed where to meet for training. In ones and twos the men would make their way to the meeting places in the jungle and mountains.

When the Japs Became Suspicious

In addition to military training the Resistance provided an espionage system which gave the Allies information of enormous value on troop movements and concentrations. Secretly leading and supporting the movement were many of the highest political, service and police leaders in Siam. As the movement spread the Japanese became suspicious, and their commander in Bangkok issued a public statement in June 1945 that he knew all about the existence of secret landing-grounds for men and arms in the North. He added that it was about time the Siamese became more co-operative.

THEY did—but not with the Japanese. They were put to the test, for they had to stay underground, often retreating, and wait for the day of rising. They carried out their orders, with the result that when the War ended they provided a first-rate organization for helping Allied prisoners who were awaiting release in their camps.

Some British officers sent to lead the Resistance owe their lives to the Siamese who, instead of turning them over to the Japanese, gave them shelter. Thus they operated with the underground movement in all parts of Siam, and at the time of the surrender they had established themselves actually in Bangkok—in the shadow of the Japanese 18th Army's H.Q.

GERMAN RADAR WAS DEFEATED BY 'TINSEL'—aluminium foil strips (known also as " chaff ") first dropped by the R.A.F. in 1942, which reflected enemy radar signals and gave the impression of numerous aircraft approaching from different directions. As shown here, the packets of tinsel, each weighing 2 oz., were released by the airman from a special chute in the plane's radio room, the strips breaking away and fluttering down independently. *Photo, Keystone*

DROPPED BY PARACHUTE, airborne lifeboats saved the lives of many air crews during the War. Equipped with mast and sail and 4-h.p. engine, first-aid outfit, rations, spare clothing, water purifying units, and other essentials, each boat is wonderfully compact. Here is one of the Royal Navy's airborne lifeboats in action. A Barracuda (1) has released its craft which, borne by three parachutes (2) descends upon the sea. The ditched airmen have clambered aboard and hoisted the sail (3). See also page 6 ; and 731, Vol. 8.

Secrets of the Navy's Parachute Lifeboat

An airborne lifeboat which could be dropped from a large bomber, yet compact enough to be carried in the torpedo-bay of a shipborne plane and strong enough to withstand heavy weather, was tried out in the Solent by naval and civil technicians of the Royal Naval Safety Equipment School. It was dropped on three parachutes by a Barracuda aircraft from a height of 700 ft. As it landed on the water three men, who had been standing by in a rubber dinghy, clambered on board, and within a few minutes were sailing smartly towards the harbour.

It is "bombed up" in the aerial torpedo bay of the aircraft. During its descent three rockets were fired electrically—one carrying out a sea anchor to keep the boat's head to wind, the other two on either beam carrying 150 yards of buoyant line for the rescued men to seize and thus haul themselves into the boat.

The lifeboat, 17 ft. 9 ins. long, and with full equipment weighing 1,200 lb., is built of two mahogany skins supported by linseed oil-soaked fabric. It is fitted with buoyancy chambers, fore and aft, which are automatically inflated as the boat leaves the aircraft, ensuring self-righting in all weathers. In a rough sea the boat rights itself from a complete capsize in 12 seconds.

Besides its mast and set of sails, it carries a 4-h.p. auxiliary engine which produces a speed of 4½ knots over a range of 120 miles. Rudder, drop keel, bilge pump, rope ladders, oars and compass are all provided, and a complete survival equipment is carried in watertight hatches. This includes water-purifying units sufficient to make 45 pints, self-heating soup, condensed milk, cigarettes, flying rations, a heliograph, first-aid outfits, supplies of warm clothing, and a radio transmitter with range of 200 miles.

The Army Camouflaged the Navy's Ships

In the summer of 1943 the Naval authorities operating small vessels in the Aegean area were concerned because these craft were easily spotted from the air. Several of them were shot up, and it was thought desirable that camouflage should be used to make them less conspicuous. The ships were being operated from the coast of Syria and the Lebanon, and so it was of the Army authorities in this area—the 9th Army—that a Naval officer one day asked for help. The Camouflage Branch immediately set to work, and although at that time the disguise of ships was a new venture to them they soon evolved a suitable technique.

Reconnaissance along the coasts of the Green Islands prior to October 1943 was carried out by caiques—familiar craft in these waters, innocent in appearance, and used principally for fishing purposes. It was possible for them to mingle with other caiques, and to go into ordinary fishing areas and harbours without attracting attention. Their movements, however, were limited, for, if they went into areas not usually frequented by such craft, they became conspicuous. In such circumstances, movement by caique had to be by night.

If, however, day movement became necessary, the craft relied upon the disguise inherent in its design, to deceive the enemy. Berthing along the shores of enemy territory had to be done by skilful siting of the craft, and as far away as possible from habitation. It was soon realized that if special camouflage could be used, giving concealment from the ground and the air, reconnaissance could be extended to more dangerous waters.

Experiments were carried out along the coast of the Lebanon, and a camouflage factory was set up at Tripoli to manufacture the equipment necessary. Having prepared some trial nets, camouflage officers went up the coast in a vessel 33 ft. long and having a crew of eight. The plan was to take the vessel out to an island and conceal it by a given time, when it could be observed and photographed from the air. Unfortunately, the vessel's engine broke down and the craft had to put into the nearest port.

A messsage was sent to the aircraft, and although only half an hour was allowed for concealment, and despite the fact that the ship's captain could not spend time finding the most suitable anchorage, the ship was effectually concealed. The plane had on board a pilot and two observers, all of whom knew the size and shape of the ship and its approximate location, but they could not find it. When the result of the experiment were shown to the Naval authorities they decided to adopt it. Because these methods were probably being used in Japanese waters the story could not be told until recently.

First United Nations Assembly Gets to Work

It was not to be expected that the Assembly comprising delegates from 51 nations meeting in London to decide the fate of the world would be altogether free of "growing pains." Tough problems were early presented, as revealed by this account, specially written for "The War Illustrated" by an impartial observer, RUGGERO ORLANDO. See also illus. pages 655-658.

THE General Assembly of the United Nations opened its first session on January 10, 1946, the twenty-sixth anniversary of the League of Nations. Few were aware of the fact that the choice of this date was in itself controversial : the difference between two schools of thought could already be noticed during the preparatory work.

One school of thought, in line with the reformist tradition of the West, maintained that errors in the past would not justify a complete break with the Geneva tradition. The other school, revolutionary and supported by Eastern Europe, believed that the best way of avoiding past errors was to deny the past and break with it. This revolutionary thesis prevailed in the clash over the most important organizational problem—whether the permanent home for the United Nations organization should be in Europe or in America. And it was clearly stated in the Executive of the Preparatory Commission by the Soviet delegate, Andrei Gromyko, that "The old world has had it once, and it is time for the New World to have it."

However, one of the convinced supporters of the Western school, the Belgian Foreign Minister Paul Henri Spaak, was expected to be unanimously elected President of the first session of the General Assembly. The Prime Minister, Mr. Clement Attlee, welcomed the Assembly in London with a speech that defined the aims of the new organization as "not just the negation of war, but the creation of a world of security and freedom." Then the deputy leader of the Soviet delegation unexpectedly proposed as president Mr. Trygve Lie, Foreign Minister of Norway. But Mr. Spaak was elected by 28 votes to 23.

Naturally the Soviet move, which had caused a division in the Assembly on the very day of its inauguration, was widely discussed. One of the most frequent comments heard was that Moscow was attempting to separate the Scandinavian countries from what the Soviet Press calls "the Western bloc." Others expressed the belief that the U.S.S.R. opposed Spaak because he is a typical representative of the Geneva tradition.

Most Powerful Body in History

Tension slackened when it came to the election of the six non-permanent members of the Security Council and of the 18 members of the Economic and Social Council. The Security Council is the most powerful body in all history. It can settle disputes, decide on economic and diplomatic sanctions and finally on peace or war. Nothing and nobody outside the Council is strong enough to obstruct it. But, according to many opinions, its work can all too easily be hampered from within. Article 27 of the San Francisco Charter demands that all decisions, except those on matters of procedure, "shall be made by an affirmative vote of seven members, including the concurring votes of the permanent members," that is to say, China, France, U.S.S.R., U.K., and U.S.A.—a provision generally known as "the right of veto" by the Big Five.

The Security Council held its inaugural meeting on January 17. It was presided over by Mr. Makin, Australian Minister for the Navy. Each delegate made a speech. Mr. Vincent-Auriol of France reminded the Council that exactly 75 years ago "the German Empire had been founded by Bismarck. We may reflect now on the fall of this empire of violence ; today marks in a very special sense the beginning of a new era of law and justice among peoples and nations."

The General Assembly debated for several days the report of the Preparatory Commission, and almost all delegates took this opportunity to reaffirm their will to cooperate loyally and make the United Nations a success. In opening the general discussion on January 14 the American Secretary of State, Mr. F. J. Byrnes, reiterated the pledge given by President Truman at the San Francisco Conference : "The responsibility of the great States is to serve and not to dominate the world."

Major Anxieties of the Moment

Speaking for Britain, Mr. Bevin laid stress on the importance of economic advancement : "The social disorders rising from the War and the failure to satisfy the physical and intellectual development of mankind may lead to still further troubles and serious conflicts. The task which thus devolves upon the Economic and Social Council is an urgent one and has just as great and important a bearing on world security and peace as the Security Council." Mr. Bevin also said his Government had decided to place the mandates in Africa, granted to her by the League of Nations, under the trusteeship system.

The Soviet delegate, Mr. Gromyko, urged the "decisive rejection of voices speaking of the Charter as already obsolete and needing revision." He uttered a warning : "The organization of the United Nations was born as a result of bloody battles against Fascism. It would, however, be a mistake to consider that military victory over Fascism removes the necessity for the further persistent struggle for the eradication and complete liquidation of Nazi-Fascism which still remains."

The Persian delegate, Seyed Hassan Taqizadeh, sounded a note of immediate concern : "We wished that, like many other fellow-members, we were attending this Assembly free from major anxieties. But we can hardly refrain from referring to the very disturbing situation prevailing in Persia. We must reserve our right to bring the question before the Assembly."

Many a delegate, and above all the American Secretary of State, had expressed the desire "to avoid casting excessive burdens upon the new institutions, especially in their infancy." However, the Persian speech was soon followed by a formal request of the delegation that "interference of the Soviet Union in the internal affairs of Persia should be brought to the attention of the Security Council." Not wanting to appear as the only defendants before the new organization, the Russian, followed by the Ukrainian delegation, asked for inquiries into the presence of British troops in Greece and Indonesia.

THUS the Security Council, less than a fortnight after its inauguration, was facing three extremely serious problems. Before meeting for the second time on January 25, the President of the Security Council received a letter from the leader of the Soviet delegation, Mr. Andrei Vyshinsky, who had just arrived in London, stating that the Persian allegation was "in contradiction with reality." The letter quoted former Persian statements, acknowledging the legality of Soviet activities in Persia, and concluded, "The Soviet delegation regards the appeal of the Persian delegation to the Security Council as without any foundation, and is categorically opposed to the consideration of the mentioned appeal."

The most dramatic meeting, so far, in the life of the organization then followed. Near Mr. Vyshinsky sat Mr. Bevin, who opposed the Soviet proposal to exclude the Persian issue from discussion, with the words, "I am very anxious that complainants should be heard by the Council, whoever they may be." Then, rather out of order, he went on to tackle also the Greek and Indonesian questions : "In the case of Greece, I shall offer no objections to the fullest investigation and discussion. Indonesia is primarily a matter for the Dutch Government," Mr. van Kleffens, representative of the Netherlands, also agreed that his Government had no objection to an investigation.

Mr. Edward Stettinius, Jnr. (the American representative on the Security Council and leader of the U.S. delegation after Mr. Byrnes' departure for Washington on January 24), submitted that the correspondence from the delegations of Persia, Soviet Union and Ukraine should be listed on the agenda of the Security Council for consideration. Further debate followed, Mr. Vyshinsky assuming that to examine a complaint should not necessarily mean it to be "considered." Mr. Bevin objected : "I do not want the situation to arise that after going through all the performance of hearing the case, somebody says that the Council cannot discuss it."

The Big Problem of Trusteeship

The President answered that it was up to the Council itself, at its next meeting on January 28, "to determine just how it shall treat this particular subject, and by its own resolution it will be able to proceed as it will wish to the consideration of these subjects."

On January 28 the Persian delegate, Mr. Taqizadeh, was admitted to the Security Council. He stated that his Government was prepared to negotiate with Moscow, but under the supervision of the Security Council. The Soviet delegate, Mr. Vyshinsky, on the same day and again at the meeting of January 30, agreed to negotiate but opposed the last Persian demand asking for the removal of the question from the Council's agenda. After four hours' spirited debate the Council unanimously approved a proposal by Mr. Bevin that direct negotiations between the two parties be started, both of them being requested to inform the Council of any result achieved, and the Council reserving its right to request information at any time. Another important decision reached in this initial stage of the United Nations' life was the nomination of the General Secretary of the organization, in the person of the Norwegian Foreign Secretary, Mr. Trygve Lie.

Amongst the many organizational questions, the problem of trusteeship aroused lively discussion. The Preparatory Commission recommended that "the States administering territories under League of Nations mandate undertake practical steps, in concert with other States directly concerned, for agreements on the terms of trusteeship." The Arab States want now to clarify the meaning of "other States directly concerned." Obviously they think it should entitle them to have a say in the thorny question of Palestine. South Africa claimed special treatment for her mandate of South-West Africa, as it was one applying to the same territory as that of the mandatory power.

The World Federation of Trade Unions, representing 70,000,000 workers, asked for a permanent seat on the Economic and Social Council. While the San Francisco Charter does not recognize representation by any body but a *nation*, many delegations are sympathetic to the claim of the workers of the world.

World Peace is Planned in London

Photo, Associated Press

Freedom's Flags Unfurled in Solemn Unity

Unfamiliar to the Londoner as to the delegates from 51 nations were many of the national flags above the entrance to the Central Hall, Westminster, on January 10, 1946: the actual San Francisco flags (see page 52) were draped inside. "Gathered in this ancient home of liberty and order," for the first Assembly of the United Nations Organization, delegates were determinedly approaching some of the weightiest problems this world has ever known. See also illus. pages 624–625.

Choice Between Life and Death to be Made—

" Our ultimate aim," said Mr. Clement Attlee, the Prime Minister, addressing the U.N.O. on Jan. 10, " is not just the negation of war but the creation of a world governed by justice and the moral law." On Jan. 12, votes were cast to elect the six non-permanent members of the Security Council: Dr. E. N. van Kleffens, Netherlands Foreign Minister, about to place his vote in the ballot box (1). Mr. Attlee in discussion with Mr. Ernest Bevin, the British Foreign Secretary (2).

Photos, N Associate

—By the Peoples of the World in Assembly

Mr. J. F. Byrnes, U.S. Secretary of State (3), addressed the delegates on January 14, when the U.N.O. debated the report of the Preparatory Commission. A bird's-eye view of the Assembly (4): in the top left corner is the Organization's emblem of world peace. Mr. Clement Attlee attended a Government banquet to the United Nations delegates in the famous Painted Hall at the Royal Naval College, Greenwich (5), on January 15. One of the many interpreters (6) at the Assembly.

Active in the Deliberations of the U.N.O.

Photos, Barratts, P.A.-Reuter, Planet News

United Kingdom representatives (1), Mr. E. Bevin, Foreign Secretary (right) and Mr. Noel Baker, Minister of State. Saudi Arabia (2), H.R.H. the Emir Feisal, Foreign Minister (left) and H.E. Sheikh Hafiz Wahba. Belgium (3), M. Paul Henri Spaak, Foreign Minister and President of the Assembly. U.S.S.R. (4), M. Andrei Gromyko, Ambassador to Washington. Norway (5), M. Trygve Lie, Foreign Minister. Canada (6, l. to r.), Rt. Hon. L. St. Laurent, Minister of Justice, Mr. Gordon Graydon, Mr. Paul Martin. Australia (7, l. to r.) Mr. Paul Hasluck, Lt.-Col. W. R. Hodgson, Prof. K. H. Bailey.

The Ordeal of Cassino

A Review by HAMILTON FYFE

I HAVE just read a book that gives a clearer, and I think truer, picture of what war is like to the soldier than any I have read before. If the War were not over I should not call attention to The Monastery (John Lane, 7s. 6d.). I don't think it is a book to be read while fighting goes on, either by the soldiers or by their relatives and friends at home. It is too true—terribly, appallingly true of the sensitive, the imaginative, those whose intellect revolts against the stupidity of war and whose nerves are constantly flayed by its dirt and dullness and danger.

The author of The Monastery, F. Majdalany, is one of those. Whether he is British-born does not appear. He is an officer in an infantry regiment, and his battalion took part in the gradual and painful reduction of Monte Cassino in the first months of 1944, which cost us so many lives and was such a wasteful delay on the road to victory.

You will remember how some people became very agitated about the ancient buildings on the top of the hill, two thousand feet above the town of Cassino, which the Germans had turned into a strongpoint, believing it could never be taken (see pages 653, 655, Vol. 7, and 88-89, Vol. 8). These critics thought that we ought not to destroy a holy place just because it happened to lie across our road from Naples to Rome and because some Germans were there. I should like to make such silly sentimentalists read this book. I should like to have put some of them just where Majdalany's battalion was for over a month, about half-way between the town and the summit.

Death in the Air All the Time

Here, in the foremost positions, which the same men held for six days at a time, it was impossible to move by day without being seen by the enemy and at once bombarded. All the hours of daylight had to be spent cramped in a narrow shelter. This could be made comfortable with blankets, and "a good proportion of the day was devoted to sleep. But with shells and mortar-bombs sleep was seldom unbroken. All a man had to look forward to at the end of the day was a meal of half-warm meat pasties and another long night of straining alertness. And all daylight activities, whether eating or anything else, had to be conducted in the lying position." Nerve-shattering indeed !

When a company was relieved after its six days, "limbs and muscles were so stiff that men frequently had great difficulty in marching out of their positions." What they marched to was not exactly luxurious. They lived in what had once been shepherds' houses reduced to "a decaying mass of rubble and battle wreckage." They shared these with large numbers of centipedes and other crawling things, "which had a disconcerting habit of dropping suddenly and silently from above, which made them even more unpleasant than shells. Shells are not nice, but you can hear them coming."

Then there was the Smell, that old familiar smell which "pervades the world of the Infantry, which is universal and haunting, the smell of death." Decomposing bodies were all too frequently encountered. Death was in the air all the time. The knowledge that they were being watched from enemy observation posts made them feel as if they were "being suddenly stripped of their clothes." They could feel the eyes watching them. They waited for the result of their being spotted. Sometimes it came, sometimes it didn't. But either way you had that feeling of insecurity, of hidden peril lurking above you.

In the darkness there was "the familiar dread which is inseparable from night-time in the line. Will there be a counter-attack ? What's hatching in the Monastery ?" As a consequence of this jumpiness there were false alarms. Lights would be reported. Perhaps they had been there, perhaps it was the sentry's strained sight which imagined them. "Sentries were always reporting lights." In any case Very lights were "a commonplace in the routine of the front line."

> Being attacked by night is particularly unnerving because you cannot tell whether there are twenty of the enemy or a whole battalion. If two machine-guns can infiltrate through your positions and open fire from behind, the most dogged temperament finds it hard to resist the impression that it is surrounded.

After the report of lights comes a good deal of sporadic firing. "Nobody speaks, unless it is just to pass a message on the telephone or the wireless. They just stood or leaned or sat motionless—and fancied they could hear their heart-beats." When the firing eased off and it became clear that nothing out-of-the-ordinary was to happen, they began to talk again. "They made the rather forced little jokes which always follow a period of fear."

Eight Hours to Dressing-Station

That is frank enough, and the author is not less straightforward in describing the dullness of the in-between times. "Life resolved itself into that deadly sameness which is the hardest thing of all to bear in war. A sustained emptiness of dull repetition, relieved only by spasms of danger and the dread that goes with it. The same old thing day after day. The same, small dull things happening time after time."

I have sensed that dreariness so often when I have been visiting troops as a war reporter. They try to hide it from outsiders. "The chances are that a casual visitor would notice none of it. He would go away and say 'Yesterday I went to see the So-and-So's near Cassino. They were in good heart. What a cheery lot they are ! Amazing how those chaps stick it !'" But I wasn't a casual visitor. I was a student of war—and human nature. I knew how they felt under their masks of cheeriness. I have seen the same sort of scarcely bearable boredom among officers at home during the past War. Planted in some out-of-the-way spot, sick of it and themselves and one another !

EVERYTHING needed on that slope of the Cassino hill had to be dragged up from the town. There were stretcher-bearer posts all along the track at intervals of two hundred yards and a dressing-station at the bottom. Casualties were handed on from one post to another, but it often meant that "a chap is lucky if he gets to the dressing-station within eight hours of being hit, or without being dropped once or twice on a wet night." If you weren't wounded, one of the torments was the scarcity of water, which had to be brought up like everything else. By rigorous rationing, half an inch of water at the bottom of a petrol can could be shared among three men for shaving. Teeth could be cleaned without water, "except for a few drops to clean the brush, and damp early morning grass does just as well." Shaving was considered necessary ; it "works wonders with one's morale." Does it in fact ? Or is that merely a tradition ? The Navy does not always need it. Submarine crews, for example, do not always shave.

Soldiers are like schoolboys in sticking to old formulas and habits—and in other ways, too. For example, a kind of game was played three or four times a day, and a dozen times a night ; a sort of duel, or "a lethal shooting match." First light mortars would get to work, with rifle grenades. Then heavier mortars, then artillery. "It was really just a great big game of cowboys and Indians, with the unfortunate difference that someone always had to die and more had to be maimed." Thus during the four and a half weeks that the battalion held that position on Monte Cassino, in spite of its having "a quiet time," over 70 officers and men were lost. "In any other arm of the Service that would be considered a lot for a period of 'doing nothing.'"

MANY of those losses were among the food carriers. Both sides did all they could to kill the men toiling up with provisions. "Above all we went for the mountain tracks and passes where we knew their ration parties had to walk . . . We poured shells all along the routes the German mules and porters had to take, for the chances are in this kind of battle that if you kill one man carrying food half a dozen men will go hungry the next day." It would be hard to write a sentence summing up more succinctly the loathsomeness, the devilishness of war.

When relief came, the battalion marched down the hill and through the town "in the way of the Infantry, their feet scarcely leaving the ground, their bodies rocking mechanically from side to side as if that was the only way they could lift their legs. You could see it required the last ounce of their mental and physical energy to move their legs at all." Yet they looked as if they could keep on moving like that for ever. Their staring eyes seemed to see nothing. No one sang or whistled, hardly anyone spoke. "Their clothes were torn and ragged. They carried their weapons every conceivable way they could be carried. Every few minutes they would change shoulders or change positions. The heavier burdens, like the Brens and the mortars, were passed along from one to another. Every man took his turn."

Back to the Final Assault

The general was waiting at the junction of the tracks in the olive groves to watch his men march in. "When they came to the place where the trucks were an officer led them off and helped them to drag their leaden bodies into the backs of the vehicles, where they collapsed in sleep. As soon as a truck was filled it rumbled off down the dusty road, taking the sleeping men from the battlefield."

At last they came to country where it was spring, and for ten days or so they rested. Then came the order to go back. The division to which they belonged was to take part in the final assault. To picture what is involved when a division takes the road, imagine, says the author, a town of 15,000 inhabitants moving in its entirety to an area fifty or more miles away.

> Imagine the town being given a few hours' notice to pack into lorries all its inhabitants, the contents of all its shops ; its petrol stocks and all mechanical stores and plant ; its business and administrative files and records ; everything, in fact, essential to its daily existence. Imagine it setting off one morning in its vehicles and by the afternoon being established in a new location that is only an expanse of fields : not only established but carrying out its normal work without anyone having gone without a meal. That is how it is when a division moves.

Well, that is certainly a bouquet for the Army, and one which it deserves. If we can harness the administrative ability which accomplishes that miracle to the tasks of Peace, tackle our industrial problems with the same quiet orderliness and forethought, we can look into the future without fear.

Keeping the Wheels of U.N.O. Smoothly Turning

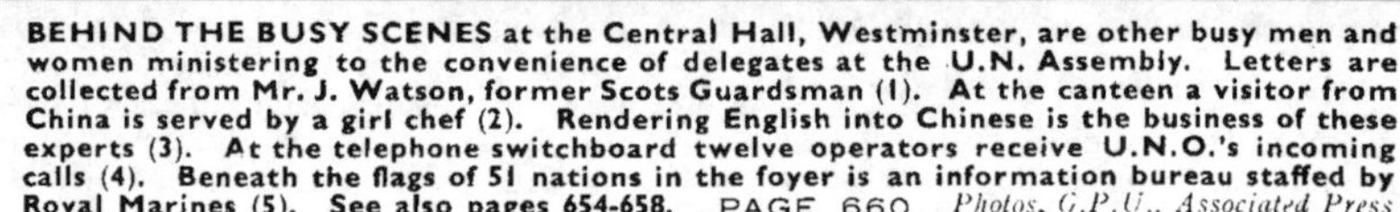

BEHIND THE BUSY SCENES at the Central Hall, Westminster, are other busy men and women ministering to the convenience of delegates at the U.N. Assembly. Letters are collected from Mr. J. Watson, former Scots Guardsman (1). At the canteen a visitor from China is served by a girl chef (2). Rendering English into Chinese is the business of these experts (3). At the telephone switchboard twelve operators receive U.N.O.'s incoming calls (4). Beneath the flags of 51 nations in the foyer is an information bureau staffed by Royal Marines (5). See also pages 654-658. *Photos, G.P.U., Associated Press*

Timber Houses From Sweden Erected in Britain

PREFABRICATED two-storey dwellings of four different types, 5,000 of which were recently ordered from Sweden, are intended for permanent use in this country: photographs in this page were taken at Abbots Langley, Herts. Swedish standards have been adopted to conform with British requirements, including party walls with brick fireplaces and chimneys (1). A house can be quickly erected on the concrete site; workmen took only 2½ hours to put up these wall panels (2). Roof tiling, glazing and painting are done by the local authority; Ministry of Works supplies cookers, washing and plumbing fixtures. Accommodation includes living-room, three bedrooms, bathroom and kitchen; a one-storey outbuilding contains additional W.C., washing, fuel and store room (3). All four types have front porches (4). Kitchens are compactly equipped (5).

Exclusive to THE WAR ILLUSTRATED

How Will the Ministry of Labour Find Me a Job?

Most of the thousands of men and women who are demobilized each week have one special target in mind—a situation. Our contributor FRANK ILLINGWORTH applied to the Ministry of Labour and National Service for employment; and in this article specially written for "The War Illustrated" he explains the system of job-finding and outlines its attendant problem.

RESETTLEMENT of labour is a mammoth problem. Millions of men and women, uprooted from their chosen professions, have to be guided back to industry along lines twisted into fantastic shapes by shortages of materials, lack of housing and uncertain international conditions. Here, an employer cannot take further employees until he can secure materials; there, a firm can obtain the materials but not the housing necessary to an increased staff.

Shifts of population, transfers of industries, demands for labour in unpopular employment—the mines, hospitals and so on—Service requirements and those of agriculture and transport; all these factors have to be fitted into the pattern of a giant jigsaw jumbled by six years of total war.

The problem rests with the Ministry of Labour and National Service; on the Employment Exchanges in every little town throughout Britain, and on the London Appointments Office and the twelve Regional Appointments Offices in the Provinces. It was to see how the organization worked that I went to the Resettlement Advice Service, and then applied to the London Appointments Office for a job, following my application from section to section until at the final desk it went into a pigeon-hole, and, a few days later, released a letter asking me to call on Messrs. So-and-So for an interview.

THE Resettlement Advice Service is the stepping stone from Service to civilian life. The Government fully realizes that men and women who have been in uniform for a number of years are out of touch with everyday affairs at home, and particularly with conditions resulting from "controls." The task of the Resettlement Advice Service is to solve their problems, and it plays a big part in finding jobs for demobilized men and women in many different fields.

Among those whom I joined in a well-furnished room was a man of thirty-five who had left a business behind in 1939. He had no money with which to buy stock, he had no idea how or where to secure the permits necessary to rebuild a war-damaged storage shed, he couldn't understand the controls governing sale and purchase, and he had come to the Advice Service for help.

The Crossroads in Resettlement

"His is a common enough inquiry," an official said later, "but some we see aren't so easy to answer, though we usually succeed. Yesterday, when a lad wanted to know the qualifications to become a lighthouse keeper we found out what they were within the hour. And a day or so ago when two young ex-Servicemen asked how to start a mobile fish-and-chip business we directed them to a Civil Defence vehicle depot where they were fixed up with a van that afternoon."

The Resettlement Advice Service is the crossroads in resettlement. Men whose questions apply to employment are summed up and directed either to their local Employment Exchanges or to the Appointments Offices which deal exclusively with men and women of the executive type. "A man might have been a lorry driver in 1939," I was told, at the Appointments Office, London, "but if Service life has developed his powers of leadership he comes to this Department for an executive job, and not to the ordinary Labour Exchanges. The best applicant for the job—man or woman—is the slogan."

I went to the Appointments Office at Tavistock Square, London, W.C.2, there to join other employment seekers in a waiting room with cubicles marked "Overseas," "Professions," etc. Here, my particulars were noted, and four days later I received a request to call for an interview.

Sympathetic Interviewer Sums-Up

The Appointments Office is divided into sections, each with a specific purpose. In one, officers from the three Services interview men who, called up straight from school, have no civil qualifications. Others deal with men with specific qualifications or aptitudes. The psychological aspect of interviewing is not overlooked. The Appointments Office works on the basis that the ex-industrial supervisor, no less than the ex-varsity man, is fully at ease only when the interviewer understands his outlook. Thus, where possible, ex-accountants are seen by interviewers with some accountancy knowledge, and pre-war works-managers are allocated to interviewers who have themselves industrial experience.

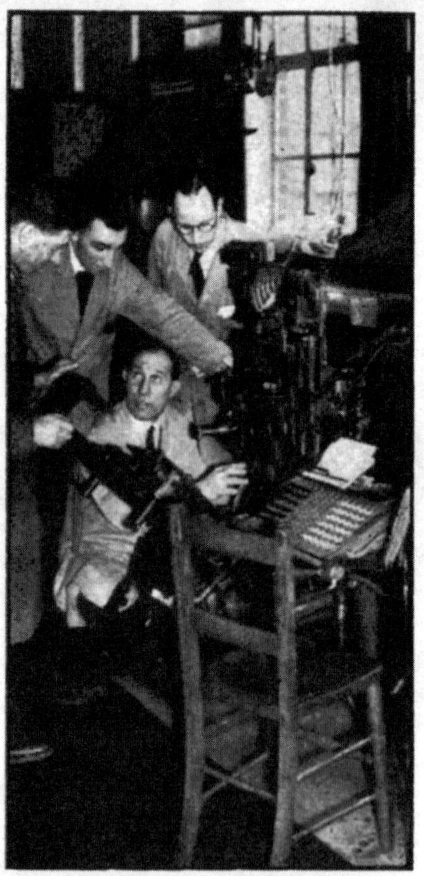

INSTRUCTION FOR EX-SERVICEMEN at the London School of Printing, S.E.1, includes all branches of the craft. Here the mechanism of a linotype machine is being explained. See also facing page. *Photo, Fox*

"Good morning! What can we do for you? Have a cigarette? Now, what is it you . . . ?" While the applicant talks, the interviewer sums him up and makes notes as to the employment he wants, his qualifications, and the salary he needs. Is he free to go anywhere? Is his bearing good, and is he self-confident? All this, and much more, is noted on a special form, and with the interview ended the Appointments Office has a complete picture of the applicant's appearance, demeanour, accomplishments, qualifications and requirements.

His "case sheet" goes to the Common Services Section—in effect, a sorting office. From here, specific professions go to the various placing sections, there to be entered on separate Registers of vacancies and applicants. In turn, vacancies arising in the Provinces converge on the London Office where, so that a man in Edinburgh can be told of a job in Bristol, and vice versa, they are sorted and circulated throughout Provincial Appointments Offices.

Next, to the "Placing Section." Here the unemployed (say) works-manager's particulars find their way into a tray opposite another containing the requirements of employers asking for works-managers. A cross-index system brings each to the other; and when the two halves more or less fit an interview is arranged. The system is well devised and is working properly. But there are snags in the matter of switching men from wartime to peacetime employment.

Such is the demand for executive posts that the London Appointments Office is taking in thirty extra staff every week to handle inquiries from all over the world. Indeed, the Registers contain more men for jobs than jobs for men—7,500 applicants against only 4,000 situations available.

'Further Educational' Schemes

What are the reasons for the gap? Geared for war, industrial assembly lines have to slow down to a very considerable extent before they can be speeded up to peacetime requirements. Many factories, short of materials and still deep in re-organization to meet changed conditions, are not ready to increase their staff commitments. In addition, years of war have denied to industry the young men who would otherwise now be skilled workers, while years in the Services have robbed thousands of once-skilled workers of their skill.

Employers want highly skilled men, and they are unable to pay high wage-rates until industry settles down again. On the other hand, the demobilized—some of them "rusty," some lacking in qualifications because they entered the Services straight from school—are asking for wage-rates commensurate with rising costs of living.

THIS is the transitional stage into which tens of thousands of men and women are being released. It is being bridged by "further educational" schemes, operated by the Ministry of Labour both for disabled and fully employable men and women, and by individual firms and employment groups. For example: the Hotel Trades Association has a scheme under which men receive pay while training for executive jobs in the Hotel Trade, suitable trainees being found employment on completion of training. And the London County Council has a school for would-be hotel and restaurant chefs.

Private employment exchanges, including those catering for individual professions, no less than the Ministry of Labour, are at the disposal of the demobilized. Next June, 12½ per cent of our total labour force will still be in the Services, against 2½ per cent before the war. Meanwhile, the Ministry of Labour employs ex-officers to tell the troops all over the world how to obtain jobs on returning home; others are busy asking employers to pull their weight by applying to the Ministry for the executives they need before they can employ more workers, and others are busy at the Appointments Offices interviewing men and women as they return to Civvy Street.

From the Services to a Civilian Occupation

THE MAN WHO IS RETURNING to the responsibilities of ordinary life needs advice on many questions as well as a job for which he is qualified. How he is assisted to secure employment is shown here step-by-step. From the Resettlement Advice Bureau (1) he may be directed either to a Labour Exchange or an Appointments Office in London or in one of the twelve regional centres (2).

He enters the London Appointments Office in Tavistock Square (3) and makes inquiries (4). Either here (5) or at his home he fills in his record of qualifications A. He is then called for an interview (6), which may last an hour, during which the interviewing officer enters his impressions on the Interview Record B. Then forms A and B are sent to a sorting office, the Common Services Section (7), to be filed into the correct category.

Meanwhile, from industry come demands for labour. The work offered, its nature and qualifications required, are noted on form C. These forms are again filed into different categories, and constant communication is maintained between London and the various regional offices. In the placing section (8) the forms A and B, relating to a particular case, and the work available, C, are compared. At this important stage every effort is made to "place" the right man for the most appropriate position before he is interviewed. Letters are sent from the placing section calling suitable candidates to be interviewed (9) for the available post. The Ministry of Labour and many private firms have organized educational courses and training schemes (10) to re-equip demobilized men for industry and the social services. "Victory in peace," stated Sir Stafford Cripps, President of the Board of Trade, on January 20, 1946, "is as hard a job of production as victory in war." However, the necessary conditions are being hastened to enable thousands more men to produce urgently needed goods. See also article in facing page.

Specially drawn for THE WAR ILLUSTRATED *by Haworth*

I Was There! *Eye Witness Stories of the War and After*

Our Great Break-Out from Stalag Luft III

How 78 Allied Air Force officers were enabled to make the great "break" from Stalag Luft III—a German prison camp in flat, wooded country near Sagan in Upper Silesia—on March 24, 1944, is told by Flight-Lieut. Ley Kenyon, D.F.C., R.A.F., in this account written specially for "The War Illustrated." His drawings, which he executed on the spot and are here reproduced, are the only authentic pictorial records of the escape-tunnel.

SINCE the completion of Stalag Luft III in the early months of 1943 four escape tunnels were dug, known to us as Tom, Dick, Harry and George. Unfortunately, Tom was discovered when its 300-ft. length was almost completed. Dick had a sad ending after months of work, when the Germans built another compound on the very spot where Dick's exit from the underworld would have been!

In our third attempt we were more fortunate. On March 24, 1944, 78 Allied Air Force officers were able to make one of the biggest tunnel escapes of this or any other war, through Harry. It took 400 men, working day and night in shifts, 15 months to complete its 320-ft. length. The brain behind this organization was a Spitfire squadron commander, Squadron-Leader Roger Bushell, spoken of by us as "Mr. X." He pitted his razor-keen wits against the enemy, and won every time during the lengthy period of precarious work on Harry.

I Forged the Essential Papers

It all had to be carried out in the greatest possible secrecy, of course. Our guards were planted everywhere round the camp to watch and follow German sentries and "ferrets"—as we called the German security guards whose job it was to look for just such underground activity as we were engaged upon. If they approached too closely the scene of operations, word or sign was flashed ahead by our watchers and work stopped until the "all clear" was given.

Several months after work had started on the digging of Harry, I was introduced into the organization—in the forgery department. It became my business to assist in the production of forged passports, photographs, rubber stamps carved from the rubber heels of boots, letters of introduction, railway tickets, travel warrants and maps. All the officers who were to escape—we budgeted for 160—were to carry with them complete official data sufficient to allow them to travel by foot or rail through Germany. And that is where I came in.

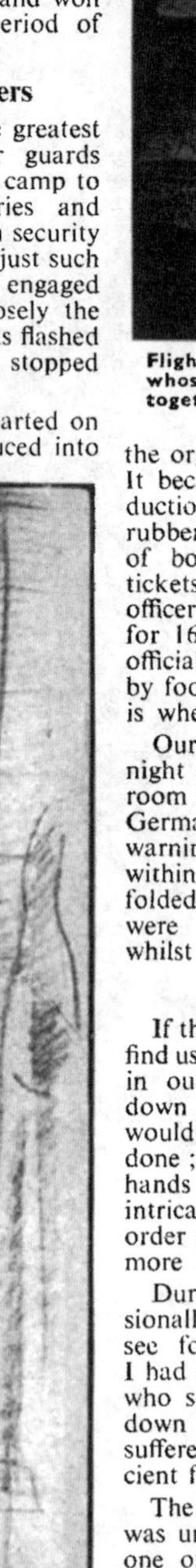

Flight-Lieut. LEY KENYON, D.F.C., R.A.F., whose sensational escape story appears here, together with his own drawings of the famous tunnel workings at Stalag Luft III.

Our forgery department worked day and night in the camp lending library, a small room in one of the blocks. In the event of a German approaching the block the necessary warning was given by our watchers, and within five seconds all the forged matter was folded up and slipped into books, which were instantly replaced on the shelves, whilst ink and pens went into our pockets.

Secret of the Concrete Slab

If the intruder entered the library he would find us innocently reading; though sometimes, in our haste, the book would be upside down! On certain days the tapped warnings would be so frequent that nothing could be done; tempers became so frayed that our hands were too unsteady to attempt the intricate work, and the chief would give the order to close shop until conditions became more favourable.

During these feverish months I was occasionally able to go down into the tunnel and see for myself the progress being made. I had tremendous admiration for the fellows who spent so much of their wakeful hours down there, 30 ft. underground. Everyone suffered physically, for there was not sufficient food to keep us up to scratch.

The entrance to the tunnel's vertical shaft was under a slab of concrete in a corner of one of the living rooms, and on the slab stood a heating stove. All this had to be lifted away each time a working shift was to go down or be changed, and, of course, it had to be replaced in such a way that it would escape the most rigorous search by the "ferrets."

BELOW the concrete slab we first dropped a shaft to a depth of 30 ft., and dug ourselves a workshop about 8 ft. by 4 ft., an air-pump room, and a dispersal chamber to congregate men or store displaced sand. When these were finished and fully equipped the tunnel itself was started, tons of fine white sand being dug out monthly and dispersed around the camp—sometimes carried out in Red Cross cardboard boxes and

AIR-PIPE MADE OF EMPTY DRIED-MILK TINS ran the full length of the escape-tunnel. Hand-operated bellows (above), made from kit bags, forced the fresh air—drawn down the vertical pipe—through to the working shift at the tunnel face; the valve apparatus was ingeniously constructed of wood and tin. *Drawing by Flight-Lieut. Ley Kenyon, D.F.C., R.A.F.*

BUILDING THE ESCAPE TUNNEL, which in places was only 24 inches square, only one man at a time was able to work at the "face" (1) where, in a position of great discomfort, he scooped away the sand for removal in boxes placed on trollies. At a half-way house (2), sand was removed from one trolly to another for forwarding. Each section had its own trucks, men and sand travelling the tunnel in three stages. A box of sand arrives at the entrance (3), for concealment within the confines of the camp. *Drawings by Flight-Lieut. Ley Kenyon, D.F.C. R.A.F.*

buried under our meagre gardens, sometimes removed in long cloth bags slung inside the trouser legs of the dispersers, who strolled round the camp and let the sand trickle out from the bottom of their tied-up pants !

Much of it was hidden away beneath our theatre. When we built the theatre the Germans allowed us to put in a sloping floor, which made it necessary for us to excavate several feet below ground-level, this giving us a fine opportunity to slip in extra sand from the tunnel unnoticed. Still more sand was hidden away in Dick ; this latter tunnel was never discovered by the Germans, and was used throughout as a hiding-place for a large quantity of our escape material.

Our Subterranean Trolly-Run

One of the most interesting features of our tunnels was the wood lining. Every inch had to be boarded in because of the looseness of the sand. Bed-boards were used for this purpose—every inmate of the camp giving up a few boards for the cause. Of course, this discrepancy in numbers had to be made up to curb suspicion, as the Germans made periodic counts of them. The splitting of the wider boards to make two was one of many ways of avoiding detection. Mortice joints were made in the ends of all boards, which were fitted in position as the tunnel progressed.

Railway lines, also made of wood, were laid, on which trollies, with metal-banded wheels, could be pulled. The trollies, manufactured in our underground workshop, consisted of wooden frames provided with a flange to hold the sand-boxes firmly during their bumpy ride. These transported man and material to the working face and were dragged by ropes made from Red Cross parcel string. An air pipe, made of dried-milk tins, ran the full length of the tunnel. This supplied fresh air to the working shift at the tunnel face, the air being forced through by a hand-pump, the bellows of which were made from kit bags, and the necessary valve apparatus from wood and tin. The inlet pipe was secreted inside the fireplace and chimney in the living-room above. The Jerry chimney-sweep must have cleaned that out a dozen times without realizing the true use of the chimney.

An electric lighting system was eventually installed by our electrician. His work was made easier by the carelessness of a German electrician who left a 600-ft. coil of electric cable unattended in a wheelbarrow ; when he returned for it, it was gone. He was later shot by his countrymen—for negligence. Approximately every hundred feet the tunnel, which was only 24 inches square, widened out to give room to officers transferring sand from one trolly to another on its transit back to the dispersal chamber. The middle section of the tunnel, passing under the anti-tunnelling sound detectors which the Germans had placed under the barbed wire, was taken deeper and the trolly lines padded to deaden all sound.

My first visit to the tunnel face was a queer experience. After descending the 30-ft. shaft and passing through the workshop I was told by my guide to lie on the hard wood frame of the trolly in the tunnel entrance. Immediately it started to move forward into the black void, and gathered speed. Seconds passed before I saw a spot of light ahead, no larger than a postage stamp. This increased in size as I rumbled forward through the stifling heat, until I was pulled into the first half-way house, lit by a wick floating in a tin of German margarine.

Then I was told to transfer to the next trolly, for the second part of the journey to the tunnel face. Here I found a worker, naked to the waist—a bomber pilot and already three years a prisoner—hacking at the sand and pushing it back to his number two, who was piling it into boxes ready for transit. I held up operations temporarily to make quick sketches of all I saw. Very quick! My models were impatient. They wanted to get on with the work. And I wanted to get back up above as quickly as possible; I had heard too often of the sandfalls under which our men were almost suffocated before they could be extricated.

BACK again in the workshop an alarm had just sounded. A tin hanging from the roof and containing stones had been rattled by a string from ground-level, giving warning of an approaching "ferret." Suddenly everything became eerily silent, and eyes were expectantly lifted to the entrance trap. Several minutes passed before the all clear was given and the rumble of the trollies and the dull noises of underground work recommenced. A new shift had come down, and the old shift ascended to clean themselves of every grain of sand and dirt in the wash-house and change into normal clothes before they returned to their own blocks—to sleep, and sometimes to eat.

Above ground, activity was intense. All the equipment for escape was being secretly manufactured, in rooms carefully guarded by our security men. Besides the forged papers, civilian clothes, made from any material we could acquire, compasses, iron rations, and route maps were turned out in sufficient numbers to equip the 160 men who had been detailed or balloted for the escape. No date for the break had been released—this remained a secret to all but a few, almost until the last hour. At dusk on March 24, 1944, that hour arrived.

Excitement was at fever pitch. Superb organization made it possible to concentrate all the escapists into Harry's block unseen by the watchful German sentries in their boxes continuously swinging their searchlights into every corner of the camp. Even the dogs were silent.

Shadowy figures sauntered across the compound in the dim light—blankets tied round their waists under their overcoats, their pockets bulging with rations and equipment. One by one they slid into the rooms allotted to them. One by one they were ushered into the tunnel room and given final instructions before descending the shaft. Mistakes were made, scares were numerous, but no sound echoed from that block throughout the night.

(Concluded in "The War Illustrated" No. 227).

The Germans Now Raise Their Hats To Us!

The grand job the British soldier is doing in getting Germany on her feet again—and how the people are responding—needs to be made known to the world. Evening Standard correspondent Richard McMillan, writing from Berlin on January 11, 1946, places his findings on record.

WE have heard enough about the black market, about fraternization, about those mythical millions supposed to be made in the sale of our cigarettes; forget, too, the recurring stories of quarrels and fisticuffs and bad feelings between the troops and civilians. Let us talk instead of the grand job the British Tommy is doing in getting Germany on her feet again. From the Germans themselves, everywhere you go, you are likely to hear more praise than blame about him.

"We cannot help but admire the British soldier for the great work he is doing," they say. "We have seen him achieving the miracle of putting some life and order back into a crushed, broken, smothered and hopeless nation." So, in case you have the idea that sideline rackets, black market and fraternization are the main preoccupations of the British Army, you will be glad to hear about the truer picture in the B.A.O.R. zone. And it will make you realize why the Germans tip their hats to our men.

A British administrative officer told me today: "The feeding of Germany, the restoration of communication on roads, railways and canals, the policing of the cities, towns and country districts day and night, the handling of displaced persons, the cleaning up of the battlefield, the disarmament of Germany, the tracking down of Nazis, the shipping and distribution of clothing, the fighting of disease, the razing of ruined towns to make way for the housing programme, the rebuilding of houses and huts and even helping in the difficult task of searching for missing P.O.W.—these are a few of the tasks that figure in the gigantic worksheet. And it is the British Tommy who is doing the job."

Hanging On By Their Eyebrows

That does not mean that our men are doing all the hard work themselves; no, they are the gaffers. They do the planning and thinking, and then there is a German slave army of P.O.W. to carry out the task. Let us begin with getting Berlin on to its wheels. After the collapse of the city last May, only 51 tramcars remained in service. Today there are more than 800. They are running smoothly.

"It is always like the last tram home. They hang on by their eyebrows; it doesn't do them any harm. But the transport system is a going concern," said a corporal. Leave Berlin and link up with the autobahn. We pass the Russian zone and run through the British zone of occupation under B.A.O.R. For hundreds of miles you pass along the repaired autobahn itself or fairly well repaired side roads.

BAILEY bridges span chasms left by German dynamiters. Many miles of roadway have been cleared of smashed tanks and rubble; thousands upon thousands of craters have been filled in; 195 Bailey bridges have been installed in the British sector in Germany; 540 miles of road have been repaired; 1,100 miles have been tar-sprayed. Away out in the wilds of Germany you will come to a long Bailey bridge. There is a solitary

REVIVING THE RUHR COALFIELDS, which before the War were capable of producing 125 million tons annually, proceeds apace, as told here. In the course of Allied air raids, 32 collieries were put out of action; here is the interior of a wrecked lamp-house once capable of charging 4,000 miners' safety lamps. In May 1945, at the time of the German collapse, only 2,000 tons of coal were shifted; now more than 11,800 tons are moved every 24 hours under the direction of the North German coal control. *Photo, British Official*

British policeman there, an M.P., keeping guard and signalling the traffic through, all part of the British policing system and traffic control throughout Germany.

Passing the Dortmund-Ems Canal, a team of German labour was trying to undo some of the R.A.F.'s handiwork. In charge was an R.E. officer. They were raising the massive wreck of a steel bridge from the canal bed. It is the same story with the railways. The Germans blew nearly 700 bridges in the British zone and we have repaired a third of them. The Germans had only 650 miles of railway in operation in the British zone when they collapsed. We have now 6,575 miles—all the work of the British soldier.

German Prisoner Teams at Work

Canals, too, have been got going again. You can now travel right down the Rhine to the sea. The story of German coal revival is a tribute to British mine experts in the Army, plus the strong shoulder of the Pioneer and Forestry Corps, who supplied the millions of pit props from German forests. In May 1945, at the time of the collapse, 2,000 tons of coal were shifted: today more than 11,800 tons are moved every 24 hours.

As you roll along the autobahn you will see a Tommy with a stick in his hand directing his German prisoner team. Under the British gaffer's guidance the Germans fell trees for fuel, lift mines, clear away the wreckage from dams and culverts and railways caused by the R.A.F. bombs. "Funny how willing they are to work," the Tommy says. "They only want to be led. They have just to be told what to do and they do it like lambs."

TWO HUNDRED FEET BENEATH HIGH HOLBORN, LONDON, brick-lined tunnels run for miles. As described below, these were intended for use in the event of invasion or other grave emergency. Now they are to house 500 tons of Government books and documents which were evacuated during the War to various parts of the country. *Photo, The Evening Standard*

THEN there is the vast clerical task of running the Occupation. British Army clerks with civilians, too, do that—and do not forget the bright little A.T.S., who have joined so efficiently in the job of showing Germany and the world how a country really should be run. The telephones, too. More than 33,000 trunk telephone calls alone are cleared by day through the British zone. And British voices call over thousands of miles of new telephone lines which have been installed within the frontiers of Germany itself. Fraternization, yes, it exists and will increase; the black market is there, but is dwindling; quarrels are bound to occur between conquerors and conquered. But don't forget that much more vital overall picture of achievement. It is the finest advertisement of our way of life we could offer the German people.

They say—and I believe they are speaking the truth—they like us for it and thank us for it. You too, therefore, might do as the Germans do and tip your hat to the British Tommy in Germany.

Our Underground Citadel Built for 10,000

A top secret during the War, this enormous shelter, 200 feet beneath a London thoroughfare, would have been used by Government executives in the event of invasion or super-bombing. For two hours, on January 10, 1946, an Evening Standard reporter trudged around the empty, echoing spaces—now being filled with the Public Records of England.

THERE were 12 of us in the tunnelled labyrinth 200 feet beneath the traffic-jammed thoroughfare of High Holborn; a representative of the Public Record Office, a foreman, five workmen, two watchmen, a liftman, an electrician and myself. Between us we made up the total population of an underground citadel that was built to accommodate 10,000.

It was here, during the War, in this top-secret, deep shelter, that thousands of Government executives would have retired to carry on the battle in the event of invasion or super air raids. It was here today that I watched workmen wheeling into the bunk-lined, electric-lit tunnels, loads of Government books and documents which had been "evacuated" to the country during the War. The public records of England are coming back to Town. And 500 tons of them will in future be housed in this underground city built to defy bombs.

Rations for a One-Year Siege

The deep shelter, built at a very high cost, but never required, has been found to be an ideal depository for some of Britain's most important archives. When war broke out the Public Record Office had to evacuate from Chancery Lane more than 2,000 tons of official books and documents which had accumulated since the days of the Domesday Book nearly 900 years ago.

"It was a colossal task," I was told today. "Contents of about 20 miles of shelving had to be transported by lorry to the country. But the job was done—not one book, document or paper was lost or damaged throughout the War." Among the 2,000 tons of documents were 500 tons of modern departmental records, which were first stored in Canterbury Prison. After the fall of France they were transferred to three depositories in safer parts of the country.

EVERY day two five-ton lorries, with Public Record Office officials aboard, draw up to the shelter entrance with their loads of records brought from three country depositories—an ecclesiastical training college near Oxford, a ducal castle in the North, and a casual ward in the Midlands. For two hours today I trudged around the empty, echoing tunnels, 200 feet beneath the road. They seemed to stretch away for miles, and possibly they did.

I saw the bunk-lined corridors, the control room from which shelterers would have been marshalled, modern kitchens which would have provided hot meals on the cafeteria system, endless rows of stools at the food "bar," and food-storage cupboards which could have stocked sufficient food to withstand a one-year siege.

When fitted with shelving the bunks' steel uprights will make perfect storage receptacles for the official records. Said the Public Record Office official: "We did not choose an underground shelter for 'safety-first' reasons. It is merely that it is available and is ideal for our purpose." Work on the shelving of the bunks will start soon. It may take months to complete. About 80,000 ft. will have to be fitted.

★—As The Years Went By—Notable Days in the War—★

1940

February 12. *First Australian and New Zealand troops in Middle East arrived at Suez.*

1941

February 6. *Benghazi surrendered to Wavell's troops; many high-ranking Italian prisoners.*

February 10. *British parachute troops captured in Calabria, Southern Italy.*

1942

February 12. *Scharnhorst, Gneisenau and Prinz Eugen dashed from Brest through the Straits of Dover and reached German ports.*

February 15. *Singapore fell to Japanese. Large-scale Japanese landings in Sumatra.*

1943

February 2. *Capitulation of remnants of German Sixth Army to Russians at Stalingrad.*

February 8. *Red Army captured Kursk.*

February 10. *Guadalcanal cleared of Japanese.*

February 14. *Russians captured Rostov-on-Don.*

1944

February 3. *Germans launched first heavy offensive on the Anzio beach-head.*

February 15. *Allies bombed Cassino Abbey.*

1945

February 7. *Conference held at Yalta, Crimea, between Roosevelt, Stalin and Churchill.*

February 13. *Budapest captured by Red Army.*

When Our Airmen Come to Earth

By CAPTAIN
NORMAN MACMILLAN
M.C., A.F.C.

The word mufti comes from the Arabic, and has a dual meaning when used in the English language. It is the title of a Mahomedan priest or expounder of law. Hence the title Grand Mufti of Jerusalem. The Concise Oxford Dictionary states that it is the present participle of the Arabic word *afta* which translates into English as "decide point of law." Those who have read the Koran will understand how closely associated are Mahomedan priests and deciders of law in Islam. Time and again Mahomet declares that he is but the mouthpiece of the Lawgiver, and as such is the messenger of absolute truth and justice.

It is curious that this same word mufti should be applied in English to the civilian clothes worn by a person who has the right to wear uniform. Presumably this usage arose from the dispensorial duties of the British soldier when stationed abroad, so that even when he went about out of uniform his status was still acknowledged by the reference to his being "in mufti."

The old school of British soldiers is associated with the word mufti. It brings to mind the Kipling era. The more common word in Britain today is civvies, associated not with the Middle East and India but with British towns made up of civvy streets, in contrast to the barracks, encampments, quarters and cantonments of military life. Yet it seems to me that the word civvies is the language of the civilian temporarily turned soldier, while the word mufti is the word of those who have made soldiering a career. That is why I use the word mufti in this article, because I know that during the course of the present demobilization many who would choose to make the Service a career are being returned to civvy street to wear mufti with regret.

Big Change From Service Life Marked by Levelling of Ranks

There is a great difference between the Service in peace and the Service in war. In war the need is for men—"bodies" has come into modern Service slang to indicate the human unit. How often has one heard the phrase spoken into a military telephone: "Can you let me have so many bodies for such-and-such a job?" The need is for men (and women) to undertake a special task in war and to concentrate upon it. Thus military education is specialized and narrower in wartime. The need for "bodies" produces the means to secure them. Instructional schools are set up to train "bodies" for their special task. In these circumstances the apt individual without high educational qualifications can "make the grade." Personality counts in war more than in peace; for in war instinctive, uneducated leadership may be more valuable than any other asset.

The graduation in Service ranks means that every man above the rank of private soldier, aircraftman, or seaman has a certain power of command, increasing in scale as rank becomes more exalted. There is thus wide scope to fit in the multifarious types of character when the Services absorb millions into their ranks. There are not the same opportunities in mufti for the millions. Industries are not run on the basis of graduated ranks. There are many fewer gradations, and often the only distinguishing characteristics are those of face and voice, and perhaps the quality and cut of clothes.

It is this that marks the big change from Service to civil life. The man who was an officer may have to give up his rank to join on level terms others who held lesser rank; he may even find himself being "bossed" by a former private. If war can reduce directors of companies to aircraftmen, and City of London solicitors of eminence to coastal gunners, peace can transform flying-officers into door-to-door salesmen, or other less distinguished citizens.

The Sunday Dispatch for January 20 told the story of Edward Nolde, driver of a No. 16 London omnibus between Victoria and Cricklewood, who six months before

B.O.A.C. STEWARD of a Sunderland flying-boat on a flight from Britain to India puts the finishing touches to a four-course meal. Cooked, and then frozen in London, it is served up hot to passengers and crew during the journey. *Photo, B.O.A.C.*

was a Flight Lieutenant wearing the ribbon of the D.F.C. with the Pathfinder Group of Bomber Command. He was with the London Passenger Transport Board before the War, and returned to it on demobilization as a bus conductor. He said, "Any man who has a chance to go back to his old job should take it. And if a man has held a commission in the Forces, any additional qualifications he has gained through his experience will soon be discovered and put to use." Good luck to him, for his sound sense, and in his appearance before a promotions board for advancement to inspector.

For the lucky men the War was but an incident in their lives. They have a lucrative post in a business that was continued in their absence. For others, like Nolde, the end of the War meant a big cut in pay. For still others there is no job waiting.

Men who have flown operationally in war have done something which has stimulated character, and brought out qualities that previously were perhaps but latent. If these men recognize this personal development in the forcing house of war, they can profit by it, provided they do not assume that it should bring them special privileges. Their privileges in the Services had to be earned by work for the Services. Their privileges in civil life have to be earned by their work in civil life. What have the men who flew gained technically during war? I would assess their gain in their categories as pilots, navigators, wireless and radar operators, and flight engineers. (Air gunners have gained in personality, but their work has no value in civil life.)

Employment in Civil Aviation Available Only to a Minority

The air lines are growing in importance. They will want pilots, navigators, flight engineers, radio and radar operators. The Government civil airfields, wireless and radar stations will require ground personnel for inspection, control and operations. Flying schools to teach civilians to fly will need pilots and ground instructors. The aircraft industry may need a few replacement test pilots, but there cannot be many vacancies here, and they will be open to special pilots with exceptional technical qualifications. Business companies will want aircraft to transport executives quickly about their business. Flying salesmen will be required to sell not only aircraft but many ranges of goods.

But all these flying jobs represent a mere fraction of the great numbers of air-trained men who are available today. It will be the minority who will survive in the scramble to remain in their new profession of aviation on the civil side. Those who wish to do so will have to take their civilian licences as pilots, navigators, wireless operators, flight and ground engineers. But that there are vacancies is witnessed by the acceptance for training by British Overseas Airways as air stewards of some 200 Air Training Corps cadets, recruited direct from civil life, with some drawn from country villages. There will also be ground staff appointments in all the air line organizations, for duty in administrative and technical capacities both at home and abroad. Here a knowledge of appropriate languages will be of value.

But the majority of our wartime airmen will have to come to earth. The recent statement by Marshal of the Royal Air Force Lord Tedder that the peacetime force must be a David and not a Goliath indicates that the reduction in the R.A.F. will enable the Air Ministry to prune severely. Expansion in air line operation and the aircraft industry will not be rapid. Indeed, the industry must first shrink to normal before its expansion can begin on the new peacetime basis.

The men who make a bargain with themselves that they will remain in aviation and make it their post-war career should first try the R.A.F. and the Fleet Air Arm, then the air lines and the aircraft industry (including the ancillary industries such as oil, petrol and paraffin, instruments, tires and so on). If they fail in these four major fields their hope is slight in the remaining air activities, and they should seek work elsewhere.

If they want to continue their wartime association with aviation, they will have opportunity to give their country part-time service in the peacetime R.A.F.V.R. or Auxiliary Air Forces (men's and women's), Royal Observer Corps and Air Training Corps, all to be administered in future under one R.A.F. Reserve Command. Thus they can make the air their hobby instead of their profession, and will be happy if they realize that half a loaf is better than no bread.

British Wings Speed Dutch Safely from Java

ENGULFED IN THE INDONESIAN TROUBLES, Dutch civilians in Batavia have been evacuated by the R.A.F. to Singapore and other places at the rate of 1,000 a day. A sick internee is lifted from a Dakota transport by medical orderlies of No. 6 Casualty Air Evacuation Unit (top). The latter did magnificent work in Burma when they flew thousands of casualties from the front lines. On the quayside at Batavia (bottom) a Sunderland crew assists women and children waiting to be rowed out to flying-boats in the harbour. See also page 579. *Photos, British Official*

The Editor Looks Back

WOULD THEY COME? Feb. 24, 1940

I saw a mountainous façade of sandbags that has shielded a West End club since September being removed the other day. Whether to make way for some other form of protection or because the committee have decided we're not going to have any raids after all, I can't say. But not the latter, I hope, as there can be no greater self-deception. Every airman to whom I have spoken believes we must be prepared to the *n*th degree for being raided in Goering's good time. I renewed acquaintance with one of the most famous of world fliers last night and found that he, too, held this opinion.

HOW strange to recall today that five months after the phoney War had started we were still speculating on the possibility of London being raided!

THIEVES Feb. 24, 1940

"I said, in my haste, all men are liars." The old Scotswoman who commented that if the Psalmist had come to her town he might have said it "at his leesure" was wise in her generation, but one has no biblical authority—so far as I know—for "all men are thieves." And yet the readiness with which the average decent person will take what isn't his'n if the chance comes is undeniable. Perhaps you read of a fishmonger who said the other day that in the black-out he had lost most of his profit by customers stealing fish as they left his premises. There is nothing that won't be stolen given the opportunity.

SIX years on, the thieves have grown from companies and battalions into armies, and you will find them where you would least expect. The latest trick I have heard about is the substitution of straw and chaff mattresses for valuable hair and wool articles of pre-War make. This, I gather, has happened in some cases where furniture was left in store. Once you discover that you are sleeping on a shoddy mattress which you had supposed to be your own woollen one, it is too late to complain. I am told that the stock explanation is, "You must have got somebody else's mattress, and he has got yours." I had this from a lawyer who was handling a particularly flagrant case of substitution. So, have a care when your mattresses come out of store.

WE WERE WARNED! Mar. 2, 1940

If there are any rich readers of my jottings let me warn them that Stalin's disciples in England, otherwise the Central Committee of the Communist Party of Great Britain (who have just done me the honour of pushing their manifesto through my letter-box), have got their eye on 'em. My millionaire readers in particular had better look out, for the likes of Mr. Pollitt, who polled 966 out of 15,460 votes the other day in Silvertown, is after them. Here's their War Aims:

> Better times for the people. Make the rich pay. No blockade on wages. No profiteering. No tightening of belts for the poor. Unity of action now against the Chamberlain Government and the millionaires.

But it seems to me that their battle is already won—won for them by the Chamberlain Government in the person of Sir John Simon. For I am one of "the people," I am a wage-earner, I am no profiteer, I am not rich, and I am just about £990,000 short of being a millionaire, yet a good deal more than fifty per cent of my total earnings are snaffled by the Government, whose Chancellor cheerfully and persistently tells me to prepare for still greater sacrifice!

WELL, most of those generous War aims of the Communists were achieved by the dire force of circumstance, and no thanks to the Communists. Indeed, it almost looks as though six years after that note was written and a "phoney peace" has dawned, we may have to re-read the first verse of Matthew xxvi, 11, which runs, as you will no doubt remember, "For ye have the poor always with you." You may also remember that when the foregoing note was written Russia was nearing the end of her attack on Finland, while in agreement with Germany she had been able to occupy half of Poland. Strange indeed have been the mutations of Soviet policy since the signing of that pact with the Nazis which preceded the starting of the Second Great War! However, we live—but do we learn?

MORE GALLIC WIT Mar. 2, 1940

One of the many delightful literary journals of France that come to my editorial desk every week is *Marianne*. The issue before me has an amusing and instructive item of immediate interest which I translate:

A sergeant and six French soldiers form the garrison of a small island in the Pacific. Every six months a ship calls with provisions and mails.

"What's going on in France?" asked the sergeant.

"We are at war."

"With whom?"

"Germany."

"Ah! With our Russian allies we ought to win easily."

"But the Russians are no longer our allies. They have even joined forces with Germany."

"What! Then we shall be up against the Germans, the Russians and the Italians!"

"No. Italy is neutral."

"Oh! Tell me, there must have been a deuce of a battle on the Maginot Line?"

"Not at all. The two most important battles were fought, one in the Arctic Circle, the other off Montevideo."

HOW vividly that little bit of jeu d'esprit brings back the strange uncertainties which marked those early days of 1940, when terrific events were in preparation and were so soon to jog the whole world into a seething state of fear, doubt and despondency. Britain's "splendid hour" was just about to strike—and today we are garnering the thanks of all those "united nations" whose future freedom Britain made possible by her incredible self-sacrifice and her steadfast stand for human liberty—"I don't think, Papa!" as Harry Tate's son was wont to remark in one of his comic sketches that were soon to be just memories of the old music halls, themselves but memories now.

THE BRIGHT-OUT! Mar. 16, 1940

"For black-out read bright-out" would seem to be the wishful thinking of those who tell us that soon the black-out will be a nightmare of the past. The idea is to rush to the other extreme and send up from London and our other great cities such a blaze of searchlights into the nocturnal sky that air raiders would be dazzled and rendered less able to spot an objective than in the black-out, while down below we should be carrying on as if it were high noon. I'm not hopeful, but if the "bright-out" were ever realized it would have a fine effect on public health, which under the black-out is certainly deteriorating . . . health of mind and health of body. Eyesight has been affected by the long unillumined periods that are now rapidly diminishing, thanks to the coming of spring and wisdom of advancing summertime.

THE "bright-out" was merely a wild dream, and all of us who lived through the horrors of five years of black-out are suffering in health today. When I think of these years and all they mean in loss of vitality and resources to the British people, my gorge rises as I read some of the unjust, ungenerous, and ignorant stuff, such as the late Theodore Dreiser and all America's isolationists have been publishing in the Press to the confusion of their fellow Americans. There can be no mutual understanding between nations so long as any measure of distrust exists on one side or the other. It exists on the other side of the Atlantic in some force, unhappily.

POSTSCRIPT

It was refreshing to read from a naturalist and council-member of the Royal Society for the Protection of Birds the other day, a tribute to the War Office—for their kindness. For, thanks to the War Department, ten square miles of English countryside near Dungeness is being preserved as a sanctuary for "all types of rare nesting birds." It will come as a relief to bird-enthusiasts (as well as a surprise) to learn that in this area, at least, Operation Pluto had no ill-effects upon wild life, "although petrol escaped from the pipe-line and fumes spread over a wide area." This will be good news to many.

A RECENT advertisement for the New York Central Railway appearing in an American magazine claims for that railroad the credit of being the first to instal troughs for watering locomotives at speed. This, of course, is nonsense. The first water-troughs (I am assured by the L.M.S.) were laid on the old London and North-Western at Aber, on the North Wales coast, in 1857, and the idea was copied by the rest of the world. But the Yankee claim is merely characteristic.

A DISTINGUISHED London medical man has bravely tried to comfort the great shaving public, especially those who find the shortage of razor blades acute in the figurative sense. He says that a blunt razor is less injurious to the face than a well-stropped one. I wonder? I seem to remember my mother's vain attempts to convince me that rice pudding was more "nourishing" than jelly. But I still prefer jelly—and will continue to keep my razors well honed and stropped.

ACCORDING to a woman educationist, few children, if left to themselves, will shudder on seeing a worm or a slug. This complex of repugnance, she assured a conference of teachers, is copied by children from their parents. The awful remedy which would seem to suggest itself is that of the grins of the fathers being visited on the children. Though not, I hope, to the third and fourth generation. Or even to the second.

A WOMAN scientist with a violent antipathy to smoking left, recently, among other bequests, £100 to the University of London "to be devoted to the needs of non-smoking students." One would have imagined that in these days of one-and-two-for-ten the "needs" of non-smokers would be virtually—and happily—non-existent.

FROM subscribers to the Wine and Food Society downwards, every member of the public with an appreciative palate will rejoice at the Government's decision to insist on the correctly-descriptive labelling of all "wines" made up in this country. Even if it calls for "Château Rickmansworth." Or—"Veuve Higginbotham."

In Britain Now : Honouring Civilian Killed

FIRST ROLL OF CIVILIAN WAR DEAD of the British Empire and Commonwealth has been placed in a shrine in Westminster Abbey, near to the Tomb of the Unknown Warrior. The four volumes, one of which is open (above), contain records of nearly 60,000 civilians whose deaths were caused by enemy action in the United Kingdom. Each day a page is turned by the Dean's verger.

LONDON'S FIRST PREFABRICATED SETTLEMENT has risen out of the ruins of Cubitt Town in the Isle of Dogs, which was almost wiped out in the air raids of 1940-41. Below, the reconstructed area which comprises 300 buildings. *Photos, Topical, G.P.U., Reuter, Keystone*

MEMORIAL TO FIGHTING FRENCH NAVY, in the form of a Lorraine Cross and anchor, commemorating the lives of officers and men lost in the Battle of the Atlantic, was unveiled by Mr. A. V. Alexander, First Lord of the Admiralty, at Lyle Hill, Greenock, on January 18, 1946. French warships recently left Greenock to return to France.

UNEXPLODED PIPE MINES are being rendered harmless in different parts of the country. These were planted underground at vital points in 1940 when Britain was in danger of a German invasion. Packed with high explosive, in an emergency they would have been electrically detonated by remote control. Sappers are here seen dismantling pipe mines in Sussex.

Askari Warriors Dressed for the Dance

WITH SPEARS AND SHIELDS FASHIONED FROM DERELICT AIRCRAFT PARTS selected from a salvage dump, Askari warriors from two Kenya battalions of the 11th East African Division—which fought so magnificently in the East African and Burmese campaigns—recently assembled for a great tribal dance, one of the most spectacular of post-War days. Among those taking part in this picturesque blend of old tradition and modern warfare were members of the Nandi, Wakamba and Jalua tribes. See also illus. page 22 ; and 619, Vol. 7. *Photo, British Official*

Printed in England and published every alternate Friday by the Proprietors, THE AMALGAMATED PRESS, LTD., The Fleetway House, Farringdon Street, London, E.C.4. Registered for transmission by Canadian Magazine Post. Sole Agents for Australia and New Zealand: Messrs. Gordon & Gotch, Ltd.; and for South Africa: Central News Agency, Ltd. February 15, 1946. S.S *Editorial Address:* JOHN CARPENTER HOUSE, WHITEFRIARS, LONDON E.C.4.

Vol 9 The War Illustrated No 227

SIXPENCE and AFTERWARDS MARCH 1, 1946

THE BRITISH COMMONWEALTH FORCE FOR THE OCCUPATION OF JAPAN (B.C.O.F.) is drawn from the U.K., Australia, New Zealand and India; its commander-in-chief is Lieut.-Gen. J. Northcott, C.B., M.V.O., of the Australian Military Forces. At a recent inspection in India of the British and Indian contingent, who were about to leave for Japan, the goat mascot of the 2nd Battalion the Royal Welch Fusiliers headed the parade. The British-Indian Division is commanded by Maj.-Gen. D. T. Cowan.

Edited by Sir John Hammerton

NO. 228 WILL BE PUBLISHED FRIDAY, MARCH 15

War Orphans Cared for in English Country Home

UNABLE TO RETURN to their homes when the War ended in Europe, large numbers of children who had been evacuated created a major problem in Britain. Through the Anglo-American Relief Fund, under the direction of Lady Gunstone, O.B.E., some of them are being cared for at The Round House, Ware, Herts., which has been converted into a nursery home. Not all are orphans; a few are "unwanted" and others cannot return because of the housing shortage.

The Round House, with some of the children at play (1). Mealtime (2) is a serious affair, but not more so than the problem of the instructional toy with which this young Canadian (3) is faced. Too small to sit at table, the youngest guest (4) is assisted to his lunch by a somewhat older companion. One of the sisters takes a party for a walk (5).

Photos, Keystone

Grim Drama of Justice at Nuremberg

By

JOHN FORTINBRAS

THE Rogues' Gallery at the World's greatest crime trial, and members of the most eminent tribunal in history, are here vividly sketched by an observer, specially for "The War Illustrated." Tense is the atmosphere of the court as there emerge details of the records of a handful of men who in complicated conspiracy betrayed a nation. See also illus. pages 559-562.

IN Nuremberg not one city but two lie in ruins. Cracked and crumbled is the once splendid acreage which comprised the walled medieval town of Germany with its red-bricked castles, keeps, watch-towers, moat-houses and churches, the town in which Albrecht Dürer the artist lived and sketched, and Hans Sachs the meistersinger wrote his verse. Around it there grew up a new Nuremberg which traded in fancy cakes and toys of impish ingenuity until armaments fever seized it and Julius Streicher launched his "Jew baiting" campaigns in "Der Stuermer." Now that town, too, has become a weary waste of rubble and upheaval.

Yet, ironically for those conspirators who promoted the Third Reich, one imposing edifice has chanced to survive almost unscathed the general catastrophe. To Nurembergers, this historic block in Fuerther Strasse goes simply by the name of the Justizgebaude (justice buildings). Elsewhere, the same buildings are being talked about today as "The Palace of Justice."

In the Court Room, the Schwurgerichts as it is called, one misses at first the veneration and solemnity associated with an English High Court of Justice. There is no judge in wig and scarlet robes, no black-gowned usher, none of that faint smell of antiquity that typifies judicial proceedings in our own country. In fact, before the Tribunal sits an atmosphere of hubbub prevails.

Twenty Strained and Miserable Men

It arises from the cine-cameras (a Russian unit is photographing every second of the trial), from the banks of white arc-lights, from the interpreters sitting behind glass panels, from the purple-robed German counsel appearing for defendants, from the strange mixture of uniform and civilian suiting among personnel of each nation's prosecuting team of learned counsel, from the earpieces or language translators which everybody wears save those in the immediate vicinity of the prosecution stand, and from the shorthand writers tapping away at their stenotype machines, recording the proceedings in four languages.

One turns from the dais where the tribunal sits—with, as its background, the four flags of the Allied Powers unfurled against pale green curtains—to contemplate two rows of strained and miserable men, twenty in all, through whose acts of infamy, alined into one vast conspiracy, the Prosecution traces the terrifying career of Nazism to its end.

THEY smile little, only uneasily. By all tokens, they represent the greatest accumulation of savagery ever perpetrated in the name of man, and the greatest humiliation to which any nation—even the German nation—has fallen. These giants, a little time ago so ruthless and inhuman, appear now as shrunken beings contemptible in the sight of freedom-loving peoples. Keitel and Jodl, the Chief of the General Staff and his Operations Chief, alone wear uniform, a plain German soldier's tunic without emblems or badges of any kind. The civilian suits of the others range from dignified dark blue, as worn by Admirals Doenitz and Raeder, to the check suiting of Frick, whilst Goering wears a pearl-grey tunic peculiarly his own.

Some hold that the faces and personalities of these men are in essence nondescript, and hardly to be distinguished from a gathering at a directors' board meeting or the members of a jury panel. But the trained observer perceives authority sharp and strongly-defined in the faces of the fighting Germans, in Doenitz, in Raeder and Keitel, not perhaps so markedly in Jodl. Just as he must detect in Goering's face an unusual plasticity, and a vitality that tallies with Hitler's description of him as a man "impatient and impulsive."

Hess, the one-time Nazi idealist, with his beetling black eyebrows, his white hatchet face and glaring eyes, is not a pretty creature. But if ugliness distinguishes one man in this rogues' gallery it is Julius Streicher, sadist and flagellator, a man with much champing jaw, and blunt, brutal, sarcastic features, a face as inhuman as the doctrine of persecution which he preached. Baldur von Schirach, the Jugend leader, still preserves a well-groomed appearance; in contrast the once debonair Ribbentrop looks gaunt and haggard, an ambassador of decadence.

Impassively behind the defendants stand American G.I.s on sentry duty. Some appear never to stop chewing gum. Their white enamelled helmets are adorned by a symbolic shield figuring Nazi emblems in shattered pieces. They wear white belts and white spats, and these, with the white batons held behind their backs in white-gloved hands, appeared first to me as more reminiscent of a military tattoo than a court of justice.

Justice Intact and Irreproachable

At the Law Courts, London, Lord Justice Lawrence, ermine-robed, seemed in his compact, vastly dignified figure to incorporate Justice and present Her intact and irreproachable to all in that hushed court. Now his Lordship sits unrobed. His bald, rounded head is graced by no Judge's wig. And the judges of the Allied Powers who sit beside him, though constituting the most eminent tribunal in history, wear none of the trappings of distinction. Mr. Justice Birkett, with his flatly brushed, lank, straw-coloured hair looks at times in his spectacles inexpressibly owlish.

One of the French judges, bald-headed and with a grey, drooping moustache, might have been born in the pages of Dickens. The two Russian judges, strongly built, younger than the other men, sit sternly upright, in their lemon-brown military uniforms.

I felt proud of Lawrence from the beginning. He follows every word spoken from the prosecution stand with a sharp mind; its penetration impresses everyone. Yet, perhaps because I have been reared in British traditions, my first reaction was to hate and decry the apparent informality of the trial. Sufficiently enlightened we may be, I thought, to dispense with the emblems of Justice, with the atmosphere, half-sacerdotal and half-historic, in which Justice exists in so many courts in England. But how much I wished that, in contrast to the easy, matter-of-fact way in which the defendants had condemned to horror and monstrous misuse millions of their fellow human beings, those same men should live for what may be the last few weeks of their lives in an atmosphere alive with the sense of retribution.

Such, in summary, were the thoughts which occupied my mind during the first few minutes of the tribunal's session on January 2, 1946, which marked my introduction to the Court. Then I began listening intently to the evidence. I heard Colonel Storey, of the American prosecution team, reading in measured tones the affidavits of witnesses to ghetto mass murders at Rovno in the Ukraine—how, as the secret police carried out their murderous missions, women ran about the streets with dead babies in their arms before they, too, stripped naked and made to lie in charnel pits, became dead.

It seemed that only with an effort of mind dare one visualize such happenings. I have heard much more terrible evidence since that day. Yet every word from Storey represented, to me, the agonies, the unmentionable agonies, of tens of hundreds of men, women and children. I heard for the first time of the infamous device at Mauthausen Concentration Camp reserved for "K" prisoners. K stands for "Kugel," German for bullet. And K prisoners included Russian prisoners of war, prisoners recaptured after attempted escapes, political and racial "undesirables," and others. All were marked for death and measured for death.

Most Terrible Evidence Marshalled

Each victim was forced to stand upright beside a metrical column, from the top of which a sliding plank was poised. When the wood moved down its socket and touched the prisoner's head the measure automatically recorded his height. Simultaneously, a mechanical attachment discharged a bullet into the nape of his neck. Often, the concentration camp authorities, the tribunal heard, had too many K prisoners on their hands to extend to all this individual and "humane" treatment. So some prisoners were sent to the "bathrooms"—hermetically sealed chambers into which poison gas concentrations were discharged.

I heard of Hitler's orders carried out in the Occupied Countries to enforce the Nazi rule by terror. If a man were suspected of any act against the Nazi regime it was the German policy to seize every member of his family and, after removing them to the Reich, to liquidate them, taking special care to ensure that no word of their death ever went back to their home town.

I heard of Einsatzkommandos, chiefs of Secret Police Units, whose function in the Eastern occupied areas was to exterminate Jews and Russian commissars. In their huge mass-scale killings of Jews, women and children were not exempted, although a difference existed in that gas vans were ordered for women and children, and with the poison being supplied by the vehicle itself a journey was arranged of sufficient duration to ensure that by the time the mass burial quarry or anti-tank ditch was reached all would be dead.

I heard also how the defendant Kaltenbrunner, Himmler's right-hand man, saw fit to encourage civilians to lynch Allied airmen who parachuted down or otherwise fell unarmed in their midst. The order to which Kaltenbrunner gave his signature said, "In agreement with the Reichsfuehrer S.S. (Heinrich Himmler) I have directed all higher police officers that all Germans shall go unpunished who in the future participate in the persecution and annihilation of enemy aircrews who parachute down."

WHILST such records are related the rest falls into the background. Americans, officers and men, in the visitors' gallery, forget the jazz music which sounds day in and day out thirty paces away from the Court, forget their gum-chewing and other indulgences. The unconventional background of the trial vanishes. In its stead the awe of Justice prevails as that of a sword brandished nakedly: a sword leaping out of an accumulation of the most terrible evidence ever marshalled by man against man.

Northern Ireland's Share in Victory

By MAJ.-GENERAL SIR CHARLES GWYNN K.C.B., D.S.O.

THE English are a forgiving and forgetful people. They are accustomed to bow to the will of a majority and, taking Ireland as a whole, the majority of the Irish would certainly like to see the partition of their own island abolished. A desire to make concessions to the wishes of the majority and to forgive and forget Eire's neutrality may become all the stronger because those fortunate enough to visit the country and to dip into its flesh-pots find the inhabitants charming and friendly.

The north can offer no such attractions, and the people, though as Irish as those of the south, can be dour enough. Moreover, it can with some justice be claimed that, despite the attitude of its Government, Eire contributed as large a proportion of its man-power to the fighting Services of Britain as did the north, and that great numbers of men and women crossed the Irish Sea to take part in the industrial war effort. To these as individuals we owe gratitude for gallant and useful service, all the more because they received no encouragement in their enterprise from their own government.

But let us not forget that the debt we owe to Northern Ireland was of a vastly different character, and that the services it rendered to the Allied cause were of immensely greater importance. The debt is all the greater because the British Government and people can claim little credit for placing Northern Ireland in a position to render those services. When established, partition of Ireland was looked on by the majority of Englishmen as a regrettable political expedient, rendered necessary by the irreconcilable aspirations of Irishmen—a grudgingly granted concession to the claims of the stubborn north.

RESOURCES Placed at Disposal of His Majesty's Government

The frontier between the two parts of the country had no military significance, and seemed to many an absurdity calculated to cause the maximum inconvenience and to present magnificent opportunities to smugglers. That it would ever become a frontier of vital strategic importance probably never occurred to anyone, for at the time the retention of the south Irish naval bases met requirements. Yet, in the event, probably no other land frontier had equal strategic value in the course of the War. In a search for sixpence the British Government had picked up a sovereign, and not for the first time in its history had unwittingly and unwillingly retained an asset of immense value which it had almost thrown away.

The first debt owed to Northern Ireland is due to its insistence on maintaining to the full the British connexion. Whether that insistence was, as some believed, inspired by bigotry and suspicion of the south or by genuine devotion and loyalty to the Empire as was claimed, is immaterial. For though both influences were probably at work full proof has been given that loyalty was genuine. At the outbreak of War the Northern Parliament without reservation placed the area enclosed by the "absurd" frontier and all its resources at the disposal of H.M. Government and accepted all the risks and hardships of war.

Eire's declaration of neutrality which denied the use of the southern ports to the Allied Navies vastly added to the strategic importance of the northern area, and as the War went on that importance progressively increased, affording as it did advanced naval and air bases for the prosecution of the Battle of the Atlantic. In particular they covered the approaches to the Clyde and Mersey, which became the main channel through which food, munitions and supplies of all sorts reached Britain, not only from America but from all parts of the world. The area was also to form a valuable training-ground for British and American troops.

ITS importance to the U.S. war effort was proved when the construction of a new port in Lough Foyle, to supplement the somewhat limited facilities at Londonderry, became one of the first tasks undertaken by the American advanced guard, the great Port of Belfast being insufficient to exploit the potentialities of the area. Obviously the area from its geographic position had the additional advantage of having a degree of immunity from air attack, although Belfast did not escape unscathed. It was to northern insistence that we owe the possession of this strategic asset which, it is to be hoped, we have learned should never be relinquished.

Small as the area was, the value of its resources should not be underestimated. Though mainly an agricultural country it contained industries of great importance. Outstanding was the great shipbuilding industry of Belfast which produced important naval units in addition to much mercantile tonnage. The linen industry and rope factories for which the country was famous were also of special value. These together with other associated engineering establishments provided a force of highly skilled artisans, which greatly facilitated the development of new war industries. Agricultural production was also intensified by increased use of mechanized implements, with the result that some eleven million pounds' worth of food could be shipped annually to Britain. The acreage under flax, always an important crop in Ulster, in particular was extended to meet the demands for the expanded linen industry and to compensate for the loss of supplies of fibre formerly imported. On the whole the industrial and agricultural effort fully equalled, if it did not exceed, anything achieved on the other side of the Irish Sea. This is the more remarkable because the Government of Northern Ireland had anxieties about the attitude of a substantial minority of the population which did not exist in other parts of the United Kingdom. It can only be concluded that the spirit of loyalty to the cause to which the country had committed itself proved infectious.

OUTPOST of Great Importance for Defence of These Islands

Without conscription or a territorial army and with the population so fully employed on War production it was obvious that the numbers that joined the fighting Services would be affected. Nevertheless many young men and women volunteered for all the Services, and recruitment for the regular regiments whose home is in Northern Ireland was well maintained.

The north certainly cannot be accused of lack of martial spirit, and it is naturally proud of the astonishing capacity it has shown for producing generals of outstanding distinction out of the small field it offers for selection. It is not difficult to find reasons why Southern Ireland should be famous for the horses it breeds, but how can we account for the fact that out of a population of one and a quarter million Ulster produced men of the stamp of Field-Marshals Alexander and Montgomery to command in the Field, and Field-Marshals Lord Alanbrooke and Sir John Dill as principal military advisers ?

When Montgomery succeeds Alanbrooke (in June, 1946) we shall have seen three men from Northern Ireland successively holding the highest appointment in the British Army, that of the Chief of the Imperial General Staff. Never has the Empire been better served in Field and Council Chamber.

Fitting as it is that the debt owed to the people of Northern Ireland should be remembered and acknowledged, it is even more essential that it should be realized that the territory they occupy forms a strategic outpost of vital importance for the defence of these islands—an asset which should never again become a counter in party politics or be thrown in the scales of appeasement bargaining. As an Irishman connected equally with north and south I do not like partition, but as a soldier I do not doubt its necessity.

SHIP REPAIRING was one of the outstanding contributions of Northern Ireland to the Allied cause. In Belfast Harbour (right) a frigate of the Royal Navy is being attended to, in a floating dock at Harland and Wolff's great shipyard. See also facing page

Photo, Northern Ireland Government

With Mighty Endeavour They Speeded the Peace

NORTHERN IRELAND parachute workers busy for the R.A.F. (1). During the Victory celebrations on May 13, 1945, crowds filled Belfast's Donegall Square (2). The Royal Irish Fusiliers (3) served in France, Italy and N. Africa. At a Belfast shipyard a giant floating crane is seen beside an aircraft carrier undergoing repairs (4).

H.M.C.S. WARRIOR, first capital ship and fleet carrier to be commissioned by a Dominions navy, has a displacement of 18,000 tons, carries a complement of about 1,000, and has accommodation for Seafire fighters and Firefly reconnaissance aircraft. She was built specially for the Royal Canadian Navy by Messrs. Harland and Wolff, at Belfast, where this photograph was taken, and was commissioned on January 24, 1946. *Photo, Associated Press*

Our Navies in the Great Change-Over

By

FRANCIS E. McMURTRIE

It is some months since the Navy Department, Washington, disclosed in broad outline the strength at which it is intended the United States Fleet shall be maintained in the immediate future. It was proposed that there should ultimately be retained in service 18 battleships, three battle cruisers, 27 fleet aircraft carriers, 79 escort carriers, 79 cruisers, 367 destroyers, 296 destroyer-escorts and 200 submarines. Of these, a substantial proportion, amounting to seven battleships, 12 fleet aircraft carriers, 58 escort carriers, 33 cruisers, 191 destroyers, 256 destroyer-escorts and 110 submarines will normally be laid up in reserve.

A further announcement has now been made by the Secretary of the Navy, Mr. James Forrestal, giving the ships which are to be assigned to two principal fleets as follows: Pacific Fleet: two battleships, nine fleet carriers, nine escort carriers, 20 cruisers, 16 destroyer-escorts, 39 submarines, five minelayers, 24 minesweepers and 45 auxiliaries of various types. Atlantic Fleet: two battleships, four fleet carriers, four escort carriers, eight cruisers, 54 destroyers, 20 destroyer-escorts, 51 submarines, five minelayers, 20 minesweepers and 35 auxiliaries.

FLEET'S Future Composition and Distribution Yet to be Decided

Behind these two fleets, ready to reinforce them at short notice, will be the "ready reserve," comprising six battleships, five fleet aircraft carriers, 18 cruisers, 40 destroyers, four destroyer-escorts, two minelayers and four minesweepers. It will be observed that in these lists there is no separate mention of America's three battle cruisers, which have presumably been counted in with the cruisers. This rather suggests that the value of the battle cruiser as a type has been somewhat discounted by war experience.

As yet there has been no indication of Admiralty intentions concerning the future composition and distribution of the British fleet. Presumably the information is being reserved for the Navy Estimates, which are normally placed before Parliament shortly before Easter. In the War there were no Estimates in the ordinary sense, the money required for the Navy being covered by token votes, passed without discussion or disclosure of any details.

It is known that certain obsolete ships are being discarded, while others have been placed in reserve or relegated to harbour service. A large number have been, or are about to be, sold or scrapped, including the ancient aircraft carriers Furious and Argus, over a dozen cruisers, more than 100 destroyers, about 40 submarines and sundry craft, such as the "Castle" and "Flower" type corvettes and the older minesweepers.

This should be sufficient to give an idea of the number of ships likely to be available for active service when needed, though the recent tendency to send to the scrapheap brand-new destroyers which have not long been launched must prevent some of the figures from being more than broad approximations.

In capital ships, the pre-war total of 15 has fallen to seven, though including the Vanguard, nearing completion. Besides this new ship, the King George V, Duke of York, Anson, Howe, Nelson and Rodney are the only British battleships which can be considered fit to fight. It would seem likely that five of these ships will be maintained in full commission in the Home and Mediterranean Fleets, leaving the other two as a "ready reserve," to adopt the American term—available either as a potential reinforcement or as reliefs for ships requiring to be refitted.

In fleet aircraft carriers the position is somewhat better, though it may not remain so unless all those under construction are carried to completion. It has been reported that five or six large fleet carriers which were building have been cancelled, together with several of lighter design. Disregarding these, it would appear that there may be available in due course seven or eight of the former and from 15 to 20 of the latter. There are also three ships of hybrid type, the Unicorn (see illus. in page 647), Perseus and Pioneer, which may be described as maintenance aircraft carriers and are extremely valuable ships.

Of the 38 escort carriers in service when the War ended, 33 have had to be returned to the United States Navy under the terms of the Lend-Lease scheme. One of the remaining five, the Pretoria Castle, is likely to revert to her peacetime status as a passenger liner plying between this country and South Africa. This would leave Campania, Nairana, Vindex and Activity available, but one of these is to be transferred to the Netherlands flag.

In cruisers there is a serious shortage, having regard to the total of 70 which the late Earl Jellicoe recommended as an absolute minimum. The post-war residue would appear to be certainly under 50, and this includes the Arethusa and Aurora, which have been mentioned as likely to be transferred to Allied navies, together with the Blake, Defence, Superb and Tiger, now completing. There is some doubt whether the Bellerophon and Hawke will be completed, so these two cruisers have been left out of the calculation. Evidently it is considered that the allocation to foreign stations of a proportion of our fleet aircraft carrier strength will more than compensate for this cruiser shortage, or the position might well be described as alarming.

Assuming that about 50 per cent of the new destroyers in hand will be completed, there should be available 150 modern fleet destroyers. How many of the "Hunt" class, corresponding approximately to the American destroyer-escorts, are to be retained in service is doubtful. Several are believed to have been condemned as the results of hard service or extensive damage, but there may be 30 or 40 suitable for duty in home waters and the Mediterranean for some years to come.

FRIGATES Assigned Under Lend-Lease Being Returned to U.S.

In submarines the position is a little more difficult owing to the complete uncertainty about the number of new ones to be completed. On the 50 per cent basis adopted in the case of the destroyers there ought ultimately to be about 120 available, but it is doubtful if so many will be kept.

Probably the later frigates of the "Bay" and "Loch" classes will be retained, to the number of about 50, but most of the "Rivers" seem likely to be discarded. All the "Captains" and "Colonies" are being returned to the U.S. navy, having been assigned to this country under the Lend-Lease scheme. About 30 sloops of recent design will also figure in the post-war fleet together with the majority of the mine-sweepers of the highly successful "Algerine" design, 100 in number.

In all these calculations the navies of the overseas Dominions have been included, as they would operate with the Royal Navy in time of war. Comparing the position with 1939, the Home Fleet was then made up of seven battleships and battle cruisers, two aircraft carriers, six cruisers, 26 destroyers and five submarines; while in the Mediterranean Fleet there were four battleships, one aircraft carrier, six cruisers, 40 destroyers and seven submarines. On the China Station were one aircraft carrier, four cruisers, 14 destroyers and 15 submarines. Five cruisers constituted the bulk of the America and West Indies Squadron (including ships in South American waters). There were three cruisers on the East Indies Station, one on the Africa Station, and two lent to New Zealand. Presumably something on a similar scale will be organized in the near future, but with more aircraft carriers and fewer battleships and cruisers in the picture.

Last Fight of H.M. Submarine Universal

CRIPPLED BY ENGINE BREAKDOWN off the Pembrokeshire coast and taken in tow by the destroyer Southdown, the Universal, on her way to be broken up, went adrift when the towing gear broke. Battling against storms for 36 hours the crew twice refused to abandon ship ; then, in a 50 m.p.h. gale, they were rescued by the Aberystwyth and Fishguard lifeboats, on February 5, 1946. The Universal had a grand war service record, sinking or damaging 40,000 tons of enemy shipping during a year's patrol in the Mediterranean. *Photo, Keystone*

Full Military Honours for Malayan Maquis Leader

COL. LIM BO SENG, an heroic leader of the Malayan resistance, was buried on January 13, 1946, at Singapore. Escaping from Malaya in 1942 he made his way to Chungking, where he was created leader of a Chinese unit of Force 136—a part of the great guerilla army, composed of Chinese, Malayas and Indians, which harassed the Japanese. Col. Seng returned to Malaya in 1943 accompanied by a small party which included British officers. Caught by the Japanese, he died in June 1944 as a result of tortures. On the steps of the Municipal Building in Singapore, in front of the table draped in white (Chinese symbol of mourning) upon which rests the bier, a portrait of the dead hero was displayed (above). The British guard of honour presented arms (below) as the bearers laid the bier on the gun-carriage.

Photos, British Official

Commemorating Our Great Desert Campaigns

IN GLORIOUS MEMORY
of the first
BRITISH LIBYAN CAMPAIGN
7 DEC 1940 TO 13 APRIL 1941
and
THE WESTERN DESERT FORCE
under
GENERAL SIR ARCHIBALD WAVELL
A TRIUMPH IN ADVERSITY

IN WHAT WAS ONCE THE PALACE OF GRAZIANI, former Italian governor, at Benghazi, on January 15, 1946, a plaque (1) in memory of the Western Desert Force under Field-Marshal Viscount Wavell was unveiled, together with another marking the triumphant drive of Montgomery's 8th Army against Rommel. The ceremony was performed by General Sir Bernard Paget, G.C.B., D.S.O., C.-in-C. Middle East, seen (2) with the senior chaplain during the dedication of the plaques, whilst the band of the Royal West African Frontier Force played (3)

Major Mysteries of the Second Great War

What General George Marshall called "the greed and mistakes of the war-making nations" contributed largely to Allied victory. Blunders of Axis policy, catastrophic in their consequences, are examined by HENRY STEELE COMMAGER, Professor of History at Columbia University. His article (condensed) is reprinted from The New York Times Magazine. See also facing page.

When Hitler embarked upon war in September 1939 Germany was unquestionably the mightiest military power in the world. And the grand strategy which dictated the application of that power was sound: the strategy of disposing of enemies and potential enemies one by one. Within a year and a half Germany had extended her dominion from the Arctic to North Africa, from the Bay of Biscay to the Black Sea. Franco's Spain was friendly; Russia was still bound to Germany by a non-aggression pact. Only Britain held out, and though Britain might fight on indefinitely it was inconceivable that she alone could reconquer the Continent.

In eighteen months Germany had won such triumphs as no nation had known for more than a hundred years. Within another year she had raised up against her the most powerful military coalition in history. And in three more years she suffered defeat more complete, catastrophe more overwhelming, than any known to history. Meantime, her Axis partner in the Far East, whose triumphs had been equally dazzling, had experienced a comparable reversal of fortunes.

How had it happened? The answer is, of course, to be found in the achievements of the great coalition—Britain, Russia, the United States, China, and their Allies. But this is a superficial answer. Why had Germany and Japan failed to realize what was bound to happen if Russia and the United States were brought into the War against them and to take adequate counter-measures?

Things Hitler Might Have Done

Theoretically, Hitler might have so conducted himself that the United States would not have felt her security threatened or the American people their principles outraged. But then he wouldn't have been Hitler. He might—quite theoretically—have observed treaties and pacts; he might have abstained from persecution of Jews and minorities; he might have established a new order on the basis of justice and humanity. Had he been the kind of leader who would have done these things, however, he wouldn't have started war in the first place. Let us try to list what seem to be the major mysteries of Axis political and military policy, and speculate about the explanations behind them.

Why did the Axis fail to co-ordinate its plans and operations? Why did not Germany, Italy and Japan launch their attack simultaneously, either in 1939 or in 1941? (See map 1, opposite page). Japan, to be sure, was not ready in 1939. But neither were Britain, Russia, or the United States. In 1939 the U.S. were, in the words of General Marshall (see page 612), "not even a third-rate military power." Britain, feverishly rearming against the German menace, was all but helpless in the Far East. Russia, eagerly signing a non-aggression pact designed to give her time to rearm, was in no position to fight a two-front war. Or—if Japan was too unready—the war might have been delayed until she was ready, in 1941. At that time, even with the rearmament programme which the War had brought on, neither Britain nor the United States was able to restrain Japan. Germany, in turn, would probably have enjoyed the same relative superiority in the autumn of 1941 that she enjoyed in the autumn of 1939.

The Axis never achieved a co-ordinated attack. They did not achieve it even after December 1941. Italy entered the War at her convenience—and we are told now that Germany never wanted her in the War at all. Japan, too, came in when it suited her interests to do so, and fought her own war. Perhaps, given the totalitarian philosophy and psychology, a common policy was impossible, for implicit in totalitarianism were racism, distrust of other peoples and States and ambition for world domination.

Why did Germany fail to invade Britain in 1940? Invasion of Britain would not have been easy. The Royal Navy still commanded the Channel, the R.A.F. was still supreme in the skies over Britain, and Britain's coastal defences—we are now beginning to learn—were even more formidable than was then supposed. Yet invasion—either a direct assault upon the beaches, paratroop landings in England or a combination of both against Eire—was not only the logical but as we now know the necessary step for the completion of the German plans. (See map 2).

Goering's Spectacular Failure

Why was it not attempted? The answers are familiar enough. Hitler had not anticipated quite so speedy or so overwhelming a victory in France and was not ready to invade. He did not have the landing craft or the organization behind them. He felt it necessary first to knock the R.A.F. out of the skies, and this Goering failed to do. And so forth and so on.

Again these are answers that tend to mystify rather than to clarify. For a decade Germany had prepared for war. Prior to the summer of 1940 everything had gone like clockwork. Why did the planning break down here? Why was the Wehrmacht not ready to invade? Why had the paratroopers not been trained for precisely this operation—as they were trained for the invasion of Crete? Why was Goering not willing to risk enough planes to ensure destruction of the R.A.F.? There were planes enough for the Balkan venture the following spring and for the all-out assault on Russia.

Possible answers suggest themselves. First, Hitler had confidence that the Luftwaffe could destroy the R.A.F. and then proceed to the disruption of British industries and communications at will; he had confidence, too, in his U-boat campaign. He was unable to imagine that a nation faced with the odds which confronted the British in 1940 would not accept the obvious fact of defeat.

Second, there is the intriguing possibility that Hitler did not want to destroy Britain—as he did want to destroy Russia. So great was his admiration—perhaps respect is a better term—for Britain and the Empire, that he preferred to have Britain come over to his side much as France had, through the establishment of a collaborationist government. His failure to plan for an invasion, his curious offer, just before the launching of the blitz, of peace with a guarantee of the Empire, his unwillingness to use all of his air power against the little island—all these suggest an indecision, a confusion of purpose, rather than military incompetence.

Why did Hitler fail to occupy Spain and thus close the Mediterranean to the Allies? In the light of later events this would seem to have been the major, as it is the most inexplicable, of Hitler's mistakes. Assuredly, he could have encountered little serious opposition from Franco's Spain. Nor could Gibraltar have withstood, indefinitely, attack from the land and from the air. Once Gibraltar was in Nazi hands Malta must have fallen, the British fleet would have been debarred from the Mediterranean and the whole of North Africa would have fallen to Italian and German armies. Italy, instead of being a liability, might have become an asset; the oil of the Near East would have been available; the Anglo-American invasion of 1942 rendered impossible. (See map 3).

What is the explanation of Hitler's failure to make so natural, so logical a move? Probably the desire to concentrate all available force against Russia was the decisive consideration. Possibly Hitler believed that the Italian campaign in Libya and his own attack through the Balkans would clear the British out of the Mediterranean in any event. Possibly, too, there were objections from Mussolini, inclined to regard the Mediterranean as his sea, Spain as in his sphere of influence.

Why did Germany attack Russia in the summer of 1941? It is scarcely necessary now to elaborate on the consequences of the German attack on Russia, or to suggest that had Hitler been victorious in Russia—as he almost was—the war would still be going on. Yet why was the attack made? It was, given the nature of Nazism, almost inevitable.

An Old Adage the Japs Forgot

From the beginning the Nazis had singled out the Bolsheviks as their greatest enemies, and the first Axis alliance was the Anti-Comintern pact with Japan in 1936. The German-Russian non-aggression agreement of 1939 was obviously a marriage of convenience. From the beginning, too, it was clear that Russia was preparing for an inevitable showdown. When Hitler invaded Poland from the west, Russia invaded from the east. The attack on Finland, the absorption of the Baltic States, the annexation of Bessarabia, were all a part of the Russian programme of defence against attack from Germany. There was thus every reason for Hitler to believe that the sooner he attacked the better his chance of success.

He did attack at what was, doubtless, the earliest possible moment. First there was Britain to deal with, and the Battle of Britain raged all through the autumn and winter of 1940-1. Then the Balkan flank had to be cleared, the British thrown on the defensive in North Africa. When the invasion of Russia came in June 1941 it was a spectacular success; in the end Russia proved the graveyard of Hitler's army and Hitler's hopes. (See map 4). Yet until Stalingrad Hitler's gamble seemed justified.

Why did Japan attack Pearl Harbour, and, having attacked, not invade the Hawaiian Islands? It is clear now that the attack on Pearl Harbour which might have been a glittering triumph was, in the end, a fatal mistake. The Japanese forgot the old adage: when you strike a king, strike to kill. They struck what was potentially the greatest naval and military power in the world—and failed to kill. They failed even to destroy the U.S. Pacific fleet.

Having decided that an attack on the American fleet at Pearl Harbour was strategically sound, why did the Japanese fail to prepare for an invasion of the Hawaiian Islands? Whatever it involved, it would have been worth the cost. For if Japan had controlled the Hawaiian Islands it is difficult to see how we could have mounted an offensive. The failure to seize Hawaii and, at the same time, the Aleutians and Dutch Harbour seems now the greatest of Japanese mistakes, perhaps the greatest of all the Axis mistakes. (See maps 1 and 5).

Where Aggressor Nations' Planning Went Astray

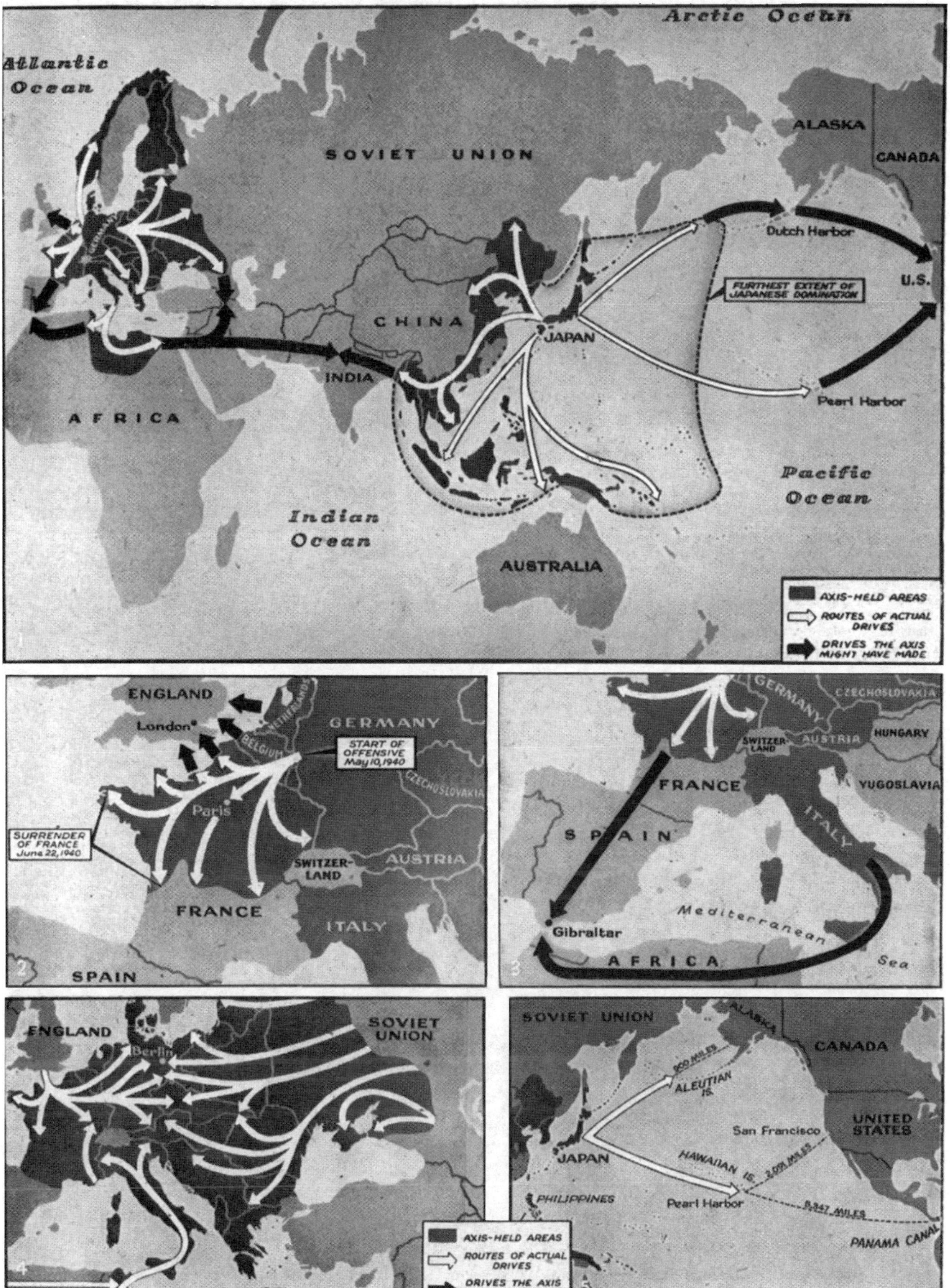

HAD GERMANY, ITALY AND JAPAN STRUCK SIMULTANEOUSLY the grand strategy indicated by black arrows (1) might have succeeded. Collapse of France in 1940 left England vulnerable to conquest (2), but Hitler hesitated and was lost. By occupying Spain and securing Gibraltar Germany might, in 1941, have closed the Mediterranean (3). When Hitler invaded Russia in that year he laid Germany open to attack from several directions (4). The Japs blundered when, having attacked Pearl Harbour, they did not invade Hawaii (5).

By courtesy of The New York Times Magazine

U.N.O. Security Council Meets for First Time

AROUND A HORSESHOE-TABLE at Church House, Westminster, on January 17, 1946, was held the first meeting of the United Nations Organization Security Council, under the chairmanship of Mr. N. J. O. Makin, Australian Minister for the Navy; Mr. Bevin (1, left) in discussion with Mr. Stettinius before proceedings commenced. General view of the Council in session (3): front row, l. to r., Mr. Modzelewski (Poland), Mr. Gromyko (Russia), Mr. Bevin (U.K.), Mr. Stettinius (U.S.A.), Mr. G. Jebb (Secretary), Mr. Makin (Australia), Senhor de Freitas-Valle (Brazil), Dr. Wellington Koo (China), Dr. A. H. Badawi Pasha (Egypt), Mr. Vincent-Auriol (France), Senor de Rosenzweig Diaz (Mexico), and Dr. van Kleffens (Netherlands). Mr. Vyshinsky (2, left) chief Soviet delegate with Dr. D. Manuilsky, Ukrainian Commissar of Foreign Affairs. See also pages 654-658.

Now It Can Be Told!

OLD LOCOS WERE FIGHTERS' 'GUINEA PIGS'

On a lonely R.A.F. Fighter Command station in Northumberland early in 1943 old railway engines, battered tanks and worn-out motor-lorries played a part in the success of the invasion of Europe. They were "guinea-pigs" for a set of experiments to test the effectiveness of R.A.F. fighters against ground targets. Data gained from these tests reduced tank-busting and ground-strafing to a mathematical formula which helped to bring victory for the Allies. The tests were arranged by ballistics experts in co-operation with the "Boffins" of Fighter Command, a team of civilian scientists acting as advisers to the Commander-in-Chief.

Rocket projectiles and all types of cannon and machine-gun ammunition were tried out against the vehicles at the fighter station at Milfield, near Alnwick, and the effectiveness of each type of attack was tabulated after constant rechecking. Finally, the civilian scientists could produce such formulae as "If one Spitfire Mark 5 attacks a railway engine with its cannon, the resultant damage will take an average of twelve man-hours to repair." These formulae, when checked with captured enemy records, frequently proved to be exact.

Another vital piece of ballistics work carried out was the evolution of a method of making maximum use of the British multi-gun fighters. When such a fighter goes into action each of its guns does not fire simply straight ahead. Each gun is set to fire on a slightly different aim, so that a "pattern" of bullets strikes a target at a given range. Intensive research into bullet "patterns" resulted in fire-power being put to the best possible use for the job in hand.

For instance, a concentrated blast of fire to tear a Nazi bomber apart at 200 yards' range might be desirable for a night fighter, but the same pattern would be wasteful and inflict less damage on, say, scattered troops at low level. A big part of the scientists task was to reduce the complicated formulae used by ballistic experts to describe the behaviour of bullets or rocket projectiles under the influence of wind and gravity.

BOMBER COMMAND AND THE WAR IN THE ETHER

A remarkable story was unfolded by the Signals Directorate of the Air Ministry at the close of 1945 of how Bomber Command fought and won the war in the ether. The R.A.F.'s objectives were the Luftwaffe's radio communications and the enemy radar—the radio "eye" which can detect and position approaching aircraft. The intention was to reduce this enemy intelligence to chaos.

BATTLE DECOYS with which we deceived the Germans included tanks (above), aircraft, lorries, invasion craft and A.A. guns (right). Pneumatic models made of barrage balloon material, these were inflated by means of a special air-pump, the "erection" occupying only a few minutes. Deflated, each could be packed in a very small space. *Photos, Keystone*

Radio counter-measures, as they are called, were first considered in 1941, and in 1942 it became feasible to employ them in Bomber operations. From then until the end of the War this extremely complicated and abstruse subject became the wholetime study of a small number of specialists who alone understood all its ramifications.

The most spectacular of these radio counter-measures introduced itself over Hamburg on the night of July 24-25, 1943, when a vast number of aluminium foil strips (see illus. in page 652) fluttered slowly down from our bombers, to settle on the city. This was operation "Window."

Each of the 791 bombers employed on the Hamburg raid dropped (in addition to its bombs) one bundle of 2,000 of these foil strips *every minute*, which mounted to 2½ million strips weighing 20 tons. Assuming that each bundle showed an echo for 15 minutes, the total number of echoes on the enemy's screens during the raid represented 12,000 aircraft.

Side by side with our enemy radar offensive was the determined effort to upset enemy radio communications operated by the Luftwaffe. This mostly took the form of "jamming," or obliterating an enemy signal with a more powerful one of our own on the same frequency. A variation was the use of German-speaking W.A.A.F. broadcasting from the U.K. on Luftwaffe frequencies, giving false information and counter-orders.

Apparatus Captured at Bruneval

In the summer of 1941 it was established that the enemy were using radar to plot our bombers for fighter interception. Calculations gave the experts its approximate position, and in December 1941 aerial photographs were obtained which led to our raid on Bruneval on February 27, 1942. It was the knowledge gained from the capture of German apparatus there that made possible the development of our counter-measures, two of which—code names "Tinsel" and "Mandrel"—were introduced in December 1942 and were an immediate success.

Developed at the Royal Aircraft Establishment at Farnborough, "Tinsel" made use of a radio-telephone transmitter with the microphone placed in the engine or in the aircraft's fuselage. Each operator was given a specified frequency band to watch with instructions to "jam" any German radio telephone he heard, and the noise the German pilot heard from our aircraft may be imagined. Every wireless operator in each bomber took part. They were trained with the help of gramophone recordings of actual night-fighter radio traffic. Valuable help came from the German-speaking operators distributed through the bomber force and

'FOLLY' THAT HELPED US TO MAKE MOSQUITOES

The Thames and Medway Canal, built by Mr. Ralph Dodd in the last century, earned the name of "Dodd's Folly" when railways reduced its value. Much of the canal was filled in before the War as part of the Southern Railway scheme to electrify the line from Gravesend to Gillingham, and it would probably have disappeared altogether but for Hitler. But the War knocked the "folly" out of its nickname. Thousands of Canadian logs were thrown into the canal to season timber for Mosquito construction.

GERMAN 'VIPER' PLANE, developed towards the end of the War but never actually used, was powered by rocket. Rate of climb about 37,000 ft. a minute, its purpose was to destroy enemy aircraft —its pilot to be ejected and descend by parachute. From the launching cradle (left) the take-off (right) was vertical. *Photos, Keystone*

from many of the Polish squadrons came a stream of valuable information as to enemy reactions to the jamming.

The intention with "Mandrel" was to jam the enemy's early warning system, the idea being that if his fighter reaction against the raid could be delayed only 20 minutes a very great advantage would be gained. Associated with this were a number of high-powered ground jammers sited along the South Coast which were intended to blind the German stations across the Channel. On the night of April 26-27, 1943, a high-powered wireless transmitter with a narrow beam-operation, code name "Ground Grocer," was established at Dunwich on the East Anglian coast, and to judge from remarks heard coming from German pilots was an immediate success. A second transmitter was later established at Deal, Kent.

The Germans found themselves forced to use very high frequencies for their communications, and jamming equipment for this was installed at Sizewell on the East Anglian coast. This produced enough noise in the enemy earphones to prevent effective control of their fighters over the Dutch coast and farther west. The operation began work on the night of July 30-31, 1943, under the title of "Ground Cigar" and remained in operation until September 17, 1944. Range limitation was an obvious objection to this, however, except as an interim measure. What was wanted was airborne equipment which would carry the jamming right into enemy territory, thus protecting aircraft of Bomber Command over the whole route to and from the target.

More investigation followed, new equipment was designed and the decision was made to equip a normal 3-flight Lancaster bombing squadron (No. 101). It was first used operationally on the night of October 7-8, 1943, in No. 1 Group, with jamming apparatus, when each aircraft carried a trained German-speaking operator as an additional crew member, whose duty it was to find and jam enemy frequencies. A normal bomb load less the weight of the operator and the equipment was also carried.

Five months had elapsed during that year before fitted aircraft were ready for the Squadron. The type of jamming is best described as a "wig-wog" noise which produced a constantly varying audible note running up and down the scale on the speech channel that was to be jammed. The receiver was an ingenious piece of equipment, specially designed for its purpose and quite unlike anything before fitted in an aircraft.

So successful was this system that the Germans were forced to use Morse telegraphy in an attempt to break through. They tried speeding up their radio-telephone messages, switching on their transmitters for only a few seconds at a time, without success. Yet another subterfuge was to transmit a continuous musical programme, breaking off suddenly to snap out an order. "Airborne Cigar" (or A.B.C., as it became known) was operated by No. 101 Squadron from October 7-8, 1943, to April 19-20, 1945.

Ghost Voice Created Nazi Chaos

The B.B.C., the General Post Office, and Cable and Wireless, joined in the "Corona" system which was to be used as a means of confusing, distracting and annoying the enemy, even to the extent of giving the German fighters instructions contrary to those which they received from their own ground controllers. Instead of transmitting "noise," as was the case with the ordinary "jamming" tactics, it was decided to use a "ghost voice"—a fluent German speaker. This was heard by the enemy for the first time on the night of October 22-23, 1943.

The target on this occasion was Kassel, and before the end of the raid there was chaos in the enemy night defence organization. A furious German ground controller was warning his aircraft to "beware of another voice" and "not to be led astray by the enemy." The "voice" not only spoke idiomatic German but could also mimic perfectly the voices of his opposite numbers. After a particularly violent outburst by the German controller, the "voice" said: "The Englishman is now swearing." The German's reply was: "It is not the Englishman who is swearing but me!"

There were many more radio devices used to counteract the enemy's frantic attempts to control the Luftwaffe fighters. Often this meant quick thinking on the part of the R.A.F. technicians who were always one jump ahead of the Germans. Right up to D-Day our technical resources were engaged in a tense fight to keep our bomber losses down to an average maximum of five per cent which was achieved.

Flying Broadcasting Station

An early attempt to deal with enemy radar by use of a warning receiver was christened "Boozer." In its original form it was simply a receiver which lit a warning lamp when the aircraft became "illuminated" by an enemy radar transmitter. The pilot changed his course until the lamp went out.

Operation "Drumstick" jammed enemy high frequency telegraph controls in the 3·0-6·0 megacycle band. "Fidget" jammed enemy telegraph commentaries and instructions to night fighters during the progress of a Bomber Command attack on the medium waveband. Enemy ground radar stations using the 300-600 megacycle band were jammed by operation "Carpet." And "Jostle" was a high-power high-altitude jammer of enemy radio-telephone communications on short and ultra short wavebands. It was in fact a flying broadcasting station, 40 times more powerful than the transmitters usually carried in aircraft.

One more device was known as "Pipe-rack," which jammed enemy radar on the 95-210 megacycle range. With all these devices, not only was the enemy pursued with unfailing vigour but radio counter-measures in Bomber Command paid a dividend out of all proportion to the capital, in terms of effort, which was invested in it.

FOREST CAMPS FOR REFUGEES

SECRET plans for dealing with many London refugees during the War—should the need have arisen—were disclosed by the Essex County Council in December 1945. The Star reported: An inner belt of rest centres—including camp accommodation in Epping Forest, where 12,000 a day could be fed and 7,000 sleep under cover—was planned.

To meet the possibility of people going out to the surrounding country at night and returning to their work during the day, a "trekker" scheme was prepared. On every road leading out of heavily bombed areas, buildings were equipped and stocked with food, and police and wardens would have acted as guides, so that evacuees would not have had to sleep "rough."

None of those special arrangements was needed, but in 526 rest centres were accommodated 80,000 homeless persons, including 39,000 from Ilford, Dagenham, Barking, Romford and Hornchurch.

How the British are Re-educating the Germans

Exclusive to THE WAR ILLUSTRATED

A New and Saner Order in 13,600 Schools

The Light of Knowledge shorn of Nazi taint is to shine in the 13,000 elementary and intermediate and 600 secondary schools in the British zone of Germany. Selection by the British Military Government of trustworthy staffs presents difficulties; a former Nazi woman teacher who has applied to be reappointed is examined (top) by Lieut.-Col. Hiscocks at his H.Q. in Dannenberg. Second from left is Major Stevens, responsible for education, seen (bottom) questioning a pupil.

British Military Government is Succeeding—

In Dannenberg, one of the most advanced areas in the British zone of Germany, our Military Police find their work diversified by occasional need to chase mischievous small boys (1), but everyone seems quite happy about it. Flight-Lieut. A. Theakston, R.A.F., helps to serve soup at an open-air kitchen (2). Burgomaster B. Roggan (3), prisoner of war in England during the First Great War, now keeps open-house for inquiring troops of the 8th Batt. Middlesex Regiment.

—In Restoring Normal Life to Germany

A lucky discovery made by Flight-Lieut. Theakston is a brown-coal mine in Dannenberg. As representative of the B.M.G. he is having it excavated and prepared for immediate working; the fuel situation, at least locally, will be considerably improved. With him (4) is his manager, Heinrich Wolter, who was in charge of the building of Hitler's hide-out in the Reich Chancellery. Private Wynne Evans, of Flint, N. Wales, shares his chocolate ration with German youngsters (5).

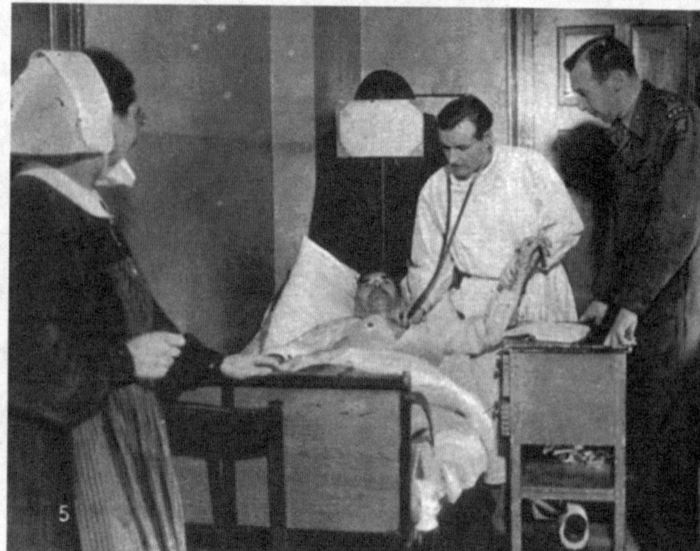

All In a Day's Work for 'Mil. Gov.'

Exclusive to THE WAR ILLUSTRATED

In charge of German Military Government Police in Dannenberg, Capt. W. E. Birchenall inspects his squad (1), newly issued with wooden truncheons. Check-up of motorists on the outskirts is a nightly routine for British troops and German police (2). Our men wait to enter Dannenberg Church as the local congregations file out (3). Flight-Lieut. Theakston inspecting a soap-making factory (4) which formerly manufactured T.N.T. Lieut. R. Bremner, R.A.M.C., tours hospitals (5).

"Burmese Outpost"

Reviewed by HAMILTON FYFE

THE nature of war books has altered. Their interest now lies not so much in the war itself, which used to give them a compelling lure, but in their writers. In such books as The Monastery (see page 659), and Burmese Outpost by Anthony Irwin (Collins, 10s. 6d.), we see how the conditions of war affect the characters, the outlook, the temper of young men; and as the future depends on what men who are now young make of it, it is both useful and interesting to learn as much as we can about them.

Major Anthony Irwin, who fought with native volunteers in Burma (see pages 648-649) and has the highest opinion of them—his book, indeed, is a plea that Britain shall not forget what they did for her—has a more vivid personality than the author of The Monastery. They are both frank about their feelings, their likes and dislikes, their attitude towards "the people at Home." But Major Irwin lays about him with a more cutting whip-lash. He shouts where his fellow-major only spoke in subdued tones. Any moment he is liable to slide off suddenly into a diatribe against something or somebody and to go on hammering away at them or it in most entertaining fashion, and as a rule with a good deal of horse sense, until he thinks of another topic.

The Collapse of Civilization?

I say "horse sense," which means intelligence based on instinct rather than ratiocination, because it seems to me that Major Irwin jumps—or should we say flies—to conclusions, instead of progressing towards them by the process of thinking things out. This is what the writer of the Foreword to his book, who appears to be one of the high-ups, a general at least, though he merely signs himself "X," must mean when he touches on Irwin's "turbulence of spirit, his mixture of rebelliousness, intolerance, consideration, crudeness, yet sensitivity and loyalty" and says that this mixture "characterizes so many of the youth of our day."

I hope that last statement is correct. I hope there are large numbers of young men like Irwin. There is plenty for them to do in cleaning up the world after the two fits of madness in which we have smashed up so much, both material and moral, of what we called Civilization. I am sure they can do it if they are given the same opportunities for peace work as they had in war. All that is needed is an understanding of their potential value, and a resolve to use it, on the part of ruling persons. If they should be treated again as they were after the First Great War, the collapse of civilization will be complete.

NOT many, it is true, had the same chances as Irwin. He was responsible for an area of the Arakan about twice the size of Middlesex, he had a thousand men under him, and a cash account of £1,000 a month. All sorts of jobs came his way and were tackled with energetic readiness:

> For a month I supplied a brigade with fresh vegetables and meat because the Army system had broken down. Three times I've built or had built a complete hospital. I've had to supply labour to build an aerodrome and more labour to build roads.
>
> And at the same time I've had to do my own job; getting information; patrolling areas of Occupation; leading Army patrols on their first sortie into enemy territory; planning ambushes; keeping the people on our side with thick slices of bread and butter; smoothing over sundry crimes that will always occur in an area occupied by any but the highest trained of Forces.

"All this for a pound a day," he finishes, and you must not think he is complaining, any more than you need imagine he swanks about what he did for his pound a day. He would not claim that he was in any way exceptional, though I think perhaps in some ways he was. Most of what he did could and would have been done by any young officer with his wits about him; but I doubt if there are many who would have started a school in an Arakan village as one of those "thick slices of bread and butter" that were required to keep the Arakanese on our side.

Irwin's School in No Man's Land

War and the nearness of the enemy had caused all the schools to close down. The father of the Headman, a Moslem moulvi (priest) and a Hadji, which meant he had performed the pilgrimage to Mecca, was anxious about the children's education (which consisted, by the way, mainly of reading the Koran), and Irwin promised him that a school should be built. The promise was kept, and amid intense enthusiasm the opening ceremony took place. No wonder he felt proud!

> I was confident that this was the first school ever to be started in the no man's land between two war-waging armies by one of those armies. The school was only a mile from the enemy and five from our own forces, and the ceremony was held under the protection of our own Bren guns . . . What could we not do for these people, and with, if only we were able to look after them in a sensible way?

But he found very little interest taken in this most commendable activity.

WITH the tribesmen he commanded he had sympathy, and that gave him understanding of them and their problems. He liked and admired them. Why they ranged themselves on our side he found it hard to know. They have no idea "what real freedom means. They know only that the British have been running their country for many years and that they have, in return for rates and taxes, been allowed to sow and to reap, to pray and to hold their festivals. Being an ignorant people, that has been, on the whole, enough for them. But I see their lot from a different viewpoint, and it will never cease to be a wonder to me that they have not turned on us and helped the Jap to kick us out."

Major ANTHONY IRWIN, M.C., whose book is the subject of this review, was responsible for an area of the Arakan about twice the size of the county of Middlesex.

Now a young man who can think like that is on the way to being an intelligent grown-up person. He will go on thinking until he realizes that all any people ask from rulers is that they should be able to go about the daily affairs of life without hindrance, getting their food, clothes, shelter and such comfort as is customary among them, without having to pay too much for the privilege of being ruled. That, of course, is not so agreeable a life as animals lead, who have no taxes to pay and are provided by nature with covering for their bodies, nourishment, dwellings and occupation; but it is as much as human beings can expect, and in fact, it is as much as the great mass of human beings do expect.

THEREFORE I suggest to Major Irwin that he should not scoff at Social Security or suppose that it will prevent us from being resourceful and destroy initiative, "making life so easy that the only mass thoughts will be turned to how more to amuse ourselves—then War, for our children." On his own showing, this is nonsense. We gave those tribes in Burma security "to sow and to reap, to pray and to hold their festivals," and they stood by us in the hour of need. Why should "marshalling the State for the benefit of the people" have on Europeans a worse effect than it had on the Arakanese? Anyway, the Arakanese had quite as much "real freedom" in the Atlantic Charter sense as the vast proportion of any European or American populations.

Why, it is the absence of security that Major Irwin himself blames for our "negative non-constructive existence" between the wars. The young distrust the older folk because "they led us into these shambles." Politically the young are "unsound" and "morally pretty lax." But, they wonder, "What guarantee is there that there will not be the same class of traitor in power after the war as there was between the wars? The man who will again say that he knew that Germany was rearming and that we should rearm, but was afraid of losing the election if he told the people the truth."

Hotel Commissionaires, V.C.

He is afraid that what he once saw outside a big London hotel—"two men in bright and flashy uniforms, standing there as commissionaires, both wearing on their left breasts the ribbon of the Victoria Cross"—he is afraid he may see that again.

> Perhaps they liked the job because it kept body and soul together. It certainly fed them and their children, but I wonder what they felt as they took a ten-bob tip from a man who had made that ten bob and millions more of them out of those Victoria Crosses. "Taxi, sir?" . . . "Thanks very much" . . . "A Company will attack and . . ." . . . "The War Office regrets to inform you that your son is dead."

Sentiment? Yes, but the right sort, the healthy sort, the sort of sentiment that will pull us through if we act upon it. Irwin is rightly furious at the spurious sentiment, the slop "that the B.B.C. allows greasy young men of doubtful extraction to fill the air with—*There's a Rainbow round the Corner* or *Humpty Dumpty Heart* or *Baby Mine*." He is entitled to be equally savage against politicians who are sentimental in a different, but quite as detestable a way. But what his demand really amounts to is that he wants security; he fears "building our lives on shallow shifting soil: we want the rock, but cannot find it."

Well, I think he has done his bit towards locating it. And I am certain that he and others like him, who have acquitted themselves well in responsible positions during war, can do a great deal to help in pulling us out of our difficulties in time of peace—if only they are given the chance.

Home Railways Revolution

Post-War Designs for Speedy Travel and Greater Passenger Comfort

Specially drawn by Haworth for THE WAR ILLUSTRATED

WAR PERIOD				POST-WAR TASKS	
ENEMY ACTION LOSSES	DAMAGE	OTHER LOSSES		URGENT	LONG-TERM
6	482	256		IMMEDIATE REPLACEMENTS	STANDARDISATION OF DESIGN
635	13314	1000		RECONDITIONING	NEW TYPE CARRIAGES
2680	16132			IMMEDIATE RENOVATION	WATER & SHOCK-PROOF WAGONS
RAW MATERIALS				COMPLETE OVERHAUL	ELIMINATION OF BOTTLENECKS
CONTRACT LABOUR				REPAIR	NEW CONSTRUCTION
				PAINTING, LIGHTING	NEW TYPE STATIONS
RELEASE OF TRAINED STAFF FROM FORCES			TIME TABLE	RESTORATION OF PRE-WAR SERVICES	

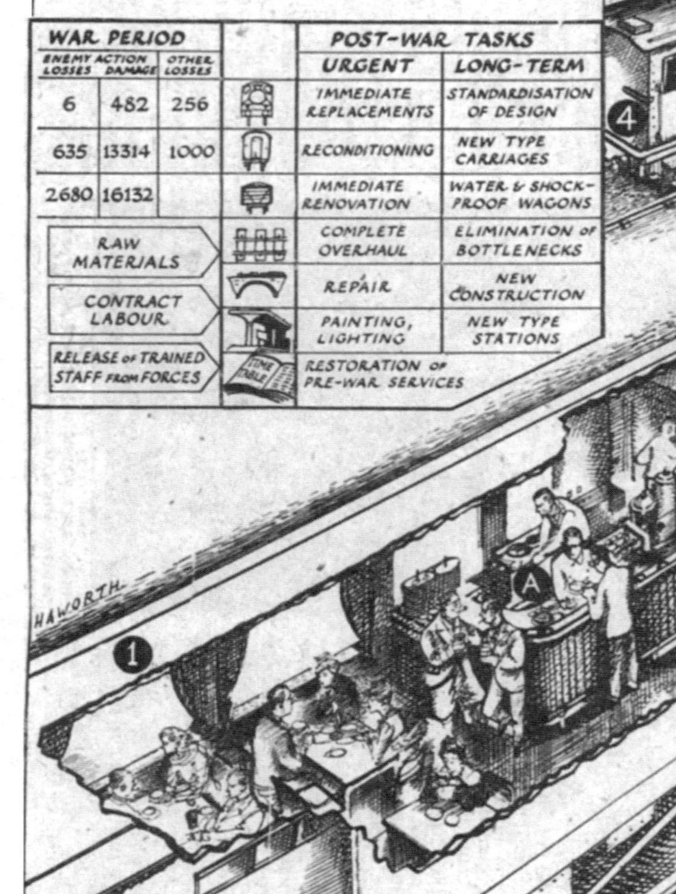

TRANSITION FROM WAR TO PEACE on British Railways involves not merely restoration to normal services, but striking improvements on the old standards. The enormity of the task is indicated in the small chart.

The main part of this drawing by Haworth illustrates the post-War design for rolling stock on the L.N.E.R., and with similar developments by **other companies** shows the progress that is being made by British railways generally. Provision is made for light meals while travelling: a post-War buffet car (1) with quick service (A). **Seating** accommodation and table arrangements are improved. The pantry (B), where the meals are prepared. **New-type** passenger coach (2) has two transverse corridors (C) and (D) in addition to the normal one. Closed compartments (E) are retained for passengers who prefer that type. Stations will be redesigned (3), and will have greatly improved refreshment and waiting rooms.

The train indicator (F) though smaller is more efficient. The **Diesel-electric** shunting locomotive (4) economizes in fuel and is easier to handle. **Electric** locomotive (5) is one of many being built. **Signal** boxes (6), an advance on the old pattern, are designed on the unit principle, and whilst uniform in appearance can be adapted to varying capacities. Section of a new London Transport carriage (7) showing one of three compartments; each has a separate door and all are joined by a through-corridor.

In the centre foreground is seen one of the new B 1 mixed traffic 4-6-0 locomotives, 400 of which have been built under the L.N.E.R. five-year plan. **Working** parts are interchangeable.

Our Firemen Carry War Methods Into Peace

Marvellous method of communication used by the British Army in the Desert Campaigns, and also by our parachute troops, the "Walkie-Talkie" takes its place in Peace as the latest radio aid to fire-fighting. It is described, specially for "The War Illustrated," by EDWIN HAYDON, until recently N.F.S. Public Relations Officer in Essex. **See also page 694.**

A WOMAN trapped on the fifth floor of a blazing factory . . . a wall, undermined by the crackling inferno, threatens to collapse and bury beneath an avalanche of debris anyone in its crumbling path . . . stalwart figures, high above the heads of the surging crowd, steel-helmeted fire-fighters limned against the crimson skyline, ask for instructions or aid. These are moments of crisis, when instantaneous communication between the keen-eyed N.F.S. officer in charge of operations at the control point—usually a radio-equipped motor-pump, van or staff car—and his men may mean the split-second difference between life and death.

Staggering through the smoking building, the unconscious woman lolling over one shoulder, a fire-fighter listens through his earphones to swift orders winging their way to him from the "chief," rapped into the hand microphone the officer holds. Another fireman, a hundred yards distant on the ground, similarly equipped with the "walkie-talkie" portable two-way radio telephone outfit, receives and passes on to a junior officer at his side alternative orders.

The officer shouts hoarsely. The crew of the nearby turntable ladder spring to action. The ladder swings into space and place as the fire-fighter, with the woman on his back, barred from reaching a window by the sea of blistering flame, thrusts her limp figure upwards through a smashed skylight to the waiting colleague crouched on the roof.

Demonstration Behind the Scenes

Surging streams of water—steaming jets at 100 lb. or more pressure per square inch—hiss from a brace of hose, manned by firemen beating back the advancing flames as, an instant later, their burdened comrade clambers down the ladder with his charge, while the watching crowd roars. Meanwhile, further radio-transmitted orders send men suddenly scattering for safety just before the east wall of the burning building disintegrates and crashes down to earth. No one is hurt—thanks to this wartime wonder of portable radio communication.

How does the "walkie-talkie"—already used successfully at several big London fires—actually work? Come with me behind the fire-service scenes. At the London Regional Headquarters of the N.F.S. a senior officer shows you around the school where officers and their drivers are being taught how to use not only "walkie-talkie" but the radio apparatus which now links—by wireless—Regional H.Q. with every "first-away" fire-fighting appliance in London—those great, red-painted motor-pumps which race to the scene of the latest conflagration—plus thirty staff cars and some seven fire-boats. He is a technical communications expert, who has dreamed of this day ever since he attended a tar-boiling job in 1922 necessitating a long water relay, and visualized the value of radio communication in establishing and maintaining immediate contact all along the thousands of feet of hose, plus boosting pumps, between the fire and the source of water supply.

A leading-fireman instructor dons the "walkie-talkie" equipment to demonstrate, while the senior officer who acts as our guide explains the various items: the haversack slung at the back which houses the battery; the small, 5-valve radio receiver and transmitter set in a steel case housed in a haversack at the operator's side, with its two-way switch and simple tuning dial easy to hand.

As the instructor plugs in the spear-like, four-foot long aerial, the officer emphasizes that the earphones are specially designed to allow them to be worn beneath a regulation steel helmet and draws particular attention to the webbed-collar "throat mike." This, it is explained, fits snugly around the neck and actually picks up the vibrations of the larynx. Advantages of this type of microphone are (1) it leaves both hands free; (2) it allows the operator unobstructed vision, which would not be the case if the mike was set in front of his mouth; (3) the throat mike is less likely to be damaged when the fireman is crawling about a building, and (4) even if a man's voice is affected by smoke and fumes a mere whisper will be heard clearly through the earphones by the control officer, who may be as far distant as 500 yards.

"WALKIE-TALKIE" RADIO EQUIPMENT as worn by the N.F.S. The small receiver and transmitter set, with four-foot long aerial plugged in, is slung at the operator's side for instantaneous use. *Photo, Associated Press*

To prove this, the officer hands you one of the headphones, linked to a demonstration set lying on a nearby bench in the big, square basement radio lecture room, replete with maps and various types of transmitters and receivers used on motor-pumps, in fire-boats and staff cars. He switches on the set and instructs the leading fireman, who is now moving around the corridors outside, to demonstrate the "whisper" technique.

EVEN holding the earphone an inch away from your head you can hear him quite clearly chanting test messages: "Zero..1..2..3..4..5..6..7..8..9..10..I am now turning, and passing the boiler room. I am now moving towards the control room. I am now returning to the radio room . . ." At first sight, as the demonstrator reappears, still speaking, you might conclude that he was slightly mad, for he appears to be talking to himself, although not a sound reaches you directly—no, not even if you move to within a foot of him. Yet, all the same, his words come clearly and distinctly through the earphone that you hold.

Watching the class of twenty N.F.S. men receiving theoretical and practical instruction in the latest radio fire-fighting technique, the senior officer tells you that to date 50 operators have been trained in the London area to use "walkie-talkie," and that sets are available at present at Regional H.Q., at all Fire Force H.Q. in the Metropolis and also at sub-area levels. Any of these sets can be swiftly sent on to a fire when requested.

The importance of absolutely accurate messages being transmitted and received under operational conditions, when misunderstood or ambiguous information might prove disastrous—or involve avoidable fire-and-water damage—is obvious. The students therefore receive intensive, practical training in the efficient transmission and reception of standard messages.

Possibility of Error Precluded

A leading-fireman instructor, demonstrating for my benefit, sat at a central control microphone which, on the fire-ground, would actually be the H.Q. of the senior officer in charge of the fire-fighting operations, and began rapping out messages. These were received simultaneously by a dozen firemen-students, all wearing earphones and sitting with their backs to him at benches lining the walls of the lecture room. They, in turn, replied over their sets in standard terms: a system which precludes the possibility of error as far as is humanly possible in an imperfect world.

It was also pointed out that one danger—that of indiscriminate and simultaneous broadcasting by several radio-equipped machines or cars at any one fire, liable to cause tremendous confusion—must be avoided at all costs. And so, normally, only one vehicle, acting as the central fire-ground control, operates at any one time.

The eventual aim is to train every member of the London Fire Force in the use of this equipment—the course takes three days—and to carry two sets of "walkie-talkie" apparatus on every fire-fighting appliance. When that day comes communication methods like field telephones, which are unsatisfactory for use in buildings because of the trailing wire; messages by hand, which are slow; by signals, which are likely to be misunderstood; by whistles or by shouting, will no longer be necessary. Experiments are now being undertaken to discover whether the portable two-way radio telephone can be used simultaneously by a fire-fighter with artificial breathing apparatus, by means of which a man can work for a reasonable period in the thickest smoke.

Research to Secure Perfection

Emphasizing that the present apparatus is still only in its experimental stage—that much research will be required to adapt and redesign it so that, for one thing, it is sufficiently sturdy to survive rough handling, drenching with water and exposure to considerable heat and to meet fully all fire service needs—the officer pointed out that this latest development is part of an N.F.S. radio communications plan in the London area which began in 1942, when Regional H.Q. was linked with fire-appliances on the fire-grounds, with fire-boats and senior officers' cars, on similar lines to the police set-up, and which is serviced by two transmitters, one sited at Hampstead and another—a standby—at Regional Headquarters.

'Walkie-Talkie' in Action at a Big Night Blaze

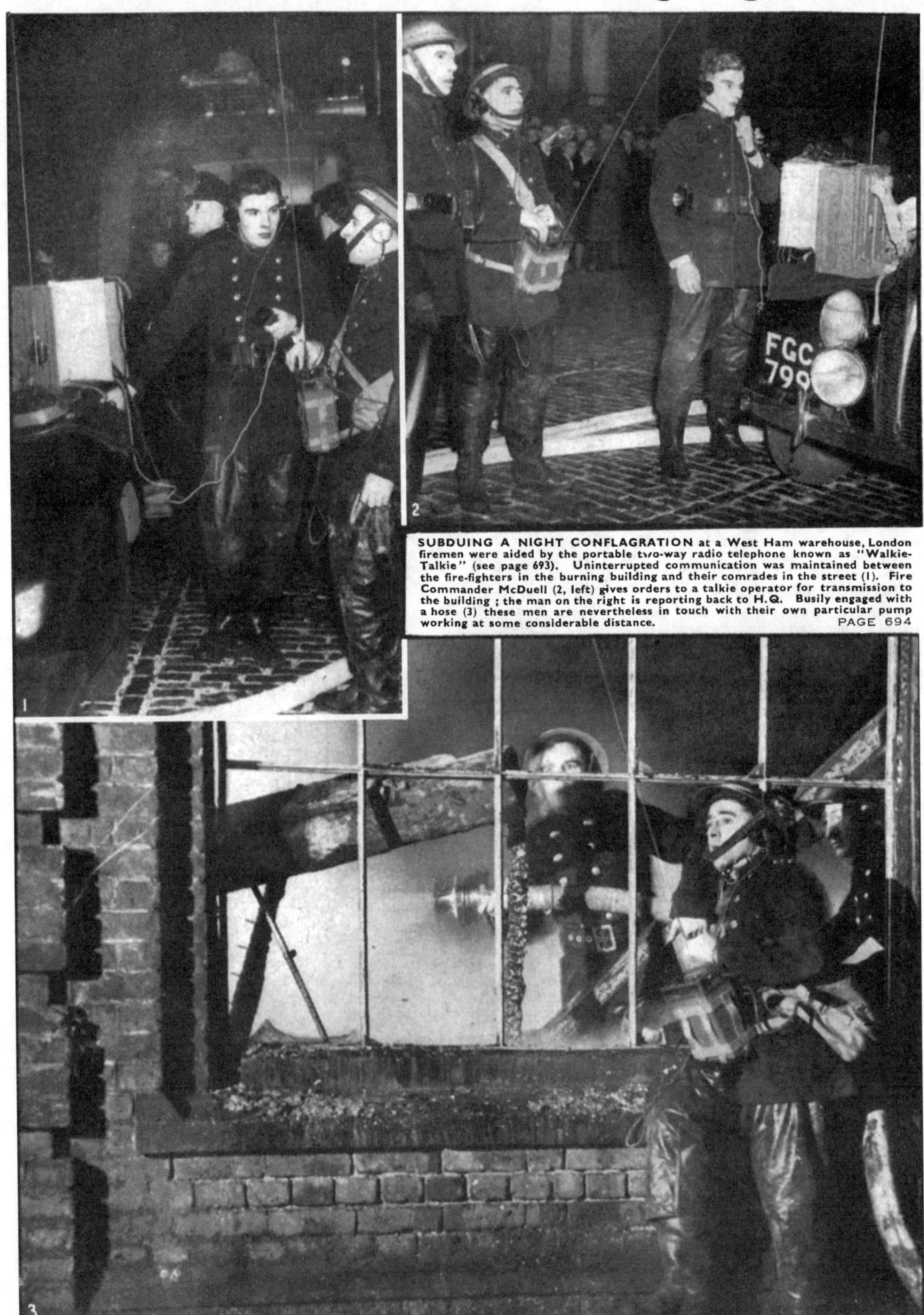

SUBDUING A NIGHT CONFLAGRATION at a West Ham warehouse, London firemen were aided by the portable two-way radio telephone known as "Walkie-Talkie" (see page 693). Uninterrupted communication was maintained between the fire-fighters in the burning building and their comrades in the street (1). Fire Commander McDuell (2, left) gives orders to a talkie operator for transmission to the building; the man on the right is reporting back to H.Q. Busily engaged with a hose (3) these men are nevertheless in touch with their own particular pump working at some considerable distance.

To Build This Railway 16,000 Prisoners Died

A SINGLE TRACK FROM SIAM TO BURMA, the notorious Bangkok-Moulmein railway (top) was constructed under compulsion of the Japanese by British and Allied prisoners of war and 100 000 native labourers, in 1942-43. Toiling for 17 hours a day in appalling conditions, in disease-ridden and pest-infested jungle, men died like flies: their last resting-place line-side cemeteries such as this (bottom) recently cleared by Jap gangs under Allied supervision. See also story in page 409. *Photos, The Times*

I Was There! Eye Witness Stories of the War and After

When the German Guns First Shelled Dover

A member of the Auxiliary Fire Service in Dover when guns at Calais shelled the town in August 1940, Frank Illingworth tells specially for "The War Illustrated" this story of the sighting shots to the first full-scale bombardment of Britain from an enemy shore, and how the Royal Marine Siege Regiment replied—in the first cross-Channel gun-duel in history.

13-YEAR OLD A.R.P. MESSENGER, one of the Clark twins of Dover referred to below, was one of Britain's youngest home-front-line "men" in 1940. The twins had the honour of being presented to the Prime Minister.
Photo, Frank Illingworth

At a few minutes past nine p.m. on Aug. 22, 1940, a heavy explosion interrupted the B.B.C. news broadcast. Three more explosions followed. My housekeeper and her husband, by name Stubbs, and I collided in a frantic scramble for the front door.

"The sireens haven't gone, have they?" demanded Mrs. Stubbs. We assured her, "No!" Silence followed the last explosion. From nearby trees the blackbirds again took up their song, and owls hooted. Slowly we returned indoors, considerably mystified by the explosions—whilst a further salvo of 14-in. shells was spanning the Straits.

Warden Brown, of the Westminster Bank, came running up, looking worried. "Wouldn't be sure," he said, "but I think that's shelling. Listen! See if you can hear the stuff coming over." He lay on his stomach in the shelter of my garden wall at Kearsney, two-and-a-half miles behind Dover, as explosions tore the heavens apart and a shrapnel shell burst low overhead. We needed no more confirmation of Brown's warning. The violent descent of several tiles occasioned Mr. and Mrs. Stubbs' hasty retreat to shelter. I rushed in for my uniform; Brown headed at the double for his post.

On my way to the fire-station I heard him warning the occupants of a car not to venture into the town. Perhaps this was not the best advice, for two shells were bursting within 800 yards of us for every one in Dover itself, but we weren't to know this at the time.

Brilliant flashes over Calais and Boulogne heralded the explosion of further four-gun salvos. The town rocked, and sullen columns of brick-dust were soaring up when I arrived at the fire-station. My arrival there was usually met with remarks unsuitable as greeting even to a junior officer such as, "Whatcheer, cock!" and "Here comes Frankie!" This time there was no banter. The men stood in anxious groups. Then someone said, "We're being shelled, sir!"

Another Salvo Shook the Town

The same atmosphere pervaded the control room. Section-Officers Baynton and Campbell, G.M. (see pages 412–413, Vol. 3); were pretending to play darts; Patrol-Officer Bill Spicer, and our Chief, Sergeant Ernie Harmer, G.M. (see page 412, Vol. 3), were pretending to read; and the telephonists' knitting needles were clicking rather faster than usual. Another salvo shook the town, and Harmer said to the girls: "You'd better get across the street into the shelter—Spicer and Baynton will take over the phones."

For a moment the girls exchanged uncertain glances. Then Miss Flack replied, "We'd rather stay at our post, sergeant." But tempers were strained; we had never been shelled before, and Harmer whipped around with the order: "I said get over the road—all of you get under ground—you'll be called if you're wanted!"

We retreated to the shelter. It might have been a Hollywood "set." Firemen, wardens, rescue men, women and children from the streets—friendliness, frayed tempers, and mixed drama. In one corner a nun soothed a screaming child while nearby a fireman from London, blown off his bicycle by a shell burst, muttered savagely. The Clark twins, diminutive thirteen-year-old A.R.P. messengers, played billiards. Two mothers, nursing their infants, edged farther along the bench they shared with a fireman. Into this scene came Fireman Forth, bringing

FOURTEEN-INCH. SHELL FIRED FROM CALAIS is seen bursting behind the National Provincial Bank (left) in the centre of Dover, in August 1940. Another wrecked the interior of St. Barnabas' Church (right). The cross-Channel bombardment of this front-line area continued, off and on, until the autumn of 1944. The excitement and devastation caused by the 1940 "sighting shots" which heralded the full-scale bombardment of this country are described above. See also illus. in page 382, Vol. 8.
Photos, Frank Illingworth, Keystone

CARPENTRY CLASSROOM IN H.M.S. FLYCATCHER, Naval shore establishment at Middle Wallop, near Andover. Servicemen with an eye to a civilian occupation are learning to make ironing-boards, cots, toys and other much-needed household articles. For those otherwise inclined there are bricklaying, commercial and other courses designed to equip them to take their part in industry. How men from the Fleet Air Arm gain their "passport back to Civvy Street" is told below. *Photo, Associated Press*

news of what was going on outside. He was covered with brick-dust and streaked with sweat, for on the way to the fire-station he had stopped to burrow for two women, the Clark sisters, whose cottage German gunners had blown to bits. "It's not too good out there," he said quietly. Civilians, we firemen had no military discipline to lean on; and I for one did not relish the idea of riding a fire-engine along streets under artillery fire.

Then Alec Campbell's raucous voice bellowed through the door: "First crew to the Catholic Church—get going!" Firemen stumbled into the night as flashes illuminated the sky over the French coast. Near the Catholic Church an ambulance was removing two sailors killed by splinters. The same shell had scattered rubble, tiles, earth and branches across the road; the stench of cordite filled the air, and through the brick-dust could be seen the gaping wall of a house near the nursing home. But there was no fire, and the crew returned to Central.

R.M. Siege Regiment in Action

The night of August 22, 1940, was not the first time we had heard shells bursting That morning I had watched German artillerymen shelling a convoy in the Straits. And ten days previously, at 11 a.m. on August 12, two sudden explosions had shaken the town, killing a man and a dog. At the time I did not recognize them as the sighting shots to the first full-scale bombardment of Britain from an enemy shore.

For three-quarters of an hour German shells crashed into the town, in up to four-gun salvos, and soared over it into the outskirts of Kearsney and River. Gun flashes over Calais, then the sharper stabs of shells exploding among our homes, showed the streets to be empty except for police and wardens sheltering in doorways.

Towards the end of the bombardment, Bill Spicer, who had been watching the flickering and reverberating heavens from the street, came into the shelter with big news: "Looks as though *our* guns are firing from the cliffs!" We went out to investigate. Sure enough, the guns of the Royal Marine Siege Regiment were in action. Brilliantly white flashes, resembling those over the French coast, flickered for brief seconds; and the roar of British long-range artillery re-echoed through the valley as the Marines opened up in the first cross-Channel gun-duel in history.

Silence had returned by eleven o'clock, and I turned for home. Groups of people were standing around the rubble. There were snatches of conversation: "One shell by the Railway Bell Hotel" . . . "One in Cherry Tree Avenue" . . . "St. Barnabas' Church has gone" . .

I cycled into a shell-hole en route to the church. A dog was running around on three legs, howling as someone tried to dispatch it. The church was wrecked. I went inside. Moonlight shone through gaping walls; brick-dust still fluttered across the rubble. The stench of cordite hung heavy over all.

Outside, a woman muttered: "When'll the Boche open up again?" She was not to know it, but the answer was, "Tomorrow and again and again for forty-nine months!"

Back to Civvy Street via H.M.S. Flycatcher

Vocational training centre for thousands of Servicemen approaching demobilization, this "stone frigate's" classrooms are filled with trainees from the Fleet Air Arm keen to succeed in civilian jobs. A visit in January 1946 is described by The Evening Standard Naval Reporter.

Aircraft still fly from this "stone frigate" on the hills outside Andover, Hampshire, but there is other important work going on inside the big hangars. Bearing a ship's name, as all naval establishments do, H.M.S. Flycatcher is the vocational training centre for thousands of men leaving the Fleet Air Arm.

I saw them at work today as tradesmen, as office workers and as craftsmen. The instructors were nearly all ratings. Leading Air Mechanic J. Harratt, who was taking a bricklaying class, said: "They are not going out as experts, but they have the idea and are very keen." In charge of one of the commercial classes was Leading-seaman John Beeby, of Northampton, who, with L.M.S. office training behind him, handled the blackboard with confidence and authority. His pupils have ambitions in such varied directions as boxing promoting, estate agency, drapery and the public-house business.

"Jack the handyman" was to be seen in most sections. Kettles, frying-pans, ironing-boards, toys and even cradles were being made by the trainees. Admiral Sir Denis Boyd, Commanding Naval Air, also toured the hangars at H.M.S. Flycatcher.

"Everything is made to work," he said, as he pressed buttons and switches in the electrical section. "Captain Ede, who was minesweeping most of the War, and Commander Rumsey, the chief instructor, are astonishing me by what they can accomplish with the men in a short time. We older Navy men welcome the opportunity to give these youngsters a flying start on the way back to civilian life."

And at the end of a month's training each man who has earned it gets a slip of paper which is signed by the captain and states that he has taken a course at H.M.S. Flycatcher. It is his passport back to Civvy Street.

WELDING particularly interests this trainee at Middle Wallop, who is within sight of the end of his service with the Fleet Air Arm. See story on left. *Photo, Associated Press*

I Saw the Burned-Out Heart of Frankfort

With a party of British and Dominion correspondents, William Forrest of The News Chronicle visited the shattered town of Frankfort-on-Oder in the Russian zone of Germany on January 30, 1946, and heard from the burgomaster the terrible story of how 12,000 people have died since peace came.

In six months of Russian occupation 12,000 people—roughly one-sixth of the inhabitants—died in Frankfort-on-Oder. The burgomaster, Dr. Ernst Ruge, told us they died "from sheer hunger." Next day the Russians produced a corrected version of his statement, which said that the 12,000 died "from all causes."

With an impressive escort of Red Army officers, led by the military commander of the town, we drove through the burned-out heart of Frankfort to keep our appointment with the burgomaster at the town hall. Dr. Ruge shook hands warmly with the Russian commander, who then presented the party of British and Dominion correspondents. We were given seats, the Russian officers sat behind us, the burgomaster's secretary prepared to take a shorthand note, and the interview began.

Before the Nazis came to power Dr. Ruge was the head surgeon in a Frankfort hospital. The Nazis dismissed him because he was anti-Fascist. He is now a member of the Social Democrat Party. We asked him to tell us what had happened in Frankfort since the end of the war, and this is what he said:

Only 24 Doctors Instead of 60

"Before the war there were 85,000 people in this town: today there are 53,000, of whom only 18,000—12,000 men and 6,000 women—are fit for work. More than 100,000 German refugees from beyond the Oder, driven out by the Poles, have passed through the town. We have also had 30,000 German prisoners of war returning from Russia. All these prisoners were ailing and unfit in one way or another—that is why they were released.

"Frankfort was the first German town they reached on their long journey home, and most of them wanted to stay here. But we could keep only four or five thousand, and of these more than half are now dead. Our means are terribly limited. We have only 24 doctors instead of the 60 we had in normal times, and the present time is so abnormal in many ways; and we have practically no medicines.

"We have ordered medical supplies from Berlin and Dresden, but so far we haven't received them, and we can't get any from the British and American zones because we can't go there to buy them. Epidemics? Yes, there has been a bad epidemic of typhoid—3,000 cases, and 800 deaths. Now there is typhus in the town—there were three deaths from it last week. For the first six months the food situation was very bad. Up to December 1 no fewer than 12,000 people died from sheer hunger."

Dr. Ruge repeated the phrase "from sheer hunger" three times. Then, with a smile for the Russian commander, he said that recently, "thanks to our Russian friends," the food situation had greatly improved. What else was there to tell? In the countryside, said the burgomaster, there had been plunderings and killings "by irregular troops without discipline or commanders." Then, on the other side of the Oder, were the hostile Poles who had driven all the Germans out and now even shot at any German who tried to fish in the Oder.

"The Poles have tried to populate their new territory with their own people, but without success," he said. "Most of the settlers who came from Eastern Poland have gone away again. Before the war 18,000 Germans lived in the suburbs of Frankfort on the east bank of the Oder—now there are only 60 Polish families there. And you can drive for miles on the other bank without meeting a soul. The villages, once peopled by Germans, are deserted. The land is empty."

In Poland's 'Western Desert'

The burgomaster's wife, who speaks excellent English, joined us, and while some of us continued to interview the burgomaster, others spoke to her. The secretary could no longer keep up her shorthand note. Thereupon the Russian commander rose and said it was time to go. We went down to the Oder and gazed across at what is now Poland. Nothing stirred there.

A year ago the swift-flowing Oder was Germany's last ditch. Today it is her closed eastern frontier. On the one side lies Poland's "Western Desert," as I heard it called in Warsaw; on the other side lies a German graveyard. After a banquet at the Russian headquarters we were escorted to Potsdam, capital of the province. Next day the Russians in Potsdam produced a verbatim typescript of our interview with the burgomaster. "The burgomaster," we were told, "has made one important correction. When he said there were 12,000 deaths from hunger he meant deaths from all causes."

Our Tunnel from Prison Camp to Freedom

One of the most sensational incidents in a German prisoner-of-war camp resulted in the break-out of 78 Allied Air Force officers. Here Flight.-Lieut. Ley Kenyon, D.F.C., R.A.F.—who was the escape organization's forger of essential papers—concludes his story which began on page 664. In the previous part he described the preparations and the agonizing wait on March 24, 1944, for the actual "break" to commence.

Those who were not concerned in the escape lay wakefully in their beds, some fully dressed, waiting for the dreaded sound of—we knew not what, perhaps rifle fire—perhaps the bark of a dog or the guttural voice of a guard. Just after dusk the fateful word "Break" was given.

Experienced tunnellers completed the last few feet and broke out into the wood on the far side of the road—beyond the barbed wire. Three ropes were run out from the tunnel exit to the edge of the wood, and a guide planted himself at the end of each to direct escapists. One rope ran south for those escaping into Czechoslovakia and the southern countries, one west for those attempting a railway passage from the local stations, and one north for those making for the northern ports and Sweden.

At intervals of two minutes man after man sped through the tunnel and emerged from its mouth, to disappear into the darkness of the wood. The searchlights kept up their groping, but could not be pivoted round far enough to pick up the tunnel exit—a possibility which had been considered when the first plans were drawn up. Sentries outside the wire passed within 20 feet of the exit but suspected nothing.

Double Guard Around the Camp

Throughout the night the work continued. Mishaps occurred which held up operations and prevented the full number of escapists from getting away. The displacing of a few wood shorings in the tunnel caused a serious subsidence of sand, and it took nearly an hour to clear the obstruction.

For the first time in several nights a bomber force from England attacked Berlin, only 80 miles to the north-west, and as usual the Germans switched off the electric supply. Everything was cast into darkness, whilst the ground around us shook with the impact of bombs. Trickles of sand dropped through between the supporting bed-boards with every blast. Ages passed before emergency spirit lamps could be passed along the tunnel, then once again the trollies moved forward with their human cargo. Extra care had now to be taken, as the guard around the camp was doubled during local air raids.

It was just before five. Dawn was breaking over the snow-covered ground when the dreaded sound came—a shot. A sentry passing near the tunnel exit saw a movement in the undergrowth and let fire with his rifle. He missed his target but gave the alarm. We in our beds knew it was the end. Within seconds hell broke loose. Hordes of German guards swarmed into the camp.

CEMETERY AT STALAG LUFT III, near Sagan, Upper Silesia—site of the ill-fated break-out by Allied Air Force officers described here. Two officers, members of a camp working-party, are seen near the impressive memorial to fellow-prisoners who perished there.

From a drawing by Flight-Lieut. Ley Kenyon, D.F.C., R.A.F.

Window-shutters and doors in all the blocks were bolted and barred—some were nailed up—and word was shouted down the corridors that no one was to move from their rooms on any pretext.

Harry's block was ransacked by the Germans. Furniture and walls were stripped in the guards' efforts to find all our escape material. Of the 160 officers who were to escape only 78 got away. The unfortunates who were left behind were driven out into the cold, paraded, counted a dozen times, and almost completely stripped by the frenzied guards in their endeavour to find everything concealed on their persons. The camp commandant, wearing pyjamas under his overcoat, stormed up and down, flourishing a revolver and thrusting all who showed the slightest signs of resistance or flippancy—German guards and prisoners alike—into the camp gaol.

Wild-eyed Huns with guns, fearful of their own responsibility and perhaps of their lives, posted themselves at every vantage point whilst the search went on. Hours passed before we were released from our blocks and the whole camp was driven on to the parade ground, where we remained until late in the afternoon. Time after time we were counted. As mathematicians the Germans were hopeless, and by the end of the day they were still arguing with each other on the final score. We, of course, used every means possible to make their task more difficult.

DEFEATING BOREDOM during their captivity at Stalag Luft III the prisoners organized Rugger matches and other sports and games. Hobbies also came in for serious attention in spite of the woful scarcity of materials. And ever-present were galling thoughts of Home and the possibilities of escape. *Photo, Flight.-Lieut. Ley Kenyon, D.F.C., R.A.F.*

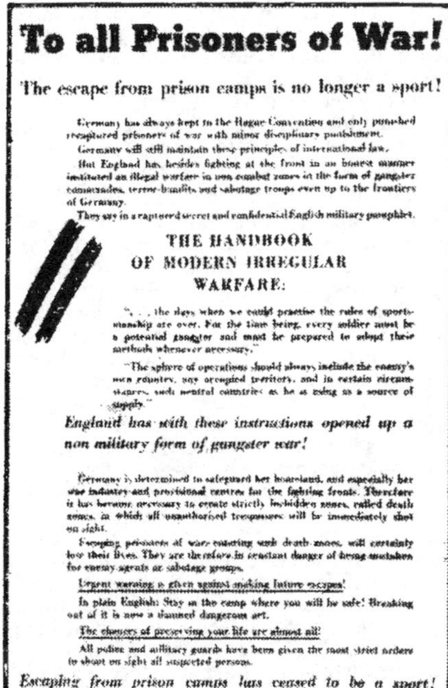

To all Prisoners of War!

The escape from prison camps is no longer a sport!

Germany has always kept to the Hague Convention and only punished recaptured prisoners of war with minor disciplinary punishment.

Germany will still maintain these principles of international law.

But England has besides fighting at the front in an honest manner instituted an illegal warfare in non combat zones in the form of gangster commandos, terror bandits and sabotage troops even up to the frontiers of Germany.

They say in a captured secret and confidential English military pamphlet,

THE HANDBOOK OF MODERN IRREGULAR WARFARE:

"... the days when we could practise the rules of sportsmanship are over. For the time being, every soldier must be a potential gangster and must be prepared to adopt their methods whenever necessary."

"The sphere of operations should always include the enemy's own country, any occupied territory, and in certain circumstances, such neutral countries as he is using as a source of supply."

England has with these instructions opened up a non military form of gangster war!

Germany is determined to safeguard her homeland, and especially her war industry and provisional centres for the fighting fronts. Therefore it has become necessary to create strictly forbidden zones, called death zones, in which all unauthorised trespassers will be immediately shot on sight.

Escaping prisoners of war, entering such death zones, will certainly lose their lives. They are therefore in constant danger of being mistaken for enemy agents or sabotage groups.

Urgent warning is given against making future escapes!

In plain English: Stay in the camp where you will be safe! Breaking out of it is now a damned dangerous act.

The chances of preserving your life are almost nil!

All police and military guards have been given the most strict orders to shoot on sight all suspected persons.

Escaping from prison camps has ceased to be a sport!

DEATH ZONES WARNING issued in the camp by the German authorities as a deterrent to prisoners contemplating a "break." See centre column, this page. *Photo, Flight-Lieut. Ley Kenyon, D.F.C., R.A.F.*

To Be Shot Immediately on Sight

The climax to this break-out? Only three officers—a Dutchman and two Norwegians—reached England. Fifty of the others were shot, in the words of the Commandant, "whilst trying to re-escape." We know better. The few that were eventually brought back to the camp told us of the days they spent in the infamous Gestapo jail at Goerlitz: of how a guard would visit the cells and read out names, whereupon those on the list would be led away never to be seen alive again. We knew that none of them would have attempted to re-escape after all his essential escape equipment had been taken from him—and probably his boots, as well. As a result of all this, severe impositions were placed upon those of us left behind. What the Germans called "Death Zones," covering practically the whole of Germany, were instituted, in which all unauthorized trespassers would be immediately shot on sight. This interesting information was presented to us in the form of leaflets planted around the camp at night, by their security men. Our guards completely lacked any sense of humour: they just couldn't face the ridicule to which they would have been subjected had they openly given us those leaflets in daylight! However, we collected the bits of paper and returned them!

Individual escapes continued, and work on our last tunnel—George—was immediately started. George was shorter but just as elaborately equipped as Harry. Its entrance was concealed under one of the 300 Red Cross box seats in the theatre, and work down there continued even during the musical and theatrical shows which were put on practically every night of the week.

How I Hid My Tunnel Drawings

In the event of the German guards deserting their posts at the end of the War, we had planned to use this tunnel to put out our recently formed commando parties to take over—if necessary with a pitched battle—all the resources such as the armoury, ammunition dump, water and electricity supplies, necessary to sustain life in the camp until our Allies the Russians arrived. But we were force-marched away from the camp in January 1945, before it was necessary to put this plan into operation.

The drawings I made in the tunnel were done several weeks before the pre-arranged date for the big break. I was asked by the committee to carry out this series to record permanently the masterpiece of tunnel engineering. I worked on them in extremely difficult conditions. Sometimes I lay on my back and used the roof of the tunnel as a drawing desk. The heat was intense, though the ingenious air conditioning pumps were operated throughout.

When the drawings were completed they were packed away into an airtight canister, made of dried milk tins, and hidden in our underground dispersal chamber for recovery when required. Months later, when we received the order to march, we were given only an hour's notice. The Russians were 30 miles away. There was insufficient time to rescue the drawings and other escape material from this chamber, which was the workshop of Dick.

Its entrance was beneath the grill of a drain in a shower-house, and the side of the concrete wall of the drain had to be removed to gain entrance to the shaft, and replaced and sealed afterwards if the drain was to be used. So we flooded this tunnel with water from the showers as a precaution against the Germans finding our documents hidden there. They remained there for another five months, surviving the occupation of the camp by the Germans, who used it as an advance military depot until they were at last forced to withdraw by the Russian advance south of the Oder.

The drawings were eventually found, unscathed, by a British officer, who was too sick to leave the camp with the main body of prisoners, and remained in the hospital. After his release he descended with other officers into the dispersal chamber. He found that the flood-water had seeped away and had not damaged the escape material. Much of this material has since been brought to England—including, of course, my drawings, which are the only authentic records of the tunnel in existence.

★—As The Years Went By—Notable Days in the War—★

1940

February 16. *H.M.S. Cossack rescued British from prison-ship Altmark in Norwegian fjord.*

1941

February 25. *Mogadishu, capital of Italian Somaliland, captured by E. and W. Africans.*

March 1. *Bulgaria joined the Axis; German troops entered Sofia, the capital.*

1942

February 27. *Battle of Java Sea began; Allies lost five cruisers and six destroyers.*

February 28. *Combined Operations raid on radiolocation station at Bruneval, Normandy.*

March 1. *Japanese troops landed in Java.*

1943

February 25. *German attack in Faid Pass-Kasserine area of Tunisia finally held.*

1944

February 16. *Second German attack at Anzio.*

February 22. *Krivoi Rog, iron-ore centre in the Dnieper Bend, recaptured by Russian troops.*

1945

February 19. *U.S. forces landed on Iwojima, Volcano Is., after two months' bombardment.*

February 26. *Flying Fortresses and Liberators made biggest daylight raid on Berlin.*

March 1. *U.S. 9th Army captured Munchen-Gladbach; U.S. 3rd Army occupied Trier.*

When Aircraft Travel Faster than Sound

By CAPTAIN
NORMAN MACMILLAN
M.C., A.F.C.

MARSHAL of the Royal Air Force Sir Arthur Harris has been credited with saying that we have seen the last of the great bombing wars employing huge fleets of aircraft for that purpose. But he has not elucidated this statement by any prophetic outline of the nature of future conflict, if such there is to be. In any case, whether there ever is another great war or not, there is as yet no real evidence that the Great Powers are prepared to give up the national sovereignty that arises from the possession of arms.

Lord Halifax, speaking in New Jersey on February 4, 1946, was reported to have said to the Americans . "Probably neither your nation nor mine would be prepared today to take the risk of leaving security exclusively to some international force." The differences between Mr. Vyshinsky and Mr. Bevin in the Security Council of the United Nations over British troops in Greece lends point to this statement, for there was never any suggestion that the British troops should be replaced by an international force.

Thus it is reasonable to suppose that the institution of the United Nations will not in the near future cause the Great Powers to give up their own armaments. However willing they may be to assist some international structure to deal with smaller disputes, they see clearly enough that their own prestige within the United Nations organization depends upon their own economic and military strength.

GREAT Nations' Triple Purpose in the Development of Aircraft

I do not propose to carry this argument into the political field. But it seems obvious that in the military field this means that there will be a continuation of armaments development by all the Great Powers. What this entails is best seen by comparing police forces with armies. Police forces have not shown any tendency to desire more powerful arms, and have played no part in armament development. Therefore if the world could be controlled from international crime by a police force, the stimulus to arms development could cease, because the police would be operating against unarmed criminals and could enforce law and order with the minimum of the simplest arms.

But the world has seen in recent decades how criminals have taken advantage of fast transport vehicles. The development of the motor-car has played a great part in crime. And against a world police force armed with simple weapons there is no doubt that the aeroplane would also be used to play a great part, and perhaps a greater part than the motor-car, in crime. Thus, any world police force would have to possess the fastest types of aircraft to suppress such criminals. For this reason and because of air transport development, it is certain that there will be a continuing progress in aircraft, whatever may be the outcome of present tendencies in the sovereignty in arms.

IT is not only the atom bomb which brings the desire to retain arms as part of sovereignty. Far more it is the existence of varying political structures among the nations. And without political unity there can be no sure foundation for a single world order. That is the goal towards which the world is moving, but until it is reached there will be manifold scientific advances in armaments, and the retention of great armed forces to strengthen the different political outlooks of the great nations.

There is therefore on the part of the great nations a common desire to develop aircraft for the triple purposes of military strength, civil transport, and police security. This means that the progress in aircraft design will be rapid, and by 1950 at the latest we should see gas turbine engined aircraft crossing the Atlantic at fast speeds and considerable heights, carrying up to nearly 100 persons (crew and passengers).

We shall have entered the era of engines of 10,000 horse-power for aircraft. When we recall that the most powerful engines used in Allied bombers during the Second Great War did not exceed 2,500 horse-power, we gain some idea of the progress in various directions that these new and far more powerful engines will make possible.

JET-PROPELLED, the all-metal De Havilland Vampire has flown at 540 miles per hour. Speed of sound is about 743 m.p.h. at sea level. See also pages 571 and 573. *Photo, Charles E. Brown*

In aircraft, engine power can be utilized in two ways. First, it can be employed to lift greater loads and numbers of passengers by making possible the construction of larger aircraft. Secondly, it can be used to attain greater speed. And it is possible to strike a compromise between these two extremes.

What has been done in recent years is best seen by the table I give in the panel below.

Year	Aircraft	Horse-Power	Speed
1938	Hurricane	1,050	335 m.p.h.
1939	Spitfire	1,050	367 ,,
1943	Tempest	2,200	435 ,,
1944	Spitfire	2,040 (with triple supercharger)	450 ,,
1945	Meteor	6,000 (about)	606 ,,
1950	?	20,000	700-800

From this table it is apparent that it is the gas turbine, commonly called the jet engine, which has produced the recent jump in speed, and which offers the possibility of reaching and exceeding the speed of sound (around 743 miles an hour at sea level).

When discussing high speeds, technicians use words that are not in common use. I mean such expressions as "compressibility" and "supersonic." And they are worth a moment to explain. Air is a gas and is therefore capable of being compressed into smaller volume by pressure, whereas water, being a liquid, cannot be compressed into smaller volume. But when air is sufficiently compressed it begins to assume the characteristics of water, and aircraft begin to experience this condition when their speed begins to approach the speed of sound.

I have seen objects in wind tunnels through which the air can be driven at speeds at and far above the speed of sound (up to nearly 1,400 miles an hour, in fact), creating a compression wave due to the pressure caused by their obstruction to the airflow. At the speed of sound this wave (which is visible both to the human eye and that of a camera) stretches out at right angles from its nose straight across the path of the object.

PROBLEMS Arising From Terrific Pressure at Supersonic Speeds

As the air speed increases into supersonic (or over the speed of sound) speeds, the wave bends progressively backwards until it is shaped like the two outward lines of a broad arrow. At some sufficiently fast speed it will completely envelop a streamlined object within a cloak of air possessing properties like those of water to a swimmer. The effect on aeroplanes of these phenomena are referred to as problems of compressibility.

Shells, bullets, some bombs and the V2 rocket all travel at speeds above that of sound. So quite a lot is known about designing for supersonic speeds. But when the complicated structures of aeroplanes are designed to travel at or above the speed of sound, many new factors arise. Wings must not flutter or they might break. Air controls must be adequate for the pilot to maintain stability at landing speed, and yet not feel solid under the terrific pressure of supersonic speed ; they must be free from all backlash or buffeting or they might break up the aeroplane in the air. The fuselage and wing coverings must be able to withstand the enormous air pressure outside, especially if fuselages are to be pressurized to enable their occupants to travel in comfort at great heights, for in this case leakages are not permissible. Rivets must not deform or break. There was some evidence of rivet looseness after the record speed runs of the Meteor in Nov. 1945. (See illus. page 477.)

PARACHUTES will have to be redesigned to stand up to the fierce strain of opening at supersonic speeds. Possibly it will be necessary to have several parachutes opening in relays, first a small one to check the initial forward speed of the disemplaning airman, then a second to reduce his velocity still further until it is safe for the final landing canopy to break open and bring his vertical descent rate down to the normal parachute landing speed of about 12 miles an hour.

Automatic anti-collision radar devices will have to be invented for jet-planes flying at these speeds. Already there has been one collision between two Meteors. Jet-bombers will have to release their bombs perhaps ten miles from the target, or use parachute check gear and release them directly over the target.

Moscow will be two aeroplane hours from London, New York four. San Francisco and Moscow will be six hours apart. Rockets will travel between them in a few minutes. The late F./Lt. J. Llewelyn Rhys, when flying bombers five or six years ago, wrote that "England is my village." Jet-planes will make Britain a village in one country called the world. This conception is mankind's only safeguard from the crucifixion of his species in the future that we face today.

Royal Navy Planes Are Dumped in the Pacific

NOMINALLY VALUED AT £6,000,000, more than 300 warplanes surplus to the requirements of the Royal Navy, stripped of all useful parts and "of no value to anybody," were recently loaded aboard escort carriers in Sydney Harbour, taken out to sea and dumped, on orders from the Admiralty. On the quayside (top) one is being swung aboard the carrier Pioneer, on whose flight deck (bottom) dismantled planes are assembled. They included American Corsairs, Hellcats, Avengers, and British Barracudas; some were new, but most had been flown. *Photos, Planet News*

The Editor Looks Back

THOSE ECONOMISTS Mar. 23, 1940

"Things no fellah can understand." In wartime their number increases beyond all computation. Most of these are concerned with the (to me) obscure, mysterious and always-wrong science of Economics. Why bank rates should go up when you expect them to go down, why shares in steel-producing companies should recede when the companies are choked with orders for their produce, why too much gold in a nation's treasury should produce a devastating slump in industry . . . these and a multitude of other queer things can be glibly explained by our "economists." But one of the things I learned in the years of the First Great War was never to do what an "economist" advises. The more distinguished he was the more surely would the event give the lie to his advice. Which is a solemn fact. Doing the exact opposite would have produced the most satisfactory result.

AND I am of the same opinion still. It may be a case of invincible ignorance on my part, but time will tell how wisely our economists have handled the great problems of finance which have recently been the chief concern of the world, and from lack of understanding I am content to leave it to time.

BUMBLEDOM Mar. 30, 1940

One never knows what actuates the official mind. I took a journey by car not long ago to witness for myself the result of a Nazi hit on a coastal object, adequately reported in the official news at the time. There were a good many sightseers already on the spot, and what seemed to be effective police control already in action. I had my camera and binoculars with me. A courteous and obliging policeman stopped my car and asked if I had either or both of these, and on being truthfully answered he relieved me of them. As I had not taken the precaution to secure an official permit to take photos at points where there might have been official prohibition (in any case I could have published none without the Censor's approval) I surrendered the apparatus in question. But a few hundred yards on I counted nearly a score of persons who had not passed along the motor road, thereby escaping police interrogation, calmly clicking their cameras and observing through their binoculars all that was to be seen. Officialism moves in a mysterious way its duties to perform.

THE episode described (so characteristic of Bumbledom) occurred at the burning of the S.S. Barnhill, off Langney Point, near Eastbourne. The young Huns often flew back to have another crack at it, but some remains of its hulk are still to be seen; and during the recent gales all along the South Coast there was an exciting moment when a drifting mine seemed about to give the old ship its coup de grâce. *But just as it came alongside and the spectators were prepared to cheer the big bang, some undercurrent swept the mine harmlessly past the wreck.*

1,000,000 PETS DESTROYED Apr. 6, 1940

To me one of the saddest bits of news in the papers today is the statement that in the first week or two of the War nearly one million pet animals were destroyed. As an animal lover, I can testify to the deep and abiding joy I have had in the companionship of a succession of half a dozen canine friends whose happy lives intertwined with my own through well nigh half a century. To the curmudgeonly ones who look upon dogs and cats as mere "beasts that perish"—wherein I fail to distinguish any tremendous shoreless gulf between them and their fellow-creatures who have learned how to wear clothes and drive motor-cars—to all such the dog-lover is stupid, sentimental, sloppy . . . so why bother about them? But to all who have had the good fortune to experience that companionship of our four-footed fellow-mortals sung by Scott, by Byron, Burns, and innumerable men and women of feeling in all ages, it is a melancholy thought that one million were destroyed—needlessly, as it would now appear—under threat of widespread air raiding, evacuation and food rationing. What an extinction of precious, humanizing affection! Let's hold on to our pets as long as possible and only in the last resort contemplate extinguishing their lives which, at best, are all too short.

THE present demand for dogs and cats as indicated by the "Wants" columns of the Daily Press, may have arisen from the rather indiscriminate slaughter. I have it on good authority that some hundreds of Eskimo dogs, or huskies, had to be "put to sleep" when the need for an invasion of Norway disappeared. They had been trained at great expense in the North of Scotland with a view to doing team work on the snowfields of Norway. It seems a pity some more useful end for them could not have been devised. Of course, they were hardly suitable as pets. The voluntary relinquishment by large numbers of our people of their dogs for War service has ended in happier manner (see page 587).

OFFICES OUT-OF-TOWN Apr. 6, 1940

One far-reaching financial effect of the large-scale evacuation so hastily undertaken by many large firms, insurance offices, banks and central organizations, at the beginning of the War is likely to be a reduced demand for London business premises after it is over. I know of one company which for many years has been paying a rental of £2,500 for its London office that is now functioning quite satisfactorily from a country house in Surrey the rental of which is only £100. If firms are able to carry on their business from country addresses where rents and rates are absurdly low by comparison with those paid in Central London, it is highly probable that they will endeavour to continue doing so when the War is over. After all, a vast amount of the office work that is conducted in London could as easily be done in the heart of Surrey or Sussex, leaving only a skeleton staff to maintain the necessary London contacts.

SO far as I can gather, my forecast looks like being at least partly realized. Several large insurance offices with which I have small dealings are still carrying on in the country quite efficiently, and if the "wide open spaces" which the bombing so quickly created round about St. Paul's are, as we have been told, in some measure at least to be turned into boulevards and green parterres before rebuilding commences, it is clear that there will not be as much office accommodation available for city offices as before the blitz. Perhaps this may result in taller buildings going up.

WAR IN PICTURES Apr. 20, 1940

No one has been more considerate than I in his criticism of our Ministry of Information. For I know something of their trouble with red-taped (no, not tabbed) Service departments. The M.O.I. must take the blame. I take off my hat to Dr. Goebbels. He may be a liar and a knave and an incarnation of all things bestial, but he knows his business better than any of the folk that have got into cushy jobs at his opposite number in London. I can get dozens of photos of what the Huns are doing in Norway, but not a single one of what we are doing. Two weeks ago I published a photo showing some German soldiers about to disembark from a Nazi transport at Oslo. It had been telegraphed to New York, and then retelegraphed to London (at a cost of sixty guineas, incidentally), and I had to pay a modest special fee for its use in THE WAR ILLUSTRATED.

NOT until America came into the War was there any real improvement in the supply of photographs. The Huns were completely our masters in this respect, during the earlier months, and only when the Russians and the Americans joined in with their better equipment and the better sense of the value of pictorial news did our M.O.I. begin to drop its antiquated notions of how the public demand for the actualities of photography should be met. Latterly the British service of war pictures was almost up to the quality though never the quantity of the American. Another way in which we lagged behind to the very last: the news reel. I went every week of the War to the News Cinema, and there were occasions when one might have thought that the only armies showing any activity were American.

POSTSCRIPT

I HAVE seldom listened to more effective broadcasting than E. M. Forster's two Sunday-night talks on India. Forster is such a master of the microphone that I imagine his scripts must rank, with "Max's," as broadcasting classics. Some years ago a colleague of mine, then at Broadcasting House, was "auditioning" a group of "buskers" (theatre-queue entertainers) for a London programme. Among the apparently would-be aspirants was a sparse-looking middle-aged man in cap and mackintosh, who sat nervously on the edge of his chair, glancing at the studio-clock. After ten minutes' agony he rose and introduced himself nervously to my colleague. It was E. M. Forster, due to go on the air! He had been shown into the wrong studio by mistake.

CELEBRATING their twentieth birthday soon is U.F.A.W.—in other words, the Universities Federation for Animal Welfare—about whose activities I wrote in a recent Postscript. In their new prospectus, gaily illustrated by "Fougasse," I read that the number of experiments performed on animals in this country has steadily increased from 311 in 1883 to "about a million per annum." This, on top of the fact that no anti-vivisection Bill has reached a second reading in either House since that very same year, is surely sufficient justification for U.F.A.W.'s continued existence and support.

STRAW in the wind? The Tartar language, one of the oldest and most complicated in the world, spoken by 30,000,000 people in Central Asia, is being translated into English—in the shape of the first Tartar-English dictionary and grammar. So far, Tartar has been translated only into Chinese.

LAYER upon layer of Nazi hypocrisy is being torn away as the war criminals' trial at Nuremberg proceeds. Latest flash of illuminating evidence comes from a Belgian witness who disclosed that the Germans collected some 3,000 tons of metal in his country by seizing church bells under an order entitled "Artistic Protection." That, I suppose, would cover Goering's looted Botticellis as well—to say nothing of the countless art treasures filched by the other Nazi leaders from the Germans themselves.

In Britain Now: Salvage for Home-Building

BLOCK-HOUSE erected at the end of Folkestone Pier during the threat of the German invasion in 1940, and nearest point to the French coast, was recently demolished. Workmen are seen using pneumatic drills on the concrete structure (right), overlooking the well-known harbour.

DEBRIS from London air-raid shelters now being demolished is ground and crushed by this plant (below) at Bridge Mills, S.E. It provides bricks, sand and concrete for new houses planned by the L.C.C. and a new basic material formed from the crushed debris is suitable for making exterior walls and partition blocks for interior walls.

MAGNA CARTA, most perfect copy of the four in existence, was returned to Lincoln Cathedral on January 24, after having been deposited in the U.S. Congress Library for seven years. It was loaned for the New York World's Fair, 1939, and travelled back in the Queen Elizabeth. Mr. R. S. Godfery, Cathedral Clerk of Works (above), using a tin-opener on the lid of the 60-lb. metal box containing it.

Photos, Hamlins, Planet News, Keystone, Fox, Topical

FAMOUS PAINTINGS, including some 800 from the Tate Gallery and 200 from the London Museum, which were stored during the War 80 feet below the surface of Piccadilly Circus, were removed on February 4, 1946. They had been housed in a disused part of the Piccadilly Tube at Piccadilly station. The pictures are here being taken up one of the escalators (above)

PREFABRICATED OFFICE, first to be erected in the City of London, has been completed on a Fenchurch Street bombed site. The building, which has 18 rooms, a water-tower and skylight ventilation, stands amid heaped concrete blocks (left). Literally built from scrap, it was erected by five men in three weeks; cost, about £2,000.

Treasures Come Home to the British Museum

FROM THEIR WARTIME REPOSITORY AT SKIPTON CASTLE, Yorkshire, where they had been for six years, 20 tons of precious manuscripts and ancient documents were returned to the British Museum, Bloomsbury, on January 30, 1946. Guarded by police and railway detectives, they were brought to London in " house-to-house " containers which were padded, locked and sealed, and are here seen on their arrival under the portico of the main Museum building. Decision had not then been reached as to the renewed public exhibition of the contents. *Photo, P.A. Reuter*

Printed in England and published every alternate Friday by the Proprietors, THE AMALGAMATED PRESS, LTD., The Fleetway House, Farringdon Street, London, E.C.4. Registered for transmission by Canadian Magazine Post. Sole Agents for Australia and New Zealand: Messrs. Gordon & Gotch, Ltd.; and for South Africa: Central News Agency, Ltd. March 1, 1946. S.S. *Editorial Address:* JOHN CARPENTER HOUSE WHITEFRIARS, LONDON, E.C.4.

Vol 9 The War Illustrated No 228

and AFTERWARDS

SIXPENCE

MARCH 15, 1946

MLLE. ANDRÉE DE JONGH, young heroine of the Belgian Underground Movement, displayed outstanding gallantry and devotion to the Allied cause by helping many R.A.F. and Allied personnel to escape from enemy-occupied territory. In recognition of this she was awarded the George Medal at an investiture at Buckingham Palace on February 13, 1946. As an additional appreciation she was presented by the Under Secretary of State for Air with a clock from a R.A.F. bomber. See story in page 731.

Edited by Sir John Hammerton

R.A.S.C. and R.E. Are Busy in Malaya

SMUGGLING and piracy along the Malayan coastline confronted the British after Japan's surrender in August 1945. Illicit traffic in opium and other drugs was unchecked throughout the Japanese occupation of the peninsula. Now Royal Army Service Corps Water Transport Units with Customs and Excise officials patrol the coastal waters ; already the Port Swettenham area has been almost cleaned up.

R.A.S.C. vessel trails a suspect junk (1) and draws alongside (2). Suspicions are justified as from the junk's hold a jar of opium is handed up to the officer in charge of the search party (3). By similar illicit means thousands of pounds worth of drugs had entered the country from Java, Sumatra and Siam.

MALAYA'S ONLY COALFIELD, at Batu Arang, starts production again with Royal Engineers adopting open-cast methods —the mines being flooded. Coal for railways and factories tipped for washing (4), water freeing it of debris (5).

Australia's Heroic 'Gull Force'

DURING the dark days that opened the Pacific War, when the Japanese rolled south in a mighty flood with all the initial advantages of tactical surprise and painstaking preparation, numerous tiny Allied garrisons isolated in the vast Pacific were perforce abandoned to sacrifice and suffering. It is true courage when a man bravely enters battle and fights to the last, knowing full well his chances of survival are indeed remote. Fine pages of heroism were written by men in circumstances such as these—by the British at Hongkong, by the Americans on Wake Island, and by the Australians on Amboina in the Moluccas.

The bulk of the Australian garrison on Amboina was made up by the 2/21 Battalion which consisted of volunteers who enlisted following the fall of France in June 1940. Other battalions formed at the same time were dispatched to the Middle East where, as members of the famous 9th Australian Division, they stood Rommel at bay outside Tobruk for more than half a year. The 2/21 Battalion, however, was transferred to the 23rd Brigade of the ill-fated 8th Division.

Early in 1941 the bulk of the 8th Division moved to Malaya, but the 23rd Brigade was detached to fill another role. Based on Darwin, it was to secure the airfields along vital lines of communication between Australia and Singapore in the event of war in the Pacific. Split into three Battalion groups, the Brigade was entrusted with the defence of Rabaul (New Britain), Amboina (Molucca Islands) and Koepang (Dutch Timor). A force of Commandos was earmarked to secure the important airfield at Dilli, in Portuguese Timor (see page 714, Vol. 6).

Five Simultaneous Landings

Based on the assumption that the great key base of Singapore would stand, the Brigade's role—which proved impossible for a force of that size—was not so greatly out of proportion at the time of its conception.

Although plans for the defence of these island airfields, so close to the Australian mainland, had been drawn up in conjunction with Dutch military authorities they could not be implemented until the Netherlands became at war with Japan.

When Pearl Harbour (December 7, 1941) at last put an end to their waiting the 2/40 Battalion group moved to Koepang, and the 2/21 to Amboina, where the small Dutch garrisons gladly welcomed their coming. Meanwhile, the force from the 2/2 Independent Company of Commandos took over the airfield at Dilli, in Portuguese Timor, despite Portuguese protests at this alleged violation of her neutrality. By December 17 the move was completed.

KNOWN as "Gull Force," the 2/21 Battalion group found a garrison of about two thousand native troops, led by Dutch officers, awaiting them on Amboina. Although comparatively lightly armed, the Dutch had two six-inch coastal guns defending the fine Ambon harbour. The only artillery the 2/21 Battalion had in support were four two-pounder guns from the 18th Anti-tank Battery.

Communications on Amboina were poor, for the island, shaped like a distorted figure eight, had only a narrow neck of land joining the two major portions, and it boasted few roads. Main communication between the airfield of Laha, north of the Ambon harbour, and Ambon itself on the south, was by boat across its waters. Two companies less a platoon of the 2/21 Battalion were entrusted with the defence of Laha airfield. The remainder of the group manned the approaches to Ambon itself. On the east of the island, the Dutch-led native troops dug in along the coast.

By ROY MACARTNEY

EIGHT hundred Australians garrisoned the island of Amboina, in the Netherlands East Indies, in January 1942 when 20,000 Japanese stormed ashore; less than two hundred remained alive at the Japanese capitulation in September 1945. The full story of the fortitude and suffering of "Gull Force"—revealed only after liberation—is told specially for "The War Illustrated."

So confident were the Japanese that Singapore would be theirs that they did not wait for its fall before beginning to roll up the thin line of garrisons astride the direct approaches to Australia. On January 23, 1942, they landed 17,000 shock troops, quickly overwhelming the small Australian garrison of 1,400 men holding Rabaul. Next on the list was Amboina.

Three days before the enemy descended in force on January 31, the Amboina garrison knew they were coming. R.A.A.F. Lockheed Hudsons had sighted an enemy convoy of approximately 40 vessels, including aircraft carriers and troopships, heading in the direction of the island. What units of the squadron remained airworthy carried out raids on the enemy, but on January 30 the squadron was ordered to withdraw to Darwin.

AMBOINA, where a depleted Allied garrison fought 20,000 Japanese for four days, February 1-4, 1942, and survivors were subjected to torture unsurpassed in the War.

SHORTLY after midnight on January 31 an enemy force of 20,000 men made five simultaneous landings on Amboina, mainly on the east coast. With the dawn, swarms of carrier-based Japanese aircraft held undisputed sway over the island, bombing and strafing at will. Within a few hours the Japanese penetrated the native troops' position west of Paso and drove down upon the Australians holding Laha airfield and Ambon. Communications between the two forces failed, enemy bombing destroying all wireless and cutting the sole telephone line.

For four days the unequal battle raged. In ferocious hand-to-hand fighting in the jungle the two companies north of the harbour denied the enemy the Laha airfield, standing squarely across its eastern approaches. Their old Lewis guns and three-inch mortars broke up every assault. Just as stubbornly, the remainder of the Battalion held the enemy at bay on the south of the harbour. Japanese warships penetrated the harbour on February 3, bringing their guns to bear at point-blank range. Like David confronting Goliath, the four two-pounder guns opened fire to engage the enemy vessels.

Thin platoons were shuffled round in the tall kunai grass in an endeavour to stem every enemy penetration; but with their ammunition spent, their dumps blasted by bombing behind them, the Allied force at last succumbed to the weight of the enemy.

By February 4, Ambon was in enemy hands and the bombardment was directed at the last Australian pocket holding out on Laha airfield. That afternoon, the Japanese swarmed across the airfield—and the battle of Amboina was at its end.

The well-planned Japanese offensive had required the Laha airfield for their next move. A fortnight later, on February 19, squadrons of their medium bombers took off from the airfield to join aircraft from a carrier task force which carried out the first smashing raid on Darwin, completely neutralizing the Australian base. At the same time thousands of enemy troops stormed ashore in Timor to seize Koepang and Dilli.

Back on Amboina, 26 Australian walking-wounded had escaped from a dressing-station at the conclusion of the battle and had taken to the jungle. Wending their way from island to island, mainly by native canoe, they at last landed on the shore of the Gulf of Carpentaria: and the story of the battle of Amboina became known in Australia. But a fog of uncertainty regarding the fate of the survivors cloaked the island for three years. Not one member of the garrison during this period was officially posted as a prisoner of war by the enemy. Then, after the Japanese capitulation, in September 1945, a story of horror became known.

Survivors Too Weak to Stand

Through these long years of incarceration the Japanese tortured, starved and subjected their prisoners to every inhuman bestiality conceivable. In the hell-camp of Tantoei tortures included the stringing-up of Australian prisoners to trees with wire cables tied round their hands, their feet just touching the ground. In this position they were beaten until insensible, revived with water, then beaten again. This went on for days, Japanese placing lighted cigarettes in the prisoners' nostrils and inflicting other devilries until death brought merciful release. Desperate attempts to escape met with ruthless treatment at the hands of the Japanese. Indeed, none managed to escape, and 17 Australians were executed during the long years on Amboina.

Another enemy trick was to place ammunition dumps in and around the prison camp. With the coming of Allied aerial supremacy Amboina was subjected to heavy attacks, and one raid found the ammunition dump, which exploded. Scores of Australian, Dutch and native prisoners, including some women and children, were killed or wounded. The last Australian medical officer in the camp was killed by bomb-blast while tending casualties. Thereafter sickness took terrible toll. Prisoners suffering from tropical ulcers were kicked and beaten about their decaying limbs. Others were forced to open picric acid bombs with hammers, thereby receiving terrible burns.

EARLY in 1945, when Allied forces were becoming victorious on all fronts, the Japanese quickened the tempo of their efforts to work the prisoners to death. Between January and August of that year, 290 Australians died, bringing the total laid to rest in their small cemetery to 428. Thus there were less than 200 fever-stricken survivors of the original 800 Australians on Amboina when the blessed relief of liberation ended their suffering. Rescue ships found most of the gaunt survivors too weak or ill to stand. The last chapter of the Amboina horror was written on Morotai, where an Australian Court Martial sentenced to death by shooting the Japanese Commander and two of his officers staffing the hell-hole of Tantoei. Thirty-two other guards will pay for their inhumanity with terms behind barbed wire ranging from one to twenty years.

This is Monty's New Job

By MAJ.-GENERAL SIR CHARLES GWYNN K.C.B., D.S.O.

WHEN Field-Marshal Viscount Montgomery of Alamein takes over the appointment of Chief of the Imperial General Staff in June 1946 the demobilization of our wartime army will be practically complete, but it is obvious that does not mean the Army will have assumed its normal peacetime shape. *Ad hoc* expedients are necessary to enable us to deal with immediate post-war commitments, and the Government has announced its short-term plans to meet the existing situation.

Under these plans it is hoped by the end of this year to reduce the numbers of trained men in the three Services to 1,100,000 plus 100,000 under training. In order to fill the places of men becoming due for demobilization or discharge, the call-up of young men under the National Service Act will be continued without prejudice to final decision as regards the adoption of a permanent system of National Service. The length of service required from new entrants will be fixed as soon as possible, but much depends on the rate of intake of voluntary recruits to the regular Services and on progress in the liquidation of post-war commitments.

Nevertheless, it is clearly essential to formulate and set in motion long-term plans for the formation of the Army we shall permanently need. That, subject to Government decisions, is probably the main task that will confront the new C.I.G.S. There can be no question, as happened after the First Great War, of the Army resuming its pre-war shape ; nor, I think, would it be practicable or advisable to aim at producing a miniature copy of our wartime army.

PROBLEM of Finding Men to Fill New Army's Ranks

In some ways the problem of giving us a new-type army is simpler than it was in 1919. Then the new weapons produced in the war had all been designed to meet trench warfare conditions and were unsuitable for mobile operations. They suggested lines on which armaments would develop, but clearly a long period of experiments and redesigning was necessary before weapons of more general utility could be produced. Premature rearmament would have only resulted in costly replacement of obsolescent types. Experiments were initiated and considerable progress was made until financial stringency ended the experiments and made drastic rearmament out of the question. The Government's assurance that no major war could occur without ten years' warning, and disarmament policy (including proposals that weapons should be limited to defensive purposes), did little to encourage invention and relegated the Army to police functions.

We have now learnt our lesson and the War has carried experiments to completion. The majority of weapons seem now to have approached final shape, although rockets, controlled projectiles and air transport may lead to further developments. Field-Marshal Montgomery should therefore encounter few difficulties in providing his new army with suitable weapons. Moreover, there seems no reason why wartime armaments not required for the normal peacetime army should not, for a considerable period at least, be stored in reserve to meet the needs of possible expansion instead of being scrapped.

The problem of finding men to fill the ranks of the new army will this time be much more difficult than that of armaments. Presumably the C.I.G.S. will remain responsible for advising as to the strength of the army we need for our own special commitments, and the military staff of U.N.O. may make supplementary demands. That we are bound to have a professional regular army voluntarily enlisted is universally admitted, but will improved conditions of pay and terms of service produce the number of recruits it will require ? Improvement of conditions is long overdue, both in justice to the men and for the credit of the State as an employer ; but unavoidably long periods of foreign service and the fact that the Army cannot offer a life-long occupation, are probably the factors that limit the intake of recruits rather than the scale of pay.

Field-Marshal Viscount MONTGOMERY OF ALAMEIN, of Hindhead in the County of Surrey, G.C.B., D.S.O.
From a portrait by James Gunn, by permission of the artist

Enlistment for short service at home (including some European stations) may attract additional recruits, but it tends to reduce the numbers willing to accept the longer engagement required to maintain a foreign service force. Although the Government has not yet decided to continue compulsory service indefinitely, if voluntary enlistment does not produce necessary numbers, it is to be hoped that some compulsory training will be adopted to facilitate the rapid expansion of the Army in times of crisis.

IN addition to recruiting problems it is certain that during Field-Marshal Montgomery's term of office the strength of foreign service garrisons and the location of our strategic reserves will be under constant review. Development in India may produce a new situation, and our War experience alone clearly indicates the necessity of reconsidering our other commitments. The War at least has made it clear that air forces cannot replace land forces as at one time it was argued might be possible ; but, on the other hand, the new spirit of co-operation that exists between the R.A.F. and the Army may materially affect the latter.

Under our existing system the C.I.G.S. is responsible jointly with the heads of the other Services for reviewing, and advising the Government on, our military policy and commitments in the widest sense. Whether that system will be maintained or changed, as some have advocated, by the appointment of an overall Chief of the Staff we do not yet know. But whatever system is adopted we can, I think, rely on the disappearance of the inter-Service rivalries and conflicting claims which regrettably existed in the inter-war period. Certainly there has been no stronger advocate of the necessity of intimate co-operation between the Army and R.A.F. and of overpowering air strength than Field-Marshal Montgomery ; he has also had exceptional experience of co-operation with the Royal Navy, and has paid tribute to the importance of sea communications in whatever enterprise the Army undertakes.

There will therefore be no lack of problems beyond those that affect our peacetime army to which Field-Marshal Montgomery will be able to apply his brains, great experience and energy. Surely he will have a say in formulating plans for the expansion of the Army in case of war, and I can hardly think that he would be content with an indefinite ruling such as the Government gave after the First Great War that the Territorial Army would in future provide the sole basis of expansion. A ruling which certainly left many Territorial officers uncertain as to the role of the T.A.

DOMINIONS' Contribution to the New Defence Set-up

Again, although the Dominions have free choice as to whether they would take part in a war or not, it is clearly desirable that the closest touch should be maintained with their military staffs ; and the fact that Canadian, Australian, New Zealand and South African troops have all fought under his command ensures that Field-Marshal Montgomery appreciates the great contribution the Dominions can make to the new set-up of Commonwealth defence.

There is, in fact, little that the experience of the new C.I.G.S. does not cover, either in command or as a Staff officer. In addition to his War service he has served in India and Palestine, [has been on the staff of a Territorial Division, a student at the Imperial Defence College, and been on the Staff of both the Camberley and Quetta Staff Colleges. It is curious, however, that he has never held an appointment inside the walls of the War Office. Will he find that a handicap ? For War Office procedure and the workings of financial control take some learning and may prove irksome. Yet it may be that a fresh mind will be more valuable than experience. The War Office has always been accused of being a slave to precedent ; and with so many new departures to be made, search for precedent might well interfere with the working of clear commonsense thought.

It is certain that the nation will expect much from Field-Marshal Montgomery, for it has realized the importance of the Army to its very existence. He will command its good wishes and confidence, but it must be clearly realized that he cannot make bricks without straw. Parsimony in defence expenditure has surely been finally proved to be the worst form of economy.

German Mounts for British M.P.s in Austria

OUR MOUNTED MILITARY POLICE in Vienna use horses formerly belonging to the German S.S. (Black Guards: see page 121, Vol. I). These animals were found, in a starved condition, near Klagenfurt. A detachment in one of Vienna's main streets (1), and grooming mounts in their stables (2). One of our men with his Austrian "opposite number" at Graz (3). *Photos, G.P.U., New York Times Photos*

How We Beat the German Bid to Block Suez

By

FRANCIS E. McMURTRIE

At the beginning of May 1941 the situation in the Eastern Mediterranean was decidedly critical. Fighting hard until it reached the beaches from which it was evacuated by the Navy, a British army of 50,000 had been withdrawn from Greece and landed in Crete. This was not accomplished without losses. Lacking adequate air cover, the crowded transports and their escorts suffered severely from the attacks of the Luftwaffe, and a number of the British and Greek destroyers which had taken a prominent part in the evacuation of troops were sunk.

It was evident that an attack upon Crete would be the next item in the enemy programme. It was most likely to take the form of a combined sea and airborne landing, which would be difficult to repel with the limited naval resources available, in the absence of anything approaching a strong air defence. Reinforcements and munitions would have to travel by the long route around the Cape, up the East Coast of Africa and through the Red Sea to Egypt. For their rapid transport to the scene of action, free passage through the Suez Canal was, obviously, indispensable.

These facts were quite well known to the Germans, who were using their utmost exertions to mass troops and aircraft for the assault upon Crete. Though it was hoped to effect a successful landing by sea, it was quite appreciated that this could not be guaranteed against naval opposition ; and in the event, seaborne invasion proved a costly failure. (See story by Commander Anthony Kimmins in page 739, Vol. 4). Instead, the enemy had ultimately to fall back on the more expensive method of an airborne descent by specially trained troops.

In these circumstances, anything which would interfere with the smooth transmission of men and materials through the Suez Canal would naturally be of the greatest assistance to the Germans. It might also have the further advantage of reducing the concentration of British naval force off Crete. To block the Canal would unquestionably simplify the problem of conquering the island. To accomplish this purpose it was decided to make use of a fresh type of mine which had recently been perfected and was being turned out in large numbers.

More than two months before, reports had been received in this country of a new design of enemy mine of the magnetic type, which could not be swept by existing methods. As far as could be gathered from captured documents and other information reaching the Naval Intelligence Division, this mine would be dropped from aircraft without the usual parachute and would resemble a bomb in appearance. Further inquiries were prosecuted without delay, eliciting the fact that the weight of the new mine was 1,000 kilogrammes, or about a ton. Goering was so pleased with this new weapon that he had been heard to boast that it would soon finish off the Royal Navy.

SENTINELS OF SUEZ are the twin towers of the 1914–18 Anzac War memorial at Ismailia, Egypt, erected to commemorate the defence of Suez by Empire troops in the First Great War. In the Second Great War the German plan to block the Canal by the use of mines dropped from the air is revealed in this page. *Photo, Topical*

To the Investigation Section of the Torpedoes and Mining Department at the Admiralty these reports conveyed a good deal. It was naturally assumed that any specimens of the new mine that might happen to drop on land instead of in the water would be set to explode on impact ; and that if any failed to do so, "booby traps" would have been provided in order to defeat attempts by our experts to render the mine harmless before dissecting it for investigation.

Specimen of the New Weapon Found and With Great Caution Examined

No specimen of the mine had been definitely identified up to the end of April 1941, when a series of heavy air raids on the Clyde and Mersey districts began. Commander F. Ashe Lincoln, R.N.V.R. (see illus. page 486), of the Torpedoes and Mining Department, had been assigned the duty of seeking for an intact mine, and proceeded with a group of specialist officers to make a thorough search in both areas. On May 6 he was successful in discovering one in the hills overlooking Dumbarton. It was at first reported by the Army as an unexploded bomb, but closer examination pointed to its being actually one of the new mines.

Another of these missiles had exploded about a quarter of a mile away, and in the crater were found a number of particles of explosive which had not detonated, together with some pieces of the mechanism. This explosive was one known as hexanite, which as a rule was never used by the Germans in bombs but only in mines ; this alone seemed to suggest that it must be a specimen of the new weapon. One of the dangerous features of hexanite is that it is ticklish stuff to handle. Contact with the bare flesh almost invariably produces a form of dermatitis. Unconsciously, Commander Lincoln exposed himself to this risk by picking up particles in his fingers to scrutinize them ; but fortunately prompt medical attention was at hand and saved him from serious consequences.

Together with one of his assistants (now Lieutenant-Commander H. F. Wadsley, G.M., D.S.C., R.N.V.R., of H.M.S. Vernon), Commander Lincoln next morning proceeded to examine the unexploded mine. To begin with, a booby trap was looked for beneath the fuse, but when the latter had been extracted there was nothing to be found under it. Not long previously a number of officers of the Vernon had lost their lives through a device of this kind behind the rear door of a mine. Bearing this in mind, the investigators took care that the rear door was eased open very gently until a finger could be inserted. Nothing at all suspicious being encountered, a torch was shone into the interior, but still there appeared to be no sign of any booby trap.

Luftwaffe Raid in Force Rendered Ineffective by Prompt Sweeping

It was at this stage that the investigators were in the greatest danger. Quite unknown to anyone outside Germany, the enemy had devised a new type of booby trap which should have operated at this juncture. It took the form of a photo-electric cell, so designed as to blow up the mine immediately either daylight or an artificial light was introduced into the interior. Providentially, it failed to work owing to a small length of wire, connecting the booby trap with the detonator, having been broken by the shock of the fall. Thus the lives of two officers were saved, and the mine was by degrees rendered harmless.

It was then dispatched by the quickest route to the Vernon torpedo school, to be dissected by the scientists attached to the department of the Superintendent of Mine Design. Working all night, these experts were able to analyse the intricacies of the mechanism and find out exactly how everything worked. After this it did not take many hours to arrange an effective method of sweeping the new mine. As there was no means of knowing where the mine would next be encountered, or in what numbers it might be found, this important information was at once disseminated in every area of naval operations.

Nor was it any too soon, for within twenty-four hours the Luftwaffe made a raid in force on the area between Port Said and Suez, and dropped a large number of the new mines into the Canal itself. Great destruction might well have been caused ; and, at the very least, traffic would have been held up for an indefinite period but for the work that had been done by naval officers and scientists during the preceding few days. As it was, the whole of the minefield was swept up in the course of the following day, though the Germans were not to know it. Had it not been for this, it is improbable that Crete would have been able to hold out for so long as it did ; and British losses in its defence would doubtless have been heavier, to say nothing of the all-precious element of time, so vital in war.

Men in Navy Blue Home from Far Eastern Service

BROAD SMILES are the order of the day when ships of the Royal Navy reach British ports from Far Eastern waters. Some of the ship's company of H.M.S. Kempenfelt (1) when she docked at Chatham wore Jap flying suits and steel helmets. The Kempenfelt formed part of the Fleet which was at Hongkong for the surrender of the Jap forces there. As the cruiser H.M.S. Cleopatra docked at Portsmouth (2) relatives and friends lined the deck of another ship to welcome her.

The Royal Navy's oldest destroyer, H.M.S. Scout (3) completed her last voyage when she arrived at Swansea after being in commissioned service for nearly 28 years, the last seven continuously in the Far East. Her Commander (Lt. D. M. Edwards), is seen with his officers and ratings (4) before bidding a last farewell to the ship, whose fate has not been yet determined. She may be converted into a training ship for Sea Scouts. *Photos, Keystone, G.P.U., P.A.-Reuter*

British First-Aid to Recovery in Hongkong

REHABILITATION HAS BEEN HINDERED by epidemics, the homeless and the orphans. Anti-Malarial Units in Vengeance aircraft of the Fleet Air Arm spray infected areas (1) with D.D.T. Waifs and strays are housed in the King's Park Orphanage, under the care of a R.A.F. Airfield Construction Unit; two of the youngsters out for a walk (2). A gaily-decorated theatre is admired by our men (3). Japanese accused of atrocities are housed in Stanley Gaol, where the British barber demonstrates just how close the hair must be cut (4).

Photos, British Official

For Your Tomorrow They Gave Their Today

KOHIMA MEMORIAL stands high above the scene of one of the fiercest and most decisive battles of the Burma campaign. Erected by men of the 2nd British Division, it is a tribute to comrades who made the supreme sacrifice in the battle of Kohima and the Imphal Road, April–May 1944. Bearing the inscription "When you go home tell them of us, and say—For your tomorrow they gave their today," it was unveiled by General Sir William Slim, then Commander of the 14th Army. See also illus. page 521. *Photo, Indian Official*

Now It Can Be Told!

FALMOUTH WAS U.S. NAVY INVASION BASE

TRAINING accommodation for more than 170 officers and 2,600 men of the United States Navy made Falmouth Sub-Command an important base for the D-Day assault. Loaded with personnel, vehicles and equipment, 38 L.S.T.s sailed to join the D-Day armada, and an average of four M.T. ships a day ferried vital transport and supplies in the invasion build-up.

Falmouth was commissioned on Sept. 3, 1939, as H.M.S. Forte. The Imperial Hotel became H.M.S. Forte II. In December 1939 a Contraband Control Base was opened. Defence Booms were laid in the harbour, St. Mawes Bay, Falmouth Bay and the Helford River, the last being removed in May 1945. First test of Falmouth's improvisation came late one night in May 1940, when ships of the Royal Netherlands Navy arrived after escaping from Holland.

Hundreds of troops passed through Falmouth on their way to France in early June 1940. After Dunkirk, thousands of troops and refugees, brought over in 243 ships, were cared for by W.R.N.S. and W.V.S. personnel and housed in cinemas and the Princess Pavilion. June also brought the first air raids against the Dockyard. In eight raids during the month one ship was sunk, two set on fire, and considerable damage was done to the Northern Arm of the Dockyard.

An Auxiliary Patrol was formed, consisting of yachts, trawlers, drifters and motor boats, guarding the harbour and the boom entrance until finally paid off in June 1945. Observation minefields, a balloon barrage and anti-submarine fixed defences also protected the harbour, and in May 1941 a Coastal Force base was set up at Coastlines Wharf. After D-Day, Coastal Force activity at Falmouth diminished, and in October 1944 the base closed down. Air raids and harbour mining activity caused several casualties during 1941.

The King and Queen visited Falmouth in May 1942, when it was decided that the port should be used as a Combined Operations Base. In July the following year it was decided that the United States Navy should take over the organization. The first U.S. contingent arrived at St. Mawes on August 18, 1943, establishing a U.S.N. Advanced Amphibious Training Sub Base in requisitioned buildings; mooring buoys were laid and five loading hards built before D-Day. The base closed in 1944.

'JELLYFISH' SAVED THE LIVES OF MANY ALLIED SEAMEN

A WARTIME invention which saved the lives of Allied seamen by enabling convoys to be navigated with razor-edge accuracy in darkness and adverse weather, "Jellyfish" was recently described in The Evening Standard.

The device, which was made by a British electrical firm, consisted of a radar buoy which actuated its own machinery, sent out secret navigational signals, and blew itself up when its job was done.

The buoy consisted of a cylindrical tank containing receiving and transmitting radar equipment and a telescopic aerial. It was sunk, and when it reached a pre-determined depth an anchor chain paid out a mooring weight and the buoy rose horizontally to the surface. The telescopic aerial extended itself, radar equipment was connected and began to work, and the buoy prepared for its own destruction by explosives.

THE NIGHT BEFORE THE NORMANDY D-DAY

WHEN the Allied invasion fleet crossed to Normandy on the night of June 5/6, 1944, it did not meet a single attack by the Luftwaffe or by enemy E- or U-boats. When our parachute troops were dropped a few hours before the assault they landed with negligible casualties, though we had expected a 25 per cent loss. After our initial landings the enemy held back his main reserves for 18 to 48 hours, and enabled us to secure a firm foothold.

These were the chief results of the greatest hoax in military history—a hoax carried out almost entirely by 105 aircraft of the Royal Air Force, by 34 small ships of the Royal Navy, and by R.C.M. (Radio Counter Measures—see full story in page 685). In the planning of Operation "Overlord" (the code word for the Normandy invasion) it was considered essential that the enemy should be made to believe that the assault would come not on the Normandy beaches but farther north in the Pas de Calais between Cap d'Antifer and Boulogne.

This was the task of R.C.M. The responsibility for carrying it out rested with Bomber Command. But long before the operational planning could be commenced, much preliminary technical work had been carried out by the Telecommunications Research Establishment. For two months before D-Day, and for the month following our landings, Bomber Command played a leading part in the hammering of German coast defences and the "softening-up" process round the French coast. The German night fighter force, based in north-west France, invariably reacted strongly to these attacks by our bombers.

Well-Rehearsed Deception

The great chain of enemy radar stations round the French coast were always equally alert. In the conviction that our technical devices were so highly developed that we could confuse the enemy into mistaking a carefully-planned feint for the real thing, R.C.M. was ready with a complicated and well-rehearsed scheme of deception.

THE scheme was in five parts, each with a separate aim but linked in one general plan. The five parts went under the code names Taxable, Glimmer, Mandrel, A.B.C. Patrol, and Titanic. Their aims were (1) to simulate diversionary attacks by air and sea away from the real assault area; (2) to provide cover for the genuine airborne landings; (3) to throw the German radar system into such a state of confusion that enemy reaction to our intentions would be delayed and greatly minimized. On the night of June 5/6 the five parts of the R.C.M. plan went simultaneously into operation, as follows:

In "Taxable," eighteen small ships of the Royal Navy steamed towards Cap d'Antifer at a speed of seven knots to suggest a landing on that part of the French coast. As enemy radar could quickly sum up the size of this force and dismiss it as not being a serious threat, one of the R.A.F.'s most experienced squadrons, No. 617—led by Group Capt. G. L. Cheshire, V.C., D.S.O., D.F.C.—flew in support. Every minute of the 3½ hours of the operation, the aircraft of this squadron dropped twelve bundles of

AMERICAN APPRECIATION OF THE PEOPLE OF FALMOUTH took practical form in the presentation of a memorial shelter built by U.S. Navy men with materials paid for by their officers. Here the shelter is being formally handed over to the town after the raising of the Stars and Stripes by the Mayor of Falmouth. *Photo, U.S. Navy*

"Window"—the thin metallized strips which produce false echoes on the enemy radar screens and so confuse their plotting.

Flying in box formation over an area 12 miles wide and eight miles deep, the aircraft had to fly in a continuous orbit gradually nearing the French coast, to give the impression of a large convoy heading slowly towards it. The effect was heightened by the Navy ships towing balloons which would reproduce a "big ship" type of echo on the enemy radar screens, and also by our aircraft jamming the German radar to prevent recognition of the "Window" deception.

Exactly the same deception was practised in a direction heading for Boulogne. In this case ("Glimmer") 16 ships were covered and "magnified" by 218 Squadron. In two areas in the Channel—due south of Littlehampton and due south of Portland Bill—twenty aircraft of 199 Squadron ("Mandrel") maintained a jamming barrage which covered the enemy's coastal radar frequencies, reduced his warning system, and screened our own aircraft.

They flew at 18,000 feet at a constant distance of 50 miles from the enemy coast and with positional error of never more than five miles from ten fixed points in the Channel, and jammed the Hun radar for hours on end. In this task they were joined by four Fortresses of No. 803 Squadron of the U.S. Army Air Corps.

In the area between Taxable and Glimmer, 29 Lancasters flew for 4½ hours in "A.B.C. Patrol" to lure the enemy night fighters away from the actual landing areas. They, too, added to the confusion on the German radar by providing between them 82 jamming transmitters. A secondary reason for this patrol was the hope (speedily fulfilled) that the Germans would mistake it as top cover for the "invasion" simulated by Glimmer.

While all this was going on, dummy airborne invasions ("Titanic") were carried out at two points—one slightly east of Fécamp, the other halfway down the Cherbourg Peninsula. Dummy parachute troops were dropped at both points; in addition, enough of the invaluable strips of "Window" were dropped to give the harassed enemy radar operators the impression that this airborne invasion was twenty times larger than it was.

The actual invasion forces sailed on their appointed course without any interference by air or sea. Through R.C.M., the enemy appreciation of the main direction of our attack was completely wrong. In R.C.M. operations on the night before D-Day only three of the 105 aircraft taking part were lost.

Secret 'War Effort' Charts Are Revealed

A series of hitherto unpublished charts which were studied daily through nearly six years of war by the Chiefs of Staff Committee were published officially a few weeks ago. Commenting on the series, The Daily Telegraph pointed out that nearly 40 charts give many new figures illustrating Britain's successes and sacrifices on land, at sea and in the air.

One shows that of 9,000 flying bombs launched between June 13, 1944, and March 30, 1945, fewer than 6,000 crossed the coast. There were 2,500 "incidents" inside the London area and 3,500 outside. Anti-aircraft fire shot down slightly over 2,000 flying bombs to beat the total accounted for by fighter aircraft. Worst weeks for long-range rockets were those ending November 30, 1944, when 40 killed 255, and March 8, 1945, when nearly 70 killed 250 people. The greatest number of rockets fell in the week ending February 15, when the death-roll was 212.

The total of men under arms rose from under 500,000 in mid-1939 to over 4,500,000 in 1944. This growth was largely at the expense of the building, textile, clothing and distributive trades, in which the number of workers shrank from 6,000,000 to 3,000,000.

A graph resembling a skyscraper shows that the production in fighter aircraft, which in September 1939 was less than 100 a month, had at the beginning of the Battle of Britain risen to 450. In 1944 the average was 900.

The production of war stores generally, taking the average index for production in 1940 as 100, rose steeply to a peak of 350 in February and March 1943, and remained at 240 in April 1945.

One of the most striking graphs is that showing the U-boat's enormous toll of merchant shipping. In 1942 it amounted to some 6,000,000 gross tons, compared with under 2,000,000 in each of the years 1939, 1940 and 1941, and had fallen to about 750,000 gross tons in 1944

In December, with America in the war one year, was recorded the first substantial excess of tonnage built over losses from all causes. Of about 1,200 commissioned, nearly 800 U-boats were sunk by July 1945; 200 were scuttled and over 150 were under Allied control. The remainder were unaccounted for.

In April 1944 the enemy's source of oil in Europe became a priority air target. In the absence of continued Allied bombing, output of oil might have recovered by August to 1,000,000 tons. Instead, by April 3, 1945, Axis oil output was down to an estimated monthly rate of 50,000 to 150,000 tons.

Other graphs show that in 1943 Canada and America consumed more milk, poultry, game, fish and eggs than in pre-war years, while Britons had less of everything except milk potatoes, vegetables and grain.

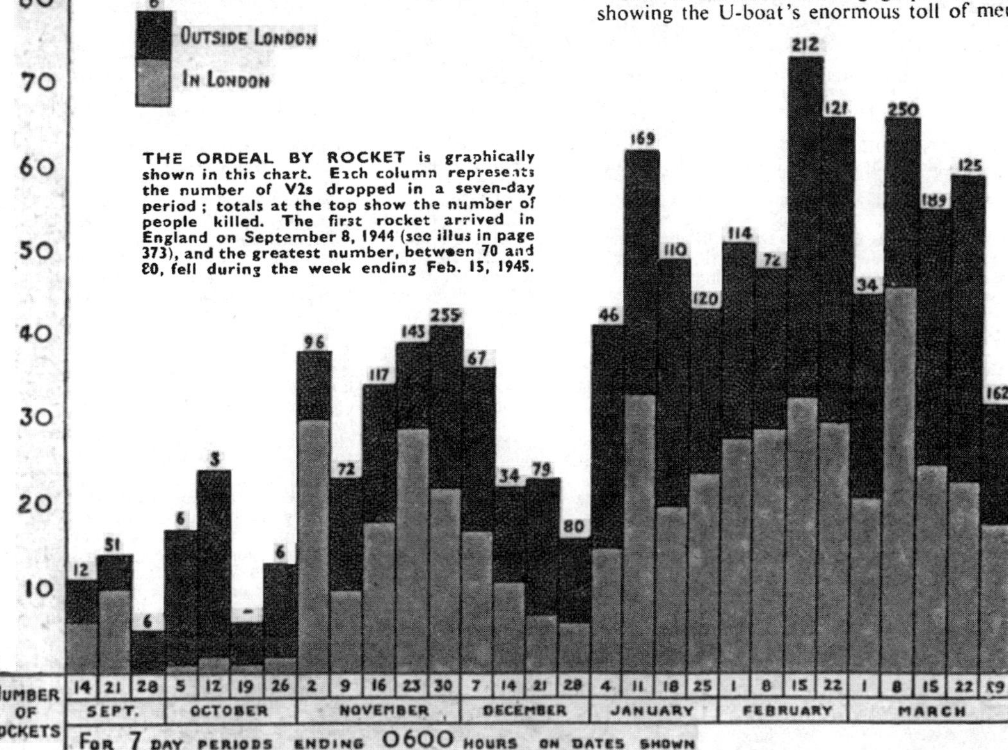

THE ORDEAL BY ROCKET is graphically shown in this chart. Each column represents the number of V2s dropped in a seven-day period; totals at the top show the number of people killed. The first rocket arrived in England on September 8, 1944 (see illus in page 373), and the greatest number, between 70 and 80, fell during the week ending Feb. 15, 1945.

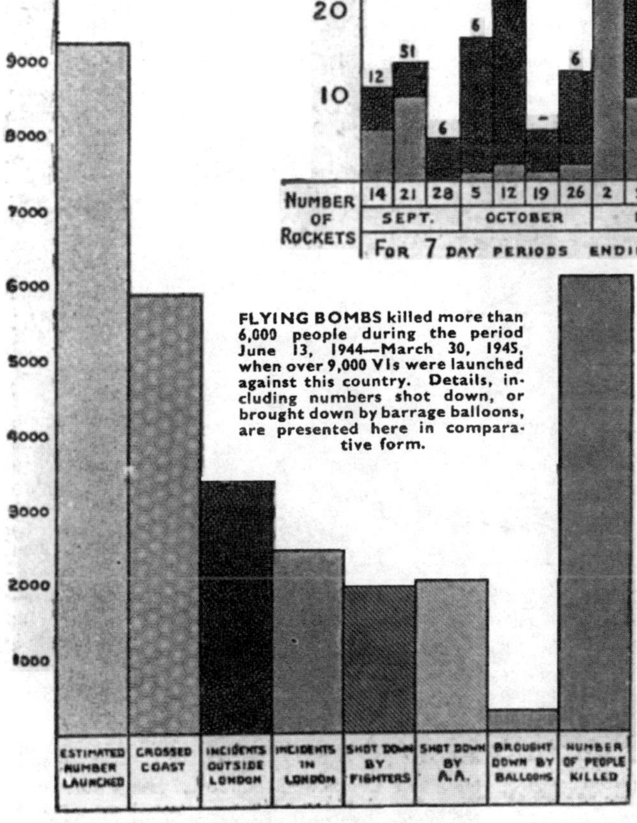

FLYING BOMBS killed more than 6,000 people during the period June 13, 1944—March 30, 1945, when over 9,000 V1s were launched against this country. Details, including numbers shot down, or brought down by barrage balloons, are presented here in comparative form.

1,000,000,000 May Face Starvation

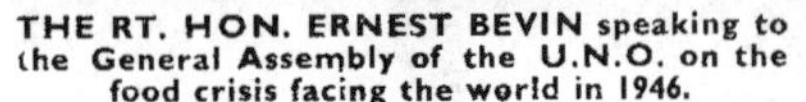

THE RT. HON. ERNEST BEVIN speaking to the General Assembly of the U.N.O. on the food crisis facing the world in 1946.

SERIOUS AND AVOIDABLE WASTE is demonstrated to the housewives of Hammersmith : bread collected from waste-bins.

CATASTROPHE of world-wide famine, in which one thousand million people might be involved, was declared a distinct possibility within a few months by Mr. Ernest Bevin, British Foreign Secretary, in a speech to the General Assembly of the U.N.O. at Westminster Hall, London, on Feb. 13, 1946. His speech, broadcast to the whole world, supported a Resolution by the Big Five—Great Britain, America, U.S.S.R., China and France—to urge the United Nations to take drastic and immediate steps to conserve supplies and to step-up to maximum the production of wheat for the coming season. He also appealed to all Governments to publish full information as to their own supplies of cereals and reveal steps they proposed to take to ensure maximum production.

The full gravity of the situation was summed up when Mr. Bevin reiterated the figures of requirements and available supplies in regard to wheat. He stated that 17,000,000 tons would be required by the importing nations during the first six months of 1946, and that the total available in the exporting countries for that period was only 12,000,000 tons. Included in these figures were the requirements of U.N.R.R.A. The deficit, shown as 5,000,000 tons, may well be increased when later figures are made available, as the situation in respect of wheat and rice had deteriorated.

He pleaded with each Nation to make the handling of the crisis a major part of their policy, irrespective of political considerations "because civilization really depends on solving this food problem and we cannot begin reconstruction unless it is surmounted within four months." Failure to make a collective effort—allowing the situation to run its course unchecked—would result in certain famine and starvation in many areas, but "maybe even with our available supplies with proper distribution and organized effort we can avoid that." Dealing with steps that could be taken to alleviate the suffering caused through disturbance of the whole economic life of the world, Mr. Bevin stated that the first consideration was to see that every ounce of food is properly used. The second step was for the "Governments to collaborate in securing adequate and fair distribution of surpluses. This must be more than a pious expression of opinion ; it must be made a part of each Government's policy."

BRITAIN is to increase her acreage of wheat to be sown this year, and anti-waste campaigns have been started. Where necessary the diet is to be modified to include less variety, as, in Mr. Bevin's words, "it was a question of survival, and the survival of the people throughout the world was a better thing than varied diet. It was better to have a monotonous diet than to have death running through the whole of the human race." He regarded the Resolution as a call to the Nations in the greatest common cause that ever faced them, and it would need all the resources, ingenuity, ability and organization to ensure that the millions of human beings might not only survive but contribute to the future happiness of mankind. Mr. Stettinius, speaking for the United States, one of the greatest of the food-producing countries, pledged the full support of the U.S.A. if the Resolution was adopted. Declaring that it was by this test that the United Nations would stand or fall, he appealed for unanimous support, and the Resolution was carried by acclamation on February 14, 1946.

FEEDING BRITAIN is the onerous task of Sir Ben Smith, K.B.E., Minister of Food (right). Among many generous food gifts from our Dominions was a consignment from Australia (above) being distributed to the elderly people of Southwark, London, by Mr. Norman Martin, Agent-General for Victoria.

Photos, Keystone, Central Press, Associated Press, Topical

Made in Britain and Welcomed the World Over

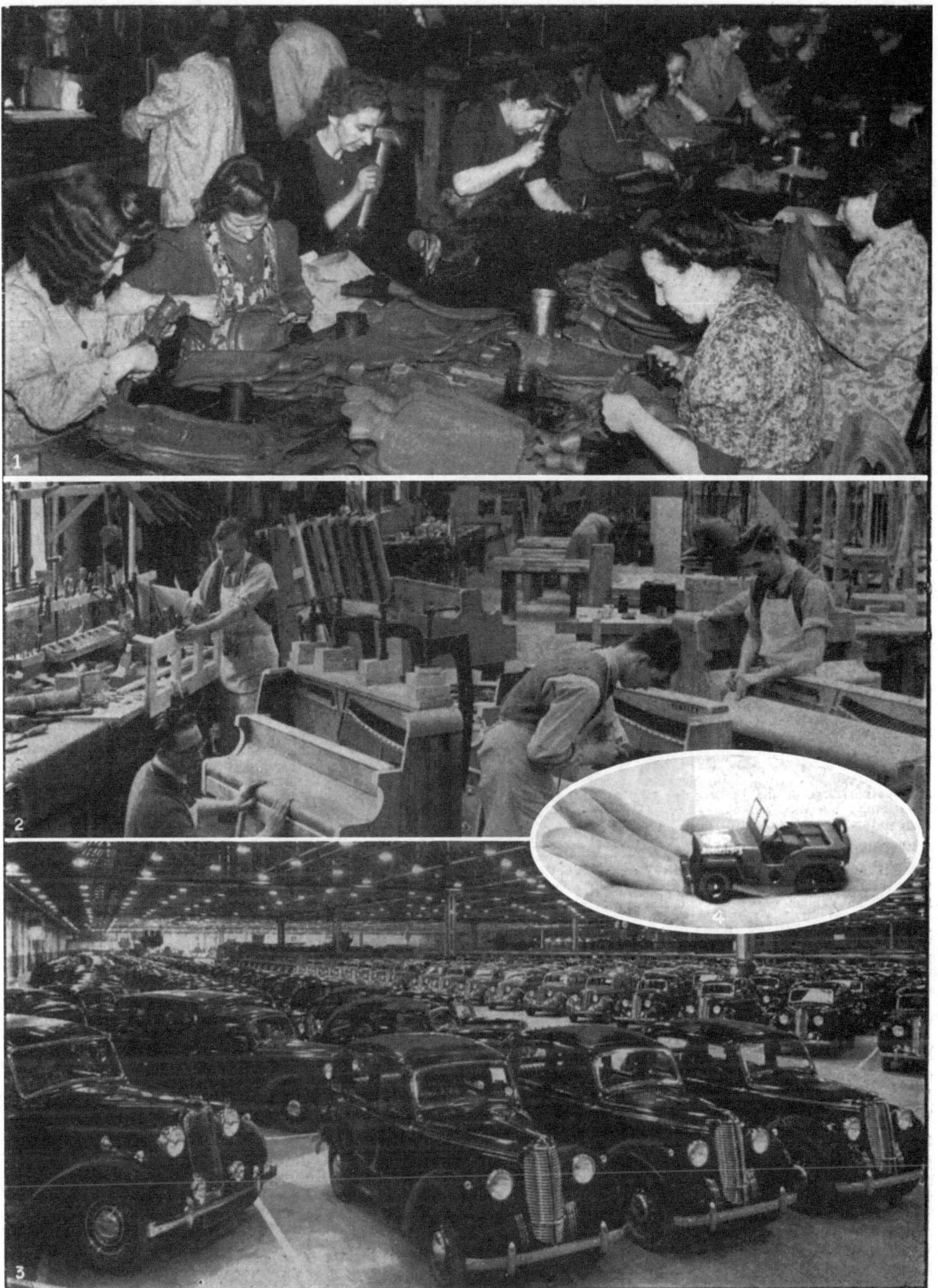

OUR EXPORT DRIVE IS GAINING MOMENTUM with more war factories turning over to peacetime production. Rubber hot-water bottles, for long unobtainable in this country without a doctor's certificate, are being made at a Streatham, London, factory (1) for overseas. Pianos are assembled (2) for foreign buyers. A former shadow-factory (3) is sending some 4,000 cars abroad each month. The toy industry is booming; thousands of model Jeeps (4) are going to America. See also page 366. *Photos, Fox, P.A.-Reuter, The News Chronicle*

Fleet Air Arm Officers on Loan to the R.A.F.

The services of many individual members of the F.A.A. loaned to the R.A.F. were magnificent indeed. Co-operation was perfect and results more than justified the partnership. Exploits of aces among the Navy's flyers ("flying fish"), some of whom helped to save Britain in 1940, are revealed in this article specially written for "The War Illustrated" by L. F. THOMPSON.

In the first R.A.F. aircraft to cross the German frontier in the War there sat a naval officer, the observer. He was Commander Thompson, R.N., and in that sortie, whose objective was the photographing of the German fleet on its way out of Wilhelmshaven, was born a co-operation between the R.A.F. and Fleet Air Arm of which some phases are little known.

Many people will remember the phrase "Fleet Air Arm aircraft operating under R.A.F. Command." It became quite familiar, and usually continued to tell how E-boats or R-boats had been sunk at night in the Channel or off the enemy coast! Sometimes it was a minelaying story, or perhaps it was part of a communiqué from Cairo at the time when the Albacores were pin-pointing desert targets for the heavy night bombers.

A less familiar aspect is that of the individual naval officer who flew in a R.A.F. squadron as part and parcel of that entity. He was "on loan," and he turned up on all sorts of odd R.A.F. missions. His hosts usually referred to him as the "blue job" or the "flying fish," and accepted him wholeheartedly into their generous companionship.

There are not so many men entitled to wear the little emblem on the 1939-1945 Star ribbon which indicates membership of "the few." With those who helped to save Britain and the world in 1940 were some F.A.A. men. Alongside Squadron-Leader (now Group Captain) D. Bader, D.S.O. and bar, D.F.C. and bar, flew such men as Sub-Lieutenant (A) R. E. Gardner, R.N., and Sub-Lieutenant (A) R. J. Cork, R.N. There were not many of these naval officers, forty at most, and the survivors of the Battle were fewer; but they had their share in that hour of glory.

Keeping Night-Long Vigil

With Britain saved from invasion came the slow building-up of the gigantic night bomber force which eventually was to strike such hammer-blows at the Reich. But in 1940-41, when listeners to the B.B.C. heard that "last night our bombers raided the marshalling yards at Hamm," it usually meant a succession of solitary aircraft keeping a night-long vigil. At the controls of that lonely Hampden, or Wellington, was quite possibly a man in darker blue uniform than the rest of his crew. The shortage of trained pilots for Bomber Command had led it also to draw on the Royal Navy's flyers. Of those early bomber-men very few indeed returned to fly again with the Fleet Air Arm.

Not all the jobs given to the "flying fish" were quite so critically dangerous or so far removed from their normal naval work. There were several officers like Lieutenant (A) J. Plant, R.N.V.R., who served in Air-Sea Rescue Walrus squadrons of the R.A.F. And others such as Lieutenant (A) "Kipper" Baring, R.N., whose sundry duties in the Middle East included the dropping of wild-looking Resistance men, garbed in long cloaks, into the Balkan mountains.

Throughout their long and bitter mining campaign against the Germans, Bomber Command had a fairly constant flow of Fleet Air Arm observers supplied to them. At one time these officers also carried out the other routine bombing missions. It was a trifle unusual for a navigator, trained in the draughty rear cockpit of a Swordfish, to find himself in the comparative comfort of a four-engined bomber. One such complained that he had to draw longer lines!

When, shortly before the Anglo-American invasion of North Africa, certain Blenheim squadrons began training in East Anglia, they each had one F.A.A. officer attached to them. One of these squadrons was commanded by the late Wing-Commander H. G. Malcolm, V.C., whose fame has been perpetuated by the Servicemen's clubs named after him. The observer attached to his squadron was Sub-Lieutenant (A) K. G. Williams, R.N.V.R. On his last heroic attack in Tunisia, Malcolm's squadron lost all their aircraft, and only six men survived.

NAVY AND R.A.F. CO-OPERATION was not confined to offensive operations during the War. Here, Fleet Air Arm mechanics and R.A.F. ground staff work together on the overhaul of a Naval aircraft operating with Coastal Command. *Photo, Fox*

Perhaps the largest transfer of aircrew on loan to the R.A.F. came at the end of 1943. This took place under the auspices of the late Air Chief Marshal Sir Trafford Leigh-Mallory, then A.O.C.-in-C. Fighter Command. It was in a field of air warfare completely new to the Fleet Air Arm, and ensured that two or three complete crews, pilot and observer, should be attached to practically every night-fighter squadron.

This gave the naval aircraft a chance they had dreamed of, to fly in Mosquitoes. It also brought them under the leadership of such aces as Group-Captain (then Wing-Commander) John Cunningham, D.S.O., D.F.C. (See page 246, Vol. 4). They soon proved their worth, and first blood was drawn by Lieutenants (A) W. Lawley-Wakelin and Williams, R.N.V.R., in January 1944, when they destroyed a Junkers 88 in one of the Luftwaffe's last large-scale attacks on London.

Apart from such defensive night-fighting, the Mosquito squadrons were sometimes called on for other duties. One squadron, stationed in Cornwall, was allocated the task of long-range day patrols in the Bay of Biscay. The object of these patrols was to protect the aircraft of Coastal Command on anti-submarine patrol from the German fighters stationed on the French Atlantic coast. Thus the "blue jobs" attached to this squadron found themselves, somewhat to their chagrin, back at their old job, as one put it, of "flying over lots and lots of water." They had the satisfaction, however, of adding to the squadron's list of successes.

D-Day transformed most of the R.A.F.'s night fighting squadrons from defensive to offensive units. Acting under the orders of Fighter Command on intruder operations, or Bomber Command on bomber support missions, the Mosquitoes went farther and farther afield. The naval aircrews shared in the resultant successes and shared, too, in the casualties. One of the best crews, Lieutenants (A) D. Price and R. Armitage, R.N.V.R., gained the award of the D.F.C. for their outstanding work at this period.

Channel Buzz-Bomb Patrol

Then came the VIs, and some of the night fighter squadrons were switched to the job of shooting them down. One of the naval crews has described the typical nightly scene when on a mid-Channel buzz-bomb patrol. "In France we could see the flares and explosions as Bomber Command went in. Just off the French coast were the German flak ships only too ready to let go with their tracer; and, in mid-Channel, as like as not, would be the flashes from a battle between the E-boats and M.T.B.s. Then the buzz-bombs would start coming and the fighters would let go with all they had, and over to the north thousands of searchlights and gun-flashes completed the picture. When everything was going at once it really looked like Hollywood's idea of war."

Towards the end of 1944 the surviving naval night-fighters returned to their own service. "Well," they jokingly told their former hosts, "we've got the invasion running smoothly for you!" The story that had begun with Commander Thompson on September 3, 1939, was now nearly ended. The service of Fleet Air Arm crews in Air Force squadrons served many purposes. Sometimes it was an end in itself. Sometimes the experience gained for the Fleet Air Arm was the dividend. Frequently it proved what the naval crews could have achieved earlier in the War had it been possible for them to receive adequate machines and equipment.

After the war of 1914-1918, the Royal Naval Air Service became part of the Royal Air Force. From their co-operation and collaboration in this last War, in particular the service of individual members in R.A.F. squadrons, the modern Naval Air Service has a high regard for the Royal Air Force, whose laurels it was proud to help to maintain.

After Devastation—Restoration

Exclusive to THE WAR ILLUSTRATED

Albania Sets Her Ravaged State in Order

In the fight against Italian and German occupation the Albanian National Liberation Army lost some 22,000 men out of a population of 1,000,000. Material damage was great: repairs in progress at Tirana, the capital (1), which was liberated on Nov. 17, 1944. Her soldiers have a first-class reputation: on parade for drill (2). At this shoemender's shop (3) old tires are used for resoling. On January 11, 1946, Albania was declared a republic, ex-King Zog being forbidden to return.

Russia's Great Hydro-Electric Power Plant—

Pride of the U.S.S.R., the Dnieper power station which the Russians blew up, in accordance with their "scorched earth" policy, when they evacuated Dnepropetrovsk on August 28, 1941, is being restored. The town was retaken from the Germans on October 25, 1943, and in the early days of 1946 work on the concrete part of the dam was nearing completion and the stage was being approached when power could again be supplied to the industry and agriculture of the Ukraine.

Exclusive t

—Will Function Again on the Dnieper's Banks

Necessary replacements include 25,000 tons of new steel sections and equipment and 175,000 tons of concrete work. Assembling the metal frame of the power station building (1). Work on one of the abutments (2) of the monster dam. Cranes carry masses of concrete and fixtures to the labourers (3). Indicating the magnitude of the power-house machinery: changing bushes for the oil master-switch (4). It is expected that restoration will be completed before the close of 1946.

Netherlands Farmlands Twice Wrested From the Sea

Exclusive to THE WAR ILLUSTRATED

Noted for heavy wheat crops, the Wieringermeer area was originally raised from the Zuider Zee by the industrious people of the Netherlands. On April 17, 1945, the Germans wantonly blew up the dikes and the land was inundated afresh. Wieringerwerf under water (1). Flood damage at Middenmeer (2). Now the breaches have been sealed and the water pumped away. No trees remained alive: replacements (3) "heeled-in" for later planting. Ploughing starts again (4).

"The Challenge of Red China"

Reviewed by HAMILTON FYFE

"THE Chinese Empire," remarked old Mrs. Voysey in the fifth act of The Voysey Inheritance, Granville Barker's play, "must be in a shocking condition." That was forty years ago. For a long time before that, and ever since then, articles and books have been filling the public mind with that same idea. I cannot remember a time when China did not seem to be "in a shocking state."

Every now and again the announcement is made that a change for the better has come. We have heard lately that a move has been made towards unity, and we all want to believe it. But we cannot help remembering how often we have been deceived. When the Chinese Empire was turned into a Republic that did not stop the private wars between feudal potentates, each with an army of his own. When a central government emerged strong enough to put down these disturbances, conditions became little less confused and disorderly. At last Chiang Kai-shek (see illus. page 498, Vol 7) rose to the top, and hope of a united China revived, especially when Japan invaded Manchuria in 1931. Now, it was supposed, the Chinese really will stand together to resist this unprovoked aggression.

But for some while past there has been an impression that their leaders were interested in an internal conflict as well as in fighting the Japanese. As in Europe, so in China there grew up a Communist Party which demanded both reforms at home and more vigorous waging of war against the Japanese. It began to look as though the government established in Chungking was using some of the arms and ammunition sent to it, not only for the purpose of striking against the common enemy, Japan, but for another purpose as well. This was the recovery of the northern province adjoining Manchuria, where the Communists had set up a system of their own.

Economic and Financial Crisis

At one period it did appear likely that the quarrel would be patched up. No difference between Communists and anti-Communists can ever be more than patched up, any more than those between Roman Catholics and Protestants in the 17th century could be. It was intelligible enough that the Kuomintang, the government in Chungking, should aim at suppressing a movement hostile to itself. What one finds very hard to believe is that Chiang Kai-shek and his colleagues should have made war on the Communist province because Tokyo was afraid of Communism.

And yet in his book The Challenge of Red China (Pilot Press, 15s.), Gunther Stein, who has been in the Far East for more than ten years as correspondent for American newspapers, says of events in 1940:

> Once more in the midst of the China-Japan war Tokyo demanded from the Chinese Government that it suppress the Communist armies . . . Once more the Kuomintang took action.

It was, of course, to Japan's interest that the Chinese should be divided into two sections fighting one another. But there seems to have been another motive for their demand. The Japanese rulers were afraid that if Communism spread in China it might, as a Jap militarist organ put it, "seriously affect Japan." For the Japanese rulers knew a good deal more about the methods of the Communists in Shantung and Shansi, the area they controlled, than did the authorities in Chungking. They felt they could deal with the rest of China so long as the Kuomintang's methods of government remained what they were.

> The lack of democracy and free speech in Kuomintang territory paralysed the people's spirit and the war effort in general. The economic and financial crisis rose and nothing effective was done to combat it. The grossly inequitable distribution of war burdens among various strata of society led to increasing popular dissatisfaction. The pathetic undernourishment of the Kuomintang soldiers and the delay of urgently needed army reforms weakened China's military power more and more.

When I made the acquaintance of Gunther Stein before he went to the Far East, he was strongly anti-Fascist. Hitler had turned him out of Germany. He detested the Nazi system. But he was certainly not a Red. I received the impression that he disliked Moscow totalitarianism almost as much as the Berlin brand. This makes me all the more ready to accept his judgement about Red China. He has no theories, no "ideology," no propaganda to put across. He simply relates what he saw and heard during a three months' visit to the Communist provinces of the Border Region.

Bewildered by Their Double Task

He went with no prejudices, no high expectations; simply as a reporter determined to discover the facts, which he set down in a convincing because unimpassioned manner, with a desire to make his readers understand why China is still "in a shocking state," and how urgently necessary it is that "American, British and Russian statesmanship should help China to become *one*."

As Mr. Stein travelled from Chungking, in the centre of the country, to the north, he noticed that the population appeared to be thoroughly mobilized.

> But it was evidently a disciplinarian and not a popular mobilization, based on suspicion rather than trust of the people, on rigid control from above rather than on any attempt to enlist voluntary co-operation. The ordinary men and women and youths I saw impressed me as even more apathetic than elsewhere in China, as though they were bewildered by their contradictory double task of facing an external enemy and an internal foe.

When the author had crossed "the lifeless, closely-blockaded border between the two halves of China," being rowed across the Yellow River, on which there had been so much trade in peaceful times and which was now deserted, he found a different spirit in the people. The farmers looked better fed and clothed; they seemed to have more livestock. Cotton was being grown; spinning and weaving went on. Schools were more numerous "and there was in general more activity in these little cave-villages, poor though they still were, than in those we had passed on the other side. The village magistrates were keen, practical men of the peasant type. They did not try to conceal defects; they talked about them freely and spoke hopefully of prospects of improvement in the near future."

Generalissimo and Mme. CHIANG KAI-SHEK at Nanking with General George C. Marshall, newly appointed U.S. ambassador to China and former U.S. Chief of Staff.

Photo, Keystone

THERE was none of the pretence which has made Americans, and Europeans too, impatient of Chinese methods, diplomatic and business; none of "those irritating and often unconquerable handicaps to mutual understanding and practical co-operation which that fateful little word 'face' still implies as it has done ever since foreigners made contact with China." What that means is, to put it more bluntly, humbug. False compliments, roundabout speeches, insincere humility, foolish pride—that is "face." In Red China, according to Mr. Stein, "it simply does not exist." This naturally makes personal relations far easier.

Michael Lindsay, son of the Master of Balliol, not a Communist himself but a fellow-worker with them, has warm liking as well as admiration for those among whom he lived with his Chinese wife in Yenan, the capital of the two Communist provinces. Life is simple there, even hard, but there is "a peculiar pioneer atmosphere of unsophisticated self-assured enthusiasm" which inspires confidence, and makes "its primitive caves teem with life and activity." Mr. Stein contrasts it with Chungking, "getting more weary, lax and helpless, its crowds looking strained and purposeless in the stale and futile commercial atmosphere of dirty streets, its officials sitting year after year in clogged, over-staffed Government offices, more undernourished and dejected as time goes on."

New Ways of Getting Things Done

Evidently, if we are to trust Mr. Stein, the new united China will have to be run by the Reds if it is to be successfully run. This does not mean that it will imitate the Russian system. "The Chinese Communists feel as grown up, after eighteen years of continuous responsibility for the conduct of armies and administrations, as the Soviet Union does after twenty-eight years. They regard the conditions under which Marxism has to be applied to China as utterly different from those prevailing in Russia." Its aim will be efficiency, not the triumph of an ideology. It will not be hampered by personal feuds and political struggles between leaders.

> The deeper I probed, the more likely I found it that relations inside the Party were largely determined by mutual frankness and a good measure of democratic procedure, which led to a harmonization of views. . . . I failed to discover any signs of dissension. . . . Every functionary seems to be freely elected by members, from the lowest organizations up.

What the Chinese Communists aimed at was to provide a system of government cheap enough for the people to finance without difficulty (such a system they have never had), and ready to take on all sorts of responsibilities that had been shirked before. They tried many new ways of getting things done. For instance, they induced both soldiers and officials to grow their own food. One district magistrate told Mr. Stein that he and his staff would not only be able to do without wages, but they would contribute largely to the public stock of grain. Thus "officials instead of drawing salaries pay for the honour of working for the government."

To sum up, it would appear that if Mr. Stein's judgement is as sound as his evidence seems to be worthy of consideration, Chiang Kai-shek's regime will have to undergo some important changes to bring it more into touch with modern ideas of democracy before we can entertain any hope of China emerging from that "shocking state" in which it has so long been existing.

Hard-Won Resurgence in Northernmost Norway

FINMARK'S STRUGGLE to fashion means of existence in this bleak Arctic region continues as more and more of the surviving inhabitants return from enforced evacuation to commence life over again. With systematic savagery the Germans destroyed all the essentials for human life.

Out of this scrapheap of War, families have improvised accommodation for themselves in face of countless difficulties. An upturned bomb-fin (1) becomes a wash-basin. A family returns by horse and cart to the ruins of Honningavaag (2). The district nurse settles down to work in the porch of the church, the only building to escape destruction in Karasjok (3).

Transport problems are not easily overcome : one of the few boats that remained undamaged is seen (4) on the Tana after landing supplies for the people of Polmark. Mines and mine-fields hinder reconstruction, and the presence of these is indicated by a warning sign (5). See also illus. page 296 ; and pages 588–589, 749, Vol. 8.

Exclusive to THE WAR ILLUSTRATED

Canada's 'Operation Muskox' is Under Way

ARCTIC CONDITIONS call for specially designed equipment to make "Operation Muskox" a success. Included are "snowmobiles" (1), tank-like vehicles with wide treads; these are fitted with plate-glass windows, heated cabins and bunks. A Dakota (2) is being warmed-up for the task of dropping supplies to those on trek. Several types of face-mask are worn (3) as protection against the cold on the 3,100-mile route from Churchill, Manitoba, to Edmonton, Alberta (see map).

Photos, New York Times Photos

A PEACETIME EXERCISE ON A WARTIME BASIS, "Operation Muskox" set out from Churchill Air Base on Febuary 15, 1946, to cover the Arctic and sub-Arctic wastes of Canada. Sanctioned by the Canadian Minister of National Defence in October 1945, it is non-tactical, although co-operating forces are to be Canadian Army and R.C.A.F. personnel. With the party are scientists and observers, and representatives of the Dominion Observatory, Meteorological Service and Survey branches.

On its success may well depend the opening-up of trans-Arctic routes and the developments of the Northern Arctic wastelands, the object being to study the movement and maintenance of vehicles and personnel by air and land co-operation in conditions varying between the barren wastes of an Arctic winter and the North-Western bush in spring. Reliance is being placed on the ability of "snowmobiles" to overcome these changing conditions, also on the new-type Arctic clothing. Equipment used is Canadian designed and built, being the direct result of Britain's overtures to the Canadian Army for similar equipment in which a number of British Lovat Scouts had been trained at Jasper during the winter of 1943-44 for the proposed invasion of Norway.

The route of some 3,100 miles (see map) commences at Churchill, Manitoba, and terminates at Edmonton, Alberta, and is to be covered by a force numbering about 45, in 12 "snowmobiles," to arrive at Edmonton on May 5, 1946. A small advanced force was sent to Baker Lake to prepare an air-strip and to establish a scientific station to obtain and dispatch meteorological and magnetic data. It was reported on February 18 that the exercise party had reached a point about 45 miles north of Churchill and was there marooned by a snowstorm and high winds.

Victims of the Inhuman Doctors of Dachau

At the Nuremberg trials a Czech surgeon, Dr. Franz Blaha, gave evidence on January 11, 1946, of "scientific" experiments on human beings which he had witnessed during his four-years' imprisonment at Dachau concentration camp. Some of these acts, perpetrated by German doctors and S.S. men on Slavs and other "inferior races," are recorded in this article specially written for "The War Illustrated" by JOHN FORTINBRAS.

TWENTY men, perhaps the worst men alive in Germany today, sat hard of face and sullen-eyed in the dock at Nuremberg, when Mr. Thomas Dodd, Counsel for the United States, interrupted the sequence of indictments of individual defendants to call as witness Dr. Franz Blaha, chief physician of the Polyclinic Hospital at Prague. The prosecutor said that his witness would give important evidence involving Rosenberg, Funk, Frick, Sauckel and Kaltenbrunner, about certain surgical operations and research work he had seen during his imprisonment at Dachau from April 1941 until the camp's liberation in April 1945.

Squarely built, clean shaven, and with a pale, studious face, Dr. Blaha repeated the oath after the President, nervously. He then stood rigid, but with mouth square-set, before being motioned to a seat. Instead of examining him immediately, the prosecutor, to save the Tribunal's time, read an affidavit subscribed to and sworn by the witness at Nuremberg two days earlier:

"In June 1942 I was taken into the hospital (at Dachau) as a surgeon. Shortly afterwards I was directed to conduct a stomach operation on twenty healthy prisoners. Because I would not do this I was put in the autopsy-room, where I stayed until April 1945. While there I performed approximately 7,000 autopsies. In all, 12,000 autopsies were performed under my direction." What lay behind those 12,000 post-mortems filled every man and woman in court, perhaps even the wretched Nazi leaders, with feelings of anguish, anger and dismay.

Unconscious in Ice-Cold Baths

To explore methods for reviving airmen who had baled out into the sea, and survivors from sea disasters, one Dachau doctor, Sigismund Rascher, a friend of Heinrich Himmler, prepared ice-cold baths in which prisoners were put and kept until they became unconscious. A rectal thermometer registered their temperatures. Each time a prisoner's body dropped one degree in temperature, Dr. Rascher or one of his assistants put a needle into the man's neck and extracted a globule of blood. This was analysed. Most men died when their body temperatures dropped to 25 degrees centigrade. One man remained conscious until 19 degrees centigrade.

IT then became Rascher's special object of research to try out various means of reviving those men who, although unconscious, were not dead when removed from their ice baths. He experimented with hot-water applications, electro therapy, artificial warmth from the sun, and what he was pleased to call "animal warmth." For this last treatment prostitutes of non-German nationality were used, and two of them were made to lie naked, one on each side of the semi-frozen body, reviving it by their own body heat.

In these experiments Dr. Sigismund Rascher used 300 prisoners. Many died in his ice baths. Of the others, the majority lost their reason and were then sent to "invalid blocks" where, in common with all patients committed to such blocks, they were "liquidated." Only two survivors, the Czech doctor told the Tribunal, were known to him from those forced into these immersion researches—a Pole and a Yugoslav. Both were mental cases.

Also designed ostensibly to save lives at sea, and more fundamentally to destroy lives at Dachau, were a series of salt-water experiments conducted on Hungarian and gipsy prisoners in the hospital during the autumn of 1944. From 80 to 90 prisoners of these nationalities were selected at varying times. They thus became hospital patients, and their treatment consisted of being locked in a room and "fed" for five days on salt water. They had nothing else to eat or drink. Periodically, Dachau's mad doctors took samples of their urine, blood and excrement. Curiously, in the light of almost every other experiment ever devised at Dachau, this salt-water test, though it agonized its victims, claimed no fatalities. The explanation for this, Dr. Blaha said, lay in the comradeship of other prisoners by means of which food was smuggled into the "salt-water cells."

Skin Stripped From Dead Bodies

Dr. Sigismund Rascher used from 500 to 600 prisoners in his experiments to determine the effects both of high altitudes and of rapid descents on parachutists. He constructed a special van, fitting it with valves and pressure pumps, so that its air density could be regulated at will, reproducing atmospheric conditions from ground level to 100,000 feet. Into this hermetically sealed van prisoners were thrust in groups of 20. Then the doctor began manipulating the valves and, with trained precision, recording data. Sometimes Dr. Blaha himself looked through an inspection window during these experiments. Invariably he saw men lying unconscious on the floor of the van. Most of them eventually died through haemorrhages of lungs or brain. Almost all coughed blood when taken out. It was Dr. Blaha's duty to clear out the bodies from the altitude van and send their internal organs as subjects for special research to a laboratory at Munich.

DR. SIGISMUND RASCHER, assisted by Dr. Wolter, forced the Czech surgeon to turn his skill to taxidermy and strip scientifically the skins from dead prisoners, taking care to remove only healthy skins, chiefly that from the back and chest of bodies which had belonged to healthy prisoners. The human skins were then chemically treated and placed in the sun to dry. Afterwards, leather-operatives and kindred craftsmen went to work, cutting the skins into special shapes and stitching and sewing them into saddles, gloves, riding breeches, house slippers and ladies' handbags. S.S. men, it was revealed, valued tattoed skins highly.

Sometimes, with the supply of skin from dead men falling off, the leather-workers became idle. Whereupon their "needs" would be suggested to Dr. Rascher, and next day the autopsy department would be presented with the bodies of 20 or 30 young people, all healthy-skinned persons ; a bullet hole neatly drilled in their neck was proof that their murderer had taken care, in killing them, not to spoil the covetable part of their skins. It was forbidden to cut up German inmates in this way. Poles, Russians and other Slav races sufficed.

A set of healthy teeth imperilled one also at Dachau. Orders would be received from the experimental station at Oranienburg, asking for skulls. Whereupon the S.S. men to whom these orders were given, replied, "We will try to get you some with good teeth." Then Dr. Blaha's department would receive a new supply of such heads. They had first to be boiled and their soft parts removed before dispatch to Oranienburg.

Polish, Czech and Dutch priests furnished the majority of victims for experiments in which 40 healthy prisoners were selected, 20 of whom were given intra-muscular injections and 20 intravenous injections of pus obtained from the bodies of diseased people.

Following the injection, the victims were denied any kind of treatment for three days. By that time their agony was intense. Their bodies, in most cases, were inflamed, and their blood-stream poisoned mortally. After the third day each group was divided into two groups of ten. One half then received chemical treatment with liquid and special pills. The other half were subjected to specialized treatment with sulfanamide, and surgical operations sometimes carried so far as to lead to the amputation of all limbs.

Nor was the treatment by pills any less diabolical. For Dr. Blaha testified that in his post-mortem examinations he found perforations of the stomach walls due to the chemical of the pills, and everyone so affected must have died in unimaginable pain.

Injected With Malaria Germs

At the personal request of Reichsfuehrer S.S. Himmler, Dr. Klaus Schilling specialized in malarial researches and established a special clinic at Dachau hospital. Between 1941 and 1945 he forcibly treated about 1,200 prisoners. Most of them, I believe, were Russians who, of all nations, suffered the worst at this concentration camp. The victims so chosen were first either bitten by mosquitoes or injected with malaria sporozoites obtained from mosquitoes. Then, with the fever developing in them, Dr. Klaus Schilling had ample scope to study scientifically the effect of various antidotes such as antipyrin, quinine, pyramidon. The death roll here was considerable. Thirty to forty patients died from malaria. Others, enfeebled by their malaria attacks, became prone to diseases, particularly the rampant "hunger typhus," which either killed them direct or qualified them for admission to the "invalid blocks." A number were poisoned by overdoses of neosalvarsan and pyramidon.

With outstretched hand, the Czech doctor identified in court at the prosecutor's request from among the Nazi war-criminals two, Rosenberg and Frick, whom he remembered having seen at Dachau to carry out an inspection. Kaltenbrunner, Himmler's chief lieutenant, who as a sick man was absent from court, had been seen there, too, by the Czech doctor. Funk and Sauckel, two more defendants, will have to establish in their defence ignorance of conditions at Dachau. But those doctors—will retribution overtake them ? It may be that their researches had some scientific value, but if Dr. Blaha's testimony be believed—and he is a surgeon of high qualifications—then these inhuman experimenters had not even the right to put forward the pretext of scientific research as an excuse for their cold-blooded murders.

IN reply to Monsieur Dubost, the French Prosecutor, who asked him if he knew the aim of the experiments the Czech doctor replied, "According to scientific rules, so far as I can judge, it had no purpose at all. It was simply a useless piece of murder, and one must be astounded that university professors and physicians were able to carry out these experiments in such a way. It was much worse than all the 'liquidations' and executions, because the victims of these experiments had their misery prolonged, by various medical means, so that the experiments might last longer and give the experimenters more time to observe their victims."

Anti-Suicide Guards are Alert at Nuremberg

AMERICAN GUARDS LOOK INTO THE CELLS housing the Nazi war-criminals at Nuremberg every thirty seconds, day and night, whilst these are occupied, as a precautionary measure against attempts at suicide. Other steps taken to prevent any of the prisoners following the example of Dr. Robert Ley, who hanged himself before the opening of the trial, include a daily search, and the removal of ties, belts and shoe-laces whenever the prisoners are returned to their cells. See also illus. pages 559-562.

Photos, New York Times Photos

I Was There!

Eye Witness Stories of the War and After

My Last Moments in H.M.S. Prince of Wales

On November 30, 1941, Prince of Wales slid into Singapore Harbour, eagerly watched and cheered by excited crowds. A few days later, riven by torpedoes and bombs, she rolled over and disappeared into the grey waters of the China Sea—her audience then the Jap airmen circling above. The tragic story is told specially for "The War Illustrated" by one of the survivors, Surgeon Lieut.-Commander E. D. Caldwell, R.N.

SURGEON LT.-CMDR. E. D. CALDWELL, R.N., was in charge of upper deck casualties when the end came to H.M.S. Prince of Wales.

We had left suddenly for a secret destination in October 1941, sped out and south to Capetown, where secrecy broke and newspaper headlines flared the news "Britain's Newest Battleship for Singapore." Urgency was apparent then in our speed across the Indian Ocean into Colombo, out again across the Bay of Bengal, and finally into the narrow, green-banked waters of the Straits.

When we arrived, Singapore was gay, brightly lit and, on the surface at any rate, confident that the advent of the Eastern Fleet would counteract and lull the insistent sabre-rattling of the Japanese war-lords. The night after our arrival a party was given in our honour. Friends were made, and future plans discussed of meetings, of tennis and golf; but these were not to be, for early the following day all leave was stopped.

It was about 3.30 a.m. on the fateful Sunday morning of December 7, when I awoke hearing "Action Stations" shouted and sounded off on the ship's loudspeakers. As I reluctantly got up and dressed I thought it was only an exercise, but on arriving at my action station on the bridge I quickly realized from the general atmosphere of tenseness that this was not the case; and on questioning someone I was told that several almost certainly hostile aircraft were reported flying in towards Singapore. The first grey light of dawn was just visible as we stood there—whispering, waiting.

Suddenly someone shouted "Look!" and pointed. There, far away and very high over Singapore itself, just dots moving in a searchlight beam, were several aircraft. I watched them, fascinated. We knew now they were Japs, and as I looked I thought, "What everyone hoped and prayed would not happen is about to happen now, for just as soon as they drop a bomb, or we fire a gun, it's another war to spread misery, death and destruction." Even as I thought this, I heard the crump-crump of bombs, answered almost instantaneously by the flaming roar of our guns. So it had happened!

Later, as we gathered round a crackling, oscillating wireless set in the wardroom, we heard of the fury and treachery of the Japanese stroke, of Pearl Harbour, of battered ships and airfields. And I think most of us felt, "Well, the Americans are in! It's round one to the Japs—but now they'll get it!"

We Were to Attack at Dawn

Gradually we began to get news of the locust-like infiltration of the Japs through Indo-China, of convoys moving south, of landings and fighting in the northern tip of Malaya. Late on the afternoon of December 8 we heard the orders we were all expecting, and as the Prince of Wales, followed by H.M.S. Repulse, led out to sea, to whatever was in store for us, we were proud of her—powerful, sombre and sinister.

I experienced that tense awareness of one's heart beating; that rather pleasurable, bitter-sweet enjoyment—I wonder is it pleasure? It's difficult to say, for I am quite sure no man gets any kick out of being shelled or bombed. I certainly don't, but I do know that these occasions give you an intense comradeship with your shipmates, and a rather selfless exaltation which appears to be pleasurable.

We went to routine Dusk Action Stations and then many of us stood on deck talking long after darkness had fallen. Where were we going? What was ahead of us? How did the Japs fight? Were they truly fanatical? Did they make suicidal attacks? (I recalled the last time I personally had seen a Jap—he was playing snooker at Edinburgh.) I talked to an old friend of mine who had joined the ship at Singapore, and we watched the escorting destroyers winking a few signals at us, then went through the screen into the bright, chattering wardroom for a drink.

Later there was a sudden silence, then the loudspeaker buzzed into activity. The Captain was going to talk to the ship's company. His well-known voice began: there was a convoy of Jap ships unloading men and material in a bay in North Malaya. They were escorted by at least two battleships, half a dozen cruisers, and many destroyers. We were going in to attack them at dawn on

H.M.S. PRINCE OF WALES AT SINGAPORE. She was Flagship of the C.-in.-C. Eastern Fleet, Rear-Admiral Sir Tom Phillips (inset). It was from here, accompanied by H.M.S. Repulse, that she left on her ill-fated mission—primarily to intercept Japanese transports. Without fighter escort, both ships met the full fury of Japanese air attacks and, as told in these pages by a survivor, were sunk on December 10, 1941, Sir Tom Phillips going down with his ship, of which this is probably the last photograph to be taken.

Photo, British Official

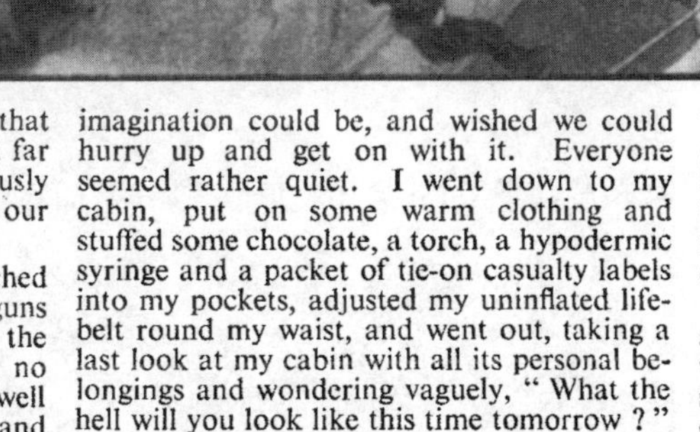

LISTING HEAVILY the Prince of Wales (left) is nearing the end. Members of the crew await their turn to slide down ropes to the safety of a destroyer (below). Of a total of 2,925 carried in the Prince of Wales and the Repulse 2,330 were saved.

Photos, Associated Press

the 10th. We had the vital element of surprise, we could do great damage, we would have to be prepared for quick retaliation and subsequent heavy aerial attack by the enemy.

Well, that was it. Someone said he'd heard the names of the enemy battleships, and this caused a run on "Jane's Fighting Ships." How many guns? What size? What have their cruisers got? We steamed northward, well out to sea, in cloudy, poor visibility, admirable for our purpose. Unfortunately, about an hour before the onset of darkness the clouds lifted, the sky cleared and shortly afterwards the news flashed round the ship that a Japanese float-plane had been spotted far off on the horizon and was quite obviously shadowing us and relaying details of our course and disposition.

We stood on the upper deck and watched it in the now fading light. Our 5·25 in. guns traversed silently and menacingly, but the range was too great and, alas, we had no fighter aircraft available. We could well imagine the excitement, the conjectures, and of course the preparations the Japanese airman's radio messages would arouse at his base. And we cursed the fact that sheer chance had revealed us in that short, clear period before darkness fell.

We were to be at our action stations all night then, and I wandered into the wardroom for supper, by now a bleak, comfortless wardroom, with pictures, books and trophies taken down and all movable objects firmly lashed, in the usual preparations for impending action. There was a cold, uninteresting help-yourself supper, the stewards and attendants being already employed on their various jobs in gun turrets, ammunition hoists and shell rooms.

I didn't feel hungry. But I thought what a curse a vivid imagination could be, and wished we could hurry up and get on with it. Everyone seemed rather quiet. I went down to my cabin, put on some warm clothing and stuffed some chocolate, a torch, a hypodermic syringe and a packet of tie-on casualty labels into my pockets, adjusted my uninflated lifebelt round my waist, and went out, taking a last look at my cabin with all its personal belongings and wondering vaguely, "What the hell will you look like this time tomorrow?"

My action station was on the Signal Deck on the bridge. I had first-aid outfits and bamboo stretchers stored there, and a telephone communicating with the other between-deck Medical Stations. I stood there for a long time, just leaning over the bridge, looking down at the dark sea with the foam creaming its way aft on our bow wave, not thinking of anything much, and occasionally drifting in and out of the upper conning tower where we could smoke and just distinguish forms to talk to in the eerie blue light. I sat on the deck and, leaning against a stretcher, dozed and woke and dozed again.

Then somebody shook me and said, "There's a broadcast just coming through!" It was from Admiral Phillips, telling us he had reluctantly decided to cancel our dawn attack. He knew how disappointed we'd all be, but unpleasant preparations for our reception would be too great to justify our going in, and we were now to alter course and turn south—that was all. I didn't quite know whether I was a bit relieved or disappointed; but I did think that it must have been a hard and also a brave decision to make.

NEXT morning as we steamed south we received news of suspected Japanese landings farther down the Malayan coast, and a destroyer was sent in to have a "look see," our aircraft also being catapulted off the ship on reconnaissance. However, nothing was found. The morning wore on. Suddenly, about 11.20 a.m., we resumed first degree of readiness, and shortly afterwards, echoing over all the ship's loudspeakers, came that harsh and insistent bugle call "Repel Aircraft!" Galvanic in its effects on everyone and dramatic in its results! Every man has his post of duty and gets there by the shortest and quickest route, probably plugging cotton-wool in his ears and jamming on his tin helmet as he runs.

We were steaming very fast now, Repulse and ourselves with our destroyers spread out well ahead of us, and suddenly I saw puffs of smoke coming from one of them. She had opened fire. Looking for the puffs in the sky I saw more and more Jap planes, and our guns started up. A signalman shouted "Look at that So-and-So coming in at us!"

I saw a heavy, twin-engined bomber fairly low over the water, coming straight in at us. The noise was unbelievable, the roar of all our 5·25 in. armament, the cracking detonation of Oerlikons and Bofors and the chattering.

ear-splitting rhythm of the multiple pom-poms. They rose through a frenzied crescendo as the bomber approached. I watched him get nearer and nearer, bigger and bigger. I was fascinated, and kept thinking " We must get him, we must get him ! " Then I saw his torpedo fall from the belly of his plane, splash into the sea, and its tell-tale line of bubbles heading for us.

Simultaneously the ship swung round to port to avoid its track, and I found myself holding my breath and gripping the rail like a vice as the torpedo passed harmlessly on its way. They were attacking us from high level, too, and a stick of bombs came screaming down ahead of us, throwing up huge pillars of water as they exploded in the sea. We avoided another two torpedo attacks on our starboard side, and as the second plane banked away there was a cheer from the guns' crews—or rather a roar—as smoke and flames began to pour from it, and then like a great flaming newspaper it dropped lower and lower till it hit the sea and disappeared. A huge oily column of smoke marked its end.

We saw another dark plume of smoke rising from the sea three or four miles astern. It was certainly nice to know that anything crashing into the sea was Japanese. Then there was a slight lull. So far, so good. We sent a signal to H.M.S. Repulse asking her if she was all right, and her Captain replied, " Yes, have already avoided 19 torpedoes." I had not time to finish the cigarette I had lit, when " Repel Aircraft " sounded off, and I saw more aircraft heading in our direction. The guns roared again and I heard a shout : " They've hit Repulse ! " I looked across and saw smoke and flames rising from her amidships. It gives you a nasty jolt to see another ship hit. I went to the intercommunicating telephone to tell the others down below, and as I clicked the receiver on there was a dull, heavy, shuddering explosion.

THE 35,000 tons of Prince of Wales lifted and settled with a slight list—a horrid, sickening feeling. Verbal comment seemed superfluous. A young Marine standing near me said, " W-was that a t-torpedo ? " and started, quite automatically I'm sure, blowing up the inflator on his air belt. Our speed dropped. The whole set-up was changing and I didn't feel awfully happy. I wondered how the medical parties between decks were getting on. The indescribable din continued. Repulse had been torpedoed two or three times now and was travelling very slowly, listing badly, and on fire, but her guns still flashed defiantly. As I watched her there was another heavy, sickening jolt—it's hard to describe—like a sudden earth tremor, I imagine. Another torpedo struck us and a huge cascade of water drenched us on the bridge. I went into the upper conning position to use the phone and find out if I was wanted below, but it was out of order.

My job was upper deck casualties, so up till now I'd nothing to do but watch it all happening. The Commander came scrambling up a ladder, said " All right here ? " and gave us his grand, tough smile. The ship shook to another explosion. The high-level bombers had hit us with a heavy bomb which crashed through the catapult deck and exploded between decks. My impressions after this were a jumbled medley. I saw the battered Repulse hit again and again, list over more and more and slip below the water, leaving hundreds of bobbing heads, boats, Carley floats and debris.

I SAW the track of a torpedo approaching, and realized that in our crippled condition it was going to hit us. It seemed a horrid inevitability waiting for the explosion that followed. I thought if only it was going to get dark soon we might escape, but it was only midday. We gave a great lurch again as the torpedo tore into us. We were now practically stationary and listing heavily to port.

I realized that we could not last much longer and had a sudden vivid flash-back of our short-lived but exciting commission—10 months full of incident, full of high lights. His Majesty the King coming on board ; the Bismarck action, with H.M.S. Hood blowing up and sinking just ahead of us ; the thrill of taking Winston Churchill across for the Atlantic Charter ; his meeting on board with the American President, Franklin D. Roosevelt, and these two great men in our wardroom ; grimmer memories of fighting, escorting a convoy to Malta, then the sudden trip out East to Singapore, to this.

There were casualties on the upper deck now and several had been brought up inside the superstructure. They were attended to, dressed and given morphia, and those that were unable to look after themselves were carried and placed inside Carley floats, for it was obvious now that we were going to sink soon. I went up top again for more morphia and looking aft through the clouds of smoke saw one of our destroyers manoeuvre alongside the quarter-deck and take off many wounded and as many others as she could manage. She slid clear as our list increased.

The foc's'le now presented an amazing sight, with hundreds of sailors standing placidly smoking and chatting on the sloping deck—they had mostly been driven up from below by the encroaching, rising water. The guns' crews on the upper deck were still at their posts, and there was nothing for the remainder to do but wait for the ship to sink. We enlisted several of them into stretcher and first-aid parties for the wounded. Someone told us there was a man with a broken leg lying in one of the compartments. We tended him, launched him and two of his pals in a float into the sea, now lapping all along the port side of the foc's'le.

I Dived Into the Oily Water

Men started climbing over the rails, and diving and jumping 30 or 40 feet into the sea below ; but " diving " off the high side of a sinking ship is a euphemism ! I took off my cap and my shoes and looked carefully round for somewhere to put them (an extraordinary action which I have read and heard of other people doing). I stood for a minute in the orderly crowd waiting their chance, and heard a sailor say to his pal, " Come on, chum, all them explosions'll have frightened the blinkin' sharks away."

The ship was heeling over more now, and I climbed over the guard rails and slid down to a projection on the ship's side. I stood there and looked down on dozens of heads, arms, and legs in the water, still far below. Then I said to myself, " Please God, don't let me be drowned ! " took a deep breath, and dived into the oily water.

A few minutes later H.M.S. Prince of Wales rolled over, her bows rose in the air, and she slipped out of sight beneath the waves.

CONTROL ROOM OF THE PRINCE OF WALES, a masterpiece of mechanical efficiency, where the Chief Engineer was kept informed of what took place in any part of the ship. After the tragedy, black specks of bobbing heads are seen in the water (left) as survivors struggle towards boats and a destroyer.

Photos, Admiralty, Associated Press

How I Saved R.A.F. Pilots from the Gestapo

Decorated by His Majesty King George VI on February 13, 1946, Mlle. Andrée de Jongh, G.M., 25-year-old Belgian girl, was instrumental in arranging the evacuation of Allied service personnel who were stranded in enemy-occupied territory in Western Europe. Here is her remarkable story, as told in an interview with The News of the World special correspondent. **See also portrait in page 705.**

When my country went to war with Germany I was able to help in a Brussels hospital, as I had studied nursing at evening classes. After the Nazis overran Belgium we soon learned something of the misery of life in occupied territory.

In the hospital I met many wounded soldiers, some Belgian, others French and English, and it was always in my mind that I could do something to help them. But the hospital was under German control. Regulations were severe, and to have helped a wounded man to escape would have meant compromising the whole of the staff.

Each day as I left the hospital and walked to my home to see my parents I read the notices posted on the walls in the streets:

"*ANYONE FOUND AIDING THE ALLIES WILL BE SHOT.*"

But still I knew that I must do something to help. My first chance came by accident. I discovered that my own sister was one of a group of patriots, working underground.

I begged her to give me work to do, and in October 1940 I was asked to obtain information about military traffic in Brussels. But I failed. The information I passed on was not what was needed. Then the hospital was closed down, and through a friend I got in touch with patriots who were hiding British troops. I was asked to get food for them, but again I knew the bitterness of defeat. Obtaining extra food was a hopeless task.

But events moved swiftly. Early in 1941 the Gestapo swooped. Many of my compatriots were thrown into prison and shot. One day I found that I was left working alone with one other friend. We planned our next move together. He knew the South of France well, and thought we could get soldiers to safety by taking them out of that country and into Spain.

The risks, we knew, would be great. But the route to the South of France and Spain was the only one still open. The Germans appreciated this, too, and they patrolled the border between Occupied France and Vichy France, helped by Alsatian dogs and mounted police. But it was worth trying. My friend went off to Bayonne to explore the route, while I was left to think out the problem of obtaining money.

Non-Swimmers Towed to Safety

It was then that I took my first great risk. I decided to go and see the manager of one of our biggest Belgian banks. I knew that if he were not with us arrest was certain. I went alone and talked to him. To my joy he was sympathetic and made available all the money I needed. Afterwards I learned that this was planned with the help of the Belgian Government in London. Messages in code, broadcast by the B.B.C., told the banks that amounts paid out would be placed to their credit in London.

In the meantime, my friend was back from Bayonne. The route was possible, and halting places had been arranged. All was now ready for our first convoy. In July 1941 the first venture was made. My friend and I collected eleven Belgian soldiers, and set off on our journey of nearly 1,500 miles. All had been provided with money and false identity cards. We wore civilian clothes, and travelled openly by day in little groups.

Our plan was simple. Along the route was a series of halting places, and at each we had an agent. One agent passed the escaping party on to the next. We knew, for instance, that we must find the priest in the village of X and give him the password. People in all walks of life were helping us; sometimes a doctor, maybe a greengrocer, or some simple person the Nazis were least likely to suspect. The orders for each day were short. "Go to the cobbler in ——. The password is 'Swallows.'"

All went well and we crossed the River Somme at night in a rowing boat. More than 800 miles to go, but we finally reached our last halting place at Bayonne. Here Spanish smugglers took over and guided the party over the mountains into Spain. The price was £20 a head. My second party was three British soldiers and six Belgian pilots. All went well till we reached the Somme.

To my dismay the boat was gone; we must be suspected. There was no going back; the only way was to swim the river. How many of us could swim? Five. What was going to happen to the other six? Luck was with us, for we found an old motor tire which, inflated, would act as a lifebelt. It worked. Silently, in the darkness, we undressed. First the swimmers slipped into the water and, with bundles of clothes on our heads, we went across to the other bank.

There was not a sound. I swam back again, and one by one we towed the non-swimmers to safety. We dried ourselves as best we could, dressed, and held a council of war. Evidently the Gestapo were after us. We decided to split into two parties. My friend took the six Belgians, and I went on with the three British, arranging to meet again near Paris.

We waited at the meeting place for some days, but the other party did not arrive, and I carried on alone. Later I learned that one of the men we thought to be a Belgian pilot was a traitor. He waited his chance and denounced my friend and his comrades to the Gestapo. Disappointment awaited me at the Pyrenees. My contact explained there was great difficulty in getting the British through Spain, but on the other side of the mountains was a British Intelligence officer who was waiting to arrange the escape route.

I set out with a Spanish smuggler to find him. The first night we walked for eight hours and then hid in a wood until darkness fell. The next night we walked for 12 hours, and when the morning came we were on Spanish soil. It was an exhausting journey up the rough mountain paths, struggling on hour after hour, fearful lest we should be ambushed, and ready at all times to dash away into the darkness.

Later I got to know that journey well, for I made it 34 times, sometimes in bitter weather and the snow up to our knees. Once we were ambushed by frontier guards, but got away. Each time we crossed the Bidassoa, which in mid-winter was a raging torrent. I met the British Intelligence officer, and for three weeks we planned the escape route. When it was done I set out on my return journey alone.

My Father Paid With His Life

With the help of the stars and a compass I kept to my path. In Paris I sent a message to my father. Quickly news came back to me. The Gestapo had arrested my mother and sister and were holding them as hostages. I could not go back to Brussels. I made my headquarters in France, and parties to be taken over the frontier were brought to me.

The work went on, but at length my father was caught, and paid with his life for the part he played. In 1942 the R.A.F. were making their big raids on Germany, and numbers of pilots were brought down in occupied territory. We knew that we must organize their escape. Bombers, using the shortest route in and out of Germany, were mostly brought down in one strip of country, which to us became known as Death Valley.

More than 400,000 men and women were brought into our organization—priests, teachers, doctors, peasants—there was room for them all. A baron organized them into groups of beaters, and each night they went out into Death Valley to find the British pilots. It was a race to get to them before they were caught by the Gestapo. The organization met with great success, but alas, the brave baron, a distinguished Luxemburg banker, was caught and executed.

For a year and a half I carried on, but then I was forced by exhaustion to hand over to another. At long last my good luck failed me. On January 13, 1943, when near the frontier, a Spanish smuggler denounced me to the Gestapo. I was taken back to Bayonne, and afterwards I spent four months in solitary confinement in various French and Belgian prisons.

Later, with thousands of others, I was to know the horror of the concentration camp at Ravensbrueck. Here two out of every three of the women captives died from their experiences. But liberation came, and once more we breathe the blessed air of freedom.

★—As The Years Went By—Notable Days in the War—★

1940

March 13. *Hostilities ended in Russo-Finnish war; armistice signed in Moscow on March 12.*

1941

March 4. *British naval raid on Lofoten Is.*
March 11. *Lease-Lend Bill passed by U.S. House of Representatives and signed by Roosevelt.*
March 13. *First of two successive night bombing attacks on Glasgow and Clydebank.*

1942

March 3. *Japanese air raids on Broome and Wyndham in Western Australia.*
March 6. *Japanese entered Batavia, Java.*
March 8. *Rangoon occupied by Japanese.*

1943

March 3. *Rzhev stormed by Red Army troops.*
March 4. *Two-day battle of Bismarck Sea ended; Japanese convoy sunk by Allies.*

1944

March 14. *14th Army across Chindwin River.*
March 15. *Allied air forces dropped 1,400 tons of bombs on town of Cassino, Italy.*

1945

March 6. *Cologne occupied by U.S. 1st Army.*
March 7. *Americans crossed Rhine at Remagen.*
March 14. *First of new ten-ton bombs dropped by R.A.F. on Bielefeld railway viaducts.*
March 15. *U.S. flag hoisted over Iwojima.*

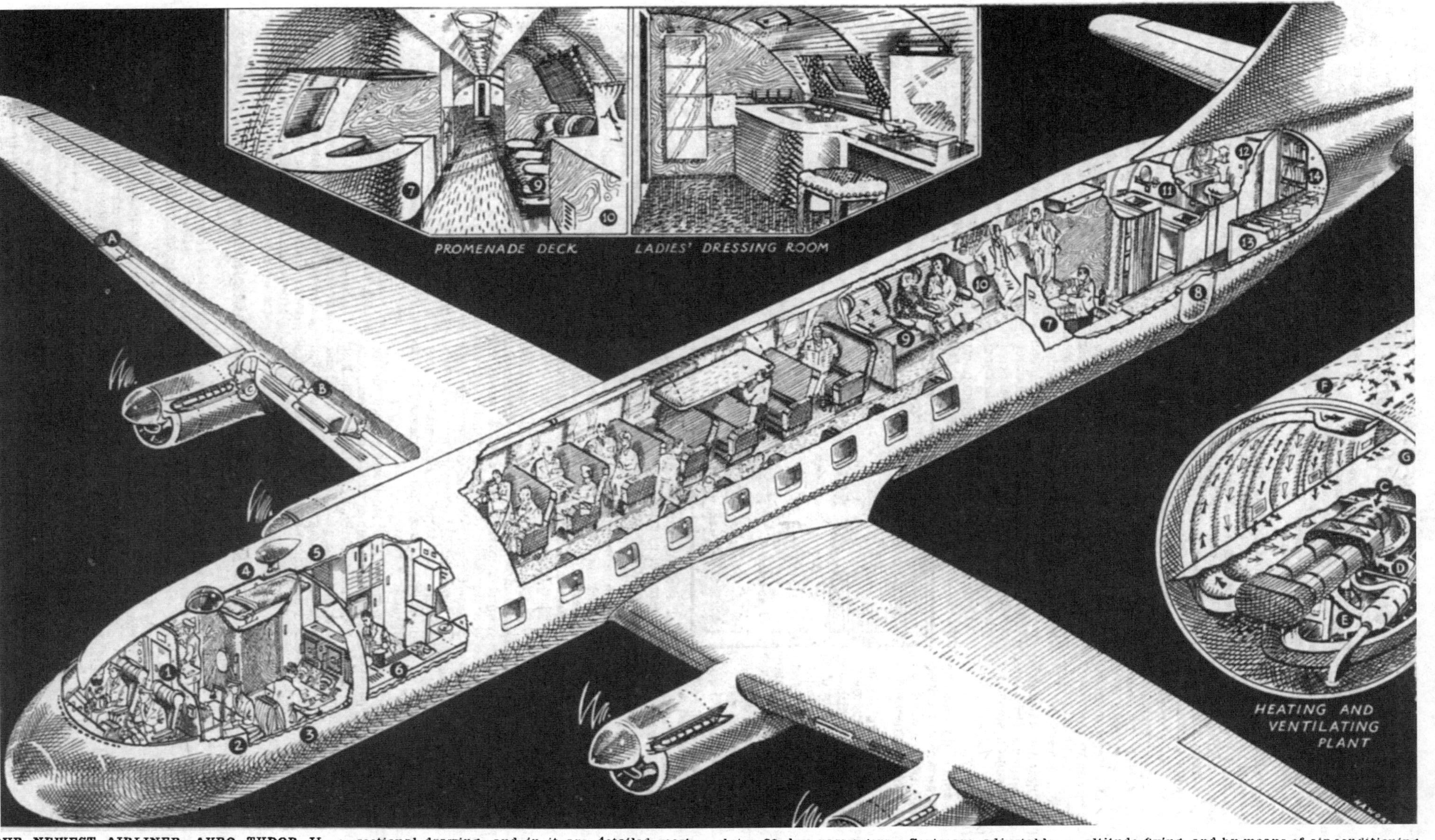

OUR NEWEST AIRLINER, AVRO TUDOR II, built by **A. V. Roe & Co.,** who produced the **Lancaster** bomber, has a wing-span of 120 feet and a length of 105 feet. Weighing 34 tons, it is powered by four **Rolls-Royce Merlin** engines and cost about £100,000 to build. Incorporated in it are the latest developments in navigational instruments, including radar, and the needs of passengers have received particular attention. **Special facilities were given by the manufacturers for our artist, Haworth,** to make this sectional drawing, and in it are detailed most of the aircraft's outstanding features.

The flight deck houses the crew; positions are shown of the captain, who is also chief pilot (1), and (next to him) the first officer and the navigator (2). Across the gangway is the engineer at his control panel. Radio officer (3), crew's rest room (4). Metal grille of safe for important articles and mail (5). Steward in the galley (6).

The main cabin accommodates 40 day or 22 night passengers. An alternative type accommodates 60 day passengers. **Seats** are adjustable to the upright position, and folding bunks are featured: one is seen being lowered into position. The promenade deck is furnished with a cocktail bar (7). Inset is a view through the entrance door (8), showing a settee (9) convertible into a bunk, and (10) a twin bunk folding cabinet. A well-appointed dressing-room for men (11), and the ladies' dressing-room (12) also shown in detail (inset). **Baggage** compartments (13 and 14). The hull of the aircraft is pressurized for high altitude flying, and by means of air-conditioning plant fresh air is constantly circulated throughout the plane.

Air is drawn into the wing and filtered at (A), cooled at (B) and circulated through the plant (inset). Used air is recirculated by means of the fan (C), in conjunction with the mechanisms (D) and (E), which add fresh air and heat respectively before distributing it through the duct (F), and finally through the grilles (G) near each seat. See also facing page.

Blazing New Trails for Air Travel

By CAPTAIN
NORMAN MACMILLAN
M.C., A.F.C.

BEFORE the War, British airliners carried flight stewards on the Continental and trunk routes, to prepare and serve the meals and generally look after passengers' comfort. Lufthansa, flying between London and Berlin, did not trouble about meals en route. For the Germans it was good enough if the passengers could snatch a hasty meal at the trim, clean restaurant at Amsterdam's airport. But Swissair, on the four hours' trip between London and Geneva, flown non-stop, carried air hostesses instead of the stewards of staid Imperial Airways.

Air hostesses were first employed on the American domestic airlines. The scheme was initiated, I think, with the idea that smart girls would give the timid passengers more confidence in flying, in the days when flying was less common than it is today. And as Swissair used American airliners it was appropriate that the air hostess idea should also be adopted, and very efficiently the Swiss girls carried out their duties. They were multi-lingual, and equally at home in Paris, London, Copenhagen or Berlin.

British South American Airlines has adopted the air hostess for the glamorous run to the River Plate. When the Lancastrian "Star Light" took off from Heathrow airport on January 1, 1946, for the first exploratory flight, with Air Vice-Marshal Donald C. T. Bennett in command, there were eighteen persons aboard, including the crew. And the crew included 24-years-old hostess Mary Guthrie, flying in the role of first transoceanic air hostess, the only woman on board. Her war career had led her to this new one. First a V.A.D. nurse attached to the R.A.F. Nursing Service, then a pilot, ferrying aircraft with Air Transport Auxiliary, and now pioneer of a new job for British women, with ports of call at Lisbon, Rio de Janeiro, Montevideo, Buenos Aires, and, in future, Santiago de Chile, all cities of Portuguese and Spanish origin and unrationed luxury.

LANCASTER Bomber Conversion for Temporary Airline Development

Fifteen days were spent on this first proving trip for the latest of Britain's intercontinental airlines. But the "Star Light" cruised at four miles a minute, and took only 28 hours 18 minutes in the air to reach Buenos Aires from Heathrow. Most of the time was spent at Montevideo and Buenos Aires in organizational work for the future of the line. (See illus. in pages 636, 640.)

It is strange to recall that, before the War, Britain had no airline flying to South America, and indeed had no aircraft suitable for this purpose. It was intended to interconnect Britain with Latin South America some day, but the date was never specified. War development of aircraft was so swift that it became possible to prepare for the opening of this route before the War was over. But it must be remembered that the Lancastrian is only a stop-gap plane, a conversion of the Lancaster bomber to temporary use for airline development. It has brought Sydney and London to a space-time of only 63 hours, but it does not carry many passengers. (See illus. pages 481, 504.)

Already the British aircraft industry is hard at work on various airliners designed expressly for civilian use, among them the Vickers Viking, De Havilland Dove, Handley Page Hermes and Avro Tudor. There are two versions of the Tudor, and recently A. V. Roe & Co., Ltd., their manufacturers, kindly gave facilities for WAR ILLUSTRATED's artist to execute the drawings of the larger type—the Avro Tudor II—which are reproduced in the opposite page. Seventy-nine of these aircraft have been ordered for use on the England-Australia, England-South Africa, and England-South America routes.

The most modern long-range airliner actually in service today is the Constellation, and British Overseas Airways are to purchase a number of these American craft for the trans-Atlantic service, an unpopular move in British industrial aviation circles, but one without immediate alternative save the operation of services less efficient than those of American airlines. Disadvantages, of course, are apparent in the dollar cost of the aircraft

MISS M. S. GUTHRIE, hostess of the Lancastrian airliner "Star Light," at Heathrow Airport, London, before its flight to South America. *Photo, P.A.-Reuter*

and the training of the aircrews; but there will be value in the experience of operating these latest American aircraft while our own types are under construction.

The significance of the Constellation to airline operation is easily shown by what these aircraft have already done and are scheduled to do. One broke the U.S.A. transcontinental commercial flight record on February 3 by flying 2,490 miles non-stop from Burbank, California, to La Guardia airfield, New York, in just under seven hours and a half with 45 passengers and a crew of seven. On February 6 the Constellation "Star of Paris," belonging to Transcontinental Western Airways, arrived at Paris from Washington with 35 passengers, making the first regular flight between the U.S. and French capitals. Carrying 30 passengers in bunks they will cut Pan-American Airways' time of flight between San Francisco and Sydney to 30 hours.

The economical cruising speed of the Constellation is 250 m.p.h. and the high cruising speed 280 m.p.h. They can fly at the lower speed from Rineanna (Eire) to Gander (Newfoundland) in 10 hours against a 50 m.p.h. wind, and maintain a schedule of 17 hours between London and New York, and 12 hours between New York and London. They have already flown from Gander to Rineanna in 6 hours 36 minutes, New York to Lisbon in 10½ hours, and New York to Hurn (Hampshire) in 12 hours 9 minutes.

When they travel at 19,000 feet their passenger cabins are pressurized to an artificial level of 6,000 feet, and so, without any discomfort to the passengers, they can travel safely above the height of dangerous conditions where wings are liable to lose their lift through distortion of the airflow caused by ice forming on them, and where engines may lose their power because ice forms within the air intakes. And a high safety factor is assured when cruising at 250 m.p.h., because the four engines need be driven at only 57 per cent of their maximum power to attain this speed.

The older American airliners cannot equal the Constellations, as is shown by the Douglas DC-4 that inaugurated American Overseas Airlines service between America and Scandinavia. En route to Stockholm, this aircraft took 22 hours to reach Copenhagen from Gander. Yet American contact with the times is shown by Pan-American Airways giving cinema shows in its DC-4s, with a silver screen fitted against the bulkhead of the flight deck illuminated by a special type of light-weight projector.

BRITISH Jet-Engined Passenger Aircraft for Atlantic Crossing

It is probable that it will take Britain another two or three strenuous years to make up the leeway, lost by the War, in her development of civil transport aircraft. But it is thought that when she does so she will be first in the field with jet-engined passenger aircraft capable of traversing the Atlantic. This would be a fair reward for all the development work in jet-planes that Britain has undertaken, and the results of which she has so freely given to America as an ally during the War. But I cannot see that the British aircraft industry has any right to suggest holding back the operational development of commercial air routes during the intervening period because it cannot now deliver aircraft with the same characteristics as the Constellation.

There must be recurrent periods of swifter development of some branches of aviation, now in one country, again in another. The British aircraft industry cannot hope to be in the van of every production development every time; and if there comes a period when it is not ahead, should British operators be handicapped because of it?

Quietly and without fuss the R.A.F. Lancaster "Aries" has made aeronautical history of a valuable navigational kind. First came her globe-circling flight, then the flights over the magnetic and geographic poles of the northern hemisphere, and more recently a record-breaking flight from England to Cape Town. It is certain that these flights are accomplished for special reasons, and have definite objects in view.

WHAT these are has not been disclosed, but it is not a difficult guess to make that they are connected with air mobility and operational efficiency of military air forces rather than development of air transport.

There is still much to be learned about navigational control in the areas of the world where it was not practised as highly as within the battle zones. And as the preventing of future war probably depends upon keeping the fighting elements out of the danger areas until they are actually required, the power of swift reinforcement by air becomes of greater importance than it ever was in the War just ended; and to that end a study of navigational geography and the behaviour of the latest navigational instruments used by aircraft has become a subject of profound technical necessity.

The Editor Looks Back

PITY THE OLD HORSE — Apr. 27, 1940

I'm really sorry to see the old horse appearing again in London streets. With Dean Farrar I have always felt that Christianity, for all its humanitarian and ennobling teaching, has no satisfactory explanation of the life and death of the London draught horse. To see those dear old things straining under their loads with no hope of anything beyond a feed of hay and a few hours' leisure in their dark stalls has often given me an acute sense of pain. Their unrewarded suffering is a mystery beyond our solving. Forty years ago, when street traffic was more confused and ill-ordered than it is today, it was not uncommon to see some poor horse standing or lying in Fleet Street or Ludgate Hill with a broken leg or damaged fetlock awaiting the slaughterer. I rejoiced in the coming of motor traction and the horse's disappearance from the thronging City streets. And now they are back again in hundreds ; the first of living things that will be maimed and slaughtered when the bombers get through. I hate the thought. Farrar was right ; our philosophy has no word of comfort for the life of the van-horse in a crowded city. And these devoted servants of man are so absolutely beautiful

IN the present confusion of traffic in London, which we may hope is only temporary, the old horse is still in evidence ; and one has sometimes to bless it for holding up the endless stream of motor vehicles and giving one's car a chance—literally a "break"—when waiting to turn left or right. Doubtless we shall yet see much improvement in the organizing of central London's daily increasing traffic. There was a time in 1919 or the following year, before traffic lights had been devised, when road conditions were even worse than they are today. I remember that on more than one occasion then it took me about 25 minutes to drive my car from Charing Cross to Ludgate Circus !

CHAMBERLAIN GOES — May 11, 1940

In the twinkling of an eye, Mr. Chamberlain's dignified demission and the instant coalescence of all political parties under the War leadership of Mr. Churchill seemed the most natural things to happen, and somehow divorced from party feeling. There are many who regret that the fates have not decreed that he who, more than any other man, saved our country at the moment of its greatest peril by a policy which, in very truth, did make Hitler " miss the bus," should have had the satisfaction of leading it to the victory in which all of us with any spirit or power of endurance so profoundly believe. But in Mr. Churchill we have the ideal War leader in whom energy, vision and experience unite to make a leader completely worthy of our confidence. The Carson-Asquith wrangle over Ireland had a good deal to do with the Kaiser's Germany deciding that the hour had struck . . . fools that they were. It looks to me that the political moves which led to Mr. Chamberlain's resignation—though I am certain he had no more loyal colleague than his successor—may have helped to decide Hitler, who knows little more about the British temperament than a Patagonian, to take the plunge. And, if that were so, events may yet prove that after all the Chamberlain crisis in the House was curiously opportune.

THIS judgement of mine at the critical moment six years ago will, I fancy, have fairly general endorsement today, where political bias does not intervene. My great regret is that political bias did intervene last year before our brilliant War leader had had the satisfaction of taking his proper place at the Peace Conference. I had hoped that party politics would have been kept out of the governance of the country at least till that crowning event. But I am a complete innocent so far as party politics are concerned.

STILL AN ISLAND! — July 6, 1940

Britain is no longer an island we have been told times out of number by writers who like to make our flesh creep in picturing the possibilities of aerial destruction. But, believe me, Britain's hope and confidence reside today in the geographical fact that she *is* an island. The infamous—the almost incredible—French betrayal has brought the enemy's airports nearer to our shores. For it would be lunacy to regard France today as other than an enemy country, since the military poltroons and scoundrelly politicians who are temporarily in power there (if such a term can be applied to creatures who have sold their souls and their countrymen into Nazi slavery) will do just as their Nazi bosses tell 'em to. Thus those of us who have homes on the South Coast can look on clear days across the Channel to a land that teems with our implacable enemies, where once we had every right to suppose only friends held sway, and from these former airports of our treacherous ally it is a matter of minutes to launch attacks upon our shores, such as the futile bombing which I witnessed yesterday.

THAT bombing did not long continue to be " futile," as anyone could see even now who visits our South Coast resorts. But most of these are enjoying a return to prosperity, for after nearly six years without a sight of the sunny waters of the Channel, and longing for that exhilaration which is borne on the salty winds, inland dwellers are crowding in their thousands to the coast once more. Only the lack of labour due to tardy demobilizing is thwarting these towns from putting themselves in better shape to accommodate visitors and regain some portion of their lost revenues. But the fact remains that Britain is still *an island, and it was because of that that we have survived through every devilment invented for our destruction.*

THE FREE FRENCH — July 13, 1940

A feeling of inexpressible sadness comes upon me when I see the fine young " matelots" of the French Navy wandering about the streets of London. It must be a terrible thing to be a sailor in a navy whose government has ratted upon its allies and has sought to hand over its splendid ships to the common enemy. For that is what the action of the traitorous Pétain-Laval junta amounts to. That they can still smile, these brave young sons of the France that was, is a proof that they have not lost heart and will yet bear their parts in voluntarily helping General de Gaulle and Admiral Muselier in the long fight which we must now envisage for victory of the France that is to be. I am sure that all Londoners who encounter these French sailors in their perambulations of our world-famed streets must have the same sort of pathetic admiration for them that I feel.

WHATEVER we may think of De Gaulle as a statesman, we can never forget —nor will History fail to remember—that the renascence of France would still have been a long way off had he not made the stand he did when he came to England to uphold the Tricolour (with the added Cross of Lorraine) as the rallying point of a Free France. It is a pity that De Gaulle lacks the personality which stirs the enthusiasm of the multitude, and the friendliness of those who come in close relations with him. I well remember him frequently lunching at the Savage Club, next door to the Free French H.Q. in Carlton House Terrace, and the air of unapproachability that seemed to envelop him at that very free-and-easy club. The Free French flag that was flying on the top of their building was so enormous that it might have been seen from a raiding plane thousands of feet up. As the neighbourhood was a favourite target for the daylight bombers, a much smaller flag was substituted for the outsize one. The whole of that historic terrace, however, suffered heavy damage, and on its frontage to the Mall it still shows its many wounds.

POSTSCRIPT

A FRIEND just home on a visit from Jerusalem was telling me the other day that his little daughter, aged four or five, has been singing a new version of an old hymn since Viscount Gort succeeded Sir Harold MacMichael as Governor :

All things bright and beautiful,
All creatures great and small,
All things wise and wonderful,
Lord Gort made them all.

"THERE are as many newspapers and periodicals in the United States," I am informed by an American contemporary, " as in all other countries of the world combined, and with only about one-sixteenth of the population." Maybe. But how many of them enjoy one-tenth the reputation of The Times, The Daily Telegraph or The Manchester Guardian ?

BRITISH troops have been warned that a drink being sold to them in the Hamburg area was made from alcohol originally intended as fuel for V2 rockets. That our own troops have an expressive name for it I have no doubt. But what of the Germans ? Might I suggest " Anti-Red Biddy " ?

AFTER reading an account of an inter-Allied celebration of Burns Nicht in Nuremberg, I feel somewhat easier in my mind regarding the future of U.N.O. For, according to one report, " the Russian found the combination of haggis and whisky 'wonderful,' and eagerly discussed the possibility of a similar thirst-provoking dish to be coupled with vodka." If it's thirst they're after, I would recommend a visit just now to the home of both whisky and haggis: Scotland.

THE blatant subtlety (there's no other way of putting it) of American advertising never fails to intrigue me. A New York women's store recently warned would-be purchasers of their nylon stockings that they must be prepared to face a " battle royal " with other would-be purchasers. " We have nylons," ran the advertisement, " but, believe us, having nylons is almost worse than not having them." You will agree, I'm sure, that the operative word here is " almost."

THE Chinese outlook is, to say the least of it, always picturesque. It has been officially announced from Chungking, for instance, that the Chinese version of Mr. Attlee's name has been changed from " Aoteli "—which is virtually meaningless in Chinese—to " Aitehlih," which can be translated as " Fostering uprightness and courtesy." I have always had a deep respect for the Chinese, but I shall be doubly careful in future not to incur their displeasure. The retransliteration of someone else's name—in a derogatory direction—is surely the simplest (and most effective) weapon of insult known to Man.

In Britain Now: Long-Distance Coaches Again

WAR-YEARS SUSPENSION of long-distance motor-coach services came to an end when the London-Blackpool route was operated again, on February 16, 1946. Passengers are seen (right) at the Victoria Coach Station, London, about to take their seats for the first journey; the driver is adjusting the destination sign.

WIVES AND CHILDREN of U.S. soldiers aboard the Queen Mary at Southampton (below) settle into their quarters for the Atlantic crossing, to be reunited with husbands and fathers. The giant liner has been converted to a "nursery" ship, and the interior in many respects resembles a well-appointed floating clinic.

FIREARMS and ammunition of all descriptions from homes throughout Britain were handed in at police stations, following the appeal by the Home Secretary (in the House of Commons on Feb. 14, 1946) to all who possessed them. Proceedings would not be taken against anyone who gave up firearms or ammunition held without a licence by March 31. Above, a police sergeant accepting a rifle to add to his varied collection. By March 1, 4,000 firearms and 50,000 rounds of ammunition had been handed over in London alone.

PLEASURE TRIPS will be a feature of the coming holiday season when the steamers Royal Eagle and Golden Eagle commence sailings from the Tower Pier, London, to Ramsgate, Clacton and Margate. The Royal Eagle (left) is being redecorated, after having served as a flak ship during the war. Both Golden Eagle and Royal Eagle helped, in 1940, to evacuate troops from Dunkirk, where a sister ship, the Crested Eagle, was lost.

Photos, Planet, Associated Press, Topical, Keystone

'Canteen Commandos' to Sail for Singapore

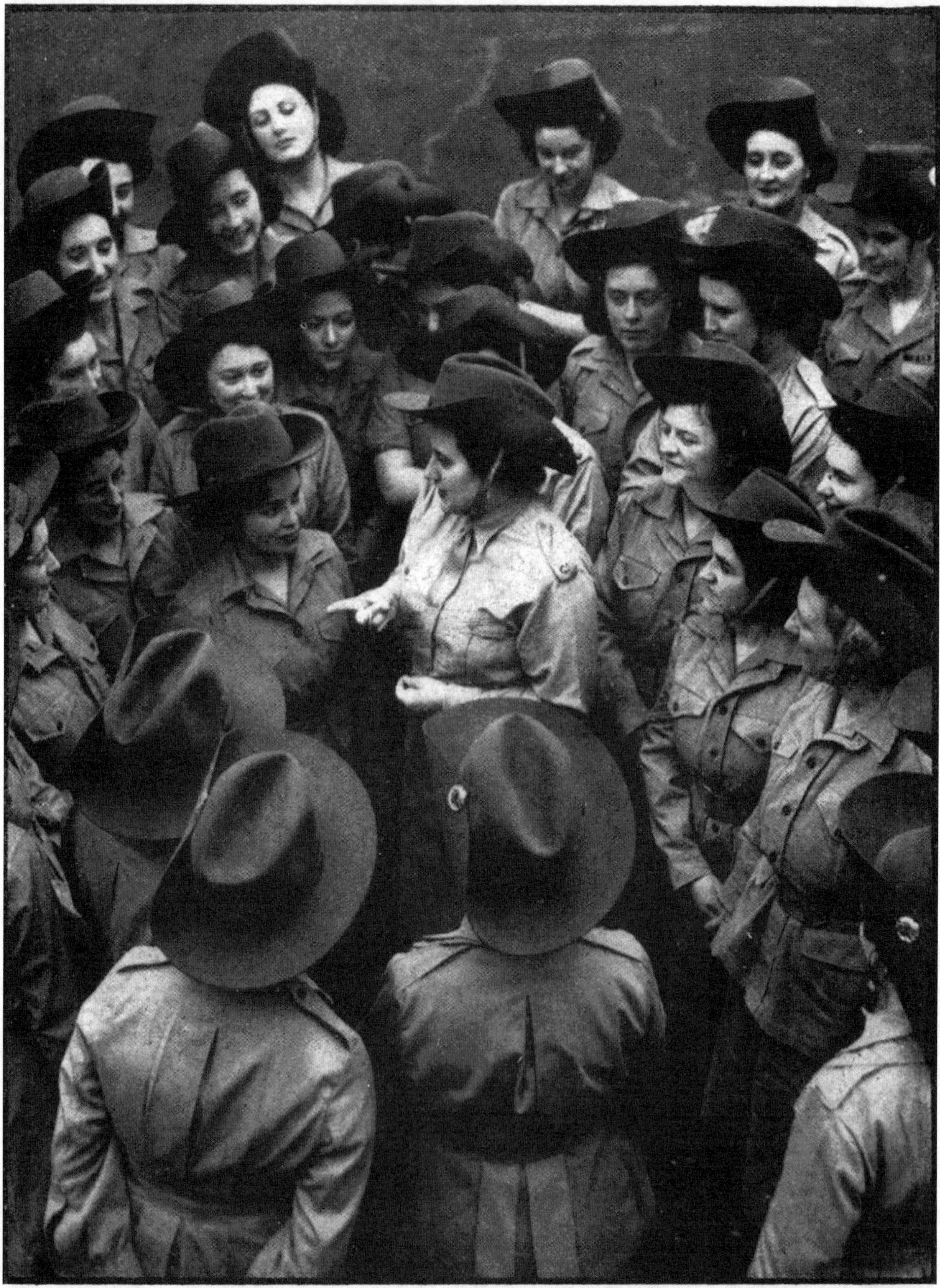

FOR THE FIRST TIME IN N.A.A.F.I. HISTORY girl members of the Expeditionary Forces Institutes (E.F.I.) will shortly be working in the Forces canteens at Singapore. Several are seen—all obviously imbued with a happy spirit of Adventure—listening to a few words of advice, after being fitted out with tropical kit at a centre in London in readiness for the voyage. Some are wearing decorations earned on the various Fronts, where they were popularly known as "Canteen Commandos."
Photo, P.A.-Reuter

Printed in England and published every alternate Friday by the Proprietors, THE AMALGAMATED PRESS, LTD., The Fleetway House, Farringdon Street, London, E.C.4. Registered for transmission by Canadian Magazine Post. Sole Agents for Australia and New Zealand: Messrs. Gordon & Gotch, Ltd.; and for South Africa: Central News Agency, Ltd.—March 15, 1946. S.S. *Editorial Address:* JOHN CARPENTER HOUSE, WHITEFRIARS, LONDON, E.C 4

Vol 9 The War Illustrated Nº 229

SIXPENCE and AFTERWARDS MARCH 29, 1946

MEN OF H.M.S. DEVONSHIRE were in jovial mood when the cruiser docked at Plymouth after one of her trooping voyages from Australia. She had also been employed in troop movements during the Pacific War, and earlier had been on escort and patrol duty in the South Atlantic. Her next and last trooping trip will be from Colombo; then the cruiser will proceed to Scotland, to be converted to a cadet training ship to replace H.M.S. Frobisher. (See pages 585, 591; also page 489, Vol. 6.) *Photo, Fitzgerald*

Edited by Sir John Hammerton

NO. 230 WILL BE PUBLISHED FRIDAY, APRIL 12

Royal Navy Barracks in Roman Emperor's Castle

FORT CASTELL DEL' OVO, in the Bay of Naples (1) where Romulus Augustulus died in 476, is now a "stone frigate" home of British sailors, who are seen at the N.A.A.F.I. canteen (2), and waiting to go "ashore" (3). The sunset ceremony of striking the White Ensign takes place on the battlements (4), beneath which the entrances to apartments (5) are named after British warships.

World's Worst Journey is Ended

By
WEBSTER FAWCETT

DRAMATIC and perilous daily flights from North-East India over the Himalayan spurs with war supplies needed by China ceased at the close of 1945. But the service will not soon be forgotten by those who blazed the trail and those who saw it through to the finish, for reasons outlined here. See also illus. pages 44-45, Vol. 8.

ONE of the most astonishing chapters in flying history began in March 1942, when the Japanese advance in Burma closed the Burma Road, so long a symbol of China's stubborn resistance. President Roosevelt promised airborne aid to China, and a handful of Douglas DC3 transports under Col. W. D. Old soon began implementing his pledge by way of the "Hump" route.

Operating from a poor airfield, with no maintenance facilities, little staff and inadequate ground crews, the pilots never dreamed that the air ferry they were pioneering from Assam across the perilous Himalayan spurs would result in more freight to China than the Burma Road had ever carried. These pilots of U.S. Air Transport Command and Chinese National Airways Corporation were flying an almost uncharted route, with no weather reporting and no fighter protection, while running the gauntlet of attack from enemy aircraft.

There was no radio beam and Col. Old's H.Q. did not possess a radio set, until a wrecked one was obtained and repaired. For the first two months the flyers did not even have oxygen equipment, although they had to fly at 17,000 feet or over. Nor did the majority of the planes have any superchargers to help them to climb the necessary height over the sabre-toothed peaks. For the first six months the weather was so bad that none of the pilots ever saw the country they were flying over—and some of them thought it was just as well!

15 Transports Lost in One Day

Yet within a year the Hump ferry was handling over 3,000 tons of freight a month. More pilots were involved than the entire U.S. air transport system had employed before the War, and traffic soon became greater than that of America's three leading airlines together. Then the R.A.F. began taking part in the regular service in July 1944, and the tempo of Far Eastern warfare quickened, daily flights amounting to 200 aircraft. In October 1944, 20,000 tons of war material was reaching China monthly over the Hump and in January 1945 no less than 44,000 tons were flown in.

One British flyer, Squadron-Leader Michael Vlasto, D.F.C. and Bar, made over 120 crossings with supplies and passengers, through electric storms, gales and snow. An intrepid Canadian, Flying Officer Murray Scott, logged 600 Himalayan flying hours, and a Chinese-Canadian pilot, Capt. Harold Chinn, actually made over 400 Hump journeys within 18 months. On one voyage 75 people were carried and set down safely, an incredible load for an aircraft normally taking only 20 passengers. When the 4,000 h.p. Curtis Commando transport went into action, larger cargoes such as jeeps, dismantled 2½-ton trucks, tanks and rows of pack-mules were carried with impunity.

BUT on one terrible day in 1945 no fewer than 15 Allied transports were lost on the Hump. The score would have been one higher had not Murray Scott and his crew fought a snowstorm for nearly seven hours in the air and then made an astonishing landing at Kunming without either flaps or brakes.

On another occasion, when five Spitfires vanished without trace and a Dakota limped home with a wing torn off by a monsoon squall, a transport pilot found himself getting weak and discovered just in time that all his crew were unconscious. Flying blind through the monsoon with erratic instruments, he had unwittingly been forced to some 30,000 feet.

Things like that were frequently happening. A young pilot finding his C46 icing-up at 12,000 feet gave the order to bale out, and when his crew had gone over the side found he could still fly the plane. He crossed the Hump alone, and five hours later landed at a Yunnan field without his crew but with his plane load intact. Another plane, India-bound from China, became iced so badly that passengers and crew were forced to jump, and then walk to the base through the jungle. It was not till some weeks later that a Chinese colonel—one of the passengers—discovered this was not the customary way of reaching India!

Then there was the exploit of five Americans who parachuted into Tibet and were royally entertained in Lhasa, before their 42-day journey home on foot and by mule. At best, a parachute jump into the precipitous mountains and unexplored gorges meant hardship and grim exposure. At worst—the secret valleys and untrodden peaks have become scrap-heaps of lost planes and graveyards of dead men.

Such was the heavy price paid for the conquest of the "roof of the world." At first it was certain death to go down in this inhospitable terrain, but after the inauguration of a Search and Rescue Squadron in October 1943 more than three-quarters of all the men who baled out over the Hump were saved. Each walk-out party brought added knowledge of the wasteland, and experience helped to develop a standard jungle kit to be dropped to stranded men with rations, medical supplies, fishing tackle and even a portable radio to help them keep in contact with the rescue planes.

Money with which to buy the good will of the hillmen, and extra shoes and socks, were not forgotten, and doctor parachutists were often dropped. As crashed crews tramped back to base, rescue planes (rarely able to land in this difficult terrain) circled over them daily, dropping supplies and guiding them on the long trek home.

The round trip to China and back was 1,100 miles. Many men flew it two or three times a week, and on one exceptional day 565 sorties were flown. As the War progressed, the pace made itself felt in the Hump run. The Allied victories in North Burma enabled aircraft to take a lower, southerly route, and 13,000 feet became the regular altitude for the mountain crossing on the newer, safer line. Over the Hump No. 52 squadron of the R.A.F. operated daily for eighteen months, flying about 15,000 hours with the loss of only one aircraft. The last mission on this worst air journey in the world was flown on New Year's Eve, 1945, by Dakotas of R.A.F. Transport Command, the American service having ended the previous September.

The end of the War made the southern route into China possible, and the saga of the Hump was closed. It had been no blind, unplanned battering at difficulties. Those who blazed this trail had been forced, by reason of enemy aircraft, to risk all on that route which meant registering a height of 17,000 feet and combating weather as bad as was to be found. But when the Burma victories brought a change for the better, those who planned the airway charted the new and somewhat safer line. On this lesser climb the Dakotas crossed the mountains at the more reasonable altitude of 13,000 feet. Even so the journey was no joy-ride for air-crews when at last the R.A.F. closed the Hump route.

IN the end, however, the ferrying of the Himalayas had become so comparatively safe that a three-year-old girl, Wendy Earl, daughter of a British missionary freed from a Japanese internment camp, was flown over the Hump to Calcutta by Pilot-Officer Peter Kearvell. Wendy Earl symbolized the new era of achievement, the conquest of one of Nature's last fastnesses.

ON AN ASSAM AIRFIELD a lorry load of material is being transferred to a U.S. Transport Command plane, for carriage over the Himalayan peaks to distant China. Always the air-crews were faced with the possibilities of having to bale out suddenly over wild country, and of risk of destruction by violent storms prevalent along the route. *Photo, Sport & General*

Fine Record of Our Colonial Troops from Africa

By MAJ.-GENERAL
SIR CHARLES GWYNN
K.C.B., D.S.O.

I DOUBT if the part taken by the troops drawn from our East and West African Colonies is sufficiently appreciated. That is hardly surprising, because there were no war correspondents specially assigned to record their achievements. In the Journal of the Royal African Society (October 1945) Mr. E. E. Sabben-Clare, a Tanganyika District Officer, has, however, given a comprehensive review of the services rendered by the African Divisions in Asia and of the circumstance of their formation. I frankly acknowledge that in this present article I depend mainly on the information he gives.

It is, I think, generally well known that normally no British units are stationed in our East and West African Colonies, and that what might be called the garrisons responsible for local defence and internal security are provided in the main by the King's African Rifles and the Royal West African Frontier Force respectively. Under pre-war conditions these had rather the character of a military police and were composed chiefly of lightly armed infantry units commanded and trained by British officers assisted by a small number of British non-commissioned officers.

Together they numbered about 20,000 men, and although they had rendered conspicuous service in Africa they had practically never been used outside it. In the Abyssinian campaign they had shown themselves more than a match for the best Italian troops, but until after the fall of Gondar the question of using African troops in Asia against the Japanese was not raised, and it was with some hesitation that the decision to do so was taken. The African is liable to home-sickness and is never happy for long when removed far from his family, and finding officers and N.C.O. instructors accustomed to deal with Africans for a force of the size needed was a problem.

EAST African Troops in Ceylon and West Africans in Burma

Furthermore, the African recruited from primitive surroundings and ignorant of any language but his own reputedly took long to train, yet obviously many new recruits would be required ; and to meet the Japanese, then at the height of their reputation as jungle-fighters, a high standard of training was essential in a force which would have to be composed of all arms. Nevertheless, when we became engaged in two wars no source of fighting material could be neglected, and early in 1942 the first East African troops were dispatched to Ceylon.

West African troops could not, however, be spared until the Allied landing in North Africa removed the danger of attack from Vichy-controlled African territory. In the event, neither East nor West Africans were required on active fronts in Asia until the beginning of 1944, though one East African brigade took part in the Madagascar landing and stayed for some time on garrison duties.

Early in 1943, as all danger in Africa had passed, it was decided to use a considerable African force in Asia. The East African contingent in Ceylon was increased to a division, and two independent E.A. brigades were formed later. A West African force of two divisions was, in the middle of the year, sent to Burma, the 81st W.A.D. being the first of the African contingents to come into action. This Division, less one brigade, operated on the Arakan front and advanced into the Kaladan Valley in order to draw off Japanese forces which might threaten the main force moving towards Akyab. Supplied entirely by air it took six weeks, cutting a track 150 miles long, to admit the passage of its guns and motor vehicles before emerging into flats round Kyauktaw.

There it took the dominating Pagoda Hill, but, ordered to demonstrate still farther south towards Akyab, only a small party of E.A. scouts attached to the Division was left to hold Pagoda Hill, and this the Japanese by a characteristic outflanking counter-stroke overran without difficulty. The main army nearer the coast had also by this time been heavily counter-attacked and held up. The Division was therefore forced to retire and fought its way back during the remainder of the dry season, often under difficult conditions, almost to its original starting-point.

WEST AFRICAN WARRIOR, armed with a machete as used on night patrols in Burma. Appreciation of the War services of such well-trained men is expressed in this page. *Photo, British Official*

Meanwhile, the third brigade of the Division had been trained as airborne troops and been chosen to form part of the long-range penetration group co-operating with General Stilwell's force. It was a strange experience for men, many of whom in Africa had never seen aircraft. With the Chindits the brigade took part in many engagements, and acquitted themselves with great credit.

IN 1944 the 11th E.A. Division also came into action. After completing its training in Ceylon it had been transferred to Chittagong in Assam, and from there, in August, it was flown to the Manipur front to take part in the counter-offensive while the monsoon was at its height. Here it became the spearhead of the attack in the Tamu area. In appalling weather it fought its way down the Kabaw Valley and captured Kalewa on the Chindwin, where it established the bridge-head over the river from which the main advance into northern Burma started. This, by general consent, was an exceptionally brilliant operation, for the Kalewa Valley presented many difficulties. On completion of its task the 11th E.A. Division was relieved by the 20th Indian Division.

Meanwhile, the 81st W.A. Division had again taken the offensive in Arakan. In September 1944 it once more advanced into the Kaladan Valley, this time, however, with porters replacing motor vehicles which had proved entirely unsuitable to the conditions. The Division gained much in mobility by the change and manoeuvred the Japanese out of prepared positions by outflanking movements directed against their communications.

There was some hard fighting in January 1945 about Kyauktaw, and after some further successes the Division at the end of the month was relieved by the 82nd W.A. Division, which had arrived in India during 1944. This Division continued the advance southward, outflanking and harassing the rear of the Japanese who were attempting to prevent the series of amphibious attacks by which new air bases along the Arakan coast were being secured.

In the amphibious operation which captured Ramree Island one of the two additional East African brigades which had arrived during 1944 took part, while the other helped to clear the area west of the Chindwin. By this time the African troops in Burma numbered 120,000 men, one-tenth of the whole army employed there. It will be seen that they had taken an important share in the actual fighting, and in addition they had rendered valuable service in the rearward organizations of the army.

PROUD of Their Service Awards and "Mentions"

To meet the great expansion of the original military forces of the African Colonies it had, of course, been necessary to extend the area of recruitment to sections of the population, sometimes the most primitive, that had never before been tapped. For example, the tribes of southern Nigeria contributed their quota, though formerly the R.W.A.F.F. had been recruited from the reputedly martial and more advanced peoples of the northern districts ; yet the new material to a surprising degree lent itself to training.

THE difficulty of finding officers familiar with African mentality was in the first instance met by drawing heavily on those employed in Government service and private enterprises in the country. Northern and Southern Rhodesia and South Africa also made valuable contributions, but it became necessary to employ officers and N.C.O.s who had never before encountered Africans.

Considering the comparatively short period they were in action the casualties among African troops were considerable, though not excessive ; 1,544 were killed or died of wounds, 4,640 wounded and 328 missing—the last figure being surprisingly small. It may be thought that Africans would have been to some extent immune to malaria and would have stood the climate better than British or Indian troops ; but it was found that they had no advantage in this respect and, as in the case of other troops, they owed much to the medical service.

Africans may well be proud of the list (not yet complete) of the Service awards they received. To date it includes 15 B.E.M., 8 M.C., 15 D.C.M., 133 M.M., and 407 mentioned in dispatches, as well as a few still higher distinctions. On the whole, it is evident that the experiment of employing Africans in Asia justified itself. But perhaps the experiment cannot be considered complete until it is seen how the returning troops will be able to readapt themselves to their African surroundings.

Turbulent Factions in India Call for Restraint

MOB VIOLENCE IN BOMBAY resulted in casualties among supporters of mutineers of the Royal Indian Navy on February 19-20, 1946, when they clashed with British troops called out to restore order: Army trucks patrolling the streets (1). The scene after police had charged demonstrating students (2) during the birthday celebrations of Chandra Bose, former head of the "Government of Free India," on January 23. Troops (3) preparing to meet rioters, and later (4) deployed across a street.

Turkey's Wartime Aid to the Allies

By

FRANCIS E. McMURTRIE

THROUGHOUT the critical days when our armies were fighting to retain their foothold on the borders of Egypt, while our fleet with difficulty held its own against superior enemy forces in the Mediterranean, Turkey was in an exceedingly awkward position. Her tradition of friendship with this country, so rudely broken in 1914, had been renewed under the rule of Kemal Ataturk.

Every effort was made by the Germans, Italians and Japanese to persuade Turkey that the cause of the Allies was a hopeless one, and that her only chance of survival was to throw in her lot with the Axis. In spite of this ceaseless cajolery, the Turkish Government remained steadfast in its attitude of benevolent neutrality towards Britain—a much more useful line of conduct than open alliance, for which the armaments at Turkey's disposal were quite inadequate. Indeed, it would have suited Germany well at one stage to have been able to treat Turkey as an enemy, as it would have given her the opportunity of occupying further Aegean bases.

In 1914 Turkey had been placed in an even more difficult position. At the outbreak of war on August 4, the political situation in Constantinople was very unsettled. A weak Government was being pressed by a strong opposition, known as the Young Turk party, to side with the Germans; but this pressure was resisted until the German warships Goeben and Breslau, fleeing from the British Mediterranean Fleet under Admiral Sir Berkeley Milne, entered the Dardanelles on August 10, and were permitted to anchor.

It was then arranged that the two ships should be sold to Turkey, but the transfer of ownership remained little more than nominal, as the German officers and men remained on board both ships. Though the Government still strove to cling to a semblance of neutrality, the decision was taken out of their hands when Russia declared war upon Turkey at the end of October. All the Allied Ambassadors quitted Constantinople on November 1, and two days later the British fleet proceeded to bombard the forts at the entrance to the Dardanelles.

One of the contributory factors in swaying the Turkish decision is known to have been the requisitioning by the Admiralty of two battleships (renamed Agincourt and Erin) and four destroyers, which were building in British yards for the Turkish Navy. Though a clause in the builders' contracts justified this measure, Turkish opinion took the view that such action should not have been taken without preliminary negotiation. In fact, the purchase of the Goeben and Breslau was held to be excused by the need for replacing these battleships and destroyers. A similar situation might well have arisen in the war which has lately concluded. There were building in British yards in 1939 four destroyers, four submarines and two small minelayers, all of which might have been requisitioned perfectly legally had the Admiralty followed the precedent of 1914. Instead, the question was opened through diplomatic channels, as a result of which the Turkish naval authorities proved willing to take a reasonable view of the matter. It being clear that British need for ships was fully as great as in the previous war, there was no difficulty in arriving at a compromise which proved satisfactory to both countries. Naturally, the enemy could only guess at the arrangement ultimately reached.

This was that Turkey should take delivery in due course of two of the destroyers, the Demirhisar and Sultanhisar, and the two little minelayers Sivrihisar and Yuzbasi Hakki. The remaining six vessels were all placed at the disposal of the Royal Navy for the duration of hostilities.

ESCORT Duties From Gibraltar to Malta Under Heavy Fire

The destroyer Muavenet, when she was completed in January 1942, became H.M.S. Inconstant, and two months later her sister ship, the Gayret, was commissioned as H.M.S Ithuriel. The submarines were the Oruc Reis, Murat Reis, Burak Reis and Uluc Ali Reis, all named after Turkish admirals. They became H.M. submarines P.611, 612, 614 and 615 respectively. All six units were built by Messrs. Vickers-Armstrongs, Ltd., at Barrow-in-Furness.

Both the destroyers figured in Admiralty communiqués in the course of the War. The Inconstant engaged a U-boat which attacked a convoy under her escort off Algiers in 1943, and succeeded in destroying the enemy submarine. And in August of the preceding year the Ithuriel was one of the ships under Vice-Admiral Sir Neville Syfret that escorted a convoy from Gibraltar to Malta in the face of savage attacks from enemy submarines and aircraft. In the course of this operation the Ithuriel rammed and sank the Italian submarine Cobalto.

No particulars of the activities of the four submarines have so far been released. P.615 was unfortunate, being sunk by a U-boat off Freetown on April 18, 1943, but the other three survived the war and have since been handed over to the Turkish Navy. It is understood that a British submarine is to be given to Turkey in replacement of the P.615, and that she will be given the name Uluc Ali Reis in memory of the lost vessel.

INVALUABLE Assistance Against the Germans in the Dodecanese

With due ceremony the Inconstant (now again the Muavenet) hoisted the Turkish colours at Istanbul on March 7; but the Ithuriel had received extensive damage through striking a mine, and has therefore been sold for breaking up, and another destroyer, H.M.S. Oribi, has been assigned to the Turkish Navy in her stead. The latter is somewhat bigger than the Ithuriel, having a displacement of 1,540 tons against the latters' 1,360 tons, but they are similarly armed, each mounting four 4·7-in. guns.

This, of course, by no means completes the record of aid furnished by Turkey during the War. When the first abortive attempt was being made to drive the Germans out of the Dodecanese Islands in the closing months of 1943, Turkish assistance was invaluable. Our warships and supply vessels made use when necessary of Turkey's territorial waters in the sure knowledge that, whatever diplomatic protest might be made, no solid hindrances would be placed in their way. After the enterprise had clearly failed of its object, British and Greek troops in Samos were able to withdraw through Turkish territory.

During the British advance into Syria the resistance of the Vichy forces was limited by the fact that they were unable to obtain supplies or sympathy from Turkey; and when a number of small craft and auxiliaries took refuge in Turkish waters after the collapse of armed resistance, these ships were promptly interned. Two were taken over by the Turkish Navy, but one of these, the oiler Adour, has now hoisted the Tricolour again. In the Turkish Navy especially, sympathies have always been strongly with this country, which in the past has repeatedly furnished it with its best ships and with the services of officers for training purposes.

TURKISH SUBMARINE Murat Reis (above) served during the War as H.M. Submarine P.612. The destroyer Sultanhisar (top), is a sister ship of the Muavenet which served with the Royal Navy as H.M.S. Inconstant for the duration of hostilities. Both the Muavenet and the P.612 have now gone back to Turkey.

Momentous Homecoming of H.M.S. Formidable

THIS 23,000-TON AIRCRAFT CARRIER arrived at Portsmouth on February 5, 1946, from the Far East, with the paying-off pennant flying from her mast-head. The enthusiasm of those greeting her from the shore is matched by her homecoming company. The Formidable left England in September 1944, and the following May fought off a Japanese air attack but was hit and set on fire. It was from her flight-deck that the first British carrier-borne aircraft attacked the Jap mainland. See also illus. page 480. *Drawing by C. E. Turner, by courtesy of The Illustrated London News*

Ex-German Warships Sail for Soviet Ports

UNDER RUSSIAN COMMAND, units of the German fleet concentrate at Kiel preparatory to leaving for ports in the U.S.S.R., in fulfilment of the Potsdam Agreement. They comprised three small destroyers, the cruiser Nurnberg (1), of 6,000 tons, the battleship Hessen, built in 1903 and now a wireless controlled target ship (2), and the naval depot ship Otto Wunsche, German members of whose crew are seen leaving (3). The torpedo boat Blitz, which operated as control vessel of the Hessen, built in 1910, was included.

Photos, British Official

France's Navy is Coming into Its Own Again

FROM BRITAIN'S SHARE OF THE GERMAN FLEET, eight destroyers of four different types were handed over to the French, in a gesture of friendship, at Cherbourg, on Feb. 4, 1946. The Tricolour flies from their mastheads during the ceremony (1). At Toulon, scene of the scuttling of the French Fleet on Nov. 27, 1942, the Richelieu (2), returned from the Far East, was in Feb. 1946 awarded the Croix de Guerre by Admiral Lemonnier who is seen (3) conducting the investiture on board, when he also decorated 80 officers and ratings.

Photos, Keystone, Planet News

U.S. 8th Army Air Force Says Goodbye to Us

"OLD GLORY" COMES DOWN FOR THE LAST TIME at Honington, Suffolk, only remaining airfield in Britain occupied by the famous U.S. 8th A.A.F. The airfield was handed back to the R.A.F. on Feb. 26, 1946, when a simple ceremony was attended by Air-Marshal Sir James Robb, C.-in-C. R.A.F. Fighter Command, and General Emil Kiel, last commander of the 8th A.A.F. in England, seen shaking hands (inset), and (above) saluting the American flag as it is hauled down to be replaced by that of the R.A.F. *Photos, P.A.-Reuter*

Limbless Ex-Servicemen Now Walk—and Work

Miracles of artificial limb-fitting are being performed at the Roehampton, Leeds and other centres, so that even those who have lost both arms and both legs become not only thoroughly self-reliant but skilled and employable again. Photographs in this and the two following pages were specially taken to illustrate this article by FRANK ILLINGWORTH.

A FEELING of immense pity surges up when first you enter a "limb-centre." How could it be otherwise when you see a young man with both arms, both legs and an eye gone, trying to play the piano with artificial limbs; an armless man learning to shave himself again; a legless one taking his first uncertain steps with a wheelbarrow?

I, with my two legs and two arms, felt self-conscious walking behind the day's quota of new arrivals—a boy of twelve who lost a leg to the Luftwaffe, a girl armaments worker who lost a hand when a faulty fuse exploded, and a score of ex-Servicemen returning to the limb-centre for further fittings. But long before you leave Roehampton or the Leeds Limb-fitting Centre, or those at Glasgow and Cardiff and elsewhere, the pity gives place to a certain knowledge that these who are maimed have a future to look forward to.

"Once they leave us they're able to fend for themselves," I was told at Roehampton. And after a day spent there, and another at Leeds among 400 men with half the requisite number of limbs, I can confirm that, given a chance by employers, the maimed can make a living.

By way of example, take the case of five armless men who left the Leeds centre together: all are in full employment; two of the quintet have earned three increments, and one, Sergeant W. Edwards of Rochdale, is a sparetime gym instructor.

He Now Shaves Without Arms

It must be stressed that the limb-centres have no part in giving the maimed a trade. Their sole purpose is to fit the armless and the legless with limbs and train them in their use. And in this they are doing magnificent work. But much depends on the man himself. "We can give him arms and legs that work," I was told, "but he's got to have the will to win through, like that fellow over there—from Tobruk. Ask him if you can light his cigarette."

Diffidently, I proffer help, and receive the reply: "No, thanks. I've got to learn to use these—er—things." The lad from Tobruk held a matchbox in a steel hand resembling a large paper-clip and a match that kept dropping from another metal "grip." He found it difficult to pick up the match because he had yet to learn how to use his hinged legs. But he said: "I'm learning fast, thanks."

WHEN possible, surgeons remove limbs at points suited to the wearing of artificial attachments. Recovered, and fitted for a limb at the centre, the soldier or civilian awaits the arrival of his new arm and/or leg. Then it is that the testing time arrives. Manipulation of the new attachment raises the old, hankering question: "Will I be able to earn a living?"

Many a man breaks down under the test; and it needs constant encouragement on the instructor's part to build up the will to win through. The case of an ex-soldier with both arms and legs and one eye missing illustrates this point. He learned to dress himself, use knife and fork, saw wood, wield a cricket bat, and type. When he faltered, the instructor was at his side: "If I can work a farm and run a pub in my spare time with one arm, you can shave yourself—arms or no arms." He shaved himself. He learned to dig, and play billiards. He was doing well, had confidence in his "attachments." Play the piano? Of course he could. His artificial legs controlled the pedals, the steel "fingers" of his right hand ran along the keys after a little practice, and those of his left hand were soon almost as good as his right.

But, blind on his left side, he could not see all the keys properly. Here was something he could not do; what else would he find to be too much for him? This small defeat threatened his whole future, until the instructor made the suggestion that he should

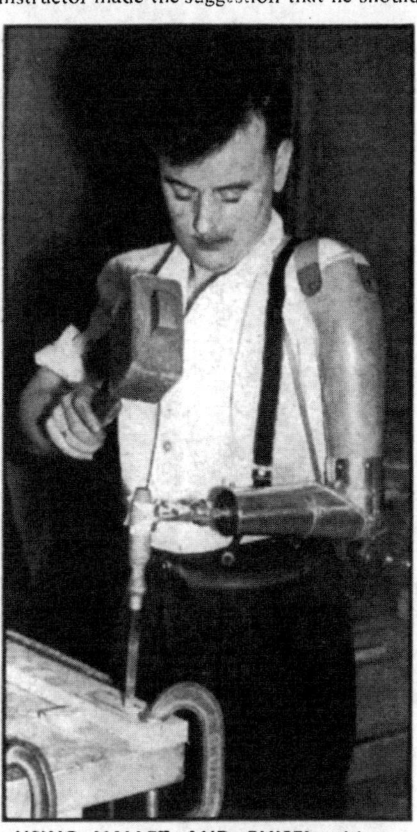

USING MALLET AND CHISEL with an artificial left arm presents few difficulties to this ex-Serviceman at Roehampton.
Exclusive to THE WAR ILLUSTRATED

sit sideways at the keys. A few hours later he was playing jazz; and today he is in full employment.

While I listened to this tale my eyes followed a young man wearing an artificial arm for the first time. Like a child with a new toy he moved from one thing to another. He used a hammer, plugged another attachment into the wrist socket and wheeled a barrow. The sink caught his eye and he washed a perfectly clean hand. With successive attachments he wielded a cricket bat, typed, planed a block of wood, slipped a few essential attachments into a suitcase, clipped his "dress" hand into the wrist-socket and went to his quarters.

Given careful selection of employment, the limbless can attain one hundred per cent efficiency. There is an instance where an employer refused the application of a legless arc-welder, with only one thumb and finger, for a change of employment—on the grounds that he was doing such highly skilled work that he could not be replaced. The armless are holding down jobs on their merits as precision instrument makers, capstan operatives and machinists; they are to be found in stamping mills, aircraft factories and spinning mills.

This is made possible by advances in limb design. Following the First Great War, many an ex-soldier put his artificial limb away in a drawer and went on the dole. Today, leather-and-metal legs contain knee mechanisms that return a flexed limb with every step, permitting ease of movement, even grace of movement.

Making 9,000 Limbs a Year

Artificial arms weigh only 3½ lb., yet offer a wide range of movement and considerable strength. At the Leeds Limb Centre, the instructor crooked his arm and said: "Tug at it; no, not like that, *tug!*" It remained as rigid as a wall. The socket and shoulder-harness remained firm, and there was no "give" in the elbow mechanism. The latter, fitted with a metal lever, is operated by a strap passing across the shoulder muscles. Flexed, they tauten the strap and release the lever; relaxed, the lever locks the elbow in whatever position the wearer favours for the moment.

A certalmid hand (made of waxed linen for lightness) for "dress" purposes and a set of "working appliances" complete the arm. The latter are designed for specific purposes. The "hook" is the general purpose attachment, but a wide range of "grips" are at the wearer's disposal.

In 1939, some 300 employees (many of them limbless), at one of the Roehampton limb-factories, turned out 5,000 limbs annually and repaired 55,000. Today, with the hospitals gradually emptying, the demand is mostly for "first limbs"; and the legless supervisor (one would never imagine him to be limbless) told me that the factory employs well over 500 trained men with an annual production of 9,000 limbs from adult to the number one child's size.

LIMBLESS children offer perhaps the saddest aspect of total war. But when amputation does not impair physical health the legless or armless child need never be a charge on the State. At Roehampton I saw a cine-film of legless children riding bicycles, somersaulting, romping like any ordinary youngsters. Indeed, it would have been hard to believe that they wore man-made legs but for the fact that they wore specially short trousers for the occasion. Surgeons from the Dominions, America and every one of the liberated European countries, who visit Roehampton to study a department of healing which is more advanced in Britain than in any other country, have seen this film.

Hope in the Future is Reborn

Meanwhile, at the limb-centres new arrivals are being told: "You can do it, but it depends on you. We can give you limbs, but YOU have to win through with them." Determination is built up by alternately encouraging and shaming the faltering man to try again. And, with success, hope in the future is reborn to blossom into certainty when the limbless man or woman walks out of the centre, certalmid hand holding a suitcase.

Therein are the "working fingers." The legless need no help in boarding train or bus taking them home. The armless need no help in opening the suitcase, placing the shaving "grips" in the bathroom, the hair-brush "grips" on the dressing-table, those for eating in the sideboard, and those for work in valise or tool-bag. All they want now, these men and women with man-made limbs, is for employers to give them the chance of proving their worth.

At Roehampton Disabilities Are Surmounted—

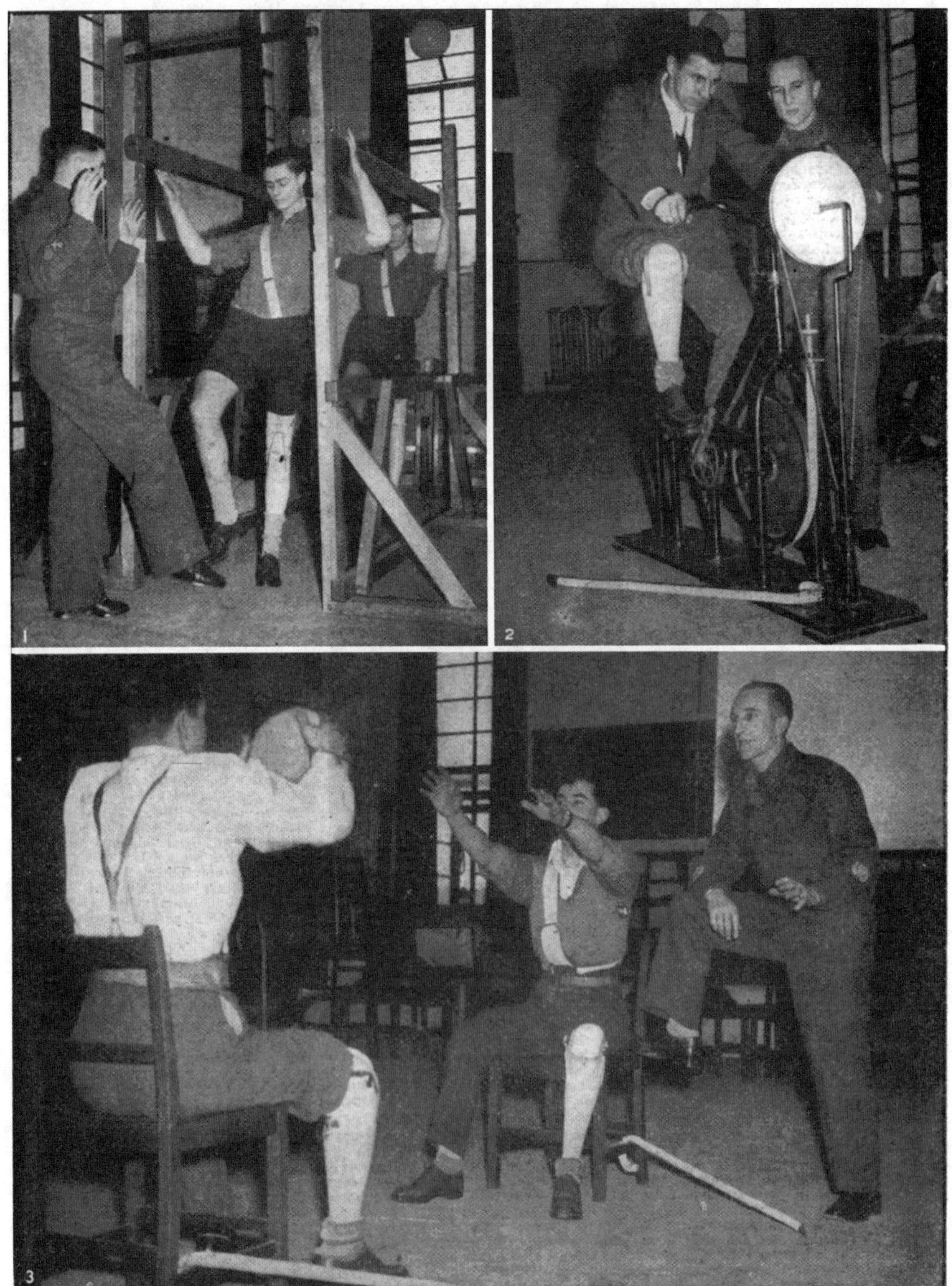

IN THE GYMNASIUM at the Roehampton hospital for Servicemen who have been fitted with an artificial limb, or limbs (see page 747), walking rails (1) assist the patient in the early stages of recovery to acquire confidence and ease of leg movement. Progress in correct and comfortable manipulation of the artificial leg is ensured through exercise on a stationary cycle (2). To strengthen muscles weakened by operations and lengthy bedridden periods, medicine ball practice (3) is carried out.

Exclusive to THE WAR ILLUSTRATED

—and Occupational Skill Triumphantly Regained

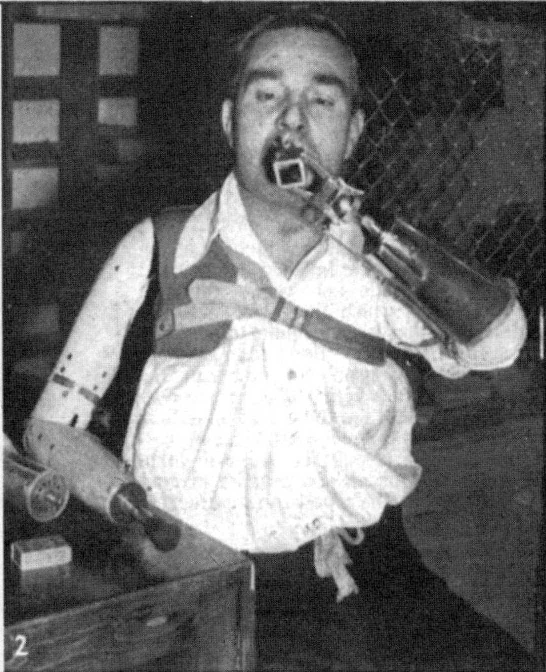

HIGHLY INGENIOUS DEVICES easily clipped to artificial arms enable pleasures and pastimes to be indulged in with little restriction. Even the more strenuous forms of gardening (1) are successfully attended to, and smoking a cigarette in the hospital workshop (2) call for no assistance.

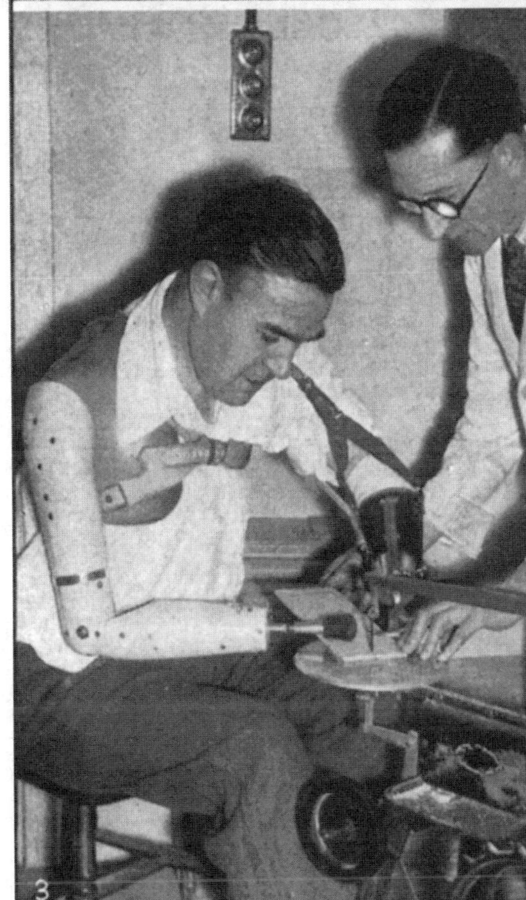

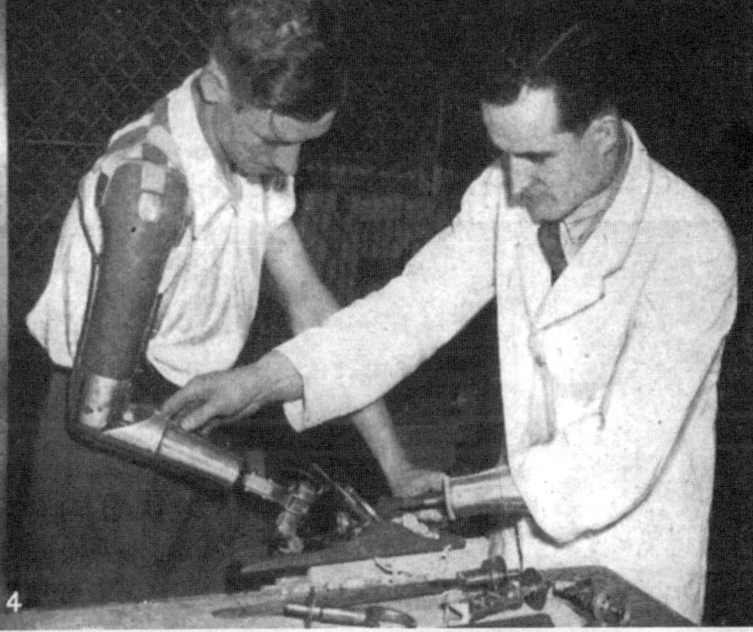

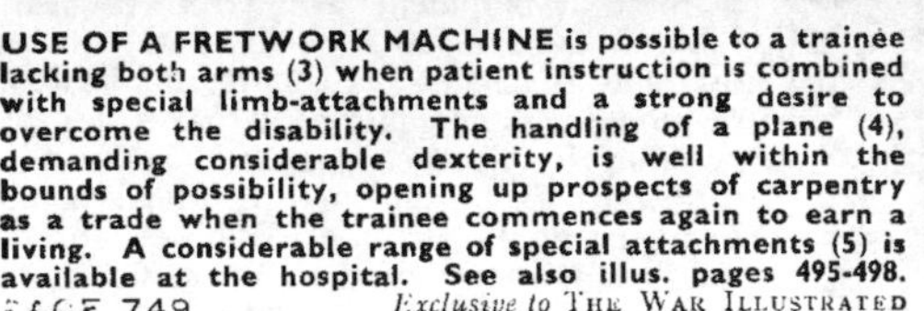

USE OF A FRETWORK MACHINE is possible to a trainee lacking both arms (3) when patient instruction is combined with special limb-attachments and a strong desire to overcome the disability. The handling of a plane (4), demanding considerable dexterity, is well within the bounds of possibility, opening up prospects of carpentry as a trade when the trainee commences again to earn a living. A considerable range of special attachments (5) is available at the hospital. See also illus. pages 495-498.

Now It Can Be Told!

HOW RADAR HELPED OUR FIELD ARTILLERY

A CONSIDERABLE amount of publicity has been given to radar as used for anti-aircraft purposes. It is now possible to reveal how the Ministry of Supply Radar Research and Development Establishment (known as R.R.D.E.) at Malvern found even further uses for it.

In both Great Wars a vast number of the casualties suffered were inflicted by mortars: those highly mobile and very formidable weapons against which the trench, wall, or usual cover, affords inadequate protection. To beat the mortar a solution had to be found to the following problem: how can the mortars be spotted with sufficient accuracy and speed to enable fire to be brought to bear on them before they are moved? In considering the problem it must be borne in mind that mortar teams make a practice of constantly changing their position in order to confuse the other side.

It was only when the War was in its fourth year that the old methods of locating, based on sound-ranging or actual visual spotting, began to be superseded. Existing methods were successful only under very favourable conditions and did not, therefore, by a long way solve the problem; with the result that mortar casualties remained high. Then radar became a decisive factor in the fight, locating mortars with such accuracy and speed that gun-fire could be brought down on the target within a very short time of the first mortar bombs falling.

Difficulty Cleverly Solved

It had been found during research that some radar sets were able to "see" mortar bombs in the same way that aircraft could be "seen." Thus, when the bomb passed through the radar beam its trajectory could be plotted and its point of origin determined. Work was urgently undertaken at R.R.D.E. by the scientists, R. G. Friend, G. H. Beeching and C. G. Tilley, on the adaptation of existing anti-aircraft radar to this use.

There was, however, one especial difficulty: owing to the limitations to vision caused by hills, etc., it was not possible for a radar set to "see" the bomb during the early part of its flight, and therefore the plot excluded the vital portion. An ingenious way round this difficulty was found by R. I. B. Cooper and W. T. Stone, who produced a device for attachment to the radar which gave location to a high degree of accuracy. A gallant attempt was made by D. R. Chick, of R.R.D.E., to produce a highly mobile equipment especially for this role. Bad luck at the end of the European war defeated the attempt, but development still continues.

The difficulty of detecting the movement of enemy vehicles and troops by night or in fog without making use of lights or flares has, to a certain extent, been overcome by radar equipment of special design. This equipment, designed by C. A. Walley, working under E. W. Chivers and Dr. A. E. Kempton, is fully mobile. It is capable of detecting the movement of vehicles, trains and bodies of troops at very considerable distances.

Warning to operators of any movement is given by a note on a loudspeaker. It is easy to imagine the effect of such a set had it been produced in time to watch certain road junctions during the liberation of France. Immediately the enemy began to move by night, a heavy and accurate concentration of fire would have descended upon them, making movement impossible.

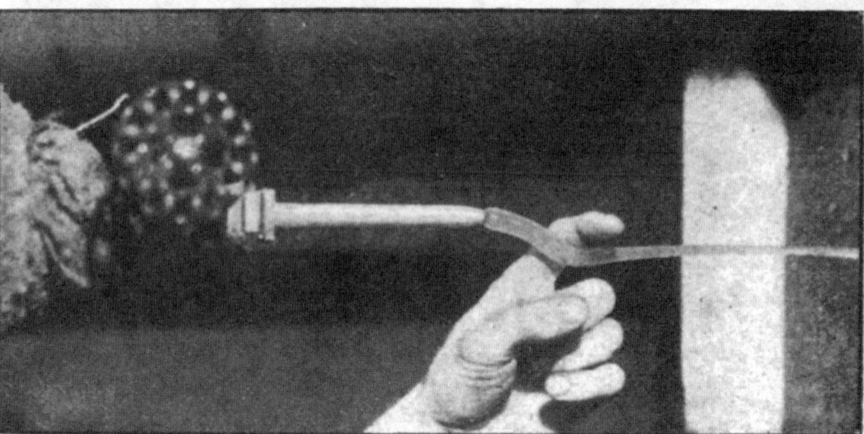

DRAGON'S BREATH—FLAME-THROWER FUEL was one of the most remarkable wartime discoveries made by the Department of Scientific and Industrial Research. A liquid, it becomes almost solid in air, and can be diverted, as seen above, without breaking the jet. It can be shot as far again as any other flame-thrower fuel and five times as much can be deposited on the target. See also illus. page 612, Vol. 8. *Photo, British Official*

When guns are bombarding small targets it is necessary for an observing officer, in a position well forward of the guns, to correct the fire by visually observing the fall of the shells on the ground. It is not difficult to realize that this method of controlling fire is impossible in darkness, fog and bad visibility, with the result that in these conditions shells cannot be corrected.

The Enemy Were Astonished

Dr. Kempton and F. J. M. Farley set to work on this problem, and radar equipment can now, in certain circumstances, take the place of the observer, inasmuch as it enables the radar operators to see on the cathode ray tube both the target and the position of the fall of the shell in relation to the target. From this information correction to range and line can be applied, until the target and the fall of the shell are seen on the tube to coincide—in other words, when the target is actually being hit.

As in the case of all radar, equipment is not handicapped by darkness and fog. On occasions during the War the enemy were astonished to find themselves subjected to heavy gun-fire which had obviously been "corrected" on to the target, when it was impossible for any observer to see more than a few yards. They did not know that the correction was being made by the use of radar.

It is interesting to note that the major part of these developments arose from the use of radar in a role for which it had not been originally designed. Such is the flexibility of modern radar equipment that it has been possible, by close co-operation between the Research Establishment at Malvern and Army users, to adapt existing sets for new roles as an interim measure in the field, while special equipment is still under development.

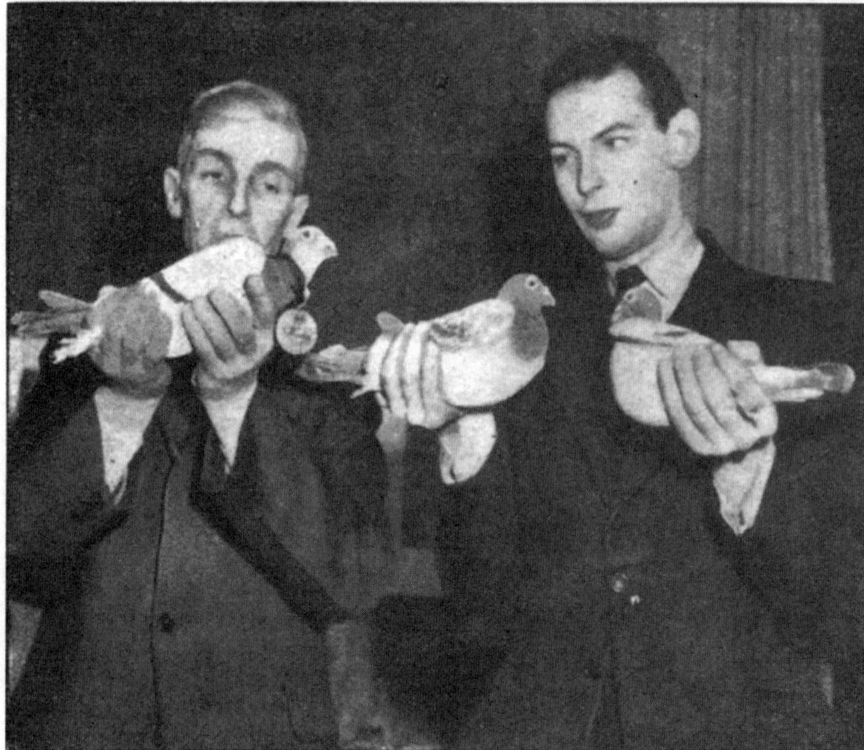

AWARD OF THE DICKIN MEDAL TO "TOMMY" revealed how this pigeon was found exhausted in Holland, having gone off its course during a race in England. A Dutch patriot kept the carrier bird until he acquired military information; this he attached to its leg, and released it. The pigeon arrived home in Lancashire on August 19, 1942, the message proving of considerable value to the Authorities. Above, the owner of the bird, with its decoration, and the Dutch patriot with two pigeons presented to him by the R.A.F. See also illus. page 696, Vol. 8. *Photo, New York Times Photos*

Decoys that Deceived the Enemy

These British devices for tricking the enemy so impressed high-ranking U.S. officers that the Americans commenced manufacture of them on their own account. Pneumatic Sherman tanks and a lorry (1) designed to deceive the Germans at 500 yards; here they are seen at 120 yards. One could be packed into a holdall a little larger than a cricket-bag; inflated in five minutes to Sherman size it weighed only 170 lb., against the 35 tons of its metal counterpart. Special anchorages prevented displacement in high winds. Dummy 25-pounder gun, trailer and towing vehicle (2), rigid when erected, looked real at 500-1,000 yards. Fake L.C.T.s (3), 160 feet long, erected and launched in six hours, were used as a decoy in a South-East coast harbour when we were preparing for the invasion of the Continent.

Photos, British Official

Our Merchant Navy Throngs With Every Tide—

Shackles and wounds of war not yet forgotten, men and ships serving under the old " Red Duster " are staging a magnificent peacetime come-back. At the Port of London 90,000 cases of Valencia oranges are seen (1) being unloaded, and (2) in the warehouse ready for distribution. Cars in increasing numbers are being exported: in the King George V Dock a lighter (3) loaded with motor vehicles in crates noses in between the Gleniffer, bound for the Far East, and the Gascony.

Photos, [illegible]
Stan[illegible]

—Through London's Gateway to the Seven Seas

Evening
one

Hub of the world's shipping, the Thames docks were on February 22, 1946, busy with the greatest number of ships—120—gathered there on any day since the War began. Tea, sufficient for two thousand million cups, constituting a record shipment, was brought to the West India Dock by the Empire Allenby: lighters (4) were landing the 106,778 chests on February 20. The King George V Dock (5), with long lines of vessels berthed for loading or discharging.

War's Ravages are Vanishing from Greece

Photos, Associated Press

The United Kingdom agreed on January 25, 1946, to provide from military stocks material for the repair of Greek land communications and the rebuilding of houses. Other material and transport are being supplied by U.N.R.R.A., but largely the reconstruction of a village depends on its inhabitants. Children shovel sand (1) for making plaster needed for the new school. Two peasants retile a cottage roof (2). The result of communal effort: a village completely restored (3).

"Carrier War"

Reviewed by HAMILTON FYFE

Few knew at the time how low our defensive strength had sunk after Dunkirk, but we have been told often enough since. Fewer still realized how weak the American Naval and Naval Air Forces were after Pearl Harbour, and not many here in Britain—perhaps not even in the United States—have yet come to a full realization of the immense effort that was required to overcome that weakness.

The most informing book on the subject that I have read appeared lately in New York, published by Simon and Schuster at $2.50. It is called Carrier War, and the writer, Lieut. Oliver Jensen, U.S.N.R., though he is concerned mostly with the war in the air, manages to give a comprehensive picture of the Central Pacific campaign from the time when the U.S. fleets were able to take the offensive until nearly the end of 1944.

It is a stirring tale he has to tell and one that in its details will be new to most British readers. Not many had the patience to follow with a large-scale map the actions of which we received such scrappy accounts; the names were so "outlandish," the strategy so hard to follow. Lieut. Jensen makes the whole series of operations intelligible and gives us much by which to remember each odd-sounding place. Truk (pronounced Trook) and the Marianas and Rabaul and Tarawa and Kwajalein have memories attached to them which will long endure. We shall never forget the enormous difficulty of clearing the Japanese out of the huge ocean areas and the innumerable islands over which they had swarmed like poisonous insects before measures could be taken to hold them in check. We shall think of the commanders, whose names have meant almost nothing to us, as vivid personalities, and of the crews they commanded as sea-rovers not a whit less daring and hard-bitten than those who made the Spanish Main famous for adventure and enterprise nearly five centuries ago.

A Thorn in the Flesh of the Japs

Here is a portrait of the admiral who led the "big roving pack of fast aircraft carriers" through all those momentous battles of 1944. His name is Mitscher. How it must have angered the Japanese to know that this thorn in their flesh was of German descent! He is:

> A gnomish man, slight to the point of being skinny. His ruddy face is wrinkled to a well-lined leather: eyes as blue as the Pacific are set beneath bushy eyebrows, which the sun has faded from reddish brown to yellow. Over them is usually perched a long-visored baseball cap, the badge of the aviation trade, which he prefers to the heavily gilded headgear of his rank. He wears horn-rimmed dark eyeglasses and an open-neck khaki shirt. . . . In other clothes he might be taken for a country doctor, although he once startled all hands by appearing from his cabin during a night action in pyjamas the colour of pimento (red) and green cheese.

We are not to imagine the Navy pilots under his command, says Lieut. Jensen, as "a grim, tight-lipped crowd with a stony heroic cast of feature and an inclination to talk sparingly in a clipped Journey's End or What Price Glory style. They are a pleasant, easy-going, affable lot, known to surface sailors affectionately as Airedales or bird-men. . . . At casual inspection they are a good deal like college boys, and save for the business in hand a great many of them would be completing courses there now."

There is a French-Canadian among them, and a Mormon from Utah; there are farm boys and city boys, there is even a poet. They are inclined to indulge in other-worldliness just before they set out on a raid. One Sunday when a big attack was in prospect, "there was a great deal of religious activity, more than there had ever been on any Sunday up to that time." Some attended both Protestant and Catholic services "just to be sure that all fronts were covered."

All these pilots had been trained since the United States were brought into the War at the end of 1941, just as the planes in which they operated had been constructed and the carriers from which the planes took off had been built during that period. The Americans "had lost one navy and were waiting on the sweat and genius of their plants and shipyards to create a new one." Not till June 1943 was American sea power reborn. Meanwhile, writes Mr. Gates, Assistant Secretary of the U.S. Navy for Air, in his Foreword to the book:

> The enemy expanded and held extensive conquests in the Pacific which constituted a real threat to our national existence. We were for months hard-pressed to keep even one aircraft carrier in operation against Japan. The situation for a time seemed very dark after the heavy losses suffered in the first months.

The seven large aircraft carriers which the U.S. had in 1941 were not in Pearl Harbour. They were fortunately at sea. But they were soon reduced to one; the only hope lay in building new ones at frantic speed. There was some doubt as to the design of these. That had been studied for more than twenty years. At first the idea of launching aircraft from a deck and having them return to alight on it was met, as all new ideas are met, with scepticism and even ridicule. "Even many of aviation's advocates foresaw little use for the new gadget save as a sort of glorified look-out or gunnery observer." However, when Britain had led the way during the First Great War, the U.S. followed and built a number of aircraft carriers.

These had become out of date. From the losses sustained in 1942 a good deal had to be learned. The vessels were vulnerable to fire, they had not sufficient anti-aircraft protection. The methods of launching, handling and recovering planes were not fast enough. "Imagination was called to work" and the result, if short of perfection, "always a little beyond the horizon," was, Lieut. Jensen claims, closer to the goal than any carriers had been up to then. At all events the Navy Department was able to describe their new carriers as "the most powerful and destructive units in the history of sea warfare." They had four principal uses. One, to find and attack an enemy fleet in the old-fashioned pattern of sea hostilities. Two, to assist in protecting their own fleets from attack. Three, they could serve as a strategic air force, pouring destruction on enemy bases, towns, and ground installations. Four, they could be used as a tactical force, bombing and firing from low level in support of ground troops. All these tasks were carried out in the Pacific War; the one which brought the most resounding successes was that of meeting Japanese defences on islands and atolls which they believed impregnable

L.S.T.s AS AIRCRAFT CARRIERS were used in the Pacific for invasion purposes. One of the light aircraft carried by these ships is about to alight on an adaptable landing strip.
Photo, New York Times Photos

Flame-Throwers Ignited the Petrol

The Japs had reason for that belief. On Betio atoll, for example, in the Gilbert Islands (see page 339), they had covered its area of one square mile with "the most intricate system of defences any island ever possessed." All round it, at intervals of twenty yards, were pill-boxed and sand-bagged machine-gun emplacements, with eye-slits opening on the beach. "Several strong-points were particularly noteworthy: block-houses built of reinforced concrete, covered with indestructible coconut logs (which are as durable and impervious as case-hardened steel), then heaped over with sand." The only way to deal with these was to pour petrol into the vents and apply flame-throwers to set it alight. Off-shore there were concrete barriers to keep out ships and tanks, while all through the shallow water were barbed wire fences to hold boats up while a murderous, concentrated fire was directed against their occupants.

Why this atoll was so important to the Japs is not explained, but they evidently set great store by it. All their precautions, however, were in vain. By the planes from the carriers everything above ground was demolished. Truk was the scene of another of their triumphs. Here was a place that everyone who knew (or thought they knew) much about it declared to be the strongest naval and air base in the world. It is called by Lieut. Jensen a "bogy." When once the Americans had established command of the air above it they were in a position to reduce it to ruins, though many of the Japanese ships there managed to get away to the Marianas, which at one time were in the news for weeks together. They were soon disposed of by the same furious concentrated attacks by carrier bombers and torpedo planes.

What comes out clearly all through is the inferior quality of Japanese naval commanders. They were out-witted, out-stripped, out-generalled by the U.S. admirals. It seems to me the best way to disillusion our late enemies, and force them to see how insane it would be for them to try to repeat their folly, would be to circulate widely among them histories of the War written by Japanese and German authors, showing up the colossal blunders their leaders made and the appalling number of lives sacrificed to their incompetence and miscalculations. Books of this kind written by British or American authors would carry no conviction. But if the peoples of Germany and Japan were told by writers of their own nationality what a wretchedly poor figure was cut by the men who planned the War, they would surely be on their guard against being bamboozled in the same way again.

As long as they had only unprepared enemies to overcome they did pretty well, though they blundered even then; but as soon as they had to withstand equal or superior forces they lost their heads. They could not stand the strain.

Lawrence at Nuremberg: A Great Judge in Action

As President of the Tribunal at the Nuremberg trial of Nazi war criminals, the authority of Lord Justice Lawrence is absolute. He embodies in himself the impartiality and the wisdom of Justice. This incisive pen-picture of a remarkable personality is by JOHN FORTINBRAS, one of the 250 special correspondents assigned to report the proceedings. See also pages 559-562, 675.

An impressive silence dominates the brilliantly arc-lit Court of the Palace of Justice, Nuremberg, before each new session of the tribunal. "Attention!" is the usher's one word of warning. Seconds later, from the judges' oak door opposite Press and Public galleries, a file of distinguished men appears.

First is the small, clerical-looking, black-haired French judge with his bald-headed, grey-moustached colleague close at heel. The two American judges, both of senatorial aspect, follow. Then, in front of lank, sandy-haired Mr. Justice Birkett and the two strongly-built, military-figured and uniformed Russian judges, there emerges a stocky, compact figure who comports himself with unconscious dignity—Lord Justice Lawrence, the President of the Tribunal.

"Attention!" is a word his personality compels. In contrast to an English High Court judge's trappings, he wears no robes and no wig; over his dark-coloured civilian suit he wears a simple black gown which hangs loosely about him until, as he sits down, he gathers up its folds, coaxing them to his sides. His bald dome of head appears to sit over his face. It is a cathedral-like dome. His features, thus inset, convey the impression of being recessed behind his wide brow and spectacles. It is not, I think, due to his pre-eminent position alone that everyone in the Schwurgerichts (the name inscribed over the Court's main entrance) senses his presence. His is a personality designed to penetrate in any assembly.

The World's Finest Judicial Brains

The tribunal deals daily with an unwieldy array of documents, mostly English translations of German originals, which are presented in evidence against the Nazi conspirators. In the case against the arch political deceiver Ribbentrop, no fewer than seventy-six documents were made available, although Sir David Maxwell Fyfe, who conducted the case for Britain, did not find it necessary to cite from all of them.

To sift the details of evidence thus marshalled requires powers of analysis and discrimination of a profundity to exercise fully the world's finest judicial brains. That Lord Justice Lawrence is so gifted is not questioned. His incisiveness stimulates, awes even, and his cool imperturbability, if not quieting to the uneasy minds of the two banks of Nazi criminals facing him, at least fixes their attention by its authority. Sometimes there is a dry humour in his comments. American correspondents, especially, admire with a smile the wry precision that characterizes many of his observations.

All of us, sorting piles of documents in the crowded, red-plush, tip-up Press seats, know to our exasperation the difficulty of seizing quickly on the one document from which Prosecuting Counsel is quoting. Our feelings were exactly expressed by his Lordship one afternoon when he interrupted proceedings to say, "I haven't found 2126 PS yet," alluding to the document previously mentioned by counsel. He added laconically, "It seems merely a matter of chance whether one finds it or not!"

He is proof against any incidents which defendants may try to manufacture. Magnificently so. I remember how, with obvious well-meaning, German counsel for Hans Frank interposed during the American prosecutors' case against the Nazis for their religious persecutions, to ask the tribunal to hear three questions, each, he claimed, of major importance to Frank. Lord Justice Lawrence nodded his agreement.

The first question was, "Is the Vatican a signatory to the Charter of the International Military Tribunal?" Second, "Did the Vatican deliver material presented to the Court as co-prosecutor?" Third, "Does the Vatican recognize the principles on which the trial is being conducted?" Upon the tribunal's replies, stated counsel, Frank's future membership of the Roman Catholic Church depended. That faith, incidentally,

LORD JUSTICE LAWRENCE was called to the Bar in 1906, became K.C. in 1925, and since 1932 has been Judge in the High Court of Justice, King's Bench Division. *Photo, Pictorial Press*

Frank (formerly notorious as Governor-General of Poland) had embraced only since his imprisonment as a Nazi war criminal.

Lord Justice Lawrence conferred quickly with his colleagues. Then, in crisp tones, he announced their decision. "The tribunal is of the opinion," he said, "that the observations made by counsel on behalf of the defendant Frank are entirely irrelevant, and any motion which they are intended to support is denied." An American radio technician, listening to his Lordship's comment, said to me afterwards "Only an Englishman could have said that without cracking a smile. They say 'as sober as a judge.' I guess he's that fellow all right!"

Sometimes his Lordship smiles. A young American prosecutor became a little involved during one session because of his fear of producing evidence "merely accumulative" and so wasting the tribunal's time. Whereupon, taken to task for being too detailed, he suggested that the witness in this case was unduly long-winded in his answers, a trait, moreover, observed in him during previous interrogations. His Lordship regarded him quizzically for a second. Then, with a quick revealing smile, he remarked, "You are examining him!"

Right at the outset, Hermann Goering and Co. were made to realize that Lord Justice Lawrence would put up with no nonsense, accept no departures from the charter of the tribunal, and admit no play-acting appeals or emotional interludes. In fact, Goering's first words when required to plead guilty or not guilty before the tribunal were: "Before I answer the question of the high court whether or not I am guilty . . ." The President interrupted, saying very forcibly, "I informed the court that defendants were not entitled to make a statement. You must plead guilty or not guilty."

His voice is richly English. It is resonant, exceptionally disciplined and clear. These qualities are enhanced as one hears it amplified through the language translator headpieces which everyone in court wears. And its timbre, so decisive, aptly portrays the alertness of the mind controlling it. If counsel should lapse for a moment or misquote a document, his Lordship will raise his eyes and inquire, "Mr. So-and-So, you said 'execution,' did you not? In my copy I read 'eviction'?"

A Just and Proper Judgement

Few in court will forget how Mr. Albrecht, one of the American delegation's prosecution team, began his country's indictment of Hermann Goering by enlarging on Goering's blandishments, as revealed in court, his ever-ready smile, his ingratiating manner, his chiding shake of the head . . . Suddenly that judicial voice spoke with penetrating clarity. "I do not think the tribunal is interested in this, Mr. Albrecht," it said.

His mannerisms are few. The most noticeable is a vigorous twiddling of his pen, which sometimes punctuates, or so it appears, his note-taking. Then, dynamically activated, his pen's handle flutters like a whirligig. His authority is absolute. He embodies in himself the impartiality and the wisdom of Justice. As President of the Court, charged with conduct of the greatest trial in human history, there could be, I think, no judicial figure more precise in mind, more fitting to represent the highest principles of civilized society in the sifting of responsibility for the most lurid saga of evil known in man's annals.

When I first sat in Nuremberg as one of the world's 250 special correspondents assigned to report the trial, I reacted to Lord Justice Lawrence by summarizing his presidency as conferring honour and distinction on the English judicial system. Today I extend that assessment. I see him as a greater figure, beyond even the personification of Justice to which English law subscribes. I see him as the judge of history, devoid of emotion, devoid of false reasoning, relentless and unwearying in his analyses to arrive at truth.

Thereby in the name of humanity, as in the name of the law, I see him presenting Justice as Justice is due to the millions of victims of Nazi-controlled Germany's reign of terror, and bringing judgement, a just and proper judgement, whatever it be, to each of the wretched men grouped as conspirators before the tribunal. The task, almost a superman's task, which this stocky, immensely dignified figure now discharges may well become a coping-stone in the edifice of peace-loving peoples. Just as it will assist materially to purge the world of evil. It is to be hoped that all nations, including the German nation, will honour one day the name of Lord Justice Lawrence.

Accused War Criminals Await Their Deserts

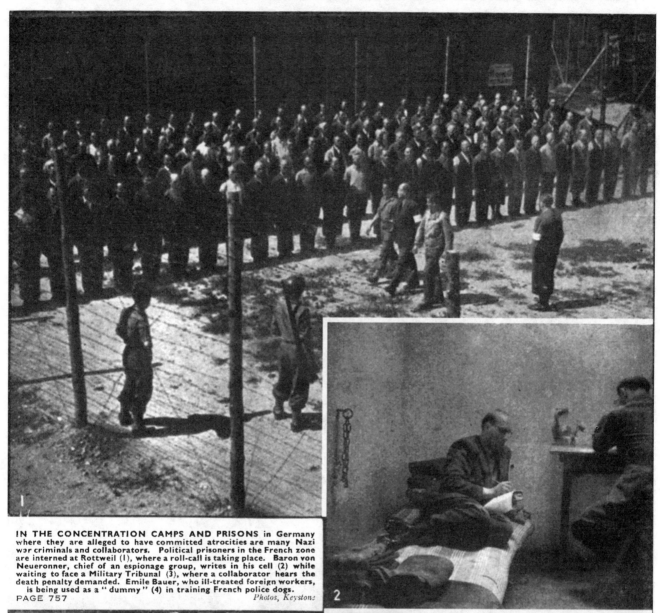

IN THE CONCENTRATION CAMPS AND PRISONS in Germany where they are alleged to have committed atrocities are many Nazi war criminals and collaborators. Political prisoners in the French zone are interned at Rottweil (1), where a roll-call is taking place. Baron von Neueronner, chief of an espionage group, writes in his cell (2) while waiting to face a Military Tribunal (3), where a collaborator hears the death penalty demanded. Emile Bauer, who ill-treated foreign workers, is being used as a "dummy" (4) in training French police dogs.

Photos, Keystone

Our Troops See Monuments of Ancient Greece

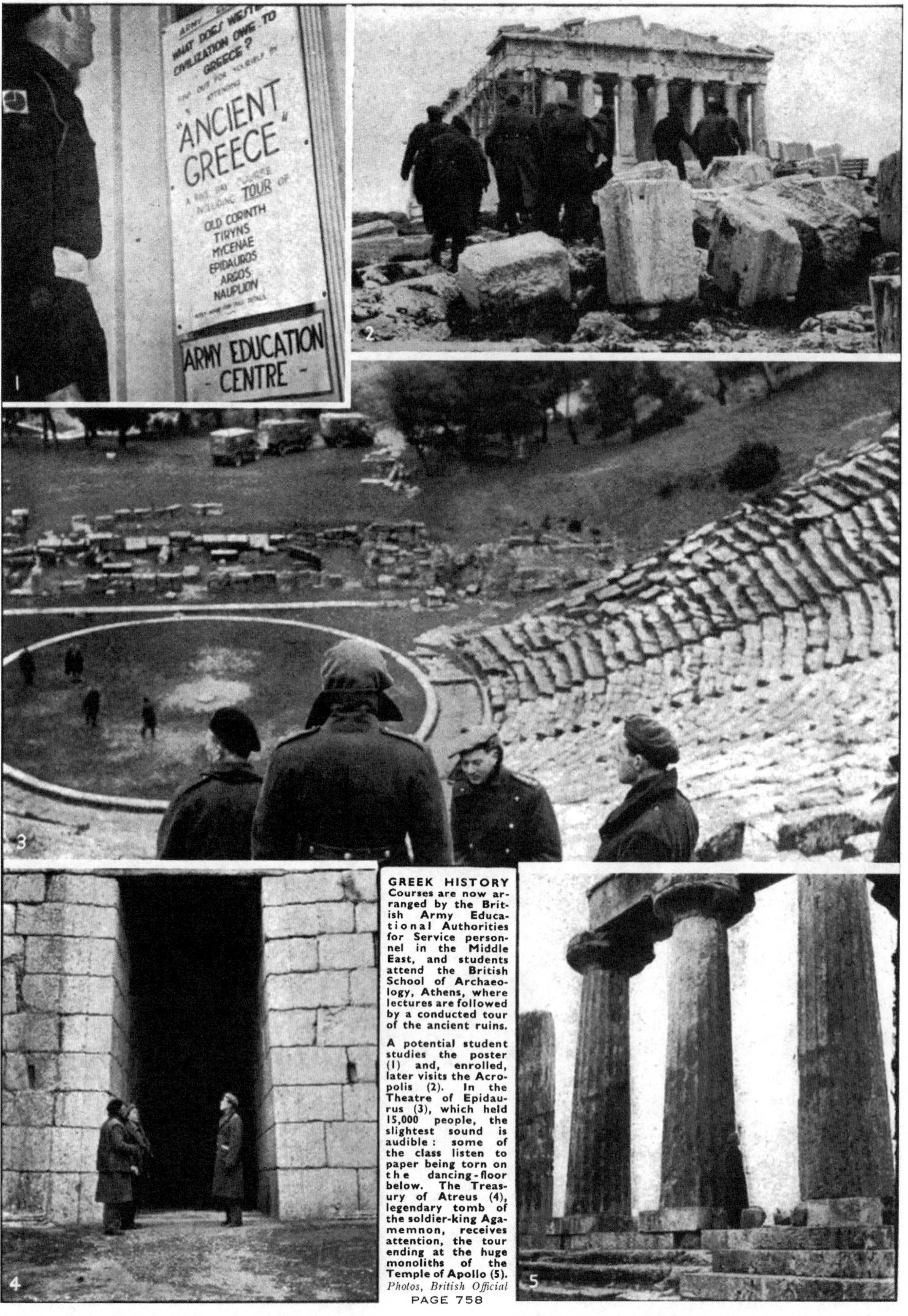

GREEK HISTORY Courses are now arranged by the British Army Educational Authorities for Service personnel in the Middle East, and students attend the British School of Archaeology, Athens, where lectures are followed by a conducted tour of the ancient ruins.

A potential student studies the poster (1) and, enrolled, later visits the Acropolis (2). In the Theatre of Epidaurus (3), which held 15,000 people, the slightest sound is audible: some of the class listen to paper being torn on the dancing-floor below. The Treasury of Atreus (4), legendary tomb of the soldier-king Agamemnon, receives attention, the tour ending at the huge monoliths of the Temple of Apollo (5).

Photos, British Official

A New and Nobler House of Commons Will Arise

THE DEBATING CHAMBER OF THE HOUSE OF COMMONS, destroyed in a bombing raid on May 10-11, 1941, is to be rebuilt: excavation for the foundations of the new building is seen in progress. Designed by Sir Giles Gilbert Scott, in conjunction with his brother, Mr. A. Gilbert Scott, it will incorporate the latest developments in acoustics, air conditioning and heating, but the Chamber will retain its unique rectangular seating arrangement to which M.P.s have been accustomed for 400 years. See also illus. pages 539-541, Vol. 4. *Photo, P.A.-Reuter*

I Was There! Eye Witness Stories of the War and After

I Fought With the Grenadier Guards at Furnes

Sixteen miles east of Dunkirk, the Belgian town was doggedly defended by a battalion of Guards infantry (7th Guards Brigade), a company of Middlesex Regiment machine-gunners and a battery of R.A. during 72 terrible hours—May 30-June 1, 1940—of German bombing and shelling. The story of this rearguard action to cover the withdrawal to the Dunkirk beaches is told by ex-Guardsman A. A. Shuttlewood.

Guardsman A. A. SHUTTLEWOOD, of the Grenadiers, relates here the heroic stand of his battalion together with men of the Middlesex Regiment and Royal Artillery at the approaches to Dunkirk in 1940.

The young officer in command of the battery of R.A. attached to our (2nd) Battalion of Grenadier Guards set up his observation post in the steeple of a church in the main square of Furnes, and from this precarious position directed the firing of the big guns under his control. Thanks to his accurate judgement the gun-crews did magnificent work, sending salvos of shells into the teeming mass of German troops and transport facing our forward companies of infantry.

Detachments of the Middlesex machine-gun company were dug-in at the southern extremities of the town, firing on fixed lines: a deadly curtain of cross-fire which prevented the Germans from making a large-scale infantry attack. Enemy mortar bombs and shells, however, rained thick and fast upon the town itself. Several hits were registered on the conspicuous target presented by the steeple; but the young artillery officer, undaunted, and miraculously unscathed, calmly carried on with his directions and corrections of range, elevation, and so on.

Our Battalion H.Q. telephone exchange was intermediary between the O.P. and the troops of guns in the battery. Occasionally, a shell-burst severed the connecting lines of cable, and members of our signal platoon promptly set off to repair the break. Fifty feet of cable vanished as the result of one direct hit. During these phases of forced inactivity, the observer descended from his steeple to compare notes with our officers. The firing was resumed on the return of the signallers and after the artillery officer's resumption of his lofty perch.

Just before dusk fell, on the evening of May 30, 1940, we heard the throb of enemy planes. They came into full view—dive-bombers. As they swooped down at us, with engines shrieking, we dived into cellars below the street level. I had time to notice that the Huns' shelling and mortar fire had subsided, as if by arrangement with the bombers. Several waves of the latter swooped, dropped their bombs and made off back to their bases. The roof shook above our heads, the stone floor beneath our feet.

"Surrender" Leaflets Dropped

Dust and pieces of whining shrapnel showered through the cellar grating, which looked out on to the street. The fumes and the sickening smell of cordite half-choked us. Thick smoke wreathed up from a petrol tommy-cooker which we had been using, but a kick from someone's boot put an end to that. It was so stifling in the cellar that we were blinded with tears and had to don our respirators.

When the planes sheered off we emerged, to view the damage. The street was splotched with what appeared to be huge flakes of snow, but which on closer inspection (minus gas-masks) proved to be leaflets. They were written in three languages, English, French and Flemish, and read as follows: "Lay down your arms, brave soldiers, for you are hopelessly beaten. You must surrender." Jerry was optimistic!

I walked along the street. It was a mass of wreckage. Telegraph poles had been uprooted, their wires strewn in all directions. Shop windows spilled their contents on to cratered pavements. Bricks and fallen masonry were everywhere. Not a single building had escaped damage. Huge holes gaped in sagging walls, roofs were shattered, and many houses and shops destroyed.

Dusk fell as I made my way to the cellar that housed the telephone exchange. I was operator on duty, and throughout the night enemy shelling continued spasmodically, with flares illuminating the darkness at intervals until dawn. Jerry must have been considerably shaken when—at 2.15 a.m. on the morning of May 31—elements of one of our forward companies made a sharp incursion into his lines and, covered by machine-gun fire, routed several strong-points with the bayonet.

Our losses were light, but that raid had a demoralizing effect on the German infantry, for it was discovered, later in the morning, that their forward troops had withdrawn some distance from their original front line. Their artillery opened again more vigorously than ever, and our lone battery replied, scoring direct hits on a number of wheeled vehicles and neutralizing some gun emplacements. We lost several men from the enemy shelling, as did the Middlesex machine-gunners.

During the afternoon, under cover of a heavy smoke-screen laid down by their artillery and mortars, the enemy infantry advanced again to their original positions; the fact that they were numerically superior to the defenders of the town was beginning to dawn on them. If they had attempted one really big attack, with all of the resources at their disposal, our small garrison would have been overwhelmed. But they lacked the nerve to try it. And we held on. Meanwhile, the mass evacuation of Allied troops from the Dunkirk beaches was in full swing.

Suddenly, the firing of our big guns petered out; only the chatter of machine-guns and the inter-

THE 13th CENTURY CHURCH OF ST. WALBURGA in the ancient town of Furnes—before the War one of the most picturesque in Belgium—whose steeple (centre) was used as an artillery observation post by a young R.A. officer during the great fighting retreat, as told in this page. At the left is the imposing Town Hall. All this was left in "almost unrecognizable ruin," when the War surged through it. See also pages 254-255, Vol. 3. *Photo, E.N.A.*

The Carrier Platoon included 20-year-old L/Sgt. Mitchell, later presented with the D.C.M. by H.M. the King at Buckingham Palace. His chief act of gallantry saved the Battalion from what might have developed into an unpleasant situation. He was reconnoitring the area on the western extremities of Furnes when the Battalion marched in from the eastern approaches in the early hours of May 30.

He saw a long string of male refugees on bicycles, heading toward the town, with blankets draped across the handlebars of their bikes. The N.C.O. halted the column by swinging his carrier broadside across the road, intending to warn them that our men were in the town and that the enemy was thought to be in the vicinity. Thereupon the leading cyclist became panicky, drew a revolver from the folds of his blankets, and fired point-blank at Lance-Sgt. Mitchell. Fortunately the shot went wide. Others of the refugees started firing then, so our N.C.O. quickly manned the Bren-gun and shot up the entire assemblage of disguised Germans. For as such they were identified in due course. By mass infiltration amongst us they could have wreaked havoc with communications and perhaps morale.

Excepting those ghastly last hours on Dunkirk's beach Furnes was the hottest spot I encountered during the whole campaign. We withdrew from the town as the beach evacuation was nearing its climax, leaving behind us almost unrecognizable ruins.

mittent crack of rifles remained. I was off duty, and was sprawled in a corner of the exchange room—I had not slept a wink for over two days, and was now too weary to sleep—when the young R.A. officer staggered into the cellar, lurched into the adjoining room (our improvised Battalion H.Q.) and slumped on to an empty orange-box which the Adjutant used for a chair. He looked very, very old at that moment. His face was drawn and haggard ; his shoulders drooped.

"That's that!" he said. "All our ammunition's gone. We blew them to hell with what we had. If only we had some more . . ." Suddenly he bowed his head, cupped his chin in his hands, and cried. Great, heart-rending sobs shook his slight body. It was not so surprising a reaction to us. Battle-hardened, we had grown accustomed to weird happenings.

A Direct Hit Shatters the Steeple

For five minutes the sobs continued. Wisely, none of his fellow-officers made efforts to console him. Then he slumped backward, and began to snore—exhausted beyond measure. He had done his task well, and was one of the most conscientious officers I have known. I felt a great admiration for him in those desperate days, and I mentally salute him now.

The dive-bombers made another attack that evening, during which the building above our cellar was destroyed and the church steeple collapsed under a direct hit. Enemy shelling was persistent throughout that night. They realized our artillery was out of action, yet they were still hesitant to make a large-scale attack. The lines of signal cable to our forward companies were shattered in places from time to time, and we set off to repair the breaks, with D3 telephones, reels of cable, earth pins, adhesive tape. At this crucial phase it was imperative that lines of communication be kept open, and we lost count of the repairing missions carried out from dusk to dawn.

As the first cold light of morning broke over the scene the Germans at last threw in what was intended to be a deciding attack. But our machine-guns stuttered continuously and waves of their infantry were mown down like corn. The hordes broke and went scurrying back to their dug-outs, from which they did not venture to stir for the rest of the day. Our Commanding Officer and two Company Commanders were killed whilst we were defending the town. An enemy machine-gun nest was responsible ; it caught the three whilst they were making a personal recce on the outskirts. As soon as the news reached us the officer-in-charge Bren carriers drove across the open country, shot up the German machine-gun crew, recovered the three bodies, and brought them to Battalion H.Q. for as decent a burial as was possible in the circumstances. For this, and other feats of bravery, he was later awarded a well-earned Military Cross.

OUR TELEPHONISTS, WEARY FROM LACK OF SLEEP, maintained communication between forward companies and the artillery observation post in the St. Walburga steeple at Furnes, until this was destroyed by shell-fire. A British gun stands silent (left) amidst empty shell-cases. "All our ammunition's gone. We blew them to hell with what we had. If only we had some more!" said the young R.A. officer. *Photos, British Official; Associated Press*

I Died at Buchenwald on Friday the 13th

In February 1946 it was announced that "The King has been graciously pleased to award the George Cross to Acting Wing Commander F. F. E. Yeo-Thomas, M.C., Royal Air Force Volunteer Reserve." At an Air Ministry conference the Wing Commander related his amazing experiences up to the time when he reached the safety of the American lines. Part of his story, in condensed form, is given here. **See also pages 410-411.**

My first trip to France was on a very difficult job. I was dropped by parachute on February 25, 1943, when we knew little about the French Resistance movement. We had a list of names, and the idea was to find out first just what really lay behind them. That was my particular task. I started getting busy in Paris and all over France sifting our information and contacting various people. I was very lucky, and managed to find five main Resistance movements in the north and three in the south. Each movement at that time was a watertight affair. None knew much about the other, for security reasons, and I had to co-ordinate their efforts, with a French officer Boisselet, who died in 1944, two days after I was arrested. He and I worked as a team, and when we came back from that trip, in April 1943, we had got these people together, knew exactly with whom we were dealing, and were able to get to work on a plan to bring the whole of the French Resistance movement under a single command.

My second trip was in September 1943, to inspect what had been done in the interim period, to see how things were progressing, and also find out just what the French required in the way of arms, supplies, and so on. At that time we knew there was a Maquis organization, but we did not know anything more about it. So that was another job—to travel all over France and visit these small, armed groups of Maquis.

Wing Commander F. F. E. YEO-THOMAS, M.C., R.A.F.V.R., awarded the George Cross for his services with the Maquis, relates his experiences here. *Photo, Central Press*

Seeing the way these men were trained, how disciplined and keen they were, I realized that if we could get supplies to them we had the nucleus of a very formidable secret army in France. I came back to England and reported what I had seen. I had the honour of an interview with Mr. Churchill and was able to tell him all about the Maquis. From then on we concentrated on sending large quantities of arms to them.

How the Gestapo Captured Me

My third trip (again I parachuted down) was undertaken in February 1944, when we were getting ready for the invasion. The idea then was to bolster-up morale, because these Resistance movements had had heavy losses, and the Germans were running them down as fast as they could. My capture came about through the arrest of one man; he was taken with a slip of paper on him. On the slip he had marked the name of a bridge, a date, and an hour. The Gestapo beat him up very badly.

They took him to the meeting-place at the hour mentioned on the slip of paper, and captured a comrade of mine and tortured him. They caught another man, too, whom I knew as Jacques, a very fine fellow; he committed suicide on the spot. And they captured a courier who was meeting *my* courier. The latter made exactly the same mistake as the original man; he had a slip of paper, inscribed "Shelley, Passy, 11 o'clock." The Gestapo said, "We know Shelley!"—that was me. My courier got the wind up and admitted that he was meeting me at 11 o'clock at Passy. And coming round a corner there I had five men on my back before I knew where I was!

On that trip I had intended to release my comrade Boisselet, who had been arrested in December, and I had organized an attack on Fresnes Prison where he was held together with a man named Baudouin, who was selected as General de Gaulle's representative in France. I had cars and arms, explosives, false papers, German uniforms, men who spoke German, to attack the prison and get these people out. I was arrested on March 21—the day before the prison was to be attacked!

My Three Weeks in Darkness

I was in Fresnes Prison for four months, in solitary confinement, and was beaten-up every morning by a German N.C.O. He used to open up proceedings by saying, "Ah! British officer! We kill you slowly!" And *bang*!—he would punch me on the jaw, then kick me in the stomach, stand back and grin, and then walk out. He discovered after about two months that I was getting information from outside. For this I spent three weeks in the darkness of an underground cell, with about a quarter-pound of bread a day and nothing else at all, not even soup. I had no bed. My coat, gloves and handkerchief were taken away. I had nothing to wash with. Fungi grew in this damp cell. There were rats, and heaven knows what. It was the only time in the whole of my experience when I felt really downhearted.

But I began to feel better when I discovered that it annoyed them intensely if I sang—"God Save the King," "Britannia Rule the Waves"—anything I thought would annoy them I sang. That resulted in a sentry every now and again clumping me with a rifle-butt. But each time he entered I saw a bit of light, which was cheering. Getting their goat gave me pleasure—but I came out of Fresnes in a very bad state.

From there I went to Compiègne, and made two unsuccessful attempts to escape. Then I went to Buchenwald, where I "died" of typhus and, by that ruse, changed my identity. I knew I was to be shot, or hanged, or something, but I wangled things with the connivance of a S.S. doctor in the "guinea pig" block. He had the wind up and I was able to play on his nerves to some extent by telling him what would happen to his wife and family when the War was over. I rubbed it in hard, and he agreed to arrange a change of identities for three of us in the "guinea pig" block where he carried out experiments on human beings.

The outcome of this plan was that I "died" on Friday, October 13, 1944—under an assumed name, of course, because here they never knew my real name. I was "resurrected" as Maurice Chauquet, a Frenchman deported for forced labour. Later, I found myself married, with two children, and it was an unpleasant job when I got back to have to see Mme. Chauquet and tell her that her husband had died of typhus, and then I had to sign all sorts of documents so that she could get a pension!

Smuggled Into Europe's Last Fascist Fortress

Feeling against General Franco ran so high that the French Government decided to close the frontier with Spain from midnight on Feb. 28, 1946. But Franco himself closed it, all along the Pyrenees, on Feb. 27. This dispatch was sent by George McCarthy, The Daily Mirror Chief Correspondent.

Two days after Franco closed his French frontier with a ring of armed men, I slipped across that bristling border. The Fascist Government which smiles on a few British journalists and politicians does not countenance certain other reporters entering Spain. It is necessary to travel underground.

So with a false name and forged papers, I was smuggled into the last Fascist fortress in Europe. Today (March 4) I have returned to France after spending five days in Spain, four of them in the Catalonian capital of Barcelona. Every train in the frontier zone is under close police supervision.

There was an anxious moment for me, after getting over the border, when a Franco detective wanted to see my papers—and I could speak no Spanish. Happily my guide,

WELL-STOCKED STREET MARKET IN MADRID, like others of its kind in Barcelona and elsewhere, offers much to the privileged classes, but brings little comfort to the majority of Spaniards, who after years of civil war and Franco's Fascist regime now find themselves without the means to buy—though bananas are plentiful. *Photo, Associated Press*

FRENCH-SPANISH FRONTIER, at Hendaye, in the Pyrenees, was the scene of hurried last-minute activity before it was closed on Feb. 27, 1946, practically severing all relations between the two countries. This action of General Franco forestalled the French Government's decision by a few hours. The tide of feeling towards Franco and his regime, which had been rising for a long time, was stimulated by the execution of several Spanish Republicans who, as refugees in France, had fought gallantly with the Maquis. *Photo, Associated Press*

who calls himself Richards, although it is not his name, was the first to be interrogated. His papers were in order. And then I got by with papers which proved that my name was José Camps, that my mother's name was Pons, and that I was born in Barcelona.

That was the only obstacle on the road to Barcelona. And in that city I found a people waiting for news from London. The men and the women of the Resistance moved around me like a protective umbrella. I travelled in the trams and in the underground and in taxis; I visited many homes; interviewed the leaders and the rank and file of the Resistance. Everywhere I was at once asked the question, "What is the British Government going to do?"

After Long Despair and Apathy

The Franco papers have suppressed news of the Allied moves against the Spanish Government, but everybody knows that a crisis exists. Unfortunately, thousands of people have accepted the newspaper propaganda that Britain is reluctant to move against Franco, and that if she does it will be to support a monarchy in Spain.

It is impossible to overrate the trust the Spanish people have in the British public. For ten years the Spaniards have fought Fascism and they are the last to be liberated. They wanted an Allied victory; they saw with mounting hopes the rise of the Labour Party at the polls; now they suffer a reaction. On every side you hear the question: "When will Britain come to our rescue?"

Do not forget that these are a people wearied by the long years of war. The best of their leaders are dead. Their successors sicken in Franco's gaols. (The number of political prisoners is unknown, but is estimated to be at least 15,000.) The workers, after years of despair and apathy, are once more on the march. And once again they look to England, the traditional home and the hope of liberty.

What goes on in Spain behind that forbidden frontier? You will find what you would expect to find in a battlefield where Fascism has triumphed. Spain today is a great prison-house, for too many a prison of the body, and for all a prison of the mind. For a rich few it is a paradise. Here every evil flourishes. Here privilege is enthroned, and here indeed may be found poverty in the midst of plenty.

The shops are full of every kind of goods, but the people have no money to buy. If you walk in the streets of Barcelona you will think at a glance that this is the most prosperous country in Europe. It is like pre-war England. The shops display windows full of eggs and hams, and sausages (there is little meat, although the rich never go without). There are oranges, bananas, nuts, raisins, and apples, wine and beer and brandy. But the great majority of the people go hungry.

There is much I cannot tell in the space of one report. But there is one thing more I want to say: The only people who look happy in Spain today are the dandified officers of Franco's Army.

★—*As The Years Went By—Notable Days in the War*—★

1941

March 24. *El Agheila occupied by Axis forces; first appearance of Afrika Korps in Libya.*
March 27. *King Peter and Yugoslav Army under Gen. Simovitch deposed pro-Axis Government.*
March 28. *British naval victory over Italians in Battle of Cape Matapan, Greece.*

1942

March 27-28. *Combined Operations raid on St. Nazaire; destroyer H.M.S. Campbeltown used to ram the main dock gate of the port.*

1943

March 20. *In Tunisia the Eighth Army launched an attack against the Mareth Line.*

1944

March 19. *Germans began to occupy Hungary; parachute troops took over airfields.*
March 22. *Announced that Japanese troops had crossed the Burma-India frontier.*
March 24. *Major-General Wingate of the "Chindits" killed in air crash in Burma.*

1945

March 17. *U.S. 3rd Army entered Coblenz.*
March 20. *Whole of Mandalay freed by British and Indian capture of Fort Dufferin.*
March 23. *Mass crossing of Rhine by British, Canadian and U.S. troops under Montgomery.*
March 28. *Russians captured Gdynia.*
March 29. *U.S. 7th Army occupied Heidelberg.*

Shall We See an International Air Force?

By CAPTAIN
NORMAN MACMILLAN
M.C., A.F.C.

It was certainly appropriate that Mr. Winston Churchill's speech of grave warning (at Fulton on March 5, 1946) should have been delivered within the State of Missouri, for there is an American expression "I come from Missouri" which is the western equivalent of the British "No flies on me!" Just as his unique career was the perfect apprenticeship for his leadership of the British peoples from May 10, 1940, almost to VJ Day 1945, so the rejection of his party by the electorate last year has given him an unparalleled position to speak frankly as a private citizen.

Mr. Churchill was one of the few British politicians who tried to halt the race to European destruction in the years leading up to 1939. Today he is a world figure endeavouring to avert global calamity. Is it not strange that he should have been reverted, in the activities of mankind, to the same position as before 1939, save that this time his rostrum faces the world and not, as then, the European cockpit alone? But his speech was not one of unrelieved gloom. It contained the hope that the United Nations Organization might this time be able to bring the nations together to work in peace in the harmony of law instead of the discord of war. He made the following proposal:

"The United Nations organization must immediately begin to be equipped with an international armed force. In such a matter we can only go step by step, but we must begin now. I propose that each of the Powers and States should be invited to dedicate a certain number of air squadrons to the service of the world organization. These squadrons would be trained and prepared in their own countries, but would move around in rotation from one country to another. They would wear the uniform of their own countries with different badges. They would not be required to act against their own nation, but in other respects they would be directed by the world organization."

Whatever support it receives from the member States of U.N.O. this is an interesting proposal, which has several important implications if carried into effect. First, and not least important, would be the change in what is called intelligence "security." In this sense the word security is used to mean the prevention of leakage of military information from the country of its ownership and from the sole possession of those of its citizens in the secret.

For, if the military aircraft of the principal member States were to be moved about from one country to another, there could be no secrecy about these machines or their equipment. This would mark a great advance in the confidence of one nation with the other nations, and all with each, if the great aircraft-designing States and the most powerful military nations really allocated their latest types of aircraft to the service of the world organization.

PRINCIPLE Whose Acceptance Would Mould the Destiny of All Mankind

But this is again precisely where the fabric of U.N.O. has shown itself inclined to be shoddy, with the risk of wearing threadbare unless most delicately handled. Who would ensure that each State really placed its latest aircraft into this pool? If some withheld their latest aircraft for national defence and gave to the world organization their obsolescent types, the power of the world organization would be no greater than that of a third-rate Power. And U.N.O. would then be no more able than was the League of Nations to prevent aggression by any Power possessing its own requisite strength, as were Japan, Italy and Germany.

If the world organization is to possess a real air force it must have the power to order its own types of aircraft from whatever source it desires, so that its equipment would be as modern as that of any independent State member. But there are the difficulties of cost; the commercialization of the organization, so that the industries of the member States would be angrily competing with one another for the orders, as one means to build up their own industrial strength; and indeed, that of the creation of a strange independent sovereign power which might be seized by unscrupulous men to impose their own conditions of life upon all mankind.

This position can be reached only through experience which will lead to the eventual creation of a one-world State, possessing a free Parliament, under which all men of all races will be able to live in accordance with the principles enunciated by Abraham Lincoln at Gettysburg; or, the apparent alternative, through the growth of a doctrinaire system, like that of Russia, into world coverage. We see, therefore, that in this suggestion Mr. Churchill was enunciating a principle whose acceptance now or in the near future would mould the destiny of mankind for centuries, even if it were put into effect only inefficiently by some nations.

THE RT. HON. WINSTON S. CHURCHILL, introduced by President Truman (left), making his dramatic appeal at Westminster College, Fulton, Missouri, on March 5, 1946, for closer Anglo-American relations and an international armed force for U.N.O. He was addressing an assembly of students, and his speech aroused world-wide comment. *Photo, New York Times Photos*

Second, if the aircraft so allocated to the world organization were to be moved around from one country to another, the bases that they used would no longer be secret from other nations, and the minds directing the military staff of the Security Council would be able to plan global strategy with the use of certain known bases. This would undoubtedly have the effect of reducing the national security of any given member State as a separate entity, and if it decided upon unilateral action it would first have to destroy the U.N.O. air detachment within its territory. This would at once disclose its intentions.

So, to prevent any such disclosure, it would be more likely to attempt to begin an act of aggression, either when its own detachment was temporarily withdrawn for re-equipment within its own territory in place of any foreign element, or when its own detachment was strategically well situated to assist in the first blow. There are, therefore, risks to be run in the execution of any such plan.

But before such a plan could be put into operation, each State would necessarily have to agree to the establishment of extra-territorial air bases within its own sovereign territory. Britain of course did this by leasing bases to the U.S.A. during the recent war. China has frequently done so in the past. It is a prerequisite of colonial ownership—one reason why the Third Reich wanted her colonies back, and why other nations did not want to return them.

But it is a new departure in international relationships to propose that a sovereign State should concede bases within its own territory for the occupational forces of a world organization. It remains to be seen what the world's reaction will be to this suggestion, which, undoubtedly, because of its cession of a part of sovereignty, its voluntary tearing down of some of the veils that cloak "security" conditions, and its relinquishment of a part of the national armed forces, would tend to create more difficult conditions for the propagation of war as a means to extension of power.

NATION That Holds Aloft the Torch to Light the Way for the World

Meanwhile, it seems clear from Mr. Churchill's speech that he regards the situation of the British Isles as one of strategic military isolation in the current political impasse. Germany was on the Rhine. Russia is on the Oder. Not much farther east. Germany had to fight to try to create a linkage through the Middle East to the Far East. Russia does not. Her linkage is there in one continuous block of territory, reaching from the Baltic to the North Pacific.

In 1942, Field-Marshal Jan Smuts forecast Britain's position after the War as that of a little island lying off the western shore of Europe. He is uncannily correct in his broad forecasts. The truth is that in the existing situation Britain is fighting a politico-military-strategic Battle of Britain almost single-handed; and Mr. Churchill, now, as then, has through his forthright speech made Britain again the nation that holds aloft the torch to light the way for all the world. Let us hope that the suggestion for an international air force will be adopted despite all its difficulties, and that through the air Russia, America and Britain may become a triumvirate of peace.

★ My friend and contributor Captain Norman Macmillan has just written to say that a rumour going round the town to the effect that he had taken his life is, happily, "exaggerated." The victim of the recent suicide, who bore the same name as our Air Correspondent, was neither known nor related to him.—Ed.

Royal Irish Fusiliers on Duty in the Austrian Alps

BRITISH OCCUPATION TROOPS not uncommonly have somewhat tedious tasks, but they carry them out with commendable cheerfulness. High up in the Austrian Alps, the Royal Irish Fusiliers guard the five-mile long railway tunnel through the Saviske Mountains to see that unauthorized persons do not travel between Austria and Yugoslavia either on foot or by the daily train from Rosenbach, near the frontier. They make the best of the available transport and use a bogey to convoy them to and from their billets. *Photo, G.P.U.*

The Editor Looks Back

'THE FAT BOY' Aug. 3, 1940

Last night I encountered a prominent West Country physician on a visit to London and found in him certain characteristics of the Fat Boy who loved to make one's flesh creep. Among other things, he told me of the terrors in store for us when Hitler's murder men can carry out his diabolic schemes (incidentally he couldn't tell me why they were not getting on with them) for the smothering of Britain with that deadliest of corrosive gases known as Lewisite. And as though that were not sufficient, the Huns are also preparing (he told me genially) to spread anthrax germs over all our pasture lands. Presumably Lewisite would wipe out the inhabitants, while the anthrax germs would destroy all live-stock for generations to come, so that he must have had a mental picture of these British Isles transformed into so much barren and poisonous soil—the great graveyard, so to speak, of the British race. After which he suggested that I might join him in a drink, but I declined, feeling more tempted to report him for giving expression to such defeatist nonsense.

THAT Fat Boy is beyond drinking now. He was a gloomy Scot, and waxed gloomier the more he imbibed the liquid product of his native land, now so much scarcer than it was in 1940. It used to have a different effect on others, whose hopes and visions of ultimate victory rose with every glass. All expert opinion which I obtained at the time scouted the gloomy pictures that Jeremiah drew for us.

TEMPORARY TYRANTS Aug. 10, 1940

Often have I remarked that in order effectively to wage war against dictators, totalitarians, authoritarians or whatever you like to call those States in which democracy is either dead or slumbering, we have to adopt some of the methods of absolutism on which they are founded if we would prevail against them. Who shall say that Britain continues as a purely democratic State today with wartime "dictators" telling us what to do whether we like it or not? We have "for the duration" willingly agreed to the abrogation of many of the most cherished rights of freedom in order to present a united front to the foe. No other method could succeed. But give the bureaucrat an inch and he'll take an ell, be he British or Boche; and from our experience of what happened during the last War and the so-called years of peace which followed it, we might well expect to have to fight for the restoration, once the war was over, of many of the rights which have been taken away from us on the plea of war emergency.

WELL, we know more about the faults of the bureaucrats today than when I wrote that; but nearly a year after the nominal end of the War there is very little sign of any let-up in the burden of bureaucracy under which we are groaning. We may still hope it is "temporary," but many things begun as temporary measures can develop a longevity which is indistinguishable from permanence.

THE LITTLE COUNTRIES Sept. 7, 1940

Looking back over the last twelve months, I have every reason to be confirmed in an opinion to which I have often given expression in the last thirty years: that small neutral states interlarded among the greater states of Europe are a constant source of danger to peace. So long as the appeal to force remains the ultimate arbitrament between the great powers, the small peoples whose right to "self-determination" was accepted in theory at the founding of the League of Nations, and didn't mean a thing at its foundering, will be no better than material for crushing between the upper and nether millstones.

Had but the Scandinavian states united to maintain their independence, with Holland and Belgium in similar union for defence—and what a different course the War would have taken! Although France, as events have revealed, was rotten or at least rotting at the core of its body politic, the neglect of Holland and Belgium to arm themselves adequately in their own defence, and their too scrupulous efforts each to maintain a neutrality utterly beyond its power, had much to do with the military collapse of France. Whatever new order the eventual victory of Britain and her Allies may produce in Europe and Asia, the theory of self-determination for the lesser nations will have to be applied in association with some effective form of co-operative defence against any aggressor power.

I HOPE I am not being too optimistic in thinking that, despite the Anglo-Soviet exchanges at the Security Council of U.N.O., in which Mr. Bevin acquitted himself so well, there is every sign that the small sovereign states are going to have fair play and good living conditions under the new world order that is coming into being. There is no denying that in times past they have been spots of trouble, which were made the excuse for the stronger powers to start hostilities.

THE DAY CAME! Oct. 5, 1940

A day will come when our air power will so outstrip that of the braggart Hun that he will venture no more on his missions of murder against our towns and villages, while we shall be able to repay him in kind with compound interest. Even now the doom of Nazi Germany is preparing on the great training grounds of Canada, whence vast aerial armadas will come to smother both Germany and Italy and all the enemies of Britain. That part at least of our Empire plan for victory was certainly confirmed by men of vision and determination.

ELIA'S BIRTHPLACE Oct. 19, 1940

A stone's-throw from my editorial office at Whitefriars the yellow leaves are falling in the Temple gardens—not to mention the lovely old masonry of the historic buildings there which, after weathering nearly four centuries of time, was no match for the H.E. bombs dropped upon it by Hitler's young barbarians. I'm glad, however, that the gentle Elia's birthplace escaped, for in all the world no greater contrast to the Nazi doctrine of brute force could be found than in the serenity and friendliness of our beloved Charles Lamb, who was born there in Crown Office Row around which the flying fragments of the bombed Inner Temple Hall were falling so recently. (As I had written that word "serenity" another Alert spells it "sirenity"!). "So perish the roses"—but their fragrance lingers on in a world that is falling about our heads.

NOT long after, in passing among the ruins, I noted with sorrow that Lamb's birthplace had gone.

SECOND GREAT FIRE Dec. 30, 1940

Though I have been a Londoner by residence for only forty years, I have known it intimately for a full half-century. In the days of my youth it was my Baghdad. And today it is one with Baghdad in most things that made it romantic to my mind. Not that these were all extinguished in the Second Great Fire of Sunday, December 29, 1940. Far, far more of the old London that I loved had disappeared ten, twenty, thirty years ago. But the finishing touch came on that horrific Sunday night.

Fire is the great destroyer; worse than high explosives; and devastation has overcome the most famous of the world's publishing centres. Makers of books whose names are famous wherever the English language is known have had their homes for generations in Paternoster Row. And books, somehow, are not like furniture and furs and frills, so that we feel something with life in it has been destroyed when books feed the holocaust. The other things don't matter so much. But that's only a fancy, especially in these days when book production has been mechanized to the same pitch as electric torches. There will be a Paternoster Row again, but it will merely be the name for a place that "ceased upon the midnight hour." I've seen enough of the new London buildings to make me love the old ones more. The modern stuff that will arise will be exactly like what I have seen in Berlin, Paris, Buenos Aires and New York. The spirit of eld which haunted the purlieus of Paternoster Row and Square, Ivy and Warwick Lanes, can never come back. And something is here for tears.

[THE END]

POSTSCRIPT

A ROCKET-DRIVEN "space-ship" has been designed by a young Frenchman who claims it will reach the moon in eight hours. What I should be more interested to learn is: What does he intend doing once he gets there? Which—as my Chinese friends would doubtless point out—applies to much high-speed travel nowadays.

AN American soldier just returned from the wars has delivered himself of this shattering dictum: "It's a great deal easier studying history than it is making it." A glib enough generalization, until one recalls that some of the greatest students of History were those who also made it. Witness Thucydides, Xenophon—and Churchill.

FROM all quarters I hear complaints that queue-breakers are more active than at any time since 1939. All the old saws about the worm turning, and the last straw, naturally spring to mind—in extenuation—and for once I agree with them. Yet for the majority of us there is virtually no way out, except grinning and bearing. That is at once the tragedy and glory of life today (such as it is), even though most of us expected cream (however synthetic) with the fruits of victory.

I so frequently complain of the continued wastage of paper that it gives me double pleasure to record what seems to me a highly commendable example to the contrary. At the Greek Exhibition at Burlington House, London, just now they are letting out the catalogues on hire. You pay a two-shilling deposit, which you retrieve on returning the catalogue as you go out.

TRAVELLING to town by train I have been both amazed and amused to observe one of our youngest Air Vice-Marshals marking, learning and inwardly digesting—Mein Kampf! The officer in question is not an acquaintance of mine, otherwise I should ask him whether he is preparing for the Third Great War, or merely trying to catch up on the Second. The old theory that we Britons always win the last round ought to be given a rest, especially in the Atomic age.

In Britain Now: Abolishing Traces of the Hun

DIVERS AT LOWESTOFT, Suffolk, search the dock-bed for unexploded German bombs and shells. One of the searchers is seen (left) coming up to report. So far a few shells have been located by these naval mine-clearing parties.

WATER-JETS AT PERRANPORTH, Cornwall, are used on the beaches to expose mines which, sown there during the War, lie deep below the sand: a converted Bren-carrier (above) hurling a powerful jet, its crew taking cover.

EXETER CATHEDRAL (left), damaged in the "Baedeker" raids of 1942, is the centre around which the city is to be rebuilt. Completed plans and models have been examined by the Minister for Town and Country Planning and await approval.

IN PARLIAMENT SQUARE, London, a bulldozer (above) assists in the clearance of air-raid shelters. It pushes the debris away after the shelters have been pounded to pieces by a heavy steel weight swung by a mobile crane. (See page 30).

Photos, Planet, Penhall, P.A.-Reuter, Keystone

'The New Britain Must Be Built on Coal'

DURHAM MINERS HOMEWARD BOUND AT DUSK, these share the burden of responsibility for putting Britain on her feet again—of repairing the deficit in the nation's coal supplies which during this winter has been recorded as 8,000,000 tons. After a strenuous day in the pits, these sturdy underground workers still have in mind the warning issued on February 9, 1946, by Mr. Emanuel Shinwell, Minister of Fuel and Power, that "the new Britain must be built on coal, or it can never be built at all."

Photo, Topical Press

Printed in England and published every alternate Friday by the Proprietors, THE AMALGAMATED PRESS, LTD., The Fleetway House, Farringdon Street, London, E.C.4. Registered for transmission by Canadian Magazine Post. Sole Agents for Australia and New Zealand: Messrs. Gordon & Gotch, Ltd.; and for South Africa: Central News Agency, Ltd.—March 29, 1946 S.S. *Editorial Address:* JOHN CARPENTER HOUSE, WHITEFRIARS, LONDON, E.C.4.

Vol 9 The War Illustrated No 230

and AFTERWARDS

SIXPENCE APRIL 12 1946

SOUTHAMPTON HONOURED U.S. SOLDIERS by the presentation on March 14, 1946, of a scroll to the 14th Major Port (Transportation Corps) U.S. Army, granting them the privilege of marching through the town with fixed bayonets, drums beating and colours flying. Detachments of the Corps, which embarked nearly 2,000,000 U.S. Servicemen for Europe, are seen marching through the Bargate, where the Mayor, Alderman H. Vincent, J.P. (left) took the salute. *Photo, Keystone*

Edited by Sir John Hammerton

NO. 231 WILL BE PUBLISHED FRIDAY, APRIL 26

Our Mightiest Carrier Slides Down to the Sea

H.M.S. EAGLE WAS LAUNCHED AT BELFAST by Her Royal Highness the Princess Elizabeth on March 19, 1946. For the Princess it was her first official visit, alone, outside the mainland ; she crossed from Greenock to Belfast in the new cruiser H.M.S. Superb (1), whose company is seen " dressing " ship in her honour. Princess Elizabeth's personal standard (2) at the masthead of the Superb, the first time it had flown at sea. The hull of the mighty aircraft carrier—sixth to be built at Harland and Wolff's yard during the War—slides down the slipway (3) after Her Royal Highness had named her H.M.S. Eagle, in traditional style (4).

Photos, P.N.A.

How U N O will Police the World

By E. H. COOKRIDGE

NUCLEUS of the High Command and General Staff of the International Police Force now envisaged by the Governments of the Five Great Powers is the Military Staff Committee of the United Nations Organization, which continued discussions in London after the ending of the First General Assembly on Feb. 14, 1946, and resumed when in New York in March. Problems in connexion with this Force-to-be are here explained.

THE charter of the United Nations does not provide for a permanent World Army. Article 43 of the charter imposes on the members of the United Nations only the duty "to contribute to the maintenance of international peace and security and to make available to the Security Council, on its call . . . armed forces." And Article 47 says that "the Military Staff Committee shall assist the Security Council in all questions relating to military requirements and command the forces placed at the disposal of the Council."

But the charter also provides that special agreements between the permanent members of the Security Council can be concluded with a view to establishing a permanent armed force, fixing its numbers, armament and equipment. The charter contains the important proviso that, in order to enable the United Nations to take urgent military measures, the member states shall hold immediately available national air force contingents for combined international enforcement action. The discussions in London of the Military Staff Committee have gone beyond the original letter of the charter. The Governments of the five great powers have agreed that it would be far better to have a permanent World Police Force—consisting not only of air contingents but also of land forces and naval units—than an improvised force called up only in the case of immediate emergency.

THE MILITARY STAFF COMMITTEE of the United Nations met for the first time at Church House, Westminster, London, on February 4, 1946. The permanent representatives of the British chiefs of staff are Admiral Sir Henry Moore (1), chairman ; Lieut.-General Sir Edwin Morris (2) ; and Air Chief Marshal Sir Guy Garrod (3). *Photo, Topical*

British and American plans submitted to the Military Staff Committee envisage a comparatively small but highly trained body of men, wearing a common uniform and serving under a world flag, the blue-gold emblem of the United Nations. Stress is laid on the need for one uniform in order to promote a spirit of fighting solidarity.

THE Military Staff Committee has to solve very many problems and it would be too optimistic to expect a quick solution. How many men, aircraft and ships are needed to police the world ? What contributions in men and armaments will each nation be required to make ? How shall the problem of command be solved ?

These problems are being discussed by the representatives of the Big Five—Great Britain, the United States, the Soviet Union, France and China. The respective General Staffs have delegated some of their most famous experts on military organization. Britain is represented by Admiral Sir Henry Moore, a former commander of the Royal Navy Staff College at Greenwich who represented Britain on many international conferences, including the 1927 Naval Conference, and was also one of the military advisers at Geneva. During the Second Great War Sir Henry was in command of our convoys to Russia and led the naval units during the Fleet Air Arm attack on the Tirpitz on April 3, 1944.

The British Army representative, Lt.-General Sir Edwin Morris, C.-in-C. Northern Command, was Director of Staff Duties at the War Office at the outbreak of the War and has wide experience in army organization. Spokesman of the Air Ministry is Air Chief Marshal Sir Guy Garrod, who organized the Air Training Corps and is now head of the R.A.F. delegation in the U.S.A.

Bearing Great Responsibility

The United States are represented by three fighting men. General George Kenney was in command of air operations in the South-West Pacific and distinguished himself in the New Guinea and Leyte campaigns. Lt.-General Ridgway took part in the invasion of Sicily and Italy under General Mark Clark. And Admiral Kelly Turner commanded the famous amphibious forces in the South-West Pacific. Two of the Soviet members, Lt.-General Vasiliev and Major-General Shaparov, were both heads of the Russian Military Mission to Britain before they were given commands of armies of the Red Army. Vice-Admiral Bogdenko commands the naval units in the Black Sea.

China has sent to the conference three of her most famous military leaders. General Shang Chen is personal chief of staff to Generalissimo Chiang Kai-shek. General Kwei Yun-Chin, at present head of the Chinese Military Mission to Britain, commanded in the Shanghai and Nanking campaigns ; he has organized the Chinese Scout Movement on British pattern, and had a big hand in training the Chinese partisans during the long war against Japan. General Sun Li-Fen was trained in an American military academy, fought in Burma and when cut off by the Japanese led his forces through uncharted jungle and mountains into India. France is represented by General Alphonse Juin, the chief of staff and hero of North Africa, and Admiral Raymond Fénard, who commanded the battleship Dunkerque and joined De Gaulle in 1940.

With these men, who have elected Sir Henry Moore as chairman, rests the heavy responsibility of working out the status of the future World Police Force. They have agreed that the force should be based on "proportional representation." On this reckoning the proportion would be four Britons, 13 Americans, 18 Russians, and so on; but when the British Dominions are included the number of sailors, soldiers and airmen from the British Empire would be about equal to those from the United States.

Although China is the most populous country of the great powers, the Chinese representatives have stated that China will not be able to supply such large numbers of trained troops, and especially sailors and airmen, as the strict interpretation of the proportional system would indicate. In practice, it appears, Britain and the United States will provide the bulk of the naval and air forces, whilst the Soviet Union will be called upon for land forces.

Our Own Conscription Problem

The respective national forces would remain in national brigades, because of language difficulties and different customs. But it is foreseen that officers and N.C.O.s will be interchanged, a measure that will certainly promote the spirit of comradeship amongst the international troops. Possible headquarters of the High Command of the World Police Force is also a subject of discussion. Disturbances in which the international army may have to intervene by order of the Security Council are more likely to occur in Europe than elsewhere. Austria or Luxemburg might provide the site for headquarters, both being central areas for the domination of the European scene and neither being a "great power."

Military colleges for officers and N.C.O.s of the World Police Force will be set up at the seat of the headquarters, where study of languages will be one of the important subjects, international law, geography and cartography some of the others. The students would also have a sort of "post-graduate" military and strategical training. The problem of new weapons, especially the atom bomb, is closely linked up with the question of future equipment of the force.

THE International Police Force will have great mobility. Its land forces will be fully motorized. A number of international garrisons and especially a chain of airfields would be established not only in Europe but also in other parts of the world.

For Britain, the establishment of the force is of utmost importance. Mr. Attlee has indicated that the problem of conscription in Britain turns on the question whether and when the International Army will become a fact. The British contribution would probably not exceed 150,000 men, and with other requirements of armed forces throughout the Empire we may need not more than a standing army of 500,000. But these estimates are obviously based on an assumption that the world will return to peace and harmony. With troubles in India, Palestine, Egypt, Indonesia, Greece, and the burden of a prolonged occupation of Germany, the prospects for abandoning conscription in Britain are remote. It may well be two years before the plan of the International Police Force will be put into practice.

Empire Armies Fought in Four Continents

By MAJ.-GENERAL
SIR CHARLES GWYNN
K.C.B., D.S.O.

IN the course of the six years of the Second Great War the Armies of the Empire fought in an even greater number of theatres and in a wider variety of conditions than in the war of 1914-18. They gained experience of Arctic and mountain warfare in Norway and Italy, of desert fighting in Libya, of roadless rugged country in Abyssinia, and of jungle fighting in Burma, Malaya and New Guinea, of bitter cold, of tropical heat and tropical rain, and of conditions where water supply was a controlling factor. To all these conditions the Army proved capable of adapting itself as well as to the more normal conditions of modern warfare in highly developed regions.

Yet despite the multiplicity of theatres there was not the dispersion of effort nor clash between the interests of the various theatres which led to so much waste of lives and power in the First Great War. Partly owing to wiser and more efficient supreme strategical control, and partly through force of circumstances, it was possible to deal with the problems of each theatre seriatim and to build up a powerful strategic reserve for the final decisive encounter. As a consequence when the Army was called on for the decisive effort it was at the peak of its efficiency both on the Western Front and in Burma, in contrast to its depleted and exhausted state when the final stages of the First Great War were reached in 1918.

REVERSE Which Would Have Shaken the Confidence of Many Armies

Nevertheless, the Army went through many dark hours. Its first experiences in France and Norway were disastrous. Owing to rapid expansion following years of neglect it was called on, insufficiently trained and inadequately armed, to face a fully prepared and war experienced enemy. Dunkirk and the abandonment of the Norwegian undertaking would have broken the heart and shaken the confidence of many armies. Except for the small and scattered garrisons in outlying stations abroad the country was without an army, and to protect the heart of the Empire from invasion and to save it from isolation it had to depend on the Royal Navy and the Royal Air Force.

How effectively those two great Services met the situation we know, but perhaps the Army has not been given sufficient credit for the manner in which it set about its task of reconstruction. It is, I think, fair to say that at the time the bulk of public opinion had abandoned all hope of the Army ever playing a decisive part in the struggle ahead. But the Army never lost faith in itself nor was shaken in the belief that, however important the role of the other Services was, final victory could not be won till the Army closed with the enemy and defeated him.

MOREOVER, it was realized by those who mattered that it was not only necessary to recruit and arm to the highest standards possible, but that it was essential to give the new army training which would enable it to meet a war-experienced enemy on something like equal terms. A new system of training was adopted which involved undoubted risks that would be unacceptable in normal peacetime training. The object was, of course, to introduce the troops as far as practicable into the atmosphere and dangers of warfare before committing them to battle. The First Great War had shown, and experience in France had confirmed, how much waste of life and loss of power were entailed in using troops under-trained and inexperienced. It may not yet be fully realized what our own army, and later the American Army, owed to the system of training devised.

While our main army was reforming in England our overseas detachments had obviously a defensive role. But Wavell's brilliant campaigns in Cyrenaica and Abyssinia proved what active defence can accomplish, and that the Army still retained offensive power. Our somewhat quixotic, and perhaps strategically indefensible, intervention in Greece again involved the Army in the bitterness of retreat, both there and in Cyrenaica. Yet in the long run, by upsetting the timing of the German attack on Russia and causing the Germans to abandon their designs on Iraq, it had far-reaching results which compensated for the losses incurred by Australian and New Zealand troops and by the Royal Navy in particular.

Lt.-Gen. SIR RICHARD McCREERY, K.C.B., C.B.E., D.S.O., M.C., who has been appointed G.O.C.-in-C. the British Army of the Rhine. This post of Army Commander (to be assumed on June 26, 1946) has been created because Lord Montgomery's successor as C.-in-C. British Forces in Germany is an airman, Marshal of the R.A.F. Sir Sholto Douglas.
Photo, Topical

NEW Theatres of War Opened When the Japanese Volcano Erupted

The regrettable necessity of dealing with the Vichy force in Syria brought the Army into yet another theatre before, in the autumn of 1941, the 8th Army was constituted and reopened the campaign in Libya. There, after a hard and fluctuating struggle, Rommel was defeated, but not decisively ; and it was discovered that in the matter of armaments we had not yet caught up on the enemy's lead. Rommel struck again, and having thrown the 8th Army on the defensive finally defeated it at Gazala, and Tobruk was lost. Once again the Army was in retreat, and Rommel perilously close to Alexandria when his pursuit was halted.

Meanwhile, the Japanese volcano had erupted and new theatres of war had been opened in Malaya, New Guinea and Burma with fresh retreats and disasters. Our defensive forces numerically, in armaments and in experience, were in no state to deal with the invader. With the Russians, also hard pressed and in retreat, summer of 1942 was the darkest hour before the dawn. But with the autumn the first streaks of dawn could be detected. Rommel's attempt to reach Alexandria was defeated, the Japanese had met their first reverse on land at Milne Bay and been thrown back from Port Moresby, and the German offensive in Russia was losing its momentum.

Finally, the sun rose over Alamein and at Stalingrad ; and henceforth it was the Allied Armies who were to open new theatres in the course of their advance to the decisive arena in Germany. They had finished with retreats, and they had now to show their qualities of resilience and to prove that armies are still the instruments with which decisive results can be achieved. Tunisia, Sicily and Italy were the new theatres, each presenting its special difficulties of terrain and each requiring amphibious operations to force an entrance—a wonderful opportunity for gaining training and experience before the immensely more formidable task of re-entering the French theatre.

RISKS of the Enterprise Were Not Realized Until Revealed on D-Day

These operations not only finally eliminated the Italian Army and Navy, diverted a considerable part of Germany's war potential from the Russian front and reopened a vital line of sea communications, but they had also restored public confidence in the Army. Certain sections of public opinion were already asking, why waste effort in the Mediterranean instead of stepping across the Channel to open a second front ? The immensity of the scale of preparations necessary, and the risks of the great enterprise failing, were, of course, not realized until revealed on D-Day. Even now it is questionable whether the patience with which the Supreme Command refused to be tempted into premature action is fully appreciated ; nor is it fully realized how disastrous would have been failure in an undertaking full of risk even after the most complete preparation.

ONCE the break-out from the Normandy bridge head was accomplished proof was finally given that the Army, with the close and full co-operation of air power, was the essential instrument for achieving decisive victory. Within a few weeks the enemy's army was shattered, France and Belgium were liberated, and the bases from which the V weapons flew were overrun. Within a year the Siegfried Line had been broken through, the Rhine crossed, and unconditional surrender of the enemy had been extorted in the heart of his own country. The same policy of patiently building up reserves and of employing them with a well-defined object was applied in Burma ; the 14th Army used at the decisive time and place and in full co-operation with air power was able in an astonishingly short time to achieve the seemingly impracticable.

Looking back on the War it may be true to say that we muddled into it, but surely on this occasion there is no justification for saying that we muddled through. Surely there was astonishing skill and patience displayed in clearing up the original tangles. All the same, many times during the War I was reminded of a remark a distinguished general once made to me. He said, "Why does our Army never arrange in manoeuvres to practise retreats ? Have we ever had a war in which we did not begin with a retreat ?" In practically every theatre that remark, unfortunately, proved true, though it was not the fault of the Army.

We Take Over from the Australians in Celebes

BRITISH AND INDIAN TROOPS of the 80th Infantry Brigade arrived at Macassar, on Celebes Island, Netherlands East Indies, from Saigon on January 31, 1946, to take over from the 21st Australian Infantry Brigade. The H.Q. faces one of the main thoroughfares of the town (top), which suffered little damage from Allied bombing and Japanese occupation. Two days later the handing-over ceremony took place in the forecourt of the H.Q. (bottom), where Australians (right) and British present arms at the changing of the guard.

Photos, British Official

Strange Story of H.M.S. Habbakuk

By
FRANCIS E. McMURTRIE
A.I.N.A.

A GIGANTIC aircraft carrier, 2,000 feet long, 300 feet across the beam and 200 feet in depth, was projected as the War was entering its third year. This floating airfield would have had hangar capacity for 200 Spitfire fighters or 100 Mosquito bombers, complete with every facility in the shape of operational and repair shops, etc. It would have been propelled at a speed of seven knots by Diesel-electric machinery with a normal consumption of 120 tons a day. Fuel capacity for 5,000 tons was to be provided, which would have given the ship a radius of action of 7,000 miles. The complement was to have been 404 officers and 3,216 petty officers and men.

The cost of one such vessel was estimated at not more than £10,000,000, due to the intended use of ice as the main structural material. This idea was put forward by the originator of the project, Mr. Geoffrey Pyke, Director of Programmes at Combined Operations Headquarters, and was based on the known difficulties of breaking up icebergs by the use of high explosive. In order that the ice should not melt, 14 per cent of wood pulp was to be mixed with it.

This material was given the name Pykrete, after its inventor. The method of manufacture devised, after various experiments had been carried out in Canada, was to spread a mush, made by mixing mechanical pulp with water, over a flat surface; it was then rolled until a uniform smooth layer three-eighths of an inch thick had been obtained. This being frozen by blowing cold air across it, Pykrete was the result. A total of 1,700,000 tons of this material would have had to be produced in one winter to build a single ship.

PROTECTION Against Melting and Bomb and Underwater Attack

It was intended that one or more of these huge carriers should operate in the North Atlantic, affording permanent protection to convoys. So impressed was Mr. Churchill with the proposal that he commented on it in the following terms: "I attach the greatest importance to the examination of these ideas. The advantages of a floating island or islands, if only used as refuelling depots for aircraft, are so dazzling that they do not at the moment need to be discussed. There would be no difficulty in finding a place to put such a stepping stone in any of the plans of war now under consideration. The scheme is only possible if we let nature do nearly all the work for us, and use as raw material sea-water and low temperature. The scheme will be destroyed if it involves the movement of very large numbers of men and heavy tonnage of steel or concrete to the remote recesses of the Arctic night." It was at the Prime Minister's suggestion that the scheme was christened Habbakuk.

Being built of 40-foot blocks of Pykrete, the interior of the structure would have been given complete immunity from any known form of air or underwater attack. The Pykrete was to have been protected from melting or erosion by an insulating skin tough enough to withstand normal weather conditions and the battering of the waves. The extent of possible torpedo damage would have been a crater not more than three feet deep and about 20 feet in diameter; while bomb damage, even though the crater might be slightly deeper, would be no more serious in its effects.

ALL the preliminary work was carried out under the direction of a special Research and Development Committee at Combined Operations Headquarters in this country. In order to test every obstacle, this committee was strengthened by calling in experts in all matters investigated. Thus there was a scientific advisory panel, concerned primarily with the properties of ice, and an engineering advisory panel, dealing with constructional problems. Prior to the institution of larger scale experiments in Canada, these panels did some very useful work on ice production and the measurement of ice properties in England. During the winter months of 1942-43, research was pushed forward energetically in Canada under the direction of Dr. C. J. Mackenzie, President of the National Research Council of Canada, and the form and general dimensions of the aircraft carrier were outlined. To examine the technical possibilities, the Montreal Engineering Company was brought into consultation.

When the Quebec Conference was held in August 1943 the Chiefs of Staff reported that they saw no use for iceberg ships in operations for the invasion of Europe. It thus became clear that any future use made of the Habbakuk project would be in connexion with the war with Japan, in which case the vessel would need to be constructed on the Pacific coast. Previously it had been planned to build it either at Corner Brook, Newfoundland, or in Seven Islands Bay, Quebec Province. Both these sites were near pulp factories, with deep water close inshore, and an open channel to the sea, besides being in sufficiently high latitude. Otherwise, the ideal site would have been the Saguenay River; but this was put out of the question by the existence of a shallow bar at its mouth.

The outstanding objection to using ice in the construction of the ship was, of course, its tendency to melt. From the outset it was clear that the larger the vessel, the slower would be its percentage rate of melting; but if the structure was to preserve its essential shape, it was important to prevent any melting at all. This was the object of the external insulating skin, together with an ingenious system of internal refrigerating ducts.

A block model of the vessel was actually constructed during the winter of 1943 at Patricia Lake. Its dimensions were 60 feet long, 30 feet beam and 20 feet depth. A wooden framework carrying the insulation was first constructed on the lake ice, gradually built up with ice blocks, and allowed to sink into the lake. A central hold contained refrigerating engines, which circulated cold air through a series of sheet iron pipes, placed immediately behind the insulation. This model weighed in all about 1,000 tons, and was constructed in about two months by a gang of 15 men. After a few initial difficulties the refrigeration system worked well, and the structure was kept frozen until nearly the end of the ensuing summer.

THE Economic Factors Finally Killed this Daring Project

Armament of the ship was to have been restricted to anti-aircraft guns. It was never fully settled whether the aircraft should be parked on deck, limiting their numbers, and leaving them exposed to enemy attack, or be stowed in the hangars, giving rise to the danger of weakening the structure by the necessity of leaving apertures in the deck.

After the Quebec Conference the United States Navy was brought into the investigation. It was then found that the Pacific coast offered little in the way of satisfactory sites. Puget Sound had too warm a climate, and Alaska was too remote. The joint board which was studying the question ultimately reported, on December 16, 1943, that the scheme involved such expenditure of effort, particularly on the Pacific coast, that it could not be undertaken without interfering seriously with plans of greater priority. Accordingly the Habbakuk project was finally dropped by the Allied authorities.

Its use in the Atlantic had been largely stultified by the employment of escort carriers in large numbers to attain a similar end. Moreover, the development of aircraft requiring longer and larger runways tended progressively to limit the value of any floating island of practicable size. Finally, and overshadowing everything else, was the economic factor, hinted at in Mr. Churchill's minute already quoted. Though the raw material might be abundant and cheap, the labour involved in handling the undertaking would have been the major item of cost; and on the basis of man-hours the verdict had to go against the project.

AIRCRAFT CARRIERS CONSTRUCTED LARGELY OF ICE, each propelled by Diesel-electric machinery and with a complement of 3,620, were seriously considered in connexion with anti-submarine warfare, and a scale model was completed in the winter of 1943, as told above, at Patricia Lake near Jasper in Alberta, Canada. The system of propulsion is indicated in the side view (top), where 13 of the 26 engine-nacelles are seen. The enormous ice drome compared diagrammatically (bottom) with the liner Queen Mary. *Drawings by G. H. Davis, by courtesy of The Illustrated London News*

H.M.S. Suffolk's Company Stow Food for Britain

WHEN THIS 10,000-TON CRUISER CALLED AT SYDNEY, Australia, en route for Home, members of her company sacrificed their shore-leave to take aboard thousands of cases of food destined for the U.K. and store these in every available space. H.M.S. Suffolk gained prominence in 1941 when, with H.M.S. Norfolk, she shadowed the German battleship Bismarck after she had slipped out from Bergen, Norway, on the chase which ended in the Bismarck's destruction in the Atlantic (see pages 580-581, Vol. 4).

Photo, Planet News

Maintaining the Peace in Troubled Trieste

ALLIED MILITARY GOVERNMENT assumed control of the Italian city and port of Trieste, on the Adriatic, on June 9, 1945, following the dispute between Italy and Marshal Tito, fomented by his demand for its cession to Yugoslavia after it fell to the 8th Army and Yugoslav troops in May 1945. The intervention of Field-Marshal Alexander resulted in an agreement by which the future of the city was left to the Council of Foreign Ministers to decide. H.Q. of the Military Government is in the Palace of Justice, where the British flag flies (1). All civil police organizations were disbanded and a new force recruited for training under the command of Major J. Henderson (2 left), who is seen with Lt.-Col. Richardson, centre, Assistant Chief of Police, and Captain T. Cawthorne, U.S.A., Chief of the Police Technical School. A mounted detachment of the new force (3). In the harbour, where clearance of defences is now almost complete (4) are the British sloop Pelican and the frigate St. Austell Bay.

Photos, G.P.U.

‘Egg and Chips Palace’ in Libya Closes Down

N.A.A.F.I. CANTEEN AT "MARBLE ARCH," on the Cyrenaica-Tripolitania border, well known to thousands of 8th Army and Desert Air Force men (see illus. in p. 484, Vol. 6), has served its last egg and chips. Some 200 miles from Benghazi and 400 from Tripoli, the canteen (1) was opened three years ago. It is close to Mussolini's "triumphal" arch (right), which British soldiers are inspecting at close quarters (2). To supply the canteen, which included a restaurant and stage, water had to be transported 120 miles from Agedabia, and then pumped into tanks (3). Bread and cakes had to be brought 200 miles across the desert. It was also a centre for bulk issue stores, which were housed in the tented section (4). For the past two years the canteen served R.A.F. Transport Command operating the Far East route. *Photos, N.A.A.F.I.*

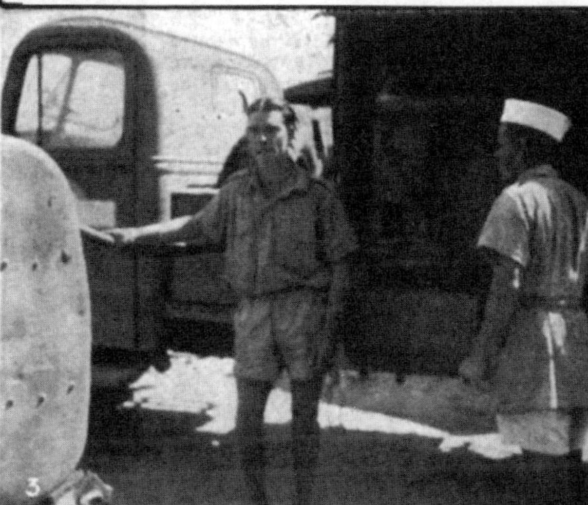

The Unarmed Army That Went Valiantly to War

Men and women of the Salvation Army exchanged peaked caps and poke-bonnets for steel helmets and for five years worked in mobile canteens, front-line dressing stations and in Red Shield clubs, hostels and hospitals, from Burma to Bremen, from the Solomons to Sollum. The story is told in this article specially written for "The War Illustrated" by FRANK ILLINGWORTH.

BULLETS whistled across Wau airfield, New Guinea, in January 1943, as the great Douglas air-transports trundled to a halt, and over the Salvation Army shack at the airfield's edge where the Australians stopped for gulps of black coffee before doubling from the planes into action. For twelve days the battle raged incessantly. Frequently, shells burst near the shack; but night and day Captain Cecil Ewan, Captain of the Salvation Army, kept the 12-gallon bath-tub of coffee on the boil. "Salvo corfee" the Australians called it. Just one typical episode in the wartime saga of the Salvationists.

The Red Shield sign of the Salvation Army appeared on every Front, from the day the first of its "soldiers" to be killed in action, Mrs. Brigadier Climpson, fell to a bomb-splinter during the 1940 retreat in France. The girls and women who in May 1944 drove mobile canteens across the swollen Rapido River in Italy, with the 8th Army spearhead, wore battledress; but over their bunks hung the familiar poke bonnets of the Salvation Army. S.A. men went ashore with the first wave at Salerno on Sept. 9, 1943 and set up first-aid posts on the erupting beaches.

All the Way to Final Victory

Their "regimental" emblem, the Red Shield, swayed back and forth in North Africa, and from Tobruk and El Alamein went across the Mediterranean with the 8th and 5th Armies to Sicily and Italy. From Greece and Crete it went with the Australians and New Zealanders to New Guinea and the Solomons. In Burma it fell back before the Japs in 1942, and then entered Rangoon with the advancing 14th Army spearheads on May 3, 1945. Soon after D-Day it landed in Normandy and stormed along with canteens, chapels and libraries all the way to final victory; at Bremen, girl Salvationists were the first to serve tea to British troops taking over the port in May 1945.

The Salvation Army is an international organization. It knows no frontiers. Normally controlled from London, contact with a great part of the S.A. was lost on the outbreak of War. The Red Shield appeared on both sides of the world's battlefronts: the Luftwaffe shattered the S.A.'s maternity hospital in London, and the R.A.F. wrecked its Berlin counterpart. And there were occasions when enemy Salvationists, advancing with German and Italian panzers, took over Allied Salvation Army posts, and vice versa.

IN both Allied and enemy countries Salvationists went into action on Sept. 3, 1939. With the first bombs, the British section set up canteens in air-raid shelters—until the Government scheme got into its stride—established first-aid posts for the injured, and hostels and canteens for the homeless. There was no lack of work to be done; but there was shortage of personnel, because the young Salvationists were called into the Forces, and many of the Commissioned members, qualified Ministers of Religion, volunteered for Overseas service.

In swinging from peace to war the Salvation Army had the advantage of a world-wide organization. There was no need to set up headquarters in individual countries before it could go into action in France or Algeria or Malaya. For example, the French Salvation Army had a fully staffed building at Arras (the B.E.F. Headquarters in 1939-40), and British Salvationists made it their base for stranded men during the retreat. It became the meeting-place for the homeless, civilians and Servicemen alike. There was an occasion when a Salvation Army colonel marched to the Arras Red Shield Club at the head of a bedraggled khaki band singing "Roll Out The Barrel!"

So it was in Burma, Singapore, Hongkong and the Pacific Islands. The organization was already there when the troops first went into battle. When they fell back, many local S.A. men remained behind to help the civil population, and ended up in internment camps. Major Harvey and Adjutant Matthews were the only two white men to stay behind when we pulled out of Penang on December 19, 1941, and Kuala Lumpur a week or so later. At Hongkong's Stanley Prison a Salvation Army man was interpreter between the Japs and the prisoners they executed. Salvationists who fell back with our Forces set up advance posts, sometimes practically in the front lines.

ON THEIR 50th ANNIVERSARY (Oct. 17, 1941) the International Staff Band of the Salvation Army performed in the forecourt of Buckingham Palace, where the bandmaster, Col. George Fuller, introduced his players to H.M. the King. *Photo, P.N.A.*

When the Australians advanced on Salamaua, in September 1943, Adjutant Edwin Robertson, senior Salvation Army Welfare Officer with the 3rd Division, tramped fifty miles a day with the spearhead troops. At some points the river water, cluttered with bodies, was undrinkable. But 32,000 gallons of coffee were served on the way to Salamaua. On the beach there a shell dropped six yards from the Red Shield Club, flinging earth over the congregation while Robertson conducted a short service.

In the New Guinea jungle, on the Kokoda Road in the autumn of 1942, Australian troops came upon a man they last saw serving coffee in Syria—Major Albert Moore of the Melbourne Salvation Army. The Red Shield Hut he established was five-days' jungle journey through the Owen Stanley mountains. Coffee-shop, church and hospital rolled into one, and served by Major Moore and a dozen Papuan Salvationists, it cheered many a Digger on the weary Kokoda Road. It was the same story in Burma and Malaya, where men and women from the Mother Country and the Dominions worked with Burman and Malayan Salvationists all the way from Rangoon to Kohima—and back again. Meanwhile, in Britain the Salvation Army prepared to link up with its sister organizations on the Continent when the invasion got under way.

Heroism of Red Shield Ladies

Some idea of the size of the organization in this country is illustrated by the fact that Red Shield canteens attended more than 650 incidents during the flying-bomb and rocket attacks alone, serving something like half a million people amid the rubble of their homes. It was my good fortune to know some of these men and women who exchanged poke bonnets and peaked caps for steel helmets. Captain Aspinall, for example. We of the Auxiliary Fire Service in Dover called him the "Salvo chap." He could be relied upon to turn up at "incidents" before the bombing was over. Time and again one saw him driving through empty streets under long-range artillery fire from Calais and Boulogne.

"You see," he would explain to us, "I want a cup o' coffee myself; but it's no fun drinking by myself, so I come out an' have one with you fellows." By a cruel trick of Fate he was killed while serving tea, when a shell crashed into the Salvation Army H.Q. Then there was Captain Harvey, whom I saw win the B.E.M. burrowing for the wounded beneath a tottering building.

The young women of the S.A. drove their canteens into the firing lines: Adjutant Rita Strickland and Miss Esther Walker, attached to an 8th Army tank division, were at Foggia, Bari (where Adjutant Gaskin was killed when the Luftwaffe bombed the harbour and blew up two ammunition ships on December 2, 1943), at Ancona, Rimini and the Rapido. Many an 8th Army man remembers them. The elderly, motherly type, unable to rough-it, did no less to maintain morale. "Nag us a bit, missus," one dejected youngster said to a Red Shield Lady, "and make it seem like home." Within a couple of minutes he was wearing an apron and lending a hand behind the counter! It was little things like that which kept a tired man going.

THE social side of Salvation Army work—the nursing, hospitals and crèches, hostels and Missing Persons Bureau—is another story. Suffice it to say that the S.A. spent well over one million pounds during the War. Its work among Servicemen in one year alone provided the troops with ten million sheets of writing paper and one hundred and fifty million cups of tea.

What of the years ahead? In Britain the aim is to "meet the immediate demand in any field until new Government schemes come into operation." And abroad? The Salvation Army has an enormous task on its hands in Europe and Asia and in the Pacific. Its 2,500 Red Shield Clubs cannot hope to cope with the millions of under-fed, the disease-ridden and the homeless; they can cater only for the comforts of the Occupation Troops. The Salvation Army is the only international organization to have survived two world wars, and its two sections—Allied, and for want of a more suitable word, enemy—have linked up again for service in the common cause.

Salvationists on Home and Overseas Fronts

S.A. MOBILE CANTEEN UNIT was at hand with hot drinks for the rescue squad (top) shortly after an L.C.C. school at Lewisham, London, received a direct hit in a daylight raid on January 20, 1943 (see page 569, Vol. 6). At the same time, at the other side of the world, Australian troops were being served with coffee or cocoa and biscuits under the sign of the Red Shield, the S.A.'s "regimental" emblem (bottom) on their way to the forward area near Mubo, New Guinea. See also facing page.

Photos, Sport & General, Salvation Army

In Mukden After 7 Months' Russian Occupation

FOLLOWING THE WITHDRAWAL of Soviet troops in March 1946 Mukden, in Manchuria, was a centre in the dispute between Chinese Nationalists and Communists. A portrait of Chiang Kai-shek outside the Nationalist H.Q. (1). Notice in garbled English adds interest to U.N.R.R.A.'s offices. (2). Russians are alleged to have removed machinery from this wrecked factory (3). Trains to Mukden crowded with refugees (4)

Japan's Emperor Makes a Break with Tradition

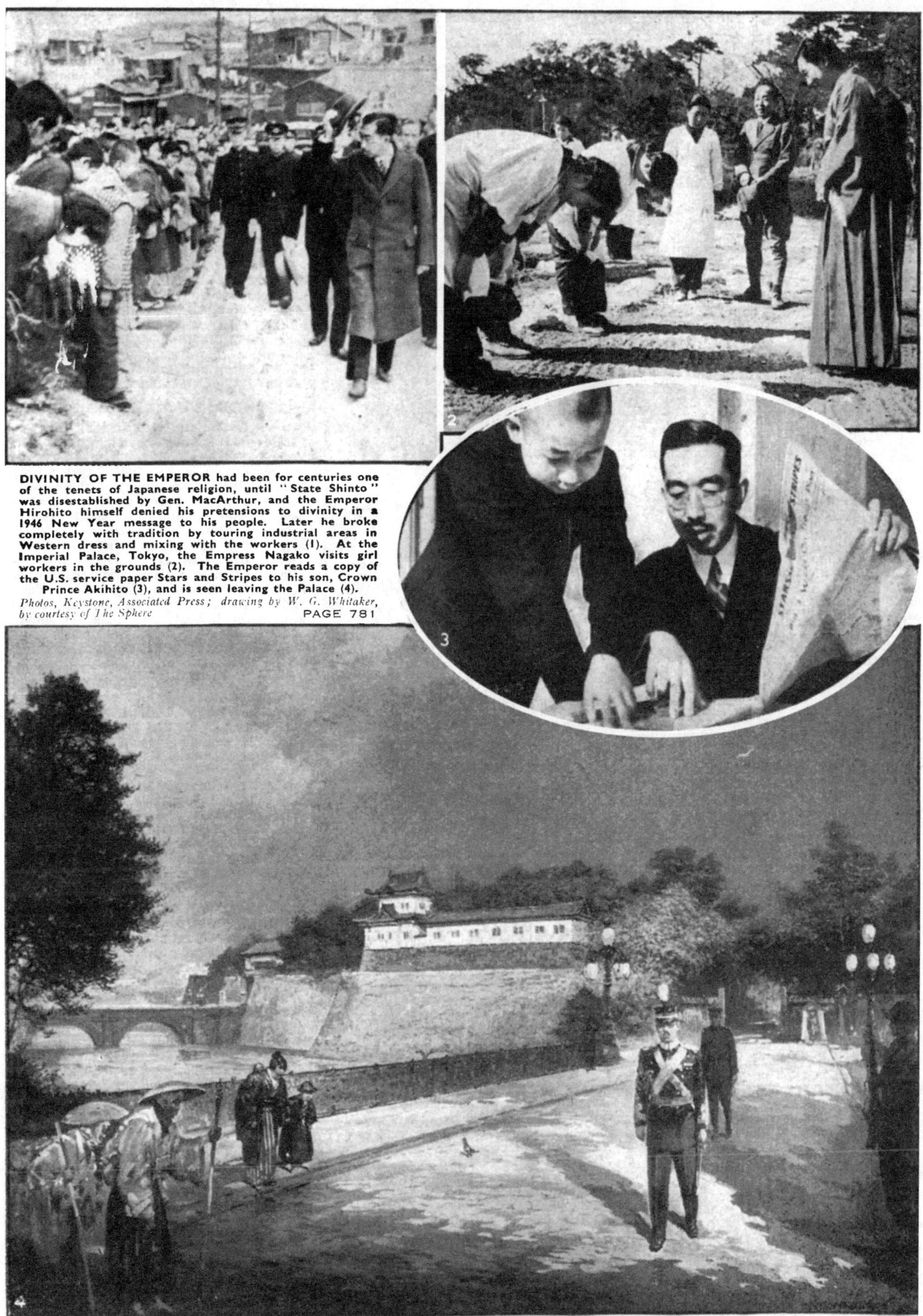

DIVINITY OF THE EMPEROR had been for centuries one of the tenets of Japanese religion, until "State Shinto" was disestablished by Gen. MacArthur, and the Emperor Hirohito himself denied his pretensions to divinity in a 1946 New Year message to his people. Later he broke completely with tradition by touring industrial areas in Western dress and mixing with the workers (1). At the Imperial Palace, Tokyo, the Empress Nagako visits girl workers in the grounds (2). The Emperor reads a copy of the U.S. service paper Stars and Stripes to his son, Crown Prince Akihito (3), and is seen leaving the Palace (4).

Photos, Keystone, Associated Press; drawing by W. G. Whitaker, by courtesy of The Sphere

How Near to Winning Were the Germans?

An enormous mass of widely scattered documentary evidence must be collated before the strategic history of the War can be written in full. Meanwhile, a thought-provoking study of Nazi strategy by the Czech expert, Lt.-Col. F. O. Miksche, who was on General de Gaulle's staff, is examined here by Dr. EDGAR STERN-RUBARTH. See also pages 682-683.

THERE have been signs of a certain self-complacency gaining ground in Allied countries whereby it is taken for granted that sooner or later Hitler would have been vanquished, anyhow. This assumption is shattered by a thorough study of the whole problem of Nazi strategy which has been made and presented in a book titled Hitler's Strategical Errors.

The author, Lt.-Col. F. O. Miksche, now Military Attaché of Czechoslovakia in Paris, was on General de Gaulle's staff during the War and, through his earlier books Blitzkrieg and Paratroops (see page 588, Vol. 6), influenced the general concept of modern warfare. His new work is available, so far, in French only (Les Erreurs Strategiques de Hitler, Payot, Paris).

Miksche's thesis, in brief, is that Hitler had at least four major chances of winning, and a fifth of terminating the war without total defeat; that, according to one's own reading, either a benevolent Providence or the Fuehrer's maniacal fixation upon political and prestige considerations prevented him from grasping these opportunities: and thus was humanity saved.

The Fuehrer's Right-About-Turn

According to Miksche, Hitler's missed opportunities were: (1) the carrying of his successful blitzkrieg in the East, in 1939, into a then unprepared Russia, there gaining and stabilizing the decisive victory he tried in vain to secure in 1941-1942; (2) the invasion of Britain, if need be with improvised means, immediately after the collapse of France; (3) the conquest of French North Africa by pushing on through Spain and securing West Africa as a base against British emergency shipping around the Cape and against a future Allied landing operation in North Africa; (4) with or without Franco's assistance, the turning of his subsequent African campaign into a major operation, saving Italy's Empire, conquering Egypt and the Suez Canal, and hitting at the British Empire in the Near and Middle East.

After having missed these four major opportunities of winning the War (all between September 1939 and June 1941), Hitler had another chance of not losing it completely, to say the least. This was by withdrawing in time—in the autumn of 1942, from which period he was in fact forced entirely on to the defensive—into the "Citadel of the Third Reich."

ANY one of these operations would have been fully in accordance with German military teaching from Clausewitz to Schlieffen and with the conclusions drawn by Ludendorff from the events of the First Great War. But at every turn the General Staff's suggestions, and Hitler's own lip-service to these teachings, were cast aside for political, psychological or propaganda reasons. The essence of all German military wisdom, always, had been the prevention of a major two-front-war; yet that is, precisely, what the Fuehrer provoked.

Resolved though he was upon eventually acquiring the industrial and agricultural resources of southern Russia, he made a right-about-turn after the conquest of Poland. One may or may not agree with Miksche as to the likelihood of Hitler's persuading the Western powers to "non-intervention" in the event of his invading Russia at that time; but by attacking Denmark, Norway, the Low Countries and France in 1940 he ensured the existence of a Western Front when he later turned again to the east and engaged the bulk of his resources in Russia.

Again, by launching his main drive eastward early in the War he would not have had to conquer the Balkans, where the aristocratic regime of Hungary, Rumanian ambitions in the Dniester delta, the old traditions of the Bulgarian rulers, and Prince Paul's Yugoslav set would have sided with a victorious attacker of the Soviet state. An isolated Turkey might then have been persuaded to come in on the side of Germany; Finland would not have missed the opportunity to recover her losses or, presumably, still have been in the field; the small Baltic states would have tried to preserve, or regain, their independence; and, in due course, Russia might in turn have had to face the nightmare of a two-front war if Japan had seized her opportunity.

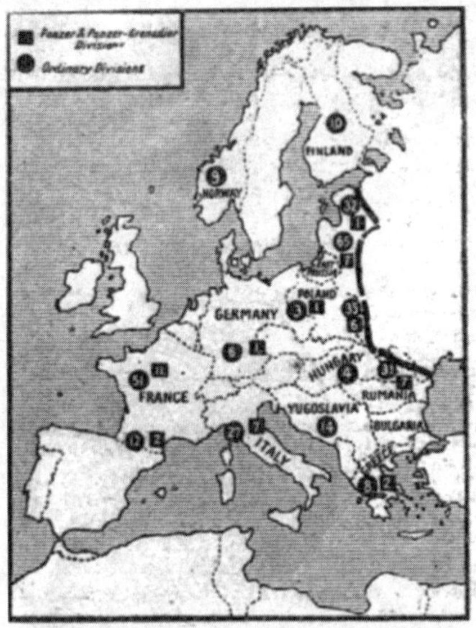

DISPOSITION OF GERMAN DIVISIONS before the Allied invasion of Normandy, showing preponderance of strength on the Russian front and armies still held in outlying regions by Hitler against advice of his generals.

As to Hitler's second failure as a strategist, even if his preliminary assaults upon Norway, Denmark, Holland and Belgium had military justification of a kind, it was his triumphant strutting at Compiegne and Paris, the irrecoverable time wasted in completely annihilating the French forces, that lost him the chance of following up Dunkirk and the conquest of the Channel coast with a lightning invasion stroke against an unprepared Britain. Fascinated by prestige considerations, possibly afraid of a later recovery of France, he committed—as Miksche puts it—the same mistake as Moltke junior in 1914, and neglected the famous Schlieffen instruction, "Make me the right wing strong."

FOR the right wing, this time, was England. The author seeks in vain for an answer to the question why a surprise invasion, whose possibilities he impressively outlines, was not tried by an otherwise over-ambitious and daring Nazi strategy; by means of parachute landings such as, in even more difficult conditions, were successful less than a year later in Crete; by landings from any available, improvised craft, and so forth. He can find only psychological reasons—fear of the unfamiliar sea, British stubbornness, superstition perhaps.

Even less explicable, if possible, appears German strategy in the Mediterranean, in the light of this searching study. The Italian Navy outnumbered by far the British naval forces available in that vital area. With 200,000 Italian troops in the north, and another 300,000, all well provided with air cover, tanks and guns in the southern colonies, our forces were outnumbered by 10 to 1, and more than 20 to 1 respectively, in 1940, and by as many as 7 to 1 in December of that year when Wavell launched his first, devastating attack. Hitler might have had a victory, if he had bolstered up his unreliable allies not with the paltry 3 to 5 divisions of his Afrika Korps but with the army later wasted in the Balkans; and if, instead of in March 1941, he had intervened in Libya in August 1940. The potential consequences—the cutting of Britain's artery, the invasion of the Near and Middle East, the menace to Russia from the south, even a join-up in India with the Japanese armies—would have justified any effort; instead, he treated the African theatre as a side-show, and lost.

Mussolini's Aid Over-Estimated

Whatever Franco's official attitude might have been, a German march across Spain, supported by Italian naval operations, and the penetration in bulk into North Africa, would have taken no more than 60 divisions: 30 for guarding France; 15, or even a mere 10, for holding the Spanish lines of communication; and another 15 to 20 might have been landed in Algeria and Tunisia by September 15, 1940. With the Straits of Gibraltar sealed, the western basin of the Mediterranean closed from Tunis and Bizerta; Africa's coast down to Dakar a base for U-boats and planes, Rommel, instead of Graziani, in command, the prospect would have been even worse for us.

If the reason for Hitler's missing that Mediterranean opportunity was the growing conviction that he had over-estimated by far the military value of his ally Mussolini, his later doom in the east was certainly due to his under-estimating the industrial capacity and resilience of Russia. That is his only excuse for having systematically rejected the advice of his generals for a timely shortening of his lines—possibly, as Miksche shows, in four different ways, by which the 3,700 kilometres of the line at the time of Stalingrad would have shrunk to 1,800, 1,650, or 1,500 respectively, and the 230 divisions he then needed for a mere holding fight have been reduced to between 95 and 110.

This, and this alone, would have given him the "masse de manoeuvre," the fresh reserves of between 50 and 100 divisions which were lacking to him at any time after the winter of 1941-42. With these he could have reinforced any menaced point, and might have prevented an Allied break-through into his huge inner fortress, embracing Denmark, Holland, Czechoslovakia and a large part of Poland, and surrounded with partly natural, partly well-planned outer defences from the Pripet to the Carpathians, through Yugoslavia and northern Italy, and along the Alpine ranges.

CHURCHILL, on September 28, 1944 (and Montgomery a fortnight earlier) rightly pointed out how much we owed "to the extraordinary blunders of the Germans." The author of Hitler's Strategical Errors does not neglect the vital importance of one date in the War—September 15, 1940, when Goering lost 185 out of 500 planes attacking London, and the British fighter force lost 25 machines and 11 pilots. "In the history of the world," says Miksche, "one does not find another victory won with such small losses and securing such a lasting success."

Photos, British Official

R.A.F. Regiment on a Weapons-Hunt in Java

Tasks of British troops in the capital, Batavia, were "made more difficult by the fact that certain extremist elements had seized arms from the Japanese," declared Lieut.-Gen. Sir Montagu Stopford, Allied C.-in-C. Squadrons of the R.A.F. Regiment have collected a varied assortment of weapons (1). Official notice printed in Indonesian and nailed to a tree (2) announces a search of native quarters; while this is being conducted a detachment covers the approaches (3).

Panama Canal Reopened to British Shipping

When Lend-Lease ended, in 1945, our Ministry of War Transport imposed a ban on the use by British merchant ships of the " Big Ditch," to save dollar currency : in one year alone—1940—Britain had paid about £1,250,000 in Panama Canal tolls. In March 1946 the ban was lifted, enabling our ships to travel again between Britain and New Zealand and Australia by this short cut. The Canal helped immeasurably in the prosecution of the War at the end of the long Pacific supply-lines. Tens of thousands of troops made the passage, vast quantities of supplies, aircraft carriers and battleships such as the Missouri (1), which just managed to scrape through each of the three systems of locks (3). A big battleship requires ten to eleven hours to complete the 50½-mile passage. Wartime defence of the Canal Zone included this 14-in. railway gun (2).

Photos,

' Big Ditch's' Part in the Allied Victory

imes Photos

More than 23,000 vessels went through the Canal during the period July 1, 1941, to June 30, 1945, cargo amounting to 45,000,000 tons. Between January and July 1945 nearly 1,500,000 tons of Army cargo alone passed from the Atlantic to the Pacific. Four destroyer escorts are seen in a lock chamber (4), with space to spare. It is only the very big ships which cause misgiving; U.S. carriers of the Medway class are too wide to negotiate the locks, and plans for another set, capable of accommodating any vessel that can be visualized at present, are being reviewed in the light of war experience. The Culebra (now called the Gaillard) Cut (5) was a long and crucial problem in the construction of the Canal, which was opened to commerce in 1914 and shortens the sea journey from Liverpool to San Francisco by 5,666 miles.

Ancient Nuremberg in the News Today

It was as the gateway through which rich trade from Italy and the East passed to Northern Germany that Nuremberg, a city of Bavaria and now site of the Nazi war-crime trials, won prosperity in the Middle Ages. In modern times its commercial importance was maintained, large factories being built outside the city walls; and under Hitler it gained notoriety as scene of the annual Nazi Party Rally.

The city's medieval aspect remained, in old walls and gateways, irregular streets and picturesque gabled houses, almost unimpaired, until the great R.A.F. raid of January 2, 1945, in a matter of twenty minutes laid most of Nuremberg in ruins.

In addition to being a commercial centre, Nuremberg was world-famous as " the home of German art," largely through the influence of the artist Albrecht Dürer (1471-1528), whose house was preserved as a museum and a centre of attraction for tourists: the house at the outbreak of the War (1) and as it is today (2). Though its ancient timber has been largely destroyed the stone and other framework remains, giving grounds for hope that some happier day, when a new Nuremberg rises from the debris (3), this fine old Gothic building where many of Dürer's masterpieces were completed may take on a semblance to its former state. See also pages 47 and 596.

Drawings by W. G. Whitaker by courtesy of The Sphere; photograph by Associated Press

Odyssey of a Brigadier

A Review by
HAMILTON FYFE

Why are escape stories always read with close interest—whether they are of convicts escaping from gaols, or democrats running away from gestapos, or prisoners of war eluding the watchfulness of their guards and making for the open country ?

They are popular, these stories, because all readers can put themselves imaginatively in the places of the fugitives. Just as girls in factories, shops or offices like novels which tell of drudges who became duchesses, so we all like a tale, true or made-up, which helps us to picture ourselves as going through adventures, taking risks, defying authority, and finally triumphing over all obstacles and regaining freedom.

Among the many books I have read about escapes from prisoner-of-war camps or fortresses I don't remember any that gripped my interest more tightly and at the same time stirred my feelings more deeply than Farewell Campo 12 (Michael Joseph, 10s. 6d.), by Brigadier James Hargest, C.B.E., D.S.O., M.C. This has now gone into a second edition and will probably, if paper supplies permit, run into several more. Its charm lies very largely in the personality of the writer, who was killed in France soon after our invasion began in 1944.

He was a New Zealander. He had fought in the 1914-18 war, then farmed in his own country and become an M.P. there, then taken a distinguished part in the 1940-41 operations in Greece, Crete and North Africa. He had the bad luck—it really was that—to be captured towards the end of the latter year. The troops he commanded were suddenly surrounded by masses of tanks ; the only alternative to surrender would have been wholesale massacre.

All One Hates Most in the World

At first Brigadier Hargest felt being captured so overwhelming a disaster that for a while his mind could hardly grasp what it meant. It seemed quite impossible that " one's command, one's freedom, one's right to think for oneself could have been taken away and that henceforth one must obey the dictates of those representing all one hates most in the world." Like every soldier who goes into battle, he had foreseen possibilities of death, wounds, incapacity, but had " never for one moment thought of capture."

> Now I was caught. But with full realization came simultaneously the determination to escape. That never for a moment left me during the next sixteen months.

Of the Germans, who captured him, he speaks well. Rommel spoke to him coldly, but courteously, though he stupidly took offence when the Brigadier did not salute him. (" I was in the wrong, but I stuck to my point," which was that he was under no obligation to do it.) Of the Italians, to whom he was transferred, Hargest formed a very low opinion. There was a major, " plump, dapper, beautifully dressed, with a tongue that chattered like a monkey's all the time." There was a prison commandant, " talkative, gesticulating, useless," who was also a liar. There were the crew of a ship carrying 2,000 British prisoners who abandoned it—and them—in a panic and tried to row away. Fortunately they were ordered back in time and sailed the ship to port.

Hargest was a good hater. He so heartily detested one of the Italian officers placed in charge of prisoners that " I have always hoped he had a perfectly hellish life afterwards, being hounded from place to place by British troops and British aircraft till at last one of the latter dropped something right on top of him." On the other hand, tribute is paid with warm-hearted gratefulness to anyone, friend or enemy, who behaved kindly. The Italian naval officers were far more sympathetic than the military, and army doctors received very good marks.

Of the French peasants and railway men who took care of him later, when he was on his way to Spain, and of several Spanish folk who helped him, the Brigadier speaks with genuine affection. Everyone with whom he came into contact liked him. He responded by opening his heart to them. Over and over again he tells how partings from those who had sheltered and guided him were " such sweet sorrow "—sweet because freedom lay ahead, sorrowful because they knew they would not meet again.

Touched Rock-Bottom in Misery

When he reached the Spanish frontier after his long journey through France, he looked back sadly, yet with joyful mind, remembering " the band of men and women who had cared for my safety with completely selfless devotion. They had exposed themselves to punishment, to certain death, if they were caught, and each one of them had spurned reward. . . . They had all said the same thing ' I am a patriot. I do it for France.' " Looking back thus, Hargest felt that he would in future wear the Legion of Honour, which had been conferred on him in 1918, " with a deeper understanding of the mystical quality that is called the Spirit of France."

It happened that a number of general officers had been taken prisoner about the same time in Africa. They were eventually lodged in a *castello* on the hills above Florence, a fortress of unusual strength, built, ironically as it turned out, by an Englishman in the early part of the 19th century. How its inmates now cursed the fancy that had made the place, with its immensely thick walls and battlements and solid masonry, so suitable for a prison !

Before he arrived there, Hargest had some most uncomfortable hours. In one camp on the coast of North Africa scarcely any of the ordinary decencies of life were provided. " Even eating and drinking presented difficulties, as we had few spoons or knives and forks among us, and drinking vessels were rare. It was an unforgettable sight to see 70 British officers clambering over a large Italian refuse dump, seeking anything that would hold liquid—old tins or bottles, and pieces of tin that could be cut into the shape of spoons." That afternoon they " touched bottom in misery," he says. But I feel sure he must have had some fun out of it, too.

Brigadier JAMES HARGEST, C.B.E., D.S.O., M.C., New Zealand M.P., whose escape story Farewell Campo 12, is reviewed here. He was killed by a shell-burst in Normandy, August 12, 1944. *Photo, Topical*

As soon as he had settled down to the dull daily routine of the *castello* the Brigadier began planning an attempt at escape. Several of his companions were doing the same thing. Two generals, whose combined ages came to a hundred and ten, managed to break out and walk for seven days, doing more than twenty miles a day, carrying heavy packs over mountainous country, before they were recaptured by the Italians.

One great difficulty was making-up costumes that would pass muster, when they were on the road, as unobtrusive civilian dress. Hargest decided to look like a French or Italian workman. Clothes could scarcely ever be bought, so jackets and caps were made out of army blankets. Then came the problem of trousers. They had to be blue. The Brigadier had only the old battledress trousers in which he had been captured. He had to find some decoction which would dye them blue.

Green walnuts, tea, coffee, " Condy's Fluid " and various berries were tried without success. Then, at last, boot polish and a bottle of ink did the trick. This mixture was brewed in a bedroom jug and poured into a bath. It turned everything in sight blue ! And all he had to clean up with were an old brick and some soap. His hands were blue for days ; he had to wear gloves to ward off suspicion.

Another headache was the necessity for forging identity cards that would deceive the police. One of the prisoners set to work on these and " rose to superb heights, from which the fact clearly emerged that, if he had not chosen to be a respectable major-general, he might have had a successful career " in the ranks of crime. His hobbies were sketching and painting, so he was allowed to have brushes, fine pens, paper, inks and colours. He copied an Italian identity card exactly, matching the paper, reproducing the crest, stamp-markings, print and the signature of the issuing official.

Excavated With Infinite Pains

He also provided photographs for the cards, by picking out from a gramophone catalogue portraits of singers which would pass for portraits of the fugitives. By a lucky chance the size of these and the paper they were printed on were like the portraits on the cards. Six of the latter were produced, so good that " it was impossible for the lay eye to tell the counterfeit from the original."

The escape was made through a tunnel excavated with infinite pains and hidden from observation with astonishing ingenuity. Eventually they reached Switzerland and thought their long ordeal was over. But they were mistaken. After a while the Brigadier's friend went off to Spain—and died there. Hargest felt he must follow and find out what had happened to him. So once more he started on a long journey, through countries more or less hostile, where he could only hope to avoid arrest by being passed on from one sympathizer to another. He came through this second severe test of nerves and physical endurance and arrived back in England. But he was never to return to New Zealand, his homeland. He lies buried in a little French churchyard at Roncamps, in Normandy.

THE SALVING OF WRECKS IN THE PORT OF LONDON is the responsibility of the Port of London Authority (see facing page). Through the courtesy of the **P.L.A. Salvage Department** our artist **Haworth** witnessed an actual operation in the Thames, and this drawing was made from sketches done on the spot.

The scene of the wreck is marked by a buoy (A) flashing a green light. A diver (B) is sent down to make an examination, and on his report the raising operation is planned.

The vessel shown here is of about 5,000 tons, and most of its cargo of coal has been removed by mechanical grabs. The remaining hull, plus mud and sand, weighs about 1,000 tons under water. A 9-in. wire hawser is worked underneath by two 120-ton lighters (C) and (D), by means of their powerful winches (E). Sometimes mud obstruction is cleared by a diver using a high-pressure hose (F). Next, lighters **N3** and **N4**, each 160 ft. long and able to lift 1,200 tons, are manoeuvred over the wreck, and in about 90 minutes 1,200 tons of water are pumped into each of them until they are low in the water. Six pairs of 9-in. wire hawsers now need to be worked into position and clamped across their decks, the clamps (G) being given extra grip by the insertion of coir rope. Each pair of hawsers is arranged as at (H), the wreck being cradled in six double loops, the strain taken by the steel gunwale plates (J).

When all this has been completed, water is pumped out of the lighters so that they lift the wreck from the bed of the river (K). Using the rising tide as at (L), the group of vessels is towed to a beaching point until high water. The slack of the 9-in. hawsers is taken up on the ebb tide, ready for the next flood tide lift. At each tide the wreck is raised farther until water can be pumped out of undamaged holds, thus securing partial buoyancy (M), further buoyancy being provided by the two big lighters. Then the wreck is towed to the beach, where temporary repairs enable her to reach dry dock.

How London River's Salvage Men Beat the Blitz

Fine feats of wreck-raising were performed by men of the Port of London Authority's Salvage Service. Nearly 40 war honours were won in this tremendous task of keeping the Port open for seaborne supplies under aerial bombardment and whilst the Thames bridges were being singled out for special attention. How this was achieved is told by Capt. MARTIN THORNHILL.

While marine engineers and scientists were grappling with the impending problem of how to cheat the deeper seas of their wartime prey, divers and salvage men were already at work in home waters. They were battling with strong currents, cutting through decks and bulkheads with oxy-acetylene apparatus, risking death from low-level air attack, from explosion, and the fouling of rescue and breathing gear.

Almost without pause from the commencement of the War to its end, marine salvage experts were toiling in the Thames and its approaches. From the first mine laid in 1939 to the last V2 fired in 1945, the blocking of this vast sea terminal was prominent in Germany's plans. Roads, railways, airfields, the focal points of troops—all these were priority targets, but none suffered the incessant, concentrated punishment which was meted out to the Luftwaffe's No. 1 objective, the Port of London.

Braving the heavy shore and air defences, the enemy succeeded in sinking or damaging hundreds of ships and small craft which were vital as carriers of food and supplies. To salve these vessels for return to duty and keep the channels and Port open for seaborne supplies were responsibilities of the Port of London Authority. The story of how these responsibilities were shouldered begins, appropriately enough, with that small but efficient pre-war body of first-aiders of the sea, the Mooring and Wreck Raising Service. At the request and with the practical support of the Admiralty, the Port of London Authority now took the whole of the Thames Estuary under its wing, supplementing the Wreck Raising Service with a special Salvage Corps of officers and crews.

And none too soon. Barely two months after the outbreak of war the enemy made history by laying the first magnetic mine from the air, in the Thames Estuary. Thenceforward the practice went on daily, or nightly, with peak efforts at frequent intervals. In the winter of 1940 magnetic mines were rained on the docks and tideway as far upstream as Richmond, and a large number of vessels which had escaped the magnetic menace in the estuary met at least a temporary fate by way of H.E. and incendiary bombs.

But the Luftwaffe had reckoned without the Salvage Department. By the end of 1940 the Department had dealt with over forty sunk or damaged ships and hundreds of smaller craft. It was a battle with time as well as the enemy. Fifty-four craft were raised within six weeks, and not once during this or later periods was any ship prevented by obstructed channels from proceeding up or down river, although five vessels might be sunk in the estuary in a single day.

The strain on the men was terrific. Again and again exhausted personnel, ashore for a brief rest, were recalled for urgent duty on the salvage vessels which were in constant danger of enemy attack, not to mention the incessant threat of mines. To add to the difficulties, normal means of communication were often disrupted.

While first-aid was being rendered to a casualty aground in the estuary, the Salvage Officer spotted an enemy reconnaissance plane obviously photographing the proceedings. When the aircraft had gone the officer decided to move his "patient" at once. With the help of other craft he succeeded in towing the vessel to a bank about four miles upriver. That night the enemy revisited the original scene in force, and dropped flares; but, finding no target, went home again, no doubt to slate the observer who had so confidently sent them on a fruitless mission.

Civilian Crews' Non-Stop Fight

"Incidents" followed one another in such quick succession that it seems unfair to make selections. Salvage crews fighting fires in bombed colliers were hindered but not deterred even by exploding ammunition. There was the 5,000-tonner mined off Southend in 1940. Broken nearly in two by the explosion, she was almost abandoned as a total casualty. In normal circumstances she certainly would have been. But these were abnormal times; the nation's need was such that everything possible must be saved. The maximum gear was mustered, the vessel raised and repaired; and in November 1942 she was helping in the North African landing.

The craft engaged in the reorganized Salvage Service were admirably adapted for their tasks. Steel bridge protective works and high-angle guns, employed to good purpose on a host of occasions, provided at least some measure of safety for these civilian crews slogging away in their non-stop fight to save and return the casualties to their urgent occasions. Superbly equipped, the salvage vessels carried divers and up-to-date diving apparatus; powerful salvage pumps and auxiliary craft were always available.

Yet there could be no text-book or rule-of-thumb for specific or even general guidance. Every wreck had its own peculiar problems, to be tackled and settled by the Salvage Officer's own experience and resourcefulness. It was experience which later on contributed valuable expert personnel and gear to the "Mulberry" scheme and the site at Arromanches (see pages 430-434 and 710, Vol. 8).

Thousands of Londoners are unaware that several of the Thames bridges also suffered considerable bomb damage. Lying in the Port of London area, these also were singled out for special enemy attention. In all, they were involved in twenty-one incidents, yet never was more than one of the busy river crossings closed at any time. Two bombs shut down Blackfriars Bridge for two days.

Although it suffered extensively from blast in 1940 and again in 1944, London Bridge was never out of action; which was fortunate, for about 24,000 vehicles use the bridge in an average twelve hours. Southwark Bridge was six times involved; the worst occasion was in May 1941, when a high-explosive bomb destroyed the north arches and closed the bridge for eight weeks.

Tower Bridge suffered most damage. Even in normal times this is London's most expensive bridge; over £31,000 is spent in a year on repairs, cleansing, staff wages, and hire of a steam tug in case of emergencies—about twelve times the upkeep cost of London Bridge. In 1940 Tower Bridge's high-level bridge was struck by a bomb which cut the hydraulic mains and put the road bridge out of action for six days. In April 1941 a parachute mine on the foreshore damaged the bascule and towers, the residences, cabins and engine-room; that incident closed the bridge for another four days.

In August 1944 Tower Bridge was "out" again for three days. In the previous month a flying bomb fell on the bridge's tug, the Naja, destroying her completely. Her crew of four were being relieved, the captain and engineer had just gone ashore, leaving the mate and stoker aboard. These, together with the fresh crew, were all killed.

Fired by a traditional sense of duty as high as that in any of the Services, P.L.A. men never cracked. Fair weather or foul, they were determined to keep the Port and its services open for the nation's weal. Nearly forty war honours have gone to men of the P.L.A. Salvage Service. Against the retaining wall of Island Gardens, North Greenwich, is a sad little cemetery where sunken craft beyond repair were temporarily dumped. Over them flutters the green wreck-marking flag. Every shattered pile, every battered wharf likely to obstruct navigation, is thus marked, and at the height of the War the Harbour Service nearly ran out of green bunting.

Since the outbreak of the War the Authority's Salvage Department has raised 32 vessels approximating 82,000 gross registered tons. All but one of 50 ships, totalling 208,000 gross registered tons, have been rendered major salvage assistance by patching, pumping and refloating. The number of smaller craft, including tugs and barges, raised from river and docks, reaches the astonishing aggregate of 252.

AFTER A DIRECT BOMB-HIT, in July 1941, H.M.S. Helvellyn, paddle minesweeper, was practically submerged in the Surrey Docks (left). Thanks to the efforts of the Port of London Salvage Department the Helvellyn's stern was later beached at Millwall (right). Feats of salvage and removal of wrecked craft of all types, to keep the Thames and its estuary open to shipping during the Luftwaffe's attacks on the Port of London, are recorded above. More than 300 vessels had been dealt with since 1939. See also facing page.

Photos, Port of London Authority

From Europe's Battlefields to Salvage Depot

AT VILVORDE, NEAR BRUSSELS, is one of the largest dumps of battlefield litter in all Europe. Thousands of abandoned and unserviceable guns, armoured vehicles and trucks are collected there, to be broken up and transported in barges to Antwerp for shipment as scrap metal to Britain. Part of the depot (1), with fragments of vehicles (2). British 17-pounder guns (3) awaiting shipment at Antwerp, where (4) scrap is being loaded. See also page 427. *Photos, British Official*

Dresden Facing Up to Reconstruction Problems

CENTURIES-OLD GERMAN CITY and capital of Saxony, famous for its art collections and the delicacy of the china made here Dresden's reconstruction is now under way. The town was target for several Allied air attacks, including a fire raid on Feb. 13, 1945, when 650,000 incendiaries showered down. Workers board trams amid the debris of Johannestrasse (1). German architects with plans for the new city (2) survey the ruins to select sites. Builders busy at the Zwinger Art Gallery (3). In the Royal Porcelain Works at Meissen (4), near Dresden, production of the famous china has restarted. Townspeople who voluntarily give up their Sunday rest to help in clearing bomb damage are served with soup (5).

I Was There! Eye Witness Stories of the War and After

How We of the Naval C.S. Handled the Convoys

"Being in all respects ready for sea, you will weigh and proceed in accordance with the following orders." Many times during the War these words were read by Merchant Navy Masters when given their final sailing instructions by the Naval Control Service. The inside story is told specially for "The War Illustrated" by Lieut.-Commander J. W. M. THOMPSON, R.N.V.R.

Lieut.-Commander J. W. M. THOMPSON, R.N.V.R., of the Naval Control Service, relates his experiences of the wartime shepherding of merchant shipping.

BEFORE the commencement of hostilities in 1939 a special department had been established at the Admiralty to be responsible for the organization of all Merchant Shipping movements. Trade Division, as this section was known, was represented in every major Allied port in the world by a Naval Control Service Officer (N.C.S.O.). At neutral ports other arrangements were made.

In September 1939 I was appointed to the Thames Naval Control at Southend, and soon found myself attached to the Convoy office, which was in the charge of a Commander R.N. It was a matter of pride in those early days that the first convoy left the Thames only two days after war had been declared. Our motto was "Sail Ships"—and we did! I remember a day in March 1940 when over 2¼ million tons (gross) of merchant shipping sailed from the London river—a record that, I believe, was never broken.

The organization at an Assembly Anchorage differed from that at a Loading Port. At the former, the N.C.S.O. relied entirely on signals received by wireless or teleprinter from other ports indicating what ships were sailing in their convoys, and he would thus be able to judge what ships were likely to arrive in time to sail from his own anchorage in the convoys that were already scheduled to sail. At a terminal port, however, the N.C.S.O. maintained close liaison with the Ministry of War Transport and the Port Authorities, so that completion dates of loading and discharge could be forecast and arrangements made for the ships' inclusion in the next suitable convoy.

Most convoys ran in regular cycles and were designated by numbers. For instance, "FT37" indicated the thirty-seventh southbound convoy from the Firth of Forth to the Thames, and these convoys, sometimes 9 knots, sometimes 7 knots, arrived almost daily. Many of the ships were loaded colliers bound up-river, but the majority of ocean-going tramps required onward routeing to Canada, South America, India, or Australia. We, having prior knowledge of their expected arrival, would be able to allocate the ships to their respective ocean convoys. Some ships would be sailing on the day they arrived, others would have to remain at anchor for four or even six days for a South Atlantic or Mediterranean convoy. Each ship was boarded by an officer on arrival and the Master told, in confidence, what would be his probable sailing date; certain details of the vessel were also obtained for use in the Convoy office.

THE Admiralty, or local Commander-in-Chief, had already promulgated convoy programmes after provision of Naval escorts and air protection had been arranged, and every N.C.S.O. concerned would know some days in advance what convoys were sailing, when, to which destinations, and the minimum speed of ships eligible for each convoy. From the details provided from other ports by signal and from information received from the London Docks, we at Southend were able to prepare a skeleton convoy cruising order of the next ocean convoy—the "Ocean Broad Front," as it was known.

Normally a Naval Commodore, with a signal staff, was embarked in a ship having good navigational aids and accommodation, and this vessel was positioned as the leader of the centre column of the convoy. Should the Commodore's ship be disabled, we appointed a Vice-Commodore to take charge, and also a Rear-Commodore in the possible event of the Vice-Commodore also being sunk or damaged. These were both Masters of two of the ships in the convoy.

Ocean convoys were always formed on a broad front, the number and depth of columns varying according to the number of ships. The Convoy officer allocated a definite position in convoy to each ship, and this was indicated by a system of Pendant Numbers—the pendants being flown by each ship on sailing. In this way Masters of all vessels could identify their relative positions in the convoy, and the Commodore and escorts were assisted in maintenance of control over the convoy as a whole. The Commodore's ship would be still further identified by the flying of the Commodore's Broad Pendant—a blue cross on a white background.

British ships with good navigational aids were usually chosen as column leaders, especially in the early days of the War. Ships with valuable cargoes (explosives, military stores, or petroleum products) were given centre "safe" positions; ships fitted with balloons were staggered so as to give the maximum protection to the convoy as a whole; ships with the best A.A. weapons were similarly placed; and vessels with anti-submarine armament and anti-torpedo nets were stationed in the wing columns and in the rear of columns.

At the Conference of Masters

Consideration was also given to the relative sizes of ships ahead and astern, and ships breaking off for intermediate ports were so placed that they could leave the convoy without causing confusion. Allowance was also made for ships from intermediate ports which might join the convoy at sea either singly or in a group.

Owing to the fact that most anchorages were protected by an anti-torpedo boom with a narrow "gate," and also to the restricted width of the war channels, the convoy could not form up on a broad front until clear of confined waters. Diagrams were accordingly included in the convoy orders (and explained at the conference of Masters which was held ashore before the convoy sailed) showing the method of proceeding to sea in single line, the Commodore's ship leading, and, on his giving the signal by flag or light, ships formed into

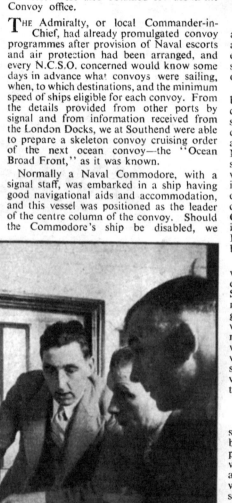

SKIPPERS OF FISHING TRAWLERS in conference at a Naval Control Service office. They are receiving instructions—upon which their own safety, among other things, depends—from the N.C. officer (left) before proceeding to the appointed fishing grounds. The workings of this wartime organization are revealed in these pages. *Admiralty photograph*

two columns, each alternate ship pulling out and taking up station to starboard.

Base convoy organization continued seven days a week, at all hours of the day and night. Sailing times were liable to be altered without notice (and were !), and enemy activity often entailed a convoy being re-routed twice during the night before it sailed.

The Commander Tore His Hair

In June 1940, with the Germans holding the French coast, passage of the English Channel was denied to ocean-going shipping. I recall the first ocean convoy that had to be sailed from the Thames by way of the Pentland Firth, with its dangerous tides, instead of through the Dover Straits. A hectic day was drawing to a close, with the ending of the conference at which the Masters of the ships sailing the following day had been briefed by the N.C.S.O., the Commodore and the Senior Officer of Escort. At about 18.30 an " immediate " signal was received from Admiralty stating that the convoy was to sail Northabout and that a revised ocean route was being sent in cipher.

This meant that all existing orders had to be scrapped, and since other ships would now be able to catch the convoy as it passed the various East Coast ports on its northward passage, the number of ships would be increased. The Convoy office was in a turmoil with messages from the anchorage being received, signals from other ports arriving, and the senior officer issuing orders in quick succession.

"Ask Tyne if they will have any joiners?" . . . "Commodore's ship has engine trouble" . . . " Ask the Routeing Officer if that new route is through yet " . . " Rangoon Star is still one wireless operator short " . . . " Humber have four possible joiners—names, destinations and speeds coming by teleprinter " . . . And then, to cap everything, C.-in-C.'s Operations Room phoned to say that enemy aircraft had mined one of the channels to be used—this meant special new routes to give a safe diversion from the dangerous area. The night ended with an ordinarily sedate Commander standing on a chair and tearing his hair whilst trying to get sense out of a North-East Coast duty officer ! By 01.00 complete new orders were ready and Boarding Officers in tugs and drifters delivered them to the ships in the anchorage. At dawn every vessel sailed according to orders, and the next two convoys were being planned in our office.

There was an afternoon in August 1944 when I was assisting at a conference being held on board a ship in the Gulf of Naples (for security reasons)—for the convoy that was to arrive two days later off Southern France and land the first troops and supplies. In Naples we were close behind the American Fifth Army Front, and we had to accustom ourselves to U.S. methods and phraseology as the U.S. Army controlled the berthing, loading and discharge of all Merchant Shipping in the port. Co-operation became a fine art and neither side let the other down.

In March 1944 the discharge tonnage for the Port of Naples—damaged though it was—was the largest in the world. We sailed convoys south, convoys "up the line" to Anzio, and all sorts of odd ones to Sardinia and Corsica as circumstances dictated and provision of escorts allowed. We also had two or three hospital ships a day to route, "up the line" or back to the U.K. or U.S.A.—each ship routed clear of convoy routes and, of course, mined areas. These are some of the typical responsibilities of a N.C.S.O. in an operational area.

I Saw Air-Raid Shelters Crumple and Collapse

At 11 o'clock on the night of March 16, 1946, the police closed Lower Regent Street, London, to traffic. Massive brick-and-concrete shelters were to be demolished by mechanical monsters working all through the night. The scene is described by Robert Waithman of The News Chronicle.

From Waterloo Place and out of side streets where they had been waiting, I saw come rumbling into Lower Regent Street on caterpillar treads a family of four great mechanical shovels, their headlights blazing like angry eyes. Half a dozen heavy lorries followed them. The cabs of the tractors and the lorries were dark green, with "Willment—Waterloo" painted across. Thirty-four men swarmed in and around them.

The tractors squared up to two of the three air-raid shelters in the middle of the street. The biggest of the four shovels went to the top end of the top shelter ; the next one crawled to the right flank of the top shelter ; the third lumbered up to the top end of the bottom shelter ; the fourth went to its left flank.

The two tractors that faced down the street were fitted with shovels; steel mouths with four savage steel teeth, each a foot long. The two at the sides of the shelters had at the end of their dipper arms not shovels but huge balls of solid cast steel, a yard or so in diameter. There was a moment of relative quiet after they were in position, then a controlled Bedlam broke loose.

At the side of the top shelter the flanking tractor began to belch flame from the row of Diesel exhausts on the cabin roof. The jib and the dipper-arm reared and the steel ball hung for a moment over the wall of the shelter and then fell. The jib moved and the ball rose and fell, pounding the top of the wall in a different place each time, and the concrete cracked beneath it. Then the jib rose higher and the dipper-arm descended and sent the ball swinging against the side of the wall.

First at the top and then lower the wall fell inwards. The wall was two feet nine inches thick, and it was solid brick and

SAILING INSTRUCTIONS, always subject to last-minute changes in wartime, were delivered to Merchant Navy skippers in a variety of ways. Normally, conferences were held at the local Naval Control Service office, some time before sailing, as explained in the story by Lieut.-Commander J. W. M. Thompson.

At other times personal delivery was the most expedient method, a N.C.S. Boarding Officer going the rounds of the vessels in the port or harbour (above). Final messages, cancelling or altering previous instructions, were occasionally passed at the end of a bamboo pole (left) from a Navel Control Service launch to the captain of a ship in convoy.

Admiralty photographs

AIR-RAID SHELTER DEMOLITION in Lower Regent Street, London, was conducted at high speed, mechanical navvies working throughout the night (1), some pounding the structures to rubble with solid steel balls (2), others scooping the masonry into lorries with great clawed shovels (3).
Photos, British Movietone News

concrete ; but it cracked and crumpled and tumbled down in jagged chunks. White dust whirled up to the white lights overhead. A greater noise began as the shovel at the top of the shelter dipped and clawed at the fallen masonry. The cab shook and lurched and yellow flame spurted from its roof while the shovel pawed and shoved the debris into place and then scooped it up and swung it over into a lorry.

We on the pavement watched and listened raptly. When the ball swung hard and the ground shook we grinned at one another. For it was good to be outside the shelter ; it was good now to hear the din and to feel the shock in the ground. As the wall came down it began to reveal notices pasted on the inside of the opposite shelter wall. HOT BATHS, one began, and another said NO SMOKING. The swinging ball moved slowly towards the shelter entrance, where the words 40 PERSONS were painted. Presently that sign too lay in ruins.

The noise of Peace went on all through the night. When the great machines and the lorries and the dusty men left on Sunday afternoon there were only roped-off hollows in the road, and now you could see clear down Lower Regent Street from Piccadilly. It looked spacious and calm.

South Africa as the British Serviceman Saw It

For the Princesses, who will be making their first journey Overseas, and for the King and Queen, who will be seeing Africa for the first time, the Royal visit next year will be one of their most memorable experiences. Wartime memories of the sunny land are conjured up by J. Heming, of The Daily Telegraph, who served there as a R.N.V.R. officer.

I CAN think of nothing which could give South Africa greater pleasure than the Royal visit which is to take place early next year. Nowhere in the Commonwealth did the War do more to strengthen the bonds that unite the family of nations of which the King is the head. The warmth of feeling for "home," as the United Kingdom is so often referred to in conversation in the Union, was shown by the remarkable welcome British Servicemen received in South Africa. From the days when convoys used to halt at Cape Town on their "round Africa" voyages, to the time last year when VJ Day found R.A.F. and Naval forces stationed there, the greatest possible hospitality was extended to our men. A typical example is the work of the South African Women's Auxiliary Service (S.A.W.A.S.), who were prepared to arrange anything from a wedding to a round of golf. Any man going on local leave had only to say how long he had and where he would like to go, and the S.A.W.A.S. did the rest. By road and rail men were whisked away to their destinations. There they were met and taken to some homely house, where they were honoured guests. One man I know went from Cape Town to the Game Preserves and Victoria Falls in Rhodesia and back, with stops in Bechuanaland. It took him a fortnight, and he was not allowed to spend a penny. In the permanent Service establishments in South Africa there was a standing list of local residents always willing at short notice to entertain men. No function was complete without at least a sprinkling from Britain.

No wonder a high percentage of Servicemen whose release became due while they were in South Africa elected to take their discharge there with a view to settling permanently in the Union. Men had little difficulty in finding employment.

Story Told in Veld and City

A striking fact concerning South Africa's contribution to the War effort emerged in a statement made by General Smuts last year. There had been no conscription ; and yet, he said, the number of men who volunteered was so great that the force sent overseas could not have been increased even with compulsory service. These volunteers came from every section of a varied population in all parts of the Union. Men of differing political views and from geographically segregated areas served side by side with soldiers from the other Dominions, from the Colonies and from Great Britain.

They have returned with a story which must by now have been told in veld and city in every part of the Union. Through all those great campaigns in North Africa and Italy, in prison camps and in the green haven of England, these virile and proud young South Africans found that there was also strength and dignity in the rest of the Commonwealth. To many this was not something they had always taken for granted. German propaganda had industriously spread the "effete Englishman" fiction.

Nowhere will the Royal party be more assured of an enthusiastic reception than at their port of arrival, Cape Town. In this city, nestling below Table Mountain and cupped in one of the most beautiful bays in the world, they know how to make festival.

I was in the ship which brought the first South African prisoners of war home, and I can see still the thousands of street lights clustered in the shadow of the mountain

SOUTH AFRICA'S TABLE MOUNTAIN, beneath which British soldiers and American sailors exchanged greetings during the War, is one of the many attractions in the Union which will interest the King and Queen and the Princesses during the Royal tour next year. Their port of arrival will be Cape Town, at the foot of the Mountain. *Photo, Marsh, Cape Town*

slopes, while above, dawn crimsoned the heights. The quays were beflagged and masses of people lined the roads. The atmosphere was electric long before the ship tied up.

The train journey up country is a memorable one. A long climb to the Karoo starts through the lovely Hex River valley and continues breathlessly on the sides of precipitous mountains. The Karoo itself, one of the sights of South Africa, is apparently a panorama of desolation—a rock-strewn plateau giving life incredibly to infinitely numerous bush plants. Yet this vast plain produces fine sheep. In Durban, which South Africans describe as their finest resort, is a shopping centre, surely the equal of any existing today. There are many modern buildings here—the skyline from the air is not unlike New York's, although, of course, smaller—and the port was of importance to the Royal Navy during the war.

Zulu rickshaw "boys" contribute to the colour of the town. Usually magnificent physical specimens, they maintain an amazing pace with their vehicles. They are very clever at adjusting the balance of their weight in the shafts so that the only energy expended is in a forward direction. They considered it was a special honour to carry a British Serviceman, which they did with gay shouts and palpitating capers.

Among other places Their Majesties will see are Johannesburg, financial and gold-mining centre, and Pretoria, the capital. Johannesburg (visitors are warned against the contraction Jo'burg) is 6,000 feet up, and new arrivals are often apprehensive about their breathlessness for a day or two. Here is the deepest gold-mine in the world—over 8,000 feet down—and some interesting native compounds. When I visited one of these with two other naval officers, a full-dress Zulu war dance was performed specially for our benefit.

PRETORIA is full of atmosphere and of contrasts. Some of the smaller edifices seem unchanged in character since they were erected during the town's inception; the Parliament buildings are magnificently conceived and finely sited. Here, as elsewhere, British officers were honorary members of the golf and social clubs. Down south, Simon's Town, the naval base, is situated on a most beautiful coastline, along which the road from Cape Town runs. This is on the east side of the Cape peninsula and faces the Indian Ocean, which meets the Atlantic at Cape Agulhas, South Africa's most southerly point, not far to the south-east. Between Cape Town and Simon's Town is Groot Schuur, the official residence of Field-Marshal Smuts, Their Majesties' host in South Africa, a handsome building in a woodland setting.

★—As The Years Went By—Notable Days in the War—★

1940

April 9. *Germans invaded Denmark and Norway; Copenhagen and Oslo occupied.*

1941

April 5. *British forces entered Addis Ababa.*
April 6. *Yugoslavia and Greece invaded; open city of Belgrade bombed by Germans.*
April 10. *British and Imperial forces in contact with enemy in Northern Greece.*

1942

April 6. *First Japanese air raids on India: Coconada and Vizagapatam bombed.*
April 9. *American resistance ended on Bataan, Philippines; Corregidor still holding out.*

1943

April 11. *In Tunisia British 1st and 8th Armies established contact near Fondouk.*

1944

March 31. *Red Army over Rumanian frontier.*
April 10. *Odessa recaptured by Russians.*

1945

April 1. *U.S. 10th Army invaded Okinawa.*
April 5. *Soviet Government denounced the Russo-Japanese Neutrality Act of 1941.*
April 6. *Russians breached Vienna defences.*
April 9. *Koenigsberg captured by Russians.*
April 12. *U.S. 9th Army crossed the Elbe. Sudden death of President Roosevelt.*

PALESTINE: THE ZIONISTS' VIEWPOINT

To "The War Illustrated" Number 222 Mr. Kenneth Williams contributed an article entitled Grasping the Palestine Nettle. Some of our Jewish readers have expressed their dissent from the general trend of his statements, in particular Mr. H. Newman, well known as a Jewish journalist. He has sent a letter of some length in which he replies to Mr. Williams. Somewhat reduced, whilst retaining the main points of his case for Zionism, his letter is reprinted below. There is no space in "The War Illustrated" for controversial correspondence; but we make this exception out of courtesy to Mr. Newman as an advocate of Zionism, and without in any way reflecting on Mr. Williams' contribution, which was written at our invitation. No further correspondence will be considered.—EDITOR

IF justice is to be the basis of human relationship, why should this elemental axiom be denied to the Jewish people? Why should this one people in all the earth be refused the cohesion which its own territory would confer?

Anti-semitism exists. Persecution of Jews continues. A third of the Jewish people—6,000,000 souls—were mercilessly slaughtered by the Nazis. Prejudice against Jews will continue so long as Jews remain a phantom, wandering people, fleeing from one country to another; tolerated, perhaps, but welcomed nowhere, resented everywhere—because they are living irrationally. The *raison d'être* of Zionism is to rationalize the relationship of the Jewish people to other nations.

The Balfour Declaration of 1917 might have been a unilateral promise by the British Government, but its terms were unanimously accepted and ratified by 52 nations, and embodied in the Mandate. The terms were specific: ". . . . recognition has thereby been given to the historical connexion of the Jewish people with Palestine and to the grounds for reconstituting their national home in that country."

The Mandatory was charged with "placing the country under such political, administrative and economic conditions as will secure the establishment of the Jewish national home (Article 2), and the necessity "to secure the co-operation *of all Jews* who are willing to assist" (Article 4) . . . the directive to the Government to "facilitate Jewish immigration" (Article 6) . . . with the additional proviso that the Administrative "facilitate the acquisition of Palestine citizenship by Jews" (Article 7).

This was an open invitation to Jews throughout the world, but Kenneth Williams roundly declares "the idea of a Jewish State in Palestine, which was never promised and is a gloss put by Zionists." Lloyd George, one of the proponents of the Balfour Declaration, declared before the Peel Commission that the intention was to give Jews the opportunity of becoming "a definite majority . . . then Palestine would thus become a Jewish State. The notion that Jewish immigration would have to be restricted in order to ensure that the Jews would be a permanent minority never entered the heads of anyone engaged in framing the policy. That would have been regarded as unjust, and as a fraud on the people to whom we were appealing."

The words of Balfour, Viscount Cecil, Wilson and others intimately concerned with the War Policy and Treaties in 1917-1922 show Kenneth Williams inaccurate. It was to be the fulfilment of 2,000 years of Jewish prayers. Twenty centuries of forcibly dispossessed homelessness was to be ended.

Over 90 per cent of the Jewish people support Zionism. They know it is the only answer. Nowhere else, except in Palestine, can Jews claim "as of right and not on sufferance" to live. The status which national cohesion would give is the one solution of the drawn-out Jewish problem. Kenneth Williams cites Mr. Bevin in an attempt to create a distinction between Zionists and Jewry as a whole. This proposition is fallacious. To *every conforming Jew* the return to Palestine is an integral and indivisible part of the Jewish faith. The prayer "next year in Jerusalem" is reiterated in the Jew's most solemn and sacred moment. . . .

Arabs have benefited a thousandfold—in living standards, health, education. They have gained. Why, then, refuse justice to the Jews who have turned malaria swamps and eroded soil into flourishing settlements, and have built beautiful cities even on sand dunes?

What is Britain's strategic policy? Arabs everywhere tell British and French to "clear out." Jews alone desire and urge that Palestine become a British Dominion. In both the last wars Arabs have fought against British and Allied interests. Ten times as many Jews as Arabs joined the Palestine forces. Jews, and not Arabs, have, through the times of war, proven themselves Britain's best friends. Expediency, no less than humanitarian ideals, demands the fulfilment of an explicit pledge—Palestine as a Jewish Commonwealth.—Yours, etc.,

H. NEWMAN

Would Bombs Alone have Beaten Germany?

By CAPTAIN NORMAN MACMILLAN M.C., A.F.C.

THE war strength of the Royal Air Force on V-Day was 1,100,000. In Bomber Command, out of 110,000 men trained, 50,000 lost their lives, 15,000 were seriously injured, and another 15,000 less seriously injured. A grave total.

In the House of Commons, Wing Commander Millington has raised the question of the recognition of the work of the bomber aircrews, who, he said, felt that the exclusion of their chief, Sir Arthur Harris, from the New Year's Honours List was an affront through him to all who served under him.

Meanwhile, "Bert" Harris has left the country to return to South Africa, where he first joined the forces in the First Great War. His last recognition was promotion to the highest air rank of Marshal of the R.A.F. There was, of course, probably only one other air appointment in the R.A.F. which he might have held, that of Chief of the Air Staff. This appointment is made by the Prime Minister, and under Mr. Attlee it went to Marshal of the R.A.F. Sir Arthur (now Lord) Tedder.

GERMAN Evidence of Effectiveness of British and American Bombing

These two notable R.A.F. commanders are exponents of air power wielded in two ways. Harris was the man who applied strategic air power, Tedder the one who wielded tactical air power. Tedder worked with the Army, and to a lesser degree with the Navy. Harris played the more solitary part, striking at Germany with the long arm of the bomber, but occasionally diverting his forces to aid the Army or the Navy when no tactical air power in existence could have done what his heavy bombers did—at Houffalize, St. Vith, Cleve, Goch, Caen, the Falaise Gap; the laying of the trail of magnetic mines ahead of the Scharnhorst and Gneisenau after they had passed through the English Channel; the destruction of the Tirpitz at anchor in a Norwegian fjord surrounded by torpedo nets; the destruction of the Mohne and Eder dams; the destruction of the railway viaducts that cut the Ruhr railways and trapped 300,000 German troops.

We all know how often in this recent War was proclaimed the triumph of combined operations, how often it was argued that all arms were needed to win the War, and how frequently the allocation of resources to strategic bombing was deplored. Harris had to fight not only the enemy, but opponents at home who did not subscribe to his views on the efficacy of bombing. Now, evidence is available from enemy sources of the results of the scientific British and American bombing of Germany. The Under Secretary of State for Air gave German evidence when presenting the Air Estimates in the House of Commons on March 12, 1946.

"In the Luftwaffe," said Dr. Speer, Reich Minister for Armaments and War Production, when under interrogation, "the shortage of fuel became insupportable from September 1944 onwards. The allocation was cut down to 30,000 tons a month, though the monthly requirements were between 160,000 and 180,000 tons.

"In the Army the shortage first became catastrophic at the time of the winter offensive of December 16, 1944. This was substantially responsible for the rapid collapse of the German defensive front against the Russian break-out from the Baranovo bridge-head. There were 1,500 tanks ready for action, but they had only one or two fuel supply units and were immobilized."

Asked if he believed that strategic bombing alone could have brought about the surrender of Germany, Dr. Speer said: "The answer is 'Yes.' The attacks on the synthetic oil industry would have sufficed, without the impact of purely military events, to render Germany defenceless." Field - Marshal Erhard Milch, head of the Luftwaffe, said: "If the oil plants had been attacked six months earlier Germany would have been defeated about six months sooner." Dr. Fischer, head of the Oil Department of the Ministry of Armaments, said: "If the air attacks had been concentrated on industry, particularly oil, chemicals, power and transportation, the War would have been over one year sooner."

THESE statements are striking confirmation of views I have frequently expressed in THE WAR ILLUSTRATED. In No. 133 (July 24, 1942) I wrote: "... the strategic disposition of air power is even more important than its tactical employment." But, on December 11, 1942, I noted the fact that "strategic air war has been forced to give way to meet the needs of tactical air war ..." On April 2, 1943, I recorded Air Chief Marshal Sir Arthur Tedder as saying: "I never subscribe to the view that the air alone can win the ultimate victory ..." Because of the conditions then existing I wrote in the same article that "The demands of the field forces and the sea forces will determine whether in the course of this War it will be possible to prove the bombing theory that a nation's will and power to resist can be crushed from the air."

And again, referring to the promised build-up of the American Army 8th Air Force, I wrote: "When aircraft like these can duplicate by day what Bomber Command does by night, the climacteric of a German breakdown will indeed be near." And on February 4, 1944, in my article appeared these sentences: "If our bombing is maintained and increased ... battered German industry will bring Hitler's downfall because it will be unable to give him arms. We can win the War by bombing."

As I have said, during the War there were two schools of thought, and exponents of two methods of attaining victory. Mr. Churchill, as Defence Minister of Britain, used both, probably as the best way to get the maximum effort from all. But the result was a trail of destruction throughout almost all Europe, and, apparently, a lengthened war.

STRUCK Blows Which Aided Equally the Western Allies and Russia

Assuredly the sacrifices made by the air-crews of Bomber Command and the 8th Air Force were not vain, for they must have reduced to a fraction of what they might have been the casualties among the surface forces. And these two strategic air forces, plus the smaller U.S.A. 15th, struck blows which aided equally the Western Allies and Russia. Without their aid, would the Red Army have been victorious? Those who heard the great bomber fleets pass out towards Germany in the day of their might must be struck by the words in Ezekiel i, 24: "I heard the noise of their wings, like the noise of great waters, as the voice of the Almighty, the voice of speech, as the noise of an host."

Soon after the end of the First Great War the American Navy and Army staged bombing tests against surrendered German warships. The Naval air tests were inconclusive. The Army bombing, under Brigadier-General William Mitchell, was not. Mitchell, too outspoken in his advocacy of air power, was dismissed from the Army in 1926, and died unhonoured before the Second Great War. During this War his name was reinstated in the American Army List, posthumously promoted to General. The Mitchell bomber was named after him.

Today we run the same risk of under-estimating future air power. The man who did most to defeat Germany from the air has gone from this country to make his home elsewhere. Presumably we have subscribed officially to the theory of combined operations. The theory of air power as an individual war-winner is not popular with the Army and the Navy. From what has already been made known about the forthcoming atomic bomb tests against surrendered Japanese warships in the Pacific, it would almost appear that the object is to prove that naval vessels can survive atomic warfare rather than to discover if atomic bombs are still more deadly than the bombs that sank the Tirpitz, the toughest warship of the German Navy. Truly, history repeats itself and man learns but little from his mistakes.

Parachute-Jumpers Safeguard American Forests

VALUABLE TIMBERLANDS THREATENED BY FIRE are sky-patrolled by trained observers, and parachutists—advance-guard of the forest fire-fighters—are dropped (1) in the vicinity of an outbreak. As protection against possible facial injury through contact with tree branches in the descent, the jumper is masked (2). Equipment includes a portable two-way radio set (3) for transmission of instructions to the nearest fire-fighting base. First intimation of a fire appears to a spotting aircraft as a dense smother of smoke (4).

Roosevelt's Old Home Preserved for Posterity

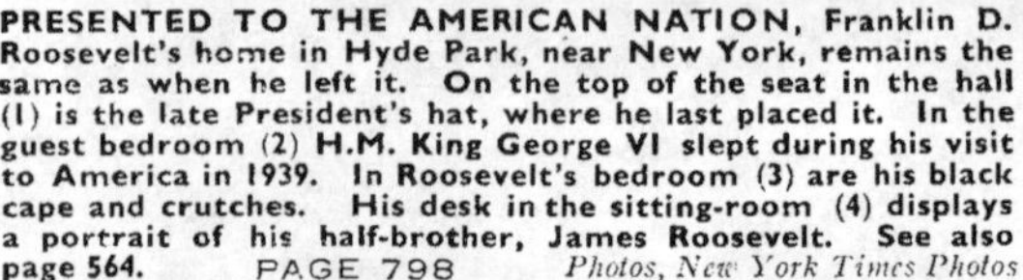

PRESENTED TO THE AMERICAN NATION, Franklin D. Roosevelt's home in Hyde Park, near New York, remains the same as when he left it. On the top of the seat in the hall (1) is the late President's hat, where he last placed it. In the guest bedroom (2) H.M. King George VI slept during his visit to America in 1939. In Roosevelt's bedroom (3) are his black cape and crutches. His desk in the sitting-room (4) displays a portrait of his half-brother, James Roosevelt. See also page 564. *Photos, New York Times Photos*

In Britain Now: A Great War-Leader Honoured

V-PARADE PREPARATIONS are being conducted with the aid of German prisoners of war. Once members of Hitler's Wehrmacht, they may have had their own dreams of marching through London as goose-stepping conquerors. Some of them are seen (above) handling stores in Kensington Gardens, where they are erecting camps to house Colonial troops who will be in the great Parade on June 8, 1946.

F. M. VISCOUNT ALEXANDER of Tunis (right), first of the country's war leaders to receive the honorary Freedom of the City of London, speaking at the Guildhall after the presentation ceremony on March 19, 1946, during which he received a token Sword of Honour—one presented to Field-Marshal Lord Allenby 25 years before. The Freedom of the City was also bestowed on Lady Alexander.

SLAKING the horse's thirst is one of the numerous tasks that befall civilian girl workers at the Royal Army Veterinary Remount Depot, at Melton Mowbray, Leicestershire. The depot, run by male Army personnel, employs civilian help to assist in the training, and to tend to the well-being, of horses until the animals are required for service elsewhere by the military authorities.

ONE OF THE LAST balloons of London's famous barrage (left) may still be seen hovering above the capital from the bombed site of the infirmary at the Royal Hospital, Chelsea, where it is being used for research on the effect of weather on radio transmission. The balloon is raised and lowered four times a day, recording pressure, temperature and humidity at 200-ft. intervals.

SPRING-CLEANING NELSON is a precarious business for the steeplejacks perched on the scaffolding surrounding the statue, nearly 150 ft. above Trafalgar Square, London. The cleaners, dwarfed by the 18-ft. figure of the celebrated Admiral, are supervised by a member of a famous family of steeplejacks who for three generations have made the difficult ascent.

 New York Times Photos, Barratt's, Fox, International News Photos, P.A.-Reuter

The Loire is Bridged Again at Nantes

PONT DE LA VENDÉE, SPANNING THE LOIRE, at Nantes, France, was opened to traffic in December 1945, after its strength and stability had been tested by locomotives, weighing 250 tons, which are seen nearing the completion of their run. A temporary structure, 700 yards long, this bridge replaces the original whose ruins are to the right. The construction, commenced in April 1945, entailed the use of 1,600 tons of steel. During the War nearly 3,000 bridges were destroyed in France by the retreating Germans and by Allied bombing. *Photo, Planet News*

Printed in England and published every alternate Friday by the Proprietors, THE AMALGAMATED PRESS, LTD., The Fleetway House, Farringdon Street, London, E.C.4. Registered for transmission by Canadian Magazine Post. Sole Agents for Australia and New Zealand: Messrs. Gordon & Gotch, Ltd.: and for South Africa: Central News Agency, Ltd.—April 12, 1946. S.S. *Editorial Address:* JOHN CARPENTER HOUSE, WHITEFRIARS, LONDON, E.C.4.